Short Story
Criticism

Guide to Gale Literary Criticism Series

For criticism on	Consult these Gale series
Authors now living or who died after December 31, 1959	*CONTEMPORARY LITERARY CRITICISM (CLC)*
Authors who died between 1900 and 1959	*TWENTIETH-CENTURY LITERARY CRITICISM (TCLC)*
Authors who died between 1800 and 1899	*NINETEENTH-CENTURY LITERATURE CRITICISM (NCLC)*
Authors who died between 1400 and 1799	*LITERATURE CRITICISM FROM 1400 TO 1800 (LC)* *SHAKESPEAREAN CRITICISM (SC)*
Authors who died before 1400	*CLASSICAL AND MEDIEVAL LITERATURE CRITICISM (CMLC)*
Black writers of the past two hundred years	*BLACK LITERATURE CRITICISM (BLC)*
Authors of books for children and young adults	*CHILDREN'S LITERATURE REVIEW (CLR)*
Dramatists	*DRAMA CRITICISM (DC)*
Hispanic writers of the late nineteenth and twentieth centuries	*HISPANIC LITERATURE CRITICISM (HLC)*
Native North American writers and orators of the eighteenth, nineteenth, and twentieth centuries	*NATIVE NORTH AMERICAN LITERATURE (NNAL)*
Poets	*POETRY CRITICISM (PC)*
Short story writers	*SHORT STORY CRITICISM (SSC)*
Major authors from the Renaissance to the present	*WORLD LITERATURE CRITICISM, 1500 TO THE PRESENT (WLC)*

ISSN 0895-9493

Volume 24

Short Story Criticism

Excerpts from Criticism of the
Works of Short Fiction Writers

Jeff Hill
Lawrence J. Trudeau
Editors

Carol T. Gaffke
Associate Editor

GALE

DETROIT · NEW YORK · TORONTO · LONDON

STAFF

Jeff Hill, Lawrence J. Trudeau, *Editors*

Carol T. Gaffke
Associate Editor

Marlene S. Hurst, *Permissions Manager*

Margaret A. Chamberlain, Maria Franklin, Kimberly F. Smilay, *Permissions Specialists*

Edna Hedblad, Michele Lonoconus, Maureen Puhl, Shalice Shah,
Permissions Associates

Sarah Chesney, Jeffrey Hermann, *Permissions Assistants*

Victoria B. Cariappa, *Research Manager*

Laura Bissey, Julia C. Daniel, Tamara C. Nott, Michele P. Pica,
Tracie A. Richardson, Norma Sawaya, Cheryl L. Warnock, *Research Associates*

Mary Beth Trimper, *Production Director*
Deborah L. Milliken, *Production Assistant*

C. J. Jonik, *Desktop Publisher*
Randy Bassett, *Image Database Supervisor*
Mikal Ansari, Robert Duncan, *Scanner Operators*
Pamela Hayes, *Photography Coordinator*

Library of Congress Catalog Card Number 88-641014
ISBN 0-7876-0756-8
ISSN 0895-9439

Printed in the United States of America
10 9 8 7 6 5 4 3 2 1

Contents

Preface   vii

Acknowledgments   xi

Preface

A Comprehensive Information Source
on World Short Fiction

S *hort Story Criticism (SSC)* presents significant passages from criticism of the world's greatest short story writers and provides supplementary biographical and bibliographical materials to guide the interested reader to a greater understanding of the authors of short fiction. This series was developed in response to suggestions from librarians serving high school, college, and public library patrons, who had noted a considerable number of requests for critical material on short story writers. Although major short story writers are covered in such Gale series as *Contemporary Literary Criticism (CLC)*, *Twentieth-Century Literary Criticism (TCLC)*, *Nineteenth-Century Literature Criticism (NCLC)*, and *Literature Criticism from 1400 to 1800 (LC)*, librarians perceived the need for a series devoted solely to writers of the short story genre.

Coverage

SSC is designed to serve as an introduction to major short story writers of all eras and nationalities. Since these authors have inspired a great deal of relevant critical material, *SSC* is necessarily selective, and the editors have chosen the most important published criticism to aid readers and students in their research.

Approximately eight to ten authors are included in each volume, and each entry presents a historical survey of the critical response to that author's work. The length of an entry is intended to reflect the amount of critical attention the author has received from critics writing in English and from foreign critics in translation. Every attempt has been made to identify and include excerpts from the most significant essays on each author's work. In order to provide these important critical pieces, the editors sometimes reprint essays that have appeared elsewhere in Gale's Literary Criticism Series. Such duplication, however, never exceeds twenty percent of an *SSC* volume.

Organization

An *SSC* author entry consists of the following elements:

- The **Author Heading** cites the name under which the author most commonly wrote, followed by birth and death dates. If the author wrote consistently under a pseudonym, the pseudonym will be listed in the author heading and the author's actual name given in parentheses on the first line of the biographical and critical introduction.

- The **Biographical and Critical Introduction** contains background information designed to introduce a reader to the author and the critical debates surrounding his or her work.

- A **Portrait of the Author** is included when available. Many entries also contain illustrations of materials pertinent to an author's career, including holographs of manuscript pages, title pages, dust jackets, letters, or representations of important people, places, and events in the author's life.

- The list of **Principal Works** is chronological by date of first publication and lists the most important works by the author. The first section comprises short story collections, novellas, and novella collections. The second section gives information on other major works by the author. For foreign authors, the editors have provided original foreign-language publication information and have selected what are considered the best and most complete English-language editions of their works.

■ **Criticism** is arranged chronologically in each author entry to provide a useful perspective on changes in critical evaluation over the years. All short story, novella, and collection titles by the author featured in the entry are printed in boldface type to enable a reader to ascertain without difficulty the works discussed. Also for purposes of easier identification, the critic's name and the publication date of the essay are given at the beginning of each piece of criticism. Unsigned criticism is preceded by the title of the journal in which it appeared.

■ Critical essays are prefaced with **Explanatory Notes** as an additional aid to students and readers using *SSC*. An explanatory note may provide useful information of several types, including: the reputation of the critic, the intent or scope of the critical essay, and the orientation of the criticism (biographical, psychoanalytic, structuralist, etc.).

■ A complete **Bibliographical Citation,** designed to help the interested reader locate the original essay or book, precedes each piece of criticism.

■ The **Further Reading List** appearing at the end of each author entry suggests additional materials on the author. In some cases it includes essays for which the editors could not obtain reprint rights. Boxed material following the further reading list provides references to other biographical and critical sources on the author in series published by Gale.

Beginning with volume six, *SSC* contains two additional features designed to enhance the reader's understanding of short fiction writers and their works:

■ Each *SSC* entry now includes, when available, **Comments by the Author** that illuminate his or her own works or the short story genre in general. These statements are set within boxes or bold rules to distinguish them from the criticism.

■ A **Select Bibliography of General Sources on Short Fiction** is included as an appendix. This listing of materials for further research provides readers with a selection of the best available general studies of the short story genre.

Other Features

A **Cumulative Author Index** lists all the authors who have appeared in *SSC, CLC, TCLC, NCLC, LC,* and *Classical and Medieval Literature Criticism (CMLC),* as well as cross-references to other Gale series. Users will welcome this cumulated index as a useful tool for locating an author within the Literary Criticism Series.

A **Cumulative Nationality Index** lists all authors featured in *SSC* by nationality, followed by the number of the *SSC* volume in which their entry appears.

A **Cumulative Title Index** lists in alphabetical order all short story, novella, and collection titles contained in the *SSC* series. Titles of short story collections, separately published novellas, and novella collections are printed in italics, while titles of individual short stories are printed in roman type with quotation marks.

Each title is followed by the author's name and corresponding volume and page numbers where commentary on the work is located. English-language translations of original foreign-language titles are cross-referenced to the foreign titles so that all references to discussion of a work are combined in one listing.

Citing *Short Story Criticism*

When writing papers, students who quote directly from any volume in the Literary Criticism Series may use the following general forms to footnote reprinted criticism. The first example pertains to material drawn from periodicals, the second to material reprinted from books:

[1]Henry James, Jr., "Honoré de Balzac," *The Galaxy 20* (December 1875), 814-36; excerpted and reprinted in *Short Story Criticism,* Vol. 5, ed. Thomas Votteler (Detroit: Gale Research, 1990), pp. 8-11.

[2]F. R. Leavis, *D. H. Lawrence: Novelist* (Alfred A. Knopf, 1956); excerpted and reprinted in *Short Story Criticism,* Vol. 4, ed. Thomas Votteler (Detroit: Gale Research, 1990), pp. 202-06.

Comments

Readers who wish to suggest authors to appear in future volumes, or who have other suggestions, are invited to contact the editors by writing to Gale Research Inc., Literary Criticism Division, 835 Penobscot Building, Detroit, MI 48226-4094.

Acknowledgments

The editors wish to thank the copyright holders of the excerpted criticism included in this volume and the permissions managers of many book and magazine publishing companies for assisting us in securing reproduction rights. We are also grateful to the staffs of the Detroit Public Library, the Library of Congress, the University of Detroit Mercy Library, Wayne State University Purdy/Kresge Library Complex, and the University of Michigan Libraries for making their resources available to us. Following is a list of the copyright holders who have granted us permission to reproduce material in this volume of *SC*. Every effort has been made to trace copyright, but if omissions have been made, please let us know.

COPYRIGHTED EXCERPTS IN *SSC*, VOLUME 24, WERE REPRODUCED FROM THE FOLLOWING PERIODICALS:

American Book Review, July, 1983. © 1983 by The American Book Review. Reprinted by permission of the publisher.—*Analog Science Fiction/Science Fact,* v. XCIX, October, 1979 for a review of 'Fireship' by Anthony R. Lewis. Copyright © 1979 by the Condé Nast Publications, Inc. Reprinted by permission of the author.—*Ariel: A Review of International English Literature,* v. 167, July, 1985 for "The Pegasus Symbol in the Childhood Stories of Sinclair Ross" by Karen Bishop. Copyright © 1985 The Board of Governors, The University of Calgary. Reproduced by permission of the publisher and the author.—*Arizona Quarterly,* v. 24, Spring, 1968 for "The Short Stories of Machado de Assis" by John Nist. Copyright © 1968 by Arizona Quarterly. Reproduced by permission of the publisher and the Literary Estate of John Nist.—*Book World—The Washington Post,* v. XXXVI, April 28, 1996. © 1996, Washington Post Book World Service/Washington Post Writers Group. Reproduced with permission.—*Books Abroad,* v. 40, Winter, 1966. Copyright 1966 by the University of Oklahoma Press. Reproduced by permission.—*Canadian Literature,* v. 47, 1971 for "No Other Way: Sinclair Ross's Stories and Novels" by Sandra Djwa. Reproduced by permission of the author.—*Canadian Literature,* n. 94, Autumn, 1982 for "The Case of Ross's Mysterious Barn" by F. H. Whitman.—*Chicago Tribune,* September 3, 1989 for "Tales of Broken Love" by Catherine Petroski. © copyright 1989, Chicago Tribune Company. All rights reserved. Reprinted by permission of the author.—*CLA Journal,* v. XXVII, December, 1983. Copyright, 1983 by The College Language Association. Used by permission of The College Language Association.—*The Commonweal,* v. LXVII, October 25, 1957. Copyright © 1957, renewed 1985 Commonweal Publishing Co., Inc. Reproduced by permission of Commonweal Foundation.—*Critique,* v. XXVI, Spring, 1985. Copyright © 1985 Helen Dwight Reid Educational Foundation. Reproduced by permission of the Helen Dwight Reid Educational Foundation, published by Heldref Publications, 1319 18th Street, NW, Washington, DC 20036-1802.—*Esquire,* v. LXXXI, April, 1974 for "Milan Kundera, The Joker" by Philip Roth. Copyright © 1974, Esquire Associates. Reproduced by permission of The Wylie Agency, Inc.—*The Explicator,* v. 41, Fall, 1982; v. 46, Winter, 1988. Copyright 1982, 1988 by Helen Dwight Reid Educational Foundation. Both reproduced with permission of the Helen Dwight Reid Educational Foundation, published by Heldref Publications, 1319 18th Street, NW, Washington, DC 20036-1802.—*Fantasy Review,* v. 7, December, 1984 for "Second Rate Vinge" by Carolyn Wendell. Copyright © 1984 by the author. Reprinted by permission of the author.—*The Georgia Review,* v. XXI, Spring, 1967; v. XXVII, Fall, 1973; v. XLIV, Spring-Summer, 1990. Copyright, 1967, 1973, 1990, by the University of Georgia. All reproduced by permission.—*Hispania,* v. XLVIII, March, 1965 for "Machado de Assis: Short Story Craftsman" by Donald M. Decker; v. XLIX, December, 1966 for "Love and the 'Causa Secreta' in the Tales of Machado de Assis" by Carmelo Virgillo. © 1965, 1966 The American Association of Teachers of Spanish and Portuguese, Inc. Both reproduced by permission of the publisher and the respective authors.—*Hispanic Journal,* v. 8, Fall, 1986. Reproduced by permission.—*The Hudson Review,* v. XXXIII, Summer, 1979. Copyright © 1979 by The Hudson Review, Inc. Reprinted by permission of the publisher./ v. III, Winter, 1951. Copyright © 1951, renewed 1971 by The Hudson Review, Inc. Reproduced by permission.—*Index on Censorship,* v. 4, Winter, 1975. Copyright Writers & Scholars International Ltd. 1975. Reproduced by permission.—*Kentucky Romance Quarterly,* v. XVIII, 1971. Copyright © 1971 Helen Dwight Reid Educational Foundation. Reproduced with permission of the Helen Dwight Reid Educational Foundation, published by Heldref Publications, 1319 18th Street, NW, Washington, DC 20036-1802.—*Kirkus*

COPYRIGHTED EXCERPTS IN *SSC*, VOLUME 24, WERE REPRODUCED FROM THE FOLLOWING BOOKS:

PHOTOGRAPHS AND ILLUSTRATIONS APPEARING IN *SSC*, VOLUME 24, WERE RECEIVED FROM THE FOLLOWING SOURCES:

Alice Adams
1926-

(Full name Alice Boyd Adams) American short story writer and novelist.

INTRODUCTION

In her fiction, Adams tends to focus upon well-educated, upper middle-class female professionals whose lives undergo transformations during their search for happiness and independence. Anne Tyler has characterized these heroines as "perceptive . . . intelligent and a bit world-weary." Adams has stated in an interview with Neil Feineman that she prefers writing short fiction to novels, and several commentators have observed that her talents are best suited to that genre. Reflecting on her economy of style, Robert Phillips has observed, "William Blake said, 'You never know what is enough unless you know what is more than enough.' Alice Adams knows the latter. She suppresses and condenses, allowing the reader to make vital connections between situation and character."

Biographical Information

An only child, Adams was born in Frcdcricksburg, Virginia, and raised by her parents in Chapel Hill, North Carolina, where her father taught Spanish at the University of North Carolina. Upon finishing high school at age fifteen, Adams entered Radcliffe College. She graduated in 1946 and worked for a New York publisher for less than a year. She married in 1947 and moved to Paris, where her husband was studying. The marriage was unhappy, but she returned with her husband to the United States in 1948. They settled in California, where he taught and continued his education. Adams worked on her writing and cared for their child, who was born in 1951. The couple eventually divorced in 1958. The following year she published her first story, "Winter Rain," in the magazine *Charm*. Adams struggled financially in San Francisco for the next few years while working several unsatisfying jobs. In 1966 her first novel, *Careless Love*, appeared in the United States, where it was poorly received, though it fared somewhat better in England the next year. Following the unremarkable performance of *Careless Love*, Adams wrote romances for the women's magazines *Cosmopolitan*, *Redbook*, and *McCall's*. In 1969 *The New Yorker* published "Gift of Grass," signalling Adams's inaugural appearance in a literary journal. "Gift of Grass" also became her first story to receive the O. Henry Prize, an esteemed annual award given to exceptional works of short fiction. Adams continued to garner recognition for her short stories, which continued to appear in magazines and journals. Many of these were gathered in the 1979 collection *Beautiful Girl*. Two more novels by Adams had also been published by the time *Beautiful Girl* was published, confirming her vocation as a

writer, despite the mixed reviews that the books received. Her 1975 novel *Families and Survivors* earned a nomination for a National Book Critics Circle Award, and the following year she received a grant from the National Endowment for the Arts. In 1978 Adams secured a Guggenheim Memorial Fellowship, and in 1982 she received the O. Henry Special Award for Continuing Achievement, an honor shared only by Joyce Carol Oates and John Updike. She continues to live in San Francisco and occasionally teaches at Stanford University and the University of California at Davis and at Berkeley.

Major Works of Short Fiction

Adams's stories often are defined by the motifs of love, loss, longing, and insecurity. In "A Pale and Perfectly Oval Moon," Adams tells of a man who becomes fully aware of his love for his deceased first wife only after he has begun a comfortable second marriage. The troubled sixteen-year-old protagonist of "Gift of Grass" secretly leaves two marijuana joints for her distraught stepfather as a form of consolation. "Roses, Rhododendron" contrasts the idealized outward appearance of a family with the actual dysfunctional state of their relations. The stories of

Return Trips, like earlier narratives such as "Beautiful Girl," revolve around individuals trying to come to terms with their past or nostalgically recalling momentous events or relationships in their lives. In the collection *To See You Again* Adams depicts older characters coping with change and pursuing paths of self-discovery. Some other common themes in Adams's fiction include the demands and value of lifelong friendships and the difficulty of sustaining romantic relationships.

Critical Reception

While Adams has written several novels, she began her career publishing short stories, and it is her story collections that have consistently earned her praise. A highly skilled writer whose craftsmanship is widely recognized, Adams has a manner that has been likened to that of a painter. As Linda Pastan stated in a review of *To See You Again*, "Like a watercolorist, she is skilled in rapidly and economically landscaping her world." Beverly Lowry, writing about *Return Trips*, also likened Adams to a watercolor painter whose "every brush stroke must be perfect" and whose "hand is lightning fast and brilliant." While acknowledging the virtues of Adams's best fiction, reviewers have commented that many of her stories share a vague similarity that renders them monotonous. Adams tends to write about a certain type of woman, with familiar settings and subjects, and in a consistent style. In addition, others have noted that some stories lack resolution or concluding insight. Despite these perceived shortcomings, Adams has earned a reputation as an authority on contemporary American women. Barbara A. Herman has summed her artistic aims: "With a sharp eye and a sympathetic voice, Adams writes about woman's coming of age in contemporary society—discovering her identity, working out her social and personal relationships, and finding a rewarding occupation. For her heroines, . . . the 'they married and lived happily ever after' ending will not suffice. Adams believes that the contemporary woman has more, or at least different, criteria for a meaningful life."

PRINCIPAL WORKS

Short Fiction

Beautiful Girl 1979
To See You Again 1982
Return Trips 1985
After You've Gone 1989

Other Major Works

Careless Love (novel) 1966
Families and Survivors (novel) 1975
Listening to Billie (novel) 1978
Rich Rewards (novel) 1980
Superior Women (novel) 1984

Second Chances (novel) 1988
Mexico: Some Travels and Some Travelers There (nonfiction) 1990
"The American Short Story in the Cybernetic Age" (essay) 1991; published in *Journal of the Short Story in English*, Vol. 17
Caroline's Daughters (novel) 1991

CRITICISM

James N. Baker (essay date 1979)

SOURCE: "Delicate Balance," in *Newsweek,* Vol. XCIII, No. 2, January 8, 1979, pp. 61-2.

[*In the following review of* Beautiful Girl, *Baker declares Adams's stories "elegant" and "artfully simple."*]

Alice Adams is something of an anachronism.

Instead of trying to dazzle us with verbal acrobatics or hammering away at ugly truths about society in the manner of many of her contemporaries, she writes elegant short stories that recall such past masters of the form as Flannery O'Connor and Katherine Mansfield. Like them, she offers fleeting, melancholy glimpses of ordinary people made extraordinary by her perception.

[The stories in *Beautiful Girl*] are old-fashioned stories, artfully simple in structure, rich in precise language and consistently moving in their examination of imperfect human relationships.

Adams puts surprising nuances into fairly standard conflicts. In **"A Pale and Perfectly Oval Moon,"** Van, cozily ensconced in a second marriage to "simply very nice" Joan, secretly mourns the death of his bitchy first wife. "Had she been shrewish on purpose so that he would miss her less?" Her most striking stories, however, tell of more offbeat relationships in which help comes unexpectedly. A disturbed teenager in **"Gift of Grass"** senses for the first time her inattentive stepfather's chronic despair and charitably hides two joints of marijuana in his desk. In the title story, a once-rejected suitor turns up in time to save the cause of his old torment—a former beauty—from the ravages of middle-age alcoholism.

Two stories—the collection's best—flicker between past and present. Two Southern brothers in **"The Swastika on Our Door,"** once so proud of their racism, intellectual superiority and self-imposed isolation at Harvard, gradually grow apart: one turns gregarious and prospers, but is forced to stand helplessly by while the other remains ascetic and dies young. In the enchanting **"Roses, Rhododendron,"** the narrator recalls how as a fatherless little girl in the 1930s she idealized a friend's family. One night, she witnessed a sudden, violent quarrel at their dinner table: "That exposed depth of terrible emotions might have suggested to me that the Farrs were not quite as I had imagined them, not the impeccable family in my mind—but it did not. I was simply and terribly—and selfishly—upset." This story about the mysteries of little girlhood—and their solutions in later life—is as stirring as the best work of Mansfield.

Alice Adams's heroines spend enormous energy looking for good men. At worst, this searching unfolds in an uninspired chronology of major loves, minor loves, and time spent with friends. At best . . . the passion is complicated with stiff doses of wisdom and affection. More is at stake than romance.

Rhonda Brammer, in a review of To See You Again, *Saturday Review (New York), March, 1982.*

Laurie Stone (essay date 1979)

SOURCE: "Short Circuits," in *The Village Voice,* Vol. XXIV, No. 14, April 2, 1979, p. 87.

[*In the following review of* Beautiful Girl, *Stone finds Adams's treatment of physical appearance refreshing, but she judges the stories trite.*]

People tend not to write about what they don't like or wish did not exist—once it was blacks, homosexuals, and strong women. The fat and slovenly are the new subversives in the culture of the fit, threatening to the *status quo* ideal, undifferentiated and almost invisibilized in our art. When is the last time you read a story about a fat person?

Fat, plump, or strange-looking characters appear with arresting frequency in the stories Alice Adams has collected in *Beautiful Girl* Adams thinks that beauty—or the lack of it—is a fundamental matter. The fat, plain, and physically unacceptable are not just neutrally other than the beautiful and thin; they are a judged and exiled population apart, Adams puts the Darwinism back in "fitness."

To Adams, appearance is destiny, but not always the predictable one. Ardis Bascombe of the title story has purposely traded her extraordinary good looks and promise for alcohol. Twenty years after her southern belle prime, we see her splendidly defy the man who would claim and recover her with the assertion that she is *still* a "beautiful girl."

In Adams's stories, people with undesirable faces and bodies turn out sometimes to be desirable. In **"A Jealous Husband,"** Martha Macmillan, whose "body ballooned out above short legs"—"the thalidomide kid" is what she sometimes calls herself—manages to have an affair that utterly unhinges her "fairly funny-looking" husband.

Fatness is not one deviation in Adams but a spectrum: a cushion from painful feelings, or an insensitive battering force, or a sign of largess, license, and freedom. Extreme thinness can be equally burdensome. In the fine story, **"The Swastika on Our Door,"** the brothers, "fat Roger" and "skinny tortured Richard," "two southern 4-F's in giddy wartime Cambridge," are sentenced by their bodies to a "violent loneliness" and a ludicrously inappropriate "marriage." Each brother defines the other, and they cannot survive apart. Fatness per se is dependent for its definition on the concept of thinness. Adams dramatizes our difficulty in really grasping the full range of human experience without freaks and borderline freaks.

Adams is at her best—surprising and clarifying—in **"Beautiful Girl," "Roses Rhododendron,"** and **"The Swastika on Our Door."** Her writing is especially vivid from the child's perspective or from the view of a recurrent type of nonfreakish woman. She grew up in the South, she is somewhat edgy and adrift, she has an eye for sensual detail and a humane and generous nature. Too generous, perhaps. Adams's narrators tend to get sappy from time to time, especially when dealing with high bathos-factor subjects like nostalgia and fat people or with romance.

The love stories **"Ripped Off," "Flights,"** and **"Home Is Where"** do not work at all for me. From story to story, the characters are reading the same books: *Moby Dick* and Jane Austen. Referring to the first moment of intimate connection, one narrator says, without irony, "He had been recognized." The endings are pat and sentimental. The women act like "women" (insecure, vulnerable); the men act like "men" (fearful of the "women," aloof). I don't think love has to be that embarrassing to observe, but if Adams, a generally intelligent and innovative writer, can't animate the romance, maybe it's time she gave it a rest.

Dean Flower (essay date 1979)

SOURCE: "Picking Up the Pieces," in *The Hudson Review,* Vol. XXXII, No. 2, Summer, 1979, pp. 293-307.

[*In the following excerpt, Flower provides a mixed assessment of* Beautiful Girl.]

[Adams] has been represented in every O. Henry Award collection for the last eight years, and her three novels (most recently, *Listening to Billie* last year) have received much praise, but to my mind her fiction fails—despite its numerous attractions—to offer a sufficiently serious criticism of the worlds she knows so well. Adams moves easily from Chapel Hill to New England to San Francisco, usually in the society of the rich: "Ardis Bascomb," the title story begins, "the tobacco heiress, who twenty years ago was a North Carolina beauty queen, is now sitting in the kitchen of her San Francisco house, getting drunk."

Adam's favorite strategy is to place an interesting woman, frequently a beautiful one marred by fat or scars or terminal illness or age, at the center of her stage, and then supply her with admires: a handsome, successful, dullish lover; a teenager disturbed but attracted by her womanly energy; an unfaithful husband who regrets their lost love; an inhibited stranger; an old college roommate; an uncomprehending foreigner. The strategy is dangerous in its tendency to endorse the already vigorous narcissism of these women. Yet Adams is clearly fascinated by the ways people find to imagine themselves, or their lovers, or their parents, as strangers do. And frequently too the result is love deflected toward strangers.

In **"For Good"** a twelve-year-old girl goes to a party with her father and stepmother, and learns that the hostess was once his mistress. The girl is drawn to this distressed woman far more deeply than to her own mother. When the woman drunkenly embraces a guest and says, "Ah, my long-lost love, why couldn't everything last?", the girl hears real desperation in this stagy remark. It's the stranger, seldom the parent or spouse, who releases the deeper emotions of Adams' characters. The oddly matched couple in **"A Jealous Husband"** restore their shaky relationship, and their own self-esteem, when she drifts into an affair with a black man. Jealousy, the husband learns, can be both erotic and narcotic. The beautiful rich woman in **"Flights"** has been scarred in the car accident that killed her previous husband; now she's vacationing with her next (a young, aggressive television producer) on the Hawaiian island of Kauai. She would be another sulky-glamorous American bitch if it weren't for the way we see her, through the dazzled eyes of a young, withdrawn resort-keeper. He's a perfect stranger who understands her inmost thoughts, intuits her fears, and suffers her pain; moreover, she understands him instantly, and deeply. Why is it that only strangers can be so perfect? A much better story, **"Winter Rain,"** describes the maturing of a young woman spending a year in Paris. She rents from a nasty old phoney-elegant Madame who frustratingly refuses to be the friend or surrogate mother the girl wishes for. Unwittingly, Madame confirms and strengthens the girl's identity. There should be more strangers like this in Adams' world.

At their best these stories explore complex relationships in a quick, deceptively offhand manner. They tend to begin with a tense problem (a wife dying, a divorce impending, a moment of wrath, an anxious move to a new place) and unravel gradually, without much climax except a muted sense of recovered balance and diminished expectation. What's too often missing is a final criticism. The woman in **"Home Is Where"** has a splendid summer romance when she returns to North Carolina to decide about a divorce; but the romance ends, the man goes off to become famous, she marries someone else. One feels neither gladness nor sorrow in such conclusions, but rather an implicit appeal of stylish melancholy: "And later I married the other man, and later still I almost got used to being happy." In **"A Pale and Perfectly Oval Moon"** the weak husband remembers his complex and difficult wife as "the most remarkable and interesting woman I've ever known." But she's dead now, and he never could convince her in life. Alas, I suppose. These closures seem mostly attempts at elegant gesture. I prefer the ending of **"Beautiful Girl"** where the former love murmurs consolingly in the drunken

woman's ear, "I want you to be my beautiful girl again," and she raises her head abruptly: "'I am a beautiful girl,' she rasps out, furiously."

The theme of love in Adams's fiction:

Nobody writes better about falling in love than Alice Adams. The protagonists of her stories, almost always women, often professional women—lawyers, art historians, illustrators, journalists—with a number of years and a good deal of experience behind them, know exactly what is about to happen: no nitwits, never victims or too gaga, they have been there before. They fall with eyes open, knowing full well that the man in question might be inappropriate—married or too self-involved ever to commit totally. Such women think they should know better. They do know better. That is the glory of an Adams heroine, she is that smart and still goes on. "Ah," she says to herself, sighing, "this again: *love*." And plunges in.

*Beverly Lowry, "Women Who Do Know Better,"
in* The New York Times Book Review,
September 1, 1985.

Alice Adams with Neil Feineman (interview date 1980)

SOURCE: "An Interview with Alice Adams," in *Story-Quarterly*, No. 11, 1980, pp. 27-37.

[*Below, Adams discusses the style, themes, and characters of her fiction.*]

[Feineman]: *I had loved Families and Survivors so much that I couldn't even finish Listening to Billie when it came out. But in rereading it, I found it a much better book than Families and Survivors.*

[Adams]: I think it is a better book, a more difficult book. As you just said, it's not instantly appealing. It was a terribly hard book to write.

In it, you define poetry as, among other things, an overreaction to experience. Does this describe your own writing as well?

Yes, I suppose the quote was more personal than a definition of poetry. All my life—and I suppose this is true of most writers—I've been accused of overreacting. People say calm down, for heaven's sake, take it easy. But I think if I did that, if I were tranquilized, I wouldn't write.

And another thing about *Listening to Billie*: I had become so bored about pretending to write about a painter when I really know nothing about painting and a great deal about writing. That's why I very consciously made Eliza a poet, and because I see an affinity between poetry and the short story and thought I could cope with Eliza's writing poetry. It would be a lot like my writing short stories.

But it would be too much to make her a short story writer?

Yes, I think so. But a lot of the things that I described Eliza doing were straight out of my own literary experiences.

You seem to be a particularly autobiographical writer, especially in the short stories like "Roses, Rhododendron," the one about Harriet. . . .

Yes, the one about the girl from the North who moves down from the South. I did a curious thing there that seemed to work out. I decided to try to write about myself and my family from the point of view of an outsider.

It seemed that you were Harriet.

Well, yes. When my father died, an old friend of mine from there wrote such a touching, incredible letter that I thought how strangely and differently she sees us from how it felt to be one of us. And that's how the story came about.

To get back to the quote about overreaction, I wouldn't call you an epic writer; you seem to take something that's far from momentous and then invest it with a great deal of importance.

It's probably not an investiture at all; I probably experienced it that way. It may not be momentous to you, but it was to me.

Is that because you're overreacting to experience?

Probably. By the way, this morning, my horoscope said I should give extremely brief answers to any questions that come my way. (*Laughter*)

You seem to be a person who can't get away from the South. In Families and Survivors, you write that these people have lived almost all their adult lives in California, yet still feel that the South is their home.

I think that's true. I've been here for so long, but I still feel transplanted. Last winter, however, I went back to the South for the first time in about twenty years and that was a rather horrifying experience. I almost instantly realized why I had left. I couldn't stand it there; it was horrible; I couldn't wait to leave. I used to think that everyone I knew there was stupid and a racial bigot and I found out I was at least half right. I couldn't wait to get out the first time and I couldn't wait to get out then.

Could we talk now about "A Pale and Perfectly Oval Moon"?

It's interesting that you pick that story. To me, one of the most significant things about it is that I couldn't sell it anywhere. It was sent to every magazine you can think of, including some very small reviews, but no one bought it. I think people can't bear to consider cancer; it scares them. And I also think there's the older woman problem.

An editor with whom I had had otherwise good experience wrote me a rejection letter that said she thought it was well-written but that Joan was more interesting than Penelope. I don't know if you remember Joan; she was the husband's girl friend and later his wife and she's not the least bit interesting—she's just a pusher who's not bright at all—so that made me feel rather defeated in that I hadn't got the story across.

I especially like the way that Penelope's love triumphs; even though she is dead, she still retains that hold over her husband's imagination.

Of course Penelope was a fantasy—that is, what one would like to think one would do. It was a form of exorcism also. I like the story; it's one of my favorites.

Which other ones do you like?

I don't know. I usually like them a lot when I finish them. I think I like **"Verlie"** a great deal—it only took me twenty years to write. I worked so hard on that story; if you think about it, there are so many ways you can go wrong with it. You can sentimentalize her in a very unfair and quite gross way and I may have done that the first few times. But I kept coming back to it and writing version after version that I knew wasn't right so I was very pleased when I finally did get it right. Another thing that happened was that I couldn't bear to have the story end badly because I was so deeply fond of her—and I couldn't resist using her true name.

Did she read it?

Oh no, she's been dead for many years. Also, she couldn't read.

How did you resolve the ending?

I filched a plot from Joyce Carol Oates. I don't know if you remember the story, but at the very end it goes back to the middle and she did that in one of her stories, which I thought was a terrific idea, especially for **"Verlie."**

You should date the stories in your anthology.

I think so, too, but quarrel with Alfred Knopf, not me. It would be interesting to know and, frankly, I can't remember when I wrote each. I've a rotten memory for that kind of thing.

Was "Verlie" written before the other two Todd stories?

Yes, it was.

It was the best of the three, I think.

I think so too. But I like **"Alternatives,"** the one that encompasses so many years. It begins in the thirties.

Is Jessica still alive in that one?

Yes.

You killed Jessica off very casually.

Well, oh, yes, I think in a parenthesis.

Is "Beautiful Girl" your favorite?

No, I like it, but it isn't my favorite.

I thought it was, because of the title.

No, someone at Knopf picked it out because they felt it was the most dramatic phrase. I do like it, though. It is different in that it is more bitter and more angry than most of the stories.

It does have a positive and interesting mother-daughter relationship.

There are a lot of those in my work. It must be a wish fantasy on my part, because I didn't enjoy a positive relationship with my mother and never have had a daughter.

"The Swastika on the Door" is another story that covers an extended number of years.

I like that story very much. It was important to me for two reasons. It was the first story that I outlined in a particular way that I've been doing ever since and it was also the first story I sold to *The New Yorker,* which, for me, was an important thing. And I had an agent at the time who was an absolute jackass and who was not interested in the least in any story he could not sell to *Redbook,* so I practically bent his arm back and said you must send this story to *The New Yorker*; I don't care if you are sure they won't buy it. I just want them to see it. Anyway, they bought it, which made me very happy.

And the outline is interesting in that it is written in five acts, as are a lot of my stories. It begins—let me go backwards. A long time ago in Chapel Hill, I took a summer course with a creative writing teacher named Phillips Russell who was doubly suspect. One, he was middle-aged—which probably means about ten years younger than I am today—and two, he was a friend of my parents, so what could he know? He thought that stories were either three or five acts and the formula for the five acts was ABDCE: action, background, development, climax, ending.

Is that an original theory?

I really don't know. But I'm doing my best to promote it. . . . In any case, I had a very strong feeling about the relationship between those two men. I knew there was a good story there somewhere and it came to me that the five-act formula would be a good one to apply to two men who had been friends—in the story I made them brothers—for a very long period of time, which is something I still like to do. I think my stories often cover a longer time span than classical stories do.

The parentheses also are distinctive

Yes, that's something I'd better stop doing. I think they were somewhat overdone in *Families and Survivors.* A wicked person could do an awfully easy parody of that.

It does seem like a case where style overwhelms content. And why Families and Survivors *seems like a better book than* Listening To Billie *at first.*

Well, it's simpler; there's less there in *Families and Survivors. Families and Survivors* now seems to me a rather simple-minded piece of social history.

Can we get back to the formula?

Yes. Action, background, development, climax, ending. The action begins with the woman finding the snapshot in San Francisco in the present and then goes backwards to Harvard in the forties and then it goes forward and they meet Ellen.

Ellen is great.

I don't know where she came from.

Do your characters become real enough to you to the point that they pop into your mind later on? Does Ellen, for instance, ever let you know that she's still in the institution and then tempt you to write another story about her?

Yes, they pop in; but no, I don't want to write about them again. There are certain prototypical figures that I've written about quite a lot. The narrator in **"Roses, Rhododendron,"** for example, is actually quite a lot like Kate in *Families and Survivors.* I know who that is and I do write about her often.

Does she know who she is?

Yes.

Are you in close contact with her?

Oh, yes.

What does she think?

She's rather flattered. The affection and the admiration seem obvious.

Are you Eliza?

To a degree. But I was trying to write about someone who is much more interesting and talented than I am. She's certainly more independent.

Smith and Daria are interesting characters.

Smith changed a great deal in the writing of the book. At first I just thought he was an archtypical, sexless, right-wing reactionary, but as the book went on, I became sym-

pathetic and finally very fond of him. And Daria is the
madwoman in the attic. I love the idea of her giving the
money away.

*It reminded me too much of my roommates in college who
became Hari Krishnas.*

I could see where it would be alarming if your sister or
wife actually gave away the money. And I would have
been terribly upset if my son had become a Hari Krishna.
But I love the idea.

*Judging from your writing, you seem to be a person who
is able to recapture the past and trace one incident's
ramifications throughout an entire lifetime.*

I remember everything that ever happened to me and I can
bear grudges for a very long time.

Do you read and like short stories?

I adore them. I especially like Joyce Carol Oates, V.S.
Pritchett, John Cheever, Laurie Colwin; I don't know—
there are so many.

*Where do you fit among them? Where do you feel your
place in literature is?*

I don't know. I don't think of my having a place in
American literature. I don't think I'm as good as they are,
but I also don't think it's important. After all, I try.

When did you start to write?

I was one of those annoying kids who wrote poetry at
four. I came from the kind of intellectual background that
made writing seem like the most praiseworthy thing to do,
so there was never anything else. My mother wanted to be
a writer and was a failed one; she was depressed, unhappy, and peripherally involved with the literary world. She
wrote book reviews for a small newspaper. Jessica, in the
Todd stories, is rather like my mother; those stories are as
close to home as I've come, I think. Aside from the guilt
and the mourning, you know, there is a real freedom for
a writer when his or her parents die you don't have to
worry anymore about hurting their feelings or embarrassing them.

Anyway, Chapel Hill was a literary place and, I gather,
still is. My son recently had to go back on a legal errand
for me and he told me that everyone there was writing a
book. So wanting to be a writer was not unexpected.

In any case, I stopped writing poetry when I went to Radcliffe. The poems were really terrible and the poetry course
I had come up there to take conflicted with some science
requirement, so I ended up taking a short story writing
class. One day the teacher called me up to his desk and
asked me what else I could do. When I told him I had never
showed the slightest talent for anything else, my writing
teacher said, "Miss Adams, you're a very nice girl. Why
don't you forget about this writing and go get married."

Unfortunately, I came close to taking his advice. After
graduation, I went to New York and worked briefly—
three months, I think—in publishing. I basically pooped
off, took long week-ends, and the like. I had this idea that
my simple presence there was sufficient.

Then I went back to Cambridge, got married, took odd
jobs to put my husband through graduate school, wrote
without taking myself seriously, had a son, got divorced,
and, after that, things started picking up slowly. I was a
rather late-developing writer: my first novel wasn't published until I was forty and I have only been able to make
my living as a writer for the last ten years or so.

I am expecting a parenthesis here to tell me how it ends.

You know . . . I started doing them—*parentheses*—for
fun and it gave me such a sense of power and control that
I couldn't stop. It established my authority and let me be
terrifically manipulative, and it gave the reader something
to look forward to. But I mostly did it for fun. And now
I must stop—no more parenthesis.

*What was that period like in-between the divorce and
getting published regularly?*

It was a very depressing period in terms of work. I felt
bleak, lonely, envious. I kept on writing, but it struck me
as an excessively neurotic thing to be doing—to be wasting
all that time on something I was not good at. I went to a
psychiatrist who told me that I should stop writing and
stay married, but I've always been a strong rebel and in
some recess of the mind, I must have thought I was good—
and known he was a fool—because I did keep writing.

I don't think it matters in the end what people tell writers;
they keep writing regardless, if they are supposed to be
writers. I have a very close friend, the editor William
Abrahams, who took me very seriously early on and behaved
as if I were a distinguished writer. There were also a few
other supportive people. Naturally, those were the ones I
chose to listen to. But it wasn't an easy period.

I remember when I published my first story, **"Winter
Rain,"** and I got divorced. I thought I would then get
published all the time, but it didn't work that way. Still,
my life improved; I gradually developed, sold a few stories,
and, six or seven years later, sold my first novel, *Careless
Love.* The reaction to it was disappointing; I was trying to
be funny and almost no reviewers laughed, except, oddly
enough, in England. So I got discouraged and went back
to the short story because I knew I was getting better at
that. I was published in *Redbook* and *The Atlantic,* as well
as *The New Yorker,* and was eventually ready to go back
to the novel.

I have a new novel coming out in September called *Rich
Rewards.* It takes place in San Francisco, but is a departure
for me because it takes place in one year and involves
politics and murder. The one I'm working on now is more
like *Families and Survivors* in that it begins in the 40's
and goes ahead. It will cover four friends and will be a lot

longer than my other books so it will take a lot longer to write. I am under no timetable and don't have a working title, but am excited by it.

During that time, I'll also be writing short stories; that's the form I love best. I don't outline novels anywhere near as carefully; they tend to get away from you and end up in quite unexpected places. Short stories don't take over in that way; there are not so many surprises. A long time ago, I began a story not knowing how it would end, but now I don't begin until I know where I'm going.

Besides, the short story is so much more rewarding. You get immediate gratification—a couple months' work and then a little wait and then it comes out and you get a lot of mail. And I'm not in the large-advance class for a novel; short stories are still more lucrative for me. But more than that, I consider them important and artistically fulfilling.

Why bother with novels, then?

You can say more in novels. Some ideas can't be compressed into a short story. In *Listening to Billie,* for example, there was a positive connection made between sexuality and political radicalism; radicals are sexy, reactionaries are sexless. I don't think I could have made that point in a short story.

When you get all that mail, are there a lot of manuscripts?

I try to avoid them. Once I saw an old college friend of mine who asked me to read her husband's manuscript. I hadn't seen him in twenty years and vaguely remembered him as a boring reactionary. He sent me an appalling short story, a hunting experience, that had NRA stamps all over it and did not send a self-addressed-stamped-envelope. I sent him back a letter telling him that all writers send self-addressed-stamped-envelopes and since most of us were pinko-Commie-pacifists, one must never put NRA stamps on our manuscripts.

Can you separate Alice Adams, the person, from Alice Adams the writer?

Less and less. I am, I would say, extremely motivated. I would like to write better and better short stories.

What about novels?

It's easier to publish novels, really. I don't worry at this point about whether or not a novel will be published. But whenever I write a short story, it's still a total gamble. I'm often surprised. I mean, I keep going back to **"A Pale and Perfectly Oval Moon,"** which I liked and was surprised that no one bought.

But I'm almost always writing on spec; no one calls me up and asks me to do anything. My editor from *The New Yorker* may call and say that they would like a new story, but that doesn't mean they will take what I send them. I get rejected all the time.

> **A shortcoming of Adams's short fiction:**
>
> Perhaps because she is used to the larger scope of the novel, Miss Adams seems sometimes to underestimate the possibilities of the short-story form. While deft and careful—her work has been represented in every O. Henry collection for the last eight years—her stories do not always dig deep enough into their subject to satisfy the interest their craftsmanship arouses. In **"Gift of Grass"** we see teen-age Cathy at a session with her unsympathetic and mercenary psychiatrist, then we follow her to Golden Gate Park where she stretches out on the grass with a joint and waits "for the melting of her despair." Now, we think, we'll find out what goes on inside her head—what is she thinking, fantasizing, remembering, wishing? Instead of telling us, Miss Adams just has her fall asleep. Of course, we know in a general sort of way what's bothering Cathy, but that's not because she's a vivid fictional character, it's because she's a recognizable type.
>
> Katha Pollitt, *"Good Ole Boys and Wistful Hippies," in* The New York Times Book Review, *January 14, 1979.*

So you have some of the same worries that a beginning writer has.

I don't have the same worries I had ten years ago but, sure, I have terrific worries. I worry about where the next short story is going to come from; I worry about if and where it's going to get published. I go through notebooks sometimes and occasionally I will rewrite an old story that was not right the first time.

How do you feel about that?

Fine. In fact, it seems like a very good thing for someone to do. Un-wasteful. A lot of writers, though, hit slumps—terrible slumps that become permanent states of decline. I worry about that, and consider myself lucky that I was a late starter.

In your books, many characters are on the outside, observing at the expense of acting. They're almost dispassionate in the sense that though life is swirling around them, they settle for observation rather than participation.

I think that's the stance of a writer.

What do you lose?

Well, I often wish I were more of a political activist, for example. But then, on the other hand, you take a writer like Grace Paley, who's so marvelous as a person and a writer. I truly wish she would be less politically active and would write more.

As you assemble more and more substantial a body of work, what do you consider your weaknesses?

I don't know. I used to think my plots were very weak, but now I am not so sure. I am not, I don't think, a self-conscious writer. I really don't know if I have a place in literature or what my strengths or weaknesses really are. . . .

I might know more in several months. I am going to teach a creative writing course for the first time. I've never done anything like it before and don't have a great love for the academic world, so I'm not sure I'll be there long. But I am going to give it a chance.

What are you going to tell your students?

I don't know. Something like: STOP SPEAKING TO YOUR PARENTS, DON'T GET MARRIED, NEVER HAVE ANY CHILDREN, AND WRITE!

Carolyn See (essay date 1982)

SOURCE: "23 Stories Form Necklace of Thought," in *Los Angeles Times,* April 13, 1982, Section V, p. 6.

[*In the following review of* To See You Again, *See praises Adams's stories as "hard and sharp and unbearably concrete."*]

The conventions for describing women short-story writers are almost as constricting as the form itself. "Wise and witty" are words used often (can you imagine "wise and witty" applied to a novel by Norman Mailer?); "Wise, witty, luminous, delicate." But just as the best women short-story writers work in unexplored realms, the words to describe their creations may not have been invented yet. (The Tlingit Indians had no word for lighter fluid.)

The jacket material describes Alice Adams as comparable to Flannery O'Connor and Katherine Mansfield, when indeed all Adams has in common with those writers is that she is also a woman and writes short stories.

It might be more productive to think of Alice Adams as comparable to Walter Cronkite, because you can believe what she says. Or to Albert Michelson, Einstein's predecessor, because of her experiments in motion, time and light, or to evangelist Terry Cole-Whittaker, because Adams insists—philosophically and intellectually—on the possibility of happiness for intelligent people. Or to Norman Mailer, because she'd knock him out in the first round.

[The stories in *To See You Again*] only pretend to be refined, or appear at first glance to fall into that category. Actually they are hard and sharp and unbearably concrete—a hammer on the carpenter's thumb. They are mostly about women, women at once "successful" and away from the center of things, preoccupied as they are with making nice dinners, accommodating decent enough husbands who usually drink too much, deciding to take "desperate" measures to keep those husbands, or choosing, like pragmatic fishermen, to hurl them back into the great trout stream of life.

Most of Adams' women are like most women, neither slave nor feminist, but something in between, taking life minute by minute, falling for an investor in a singles bar (because he—or in spite of the fact that he—describes himself as a gambler), going on with a company dinner even after her husband takes a little nap in his dessert plate, and paying some attention to sexuality. Whom are we attracted to, and why, and how does that, how should that, affect our lives?

Each of the 23 stories here is important and fine; as they progress, they make a necklace of thought. Timing is everything and nothing in our lives, Adams seems to be saying.

In **"By the Sea"** a young, not-dumb waitress makes what the reader may see as a big mistake. She passes up an opportunity to be loved by a very rich man—partly because he has a birthmark on his neck, partly because he's so nice she's repelled by him—that's not how men are supposed to be.

In **"A Wonderful Woman"** one of those wonderful women we all know and try to be has had to wait a full 60 years to be happy, to fall in love. She arrives alone at a hotel for a rendezvous and her lover appears to have stood her up. Will she be able to stand it? Can she—after a dull husband, a cruel lover a life of dutiful motherhood and virtue all around—stand not just another rejection, but another disappointment, another of life's dull slaps? But being "wonderful" carries its own rewards, Adams assures us, whether the one we love shows up or not.

The thin membrane that separates all of us from happiness—how it cuts us off, wraps us up, miraculously opens up so that we can step through into light—that is the subject of these stories. In **"Legends,"** a truculent woman sculptor waits to be interviewed, not as an artist, but as part of a legend. She and a (fairly) famous composer have had a long and much-chronicled affair. She hates to rehearse the same old facts, wishes "they" would ask about her own work.

We find that the reason she resists the old "legend" is because she believes her beloved composer really loved someone else all these years—her attachment, her obsession, her tenderness, her loyalty, may have been poor replacements for what her lover may have really wanted: that small blonde cutie who dumped him long ago. But—just one of a series of small, surprising, "happy" endings—the interviewer has wanted all along to talk about her work. "I had a marvelous time," the sculptress tells us.

It's not that the world isn't full of treacherous, gray-faced men who try to play good women off against each other, or fork-tongued Southern belles, or betraying dads who leave their homes and money to the last of the live-in stepmother instead of their bereft and unloved children. But for every traitor, Adams suggests, there are friends who have our interests at heart, cousins to cheer us up, husbands whose very infirmities may be loving bonds to hold their wives to them.

And beyond all that, each of us has a secret well of happiness that we may luck into, maybe when we have the courage to leave a relationship, like the woman who deserts the investment-gambler. Maybe when the very worst has already happened to us, and so our lives become paradoxically safe. Or maybe when we get lucky, the timing is right instead of wrong. At almost the end of this collection comes the companion piece to the luckless waitress who has made the wrong choice.

In **"At First Sight"** Paul, an unattractive little boy, falls madly in love with a blonde grown-up who is destined to become his stepmother, but not before she has (irrevocably?) wrecked his life. Paul holds a grudge, to put it mildly, against his pretentious, loveless childhood home, his philandering dad, the heartbreak and suicide that have almost destroyed him. But wait a minute! Time passes. Good people exist too; they even exert an influence. And Paul, cranky, orphaned, loveless, homosexual and ugly, has his chance at a happiness as blinding and authentic as his suffering has ever been.

Not very witty at all, these stories are "terrible as an army with banners," strong as Spencer Tracy in the old days, and glorious as the Fourth of July.

William Buchanan (essay date 1983)

SOURCE: A review of *To See You Again,* in *Studies in Short Fiction,* Vol. 20, Nos. 2-3, Spring-Summer, 1983, p. 143.

[*In the following review of* To See You Again, *Buchanan discusses common characteristics of Adams's stories and comments on comparisons of her writing with that of Flannery O'Connor and Katherine Mansfield.*]

[*To See You Again*] collects nineteen stories, a majority of which first appeared in the *New Yorker* and reflects the milieu of many of its readers: the educated, the talented, the well-to-do, the divorced, in their pursuit of pleasure, mostly extra-marital sex and cocktails. Most of them end on an affirmative note. Several are told in the present tense, with a hazy atmosphere where bits and pieces drift in and out of view, something approaching a stream of consciousness technique. Others (the majority) are told in a more straightforward manner and have a plot. Here are some that seem typical: An unhappily married woman substitutes for a semester teaching in a junior college, where she has a student "so beautiful [she] hardly dare look at him." He disappears the last day of class without saying good-bye. That night she sees an actor on TV who looks just like her student but twenty years older. She takes satisfaction in thinking that his beauty will pass into mere handsomeness. A talented but homely artist assumes people are interested in her mainly because of a celebrated love affair with a composer, one who actually ceased to be productive well before his death. She is made happy by a woman interviewer who shows real appreciation of her own work. A middle-aged woman, divorced, has an affair

with a lawyer in a similar situation. During their weekend at Las Vegas she discovers he is really counting on making money by gambling and depending on her help. She makes a hasty escape. An airline loses the luggage of a woman recently widowed and returning from a vacation. The luggage contained diaries she kept in the period following her husband's death. She decides she should not regret the loss; she must not cling to the past.

The blurb on the jacket suggests a comparison with Katherine Mansfield. This comparison seems apt. Both use mainly women protagonists, and their stories show a very feminine concern for the quality of relationships and moods. Understatement predominates, Mansfield being the subtler of the two. Ms. Adams's stories are told in a more casual, not to say sloppy, manner.

The blurb goes on to suggest a comparison with Flannery O'Connor. This comparison does *not* seem apt. There is nothing feminine about Ms. O'Connor's stories. In [*To See You Again*] there are no powerful, obsessed characters, no strong tension of moral dilemma. Ms. O'Connor presents the grotesque and the demonic in a way that strongly implies the glory of their opposites. Impersonal or complacent rationalists fare badly in Ms. O'Connor's fiction. None of those concerns are found in Ms. Adams's stories. We might say that whereas Ms. O'Connor shows us lost, violent souls, Ms. Adams gives us hollow ones, living quietly desperate lives, objects of her unsentimental affection.

Linda Pastan (essay date 1983)

SOURCE: A review of *To See You Again,* in *American Book Review,* July, 1983, p. 4.

[*Here, Pastan maintains that Adams's attention to character and detail enable her to skillfully reveal "the whole of an emotional life" in each story.*]

Though the titles of Alice Adams' books often sound like the names of popular songs, the books themselves are beautifully crafted tales of the complexities of modern life, particularly for women. It is difficult to publish a collection of short stories these days, and Alice Adams has paid her dues to the market place with some very good novels. But it seems to me that the short story is her true métier. Like a watercolorist, she is skilled in rapidly and economically landscaping her world. The layers of oil color, though not beyond her ability, seem less suited to her temperament.

To See You Again is a collection of nineteen stories whose protagonists are women, nearly all of whom live in or near San Francisco, though there are occasional forays into Mexico which seems here almost to be a suburb of San Francisco. In most of these, some precipitating event both frames the story and acts as a kind of window through which the whole of an emotional life can be observed. These events can be trivial: the loss of a suitcase, an unscheduled stop by an airplane near a character's home town, the glimpse of a woman across a restaurant who looks like some other woman, long forgotten. But in each case the event leads to a small epiphany, in which at least the possibility of change is opened.

In **"The Break In,"** for example, a woman and the man she is to marry must deal with the vandalizing of his beautiful house near Lake Tahoe.

> Watching him, looking up from time to time as she fails to concentrate on her book, Cynthia has a sudden and curious perception, which is: Roger had actually enjoyed everything about this break in—the dramatic suspense of the drive up, the speculations as to what they would find, wondering about who had perpetrated this misdeed. Even, looking back, she feels that he was slightly disappointed that it wasn't worse. He is the proud rescuer of his house, like a man who has restored his wife's honor.
>
> A few minutes later this view seems somewhat unfair— or not entirely true. But as it retreats from her mind another, simpler thought enters, a single sentence: I cannot marry Roger, or his house.

Such simple but crucial sentences enter the minds of many of Adams' characters. "It was not until I was in the taxi, heading home from the airport, and thinking with foolish pleasure about my check for twenty-five dollars, that I realized that my notebook was in the missing suitcase, along with the stained robe and the other things I didn't much care about. And in that moment of understanding that my notebook could be gone forever, I did not see how I could go on with my life."

It is interesting, however, that in the strongest of the stories, **"Snow"** and **"At the Beach,"** there is no such precipitating event. Instead, a group of characters is illuminated by almost casually interacting with each other. Nothing really happens in these stories, yet everything is revealed.

Alice Adams has a shrewd ear, as well as an accurate eye for the telling detail, the revealing though offhand remark. She is also skillful at using street names and descriptions of dress to do some of the work of character delineation. In fact small descriptive passages often are used to set up a whole mood of expectation, as in this paragraph from **"At the Beach"**: "The arrival of the elderly couple down at the beach, at almost precisely noon each day, is much noticed; it is when they look, perhaps, most splendid. In trimdark bathing suits, over which they both wear white shirts, in their hats and large dark glasses, advancing on their ancient legs, they are as elegant as tropical birds— and a striking contrast to everyone else on the beach, many of whom wear bright colors. One woman in the Chicago group has a pea-green caftan that literally hurts Amanda's eyes."

Inevitably, some of the stories in *To See You Again* are weaker than others, though none of them are bad. It is probably best not to read them all at once, for certain stylistic tics, the frequent use of parentheses for example, can

become annoying in large doses. And the way the stories move is similar enough to occasionally be predictable.

Still, the cumulative effect of the book is to make the reader feel as though he knows The San Francisco of Alice Adams in the special way one knows a place inhabited by friends. This San Francisco is a city full of lovers falling in and out of love, of small intimate restaurants where white wine is consumed on rainy afternoons, a city filled for the most part with very grown-up people, growing accustomed to pain. One of the characters in **"Truth Or Consequences"** says about a boy who had a deep effect upon her, "He could be another sort of person altogether; he could be as haunted as I am by everything that ever happened in his life." The reader too will be haunted by the characters Alice Adams has made so abundantly real by the grace, intelligence, and honesty of her prose.

It is refreshing and hopeful to find a writer in this day and time who, although recognizing love's possibilities for destruction, can still write about the ways in which love, both sexual and platonic, is akin to salvation.

Susan Wood, "Stories of Love and Loss," in The Washington Post—Book World, *January 21, 1979.*

Anne Boston (essay date 1986)

SOURCE: A review of *Return Trips,* in *The Times Literary Supplement,* No. 4322, January 31, 1986, p. 112.

[*In the following review of* Return Trips, *Boston asserts that Adams's stories are monotonous in their unvarying treatment of individuals trying to come to terms with their lives.*]

Going back, especially to the place where you were happiest, is usually a mistake, as more than one character discovers during the course of these stories by the American author of the novel *Superior Women.* The strongest afterimage [in *Return Trips*] is left by the story **"Molly's Dog"**, in which a "newly retired screen writer" makes a "return trip" to Carmel, where she often stayed with lovers in the past. But this time she is going with her gay friend Sandy, and she realizes beforehand that she is wrong to go: not because the place has changed but because she has. Now, older but little wiser, she finds herself literally dogged by a mongrel which, befriending them on the beach, gallops desperately after the car as they drive off. "But why didn't we go back for the dog?" she can't help crying later—provoking a final argument with Sandy, and the painful surfacing of regrets for a lifetime's missed opportunities.

Alice Adams is a confirmatory rather than a revelatory writer. Summings up, not surprises, are the essence of these brief lives called into account by cutting from present to past and back. Several stories cover a decade or more, and require a fair amount of background detail, making them more like preliminary sketches for novels.

The title story, for instance, starts maybe fifteen years ago with the narrator's first, most intense love affair, doomed by Paul's illness and early death; flashes back further still to her childhood in the South, which she loved despite her mother's unhappiness; shifts briefly to her two marriages; and one ends with the unplanned visit to her childhood home which has evoked all these memories. This is a lot of ground to cover in twenty pages, and Adams is driven to explain almost apologetically through her narrator:

> A very wise woman who is considerably older than I am told me that in her view relationships with people to whom we have been very close can continue to change even after the deaths of those people, and for me I think this has been quite true, with my mother, and in quite another way with Paul.

Adams is interested in old age: the accumulation of experience fits her theme, and her elderly characters are also her liveliest. In **"Waiting for Stella"** a group of old people wait for Stella's husband, who is very late for lunch, a few weeks after her death; always irritatingly over the top in life, now she insistently reminds them of their own mortality through her absence. Elsewhere, Adams's assessment of the "emotional reality of women's lives today", as the blurb would have it, is characterized by a kind of defensive introversion: one character describes herself as a depressive, and anxiety is often the dominant emotion.

After *Superior Women,* the landscape of **Return Trips** (Alice Adams's first short story collection to be published here) is disappointingly flat. In the absence of humour, sensitive observation and accurate description are not enough to compensate for a prevailing sameness of tone. Perhaps this is partly a result of the way the book was conceived—short stories written to a theme are liable to turn into a series of exercises, consciously doctored to fit the prescribed boundaries: a trap which this collection doesn't always escape.

Lee Upton (essay date 1989)

SOURCE: "Changing the Past: Alice Adams' Revisionary Nostalgia," in *Studies in Short Fiction,* Vol. 26, No. 1, Winter, 1989, pp. 33-41.

[*In the following essay, Upton analyzes the function of nostalgia in Adams's short stories.*]

Alice Adams extends upon and recasts our definitions of nostalgia. Dispossessed, the female characters in her short fiction turn to their memories as their most volatile, and promising, possessions. These women rechart their lives, actually returning—imaginatively and, more often than not, physically—to past landscapes. This hunger for retrospectives emerges as a peculiar form of nostalgia. *Nostalgia,* with its semantic reference to *homesickness* and its root in the Greek *nostos* ("return home") and *algos* ("pain"), becomes a revisionary impulse. As Adams' narrator of the title story of **Return Trips** has been told by "a very wise woman": "Relationships with people to whom we have been very close can continue to change even after the deaths of those people. . . ." Adams' characters may, in a sense, change their past, for memories allow them to alter even their relationships with the dead. For Adams, the past is alive and may be made well. She allows her characters to go homeagain, inevitably to transform their relationships to the past and to confirm or renegotiate current choices.

Characters in Adams' short fiction may be involved in a form of nostalgia that resembles what Fred Davis calls "interpreted nostalgia," in which "the analysis of the experience, however rudimentary, fleeting, or mistaken, comes in some part to be fused with the primary experience itself, causing it to become something more than a mere proclamation of, or even dialogue upon, past beauties and lost virtues" [*Yearning for Yesterday: A Sociology of Nostalgia,* 1979]. If Adams imagines the past as a living tissue and, as such, alterable, her characters, nostalgically casting backward, suffuse memory with their desires. As the past permeates the present, these women seek to construct an image of memory that is pervaded with renewed intensity. Not only does Adams explicitly define some of her characters' longings as nostalgic, she alters her readers' perceptions of nostalgia. The past may be probed and rewritten even as it haunts these characters.

By labeling as "nostalgic" Adams' vision within the short story, her preferred genre, I realize that I risk connecting this fiction with wistfulness and sentimentality, associations that have accrued to the idea of nostalgia. Yet Adams finds in nostalgia profound reflections upon women's sense of homelessness and cultural displacement, their "homesickness," and in turn explores the projection of past images as desired guides.

In exploring retrospectives, however, Adams would have us recognize that we do not engage in nostalgia without risk. She isolates three relationships to the past that I have chosen to call *static, vertiginous,* and *revisionary.* Static nostalgia is the most limited evocation of the past—passive, untransformative. Vertiginous nostalgia is its radical opposite—a tendency to be absorbed by the past yet continually to rewrite memories without accepting any past choices. Through revisionary nostalgia, however, Adams discovers in longing for past conditions an active source of renewal; the personal past becomes a living force. The middle-aged and older woman creates a relationship, occasionally even a form of romance, with an image of herself as a younger woman. Anxious for a redeeming image of a past psychic "home," such characters are finally homesick. Through their nostalgic impulses, they would shelter the vulnerable young women they had been at the moment when their earlier pleasures were disrupted.

The title story of Adams' first collection of short stories, **"Beautiful Girl,"** posits a woman's relationship to her past that may serve as a useful introduction to Adams' conception of a static nostalgia. Ardis Bascombe, middle-aged and alcoholic, cannot progress beyond imagining herself as a Southern belle. She keeps "A large portrait of her[self] . . . framed on the kitchen wall: bare-shouldered, in something gauzy, light—she is dressed for a formal dance, the Winter Germans or the May Frolics." Tellingly, at the story's conclusion, Ardis Bascombe cries out to a man who has attempted to rescue her from alcoholism: "I am a beautiful girl"—a cry signalling her refusal to move beyond an early and prescribed identity. Self-forgetful, Ardis Bascombe neither lives actively within the present nor truly encounters past dynamics, but remains oddly suspended between past and present. We come to recognize Ardis Bascombe as if she were Adams' variation of a frog prince. Here, however, we have a frog princess who will not metamorphose. Adams moves beyond the simple cliché of the faded Southern beauty queen who clings to the past, for Ardis Bascombe's case is more desolate. Neither reflecting upon the past nor actively choosing to live within the present, she will not rescue herself or accept rescue from another. Adams' characters, paradoxically, often must learn to *keep up* with their pasts. The past, like the present, requires creative stewardship.

A contrary danger exists for still other Adams' characters in their relationships to the past. They may suffer a form of vertigo through conjuring in despair alternate versions of their earlier lives. Ceaselessly rewriting their pasts, they find the present uncontrollable. After five marriages, the cleaning woman in **Return Trips**'s **"Alaska"** cannot be sure if her current husband will turn into an earlier, violent husband of the same name. Avery of **"Alternatives"** in **Beautiful Girl** remains "plagued with alternatives; she constantly rewrote her life into new versions in which she did not marry Stanley. Or Christopher." Avery's revisions negate past choice; she disowns rather than illuminates her actual past. If retrospectives are like a writer's revisions to Adams, Avery is a writer who continually blue pencils her choices.

I have isolated these attitudes—a failure reflectively to analyze past images, on the one hand, and a continual revision of the past, on the other—as two particular dangers about which these stories instruct us. Yet often Adams pits her characters in a third movement, working between these two extremes, recognizing the omnipresence of the past within contemporary choices, considering alternate scenarios, but finally honoring and meditating upon a selected past image. Characters, after returning to the landscape of their pasts, both imaginatively and physically, may begin to reclaim and re-envision the present. As Annis Pratt has found in her remarkable study of archetypes in women's fiction. [*Archetypal Patterns in Women's Fiction,* 1981], "The older woman hero['s] . . . goal is to integrate her self with herself and not with a society she has found inimical to her *desires*" (emphasis mine). Aware of their desires, Adams' characters seek to make a connection with extended aspects of selfhood through their very longing for their personal pasts. Rather than necessarily integrating

an earlier self, however, they may envision an earlier other self as simultaneously coexisting, a self that may be recovered and "visited." In **"Roses, Rhododendron"** a woman's letter to a childhood friend signals her own reconnection to a second, chosen family and a renewed image of the past. In **"Elizabeth"** a remarkable older woman's legacy continues to link the lives of the two younger people who were her friends. The widow of **"Lost Luggage"** cannot reclaim the notebook that recorded her grief. Only when she records the past, particularly the early past, acknowledging herself to have been "a searching woman," does she recover from her anxiety.

"Home Is Where" in **Beautiful Girl** explores Adams' third order of nostalgia: the female hero re-envisions her present through her very longing for a positive image of the past. While on one level the story is an exploration of fear (Adams' protagonist is fearful of her husband, fearful of her lover, fearful for her son's future), nostalgia makes change possible. Prompted by nostalgia, an emotion so strong that she fears she "would die of longing for home," she returns to her small Southern hometown. Through her return and a summer romance, she routs her central anxiety. Yet the distant past is only a brief anodyne; while the past fortifies this woman, it also challenges her. Remembered pleasure draws her into a new relationship to her past and to her present until she "almost got used to being happy." Her susceptibility to the past—her longings that Adams explicitly defines as nostalgic—determines her strengths.

Here as elsewhere, Adams limns the peculiar dominance of memory. That memories involve reflection and interpretation we readily acknowledge, but that we may symbolically change the personal past—that the past radiates through our present and thus, like the present, remains permeable, open to change—is one of Adams' more provocative arguments. "I remember everything that ever happened to me," Alice Adams told an interviewer. The line might have been spoken by one of her characters, one who would be made to come to terms with the force of memory. In Adams' fiction, memory may provoke creative disruption, emerging as a reason for and even as a means of travel. Engaging in nostalgic journeys, her characters do not often find escape but possibilities fraught with potentials for both healing and hazard.

Adams' latest collection, **Return Trips,** is her most developed in its exploration of nostalgia among women who transform their pasts, and even heal a past as it coexists with the present. Often her older women have gained some degree of social power and financial stability. They must now develop a renewed relationship to the past in which as younger women they were far less powerful within a cultural context but perhaps more independent of social strictures. These female characters may choose to creatively reenact the past, even symbolically to rescue the past, providing a new home for stray aspects of their identities.

An attempt to reimagine and reencounter past choices emerges in the title story of **Return Trips**. A woman recalls an early affair after which she became a professor of contemporary history—a particularly significant occupation, for, like so many of Adams' characters, she is a historian of the personal past. Even the strong continuing influence of her dead lover, however, is not a genesis point but part of a complex of images, a further extension of an earlier sensual memory and a manifestation of her longing for her dead mother. The narrator's feelings toward Paul, who died of a heart condition, are reflected within her current marriage to a doctor. Her memories of her own mother, in turn, are mirrored by her attitude toward an older woman, Popsie Hooker. Through this web of associations we learn that the past is, after all, not past for this character.

The narrator performs "an expurgatory ritual of sorts," returning to her hometown as a means of testing her mother's emotional legacy. Latent within her final decision to visit Yugoslavia—and to take her husband, a doctor, with her—is the narrator's attempt symbolically to heal Paul. With her doctor-husband she would visit the area where Paul was hospitalized for a condition that is now surgically treatable. In returning, then, to the source of a passionate egalitarian relationship, Adams' narrator reads backwards, tracing through the strata of relationships. While it is futile to believe that the dead can be rescued, **"Return Trips"** suggests that the protagonist would effect her own symbolic rebirth. By honoring the past and therefore honoring her own earlier identity, she enacts her own rescue.

Adams continually explores the curious role of expectation, for she is interested in remarkable homecomings, the second chance for characters of appetite and will. Her characters' failures, however, may occur through inattentiveness to their own pasts. This theme of nostalgic self-recovery—as an unfulfilled promise—is especially prominent in **"Molly's Dog"** of *Return Trips*. Molly Harper, we learn, was once a poet, a fact briefly noted at the story's beginning. She has recently retired from screenwriting, an occupation taken up when the financial hazards of a poet's life became particularly enervating. In turning again to serious writing, she is at a point of return—return to an earlier vocation, to the sustaining activities of a younger self. While she and a friend vacation in Carmel, a site associated with her more romantic youth, she also must psychically "return" to her earlier self, the young poet she has abandoned.

Yet Molly Harper cannot initially honor her earlier self: she characterizes the young woman she was as "very silly." In talking to Sandy, a friend who accompanies her, she reveals her distance from the past: "You wouldn't believe how stupid I was, as a very young woman . . ." Her acceptance of her past moves only so far as "tolerance":

> How eagerly self-defeating she had been—how foolish, in love. But she felt a certain tolerance now for that young person, herself, and she even smiled as she thought of all that intensity, that driven waste of emotion. In many ways, middle age is preferable, she thought.

Her dismissal of the past is followed by Adams' introduction—within the very next sentence—of a dog, a symbol of that unrecovered, still suspect, only "tolerated" portion of Molly Harper's past. In the stray dog, Molly Harper

projects her own stray identity and her buried nostalgia for her earlier life. The dog is identified repeatedly by its "tall ears." (Characters who listen well tend to be rewarded in Adams' fiction.) Molly Harper sees the "long-legged, thin-tailed dark gray dog, with very tall ears—a shy young dog"; it "seemed to smile" and to exhibit a "certain shy independence." The dog's "happy frenzy" and "sheer delight," the haunting image of the dog chasing after her car and then receding—all reflect Molly Harper's unconscious knowledge of her devalued earlier self's independent pleasures and their consequent loss.

Molly Harper makes a return trip not only to Carmel but, through rereading, to E. M. Forster's *Howards End*. The novel is referred to otherwise in Adams' novel *Rich Rewards* as the "old favorite book" of Daphne Matthiessen, Adams' most amply rewarded protagonist in either her novels or her short stories. Daphne Matthiessen is allowed a happy ending, returning to the promises of her early past. Molly Harper, however, is nowhere so lucky. *Howards End,* with Forster's epigraphical and textual injunction "Only connect," may be a message to the aging woman who has disowned her younger self. The novel, furthermore, serves as a vehicle of communication between Molly and her traveling friend, with whom she eventually strains her relationship. Finally, in rereading the Forster novel, Molly Harper rereads her past choices and yet, ironically, fails to "connect" with her earlier self. Nostalgia itself is projected in Adams' fiction as a form of rereading and renewed connection. To "read" one's life, one must discover meaning; here, making sense means making new "readings" of nostalgic images. These characters must "only connect" with the force of their personal pasts, frequently to "rehouse" their earlier selves.

For Adams, recognizing and honoring connection to the past is a prerequisite to her characters' continued development. The *more past*—that is, the older—these women are, the more complex is their perspective. If they can maneuver between forever failing to imagine any revisions in their relationships to the past and between endlessly imagining alternatives to the past, if they can accept their earlier selves without condescension, they may actually make their way to an almost-happy ending. Dwelling on the past, that action we are told hobbles us, does not simply become a significant integer of these protagonists' stresses but determines their potential for serious growth.

Through characters who look with longing toward the past, Adams returns us to the fundamental meanings of *nostalgia*. In the *Oxford English Dictionary*, the word is initially defined as "A form of melancholia caused by prolonged absence from one's home or country; severe homesickness." Surely pain and longing for home are evident in these stories; the loss of actual homes runs like a lietmotif through much of Adams' fiction. As Fred Davis points out, our current definition of "nostalgia" has suffered "the gradual semantic deterioration of its core referent of *homesickness*." Adams, however, returns homesickness and actual homes to her own explorations of nostalgia. For Adams, creative memory must finally become the actual home; her characters are "inhabited" as much as they are the inhabitants of their homes. More than explorations of domestic environments, and certainly not simple representations of women's claustrophobia, her homes are images of nostalgia as transformative.

Two stories, in particular, illuminate this theme. In **"Berkeley House"** of *To See You Again,* Charlotte O'Mara (a contemporary Scarlett O'Hara whose Tara is on the auction block) responds to the sale of her childhood home by her Southern stepmother as if she were being "deracinated": "'Love' was too simple a word for her feelings about that house. She has reacted to its sale with rage and anguish, with an acute and wild sense of loss. . . ." The house's actuality has not haunted her so much as her own memory—and her need for a psychic home. For years, her dreams had taken place in the house of her childhood. Yet at the story's conclusion, Charlotte O'Mara no longer dreams of her house. Only superficially, however, may we take the disappearance of the house dream as an indication of health. More complexly, the protagonist's loss of the dream signals her inability to imagine a renewed context for herself, registering her further isolation. We learn to recognize Charlotte O'Mara by one of her most persistent attitudes: regret.

Illuminating **"Berkeley House"** is Adams' closing story in *Return Trips,* a story that presents nearly the same plot signatures. In both, houses are put up for sale by stepmothers, and protagonists are haunted by dreams of their childhood homes. In **"My First and Only House,"** however, the narrator, unlike Charlotte O'Mara, discovers her power through nostalgic memories of the home in which she lived for her first sixteen years. Her cultivation of a nostalgic image is more enriching, finally, than Charlotte O'Mara's renunciation of nostalgia. The narrator of **"My First and Only House"** distinguishes between the sterility and unhappiness of the actual past and a nostalgic image that she has created. The actual house of the past had been owned by the father, who may dispose of it as he pleases. (The stepmother in Adams' fiction is not cruel so much as distanced, somehow beside the point.) As a daughter, the narrator must discover her own shelter.

After the narrator returns to the actual house, she finds it "freshly painted, viewless" and in its actuality "non-existent" to her. As she has it, "it is not where I live." Her revisionary nostalgia creates another imprint, a fictional transformation: "I live in a huge, mad house with the loveliest view. With everything in bloom." She transforms her memory of her first house into a natural arbor, profuse with possibility. Without deluding herself about the conditions of loss that she first encountered there, she transmutes an image of home.

At such a point of emphasis—Adams' last story within her latest collection—**"My First and Only House"** acts as a paean to revisionary nostalgia. No less surprising, the story performs as Adams' own textual return to earlier motifs: she makes a return trip to Chapel Hill, that Southern college town of which she writes in much of her fiction, and returns as well to echoes of former characters. (Verlie, one of the

most moving characters in *Beautiful Girl,* Adams' first short-story collection, is reintroduced in a parenthesis.) Adams also returns in this story to her common subject of nostalgia and its imaginative transmutation.

If "fate . . . tends to reward happiness rather than virtue," as Adams writes in **"Lost Luggage"** in *To See You Again,* many of these characters reveal their very distrust of cultural conceptions of virtue for women. Nostalgia of some sort may be particularly dynamic for women who are burdened by social standards of behavior inimical to both their self-growth and self-pleasuring. Yet even as Adams' characters survey their losses, they may attempt to create images of happiness. Traveling in the southern United States or frequently in sunny countries, they engage in their own reeducations. These women remind us of the capricious quality of memory as they creatively recast the past, longing for reconnection with their earlier identities, seeking fulfillment. They do not forget actual losses and deprivations; they seek reinterpretation of the past rather than its renunciation.

As Alice Adams herself has gained increasing recognition, it is her style that critics most often praise. Through these highly crafted stories, Adams has attained a reputation as something of a writer's writer. At least twice she has been called a "watercolorist" of prose. While we most often think of watercolor as a medium that does not permit revision, the contrary tension in Adams' short fiction arises from its very focus upon revision. Her "content" often traces acts of rewriting, recasting, returning to longed-for conditions within the personal past.

> The characters in Alice Adams's novels and short stories are almost constantly traveling, on the road, on the move—changing jobs, moving from home to home, relationship to relationship, with the improvisatory skill of veterans of the 60s.
>
> *Michiko Kakutani, "Books of the Times,"*
> *in* The New York Times,
> *August 21, 1985*.

Retrospectives challenge both this author and her readers. Like Molly Harper, we must be rereading, here rereading Adams, or else we may misunderstand the world she evokes—as one reviewer has in labeling Adams' fiction as a vehicle for "sanctified selfishness," [Jane Larkin Crain, "Sanctified Selfishness," *The New York Times Book Review,* February 26, 1978]. More accurately, Adams' stories investigate, even make a virtue of, self-recoveries enacted through nostalgic impulses. Characters attempt forays into the past, imaginatively re-encountering images of their most vulnerable earlyselves. Nostalgia, complex and revisionary, is here not a minor emotion of a minor literature; homesickness (nostalgia's roots in *pain* and *longing for home*) occurs among women with desires that overwhelm the narrow conditions of their present lives.

"I hate a listener with a memory," Folly proclaims in Erasmus's *The Praise of Folly*. Adams often writes of good listeners who would cultivate their own extraordinary memories. That so many of her characters are not only haunted by their pasts but intent on maintaining an active relationship to the past, a form of imaginative housekeeping, may in part account for the complex power of Adams' characters and her richly layered narratives in which homecomings are always challenged with risk.

Kirkus Reviews **(essay date 1989)**

SOURCE: A review of *After You've Gone,* in *Kirkus Reviews,* July 15, 1989, p. 1008.

[*In the following review of* After You've Gone, *the critic finds that most of the stories in the collection are weak, although a few are "jewels."*]

It's too bad that Adams titled [*After You've Gone*] after the weakest of the 14 stories here—a smug monograph narrated by a jilted lawyer and directed at her poet ex-lover—because it may discourage Adams fans from delving further to sift out a few scattered gems.

In **"Fog,"** for instance, as a small mishap redirects that start of a San Francisco dinner party and ends up changing the course of a few lives, it's pure Adams, toppling the exquisite social order to get to the dark—and often funny—truths below the surface. In **"Ocracoke Island,"** elderly professor Duncan Elliott, on a visit to Manhattan, is a stirring, sharply etched character as he plods from meeting to meeting, worrying about his dental problems and spreading his tale of woe: recently, his fourth wife, Cath, has run off with another man to live on Ocracoke Island, a place that now looms large in Duncan's imagination. And **"1940: FALL,"** like an earlier Adams story, **"Roses, Rhododendron,"** deftly captures a childhood memory about belonging, at least temporarily, to someone else's world. At her best, then, Adams knows just how to put love through the prism of social convention so that it shimmers back at us refracted into its separate parts—lust, pity, jealousy, need. But too often the kind of narrative shorthand she increasingly relies on (where physical descriptions fill in for emotions and memories are weightier than actions, and all the missing pieces are explained with parentheses) gets in her way. Stories like **"A Sixties Romance"** and **"What to Wear"** are so thin and mannered that they might be Adams parodies.

Overall, worthwhile for those willing to sort the jewels from the strass—when she wants to, Adams can really sparkle.

Catherine Petroski (essay date 1989)

SOURCE: "Tales of Broken Love," in *Chicago Tribune,* September 3, 1989, p. 5.

[*In the following review, Petroski appraises the themes and characters of the stories in* After You've Gone.]

Alice Adams' new collection of short stories, [*After You've Gone*], is the work of a writer at the height of her powers—lucid, confident, refined, adept, provocative, perspicacious, startling and satisfying.

Adams is among the most triumphantly feminine, if not militantly feminist, writers working in a form sometimes considered the special preserve of female writers. In years to come, these stories may well be valued for extra-literary reasons, for they record the milieu and concerns of a particular generation of women in a certain social stratum.

To rush Adams' stories to the vault of literary and social history, however, would do a disservice to both author and readers, for thisis fiction full of characters who take the daily risk of breathing, who often stumble, routinely have their hearts broken, gather themselves and forge ahead.

Many of the stories in *After You've Gone* share elements with the title story, which appeared in the 1989 O. Henry Prize anthology. As this story of a broken love affair unfolds, and the deserted woman who narrates receives ever more curious letters from her younger replacement, the narrator's bond to the younger, naive woman—not unlike her earlier self—evolves through disbelief, anger and bitterness to pity and recognition.

The collection's last story, **"Your Doctor Loves You,"** is both precipitated by, and the occasion of, love gone awry. As expansive and evocative as a mini-novel, this is the story of a woman just getting a divorce who rediscovers how frightening, hazardous and mysterious the process of establishing relationships is. Readers may feel a visceral response to her vulnerability and to the incredibly disengaged and self-absorbed man who briefly comes into her life.

In general, Adams' male characters are not a terribly appealing lot; the women are the positive forces in this universe. However, several stories here have male point-of-view characters, if not exactly protagonists.

"Ocracoke Island," another broken-love story, tells of a professor named Duncan Elliot whose young (third) wife leaves him, running off with a dashing Irish poet who had read on campus. Visiting New York, Duncan has the three meals a day with different people from his past (a former student, an English critic who is an old friend, and finally, a former wife) and in so doing confronts not only his past but also his mortality and inadequacies, perhaps for the first time.

Several stories of uneasy co-existence—**"Traveling Together,"** **"A Sixties Romance,"** and **"The End of the**

Themes in Adams's fiction:

Alice Adams's heroes and heroines are ever on the lookout for means of trading current attachments, selves, environments, repressions for something fresher. When they review a canceled marriage or revisit a childhood scene, they're moved less often by nostalgia than by longing to confirm the absolute pastness of the past—to prove to themselves that yesterday can't lay a glove on them. . . .

Lots of moving on, in short. Miss Adams's manner is good-humoredly ironic and understated, and she's a deft social observer. . . . Readers in north central middle age will doubtless be heartened, moreover, by the lively desire and splendid resiliency of this author's senior citizen–changelings. . . . And it's at least arguable that the short story is, finally, a happier form for Miss Adams's gifts than the novel. Moral vacancy, nervous shuttling in and out of relationships, weightless life commitments and plans—these items are better suited to brisk, won't-take-a-minute short stories than to the huff and puff of noveleso.

Benjamin DeMott, "Stories of Change," in
The New York Times Book Review,
April 11, 1982.

World"—deal pointedly with the difficulties people have in sustaining relationships and why, given the difficulties, they persist in them. One troubling story, **"What to Wear,"** ostensibly is about a woman deciding how to dress to visit a former lover in a psychiatric ward; it raises tough questions about the effect people have on each other, and about how we show surface concerns that displace our real ones.

The other major strain running through the collection is the theme of old friendships—especially childhood friendships and their impact (or lack of it) on later life—and the unpredictable results when these friendships are renewed. **"Child's Play"** explores, from two young girls' point of view, the twin mysteries of alcoholism and their parents' friendships; in **"Tide Pools"** a woman becomes caretaker for her childhood friend, who has inherited her parents' alcoholism. **"Favors,"** a male variation on the theme, is a fascinating story about the ranking of commitments—what allegiance takes priority over what other allegiances—as an unlikely set of circumstances puts to the test the long-standing friendship of two men.

Two more general concerns also run through the stories: the characters' capacity for self-deception and the tremendous dispersion of energy that occurs in relationships that are not always mutually beneficial.

The quintessential Alice Adams' scene takes place in a gorgeous, capacious house high in the California hills—say, at a party of literate, attractive, affluent people who have known each other for a long time (often in variously combined, intimate relationships). But despite an abundance of wonderful food, wine, conversation and other reassurances of the good life, these people find themselves vaguely ill-at-ease and essentially isolated.

Ah, well, the existential condition, one might say; this is nothing new. But when the power of fiction takes over, as it does in Adams' stories, nothing, including the reader, is ever quite the same.

Ron Carlson (essay date 1989)

SOURCE: "Clobbering Her Ex," in *The New York Times Book Review,* October 8, 1989, p. 27.

[*In the following essay, Carlson judges Adams's stories in* After You've Gone *stylistically polished but emotionally and psychologically unsatisfying.*]

The 14 short romances in Alice Adams's new collection [*After You've Gone*] are—with two exceptions—about women. These women are professionals (lawyers, painters, college deans, authors, political activists, architects, psychologists, physicists, sculptors) who live in the up-scale world of gracious houses in cities from California to Maryland. They travel to Italy with lovers and on lecture tours without lovers, and to Mexico with and without their husbands. They love cats. Their closest friends are women. And, as the bittersweet title of the book suggests, they've had some trouble with men. But they're almost all *better* now.

The title story is a letter from a lawyer to her former lover, a well-known poet, who has recently run off to Oregon with a young woman. (Poets run off with young women twice in this collection.) This is a wonderfully cultivated revenge story. Her epistle inventories her life now, notes that the poet's new young woman has been writing to her almost daily and then steps up and clobbers him with sage advice. Here is clearly a superior woman (she wishes he hadn't taken his copy of Moby-Dick) on the righteous edge of being smug, a woman who has washed one man out of her hair and is better for it.

All but two of the stories are written in the third person with a kind of standard opening, including a character introduction. Consider these samples from the first paragraphs of six stories: "Zelda Hoskins, a pretty, light-haired young woman from Toronto"; "skinny, scared, precocious Prudence Jamieson and pretty, placid, trustful Laura Lee Matthews"; "a woman named Antonia Love. She is a painter, middle-aged, 'recently successful'"; "Roger Michaels, an architect, on meeting a woman named Julia Bailey, a mathematician"; "Sheila, who teaches Victorian literature at a local university"; "Susan Quince, a dean in a small women's college."

The effect of such writing is perceived as a kind of glib omniscience; an author being facile. Reading the stories becomes like reading about people in stories and not—as in the best realistic fiction—about people we know. Ms. Adams compounds this slightly by giving arch names to some of the men: Bynum, Braxton, Reeve, Jasper, Grantly and Egon.

Many of the stories in *After You've Gone* evoke a strong sense of nostalgia, and the characters and events have soft contours, as seen through the lens of time passed. In the best of these stories, this essence is created with simple lyric imagery, as in **"Child's Play,"** an ambitious tale about alcohol and friendship: "The Jamieson pool was ideal for summer-night parties. Sophia's maid would leave bowls of potato salad in the icebox, and at suppertime Dan would build a fire down by the pool. . . . They would all be sitting around on steamer rugs, on the summer dew-damp ground, as fireflies drifted through the darkening evening air. As flirtations and arguments grew heavier with drink."

One of the strongest stories is **"Lost Cat,"** in which a woman's search for a pet brings to her mind her worst fears: losing her lover and getting cancer. It is one of the shortest stories in the book and has one of the few unsettling endings: neither self-satisfied nor improved, the woman (who, ironically, is a psychiatric social worker) faces the fact of permanent uncertainty.

Reading and rereading this collection, I was struck by Ms. Adams's facility as a writer. We fly over the terrain of most of these discreet stories comforted by the overt skill of our pilot—yet we arrive at the endings with only a vague sense of having been close to anything.

This doesn't mean that the book won't have plenty of friendly readers. *After You've Gone* does radiate—in a way that's often more successfully achieved in novels—a kind of knowing familiarity with estrangement and the blessings of time. But it seems an unusual collection in light of the many stories being published today that bring their characters alive with an edgy immediacy. While I admire the cool surfaces of Alice Adams's stories, they leave me wanting more heat. In so much contemporary fiction, characters are leaping wildly from the frying pan into the fire, but in Ms. Adams's world they only get to remember the flames.

Greg Johnson (essay date 1990)

SOURCE: "Some Recent Herstories," in *The Georgia Review,* Vol. XLIV, Nos. 1-2, Spring-Summer, 1990, pp. 278-88.

[*In the following excerpt, Johnson commends Adams's depiction of women's relationships—romantic and platonic—in* After You've Gone.]

In *After You've Gone,* Alice Adams' tenth book of fiction, the typical character is an intelligent, career-minded woman whose personal history includes a series of failed relationships with men. Her heroines tend to hold feminist ideals—generally they are self-supporting, intellectually autonomous, and politically liberal—but fail to practice these ideals when choosing and relating to their male partners.

> **On women in Adams's fiction:**
>
> Adams' heroines reach for survival. Though her protagonists sometimes consider suicide, long "popular" with some women writers and their female protagonists as a final attempt at control, it is not a method of success for Adams' survivors. Her heroines take more positive action. They resolve not to be victims. They positively assert their own personalities through an occupation or a task as both a survival skill and a means of defining self.
>
> *Cara Chell, "Succeeding in Their Times:*
> *Alice Adams on Women and Work,"*
> *in* Soundings, *Spring, 1985.*

As the title of a recent bestselling self-help book would have it, they're smart women who make foolish choices. (The first clue to their emotional dependency, at times verging on desperation, is in the volume's title, which suggests wistful melancholy rather than jubilant independence.) The title story is representative: a successful lawyer has been abandoned by her handsome lover (a charismatic poet whom she has supported financially) in favor of a younger woman. An epistolary letter addressed to the poet but probably never mailed, **"After You've Gone"** is both sarcastic and affectionate, embittered and fair-minded. But if the woman's recollections and present resolve to do better suggest her intelligence and renewed self-esteem (she has since become involved with another man—"a more known quality than you were," she tells her former lover), they also betray her lingering investment in the past relationship.

Similarly, the heroine of **"On the Road,"** Brendan Hollowel, is a renowned scholar trapped in a loveless marriage to a Washington attorney. The story follows Brendan through one of her lecture tours, during which she is approached by a handsome stranger. She rebuffs him, but then finds herself "headed for the elevator, hurrying like a schoolgirl, or some classically frustrated, quite deranged spinster lady." Seeking solace in sisterhood, she discovers that her friendships with women are charged with negative rather than positive energy. "Aren't women supposed to be nicer to each other these days?" she asks herself in despair. "To be less rather than more competitive? In a discouraged way she decides that in some instances, at least, the grounds for competition have simply shifted, if ever so slightly." Like several others in this volume, this story seems to stop rather than end, with Brendan's conflicts still unresolved, her life quite likely to continue in the same melancholy groove.

Not all of Adams' stories feature such grim portrayals. In **"Favors"** a young woman who has recently entered a rash marriage takes a step toward maturity through getting to know an elderly but fiercely committed political activist. And **"Tide Pools"** describes the nurturing reunion of two girlhood friends. Judith is a cautious, self-sufficient woman, a divorced college professor living alone, yet she renews her childhood affection for the ebullient Jennifer, whose subsequent life has been marked by several failed marriages and a dependence on alcohol. As adults, the two women support but do not judge one another, and by the end of the story Judith can say, "all things considered, even living alone, I really feel better and better . . . , and I think I have never been so happy in my life."

Although love generally brings to Adams' women the "Deep, irremediable scars" mentioned on the last page of **"A Sixties Romance,"** it also deepens their self-awareness and leads to a self-sufficient, if emotionally brittle, maturity. These women combine fragility and strength, and their emotional hesitations are effectively suggested by the author's prose style, which is both deft and delicate, ironic and questioning. With its numerous intelligent but melancholy ladies, and its equally numerous handsome heels to whom they seem in thrall, *After You've Gone* might well displease the most militant fringes of feminist criticism; but it's an honest, wise, and finely written book.

Barbara Frey Waxman   (essay date 1990)

SOURCE: "Beginning the Journey to Selfhood in Middle Age," in *From the Hearth to the Open Road: A Feminist Study of Aging in Contemporary Literature*, Greenwood Press, 1990, pp. 45-94.

[*In the following excerpt, Waxman interprets "A Wonderful Woman," "Lost Luggage," and "To See You Again" as belonging to the* Reifungsroman *genre because they are stories in which middle-aged characters discover their self-identities and determine new directions for their lives. In the introduction to her book, Waxman defines* Reifungsroman *as the "novel of ripening—opposing its central tenet to the usual notion of deterioration in old age."*]

With good reason the short stories of American writer Alice Adams have appeared regularly in the prestigious annual O. Henry Award Collections. [In a review of *To See You Again*, *Baltimore Sun*, April 4, 1982] Robert Michael Green describes her gifted writing: "At its best, Alice Adams's reportorial style reminds us of Saroyan, Katherine Mansfield, and Hemingway's most innocent (and charming) stones. That's good company." Adams's concern in her fiction with the experiences of aging and emotions of middle-aged women also puts her in the company of Doris Lessing; her middle-aged heroines, like Lessing's, travel on psychic journeys to themselves, "ripening" or acquiring the greater maturity and wisdom that characterize women of *Reifungsroman*. During the 1970's—when *The Summer Before the Dark* was published—and into the early 1980's, Adams wrote a series of short story gems that were collected, titled *To See You Again*, and published in 1982. Several of the stories in the collection are *Reifungs-roman* in miniature, and three that depict middle-aged women, **"Lost Luggage," "A Wonderful Woman,"** and the title story, **"To See You Again"** enable readers to experience middle age intensely.

To Adams, middle age for women is often synonymous not with complacency and boredom, but with upheaval in longstanding relationships and with the brave formation of new relationships; Phyllis L. Thorn has observed that Adams "writes especially well of people in their middle years whose marriages have come apart through divorce or death, . . . whose new 'relationships' are tentative and frightening as well as loving, rich, and rewarding" ["Stories of Middle Years and Fresh Beginnings," *Seattle Times*, May 9, 1982]. Thorn's words aptly describe the situation of the heroines in these three stories. The first two depict middle-aged widows embarking on literal and psychic journeys that promise adventure and self-discovery, a typical pattern in *Reifungsromane*. Benjamin De Mott has hailed this fictional widow-adventurer as the "new-style picaresque heroine" and notes that in depicting such heroines, Adams is able to explore "the feelings and impulses . . . [that] lie close to the core of contemporary emotional life" ["Stories of Change," *The New York Times Book Review*, April 11, 1982]. The third story gives us a portrait of a woman not literally but virtually widowed through the mental illness of her husband. She embarks on her journey of self-discovery not by traveling but by taking a job, during which she develops a crush on a young man, In the first two stories especially, the two women start out anxious about the experiences they arc to have, but emerge sounder for them, more self-confident and self-knowledgeable. The third story's protagonist has only an internal journey, a set of fantasies reminiscent of Kate Brown's and Jane Somers's rich inner lives. Yet she, like Adams's other two heroines, also changes, becoming more optimistic about her old age, even if middle age's obstacles to happiness seem formidable to her. As De Mott wryly observes, "Readers in north central middle age will doubtless be heartened . . . by the lively desire and splendid resiliency of this author's senior citizen-changelings." De Mott's tinge of flippancy here probably reflects his own uncomfortable, stereotypical thoughts about aging. He fails to give Adams credit for creating appealing, courageous middle-aged heroines who have the power to change not only themselves, but also readers' common notions of middle age for women.

Felicia Lord is the "wonderful woman" of that ironically titled story. The irony of the title is that while everyone considers her a wonderful woman who copes admirably with the death of her husband and other major difficulties, Felicia disparages her own conduct, insisting she has not acted out of choice or strength of character: "Wonderful is not how Felicia sees herself at all; she feels that she has always acted out of simple—or sometimes less simple—necessity." There is a clear discrepancy between the way she perceives herself and the way others perceive her, especially as the narrator encourages readers to see Felicia in attractive terms, with positive observations filling the opening paragraphs; she is pretty, a "stylish gray-blonde," and strong, a "survivor" of marriage to an alcoholic artist manqué (now dead) and five children (now grown) and of a love affair with a Mexican man, ending in an abortion. In short, she is a determined, complex, active woman whose creative yet unpretentious bent is summed up when the narrator describes her as "a ceramicist who prefers to call herself a potter." Felicia's self-disparagements, conveyed through third-person limited omniscient narration, seem misplaced beside such praise. The narrator does not directly explain the discrepancy between internal and external assessments of Felicia, an omission that, as Elizabeth Forsythe Hailey has suggested, is typical of Adams's reportorial style: "Writing in a deliberately flat style, she refuses to tell you what she expects you to discover for yourself." However, it is clear that Felicia is not accurately or fully acquainted with herself.

In the course of this story Felicia's self-disparagement and ignorance of herself end as she undergoes intensive self-examination while she waits for her lover in a San Francisco hotel. While waiting and wondering whether he will appear for the rendezvous, Felicia, like Kate Brown and Jane Somers, has "remembrances of sex and loves past," a common element of *Reifungsroman*. This scrutiny of her past enables her to acknowledge her strength, her ability to survive alone, and her basic wonderfulness. Like an enthusiastic and idealistic 16-year-old, she feels exhilarated about her new romance; her future seems brimming with possibilities. Yet the opening sentence suggests that like a naive and vulnerable 16-year-old, she initially fears the failure of this relationship with a man, as she embarks on it "at her age"; her self-deprecating tone in this last phrase is also a reprise of the old attitude that love is for the young and old love is somehow inappropriate. However, reviewing her rich history of romantic attachments allows her to see that she has successfully weathered romantic crises and is equipped either to venture into new love in middle age or to meet her future without a romantic relationship. The traditional borders between the emotional domains of youth and age become blurred in Adams's depiction of Felicia's romantic feelings.

Adams scrutinizes Felicia's panic at the thought that this meeting and this relationship will fail. Self-conscious and insecure in this new "inappropriate" role, Felicia feels less sure of "what she is about" than the bellboy who, she paranoically thinks, smiles knowingly at her. The narrator describes her unsettling emotions, her disorientation in this role of lover at age 59, through physical sensations: Felicia feels a "dizzying lurch of apprehension . . . intense in its impact," and "suddenly quite weak," she has to sit down. As she looks out the window in her dizzy state, even the rooftops have a "crazy variety," reflecting and increasing her disorientation. Felicia's thoughts leap from crazy roofs to questions about her crazy relationship with Martin, a risky departure from her customary kind of man. This "farming sailor" defies her usual categorizing; Martin is "entirely new to her." Is this, she wonders, an imprudent decision by a formerly wonderful, sensible woman—inappropriately daring for a woman just short of 60? Is this a false start on the road to true *reifung*, such as Kate Brown experienced in her liaison with Jeffrey Merton? And is San Francisco an inappropriate place for this meeting, given its role in her past relationships, the history that she is about to reminisce over? As she waits for Martin, questions and doubts punctuate her inner monologue, mirroring her society's assumptions about youth and age: her romantic feelings and risk taking are deemed embarrassing for one of her "advanced" age. Her fear of failure, then, comes not only from her sense of personal inadequacy, but also

from her sense of having overstepped social bounds by reaching for "youthful" pleasures; images of natural catastrophe express her fear of the consequences of this "unnatural" liaison that tampers with nature: "Supposing she isn't 'wonderful' anymore? Suppose it all fails, flesh fails, hearts fail, and everything comes crashing down upon their heads, like an avalanche, or an earthquake?" The doubts that strike her are reminiscent of Jane Somers's dismay as she stands in front of the mirror naked, sees her juiceless body, and fantasizes making love with Richard. Readers increasingly sympathize with Felicia as the waiting period stretches out, sharing her dismay that she may have been abandoned. The doubts, the excitement, the suspense, and a virus combine to make Felicia sick.

Some of Felicia's doubts during this interminable waiting period are eased by the arrival of Martin's telegram informing her that a "crazy delay"—the word "crazy" linking the telegram with the crazy San Francisco roofs and her sense of the craziness of planning such a rendezvous at all—will keep him from her for a few days. The delay enables her to consider whether the liaison itself is crazy, allows her to be sick and convalesce, and gives her time to reexamine her past in order to reassess herself and prepare for her future.

She experiences in abbreviated form (appropriate to the short story) Kate Brown's momentous summer of illness, introspection, and maturation. Felicia reviews her courtship and marriage to Charles and her mothering of their five children, her love affair with Felipe (a false start on the path to maturity), and the recent history of her passion for Martin. As she takes to her bed and reminisces, she feels older, no longer like the romantic 16-year-old for whom the silk and lace lingerie she wears is appropriate, but instead decked out like "an old circus monkey,"— echoing Kate Brown's self-description when ill and aging like a thin, sick monkey. Felicia imagines that the bellboy grins at her with malice and contempt, seeing her as "an abandoned woman, of more than a certain age." She fantasizes her illness spiraling to death and herself becoming "an unknown dead old woman" in this hotel room. Old age, illness, helplessness, abandonment, death: she faces squarely in this fantasy some of the grisly myths about senescence, gathering strength to puncture them.

Moreover, as she remembers her past, Felicia demythicizes it. This demythicizing is necessary so that her past will not have the power to thwart newly developing aspects of her future. First she remembers her fairytale courtship with her husband during the glamour of wartime: brief leaves, dancing all night in elegant hotels, the marriage proposal during a champagne breakfast; Adams selects the concrete details of the reminiscence carefully to suggest its romanticized quality in Felicia's mind. Then Felicia, like Jane Somers, confronts the real emptiness of her marriage, her lack of love for her dead husband; "having seen the lonely, hollow space behind his thin but brilliant surface of good looks, graceful manners," Felicia remembers feeling so sorry for this despairing failed artist that "it was then impossible to leave him." Similarly, Kate Brown contemplates her husband's weakness for affairs with younger women and recognizes the flaws in their marriage. For Kate, Jane, and Felicia, the starry-eyed view of marriage is gone. Felicia dismisses one of her youthful illusions, "a dream of a courtship, and then a dream groom."

As part of her assessment of her marriage, Felicia, like Kate Brown, also scrutinizes her role as a mother. She does not see herself as a good mother, not having liked young children, and is grateful that she has gone beyond the role so that she can see her grown children "with great fondness, and some distance." Unlike Kate, Felicia experiences no empty nest syndrome. She simply dismisses another of her life's myths, that of her being the devoted mother of five. Again she is confronted by the undeniable flatness of her married life: if children are at the center of their marriage and Charles married her mainly to be the mother of his children, she has not discharged her maternal role so "wonderfully."

Felicia also reexamines her "ideal" romantic relationship with her Mexican Communist artist-lover Felipe, whose macho, radical style swept Felicia off her feet. Their passionate affair results in her pregnancy, an emotionally agonizing abortion in San Francisco, and, finally, Felipe's return to his wife. Another dream is shattered: a dream of passionate romance: "And she thought, 'Well, so much for my Latin love affair.'" She is gradually realizing how well she has survived, summoning strength, courage, and the will to go on. Phyllis L. Thorn observes this resilience in many of Adams's female characters: they are "courageous and resourceful people with an appealing talent for starting over and making new beginnings." As she reexamines her history and learns to appreciate her own emotional stamina, Felicia is also convalescing from her physical illness. Her physical recovery reinforces the idea that she is becoming more self-knowledgeable and more self-congratulatory.

The most challenging aspect of Felicia's reminiscence concerns the new history of her relationship with Martin, whom she has known for only a few months. It is too soon to know and trust him, she realizes, yet here she is in San Francisco waiting to meet him. He has asked her to marry him, a proposition that she knows requires mutual trust, but now she ironically doubts whether he will even show up at the hotel. Finally she faces the possibility of a future without him. It may hurt at first, "the possible loss of such a rare, eccentric and infinitely valuable man," but with her history to buttress her, Felicia "realizes that she can stand it, after all, as she has stood other losses, other sorrows in her life. She can live without Martin." Felicia reaches this conclusion out of conviction; she realizes that she is not just whistling in the dark after having reviewed her painful history and track record of survival. She can live alone comfortably. And readers nod approvingly as she goes out to a nice dinner by herself, acknowledging that to dine alone is "really not so bad." However, feelings of weakness and childishness return when, back at the hotel, she is disappointed that Martin has still not arrived.

Like Lessing, Adams uses a dream to explore further Felicia's conflicts and ambivalence about her newly ac-

knowledged autonomy; dreams are central to the heroine's self-examination in most *Reifungsroman*. She dreams a man comes to her room at night and although thrilled to see him, she is not sure who he is: "Is it her husband Charles, or one of her sons? Felipe? Is it Martin? It could even be a man she doesn't know." She confesses that the dream saddens her, perhaps because in it she is so happy to see the man, suggesting that despite her struggle for autonomy, she is dependent on men for happiness, after all; or she may be saddened because in the dream Martin is identified with the other men in her life with whom her relationships turned out to be disappointing or limited. Her ambivalence about solitude versus male companionship is evident in either interpretation of the dream.

This ambivalence in her dream life is overtaken by Felicia's increasing enjoyment of her own companionship during her waking hours. She appraises herself in the omnipresent mirror of the *Reifungsroman* and sees, more optimistically than Jane Somers, "a strong healthy older woman." She no longer waits passively in her hotel room for her lover, but tours San Francisco, pleased by her own company. By the time Martin arrives, Felicia has matured by facing her past, becoming comfortable with her present aloneness, and recognizing her own strength for the future.

Martin's arrival in the middle of the night is like her dream: she cannot at first identify who he is. When she does, she is glad to see him. Yet she has learned that her future is not contingent solely upon him or this relationship. Regardless of what may happen in her relationship with Martin, Felicia ends her story confident that she will again be a survivor—finally giving herself credit for being one—a survivor with many options before her. Felicia Lord acknowledges herself "lord" of her own destiny. By empowering Felicia in this way, Adams is no longer giving credence to American society's dualistic notion of youth as an epoch of power and choice and middle age as a time of increasing disenfranchisement and dependency, particularly for women.

Janet Stone Halloran could be Felicia Lord's sister. The protagonist of **"Lost Luggage"** describes in a first-person narrative some of the same experiences and thoughts that Felicia has, although she appears to be more self-confident at the beginning of her story than Felicia. Like Felicia, Janet is middle-aged and recently widowed. When the story opens, she has just returned from her first vacation alone, for which she congratulates herself with "more than usual self-approval; you could call it pride or maybe hubris, even." She has enjoyed her own companionship, socialized with other people, successfully negotiated the practical details of traveling. She seems to have adjusted to her middle age, as indicated by her pleasure in her appearance: "I was brown and silver, like a weathering country house, and I did not mind the thought of myself as aging wood." Janet counters the stereotyped images of deterioration, gray hair, increasing wrinkles, and sagging flesh with these lovely images of physical aging as ripening or enhancing one's appearance. Adams has also written positively about her own middle age and gray hair in an autobiographical sketch for *Vogue*, "On Turning Fifty": "My fifties . . . are the best years of my life, so far . . . and . . . given the proper lighting and a sympathetic photographer, grey hair has a wonderful sheen."

Janet's positive mental outlook initially prevents her from becoming upset over the airline's loss of her suitcase. As the story unfolds, however, she has an emotional relapse triggered by the lost suitcase, a crisis that she has to resolve and whose resolution strengthens her for her future alone. In describing her crisis to the reader, Janet's narrative travels back and forth between her past marriage to Walter and his death, her recent past at the Mexican resort, her present in her San Francisco home, and her future hopes and schemes. The familiar pattern in the *Reifungsroman* of the flashback or reminiscence to analyze and reassess an important marital or sexual relationship from the past before building a new life, present in Felicia Lord's, Kate Brown's and Jane Somers's stories, is central to this story too.

In a sense, as she confronts her literally lost luggage in her present, Janet is also reexamining, in most cases to jettison, the figurative baggage from her past life: her formerly important relationships, values, priorities, even her traditional methods of meaning making in language. Jettisoning as a practice of the middle-aged is explored in articles on aging in popular magazines, but Adams's heroine practices it uniquely in her use of language. To rethink and dislodge meanings stereotypically associated with terms like "gray hair," "widow," "older woman," and "woman alone" frees her language to acquire new meanings, frees her to create new associations for these terms. Kate Brown freed her language during her "cow sessions." Janet's analytic method of sifting through her past and redefining her life is also patently linguistic; she writes her analyses in a large daybook or journal, like Jane Somers and Caro Spencer. Janet's journal is the one item that she really misses in her lost suitcase, until she realizes that what it contained, its meanings, or any meaning need not depend upon what is actually carried, preserved in writing, or handed down, as if in one sacred vessel, one compendious, universal, canonical volume. She realizes that because it is a process, not a "thing," meaning can be continually recreated, reconceptualized, and particularized. This realization prompts Janet's decision to buy not the duplicate of the lost daybook, but the first of several smaller, more portable and more "losable" journals and to fill the first one with new impressions of her Mexican vacation and her life; she will not attempt to reconstruct the original lost jottings. Like Janet in her journals, Adams in this story also creates new meanings for widowhood and middle age.

As she reminisces about her courtship and marriage to Walter, Janet acknowledges what none of her friends had known because Janet is a reserved person. She establishes an intimate tie with the reader by confessing to a failure of love in her marriage, only a lack of money having prevented divorce. They had married "for love (well, sex, really)," but the mutual attraction had faded and left Janet a lonely woman who read obsessively while Walter indulged a penchant for owning expensive cars. She recalls her lack of sympathy for Walter and his hobby with some guilt

because of his early death. Guilt is a major item of Janet's baggage from the past that she has to deal with now. In addition, her recollection of their last vacation together at the Mexican resort reveals much about the emptiness of their relationship and about her former conventional attitude toward aging. During their last vacation, both had experienced "a miasma of incommunicable depression" whose source, she determines, was the thought of their aging together, growing apart and deteriorating: "Our slowing middle-aged flesh seemed to parody its former eager, quick incarnation. . . . Is the rest of our life together, if we stay together, to be such a process of attrition?" Janet's association of aging with a repellent deterioration acts as a metaphor for the deterioration of their repellent relationship. She conjectures that if one's life is not going well or if it is worsening, aging does not seem to improve it, but merely to mock a person with the contrast to what her life had once been. Without a newly rekindled passion or strengthened identity and purpose to offset its decaying powers, such as Jane Somers, Kate Brown, and Felicia Lord acquire, aging may well become a depressing process of attrition. However, Janet must recognize the deterioration of her relationship with Walter, which aging seemed to aggravate, before she can begin ripening.

At the Mexican resort, Janet records her reminiscences and analyzes them in her daybook; her daybook also records her observations in the present of the other guests at the resort as well as her fantasies about her future as a single woman. By writing in the journal, she can move beyond the initial tendency of the newly widowed to whitewash or idealize the marriage, "to remember . . . [only] the good times between us," so that by the end of her vacation her perspective has become wider and more accurate: "I could remember the good days quite as easily as the bad." She acquires an honest appreciation of Walter and their limited marriage and can even feel the injustice of his early death. She also discovers the important role of writing in her daybook to widen her perspective on her marriage and Walter's death and to chart her progress in mourning and adjusting to widowhood. She emphasizes her preoccupation with the effects of writing on herself by mentioning how moved she had been by Doris Lessing's protagonist Anna and her efforts to understand her life through her scrupulous journal keeping in *The Golden Notebook*. Janet also refers readers to passages in her own journal that, when compared, illustrate her progress, beginning with an early nightmarish scene after Walter's death in which she records her viewing of Walter's body in the funeral home and ending with her calmer reflections about her present and her enthusiastic hopes for her future. Unlike the "process of attrition" she had foreseen in her relationship with Walter alive, she is as a widow now able, in part through therapeutically writing in her journal, to trace the healing return "to my old self, competent and strong" and to foster new self-growth.

With this strong self as a foundation, Janet assumes a "youthful" outlook toward the future, envisions herself "turning [her] life around": "I would experience an exhilarating sense of adventure . . . I could even, I imagined, find a big house to share with some other working women, about my age—not exactly a commune but a cooperative venture. Such prospects excited and to a degree sustained me." Middle-aged Janet confidently imagines herself as a single working woman, a role that blurs the borders between youth and age by invoking images of smart young *Mademoiselle* businesswomen; and the borders are further blurred by her reference to the commune, youth's challenge to the nuclear family. She does not fantasize about the presence of a man in her future, deciding after observing the conduct of another older single woman at the Mexican resort that the old woman she wants to become is not one who talks too much as if to compensate for not being part of a twosome, or one who buys the company of younger men by paying for their drinks. She will enjoy her singleness, like Felicia.

Because Janet gives the reader much evidence to believe in her new strength, independence, and optimism, the reader is jolted by her severe panic when, back in San Francisco, she realizes her daybook is in her missing suitcase and she may never see it again. She uses a dramatic analogy to describe her panic: "I did not see how I could go on with my life. Everything within me sank. It was as though my respirator, whatever essential machine had kept me breathing, was cruelly removed." The panic is a physical assault, like Felicia's dizzying, weakening lurch of apprehension as she considers the possibility that Martin has abandoned her. Neither woman gives herself credit initially for being able to survive without external support. Janet feels these lost jottings are her lifeline, protecting her from emotional collapse.

Yet as Janet finally discovers, after it becomes apparent that the airline will never locate her luggage, the lost jottings are not so important; it is the process of writing her thoughts down, making connections, making meaning, that matters. Writing in the journal is always a happy time for her as she focuses on herself and sifts through recent or distant events to create meaning out of these experiences. Writing enables her to take charge of her own emotional life.

Janet learns the importance of the process of constant recreating, making new meanings in her life that are not dependent upon those meanings she has inherited and preserved, that baggage she has carried. With this realization, she can resolve her crisis: she will buy a new notebook and start to write again. In deciding to replace the large, bulky, expensive journal with a small, compact one for her journey on the open road of her future, middle-aged Janet is jettisoning: she jettisons excess baggage, a bulky journal into which she had thrown some of her bulky, burdensome, no longer relevant feelings, such as guilt about Walter, feelings that she no longer needs to carry with her. Jane Somers and Richard Curtis could have benefited from a similar jettisoning. Janet learns that if she can continue writing—because writing is like living: engaging, experimental, full of risk taking—then what literally happens in her life is almost immaterial. Whatever happens, she will be able to embrace it, absorb it, make sense of it. Writing in her notebook gives Janet dominion over her life.

What the notebook and the process of writing mean for Janet, Adams seems to hope reading the story will mean,

vicariously, for readers: an aesthetic, therapeutic experience and analysis of loss, widowhood, and adjustment to a single middle age. That Janet titles the newest chapter in her life, her first entry in her newly purchased journal, **"Lost Luggage,"** the same title that Adams gives her story about Janet, suggests that Adams means us to see this connection between Janet's writing and our reading of Adams's writing.

Janet ends her narrative with a more solidly anchored self-confidence. She had begun her narrative congratulating herself for looking well as a middle-aged widow and for having survived her first vacation alone. She ends it by quietly stating that she will carry her portable notebook with her during any future trips, testifying to the importance of writing in her life and to her new mobility after some mid-life jettisoning. But the confidence of her very last words, "even if the book were to be lost, the loss would be minimal," testifies to her realization that the power and freedom of her writing to create new meanings in her life reside not in the daybook or in the words, but in herself. She knows now that her "strong-as-Stone" (Stone is her maiden name) strength and happiness have been self-won. The fact that she cheerfully takes on a part-time job and a paying house guest near the end of the narrative suggests that she is on her way to fulfilling the exhilarating vision she had had in Mexico of her future as an older woman alone. That she is optimistically future-oriented is further suggested by her declaration in the final paragraph: "I don't plan to go back to that particular Mexican resort; I believe that it has served its purpose in my life." This twice-visited resort now becomes a part of Janet's past, a chapter of her life's journal jettisoned by the writer to ready her for new jottings and new travels. With its firmly cheerful futurity and its challenge to conventional ways of making meanings about middle age, **"Lost Luggage"** justifies critic Norbert Blei's claim that Adams's writing "can change our lives" ["The Art of Alice Adams," *Milwaukee Journal*, May 16, 1982].

Adams's vision of aging is more ambivalent in the last story of her collection, the title story, **"To See You Again."** The middle-aged heroine of **"To See You Again,"** Laura, in a first-person narrative reveals how acutely she is aware of her own and other people's ages and the aging process itself. She, like many in American society, sees age as a major constituent of identity, not always with happy consequences. She dislikes herself because she is old in comparison to a 19-year-old man named Seth, with whom she has become infatuated while teaching an English class at Cornford. Advancing age, on the other hand, will diminish her husband's bouts with severe depression, gradually ending her intermittent widowhood. Aging may also improve her interactions with Seth, decreasing the social disparity between their ages. Although Laura experiences despair partly because of her age, by the end of her story she nevertheless imagines a better future in which the burdens of her middle age will be lightened by her entry into old age.

Laura divides her first-person narrative into four segments: one concerning Seth and her feelings for him, representing her false start on her journey to true *reifung*; a second concerning an older male friend, Larry Montgomery; the third concerning her husband Gerald, with the *Reifungsroman's* familiar reminiscence of courtship and review of marriage; and the fourth concerning a fantasy she has about her future with Gerald and Seth, inspired by a play she sees on television. As she moves through all four segments, she also journeys backward and forward along the age continuum, acquiring a perspective on youth, middle age, and old age.

Laura is more obsessed with the inappropriateness of her feelings for Seth than is Felicia. Felicia merely smiles over her 16-year-old-in-love feelings, unseemly for a 59-year-old woman, but Laura feels it is scandalous and shameful for a middle-aged woman like herself to have a crush on a youth. Her discomfort is evident in her every phrase. She tells us that she is "cruelly older than Seth" and imagines how repelled he must be by her age. She censures herself in the middle of imagining the "act of love" with him; "the very idea [is] both terrifying and embarrassing" because she would be exposing her repulsively middle-aged body to his youthful eyes: "How old I must seem to him! Revolting, really, although I am in very good shape 'for my age.' But to him revolting—as I sometimes am to myself." Laura's words convey her self-loathing, the distaste for her aging flesh that Jane Somers intermittently feels when gazing in the mirror. And Laura does not attain the self-approval in middle age or self-confidence about her old age that Kate Brown and Adams's other two heroines do. She thinks dualistically about aging, and her dualistic imagery reflects her pessimism, as she compares her middle age to the cold of San Francisco, which she then contrasts to Cornford's "adolescent summer—urgent, flushed." Her imagery associates a cold, impassive sterility with middle age while it assigns to adolescence the ripening warmth of insistent sexual passion.

As obsessed as she is with their disparity in age and her aging body, Laura is even more obsessed with the youthful beauty of Seth as she repeatedly describes to us his red-gold curls, green eyes, and bright sensitivity. His beauty seems to increase her own self-loathing as well as her pain at losing him when the semester ends. The barrier between youth and age seems unassailable as the "silly, fatuous" girls, his classmates, literally and metaphorically obstruct her last view of Seth in the classroom; they are her victorious rivals, Seth's peers. Laura tells us that she has put her feelings for Seth in perspective, but her words also suggest that she is still by her feelings for him: "Not quite anguished—I had had worse losses in my life (I have them still)—but considerably worse than 'let down' was how I felt." The only way she can cope with both the age issue and losing him is to fantasize about seeing him in the future, an older, still handsome man, but showing the effects of aging, like herself ("maybe in middle age he will be heavy? I wistfully considered that"). No longer a breathtakingly young and beautiful boy, an older Seth would somehow be more "equal" to her, less idealized.

In the second segment of her narrative, Laura's thoughts turn to Larry Montgomery in an effort to understand both how Seth would feel about her if he knew of her infatuation and what she herself would like from Seth: "Larry is exactly as much older than I am as I am older than Seth. He has what Gerald describes as a crush on me." Like Laura herself, Larry is well preserved: "Larry looks at least ten years younger than he is, trim and tan, with lively blue eyes and fine silver-white hair." Through her comparison of the two relationships she learns that she, like Larry, may have at times acted curtly toward the object of her adoration because she was terrified of revealing her affection for him. She also learns that a sexual affair is probably not what either she or Larry would want: "a stray motel afternoon with Larry was as unimaginable as it would be with Seth. Larry just likes to see me, to be near me, sometimes—and very likely that is what I feel for Seth, pretty much?" The question mark at the end of her sentence suggests that Laura is still in the process of analyzing her feelings in order to understand herself; she is not sure what she wants, or could have, from Seth. She imagines herself domesticating her unruly sexual feelings for him, which she so disparages, by making Seth a family friend and inviting him to her home. As Laura seeks answers to her questions about Seth, gaining knowledge about her identity and a direction for her future, she is mentally ripening, like most protagonists of *Reifungsroman*.

Important to this ripening process is Laura's probing in the third section of her narrative into her marriage to "sad fat" Gerald, a successful architect who has given her a "most precariously balanced . . . 'good life.'" Her marriage to this severely depressed man has been a cold one, and his bouts with depression have undermined Laura's self-approval: "one problem about living with someone who is depressed is that inevitably you think it has to do with you, your fault, although you are told that it is not." That her self-esteem has been eroded by Gerald's illness is evident in her self-demeaning fantasies about the beautiful Seth. Her contrasting of Seth and Gerald only intensifies her despair about herself, her husband, and her marriage. Gerald's fat old man's body and "heavy as boulders" depression contrast with Seth's thin boy's body and sprightly, elfinlike personal qualities. Even the language she uses to describe her home reflects her view of Gerald and their marriage; their kitchen has an atmosphere of "immaculate" sterility, and she, passionate and angry at being deprived of a passional life, imagines herself countering that sterility by painting it red.

Following the pattern of *Reifungsroman*, Laura also goes back in her memory to their youth and courtship, which offer another painful contrast to the present. Gerald was then "so beautiful, so dark and thin, . . . so elusive"—qualities of youth that remind us of Seth; and Laura was also young, "a silly undergraduate with a crush on a future architect." The contrast between this past and the present that greets her as she returns home from her final class—Gerald has descended into another depression—dismays her. All that she really has to comfort her is the statement of Gerald's psychiatrist: "With age the cycle [of his bouts with depression] may well lengthen, and the severity of each attack will decrease." The psychiatrist's words—like Lessing's and Adams's messages generally—challenge our common association of the aging process with increased depression and despair. That aging may cure Gerald gives Laura something to look forward to, but her question is, will it come soon enough? Laura's words betray her impatience and escalating despair: "age could take forever, I'm not sure I have that much time." The edgy tone of these words implies that she is enduring an unbearable situation and can only continue to do so a little longer. Time is not passing quickly enough—a phenomenon present in *Reifungsroman* about middle age, but even more common to *Reifungsroman* about old age—to cure Gerald, salvage her marriage, and bring Laura some contentment.

To distract herself from the slow passage of time, Laura has only her imagination, which she trains in the fourth section of the story on a television play that she is watching. The play comforts her because in it is an actor who strongly resembles Seth—the obsessed woman sees the face of this youth everywhere—as she imagines he will look in older middle age. She says, "Oh, so that is how he will look: gray, slightly overweight but *strong*, with a brilliant smile, and those eyes." She soothes herself by fantasizing a future meeting with the older Seth, whom she will finally be able to look at because he will have become "merely handsome." Aging has its benefits after all: not only does it cure people of the depression and despair that often assail them in middle age, but it also equalizes people's original endowments of personal beauty. This prospect offered by Laura's fantasy gives her something to look forward to: "And at that time, your prime and our old age, Gerald's and mine, Gerald will be completely well . . . no more sequences of pain. And maybe thin again. And interested, and content. It's almost worth waiting for." What a pretty fantasy, readers think—"and they lived happily ever after," ripening into an old age that is a blessed release from the disappointments and despair of middle age.

But there are two further considerations: one, this is a fantasy that will probably never come true; and two, Laura uses the word "almost": if a perfect fantasy is not completely (as opposed to "almost") worth waiting for, what is? Instead of being a comfort to Laura, this fantasy's contrast to reality may be too painful for her to enjoy or believe in. Perhaps she is not able to wait anymore, meaning her patience and ability to endure her trials have run out in mid-life. She may have lost the fight against "disillusionment . . . [and] 'the sheer fatigue of living'" [Paul Gray, "Balances," *Time*, April 19, 1982]. Because she had said, "age could take forever, I'm not sure I have that much time" to wait for the end to Gerald's illness, readers are left at the end of the story with an uneasy feeling about Laura's fragile lease on life, a sense of her inching toward suicide. Old age will be easy for her to embrace, it seems, if she can just make it through a beastly middle age. She has not had the advantages of new love that Jane Somers and Felicia have: their exhilaration and rejuvenation contrast with her despair and shame over her infatuation with Seth; pleasure and happiness seem far removed from Laura's life. Nor does she have the resource of writing in a journal, which improves the tenor and direction of Janet's life. Writing in a journal as a way of coming to terms with the conditions of one's life would be more

constructive than escaping from those conditions as Laura does through her fantasies. She seems almost as afflicted by inaction as her clinically depressed husband, achieving no pragmatic resolution of her current problems and foreseeing none in the short run. All is in abeyance till old age. Laura's story ends with her passive resignation to a barely tolerable situation, one that prevents her from garnering the happy fruits of ripening self knowledge and maturity. In **"To See You Again,"** Adams presents middle age as a time for reassessing one's life and depicts through Laura some likely results of such a reassessment: self-knowledge and ripening maturity, but also confrontation with failures, losses, and disappointments that may be paralyzing, more difficult to bear, and more treacherous than the challenges of old age.

It is curious that Adams chose to end her volume with this story and to give the collection the title of this story. Its ambiguous message about the aging process departs from the unalloyed optimism about middle age in Janet's and Felicia's stories and in other stories of the collection about old age. The story suggests that the period of middle age may be particularly trying and turbulent. And through the story, readers can understand how we torment ourselves on the issue of age—how we denigrate ourselves and others because of the meanings we attach to words like "middle-aged." Perhaps Adams chose to end her book with Laura's story because she is not a whitewasher of reality. That middle age requires some difficult transitions and adjustments to losses is amply attested to also by the struggles of Kate Brown, Jane Somers, Janet, and Felicia. These transitions and adjustments demand of the protagonists real courage and strength of character. What is, nevertheless, evident in these fictional heroines is their authors' belief that many women can develop and unearth rich reserves of courage and strength within themselves.

FURTHER READING

Biography

Herman, Barbara A. "Alice Adams." *Contemporary Fiction Writers of the South: A Bio-Bibliographical Sourcebook*, edited by Joseph M. Flora and Robert Bain, pp. 11-21. Westport, Conn.: Greenwood Press, 1993.

> Divided into the following sections: biography, discussion of themes, survey of Adams criticism, and primary and secondary bibliographies.

Criticism

DeMott, Benjamin. "Stories of Change." *The New York Times Book Review* (11 April 1982): 7, 17.

> Referring to the fact that most of the characters in the stories in *To See You Again* seek to alter their lives, DeMott states: "Practically everybody in sight is wild to start over. The change-obsessed members of Miss Adams's audience . . . will surely be amused for a time, but

there's a chance that even they may find the performance a shade too monotonic before the end."

Flam, Jack. "Savoring the Flavor of Everyday Life." *Wall Street Journal* (13 November 1989): A8.
    Negative assessment of *After You've Gone*. Flam declares that Adams's stories are insubstantial.

Kakutani, Michiko. "Books of the Times." *The New York Times* (21 August 1985): C17.
    Comments that *Return Trips* tends to focus on "intelligent, well-heeled women, now in late middle age, who have long since traded the domestic loyalties of the 50s they were raised on for the more selfish imperatives of society today." Kakutani also notes that "Adams herself writes about their emotions and the shape of their lives with clear, omniscient skill, summarizing patterns of behavior and ironies of timing with candor and dispassion."

Lowry, Beverly. "Women Who Do Know Better." *The New York Times Book Review* (1 September 1985): 5.

Applauds Adams's rendering of female characters in *Return Trips*. According to Lowry, Adams's women "are not morbid people, only smart and anxious, pensive and extremely touching."

Phillips, Robert. "Missed Opportunities, Endless Possibilities." *Commonweal* CX, No. 6 (25 March 1983): 188-90.
    Review of *To See You Again* in which Phillips observes that in her stories Adams "suppresses and condenses, allowing the reader to make vital connections between situation and character."

Pollitt, Katha. "Good Ole Boys and Wistful Hippies." *The New York Times Book Review* (14 January 1979): 14, 27.
    Finds *Beautiful Girl* pleasing but suspects that the stories in the collection did not sufficiently challenge Adams's skill as an author.

Wood, Susan. "Stories of Love and Loss." *The Washington Post—Book World* (21 January 1979): G3.
    Praises Adams's sensitive depiction of "human desire and frailty" in *Beautiful Girl*.

Additional coverage of Adams's life and career is contained in the following sources published by Gale Research: *Contemporary Authors,* **Vols. 81-84;** *Contemporary Authors New Revision Series,* **Vol. 26;** *Contemporary Literary Criticism,* **Vols. 6, 13, 46;** *Dictionary of Literary Biography Yearbook, 1986;* **and** *Major 20th-Century Writers.*

Carlos Fuentes
1928-

Mexican novelist, short story writer, playwright, screen-writer, critic, and essayist.

INTRODUCTION

Fuentes is regarded by many as Mexico's foremost contemporary fiction writer. His abilities in the short story genre have been acclaimed by critics, though his short fiction has generally received less attention than his novels. Nonetheless, Fuentes's overriding literary concerns are the same in both genres; in both he explores the issue of Mexico's national character and attempts to more firmly establish the country's cultural identity. To accomplish this, he incorporates myth, legend, and history into his work, probing the past events of his homeland and the essence of modern Mexican society. His short fiction features unusual treatments of time and the use of fantastic, seemingly supernatural, events. He is also known for the ironic twists that he frequently places at the conclusion of his short narratives. His deft handling of this classic short story tool has helped to establish his strong reputation in the genre.

Biographical Information

Fuentes was born in Panama City, Panama, the son of a Mexican career diplomat living abroad. Because of his father's work, Fuentes spent much of his childhood in foreign countries, including the capital cities of many Latin American countries and also Washington, D.C., where he lived for much of the 1930s. He attended high school in Mexico City and later entered the National University of Mexico. While studying law there, he published several short stories and critical essays in journals, thereby launching his literary career. After graduating from law school, Fuentes travelled to Geneva, Switzerland, to study international law, and in 1950 he began a diplomatic career that has included two appointments to Mexico's Ministry of Foreign Affairs and the position of Mexican ambassador to France from 1975 to 1977. In 1959 he married Rita Macedo, a film actress. The marriage lasted ten years, and in 1973 he married Sylvia Lemus. Fuentes has three children, a daughter from his first marriage and a son and a daughter from his second. In addition to his writing and his diplomatic assignments, he has served as a lecturer at universities all over the world, including the University of Paris and Columbia University.

Major Works

Los días enmascarados (*The Masked Days*), Fuentes's first collection of short fiction, appeared in 1954. The book contains two stories that have received significant critical

attention: "Chac Mool" and "Tlactocatzine, del jardin de Flandes" (which has been translated as "Tlactocatzine, in the Garden of Flanders" and "In a Flemish Garden"). Both stories reflect the author's fascination with Mexican history and his use of fantastic occurrences to demonstrate the continuing influence of the past. "Chac Mool" takes its title from an ancient rain god sacred to pre-Columbian Indians in Mexico. A statue of the god is obtained by the protagonist Filiberto, a contemporary Mexican who collects native art. After installing the statue in his basement, the Chac Mool seems to come to life, disrupting Filiberto's existence and eventually killing him. Much of "Chac Mool" is related in the form of Filiberto's diary, and this form of epistolary narration is employed in a number of Fuentes's stories. "Chac Mool" also incorporates the commentary of Filiberto's friend who first thinks the tale of the living god is the product of Filiberto's imagination. This theory is brought into question, however, by the story's surprising conclusion. "Tlactocatzine" is also set in Mexico in the mid-twentieth century. A man named Carlos moves into an old house in Mexico City and soon encounters an old woman in the garden of the residence. She turns out to be Carlota, the wife of Maximilian, the short-lived Hapsburg emperor of Mexico in the 1800s. At the story's conclusion, Carlos finds himself trapped in the garden with Carlota, unable or unwilling to return to the present-day realities he finds unpleasant. A similar situation unfolds in the novella *Aura,* published in 1962. Here, the main character Felipe becomes a secretary to an old woman who lives with her young niece, Aura. Felipe and Aura become lovers but, in the end, the old woman and Aura seem to be one person, and Felipe comes to believe that he is some kind of reincarnation of the old woman's deceased husband, a former Mexican military leader.

Fuentes's second major collection of stories *Cantar de ciegos (Song of the Blind)* signaled a new development in his short fiction. The narratives show less concern with historical figures and supernatural elements, instead featuring detailed character studies of individuals in contemporary society. "Las dos Elenas" ("The Two Elenas") concerns a mother and daughter who seemingly have different attitudes in many things—the daughter expressing a cosmopolitan openness to new experiences, the mother upholding a more conservative code of behavior. The story's conclusion, however, contains a surprise that shows both women's actions are at odds with their statements. An unexpected conclusion also figures in "La muñeca reina" ("The Doll Queen"), in which the nostalgic narrator attempts to return to his youth by finding a girl he knew when he was a child. When he does track down the woman, the result is more grotesque than idyllic; she is now physically deformed and is kept hidden by her parents who cannot accept her imperfect condition. The theme of compromised ideals runs through many of the stories in the volume. The narratives seem to suggest that those who cling to sentimental notions or espouse sharply defined codes of conduct are prone to ironic twists that leave them disappointed.

The works in Fuentes's later short fiction collections have received less critical attention than his early stories. He has continued to experiment with the genre, however, focusing primarily on novellas and extended narratives. *Constancia y otras novelas para vírgenes [Constancia and Other Stories for Virgins]* again employs elements of the supernatural while presenting characters that are obsessed by past events, both historic and personal. *The Orange Tree* takes a panoramic view of history, using five novellas to address such topics as the conquest of Mexico by Hernán Cortés, Columbus reconsidering his discovery of the new world, and Roman rule in ancient Spain.

Critical Reception

Fuentes's short fiction has been well-received. While his novels have sometimes been criticized for being inaccessible and overly intellectual, the stories have received nearly universal acclaim, partly due to their brevity and the classic short story mold that Fuentes employs. At the same time, the unusual mix of bizarre occurrences, social commentary, and mythological allusions have given critics much to puzzle over. "Chac Mool" has been analyzed as a prime example of fantastic literature, and surreal eruption of the past into the present in this and other stories

has invited many critical explanations of the author's intent. Several studies have linked Fuentes's characters to various archetypal figures, including those of the Great Mother and the witch, with *Aura* being the focus of many of these analyses. The depiction of females in the stories has also generated a fair amount of criticism; several observers have praised Fuentes's work for making transparent the power struggles which create inequalities between the sexes. Of the few negative comments about the stories, the one most often heard is that Fuentes occasionally places too much emphasis on making satiric political statements. Because of this, some critics claim, certain stories become less effective as fiction. Complaints of this kind are rare, however. Fuentes has assumed a respected position among contemporary short story writers.

PRINCIPAL WORKS

Short Fiction

Los días enmascarados [*The Masked Days*] 1954
Aura (novella) 1962
Cantar de ciegos [*Song of the Blind*] 1964
Dos cuentos mexicanos [*Two Mexican Stories*] 1969
†*Chac Mool y otros cuentos* [*Chac Mool and Other Stories*] 1973
†*Agua quemada* [*Burnt Water*] 1980
Constancia y otras novelas para vírgenes [*Constancia and Other Stories for Virgins*] 1989
The Orange Tree (novellas) 1994

Novels

La Región más transparente [*Where the Air the Air is Clear*] 1958
Las buenas consciencias [*The Good Conscience*] 1959
La muerte de Artemio Cruz [*The Death of Artemio Cruz*] 1962
Cambio de Piel [*A Change of Skin*] 1967
Zona Sagrada [*Holy Place*] 1967
Cumpleaños [*Birthday*] 1969
Terra Nostra 1975
La cabeza de hidra [*Hydra Head*] 1978
Una familia lejana [*Distant Relations*] 1980
El gringo viejo [*The Old Gringo*] 1985
Cristóbal nonato [*Christopher Unborn*] 1987
La Campaña [*The Campaign*] 1990

Other Major Works

The Argument of Latin America: Words for North Americans (nonfiction) 1963
Pedro Paramo (screenplay) 1966
Tiempo de morir (screenplay) 1966
Los caifanes (screenplay) 1967
Paris: La revolución de mayo (nonfiction) 1968
La nueva novelo hispanoamerica (criticism) 1969

Casa con dos puertas [*House with Two Doors*] (nonfiction) 1970

Todos los gatos son pardos (play) 1970

El tuerto es rey (play) 1970

Poemas de amor: Cuentos del alma (poetry) 1971

Tiempo mexicano [*Mexican Time*] (nonfiction) 1971

Cervantes; o, La crítica de la lectura [published as *Don Quixote; or, The Critique of Reading*] (nonfiction) 1976

Orquídeas a la luz de la luna [*Orchids in the Moonlight*] (play) 1982

High Noon in Latin America (nonfiction) 1983

On Human Rights: A Speech 1984

Latin America: At War with the Past (nonfiction) 1985

Gabriel García Marquez and the Invention of America (criticism) 1987

Myself with Others: Selected Essays 1988

The Buried Mirror: Reflections on Spain and the New World (essays) 1992

*This volume is made up of two stories originally published in *Cantar de ciegos.*

†These collections contain stories published in previous volumes.

CRITICISM

Joseph Sommers (essay date 1966)

SOURCE: A review of *Cantar de ciegos,* in *Books Abroad,* Vol. 40, No. 1, Winter, 1966, pp. 69-70.

[*Sommers was an American educator and critic whose books included* After the Storm: Landmarks of the Modern Mexican Novel *(1968). In this review of* Cantar de ciegos, *Sommers praises the "wide ranging variety" of the stories in the collection.*]

One of Mexico's most accomplished young writers (born in 1928) confirms his admirable penchant for experimenting, almost always successfully, with new themes and styles, in this second volume of short stories [*Cantar de ciegos*].

Equidistant between earlier fictional works—the novel *La región más transparente* and the novelette *Aura*—this new volume has points of contact with both. Primarily, however, *Cantar de ciegos* stands on its own merits: wide-ranging variety of tone and treatment; remarkable blend of universality and sophisticated cosmopolitanism; peak moments of incredibly biting satirical humor (not excluding a touch of obscenity); and the common denominator of underlying anguish implied in the title.

Echoes of *Aura* and the exploration of fantasy are present in the richly textured mood story, **"La muñeca reina."** A mature narrator's efforts to recapture youthful moments of lyric beauty with a girl of his adolescence terminate in horror verging on the grotesque.

Readers of *La región más transparente* will be prepared for the urbane, rapier-like repartee of Fuentes's middle class intellectual types in several other stories. Here his characters are mordant in their cynicism, ultra-modern in their familiarity with avant-garde literature, art and cinema, and destructive in their evaluation of established morality, particularly as regards sex.

Weakest of the stories are **"Las dos Elenas"** and **"Vieja moralidad,"** in which modern technique and clever endings do not compensate for superficial treatment of the essential themes. The two finest creations, **"Un alma pura"** and **"A la víbora de la mar,"** are clearly situated in time and place, although independent of the historical framework so vital to the author's novels. In both stories, protagonists from contemporary Mexico are placed in cosmopolitan international environments as they trace their personal quests for self-definition. It is interesting to note that, although the narrations differ in tone and mood, both end in personal tragedy and breakdown of self.

The world of characters and situations in this collection is seen from widely varying perspectives. Within its composite structure, the individual, be he from the provinces, Mexico City or Europe, faces a modern society which isolates him, and against which his prepared defenses—personal and cultural—are inadequate.

Whether their goals be happiness, artistic creativity, some form of self-expression or a mere raise in salary, the characters on Fuentes's brilliantly lit stage usually have meaningful but frustrating encounters with deceit and despair.

Richard M. Reeve (essay date 1971)

SOURCE: "Carlos Fuentes and the New Short Story in Mexico," in *Studies in Short Fiction,* Vol. VIII, No. 1, Winter, 1971, pp. 169-79.

[*Reeve is an American critic and educator and the author of* An Annotated Bibliography of Carols Fuentes *(1970). In the following essay, Reeve traces the trajectory of Fuentes's short fiction, noting his preoccupation with Mexico's colonial past.*]

If asked to list the important Mexican short story writers of today, one would no doubt call to mind the names of the dual deities of short fiction. Juan José Arreola and Juan Rulfo, who during their heyday in the mid-fifties represented the universal-fantasy tendency on one side and the rural-realistic on the other. The third member of this prestigious trinity, and one whose star is in continual ascent, is novelist Carlos Fuentes. Unprecedented success has greeted almost all of Fuentes' novels: numerous editions, translations into more than a dozen languages, purchase of film rights and winning of the coveted Biblioteca Breve prize in Spain. He is one of the rare Latin American writers who can live from his pen. Fuentes plays to the hilt his role of the grand novelist, center of attention, much sought after speaker (and visiting professor), and frequently interviewed expert on everything and anything. His contacts with Latin American and European writers are legion, and he additionally claims intimate ties with such contemporary North American literary giants as Norman Mailer, Arthur Miller, and William Styron. Recently I had the occasion to review an anthology of Mexican short story writers all of whom were under thirty years of age. In the introduction each contributor was asked to list his literary influences. With but one or two exceptions, all refused to cite the Mexican narrators of the previous generation, but the influence of Carlos Fuentes was easily detected in the works themselves. And Juan Rulfo [in *Narrativa joven de México,* 1969]; in one of his rare interviews has observed, "Carlos Fuentes is the foundation of all of today's young literature in Mexico. All the writers want to be like him."

Fuentes' talents, however, do not lie exclusively in the novel. Indeed, he began and ended his first decade of writing with collections of short stories—each very popular and each the center of a heated polemic. Many reviewers have called attention to the structure of Fuentes' novels, which often consist of loosely connected episodes not unlike short stories. One critic of the novel *The Death of Artemio Cruz* goes so far as to suggest that a lazy reader might skip the chapters told in the first and second person and enjoy the novel reading only those related in the third person [Isabel Fraire in *Revista Mexicana de Literatura,* julio-agosto 1962]. Carlos Valdés, a Mexican short story writer of considerable note, calls Fuentes "a magnificent painter of small sketches, but a doubtful muralist of unlimited spaces" and suggests that Fuentes' real future belongs in the short story genre ["Un virtuoso gratuito," *Revista de la Universidad de Mexico* XVI, 1962].

For most Mexicans, Fuentes burst upon the literary scene in December of 1954. His book of short stories **The Masked Days (Los días enmascarados)** no sooner reached the bookstores than it became embroiled in a heated controversy over its language and themes. Fuentes was accused of taking too many liberties with the Spanish language—an accusation raised with almost every succeeding book. Fuentes on numerous occasions has speculated that the Spanish language needs renovation from its fossilized state, and a critic has praised Fuentes' *Where the Air is Clear (La región más transparente)* for containing the most extensive vocabulary ever found in a Mexican novel [José Emilio Pacheco, *Estaciones* III, 1968]. The second accusation against the short stories was that they were not "Mexican" enough. This allegation, while true for several pieces in the collection, is not based on fact when considering the totality of the book. Granted, the stories avoid the long-popular topic of the Mexican Revolution, its causes, results, or actual episodes. Fuentes in these stories was more closely aligned with the fantasy and satire of Arreola, who, incidentally, was the director of the series that published Fuentes' book, although the compositions have been classified as "wilder, rawer and more precolumbian" than those of Arreola. [Anonymous, "Fifteen Young Mexican Writers," *Recent Books in Mexico,* 1957].

The common theme that unites most of the stories in Fuentes' first book is the inescapable past. In **"Chac Mool,"** undoubtedly Fuentes' best known short story and a great favorite with compilers of anthologies, a Mayan rain god returns to life and enslaves his former owner. The latter's desperate attempt to flee from the idol by running away to Acapulco is thwarted when he drowns while swimming—the rain god can still control the elements. This piece, told in the form of a diary that is read by a friend of the dead man, has all the earmarks of a psychological study instead of fantasy until the friend also meets the idol face to face.

The fifth story in Fuentes' book, **"By the Mouth of the Gods,"** also illustrates the influence of the inescapable pre-hispanic past on another resident of Mexico City. After defiantly cutting the mouth from a portrait of an Indian in the art gallery of the Palacio de Bellas Artes, the narrator finds himself pursued by a pantheon of Aztec gods. (The painting incidently was by Tamayo, one of the Mexican artists that Fuentes most admires). The pursued locks himself in his hotel room, number 1519. The number itself is but another example of Fuentes' subtlety in presenting pre-hispanic elements—1519 marked the year that Hernán Cortés landed in Mexico. After a narrow escape from the gods in the hotel basement, the "art lover" is lured from his room, according to Fuentes' tongue-in-cheek satire, as only a Mexican could be—by denying his manliness (*machismo*): "This was the ultimate insult! They had ripped away the last shred of my dignity, my social position, my entire free will. Now they were attacking my sexual prowess. I thrust open the door . . .". He is then stabbed in the abdomen in a manner recalling the Aztec human sacrifices. Another element of fantasy that Fuentes effectively employs is giving life and personality to the lips that were cut off the picture. For a time they fasten themselves to the narrator's mouth and cause him to criticize various levels of Mexican society. The theme of social criticism, which makes itself manifest for the first time, is present to a greater or lesser degree in all of Fuentes' books. This has made him most unpopular in certain government and upper-class circles.

"Tlactocatzine, in the Garden of Flanders" is another story in this collection in which elements from the past destroy a modern Mexican. This destructive force is more recent, coming from the nineteenth century. A first-person narrator relates in his diary his experiences in a haunted house in the center of Mexico City. He is taking care of the old mansion for a friend when he is confronted with the phantom of Carlota, the mad empress, wife of Maximilian. Although the conclusion is somewhat ambiguous, it appears that she lures the narrator to his death. Carlota, made famous in the literature of the previous decade by Rodolfo Usigli in his play *Crown of Shadows,* will not soon be forgotten by Fuentes. She will appear as the principal protagonist of another short story in 1956, and will be mentioned several years later in the novel *Where the Air is Clear;* and finally Fuentes himself, in a phonograph recording, treats the listener to strains from "Adiós Mamá

Carlota," the insulting song sung by the Juarists based on the melody of *La Paloma,* the empress' favorite musical composition.

In tracing the theme of the destructive past, it is necessary to leave Fuentes' first book for a moment and examine a forgotten short story he published in 1953. The title is **"Panther in Jazz,"** and curiously Fuentes never mentions it nor has he ever collected it in a book. The victim appears to be a North American student, although the reader can never be sure. The pursuer is a panther escaped from a local circus and lodged in the student's bathroom, or so the boy believes—he thinks he hears growls but never actually sees the animal. The frantic young man listens intently at the door for any sound, and finally, as he loses his mind, he kidnaps a child, tosses it into the bathroom, and seals the door. The student never seeks outside help; calling the police never seems to enter his mind. It is as if he were a primitive man, naked and alone, facing the dreaded beasts of the jungle. Fuentes' interest in popular songs can be observed in this piece with the lyrics from the tunes reinforcing the theme, but also serving as comic relief: "Bingo, bango, bongo, I don't want to leave the Congo," and in another part "Animal crackers in my soup."

Another forgotten short story, **"Errant Wheat,"** which was published in a Mexican university magazine in 1956 [*Revista de la Universidad de Mexico* XI, September 1956], also treats the theme of the inescapable past, but in an unusual and non-Mexican manner. The scene is Palestine during a recent Arab-Israeli conflict—no doubt the war of 1948 since the story appeared two months before the campaign of 1956. An Arab plane is strafing the countryside while Jewish soldiers string barbed wire. The narrator returns from a distant past of almost two millenniums. He is Lazarus, brother of Mary and Martha, whom Christ raised from the dead. But Fuentes' Lazarus is anything but a contented disciple of Jesus. His raising made him immortal, and now he roams the world as a kind of wandering Jew, incapable of experiencing human emotions or physical satisfactions relating to love or eating. Lazarus is not mentioned by name in the earlier pages, but Fuentes gives the reader enough subtle clues to deduce his identity. "No one saw him grow up," "He had always been there," "Even the old men were used to seeing him there." In another scene Lazarus covers his face with a napkin, recalling his appearance in burial clothing at the moment of his return from the tomb. He laments his raising: "Why did I have to be the proof of a Divinity?" he wails, and even darkly suggests that the resurrected Christ is no happier in His immortality; in fact eternal life is a hellish fate. Lazarus reaches out from the past and somehow infects his companions with his cursed immortality. Jews as leading characters, while rare in Mexican fiction, are not new in Fuentes' writings. They appear as early as 1949 in his first known published story, **"Rancid Pastry."** [*Muñunu* XXXVI, November 1949]. A boy returning home to New York City meets and rejects his mother and the Jewish heritage she represents. For the moment it seems that he has overcome his past by denying it, although in doing so he destroys his mother.

In the spring of 1962 Fuentes published his magnificent novella, **Aura.** Unfortunately, as far as the critical reception of the piece is concerned, it appeared almost simultaneously with Fuentes' controversial major novel, *The Death of Artemio Cruz.* The reviewers' attention was diverted to the novel, probably Fuentes' fined. Significantly, many of the most perceptive reviews of the novella are of the second or third printings, after the furor of *Artemio Cruz* had died down.

Aura, too, is the history of an individual's destruction by elements from the past. An impoverished young history teacher answers a newspaper ad and find himself in the old quarter of Mexico City. The 109-year-old widow of one of Maximilian's generals wants her husband's memoirs compiled for publication. The salary is most attractive, as is Aura, the young niece of the widow. The historian is swept along through a series of bewildering episodes of black magic and strange love makings with the girl, finally falling victim to the powers and love potions of Consuelo, the ancient widow. The historian confronts the past not only in the duality of the old woman and Aura, but also in his reincarnation as the widow's husband. As he stares at a faded photograph of the general and Consuelo, he sees Aura and himself: ". . . but it is she, it is he . . . it is you!". Consuelo, who lives in a musty household surrounded in the interior by furnishings from her nineteenth-century world and on the outside by modern steel and glass skyscrapers, represents Mexico's past, which refuses to enter the present day stream of events. As with the owner of the Mayan idol, the defacer of the painting, the contemporary student, the immortal Lazarus and many other character creations by Fuentes, the modern man succumbs to the omnipresent past—he is unable to accept its challenges and is in turn destroyed. Even Fuentes' first novel, *Where the Air is Clear,* follows the same pattern: Ixca Cienfuegos, a mysterious and symbolic Indian, overcomes an ex-revolutionary now turned banker who represents the present, and also a soul-searching young intellectual who stands for Mexico's future.

Ten years passed between the publication of Fuentes' first and second books of short stories. During this decade he acquired an international reputation with three major novels and a short novel (all translated into English) before returning to the short genre with **Song of the Blind (Cantar de ciegos)** in 1964. The past is no longer the overriding theme of the work—it surfaces in only two pieces. The book as a whole signals a new direction in Fuentes' writing and in that of the Mexican short narrative in general.

"Doll Queen" is a short story of transition that represents both the old and the new tendencies. The theme is the search of a man for his past, specifically for a young girl he had known as an adolescent. The world of his childhood is recreated in his mind; and by retracing the places they had frequented, he finally finds the child again—still a child in physique, now transformed into a hideous little hunchback. Nevertheless, we can note a number of changes in Fuentes' writing techniques—the story is longer than most of those in the earlier book. The author now develops his characters more profoundly. They become more human and believable, less caricatures or types, as more time is devoted to their background and details of their present activities. Fuentes now gives us people who live rather than puppets who symbolize an idea or are employed for purposes of satire.

Another story illustrating the duality of Fuentes' early and later periods is "**A Pure Soul**." A young Mexican student has left his family and in particular his adoring younger sister for advanced studies in Geneva. (Of interest are two autobiographical elements: Fuentes also studied in the same Swiss city and has a younger sister). The narration is told mainly by means of flashbacks as the sister arrives in Switzerland to retrieve her brother's body after his suicide. She speaks to her brother as if he were still alive and could hear her in a manner that recalls Camilo José Cela's "Mrs. Caldwell Speaks to her Son." Because of its insight into the brother and sister relationship and the intimate tone of the whole work, this story is one of Fuentes' most successful. It has also been made into a motion picture.

It is the other stories in the collection, however, that really mark a new trail in Fuentes' narrative career and pinpoint his role as an innovator of Mexican fiction. In "**The Two Elenas**" and "**Fortune Always has Her Way**" we observe the complete absence of his pre-occupation with the past. Gone, too, is the satire and social criticism of *The Masked Days*. The plots of both stories are thin—what is essential are the marvelous character portraits. Elena is a vivacious wife who is constantly seeking new excitement; she is intrigued with North American jazz musicians, the Black Muslim sect, and Beat painting. Her uncomplaining husband realizes that it is her nature always to be interested in some new fad. A friend asks her why she remains faithful to her husband: "Elena answered that nowadays infidelity was the rule . . . she meant that now fidelity was the rebellious attitude." This piece was filmed in 1964 with Julissa, Fuentes' stepdaughter and Enrique Alvarez Félix, son of actress María Félix, playing the leading roles. Elena portrays the same passion for motion pictures that Fuentes does in real life. Ever since seeing *Jules et Jim*, Elena wants her husband to invite another man into their home. She is planning to view "a mythological western: *High Noon*" and has recently attended a private showing of Luis Buñuel's *The Exterminating Angel*. (Fuentes' second novel is dedicated to Buñuel).

The other story, "**Fortune Always has Her Way**," refers to the fickleness of life. As a character observes, "I have done what I could, and Fortune what it has wanted to do." The fascinating character who is the center of this work is a Beat painter who has enjoyed the favors of dozens of women only to be rejected by the one who really intrigues him. His most recent creation is a painting of a jar of instant coffee: "NESTLE CAFE INSTANTANEA SIN CAFEINA, HECHO EN OCTLAN, JAL. MARCA REG." It is probably no coincidence that Sevilla, the painter, resembles Fuentes' good friend, next door neighbor, and famous Mexican artist, José Luis Cuevas. Incidently, it is "**The Two Elenas**" that is dedicated to Cuevas, not this one.

The uniqueness of these two stories is the focus upon individuals rather than themes. Also Fuentes seems to have chosen to write pieces for sheer entertainment in and of themselves. He has opted for mid-twentieth-century types who are universal rather than Mexican in their concept and interests. Except for a few minor details, the stories could take place anywhere in the world. Fuentes has also returned to the high society and International Set, which he so successfully pictured in his first novel, a group that Fuentes with his well-to-do family background and riotous youthful escapades knows very intimately. This novel, *Where the Air is Clear*, first published in Mexico in 1958 and widely reprinted and translated, signals the end of the rural novel, often based on the Revolution, and the emergence of the city as the focal point of Mexican and Latin American life. Many critics, among them Cuban novelist Alejo Carpentier, have underlined Fuentes' significance in the rise of the urban novel [in *Tientos y diferencias*, 1964]. What he did in his novel, Fuentes does in these metropolitan short stories. Not that he is the first or that there are not many earlier examples in this genre, but Fuentes' prestige and his acquaintance with urban high society have made his contributions very visible to the young generation of writers.

"**Old Morality**" is another short story that in its choice of hero and theme may well have influenced such young Mexican writers as Gustavo Sainz and José Agustín, who while in their late teens and early twenties became famous in Mexican letters with their novels and short stories depicting problems of adolescents. Alberto in Fuentes' narration is a teenager who lives a life of innocence on a farm in Michoacan with his grandfather and the old man's mistress. The boy's old-maid aunts from the city obtain legal permission to liberate the boy from this degrading influence; they, in their turn, seduce the handsome youth. The latter soon becomes bored with the city and writes his grandfather, "Come and get me, please. I think there is more morality on our rancho. I'll tell you all about it." This is probably one of the most humorous pieces that Fuentes has written, although the humor tends toward irony. Alberto is presented in a very sympathetic manner as are most young men in the fiction of Fuentes. The author seems to suggest that time and society corrupt the innocence of youth. One can see examples of this in Fuentes' first three novels, where the young men Federico Robles, Jamie Ceballos, and even Artemio Cruz, all succumb to the corrupt ways of the world upon reaching manhood.

Another contemporary Mexican described in this book is the innocent abroad who is deceived by foreigners. In "**Sea Serpent**" Isabel Valles climbs aboard an ocean liner off the port of Acapulco for her first ocean cruise. Although she is in her thirties, awkward and self conscious, she is swept off her feet by a charming Briton who marries her only to turn out to be a North American confidence man who escapes with her money. As in most of Fuentes' books, North Americans come off second best as admirable people. They always manage to swindle or exploit their more innocent Latin counterparts. Another character in the story is Mrs. Jenkins, an old maid school teacher from Los Angeles, who is a formidable candidate for the "Ugly American" award in both appearance and actions. She is thought to weigh ninety-eight kilograms, and several times is compared with an elephant. Another passenger calls her a "pink zeppelin of liberty". Her language is most unbecoming a teacher or a lady, and she delights in criticizing the United States: "Jack Paar is our Homer and Fulton Sheen our baby sitter . . . in San Quentin we'll fry Chessman." With the British crewmen and numerous North Americans speaking English, whole paragraphs are in this language. Critics of this book and many others by Fuentes have often complained that a reader must be bilingual or even trilingual to understand them. Fuentes' usage of English, even slang, is nearly perfect.

Another stylistic feature of this story is its unusual structure. There is no division into chapters but rather an alternating of scenes in a most distinctive manner. First come the scenes treating the adventures of Isabel Valles, which make up the bulk of the action. Alternating with these are other scenes that in all but one instance are straight dialogue between two sailors. Functioning like a Greek chorus, they always comment upon Isabel or inform the reader of events not depicted. Only in the final scene is the pattern broken, and the reader for the first time follows the scheme of the confidence man. This story is dedicated to Fuentes' friend the Argentine novelist Julio Cortázar. No doubt Fuentes recalled the latter's *The Winners*, a novel whose action also takes place on board an ocean liner.

In **"Song of the Blind"** Fuentes has departed from his Mexican themes, settings and characters. Elena and the artist, Sevilla, for example, are universal in their way of life and preoccupations. Alberto and his relatives are very Mexican, but his worries are those of a harried adolescent. Whereas in his first stories Fuentes had been a follower, essentially of Arreola's fantasy, although a very capable follower, in **"Song of the Blind"** Fuentes forms the vanguard of a new trend—to make stories interesting for their own sake. There need be no underlying social or political criticism nor reliance upon the overwhelming forces of nature, themes which have been so prominent in the regional literature of Latin America. Mexico's mythical past is also forgotten.

More than six years have passed since Fuentes has published a short story—several novel fragments have appeared during this time, but they belong to another genre and were not conceived as short fiction even though they may stand alone. We might ask ourselves what will be the direction of Fuentes' future short narratives? Studying the evolution of his literary career and analyzing several recent publications, one can put forth a few intelligent speculations. First we may expect to see even more universal or international characters. This reflects Fuentes' lengthy residence abroad in recent years. In his novel *A Change of Skin* (1967), one of the four principal characters is a Mexican girl, another a Mexican who has lived abroad much of his life, a third a Jewish woman from New York City, and the fourth, a German. In Fu-

---

Master of the Short Story:

With *Cantar de Ciegos* [Song of the Blind], Fuentes keeps an old promise. He shows he is one of the few Latin American writers who have completely mastered the strict discipline of the short story. Fuentes' tales have a mystery, a morbid elegance, an aura of things forbidden, which his more literal and mechanized novels often lack. The short story lends itself perfectly to the sudden stroke, the brilliant pirouette which he cannot resist. It is sleight of hand, and Fuentes handles it as if he had invented it.

Joaquin Mortiz, "Morbid Elegance," Atlas, Vol. 13, No. 1, January, 1967, pp. 58-9.

---

entes' most recent short novel, *Birthday* ("Cumpleaños"), which appeared in late 1969, his characters are a French university professor residing on the Adriatic coast and a British family in Hamstead, England. Not once is Mexico even mentioned. A third selection from 1968, "Flesh Spheres, Grey Eves Along the Seine," at first glance seems to be a short story, but Fuentes advises me that it is part of a novel now under construction. The setting is Paris. These latter two works especially mark another change of direction—away from the real people and places of **"Song of the Blind."** To a degree, they are a return to fantasy, but not on the elementary level of his first short stories, in which perhaps one natural law suddenly changed. These recent books picture a mysterious surrealistic world full of symbolism, contamination of levels of time and meaning, speculation on metaphysical problems such as the meaning of reality or the probability of reincarnation. They leave the reader with multiple possibilities for interpretation.

The Mexican critic Emmanuel Carballo has stated [in *Excélsion*, 1 junio 1969] that Fuentes is "the writer responsible for the Mexican prose of the last few years, a man of the Vanguard, he is three steps ahead of the other writers of his time." Regardless of which direction he takes, we can rest assured that Carlos Fuentes will continue to produce short fiction of top quality, at the same time experimenting with new and exciting techniques; all the while baffling his readers, teasing the critics, and teaching his numerous literary disciples.

Richard J. Callan (essay date 1971)

SOURCE: "The Jungian Basis of Carlos Fuentes' *Aura*," in *Kentucky Romance Quarterly*, Vol. XVIII, No. 1, 1971, pp. 65-75.

[*Callan is an American critic and educator. In the following essay, he uses Jungian analysis to analyze the various symbols in Fuentes's novella* Aura *and sees the narrative as "ritualistic."*]

Aura is an intriguing *novella* with three characters, or perhaps only one, and a conclusion that seems disconcerting. Felipe Montero, twenty-seven years old, single, a student and teacher of history, answers an ad for a young secretary who knows French. He finds a very old woman, Señora Consuelo, who lives with her niece, Aura, in a house lit only by candles in the old center of town. The job consists of revising and finishing the memoirs of her husband, General Llorente, who played a small part in the Second Empire of Mexico. The young man accepts the financially attractive offer largely because of the lovely and entrancing Aura. He is to remain in the house until the work is completed. The next day when he observes Consuelo's absolute control over Aura and assumes that she keeps her niece at her side as a means of recovering her youth, he realizes that it is up to him to rescue the girl from such an abnormal life. A trace of abnormality, negligible at first, develops rapidly until it becomes evident that the two women are one and the same person. In the last scene, Felipe embraces Aura believing that Consuelo is away, but the girl has now become the old woman and he remains in her arms. He has also come to recognize that he is General Llorente. The concept of a woman, age-old but ever young, immediately calls to mind standard symbolic figures such as Mother Church, or the goddess Natura, and when we learn that Consuelo/Aura renews herself through animal sacrifices, we are reminded of the ancient nature cults and their Great Mother goddesses: Venus, Cybele, Ishtar. Proceeding along these lines it may be noticed that the plot presents some elements of an archetypal situation, the dragon fight: a young man's attempt to rescue a damsel in distress. The theme of the dragon slayer has been interpreted by analytical psychology to correspond to a specific stage in psychic development: the initiation into manhood. In a wide sense, it is patterned on the rites of sacrifice, death and rebirth, successive forms of which, repeated at intervals throughout life, enable consciousness to expand and renew itself, on its path to wholeness. The purpose of such ritual rebirths and renewals, according to Jungian psychology, is to release or liberate psychic energy from the unconscious. The dragon fight has a corollary aim for the young Ego: to differentiate the Anima, or the creative, *animating* aspect of the unconscious from the total unconscious, which is experienced as a power at once protective and destructive, but in both cases overwhelming to consciousness, and is personified in the universal figure of the Great Mother. The task of the young "hero," expressed in myths, literature and dreams, is to rescue a "princess" by penetrating into the lair of her captor, confronting and vanquishing it; he then carries her off in triumph and marries her, which means that he takes possession of the psychic energy she represents.

Initially, Felipe Montero's adventure exemplifies the "heroic" stage, of psychic development, wherein he is to separate Aura, his Anima, from Consuelo, the Great Mother. The archetypal structure of the *novella* depicts him entering into the unconscious, the realm of the Mother, when he goes to see Consuelo. Her house is hidden in the heart of the city, another, on Donceles Street;

doncel was the term for a young lord before he had received armor. The street name suggests that this is the place for youths to begin their ordeal and become "heroes." Before entering what will be a pitch dark hallway, Felipe stops and looks back over his shoulder at the "undifferentiated world outside." Differentiation of the Anima is now in order. Consuelo later restates this when she corrects him regarding the gender of her rabbit: "Ah, you're not able to distinguish yet."

Fuentes has surrounded Consuelo with many symbols of the Great Mother, and particularly those that are associated with Hecate. This was one of the Greek goddesses of the underworld (an obvious equivalent of the unconscious); among her attributes were a key, a torch, witchcraft, dogs—she was often depicted as dog-headed. Like most Great Mothers, she was an earth deity associated with darkness and fertility, with cereals and prolific animals such as rabbits, goats, mice. The doorknocker of Señora Consuelo is the head of a dog that looks like a canine fetus. The inside of her house is dark and heavy with dampness, like a cave. She has an indoor garden of forgotten plants once used in necromancy, deadly nightshade, henbane, bittersweet and other poisonous herbs. Her pet companion is a rabbit, Saga by name, which she explains means "sabia," the wise one, alluding perhaps to the allwise Mother, Sophia-Sapientia. Her bed is full of crumbs; there is a nest of mice in one corner of her room. She is also connected with other animals: cats, which as a bride she used to sacrifice to arouse her husband's sexual appetite, rats and a goat which she and Aura slaughter in the kitchen. Psychologically these theriomorphic symbols represent the libido or psychic energy contained in the unconscious. A key hangs around Consuelo's neck; it belongs to the chest containing the Llorente papers and she entrusts Felipe with it, later referring to it several times. There is a second key in this tale, Felipe's latchkey; the phallic significance of this object, as he opens Aura's fingers and presses it into her hand, foreshadows their sexual union; it is by this key that he recognizes her on the night she comes to him in the dark. These phallic keys, like Hecate's, open the treasure chest of the unconscious that houses the energy needed for psychic growth. The domain of the Great Mother is of course a holy place; likewise the old lady's bedroom with its religious articles and votive candles is a "santuario." The torch that Hecate often carries corresponds to the candelabrum that Aura holds as she stands waiting for Felipe.

The role of the Anima is to supply guidance for the hero, an Ariadne's thread, through the labyrinth of the unconscious. In much of the story, Aura serves as Montero's guide in the dark house. The conflict develops on the second day when he sees the two women together and wonders what keeps the girl subjected to her aunt. Perhaps Aura expects him to rescue her from the chains imposed on her by the crazy old lady? The girl's pure beauty has captivated him from the start. Now, bolstered by the meritorious idea of setting her free, he allows himself mentally to claim her as his own. He feels that she will guess his intention and come to his room later—as indeed she does, being a figment of his mind.

Carl Jung defines the Anima as the archetype of life, because it inspires man to do and to achieve things contrary to his innate passion for idleness. Felipe, spurred by the new job, begins to work on his long untouched History of the Conquest, in addition to doing Señora Consuelo's work. His new drive may be due unconsciously to the stimulating proximity of a beautiful girl. At any rate, Aura has many Anima qualities. For instance, while she is very real and tangible at night, at other times she becomes elusive and unpredictable, turning up suddenly beside him, disappearing into thin air, acting withdrawn and sometimes looking right through him, oblivious of his presence; she appears young and virginal at one time, at another she seems middle-aged; she can be demur as well as provocative and shameless, and she is always a little beyond reach. These are some of the contradictions that make the Anima so fascinating, for, like all archetypes, she is endowed with mana and irresistible.

Aura is green-eyed and always clad in green; so was Consuelo according to her husband's papers. Green is the life color and is commonly associated with the Anima. The General also said that his wife irradiated life. Toward the end of the story, Felipe urges Aura to leave the old lady, saying she is hardly more than a cadaver: "She has more life than I do" exclaims the girl. Indeed, this is equally true psychologically, for while the Anima is the archetype of life, the actual source of its vitality is the Great Mother, the total unconscious.

In one of the old photos that Felipe finds, Llorente's young wife appears against a backdrop of the Lorelei rock on the Rhine; the siren of that rock, who sang sailors to destruction, is a prime example of the Anima manifestation. The sea imagery by which Aura's unusual eyes are highlighted, makes of her a Venus born of the waves: ". . . those sea eyes that seem to billow, that sparkle like foam, then recover their green calm, then become dilated again like a surging wave." Jung has noted that water and the sea are the most common symbols of the unconscious, and that typical Anima figures are sirens, water sprites and other creatures that rise out of the deep, like Venus.

The Anima personifies man's unconscious and suppressed femininity; eventually he will want to raise to consciousness this *other half* of his psyche in order to achieve a more balanced personality. On the morning after his second night with Aura, having discovered that the aunt has been in the room all along, Felipe has a premonition that he is "seeking his other half." If this is an allusion to a man's search for his feminine half, it can only be a fleeting intuition, because this is a goal for the second half of life, and Felipe is at an earlier stage.

The matter of death and rebirth is also discussed in this *novella*. Arguing that Aura should leave her aunt because the old woman is trying to bury her, he tells her: "You have to be reborn, Aura." To which she replies: "One has to die before one is reborn. No. You don't understand." Montero has shown that he does not understand the need for sacrifice, symbolic or otherwise, and as a result his initiation is to be a failure. He does not "slay the dragon,"

like a true hero, he does not even confront her (Consuelo). True, he thought of doing it: "Why don't you have the courage to tell her that you love the girl? Why don't you go in and tell her, once and for all, that you are going to take Aura with you when you've finished the work?" But he goes to his room instead and reads in the Llorente papers about how she used to kill animals for generative purposes. Once the General found her with her legs outspread and her skirts thrown up, throttling a cat; she had explained that torturing cats and sacrificing them was her way of stimulating their love, and Llorente admitted that it worked. The young woman's posture suggests the ritual exhibitionism of a fertility goddess; sacrificial death is often symbolic of sexual union and represents fecundation. It is invariably connected with agricultural worship of the Great Mother.

Thereupon, Felipe hurries downstairs to speak to Aura about her aunt, and discovers her in the kitchen spattered with blood, slitting the throat of a goat and skinning it. Sickened by the odor and outraged at the sight of Aura's servitude, he races to Consuelo's room intent on accusing her of avarice and tyranny; he finds that the old woman is performing the same motions, killing and skinning an imaginary goat, obviously instigating the butchery from her room. He returns to his room in panic, blocks the door with his bed as if he were being pursued, and throws himself on it, exhausted. Not the doings of a hero. The need for self sacrifice has not penetrated his conscious mind; his Anima performs that which he should be doing himself, but which causes him nausea: for the goat that is being slain stands for him, and he should partake in the rite. He has neither stood up to the Great Mother nor propitiated her with blood.

Next, in a feverish nightmare, he sees Consuelo crawling toward him from out of a dark abyss, moving her bony hand, advancing until her face with its bloody, toothless gums touches his own and he screams; now she retreats, waving her hand and sowing into the abyss the yellow teeth she takes out of her bloody apron. Aura is there too, her skull shaven, laughing silently with the old woman's teeth superimposed upon her own. Her bare legs break off and fall into the ravine. These gruesome visions of Consuelo and Aura portray the negative character of the Great Mother, which signifies the primordial human fear of life. The abyss is her devouring womb, the maw of the grave; sowing the teeth and the phallic legs suggests a fertility rite for which the victim is indicated when Aura looks at Felipe and laughs. Bloody gums, wizen mask, bony claws, are common characteristics of the Terrible Mother; the double row of teeth, and the skull, bare like that of a vulture, likewise betoken her devouring and deadly nature. They are well suited to Aura, for the meaning of her name is "vulture." (The vulture is an obvious and universal symbol of the Death Goddess). All the gore and horror are not mere theatrics; they express "man's experience of life as a female exacting blood," and the Terrible Mother of ancient myths turns up in the nightmares of modern men and women.

In short, Felipe has not exhibited the bravery and aplomb expected of the hero. What has happened to his Anima when he needed her? The dinner bell awakens Felipe from his nightmare; beside his plate he finds a little naked doll made of cloth and stuffed with flour that spills out of its shoulder. He eats his cold meal, the usual kidneys, tomatoes and wine (all aphrodisiacs), while fingering the revolting little doll with his left hand. When he realizes what he is doing he drops it in disgust with the uneasy feeling that it may carry some contagion. It is a sacrificial figurine connected with a fertility rite—possibly the victim of an Aztec heart removal—and its "contagion" is his identity with it.

On his way to Aura's bedroom he visits the inside garden and examines the baneful and narcotic herbs once grown by Consuelo and now by her niece. Narcosis or any diminution of consciousness is foremost in the province of the Terrible Mother's dealings with mankind. Aura seems to have changed when he sees her; she is no longer the girl of yesterday; her features have hardened and she looks to be forty. She wears a gay grimace, a sad smile that expresses such contradictory feelings that he is reminded of the bittersweet plants he just saw in the garden: what the author is picturing here may be the expression of sentimental resignation of the sacrificer that Jung describes in *Symbols of Transformation*.

Aura insists on enacting a peculiar ceremony: she washes his feet, dances with him to the rhythm of a song they both sing, then breaks a wafer made of flour which they both consume. Next she lies on the bed with her arms outstretched in the shape of a cross, and Felipe falls upon her body: "Aura will open up like an altar." It seems clear that this little ritual represents a sacrifice in which Felipe is the victim that winds up on the altar. Although there are Christian allusions, because a large Mexican crucifix dominates the bare room, the passage probably refers to one of the Mexican Indian fertility rites in which washing and bathing, dancing and singing, often figure prominently, and in which tortillas and effigies of the gods, made of flour, are consumed. At the spring festival honoring Cinteotl, the Aztec goddess of corn and fertility, a youth or maiden was attached to a cross and shot by arrows, which in this context is symbolic intercourse to impregnate the deity, impersonated by the victim, and to renew the vegetation. Felipe's second tryst therefore establishes Aura as a Great Mother and himself as the victim of a fertility rite in her honor. The Anima is fading back into the unconscious, indicating regression on his part. The hero reverts to his position as son-lover of the Great Mother. He represents the grain of corn that dies to fertilize the earth and is reborn in the spring (Adonis, Tammuz, etc.), a myth corresponding to a psychological stage preceding that of the "hero."

The setup of Consuelo's household now begins to look like a trap, where the spider-like Feminine schemes to ensnare the unwary man, which is how the unconscious appears to consciousness, by nature masculine. The epitaph of *Aura* is well chosen: "Man hunts and struggles. Woman intrigues and dreams; she is the mother of fantasy, of the gods. She possesses second sight. . . . The gods are like men: they are born and they die on a woman's breast" (Jules Michelet). This, also, is a stereotype male experience of the feminine, of the "otherness" of all that is not consciousness. Thus Montero, the hunter (for such is the literal meaning of his name) ventures into the realm of the Feminine with the potential of mastering it and emerging in glory like the sun hero. He intends to struggle for the Anima, for the emancipation of consciousness, but the dragon takes the initiative and he is disarmed. The Anima, at first virginal, soon takes on qualities of a courtesan and merges into the unconscious, to which he capitulates, victim of his instincts and impulses. (Sexuality is only one of the regressive forces and should be understood symbolically here.)

Felipe awakens later that night to find Aura standing at the foot of the bed; as soon as he opens his eyes she begins to withdraw into a dark recess of the room to join Consuelo who has been sitting there all the time. Arm in arm they leave together, and he is not to see Aura face to face again. The next time they meet she wears a green veil. Now for the first time, he speaks to her about running off with him and proposes leaving that day. "If you like" she assents. It is not too late—but he retracts: "Well, not yet perhaps. I'm engaged to do this work. When it is finished . . . then we'll go." Loyalty to the Mother imago holds him fast. Unable to break away, he cannot be reborn through self-regeneration as in the hero myth. Thus, when he goes to Aura that night, this time in Consuelo's room, he takes her in his arms "without thinking, without distinguishing"; and when the moon shines through a crack on her white hair, on her shriveled face and toothless gums, he sees the small, wasted body of Consuelo quivering slightly because he holds it and loves it, and because he has returned ("porque . . . tú has regresado", which might also be phrased: because he has regressed). Then, with his eyes open, he buries his face in the silvery hair of Consuelo, whose name means consolation, a pre-eminently motherly attribute. There is no struggle. In surrendering to the old woman, Montero yields to a longing for death or inertia, as several references to his passivity have foreshadowed; (for example, his delay in getting started on the projected History of the Conquest). The fact that Felipe fails his initiation is not unexpected; to experience this process at the age of twenty seven indicates that he has known previous failure: "Time and again the failure of the dragon fight . . . proves to be the central problem for neurotics during the first half of life and the cause of their inability to establish relations with a partner."

According to this interpretation, the story may be understood in either of two ways: First, the events up to the second night happened to Felipe but everything else is a phantasmagoria, beginning with his first dream, the first in many years, and that a nightmare. The Aura he knows thereafter is out of character with the timid girl he first met: he "awakens" from the nightmare with a cry to find Aura lying, naked and succubus-like, on top of him. This erotic dream is presented as fact, throwing the subsequent action into the domain of revery. The second view, preferable and more likely, is that the entire story is a hypnagogic drama like the famous one that Jung analyzes in

Symbols of Transformation. It further resembles the Miller fantasies in having an abortive outcome. In this case there would not be three persons in the list of characters, nor even two, but only Felipe Montero and his archetypes, which according to Jung [in *Archetypes*], "appear as active personalities in dreams and fantasies."

The wealth of symbols that normally accompanies an archetypal transformation is reflected in those that Carlos Fuentes has allotted to the situation he dramatizes. For example, in Consuelo's bedroom there are holy pictures, which besides their religious symbolism, carry a psychological significance peculiar to this tale. Christ and Mary are symbols of the Self and of the Good Mother. St. Sebastian, often depicted with arrows piercing his body, is analogous to the slaves who were shot with arrows for the feast of Cinteotl, and bears a similar connotation. St. Lucy, a martyr whose eyes were gouged, foreshadows Felipe's first nightmare about a face with empty eyesockets; such a face is that of the Terrible Mother, all the more because it lacks the eyes of consciousness. St. Michael Archangel is a renowned and successful dragon-fighter. A central picture on the wall represents devils *piercing* the damned with tridents, and *violating* women, bordered by blood and viscera—perhaps the hearts of Aztec sacrifices. The viscera also points to the daily fare of kidneys.

Again: the text is peppered with allusions to the Self, which is the center of the psyche and the goal of psychic development, commonly represented by symbols of wholeness and balance: circles, symmetrical mandalas, crosses, and other images of quaternity. Such symbols exert a uniting influence on the psyche at all stages of life, and especially in times of confusion. At the first meal, Montero dines alone with Aura; nevertheless, four places are set. A circle of light is cast on the table by the candelabrum placed in the center, surrounded by a circle of shadows. In Aura's room a great circle of light illuminates the bed on which she will stretch out in the shape of a cross; a crucifix also falls within the lighted ring. The colors symbolic of the four psychic functions are also highlighted: yellow, blue and red ribbons bind the three bundles of the Llorente papers, and green, the color of sensation, trails through the pages each time Aura's name appears. And again: throughout the *novella* there is constant tension and contrast between light and darkness, suggesting the tension of opposites in the psyche that produces psychic energy.

With the discovery that he is Llorente, Felipe is thrown into a world that is eternal. He promptly repudiates conceptual time, dismissing his watch as a useless and deceptive measure of time, and thereby accurately projecting his experience onto a transpersonal and universal level. The *novella* concludes on a note of hope. Consuelo puts her arms around Felipe, saying "She'll come back. . . . I'll bring her back," meaning Aura—the Anima. Impelled by her, he may attempt the process again.

In offering this interpretation of *Aura* I am in no way suggesting that it is the only possible one, because the text is rich in mystery and allows undoubtedly for many readings; nor is this one exhaustive. As to whether or not Carlos Fuentes knew what he was doing, I am inclined to think that he did, and, furthermore, that he enjoyed adapting and transposing into his tight little "case history" as many facets as possible of *Symbols of Transformation* and like Jungian studies.

Anthony Julio Ciccone (essay date 1975)

SOURCE: "The Supernatural Persistence of the Past in *Los días enmascarados* [The Masked Days] by Carols Fuentes," in *Latin American Literary Review,* Vol. III, No. 6, Spring/Summer, 1975, pp. 37-48.

[*In the following essay, Ciccone focuses on three of Fuentes's stories from* Los días enmascarados *in order to discuss the author's treatment of temporality and the supernatural.*]

Carlos Fuentes, the brilliantly successful Mexican author, is a novelist, playwright and short-story writer. In the period of fifteen years, 1949-64, he wrote seventeen shorter narratives. Besides his two collections, *Los días enmascarados* (1954) [*The Masked Days*] and *Cantar de ciegas* (1964) [*Song of the Blind*], he published four uncollected stories: "**Pastel rancio**" ["**Rancid Pastry**"], "**Pantera en jazz**" ["**Panther in Jazz**"], "**El muñeco**" ["**The Doll**"], and "**Trigo errante**" ["**Errant Wheat**"]. These works, written between 1949-57, the era before *Los días enmascarados* (1954) and that immediately preceding *La región más transparente* (1958) [*Where the Air is Clear*], have never been incorporated into an anthology. "**Pastel rancio,**" published on November 26, 1949 in the newspaper, *Mañana,* deals with a son's rejection of his Jewish mother, whereas "**Pantera en jazz,**" which appeared six months before *Los días enmascarados,* presents the nightmarish situation of a young man who believes he has been transformed into a panther. In a different vein, "**El muñeco**" written in 1956, depicts the plight of the mad Empress, Carlota. Lastly, "**Trigo errante,**" which was published six months later, portrays the cyclical existence of the Biblical character, Lazarus, after his resurrection by Christ.

These four tales represent an experimental period in the author's career. Much of the thematic and technical material which he introduces in these narratives will be employed, in more complex form, in subsequent works. Hence, we notice that the theme of familial discord, which was present in his first story, is accorded a greater importance in *Cantar de ciegas* (1964) and in *Zona sagrada* (1957) [*Home Base*]. Similarly, "**Pantera en jazz,**" introduces a type of protagonist who will become progressively more significant in Fuentes' art, namely, the unmarried protagonist whose emotional unfulfillment engenders psychological maladjustment, an unreliability of perception and a tendency to over-indulge in fantasy. "**El muñeco,**" in effect, is the thematic precursor to "**Tlactocatizine, del jardín de Flandes**" ["**Tlactocatzine, from the Flemish**

Garden"] and to *Aura* (1962). Finally, the topic of cyclical reincarnation, found in "Trigo errante," is essential to the description of the fantastic occurrences in *Los dias enmascarados,* in *Aura* and in *Cumpleaños* (1969) [*Birthday*].

The six stories of Fuentes' first collection, *Los días enmascarados* (1954), may be divided into two categories. In the first classification we find three tales which may be considered social parodies. They are: **"Letanía de la orquidea"** [**"Orchid Litany"**], which explores the problem of human greed, **"El que inventó la pólvora"** [**"Explosive Invention"**], a parody of our ultra-modern, technological time, and **"En defensa de la Trigolobia"** [**"In Defense of Trigolobia"**], which satirizes the vacuity of political rhetoric.

The three remaining narratives depict the fantastic persistence of the past in twentieth-century Mexico. In referring to these stories Fuentes [quoted in *La voz,* 2 diciembre 1962] maintains that: "Son cuentos fantásticos, (. . .) en que relato la reaparición de las formas extintas, ocultas en el subsuelo." [They are fantastic stories, (. . .) in which I relate the reappearance of extinct forms, hidden in the substratum.] Critics, in turn, often suggest that the title, *Los días enmascarados,* demonstrates the author's preoccupation with the Pre-Cortesian indigenous past of Mexico: "'cinco enmascarados/con pencas de maguey,' había dicho el poeta Tablada. Cinco días sin nombre, días vacios durante los cuales se suspendía toda actividad—frágil puente entre el fin de un año y el comienzo de otro—. En el espíritu de Fuentes, sin duda, la expresión tiene además un sentido de interrogación y de escarnio: qué hay detrás de las máscaras?" ["'five days masked by maguey leaves,' the poet Tablada had said. Five unnamed days in which all activity was suspended—a fragile bridge between the end of one year and the beginning of another. Undoubtedly, in Fuentes' tradition, the title further suggests an aggressive questioning of, What is there behind the masks?"] [*Siempre,* 24 de mayo 1967]. Thus, the supernatural survival of the Pre-Hispanic era is presented in **"Chac Mool"** and in **"Por boca de los dioses"** [**"By the Gods' Mouth"**]. On the other hand, **"Tlactocatzine, del jardin de Flandes,"** is concerned with the continuation of the nineteenth-century epoch in modern-day Mexico.

In the course of this critical study, significant attention will be accorded to the artistic techniques of narrative person, time and space. Consideration will be given as to the efficacy of these techniques in evoking the literary fantasy of supernatural reincarnation found in these stories. Since the element of reality-irreality is a recurrent concern in much of Fuentes' art, an analysis of it in these three tales will provide an essential insight into this aspect of his art.

The three works to be considered, **"Chac Mool,"** **"Por boca de los dioses"** and **"Tlactocatzine, del jardín de Flandes,"** share certain characteristics. All have a first-person narrator who is a bachelor. The action of all of them takes place in Mexico City. **"Chac Mool"** and **"Tlactocatzine, del jardín de Flandes"** are related in a diary form. The

space in all three has psychological significance for the narrator and the place becomes a point of convergence for diverse temporal and spatial realms. This point may be termed a *zona sagrada:* a "site" which is not divorced from time. At the end of each story the narrator is trapped in this closed spatial locus. In all three, especially in **"Chac Mool"** and in **"Tlactocatzine, del jardin de Flandes,"** there is the use of calendar chronology to suggest logical order. While implying a conventional conception of time, other elements are working which subvert the temporal scheme. Thus, the reader is led to conclude the illogical through the distortion of the logical. Fuentes' first concern when dealing with space is place, and often in his works he mentions a specific site as a focal point. As such, a certain location may possess specific historic significance. In other instances, its significance is not historical; nonetheless, it is integral to the development of artistic fantasy as a form of *aleph:* a meeting zone for diverse temporal and spatial realms. This *aleph* would include that space which may be designated as ordinary and which is the site for logical actions. Oddly enough, the *aleph* would, conversely and concurrently, be the location of the extraordinary space in which fantastic events occur.

Of all the stories in *Los días enmascarados,* "Chac Mool" is the best known and most widely commented. Fuentes recalls [in an interview in *Siempre,* 25 de mayo 1962] that the inspiration for it came from a newspaper account in 1952. It told of the events surrounding the shipment of the Aztec idol, the rain god Chac Mool, to Europe. In its transatlantic voyage it supposedly engendered many storms. This led the author to conclude: "Los datos de la nota roja aicanos: hasta qué grado siguen vivas las formas cosmológicas de un México perdido para siempre y que, sin embargo, se resiste a morir y se manifiesta, de tarde en tarde, a través de un misterio, una aparición, un reflejo. La anécdota gira en torno a la persistencia de nuestras viejas formas de vida." ["The accounts focused my artistic attention upon a fact evident to all Mexicans: to what extent do the cosmological characteristics of a bygone Mexico survive and become manifest through a phenomenon, an apparition or a reflection. The tale is concerned with the persistence of our ancient modes of life."]

"Chac Mool" relates incidents in the life of Filiberto, the principal character and one of the story's two narrators, who has unexpectedly drowned in Acapulco during Holy Week. Filiberto's friend goes there in order to bring the body back to Mexico City. In the course of the return trip, he decides to read Filiberto's diary. In it Filiberto relates that he bought a statue of the Aztec god Chac Mool in the Lagunilla market. He placed it in the basement of his house. By causing a series of floods in the basement, Chac Mool manages to surround himself with water, his natural element, and thereby to regain life. Once alive he becomes Filiberto's tyrannical master. Filiberto attempts to escape to Acapulco, which results in his death by drowning. His friend believes that the diary represents the record of an insane individual who has committed suicide. Upon arriving at Filiberto's house he is met by the reincarnated Chac Mool, who tells him to have the corpse placed in the basement.

The thematic premise of "**Chac Mool,**" the omnipresence of the Pre-Cortesian Aztec past in modern-day Mexico, is demonstrated by the fantastic revival of the Aztec god, Chac Mool. The artistic use of point of view, space and time are essential to the development of this fantastic literary topic.

The narrative mode of this story is in the form of two first-person narrators. The first is Filiberto's friend, who recounts his own impressions of Filiberto and whose narration furnishes an artistic frame in which the events described in the character's diary are interpolated. Thus, the friend's narrative accounts encompass Filiberto's presenting a perspective of paralleling verisimilitude to Filiberto's implied fantasy. His possible insanity, hence unreliability as a narrator, is alluded to in various instances.

Thus, if Filiberto is mistaken in his sense of perception, what he relates is equally erroneous.

The first suggestion of the personage's dubious sense of perception, engendered by emotional traumas, is contained in the early part of his diary. The character has reached forty years of age and senses that at this point he has uncontrollably started to decline. He confesses a sense of bewildered estrangement from his surroundings and past: "Desfilaron los años de las grandes ilusiones, de los pronósticos felices, y, también, todas las omisiones que impidieron su realización. Sentí la angustia de no poder meter los dedos en el pasado y pegar los trozos de algún rompecabezas abandonado. . . ." ["The years passed of grand schemes, of happy predictions and of all omissions which hindered success. I felt the anguish of not being able to grasp the past and thus collate the pieces of some discarded jigsaw puzzle."]

This is the first of a series of references to Filiberto's preoccupation with the past. Previously, he had expressed his memories of adolescence, a segment of his life which presented ample opportunities for friendship and fantasizing about the future. At middle age, however, Filiberto is practically alone in life, possessing only a few friends. Moreover, he readily concedes that he has not attained any considerable degree of success in his career. Sensing himself as an alienated, mediocre individual, the character directs his fantasy away from the future and develops a consuming interest in the Aztec past of Mexico. In the a the solace which is denied him in his lonely bachelorhood. He relates that one of his friends, aware of his interest in this area, observed that Christianity in Mexico is tantamount to ritualized Aztec religion as Filiberto himself confirms in his declaration: "Pepe conocía mi afición, desde joven, por ciertas formas de arte indígena mexicano. Yo colecciono estatuillas, ídolos, cacharros. Mis fines de semana los paso en Tlaxcala, o en Teotihuacán." ["Pepe knew of my fondness, since my youth, for certain forms of indigenous Mexican art. I collect figurines, idols and pottery. I spend my weekends in Tlaxcala or Teotihuacán."] Indeed, his involvement even evokes in him a feeling of guilt: "su mueca parece reprocharme que le niegue la luz" [". . . his grin seems to reproach me for denying him light"].

His anthropomorphic transformation of the statue is further revealed in subsequent entries in the diary in which he describes it as emitting cries during the night, of developing a flesh-like quality, and of acquiring hair on its body. Throughout his entries Filiberto expresses his misgivings regarding his own powers of objective observation when influenced by his imagination. His friend notices, while reading the diary, that there is a segment which contains no entry for three days. After this lapse, an account appears written in a child-like scrawl:

> "Hasta hace tres días, mi realidad lo era al grado de haberse borrado lo que era movimiento, reflejo, rutina, memoria, cartapacio. Y luego, como la tierra que un día tiembla para que recordemos su poder, o la muerte que llegará, recriminando mi olvido de toda la vida, se presenta otra realidad que sabíamos que estaba allí, mostrenca, y que debe sacudirnos para hacerse viva y presente. Creía, nuevamente, que era imaginación; el Chac Mool, (. . .) parecía indicarme que era un dios, . . ."

> ["Even up until three days ago my reality had erased that which was movement, reflex, routine, memory, and memorandum. And then, like the earth which one day quakes to remind us of its power, or death which recriminates my life-long disregard of its inevitability, another unfettered reality, which we knew existed, presents itself and jolts us in order to gain life and presence. Once again, I believed that it was my imagination: Chac Mool, (. . .) seemed to indicate to me that he was a god, . . ."]

Thus, we see Filiberto's estrangement from conventional foci of reality. In his mind the statue of Chac Mool is transformed into an actual fantastic entity which he regards as his tyrannical master and which serves ironically to fill the void of solitude in his life.

The site for the fantastic reincarnation of Chac Mool is Filiberto's home. It represents what might be designated as a *zona sagrada,* a location integral to this fantastic occurrence. The house may be described as poetic space, that is, an area whose significance and extent are determined by perception of the individual.

Gaston Bachelard defines the concept in this manner: "Space that has been seized upon by the imagination cannot remain indifferent space subject to the measures and estimates of the surveyor. It has been lived in not in its positivity, but with all the partiality of the imagination. Particularly, it nearly always exercises an attraction. For it concentrates being within limits that protect. [In *The Poetics of Space,* 1969.]" The space of the house as perceived by Filiberto is vital to the fantastic reincarnation of Chac Mool. In describing his home Filiberto says that its mournful appearance and architecture are reminiscent of the Porfirio Diaz era. The enormity of the house and its occupation by the lonely personage serve to remind him of his personal past with his parents, a contrasting and more felicitous portion of his life. As such, he is psychologically dependent upon the house and cannot or will not leave it. Its anachronistic semblance serves not only as a constant reminder of bygone years but also as a visible ambience for temporal regression. In the house's *zona sagrada* the convergence of temporal and spatial planes is possible.

Initially, the house may remind Filiberto of the pre-Revolutionary past of his parents, and thus gratify his psychological dependence on that realm. However, by placing the statue of Chac Mool in the basement. Filiberto has projected his temporal preoccupations further into the past. In effect, he has accorded his home the aura of the Aztec temples which he visited at Tlaxcala and Teotihuacán. Now the space of the basement becomes influenced by the conception which he had previously formed of the Aztec gods. Since he placed Chac Mool in the basement and since the cellar invariably symbolizes the site of illogical actions and repressed evil, it is only appropriate that the inhabitant of that realm be equally malevolent. Filiberto's room, in contrast, located at the top of the stairs, represents the realm of Reason. Therefore, when the personage relates that Chac Mool has taken up residence in his bedroom, the implication is that Evil has proven more powerful than Reason and has achieved dominance. Once in control, Chac Mool may proceed to convert the house into an Aztec temple. According to Filiberto, this is accomplished by intermittent floodings of the house, by animal bones strewn in the bedroom, and by the constant odor of blood and incense.

Chac Mool, as the god of rain, controls water in all its forms. Hence, he may cause a water pipe to burst or a sewer to flood his temple. His control of water extends far beyond the limits of his temple as evidenced by an incident in Filiberto's office in which: "Un guasón pintó de rojo el agua del garrafón en la oficina, con la consiguiente perturbación de los labores. He debido consignarlo al director, a quien sólo le dio mucha risa. El culpable se ha valido de esta oportunidad para hacer sarcasmos a mis costillas el dia entero, todos en torno al agua. Ch, . . . !" ["A prankster threw red coloring in the office water cooler, resulting in the workers' excitement. I had to report it to the boss who only laughed a lot. The culprit, and all of them around the water cooler, took advantage of this opportunity to make snide remarks behind my back all day long. Ch, . . . !"]. The incident is significant in several respects. Firstly, it serves to introduce the motif of water which is recurrent in this story, specifically water as aligned with spatial coordinates: in the office's water cooler, the house's basement, and the plaza's public fountain. Also, Chac Mool floods Filiberto's house with water and the latter ultimately drowns while swimming in Acapulco. Both of these are instances of water in spatial contexts. Moreover, the fact that the water is red within the cooler serves as a foreshadowing of Filiberto's unexpected death in an equally enclosed bay of water in Acapulco. By closed spaces we mean enclosed areas which imply confinement. Filiberto's escape to Acapulco is an instance of a closed space, a circular journey, inasmuch as he is ultimately brought back to Mexico City. Conversely, his sense of solitude and alienation is another instance of closed space: an individual living within the boundaries of his own being and deprived of significant psychological relationships. In "**Chac Mool**" there is an inherent ambiguity between

closed and open spaces. Open spaces are those which permit freedom from any predetermined course. Ironically, in this story closed spaces proffer freedom and openness while concealing their inevitable confinement. Thus, the closed space of the house is transformed from a human abode into the fantastic dwelling of an Aztec god, through Filiberto's imaginative powers, his knowledge of and interest in indigenous culture and his psychological dependence on the past, thereby effecting the change.

The time element of this story functions less conspicuously than that of space. The diary, in one respect, suggests a linear, calendar progression of time covering a span of several months from Chac Mool's purchase to Filiberto's death. In contrast to this conventional temporal pattern, there is a regressive temporal plan. This is presented in the form of the character's intense interest in all segmedirect opposition to the time spent at his job is that of his leisure, which focuses upon an ancient era. The coexistence of these two disparate times in Filiberto's mind is essential to the concurrency necessary for Chac Mool's reincarnation. Again the inherent ambiguity between the two realms of past and present ultimately allows the former to achieve dominance in Filiberto's perception. Hence Chac Mool's fantastic reincarnation is a result of the omnipresent past which Filiberto causes to regain life through his imaginative complicity.

The next story whose thematic premise is the supernatural survival of the Pre-Hispanic past in twentieth-century Mexico is "**Por boca de los dioses.**" The initial reading of this work may cause confusion because of its inherent structure. The events recounted in this tale are related through the consciousness of an individual from the Aztec present who lives in, and views, the twentieth century as an inexplicable, oneiric future. In one respect, all that is told seems more fantastic than realistic. This, however, is the key to our understanding of the story. In contrast to the other stories in *Los días enmascarados,* "**Por boca de los dioses**" unfolds in a dream-like atmosphere. This characteristic is essential to the work's theme as it accentuates the fluidity of temporal categories in Mexico. Thus, the prose is an essential technique in demonstrating the oneiric quality which Fuentes considers inherent in Mexico's time scheme.

In "**Por boca de los dioses,**" Oliverio, the first-person narrator, is an *aficionado* of painting. Upon one of his visits to the Museo de Bellas Artes he meets an old friend, Don Diego. While visiting the museum, they enter into a heated discussion concerning a Tamayo painting dated 1958. Oliverio rips the mouth from this painting. Don Diego protests and Oliverio hurls the old man to his death from an upstairs window. He returns to his hotel with the mouth and later that day places it on his lapel. From this advantageous position the mouth forces him to do and to say things beyond his control. It eventually leads him to the hotel's basement to witness the Aztec rites. Frightened, Oliverio escapes to his room. Tlazol, the goddess of lust and confession, comes to his room and by belittling his masculinity angers him into opening the door. She then proceeds with the Aztec ceremony of human sacrifice.

Thus, **"Por boca de los dioses"** presents the theme of the survival of the Aztec past in all historical epochs in Mexico. Time, in this context, is considered by Fuentes to be a composite of the three generally conceived separate realms: past, present, and future. As such, the story recounts events which occur in the twentieth century in Mexico but which are viewed as past occurrences in the Aztec present. The opening segment of this tale presents Oliverio at the moment of his sacrificial death. Therefore, the prose of the first two and a half pages represents his thoughts in a first-person, stream of consciousness technique. These thoughts, moments before his death, reveal all the incidents prior to his sacrifice. Hence, we learn that Oliverio sought to escape this end by entering the future of the twentieth century. In the future, he confined himself almost exclusively to his hotel room in an attempt to avoid the constant contact with the superficially disguised Aztec essence of Mexico City: "Vengo huyendo de ellos, de sus formas menores, y están aquí, gigantes sin más dimensión que la cólera cortés y el son reticente de las guitarras. En las calles, me miran feo, pisan mis pies, me empujan, me pintan violines y me tocan el claxon, ¡ay de observar a sus mujeres, ay de rehusar sus alcoholes, ay de demostrar que mi cerebro y mi memoria no laten a su compás!" ["I come here fleeing from them and their short statures, and here they are giants, aggrandized by their courteous anger and the reticent sound of their guitars. On the street, they look crossly at me, step on my feet, humiliate me and sound their horn. Oh, the sight of their women, oh, the thought of refusing their liquor, oh, how to show them that my mind and memory march to a different drum!"] The prose in this story possesses an oneiric semblance inasmuch as it represents events and places which are recalled through memory and are devoid of spatial and temporal limitations. Oliverio's perspective or point of view of the twentieth century is fantastic, in that it views the present and the future of modern-day Mexico as a series of reiterations from the past. In this respect, he considers the receptionist of his hotel as evidencing a frustrated need to express her indigenous past. Also, upon entering a department store he perceives the telephone operator as resembling an Aztec maiden praying at the foot of the altar. When he is about to leave the store he notices that she has been strangled with telephone wires. The significance of his intuitively foreseeing this untimely occurrence indicates the fantastic basis of his perspective, which enables Oliverio to conceive the present and the future as those realms which have already happened. From this perspective Oliverio can likewise discern what belongs to the Aztec present. Therefore, he immediately recognizes the mouth in Tamayo's painting as: "(. . .) distinta, como voluntariamente alejada de lo que pueda hacerla feliz. Distinta, mexicana, excelente . . ." ["(. . .) different, as if voluntarily separated from that which could make it happy. Different, Mexican, excellent . . ."] Oliverio reasons that the mouth, like himself, is an entity of the Aztec present which exists in modern-day Mexico. The mouth is for Oliverio the overt manifestation of the Aztec gods he wishes to escape. Once it has affixed itself to his body it can force him to warn the modern-day inhabitants of Mexico City of the omnipresence of their

Aztec heritage. It can also compel Oliverio to witness rites he wishes to escape, and ultimately it ensures his sacrificial death.

Oliverio's hotel, the fantastic site for these occurrences, permits the convergence of these temporal and spatial planes. His hotel room, which bears the number 1519, has a historical significance for Oliverio. It signifies Cortes' entry into Mexico and the end of the Aztec world. Through his fantastic conception Oliverio is able to regress temporally. Thus, 1519 does not signify the end of the Aztec domain but, in an inverse manner, the resurgence of Aztec rites. As such, his room, located at the top of the stairs, symbolizes a sacrificial altar in which the inevitable ceremony will occur. The basement of the hotel represents the original indigenous substratum upon which successive layers of European culture have been superimposed. The elevator connecting the basement and his room is seen through Oliverio's fantasy as the medium by which access to the Aztec present from the future is maintained. By descending into the basement Oliverio encounters the initial stages of the ceremony which will be completed at the top of the sacrificial altar, his room.

The mode of narration and the spatial components of **"Por boca de los dioses"** are as fantastic as the time element, which has a dual basis. In one respect, there is a reference to a time which proceeds in a linear, calendar fashion. The twentieth-century Mexico which Oliverio enters is the result of the progression of many centuries of historical epochs. In direct opposition to this temporal scheme is that which considers time in a mythic context, a fluid realm lacking distinctions between past, present, and future. In this unique Mexican time all three realms attain the same parity of existence. Consequently, Oliverio may choose to escape to the twentieth century while considering it from a past perspective of the Aztec present. In the omnipresent Aztec realm his sacrificial death can be consummated. Thus, the mouth inevitably symbolizes the persistence of this Aztec heritage despite the progression of calendar time. **"Por boca de los dioses"** and **"Chac Mool"** are distinct literary entities; however, they reveal markedly similar depictions of Mexican time as a continual reiteration of the past.

The last story to be considered in this critical study is **"Tlactocatzine, del jardín de Flandes."** Like **"Chac Mool"** and **"Por boca de los dioses,"** this work presents the subject of the past's supernatural persistence in modern-day Mexico. In this particular instance it is not the survival of the Aztec era but the continuation of the nineteenth-century Hapsburg epoch, in the person of the Mexican Empress, Carlota.

The first-person narrator and principal character of **"Tlactocatzine, del jardín de Flandes,"** Carlos, is invited by a friend to live in an old house on Avenida Puente de Alvarado. The friend asks Carlos to live there in order to imbue the house with human warmth. Carlos agrees and is especially impressed with the house's library and its glass doors, which face a garden of evergreens. One rainy day, while looking at the garden, he notices an old woman there. Upon his approaching the doors of the garden she suddenly disappears. Later that same day he receives an enigmatic message in Nahuatl: "Tlactocatzine." On a subsequent occasion he attempts to talk with her. To his surprise he discovers that she is Carlota, the reincarnated Mexican Empress. He attempts to flee the garden but finds that the doors leading back to the house are locked. At this moment he realizes that he is fated to love the resurrected Carlota.

The narrative mode of this work is furnished in a first-person, diary account. Like the narrators of the two previously discussed works, Carlos may be considered unreliable in that he is extremely susceptible to the suggestions of his imagination. His susceptibility to his imagination is in large part augmented by his momentary solitude in this enormous, unfamiliar old house. Having no one else with whom to communicate, Carlos must inevitably resort to fantasy in order to fill the psychological void which he senses around him. In addition, he demonstrates a noticeable distaste for his surroundings and is therefore prone to fantasize in order to escape what he deems unpleasant in his twentieth-century environment. His imaginative conception of the house is first influenced by his friend, Brambila, who informs him that it has been uninhabited for forty years and that it possesses a discernible chill which is not present outside. Brambila further influences Carlos by describing the house as: "(. . .)-historia, folklore, elegancia reunidos" ["(. . .)-history, folklore, and elegance all together"]. Upon seeing the house, Carlos confirms his friend's observations concerning its unique attributes. Once within it, he comes to consider it as a sanctuary which removes him from the present-day turmoil of Mexico: "Aquí se está lejos de los 'males parasitarios' de México. Menos de veinticuatro horas entre estos muros, que son de una sensibilidad, de un fluir que corresponden a otros litorales . . ." ["Here one is far from the 'parasitic evils' of Mexico. Less than twenty-four hours inside these walls, which are of a sensibility of movement which belongs to other shores . . ."] The following day his fantasy and his desire to be distant from Mexico cause him to see the garden in these terms: "Y la lluvia misma remueve, en el pasto, otros colores que quiero insertar en ciudades, en ventanas; de pie en el centro del jardín, cerré los ojos . . . , (. . .) Era un paisaje ficticio, inventado. El jardín no estaba en México! . . ." ["And the rain itself stirs up colors in the grass which I want to insert in cities, in windows; standing in the center of the garden, I closed my eyes . . . , (. . .) It was a fictitious, fabricated landscape. The garden wasn't in Mexico! . . ."] Throughout his stay in the house Carlos finds himself recalling the past in all its forms. He is especially aware of his ability to remember those aspects of the past which are directly associated with Maximilian's Empire. The house presents a preferable alternative, in the form of a nineteenth-century semblance, to the demoralizing world of the twentieth century. In this respect, Carlos expresses an uncontrollable need to remain within the confines of the house and to stare endlessly into the fictitious garden of his conception. He further implies that this process of fantasizing is not restricted to the garden alone but is applicable to the interior of the house as well: "Esas

pisadas lentas, siempre sobre hojas secas, creía escucharlas a cada instante, sabía que no eran ciertas, hasta que sentí el mínimo crujido junto a la puerta, y luego, el frotar por la rendija" ["These slow footsteps, always on dry leaves, which I believed I heard at every instant and which I knew weren't real, until I heard the slight creak near the door and the swish across the doorsill."] In this state of imaginative suggestion Carlos believes that he encounters the reincarnated Empress, Carlota, thereby demonstrating his separation from conventional norms defining reality. The progressive psychological movement by Carlos from the twentieth-century present to the nineteenth-century past is amply noted throughout the story. Upon first seeing Carlota, Carlos believes she is an intruder who has mysteriously managed to enter the enclosed garden. However, in his subsequent description he corrects his initial impression: "(. . .) en sus ojos no había ojos . . . ; (. . .) No, no diré que cruzó la enredera y el muro, que se evaporó, que pentró en la tierra o ascendió al cielo; . . ." ["(. . .) her eyes were vacuous . . . ; (. . .) No, I will not say that she crossed the enclosure and the wall, that she evaporated, that she descended into the ground or ascended into the sky; . . ."] His ephemeral perception of Carlota continues to the extent that he comes to doubt not only his eyes but his sense of touch as well: "(. . .) y la anciana me tomó de las manos, las besó; su piel apretó la mía. Lo supe por revelación, porque mis ojos decían lo que el tacto no corroboraba: . . ." ["(. . .) and the old woman took my hands, she kissed them; her skin pressed against mine. This was revealed to me because my sight and sense of touch were not in agreement: . . ."] In their last encounter in the garden, Carlos expresses his total confinement within the fantastic realm of this nineteenth-century site: "(. . .) sus ademanes son reiterativos y delatan satisfacción. Satisfacción de carcelero, de companía, de prisión eterna. Satisfacción de soledades compartidas" ["(. . .) her gestures are repetitive and evince satisfaction; the satisfaction of a jailer, of companionship, of an eternal prison; the satisfaction of a shared loneliness."] Thus, the solitude which Carlos felt as an alienated dissatisfied individual of this century is alleviated through the fantastic contact with a person from a previous and more desirable era.

Essentially, the space of the house on Puente Alvarado serves to support Carlos' fantastic imaginative perspective. The name Alvarado has historical importance in that it represents the name of the officer who assisted Cortés. Furthermore, the house located on this avenue is in the style of the Empire of Maximilian. The two are anachronistic reminders which Carlos perceives as spatially together. They represent two divergent historical epochs which, although separated by hundreds of years, are united in his conception. Essentially, the house becomes the sacred zone which permits the coalescing of divergent space and time planes of Mexican culture. Carlos, through his fantasy interprets the space of the house and its environs in a double basis. The house's exterior remains within the turbulent, modern-day Mexico City. Its interior and the garden, (the latter, mentioned in the title) conversely, assume the coordinates of

Flanders in the nineteenth century and thereby represent the tranquility of a small, European milieu of a bygone era. The garden and the interior of the house both represent closed space; hermetically sealed areas which resist the assault of time and preserve the past. The locked doors leading to the garden represent Carlos' own confinement within himself, his isolation from others. In effect, Carlos retains two alternatives: he can look out onto Puente Alvarado and feel repelled by what he sees in modern Mexico City, or he can look out at the garden in the hope that he may eventually inhabit it. In this story, as in "Chac Mool," there is an inherent ambiguity between closed and open spaces. Open spaces are those which permit unrestricted movement. The space outside the house on Puente Alvarado represents such a sense of freedom. Ironically, though, Carlos feels encumbered by the openness of a modern metropolis and therefore seeks refuge in the closed space of the garden. The garden, on the other hand, proffers freedom in the form of escape from a modern environment, but is a sphere of captivity. Within the house itself, Carlos' conception transforms the space into distinct categories. The living room, because of its proximity to the library and garden, is more readily permeated with the aura of the previous century. His bedroom, conversely, represents the realm of reason and the absence of fantasy. In the course of the story, the delivery of mysterious messages in his room indicates a substitution of illogical imagination for logic. The evergreens in the garden symbolize perennial rebirth of the past. Therefore, their presence in the house, in the form of an overpowering scent, is an indication that the previous century does not exist exclusively within the confines of the garden, but in the house as well. At this point, the fantastic reincarnation of Carlota in the twentieth century becomes possible.

Time, like space, in "Tlactocatzine, del jardín de Flandes" has a dual basis. The daily entries in Carlos' diary infer a linearly progressive calendar expiration of five days. This temporality is most compatible with the modern world of Mexico City which exists outside of the house on Puente Alvarado. In contrast to this ordinary temporal scheme is a regressively oriented one. A prime example of these two divergent temporal planes is symbolized in the relationship of Carlos and Carlota. Carlos is a young individual from the twentieth century who is the temporal antithesis of Carlota, the old woman of the previous era. Nonetheless, these two antithetical extremes merge through Carlos' constant preoccupation with the past of the Emperor Maximilian. During his hermetic stay within the house, he focuses his attention on this bygone era. The parity of importance which Carlos accords to the present and to the past enables the latter to achieve dominance. Thus, the inherent lack of distinctions between these divergent temporal concepts in his perspective as narrator-participant assures Carlota's fantastic reincarnation. At the end, Carlos is Carlota's prisoner within the confines of the previous century.

In conclusion, in the course of this study attention was given to the four unpublished stories which preceded this collection in an effort to indicate their contributions to the thematic scope of Fuentes' later work. Consideration was

also given to the author's literary premise, the supernatural persistence of the past in present-day Mexico, and to the use of the artistic techniques of narrative person, time and space in depicting this fantastic subject. As has been shown, the imaginative complicity of the narrator-protagonist in conjunction with a *zona sagrada* and a particular time scheme enable the supernatural event of reincarnation to occur. Lastly, some emphasis must be given to the importance of these three stories with respect to Fuentes' subsequent fiction. The theme of cyclical existence, first presented in "Trigo errante" and later expounded in "Chac Mool," "Por boca de los dioses" and "Tlactocatzine, del jardín de Flandes," influenced the topical basis of *Aura* and *Cumpleaños.* Of the three tales analyzed in this study, "Tlactocatzine, del jardín de Flandes" has proven to be the one which had the greatest impact on the author's later career. After *Los días enmascarados,* Fuentes expressed no literary interest in the Aztec era of Mexico. The Hapsburg past and the correlated theme of undying love, conversely, continued to draw his attention. Thus, he admitted to Emmanuel Carballo the significance of "Tlactocatzine, del jardín de Flandes:" "Es un cuento importante no sólo dentro de *Los días enmascarados* sino en el conjunto de mi obra y mis preocupaciones. En él intento recrear la historia, sin caer en los vicios propios del reportaje sobre el pasado. El pasado aparece allí como nostalgia, como espíritu que actúa sobre el presente e influye en sus proporciones y texturas. Es un cuento sobre la perseverancia del amor a través de los años. Este tema lo vuelvo a tratar en una narración más o menos extensa que publicaré pronto: *Aura*." ["It is an important story not only with respect to *Los días enmascarados* but also in the context of my work and my interests. In it I seek to recreate history, without falling into the very faults of reporting the past. The past, in this story, is depicted as nostalgia, as a presence which acts upon the present and influences its proportions and qualities. It is a story about the persistence of love throughout the years. I will treat this theme again in a more or less extensive narrative which I will publish soon: *Aura*."]

Hence, **"Chac Mool," "Por boca de los dioses"** and **"Tlactocatzine, del jardín de Flandes,"** although three distinct literary entities reiterate Fuentes' basic premise of the supernatural survival of bygone epochs in twentieth-century Mexico and influence the course of the author's subsequent literary preoccupations.

Evan Connell   (essay date 1980)

SOURCE: A review of *Burnt Water*, in *The New York Times Book Review*, Vol. LXXXV, No. 42, October 19, 1980, pp. 9, 34, 36.

[*Connell is an American novelist and author of short stories and nonfiction whose books include the novels* Mrs. Bridge *(1959) and* Mr. Bridge *(1969), as well as the collected short story volume* St. Augustine's Pigeon *(1980). In the following review of* Burnt Water, *he praises Fuentes for his ability to fully describe the destitution of the working class near Mexico City, though he finds certain stories in the collection to be less successful than others.*]

Reading these 11 stories is somewhat like watching people on a carousel—individuals you won't see again. Urchins, landlords, working men, whores, servants, cripples, spinsters, revolutionaries, decadent gentry—all come whirling past and swiftly disappear. Two or three or four return long enough to be recognized, then almost at once they curl out of sight.

What remains after you close this book? More than anything else a sense of turbid, vital, gamy, rhythmic human life in Mexico City. Those people who seemed so distinct and unforgettable as they rode by—laughing, waving, shouting, rising and descending with the motion of the gilded wheel—how quickly they dismount and walk away, leaving behind not the singular imprint of personalities we have come to know but an irregular communal web of tracks. Maybe this is as it should be. Possibly this is what the author intended.

In a prefatory note Carlos Fuentes states that he owns an imaginary apartment house in the center of Mexico City whose tenants are the characters we meet: "True, some have fled to the countryside, others are living abroad, some have even been evicted and now wander in the internal exile of the 'belt of misery' surrounding this great, can-cerous stain of a smog-ridden, traffic-snarled metropolis of seventeen million people."

So the apartment house, Casa Fuentes one might say, has been designed to function as does a ship, or the plague, or the remote country estate in murder mysteries—that is, by isolating the characters it unifies the story. Now in some cases such a narrative device can be useful, even obligatory, but here it makes very little difference. Toward the end we recognize Luisito, General Vergara and others who spoke their lines earlier, but these cameo reappearances seem gratuitous rather than integral, as though Fuentes felt obliged to demonstrate the truth of his preliminary note. The genuinely unifying factor—the authentic apartment house—is Mexico City itself.

Gringo visitors to that extraordinary place tour the majestic museum of anthropology, the university, the Zona Rosa, the flea market, Rivera's home, nightclubs, restaurants, expensive shops. This is not the stuff of *Burnt Water*—which is a translation of *atl tlachinolli*, a Nahuatl phrase referring to the ancient lake guarded by volcanoes, the site of present-day Mexico City. Tourists scarcely exist for the people of Carlos Fuentes's world, just as the habits, jobs, problems and loves of his *ciudadanos* are quite unknown to the usual tourist. The Sunday afternoon rodeo, for example, in **"The Son of Andrés Aparicio,"** has nothing to do with calf-roping or bronc-busting and most certainly would not be listed on your basic guided tour. Nor will the motorcoach pause long enough for you to chat with Sr. Federico Silva, the mandarin, in his sinking, tilting apartment crushed between two skyscrapers. You are not likely to meet young Alberto's three concupiscent aunts, or El Burro of the Hawk Brigade, or Plutarco in his Eisenhower jacket and red Thunderbird, or observe Manuelita with her 20 dogs in the cathedral.

Nor is it likely you would be admitted to **"The Doll Queen"**'s sickening bedroom embellished with worn-out shoes, ancient toys, wrinkled balloons, tuberoses, gardenias, desiccated cherries and jars of dried candy illuminated by smoky sputtering candles: "the small coffin supported on blue crates decorated with paper flowers, flowers of life this time, carnations and sunflowers, poppies and tulips . . . between the black silk sheets, on the pillow of white satin, that motionless and serene face framed in lace, highlighted with rose-colored tints, eyebrows traced by the lightest pencil."

Mr. Fuentes has an uncommon ability to dislocate your stomach. Fortunately he does not depend on this talent. He does not spiral above such putrescence with the ghoulish fixity of a buzzard; if he did, he would be unbearable because his writing is almost humorless. He understands, of course, when something is absurd, but this knowledge does not cause him to laugh. Indeed, he seems reluctant to smile.

His narrative style—with few exceptions—relies on the irruption and juxtaposition of different kinds of awareness, a technique perhaps derived from the methods popularized by Joyce. As a result, he is sometimes labyrinthine, though not so tortuous that one gets impatient. Now and then, as in **"The Cost of Living,"** he switches to a flinty style reminiscent of Ernesto Hemingway: "The girl continued walking ahead of him with short hurried steps. She waggled her hips beneath a white skirt. She looked in the shop windows out of the corner of her eyes. Salvador followed her at a distance," etc. It's a good story and the staccato prose is not objectionable, only a bit self-conscious. His elliptical sentences flow more naturally.

Mr. Fuentes is least effective when trying to generate a mood of horror, as in **"Chac Mool"** where a government clerk buys a pre-Columbian stone idol which he puts in the cellar. Slime develops on the base of the idol, moss covers it, gradually the stone becomes fleshy, and we realize that Chac-Mool is turning into some sort of Mexican Dracula. The creature is vigorously described: "standing erect, smiling, ocher-colored except for the flesh-red belly. . . . The lower teeth closed tightly on the upper lip; only the glimmer from the squarish helmet on the abnormally large head betrayed any sign of life. Chac Mool moved toward my bed. . . .'"

At this point those who enjoy shuddering are entitled to a premonitory tremble, although crustier readers may pause to ask how Mr. Fuentes will resolve a plot that can only get sillier. Well, his intention is to establish more than one level, and in this case he wants to evoke—along with the horror—the sound of Mexico's ancestral voices. So, if you are not satisfied with the dénouement, at least you can reflect on the immanence of prehistoric gods.

"In a Flemish Garden" also partakes of horror. We have a deserted mansion with the necessary chill: "a penetrating cold . . . particularly noticeable in contrast to the temperature outside." We have the garden choked by sinister vines, flowers "permeated with a mournful perfume, as if they had been gathered from a crypt after years among dust and marble," and the apparition of a little old white-haired woman, her face concealed by a black lace coif, who turns out to be the ghost of the Empress Carlota.

Carlos Fuentes is a skillful writer with an original mind, so that even his Gothic stories are worth reading; but he writes better and more memorably when he lets go of the monkey's paw.

"The Old Morality," concerning Alberto's liaison with his aunts, is told with understanding and affection for all of the characters, even the desperate, prissy middle-aged women. They have come to take Alberto away from his grandfather because the old man is enjoying life tremendously, thanks to a young housekeeper named Micaela:

"Grandfather is leaning with both hands on the head of his cane; his cigar is between his teeth, and he's puffing smoke like the express to Juárez. Micaela is standing with her arms crossed, laughing, in the kitchen door. The three aunts are sitting very stiffly on the wicker sofa. All three are wearing black hats and white gloves and are sitting with their knees pressed tight together."

They have obtained a court order, so off goes Alberto to live with Aunt Benedicta—who very soon is rubbing him with liniment and bathing him. From there on it is downhill all the way, or uphill—Alberto himself cannot be sure. Aunt Milagros arrives for a visit, slips into his room and begins stroking his hair. Wouldn't he like to come stay at her house a while? Alberto, somewhat uneasy, writes to Grandfather, but then cannot decide whether to send the letter.

It's a delightful story showing Mr. Fuentes at his most light-hearted.

At his deepest, or most tragic, he abandons the ambulatory stone idols and ghostly old ladies in order to describe what truly touches him: the belt of misery around Mexico City where men hunt rabbits and toads to eat, where a temporary job as a flute player with a little band seems like a miraculous stroke of luck, and a woman's most valuable possession is an old photograph in which her husband—who was a stable-hand—may be seen standing not far from President Calles. Here, among these cardboard and corrugated tin shacks on the greasewood plain, beneath a noonday sun which Mr. Fuentes likens to a yellow chili pepper, boys and girls discover what they are, as well as what they can never be; and it is enough to make you understand, perhaps for the first time, why there are revolutions.

Gloria B. Durán (essay date 1980)

SOURCE: "*Aura* and its Precedents in Fuentes's Earlier Works," in *The Archetypes of Carlos Fuentes: From Witch to Androgyne*, Archon Books, 1980, pp. 43-63.

[*Durán is an American educator and critic. Here, she presents a survey of critical responses to* Aura *and offers her own analysis of the novella. Durán finds that Fuentes uses the figure of Aura/Consuelo as an archetypal witch or, more accurately, a sorceress. The critic argues that this figure encompasses both creative and destructive elements and serves to address the human need to transcend space, time, and identity.*]

Aura: The Plot

Aura is a fairy tale for adults set in the enchanted land of Mexico City today. The hero, Felipe Montero, is a young historian who answers a newspaper advertisement which he feels is directed specifically to him. He finds himself in the shadowy, old mansion of an indescribably ancient woman, Consuelo Llorente. Immediately Felipe is hired to edit the memoirs of Consuelo's husband, the dead General Llorente, and is introduced to Consuelo's niece, Aura, a beautiful young girl of twenty. These are the only human inhabitants of the mansion. The others are animals, either seen or heard—a huge rabbit, the pet of Consuelo, and the cats and rodents whose presence is made known to the hero only by their sounds.

In the swiftly moving story, Felipe falls in love with Aura at first sight and before the next night has passed, she comes of her own accord to share his bed. Yet to his dismay he soon realizes that Aura is more automaton than woman, that her very motions echo those of her aunt. And he at first imagines that she is held prisoner by the old woman.

But little by little the general's memoirs reveal the truth of the matter. Consuelo, in her desperate longing to have a child, had resorted to herbs and magic until she could create a child of the spirit if not of the flesh. In some way, Felipe realizes, Aura is a creation of the "aunt." And she is an imperfect creation. When he sees Aura again only one day has passed, yet she has aged by twenty years. But his love for her has not diminished. The study of the memoirs, especially the photographs of the dead general and the young Consuelo, gradually lead him to an even more amazing revelation. *He* is in fact the general reincarnated, and Aura is the young Consuelo. In his last night with Aura the mask of youth of the widow is stripped off completely as moonlight reveals her again as a wrinkled hag. She can only summon forth the form of Aura for three days, she confesses. This is the limit of her powers. But with Felipe's help, they will try again to bring back the image of her lost youth.

The Archetypal Pattern

If we reduce *Aura* to its basic components—old witch, beautiful young girl who is a ward of the witch, young stranger who falls victim to the old woman, crumbling mansion as setting—we see that the pattern is duplicated in a number of works of literature with only slight variations. Perhaps most notable are Pushkin's *Queen of Spades,* and *The Aspern Papers* by Henry James. But whereas in the case of Fuentes one may point to the influence of the earlier works with which Fuentes, in his letter of 8 December 1968, confesses a familiarity, in the case of James it is impossible to prove any knowledge of the work by Pushkin. Yet, as I have indicated in an earlier [unpublished] study, the coincidence between these works is not unusual.

Jung has told us that when dealing with archetypal characters and their attendant myths, the risk of duplication is always present. Pierre Benoit, for example, was accused of plagiarizing H. Rider Haggard "because the accounts of the heroine in Haggard's *Wisdom's Daughter* and Benoit's *L'Atlantide* were disconcertingly alike." This is true because in dealing with fantasies of this kind, the details of character are insignificant. Such stories do not deal with individuals as such, but rather with overwhelming forces in the human psyche which are essentially the same in everyone. Their inspiration is philosophical or religious and has little to do with the vagaries of individual personality. Thus Joseph Sommers has stated [in *After the Storm,* 1968]: "A fair general statement would be that the conceptual basis of *Aura* is rooted in the eternal mysteries which overcome man." Although he does not mention Pushkin, he traces the work's literary paternity to Edgar Allan Poe and the English gothic novel, and asserts

that "despite the indirect vision it projects of the Mexican experience, [it] is more suggestive of European and American heritage than of its Mexican forebears. Fuentes himself in his letter of December 1968 also cites influences in *Aura* from other Latin American novelists, notably José Donoso's *Coronación* (which is also based on the archetypal pattern of the young and old female inhabitants of a mansion.)

The fact that *Aura* is a comment about life, about man's destiny and not about what happened to an individual, Felipe Montero. In an interview with Fuentes [in *Books Abroad* to (1966)], Sommers contrasts this work to *The Death of Artemio Cruz* where man, who is capable of rational choice, determines his own destiny. *Aura,* according to Sommers, is the other face of the coin, where "the blind side of man is portrayed; he is a prisoner of the occult forces of irreality, phantasy and myth." Fuentes concurs in this analysis and adds that in *The Death of Artemio Cruz* he had relied on the illumination of historical analysis. In *Aura,* he depended upon "the multilayered suggestivity of literary style."

I might add that the two conflicting elements of Fuentes's earliest novel, *Where the Air is Clear,* the realistic development of character and rational political commentary (the major emphasis) and the minor note of magic and fatalism—to be discussed later in this chapter—are finally isolated in these two separate novels, both published in 1962. *The Death of Artemio Cruz* carries the major theme in its concern with the Mexican revolution and its development of the character, Artemio Cruz, out of his prototype in Federico Robles. *Aura* carries out the other theme of modern Mexico born out of the ancient one and returning to it, a theme first interpreted by Emir Rodríguez-Monegal in an article in *Número* ("El mundo Mágico de Carlos Fuentes," *Número,* 2d ser. 1 [1963]), which appeared a scant year after the publication of *Aura.*

Los Días Enmascarados

In the discussion of *Aura* I shall need to refer to all of its precedents, not only Fuentes's major, first novel, but also his earlier book of short stories, *Los días enmascarados (The Masked Days),* first published in 1952. We may judge the similarity of this work to *Aura* by the commentary of Robert Mead, Jr. [in *Books Abroad* 38 (1964)]: "*Los días enmascarados* is in the cosmopolitan vein of Jorge Luis Borges, and is written for sophisticated readers. Life is a comedy played against a serious and somber background, in which the author presents man as struggling unsuccessfully against forces far stronger than himself." In one of these stories, **"Tlactocatzine, del Jardín de Flandes,"** the similarities with *Aura* are striking. The story, too, is a tale of an old mansion in Mexico City with a mysterious garden. Told in the first person, it narrates the hero's encounters with an intruder, a wrinkled hag in historical costume. Like the garden in *Aura* where strange, medicinal herbs are grown, this one is permeated by the odor of *Siemprevivas,* (literally "alive-forever," the Spanish for forget-me-nots).

The hag or witch, by means of letters, invites the narrator to a midnight tryst in the garden where he feels in her hands the coldness of the tomb. He tries to escape the mansion, but finds the door locked against him. The hag now calls him "Max" as well as "Tlactocatzine," speaks German as well as Nahuatl, and reminds him of their walks in the garden of Flanders. When he examines the shield on the locked door, he perceives a crowned eagle that seems to have the profile of the old woman. The suspicion with respect to her identity is confirmed when he reads the inscription on the shield, "Charlotte, Kaiserin von Mexico."

To summarize, therefore, we have in this story an atmosphere of increasing unreality. The mansion, which at first is merely beautiful and archaic, actually could exist in Mexico City. But when we discover that it rains always in the garden when the sun is shining in the outside world, we are put on guard. The tale becomes increasingly less real and more subjective. The creature who inhabits the garden is merely hinted at in the first reference: "one might almost say that slow steps are heard with the weight of breath among the fallen leaves."

But gradually, she grows to a certainty. At the conclusion her personality invades the entire house and imprisons the narrator forever. There is no escape from this symbol of the past who seems to be part Aztec princess and part Charlotte, wife of the emperor Maximilian. The latter figure is superimposed on the former. In a way, Charlotte is almost as much a prisoner of the earlier primitive archetype as is the narrator. She too has been caught by history and in turn must prey on others, must find new Maximilians, new victims. For the narrator she embodies "the satisfaction of the jailer, of eternal prison, satisfaction of shared solitudes".

The probability that **"Tlactocatzine,"** which we know was written together with the other stories of the collection "in some haste" as reported by Luis Harss and Barbara Dohmann (*Into theMainstream* [New York: Harper and Row, 1967]) was in fact the rough draft for *Aura* is suggested by the December letter from Fuentes (included in the Appendix) in which he discusses the germinal idea for the novel.

After enumerating the long line of witches who appear in his works from **"Tlactocatzine"** to "the old Ludivinia," shut up in the only room of a burned down mansion in *The Death of Artemio Cruz,* he adds:

> But if I am totally frank, this obsession was born in me when I was seven years old and, after visiting the castle of Chapultepec and seeing the portrait of the young Charlotte of Belgium, I found in the Casasola Archive the photograph of this same woman, now old, dead, placed inside her cushioned, iron coffin, dressed in the nightcap of a little girl; the Charlotte who died, insane in a castle, the same year I was born. The two Charlottes, Aura and Consuelo. Perhaps Charlotte never found out that she was growing old. Until the very end she wrote love letters to Maximillian. A correspondence between ghosts.

The empress Carlota (Charlotte) is clearly the inspiration for both these tales. And how well she conforms to the idea of the animal! She is youth and age (since Fuentes sees her image at both extremes of life); as an empress she represents power; and as a woman insane she is the perfect symbol of our irrational, hidden nature. For Fuentes as a Mexican, moreover, Carlota would represent the European domination of the past, and would thus repel him. Yet as a beautiful and tragic woman, she could not help but also attract a sensitive child of cosmopolitan background.

Jung has told us that the first manifestation of archetypes is often identified with personal experience; that in the case of archetypes in children under the influence of therapy, "the identity breaks down and is accompanied by intensification of the fantasy, with the result that the archaic or mythological features become increasingly apparent." ["The Psychology of the Child Archetype," *Essays on a Science of Mythology*, 1969.]

This obviously is the case history of Carlota in her metamorphosis in Fuentes's mind from portrait to ghost. His brief commentary on the role of Carlota, "correspondence between ghosts," indicates his very subjective relationship to the archetypal character. In Fuentes's mind Carlota is already a ghost corresponding with the "real" ghost of her husband. In **"Tlactocatzine"** Charlotte is even aware, momentarily, that hers is a correspondence between ghosts: "Ah, Max, answer me, the forget-me-nots that I take you in the afternoon to the Capuchin crypt, don't they smell fresh?"

Again, in commenting on *Aura* to Harss and Dohmann [in *Into the Mainstream,* 1967] Fuentes uses the same word, *fantasma*, ghost. "Every story is written with a ghost at your shoulder." In *Aura* the ghost is Woman. What does the word *ghost* mean or suggest to Fuentes, that he repeatedly applies it to the archetypal figure of Carlota-Aura? It has, of course, many connotations, but perhaps chief among them are death, the past, and the supernatural, ideas which are also associated with the anima.

But the use of the word *ghost* is unfortunate in that Harss and Dohmann then proceed to judge *Aura* as a ghost story, a genre whose requirements of suspense it fails to fulfill. "For a meaning to be revealed," they say, "it must first be withheld." One of the problems with *Aura* seems to be that the "ghost" is too close to the archetypal figure, and although the meaning may not be "handed out," as the critics charge, it is suspected by the reader from the beginning.

The Themes in *Aura*

The problem at hand, therefore, is why Fuentes, with all his literary dexterity, uses in *Aura* (and elsewhere) an undisguised archetypal figure which is so vulnerable to criticism. I would postulate that at least part of the reason lies in his didacticism. Since the significance of the archetypal figure is more obvious than that of a character complicated by an involved personal history, Fuentes, when he wishes to be sure of making a point, utilizes the former as a kind of literary shorthand. And this point, to which he sacrifices character development, is usually of a philosophical or social nature. If this postulation is correct, I am in opposition to Robert Mead, who, in commenting upon *Los dias enmascarados,* asserts that "absent from it is the intense preoccupation with social problems which characterize most of his later work" [*Books Abroad* 38 (1964)].

In support of my interpretation of the motivation behind Fuentes's less realistic fiction is a statement Fuentes made to Sommers [*Books Abroad* 40 (1966)]: "*Aura,* despite its basis in a highly subjective, even phantasmagoric view of reality, ultimately implies and reveals an external world." The fact that many of Fuentes's works do not reflect the external world as we know it does not indicate, therefore, . . . that they are not concerned with reality or with social problems. Even Harss and Dohmann recognized that *Aura* was intended as a parable (as well as a ghost story). And Emir Rodríguez-Monegal in the already referred to article from *Número,* found that *Aura* symbolized "the reconstruction of the Mexico of the old days of privilege upon the structure of today's modern and insolent Mexico."

This theme of the old built upon the new, the old returning to haunt the new, is again the theme of ghosts. And although *Aura* may not be a good ghost story, it is, I believe, intended as very much more than a mere ghost story. External reality, as in the case of **"Tlactocatzine,"** gradually withers away. But the attempt is not so much to shock, as to make the reader more fully aware of only half-suspected truths.

The Problem of Reality: Conscious Versus Unconscious. Our first intimation that **Aura** will not deal with the recognizable world of Mexico City in 1962 is provided by the narrator's observation that the house in question is located in the old center of the city! "You always thought that nobody lived in the old center of the city."

Thus he discovers that the past lives on, generally unnoticed, in the heart of the city—and by implication, in the hearts of its inhabitants. The theme of superimposition of personalities and cultures is also foreshadowed by Felipe's discovery that in this old *barrio* house numbers have been changed many times, new ones superimposed on the old which are nevertheless still visible.

The normal world of today begins to fade rapidly as he relates:

> before going in you take a last look over your shoulder, frowning at the long line of stalled buses and cars that groan, honk and pour forth the crazy smoke of their haste. You try, uselessly, to retain a single image of this outside indifferentiated world.

The last adjective, "indifferentiated," suggests the fuzziness, the unreality of the normal, daylight world Felipe has left to enter the real, but shadowy, one of the old mansion. Once inside its portals, the borderline between

real life and the world of dreams becomes increasingly tenuous. According to Robert Mead, "the reader ends by thinking that the entire story, from beginning to end, is a long dream, a chain of events which are born, live and die in the imagination of Felipe Montero."

But the problem is not dream versus reality, but dream versus consciousness. Felipe in this dream world is learning truths to which the daylight world of the conscious ego may blind us. Thus the theme of *La vida es sueño* (*Life Is a Dream*) is clearly echoed in **Aura**; we learn from our dreams, and dreams themselves reveal an often hidden and fundamental part of reality. But there is a significant difference in the basic assumptions of Calderón and of Fuentes. In the great drama of the Golden Age life may be a dream, but the consequences of man's behavior in his dream are awesome. It is a dream dreamed in order to allocate to each of us our final place in eternity, whether this be paradise or eternal condemnation. It is a dream which is a vestibule to a permanent reality. Thus Calderón's conception of the dream is predicated on free will and personal responsibility. There is an imperative need to act wisely and generously in the knowledge that one is being judged.

But if life becomes merely a dream, as in *Aura,* if there is no hereafter of an extra-worldly nature, but only a perpetual reincarnation in this dream world (a theme to be discussed shortly), there is no need to assume free will. In fact the idea suggested by the word *dream* is diametrically opposed, for the modern mind, to the ideas of free will and individual responsibility. If something is only a dream, we are not responsible for our actions—which are viewed as the automatic product of our unconscious. In dreams the course of events often seems predetermined, therefore, with little place for the dreamer's personal choice. Thus *Aura* is far closer to the dream as we know it than is *La vida es sueño.*

There is a shadow of fate, of inevitability, of nightmare at times rather than dream, in **Aura** from beginning to end. In the third sentence of the novel, we read that the newspaper advertisement that sends the hero to the old mansion "seems directed to you and only you."

The Matter of Fate. The narrator walks into the trap which is first baited by money (his need for the salary of nine hundred pesos) and secondly by Aura, whose green eyes enchant him immediately. He says to himself: "Don't fool yourself; these eyes flow, they are transformed, as if they were offering you a landscape that only you could guess or desire. Yes, I am going to live with you."

Then the trap is sprung. Felipe understands that "this house will always be in darkness." He hears the plaintive cries of the cats, whose very existence, as well as that of the garden where drug-producing plants are grown, the old woman denies; he surprises Consuelo muttering secret words before her altar with its picture of hell, and still he does not seem to react. He is apparently overwhelmed by curiosity as well as infatuation. In the last scene we may recall that Felipe is in bed with the old hag and makes no attempt to escape. Yet by this time all illusion of beauty is gone. Nevertheless, he embraces her: "You plunge your face, your open eyes, into Consuelo's silver-white hair, and Consuelo will embrace you again when the moon is out of sight.

The Role of Love in Aura. We have already seen in the discussion of the anima that this archetype always carries a suggestion of fate, of inevitability. In *Aura*, she draws Felipe to her home and, in part through her incarnation of Aura, keeps him there. He is troubled by attraction to Aura and on the conscious level rationalizes and tells himself that he really wishes to rescue her from the spell of the old woman. But on the unconscious level he understands that his real motive for remaining is his need for Aura.

Felipe, we must remember, is a modern man, a rootless intellectual who lives in the "labyrinth of solitude" that Octavio Paz describes, where each man is keenly aware of his isolation from other individuals. In Paz's chapter entitled "The Dialectic of Solitude" he states:

> What we ask of love (which, being desire, is a hunger for communion, a will to fall and to die as well as to be reborn) is that it give us a bit of true life, of true death. We do not ask it for happiness or repose, but simply for an instant of that full life in which opposites vanish, in which life and death, time and eternity are united. . . . Creation and destruction become one in the act of love, and during a fraction of a second man has a glimpse of a more perfect state of being [*The Labyrinth of Solitude,* 1961].

Such a penetrating analysis of love by a writer who has had a profound influence on Fuentes does much to explain the pull of fate on Felipe Montero.

For Felipe, Aura symbolizes the therapy of love, a fusion with someone outside himself. And since his desire is in itself part of the masochistic desire for self-destruction (also studied by both Freud and Jung), the "desire to fall and to die" of which Paz speaks, the dual figure of Aura-Consuelo satisfies both sides of Felipe's craving. Paz has also called this "hunger for communion," and the religious aspect of the sexual act is underlined by Fuentes. Aura's bedroom becomes a church in metaphor: "And you enter this empty bedroom where a circle of light illuminates the bed, the huge Mexican crucifix . . . ."

And again:

> You fall on Aura's nude body, on her open arms, stretched out from one end to the other of the bed, like the black Christ that hangs from the wall with his scarlet silk wrapped around his things, his knees open, his wounded side, his crown of thorns set up on a tangled black wig with silver spangles. Aura opens up like an altar.

Sommers, too, points out the black Christ and the analogy between sexual intercourse and Christian communion. Aura even places on her thighs a thin wheat biscuit suggestive of the holy wafer. Summarizing this scene, Sommers comments:

> Blacks arts, expressed in distorted religious symbols, generate a power superior to that of the intellect . . . The stature of man is diminished for he commands no resources to cope with the mysterious forces which intrude on his consciousness and on his life.

Yet the stature of man does not seem to be relevant in *Aura.* Felipe is not concerned about stature. Like Paz's lonely Mexican, he is concerned about reality and real existence, and his one way of achieving this is by fusion with something outside himself.

This fusion in the minds of today's young students is found in sex and religion. That this is the key to meaning in life is also mentioned by Father Greeley [in *New York Times Magazine,* June 1, 1969]. He quotes one student as saying: "The only place where we are going to find ourselves is in deep relationships with others and that means either religion or sex and maybe both." Father Greeley comments:

> The religious experience in the final analysis is seen as 'ecstatic,' that is to say, that it, like sex, takes a person out of himself and brings him into contact not only with other human beings but with the 'creative powers' which presumably underpin the cosmos.

But if Sommers emphasizes the negative aspect of Felipe's religious and sexual experience, it is only natural in that Fuentes himself has laden it with many of the ninteenth-century, romantic symbols of the Black Mass, the description of the wafer, the black Christ, etc. As a demonologist, he has not, in fact, clearly defined the nature of Consuelo's powers and thus has confused the moral significance of Felipe's love relationship with her. Talking to Harss and Dohmann [in *Into the Mainstream,* 1967], Fuentes seems to equate Consuelo with the ghost of Woman, "the keeper of secret knowledge, which is true knowledge, general knowledge, universal knowledge." And yet, Consuelo, as we have seen, acts very much like a fairy tale witch with her casting of spells and her sacrifice of cats. There are even innuendos that through black magic she is casting an evil spell on Felipe:

> You eat mechanically, with the doll in your hand . . . without realizing, at first, your own hypnotized attitude, only later glimpsing a reason for your oppressive nap, your nightmare, finally identifying your somnambulist movements with those of Aura, with those of the old woman: staring with disgust at this horrid little doll that your fingers caress, where you begin to suspect there may be a secret sickness, a contagion.

Thus Consuelo uses effigies for magic purposes; also the presence of the rabbit Saga (sagacious?) strongly suggests the familiar or witch's assistant, whose historic function has been to focus the witch's power. There is also the implication that Consuelo has fallen into the sin of rebelling against God. General Llorente, in his memoirs, writes: "Consuelo, don't tempt God . . . the devil was once also an angel."

Does all this indicate that Consuelo is in fact a witch? And if so, what would this signify with respect to the spiritual development of Felipe?

A Definition of the Witch. This question can only be answered by recourse to a stricter definition of the term *witch* than I have hitherto provided. According to Hill and Williams, authors of *The Supernatural,* the term should really be applied only to a very limited group of individuals. As they understand the term, even if Consuelo had sold her soul to the Devil by means of a pact, she would still not necessarily be a witch. Rather she seems to belong to the ancient tradition of sorceresses "who may cast spells, charms, and hexes and stir up love potions." "Providing his end is selfish . . . that the sorcerer's motive is to gain riches, power or pleasure for himself, in this world," he is sorcerer and not witch [Douglas Hill and Put Williams, *The Supernatural,* 1965].

Such sorcerers, they say, are pagan, not anti-Christian, and were in fact critically regarded by the church as private practitioners of magic, but not seriously persecuted until the mid-fifteenth century.

In order to distinguish between these suspicious but not really demonic women and real witches, Hill and Williams use the yardstick of intent. The real witch was an agent of the devil, "not one of his customers, used her magic to serve the devil's own purposes, not her own. . . . Her principal function was the worship of the devil, which involved the conscious repudiation of God and the Christian faith."

One of the sources of confusion as to the love ritual in *Aura* seems to be that sex also played a fundamental role in all witch ceremonies, as did various involved perversions and obscenities. But this was pure sex, often grotesque, with no question of love. We need only read accounts of witches' covens and black masses to see how radically different they were from anything found in *Aura.* (Fuentes confuses the picture by his references to the desecration of the Host and the Black Christ—elements of the Black Mass, which according to many authorities is virtually a literary creation and did not grow directly out of the tradition of witchcraft.) Like all sorceresses, therefore, Consuelo uses magic for her own selfish purposes, in this case to reincarnate her youth and thereby recreate love. Richard Callan [in *Kentucky Romance Quarterly* 18 (1971)] compares her to the Greek fertility goddess, Hecate, mother of witchcraft who had as her symbols dogs, goats, mice, and torches—all the items we find in the cavelike abode of Consuelo. Rather than exacting Felipe's soul, she gives him a new one, or rather reveals through her love his true soul and his true face which also had belonged to her husband, the general.

The Theme of Personal Identity. Harss and Dohmann attribute *Aura*'s popularity with its author to its frontal attack on the theme of personal identity. As we see in Fe-

lipe's metamorphosis, this attack certainly exists. But it is an attack that denies the problem rather than wrestling with it. Felipe, when he understands that he is in fact the general, experiences a crisis of vanity, or initial horror that his hitherto private face is really that of someone else. "You hide your face in the pillow trying to keep the air from tearing away your features which are yours, which you want for yourself". But he seems to accept without a struggle his psychic identity with the general, "waiting for what has to come, what you can't prevent."

His confidence in the rational world where I am I and not someone else is entirely gone. On one level we may know, as Professor René Dubos points out [in *Columbia Forum* 12 (Spring 1969)], that "the individuality of a person living now is different from that of anyone who has ever lived in the past or will live in the future," that our personalities are shaped by the peculiarities of genetic endowment and the individual response to the total environment. But on the deeper, unconscious level that Felipe has entered, all this is irrelevant. Almost with relief he accepts the idea that he is the general, and speculates on the nature of time which has given him an identity out of the past.

The Nature of Time in **Aura.** Through spiritual and bodily fusion with Aura, Felipe has apparently experienced something positive, ineffable, which can be compared not to the Black Mass but to the Mass itself. The real Mass, if properly understood, is, in the words of Jung [*The Archetypes and the Collective Unconscious,* 1959] "a participation in the transcendence of life which overcomes all bonds of space and time. it is a moment of eternity in time."

In like manner, Paz and Father Greeley have told us, man seeks fusion in love with the outside world. And he desires not only fusion in space, but also fusion in time. The dichotomy between chronological "normal" time with its generative feeling of unreality and subjective, eternal time, Paz says, "is expressed in the opposition between history and myth, or history and poetry." Love is "only an instant of real life in which the opposites of life and death, time and eternity, fuse."

The love scene between Aura and Felipe, therefore, is dominated, as is the entire novel, not by a search for identity but rather by a secret longing to lose our painful identities in an eternal world of space and time outside previous experience. In the anima, young and old, maiden and mother, is incarnated a magical conception of time which finally penetrates Felipe's being. Realizing he is now a new person, Felipe says:

> You don't look at your watch again. It is a useless object falsely measuring a time determined by human vanity, these little hands that tediously measure off the long hours invented in order to disguise the real passage of time, which races with an insulting and mortal swiftness that no clock could measure.

He seems in these words to regard himself from a vantage point outside time, a vantage point that makes normal concepts absurd: "A life, a century, fifty years, it will no longer be possible for you to imagine such lying measurements."

The ending of the novel is ambiguous, and although we realize that normal concepts of time are displaced, precisely what we are to substitute in their stead is left to the reader's imagination. There is, of course, the possibility that Felipe is only a ghost summoned by Consuelo, much as Aura has been materialized by her; that, like the narrator in Borges's "The Circular Ruins," he is himself only a dream. There is also the postulation of Richard Callan [*Kentucky Romance Quarterly* 18 (1971)] that the whole story is a "hypnagogic drama of Felipe Montero, similar to the fantasies studied by Jung. My own feeling is that it is almost useless to divide Fuentes's characters into "real" and "unreal" categories since they all participate equally of the world of myth, are all outside time and inside immortality. Specifically, Felipe is a new reincarnation of a prototype that had previously existed as General Llorente. In one of his conversations with Aura, for example, there is talk of death and rebirth: "You have to be reborn, Aura," he says. And she replies, "One must die first in order to be reborn". Reincarnation is also the assumption in many other stories dealing with the anima (as for example H. Rider Haggard's *She* and Poe's "Ligeia"), and, perhaps even more important in dealing with Fuentes, it is also to be found in the ideas of Nietzsche.

Felipe seems to know his role and to accept it fatalistically because it is a repetition. He has done it all before. Thus the "tú," the second person, familiar form in which the story is written, may be interpreted as his older, wiser, unconscious self who is privy to the secret of fate, who observes Felipe's movements from the vantage point of past experience. He knows precisely what Felipe is going to do because he has already done it in a previous existence. Thus, although the narrator speaks frequently in the future tense, there is a strong element of the past; it is an inevitable future.

Summary of Conclusions Relating to *Aura*

On the psychological plane, therefore, the character of Aura-Consuelo is an excellent example of Jung's anima, the archetype of life. Aura, with her green eyes, pictured against a green sea (the photo taken of her by General Llorente), youthful, ancient, wise and seductive, is a composite of life-giving symbols. Offering Felipe the hidden powers of the unconscious as *femme inspiratrice*, she at first spurs him on to a burst of energy in his research and writing. But as Richard Callan points out, Felipe fails the challenge offered him by the anima, fails to slay the dragon of Consuelo, who represents the fatal attraction of the unconscious. Instead of reasserting his ego, Felipe Montero, whose name means *hunter*, fails the test. (Given Fuentes's fatalism, of course, this was predictable from the start.) Montero succumbs to the consolation (epito-

mized by Consuelo whose name means *consolation*) of the Great Mother figure. Unable to rescue the anima from the engulfing form of the great feminine unconscious, he enters the world of Aura, whose name can mean *vulture, gentle breeze, breath,* or *dawn*. But Felipe chooses the dark side of her nature and pays for his choice by loss of personal identity.

On the level of historical symbolism, the theme of *Aura* implies the takeover of the new by the old, and specifically the reconquest of modern Mexico by the ghosts of her past, a theme that Fuentes had already developed in *Where the Air is Clear,* and repeats again and again. So viewed, the resemblance of Aura to the figure of witch is emphasized, and she can only be regarded negatively.

Yet the meaning of *Aura* goes beyond the parochial experience of Mexico. The roots of *Aura,* as I have pointed out, are universal. The message has an almost biblical theme. As Jung says of the anima [in *The Archetypes and the Collective Unconscious*], she "is full of snares and traps in order that man should fall, should reach the earth and entangle himself there, and stay caught, so that life should be lived."

Herein lies the great danger of the anima figure. Though she is irresistible as muse and young maiden, we have seen that she has as her negative pole the all-embracing figure of the Great Mother. (The relationship between anima and the other denizens of the collective unconscious are traced in detail by Erich Neumann, one of Jung's leading disciples, in *The Great Mother* [Princeton: Princeton University Press, 1955.]) As Neumann points out, the anima stands like a beacon on the threshold of the collective unconscious, and her blinding light conceals the dark form of the elemental female who lurks behind her. In psychoanalytical terms, Felipe succumbs to the pull of the uroboric unconscious represented by Consuelo, the Great Mother, relinquishes his precious ego with hardly a struggle and slips back with relief into the original state of unconsciousness and death.

In conclusion, therefore, whether we designate Aura as witch or sorceress, it is clear that her powers are both destructive and creative. This is the reason why Fuentes's attitude to the anima figure is ambiguous. She both attracts and repels him. He feels a compulsion to repeat her image again and again, perhaps hoping that some day she can be seized and tamed. Aura is the model for a later short story, **"La Muñeca Reina"** (**"The Queen Doll"**) from *Cantar de ciegos* (*Song of the Blind,* 1964), which gives a fairly realistic treatment of the deformation by time of a beautiful young girl who becomes a thing of repulsion. Still another story in the same collection, **"Las Dos Elenas,"** has its roots in *Aura,* with its treatment of the dual attraction of the old mother-in-law and the young bride for the modern, but confused, young Mexican narrator.

John S. Brushwood (essay date 1982)

SOURCE: "*Los dias enmascarados* and *Cantar de ciegos*: Reading the Stories and Reading the Books," in *Carlos Fuentes, A Critical View*, edited by Robert Brody and Charles Rossman, University of Texas Press, 1982, pp. 18-33.

[*Brushwood is an American critic and educator specializing in Mexican, Mexican American, and Spanish American literature. In the following essay, he examines the reading experience of two Fuentes story collections and proposes a new ordering for the stories so that would make the volumes more effective. In the process, he analyzes the narrative techniques employed by Fuentes.*]

Several characteristics of Carlos Fuentes' fiction vie for attention in any analytical consideration of his work. Stylistic virtuosity, the joining of past and present, what it means to be Mexican, his commentary on the human estate, all readily come to mind. On the other hand, if one thinks in terms of what actually happens to a reader during the experience of a Fuentes narrative, the desire to know how the story turns out is as important as any other facet of the act of reading. Most of Fuentes' short stories, individually analyzed, show how skillfully he uses the enigma code [a term from Roland Barthes's *S/Z*, 1974]. However, it is possible to reveal certain details of the narrative process, in separate stories, and still not describe adequately the experience of reading either *Los días enmascarados* or *Cantar de ciegos* as a total work, leaving the stories in the order of presentation. In other words, the experience of reading a volume of stories is different from reading the stories separately. It seems possible that, by combining analysis of individual stories with analysis of each volume as an entity in itself, one may illuminate some aspects of Fuentes' narrative technique and gain some insight into the success or failure of volumes of stories.

Fuentes' short fictions show him to be rather traditional in his penchant for resolution, even though the resolution may sometimes take for granted an element of unreality. Very often his stories end with an ironic twist reminiscent of de Maupassant or O. Henry. This resemblance is largely confined to the denouement, of course, since the story material into the narrative we read) is highly original, complicated, and variable from story to story with regard to details of technique. Manipulation of focus is probably the most important technical phenomenon in Fuentes' narration. The relationship of focus to denouement may be an important key to understanding how his fictions work or, one might say, how his narratives ensnare the reader and turn him around at the end. Four of the six stories in *Los días enmascarados* and five of the seven in *Cantar de ciegos* depend in some fashion on a first-person narrating voice; however, these voices function in very different ways, and they also relate to the denouement in different ways. In stories not dependent on a first-person voice, the focus of narration is still related, in important ways, to the resolutions of the narratives.

"Chac Mool," the first story in *Los días enmascarados,* has become a kind of Fuentes showcase because it combines the author's predilection for fantasy and his interest in joining two periods of time—or better, showing how the past continues to be a vital factor in the present. Another characteristic—the recurrence of first-person narration—may be added to this complex of typical attributes. The framing narration is by a first-person voice who reads the diary of a deceased friend, thereby conceding the focus of narration to the friend. However, the framing device acquires uncommon importance at the end of the story, when the first, apparently external, narrator reasserts his role and discovers (reveals) that his friend, who died by drowning, has been replaced in his own house, by a vitalized idol—Chac Mool, a pre-Hispanic deity associated with rain.

Unquestionably, readers who know something about Acapulco and the pre-Hispanic pantheon approach "**Chac Mool**" with a richer "repertory" (Wolfgang Iser's term [from *The Act of Reading,* 1978]) than those who do not. However, Fuentes employs several strategies (also Iser's term) that compensate for the possible deficiency in shared information, the most effective is identification with the first narrator, with whom the reader may experience the second narrator's diary account. By sharing the first narrator's experience, one may feel himself a participant in the narration, and is puzzled by the circumstance just as the first narrator is puzzled.

The story early poses the question of why Filiberto drowned. Once within the diary, a reader may expect to discover the explanation. In fact, the basic narrator takes an important step toward satisfying reader curiosity when, halfway through the story, Narrator One observes that, at a certain point in the diary, Filiberto's handwriting shows signs of nervousness or instability, although it has been normal up to this point. This advice is an essential communication between Narrator One and the text reader (really coreader of the diary, along with Narrator One), since the printed text cannot reflect such a change. Reader anticipation is heightened, but the diary itself never answers the question. It is the first narrator, to whom the reader is attached from the beginning, who resolves the enigma. Narrator One is no longer just the reader of a diary, no longer a simple carrier of the enigma; he becomes an essential actor in the narrative. When he arrives at his friend's house with the body of the deceased, he is greeted by a Chac Mool who has displaced his owner as master of the house. The resolution incorporates fantasy, but it is no less a resolution. According to Tzvetan Todorov's exposition [In his *The Fantastic,* 1975], the fantastic changes into the marvelous at the end of this narrative. At this point, the reader shares knowledge with Narrator One, but not experience.

It is commonplace—one might even say it is fashionable—to comment on Fuentes' theme of *mexicanidad* (Mexicanness). This theme is certainly apparent in "**Chac Mool,**" since the story refers to both Mexican myth and contemporary Mexican life. Dauster makes an even more specific observation with reference to the appearance of

Chac Mool at the end of the story. The former idol now seems not only to be a living person in charge of the house, he also uses some of the most vulgar symbols of contemporary society (lipstick, cheap lotion, etc.). Dauster takes this awkward contrast to be a commentary on modern Mexico [In "La transposición de la realidad en las obras cortas de Carlos Fuentes," *Kentucky Romance Quarterly* 19 1972]. A similar concern for *mexicanidad* characterizes two of the remaining five stories in *Los días enmascarados*, **"Tlactocatzine, del Jardín de Flandes"** and **"Por boca de los dioses."** Genevieve Mary Ramírez discusses the book as if it were divided into two parts, one consisting of three stories clearly referring to Mexico, and another of the remaining three stories that, for different reasons, seem almost generically distinct from the first group [in *Evolution of Thought in The Prose Fiction of Carlos Fuentes,* 1977]. Ramírez comments on the latter set and points out all the possible ways they may refer to Mexico. She also notes that the basically "Mexican" stories are the first, third, and fifth. In other words, the two sets are intercalated, not separated. As a result, the experience of reading *Los días enmascarados* as a total, logically arranged literary work is quite different from reading individual stories or one of the two sets.

"En defensa de la Trigolibia" comes as something of a shock, in sequence following **"Chac Mool."** It is a political allegory on the values cultivated and defended by two superpowers, presumably the United States and the Soviet Union. It has few characteristics of fiction or even of narrative. Its tone is that of commentary on world politics, with humor afforded by clever wordplay that satirizes bureaucratese but tends to negate its own effect by becoming tiresome before the end of the piece. Generically, it is more like satirical political journalism than a story. Ramírez says it is "written almost in an essay style." It has neither characterization nor story line; phenomena such as focus of narration or story-time versus narrative-time are not relevant to this allegorical sketch. Its final sentence-paragraph, "This is the defense of Trigolibia," actually constitutes a summary of what has gone before. It does signify, of course, that what has gone before is the writer's interpretation of the defense of Trigolibia; it is the way he sees the situation.

This disembodied voice confronts the reader at the outset: "Trigolibia is the supreme value of the Nusitanians." A reader just finishing **"Chac Mool"** has already been removed from the intimate association with Narrator One, in the first story. However, the exterior commentator of **"En defensa de la Trigolibia"** most likely jars one into a different mood altogether. In the first few moments of reading, the play on terminology may suggest the possibility of some kind of fantasy, but the allegory becomes apparent shortly thereafter. The repertory activated in the experience of this essay is totally different from that of **"Chac Mool." "En defensa de la Trigolibia"** calls for no knowledge at all of Mexico or of mythology; its referent is global politics. Furthermore, the commenting voice need make no effort to compensate for the lack of information on the part of the reader; he assumes the referent is familiar to all. His strategy, therefore, is to satirize by

inventing a system of terms, and oversimplifying a complex situation. The reader must change his own strategy completely. Instead of using the procedures necessary for participation in a joining of reality and fantasy, he must now adapt to an interpretation of allegory, in a manner that is more intellectual than emotional. In the process, one becomes aware of Fuentes' commitment to political awareness, and this fact relates back to **"Chac Mool"** by emphasizing the aspects of the first story that suggest social commentary. The end of the second piece—that is, the final sentence quoted above—emphasizes its expository nature, for it is in no way a denouement. In one sense, it is typical of the author, an excellent essayist who frequently becomes discursive in his fiction. However, it is certainly not typical of Fuentes to terminate narratives on an anticlimactic note.

The nonfiction character of **"En defensa de la Trigolibia"** initiates the seesaw experience created by intercalating two sets of stories in *Los días enmascarados*. The third story, **"Tlactocatzine, del Jardín de Flandes"** belongs to the same group as **"Chac Mool."** Indeed, once the reader has adjusted to the second story, the third will be just as great a shock in its turn. A diary account is the form of the narration; however, unlike **"Chac Mool,"** this story does not use a narrator intervening between the diary and the reader. Consequently, the effect is different; narrator and reader both conform to different strategies. To a considerable degree, the reader of **"Tlactocatzine"** is in a position corresponding to that of Narrator One in **"Chac Mool."** The difference between the two stories is especially important in the denouement because the story of the diarist is left incomplete (we do not know what happens to him). As a result, full emphasis falls upon the unusual circumstance that he narrates.

The narrator is given the opportunity to live in an old house in Mexico City. Within the house, closed off from the hubbub of contemporary city life, the diarist finds himself confronting a fantastic situation involving the presence of a ghostly woman. The denouement reveals that she is the Empress Carlota. A number of clues precede this revelation, but the practiced reader of Fuentes cannot be certain at what point he knows her identity, because the study naturally reminds one of *Aura* and of Fuentes' interest in the period of the French Intervention. What is absolutely certain is that the repertory makes requirements of the reader similar to those in the experience of **"Chac Mool."** Interestingly enough, the intercalcation of **"En defensa de la Trigolibia"** may well add a dimension to the reading of **"Tlactocatzine."** Since the political satire tends to point out the author's interest in the state of society—even with the reflective reference to **"Chac Mool"**—one is now tempted to look for similar significations in **"Tlactocatzine."** They are far from plentiful. It is possible to read the total situation as referring to the struggle between the persistence of the past and the willful destruction of it by modern Mexico, because the diarist speculates that the owner of the house may have bought it with demolition in mind. The strategies used in the narration do not encourage the search for such meanings. The focus of narration leaves one confronting the event that established the identity of the mysterious woman and, at the same time, asking if there is a rational explanation of her presence. The empress' name is apparent over a coat of arms; as for the rest of it, one must choose between the uncanny and the marvelous, as Todorov defines the alternatives. The diarist makes no choice; he just states the case. Obviously, this experience of fiction alters a reader's set of procedures for understanding, as contrasted with the political satire that immediately precedes.

The seesaw swings again with the reading of **"Letanía de la orquídea,"** though the change is not as abrupt. This fourth story begins with an unidentified voice speaking to an unidentified hearer: "Mira, vé: ya empezó el invierno" ("Hey, look: winter has already begun"). One surmises, on the basis of the language, that the speaker is not Mexican. The next sentence reveals that the scene is Panama. For the rest of the story, a voice outside the narrative relates events from the viewpoint of Muriel, a character based on the tropical prototype. Fuentes' prose style is mildly disconcerting because of its heavily rich imagery. No one would deny the author's lyricism, of course, but the richness in **"Letanía"** seems unusual: "Visceral light, yellow as rain when it mixes with dust. . . . The windows shook until sounding a reticent dactyl." Readers may well not know how to react to this stylistic procedure—could it be some kind of parody on intensely poetic prose? The portrait of Muriel develops schematically as he does typically tropical things. An allegory is taking shape, though one may not be immediately aware that such is the case. The stylization of Muriel crosses into fantasy when his coccyx sprouts an orchid. The clincher of the allegory comes when he decides to grow orchids for sale and the plant itself causes his death. So Muriel is Panama; the highly figurative language which may have been disconcerting early in the experience of **"Letanía"** now becomes part of the façade that disguises the Panamanian tragedy. As one finishes this story, a return to the beginning of it is almost inevitable because the interpretation comes to fruition only at the end, and one needs to reconsider the process of development. The referent is in fact not so much life in Panama as it is the Panamanian circumstance. The reader participates not by understanding Muriel as a human individual, but as the symbol of a political situation. Fuentes has avoided an essay, but the narrative clearly indicates the importance of social commentary in his work.

The element of fantasy is the most important similarity between **"Letanía de la orquídea"** and the story preceding it, as well as the one following it. For the reader of the volume *Los días enmascarados,* fantasy probably establishes itself, by the time these four stories are read, as the primary characteristic in common. Only **"En defensa de la Trigolibia"** requires accepting an entirely different referent and an equally different set of strategies. The fifth story, **"Por boca de los dioses,"** reaffirms the importance of fantasy and returns to the referential complex of **"Chac Mool"** and **"Tlactocatzine."** It involves awareness of contemporary Mexico, of modern art as contrasted with the art of the colonial period, and the present-day influ-

ence of the pre-Hispanic past, in the person of Tlazol, a goddess who is associated with filth and also—in a way very important to this short story—with cleaning up and forgiveness or expiation. Suggestions of allegory abound—modern impatience with tradition; modern Mexico assassinates its colonial self and the pre-Hispanic component persists, even dominates the present; the protagonist descends into the nether regions. The actual experience of reading **"Por boca de los dioses,"** however, does not exact quite so systematic an interpretation.

The narration is by a first-person voice who is the main character in the story but who tells it retrospectively. This time of narration is important because he appears to recount his own demise as the denouement: "Tlazol embraced me in a spasm devoid of sighs. The knife remained there, in my guts, like a pivot out of control, turning by itself while she was opening the door to the caravan of minute sounds of wings and snakes that were gathering in the hall, and twisted guitars and internal voices were singing". If one assumes the factual existence of the I-narrator, he must have survived this incident. Therefore, our strategy must be capable of dealing with fantasy on more than one level.

The narrator describes himself in a nightmarish situation at the beginning of the story—an introduction in parentheses. Then the narration appears to turn to real events occurring in a real world, related in the first person by Oliverio. However, this apparently real-life situation requires an adjustment on the reader's part when Oliverio removes a pair of lips from a Tamayo painting. They accompany him and speak; the narration becomes almost as if Oliverio were narrating the story of the lips. This phenomenon must be appreciated along with the intervention of Tlazol who, in the final scene, functions in an apparently definitive way; however, the scene ends in a kind of surrealistic suggestiveness that recalls the opening scene, which was parenthetical. Among other considerations, one must keep in mind the possibility of a Tamayo painting brought to life. **"Por boca de los dioses"** is the least resolved of all the stories in this volume, except insofar as resolution may take the form of dissolution.

The final story, **"El que inventó la pólvora,"** returns to social commentary of the direct kind. It is a satire on consumerism—a society in which products are less and less durable and the motto is "use everything," until the cataclysm occurs. The narration is in first person by the only character, the survivor, who relates the process of deterioration retrospectively, then shifts to present tense as he tells how he sits on the shore of a newly made sea and starts a fire by friction. The impact of this denouement must have been considerably greater in 1954, when the volume was published, than it is today, since the possibility of such a return to primitivism has now become a commonplace. The commentary on consumerism, on the other hand, seems even more vital now.

As a work of fiction, **"El que inventó la pólvora"** is of little consequence. It is more of a satirical essay, lightly fictionalized—or one might better say "narrationized." Its referent is a widely recognized social phenomenon that requires no special strategy to compensate for a difference in repertory between author and reader. In this respect, it is probably the most effective communication, over a wide range of readership, of all the stories in this first volume. It certainly is not a typical Fuentes story, however, and it ends the book on a rather strange note. (One might, of course, note the intensification of destruction, followed by a new beginning, and so make an association with *Terra Nostra*.)

Any one of the stories in *Los días enmascarados* is noteworthy for the steadily increasing intensity that the narrators manage to achieve—even in those pieces that belong only marginally to the short story genre. The volume, experienced as a single work, does not share this characteristic with its six separate parts. Quite to the contrary, the volume destroys the possibility of increasing intensity by persistently changing the functions the reader has to perform, so creating a seesaw effect of reading two kinds of texts and moving back and forth from one kind of experience to another.

Since the effect of increasing intensity—concluding, in five of the six selections, with an ironic denouement—depends largely on the manipulation of narrating voice and focusing eye, it is interesting to speculate on how else the stories might have been arranged. If one were to take into account the active role of the reader (the extent to which the reader becomes an accomplice of the narrative strategy), **"Chac Mool"** would undoubtedly be the opening story if one wished to begin with the highest degree of involvement. **"Por boca de los dioses"** would follow, the **"Tlactocatzine"** would be third. This ordering would have the disadvantage of running counter to the increasing intensity of each individual story, since the reader of this proposed sequence would feel less and less involved. However, it would have the advantage of preparing the reader to go on to the other stories which might be arranged with **"Letanía"** first, followed by **"El que inventó la pólvora"** and then by **"En defensa de la Trigolibia,"** so continuing to move toward less reader involvement by increasing the intensity of author commentary. There is a strong argument for omitting the last three stories in the above scheme—that is, for publishing them separately or for identifying them as a separate unit in the volume with the other three. In such a case, the three stories in the first group might be placed in the reverse order to allow reader involvement to increase during the experience of reading the unit of three. Placed in whatever order, in a separate section, the satirical pieces would still retain much of the chief effect of their presence: to emphasize certain social concerns and to needle reader consciousness with respect to the author's social awareness as communicated in the other three stories.

When Richard Reeve characterized *Cantar de ciegos* as "the mosaic world of modern Mexico," he clarified this allusion to the book's "Mexicanness" by saying that Fuentes had earlier dealt with the question of "what is Mexico?" and, in the new volume of short stories, turned to a consideration of "who are the Mexicans?" ["El mundo mosaico del mexicano moderno: *Cantar de ciegos,* de Carlos Fuentes," *Nueva Narrativa Hispanoamericana* 1, No. 2 (September 1967)]. This explanation sheds some light on the tendency to think of this book as a kind of turning point in Fuentes' work, even though his narratives from the first to the latest have much in common with each other. There does appear to be a shifting emphasis—a change somewhat less radical than a transition—in Fuentes' work, with regard to the extratextual reality that constitutes the referent. One might say that the persistence of the pre-Hispanic past in the present becomes a less important factor than it was in *Los días enmascarados* and *La región más transparente;* on the other hand, *Cambio de piel* alone is enough to prove that he has not totally given up his concern for "what is Mexico?" in spite of the obvious universality of that novel. The sense of difference between the first volume of short stories and *Cantar de ciegos* is created partially, of course, by some shift in emphasis; however, the difference is even more clearly the result of greater consistency in the author's act of communication, manifested especially in the intricate manipulation of narrating voice and focusing eye. While these strategies do vary in some ways from story to story, *Cantar de ciegos* does not challenge the reader, with respect to "accepted procedures," as frequently as *Los días enmascarados* does.

"Las dos Elenas," the first story in *Cantar de ciegos,* takes its title from the names of two women, mother and daughter, whose contrasting characters affect the actions of the first-person narrator. Elena Senior is an attractive, middle-aged, society matron. Her daughter, the wife of the narrator (Victor), is a caricature of "modern" woman, in her dress, her interest in art and her advanced ideas. She even proposes that she needs to live with two men in order to feel fulfilled. She insists on discussing this possibility when she and Victor have Sunday dinner with her parents.

The narrative actually begins with a commentary by Elena Senior on this particular point. Addressing herself to Victor, she lists her daughter's manias and pronounces all of them at least minimally acceptable up to, but not including, her explaining to her father that she wishes to live with two men. Although Victor is the first-person narrator, this fact does not become apparent until after his mother-in-law has stated her case. The procedure is a very important aspect of the narration because the negative attitude toward Elena Junior is established by her mother, not by Victor. The story develops then in the words of Victor, and it is mainly a characterization of Elena Junior through his reporting of what she said and did. The narration is in the past tense until the last paragraph when Victor, having taken leave of Elena Junior, who is going to spend the entire day painting, turns his MG toward Lomas de Chapultepec, where he knows Elena Senior and his own fulfillment are awaiting him. The irony of the denouement is greatly intensified by the fact that Victor never criticizes his wife. His mother-in-law's exposition, at the beginning of the narrative, establishes the base of Elena Junior's characterization and, incidentally, of her own. One may not notice immediately that her initial statement reveals her as very permissive, though there is a point beyond which she will not allow the façade to be further destroyed.

"**La muñeca reina,**" the story that follows, is quite different in theme, but the strategies are largely the same. A first-person narrator tells the story and also sees what happens. A change of tense is important because it moves the narrative voice from a retrospective position outside the narrative to an actually present time within the narrative. Such a change has an important effect in the last paragraph of "**Las dos Elenas,**" so it is hardly surprising in "**La muñeca reina,**" except possibly because it is even more important.

The story tells of the narrator's wish to relive the time of a cherished memory—the friendship of a young girl. Taking advantage of a clue, he finds her (now after many years), but the discovery is grotesque. The change of tense makes the idealized memory a past reality; the actual discovery is in the present: "I ring the bell. The shower becomes heavier and insistent." The sense of actuality created by the use of present tense comes close to making the narrator a dual personage. In the years intervening between the memory and the present, he has become the seeker rather than the sought. "**La muñeca reina**" has some of the spectral quality that characterizes three of the stories in *Los días enmascarados;* however, the denouement does not depend in any way on fantasy. It is rather a case of irony created by reality asserting itself.

The exterior reality to which "**Fortuna lo que ha querido**" refers is notably similar to that of "**Las dos Elenas.**" An artist successful in both painting and sexual conquest is characterized by inconstancy in both fields of endeavor. The subtlety of the narration is extremely attractive. The narrator does not refer to himself in a first-person form until the last paragraph of the narrative; however, his involvement with the protagonist may be felt earlier. The position of the narrator is outside the narrative, and the voice speaks in third person, but a tense change suggests a relationship that is not wholly omniscient. After providing the reader with a good deal of information about the painter—all in simple past tense—the narrator suggests a closer relationship with the artist by inserting a present perfect: "He left the hotel after the '63 exhibit. *Alejandro has always suffered feverish collapses* after presenting a new collection of paintings . . ." (my emphasis). Given this relationship between narrator and protagonist, it is appropriate that readers not know the reason for all of the latter's actions. At the end of the narrative, he turns away from a meeting with a possible conquest. The narrator does not explain why he makes this decision. It may be that he esteems this particular woman too highly to settle for just another affair; it may be that he fears rejection. Presumably the narrator does not know. He reaffirms the relationship already suggested by saying at the end of the narrative: "A while ago I reminded him that he was already thirty-three and that he should think of marrying someday. Alejandro just looked at me sadly."

With the exception of some place names, there is little to identify the first three stories in *Cantar de ciegos* as Mexican. The first and third have as their referents two internationally recognizable aspects of modern society; "**La muñeca reina**" may appear less familiar because of its grotesque denouement, but it could happen in many other countries as well as in Mexico. "**Vieja moralidad,**" the story that follows "**Fortuna lo que ha querido,**" is slightly more specific in its cultural reference, though not enough to require special preparation or compensation through particular strategies. The protagonist's grandfather is a *republicano juarista,* a clergy-baiter. The old man's heterodoxy allows him to maintain a female companion in his rural home. He is also the guardian of Alberto, his adolescent grandson, who narrates the story. A covey of sanctimonious aunts rescue Alberto from this morally reprehensible environment. They take him to the city (Morelia) and install him in the home of one of the good ladies, where he may be properly educated, both formally and informally. In the course of events, he becomes his aunt's youthful lover, with a second aunt somewhat less than figuratively waiting on the sidelines.

The first-person narrator functions in this story very nearly as he does in "**Las dos Elenas.**" The narrative begins with the grandfather speaking, actually berating the seminarians who pass by his house. He reveals his anticlericalism and then the narrating role of Alberto becomes apparent. The boy tells what happened up to and including the amorous overtures of the second aunt. By this time, one is already appreciating the irony of the switch in moral rectitude. But still another irony is to come. Alberto reports that he wrote a letter to his grandfather, asking him to come to get him because Alberto thinks there is probably more morality in the country. Then switching to present tense—just as Victor does, in another intrafamily moral irony, at the end of "**Las dos Elenas**"—Alberto says, referring to the letter, "Pero todavia no me decido a mandarla." The ironic situation, therefore, is left intact—in progress, one might say—even though it functions as a resolution in the narration.

"**El costo de la vida,**" the fifth story, presents the first real problem regarding the aesthetic consistency—or equanimity—of *Cantar de ciegos.* Both repertory and strategies are different from those of the preceding selections. The protagonist, a member of the lower middle class, economically speaking, has more problems than he has means of coping with them. A series of unpredictable circumstances leads to his death. The narrative offers no problem of credibility if one is reasonably aware of circumstances in contemporary Mexico; less informed readers may find much that seems strange (e.g., the deplorable economic condition of a school teacher), and may become so involved with this novel-of-customs aspect of the story that they may lose contact with its more general significance. The narrating voice uses third person, and though large parts of the story are focused from the point of view of Salvador, the protagonist, the effect is very different from the ironies produced by the first-

---

Novels vs. Short fiction:

[David L. Middleton]: *Don't you believe that one or the other, the novel or the story, shows your talents better?*

[Carlos Fuentes]: I don't know. They're very different. They permit you to express yourself in different ways, and to focus on certain aspects of writing with greater intensity. I have a couple of books of short stories in preparation.

How do you work on them? In relation to your longer fiction, that is? Do you work on short stories for a sustained period of time and then switch over to the novel?

They're "wound" with the novels in a way . . . intertwined. When I'm stumped with a novel, I go into a short story, and then back into the novel. That sort of thing.

Maybe there's a complementary function served for you by that kind of work habit.

They feed one another. They do, they do. I feel comfortable with both forms. These are many things I can't possibly say in a novel. Sometimes I include short stories in a novel. I don't know whether that's good form, but I like doing it.

Carlos Fuentes with David L. Middleton, "An Interview with Carlos Fuentes," Southern Review, Vol. 22, No. 2, Spring, 1976, pp. 342-55.

---

person narrator position. In **"El costo de la vida,"** the irony is created by outside reporting of contingent circumstance.

Analysts of Fuentes' short stories are generally not very kind to **"El costo de la vida."** Reeve says "being a chapter of the unpublished novel *La patria de nadie,* this story never achieves an identity or unity of its own"; Dauster considers it "the least successful story in the volume"; Ramirez calls it "the weakest story in the collection." When removed from the context of the volume in which it appears, **"El costo de la vida"** seems not to deserve such negative regard. The extratextual reality to which it refers recalls the author's *La región más transparente.* The narration accomplishes all that is normally required of a successful short story. The narrative begins at a point in the basic story where the character and circumstance of Salvador may be rapidly glimpsed. A basic conflict is established early—between the depressing demands of his struggle to survive and his desire to live with some degree of joy. The events that take place subsequently all intensify this conflict. He asks for assistance from his father; he brings back memories of his Golden Age; in conversation with his old buddies. He picks up a girl and goes with her to Chapultepec (a clear evasion of obligation to his sick wife). He gets a job as a taxi driver in order to meet his financial obligations. This careful intensification of the basic conflict adds

impact to the denouement when, in an act of friendship, Salvador meets death unexpectedly. In the words of a less skillful writer, this story might indeed have become too diffuse. Fuentes employs several strategies that avoid this result. The principal one is unabashed control of the narration, even to the point of summarizing scene—in addition, of course, to the expected balancing of scene and summary. For example, a paragraph from the episode of reminiscing with friends takes this form:

> And Alfred remembered that when he graduated the family gave him the old car and everyone went out to celebrate in a big way by club-hopping all over the city. They were very drunk and Raimundo said that Alfredo didn't know how to drive and he began to struggle with Alfredo to let him take the wheel and the car almost turned over at a traffic circle on the Reforma and Raimundo said that he wanted to throw up and the door opened and Raimundo fell out onto the street and broke his neck.

Given the impact of **"El costo de la vida"** when it is read and analyzed outside the context of *Cantar de ciegos,* one may reasonably conclude that the adverse reaction it creates when read as part of the volume is probably caused by the eccentricity of its strategies (as compared with the preceding stories).

The sixth story, **"Una alma pura,"** recovers the equilibrium and appears to be universally admired. The narrating voice belongs to the protagonist's sister. He was a Mexican expatriate who went to Europe because the cultural ambience of his native country was not to his liking. The past tenses in the preceding sentence indicate the time situation in the narrative. The sister addresses her brother, now deceased. The present time of the story is the hours immediately preceding her departure by plane to accompany his remains on the return trip to Mexico. Her reminiscence, addressed to him, narrates the story of his chaotic and ultimately unsatisfying life abroad. Naturally, it happens in the past, and is so differentiated in her narration. She tells his story and characterizes herself. Leaving the reminiscence and focusing on the present, just before departing, she is granted the opportunity to know—via a letter handed her—the last words of her brother. Ironically, in spite of the relationship she claims, she destroys the letter without reading it. The narration again is resolved but, in a sense, unfinished.

The final work in *Cantar de ciegos,* **"A la vibora de la mar,"** is really best thought of as an addendum to the volume. Its length sets it apart because it runs to seventy-three pages; the other six pieces average about twenty pages each. The repertory is somewhat different from the short stories, although its referent is a cosmopolitan society. The shipboard scene (a vacation cruise) suggests the ship-of-fools motif, and the dedication to Julio Cortázar recalls his *Los premios.* Fuentes' story is focused on the innocence of a Mexican woman tourist and the confidence men who deceive her and take her money. The story, carefully worked out by an external narrator using third person, is a tragicomedy. Riotously funny at times, the narrative ends with the woman's tragic realization that she has been exploited not only in terms of her money but, even worse, in terms of her affection. The fact that **"A la víbora de la mar"** functions as an addendum to the volume does not mean it is inferior to the rest. It stands separately, might well have been published separately, it is fortunate for the aesthetic consistency of *Cantar de ciegos* that it appears last.

Considering *Cantar de ciegos* as a total experience, one might argue reasonably that **"El costo de la vida"** is poorly placed. Using the same rationale that suggested the rearrangement of stories in *Los días enmascarados,* a preferable ordering of the later volume might be **"Las dos Elenas," "Vieja moralidad," "Fortuna lo que ha querido," "Una alma pura," "La muñeca reina," "El costo de la vida,"** and **"A la víbora de la mar"** still in the place appropriate to a separate work. This ordering gives maximum importance to similarities among the first-person voice strategies. However, the rearrangement would not make as much difference as in *Los días enmascarados,* because the variations in repertory and in strategy are much less abrupt and less radical in *Cantar de ciegos.*

The suggested rearrangement of *Los días enmascarados* would make the book seem a mature work; the present ordering creates the impression of a series of exercises. By placing together the stories in which Fuentes' narrative ingenuity is most effective, the reader's aesthetic act in realizing the narratives is more complete. The remaining pieces could still establish the author's expository gift without distorting the experience of the first set. Since the stories depend on the author's use of first-person narration, ironic revelation, and a combination of the two, these strategies function most efficiently when the reader understands, throughout a series of stories, that he is expected to use the same procedures in appreciating the experience. To a very considerable extent, this purpose is accomplished in *Cantar de ciegos*. Indeed, the rearrangement of the second volume, suggested above, might be more beneficial to **"El costo de la vida"** as a separate unit than it would be to the volume as a whole (its merits would be freed from the restraints imposed by the use of strategies that are different from those in the selections preceding and following). The other selections (always excluding **"A la víbora de la mar"** because of its length as well as for the narrative procedures used) enjoy a common set of strategies, based on Fuentes' handling of the narrating voice and the focusing eye, that create consistency in the aesthetic experience. These stories are, for the same reasons, closely akin to the three selections in *Los días enmascarados* that can unquestionably be called short stories.

Wendy B. Faris (essay date 1983)

SOURCE: "Short Fiction and Theater: Magical Realism, Symbolic Action," in *Carlos Fuentes,* Frederick Ungar Publishing Co., Inc., 1983, pp. 69-100.

[*Faris is an American critic and educator. In this excerpt from her book-length study of Fuentes's work, she comments on the elements of magical realism that she detects in* Aura *and in Fuentes's short fiction collection* Burnt Water.]

Fuentes has always been fascinated by what he calls "the world of the second reality": "I have always attempted to perceive behind the spectral appearance of things a more tangible, more solid reality than the obvious everyday reality." He claims that this continuing interest stems from his childhood taste for authors like Robert Louis Stevenson and Edgar Allan Poe [quoted in Emmanuel Carballo's *Diecinueve Protagonistas de la literatura mexicana del siglo XX,* 1965]. For him, "reality is reality plus its mirrors. . . . All reality duplicates and prolongs itself magically." In this kind of "magical realism," supernatural events appear to grow out of the environment rather than descending upon it from beyond. This sense that reality is opening out into a fantastical domain is particularly strong in the novella *Aura,* where Fuentes expands an apparently ordinary newspaper advertisement in a magical way.

Fuentes uses magical realism in two distinct but related capacities: to underline extreme psychological power and to suggest the presence of ancient cosmic forces. The rooms in *Holy Place* and the house in *Birthday* (another novella), for example, are invested primarily with emotional energy rather than with supernatural presence. The final metamorphoses in these works thus represent personal psychological force rather than divine power. The same is true for the terminal magic in *Aura:* it is primarily human enchantment. In *A Change of Skin* on the other hand, the scene in the pyramid, like the scene in *Where the Air is Clear* where Norma Robles is destroyed by fire, suggests the existence of more impersonal powers. In *Terra Nostra* and *Distant Relations* the sources of magic are less easily identified; miracles happen and people react. Events seem emblematic rather than motivational.

In discussing Aztec civilization, Fuentes contrasts the Mexican gods who are not like men with the classical deities who are. The Mexican gods are "the other; a separate reality." This separation provokes a "paradoxical encounter between what can't be touched or affected by men (the sacred) and the human, physical, and imaginative construction of those sacred spaces and times" [*Tiempo Mexicano,* 1971]. Fuentes's distinction between the world of men and the world of gods, then, roughly corresponds to the psychological and the cosmic kinds of magic in his fiction.

Alejo Carpentier has argued in his well-known discussion of *"lo real maravilloso"* ("the marvelous real") [in the introduction to *The Kingdom of this World*] that indigenous American culture and nature provide its writers with a wealth of surprising images. They constitute a spontaneous, homegrown kind of surrealism that contrasts with the artificial variety practiced by European surrealists. Instead of deliberately juxtaposing a sewing machine and an umbrella on a dissecting table, for example, or covering a spoon with fur, the American artist may simply describe what his environment contains, a colonial baroque church facade where an angel plays the maracas or a local legend in which a condemned popular leader transforms himself into a bird and takes flight as he is executed.

As we have seen, Fuentes draws much of his magic from Mexican mythology. Our surprise at the juxtaposition of seemingly incompatible images in his fiction often results from the proximity of two different cultures, from the intrusion of ancient beliefs or figures into modern scenes. It is almost as if the ancestral presences that lurked behind the scenes in *Where the Air is Clear* come out into the open in **"Chac Mool,"** *Aura,* and *All Cats are Gray;* and Fuentes's description of his fantastic stories as recounting "the reappearance of extinct forms, hidden underground," recalls Teódula's ancestors hidden under the floor in *Where the Air is Clear.* This exposure to other worlds or second realities of myth and magic occasionally lends Fuentes's work a dreamlike quality in which unreal events take place without rational explanations. When he says [in "El otro K"] that a novel by the Czech writer Milan Kundera will only exist fully if the reader "knows how to open the windows of dream it contains," Fuentes suggests the kind of participation many of his own texts require. He has set the windows of dream in his house of fiction.

According to Tzvetan Todorov, texts in the fantastic mode must inhabit that region of uncertainty between the uncanny, which seems strange yet can be explained by the laws of the universe as we know it, and the marvelous, which violates those laws. It thus operates on the frontier of two genres. The fantastic only lasts during the reading process, Todorov argues, because a reader opts for either the uncanny or the marvelous after finishing the text. Fuentes's works range from the uncanny to the marvelous, and often play between the two. Many of them, like *A Change of Skin, Holy Place,* and *Birthday,* are difficult to classify since marvelous events may be interpreted as dreams or hallucinations. With regard to Fuentes's shorter fiction, the earliest stories establish themselves as marvelous with clearly impossible events. *Aura,* on the other hand, fits well into Todorov's category of the fantastic. Indeed, as we shall see, much of *Aura*'s effect depends on its atmosphere of incipient magic and on the reader's consequent suspension between the uncanny and the marvelous.

The Witches of Desire: *Aura*

Fuentes's fondness for "the world of the second reality" attracts him to witchlike figures, for they seem able to communicate with that world. *Aura* might be called Fuentes's "portrait of the artist as an old witch" or enchantress, a subject he will pursue at greater length in *Holy Place* and which he prefigured in *Where the Air is Clear* with Teódula Moctezuma. I say "portrait of the artist" because Consuelo's creative power, like that of an artist's, is enchanting and frightening. She pursues a "second reality," "the infinite of desire and the imagination," as does Fuentes himself.

Aura, like the future-tense sections of *The Death of Artemio Cruz,* begins by appearing to address the reader directly: "You're reading the advertisement: an offer like this isn't made every day." Fuentes underscores the initial impact of the second person narration by starting with the very words that implicate readers explicitly, "You're reading," as indeed we *are.* As in *The Death of Artemio Cruz,* though we realize soon enough that the narrator is "really" talking to himself, the direct address challenges us and draws us quickly into his story. We identify with the "you" and experience the increasingly bizarre events of the story through his eyes.

The narrator, a young historian named Felipe Montero, answers an advertisement that seems tailor-made for him. An old woman, Consuelo, wishes him to edit her dead husband's papers in return for room and board and an attractive salary. As Felipe reads the papers, which contain love letters from General Llorente to his young fiancé, Consuelo, he becomes increasingly enamored of Consuelo's elusive niece Aura, who lives with her aunt. At the end of the novel, as Felipe clasps Aura in his arms, she has become the old aunt, and he himself the long dead husband. *Aura* is thus the portrait of a need—Consuelo's need to feel young and loved again, like that of Artemio Cruz, a need to deny time's annihilating force. The magical transformation underlines the urgency of her desire.

The story builds masterfully toward its final conflation by means of an increasing number of connections between Aura and Consuelo, together with hints that Aura is aging. This progression, combined with a haunting atmosphere and delicately bizarre images, make *Aura* one of Fuentes's most successful works. In the love letters he reads, Felipe learns that Consuelo is fifteen, Aura's age, when she first meets General Llorente; the general speaks of her green eyes and green dress—like Aura's, the color of youthful passion. Just after this, Felipe says: "Now you know why Aura is living in this house: to perpetuate the illusion of youth and beauty in that poor, crazed old lady. Aura, kept here like a mirror," a mirror Consuelo creates, not one that creates *her.* Then Felipe puts the manuscript aside and goes down to find Aura. Shortly thereafter, he has a dream where Aura "turns toward you and laughs silently, with the old lady's teeth superimposed on her own." Felipe's dream, in addition to signaling his growing awareness of the convergence of the two women, might also suggest his participation in the process.

As the story progresses, the identification of the two women becomes more intense. Aura asks with a "warm voice" in Felipe's ear whether he will swear to love her forever, "even though I grow old? Even though I lose my beauty? Even though my hair turns white?" After Felipe swears that he will, he reaches out to touch Aura, but she has gone to sit at the feet of Consuelo, who has apparently been watching their lovemaking and "moves her head in rhythm with the old lady's: they both smile at you, thanking you," before leaving together. Near the end of the novella, when Felipe finishes the memoirs of

General Llorente and looks at the photographs that follow them, he sees Aura in the pictures of the young Consuelo. In the second photograph, she appears with the general:

> Aura doesn't look as young as she did in the other picture, but it's she, it's he, it's . . . it's you. You cover General Llorente's beard with your finger, and imagine him with black hair, and you only discover yourself: blurred, lost forgotten, but you, you, you.

Felipe's discovery of himself in General Llorente prefigures the final scene where he again swears to love the woman he holds in his arms forever. He has become the General, saying to himself, "You love her, you too have come back" in a triumph of love over time, "when the memory of youth, of youth re-embodied, rules the darkness."

From the beginning of the tale, haunting details suggest that mysterious forces may be at work. Felipe feels as if the advertisement is intended especially for him—and no one except him answers it, even though the salary is attractive. The front door of the old house has a knocker with a dog's head that seems as if it were grinning at him. It "opens at the first light push of your fingers." As he enters the house and smells a "thick drowsy aroma," he feels as if he were entering some uncanny domain, leaving the real world of the street behind, and tries "to retain some single image of that indifferent outside world." Hints of black magic appear with the presence of killed—sacrificed?—animals and fetishlike objects. One night Felipe hears "the painful yowling of a number of cats"; the next morning he gets a brief glimpse of a group of cats, "all twined together, all writhing in flames and giving off a dense smoke that reeks of burnt fur." Later on, Felipe comes on Aura beheading a goat while Consuelo performs some kind of ritual. Another night, he finds a strange naked doll "filled with a powder that trickles from its badly sewn shoulder" beside his plate. He suspects it of containing "a secret illness, a contagion"—a love potion? we wonder. One early incident seems particularly significant in this context. When Felipe first meets Consuelo and she is explaining the editing project to him, she has a rabbit beside her. It goes away, and when Consuelo calls it, "'Saga, Saga, where are you?'" Felipe asks, "'Who?'" Consuelo then replies, "'My companion.'" "'The rabbit?'" asks Felipe. "'Yes,'" says Consuelo, "'She'll come back.'" Just after this, when Felipe hesitates at Consuelo's stipulation that he must live in her house to do the editing, Consuelo summons Aura, who appears instantly "without the slightest sound." Consuelo then says, "'I told you she'd come back.'" When Felipe, confused, asks again, "'Who?'" Consuelo replies "'Aura. My companion. My niece'." She seems to have changed rabbit into niece in her moment of need. Consuelo, then, is a witch, who possesses or creates Aura to seduce Felipe for her. And as Felipe is drawn into her magic circle, so too the reader is drawn deeper and deeper into the increasingly magical story.

That Felipe follows at all, and ultimately succumbs to Consuelo's desire, suggests not only the power of her magic, but also the universal nature of such desire itself. Felipe's sense that he is destined for this job indicates perhaps his natural attraction to the house on "Donceles"—"Maidens"—Street. When he looks for the first time into Aura's green eyes, he thinks:

> They surge, break to foam, grow calm again, then surge like a wave. You look into them and tell yourself it isn't true, because they're beautiful green eyes just like all the beautiful green eyes you've ever known. But you can't deceive yourself: those eyes do surge, do change, as if offering you a landscape that only you can see and desire.

In Aura's green eyes, Felipe recognizes a landscape of rejuvenation. Finally, of course, Consuelo's desire for youth and love must also be Felipe's and Aura's—and everyone's: to be loved even when we are old. In the closed realm of desire that is Consuelo's house, time seems to bite its tail, to approach a circular pattern where events repeat themselves. At the end of the novella, Consuelo promises Felipe that together they'll bring Aura back; and near the beginning Consuelo's face looks "so old it's almost childlike." The time of aging is not strictly one directional here.

In addition to the universal archetype of the witch or enchantress (and the strangely wonderful powers of desire she commands), *Aura* also reflects a particular aspect of Mexico's history. A historically oriented interpretation of the novel might emphasize not the triumph of love, but the tyranny of the past. In her musty old house, Consuelo's power over Aura and Felipe can be seen to represent colonial elements in Mexican society that have survived beyond their natural term. Like the ancient Aztec presences in *Where the Air is Clear,* this survival—the marvelous power of the past—is both terrifying and admirable. Rodríguez Monegal [in *Narredores de esta américa* II] suggests that Consuelo "symbolizes the reconstruction of old Mexico on top of the insolent and modern structure of present-day Mexico. . . . The memory of a dead time is embodied and lives, even though it be a monstrous life."

The isolation of the house and its special atmosphere removes *Aura* from the contemporary scene that pervades much of Fuentes's work. Manuel Durán points out [in *Triptico Mexicano,* 1973] that in *Aura,* allusions to the commercial world serve principally to establish a contrast between the outside city streets and the interior of the house. The novella thus remains "at the edge of the almost irresistible contamination" by pop art in Fuentes's texts. According to Durán, Fuentes seems to be saying that there is a limit to this contamination and that limit is the sacred. Its magic fires do not admit neon rivals. What "contamination" there is comes from other earlier—Fuentes might say eternal—sources.

Aura is frequently compared to *The Aspern Papers* by Henry James. There, a young man in search of a valuable set of papers goes to live in a mysterious old house with an old woman and her niece. When the old woman, who has an uncanny hold on her niece, dies, the niece offers herself in marriage as a condition of the young man's access to the papers he covets. But the young man refuses, and, in contrast to what happens in *Aura,* past remains past and desire unsatisfied. There are also a number of striking parallels between *Aura* and "Rappacini's Daughter" by Hawthorne: they share the old house, the mysterious garden, the mortally seductive charms of a feminine inhabitant for the young male guest. (In the case of "Rappacini's Daughter," it is the young woman's father rather than her "aunt," who "creates" her, perverting nature with his science.) It would seem that for James, and even more for Hawthorne, the powers represented by the witchy women are demonic or destructive and therefore to be avoided, whereas for Fuentes, they are fascinating, even attractive, because they open onto the "world of the second reality," which provides an alternative to our own.

As I have suggested earlier, *Aura* seems to be a classic example of magical realism, where the magical grows out of the real. Here the psychological reality of the desire for eternal youth and love motivates a magical event. As General Llorente wrote prophetically to Consuelo in a letter, *"Que ne ferais-tu pas pour rester toujours jeune?"* (What wouldn't you do to remain forever young?) In its progression through increasing strangeness toward a final fantastical transformation, the very texture of *Aura* illustrates the genre.

. . . . .

Scenes from the City: *Short Stories*

The stories in *Burnt Water*—the first collection by Fuentes in English—illustrate Fuentes's characteristic concern with public and private realms; but here, confrontations in private apartments or rooms prevail over visions of streets, markets, churches, plazas, or parks.

The title *Burnt Water,* as Fuentes explains in his introductory note, is the translation of an Aztec expression describing the volcano-ringed lake surrounding the ancient city of Tenochtitlán, the predecessor of modern Mexico City. This striking image continues Fuentes's penchant for the paradoxical fusion of contraries, his fondness for luminosity and for the persistence of ancient traditions in contemporary Mexico. It recalls that similarly evocative image in *Where the Air is Clear,* when Federico Robles's eyes are "fugitive with light, trembling, like turquoise wings aflame in darkness."

Taken all together, these stories resemble a fresco of life in Mexico City, but a fresco whose separate scenes fit into niches like those in Orozco's decoration of the city's National Preparatory School. Moreover, Fuentes's vision often penetrates the surface of this cityscape to reveal different cultural layers so that we can imagine this text, like the larger mural of *Where the Air is Clear,* as a palimpsest. The principal superimposed inscriptions come from Aztec times, from the Colonial period, from the pre-Revolutionary era of Porfirio Díaz, and, of course, from recent years. This layering makes the passage of time

visible in space and reveals Fuentes's historical consciousness, his desire to bring the past forward to the present. Once again, two influential precursors are Faulkner and Octavio Paz. Fuentes has said that "in Faulkner everything is in the chronic present. Even the remotest past is present" [quoted by Luis Harass and Barbara Dohmann in *Into the Mainstream,* 1967]. For Paz, "past epochs never vanish completely. . . . Sometimes the most remote or hostile beliefs and feelings are found together in one city or one soul, or are superimposed like those pre-Cortesian pyramids that almost always conceal others" [*The Labyrinth of Solitude,* 1961].

The notion of layers recurs throughout Fuentes's stories; these layers may implicate times, places, or people. In **"Mother's Day,"** when General Vergara and his grandson are raising hell in a bar, they are also reliving the General's war experiences: "Yaqui Indians faithful to Obregón had hidden in those holes, be careful, don't spill that cold brew, and everyone was staring at us as if we were crazy, a loudmouthed old man and a kid in his pajamas, what's with them? there they were, ramming their bayonets into the bellies of our horses . . . ." The entire story of **"The Doll Queen"** concerns the narrator's troubled imposition of past memories on present realities. He is clearly "in search of lost time," and even looks for it, as Proust's Marcel does, in parks. **"In a Flemish Garden"** inserts a Belgian garden, even Belgian weather, into Mexican soil and atmosphere: "The very rain stirs colorings in the grass I want to identify with other cities, other windows." After this vision, the narrator rushes to the opposite side of the house and looks out the street-side window to see "a blast of jukeboxes, streetcars, and sun, the monotonous sun. A Sun God without shading of effigies in its rays, a stationary Sun Stone." But when he returns again to the garden, the rain is still falling. Different ages in the city's life are consistently juxtaposed through descriptions of buildings or memories. The characters in **"Mother's Day," "The Two Elenas,"** and **"These Were Palaces"** all live in old buildings that have been altered in some way through time. In **"Palaces,"**

> it was little Luisito who did the talking, it was he who imagined the city as it had been in colonial times, it was he who told the old woman how the Spanish city had been constructed, laid out like a chessboard above the ruins of the Aztec capital.

"The Mandarin" thinks to himself that "only those who can perceive the nocturnal scent of the lost lake really know this city." A few pages later, he feels ashamed "that a country of churches and pyramids built for eternity should end up contenting itself with a city of shanties, shoddiness, and shit." This character's face, like the city he inhabits, is layered as well:

> His features were so markedly Oriental that they obscured the Indian mask underlying them. It happens with a lot of Mexican faces. The stigmas and accidents of known history recede to reveal the primal face, the face that goes back to Mongolian tundra and mountains.

In this way Federico Silva was like the lost perfume of the ancient lake of Mexico: a sensitive memory, practically a ghost.

Another kind of "layering" is the doubling, the confusion of identities, that occurs in **"A Pure Soul."** There Juan Luis superimposes his sister Claudia onto his lover Claire so that he can possess the forbidden Claudia in the flesh of the accessible Claire. Here as in many of his works, Fuentes creates a modern version of the myth of Quetzalcóatl, who fled Mexico after being tricked into incest with his sister. (Juan Luis lives in Switzerland.)

Thc Mool," records the "takeover" of one Filiberto by a statue of the ancient rain god—the Chac Mool—he had bought at the flea market. The Chac Mool has emerged into the twentieth century, come alive, so to speak. But with this life comes old age—and presumably death. **"In a Flemish Garden"** similarly describes the occupation of an old mansion's garden by the ghost of Charlotte, the wife of King Maximilian (who after the French invasion occupied the Mexican throne from 1864-1867, before being executed by Juárez). Here this ageless "witch" achieves virtually the same thing that Consuelo does in *Aura*—the revival of her husband through a young man.

These first two stories are fantastical, even allegorical. They come from Fuentes's early collection, *Los días enmascarados (The Masked Days,* 1954). Because, like *Aura,* they contain eruptions of the fantastic into everyday life, these early stories can be included in the general category of magical realism. With its resemblance to parable, its metamorphosis, and its intrusion of an ancient deity into the modern world, **"Chac Mool"** bears a striking resemblance to two stories by Julio Cortázar, "Axolotl" and "The Idol of the Cyclades." The tales warn modern children not to play with sacred ancient fire for it may still be smoldering and ready to ignite. These stories, together with novels like *Where the Air is Clear* and Carpentier's *The Kingdom of this World,* seem to constitute a kind of subcategory of magical realism that asserts the continuing power of ancient beliefs and their attendant rituals.

The rest of the stories in *Burnt Water* portray various psychological or social deviations; they are not magical, but often very strange. **"The Two Elenas," "A Pure Soul," "The Doll Queen," "The Old Morality,"** and **"The Cost of Living"** originally appeared in the collection *Cantar de ciegos (Songs of the Blind,* 1964). The title and the epigraph for *Songs of the Blind* come from a blindman's begging song that ends the fourteenth century *Libro de buen amor (The Book of Good Love)* by the Archipreste de Hita: "We cannot earn it / With these leprous, blind, / Poor, and crippled bodies." (What the blindmen cannot earn is a bit of breakfast.) The lines suggest, in addition to the two physically deformed characters in the book, a controlling image of emotional deformity. Many characters are misfits; others simply do not tolerate ways of life that differ from their own. Their "blindness" and isolation contrast implicitly with the vision that sees them all.

In "Mother's Day," a young man admires the vitality of his grandfater, who fought alongside a number of revolutionary leaders, changing his loyalties—like Artemio Cruz—as the leaders rose and fell. In this story we sense the frustration of postrevolutionary generations who feel they've missed the only real "boat" in modern Mexican history. They have been born too late and have to take the leavings of the Revolution—memories of the fight or wealth made in its aftermath. In **"The Two Elenas,"** a man lives with his wife, who toys with the intriguing idea of a *ménage à trois,* while—unbeknownst to her— he sleeps with his mother-in-law. **"A Pure Soul"** concerns another triangle, this time involving the tortured though not overtly incestuous love of a sister, a brother, and his fiancé. **"These Were Palaces"** describes life in the run-down apartments that now occupy what was an ornate palace. It concentrates particularly on the emotional affinity between a little boy in a wheelchair and a crazy old woman who looks after stray dogs. In contrast to the people who live in this ruin, **"The Mandarin"** keeps up his splendidly outmoded residence—even though it is flanked on both sides by skyscrapers—until he is finally robbed and murdered. A similar brutality ends **"The Cost of Living,"** when a teacher is knifed to death for attempting to distribute leaflets calling for a strike. In **"The Doll Queen"** a young man seeks out a former childhood playmate, only to discover that her parents have buried her alive so to speak in their apartment because she is now a cripple. Since Amilamia's parents now think of her as dead, they worship her as she used to be in the form of a doll enshrined on a baroquely decorated altar—a grotesque perversion of the Mexican Day of the Dead festivities when families construct elaborate altars to honor recently deceased relatives.

Except for **"Chac Mool," "The Old Morality"** is perhaps the most schematic story in the collection. It recounts the disruption of an eccentric but happy household by traditionally moral but inwardly corrupt meddlers. As Manuel Durán has pointed out, the provincial atmosphere, with its moral and sexual hypocrisy, links it with *The Good Conscience.* The young Alberto lives contentedly with his grandfather Agustín and Agustín's scandalously young lover on their ranch until his dead mother's three sisters get the juvenile judge to declare the place an "atmosphere of shameless immorality." He then goes to live with his unmarried aunt, who seduces him. This he half enjoys, claiming that the severe spinster has softened through sensual affection. Thus, although he thinks that on the whole he prefers life back at the ranch, he can't quite decide to send his grandfather a letter saying, "Come get me please. It seems to me there's a lot more morality at the ranch."

In addition to professing a worn-out moral code, the aunts, called Milagros (Miracles), Angustias (Anguish), and Benedicta (Blessed), talk like old morality plays. They are introduced like stock characters and act accordingly, calling Grandfather Agustín "blasphemer," "heretic," "whoremonger." The same is true for Agustín, Micaela (Agustín's mistress), and an attendant group of priests; everyone repeats the same routines and rather enjoys them. Agustín shouts daily insults at the priests; they leer at Micaela and run away when Agustín lifts Micaela's skirts, and the narrator observes how "about the same things happen each day and we're all very happy." This is true comedy in the sense that an ebullient round of life goes on; but it has a message, too: "immorality"—which may in the end be regenerative—is dressed up as "morality." The story recalls *Huckleberry Finn* in its contrast of the natural and spontaneous life with the cleaned and pressed (and repressed) "moral" life. And there's even an aunt to do the "sivilizing."

Fuentes occasionally creates a specific connection among the layers of his verbal city. A voice that records a collective memory, speaking for someone more than its owner, appears in several stories. In **"The Doll Queen,"** for example, Amilamia's parents beg the narrator to recall her for them. In **"These Were Palaces,"** Luisito seems to possess a kind of collective memory and imagination. He remembers his own past in a big house his family once owned before they moved to Mexico City. But he also "remembers"—imaginatively—the crumbling palace they now inhabit as it once existed: Old Manuelita

> made a great effort to remember everything the boy told her and then imagine, as he did and when he did, a majestic palace: the entryway before there was a lottery stand, the carved marble facade stripped of cheap clothing stores, . . . free of the advertisements that disfigured the ancient nobility of the building.

And later on, when she is alone in her room, Manuelita "rereads" these texts: "This is the way she communicated with him, by remembering the things he remembered and forgetting about her own past." Luisito and Manuelita share a hidden communal memory that comforts them because it allows them to escape from their drab lives.

This memory is similar to the memory they imagine their stray dogs might possess, both of them "carnal" and "incandescent," though in different keys. After Luisito watches some boys cut off one dog's tail, he looks at the other stray dogs and says to his little sister that "the dogs of the sun" are "telling each other something, . . . these dogs are going to remember the pain of one of their own pack, . . . but Rosa María's shoe-button eyes were like stone, without memory." Luisito's sister clearly lacks his sense of communal memory. The expression "dogs of the sun" implies that their communicative force survives from Aztec times. The dogs will add the recent cruelty of these teen-agers to all their past sufferings.

Later on in the story, Luisito wants to keep his mother from gossiping about the fracas Manuelita caused by bringing her stray dogs into the church for comfort. He does this by threatening to reveal some old letters his mother wrote—but did not send—in which she painted a falsely rosy picture of her life to an old flame. These letters, like his and Manuelita's stories, are really imaginary narratives that grow out of memory and desire. He joins his mother to Manuelita by telling her that everyone needs such imaginary worlds to survive the one they

inhabit. The imaginative narratives of Luisito and Manuelita—and the hypothetical memory of their dogs—can be seen as a paradigm for Fuentes's conception of narration itself which, as we shall see again in **"The Son of Andrés Aparicio,"** thrives on collective memory. Fuentes implies that this kind of memory is particularly strong in Mexico City: "In a place that had been a palace centuries ago little Luis found it easier to imagine things, and remember."

It seems appropriate, then, that this volume which records the collective voice of Mexico City should end with a story that pays homage to Pablo Neruda and specifically to Neruda's poem, *The Heights of Macchu Picchu,* for that poem proclaims its intention to speak for the voiceless multitudes who built the ancient fortified city of the Incas. **"The Son of Andrés Aparicio"** follows Bernabé Aparicio from outings with friends in his poor barrio through a love affair which even he perceives as rather dreary to his association with the "Chief" of an underworld organization that lives off crime and terror. Words from *The Heights of Macchu Picchu* appear (unidentified) at two crucial points in the text. Several significant details draw the two works even closer together: Macchu Picchu is an ancient citadel built of stone on stone; the Chief's house—located in the section of Mexico City called Pedregal after the stone on which it is built—resembles a modern fortress, in monumental style, with cement ramps and a sunken pool; it, like Macchu Picchu, was built for the rich by the poor. Pedregal is in one sense then a lost city, not as Macchu Picchu was before its discovery, but before the journey of the poet to recover its massed voices. But the primary lost city here is the barrio where Bernabé grew up: "It had no name and so it didn't exist as a place." It corresponds to the modern urban wasteland Neruda's climber leaves behind in his ascent toward the heights.

Let us return to the actual quotations from Neruda. When the Chief commands a token theorist in his band to read aloud "any book at all, the one he liked most," the theorist then reads "in a trembling voice" three sets of lines from Neruda's poem. The last ones, "Stone within stone, and man, where was he? / Air within air, and man, where was he? / Time within time . . ." signal the awakening of a social conscience in Neruda's poet/climber/quester when he contemplates Macchu Picchu as he begins to assume his role of literary spokesman for the nameless masses. The lines herald the end of the poem where, "I come to speak for your dead mouths," where he invites these mouths to "speak through my speech, and through my blood." But Bernabé is not ready yet; when the Chief asks him, "Did you understand anything, boy? Bernabé shook his head." The Chief burns the book, but that cannot erase the language of conscience. For like the proverbial mole of the revolution, it resurfaces. After Bernabé learns about the Chief's past harassment of his father, "he dreamed, unable to separate his dream from a vague but driving desire that everything that exists be for all the earth, for everyone, water, air, gardens, stone, time," and wakes up with Neruda's phrase, "And man, where was he?" in his mind. The dream is a dream of solidarity. It, like Neruda's words, and the stray dogs in **"These Were Palaces,"** signals a connection with past injustice.

Once again, narrative depends on personal memory. At the beinning of the story, Bernabé has not been able to put his thoughts into words because, above all, "he couldn't remember his father's voice." In a pep talk to his terrorist Hawk Brigade, designed to whet its appetite for student blood, the Chief subverts Neruda's constructive sense of solidarity. He appeals to the street boys' resentment against the rich, encouraging them to "get your revenge for . . . the abuse you've taken all your miserable lives." He invokes memory of past injustice to divide and destroy, not to unite and reform. From the Chief and his second, both, we hear the philosophy of the "fat man" in *The Death of Artemio Cruz:* dominate or be dominated. The journey of the poet in *The Heights of Macchu Picchu* culminates in his assumption of speech for the dispossessed. Bernabé's journey ends less decisively. In order to survive and not revolt, he must suppress and forget. In this atmosphere, even his mother's words "meant the opposite of what they said." Nevertheless, he is grateful that his mother gives him "his father's most handsome suspenders, the red ones with the gilded clasps that had been the pride of Andrés Aparicio." They are presumably a sign that he may eventually inherit his father's passion for reform along with his red suspenders. And so he ends up poised between his own desire for comfort and the memory of the injustice his father fought, between his mother's meaningless words and his father's red suspenders.

In echoing Neruda, in "rewriting" *The Heights of Macchu Picchu* in prose so to speak, even including a fragment—a stone—from the earlier structure, Fuentes achieves in his text a literary equivalent of the architectural layers in the Mexico City of the stories, with its palaces turned apartment houses, its lake covered by asphalt. The record of historical time informs the arrangement of literary space, for the writer's page, like the Mexican soil, is a palimpsest, covered with successive cultural texts. And the recognition of past inscriptions enlivens recent creations.

Cynthia Duncan (essay date 1986)

SOURCE: "Carlos Fuentes' 'Chac Mool' and Todorov's Theory of the Fantastic: A Case for the Twentieth Century," in *Hispanic Journal,* Vol. 8, No. 1, Fall, 1986, pp. 125-33.

[*In the following essay, Duncan attempts to place Fuentes's story "Chac Mool" within the tradition of "fantastic" literature as the term is defined by the critic Tzvetan Todorov. While Todorov reserves the genre for certain writings of the eighteenth and nineteenth centuries, Duncan believes that "Chac Mool" and the work of other Latin American writers also fit Todorov's definition of fantastic literature.*]

Tzvetan Todorov, in his landmark study *The Fantastic: A Structural Approach to a Literary Genre* [1975], offers one of the most restrictive definitions of the fantastic to date. Unlike some others who have bandied this term about and contributed to a vague and ambiguous usage of it, Todorov insists on limiting the type of literature which can properly be called fantastic. Perhaps for this reason, his interpretation has met with great favor among today's scholars and his conception of the fantastic has become the model against which many works of fiction are judged. It is somewhat ironical to note, however, that in an age when fantastic literature is appreciated and studied as an art form by greater numbers than ever before, Todorov claims that it no longer exists as a genre. According to this structuralist critic, the fantastic is confined to a specific moment in historical time: it existed only from the end of the eighteenth century through the end of the nineteenth. As he puts it, "literature of the Fantastic is nothing but the bad conscience of this positivist era."

Contemporary readers can, of course, enjoy and even identify with characters and situations out of the past, but in order for the fantastic to be most effective, it must recreate the world of the reader as faithfully as possible. The fantastic is the irruption of the unreal, the inexplicable, into the real world which is governed by certain laws of nature and logic. When these laws are violated, leaving no rational explanation for what has occurred, the fantastic comes into being. Todorov sees this condition as "the very herart of the fantastic." He states:

> In a world which is indeed our world, the one we know, a world without devils, sylphides, or vampires, there occurs an event which cannot be explained by the laws of this same familiar world. The person who experiences the event must opt for one of two possible solutions: either he is the victim of an illusion of the senses, of a product of the imagination—and the laws of the world remain what they are; or else the event has indeed taken place, it is an integral part of reality— but then this reality is controlled by laws unknown to us.

Clearly, the fantastic event would give rise to greater doubt and hesitation in the reader if it were to occur in a contemporary setting rather than in a musty nineteenth century drawing room where literary convention leads us to expect ghosts and goblins. According to Todorov, the reader's vacillation between rejection and acceptance of the inexplicable as part of reality is the *sine qua non* of the fantastic. Therefore, it stands to reason that the twentieth century should be capable of producing some of the best fantastic literature, since it would call into question the reader's own world rather than that of past generations.

Todorov's claim that the fantastic is a dead genre overlooks the abundance of fiction that has emerged in recent decades in Latin America, where the fantastic is undeniably alive and flourishing. Writers such as Jorge Luis Borges, Julio Cortázar, and Adolfo Bioy Casares have achieved universal recognition as masters of this genre. In Mexico, the fantastic has never had the immense popularity it has enjoyed in the River Plate region, yet it is an important vehicle of self-criticism and self-examination for the Mexican writer who challenges the narrow conception of reality that has come to characterize our century. It is not merely a literary game, but an alternative view of the world. Carlos Fuentes, who is today one of Mexico's most famous and prolific authors, began his career as a writer of fantastic tales in this vein. Of them, **"Chac Mool,"** has become a classic in Mexican literature. It is also a classic example of the fantastic as defined by Todorov and clear proof that the genre is still cultivated by talented writers in our century.

Todorov sums up his conception of the fantastic by stating:

> First, the text must oblige the reader to consider the world of the characters as a world of living persons and to hesitate between a natural and supernatural explanation of the events described. Second, this hesitation may also be experienced by a character; thus the reader's role is so to speak entrusted to a character, and at the same time the hesitation is represented, it becomes one of the themes of the work—in the case of naive reading, the actual leader identifies himself with the character. Third, the reader must adopt a certain attitude with regard to the text: he will reject allegorical as well as 'poetic' interpretations. These three requirements do not have an equal value. The first and third actually constitute the genre; the second may not be fulfilled. Nonetheless, most examples satisfy all three conditions.

A close examination of **"Chac Mool"** will reveal how the story meets these three fundamental requirements.

Fuentes's tale is set in modern-day Mexico City and features as its protagonist a seemingly ordinary inhabitant of the capital who blends in with the thousands of educated, middle class Mexicans who are his neighbors there. One finds passing references to immediately recognizable, real places, such as the "Lagunilla," a famous flea market in Mexico City, and to other cities such as Acapulco, Tlaxcala and Teotihuacan. The daily routine of Filiberto, the lonely middle-aged bureaucrat who is the central character and narrator during most of the story, is described in detail. His unrewarding office job, his nightly outings to cafes where he searches for companionship but rarely finds it, his petty interests and preoccupations, and his solitary existence in a spacious but shabby old house are outlined for the reader in Filiberto's diary. Like most fantastic stories, **"Chac Mool,"** begins with the complete absence of fantastic elements but, once Filiberto's character has been clearly drawn and an appropriate setting has been created, inexplicable events begin to occur.

Filiberto is an avid collector of indigenous Mexican art and one day he is delighted to find a life-size replica of Chac Mool, a pre-Colombian rain god, in the marketplace. He is able to buy it at a modest price because it appears to be a modern reproduction. He humorously records in his diary that the vendor had anointed the stomach of the god with tomato catsup "para convencer a los turistas de la autenticidad sangrienta de la escultura." Filiberto installs the statue in the basement of his home, but it seems to bring him bad luck. The plumbing in the house stops working, the pipes constantly break, and the basement is always flooded. The idol quickly becomes covered with mildew and mold, which gives him an uncanny human look. Filiberto begins to experience the first subconscious tremors induced by the incursion of the fantastic when he writes "Le da un aspecto grotesco, porque toda la masa de la escultura parece padecer de una erisipela verde . . . ." Thus, Todorov's conditions for the fantastic are met when the central character begins to experience hesitation about the nature of events portrayed in the tale, and the reader shares this feeling. Because the story is set in the recognizable world, poetical and allegorical interpretations do not influence the reader's attitude, and he is able to experience the full impact of the fantastic.

Fantastic elements gradually enter the story, creating a mood of doubt and tension for both the main character and the reader. For example, Filiberto's diary slowly changes tone and style after the acquisition of Chac Mool. Previously, he had dwelled on anecdotes about his daily life, and the passages tended to be long, elegantly written, and marked by strong currents of loneliness and nostalgia for the past. After Chac Mool comes into his possession, Filiberto begins to feel uneasy, and the entries in his diary are characterized by short, choppy sentences which hint at strange happenings but, at the same time, attempt to explain them rationally. Filiberto becomes increasingly divided: intellectually he rejects the possibility that a statue can come to life, but emotionally, he fears that such a thing could happen. The style of his diary reflects his state of mind as he tries to deal with this internal conflict. For example, Filiberto first describes Chac Mool as a lifeless statue, but as the narrative progresses, he attributes more and more human qualities to the idol until, finally, he is convinced that the rain god actually lives. In the beginning, he relates that he collects "ciertas formas del arte indigena mexicano" and that he spends his free time searching for "estatuillas, ídolos, cachorros." He has a possessive attitude toward Chac Mool and the other pieces in his collection: he calls them "trofeos" and speaks of the rain god as "mi Chac Mool." He considers all of his belongings in the same light; when the basement floods, Filiberto records: "El Chac Mool resiste la humedad, pero mis maletas sufrieron . . .", as if these items had equal importance to him. Filiberto calls Chac Mool "una pieza preciosa", a "simple bulto agónico" and "una figura", all inanimate terms, but he also begins to see human characteristics in the status as soon as he installs him in his home. He writes, after he has placed the statue in the basement, "su mueca parece reprocharme que le niegue la luz." The verb *parecer,* commonly used throughout the first part of the narrative, is important. As long as Filiberto believes that Chac Mool cannot possibly come to life, he is hesitant to commit himself in writing by using a more concrete and definite verb. Rather than stating emphatically that an event *did* happen, Filiberto says that it "seemed" to have happened. He continues to think of Chac Mool as "la escultura" while at the same time he visualizes the stone as skin: "parece padecer de una erisipela verbe." He is confronted with daily indications that the statue of Chac Mool is coming to life, yet the stronger the proof, the more inclined he is to deny it. He states, "No quiero escribirlo: hay en el torso algo de la textura de la carne, lo aprieto como goma, siento que algo corre por esa figs to hear strange noises in the night, he dismisses them as fantasy, but his diary entry reveals nervous strain: "Desperté a la una: había escuchado un quejido terrible. Pensé en ladrones. Pura imaginación." When rain-water floods his house, he writes, "Es la primera vez que el agua de las lluvias no obedece a las coladeras y viene a dar en mi sótano. Los quejidos han cesado: vaya una cosa por otra." The water motif, which always accompanies Chac Mool in the text, appears in various forms throughout Filiberto's narrative and provides clues for the reader that something inexplicable is taking place: Filiberto mentions the broken water pipes, the rain, the water he carries from a near-by fountain, and finally, the ocean, which is the scene of his death. Most of the water images are related to Filiberto's growing doubt and hesitation. For example, he covers the statue with rags to protect it from water damage, but a short time later, he discovers, "Los trapos estan en el suelo." His only comment is "Increible", which shows his reluctance to reach a decision about the nature of events he is witnessing. Nevertheless, his perception of Chac Mool has changed. He is no longer a statue—he has become a god: "Chac Mool blando y elegante, había cambiado de color en una noche; amarillo, casi dorado, parecía indicarme que era un Dios, por ahora laxo, con las rodillas menos tensas que antes, con la sonrisa más benévola."

As Todorov points out, the hesitation induced by the emergence of the fantastic is usually of a limited duration. Once the doubt is resolved in the narrative, it moves into a neighboring category: if there is a logical explanation for the phenomena described, it belongs to the uncanny, and if the phenomena is accepted as a natural occurrence, it belongs to the marvelous. In **"Chac Mool,"** Filiberto attempts to explain events with rational arguments, but they fail to resolve his doubts. Eventually, he must admit that the seemingly impossible has come to pass. He writes, "No cabe duda: el Chac Mool tiene vello en los brazos." This is the first time Filiberto does not preface his remarks with the verb *parecer*. Significantly, this same night, Filiberto awakens to find a living Chac Mool hovering over him. The scene is reminiscent of one from a gothic horror tale. The senses are on edge, sharpened by fear, and doom seems to hover in the air. However, the scene ends not with death, but with a sudden rain storm, which temporarily dissolves the spell of the fantastic:

> El cuarto olía a horror, a incienso y sangre. Con la mirada negra, recorrí la recámara, hasta detenerse en dos orificios de luz parpadenate, en dos flámulas crueles y amarillas.
>
> Casi sin aliento encendí la luz.
>
> Alli estaba Chac Mool, erguido, sonriente, ocre, con su barriga encarnada. Me paralizaban los dos ojillos, casi bizcos, muy pegados a la nariz triangular. Los dientes inferiores, mordiendo el labio superior, inmóviles; sólo el brillo del casquetón cuadrado sobre la cabeza anormalmente voluminosa, delataba vida. Chac Mool avanzó hacia la cama; entonces empezó a llover.

> **Fuentes's concern with time:**
>
> I am extremely fascinated with and worried about the problem of time. Juggling all the possibilities of time, the repertories of time with which we are faced, it is my conviction that the time which has been imposed upon us—the linear time of the West, the calendars of the West— these times are totally insufficient and do not render the full reality of life and of time. There can be other times. There are other possibilities of life and civilization, outside the reductivist sense of time of the industrialized West. I naturally go to the myth as the most convenient example of another time, a time which conceives itself in a perpetual present, one that is not alienated by the pursuit of the future, a future that we can never reach. I think the bane of the modern industrial civilization of the West is its reaching out for a future which is always around the corner.
>
> *Carlos Fuentes, in an interview with Jonathan Tittler,* Diacritics, *Vol. 10, No. 3, Fall, 1980, pp. 46-56.*

This is a turning point in the story, for the reader must now come to a conclusion that will account for Filiberto's experience and once a conclusion is reached, the story is no longer fantastic. The reader may choose to believe that Filiberto is mad, that he has imagined the episode, or that it is some kind of fantasy, but the story is not structured to allow the reader to believe, for more than an instant, that Chac Mool has indeed come to life. Parenthetical statements, made at the beginning and the end of this entry in the diary by a second narrator, encourage the reader not to trust Filiberto. This other, seemingly objective narrator voice offers a temporary refuge of sanity and calm and allows the narrative tension, which Filiberto's revelation had created, to dissipate. The reader grows wary of Filiberto's remarks and the remainder of the story is understood to be the product of Filiberto's imagination.

The narrative moves into the marvelous when Filiberto overcomes his terror and accepts Chac Mool as a companion. He notes, "Chac Mool puede ser simpático cuando quiere . . .", yet Filiberto comes to resent the rain god's interference in his life. He neglects his work and is dismissed from his post, he loses contact with his friends, and he becomes the prisoner of Chac Mool when a role reversal takes place and Filiberto is forced to act as a servant in his own home. When an opportunity arises to escape the watchful eye of the rain god, Filiberto runs away to Acapulco. where he drowns. His diary ends a few days before his death, and one of the last entries contains a reference to a threat made by Chac Mool to kill him should he try to flee.

If Filiberto were the only narrator in the story, the fantastic would cease to exist when Chac Mool comes to life, since this supernatural event is portrayed without further doubt and hesitation on the part of the main character. At the same time, the reader's uncertainty comes to an end when he is confronted with Filiberto's startling revelation. The tension, which had been steadily building in the narrative, is diffused by the marvelous descriptions of the living rain god and his relationship with the hapless Filiberto. However, there is a second narrative voice introduced into the story when a nameless friend travels to Acapulco to collect Filiberto's body and discovers the diary. Through this new narrator, the reader is exposed to a series of logical explanations that counterbalance Filiberto's allegations, and a new feeling of doubt and hesitation arises as the story once again wavers between a natural and supernatural explanation of the events described in the diary. In this way, Todorov's three conditions for the fantastic are met a second time in the story, although tension is purposely kept at a minimum now so that the reader will be off guard when the story reaches its true climax.

As the friend reads Filiberto's diary, his reactions mirror the process which Filiberto had undergone when confronted with the fantastic. At first, he tries to analyze the situation logically: "No supe qué explicación darme; pensé que las lluvias excepcionalmente fuertes, de ese verano, lo habían crispado. O que alguna depresión moral debía producir la vida en aquel caserón antiguo, con la mitad de los cuartos bajo llave y empolvados, sin criados ni vida de familia." Because there is no clear explanation, he dismisses the problem—"No quise volver a pensar en su relato"—but he becomes obsessed with what he does not understand. This narrator, more so than Filiberto, is characterized by a detached, logical attitude toward life. He raises a number of questions about Filiberto which make the reader hesitant to believe anything written in the diary, but confident in the friend's ability to sort out the truth. Excerpts from Filiberto's diary reveal that he lost his grip on reality, but the second narrator's comment remain cool and analytical. He notes: "La entrada de 25 de agosto, parecía escrita por otra persona. A veces como niño, separando trabajosamente cada letra; otras, nerviosa, hasta diluirse en lo ininteligible." This narrator assumes the task of putting Filiberto's story in proper perspective. He says, "Pretendí dar coherencia al escrito, relacionarlo con exceso de trabajo, con algún motivo psicológico", but despite his efforts, he fails: "Aun no podía concebir la locura de mi amigo."

Unlike Filiberto, who gradually came to accept the inexplicable as part of reality, the second narrator leads the story toward the realm of the uncanny by explaining the fantastic events described in the diary as "madness." Indeed, this explanation would be perfectly acceptable to the reader, as well, and the fantastic could be dismissed were it not for the final, unexpected scene of the story, where the second narrator comes face to face with a character who may or may not be Chac Mool. When the friend arrives at Filiberto's house with the corpse, he is greeted at the door by a stranger. Doubtlessly, this stranger closely resembles the description of Chac Mool in the diary, yet the final image is vague and ambiguous. The narrator is taken aback by him: "Su aspecto no podía ser más repulsivo; despedía un olor a loción barata; su cara, polveada, quería cubrir las arrugas; tenía la boca embarrada de lápiz labial mal aplicado, y el pelo daba la im-

presión de estar teñido." This scene differs markedly from the one in which Filiberto discovered Chac Mool leering at him in his bedroom, in the middle of the night. There is less overt horror, but much greater hesitation on the part of the character and the reader. The concluding lines of the story are highly suggestive, but open to various interpretations: "Perdone . . . no sabía que Filiberto hubiera . . ." / "No importa; lo sé todo. Digales a los hombres que llevan elcadáver al sótano." Thus, the reader is left to form his own opinion about this final turn of events, but he will undoubtedly experience hesitation between natural and supernatural explanations; as long as he hesitates, he is in the presence of the fantastic.

In Latin America, where fiction is often judged by its social content rather than its form, the fantastic has sometimes been criticized as "escapist" literature because it is not always grounded in socio-political issues. **"Chac Mool,"** however, is part of an important new trend that began around mid-twentieth century: it is a fantastic story with a clear social message. For Fuentes and others, the fantastic is not a way of escaping reality but, rather, of penetrating it and uncovering new dimensions. **"Chac Mool,"** for example, reminds the Mexican that the past is not dead, that indigenous Mexico has not been smothered and buried under the mask of European culture and that it will come back to haunt him until he confronts it and learns to deal with it in a more direct and honest way.

Chac Mool is portrayed by Filiberto as a character who is bitterly resentful of the present. He was once a god, a highly respected deity but, in the intervening centuries, he has been desecrated and forgotten. He resents the attitude of modern Mexicans who have abandoned their nation's indigenous heritage and are ignorant of their cultural history. Filiberto is guilty of this crime: he has purchased Chac Mool as a curiosity piece, and has treated him irreverently. He has no real knowledge of the culture that Chac Mool represents and he feels no spiritual bond to him. Ironically, as Chac Mool gains vitality and becomes a living being, he loses the immortality he had as a statue and grows old and corrupt. He loses his dignity and divine poise, and develops bourgeois tastes. The humanization process is one of corruption, for when Chac Mool gave up his ancient ways and adapted to the twentieth century, he lost his identity. At the end of the story, he is a culturally hybrid character who, rather than benefitting from the blend of two heritages, adopts and maintains the worst characteristics of both. He is treacherous, despotic and fickle, a pathetic imitation of something totally alien to his essential being.

"Chac Mool" is not an allegory, but it does have a symbolic interpretation. The rain god of the story's title can be seen as the representative of many contemporary Mexicans. Like them, he turns his back on his indigenous heritage, and comes to have the same values as those he earlier criticized for disparaging the importance of native cultures. The transformation which Chac Mool undergoes is not unlike the change millions of Mexicans have experienced since the Conquest: it is an act of self-deception and self-denial which has crippled the Mexican psyche and blocked the emergence of an authentic national identity.

The fantastic clearly does exist in the twentieth century, but it has changed to meet the needs and tastes of a modern society. Today's reader, who is familiar with the literary conventions and cliches of earlier fantastic tales, must be caught off guard if he is to experience hesitation between the natural and supernatural. Therefore, the fantastic has developed into a more subtle, more sophisticated art form, and has acquired more symbolic and metaphysical implications. For many writers like Fuentes, it is also an excellent vehicle for expression of social concerns and an effective tool with which to reshape Latin American reality.

Janet Perez (essay date 1987)

SOURCE: "Aspects of the Triple Lunar Goddess in Fuentes' Short Fiction," in *Studies in Short Fiction,* Vol. 24, No. 2, Spring 1987, pp. 139-47.

[*In the following essay, Perez examines how Fuentes uses the ancient myth of the "White Goddess" or "Mother Goddess" in his short fiction.*]

Any reading but the most superficial will reveal the special, symbolic nature of female figures in Fuentes' works. Few of his women characters can be classed as mimetic portraits of individuals drawn from life, although there is usually a mixture of elements drawn from reality with ingredients of the mythic, magical or occult. The real tends to give way before the unreal at the story's end, which strikes a note of the mysterious or unexplained. Several critics have noted Fuentes' interest in the occult, and Gloria Durán [in *The Archetypes of Carlos Fuentes,* 1980] has studied his interest in witches, seeing them as a projection of the Jungian anima. Insofar as the anima subsumes a full range of types (including the goddesses of antiquity), this is unquestionably accurate. However, since in the broadest sense all female figures may be considered aspects of the anima, examination of clearly allegorical feminine figures from the vantage point of mythic criticism should prove fruitful, for elsewhere Fuentes has displayed a broad familiarity with major myths and their variants. This essay will focus upon several tales in English translation which display certain features of the triple lunar goddess and her cult. Women in these stories exemplify two or more phases of what Robert Graves calls the White Goddess, the triple goddess of birth, love and death, visibly manifest as the new, full, and old or waning moon. Worshipped under countless titles, the goddess is associated with an array of attributes, sacred animals and emblems. Her cult is inextricably bound up with that of her son (also her husband), a sacrificial figure periodically slain and revived or reincarnated in a successor.

Graves [In his *The White Goddess,* 1966] avers that Celts, Greeks and Hebrews were all originally worshippers of the Great Goddess or Mother Goddess, one of whose names was Diana, and whose cult involved sacrifice of the male (later modified to ritual castration, mutilation or laming) and ritual eating, as described by Frazer in *The Golden Bough.* Other personae of the goddess were Danaë, Alphito, Demeter, Ceres, and Albina (regarded by Frazer as Demeter or her double, Persephone). Graves equates these with the White Goddess who is identified with Jana/Diana/Dione/Juno. Jupiter was her husband, but before that, her son. In the *Golden Ass* of Apuleius, Lucius invokes the White Goddess under several names, mentioning a variety of epithets and attributes, as summarized by Graves: "Dame Ceres, original and motherly source of all fruitful things . . . thy daughter Proserpine . . . the celestial Venus . . . sister of the god Phoebus [i.e., Athene]." Her "divinity is adored throughout the world, in divers manners, in variable customs, and by many names: The Mother of the Gods, Minerva, Venus, Diana, Infernal Proserpine, Ceres, Juno, Bellona, Hecate, Rhamnusia and Isis." Among additional relevant personae is Hera (Greek counterpart of Juno), an early death goddess who had charge of the souls of sacred kings, a form of sun god with many incarnations, including Bran, Saturn, Cronos, Orion, Samson, Cuchulain, Romulus, Zeus, Janus and Hermes, among those listed by Graves. The hero-god acquired royal virtue by marrying the queen (or White Goddess), eating some part of his dead predecessor, and in turn was succeeded at New Year by a reincarnation of the murdered king who beheaded him in an alternate eucharistic sacrifice. Each king or sun-god was the beloved of the reigning queen or Moon Goddess. All were borne by, married to and finally laid out by the White Goddess, the layer-out being the death goddess Hera Argeia.

Cirlot identifies Hecate as a symbol of the Terrible Mother, a deity who devours men, a personification of the moon or evil side of the feminine principle, responsible for madness, obsession and lunacy [*A Dictionary of Symbols,* 1962]. Her attributes include the key, dagger and torch. Triform Hecate (with three heads) presided over birth, life and death—past, present and future. As the Terrible Mother, she signifies death and represents indifference to human suffering, the cruel side of Nature. Among her symbols are [according to Graves] "water, the mother of waters, stone, the cave, the maternal home, night, the house of depth." Hecate was associated by the Greeks with the Moon, crossroads and the lower world, the number three, and the powers of witchcraft and magic. Artemis (the Roman Diana), Mistress of Wild Beasts, but also patroness of girls and hunters, was associated with Demeter, earth-goddess and goddess of fertility and vegetation, and her daughter Persephone (being identified by some with the latter), and with the harvest goddess Cybele. Aphrodite, called by Aeschylus the first cause of vegetable fertility, was also represented as the mistress of wild beasts, but inspired them with lust, putting desire in animals, men and gods. She is goddess not of spiritual love but irrational sexuality. Venus, associated in astrology with the Moon, with Mars, and with copper, is related symbolically to both spiritual love and mere sexual attraction. The white Moon Goddess's sacred number is thirteen, "insofar as her courses coincide with the solar year, but fifteen insofar as the full moon falls on the fifteenth day of each lunation. Fifteen is also the multiple of three and five: three expressing the three phases of the moon, and the Goddess's three aspects of maiden, nymph and hag, and five expressing the five stations of her year: Birth, Initiation, Consummation, Repose and Death." Nine is the prime Moon number. The Moon Goddess is associated with water (the moon draws the tides), hence with dampness or humidity. The White Goddess controls the winds, and it is an axiom that "she is both lovely and cruel, ugly and kind; she is Goddess of Life-in-Death and Death-in-Life." The three Fates are a divided form of the triple goddess, appearing in Greek legend also as the three Muses and the Parcae. The three Graces are explained as the love goddess Aphrodite in triad.

Fuentes has incorporated a surprising number of these attributes of the White Goddess into the stories examined here. Most important of her many faces are those of Diana and Hecate, but aspects of Demeter, Hera and Venus-Aphrodite are also present. **"In a Flemish Garden"** (**"Tlactocatzine"**) has the greatest use of mythic detail, but the others have sufficient parts of the mythic structure to permit identification, despite the absence of elements (two instead of three phases of the goddess, for example, or a failure to consummate the sacrifice of the male, or absence of the goddess's recognizable companions or familiars). Fuentes has implicitly related the genesis of *Aura* (whose protagonist is clearly the White Goddess) and that of **"In a Flemish Garden,"** which chronologically preceded the novelette. In a letter to Gloria Duran (8 December 1968) he recalls viewing the portrait of Charlotte of Belgium in Chapultepec Castle at the age of seven, and later finding in the archives a photograph of an enormously aged Charlotte in her coffin. "The two Charlottes: Aura and Consuelo. Perhaps Charlotte never knew she was growing old. Until the end she wrote love-letters to Maximilian." This episode from Mexico's history, the result of Napoleon's ill-fated venture of New World empire, is more specifically relevant to **"In a Flemish Garden,"** wherein several details point clearly to the cult of the triple goddess.

Narrated from the perspective of the male protagonist, this tale is set in an old mansion characterized by "a certain lack of human warmth in . . . rooms which had been empty since 1910." Forty years later, despite its sub-tropical location, the house emanates "a penetrating cold . . . particularly noticeable in contrast to the temperature outside." Even more clearly than the darkened home of Consuelo (*Aura*), this is a cave, with a climate different from that of the world outside: "We don't notice the seasons in Mexico City; one fades into another with no change of pace. . . ." "Today, in this place, I have with a kind of Nordic indolence noted, not for the first time, the approach of autumn." The story is written in diary form, with the foregoing entry corresponding to September 20, the day before the autumnal equinox. The cave, of course, is symbolic of Hecate in her dimension of Terrible Mother. The garden exhibits its own separate climate: "A grey veil is descending over the garden . . . a few leaves have fallen from the arbor . . . and an

incessant rain is fading the greenness, washing it into the soil." Water, likewise an attribute of the moon goddess, reiterates the separation of the enclosed space and external world: "If in the house I seemed to caress the skin of a different world, in the garden I touched its nerves." Beyond the rather obvious conventions of the attenuated Gothic tale, a second symbolic level alludes to 19th-Century Mexican history, and a third to myth, a timeless mélange where Aztec deities and the triple goddess of classical antiquity inhabit the same space. The melancholy and misty light belongs to the Gothic context as well as to the domain of the moon goddess, with the "verdant growth of the vines . . . not that of the burnt earth of the plateau" coming from the sphere of Demeter/Hecate. The figure which appears ("a small body, black and hunched") might be the stereotypical witch: a little old woman, "at least eighty," "wizened, slim, clad all in black." Unobtrusive symbols of the moon goddess appear: "Her skirts brushed the ground, collecting dew and clover" (both moisture and the trefoil being attributes of this deity). Her totally black garb, tangled white hair, "her bloodless lips, the paleness of her flesh" suggest a death's-head, an impression reinforced by "her hawk-like features, her sunken cheeks, reflected like the vibrating planes of the reaper's scythe" which evokes the old, waning phase of the moon-goddess, the goddess of death, as does her customary hour of appearance, at sunset. Unexpectedly, she appears next—if only fleetingly—as girl or maid, skipping about, pantomiming, until the narrator's intrusion ends the childish activity, and he again faces the old woman and a penetrating cold (a fairy-tale attribute of moon queens).

This female figure thus represents at least two aspects of the triple goddess—the old and the new moon, Death-in-Life and Life-in-Death, and it becomes increasingly obvious that the narrator possesses attributes of the sun-god: he is a "handsome blond" with an Apollonic identification with the arts, and the character of victim. He receives a cryptic message, one word on elegant old rosewood paper: "Tlactocatzine," followed by a second missive, whose author is the moon goddess in her third phase of maturity, love and fulfillment. She addresses him as beloved, writing, "The moon has risen and I hear it singing; everything is indescribably beautiful." But the icy cold of this figure is stronger than the warmth of love, and her hands, "nothing but wind—heavy, cold wind"—are controlled by the White Goddess. In this apparition, she is enveloped in a white lunar light. Not only is the narrator confused by her with her lost love, Max, but he becomes her victim, her prisoner, sealed within the mansion whose door is covered with "a thick red lacquer. In the center, a coat of arms glimmers in the night, a crowned double eagle, the old woman's profile, signaling the icy intensity of permanent confinement." The eagle on the coat of arms belonging to the late Maximilian—the old woman's husband whom the narrator is to replace—represents the Aztec sun-god, and is considered the king of the air as the lion is king of beasts. The Aztec title "Tlactocatzine" is the name used by the Indians to welcome a ruler they confused with the sun-god.

In **"The Two Elenas,"** the myth's more negative aspects are missing. What is preserved is primarily the mythic structure and the colors of the White Goddess: white, black, red. Here the idea of succession or substitution of the husband (emphasized by Frazer and Graves as central to the Goddess's cult) is seen first in the daughter's suggestion of a ménage à trois with a mutual friend and then in the establishment of a sort of identity between mother and daughter through their sharing of the same man (the mother is mistress of her daughter's husband). In this variation on the mythic original, the White Goddess is both wife and mistress/mother-in-law to Victor, a relationship sufficiently similar to the myth to evoke the archetype. The elder Elena (whiteness dressed in black) echoes the daughter's enunciation of the theme of the replacement of the sacrificial husband with his cyclic substitute, since her own aging mate—the old year—has yielded his place to the younger counterpart. The third aspect of the goddess, the hag or old moon, is absent, and a brittle modernity has replaced recognizable emblems of the goddess in what is essentially a degraded or reductive version of the myth.

"A Pure Soul" is narrated from the perspective of one of the female characters after the demise of the male victim. Claudia, the narrator, is Diana by reason of her virginity and hostility to marriage, Athene by virtue of being sister to the sun-god/sacrificial hero and her devotion to learning. Their mother is "la Llorona," the weeper (not only an Aztec myth, but a principal facet of Isis, as well as the grief-stricken Demeter in search of Persephone). Claire, with whom Juan Luis falls in love, is Venus-Aphrodite, fulfilled love, light (as her name indicates), the full moon, maternal urges. The three women, collectively, are a triad comprising maid, nymph and crone, or the central phases of the pentad, initiation, consummation, repose. But Claudia is also Hecate, according to another reading of the story, the dark side of the moon (or reverse of Claire), the evil side of the feminine principle, the devourer of men, who by her letters and psychological manipulation provokes the hero's suicide. This is a degenerate derivation of the myth, in which the mother-son incest motif has been replaced by a potentially incestuous brother-sister relationship. Juan Luis—who is Apollo because of his involvement with fine arts, music, poetry, eloquence and numerous amours—is a solar hero, sacrificed because Claudia, jealously, would rather see him dead and hers forever than lose him. This motivational change is a substantial modification, although the external structure of triple goddess and sacrificial solar hero is retained.

"The Doll Queen" provides a recognizable variation upon the mythic theme. Likewise narrated by a male protagonist, it recounts his impulsive attempt to locate a long-lost childhood friend, seven-year-old Amilamia who fifteen years earlier used to talk to him in the park. As his memory reconstructs Amilamia, she is an idealized version of the child or maid, associated with several symbols of the White Goddess: she appears in a "lake of clover," water and three-leaved plants revealing the moon goddess. She wears a white skirt, and invariably carries a pocketful of "white blossoms" (which Graves explained were used for

casting spells). Amilamia is remembered in the wind, "her mouth open and eyes half closed against the streaming air, the child crying with pleasure" (the White Goddess traditionally controls the winds). She is also something of a nature goddess, "sitting beneath the eucalyptus trees," "lying on the grass, baring her belly button to the sun; weaving tree branches, drawing animals in the mud," and "imitating the voice of birds, dogs, cats, hens, horses." The second stage of the Goddess, nymph or goddess of love, is not explicitly present but hinted at in two ways, as a dream of the narrator, "the women in my books, the quintessential female . . . who assumed the disguise of Queen . . . the imagined beings of mythology", and also as a potential of Amilamia/Aphrodite, clearly suggested when their last romp suddenly acquired erotic undertones: "Amilamia was on my chest, her hair between my lips; but when I felt her panting breath in my ear and her little arms sticky from sweets around my neck, I angrily pushed her away and let her fall."

The remembered garden has some of the magical, past-in-present qualities of the house of the Flemish garden for there, "as if by a miracle, one had succeeded in suspending the beat of the surrounding city, annulling that flood tide of whistles, bells, voices, sobs, engines, radios, imprecations." After Amilamia has disappeared from the garden—a microcosm of earth—and the hero goes to seek her, there are certain analogies with Demeter's search for Persephone (and Amilamia *is* Persephone), or Orpheus' seeking Euridyce. The hero must figuratively descend to another world: "I would have to cross the garden, leave the woods behind, descend the hill . . . cut through that narrow grove" and cross a busy avenue which is a figurative Styx with its "flood tide" of noise and the requirement of waiting (as if for the ferry-man) to "cross to the other side." What he finds is a "gray suburb," "dead-end streets," a house closed almost like a tomb, with "heavy entry door, two grilled windows with closed shutters . . . topped by a false neoclassic balustrade." This Greek motif, like the caryatids and Ionic capitals adorning the mansion of **"In a Flemish Garden"** subtly indicates the presence of myth beneath the surface of the narrative. Beyond the door, he detects "harsh, irregular breathing," betraying the presence of a sort of Cerberus (watch-dog of Hades) whose function, true to mythic prototype, is to prevent intercourse between the worlds. Leaving after his first unsuccessful attempt at "penetration" the narrator narrowly escapes being a sacrificial victim: "A piercing scream, followed by a prolonged and ferocious blast of a whistle, saved me in time. Dazed . . . I saw only the automobile moving down the street."

Returning under the pretext of doing an assessment, he encounters a woman of fifty, "dressed in black and in flat black shoes, with no makeup and her salt-and-pepper hair pulled into a knot", with eyes "so indifferent they seem almost cruel." She carries a chaplet, an old-fashioned rosary, which may be interpreted as a key, for Cirlot points out the "morphological relationship between the key and the. . . anserated cross." The witch-like appearance and key identify the woman with Hecate, as does the suggestion of cruelty. The woman's only adornment, "a silver crucifix dangling over her dark belly," is another key and also a moon symbol, since silver is considered lunar. This is the Terrible Mother, associated with cruelty, indifference to suffering, and the lower world or death (i.e., Hades). Despite insistence on the shadows and darkness of the house, its being termed "almost uninhabited", a clue which indicates Amilamia's continued presence in the tomb-like abode is a symbolic fruit "where little teeth have left their mark in the velvety skin and ocher flesh", not eaten but bitten, as in the case of Persephone and the pomegranate.

The description of the other guardian does nothing to dispel the notion that he is a monster of the ilk of Cerberus: "heavy shoulders and hidden eyes . . . scarcely visible behind swollen, wrinkled lids as thick and drooped as the neck of an ancient turtle . . . greenish hands" and hair "like the bottom of a barnacle-covered ship." His breathing evokes a dragon's hoarse breath, and he has a "choking voice that issues from his belly instead of his larynx." An "asthmatic old bear" who wears a "turtle's mask," he is clearly a composite, a mythological beast like the three-headed hound of Hades with snakes protruding from its neck and shoulders. Forced to confess the real motive of his visit, the narrator is taken to view the funereal chamber holding the dolls and forgotten toys of Amilamia, with the scent of flowers of death and in the center the small coffin with "the doll queen who presides over the pomp of this royal chamber of death." Almost nauseated and convinced that Amilamia died long years before, he leaves, but returns months later intending to give the child's card to the bereaved parents. As he approaches the door, several motifs evoke the goddess of fertility or vegetation: "Rain is beginning to fall . . . bringing out of the earth with magical immediacy the odor of dewy benediction that stirs the humus and quickens all that lives." In the dwarfish, deformed body of the "misshapen girl" he finds in a wheelchair, with a "hump on her chest," is incarnated a degradation of the myth, perhaps mentally retarded (if this is the meaning of the comic book). The guardian reacts as Cerberus to prevent her contact with the outsider: "Get back! Devil's spawn! Do I have to beat you again?" Persephone imprisoned, prematurely arrested at an infantile stage of development, she is the goddess of Death-in-Life, as the doll was Life-in-Death.

Lighter and more parodic, **"The Old Morality"** retains the skeletal structure of the myth of the youthful hero and triple goddess, the closed mansion and mother-son incest pattern. Narrated by an adolescent, it recounts his "rescue" from the "immoral" guardianship of his grandfather (a variant of Zeus, thundering his anger, shaking his cane, with a "lion's mane" and "wild beard" and young concubine). Characterized by the local press as a "land raper" and by the boy as "a wild bull with the priests and newspapermen" (lions and bulls being two forms assumed by the sun-god), the grandfather is a free-thinker whose main diversion in his old age—excepting lechery—is yelling at seminarians. He is powerless to retain his grandson when the boy's dead mother's three sisters arrive with a court order to remove him from the un-Christian household. The three aunts are obviously a triad, resembling the Furies or Parcae (in the boy's sketches they are the "sharpest-nosed and noisiest birds"). All three dress in black, with black hats and white gloves, and are almost indistinguishable. Their resemblance to harpies is stressed by the grandfather's epithet, "cockatoos."

Aunt Benedicta, consoling her lonely spinsterhood by raising Alberto as a Christian gentleman, plays the role of mother, even undressing and bathing him: "You're just a child. Pretend I'm your mother." But the bathing leads to caressing in the bath and eventually to an incestuous affair. Benedicta changes from a Hecate figure or goddess of Death-in-Life to a love goddess: "how that stiff woman in mourning who came to the ranch has changed . . . Benedicta knows how to be affectionate, too, and she has very smooth skin and, well, different eyes—bright and very wide—and she's very white." Cyclic rotation of the son/husband (who replaces a predecessor and is in turn replaced) is inverted at the end, as "Aunt Milagros, with her trembling eyelid, came to my room and began to stroke my hair and ask me if I wouldn't like to come stay a while in her house." The three members of the triad will rotate the hero-victim between them.

Fuentes may have written a deliberate spoof or burlesque of this mythic pattern of hero-victim and triple goddess in **"A la víbora del mar"** (**"To the Sea Serpent"**), the final tale of *Cantar de ciegos,* which was not translated. It involves role reversal and sexual inversion as a trio of homosexuals trick a naive spinster into marrying one of them (neither youngest nor oldest, but the central figure or "love-god"). In an obviously cyclical confidence game, a series of previous victim-brides have been conned into giving their money to the husband and have then been murdered or abandoned. Isabel commits suicide upon realizing how she has been duped. Inversion, of course, is a standard technique of parody, and the inverted elements all belong to the archetypal pattern. Other elements associated with the White Goddess are present, especially the moon and water, since the action takes place on an ocean liner, and the "sea serpent" is both a mythological allusion to the Goddess's reputed primeval copulation with the World Snake and to the biblical snake-as-trickster myth which here denotes the victimizer.

Fuentes is a self-conscious writer, an admirable critic and literary theoretician who is frequently well aware of the mythological or other sources of his inspiration. Being well-read and reasonably fluent in English, he may have been familiar with *The White Goddess* or *The Golden Bough,* or may have gone directly to original mythology sources. Whether or not he is conscious of the full extent to which he has incorporated the figure of the White Goddess and her cult into his narratives, the archetype provides a key to understanding his artistry, and might be applied fruitfully not only to the tales analyzed here, but also to those of his novels which are particularly accessible to mythic analysis, for example *Sacred Zone, Change of Skin,* and *Cumpleaños* (Birthday). The appropriateness of mythic analysis of Fuentes' works using

Aztec deities as the archetypes has been repeatedly demonstrated. Classical mythology must be considered as a comparably significant source.

George Gordon Wing (essay date 1988)

SOURCE: "A Gallery of Women in Carlos Fuentes's *Cantar de ciegos*," in *Review of Contemporary Fiction*, Vol. 8, No. 2, Summer, 1988, pp. 217-24.

[*In the following essay, Wing analyzes the female characters in* Cantar de ciegos, *noting that they are different from the sentimental female characters in Fuentes's novels. Instead, the critic finds that the women of the short stories are similar to the men—"incapable of mutual love or shared equality."*]

It was José Donoso who first drew my attention to what are central features of the six short stories and the novella that Carlos Fuentes published in 1964 as *Cantar de ciegos* (*Song of the Blind*). Donoso finds in them a common theme—"the withdrawal of human beings from basic feelings." Fuentes's characters no longer recognize themselves in traditional concepts such as "love," "hate," "justice," etc. They find these abstractions useless precisely because they exist prior to and independently of concrete experience which might make them meaningful. Consequently, neither a fixed order, nor a rational organization of society, nor a transcendent purpose are possible for Fuentes's characters, who are adrift in a world of instants and tropisms. Donoso says [in *Siempre* 604, 20 January 1965] that the hero of *Cantar de ciegos,* without any firm convictions, tries to enjoy life without committing himself—his positive values are embodied in the words "cool," "étranger," "outsider." He is a person capable of seeing clearly everything that takes place around him without being moved by it emotionally.

With the exception of one story, all of Fuentes's characters are immersed in a mass-consumer society. As Fuentes has said in an essay [in *Mundo Nuevo* 1 (July 1966)], the Mexican is now the contemporary of all men, but only to be confronted with all of the problems inherent in mass society. After describing at length its contradictions, Fuentes makes an observation that seems paradoxical: "We participate apocryphally in modernity." It is from this apparent paradox that Fuentes's realism derives a peculiar flavor. In speaking of realistic plays, especially modern ones, Arthur Miller has suggested that all of their great themes might be boiled down to a single sentence: "How may a man make of the outside world a home?" [in *Atlantic* 197, No. 4 (April 1956)]. In the prose fiction of *Cantar de ciegos,* it is indeed the underlying theme as well as the major problem confronting all of the characters, a problem exacerbated by the essential split between modernity and tradition, a split internalized and reflected in their behavior. Above all, it generates a subtheme common to all of the works of *Cantar de ciegos—plus ça change, plus c'est la même chose.* The realization of this theme is due to Fuentes's talent for depicting so graphically the visible configurations of contemporary life, the manners and morals of an apparently nontraditional society. Just as important is Fuentes's gift for expressing the split between the surface and what is relatively unchanging in Mexico. Fuentes accomplishes this in a variety of ways—structure, psycho-social analysis, dialogue, etc.— but what Joseph Sommers has said of Fuentes's methods of characterization in *Where the Air Is Clear* applies equally as well to *Cantar de ciegos*. He subordinates, says Sommers, psychological analysis to "experience, traits and thoughts which are susceptible to broader reference in the world outside the character." In short, "his interest lies more with representative qualities than with psychological idiosyncrasies." [*After the Storm,* 1968].

Isabel Valles, the protagonist of the novella, "**A la víbora de la mar**" (**To the Snake of the Sea**), might well serve as a touchstone for measuring Fuentes's other female characters. Isabel, who has inherited money, is now the owner of a boutique in the fashionable Pink Zone. A fortyish spinster and virgin, her life extends no farther than the store where "she sells beautiful things to beautiful people" and her apartment where she lives with a maiden aunt. Apart from the movies, church, and lunch (alone) at Sanborns, she has no social life. She lives in a world of repression, rigidity, and dullness—one of alienation and willed "claustrophilia." On the one hand, she is presented as a typical product of consumer society, and on the other, as one of its pathetic victims. Although her external life is patterned by this society, her super-ego survives from a much more traditional and puritanical way of life. In short, she is immersed in consumer society but somehow she is not really of it.

Persuaded by her aunt to take a vacation after fifteen years of continuous work, Isabel opts for a cruise on a British liner from Acapulco to Miami. It is apparent that she is extremely apprehensive and has a revulsion toward close contacts either emotional or physical. Courted by an American confidence man, however, Isabel gradually overcomes her fears and regrets. By playing on her snobbery and lack of self-confidence, he tricks her into a false marriage, after which he induces her to give him the money she has brought with her, an outrageously large sum for such a short cruise. He then has his homosexual lover court her to make her feel guilty, unworthy, and inferior. Finally, he allows her to discover the two of them in bed, a fact he knows will destroy her. In all probability, she commits suicide by drowning. One might say that in large part her tragic flaw was to have believed in the reality of the concept "love" in the abstract without ever having experienced it.

At first glance, it might seem that Elena, the young wife of the story "**The Two Elenas**," has nothing in common with Isabel. Elena seems to be the prototype of the completely "liberated" woman of the sixties who delights in flaunting behavioral patterns and ideas that run counter to those of her mother's generation. Nevertheless, she too avoids close involvements, but the outward patterns of behavior and ideas she uses to maintain distance are much more typical of advanced consumer societies than those of Isabel. Christopher Lasch has argued convincingly that the great malady afflicting the United States (and by extension other contemporary post-industrial societies, including Mexico) is narcissism. What needs to be stressed is that in these societies, paradoxically, the narcissist becomes socially and sexually promiscuous in order to *avoid* all close involvements [*The Culture of Narcissism: American Life in an Age of Diminishing Expectations*, 1968]. Elena is doubtlessly a narcissist of the type described by Lasch, but she is also, to go back to Fuentes's phrase, living modernity apocryphally. To begin with, for all of her apparent "emancipation," Elena is unable to transgress a traditional moral code that is at odds with most of her behavior. She is completely faithful to her husband, and the fact that it is impossible for her to be sexually promiscuous is very significant, since the aesthetic effect of the story depends largely upon the different sexual attitudes of the three principal characters.

To Elena, reality tends to be merely "role playing," "the presentation of self in everyday life" (the title of Erving Goffman's book), although her "self" is little more than a series of predictable responses to random stimuli from the world around her. Her husband, the narrator, says that what he loves most about her is her "naturalness," but the reader soon realizes that his statement is deliberately ironic. The fact is that for Elena, [as Lasch terms it] "the only reality is the identity she can construct out of materials furnished by advertising and mass culture, themes of popular film and fiction, and fragments torn from a vast range of cultural tradition, all of them equally contemporaneous to her mind." In fact, the only sustained dramatic conflict (more apparent than real) in this story springs from Elena's faddish obsession with *completing herself* (*complementarse*) by acquiring a permanent lover, a notion that occurred to her only after seeing Truffaut's *Jules et Jim*. She tells her husband that he will have to buy her a sailor suit like that worn by Jeanne Moreau in the film, only to declare a few moments later to a mutual acquaintance that she remains faithful to her husband because unfaithfulness has now become the norm. In short, the super-ego that dictates her most profound behavior belongs to another era.

Fuentes sets up a deliberate contrast between mother and daughter, providing the reader with a catalogue of their respective activities. The mother, married to a boorish *nouveau riche*, dutifully follows the routine common to upper middle-class housewives: trivial, conformist, and snobbish. But the daughter, too, adheres to a routine that is only superficially more flexible: painting and French lessons, meeting with some Black Muslims, going to jazz, cine clubs, etc. It is obvious, however, that for all of her so-called "liberation," she too is trivial, conformist, and snobbish. Attracted to all the latest fads, she is flighty and shallow; she belongs to what Alfred Rosenberg has called in another context, "a herd of independent minds." [*The Tradition of the New*, 1965]. It is the husband, "cool" and condescending, who after an amusingly subtle seduction scene, enjoys the sexual favors of his mother-in-law—he is the one who *completes* himself.

It is in "**A Pure Soul**," however, that Fuentes gives us his most memorable portrait of a contemporary, intelligent,

and apparently liberated young woman whose "inability to make of the outside world a home" results not only in her own withdrawal from life but also in her willful destruction of her brother and his mistress, although she protests her innocence. Claudia, the narrator, evokes an idyllic childhood and adolescence with her brother in which an incipient incestual relationship becomes obvious. After graduating from the university, however, her brother goes to Geneva to escape from what he considers the confinements of Mexican society, although the reader realizes that he is at the same time fleeing the incest taboo. When he writes to Claudia of his numerous transient love affairs, she is ecstatic, for it is as if she were enjoying them vicariously, especially since she knows they are ephemeral; they do not threaten his love for her. When he takes a permanent mistress, however, Claudia manages by subtle (but not really innocent or pure) means to entrap him, for to let him go would devastate her. The subtle maneuvers she uses are quite sufficient to keep him from really loving anyone else. It is almost certain, moreover, that by lying to his mistress about an incestuous relationship with her brother that was never consummated, she is responsible both for the mistress's suicide and, unwittingly, that of her brother. Winner takes nothing in this hair-raising story.

Critics have said of "**The Doll Queen**" that it differs radically from the other stories. Nevertheless, it has as its main theme, as do so many others, the search for identity in a past that is pure nostalgia. The narrator seeks out a little girl with whom he had passed many pleasant hours in a park years before. Unfortunately, he succeeds in his persistent attempts to find her. Now grotesquely deformed, she is forbidden by her parents to leave the house or to have friends. In fact, her parents have constructed an elaborately adorned coffin in which they have placed a doll that resembles her as she was as a child. One might say that the parents, imbued with the values of consumer society, prefer her dead rather than ugly. To use Veblen's phrase, there is "conspicuous consumption" in social relations that are independent of economics as such. Even more significant is the fact that the child, now a woman, cynically accepts her horrible fate. The lack of love and compassion of her parents seems to her merely an extension of a normal condition of the society in which she lives.

In "**The Old Morality**," the only story not set in Mexico City, three sisters from Morelia, pharisaic and self-righteous women dressed in black, come to "rescue" their nephew from his grandfather, who lives with a young mistress on his ranch. The grandfather, an atheist and old-fashioned liberal, gives his fourteen-year-old grandson no opportunity for formal schooling and also, according to the aunts, provides him with the worst kind of immoral and sinful examples. The boy's life is spontaneous and natural, though, compared to that of his aunts, who live in a narrow ultra-Catholic atmosphere of repression. Taken to Morelia to be brought up by his maiden aunt, a spinster in her mid-thirties, the boy, Alberto, is bored, although he remains "cool" and intelligently anticipates every wish and command of his aunt, while feeling no real affection for her. Naturally, he is obliged to take religious instruction, but during his first confession he is so innocent that he has to invent sins he has merely intuited as such from films he has seen. His aunt is extremely angry with him for having tried to fool the priest, since she would have preferred him to have described the sexual relations between his grandfather and the mistress so that she could enjoy them vicariously. When she prods him, he replies naïvely that, yes, they always sleep together. He even quotes his grandfather, without having understood him, that "a man who sleeps alone dries up. And a woman too." This reply merely arouses further the repressed prurience of the aunt and serves to release the bottled-up emotions that gradually surface as hysterical behavior with sexual overtones. When, inevitably, she seduces the boy, although he never fully understands the subtleties of her sexual behavior, he finds it all so enjoyable that he cannot bring himself to ask his grandfather to take him back to the ranch. Although one sees the aunt through the eyes of the boy, who enjoys her sexually without really loving her, it is impossible not to suspect that Fuentes admires her more than he does the urban middle-class women of the other stories. It is as if, paradoxically, her incest represents not only a gesture of despair but also a thrust toward natural behavior for which most other channels are closed in the stifling atmosphere of traditional society.

The protagonist of "**Fortuna lo que ha querido**" ("**What Destiny Wanted**") is a man incapable of genuinely human relations with anyone, an artist who lacks both imagination and feeling, who is not above plagiarism or spouting absurd theoretical clichés. He would like to believe his life and his art are hermetically sealed off from each other. In the last analysis, however, they are two sides of the same coin. It just happens, for example, that his mistresses, or rather the women he uses and debases, are almost without exception wives of his critics and friends. They all serve as masochistic foils for his misogynous and sadistic behavior. Their amorality springs in large part from their snobbishness, a hero worship of which he is unworthy. Perhaps it is also boredom that is responsible for their abjection and self-debasement, their willingness to be abused and insulted by him for his own selfish pleasures. Love and compassion, as in so many of these stories, are virtues of neither the women nor the men. When, at the end of the story, the artist does meet a North American woman who might present a challenge to his lack of humanity, might disturb his withdrawal from basic feelings, he rejects her. In summary, we might see this artist not only as a symbol of male indifference and condescension, but also as a symbol of a kind of symbiotic relationship between this type of macho and the women who, in most of the stories of *Cantar de ciegos,* accept this relationship as normal.

There is only one point I should like to make concerning "**El costo de la vida**" ("**The Cost of Life**"), the most Hemingwayesque story of this volume. The protagonist is a lower middle-class school teacher who spends a day teaching, lunching with a group of old friends, attending a meeting of his fellow teachers who vote to strike, get-

ting a job moonlighting as a taxi driver, and picking up a girl—all with his working wife sick at home in bed. The protagonist seems to feel no strong emotions about anything, not even about the proposed strike, a strike that ironically leads to his death. One of the points most relevant to my study hinges on the fact that the protagonist has married a woman of a social class somewhat higher than his own. Although they are in dire economic straits, they refuse to live in an extended family with relatives. In short, they have opted for the nuclear family, largely because of his wife. In this respect, then, they too are very much immersed in contemporary society.

In his first novel, *Where the Air Is Clear* (1958), Fuentes gives a vast panoramic vision of Mexico of the 1950s, a society whose roots he traces back to a partial failure of the Revolution of 1910. In a sense, Fuentes took as his subject the history of a period during which Mexico was being transformed from an essentially rural society into one dominated by urban capitalism. Although Fuentes has drawn his characters from the highest and the lowest social classes, it is the new middle-class that occupies center stage. Fuentes's own opinion of this new class is most nearly expressed by the courtesan Natasha:

> The new rich who don't know what to do with their money, and that's all they have the way a crab has a shell, but they don't have the circumstances, how should one say . . . of the development which in Europe gives the bourgeoisie a certain class. Of course the bourgeoisie in Europe *is* a class; it is Colbert and the Rothschilds, but it is also Descartes and Montaigne and they produce a Nerval or a Baudelaire who reject them.

Certainly no other Spanish American novelist has given us a more complete picture than has Fuentes of what Lionel Trilling has called "manners": "a culture's hum of buzz and implication . . . the whole evanescent context in which its explicit statements are made . . . that part of a culture which is made up of half-uttered or unuttered expressions of value." It follows, then, that "they are hinted at by small actions, sometimes by the arts of dress or decoration, sometimes by tone, gesture, emphasis, or rhythm, sometimes by the words that are used with special frequency or a special meaning" [*The Liberal Imagination,* 1953].

Even a cursory glance at Fuentes's portrayal of the new middle-class reveals its snobbery, its inordinate love of money, and its undeserved self-assurance. One of the central characters of *Where the Air Is Clear,* Federico Robles, has made good use of his revolutionary experience to amass a fortune and accumulate power. He has married a ruthless social climber with whom he lives in a loveless union, and their lives, in McLuhan's words [in *Dos Passos: A Collection of Critical Essays,* ed. by Andrew Hooks, 1974], are dramas of "pathos of those made incapable of love by their too successful adjustment to a loveless system."

In *The Death of Artemio Cruz* (1962), the central character does have what might be called an early "idealized" love affair, but as Keith Botsford has commented:

As a man, Artemio has not made much contact with other human beings. This novel is so much his book not only because he relates the story, but because he is alone in the profoundest sense; he is not merely the only protagonist, he is also alone within himself. For Artemio is the portrait of the Mexican *macho*—the he-man and narcissist, deflowerer of womanhood, tamer of bulls, wild horses, and all that. Today that macho is an utter fake. Money is the only object of his desire; politics and power its sublimation. For those without a hope of either money or power, there is still the image of the *macho*. Like all soi-disant Latin virility, it is a blend of impotent talk, childish rage, pasted-on moustaches, and an atrocious ignorance about women. The modern *macho* is more concerned with his deodorants and brilliantine than with sex ["My Friend Fuentes," *Commentary* 39 Feb. 1965].

In his major novels of the fifties and sixties, as well as in *Cantar de ciegos,* Fuentes has indeed portrayed a variety of macho types. In the novels, however, Fuentes has also created some extremely sentimentalized heroines who represent for the macho the epitome of natural wisdom and innocence. In *Cantar de ciegos,* on the other hand, Fuentes does not depict any idealized women. Rather, he shows his male and female characters, incapable of mutual love or shared equality, as people who more often than not are locked into grotesque symbiotic relationships. In his major novels of this period, Fuentes's main theme is the partial failure or betrayal of the Revolution of 1910, a theme expressed explicitly in long discursive passages. In *Cantar de ciegos* the theme is implied in the bleak portrait of post-Revolutionary Mexico. Fuentes's criticism of the abuse of power, principally the exploitation of women, his presentation of problems of personal authenticity and identity represent ethical judgments with far-reaching implications. Mexico, Fuentes is both suggesting and warning, has reached a stage in its history where the Mexican might welcome, or look upon with indifference, an increasing abuse of power at the broader levels of the economy or politics, for this abuse would be but a "natural" extension of his private life.

M. E. de Valdes (essay date 1988)

SOURCE: "Fuentes on Mexican Feminophobia," in *Review of Contemporary Fiction,* Vol. 8, No. 2, Summer, 1988, pp. 225-33.

[*In the following analysis of the story "Mother's Day," Valdes describes how Fuentes portrays masculine characters who stereotype the females in their lives, allowing the women only one of two roles, that of the virgin mother or that of the whore. The critic concludes that Fuentes's story effectively portrays the emptiness and violence that are related to these stereotypical views.*]

"**Mother's Day**" is a long short story (thirty-three pages) by Carlos Fuentes included in a collection of his short stories with the title *Burnt Water* translated by Margaret Sayers Peden. This short story focuses on the empirical

and verisimilar reality of present-day Mexico City. What makes it a significant ideological text is its concentration on the Mexican male's "feminophobia." Although feminophobia is not in any way limited to Mexican society, it has taken on a unique form of institutionalization in this society. In general terms throughout the patriarchal world for those who are caught up in this psychotic state, there are basically two personae for women: the virgin mother and the whore. In Mexico these personae have become symbols of good and evil.

In this narrative three men and their aging servants live alone in a large and ostentatious house in the Pedregal district of Mexico City. The old general of the Mexican revolution, Vicente Vergara, who is at the time of the narrative action about seventy years of age, rules the house he shares with his son and grandson. The son, Agustín Vergara, is a polished, suave lawyer whose every gesture is an imitation from scenes from sentimental cinema, especially from the roles played by Arturo de Córdova; he is about fifty years old. The grandson, Plutarco Vergara (named after the general, turned president, who founded the forerunner of the Party of the Institutionalized Revolution [PRI], Plutarco Elías Calles), is nineteen years old in 1965 and thirty-four at the time of the narration in 1980 when he remembers the extraordinary days of his "liberation."

There are no women in the house. Clotilde, the grandmother, died years before, still a young woman; Plutarco's mother, Evangelina, also died a young woman; she was killed before her son was five years old. Although long since dead, both women have a presence in the house: Clotilde is venerated as a household saint in the manner of the Virgin of Guadalupe; Evangelina is mourned as the innocent whore who had to be killed. Both women are commemorated in the yearly visit on Mother's Day, May 10, to the French cemetery where they are buried side by side.

The time of the narration is set in April and May of 1965, the place is Mexico City, its streets, its low barrios, and the opulent Pedregal. The story's first page is narrated in a free-indirect style that establishes the framework for the more intimate characterization of the grandfather, the General, Vicente Vergara. The rest of the story is narrated entirely in the first person by the now-mature grandson Plutarco, looking back some fifteen years to the days when he was nineteen. The narrator probes into the past in a deliberate attempt to understand the present. After the initial four pages of first-person narration, the text's narrative presentation is counter-pointed by dialogue on every page. The dialogue is all between the three men; the women are not remembered as speaking because the narrator was only five when his mother died and was not yet born when his grandmother died. The longest dialogue sequence is between the grandfather and the grandson; a shorter but highly charged sequence comes at the climax between the young man and his father.

The institutionalized social symbol of the virgin mother in Mexico is, of course, the Virgin of Guadalupe. She permeates all sectors and classes of Mexican society and, as a social symbol rather than a religious one, contributes to the denial of individuality to Mexican women. This does not mean that there are not millions of Mexicans, women and men, who daily turn to the *Guadalupana* as an essential refuge against the harsh realities of life, for this is certainly the case. What we are concerned with in this study is not the *Guadalupana* as the focus of religious piety, but the social symbol of the virgin mother, that is, maternity without sexuality. This bifurcation of procreation and birth symbolically makes all women guilty of having been blemished by sexual intercourse in order to become pregnant and give birth.

The text of this story explicitly presents the *Guadalupana* as a social symbol and not as the object of religious piety: "After our love for the Virgin and our hatred of the gringos, nothing binds us together more than a treacherous crime" says the old man. His grandson reminds him of his life-long antagonism to religion and the church. The old man responds: "The Virgin of Guadalupe is a revolutionary Virgin; she appeared on Hidalgo's banners during the War of Independence, and on Zapata's in the Revolution, she's the best bitchin' Virgin ever."

The old man is correct historically. Both Hidalgo and Zapata's troops fought under the banner of the Virgin of Guadalupe for the obvious reason that the European transplant had taken root in Mexico by merging with the Aztec goddess Tonantzin, but beyond historical accuracy he is sociologically correct when he says: "She's the best bitchin' Virgin," which is the translator's rendering of the expression "a toda madre." In the colloquial Spanish of Mexico it means "the best" and its application to the Virgin of Guadalupe as a revolutionary symbol means she is powerful. One cannot fail to see the humor in the expression.

Just as the old man respects the power of the Virgin as a social symbol, rather than a religious figure, he also has created a cult to his wife who, with the passage of time, has become a sexless symbol of purity, motherhood, and domesticity. The grandson observes the old man in his bedroom as he looks on his ancient wardrobe with affection. Every time the grandfather opens it, he is reminded of his wife Clotilde: the smell of her clothes, the memory of her bustling about the house; this nostalgia is encapsulated in the image of ironed and starched linens neatly folded on the shelves. The middle-aged narrator recalls these experiences from his youth in an attempt to gain some insight into the significance of the woman who was also his grandmother: "This ancient young woman who was my grandmother looks like a little doll. The photographer had tinted the photograph a pale rose, and only the lips and cheeks of Doña Clotilde glow in a mixture of shyness and sensuality. Did she really look like that?" The grandson's question is answered indirectly: "'Like something out of a fairy tale,' the general says to me. 'Her mother died when she was a baby, and Villa shot her father'." When Plutarco asks, "You didn't take advantage of her, just because she couldn't protect herself?", the old man's response is instantaneous: "He glared at me and abruptly cut off the light." Plutarco has seen a girl with youth and sensuality

in the old photograph and has asked his grandfather not about his grandmother, but about the young girl. He has inadvertently broken the taboo and has made an allusion to her sexuality. Plutarco has female sexuality on his mind; he wants to have his mother as his sexual partner: "I would have liked a relationship with a real lady, mature, like my father's lover, not the 'proper' girls you met at parties given by other families, filthy rich like us. Where was my Clotilde to rescue, to protect, to teach, to love me? What was Evangelina like? I dreamed about her in her white satin Jantzen bathing suit." The sexual fantasy of Plutarco of making love to his mother, or a mother substitute, is in striking contrast to the rigid separation of motherhood and sexuality which the old man observes.

The hidden skeleton in the family closet—the murder of Evangelina, Plutarco's mother, by his father—is confessed by Agustín himself in the climactic dialogue. Evangelina is embued by all three men with sensuality. The father-in-law portrays her as a whore, her husband as the victim of her attractiveness, and for the son who does not remember her, she is the object of sexual desire. None of them, however, are prepared to think of her except through the stereotypes of their own obsessions: whore, sentimental heroine, or sex object. She appears for the first time in the story through the narration of Plutarco: "I was thirteen when one of my classmates at the Revolution High School showed me a photograph of a girl in a bathing suit. It was the first time I'd ever felt a twinge of excitement. Like Doña Clotilde in her photograph, I felt pleasure and shame at the same time. I blushed and my classmate, guffawing said, Be my guest, it's your mommy." To Plutarco his mother is the central figure in his sexual fantasies from puberty through adulthood. In the dialogue between the old man and his son Agustín, Plutarco hears this description of his mother: "When you married a whore, you dishonored only yourself." Later when the old man and Plutarco are in the brothel, he asks if his mother was like the prostitute Judith:

> "Was this what my mother was like, Grandfather? A whore like this. Is that what you meant? . . . Did she put the horns on my father?"
>
> "He looked like a stag when she got through with him."
>
> "Why did she do it?"
>
> "She didn't have to, like this girl does."

Finally, Evangelina receives her most enigmatic characterization by her husband as reported by Plutarco. He said that "my mother had not taken proper care of me, she'd been dazzled by the social scene. . . . It was inevitable that it would impress Evangelina, a beautiful girl from the provinces who'd had a gold tooth when he first met her, one of those girls from the coast of Sinaloa who become women while still very young, tall and fair, with eyes like silk, and long black hair, whose bodies hold both night and day, Plutarco, night and day glowing in the same body, all the promises, all of them, Plutarco."

The dance band was playing "Little sweetheart mine, pure as a newborn child" when Agustín met Evangelina at the Mazatlan carnival. She told Agustín as she kissed him for the first time, "I like *you,* you are the tenderest, you have handsome hands." And then at the climax of the discussion between father and son, Agustín confesses: "Evangelina was so innocent, so without defenses, that's what galled me more than anything, that I couldn't blame her, but I couldn't forgive her either." So he strangled her to death in keeping with the B-class cinema he had imitated all his life. To add effect to his confession he put on the phonograph record with Avelina Landín's sentimental clichés of Mexican popular culture: "something about silver threads among the gold." Then Agustín fell into an armchair in perfect simulation of Fernando Soler's melodramatic acting in the film *Soulless Woman.* Of the three portrayals of Evangelina, the most shallow and empty is that of Agustín; she has been turned into the victim of a sentimental, cliché-ridden, melodramatic cinema: the unfaithful wife whose death restores the husband's honor.

The old man could only see women as either mother or whore, but Agustín tried to live the clichés of the cinema and was never able to experience anything authentically. Plutarco saw through his mannerisms: "I felt sorry for him; these were gestures he'd learned at the movies. Every move he made he'd learned at the movies. Everything he did was learned, and pompous."

The viewpoint of the narrator, Plutarco, is also empty but in a different way:

> Now that I'm past my thirtieth year, I can remember that night when I was nineteen as if I were living it again, the night of my liberation. Liberation was what I felt as I fucked Judith, with all the mariachis, drunk as hell, in her bedroom, pumping and pumping to the strains of the ballad of Pancho Villa's horse, "in the station at Irapuato, broad horizons beckoned," my grandfather sitting in a chair, sad and silent, as if he were watching life being born anew, but not his, not his ever again, Judith red with shame, she'd never done it that way, with music and everything, frozen, ashamed, feigning emotions I knew she didn't feel, because her body belonged to the dead night, I was the only one who conquered, *no one shared the victory with me, that's why it had no flavor,* it wasn't like those moments the General had told me about, moments shared by all, maybe that's why my grandfather was so sad, and why so sad forever was the melancholy of the liberation I thought I'd won that night. (emphasis mine)

At the end of the story, Plutarco recalls standing between his father and his grandfather at the graves of his mother and his grandmother the next Mother's Day after the "liberation" when he found out the truth about his father's drug dealings and the murder of his mother: "My grandfather sobbed again, and uncovered his face. If I'd looked at him closely, I'm sure I would have asked myself for whom he wept so bitterly, and for whom he wept more, his wife or his daughter-in-law. But at that moment I was simply trying to guess what my future would be. We'd gone to the cemetery without mariachis this time. I would

have liked a little music." Plutarco now knows the meaning of living in isolation: "No one shared the victory with me, that's why it had no flavor." These are the words the mature Plutarco uses to describe the emptiness of his sexual performance with the prostitute Judith with musical accompaniment: a false sense of participation. As he stood in the cemetery not knowing what was to become of his life he would have preferred some company, some musical accompaniment there also; the void he now felt was a consequence of his isolation even in the intimacy of sexual intercourse.

The three men are of three different generations and each has a very different viewpoint of women. To the old man they are sexless mothers or whores, to the father they are clichés from sentimental cinema, and to the young man they are sexual objects with only one purpose and function. What all three men have in common in their attitudes toward women is that they are all incapable of knowing one. The barrier between man and woman is built up through the institutionalized stereotypes and roles that govern the behavior of both sexes.

But there are numerous occasions when these sexual objects speak, think, and express feelings that are not intended for the sole gratification of the male. Herein lies the root of feminophobia: this "other," who is not a man, who has breasts and a vagina, has to be depersonalized, must be a type rather than a person. The two most powerful and time-honored forms of depersonalization are the virgin mother and the whore; one is all nurturing support and is venerated, the other is only a sexual object and is abused; neither thinks. All three male characters in this story operate through the depersonalization of the women in their lives. All three have to assign roles to them so that they can function in their feminophobic world. We have noted how the old man assigns the standard roles of virgin-whore syndrome, and how his son Agustín has recast women into trite plots, but for the grandson, Plutarco, the search for the mother in women has led to an emptiness. His sexual obsession is expressed through symbolic transference of the gardens of the Pedregal. High walls are like a chastity belt and open flowers like the genital openness of the whore: "They sowed the rock with dramatic plants, stark, with no adornment but a few aggressive flowers. Doors locked tight like chastity belts, Grandfather, and flowers open like wounded genitals, like the cunt of the whore Judith that you couldn't fuck and I could, and what for, Grandfather." He is the only one of the three to realize that the self without the other is false, and consequently sexual intercourse with a woman who is not a person is the same as fornicating with an inflated plastic doll: "And what for, Grandfather."

The structure of the story is a subtle play of relationships: between grandson and grandfather, between grandfather and father, and, finally, between father and son, and the core of these relationships is their exercise of power. This structure is one of generational juxtapositions in the context of the power struggle that is life in Mexico. The first set, Vicente-Plutarco, engages the generational poles, a man from the end of the last century who came out on top of the revolution contrasted with a man from the beginning of the second half of the century. The second set, Vicente-Agustín, exemplifies the generational clash between the viewpoint of the ex-revolutionary with that of a modern businessman. The third set, Agustín-Plutarco, presents rejection and nostalgia for the loss of a mythical vitality.

It is significant to remember that the story is narrated from the point of view of Plutarco who gives present-day values to the three sets of relationships. There is, therefore, a profound admiration on the part of the young man for the spontaneity of the grandfather and a fantasy of being able to relive the revolution with him. This is a nostalgia for the revolution and the desire for the power to kill, pillage, rape, and castrate those who stand in his way. Plutarco reports on the relationship between his grandfather and father as one where there is only disdain and arrogance on the part of the old man because Agustín never proved himself. On the part of Agustín there is the distaste for the old man's crudeness and an abject servility to him. Finally, the relationship Plutarco presents as existing between himself and his father is one of pathetic sympathy on his part and self-serving melancholy in the older man.

The wealth of the family, it must be recalled, is entirely derived from the abuse of others; first, through the spoils of war and subsequently from drug-trafficking. The ostensive victim of these relationships is Evangelina and, by extension, Mexican women, but at the most intensive level of reality the three male characters are also victims of abuse in the societal power struggle which they expiate in their feminophobia. This is a social system where the rule is exploit others or be exploited by them. The essential point is that feminophobia is only incidentally about sexual differences and is fundamentally about power: the power of authority, of force, of money, of domination of the other through any and every means available. The raw use of power that is prepared to abuse or to kill in order to win is the fine narrative thread that runs through the story. And the symbolic demonstration of power is made manifest by the veneration and abuse of women. Feminophobia was born of sexual repression by medieval introverts, but it has become institutionalized in cultures where the power struggle is always just beneath the surface. It is fitting that the only one of the three who knows that he is caught up in a system of domination of women is Plutarco. When Agustín sobs to Plutarco, "You and I, Plutarco, what battles are we going to win? what women are we going to tame? what soldiers are we going to castrate? you tell me. . . . He laughs and says, let's see whether you can do what I did, now that it can't be done any longer, let's see whether you can find a way to inherit something more difficult than my money. Violence with impunity", he is crying of his own desperate search for power. Since he could not match the old general through his open violence in war and sexual domination, he chose the role of the dishonored husband and murdered his wife.

The power struggle in Plutarco is all in the past; from the point of view of the narration, some fifteen years after the events being narrated, it is all over. There remains only

the melancholy of the person who surveys the bleakness of his life without knowing how to overcome the fact that the other that hwill remain absent from his life is the woman as person rather than as pedestal or vagina.

The popular culture of Mexico with its ongoing alternating attitudes of servile passivity or superiority toward the United States runs throughout the story as a subtle reminder that Mexico as a society sees itself bound up with a fate similar to that imposed on women. Mexico, as a participant in the economic and political reality of the North American hemisphere, is also caught up in the power syndrome, the either/or law of life: abuse or be abused. This is an ethical malaise that ultimately destroys both. Few writers, however, have been able to express the deepest fears of their culture with the power, the insight, and the effectiveness of Carlos Fuentes. The short story **"Mother's Day"** is not an isolated example of this cultural truth, but it is the literary achievement of Carlos Fuentes to present female stereotyping as the social manifestation of the male characters' pathological distortion of reality.

Michael Kerrigan (essay date 1994)

SOURCE: "In Realms of Gold," in *Times Literary Supplement,* No. 4758, June 10, 1994, p. 23.

[*In the following review of* The Orange Tree, *Kerrigan comments on Fuentes's innovative treatment of time and the author's attempt to "reanimate history" in the collection.*]

Carlos Fuentes established his international reputation over three decades ago, with *The Death of Artemio Cruz* (1962). That novel goes in search of the identity of a protagonist who is modern down to his Volvo, and Mexican down to the parasites in his gut, but the quest ends up taking in a past of conquest and revolution, and looks far beyond Cruz's native Veraeruz to the shores of the Mediterranean. Like the stars Cruz sees overhead—"only the ghost of the light that began its journey countless years ago, countless centuries"—the past informs the present. Its churches the reconsecrated shrines of Indian deities and its public buildings based on Spanish models, modern-day Mexico is unthinkable without this past.

Not that history is necessarily glorious or even dignified, nor can it be relied on for comfort or support. The grotesque story of Queen Joanna of Spain stands as both example and fable: allowed sole possession of her philandering husband only by his death, she roamed the land with his cadaver, wandering dementedly from monastery to monastery, shunning convents in her terror that even in death he might prove unfaithful. Faced with the prospect of lugging such an uncomfortable history about with them, many in Latin America and Spain have sought to deny the past. Fuentes, however, has always urged them to acknowledge and embrace it, to carry the corpse, however unappealing. The imaginative task he has pursued in an extensive and inclusive corpus of fictional work has been the exploration of what he sees as a distinctive Hispanic condition. Rummaging through the historical archives of Spain and Spanish America, leafing through its literature, poring over old masters, Fuentes has sought to reanimate history and reveal the Hispanic world to itself. It is a paradoxical world in which time plays tricks, in whose present the past everywhere comes blazing through. It is a world whose America contains its Europe and its Europe America. Its articulation has required innovative, often difficult forms— most controversially the fathomless epic of allusion Fuentes invented in *Terra Nostra* (1975), for some critics a glorious El Dorado of Hispanic culture and life, for others a vast Escorial of barren academicism.

A novel in five novellas, **The Orange Tree** is a more manageable work altogether, and it provides the English-speaking reader with an excellent introduction to these realms of gold. Stout Cortés stands at the centre of the first story, a savage personification of the European will to conquest. There is more to him than rapacity and lust, however, and less force to his will than he himself could have imagined. These are important themes in a book which finds in history a cycle of conquest and resistance which changes conqueror as much as conquered. The orange tree provides a recurrentemblem for this process. Its name derived from the Arabic *narandj*, the orange was native to the East. Its delicious, fragrant fruit, round and red as the sun or a gold coin, was brought back as booty by Syria's Roman invaders. When they set out to conquer the wild Celtiberians, the orange went with them. In the fullness of time, conquered became conquistadors, and the tree completed its westward journey, It ran wild in America, and its fruit acquired a different, more bitter taste. Taking five years to reach fruition, it could symbolize patient endurance; sleeping and gaining strength in winter, it drew life from death.

The first narrator in **The Orange Tree** speaks from his tomb, having just died of plague, but that is logical enough, once you accept the cyclical view of time at work. Death is where all the ladders start; for the Aztecs, it was the only guarantee of continuing life, the darkness that executes the sun and clears the way for a new dawn; for Fuentes, it is the path to understanding and the obvious place to begin. It is, none the less, strange to read a story which moves from experience into innocence. Cortés's interpreter, Jerónimo de Aguilar, is a wilfully unreliable narrator, telling his tale backwards, a caprice which cannot, however, make up for the authorial power he has lost. For a brief moment the only man capable of representing one world to another, he has fancied himself holding history in his hands and shaping events. Mistranslating Cortés's self-serving blandishments as the dire threats they concealed. Jerónimo offered Moctezuma the chance to avert catastrophe, to see the true nature of the brigand he was welcoming as a god. But the Aztec refused to see; his ancient fatalism was unready to comprehend a man like Cortés, a European who never doubted his freedom to fashion his own destiny.

Yet was Moctezuma really so mistaken? asks Fuentes. Did Cortés really make history, or did history make him? A strikingly unreflecting man in this tale, Cortés acquires an appreciable psychological and moral dimension only in the second, in which his two sons tell his story after his death. "Is reality only the sum total of physical events?" the Roman general Scipio wonders, in **"The Two Numantias,"** the third story here: "Are mental events only and always consequences of those material acts? Do we fool ourselves by thinking that it's the other way round . . . ?" The Cortés who emerges in his sons' accounts is an unexpectedly tragic figure, his relationship with the land he conquered intimate, compelling and finally self-destructive. Mexico changed him, though that change is plainly registered only in his children. Both named Martín, one is legitimate and white, with all the sense, pride and entitlement that entails, and the other illegitimate, born to Cortés's Indian mistress and hence the first *mestizo*. Together they are the first modern Mexicans, and the first to revolt as Mexicans against Spanish rule.

Hard as they have striven to overturn his work, the Martins represent part of their father's story, what he was and what he accomplished. Rather than asking what posterity has done for us, we have to see, implies Fuentes, that it is only in time and in other people that we are created at all. The notion of sacrifice is crucial to Fuentes as it was to the Aztecs, though it can take many different forms. There are the innumerable roads not taken: "What would have happened if what did happen didn't?" asks Jerómino, "What would have happened if what did not happen did?" There are the thousands who must live in poverty so that Artemio Cruz can have his wealth and power, their anonymity the price of his ego; there are the men who, in *Terra Nostra,* spend their lives building a royal mausoleum. And there are the warriors of Numantia who kill themselves so that their women and children can eat their flesh. We are part of a cycle of death and rebirth, Fuentes suggests; the idea that we exist as individuals is a problematical one.

The discovery of the New World shattered Spain's sense of itself, overturning all assumptions, and complicating everything with the revelation that things could be quite otherwise. To a nation which had laboured long and hard to establish a single, "Spanish" culture, purified of every trace of Moor and Jew, which offered sacrifices in the shape of heretics to the honour of One Holy, Catholic and Apostolic Church, the discovery of a second world came as a profound shock, especially when this world was so full of strange peoples, plants, animals and other "things not mentioned in the Bible." However unsettling that shock, the Spaniards hurled themselves into the task of possessing this world as if their lives depended on it; as if, indeed, something vital to life had been lost with the denial of multiplicity at home, something which now had to be sought abroad. This common project would do more than anything else to unite the rival kingdoms of Iberia into a single Spain.

In our own time—time measured out to the minute by a digital watch—an Irish actor, Vicente Valera, the protagonist in **The Orange Tree**'s fourth tale, dies during a visit to Acapulco. As he looks at the whores he has gathered around him, he feels, for the first time, how artificial and provisional is the person he has been:

> In all of their eyes, I saw a time which disregarded my individuality. Above all, I saw those Mexican children and felt afraid of escaping from my own more or less protected individuality, constructed with a certain care and lots of patience so I could face a helpless humanity in which circumstances neither respect nor distinguish anyone.
>
> I realized what had happened. In death, I had become a Mexican.

Once more, however, the American dimension offers the European gain as well as loss. Poor and powerless as he may be, buffeted as he is by a violent, uncomfortable history which affords him no individual recognition, the Mexican has a share in a collective immortality. As Jerónimo puts it, "the greatness of power fell; the small lives of the people survived." The challenge and the opportunity *The Orange Tree* presents its reader are those of escaping from "a more or less protected individuality" into a wider existence of multiple possibility and a cyclical history which holds past and present in simultanity and in ceaseless renewal. It is difficult to maintain negative capability faced with so many alternative possibilities; the temptation is always to reach for synthesis; reading such a history it is hard to resist trying to square the circle. But the rewards are immense: each of its five short novellas reflecting and refracting the last, *The Orange Tree* contrives to project—if only in image, in hints and suggestions—the story of a world. The most important stories, the novel implies, are the interminable annals of the poor. What strikes the reader first in Fuentes's work may be his erudition and intellectual rigour, but what remains in the mind is his sympathy, his concern to commemorate the countless lives sacrificed in pain and obscurity so that we might live.

Amanda Hopkinson (essay date 1994)

SOURCE: "Out of Juice," in *New Statesman & Society*, Vol 7, August 26, 1994, pp. 37-8.

[*In this review of* The Orange Tree, *Hopkinson finds Fuentes's ideas "predictable" and "tired" and declares that the book is only partially redeemed by its humor.*]

Carlos Fuentes needs little introduction. The hype on the covers of his novels, plays and essays lists his prizes and awards, his global scattering of posts as Mexican ambassador and as professor. It was during his post at Cambridge in 1992—the quincentennial of Columbus' landings—that he delivered the lectures that form the nucleus of these five novellas: perhaps that is why they have a familiar, not to say a jaded, ring.

The Orange Tree is the hand holding these five fingers, dipping into the stages of colonialism that have afflicted the "other" (southern) America. The orange seeds brought to Spain with the Moorish conquest had put down deep roots

by the time, 700 years later, that the Inquisition declared in 1492 for the final expulsion of infidels: Arabs and Jews. In the same year, Columbus in his journals was propounding strange theories about how to stand an egg on its end and a pear-shaped world on its stalk or "nipple" at the Equator. Preparing to sail the globe and square the circle, turning the tiny islands of the Caribbean into the great lands of Japan and China, he found himself tossed into the shores of Paradise, "a Jerusalem at the earth's centre."

The orange trees threw out new branches in the new world at the new conquest. For Columbus was but a preliminary skirmish in what became a repetitive war of attrition and possession. The first tale is told in the words of Jerónimo de Aguilar, the Spaniard who survived the first landing on the eastern seaboard of Mexico to become Cortés' interpreter. Soon, however, he found himself superseded by the Janus figure of la Malinche/Marina, the multilingual expert who (in Fuentes' version) superseded even his capacity for treachery and deception.

Having betrayed the Aztec emperor Montezuma with Cortés, la Malinche became the mother of the *mestizo* race, a new Eve in the Garden of Eden that would decline into being the Valley of Mexico—cradle of the most polluted city in the world.

This fable is so familiar it needs little elaboration. That the "fruit of the tree of knowlege of good and evil" turns out to be an orange is no more a poetic licence than the European convention that it should be an apple. What palls in this New World version of the Old Testament tale is the lameness of the retelling, the limpness where tautness is vital.

The pity of it is not that Fuentes cannot write. He can, if better elsewhere. But his settings, which move from the legacy of Conquest back into Roman Spain and forward into the cheap takeover of the original earthly Paradise by the Japanese-owned Paradise Inc and its programme of "team spirit, Cristóbalsan, company loyalty, yoga every morning, Valium every night", are so predictable. Where the ideas are tired, the writing falters.

Columbus' tropical nipple of the world is Fuentes' nibble at a golden globe, recurring in a crescendo of mammary metaphors. Refusing the role of narrator, putting politics into the mouths of historical characters, Fuentes cannot deflect what emerges as merely banal. Whether the *canard* that Columbus embodied the Wandering Jew after all, or the attack on the US for its appropriation of the name "America," these well-rehearsed arguments lack originality.

What saves *The Orange Tree* are the redemptive passages of humour and wit. Sailing over the standard late 20th-century Apocalypse of a world drowning in its own sewage and pollution is the ridiculous reincarnation of Snow White's seven dwarves in a yachting brothel. And trumpeting back at the rhetoric, in the arcane vocabulary of Scipio Aemilianus, are the belligerent elephants of the African king Masinissa. Blessed be the unexpected, along with odd throwaway sentences that recall the best of Fuentes' other incarnations as *The Old Gringo* or *Christopher Unborn*.

Carlos Fuentes (essay date 1996) *

SOURCE: "A Son of Scheherazade," in *Book World—The Washington Post,* Vol. XXXVI, No. 17, April 28, 1996, pp. 1, 8.

[*In the following essay, Fuentes describes his perceptions of the short story and his literary influences in the genre. In the process, he discusses his desire to mesh the "realistic" with the "fantastical" and how this desire resulted in the stories "The Doll Queen," "Chac Mool," and "A Garden in Flanders."*]

The novel is an ocean liner; the short story, a sailboat hugging the coast. Writing a novel requires an Olympic team. Singular as he or she may seem, the novelist is a team of painters, city planners, gossip columnists, fashion experts, architects and set designers; a justice of the peace, a real estate agent, midwife, undertaker, witch and high priest, all in one.

The short story writer, on the other hand, is a lonely navigator. Why this fidelity to solitude? Why this need to be in sight of the coast? Perhaps because storytellers know that if they do not tell the tale this very night, near the beach, with no time to cross the ocean, there might be no tomorrow. Every storyteller is a son of Scheherazade, hurrying to tell his story so that death can be postponed one more time.

In the short story—child of the thousand and one nights—urgency and brevity embrace. But brevity does not exclude depth or impose measures. The short story is not a pygmy novel. It is an object with its own totality, integrity and beauty. It has its own epiphanies (not, perhaps, the revelations to be found in those rare instants of Joyce or Proust). The short story must reveal its beauty, its meaning, its intensity almost instantaneously, visibly, says Sean O'Faolain, like a child's kite in the sky: "a small wonder, a brief, bright moment."

Yet in postponing death, the short story can display an art as varied as the art of Poe, Gogol, Chekhov, Maupassant or Flannery O'Connor. I like to keep in mind the lessons of two great Latin American masters of the genre, the Argentines Julio Cortazar and Jorge Luis Borges. Cortazar translated the complete works of Poe into Spanish and was keenly aware of Poe's mandate for immediacy in the tale. Cortazar excelled in giving his stories that sense of the immediate: A visitor to an aquarium discovers his own face in that of an *axolotl*; a house is taken over, inch by inch, by invisible forces; an Aztec is sacrificed in a pyramid while dreaming that he is being operated on in a modern hospital where a man being operated on dreams that he is being sacrificed in a pyramid. Cortazar's stories are discreet units, closed in on themselves.

Borges, on the other hand, conceives stories that open onto other stories, creating interrelated narrative constellations: His whole work is a garden of forking paths. His literature is made of great themes that disguise one another, like the mythical cities of "Tlon, Uqbar, Orbis Tertius," hidden behind the screens of time, sustained by memory and created only by language. Borges's story of "Pierre Menard, Author of the Quixote," is the greatest example of this art of prolonging by concealing. Menard, a minor notary in the French provinces, decides to rewrite Cervantes's novel. But all he does is copy it word by word. Yet the work is new, because in rewriting *Don Quixote,* Menard has taught us to read *Don Quixote* in a new way, with everything that happened between the publication of the novel in 1605 and the present-day reading as the new context of the narrative. Borges reveals, through his technique, that the past has its own novelties, and that the next reader of *Don Quixote* will also be its newest reader.

It is difficult in Latin America to write short stories without keeping Borges and Cortazar in mind. One writes discreetly, each story a self-contained unity; the other indiscreetly, each story harking back and forth to other stories. But whether you belong to the family of Cortazar or that of Borges, a writer is constantly seduced into giving stories either a "realistic" or a "fantastical" mode. In my own case, I have always been attracted by the possibility of discovering the fantastic in everyday occurrences or unearthing the reality that underlies even the most fantastic tale. I guess this comes from my early reading of Cervantes, once more, who is thoroughly and perpetually modern in his total disregard for genre, in his mixing of languages and his refusal to establish a border between fantasy and reality. Are the windmills really giants? Is the princess Dulcinea really the peasant girl Aldonza? Are the puppets menacing Moors? Or is it the other way around?

Another writer whose work I read early, and that made an impression on me, was Balzac, particularly his *Wild Ass's Skin* (*La peau de chagrin*). Its narrator wished to be the notary public of French social classes and "carried a whole society" in his head, but he also carried ghosts, myths, fears and unexplainable occurrences—in the novel a wild ass's skin fulfills desires but shrinks every time it grants them, until, at the end, it takes the hapless owner's life and disappears.

For me, the most fantastical tales have come from the most commonplace observations. When I was a very young man, I went twice a week to the Cinema Club at the French Institute in Mexico City, there to discover the thrilling visions of Buñuel, Pabst and Murnau. On the way home one day, I stopped in wonderment at the first-floor window of a shabby green apartment house. There, I saw a scene as poetic, fluid and oneirical as anything in German expressionist films. In a casket in the center of the living room lay a little girl, most probably a porcelain figure, but maybe, really, a small corpse dressed in white silk, her hands joined in prayer, her coffin smothered in roses, surrounded by burning candles.

But when in the morning, driven by curiosity, I went back to the apartment house, the view inside the living room was utterly transformed. The coffin and its occupant were gone. A maid was cleaning the place with a Hoover vacuum. The furniture had come straight from Sears. In the evening, the funeral scene came back to mind, and then again, night after night. . . . Until I wrote a story, **"The Doll Queen,"** in which a young man sets out to discover the whereabouts of a little girl he played with inthe park 15 years before. And thereby hangs a tale.

My first published short story, **"Chac Mool"** dates from 1953. It is the tale of Filiberto, a minor Mexican bureaucrat who indulges a fancy for collecting pre-Hispanic sculpture. He comes upon a statue of the Mayan rain god, Chac Mool, in a flea market, takes it home and puts it in the basement. Promptly, unseasonable rains begin, the basement is flooded and the statue becomes flexible, sensitive, movable . . . and demanding. The bureaucrat flees to Acapulco, where he is drowned. A friend brings the coffin back to Filiberto's house. A perfumed, overdressed Mexican Indian opens the door and says, "I was expecting you."

The basis of this story is a newspaper item I read in Europe in 1951, when a big exhibition of Mexican art crossed the Atlantic. Among the objects exhibited was the Chac Mool, the beautiful reclining figure that inspired many of Henry Moore's statues. When Spanish peasants from a drought-affected region found out that the Mayan rain god was in Paris, they sent small amounts of money to be put on the belly of the deity, hoping for a downpour. It promptly began to rain in Spain. And when Chac Mool crossed over to England, one of the worst storms to hit the Channel accompanied the god's travels.

Another of my first stories, **"A Garden in Flanders,"** is based on the short-lived empire of Maximilian of Austria and his wife, Carlota of Belgium, in Mexico. In an abandoned old mansion in Mexico City, Carlota's ghost haunts a visiting caretaker, taking him for Maximilian. Outside, the Mexican sun shines. Inside, a Flemish garden lives in perpetual winter, under a permanent drizzle.

This fantastical dimension of history has not clouded, I hope, the contemporary vision of Mexican society present in many of my novels and stories. The destiny of my city, Mexico City, has haunted me as much as Carlota's ghost. A nostalgia for the place that was; a requiem for "a city whose nights held the promise of the morning to come"; a cry of pain for the vast, smog-ridden, overpopulated, garbage infested megalopolis of today, runs through many of my stories. And alongside, a portrait of the humble, the humiliated and offended, as well as of the authoritarian clans that have defaced the city but have not managed to extinguish its spirit.

Yet, whether the tale is tender or angry, "real" or "fantastical," at the end a question must hang over it, a perfume must linger, permitting the story to be complete, but to remain open. After all, if a story is a declaration against death, its author is nothing if not a perpetual convalescent.

FURTHER READING

Bibliography

Reeve, Richard M. "An Annotated Bibliography On Carlos Fuentes: 1949-69." *Hispania,* Vol. 53 (October 1970): 595-652.

Focuses on criticism published primarily in Mexico and the United States with less attention paid to works from other areas of Latin America and Europe.

Criticism

Carter, June C. D. A review of *Burnt Water. Latin America Literary Review* IX, No. 19 (Fall-Winter 1981): 66-8.

Favorable review that finds the book to be "public evidence of Fuentes' meritorious skill in short fiction writing."

Chrzanowski, Joseph. "The Double in 'Las Dos Elenas' by Carlos Fuentes." *Romance Notes* XVIII, No. 1 (Fall 1977): 6-10.

Argues that Fuentes transcends the stereotypical use of "the double" because of a surprise ending that deepens the characterization in the story.

Donoghue, Denis. "Safe in the Hands of the Uncanny." *New York Times Book Review* (8 April 1990): 15.

Reviews *Constancia and Other Stories for Virgins* noting the "bizarre and the uncanny" elements used by Fuentes to disarm the reader's expectations. Donoghue also discusses Fuentes's work in regard to the concepts of post-modern literature.

Duncan, Cynthia. "The Living Past: The Mexican's History Returns to Haunt Him in Two Short Stories by Carlos Fuentes." In *The Fantastic in World Literature and the Arts: Selected Essays from the Fifth International Conference on the Fantastic in the Arts,* edited by Donald E. Morse, pp. 141-47. New York: Greenwood Press, 1987.

Analyzes "Chac Mool" and "Tlactocatzine" and describes the way Fuentes uses the fantastic to demonstrate a means of coming to terms with Mexico's history.

Fuentes, Carlos. "On Reading and Writing Myself: How I Wrote *Aura.*" *World Literature Today* 57, No. 4 (Autumn 1983): 531-39.

Discusses the original inspiration for his novella, including a young girl he met in 1961 who eventually killed herself twenty years later.

Gyurko, Lanin A. "Pop Art and Pop Life in Fuentes' 'Fortuna lo que ha querido'." *Horizontes* XXIII, No. 5 (October 1979): 5-20.

Analyzes Fuentes's story from *Cantar de ciegos,* focusing on his depiction of the Mexican artist and the nation's consumer-oriented society.

Knapp, Bettina L. "Fuentes: 'In a Flemish Garden,' A

Parapsychological Happening in an Architectural Context." In *Archetype, Architecture, and the Writer*, pp. 125-46. Bloomington, Ind.: Indiana University Press, 1986.

Lengthy analysis of the story that focuses on the mansion where it takes place.

Kooreman, Thomas E. "Reader Interest in *Aura*: A Search for Confirmation." In *In Honor of Boyd G. Carter,* edited by Katherine Vera and George R. McMurray, pp. 25-34. Laramie, Wyoming: Department of Modern and Classical Languages of the University of Wyoming, 1981.

Assesses the method of storytelling in *Aura,* declaring that the "consistent use of innovative narrative techniques creates an acceptable reality while intensively involving the reader."

Mortiz, Joaquin. "Morbid Elegance." *Atlas* 13, No. 1 (January 1967): 58-9.

Reviews *Cantar de Ciegos* maintaining that Fuentes is "one of the few Latin American writers who have completely mastered the short story."

Rojas, Nelson. "Time and Tense in Carlos Fuentes's 'Aura'." *Hispania* 61, No. 4 (December 1978): 859-64.

Concentrates on the "special version of time" in the novella and the Spanish verbal system that the narrator uses to communicate the story. Rojas argues that Fuentes achieves a unique narrative accomplishment by presenting the story as a series of fleeting instants.

Tyler, Joseph. "'Chac Mool': A Journey into the Fantastic." *Hispanic Journal* 10, No. 2 (Spring 1989): 177-83.

Places "Chac Mool" in the context of fantastic literature and traces Fuentes's debt to Argentinian author Jorge Luis Borges.

Van Delden, Maarten. "Carlos Fuentes' *Agua Quemada*: The Nation as Unimaginable Community." *Latin American Literary Review* XXI, No. 42 (July-December 1992): 57-69.

Examines the manner in which the collection depicts the divided nature of Mexico.

Williams, Shirley A. "Prisoners of the Past: Three Fuentes Short Stories from *Los días enmascarados*." *Journal of Spanish Studies* 6, No. 1 (1978): 39-52.

Outlines the themes in *Los días enmascarados* and explains their role in subsequent fictional works by Fuentes.

Milan Kundera
1929–

Czechoslovakian novelist, short story writer, essayist, playwright, and poet.

INTRODUCTION

Kundera is considered one of Europe's outstanding contemporary writers. He is frequently labeled an Eastern European "dissident" writer despite his insistence that his works are not inherently political or propagandistic. Rather than serving as ideological puppets, Kundera's characters are usually vulnerable individuals whose views and lifestyles are challenged through events and dilemmas in their personal lives and in society. His single collection of translated stories, *Laughable Loves*, contains several recurring themes: the ambiguousness and mutability of individual identity; the consequences of the games that individuals play in the name of love and lust; the prevalence of the social masks that people wear to disguise their true motives and to gain approval from others; and the ironic backfiring of human plans. Kundera discovered his approach to writing while working on these short stories. As he stated in an interview with Jordan Elgrably, "My writing took flight with the first story for *Laughable Loves*. This was my Opus 1. Everything I'd written prior to it can be considered prehistory."

Biographical Information

Kundera was born and raised in Brno, Czechoslovakia. His father was a well-known pianist who collaborated with the celebrated Czechoslovakian composer Leoš Jănaček. Although he once studied piano and stated that "Jănaček's music [was] for me the first revelation of art," Kundera decided at age nineteen that music was not his true vocation. He left Brno in 1948 to study scriptwriting and directing at the Film Faculty of the Prague Academy of Music and Dramatic Arts. At this time Kundera, like many other idealistic and progressive students who had experienced the horrors of World War II, joined the Czechoslovakian Communist party. He began teaching cinematography at the Prague Academy in 1952 and published his first book, the poetry collection *Člověk, zahrada šírá*, a year later. He published two other collections of poetry while working at the academy but later renounced all of these early works as adolescent and insignificant. During the early 1960s Kundera earned recognition as an important literary figure in his homeland for his 1961 critical study of the Czechoslovakian novelist Vladislava Vančury entitled *Unemí románu*, his 1962 play *Majitelé klíců* (*The Owners of the Keys*), and the 1963 short story collection *Směšné lásky* (*Laughable Loves*). He served on the Central Committee of the Writer's Union and the editorial boards of the journals *Literarni noviny* and *Listy*.

Despite his reputation as one of Czechoslovakia's most notable writers, Kundera encountered resistance after submitting the manuscript of his first novel, *Žert* (*The Joke*), to a Prague publisher in 1965. Due to the perceived negative political implications of the book, Kundera spent two years battling the censorship board before *The Joke* was published in its original form in 1967. During the Prague Spring of 1968, when the push for cultural freedom reached its zenith and writers and intellectuals enjoyed fewer restrictions, Kundera's novel was enormously popular. Prior to the Prague Spring many writers and artists were attempting to speed reform and liberalize cultural policy by creating ideologically challenging works. In his opening address to the Fourth Czechoslovak Writers Congress in 1967, Kundera candidly admonished censorship and other repressive tactics used against Czechoslovakian writers. While his speech had been approved in advance by the Czechoslovak Party Central Committee, it was considered very controversial by government bureaucrats and some writers. Kundera's status as a writer and citizen changed radically when Czechoslovakia was invaded by Russian forces in 1968. He was expelled from the Communist Party, released from his teaching position at the Prague Academy, and his works were removed from libraries and bookstores. Kundera eventually lost the right to publish in Czechoslovakia. He finally fled his native country in 1975 after being offered a teaching position at the University of Rennes in France. In 1979 the Czechoslovakian government, in order to ensure that Kundera could never repatriate, revoked his Czechoslovakian citizenship. With the 1984 publication of *L'insourenable l'égèreté de l'être* (*The Unbearable Lightness of Being*), which garnered considerable praise and later was adapted to film, he achieved international renown. Kundera lives in Paris.

Major Works of Short Fiction

The stories in *Laughable Loves* were drawn from the trilogy *Směšné lásky, Druhý sešit směšných lásek*, and *Třetí sešit směšných lásek*, collections that address the illusory nature of love and the consequences of using sexuality to gain power and influence. In "The Hitchhiking Game," one of the best known stories, a young couple engage in role-playing while on vacation. The woman, usually very inhibited and conservative, pretends she is a prostitute and at the man's urging performs a striptease on a table in a disreputable hotel. While the game begins innocently, this behavior leads to identity crises for the participants, as the woman painfully reveals when she pleads at the end of the story, "I am me, I am me, I am me. . . ." The story "Edward and God" is informed by the theme of duplicity and by Kundera's encounters with Communism. Here, a young atheistic man pretends to be godly in order to win a desirable woman's affection, but his show of religiosity lands him in trouble with his supervisor, an unattractive woman who is a fervent Communist. In order to ensure his continued employment, the young man finds himself seducing his boss— who disgusts him—with little idea of how to end this entanglement in the future.

Critical Reception

The artistic conception of *Laughable Loves* is a topic common to several critical studies of the collection. Commentators have insisted that the stories, while self-sufficient, assume much more meaning when examined in relation to each other and the volume as a whole. Furthermore, some critics have asserted that *Laughable Loves* anticipated the novel *The Book of Laughter and Forgetting*, which employs related but largely independent narratives to illustrate several prevailing themes. Another subject of discussion is the perception of male chauvinism in Kundera's narratives. A few reviewers have found his depictions of women to be misogynistic, though John O'Brien has responded that the intention of the author was, in fact, to expose damaging attitudes toward women. Many readers have remarked on the prominence of sexuality in Kundera's stories. Mark Sturdivant has commented that "sexuality becomes a vehicle for expressing a variety of interwoven threads of commentary upon

human characteristics, and for ultimately casting a pall of hopelessness and meaninglessness over mankind's fundamental existence." Agreeing, Maria Banerjee has stated that "the laughter resounding in these tales of erotic debacle is never quite free of the admixture of sadness that turns it into a grimace." Summing perhaps the unifying motif of the collection, Elizabeth Pochoda has observed: "There is in *Laughable Loves* this persistent and illusory connection between love and certainty. The would-be seducers attempt to circumvent the habitual oppression of their daily lives through love because love is voluntary, or so they think. . . . The characters who push hardest for certainty in love are the most laughable and the most disappointed. They take a holiday from one form of tyranny and unwittingly uncover another, their own."

PRINCIPAL WORKS

Short Fiction

Směšné lásky [Laughable Loves] 1963
Druhý sešit směšných lásek 1965
Třetí sešit směšných lásek 1968

Other Major Works

Člověk, zahrada šírá (poems) 1953
Poslední máj (poems) 1955
Monology (poems) 1957
Unemí románu: cesta Vladislava Vančury za velkou epikou (criticism) 1961
Majitelé klíčů [*The Owners of the Keys*] (drama) 1962
Žert [*The Joke*] (novel) 1967
Dvě uši dvě svatby (drama) 1968
The Joke [with Jaromil Jires] (screenplay) 1968
Ptákovina (drama) 1968
†*La vie est ailleurs* [*Life Is Elsewhere*] (novel) 1973
†*La valse aux adieux* [*The Farewell Party*] (novel) 1976
†*Le livre du rire et de l'oubli* [*The Book of Laughter and Forgetting*] (novel) 1979
Jacques et som maitre: Hommage a Denis Diderot [*Jacques and His Master*] (drama) 1981
†*L'insourenable l'égèreté de l'être* [*The Unbearable Lightness of Being*] (novel) 1984
L'art du roman [*The Art of the Novel*] (criticism) 1986
L'immortalité [*Immortality*] (novel) 1990
Testaments Betrayed: An Essay in Nine Parts (criticism) 1995

*Seven of the ten stories contained in these collections were translated into English and published as a single volume, *Laughable Loves*, in 1974.

†These novels were published under the following titles in Czech (the language in which they were originally written) after the publication of the French and English translations: *Zivot je jinde* (1979), *Valčík na rozloucenou* (1979), *Kniha smíchu a zapomnení* (1981), and *Nesnesitelná lehkost bytí* (1985).

CRITICISM

Philip Roth   (essay date 1974)

SOURCE: "Milan Kundera, the Joker," in *Esquire,* Vol. LXXXI, No. 4, April, 1974, pp. 85, 178, 182, 184.

[*A prominent and controversial figure in contemporary American letters, Roth draws heavily upon his Jewish upbringing and his life as an author to explore his predominant thematic concerns—the search for self-identity, conflicts between traditional and contemporary moral values, and the relationship between fiction and reality. The scatalogical content of some of his works and his satiric portraits of Jewish life have inspired a considerable amount of critical debate. Roth wrote the introduction to the English-language edition of Kundera's* Laughable Loves. *In the following excerpt, he comments on the seriousness underlying the eroticism in Kundera's stories.*]

Erotic play and power are the subjects frequently at the center of the stories that Kundera calls, collectively, *Laughable Loves*. To be sure, sexuality as a weapon (in this case, the weapon of him who is otherwise wholly assailable) is to the point of *The Joke* as well: to revenge himself upon the political friend who had turned on him back in his remote student days, Ludvík Jahn, released from the coal mines at last, coldly conceives a plan to seduce the man's wife. In this decision to put his virility in the service of his rage, there is in Kundera's hero a kinship to characters in the fiction of Mailer and Mishima—the vengeful husband, for example, in Mishima's *Forbidden Colors,* who engages a beautiful young homosexual to arouse the passion and then break the hearts of the women who have betrayed and rejected him; or the Greenwich Village bullfight instructor in Mailer's "The Time of Her Time" whose furious copulations seem to be aimed at producing pleasure for his partner in the form of punishment. What distinguishes Kundera's cocksman from Mailer's or Mishima's is the ease with which his erotic power play is thwarted and then turned into yet another joke at *his* expense. He is so much more vulnerable, of course, in good part because he has been so crippled by ostracism from the Party and imprisonment in the penal corps (compare the limitless social freedom of Mailer's Americans, O'Shaugnessy and Rojack) but also because Kundera, unlike either Mailer or Mishima, seems even in a book as bleak and cheerless as *The Joke* to be fundamentally *amused* by the uses to which a man will think to put his sexual member, or the uses to which his member will put him; and this amusement, mixed though it is with sympathy and sorrow, leads Kundera away from anything even faintly resembling a mystical belief or ideological investment in the power of potency or orgasm.

In *Laughable Loves* (translated from the Czech by Suzanne Rappaport), what I have called Kundera's "amusement" with erotic enterprises and lustful strategies emerges as the mild satire of a story like **"The Golden Apple of Eternal Desire,"** wherein Don Juanism is depicted as a sport played by a man against a team of women, oftentimes without body contact. Or it emerges as a kind of detached Chekhovian tenderness in the story about the balding, thirtyish, would-have-been eroticist, who sets about to seduce an aging woman whose body he expects to find disgusting, a seduction undertaken to revenge himself upon his own stubborn phallic daydreams. Narrated alternately from the point of view of the thirty-five-year-old seducer and the fifty-year-old seduced, and with a striking air of candor that borders somehow on impropriety—as though a discreet acquaintance were suddenly letting us in on sexual secrets both seamy and true—this story, **"Let the Old Dead Make Room for the Young Dead,"** seems to me Chekhovian not merely because of its tone, or its concern with the painful and touching consequences of time passing and old selves dying, but because it is so very good.

> Kundera is an explainer, . . . everything is discussed and expounded [in *Laughable Loves*] both among the characters and by the author. One of the stories is called "Symposium", and the title could apply to most of them. They make lively reading, but something is missing if you consider them as fiction.
>
> —*Gabriele Annan, in "The Central European Lover," in* The Times Literary Supplement, *July 21, 1978*.

Finally, in **"The Hitchhiking Game,"** Kundera turns to one of those jokes he is so fond of contemplating, the ones that begin in whimsy and end in trouble. A young couple off for a vacation together decide on the way to their destination to play at being strangers, the girl pretending to be a hitchhiker, and her boyfriend just another man passing in his car. The ensuing confusion of identities, and the heightened eroticism this provokes in the lovers, with its scary sadomasochistic edge, is not so catastrophic to either of them as his joke turns out to be for Ludvík Jahn; still, simply by fooling around and indulging their curiosity, the lovers find they have managed to deepen responsibility as well as passion—as if children playing doctor out in the garage were to look up from one another's privates to discover they were administering a national health program, or were summoned to perform surgery in the Mt. Sinai operating room.

What is laughable, in Kundera's Czechoslovakia, is how grimly serious just about everything turns out to be, jokes and games and pleasure included; what is laughable is how terribly little there is to laugh at with any joy.

Paul Theroux (essay date 1974)

SOURCE: "Small Novel, Large Stories," in *The New York Times Book Review,* July 28, 1974, p. 7.

[*An American expatriate living in England, Theroux vividly captures in his fiction and travel books the experiences of displaced individuals and the cultures of exotic lands. An important motif in his work concerns the outsider who can discover his identity only in a foreign land. In the following review, Theroux argues that Kundera's stories were shaped by the political context in which they were written.*]

When he wants to annoy the cultural commissars on his occasional visits to the Soviet Union, the superb Turkish novelist Yashar Kemal—southern Anatolia's William Faulkner—says, "Well, Socialist Realism is basically anti-Marxist. . . . " It is also, in the right hands, a great recipe for comedy: The po-faced deflation in bureaucratic gibberish, the rigidity that seems designed to collapse amid howls of laughter from its own weight. Understandably, the Czechs are embarrassed by the attention shown to their deflations especially after the heroic fiasco of "the Prague Spring." And Philip Roth points out in his introduction to *Laughable Loves* how skeptical Czech writers are when a foreigner expresses interest in them, as if the predicament is more important than the work and that any outside expression of praise can only be patronizing. Roth quotes the Czech novelist Ludvik Vaculik's lament about foreign critics judging Czech writing according to how it "settles accounts with illusions about socialism."

"I would think," Roth writes, "that like Holub and Vaculik, Milan Kundera too would prefer to find a readership in the West that was not drawn to his fiction because he is a writer who is oppressed by a Communist regime. . . ." Yes, but it is as hard to ignore the origins of the comedy in Kundera's fiction as to set aside the circumstances and concentrate on the purity of diction in the poetry of Ho Chi Minh or the Bard of Peking, who writes poems when he is not killing off his opposition.

The fact is that Kundera, who is a magnificent short-story writer and a reasonably good novelist (I am going on the evidence of *Life Is Elsewhere*; Roth has a high opinion of *The Joke*), depends for his effects on the ridiculous strictures set up by a Socialist government. You have first to assume that the hacks in the Czech Government believe they have created a Socialist paradise; after that, everything they do is funny. A writer who keeps his sanity long enough to ridicule his oppressors, who has enough hope left to make this ridicule into satire, must be congratulated. And Kundera's humor is impossible elsewhere. One can't imagine his particular situations growing out of anything but a combined anger and fascination with the cut-price Stalinists who have the whip-hand in Prague, "that city," he says, "of defenestration. . . ."

The stories are bound up with politics, and even when politics is never mentioned, as in "**The Hitchhiking Game,**" it enters the story as a kind of fatigue: why else would this pair be behaving like this if it weren't for the fact that their famished imaginations are the result of political frustration? He is more specific in other stories, because his best humor always seems to be rooted in authority situations: in "**Nobody Will Laugh**" Mr. Klima is a wise-cracking victim of the art wing of the party (who want him to praise a bad article); in "**Edward and God,**" a comedy quite as good as any of Roth's, the jokes are based on official disbelief in God, and it is impossible to appreciate the complexity of the humor until one takes into account the whole attitude toward religion in a Marxist society. Only then does the wry figure of Edward, discovered blessing himself (because he wants to be a believer) become funny. . . .

Life Is Elsewhere is a small achievement next to *Laughable Loves,* the stories. Roth finds them "Chekhovian." I think he's wrong, but this is a measure of his enthusiasm, not a critical judgment, and I would be very surprised if a better collection of stories appeared this year.

Amid stern actualities, Kundera gamely concocts . . . stories about people playing games. Games—fictions, like these stories—that turn serious: between young and aging lovers, or art-historians, or a would-be lover and his fancied's God. 'Nobody will laugh'; no, because bravely laughing is, in these fictions, only to stop yourself crying.

—*Valentine Cunningham, in the* New Statesman, *June 9, 1978*.

Anatole Broyard (essay date 1974)

SOURCE: "Between the Iron Bedsheets," in *The New York Times,* Vol. CXXIII, No. 42,567, August 10, 1974, p. 27.

[*Broyard was an influential American literary critic who, during his career, contributed book reviews to the* New York Times, *served as editor of the* New York Times Book Review, *and lectured on sociology and literature at the New School for Social Research. In the following review, he finds Kundera's stories overrated and merely "passable."*]

It seems to me that dissident writers from Iron Curtain countries are generally overestimated in the United States. We praise them for their moral courage, and overlook their literary lapses. Their fiction takes on for us a tension of personal risk and political drama that obscures its mediocrity as art. We feel the anguish of the writer's position and transpose it to his work. In a simple inversion, the censor's disapproval is regarded as a guarantee of quality. There is a naive assumption that a man would not risk his career or his life to write a bad book.

If the style of the writer is pedestrian, we attribute this to the translator or to the author's using the idiomatic richness and resonant ambiguity of his native tongue so cunningly as to defy translation. Bemused by the exotic or the unfamiliar, we are like vacationers determined to enjoy a trip to a foreign country even if its only novelties are negative ones. We tell ourselves that the experience is therapeutic.

Overfond of Philosophy

Passable is the word I would use to describe most of the stories in *Laughable Loves,* by the Czech author Milan Kundera. He explains too much and, for a writer of fiction, he is overfond of philosophy. One of the virtues of fiction is its evocation of the essential *mystery* of life, and philosophizing can only muddle this. It also pushes the writer's style toward the pontifical, resulting in sentences like this one: "Our story does not intend to be crowned with effect of so ostentatious a paradox."

"**The Hitchhiking Game**" is an interesting gift in a poorly wrapped parcel. During their vacation, a young man and his girl friend playfully assume the roles of a driver and a casual pickup. The girl has always been inhibited and her lover has tended to idealize her innocence at the expense of her sensuality. When they find themselves "liberated" by their game, it is exciting. They are reluctant to relinquish it, and gradually the game becomes an obsession. They feel that they are experiencing each other in a purely physical sense for the first time and their lovemaking is intense—so intense that it strikes the girl as a threat to her identity. "I am me, I am me, I am me . . ." she sobs afterwards, and her lover, infuriated by her betrayal of herself, retrospectively shocked with the typical priggishness of the possessive, blames her for his disillusionment.

"**Let the Old Dead Make Room for the Young Dead,**" was Mr. Kundera's best story, but for all its good moments, it has a clumsiness as art that reminds one of the clothing men wear in his country: the square cut, padded jackets with overlong sleeves, the shapeless trousers that deny the human form inside them. The story deals with a 35-year-old man who fears that the "balance sheet" of his life shows a deficit. He has experienced almost nothing, especially in the case of women, who suddenly become for him "the one legitimate criterion of life's *density.*"

When he re-encounters a woman with whom he spent one night some 15 years ago, he mourns the fact that, at the time, "she defied his imagination" and he could not assimilate her. Now she has returned to Prague, where he lives, to visit the grave of her husband, for she cherishes the "memorials" of her life as much as he regrets the fleeting emptiness of his. Though she is 50 now, he is determined to reach again for the essence that eluded him, while she weighs the security of her memorials against the throb of the present. For both of them, the reunion turns out to be an embracing not only of each other but also of life itself.

"**Nobody Will Laugh**" is supposed to be a satirical portrait of Czechoslovkia's intellectual bureaucracy, but it is such a tangle of silly improbabilities and its central character is so stunningly uninteresting that the party hacks and bureaucrats become heroes by default.

"**The Golden Apple of Eternal Desire**" is about compulsive girl-chasing, a theme that ought to have reached retirement age even in Czechoslovakia, where the difference in cultures has not succeeded in giving it a fresh turn. Mr. Kundera tried to romanticize his jaded characters with a platonic notion of "absolute pursuit" that transcends even consummation, but nothing can redeem the puerility of two men who collect girls' addresses as small boys collect baseball cards.

Sexual Behavior Is Focus

"**Symposium**" and "**Doctor Havel After Ten Years**" are both set pieces, mere vehicles for some unremarkable aphorisms about sexual behavior. Occasionally, "**Symposium**" rises to a certain stodgy sublimity, but both stories are little more than pseudo-sophisticated psychologizing, thinly disguised as fiction. In sexual decadence, the Czechs cannot compete with the government-encouraged strides of democratic societies.

"**Edward and God**" is one of those stories that sound better in summation. Edward is a young teacher whose job is jeopardized by the fact that he has been seen in church and that this is "improper" behavior in the eyes of his officially atheistic superiors. Edward goes to church, however, only in order to seduce the devout Alice. In a switch reminiscent of Mack Sennett or the Marx Brothers, he ends by rejecting Alice and becoming the lover of the haglike directress of his school.

This might be amusing if Edward were not so humorless himself. In fact, this is one of the failures of most of Mr. Kundera's characters: they don't react to themselves reacting, in that luxury of consciousness that modern fiction usually enjoys. They seem to be cramped somewhere between fatalism and literal-mindednss, as if they had forgotten, under pressure, the immense range of human possibility.

Robert C. Porter (essay date 1975)

SOURCE: "'Freedom Is My Love': The Works of Milan Kundera," in *Index on Censorship,* Vol. 4, No. 4, Winter, 1975, pp. 41-6.

[*The author of* Milan Kundera: A Voice from Central Europe *(1981), Porter is an English educator specializing in Russian literature. In the following excerpt, Porter discerns an overarching pattern in the stories of* Laughable Loves.]

Between 1963 and 1968 Kundera produced ten short love stories, which depict the comic as well as the tragic side of human relations. In 1970 eight of them appeared in a collected edition, the author having decided to omit two which he had come to regard as weak. Examining the original ten stories we find in them a philosophical progression which is taken up and developed in the novels.

The ambiguity of individual identity is a major theme in [*Laughable Loves*]. The players of amorous games slip into roles with great ease; one Pirandellian disguise follows another, and we are again subtly reminded that a society that has produced millions of "instant" Communists actually encourages pretense and hypocrisy.

—Ivan Sanders, in the New Republic, *September 7, 1974.*

An article by Milan Blahynka (*Plamen* no. I, 1967) discusses at length the first two volumes and discovers in them a system of theses and antitheses; the first three stories are concerned with a hero, frustrated in love and forced to deceive others. A young man is in love with a beautiful singer who refuses to requite his love, so he has a friend pose as an impresario, the fake impresario falls in love with her, but cannot reveal his true identity or his love, and the hero remains frustrated—the girl he loves has lost her heart to a man who does not exist. The second story involves a young composer pouring out his heart into a piece of music for the girl he loves; but she finds the composition false and insincere, not knowing that she is the inspiration for it. To compound the irony, her husband writes poetry which the musician finds false and insincere, but she and her husband actually write it between them. The third story concerns a young university lecturer in Prague. The young man is badgered by the author of a worthless publication to write a review of it. But the lecturer is reluctant to do so because he feels the work is so bad—and yet he lacks the moral courage to tell the man so. Anyway, he has suffered at the hands of publishers himself. Finally, to get rid of the persistent author he accuses him of making sexual advances to his girlfriend. This merely brings the author's strong-willed and indignant wife into the action. The result is that the young lecturer loses his job, his flat and his girlfriend.

In each story the love is sincere and yet it is either doomed from the start, or becomes more hopeless by the heroes' attempts to deceive others, to control their lives and thus to enhance their own happiness. In the first story, **'I, a mournful god'**, the hero/narrator actually tells us:

I don't write, I *live,* and speaking frankly, I despise authors of events on paper, I despise them for the sweaty describers of life they are. On the other hand, I venerate authors of events lived in life—I count myself amongst these. There are two kinds of people in life: authors of life and puppets of life.

This sums up the thesis of the first three stories. All three heroes try to be authors of life and are hoist with their own petard.

In the second volume we have an antithesis. In these three stories the heroes are more or less satisfied in love, or in their love adventures, but insist on tampering with the emotion. The best of these stories has appeared in English under the title **'A game of make-believe'** (*New Writing in Czechoslovakia,* Penguin 1969). A young couple are on a motoring holiday, alone together for the first time. The girl pretends to be a hitch-hiker, the man picks her up and readily falls into the role of lecherous motorist. The game escalates and results in the girl acting the part of a whore and becoming completely divorced from her former self:

The girl's sobs soon turned into crying out loud, and she kept repeating that pitiful tautology countless times: 'I am me, I am me, I am me . . . '

The young man had to summon sympathy to his aid (he had to summon it from a long way off, for there was none near by), to try and quiet the girl. They still had thirteen days of their holiday left.

If the first volume of stories shows the authors of other people's lives failing, their conceit getting its just deserts, volume two shows that people are not even the authors of their own lives, for even when all is going well between two human beings a new dimension may suddenly emerge, a game may become too real, a joke become a tragedy.

The third volume, however, presents us with a synthesis. Man, unable to control others' lives, and then unable to control his own, must come to terms with the world and with what freedom he has. There were originally four stories in this volume: **'Let the old dead make way for the young dead'**, **'Symposium'**, **'Edward and God'** and **'Doctor Havel ten years later'**. Each of these stories involves people making their peace with the contradictions in human relationships. They may well discover new elements in themselves and others; they may well decide that complete happiness and requited love are illusions; they may realise the limitations on their own freedom; and yet there is, at the end of the day, a feeling of contentment and assurance which is sought after in vain in the two earlier volumes.

The title **'Symposium'** has its original meaning here— 'drinking together'. In a provincial hospital a group of doctors and nurses are on night duty, drinking and discussing women. Doctor Havel is a notorious womaniser. We see in this character an example of contentment and perhaps resignation in the face of paradox and even defeat: Havel tells us that his greatest success with women concerned his being rejected once by a girl who usually slept with anybody—obviously, he argues, he must have been something special for her! One character, Elizabeth, nearly gases herself and we do not know if it is accidental, or a genuine suicide attempt. Several theories are advanced, but no one truth emerges. Certainly, she was keen to seduce Havel and failed—as he says himself—'I refused Elizabeth precisely because I don't know how to be free. Not sleeping with Elizabeth is in fashion.'

The main event in the story is tragic—someone nearly dies: and yet from this all the characters derive a certain satisfaction. Flejšman is happy in his belief that Elizabeth attempted to take her life for love of him; Elizabeth herself gains precisely the romantic kudos she lacked at the beginning of the story. And yet true motives are not revealed and in emotional terms, the characters resolve very little. Significantly, the last chapter is entitled (in English) 'Happy End'.

'Edward and God' concerns a young teacher who starts going to church in order to impress and ultimately seduce his devout girlfriend. He gets into trouble at school for going to church, his girlfriend hears of his persecution and bestows her favours on him as a reward for his faith. Edward suffers from pangs of conscience, returns to church, the face of God appears before him and: 'Look! Yes! Edward is smiling. He is smiling and his smile is a happy one . . . ' Again the contradictions that beset human relationships are faced up to and the result, if not happiness, is at least contentment.

[*Laughable Loves* is] a book of stories which are funny, erotic, playful, charged with wisdom and melancholy, worthy to bear real comparison with Chekov. Kundera is masterful and out of his own darkness he brings such delight and such subtle appreciation of life that you forget the context—as I'd guess he would want you to—and pay attention only to the quality of these stories.

—*Melvyn Bragg, in* Punch, *July 12, 1978*.

The final synthesis in this cycle of short stories is emphasised by the presentation of the 1970 edition. Two of the weaker stories were omitted—one from volume one and one from volume two; one of the stories from volume two was shifted to volume one and one from volume three to volume two. This rearrangement would seem to strengthen the thesis (deception) in volume one, the antithesis (self-deception) in volume two and the synthesis in volume three.

The final synthesis is realised by the increasing sophistication of humorous devices throughout the stories. The comic element in the earlier stories is, on the whole, based on irony, especially ironic incidents of the characters' own making—quite simply, things done in spite never turn out right. The result is to alienate the characters one from the other whilst at the same time allowing

the reader to sympathise with and understand all. In 'Symposium' a fuller range of comic devices is brought into play—bathos, bawdry, puns, and more especially, 'comic visuality'. The story is broken up into 36 very short chapters bearing titles apparently plagiarised from the silent film e.g. 'A call for help', 'The doctor's theory', 'The uncertainty of all things', 'Happy end'. The overall effect is to speed up the action and make it seem 'jerky', yet the events of the story are all perfectly rational and even everyday. There is no embroidery and no hint of the grotesque.

Roger Rosenblatt (essay date 1975)

SOURCE: "The Only Game in Town," in *The New Republic,* Vol. 173, No. 10, Issue 3165, September 6, 1975, pp. 29-30.

[*An award-winning journalist, Rosenblatt has been a columnist and editor for the* New Republic *and the* Washington Post *and has served as a senior writer for two major national news magazines,* Time *and* U.S. News and World Report. *In the following review, he maintains that the attempts of characters in* Laughable Loves *to assert themselves results paradoxically in confusion and unhappiness.*]

The downfall of the university lecturer in Milan Kundera's **"Nobody Will Laugh"** occurs because our young hero is feeling good enough to tell white lies and crack small jokes. Celebrating the acceptance of an article in a learned journal, he deludes an admiring scholar into believing that the admirer's own (crackpot) work is worthy of publication. The admirer beseeches and pursues our hero who lies and kids some more in a De Quincey-like progression, eventually involving his girlfriend, the admirer's wife, his university department and the local government in his practical jokes. When all pranks have been played and laid out, the lecturer is without girlfriend, promotion, job, civic standing or scholarly reputation, though he partly comforts himself by observing that his story has been "of the comic variety."

All seven stories in Kundera's *Laughable Loves* are "of the comic variety," bearing the same categorical stillness of the lecturer's observation. Comedy and love are the bright-colored filters through which we watch various characters move toward and away from each other; but here the filters overlap, diminishing their own brightnesses and darkening the objects under glass. Love sobers comedy; comedy troubles love. People, of course, prevail, usually making the worst of their possibilities. "The truth is that they aren't *our* stories at all," protests the hero of **"Nobody Will Laugh,"** "that they are foisted on us from somewhere outside." But the stories are indeed their own, they the comic-dangerous, stumbling about like drunks on a boat.

For Kundera massive confusion is the essential human state, the only circumstance where things are clear. Stalinism was more dangerous than fascism, he told Antonin Liehm in *The Politics of Culture* because "it began as the advocate and gradually converted it into the opposite: love of humanity into cruelty, love of truth into denunciation, and so on." Under such a regime uncertainty and flux become standards of survival and excellence; and if there is no sense of humor permitted, the sense of paradox is undeniable. But paradox to the core: reconciliations formed in the objective eye, and not always in the eye of the beholder. In **"The Hitchhiking Game"** in which a girl plays tramp for her boyfriend in order to test herself and please him, the boyfriend recoils at the lascivious mask on the face of his beloved: "These two images showing through each other were telling him that *everything* was in the girl, that her soul was terrifyingly amorphous, that it held faithfulness and unfaithfulness, treachery and innocence, flirtatiousness and chastity."

Like the lecturer's pranks, this game of pretence is no game. The boyfriend is disgusted by the disorder he finds, disgust both natural and stupid. He wants order like the mad vet in Ralph Ellison's *Invisible Man,* and the order he wants—plain girl, plain style, predictable action, domestic tranquility—this is the order of real confusion (and the basis of comedy, as Henri Bergson proved). Part of the paradox himself, the boyfriend, logically, does not approve of paradox. Fun's fun, but not when you lose your perspective.

Of course the loss of perspective is what Kundera wishes for us—at least the loss of a perspective that protects us from one out of our smug control. We say that perspective allows self-mockery, but as Kundera demonstrates, there is a great mocking universe, wider than the grin is wide, in which all jokers become part of all jokes. This universe, that piles paradox on paradox, is no laughing matter. It is the heart of seriousness, the essential frame of reference walled by mirrors, where most of Kundera's characters wind up neither laughing nor loving.

This is where Edward of **"Edward and God"** winds up, longing for God, "for God alone is relieved of the distracting obligation of *appearing* and can merely *be*. For He solely constitutes (He Himself, alone and nonexistent) the essential opposite of this unessential (but so much more existent) world." Early in the story Edward tries to woo the virgin Alice to bed, but Alice says no, leaning on piety. When Edward finally succeeds (because Alice is attracted to his feigned holy living), he discovers that Alice's allure was her faith; hypocrite to the hilt, he rejects her for commandment breaking, and then, naturally, regrets his rejection. In the end Edward does not believe in God, but very much believes in the ideal of the essential. After the last laugh (on him), he wants to take things seriously.

Kundera's happier people (Dr. Havel of **"Symposium"** and **"Dr. Havel After Ten Years"** and the two gallants of **"The Golden Apple of Eternal Desire"**) never quite reach the last laugh. Something in their make-ups, akin to art, keeps them from pursuing the jokes they make and the

jokes they are down to logical consequence. These people are artists of the beautiful, in Hawthorne's sense, making art of love, of erotic love in particular ("It is an art," Dr. Havel tells his apprentice) and art of comedy. Holding both love and laughter in perpetual abeyance, they live lightly but well: examples and perpetrators of the grand confusion Kundera celebrates. They have stamina, the salient gift of lovers and comedians.

As for the others, they fall precisely because they strive to reach conclusions: to make professor, or a girl; to find and inhabit one solid state of happiness. Our young lecturer of **"Nobody Will Laugh"** is a great kidder, a master of disguises. He tells his Klara that all his hoaxes were not lies but ways of making the truth palatable, which is so. Yet the strategy was devised by a man on the make, whose essential truth lay in his believing that words could control destiny. He too wants order, and so, satisfying the universal paradox, eventually finds himself not only out of order, the order he sought to conquer, but unaware of his ostracism.

What people see with their eyes, as opposed to what they dream to see, is Kundera's way of opposing paradoxically awareness and unawareness, youth and age, ignorance and knowledge, foolishness and wisdom—and perhaps central to the world of games, winners and losers. Alice insists that the room be pitch black when she and Edward make love, so Edward's fantasies of her body remain intact. In **"Let the Old Dead Make Room for the Young Dead"** the young man recollects his one-night affair with a woman he coveted for months; she too kept the room dark, and it seemed to him that he was making love "with someone spurious or else someone quite unreal and unindividuated." In both stories darkness keeps bright "the golden apple of eternal desire," but here the brightness has a sad tint. Where all is in the dream, nothing is realized except disappointment; people only see clearly that which repulses them.

Meanwhile the survivors keep their innocence, which in Kundera's terms means nominal experience. They are "experienced" love-makers—that is all they care to do— stay young making love, or grow old and fat making love; and for all their brief encounters and pick-ups remain joyously at ease with the comedy they perform. But who is to laugh at them? If these loves are laughable, which ones are not? Kundera chose love to propel his confused people because love makes a world where there is no escape from clichés.

"There is no escape from a game" either, says Kundera, which is sort of a cliché too. Clichés, after all, are things too true that we consider false; another paradox. *Laughable Loves* is a cliché itself: a planned piece of literature starting with the small titter of the hitchhiking game and working up to God as belly laugh. Needless to tell, **"The Golden Apple"** falls in the middle—a cliché of structure. But nothing to fret about or try to solve. What counts, as Kundera shows us, is tenderness, as usual; that and the resolute nonsense of our need for love.

C. L. Chua (essay date 1975)

SOURCE: A review of *Laughable Loves,* in *Studies in Short Fiction,* Vol. XII, No. 4, Fall, 1975, pp. 419-21.

[*In the following positive review, Chua surveys some of the themes in* Laughable Loves.]

[*Laughable Loves*] is a decidedly provocative and worthwhile volume of short stories; they challenge our imagination and exercise our intellect. These stories first appeared in their native Czechoslovakia in 1969, and American readers might have caught glimpses of them in *American Poetry Review* or *Esquire*. Here they are in a highly readable translation by Suzanne Rappaport, chaperoned by a substantial and sympathetic introduction from Philip Roth.

The title of the anthology (**Smesne Lasky** in Czech) is aptly descriptive. Kundera's laughs, however, are remote from *Playboy's* party ribaldry. Certainly his humor does stem from sexual foibles, and his stories do deal with bed manners in contemporary Czechoslovakia. However, sexuality for Kundera is as existentially important as it is for Mailer; but where Mailer's sexual heroes tend to be clad in angst, Kundera tricks his lovers up in an ironic wit reminiscent of Maupassant. Further, Kundera's erotic gamesmanship, rather like Benjamin Constant's, deals in themes of identity and illusion to which he adds some deft Pirandellesque touches; moreover his symbolism moves persistently towards social commentary. Such comparisons, however, are invidious. The quality of Kundera is nothing if not original.

The first story, **"The Hitchhiking Game,"** shows us a rather conventional young couple who playfully take on pretended romantic roles. She becomes a hitchiker; he picks her up. As they improvise their *commedia dell'arte,* the roles begin to invade the reality of the actors (one recalls Kundera's connections with the Prague Film School); the unnamed man and woman discover unexpected erotic identities in themselves which build up to the moment of climax. When the woman wishes to end the game and recover her "real" identity, piteously crying "I am me, I am me," they find that reverting to their so-called natural and real selves necessitates an artificial and pre-planned effort—a kind of role playing.

Underlying this psychologically intricate episode, one senses an undercurrent of social allegory. Imagistically, the young man's life is a "road . . . drawn with immaculate precision." Although he drives a sports car, "the terrible thought of the straight road would overcome him." To play the hitchhiking game is to detour off this road mapped out for him by his society, and he finds a spontaneity at once irresistibly tempting and dangerously anomic.

But perhaps Kundera's most politically allegorical story is **"The Golden Apple of Eternal Desire."** The story is deceptively lightweight at first glance. Martin, its protagonist, is a happily married man who persists in chasing every skirt in sight. In the course of the story, his friend the narrator comes to perceive that Martin is a sort of harmless mythomaniac about his amours and realizes that Martin's pursuit of women is a necessity for his sense of self, an activity by which he gains an identity through participation in an archetypal endeavor. But this banal erotic comedy is laced with a rather grim political allegory. In his description of the sexual chase, the narrator uses an odd terminology. When they obtain a girl's phone and address, they call it a "registration." A date is a "contact," after which matters may proceed to the consummately desirable "arrest." The analogy between the sexual chase and the police state emerges. ("Alibi," "heretic," "apostate" are some of the other terms that develop this parallel.) And the implied critique of the police state is clear. Like Martin, the police state has to pursue some quarry to obtain a sense of identity; if there is no quarry, one must be invented to justify the pursuer's existence. Kundera's allegory points up the hollowness of a police state which must resort to inventing crimes and criminals to maintain its sense of potency. Many police states, like Martin's compulsive amours, are redundant and illusory. Martin *is* happily married; Czechoslovakia (or Chile) *is* capable of prosperity and populist government.

"Let the Old Dead Make Room for the Young Dead" describes the re-encounter of a 35-year-old man and a 50-year-old woman who had made love to each other fifteen years ago. Here Kundera touches on the theme of time with an irony reminiscent of Resnais; and after some painfully protracted foreplay, the lovemaking that eventuates savors of the unwholesome and the necrophilic. **"Nobody Will Laugh"** presents us with a Slavonic Lucky Jim and shows us that fancy and imaginativeness are impossible in Czech academia. (Depending on one's own experience, one may wish to conclude that Amis' Merrie England is less or more truthful a locale that Kundera's Czechoslovakia.) Only its irony and its remarkably humane point of view avert the tragic emotions and turn this story towards wry comedy.

"Symposium" parodies Plato's matter and method and introduces a Dr. Havel, the most Don Juanish of Kundera's lovers. Following upon that, **"Dr. Havel After Ten Years"** is a *jeu d'esprit* erected upon an aging Don Juan and poses the conundrum that sensuality is more of the mind than the flesh, that a Don Juan's legend will metamorphose his ugliness into beauties, his corpulence into comeliness.

The last story of the book, **"Edward and God,"** is a complex and teasingly ambiguous tale about a young atheist teacher who pretends to be religious to gain his girl friend's favors. His public display of Christianity, however, gets him into trouble with his female superintendent. As a tactic of self-preservation, Edward has to continue to play the role of a Christian on the brink of apostasy. He is then compelled to seduce his repulsive superintendent and only manages it when her incantation of the Lord's Prayer manages to overcome an untimely flaccidity on his part. As we may expect, Kundera ends his story on an enigma (and an epiphany) in which a thoroughly defeated and steadfastly infidel Edward oddly does find God and transforms his sorrow into joy.

In sum, these seven stories are uncommonly good. Characterization is solid, psychology subtle, situations and plots as simple or complex as the desired effect requires. Admittedly, Kundera's canvas is not large. His protagonists are almost exclusively drawn from a sensuous layer of intelligentsia, a white-collar fringe of socialist society. They are philandering bureaucrats, perky academics, bibulous doctors, jobless teachers. They share the common trait of imaginativeness in their approach to eros. They love in an all-too-familiar world of modern monolithic, where spontaneity and originality are impermissible, and where creativity can only flourish by subterfuge. No wonder, then, that Kundera has attracted significant notice in France where his novel, *Life is Elsewhere,* won the Prix de Medicis and where both Sartre and Aragon may praise him.

D. J. Enright (essay date 1978)

SOURCE: "Ping-pong," in *The Listener,* Vol. 99, No. 2563, June 8, 1978, p. 746.

[*An English poet, novelist, and critic, Enright is sometimes associated with a group of authors—Kingsley Amis, John Wain, Philip Larkin, Robert Conquest, and Elizabeth Jennings—whose concerted dissent from tradition earned them the informal moniker The Movement. Well known as a literary critic, Enright's reviews have appeared in the* New Statesman, Encounter, *and* London Magazine. *In the following review, he focuses on Kundera's depiction of deceit and manipulation in relationships.*]

Generically, these stories form another set of Games that People Play, better done than most—though possibly in this sphere the better is still the enemy of the good. Milan Kundera's characters are conscious of what they are doing—it would hardly be a game if they were not—but this doesn't prevent them from doing it. Thus a contemporary Don Juan points out that contemporary Don Juans no longer *conquer* but only *collect:* they are not tragic since they cannot 'sin' and be damned, and things are made rather easy for them. Eroticism has become 'like breakfasts and dinners, like stamp-collecting and ping-pong, if not like a ride on the streetcar or shopping'. This makes the characters, for all their industrious ingenuity, one-dimensional in a special sense.

Dr Havel, quoted above, figures in two of the strongest stories here, and is a master stamp-collector, a connoisseur of woman-flesh—to which one must add that woman-soul does come into it, as a sort of tertiary sexual characteristic. These stories are funny, in a bleakish way, because the best-laid schemes can go agley: when a lot of people are playing, not everybody wins all the time—and even one's primary sexual characteristic may let one down on occasion. Otherwise the stories would amount to no more than a dreary male-chauvinist manifesto (manifesto: another word that will have to go), for while the females here are also players in the game, they are relatively docile, passive, scarcely made of such stern stuff as Donna Anna, let alone Clarissa Harlowe. Which, I suspect, is the burden of the author's not wholly concealed complaint.

From this book, as from Kundera's recent novel, *The Farewell Party,* the reader might receive a fairly reassuring picture of life behind the Iron Curtain as consisting largely of sex and spas. But an edge is given by glimpses of something else: the state, which has taken over some of the functions of God, notably damnation—though Kundera, himself now living in France, chooses not to make much of this, perhaps (as Philip Roth hints in his introduction) because he wants to be read as a writer rather than a victim of a régime. So maybe you don't go to hell, or even Siberia, but you can be rusticated, like the young Czech in **'Edward and God'**, an expertly turned story, who is so amused by the sight of a fellow-student in an attitude of histrionic grief that he roars with laughter at her. Stalin had died the day before, an event which the youth slept through unknowingly. He is denounced, expelled from the university and sent to work in a village. (This is reminiscent of the joke in *The Joke,* Kundera's celebrated first novel, where the hero's career is ruined by a flippant postcard he sends his earnest girlfriend: 'Optimism is the opium of the people!'). Tragedy, though not a desire for revenge, is averted: 'As a farmer I earn more, and contact with Nature protects me from the scepticism to which city-dwellers are prone.'

Similarly, in **'Nobody Will Laugh'**, a harmless white lie leads through self-pleased stratagems to an increasingly tangled web of trivial deceit, and then to political disgrace: circumstantial evidence suddenly swells into 'a totality of significant testimony about your character and attitude'. Again, the hero is in no danger of damnation, he only loses his girl and his job: 'my story was not of the tragic sort, but rather of the comic variety.'

'It's quite marvellous the way you are able to turn water into wine,' a woman doctor tells the chief physician whose current mistress she is. He has at some length (the story is called **'Symposium'**) explained why he was rejected by a girl who had slept with everybody else on the premises, including the undertaker: she 'honoured' him by choosing him to reject, and this he considers his greatest erotic triumph. When sex gets too easy, you have to tart it up with mental gymnastics. And what Kundera is doing, no doubt adeptly, is turning wine into water. We may think he looks very much like a disappointed idealist. One of hell's minor furies is the person whose high expectations have been casually scorned. The question is, can you hope to drive out trivialisation or even dent it by being, however sophisticatedly, trivial yourself?

Mark Sturdivant (essay date 1985)

SOURCE: "Milan Kundera's Use of Sexuality," in *Critique,* Vol. XXVI, No. 3, Spring, 1985, pp. 131-40.

[*In the following essay, Sturdivant suggests that Kundera uses sexuality as a means of expressing the futility and desperation of life.*]

In examining the work of Czechoslavakian author Milan Kundera, critic Philip Roth observes that "almost all [Kundera's] novels, in fact all the individual parts of his latest book, find their dénouement in great scenes of coitus" (afterword, *The Book of Laughter and Forgetting*.) Indeed, in Kundera's most recent effort, *The Book of Laughter and Forgetting,* the novelist follows a pattern earlier established in his highly acclaimed novel *The Joke* and his collection of short stories *Laughable Loves* by depicting sexuality as "the focus where all the themes of the story converge and where its deepest secrets are located." Kundera views sexuality and eroticism as "the deepest region of life" and therefore feels that the question of mankind's *raison d'être,* when "posed to sexuality, is the deepest question." In the expression of this belief in his three aforementioned [books], sexuality becomes a vehicle for expressing a variety of interwoven threads of commentary upon human characteristics, and for ultimately casting a pall of hopelessness and meaninglessness over mankind's fundamental existence.

Perhaps the most obvious role of sexuality in the portrayal of man involves the presentation of the characters' innermost concerns and desires, as sensed by the omniscient narrator, in scenes either during or intimately related to the sexual act. A clear example of this device, one which explores what might be termed "the sexual mentality" rather than the act of intercourse itself, arises in the story **"Symposium"** in *Laughable Loves*. In accordance with the chief physician's statement that "in eroticism we seek the image of our own significance and importance," Nurse Alzhbeta, a woman with "a hideous face but a beautiful body," protests against what she considers the "sheer absurdity and injustice" of her physical fate by performing a mock striptease. Her frustration and agony increase as a doctor to whom she "brazenly [makes] advances" harshly rejects her, causing her striptease to become increasingly blatant; this progression expresses the character's emotions via a sexually related action. . . .

Perhaps Kundera's most straight-forward presentation of this inability to establish psychological and physical unity occurs in the opening short story of *Laughable Loves,* **"The Hitchiking Game."** In this story, the young, unnamed female initially believes that her boyfriend "never [separates] her body from her soul" and that "she [can] live with him wholly." However, Kundera suggests the implausibility of such an attitude in a game which the couple choose to play: through changing identities, and fueled by mutual possessive jealousy and relentlessly heightening eroticism, the two characters' thoughts and actions offer another example of the author's viewpoint expressed via sex-dominated circumstances. To her boyfriend, the girl grows more attractive physically as she "[withdraws] from him psychically"; for as he muses that the illusion of her co-existing goodness and beauty which "he worshipped" is "real only within the bounds of fidelity and purity" and that "beyond these bounds she [ceases] to be herself," the young man realizes that "the girl he loved was a creation of his desire, his thoughts, and his faith and that the real girl now standing in front of him [is] hopelessly alien, hopelessly ambiguous." As "the game [merg-

---

es] with life," the two characters—the girl a prostitute, the boy her client—plunge into frenzied intercourse in which "there [are] soon two bodies in perfect harmony, two sensual bodies, alien to each other." This sexual act causes the girl to acknowledge her irreversible mind/body duality as she, feeling "horror at the thought," realizes that "she [has] never known such pleasure" as that which she experiences beyond the "forbidden boundary" of "love-making without emotion or love.". . .

Although *The Joke* may carry a more fervent political statement than *Laughable Loves,* the final story of the latter book—**"Edward and God"**—seems to present the author's thesis on human existence in its most forcefully despairing form. Thus, this second example of the third prong of the author's approach serves as both an ultimate declaration and as an exemplary fusion of the earlier two prongs toward the final destination of Kundera's thesis. In this tale, a lighthearted outlook on sexuality—an approach which might be expected from a book entitled *Laughable Loves*—dominates the beginning of the story as Edward, the protagonist, feigns piety and religious conviction in hopes of establishing sexual relations with the beautiful yet "very reserved and virtuous" Alice. Circumstances favor Edward as party members persecute him for his "religious beliefs," causing Alice in admiration to become "warm, and passionate" and agreeing to prove her affection for Edward by visiting his brother's cottage, "where they could be alone." At this point, the reader, probably awaiting the "Fall of Edward," is not disappointed; however, the use of Edward's long-sought sexual encounter with Alice as the actual catalyst for this decline serves to magnify the extent of his misery and to accurately demonstrate the true magnitude of meaninglessness with which Kundera associates the human condition. Edward indeed meets success in his sexual endeavors, yet, as he realizes, "Alice's unexpected turnabout had occurred independently . . . of his argumentation . . . of any logical consideration whatsoever." Representative of Kundera's belief in the farcical nature of human events, the fulfillment of Edward's consummate desire rests "upon a mistake," and Alice's change of heart had "been deduced quite illogically even from this mistake." Furthermore, representative of Kundera's practice of revealing his characters' most fundamental beliefs in scenes of coitus or some other sexually related situation, Edward is haunted by thoughts of "those long, futile weeks when Alice had tormented him with her coldness" in that Edward now is irritated by "how easily and remorselessly she [is] now betraying her God of No Fornication." Kundera's emphasis on an inescapable mind/body duality, accompanied by an inability to achieve satisfaction in either state, again emerges as Edward realizes that he much favors the "old" Alice, whose "beautiful simplicity of her looks seemed to accord with the unaffected simplicity of her faith, and [whose] simple faith seemed to be a substantiation of her attitude" however, he now "[feels] no joy at all" upon viewing her as "an accidental conjunction of a body, thoughts, and a life's course." Therefore, in an episode marked by demonstration of the fluid and cyclic characteristics of Kundera's overall analysis through sexuality, Edward masters his newly-acquired outlook—using "the words 'disgust' and 'physical aversion'" to attack his lover—by sending Alice home on the train.

The thoughtful reader now may recognize the abnormal (for a Kundera character) degree of control which Edward yields, a characteristic seemingly in direct opposition to the author's attempt to present human existence as farcical, meaningless, and hopelessly uncontrollable. However, Edward's dominance over the course of Alice's departure proves quite misleading: earlier in the story, Edward receives harsh admonitions from the Communist Party Organization in his town but manages to avoid serious disciplinary action through clever lies, which indicate his self-declared failure to "take them seriously." However, the very depth of knowledge which distinguishes Edward from most Kundera characters creates a new degree of meaninglessness and hopeless relegation to life without control, for not only is his existence plagued by these factors, he realizes and understands that "the shadow that mocks remains a shadow, subordinate, derivative, and wretched, and nothing more." Kundera seems to demand "What else can knowledge accomplish?" as Edward realizes that "what [has] happened, [has] happened, and it [is] no longer possible to right anything."

An ideal conclusion—yet Kundera apparently feels that additional "circumstantial evidence" will better hammer home his thesis. Therefore, after depicting Edward as reasonably content with his routine of sex with the directress of the Communist Party Organization (yes, yet another twist in plot) and of solitary walks, Kundera uses parenthesis to imply direct author–reader contact as he invites the reader to join him in viewing Edward visiting the local church. This final scene in *Laughable Loves,* involving Edward while sitting in the quiet sanctuary suddenly smiling a broad smile in the midst of his sorrow, might be interpreted three ways. However, two of the possible interpretations are apparently refuted by evidence given in context, leaving the third as the plausible, forceful, and rightful conclusive analysis of Kundera's evaluation of human existence. And as in his oth-

er works, the author's conclusive statement evolves from thoughts and actions based on sex-related relationships. The first of the possible renditions holds that Edward indeed sees "the genuine living face of God" and thus smiles in rapture. However, Kundera earlier insists that "Edward did not believe in God" and assures the reader that "our story does not intend to be crowned with the effect of so ostentatious a paradox"; these inserts, coupled with another author-to-reader statement in parenthesis describing God as "alone and nonexistent," severely damage the credibility of this first interpretation.

Secondly, upon recalling Kundera's penchant for surprise and his belief in man's inability to clearly judge events affecting his life, the reader might interpret the author's purpose for the final scene as "the last word" concerning Edward's lack of true judgment as he is ultimately deceived into a belief in God. Once again, however, the arguments refuting the first explanation are applicable in this case, and seem to overpower additional opposing suggestions such as the possibility of Kundera's description of God as "nonexistent" being more accurately analyzed as the author's depiction of God as a spirit rather than a member of "this unessential (but so much more existent) world."

This leaves only a third evaluation, a stance supported both by the intricacies of the final scene as well as by the story, and its foundation of use of sexuality, as a whole. This final interpretation holds that Edward, in his tragic awareness, realizes the full magnitude of the hopelessly farcical and meaningless connotations of human existence and crosses The Border [described by Kundera as "a certain imaginary dividing line beyond which things appear senseless and ridiculous"] as he smiles a smile not of "imitation laughter" but of "original (the Devil's)" laughter (*The Book of Laughter and Forgetting*), the laughter of hopeless despair. Supporting this explication of the last page of **"Edward and God"** and of *Laughable Loves,* the portrayal of Edward as cognizant of man's position continues as he is "too bright to concede that he [sees] the essential in the unessential." But he nonetheless longs "for God . . . the essential opposite of this unessential . . . world," for he is "too weak not to long secretly" for a means of removing his burden of knowledge and subsequent sorrow, which has developed via his various sexual encounters. Despite this hope, he soon recognizes that which Kundera has earlier told the reader—that God is nonexistent—and the depth of his and mankind's ignominious fate is mirrored in the terrible irony of the narrator describing this revelation as the emergence of "the genuine living face of God." The narrator, whose view now lacks the tone of intimacy earlier described in Kundera's comments in parenthesis, sadly misinterprets Edward's smile as "happy"; a more accurate approach, signified by a sense that Kundera inserts his comments since it does not smoothly follow from the previous statement (Edward as "too weak not to long secretly for the essential"), emerges in the thought that "a man lives a sad life when he cannot take anything or anyone seriously."

Kundera needlessly urges the reader to "keep him (Edward) in your memory with this smile."

Maria Němcová Banerjee (essay date 1990)

SOURCE: "*Laughable Loves;* or, The Impossible Don Juan," in *Terminal Paradox: The Novels of Milan Kundera,* Grove Weidenfeld, 1990, pp. 52-73.

[*In the following essay, Banerjee contrasts Kundera's portrayal of the Don Juan myth with traditional versions.*]

Laughable Loves was the first of Milan Kundera's works to reach American readers. It was published in New York in 1974, with an introduction by Philip Roth, while its author was still living in Czechoslovakia. But all seven stories that make up the volume were written much earlier, between 1959 and 1969, during that marvelous decade of Czech culture which was also a time of great artistic ferment for Kundera. Originally, the title *Směšné lásky* (*Laughable Loves*) linked a series of ten short stories issued in three separate "notebooks," the last of which saw print in 1969, during the final gasp of Czech literary freedom. In the definitive form achieved after several authorial interventions, stripped down to seven entries rearranged in a sequence that highlights the emotional counterpoint between laughter and pathos, *Laughable Loves* prefigures the structural archetype of Kundera's later, elliptical novels.

In his dialogue with Christian Salmon, Kundera offers his quintessential definition of the novel as "a meditation on existence as seen through the medium of imaginary characters." And when his interlocutor objects that by so broad a definition even *The Decameron* could be called a novel, Kundera retorts, "I won't be so provocative as to call *The Decameron* a novel. Still, that book is one of the first efforts in modern Europe to create a large-scale composition in narrative prose, and as such it has a place in the history of the novel *at least* as its source and forerunner." Granting Kundera the same latitude he himself gives Boccaccio, we may discuss *Laughable Loves* as an experimental link in the sequence of his novels and a source of some of his important themes.

Though *Laughable Loves* obviously lacks unity of action and has independent sets of characters (the single exception being Dr. Havel, who connects the fourth and sixth stories), the series achieves internal coherence as a reflection on the paradoxical entanglements of three major themes. These themes, first raised in the opening trio of stories to be more fully developed in the remaining four (all of which date from the last stage of composition), are: the uneasy nature of truth in an age of easy certainties; modern Don Juanism; and the discord between body and soul in erotic situations. While the book employs a diversity of narrators, the perspective on the action throughout is one of irony, which Kundera considers "consubstantial" with the spirit of the European novel.

Men and "love" in *Laughable Loves*:

[For] many of the young men in Kundera's stories love comes primarily in the form of sexual conquest, and promises adventures outside of the life plan, a rare chance to experience the unexpected and to acquire a sense of power. Fair enough, we are led to say, and why, when so much else is denied them, shouldn't love be the one reliable measure of a life's value? There is in *Laughable Loves* this persistent and illusory connection between love and certainty. The would-be seducers attempt to circumvent the habitual oppression of their daily lives through love because love is voluntary, or so they think. But the punch lines and the narrative lines of these stories generally unite to show them that there is destiny in love as in everything else even if generated by one's own black box. The characters who push hardest for certainty in love are the most laughable and the most disappointed. They take a holiday from one form of tyranny and unwittingly uncover another, their own.

                    Elizabeth Pochoda, in The Nation,
                              September 18, 1976.

The laughter resounding in these tales of erotic debacle is never quite free of the admixture of sadness that turns it into a grimace. But the narrative tempo is *allegro con brio,* and the resourceful narrators manage to maintain a posture of playful brightness even when the action explodes in their faces. This is particularly true of the opening entry, **"Nobody Will Laugh,"** which is told by an unlucky jester caught in a society where laughter has been suspended. At the beginning of the story, he is a successful university lecturer in art history who finds himself comfortably in possession of a beautiful mistress named Klara. By the end, she has turned against him and left him "because a man who lies can't be respected by any woman."

This reversal originates in the narrator's unfortunate attempt to evade the truth, an instinctive, dubiously motivated reaction that might even be construed as a sudden access of kindness. As a professional art historian, he is being badgered for a critical appraisal by an amateur scholar who has written an utterly worthless, derivative article about a well-known nineteenth-century Czech painter. Since he is at core a man of strict intellectual standards, the narrator cannot praise Mr. Zaturetsky's pedantic drivel, but there is something within him that rebels against the thought of playing executioner of the little man's plodding hopes and ambitions. Unfortunately for both of them, Zaturetsky is relentless in his pursuit of the punishing truth, and he finally manages to corner his unwilling critic, who has been playing an elaborate game of escape from his would-be victim. Zaturetsky even tracks down our hero's private retreat, a bachelor flat where he keeps Klara under wraps. When this carefully preserved separation between public obligations and secret pleasures crumbles, indulgence gives way to spite, and he falsely accuses the little man of trying to seduce Klara. The situation becomes grave when Zaturetsky's personal outrage escalates into an accusation of slander that is instantly submitted for investigation and eventual judgment by the neighborhood committee of comrades, which keeps a tight watch over socialist morals.

The inventive fibster soon discovers that all around him expected laughter has frozen into rigid indignation. He cannot even persuade his mistress that a personal code of integrity lies concealed under the elaborate structure of deception he has erected. Klara will not understand the distinction between the lie in the heart and the lie on the lips, and she urges him to get everyone out of trouble by satisfying Zaturetsky's craving for scholarly approval. Even though he feels himself driven to a fall by the laughable lie of his own creation, our hero resists her expedient advice and instead proceeds to tell Zaturetsky's wife what he really thinks of her husband's article. But that long-suffering woman harbors a pathetic faith in her partner's vocation that makes her utterly impervious to the truth at hand, and in the end the liar turned truthteller *in extremis* finds himself surrounded by distrust. To cap it all, his mistress accuses him of being a "stereotyped cynic" to justify dropping him. In the "chilly silence" that descends on him after that parting shot, the newly self-aware narrator consoles himself with the thought that he is a lonely comic spirit stranded in a world of banished laughter.

In this overture to a cycle of tales where, as Philip Roth tells us [in his introduction to the collection], "*erotic* play and power are the subjects frequently at the center," the love interest stays in the background. It is a losing stake, thrown almost casually into a game of make-believe played at the extreme edges of the problem of truth. In positing a disjunction between intellectual truth and the pleasures of Eros, which are the chosen domain of the nonserious spirit, this story, the only one Kundera preserved from the first notebook (1963), anticipates the masterly "**Symposium**" (1969).

In the book's definitive sequence, "**Nobody Will Laugh**" and "**Symposium**" frame two stories about the pursuit of sexual love, both published originally in 1965. "**The Hitchhiking Game**," the third of the series of seven, places a physically confident young man of twenty-eight opposite a woman six years younger who is only just discovering her body's potential to give and receive pleasure. The two have been lovers for a year, but she is still anguished about her lack of sexual ease. Imagining her reserve to be an obstacle for her lover, whom she adores with a jealous passion, she never suspects that he cherishes her shyness as a sign of innocence. While driving together on the first day of a holiday trip to the mountains, they inadvertently stumble into an adventure of erotic exploration, a dangerous game of masks that will throw their love off course. Attempting to imitate the kind of sophisticated flirtation she thinks he enjoys when he is away from her, the young woman pretends to be a hitchhiker and assumes the suggestive manner of an easy pickup. At first reluctantly, then with mounting ferocity, the young man responds to her provocative double-talk by escalating the verbal game into gesture. At the end of the road down which imagination leads them, they stand opposite each other in a hotel room,

two faceless bodies topped by masks. Their lovemaking is a grappling in the dark, neither of them knowing the other who lies in this harsh embrace while the body's pleasure feeds the pain it inflicts on the exiled soul.

Roth writes that this "confusion of identities, and the heightened eroticism [it] provokes in the lovers, with its scary sado-masochistic edge, is not so catastrophic to either of them as his joke turns out to be for Ludvik Jahn." Perhaps so. It is true that the private catastrophe that results from this brutal *marivaudage* remains locked behind a bedroom door. But it seems to me that Roth, who sees the grimness of these tales in the long shadow society casts over the erotic game, misses the metaphysical dimension of Kundera's dark vision of the comedy of the sexes.

The theme of Don Juanism makes its first appearance in "**The Golden Apple of Eternal Desire**," the second of the seven tales. Here Kundera's Don Juan is Martin, a man who has just crossed the threshold of forty, and is married and in love with his wife. His chronicler is a younger friend, a scholar by profession, and by predilection a student of the discipline of the erotic chase that Martin exemplifies and teaches. This unnamed narrator casts a reflective eye on the action as it unfolds within the time span of a single Saturday afternoon. The master, with his disciple in tow, embarks on the road of sexual adventure that will take them from their starting point in Prague, from village to village, to their appointed goal at a small-town hospital where two nurses are awaiting them.

Behind the wheel of a rented Fiat, the obliging pupil drives along, compelled by the imperious desire for adventure that resides within the older man sitting in the passenger seat beside him. The undivided quality of his master's will fascinates him like a force of nature. For his part, he knows he has been tricked into joining the action: the preceding Monday, when they met one of the nurses in Prague, Martin had managed to snatch a rare book about Etruscan culture from his hands and slip it into her bag while negotiating the weekend rendezvous. The prospect of reclaiming that book taints his own motivation with a distinctly scholarly duplicity. He admits to himself that unlike Martin, he is a mere "dilettante," a man "*playing* at something which Martin *lives*." "Sometimes," he reflects, "I have the feeling that the whole of my polygamous life is a consequence of nothing but my imitation of other men." Yet he also acknowledges that playful imitation has been the controlling value of his life, an imperative of sorts, to which he has consistently subordinated all his personal interests and desires.

Martin and his narrator/companion represent Kundera's first variation on that mythical pair of sexual adventurers, Don Juan and his servant, whose name keeps changing with each new version of the story while his master's remains fixed forever. Don Juan's man is called Catalinón in Tirso de Molina's *The Playboy of Seville; or, Supper with a Statue* (1616?), becoming Sganarelle in Molière's *Dom Juan* (1665), and thereafter Leporello in Lorenzo Da Ponte's libretto to Mozart's opera *Don Giovanni* (1787). Kierkegaard, in an essay on Mozart's tragicomic opera, observed that "there is also something erotic in Leporello's relationship to Don Juan, there is a power by which Don Juan captivates him, even against his will" ["The Immediate Stages of the Erotic or the Musical Erotic," *Either/Or,* translated by David F. Swenson, 1944]. This brilliant perception sheds indirect light on the bond that unites Martin and his friend. They are attached to each other by something that approximates but does not quite match the power of erotic seduction. Rather, they are inseparable as two game players are, who need each other to carry on with the game. Martin, whom his companion posits as the natural Don Juan, serves as a talismanic figure in whose living presence the illusion of physical authenticity is preserved, and he in turn uses his friend, always so obedient to the call of his master's unquestionable desire for women, as the mirror that will return a reassuring image of his own fabulous potency. Both are caught in a shared delusion of a perennially conquering male sexuality.

Kierkegaard heard in Mozart's opera the "opulent moment" of sensuousness rising above the dread to which Christian spirituality had consigned it. He interpreted *Don Giovanni* as the supreme classical expression of the Don Juan myth, capturing in all its ideality, as only music could, the "daemonic joy of life" that is Don Juan's gift to women. Kundera's treatment of the myth in **Laughable Loves** is essentially antimusical, charting an aggressively intellectual territory at the opposite pole from the Mozartian spirit of immediacy as Kierkegaard defined it. In Da Ponte's libretto, it is the servant Leporello who recites the famous catalogue of Don Giovanni's conquests, an "epic survey of his master's life," Kierkegaard calls it, whose tantalizingly incomplete tally of 1,003 invites the imagination to lose itself in an ever-expanding prospect of seductions to come. Kierkegaard conceived Mozart's Don Giovanni as "handsome, not very young," and placed his age at thirty-three, "the length of a generation." Martin, at forty, falls well within that span, in our contemporary reckoning. But Kundera's variation on Leporello clearly breaks away from the original mold. In the opera, Don Giovanni's power over Leporello is such that the servant can almost be assimilated to his master, even becoming "a voice for Don Juan." In the first scene of the second act, Don Giovanni and Leporello exchange costumes; the servant, instructed by his master, dons the mythical hat with white feathers, the broad cloak, and the sword of the sexual conquistador to woo the discarded Elvira, while the real Don Juan borrows his servant's clothes to seduce Elvira's maid.

The type of the great aristocrat slumming, *le grand seigneur qui s'encanaille,* was familiar to Parisian playgoers in the waning decades of the eighteenth century. Beaumarchais, whose comedy *The Marriage of Figaro* Da Ponte had adapted for Mozart a year earlier, in 1786, used the type *con brio,* provoking dangerously ambiguous laughter in the urbanized aristocratic audience. Don Juan also takes advantage of his servant one time too many, since for him too, it is growing late for such tricks. In his socialist Bohemia, Kundera's Don Juan retains no servant to compile the record of his amorous exploits. He is reduced to being his own accountant, but he requires a secondary male presence at his heels to witness the actuarial function that rivals and ultimately overwhelms the primary activity for which Don Juan's sword once stood as guarantor and metonymic emblem.

Martin is a highly theoretical quantifier of women. He has invented an elaborate verbal technique for targeting and pinning down his prey, and this is the essence of the art of seduction he teaches his disciple. In describing the two initial stages of his strictly codified, systematic approach to women, he deliberately uses the abstract, latinate words *registrá* (registration) and *kontaktá* (contact), words a pollster might use in preparing a survey. Martin's erotic foreplay is a cerebral activity that imitates the precision of a laboratory experiment, within a time frame arbitrarily limited as in a bureaucratic schedule. The adventure of the high road to sexual conquest starts in Prague at 2:00 P.M. and ends there before the stroke of 9:00 so that Martin, a devoted husband, can play a promised game of cards with his wife. The interval thus circumscribed is spacious enough for the two men to duly register and contact a number of new women on the way to the predetermined assignation with the nurses. The sexual consummation is postponed to a hypothetical future as the new contacts are carefully tucked away in Don Juan's impressive file.

Philip Roth has compared the Don Juanism in this story to "a sport played by a man against a team of women, oftentimes without body contact"—a witty metaphor that effectively expresses Roth's sense of the tale as a "mild satire" on Don Juanism. Martin's intellectual invention compares favorably with the typical spectator sport that middle-aged men commonly indulge in on Saturday afternoons, in New York as in Prague, seated before their television screens. But it seems to me that Kundera's tale has a deeper bottom than mild satire can fathom. The reflective narrator who watches Martin's game while also participating in it is contemplated from an even greater distance by the all-seeing yet unseen author. It was Kundera, after all, who gave the tale an epigraph from Pascal's Pensée 139, on *divertissement:* ". . . ils ne savent pas que ce n'est que la chasse, et non pas la prise qu'ils recherchent" (". . . they do not know that they seek only the chase and not the quarry"). The hunt, that quintessentially aristocratic sport of the seventeenth century, is Pascal's elected metaphor for the concept of *divertissement,* which he defines as "une occupation violente et impétueuse qui les détourne de penser à soi" ("a violent and impetuous activity that deflects men from thinking about themselves"). In Kundera's fiction, sex, not sport, is the privileged trope for the obsessive chase after nothingness that drives human beings away from the thought of death, which seems unbearable when all sense of God has been voided in the head. But Kundera insists on retaining the original, nonmetaphoric meaning of the word *divertissement,* which denotes a frivolous kind of entertainment. Frivolity assumes the value of a philosophical concept in Kundera's world. It functions as a snare for the spirit of gravity, or as an acid test for questions of the order Pascal raises in his meditation on the misery of the human condition in the absence of God.

By the end of the mock-epic narrative, Martin's reflective companion will have understood the illusory nature of his master's activity. At bottom, Martin is a mere imitator, just like his pupil, even though his game may be constructed from a real memory of his younger self. The narrator voices off abruptly at the moment when his cameralike eye has trained its lens on Martin, and himself at his side, traveling the road of return, suspended in futile animation within an ephemeral present quickened by elusive anticipation. Stoically faithful to the obligation of frivolity that Kundera likes to impose on his most conscious male characters, the disingenuous companion of borrowed adventure cuts off the inconclusive action with a fine verbal flourish, pinning down the forever receding object by naming it The Golden Apple of Eternal Desire. The sexual connotation of the symbolic apple lingers on within the word like a precious essence, even though Eve herself has become the vanishing point of an illusionistic prospect. The allusion to the primal sin in the lost garden, whose grave echo was heard in the Pascal epigraph, dissipates in the advancing twilight.

Kundera's Don Juans are haunted by the pathos of imitation and the consciousness of living a parodistic derivative of a once charismatic identity. In *Laughable Loves,* the perfection of the type is the intellectual and sexually practiced Dr. Havel, a man of wit who figures as the lead character in two of the stories. The first of these, **"Symposium,"** takes the form of a miniature drama in five acts, built around the twin questions of love and death. Like the Platonic dialogue from which it takes off, it is primarily a drama of ideas. Talk occupies the foreground while a single event, Alzhbeta's questionable suicide attempt, occurs in the background and is brought forward for commentary, somewhat like Alcibiades' failed seduction of Socrates in Plato's text. The conversation, which engages three men and two women, plays itself out during an improvised party in a hospital staff room. Dr. Havel and the sex-starved nurse Alzhbeta are both on duty, and they are joined by three colleagues: the chief physician, a bald, aging, happily married philanderer; his attractive younger mistress, who is also a doctor; and the handsome young intern Flaishman.

The atmosphere inside the room is licentious and charged with crisscrossing currents of sexual tension. Alzhbeta, a mature woman whose beautiful body is topped by a repulsive face, desires Dr. Havel in particular and all men in general, only to be rebuffed by the three who are present. Flaishman, the would-be romantic, is drawn to the woman doctor and believes he has read the signals of his imminent success in her vaguely flirtatious manner. But she, whom her lover the chief physician has dubbed Diana, "cold, sportive, and spiteful," in the second act, will take sexual aim at her lover's friend Dr. Havel in the fourth act. The chief physician, also ranked as the senior libertine of the group, delivers himself of a tongue-in-cheek panegyric to Platonic love in the first act, having earlier expressed the opinion that "eroticism is not only a desire for the body, but to an equal extent a desire for honor. The partner, whom you've won, who cares about you and loves you, is your mirror, the measure of what you are and

what you stand for. In eroticism we seek the image of our own significance and importance."

In postulating a solipsistic Eros, the chief physician has undermined the basic assumption behind the doctrine of philosophical love Diotima once taught Socrates. Plato's Eros is a force that unites two selves in the pursuit of a good higher than either of them can contain or muster in isolation. Diotima taught that the function of Eros was "that of procreation in what is beautiful, and such procreation can be either physical or spiritual" [Plato, *Symposium*]. Before bidding the physical realm of being farewell, the woman of Mantinea restored its essential dignity to the human body, by appropriating it as a central symbol of vitality in her myth of the philosopher's quest for truth and beauty. By contrast, Alzhbeta's body is held in contempt by the assembled sophists, whose practice of love is mired in mockery and whose discourse never rises above the level of *doxa.*

Alzhbeta is reduced to making imaginary love to herself in a sad mock striptease, which she performs fully clothed in the second act, to the embarrassment of those present. She leaves the room an offended woman, having unwittingly swallowed a dose of sleeping pills administered by Havel instead of the pep pill she had asked for. The truth about Alzhbeta's ensuing brush with death by gas inhalation is never established in the text. The chief physician calls it a fake suicide attempt staged to attract Havel's attention. Flaishman considers Alzhbeta's unrequited love for him the cause of a real suicide attempt that fans the flame of his erotic conceit. The woman doctor argues that it was a mishap: Alzhbeta's coffee water boiled over and extinguished the gas burner after she fell asleep. Dr. Havel affirms that Alzhbeta's intent was to offer her body to death since the living would have no part of it.

Death as the substitute lover is an image from Dr. Havel's myth about himself. In the first act, referring to his friend's sexual omnivorousness, the chief physician says, "You're like death; you take everything," and urges Alzhbeta's body upon him. In the second act, he reiterates that definition—"Havel is death"—contradicting the woman doctor, who says that "Havel is Don Juan. He's not old, but he's getting old." This exchange prompts Dr. Havel to deliver a brief discourse on "the end of the Don Juans."

> "If I should pass judgment on whether I'm Don Juan or death, I must incline, albeit unhappily, toward the chief physician's opinion," said Havel, taking a long drink. "Don Juan. He, after all, was a conqueror. Rather in capital letters. A Great Conqueror. But I ask you, how can you be a conqueror in a domain where no one refuses you, where everything is possible and everything is permitted? Don Juan's era has come to an end. Today, Don Juan's descendant no longer *conquers,* but only *collects.* The figure of the Great Collector has taken the place of the Great Conqueror, only the Collector is no longer really Don Juan at all. Don Juan was a tragic figure. He was burdened by his guilt. He sinned gaily and laughed at God. He was a blasphemer and ended up in hell."

In quite another context, Kundera has called Prague the city of endings. It is the same city that had turned festive for Mozart when it saw and heard the world premiere of his *Don Giovanni* in 1787. With an uncanny sense of time and place, Kundera has brought the mythical playboy from Seville to die of exhaustion in an anonymous hospital not far from the old imperial town that was once the stage of his most refined triumph. Almost two centuries after Mozart, Kundera sees the defiance of death (in the form of the Commander's statue), and the subsequent descent into hell, as a verbal metaphor that evokes nostalgia rather than dread. He ushers his Don Juan to extinction with a flourish of talk aimed at chasing away a yawn, and not, like Tirso de Molina, with one last stab of the fabled blade into the empty air [See Tirso de Molina, *The Playboy of Seville; or, Supper with a Statue*].

Like Don Quixote and Sancho Panza, the tragicomic myth of Don Juan is a legacy from the crepuscular glory of Spain's Golden Age. In the original play, Tirso portrayed Don Juan as a trickster, a feckless young man without a thought for death. "Plenty of time for that" is his refrain-like retort to all sermons. The fatal shaking of hands with the statue of the dead Commander is more a gesture of bravado than of blasphemy. It is above all an instinctive expression of the caste value of physical courage, the only virtue this aristocratic clown honors. But though his appetites may enjoy complete license, his mind is not yet libertine. "Let me send for a priest at least; I want to confess and be absolved" he cries on his way to hell.

It was Molière who first developed the intellectual potential of the type in his comedy *Dom Juan*. His hero believes in nothing save his own reason. "I believe two and two make four, Sganarelle, and four and four make eight," he declares, mocking his superstitious servant. He is the ideal *grand seigneur* after the Fronde, untrammeled by feudal obligations and chafing at the tightening grip of authority. Molière endows him with a pursuing wife, Elvira, a woman no sooner wed than abandoned. Dom Juan argues the case for his boundless appetite for women and his need for variety on the basis of a convenient definition of Nature. He does not wait to be challenged to supper with the statue but initiates the invitation himself. Before going down under the Commander, he has one final chance to reject Elvira, when she enters as a veiled figure of Repentance, soon to be changed into the image of Time the Reaper, with scythe in hand. Arrogant to the end, the aristocratic libertine defies the moral connotation of death twice, once in the form of Repentance the temporal worm, and then as Damnation, the eternal one.

In Mozart's music for Da Ponte's libretto of *Don Giovanni,* Don Juan emerges in his fullest incarnation, brilliantly modulating the tension between the tragic and comic modes that was inherent in the myth from the start. Don Giovanni is the lyric embodiment of the phallic illusion that death can be conquered in the repetition *ad infinitum* of the small death of sexual consummation, when time, in its relentless thrust, is seized and held fast against the vertiginous beat of a woman's heart. If Mozart's Don Juan blasphemes, it is with the conviction of his loins, and not, like Molière's libertine, with his head.

Dr. Havel's postmortem invocation of the Don Juan myth alludes to all three classical versions of the hero—the conquistador turned playboy, the licentious blasphemer, and the genius of seduction—only to negate them in the type of the Great Collector. On Havel's argument, Don Juanism is a practical and philosophical impossibility. The Great Collector, the image of a Don Juan defeated by the absence of resistance, is contaminated by death long before his term on earth is up. Once his heroic antagonism with death has been demystified, the Great Conqueror assumes the attributes of his hated enemy. Dr. Havel admits to being "at most a figure of comedy," but it is a comedy corroded by sadness, without the expansive vitality of the Spanish archetype. "Only against the historical background of his tragic gaiety can you to some extent perceive the comic sadness of my womanizing existence," says Havel, admitting an awareness of his own lack of authenticity.

It is revealing that Havel, whose body is at its sexual apex in **"Symposium"** even as his mind sounds the death knell of the Don Juan myth, should be almost frantic to resurrect that myth when we meet him again in **"Dr. Havel After Twenty Years."** At this late stage in his career, he is a married man who has just developed gallbladder trouble. He finds himself wifeless on the tiny stage of a provincial spa, where he has gone to take the waters, and where he discovers to his dismay that his reputation as a Don Juan has preceded his anatomy down the road to decay. In his new vulnerability, he must endure the humiliation of being handled with businesslike indifference by a young masseuse administering water therapy. Even though he has long known that Don Juanism has lost its epic status, he now experiences a pathetic need to practice it again. This longing is not quite a desire for women but rather a violently childish caprice for something of himself that now seems gone forever. In his hour of need, the two subordinate characters from the old myth come to the rescue of the aging Don Juan: Leporello, in the familiar form of a younger disciple, and Elvira, the pursuing wife. In Kundera's variation, the wife is a glamorous movie star whose devotion to Havel is fed by a smoldering jealousy of his philandering. When she makes her appearance in the town, the provincial public is mesmerized by her unquestionable beauty and the magnitude of her fame. Riding the comet tail of that mirage, Havel slips back into the highest orbit of his former identity. Once again, all women are accessible to him, and he happily harnesses his verbal technique to his derivative charisma as the man in possession of a mysterious and beautiful wife.

Feeling reinstated in his mastery, Havel turns playfully malicious. His young friend and admirer, a local journalist, has succumbed to the seduction of his Don Juan reputation and has solicited his expert opinion on the worth of his current erotic interest, a young woman with whom he is starting to fall in love. In a *tour de force* of verbal mystification, Havel succeeds in redirecting his friend's attention to the frankly middle-aged Dr. Frantishka, whose expressive legs and manner of walking, he claims, possess a beauty far superior to "ready-made prettiness." The kindly woman doctor is in reality the embodiment of everything maternal, a category of femininity that stands at the opposite pole from the erotic in Kundera's world. She will keep on babbling about her grown son even as the baffled young journalist is making love to her. When the obedient disciple reports back to his master on this experience, Havel launches into a discourse on the role of words in making the most casual sexual encounter uniquely memorable. "They say of me that I'm a collector of women," explains the *ci-devant* Don Juan turned erotic sophist. "In reality, I'm far more a collector of words."

Its essential physicality infected by words, the Don Juan myth in *Laughable Loves* is also touched by a corresponding erosion of gender privilege. Woman, after all, no less than man, can play at being the Great Collector, and "death" (*smrt*) is female in Czech, as in the Romance languages. In the two remaining stories of the cycle, Kundera shows two mature women exercising a highly contemporary equality with men in the matter of sexual adventurism. In Kundera's fiction, supremacy in that domain belongs to technique, which goes with age and experience. But his erotic women seem to have a greater capacity than the men for slipping into blasphemy.

In **"Let the Old Dead Make Room for the Young Dead,"** a story that belongs to the same 1969 cycle as the Havel diptych, a woman of dignity, a widow of ten years well into her fifties, surrenders herself to a man twenty years her junior. The event occurs during her trip to a small town to visit her husband's grave. But when the widow arrives at the cemetery, whose path she knows so well, she finds that "where the gray sandstone monument with the name of her husband in gold lettering used to be, precisely on that spot (she confidently recognized the two neighboring graves) now stood a black marble headstone with a quite different name in gilt." The cemetery administration explains that her ten-year lease on the grave has expired and was canceled automatically, without notice, because of overcrowding. The operative rule, they say, is that *"the old dead ought to make room for the young dead"*. This statement of necessity couched as an upbeat slogan in the style of a mass society with futuristic ambitions, offends her spirit of reverence. Yet before the day is over, she herself will fling memory and self-respect to the winds for the sake of one last moment of sexual pleasure. She will give herself to the younger man who made love to her inexpertly once before, fifteen years earlier, when she still wore the halo of sexual grace.

The widow's conscious choice of sex above honor, the stepping over sacred memorials to the past and to the dead, recalls the blasphemous wooing in the cemetery that Pushkin imagined as the scene of Don Juan's greatest triumph. Kierkegaard, having postulated a reflective seducer, a master of "the beguiling, systematic, continuous seduction," as the romantic counterpart to the classical Don Juan, ruled Byron's Don Juan a failure because his seduction "extends itself epically." Writing in 1843, he did not know Pushkin's one-act play *The Stone Guest* (1830), where the romantic type of Don Juan achieves its ideal

---

---

expression. In that drama, Doña Anna is the widow, not the daughter, of the Commander Don Juan has slain, apparently without any particular intent: "When hard by the Escurial we met, / He ran upon my sword-point and expired, / Just like a dragon-fly upon a pin." Don Juan first courts Doña Anna disguised as a monk, while she is at her devotions in front of her dead husband's monument. But the erotic will of this intensive seducer requires that he snatch the widow from the embrace of death and possess her in his own name, with his true identity unmasked. In the culminating fourth scene of the drama, which fuses the adventure of seduction and the confrontation with the statue, Don Juan and Doña Anna are both supremely conscious of the shadow of death at their shoulders, and they end by sinking into the ground in a mutual embrace. "Ah, what is death? For one sweet moment's tryst / I'd give my life without a murmur," Don Juan whispers to Doña Anna, who hesitates on the brink of surrender. He throws his defiance of death at her feet as his ultimate forfeit in a game where she hazards her feminine honor. But his victory over her, anticipated in the kiss she allows him just when the statue knocks at the door, is as much an expression of her tender pity for him ("And so you are concerned about the life / Of poor Juan!") as of her pride at having secured such a pledge of passion.

In Kundera's treatment of the wooing-over-the-grave motif, the woman's surrender also represents a collapse from the maternal into the erotic, but it is accomplished in a psychic atmosphere tainted by cynicism and vindictiveness. Kundera's fifty-five-year-old widow, who is also the mother of a demanding adolescent, harbors no illusions about the sexual moment she is about to share with this man from her distant past, almost a stranger to her now, but in whose memory she is enshrined as an elusively beautiful image. "She knew men and their approach to the female body. She was aware that in love even the most passionate idealism will not rid the body's surface of its terrible, basic importance." Neither of them really believes his tempting assurance that "she was still beautiful, that in fact nothing had changed, that a human being always remains the same." She, in particular, is painfully lucid about her body's inadequacy for the task to which their mutual greed for a taste of the past compels her. Like Pushkin's Doña Anna, she must choose between the moment's seduction and her honor, though in this case the memorial she is about to betray is more "her memorial, which this man beside her had honored for fifteen years in his thoughts," than her husband's. She suddenly visualizes her "son–enemy" as a monster of youthful egotism denying her the last vestiges of sexuality and pushing her closer to her grave. It is he, the living ghost, rather than her buried husband, who stands at her shoulder with a forbidding *memento mori* countenance while she hesitates. When she finally gives in to her insistent seducer, she inwardly hisses at her invisible son the blasphemous words *The old dead must make room for the young dead, my boy!*, and with that profane thought, she turns to her last joyless lovemaking. Kundera, like Pushkin before him, interrupts the erotic scene at the moment of her yielding, but not before he has changed the embracing lovers into an obscene vision of carrion flesh mating over an open grave.

The last of the stories, **"Edward and God,"** is the adventure of a seducer who, entangled in an irresistible combination of social necessity and his own hypocrisy, becomes a blasphemer in spite of himself. Edward begins by courting Alice, a young woman whose anachronistic religiosity forbids sexual consummation outside marriage. In order to achieve his end, he feigns a vague yearning for Alice's God, which immediately heightens her interest in their relationship. He goes with her to church, carefully mimicking her pious gestures with the studied mien of a Tartuffe. But soon his devotion is duly noted by the powers that be, and since this is a small town in the late fifties, he is hauled before a committee of socialist inquisitors at the school where he teaches.

The school directress is a fanatical Communist who was the cause of Edward's older brother's expulsion from the university years earlier, when he made light of her extravagant display of grief over Stalin's death. Now she is an ugly spinster "with the greasy black hair of a gypsy, black eyes, and black down under her nose", and with a secret penchant for young men. In imminent danger of being driven out of his job, Edward summons his powers of hypocrisy. This time he plays the other side of the coin of his putative faith in God, reinterpreting the theology of doubt with which he had courted the reluctant Alice as a crisis of a convinced Communist assailed by irrational religious belief. He explains to the committee that in spite of all the arguments his well-trained reason may advance, he cannot get rid of his faith in God. "You see, comrades, I'm telling it to you the way it is. It's better that I confess to you, because I don't want to be a hypocrite. I want you to know what I'm really like," he tells them, hanging his head.

This ostentatious demonstration of sincerity touches a responsive chord in the directress's gypsy heart. She takes Edward under her wing as her special pedagogic project, and he soon realizes that the game has slipped out of his control and that he is now a pawn in her erotic power play. The stage is thus set for the grotesque scene in the bachelorette flat where the directress has lured him for the kill. Entangled in the strings of his virtuoso lies, Edward is forced to confront the consequences of his words, and when the moment of truth ripens to the point where rhetoric must yield to action, Edward fears that "his body would sabotage his assiduous will." The anguish of physical impotence is holding him in a deadly grip when in a sudden inspiration he seizes upon the power of blasphemy to stiffen his faltering desire. Acting out the role of a religious man about to overstep the barrier of mortal sin, Edward commands the atheist woman to assume a kneeling posture and pray, "so that God may forgive us."

> As she uttered the words of the prayer, she glanced up at him as if he were God Himself. He watched her with growing pleasure: in front of him was kneeling the directress, being humiliated by a subordinate; in front of him a naked revolutionary was being humiliated by prayer; in front of him a praying lady was being humiliated by her nakedness.

Edward, master of the easy lie, who has devised this farcical scene of make-believe blasphemy out of extreme expediency, is suddenly transformed into a master of erotic sadism. Intoxicated by "this threefold image of degradation", he finds that he can now command his body at will. The double-edged blasphemy performed at cross-purposes by the believing Communist and the assumed Christian acts like a magic philter to release Edward's sexual drive.

The conquest of Alice, which follows in the next section, is almost a letdown for Edward after the satanic high he has reached with the directress. Alice gives herself to him because she sees him as a martyr suffering at the hands of the Communist system she hates. But Edward, who knows better, is disappointed in the second prize his hypocrisy has won for him. He secretly reproaches Alice for so easily betraying her once all-powerful God of chastity.

Edward's story is told by a discursive narrator whose ironic manner recalls the narrator/participant of **"The Golden Apple of Eternal Desire."** This time, the final click of the camera delivers a double exposure of Edward: as he sits alone in an empty church, "tormented with sorrow, because God does not exist," the shadow of a smile is superimposed on his face, with its solemn mask, for the grieving hypocrite senses "the genuine *living* face of God" emerging from the depths of that sorrow. The narrator treats Edward's sad face as a photographic pentimento and begs his readers, "Please, keep him in your memory with this smile," having already implicated us all in Edward's condition with a dramatic sigh in the manner of

Gogol: "Ah, ladies and gentlemen, a man lives a sad life when he cannot take anything or anyone seriously!"

The world of Edward, which he shares with Martin and Dr. Havel and all the other sophistic lovers and their victims, is a small socialist country with sealed borders, where a man can travel from the center to the periphery and back again in the space of a single afternoon. On that radically reduced *theatrum mundi,* men and women pursue each other, striving to recapture a sense of their own centrality by escaping the dull anonymity of their social condition into the illusion of a privileged sexual moment. But in the place of sensuality they find only a phantom freedom, a verbal artifact that functions as the dialectical negation of a ubiquitous external power that has posited itself as the only permissible image of God.

Michael Carroll (essay date 1992)

SOURCE: "The Cyclic Form of *Laughable Loves,*" in *Milan Kundera and the Art of Fiction,* edited by Aron Aji, Garland Publishing Inc., 1992, pp. 132-52.

[*In the following essay, Carroll considers* Laughable Loves *as a short story cycle, in which awareness of the interrelationship of the stories is essential for a full understanding of each individual narrative and the collection as a whole.*]

The fiction of Milan Kundera has inspired an avalanche of critical attention in recent years; in fact, as we come to realize the importance of his work, Kundera studies are becoming, as this volume evidences, something of a "growth industry." The works that have attracted the greatest critical attention are his most recent (and most fully realized) offerings: *The Book of Laughter and Forgetting* and *The Unbearable Lightness of Being.* However, in order to understand Kundera's work as a whole, we must turn back to his earliest fiction. We must do so, first of all and most obviously, because there is a thematic nexus that links all of the works of any given writer's *oeuvre;* naturally, we find that these works as a whole are characterized by certain (we might say "Kunderan") preoccupations. Second, we must do so in order to understand the aesthetic trajectory of his career, for these works not only represent a continuation of the traditional function of prose fiction as thematic exploration through what Kundera (in *Art of the Novel*) refers to as nondidactic discourse: they also continue another tradition, that of formal complexity and experimentation—the tradition of, to name a few, Conrad, Kafka, and Nabokov. Kundera's aesthetic trajectory is best understood by turning to his very first work as a fiction writer, *Laughable Loves,* a work which serves as the aesthetic prototype for *The Book of Laughter and Forgetting* and to some extent *The Unbearable Lightness of Being.* Unfortunately, the importance of this early work is generally overlooked; this is in part due to the fact that until quite recently a definitive English-language edition has not been available.

Laughable Loves has, for a contemporary work, a rather involved publication history. As Kundera himself remarked in an interview with Lois Oppenheim [in *Review of Contemporary Fiction,* 2 (1989)], his first short story **"I, Sad God"** (1959), marks the end of his career as a poet and playwright and the beginning of his career as a fiction writer. In 1963, this story and two others (**"My Nurse Above All Others"** and **"Nobody Will Laugh"**) were published (by Cekoslovensky Spisovatel, the Czech state publishing organ) in a single volume, entitled *Smesne Lasky* [*Laughable Loves*]. In 1965, a *Second Book of Laughable Loves* was published: it included **"The Golden Apple of Eternal Desire," "The Herald,"** and perhaps the most renowned Kundera story, **"The Hitchhiking Game."** In 1968, a *Third Book of Laughable Loves* was published; it included **"Let the Old Dead Make Room for the Young Dead," "Symposium," "Edward and God,"** and **"Doctor Havel After Ten Years."**

The three separate books were published for the first time as a single volume in 1970—the last book by Kundera to be published in his native land (although with the Czech revolution of November 1989, there can be no doubt that Kundera's works will once again be available in his own country). In this edition, Kundera eliminated two of the stories (**"My Nurse Above All Others"** and **"The Herald"**) but otherwise retained the same order and the tripartite structure, which is indicated in this volume by upper case Roman numerals and a blank page between each volume.

Also in 1970, Gallimard Publishers released a first French edition of *Risibles Amours*. Kundera decided to drop yet another story (**"I, Sad God"**), leaving seven of the original ten. For the first French edition Kundera also eliminated the tripartite division indicated by the Roman numerals and inverted the ordering of the last two pairs of stories, forming what would be the final, intended arrangement:

Nobody Will Laugh

The Golden Apple of Eternal Desire

The Hitchhiking Game

Symposium

Let the Old Dead Make Room for the Young Dead

Doctor Havel After Ten Years

Edward and God

The French edition was followed by Polish and Italian editions, and in 1974, the first English-language edition (Knopf). However, this first English edition (as Kundera points out in an *Poznamka autora* [Author's Note] which accompanies the 1981 Czech-language edition published in Toronto) presents the stories in an arbitrary order. During this period just before his emigration, Kundera had a difficult time managing his affairs. The arrangement for the English edition was done, as he points out, without his knowledge, and he was not happy with it. The first English edition obscures the relationship between *Laughable Loves* and the work for which it served as a prototype, *The Book of Laughter and Forgetting*. This is no small matter, for Kundera's fiction, like that of James Joyce, is characterized by an almost obsessive concern for the architectonics of narrative form. To read the stories of *Laughable Loves* in random order is no more critically acceptable than it would be to read Joyce's *Dubliners* in like fashion. In any case, this first English edition was reprinted for the first time by Penguin in 1975 and then reprinted (according to the publishing information in the revised edition of the text) nine times between 1980 and 1988.

In 1979, Gallimard provided Kundera with the opportunity to revise, resulting in a definitive French edition. The ordering of the stories was the same as that of the 1970 French edition, but Kundera made a number of relatively minor textual changes. In 1981, the firm 88 Publishers (located in Toronto) published a definitive Czech edition, and in 1987, Penguin published the first definitive English-language edition, which followed the ordering of stories indicated in the Gallimard.

When read in its intended arrangement, *Laughable Loves* is a work with a totalizing form. This was apparent even before the work was at last completed. After the second volume of *Laughable Loves* was published, a number of Czech reviewers pointed in one way or another to the volumes' common thematic center. Juri Opelik, for instance, noted [in a review in *Listy* 15 (1969)] that the stories use the theme of sexuality to examine problems of ideology. Another Czech critic, Milan Blahynka, noted [in a review in *Plamen* 1 (1967)] that the first two volumes of *Laughable Loves* can be seen as having an overall dialectic pattern. And in an article on Kundera published in 1975, Robert Porter extends Blahynka's notion of a dialectical pattern in the cycle to include all three volumes. According to Porter, the first volume of stories center on characters who fail in their efforts to control the lives of others, while the second volume demonstrates that people are not even capable of controlling their own lives, for "a new dimension may suddenly emerge, a game may become too real, a joke become a tragedy." In the third volume, Porter sees a synthesis: having shown that man cannot control the lives of others or, for that matter, his own, man must now "come to terms with the world and with what freedom he has" ("Freedom Is My Love," *Index on Censorship* 4, No. 4, 1975). In very schematic terms, then, Blahynka and Porter correctly identify the thematic unity and complex interplay of parts in this work.

The arrangement, the unity, and the interplay of discrete narrative units in *Laughable Loves* is not, of course, unique. Forrest L. Ingram, in a ground-breaking study entitled *Representative Short Story Cycles of the Twentieth Century: Studies in a Literary Genre,* brought critical attention to bear on a number of notable cycles such as *Dubliners, The Hunger Artist,* and Steinbeck's *The Pastures of Heaven.* Ingram defines the story cycle as a "set of stories linked to each other in such a way as to maintain a balance between the individuality of each of the stories and the larger unit." An important element of this fundamental scheme is a dynamic tension between the independence and the inter-dependence of the constituent parts—a structural ambiguity. Every story cycle, says Ingram, is characterized by a "double tendency of asserting the individuality of its components" while simultaneously asserting "the bonds of unity which make the many into a single whole." The individual units of the cycle are discrete in that they have their own beginnings, middles, and ends, and that they can be read as complete works in and of themselves—they can stand up on their own without the contextual support of the cycle. The totality of the cycle, on the other hand, results from what Ingram calls the "dynamic patterns of recurrence and development."

The patterns of recurrence may be of several varieties; for example, a thematic axis—in the case of *Dubliners,* the "paralysis" of Irish culture. Certain characters or character types may also provide a repetitive pattern, as with Nick Adams in Hemingway's *In Our Times,* who, as Susan Garland Mann notes in her study of this genre, serves as the work's "most explicit unifying device". The pattern of development, on the other hand, may assume the same forms but in a way that creates a linear trajectory and thus a kind of mega-narrative for the cycle: in *Dubliners* the characters become progressively older as one moves through the cycle; more significantly, as Brewster Ghiselin observes [in "The Unity of *Dubliners,*" *Accent,* Spring, 1956], there is a discernible "movement of the human soul, in desire of life, through various conditions." And in Faulkner's *The Unvanquished* Ingram observes a "logically sequential development of action" as one moves from story to story. The twin patterns of recurrence and development, then, account for a cycle's unity, and these patterns are set in opposition to the independence, the sense of self-containedness and closure, of each of the constituent narrative units. It should be noted that none of this need be symmetrical—some stories in a cycle may be fiercely independent, even to the point of seeming out of place. Other stories may form subsets, a strategy that is an important part of Kundera's two cyclic works: the stories **"Symposium"** and **"Dr. Havel After Twenty Years"** establish the only instance of narrative continuity (in the usual sense) in *Laughable Loves;* this is likewise true of Parts Four and Six of *The Book of Laughter and Forgetting.* In this instance, a particular bonding of stories gives the work added coherence to stabilize, as it were, the contrasting pull of disunity. On the other hand, as Gerald Kennedy points out in his study of the short story cycle [in "Towards a Poetics of the Short Story Cycle," *Journal of the Short Story in English* 11 (1988)], clusters of stories within a collection "may give special attention to a particular idea; in effect, such combinations form a sequence within a sequence." This is precisely what Maria Banerjee observes in her recent essay on a pair of stories in *Laughable Loves.* She notes that in **"The Golden Apple of Eternal Desire,"** and **"Doctor Havel After Twenty Years,"** Kundera makes explicit use of the Don Juan myth ["The Impossible Don Juan," *Review of Contemporary Fiction* 2 (1989)]. In the former story, we find a variation on that "mythical pair of sexual adventures, Don Juan and his servant" and in the latter, the young editor is reminiscent of Don Juan's servant while Havel's wife reminds us of the pursuing spouse, Elvira.

Another important aspect of Ingram's theory is the notion of a "spectrum" of story cycles, which in turn suggests three sub-genres: the composed, the arranged, and the completed cycle. The composed cycle is one which the author "had conceived as a whole from the time he wrote its first story," and as such the author composes his work according to the demands of a "master plan." The arranged cycle is at the other end of the spectrum, consisting of stories "which an author or editor-author has brought together to illuminate or comment upon one another by juxtaposition or association," and they are obviously the "loosest" of story cycles. The third sub-genre that Ingram describes is the "completed" cycle, which consists of stories that are

> neither strictly composed nor arranged. They may have begun as independent dissociated stories. But soon their author became conscious of unifying strands which he may have, even subconsciously, woven into the action of the stories. Consciously, then, he completed the unifying task which he may have subconsciously begun.

Two notable examples of the third type, the completed cycle, are found in Kafka's *Ein Hungerkunstler* and Eudora Welty's *The Golden Apples*. Although the stories of Kafka's cycle were written over a period of four years, and despite the fact that one of the four was previously published, it is also true that Kafka carefully selected the stories he wished to include in a single volume and that he firmly insisted that the stories be arranged in a particular way. Welty likewise had strong feelings about the arrangement of her story cycle, and her comments on the composing process in the case of cyclic form are revealing. "All this time in the back of my head," Welty says, "these connections had worked themselves out. I had just go get the clue, like a belated detective . . ." (*Conversations with Eudora Welty,* edited by Peggy Whitman, 1984).

Apparently, the cyclic mode of composition was ingrained in Kundera as an aesthetic practice before he even turned to fiction. Kundera's father was a noted music professor, and Kundera himself was a musician and composer during the first phase of his artistic carrer. In *Art of the Novel*, Kundera goes to impressive extremes to demonstrate that the architectonics of his literary works are derived from his musical ideas. In discussing one of his early compositions, he notes that it

> was almost a caricature preview of the architecture of my novels, whose future existence I didn't even faintly suspect at that time. That Composition for Four Instruments is divided—imagine!—into seven parts. As in my novels, the piece consists of parts that are very heterogenous in form. . . . That formal diversity is balanced by a very strong thematic unity: from start to finish, only two themes . . . are elaborated.

These cyclic tendencies carried over to Kundera's first literary efforts: as Opelik notes, **Laughable Loves** bears

considerable resemblance to Kundera's lyric cycle, *Monology*. In this respect, Kundera's literary career parallels that of two other notable writers: James Joyce's poem-cycle, *Chamber Music,* is clearly a prelude to *Dubliners;* William Faulkner's *Visions of Spring Day* may likewise be viewed as a formal experiment that paved the way for *Go Down, Moses*. In this regard, all three writers may be said to possess what P. M. Kramer, in her work on cyclic form, has called a "cyclic habit of mind" [*The Cyclical Method of Composition in Gottfried Keller's "Das Sinngedicht",* 1939].

Given that Kundera wrote the stories of **Laughable Loves** over a ten-year period and that the final form of the work came to him in the process of composition, arrangement, and rearrangement, it seems clear that it may be regarded as (to use Ingram's "spectrum") a *completed* cycle, and that his experience in the creation of this work inevitably influenced the form of *The Book of Laughter and Forgetting,* a much more aesthetically ambitious and unified work—a *composed* cycle. As Kundera himself said in a 1983 interview, in the process of eliminating three of the original ten stories and arranging the final version, "the collection had become very coherent, foreshadowing the composition of *The Book of Laughter and Forgetting*" ("The Art of Fiction LXXXI," *Paris Review,* Summer, 1984). This makes it all the more apparent that to read the stories of **Laughable Loves** in random order would be to disregard the authorial intent and the aesthetic coherence of this work.

The question of response, important in the study of any literary form, is particularly important in the study of cyclic texts, for their generic nature is not signaled by any traditional code—and yet, they elicit in the reader, in the process of successive interpretive activities, a *sense* of their generic nature. They provide for a particular kind of literary experience. As Ingram points out, the stories of a cycle are connected in such a way that the "reader's experience of each is modified by his experience of others." Further, "while each story in a cycle may be relatively simple, the dynamic of the cycle itself often poses a major challenge to the critic. . . . Shifting internal relationships, of course, continually alter the originally perceived pattern of the whole cycle." In spite of this statement, however, Ingram's analyses of various story cycles do not attempt to reconstruct this dynamism: Ingram's "fundamental assumptions," as he puts it, are in keeping with the New Critical formalism of Cleanth Brooks. Thus, as Gerald Kennedy notes in a recent article on the "poetics" of story cycles, Ingram treats the "unity of those works as an intrinsic feature of the writing rather than as a function or product of his own reading." Nonetheless, Ingram is absolutely correct in pointing to the "challenge to the critic" which is entailed in such an endeavor. The challenge is that of tracing a hypothetic reading activity as it moves through the maze of textual connections.

What happens when we read, and more particularly, what happens when we read a cyclic text? The most satisfying answers, it seems to me, are to be found in phenomenology, particularly in Wolfgang Iser's adaption of Husserl's foundational concept, protension and retention:

> . . . throughout the reading process there is a continual interplay between modified expectations and transformed memories. However, the text itself does not formulate expectations or their modification; nor does it specify how the connectability of memories is to be implemented. This is the province of the reader himself, and so here we have a first insight into how the synthesizing activity of the reader enables the text to be translated and transferred to his own mind. This process of translation also shows upon the basic hermeneutic structure of reading. Each sentence correlate contains what one might call a hollow section, which looks forward to the next corrolate, and a retrospective section, which answers the expectations of the preceding sentence (now a part of the background). Thus every moment of reading is a dialectic of protension and retention, conveying a future horizon yet to be occupied, along with a past (and continually fading) horizon already filled. . . . [*The Act of Reading,* 1978]

In her essay on cyclic form, Agnes Gereben discusses a similar phenomenon, although her grammatics are on the level of narratological units rather than the sentence and are thus even more well-suited for our purposes. She refers to this feature as the "network of cross-reference" in cyclic texts. As she explains it, if a prior narrative unit of a given story cycle contains, for instance, "an objectified simile, a situation, an attitude or value," and this given element reoccurs in a later narrative unit, then there is no 'vacuum' in the reader's mind where it tries to find its location, but it 'triggers' a field in it that has already been conditioned" ["The Syntactics of Cycles of Short Stories," *Essays in Poetics,* 1 (1986)].

Regarding *Laughable Loves,* a good place to start is in the middle, for by doing so we may trace several strands of the dialectic of retention. The title of the third story, **"The Hitchhiking Game,"** demonstrates how textual structures such as sub-titles and prefaces may serve as a key to form and meaning, for it announces that we shall most likely be presented with characters who are game players, and with this a pre-conditioned field is "triggered." That is, even by the second story of the cycle (**"The Golden Apple of Eternal Desire"**) a perceptible pattern of games, established in the first story (**"Nobody Will Laugh"**), becomes evident. In the protagonists of the first two stories, Klima and Martin respectively, we have the repetition of a character type in that they are both deeply involved in "games" that are hopelessly and pathologically out-of-control. In Klima's case the problem is so severe that it is not so much that he is playing a joke as it is that *he* is being *played by* a joke. He continues in his refusal to write a review of Zaturetsky's article and thus embarks on a peculiar game of hiding from the man. His motivation in this regard is complex: he enjoys Zaturetsky's adulation of him, and as a result he has no desire to devastate the man by rejecting his mediocre review. More importantly, however, he is intimidated by Zaturetsky's strong will, and more importantly still, there is his love for the "game"—a game that turns the respected scholar into a child lost in a fantasy world. In his delight at having

successfully eluded Zaturetsky through a series of ruses, Klima exclaims, "I longed to put on a bowler hat and stick on a beard. I felt like Sherlock Holmes or the invisible man . . . I felt like a little boy." His game inevitably leads to his downfall—to the examining committee and dismissal (an institution and an act that are repeatedly portrayed in Kundera's fiction).

Martin's game is likewise compulsive and out of control, and, like Klima's, regressive in nature: womanizing is Martin's way of denying that he is getting old. As the narrator explains, Martin has "the most regular sort of marriage" and "above this reality (and simultaneous with it), Martin's youth continues, a restless, gay, and erring youth transformed into a mere game." In these two stories, then, the reader finds a repetition, the simultaneous presence of similarity and difference: the game played by Martin in **"Golden Apple"** is, first of all, an ironic inversion of the one played by Klima, for in Klima's game of lying and avoidance, it is he, Klima, who is the prey while Zaturetsky is the pursuer; conversely, it is Martin who is the pursuer and women—women of all kinds—who are the prey. Furthermore, the reader's initial recognition of cyclicity informs an act of protension: the reader will be inclined to expect more of the same, and the ensuing narrative units will be read with the suspicion that recurrent themes, character types, and tropes may be lurking therein. Iser calls this the "the consistency building habit which underlies all comprehension." Thus, the observation of a thematic connection between the second and the first stories leads inexorably to other connections, leads to the filling of conceptual "gaps." The reader has begun to intuit the genre.

And thus, to return now to where we were—at the beginning of the third story, **"The Hitchhiking Game"**—the reader enters the story preconditioned by the game motif. The game played by the young man and his girl (the characters in this story are weirdly anonymous) is yet another kind of game: he pretends to be the type of man who uses women as mere instruments of pleasure, while she, at first coerced by the young man but later doing so of her own volition, plays the role of the freewheeling, lascivious woman. As different as this game is from those played in the previous two stories, there is yet an underlying similarity: Martin pretends to be a young man merrily going about the business of sowing his wild oats while he is in fact a middle-aged married man; Klima, the college professor, pretends to be a prankish schoolboy. It is furthermore noteworthy that the young man provides another example of the regressive personality type, for his desire to be the "heartless tough guy," we are told, is rooted in the "childish desires [which] withstand all the snares of the adult mind and often survive into ripe old age." Through this psychological profile, the underlying similarity between the regressive types—Klima, Martin, and the young man—emerges quite unmistakably. And as in the case of the game played by Klima, the young couple's game of make-believe along with their lack of foresight soon gets out of control and leads to yet another downfall. For Klima, that downfall is the destruction of a career; for the couple in the present story, it is the destruction of a relationship. This game motif continues through a number of other stories in the cycle, in particular the "Havel stories," both of which revolve around cruel hoaxes.

At this stage of the cycle another thematic gestalt begins to emerge: the related notions of womanizing, eroticism, and sexual identity. The successive kinds of womanizing which become apparent as one moves through the cycle forms an ironic sequence: in the first story, we have a man (Zaturetsky) who is in no way a womanizer but who is nonetheless accused (by the playful Klima) of being one. In the second story, we have a skillful lady's man (Martin, who has gone so far as to create a bizarre kind of science of the activity, replete with its own jargon) who would be a full-blown womanizer were it not for his essential conventionality and his guilty regard for his wife. And in the third story, we have a young man who fantasizes about being a lewd, whoring tough-guy, a womanizer of the worst kind, while he is actually a typical young man in a typical monogamous relationship.

It is in the fourth story, **"Symposium,"** in the character of Alzhbeta, that the reader finds thematic and imagistic elements which enable him to once again cast back through the text in order to form a larger constellation of meaning. When Alzhbeta performs a mock strip-tease for a rather uninterested group of doctors, the resultant image strongly echoes the young woman's strip-tease in **"The Hitchhiking Game,"** a fact which points to the special power of mental imagery in the process of constructing text totality. And yet, even as the reader notes this similarity, there are also a number of discernible and significant differences. The young woman of the previous story has to assume the role of the whore in order to feel comfortable with her sexuality. Alzhbeta, on the other hand, is fully at ease with her body—indeed, her only problem seems to be getting someone to take notice of it, and thus she cries out "Look at me! I am alive anyhow!. . . . For the time being I am still alive!" This refrain clearly recalls the "pitiful tautology" of the young woman: "I am me, I am me . . ." The ironic inversion (a trope repeatedly invoked as the spokes of the cycle come together), however, is that while Alzhbeta wants her sexuality to be noticed, the young woman wants her lover to *forget* her sexuality (manifested in her role as the whore) and recall her inner, personal identity.

The endings of narratives—cycles included—hold a position of particular importance in terms of the reading process. At the moment of textual closure, the process of protension has ceased, for there is no more text for the reader to anticipate. At this juncture the reader's attention becomes fully retentive, and the text becomes less a temporal and more a spacial entity: as Elaine Torgovnick notes, the text now "seems to pose before our eye to assume its geometry" [*Closure in the Novel*, 1981]. The activity which takes place at the point of closure, a point at which the reader looks back into the text with the desire to grasp its totality, is best described by Barbara Smith's term, "retrospective patterning" [*Poetic Closure*, 1968]. The term is apt, for it encapsulates the paradoxical combination of dynamism (retrospection is an activity, a mental process)

and stasis (a pattern is a static entity). The patterns that congeal, to return to Ingram's theory, may either be linear or repetitive—what Ingram calls "patterns of development" and "patterns of recurrence" respectively. Furthermore, entirely new thematic configurations may be triggered by the activity. As Iser notes, a basic element of the reading process, is this succession of gestalt formations; furthermore, "each gestalt bears with it those possibilities which it has excluded but which may eventually invalidate it." Acts of memory and reinterpretation within the reading process, then, can allow for a conceptual realignment of text which had already been conceptualized. The parts of a cycle are indeed, as Ingram says, like the moving and shifting parts of a mobile.

Placing the reader at the end of the cycle—that is, at the seventh and final story, **"Edward and God"**—we can observe a number of ways in which the thematic gestalten which evolve during the process of moving through the cycle become "retrospectively patterned." To return to our discussion of the various female characters in the cycle, Chehachkova, the major female figure of the seventh story, is, at first, completely unlike any of the other female characters we have encountered thus far. She is, first and foremost, a dedicated Communist. But when she decides to confess her innermost beliefs, she reveals that she holds a transcendental view—albeit a kind of socialist transcendentalism. Chehachkova espouses a belief in something beyond the self—"man is not in this world for his own sake." At this point a linear pattern in terms of the representation of women in the cycle is revealed: as we have moved towards the end of the cycle, the female characters become progressively more inclined to make pronouncements as per the possibility of transcending mortality. Consider the woman in the fifth story, **"Let the Old Dead Make Room for the Young Dead,"** who sees her son as an extension of her life and who believes that a man's accomplishments transend his physical being. Consider also Doctor Frantishka (from the sixth story, **"Dr. Havel After Twenty Years"**), who makes similar proclamations to her young lover. Given this trend, it seems with the title **"Edward and God"** that perhaps we have been inevitably led to the transcendent word and concept *par excellence*. And indeed, the story ends with Edward in a church. And though the narrator notes that the story does not end with "so ostentatious a paradox" as Edward's religious conversion, he does long for the God who does not exist.

Chehachkova is furthermore related to other female characters in the text in that she too will strip before the examining eye of the male. She is thus the final link in a chain of women (*enchained* women) who are put time and again in this (usually compromising) position. And like the women in **"The Hitchhiking Game"** and **"Symposium,"** she wants her partner to see not merely her appearance, but her inner essence, and thus her cry—"I am not a boring woman! That I am not"—is but another version of Alzhbeta's "Look at me . . . I am alive" and the young woman's lament, "I am me!" Moreover, her male counterpart is much like the other male counterparts in that he finds a certain excitement in subjecting women to degradation. The scene in which Edward forces Chehachkova to kneel naked before him while reciting the Lord's Prayer clearly recalls the strip scene in **"Hitchhiking Game,"** but with (yet another) ironic inversion: whereas the young man in the previous story got his thrills by making his lover act like a whore while doing a striptease, Edward wants Chehachkova to behave like a devout Christian (fitting, for she is indeed a Stalinist nun). In both cases the result is the same—degradation for the female, excitement for the male.

Thus, at this late juncture in the cycle yet another thematic gestalt emerges, a socio-sexual one triggered by the repeated female image—the "games" the various male characters play are often at the expense of women. This is most obviously the case in the Havel stories and **"The Hitchhiking Game."** However, upon reconsideration and a realignment of what Gereben calls "the network of cross-reference," it is true of other characters in the cycle as well: consider the way Professor Klima toys with Klara, offering her false promises of a better life. Or Martin, who thinks nothing of "registering" a woman, making a date, and then leaving her in the lurch, and thus Martin is another punishing womanizer. Or the male protagonist of **"Let the Old Dead Make Room for the Young Dead,"** whose sexual desire "was mixed with the desire to debase" the woman from his past.

Of the various forms of closural patterns, the most relevant, of course, to the cycle is what Torgovnick, in her catalogue of closural activities, calls *circularity,* which occurs when the ending "clearly recalls the beginning in some way, perhaps in its language or in situation." In *Laughable Loves,* this occurs through character, for Chehachkova's male counterpart, Edward, is almost a re-enactment of Professor Klima. Like Klima, Edward experiences an exhilarating moment of freedom when he does something he knows he shouldn't—in this case attending a Catholic Mass. In the church, Edward could not resist a "compelling desire" to kneel, to cross himself, in short, to "do something he'd never done before," and in so doing he feels "magnificently free." And like Klima, he is a teacher, one who is, moreover, under the scrutiny of those who doubt he is fit to teach. Edward's story is also one of persecution and that peculiar Stalinist institution, the examining committee. Finally, as in the case of Klima and other characters we have discussed, Edward finds that once one has started a game, it takes on a life of it own and sweeps one along with it, whether one wishes it to or not.

The more political nature of **"Edward and God"** (overt references to the death of Stalin, the revolutionary generation, and the polarized nature of Czech society after the revolution) along with the way it mirrors the first story of the cycle together set the stage for textual realignment and transformation. In the final story, the examination of political structures re-emerges, retentively reactivates similar material in the first unit of the cycle, and, as though illuminated by refracted light bouncing back and forth between the opening and closing units, the political ramifications (dormant in the reader's consciousness since Klima's ordeal with the examining committee) of the intervening units become emphasized.

Take "**The Hitchhiking Game**." The young man, as we have seen, is drawn towards the brutal results of his fantasy. But what lies behind the game? What is the motive? "The main road of [the young man's] life," we are told, "was drawn with implacable precision. . . . Even two weeks' vacation didn't give him a feeling of liberation and adventure; the gray shadow of precise planning lay even here." When he decides to take the road which leads to some place other than their all-too-planned vacation, it pushes the game "into a higher gear," but it also stands as a decisive move towards freedom, a break with the gloomy and monotonous "plannedness" of things. The girl's willingness to play the game and become the fantasy woman, the woman of *"happy go lucky irresponsibility,"* is similar: ". . . she had quite a tiresome job . . . and a sick mother. So she often felt tired. . . . She didn't have particularly good nerves or self-confidence and easily fell into a state of anxiety or fear."

An important part of their motive, then, is to escape the dismal limitations of their life. Once the reader comes to this realization, it can be connected with what he has read in other parts of the cycle, and this thematic gestalt absorbs other units of text. Thus, Martin's womanizing seemed at first to be largely a matter of trying to deny the aging process and the ineluctable forward march of time. But we will also remember that he is a married man with a job, and his erotic games must be cut short so that he can get home by the matrimonially-imposed deadline of 9:00 p.m. And so he too plays a game not only because of his regressive personality, but, at least in a limited sense, as a bid for freedom. Dr. Havel reveals similar motives when he rationalizes his rejection of a woman (a bizarre move for a confirmed womanizer). He first states that, given his predictable behavior, he should have slept with her: "All the statistics would have worked it out that way." And then he quickly adds that "perhaps for those very reasons, I don't take her. Perhaps I want to resist necessity. To trip up causality. To throw off the predictability of the world's course through the whimsicality of caprice." As Banerjee notes, Don Juans do what they do in order to escape "the dull anonymity of their social condition." Much the same is true of the male character of the fifth story ("**Let the Old Dead Make Room for the Young Dead**"), whose desire to recapture the past is the flip side of his reconciliation to his "not too exciting life . . . and the monotonous rowdiness which surrounded him at work." Furthermore, Klima's game with Zaturetsky, a game which initially seemed to be a manifestation of a regressive personality, is now opened for re-conceptualization and can become part of a new thematic configuration, one based on a social rather than psychoanalytic model. After all, early in that story, after he had been more-or-less ordered to follow standard procedure and write a nasty letter to Zaturestsky trashing his work, Klima thinks to himself, "why should I have to be Mr. Zaturetsky's executioner?" Thus, Klima's game may also be seen as an attempt to break away from narrow organizational limits.

It is clear that these characters share similar motivations. They all seem, as Havel articulates it (speaking, as it were, on behalf of the other characters), to want to "derail life from its dreary predictability." Those games may thus be viewed as originating in a desire to break free from a rigid social order, and thus those game-players may be driven not only by psychopathological conditions, but also by their discontent with the social arena in which they play. They are trapped by routine, and the reader's recognition of this reinforces the deepening impression that the effects of social and political conditions on the individual is a central theme of this work.

This dynamic, in terms of response and closure, illustrates the operation of "retrospective patterning," which in this case encourages the emergence of a thematic gestalt that is political in nature: in the final conceptualization, when one lifts the photographic plate from the chemical bath, a portrait of a politically-oppressive society is seen to have developed. However mild, ironic, and subdued that portrait may be, it is nonetheless unmistakably *there*. It is important to note, however, that the characters of *Laughable Loves* are never more than dimly aware of their collective malady, and this very lack of awareness emerges as an important corollary of this thematic core. Character after character, one realizes in retrospect, is peculiarly blind to his own motivations and to where his actions lead. Certainly, Edward moves blindly towards disaster, as do the young man ("**Hitchhiking Game**") and Martin. This blindness is perhaps most apparent in the very first story, "**Nobody Will Laugh**." Klima himself puts it in no uncertain terms: "man passes," he says, "through the present with his eyes blindfolded. . . . Only later when the cloth is untied can he glance at the past and find out what he has experienced and what meaning it had." Which, it occurs to me, may be taken as an allegory for the reading process itself, particularly in regards to the dialectic of retention and closural activities. The reader must, if he wishes to pass through the text at all, proceed at least partially "blindfolded" with the understanding that meaning generally emerges in retrospect.

As with *Laughable Loves,* Kundera's later work, *The Book of Laughter and Forgetting,* may be described as having a cyclic form; a number of critics have commented upon this in terms that clearly resemble Ingram's definition. John Updike, for example, notes that the book is "more than a collection of seven stories yet certainly no novel" [*Hugging the Shore,* 1988]. In like fashion, Terry Eagleton points out that the "structural subversiveness" of this work "lies simply in the loose consciousness whereby they encompass *different stories,* sometimes to the point of appearing like a set of *nouvelles* within the same covers" ["Estrangement and Irony," *Salmagundi* 73 (1987)]. R. B. Gill, in an explicit comparison of *The Book* and *Dubliners,* suggests that it is best regarded not as a novel "in the usual sense, [but as] a series of parts, one could call then stories, each thematically related to the others, a series of variations on a theme" ["Bargaining in Good Faith: The Laughter of Vonnegut, Grass, and Kundera," in *Milan Kundera and the Art of Fiction,* ed. Aron Aji]. And as David Lodge notes in a statement that reveals the way in which the critic must inevitably deal with cycles, "the only way to deal, critically, with *The Book of Laughter and Forgetting* is to review its textual strategies in the order in

which they are experienced by the reader" ["Milan Kundera, and the Idea of the Author in Modern Criticism," *Critical Quarterly,* Spring-Summer, 1984].

For all their similarities, there are also significant differences between these two works. Perhaps the most important and innovative of those features is *The Book*'s "polygeneric" character. The stories of *Laughable Loves* are, in and of themselves, short stories of a relatively conventional sort. By contrast, *The Book* is made up of seven Parts which in turn are fragmented in that they constitute a generic smorgasbord: informal essay (history, musicology, philosophy), the fantastic, and autobiography. As Herbert Eagle remarks [in "Genre and Paradigm in Milan Kundera's *The Book of Laughter and Forgetting,*" in *Language and Literary Theory,* edited by Benjamin A. Stolz and others, 1984], Kundera is a writer whose mastery covers a number of widely divergent genres aside from fiction—poetry, the essay, and, in the Czech tradition, *feuilletons.* "In this diverse *oeuvre,*" Eagle notes, there are persistent themes that, in *The Book,* Kundera explores in a format which allows him to write "in all of his favorite genres simultaneously. . . . " Thus, while *The Book* is certainly in cyclic form, it is not, to be precise, a *short story* cycle, and it thus exceeds its generic identity (perhaps it is more accurate to call it a "polygeneric cycle"). *The Book* also obviously differs from *Laughable Loves* in that it is peppered with statements which address the problems of fictional discourse, a genre which has come to be termed metafiction. As Charles Molesworth asserts [in "Kundera and *The Book:* The Unsaid and the Unsayable," in *Milan Kundera and the Art of Fiction,* ed. Aron Aji] "*The Book,* in addition to its thematic unity, has a structural unity that is achieved by its "concern with itself as a novel".

Furthermore, the nascent political concerns of *Laughable Loves* find fruition in *The Book,* Kundera's first work as an exile. The former work, to be sure, has a political element, for as Jeffery Goldfarb notes [in *Beyond Glasnost,* 1989], "The stories in *Laughable Loves* are [Kundera's] most explicitly non-political," and yet "they are about the ironies of domination and subjugation." In all these instances, however, the critique is a veiled one. *The Book,* on the other hand, attempts a much broader critique: problems of cultural heritage and national identity are explored in conjunction with a dominant event (the 1968 invasion) and a dominant theme ("organized forgetting").

Finally, the apparent aesthetic design of *The Book* makes it an example of what Ingram calls a *composed* cycle, while *Laughable Loves* is a *completed* cycle, one of "looser" design. This generic distinction is mirrored in the different quality of aesthetic experience which these works elicit in the reader—what Iser calls the "generic control of aesthetic response". Furthermore, in his essay on Kundera, Lodge claims that "whereas in *The Joke* Kundera displayed, at the first attempt, his mastery of the modernist novel, *The Book of Laughter and Forgetting* is a masterpiece of postmodern fiction . . ." Similarly, I would suggest that *Laughable Loves* may be viewed as a modernist cycle, while *The Book* may be viewed as a post-modernist one.

In his later work, *The Unbearable Lightness of Being,* Kundera combines his novelistic tendencies (*The Joke, Life is Elsewhere, The Farewell Party*) with his cyclic ones, thus affecting a fusion of his various experiments with narrative architectonics. Kundera accomplishes this by returning to the essay-mode used to such great advantage in *The Book* and interweaving the essayistic sections (which are thematically anchored in the Nietzschian concept of the eternal return) with fictive events (rooted, as in *The Book,* in the 1968 invasion) concerning four central characters who serve as alternating focal points for the novel's seven parts.

As successful as Kundera's more novelistic works are, I would suggest that his two works in cyclic form are even more so, largely *because* of their cyclicity. Because of its paratactic superstructure, cyclic form seems to have certain advantages in describing social situations that are characterized by fragmentation and anomie and/or a narrative consciousness characterized by these qualities. As Mann notes, cycles are "especially well suited to handle certain subjects, including the sense of fragmentation or indeterminacy that many twentieth-century characters experience." And as Stevick suggests in his comments on Hemingway's cycle *In Our Time,* cyclic form may be a cognate of a given ideological construct:

> Explicitly developed progressions between narrative units imply a great deal, one hardly realizes how much until one notices their absence: they imply a coherence within the fictive world that is physical, epistemological, and moral. Most of these coherences Hemingway did not believe in and would not counterfeit. The interchapters of *In Our Time* in their relation to the stories that occur between them, are examples of a lack of faith in coherence made into a structural principle. [*The Chapter in Fiction: Theories of Narrative Division,* 1970]

Certainly, the cycle has an advantage over the novel in this regard in that it shows a broad cross-section of characters who, as in **Laughable Loves,** are *isolated* from one another, quite different from one another, and yet have similar, socially-determined problems.

Perhaps the two most notable story cycles are Joyce's *Dubliners* and Sherwood Anderson's *Winesburg, Ohio.* One must first note the uncanny similarity between the work of Joyce and Anderson. As Martha Curry points out, it is indeed an incredible coincidence that in the first decade of the twentieth century Joyce wrote a sequence of interrelated stories "depicting the drab, isolated, and frustrated citizens of Dublin and that in the next decade Anderson wrote stories of the same kind of people in a small Midwestern town" ["Sherwood Anderson and James Joyce," *American Literature* 52 (1980)]. What is even more remarkable is that in spite of the affinities between these two works, Anderson, as Curry goes to great lengths to demonstrate, was unaware of *Dubliners* at the time. This strongly suggests that cyclic form is conducive to the fic-

tive rendering of a certain type of experience—what Joyce referred to as "paralysis" and what Anderson called the "starved side of American small town life." The formal similarity of the two works is furthermore interesting when one considers the differences between Joyce and Anderson. Joyce, on the one hand, was well-versed in aesthetic theory and often drew on this theoretical knowledge in his practice as a writer. Anderson, on the other hand, though well-read and not at all the naif he has often been regarded as, was "almost completely ignorant of aesthetic theory" (Curry). It seems, then, that even though Joyce took the "high road" of academic knowledge and Anderson took the "low road" of a strong aesthetic intuition, they both had a similar point-of-departure (anomized characters as subject) and the same point-of-arrival (cyclic form).

Another analogous work in this regard is Richard Wright's *Uncle Tom's Children,* which has been called "Wright's *Dubliners*" [Craig Hansen Werner, *Paradoxical Resolutions,* 1982]. In this work, Wright presents a varied cross-section of Black Americans in their struggle against oppression. The discrimination and violence faced by Black Americans is such that when one compares it to the struggles of other nationalities, one does so at the risk of trivialization. Nonetheless, it is a struggle that is not without its similarities to the Irish situation portrayed by Joyce or the Czech situation portrayed by Kundera. Wright's cycle is characterized, as is *Dubliners,* by a linear pattern of development in which each protagonist is older than his predecessor in the cycle. The first stories in this work take particular advantage of the fragmentation effect of cyclic form by showing the futility of isolated struggle while the closing stories, paralleling the reader's sense of totality, suggest the possibilities of social consciousness and collective action. As in other cycles, Wright's is characterized by what Ingram calls a "pattern of development" and what I have elsewhere called a mega-narrative: we see a trajectory which parallels the African-American's quest for freedom. As McCall points out, in each of the four stories Wright "broadens the areas of responsibility on the part of each succeeding main character, moving from boy to community leader, from victim to victor, so that the stories will compose a rising tide of militancy" [*The Example of Richard Wright,* 1969]. And again, such a social portrait seems to find its best expression in cyclic form.

Both **Laughable Loves** and *The Book* have much in common with these works by Joyce, Anderson, and Wright. For example, R. B. Gill notes a number of affinities between *The Book* and *Dubliners.* In addition to their shared formal characteristics, "both books are the work of an exile trying to make sense of his lost country and of his reasons for leaving it. Both are realistic appraisals of the paralysis that has afflicted their homelands." Furthermore, all four of these writers have endeavored to provide, among other things, a portrait of an oppressive society. They were all, in one way or another, exiles—Anderson, in a figurative sense, an exile from the trappings of small-town America; Joyce, an exile by choice from his stultifying and provincial homeland; Wright, also an exile by volition, living out the last decade of his life in France in a gesture that he had given up on the possibility of change

---

On the gravity of Kundera's themes:

Although his subject [in *Laughable Loves*] is sexual love, the reticence with which [Kundera] describes his settings, the focussing on problems of truth, reality and dissimulation in personal relations hints at wider concerns. He is an expert on the games people play to probe the limits of love or sexual involvement and the fixes that fantasy can lead into. All the stories start with a deliberate step into untruth, and resolve with the dangers that lie outside prosaic paths. Toes are dipped into the whirlpools of deception and withdrawn frostbitten; or lost altogether. The sparseness of the setting emphasises the philosophical sophistication of the tales and points to sterner implications.

Mary Hope, in the Spectator, *June 10, 1978.*

---

in America; and Kundera, who, as it were, purchased his exile (also to France) through the very act of writing. After the 1970 publication of *Laughable Loves,* the Czech regime banned Kundera's works, and *The Book of Laughter and Forgetting,* published in 1979 while Kundera was living in France, caused the regime to exile him *in absentia*. All of these writers created works that portray what might be termed "anomized" or "paralyzed" societies as viewed by the self-exiled artist; and all these works are cycles.

To say that cyclic form is suited to a particular cultural experience and intent on the part of the author may seem to be overstating the case; after all, there are any number of novels which depict such societies, and thus it would be premature to postulate something akin to a scientific law of literary form regarding story cycles (or for that matter, any other literary phenomenon). On the other hand, I think that the affinities outlined above strike one as being something more than coincidence. Specific literary form, specific generic types, the above evidence suggests, have sociological cognates.

Which brings us to the question of genre itself. One problem with arguing that *The Book* is an example of the cycle genre is that Kundera himself prefers to call it a novel. In his view, the novel as genre is not identified by narrative continuity or for that matter any other structural feature. As he puts it, it is a mistake "to regard a certain stereotyped structure as the inviolable essence of the novel" (*Art of the Novel*). Rather, he defines it in terms of its spirit of inquiry (which he finds particularly evident in Diderot and Sterne) and its ability both to absorb and to undermine other, dogmatic discourses.

So which is it—novel or cycle?

A generic designation is not important in and of itself. As Todorov notes, "categories have merely a constructed existence," and as a result, a work can manifest "more than one category, more than one genre" [*The Fantastic,* translated by Richard Howard, 1973]. The importance of generic designation is its heuristic value in relation to one's

purpose. Mine has been to reveal the formal complexity of *Laughable Loves,* its role in Kundera's aesthetic development, the nature of the reading experience it elicits, and its similarities, in purpose and form, to a number of other notable works.

Fred Misurella (essay date 1993)

SOURCE: "Amid Chaos, the Survival of Form: *Laughable Loves,*" in *Understanding Milan Kundera: Public Events, Private Affairs,* University of South Carolina Press, 1993, pp. 162-90.

[*Misurella is an American educator and critic. In the following excerpt, he suggests that* Laughable Loves *revolves "on the theme of our helplessness before external events and the inadequacy of language as a tool in controlling or understanding them."*]

[An] interest in ironic play, polyphony, and thematic variation as the basis of his concept of the novel's form has led Kundera to regard *Laughable Loves* as a novel in seven parts, although it began as a collection of ten separate stories published in three separate volumes in Czech. In *The Art of the Novel,* while discussing how frequently he resorts to seven-part structures in his novels, he says he eliminated three of the original ten *Laughable Loves* stories and "the whole thing became very coherent, in a way that prefigured *The Book of Laughter and Forgetting*: the same themes (especially the hoax) make a single entity out of seven narratives, the fourth and sixth of which are further linked by having the same protagonist, Dr. Havel. In *The Book of Laughter and Forgetting,* too, the fourth and sixth parts are linked by the same character: Tamina." So *Laughable Loves* might be appropriately titled as *The Book of Laughable Loves,* and in fact, according to Kundera, at his request the work carries just that title in its German and Spanish versions.

If, as he says, the hoax works as a principal theme in the book, we can extend that idea by conceiving of it as a novel about mistaken beliefs: in the self, in relationships, in human character, and, ultimately, existence, at least existence as exemplified in ideological traps such as religion and political philosophy. But *Laughable Loves* works also, and more importantly, as all of Kundera's novels do, as a higher mediation on faith in relation to language and reality. Time and again Kundera has shown how language, our primary tool in understanding and remembering, is, in and of itself, a fallible keeper of truth simply because it not only reflects reality, but through the lies of fiction creates a reality of its own that may be more believable— and more dangerous. So in *Laughable Loves* we go from **"Nobody Will Laugh,"** a story about lying and "making it" through **"Edward and God,"** a story about faith and "making it," both of which show the lie somehow betraying the liar with a new reality. Between those two stories Kundera portrays men and women using and abusing each other for their own purposes at all ages, from youth in the beginning to age at the conclusion, the two functioning as bookends for the various stages of adult human experience. In all stories love and sex at their least serious become the field on which highly metaphysical questions and fictions of self, existence, love, and God are debated. In **"Nobody Will Laugh"** the narrator Klima states the human problem succinctly, lamenting our inability to control the stories of our own lives: "They aren't *our* stories at all," he says; "they are foisted on us from somewhere *outside*." If the idea sounds suspiciously similar to the one that Jacques repeats from his former captain, we can point to it as an example of Kundera's consistency and underline Klima's words as another variation on the theme of our helplessness before external events and the inadequacy of language as a tool in controlling or understanding them.

"Nobody Will Laugh"

[In **"Nobody Will Laugh"**] Klima, an instructor of art history, sits at home with his lover, Klara, a young woman of "excellent" family, and celebrates his recent success, the publication of a study in an important visual arts magazine, while reading a letter from another scholar. The letter, from a man named Zaturetsky, asks him to review an article for publication in the same magazine that has accepted Klima's for publication. Next morning Klima reads Zaturetsky's article and finds it laughably earnest, full of platitudes, and as scholarship essentially worthless. Then the editor of the arts journal calls, encouraging Klima to say something short and negative because, he says, Zaturetsky keeps badgering them, insisting that they do not understand him and that only an expert such as Klima could appreciate his research. Flattered by Zaturetsky's good opinion, and angered because he had difficulty getting his own work published in the journal, Klima can not bring himself to write the negative evaluation. Instead, he gives a vague promise to the editor and writes to Zaturetsky himself, flattering the man at the same time he says that other specialists suspect his own opinions and that therefore his recommendation would, in the end, work against the article. Mailing the letter, Klima thinks he can forget about the article and the man, but, as he ruefully says, Zaturetsky did not forget him. There follows one of those long, complicated plot mazes Kundera runs his characters through in order to make us laugh, see the irony of frivolous behavior turned into life-changing fate (as he did with Ludvik in *The Joke*) and good intentions working against the good of those intending.

Zaturetsky confronts Klima at one of his lectures, asking for his review, and Klima, seeing stubbornness and asceticism written in the lines of the man's face, promises "something vague." Instead of writing the review, however, he avoids Zaturetsky, changing the days of his lectures, asking the department secretary to lie about his whereabouts, until Zaturetsky, stubbornly seeking him out, complains to the dean and finally receives the address of Klima's apartment in Prague. In a scene baring one of Kundera's favorite themes, and one filled with potential comedy as well, Zaturetsky invades Klima's privacy: banging insistently on the apartment door while Klara sits alone,

he forces her to respond at last and leaves a note to remind Klima about the review. From this point, the meeting of inept scholar and beautiful young protégée, the curve of Klima's fate turns irrevocably downward.

Zaturetsky arrives at the university again a few days later, asks Klima for the review, and Klima, seeing the man's mundane, ascetic nature as material for a joke, accuses him of making sexual advances to Klara at the apartment. Enraged, Zaturetsky denies the accusation, saying he has a wife and family, and threatens to get even as Klima, believing his own lie for a moment, dismisses the man triumphantly, believing the matter finished. But a few days later Klara receives a note from Mrs. Zaturetsky demanding that she come to her apartment to explain the accusations against her husband. Of course, Klara does not go, but in short order Mrs. Zaturetsky attempts to find Klima at the university and then she and her husband seek Klara at her job. Both attempts fail, but when Klima's department chairman calls him into the office to discuss the renewal of his contract, the Zaturetskys' presence hangs ominously over the meeting. The chairman tells Klima that his article has offended the dean and that the dean, because of Zaturetsky's complaints, now thinks Klima has missed his lectures for months. Klima tries to dismiss the complaints as frivolous or untrue but, at home that night, he finds a letter from the local Party committee asking to see him.

At the meeting Klima learns of complaints about Klara's presence from other tenants, hears about his "missed" lectures, and listens to the accusations of the Zaturetskys. Most ominous, perhaps, in light of what we know about Ludvik Jahn from *The Joke,* one of the committee members refers to Klima as an intellectual and sees him as refusing to help his fellow worker, Zaturetsky. With his job clearly threatened, and the slope of his fate seeming to slide downward, Klima searches for basic values and discovers the importance of his love for Klara. But with complaints from the other tenants and their privacy invaded by Zaturetsky, she can no longer live with him, and so they meet at a borrowed apartment. In a scene reminiscent of the ones between Lucie and Ludvik in *The Joke,* Klima learns that Klara feels uncomfortable meeting him in the apartment and they argue over the review he has to write. Pragmatic, she tells him to solve his problems by praising Zaturetsky's article, but in a second statement about his basic values, Klima insists that he cannot lie or joke about his work. In order to save himself and Klara, however, he asks Mrs. Zaturetsky to his apartment. Finally telling the truth, he says that her husband's article is scientifically worthless and reads passages from it along with passages from other writers to show its lack of originality. She leaves, stunned, but although the matter of the Zaturetskys seems at rest, Klima learns from Klara that the descent of his life has really just begun. Having spoken to the editor of the visual arts journal herself, she has learned that Klima will not continue at his teaching post, and she implies that the editor will now get her the job Klima himself had promised her. Shaking his hand "clearly for the last time," Klara leaves. Alone, now facing the loss of the two things he has considered most important to him, Klima looks at recent events and, resilient, still finds amusement. Having told Klara earlier that life's purpose is to entertain, he can now find comfort in the thought that his story is comic rather than tragic.

"THE GOLDEN APPLE of DESIRE"

If **"Nobody Will Laugh"** contains in miniature many of the elements of Kundera's first novel, *The Joke*, **"The Golden Apple of Desire"** contains elements of his two most recent novels: in its title a major image from *Immortality* and in character and event the married Don Juan theme so powerfully developed in *The Unbearable Lightness of Being*. In addition, this second **Laughable Loves** story handles a pair of picaros, as does *Jacques and His Master*, and endows them with contrasting attitudes in the manner of Professor Avenarius and the caricature Kundera draws of himself in *Immortality*.

The narrator, apparently an art historian, sits in a Prague café leafing through a rare book on Etruscan culture and waits for his friend Martin, who can do what the studious narrator finds impossible: he can stop any woman on the street and engage her in flirtatious conversation, although he often stops at talk and passes her on to his friends. With the theme of language underlined by the narrator's comments, Martin arrives and Kundera moves on to the second part of the story, appropriately called "The Adventure Begins." Seeing a beautiful young woman at a nearby table, Martin follows her to the cloakroom and, looking for a prop, takes the narrator's rare art book, says it is too heavy to carry, and drops it into the woman's bag. They talk, Martin learns that she works as a nurse in a country hospital, and, after the three walk together to her bus to the country, he promises that he and the narrator will drive to the hospital on the following Saturday to retrieve the book. As the section ends we learn that Martin, who has recently turned forty, has a young wife at home. He loves her and fears her, the narrator tells us, and immediately Martin tries to invent a story he can tell her to get out of the house. In this way both characters reveal themselves as trapped—one by life, the other by art—and both look to language and the imagination as a means of escape.

The narrator borrows a car and the two drive to the nurse's country town. Along the way to meeting her they stop several women, and the narrator explains Martin's stages in the game of seduction: "registration," "making contact," and what the narrator refers to as the "last level," presumably sex, the exclusive interest in which he passes off as a trait of "primitive" men. But the more refined, stylized pursuit that Martin and the narrator practice has its ridiculous side as well, for clearly, as the "adventure" of the day continues, we see the two men as ineffectual: romantics chasing beautiful maidens in a dreamlike game of words whose world is the only reality they can control.

They meet the nurse, retrieve the narrator's book, and arrange to meet her and her girlfriend after work, at seven o'clock. Martin convinces the nurse to arrange for the four of them to go to a lakeside cabin, but as he and the narrator walk about the town to occupy the time, Martin says they have to leave for Prague by eight so he can play his customary Saturday night game of cards with his wife. Nevertheless, despite only an hour alone with the young nurses, Martin feels they have time to seduce them. Meanwhile, they "register" and "make contact" with two other women, both of whom promise to meet them in a few minutes but do not return. As the afternoon passes, we come to see how much these two Don Juans are really Don Quixotes in disguise and how, despite the lure of desire that Martin lives for and that the narrator only imitates, they have no real, physical amorous goals. They lie, to themselves and others, anticipating future adventures, eagerly planning for them, but never attaining the last level of fulfillment in them. After yet another of the women they talked to does not meet them as agreed, the narrator speculates that she did not return because she believed the fiction they concocted about shooting a film on the subject of Etruscans in Bohemia. He says that it might have gone better for them if she had not believed their story. He then discusses the danger of too much faith, saying that when people believe in something completely, their faith will "turn it into something absurd," a fair comment, it seems, on the adventure the two men constantly pursue.

They return to meet the nurses at seven o'clock, park near the hospital gate, and the narrator watches for them in the rear view mirror. He sees the two nurses, obviously dressed and eager to meet them, emerge from the hospital gate. Caught up in his thoughts about the danger of too much faith, the narrator sees his friend as a forty-year-old married man playing the game of youth without knowing it. Looking at his own behavior, he considers himself more ridiculous than Martin because he knows they are merely playing: "Why at this time should I behave as if an amorous adventure lay before me, when I know that at most a single aimless hour with unknown and indifferent girls awaits me?" Without informing his friend that the nurses are there, the narrator drives away, assuring Martin that they will not arrive.

In the final scene the narrator, feeling guilty, wonders whether he can ever give up the "gestures which signify youth" for him. As they discuss a female medical student "invented" by the narrator for possible future adventure, he and Martin discuss passing her between themselves and decide to impress her by saying that Martin is an athlete. Martin sees it as "in the realm of possibility," although he is unathletic and forty years old. The story ends pathetically, with the friends' mutual, implausible lie imposing itself upon the narrator's story, or fiction; he describes the joining as a "beautiful, ripe, shining apple" dangling before them. As they follow it down the road toward the sunset, the narrator calls it **"The Golden Apple of Eternal Desire,"** an image that some twenty years later, at the end of *Immortality*, Kundera, with ironic purpose, would resurrect as a brightly colored ball floating above a mirrored swimming pool in Montparnasse: Narcissus meeting Helen, a sign of Goethe's "eternal feminine" drawing us on.

"THE HITCHHIKING GAME"

If **"The Golden Apple of Eternal Desire"** leaves its two main characters permanently on the road in the midst of the perpetual and futile game of the chase after women, Kundera uses the next story [**"The Hitchhiking Game"**] to carry on that theme, this time as a variation, making a woman part of the journey. A young couple traveling in a sports car sees the gas gauge turn toward empty and, after some flirtatious conversation about hitchhikers, stop for fuel at a station. As they wait for service, the young woman goes into the woods behind the station to relieve herself, and the young man reflects on her purity, as he calls it, because she speaks so shyly of her body functions. Charmed, he realizes that at her young age the shyness soon must pass.

The next section of the story elaborates on the young woman's reflections as she walks into the woods and steps behind a bush to, as Kundera says, give "herself up to her good mood." Angry about her shyness, she longs to feel more free about her body, reminding herself that the body we receive at birth is just one out of millions of possibilities, making it random, impersonal, and strictly on loan. For the moment at one with her body, she loves her traveling companion because he accepts her wholly, in no way encouraging the usual dualism of body and spirit from which she suffers. But, like Tereza in *The Unbearable Lightness of Being,* the young woman is jealous also, worrying about keeping her lover, fearing that he will leave her one day for a more physical woman, one more comfortable (and in harmony) with her body. After she leaves the woods, instead of returning to the car, she walks along the highway in the direction they are traveling. The young man catches up, and she waves; he rolls down his window to ask if she needs a ride. Smiling flirtatiously, the woman says she does and enters the car. In that way, lightly, innocuously, the hitchhiking game begins for these two travelers, a game, or fiction, that goes to the heart of self and what Kundera might call its various possibilities.

Driving, they continue to flirt, as if they really are strangers, and although the young man, through tenderness, attempts to reestablish their normal conversational tone, the woman insists on the new one. She imagines herself as seeing her lover now as a different person, the man he is with other, more free-living, women. Jealous, she continues to flirt with him and ultimately, caught up in her act, suffers because, as with the narrator of **"Nobody Will Laugh,"** the fiction comes to dominate their reality. Playing a "role out of trashy literature," she provokes her young man to respond in kind, and the two find themselves, almost against their will, playing out the game. The young man turns off the road, taking another direction from the one they are traveling, and suddenly, but separately, both experience a refreshing rush of freedom from the ordered, frustrating existence they have lived till then. Seeking light-heartedness and irresponsibility, they drive into an unknown country town and take a room for the night. The game continues, increasing its hold on them moment by moment, and the young man wonders whether he now sees his lover's real self, freed from inhibition by the roles they are playing. She feels different herself, shameless, without history or obligations and, at last, the woman she wants to be, and that she imagines her lover wants her to be: a pickup for whom *"everything"* is *"permitted."*

In their room after dinner, they play out the conclusion to the game. The young man, angry that his girlfriend performs the role of whore so well, speaks to her coarsely, refusing to kiss her and giving her money to force her to humiliate herself through obscene gestures and motions. She tries to reassert her normal behavior, but he continues to treat her like a bought woman, and in a scene with the emotional brutality of Ludvik Jahn's sexual punishment of Helena in *The Joke,* aggressively pulls her into bed, where their sex, a complex mixture of anger and impersonal desire, yields a moment that Kundera describes as one with "two bodies in perfect harmony, two sensual bodies, alien to each other." The young woman, having experienced what she has always most dreaded, sex without love or emotion, admits to herself that despite her horror she has experienced sexual pleasure like no other in her life. Frightened by what she has learned about herself, she lies in the dark beside her young man, both their masks off now, and cries out "I am me, I am me," while her lover, searching for compassion ("from afar," Kundera tells us), tries to comfort her. For both of them, however, the game that began so innocently, spontaneously, has irrevocably changed their lives as well as their love.

"SYMPOSIUM"

Appropriately, after two explorations of the nature of physical desire, Kundera turns to present a parody of the most famous Western work on ideal, or spiritual, love, Plato's *Symposium,* a philosophic dialogue that treats love from the perspectives of myth, poetry, reason (really false, sophistic reason), and comedy before giving itself over to Socrates's discussion defining love as intellectual rather than physical, a desire for beauty in its ideal form.

Our concept of Platonic love originates in this dialogue, and Kundera performs a parodic variation on it [in **"Symposium"**] by staging a discussion of love in a hospital, place of bodily breakdown and repair, that decidedly emphasizes the physical even as it comically belies the validity of that very solid source of erotic power. Immediately breaking down any possible realistic reading of the story, Kundera separates it into acts instead of chapters and sets the scene of the staff room at "any hospital in any town that you like." What's more, he makes obvious authorial intrusions with ironic titles to the sections of each act, and in introducing his characters says that they have gathered there under "less than important" pretexts, presumably to drink and chat, but also, we must remember, because the author has put them there arbitrarily. With the stage set, characters introduced, and, by means of parabasis, the author's presence very firmly announced, the drama begins.

Dr. Havel and Nurse Alzhbeta sit in a hospital staff room drinking, although they are on night duty, with three other physicians on the staff: the chief physician, elderly and bald; a thirty-year-old woman doctor from another ward; and Flaishman, the youngest of them, a ward intern whose naïve self-centeredness makes him one of those angelic innocents Kundera has treated so frequently and ironically in his fiction. The others have various degrees of experience, fitting for their years, and although the evening passes with what Kundera calls "appreciative chatter," we learn of some tensions. Alzhbeta has drunk too much and begins to flirt with Dr. Havel, whose response sets off whatever drama the evening will have. Complaining that as a nurse Alzhbeta should understand the limits of the flesh, Havel criticizes her desire, a vitality that he calls "incorrigible," and declares that her body movements make his head spin. "Those boobs of yours are ubiquitous—like God!" he says, ordering her to leave him alone and go about her business of injecting patients. When she leaves to do just that, the chief physician wonders aloud why Havel refuses the nurse's advances when normally, like death, he will, as the chief says, "take everything."

The two phrases, about Alzhbeta's breasts and Havel's desire, combine to state the basic metaphysical themes that Kundera handles in this story, ironically joining (and inverting) the spiritual with the physical and the erotic with the eternal. During a discussion that reinforces this yoking of opposites, the chief physician speaks of his greatest amorous success as one with a sexually experienced woman who refused to go to bed with him. He describes her refusal as a sign of lifelong commitment since he was her "first and last" refused man. The banter continues, with Havel admitting he does not know why he rejects Alzhbeta, since he has slept with uglier, more aggressive women, and he finally blames it on caprice, raising that capriciousness to a philosophic level by calling it a "scrap of freedom" in a "world of iron laws." The three drink to freedom, and at that moment, young Flaishman enters the room, having gone off to buy a bottle of champagne.

Immediately, Havel and the chief physician take advantage of the intern's youthful egotism, claiming that for months Alzhbeta has wanted him while he has ungallantly looked the other way. Flaishman, described as slow, not because of clumsiness but because of preoccupation with his inner self, replies that he is not interested in the nurse and absolves himself from guilt, saying he is not responsible for pain he causes involuntarily. At this point Alzhbeta returns to the room, drinks champagne, and the chief physician voices one of Kundera's most prominent themes: Ignorance absolves no one, not even innocents, since "Ignorance is a fault," and man bears responsibility for it. It is a theme Kundera would turn to again in other books, and the reader may recognize in Flaishman the same self-conscious innocence (and the same attachment to his mother) that motivates Jaromil in *Life Is Elsewhere*. The woman doctor defends Flaishman, and he takes it as a sign that she is interested in him. She has apparently intrigued him since they met, and when she goes to the window and declares how lovely it looks outside under the full moon, he takes her comment as a hint that she wants to be with him in the open air. He leaves the room, his chest swelling with absolute certainty that she will follow him, and enters the garden to await her. Knowing that a great love

experience is imminent, he leans against a tree and smokes, romantically seeing himself in the garden at the same time; but when he turns toward the sound of footsteps behind him he finds, rather than the woman doctor, the chief physician out to relieve his bladder. As "Act One" ends, this sudden change from romance to biological necessity comically underlines the dualism in Flaishman's (and we might say European) self-consciousness.

In "Act Two" Kundera accentuates the duality. Flaishman and the chief physician return to the staff room to find Alzhbeta, drunk, in the midst of a mock striptease that creates one of the most memorable parodic scenes in Kundera's fiction. With her body everywhere in the room, "like God," she circles the other characters, revolving especially about Havel, who sits with his head down as if attending a funeral. Alzhbeta encourages him to look at her, saying that she is vital, alive, at least temporarily, and, at that comment, the narrator describes her backside as "splendidly formed grief" dancing close to Havel, who, despite her encouragement, keeps his eyes turned to the floor. In pantomime she removes all her clothes, and, on tiptoe at the end of her dance, in the "glory of her fictional nakedness," stares down at her body, self-involved in the same way Flaishman is when he studies himself internally or stands in the garden waiting for romance to begin.

Exhausted finally, Alzhbeta collapses at Havel's feet and asks for pep pills to provide more energy. He gives her a sleeping pill instead, and when she, more tired and drunk, tries to sit on his lap, he moves his legs so she falls to the floor. Embarrassed, Alzhbeta decides to go to bed, calling the others beasts and idiots for having laughed at her. After she leaves, the doctors continue their banter. When the woman doctor refers to Havel as a Don Juan, the chief physician disagrees, again likening his colleague to death. Havel agrees with the chief physician's assessment. In a long analytic speech that lifts the consideration of love to a mythic level, he says that Don Juan is no longer a valid figure because in his time he conquered convention and innocence, defying death and God for sexual pleasure, while today's more liberal conventions would make him a collector with no tragic import. Claiming to be a mere comic figure himself, Havel says that whatever small grandeur he possesses exists only against the "background" of Don Juan's "tragic gaiety." The woman doctor compliments Havel on his fine speech, noting that it contradicts his claim to a humble masculine role. Calling him an "old fraud," she remarks on the beauty of the night, and Flaishman, once more misreading her comment as a signal, excuses himself to go into the garden. But as "Act Two" ends, Flaishman again finds something unexpected. Sure that romance is imminent, he smells gas as he leaves the building, tracks it to the nurses' quarters, and finds Alzhbeta lying on her couch, unconsicous and naked, with the unlit jet to the gas stove on. He opens the window and calls the others to help save her (as they do), but not before seeing, in yet another inversion (death made to look sexual and beautiful), just how lovely her body really is.

In "Act Three' Kundera begins to unwind the story, even as he continues the philosophic explorations. With Alzhbeta's life saved, the three doctors and Flaishman debate what happened in the nurses' room, disagreeing as much about the experience of death as they did earlier about erotic ones. As they debate, Kundera turns Alzhbeta's body (and her handling of it) into a sign for which each speaker seeks to find some meaning. Flaishman, self-absorbed romantic that he is, believes that Alzhbeta tried to kill herself out of love for him, condemns his egocentricity for not responding to her, and, reversing his earlier thinking, accepts responsibility for the unintended pain he caused. The chief physician, still superficially clever, believes Alzhbeta set up the suicide without intending to achieve it; she undressed, he says, turned on the gas, and, to tempt Havel, left the door to her room open so that he would discover her and see her beautiful body. Havel shrugs in resignation, saying he believes Alzhbeta intended to kill herself but not for him alone; everyone, not just Havel, refused her, he says, and she intended to be found naked, glorious, slipping into "intercourse with death," so that those she left behind would be envious and long at last for her underestimated body. Practical, the woman doctor refutes the other opinions, saying Alzhbeta gassed herself by mistake. She had returned to her room, finished the striptease; this time removing her clothes for real, then put on coffee to await Havel, who she thought would arrive when the other doctors left for the night; tired, she fell asleep and the water for the coffee boiled over to put out the gas flame. Havel objects to this theory and asks for an explanation of Alzhbeta's comment about being alive, if only temporarily. The woman doctor, having previously called Havel a fraud for his fine talk about Don Juan, tells him that ninety-nine percent of all statements have no meaning; that is, they are fictional. Whether Kundera intends her comment as his central theme or not, he ends "Act Three" ironically with a view of patent self-delusion: Flaishman again, seated in his parents' garden, feeling words like "beloved" and "death" filling his chest and lifting him as if he wore wings (the angel motif again), and believing that in Alzhbeta he has at long last found absolute love.

To corroborate that theme, "Act Four" presents a scene of completely idle chatter. Late at night the woman doctor returns to the staff room, claiming she cannot sleep. She and Havel talk, each claiming a lack of sexual interest in the other, primarily because of their shared affection for the chief physician. Echoing Plato, Havel says friendship between men is much more important than erotic love of women, and he goes on to say that he sees his own future in the chief physician's pretentious behavior. With the decay of the body that comes with age, he says, a man must pretend, creating "everything that he no longer is." The woman doctor understands and agrees that she too could do nothing to harm the chief physician. But their shared affection for the chief becomes the primary motive for their betrayal of him. Havel would do nothing to harm him, the woman doctor says, so "I can depend on you. I can make love with you." She sits on Havel's knee and unbuttons his shirt. In a parabatic aside that makes up a section heading, the narrator asks a question whose answer is obvious, "What Did Dr. Havel Do?" In a teasing response the narrator also says, "Ah, that's some question."

Since the answer to that question is not in words but in imagination and (as we imagine it) action, it is fitting that Kundera makes the final act of his philosophic drama revolve around a set of inventions and imaginations that in all likelihood will not be realized. He begins with Flaishman offering flowers to Alzhbeta and just avoiding the impulse to ask her to marry him. Overcome with the grandeur of his feeling, he thanks her for existing, squeezes her shoulder, and leaves to go back on duty. In the staff room he finds Havel, the chief physician, and the woman doctor still debating the suicide. Alzhbeta has confirmed the woman doctor's theory about the water boiling over, but the chief physician reminds them she could be lying since people who attempt suicide are regularly sent to asylums in their country. With the truth thus undermined, even from its source, the three continue to disagree, with each reversing a previously stated opinion. The chief physician now thinks Alzhbeta might have intended to kill herself; the woman doctor, in order "to make the world more beautiful," says they should agree; and Havel, feeling guilty about the previous night, claims that only love, not friendship, is important enough to be worth a suicide. The story ends with Flaishman, ever living in his illusions, hearing the woman doctor exclaim, as she looks through the window to a beautiful day, that she is happy to be alive. Once again, he interprets her words as a romantic signal, feels grateful for having settled his feeling for Alzhbeta with flowers "and some nice words," and (but we are left to imagine this, nothing more) excuses himself to go into the garden. The story begins again, Kundera tells us, but with Flaishman feeling stronger, older, having received a most romantic (and questionable) gift, a "splendid . . . invigorating death" that, along with love, has been investigated and debated from positions similar to those in Plato's *Symposium:* myth, poetry (Flaishman's emotions), specious reasoning (all that empty talk, especially about Alzhbeta's "suicide"), and, a Kunderan specialty from beginning to end, ironic comedy.

"LET THE OLD DEAD MAKE ROOM FOR THE YOUNG DEAD"

"**Symposium**" is perhaps the high point of *Laughable Loves* so far, its joining of farce with philosophic seriousness a key to Kundera's stated ambitions for fiction, while the three stories that follow serve as a coda of sorts, further exploring meaning through the experience of love, the memory of love, and the language that attempts, but finally fails, to encapsulate them.

From a discussion of the search for truth and reality in love and death, Kundera moves to a discussion of reality itself, especially in relation to human character. In "**Let the Old Dead Make Room for the Young Dead**," an autumnal story, he presents a pair of former lovers, meeting again in a small Czech town after fifteen years, who make the futile attempt to bring together their younger with their present selves. Complicating the situation, both have reached crisis points in their lives, moments when they are made painfully aware of the passage of time and the increased imminence of their deaths.

The woman (we never know her name) has come to this small town where her husband lies buried only to find out that the lease on the land that holds his grave has run out and the authorities have removed the body and headstone and replaced them with the remains of another. When she complains that the authorities should have let her know that the lease had run out so she could renew it, an official mutters the words that become the title and motif of this story: *"The old dead ought to make room for the young dead."* The woman wanders about the town, filled with remorse for her loss and her carelessness, and upset because she knows her son, who still loves his father, will accuse her of forgetting him. Looking to pass the time until her bus leaves for Prague, she meets a younger man with whom she spent a night some fifteen years before. He, twenty years younger than she but preoccupied with his own advancing age (thirty-five) and the signs of an inevitable bald spot on his head, almost passes her by until he recognizes her smile. As he talks to her, he feels the whole experience of the single night they spent together return. With all the cafes filled and dirty, he invites her to his apartment for coffee, and there the drama of four selves in two characters plays itself out in a single room that calls to the characters' minds another, smaller one they had made love in fifteen years before.

In an elegiac tone much like the one he uses in "The Middle-Aged Man" section of *Life is Elsewhere* and "The Dial" in *Immortality* (both are "guest-house" chapters, separate structures that are yet still part of the formal estate that makes up the world of the novel they inhabit), Kundera tells us something about the man's memory of the woman. She had been beautiful, not only older but married to an older man, more experienced, and therefore mysterious to him. After several meetings in small cafés, she had agreed to meet him in his room. Overwhelmed to be with her alone, he could not act naturally or confidently, and because of his inexperience she had to lead them into the act of love. Shamed, he had turned off the lights before they undressed and, although they were sexually intimate, he could not see her face. Now, like Rubens in *Immortality,* in the midst of evaluating his life and seeing it as pitifully uneventful, he realizes he made love to an important woman without knowing her, and seeks to redress that essential emptiness in their second meeting.

Looking at her, hearing her talk about annual visits to her husband's grave on All Soul's Day, the man analyzes her appearance and sees that with wrinkles of age, gray hair, and sagging skin, the woman eludes him still because she is not what she was. But in a narrative moment that looks forward to the genesis of *Immortality,* Kundera has the man offer the woman some cognac, and the charm of her gesture as she refuses transports him, allows him to glimpse her younger self again, in the way he recognized her through her smile when they met on the street. Moved to pity as well as recognition, he talks of the terrible trail of a life passed too swiftly, as well as the end that beckons to everyone. But she responds to his gravity without a touch of sympathy, calling his remarks "superficial." To the woman, the narrator tells us, life has meaning in the work humans do, not in their bodies that so quickly decay.

She speaks of her own work as an organizer of cultural programs and as a mother giving "everything that a mother can" to her son while she, in age, quietly slips into the background of his life. From that statement Kundera continues to provide details of her life with her son: he has subjugated her (while other men have failed), forcing her into the confines of a proper widow's role by detesting everything youthful and sexual about her until she gave in finally, telling herself that although he nudged her toward the grave, she could live beautifully through him.

The man accepts her argument, seeing it as consistent with his impression of her as a woman intensely interested in beauty and opposed to ugliness and bad taste. He recalls their one night together, her grace and frankness a contrast to his own awkwardness and shame, and thinks of her as beyond his imagination even though they had made love. Her whispered words and the features of her face eluded him in the dark, and after their shared emotions he could only think of her as mysterious and "unreal." He tells her about his experience, and she interprets his account as proof that the worth of a human life is best measured in its extension beyound the self into the memories and experiences of others. Enjoying this perception, she wonders as he strokes her hand whether he touches the skin of the woman he talks to or the woman about whom he talks. At the same time she perceives her own multiple self, acknowledging that she likes this man better than the inexperienced youth she went to bed with fifteen years before.

He embraces her and she, aware of her body's age and mortality against his memory of her youth, resists, begging him not to destroy the "memorial" of her erected in his mind. He lies, telling her he still finds her beautiful, even though he admits to himself that making love will end for him in disgust. His desire for what she was, for his memory of the woman who eluded him in youth and who has remained a mystery for him through the years, becomes a symbol for everything his life has lacked; finally, it overwhelms his physical revulsion. He tells her not to fight him, aware only that should they make love today he will finally see her face and, perhaps, read the expression he lost in the dark fifteen years before. At the same time he wants "to debase this reading immediately," and he realizes that he desires her now because the disgust that follows will allow him to put the lie to all she has represented through the years: the opportunities lost, the experiences missed, the pleasures never enjoyed; his disgust would render them all as "dust," mere images of memory or desire, "doomed to destruction."

The woman still resists but, regretting the loss of her husband's grave site and seeing her son in the man's face, feels enraged at the trap her age, the widow's role, and her son's expectations have erected around her. She declares to herself the end of all memorials. The "old dead must make room for the young dead," she thinks, repeating the cemetery official's remark, "and yes, my boy, all memorials [are] for nothing." In a complete loss of the faith that has sustained her through the years, she decides to favor physical life over memorials. She will make love to the man, the last "who would appeal to her and whom, at the same time, she could have" because things outside herself, other people's thoughts and memory have no real importance now. She gives in and, in a moving narrative moment filled with the intimacy of shame and self-knowledge, begins to undress. Kundera concludes the story ironically, a grimace of despair slightly leavened with bitter laughter over what the two characters will not only feel but see: "This time the room was full of light."

"Dr. Havel after Twenty Years"

Another autumnal story about the body's mortality and the way the spirit combats decay through language, **"Dr. Havel after Twenty Years"** does a variation on the previous story's motif of love in age. In this version, however, Kundera has age make love with youth and shows how, because of language's abilities to alter and create reality, youth, rather than age, feels privileged.

Twenty years after the events of **"Symposium,"** Dr. Havel, now married to a beautiful, well-known actress with a film just appearing in the theaters, finds himself with gallbladder problems and taking the cure at a small spa in the country. His wife, despite her beauty, feels jealous because of Havel's well-known, and well-deserved, reputation as a lover, but to his disappointment he finds himself overlooked by the women at the spa. When, at the suggestion of Dr. Frantishka (Havel's female physician), the young male editor of the spa's newspaper comes to arrange an interview, not with Havel but his wife during one of her visits, Havel reads it as a sign of how low his reputation has sunk.

However, the editor, who has heard about Havel's conquests and is insecure about his own erotic abilities, asks the older man to meet his girlfriend and evaluate her from his expert point of view. Dr. Havel agrees, and finds himself repelled by what he calls the young woman's small-town looks—she is thin, with freckles around her nose—and especially her talkativeness. Embarrassed, the editor defends his girlfriend as being "nice," but Havel replies that dogs, canaries, and ducklings can also be nice. He urges the editor to cultivate his taste by throwing "small fish back into the water" and learn to find true erotic beauty by seeking the unusual. Genuinely loving the young woman, the editor nevertheless accepts Havel's judgment and, when he meets the beautiful Mrs. Havel, becomes convinced he has taken a lesson from a master.

In the meantime, Havel, seeing new respect from others as he walks through the spa with his wife on his arm, feels more confident about himself and, in a playful mood, recommends Dr. Frantishka to the editor. She does not conform to the "ready-made prettiness" of small-town tastes, he says, and possesses very "expressive" legs. Urging the editor to listen to what those legs are "saying," Havel plants the seed of desire in the editor's imagination, just as his wife's presence creates attention from two of the women who previously spurned him. The love scene between the editor and Dr. Frantishka takes on a central role, ranking as one of the funniest that Kundera has written. In a sweet yet farcical variation of the son and lover motif he treated in **"Let the Old Dead Make Room for the Young Dead,"** Kundera describes the editor fighting to maintain his sexual ardor as Dr. Frantishka, more talkative than his girlfriend, babbles about her children: "Beautiful, beautiful!" she calls them; and when the editor, striving to maintain physical passion, says how much he wanted to make love to her when they first met, she replies by comparing him to her son: "That kid wants everything too." Finally, their sex at last completed, she gives his hair a matronly stroke, saying he has a "cute little mop" just like her son's, although Kundera, humanely and in good humor, describes her as feeling younger and, with gratitude, "foolishly good."

The story ends with Havel and the editor meeting next day. Havel's wife has returned to Prague and the doctor himself awaits another woman. The editor, slightly ashamed of his experience with Frantishka, hides it at first, but eventually provides details when Havel questions him. Enthusiastic about his own prospects now, Havel responds positively to the tale of Frantishka's conversation. He tells the editor that bodily pleasure felt in silence only grows "tiresomely similar," making one woman become like all the others. Yet we seek sexual adventures, he says, "to remember them" and, anticipating a theme from *The Book of Laughter and Forgetting,* Havel adds that it takes language, words spoken "at this most banal of moments," to make the sexual experience unforgettable. Although he is known as a collector of women, Havel tells the editor he has a different assessment of himself. Baldly stating one of Kundera's most prominent ideas while underlining the thematic role of language in *Laughable Loves,* he says, "In reality, I'm far more a collector of words"—that is, words spoken during coitus—than of women. Ironically, he follows that self-assessment by walking away hand in hand with a young woman he has met at the spa. Described as resembling a "riding horse," she heads with him toward the spa promenade where, presumably, instead of listening to her words, he will treat her like a prize possession and show her off.

"Edward and God"

In *Immortality* Professor Avenarius says that most men, given the choice, would rather be seen with a beautiful woman than sleep with her, and Havel, the self-proclaimed "collector of words," serves to confirm that assessment at the end of the previous story, making him a collector of images (and self-images) as well. As Kundera probes the reality behind the lies of language in *Laughable Loves,* he moves through various shadowy areas of philosophic truth, and in this last story of the collection he takes as his final topic the essence of the self as it relates to religious and ideological faith. A companion piece to **"The Hitchhiking Game,"** it is perhaps the most ambitious of the stories in this book, one that embodies most of the narrative techniques and themes that we associate with Kundera in his novels: parabasis and authorial intrusion, variation, social and physical necessity as a method of character motivation, use of theatrical tableaux, gravity of subject handled with light technique, parody of ideological innocence, irony, and finally laughter at the way fate turns against the best human intentions. In its concern with Communist Party guilt and restitution it parallels *The Joke* and *Life Is Elsewhere;* in its exploration of the trap that life has become it looks forward to *The Farewell Party* and *The Book of Laughter and Forgetting;* and in the farce it makes of the mysteries (and lies) inflating and deflating reputations as well as love affairs it joins *The Unbearable Lightness of Being* and *Immortality.*

Edward, a schoolteacher, not by choice, visits his brother in the country to discuss problems he will have in obtaining a teaching position from a school supervisor, Miss Chehachkova, a party zealot who many years ago caused Edward's brother to lose his status as a university student. for behaving with unbecoming levity after Stalin's death. Edward's brother was forced to leave Prague and work in the country as a result of Miss Chehachkova's denunciation, but he has adjusted well to his fate, acquiring a house, a family, a dog, and a cottage. Edward's brother tells him not to worry about the supervisor, saying that she has always gone after young men and so she will probably look favorably on him. She may even wish to redress the old wrong she did to him, he says, believing that even party zealots possess consciences.

Edward has just graduated from a teacher's college, and to his relief he finds that his brother is right about Miss Chehachkova. Tall, ugly, with black eyes and just a hint of a black moustache, she responds well to Edward and succeeds in finding a teaching position for him. The position, Kundera says, makes Edward "neither happy nor sad," since he puts a teaching career in the category of the "*unserious*" things in life, principally because it did not fit what he considered to be his true nature and he did not freely choose it. Rather, external conditions, such as the accident of academic and party affiliations (and successful performance during examinations), had chosen him for the career. Thus, he sees chance as the primary cause of his occupation, and because of that he regards it as "laughable," a key word in terms of the title of the book and the theme of this particular story. Kundera explains further: "What is *obligatory* was unserious (laughable) . . . what is *non-obligatory* was serious," and so chance, operating as necessity through Edward's grades, party membership, and scores, leads Edward into his career, allowing him no freedom of choice. But Kundera reveals the non-obligatory and serious side of Edward's experience through his love life, in this case a beautiful young woman whom he meets at school.

However, the young woman, Alice, believes in God, presenting a difficulty for Edward. Saying she could not live without meaning, Alice asks Edward whether he has religious faith, and as he, not wanting to lose her, struggles for a fitting reply, encourages him to speak honestly. Without such honesty, "there wouldn't be any sense" in their being together, she says. Edward confesses to religious doubts but goes to church with Alice on Sunday and finds himself moved by the ceremony. Emotionally compelled to kneel on the floor, he feels "magnificently free" at the same time, perhaps because in religious faith he senses the operation of choice rather than necessity. He lies, telling Alice he no longer harbors doubts about God, but unfortunately, as they leave the church together, with his soul "full of laughter," Miss Chehachkova passes and sees them on the steps.

When he meets the supervisor at school during the week, he explains his presence at church by citing an interest in baroque architecture. Clearly, Miss Chehachkova does not believe him, and therefore he excuses himself from church with Alice the following Sunday. Annoyed, she criticizes his wavering belief, and Kundera, in a parabatic aside that prefigures the technique of the novels that come afterward, describes how Edward burns with desire for Alice's body while the Seventh Commandment, forbidding adultery, remains Alice's primary means of testing her faith. The other nine commandments, Kundera says, about honoring parents, not killing, and not coveting neighbors' goods or wives, seem self-evident to her, while the seventh is inconvenient and therefore requires commitment. Using faith to fight her, Edward raises the issue of a less forbidding New Testament God allowing and encouraging love, even including sex. He quotes St. Paul, "Everything is pure to the man who is pure at heart" and refers to Augustine's "Love God and do what you will." When Alice continues to refuse him, romantically and sexually, he begins to exaggerate his religious zeal, accusing Alice of being too complacent to be truly religious. Finally, performing what amounts to a parody of faith, he ostentatiously crosses himself before a crucifix in the street. A woman janitor from his school sees him, reports him to the Party Committee, and, as Kundera says, making use of a pun on ideological as well as religious faith, "Edward realized that he was lost."

Called before the committee, presided over by Miss Chehachkova, Edward feels overwhelmed by the situation. He cannot, like Ludvik Jahn, bring himself to call his actions a joke because he is sensitive to the gravity with which the committee members regard the situation. Instead, he asks permission to be frank, and the supervisor, echoing Alice when she and Edward discussed religion, tells him he must be frank or else there is no point in their meeting. Gratified, he confesses that he does in fact believe in God even though he does not want to, since religious faith has no place in modern life. Acknowledging the contradiction between what he knows and what he believes, Edward simply hangs his head and says he feels that "He exists." Sympathetic, probably because Edward is a young man, Miss Chehachkova urges the committee to give reason a chance to defeat faith and promises to take charge of his reeducation.

At this point some readers may begin to see Edward as a manipulator of women, playing on their political and religious beliefs for his own gain. Perhaps. And, consistent with that viewpoint, Kundera tells us that Edward felt relieved to be in the supervisor's hands, resolving immediately to gain her favor "as a man." But let us not forget that the social, political world manipulates him, and he must defend himself against it any way he can. From that viewpoint the women also manipulate Edward, and we should remember that with this story's title Kundera has set out to examine, though irony, the larger philosophic issue of belief; erotic romance happens to be the field upon which he studies it.

Alice and Miss Chehachkova represent two possible directions for personal belief to take in life, as well as two possible sources of manipulation. Edward is caught between them. Discussing the Communist Party and the pain that she admits it has caused, Miss Chehachkova gives a clear variation on Alice's statement about God: Without something other than herself to believe in, she says, "I couldn't perhaps live at all." Edward asks about her personal life, whether it could not be satisfying in and of itself, and her bitter smile makes him see her evident loneliness and passion, with political commitment being an inadequate substitute for love. They go on to discuss the nature of belief and recognize the impossibility of joining religion and Communism. Miss Chehachkova, responding to the intimacy of her pupil's sympathetic attention, tells Edward that she likes his youth and especially likes him. At this moment, as Kundera points out, something important happens: the trap Edward has been working so hard to construct for his supervisor suddenly springs, but not on her. Instead, it closes on him.

Edward replies to Miss Chehachkova's statement by saying, "not too expressively," that he likes her also. She reacts with surprise, saying she is an old woman, and Edward feels obligated to deny it, calling her sense of age "nonsense". She tells him not to lie. He says, seemingly sincere, that he finds her pretty, that he likes women with black hair. The scene, humorous and wrenching at the same time, reads very much like a passage from Witold Gombrowicz, with Edward feeling himself pushed deeper and deeper into a performance made necessary by the situation, even as he plays (to himself) the character of the freewheeling Don Juan. When the directress asks why he has never spoken to her about his feelings before, he delivers a plausible response, but one that only makes things worse for him. People would have thought "I was sucking up to you," he tells her, and she replies that he should not be ashamed: "It has *been decided* that you must meet with me from time to time." That their meetings are obligatory places them under Edward's category of the "unserious" or laughable; more important, as the story develops, the scene itself signals a drastic turn in Edward's fate, placing him solidly in the Kafkan realm of what Kundera calls the "horror of the comic," where the jaws of necessity have sprung closed on his freedom. But Edward does not know that yet, and as he leaves, Miss Chehachkova strokes his hand, sending him home like a successful Don Juan, "with the sprightly feelings of a winner."

For a time Edward's sense of his situation seems correct. He has become the stuff of legend among his friends, and the virtuous Alice, now perceiving him as a martyr for his religious beliefs, agrees to spend a weekend in the country with him. But before that occurs he meets again with the supervisor in her apartment, and he learns that, for her too, principles fall easily before passion. In a parabatic

passage that lays out the theatrical as well as philosophic content of the following scene, Kundera reminds the reader how fallible is man's sense of his future before the workings of external forces: "A man imagines that he is playing his role in a particular play, and does not suspect that in the meantime they have changed the scenery without his noticing." Finding himself in the "middle of a rather different performance," he must, in all innocence, improvise his actions and his words, with the plot now inevitably working against him. Such is Edward's experience with his supervisor.

Feeling confident when he arrives at her apartment, Edward finds himself trapped by what Kundera calls *"The change of program"* and realizes that the bottle of cognac, the intense look in Miss Chehachkova's eyes, and their increasingly personal rather than ideological conversation will lead them directly into each other's arms. Repelled by her ugliness, Edward feels his livelihood threatened, and as he leads her around the room in a romantic dance, drinks glass after glass of cognac to numb himself against his feelings.

The comic and philosophic point to the scene, of course, is that Edward *must* make love to Miss Chehachkova in order to keep his job, "unserious" though he thinks it may be. Touching her breast, he gives himself up to "irreversible necessity", placing the scene (and himself) in the realm of the laughable, despite the genuine terror he must feel when his body rebels against the moment's needs. With the supervisor standing naked before him, he finds he must improvise, and he calls upon religion to cover this physical lack of desire. Declaring their actions sinful, he demands that she kneel, clasp her hands, and pray, and the "threefold image of degradation", as Kundera calls it, excites him at last. As she finishes her prayer, he lifts her off the floor and carries her to the couch.

Kundera follows Edward's near physical failure with a scene about a spiritual one. The next weekend Edward travels to the country with Alice and finds, now to his dismay, that she no longer feels reluctant to go to bed with him. The change bothers rather than enchants him because it occurs independent of his efforts and without any acceptable logic. In fact, as Edward analyzes it, Alice will sleep with him now because of a mistaken belief that he has been martyred for his religious beliefs. Yet if he did not betray God before the Party Committee, Edward wonders, why should she betray her religious principles (as the supervisor did her political ones) before Edward? With such doubts in mind, he speaks to his brother, who turns the table of ethics on him and his own actions. When Edward tells about his seduction of Miss Chehachkova, Edward's brother disapproves, saying that whatever else he has done, he has never lied. In reply Edward talks of the madness of speaking truthfully to a madman. Seeing the world as insane, he says, "If I obstinately told the truth to its face, it would mean that I was taking it seriously". And taking the world, or a madman, seriously, Edward tells his brother, would make him unserious (or laughable) and mad himself.

On Kundera's depiction of emotion:

The stories [of *Laughable Loves*] mostly turn on the ambushes lying in wait for lovers in the distinctions which [Matthew] Arnold sketched between 'what we *say* we feel, what we *think* we feel', and 'what we feel indeed.' Arnold assumed, however (following the Romantics) that what we feel 'indeed' is an unchanging quantity, an authenticity buried at depth, which we reach by careful probing through the strata of pretence. But Kundera is a sceptic of an earlier generation, and suspects that emotion is more kinetic than static, generating reality through pretences and pretences through reality. His lovers are all in pursuit of their moment of authenticity, when their soul will encounter their loved one's in utter nakedness, and they will know what it is they 'feel indeed'; but what makes their loves 'laughable' is how often they act themselves into authenticity, and manufacture what they wish to feel from what they only say and think.

Felicity Rosslyn, in "Czech Neo-Classicism,"
The Cambridge Quarterly, *Vol. 11,*
No. 3, 1983.

The conversation reaches the heart of Edward's feelings and, we might say, relates the primary question in Kundera's fiction: What is the real value of truth, beauty, and human goodness in an insane, chaotic world made comprehensible only through fictions? Having realized his physical desires at last, Edward becomes obsessed with Alice's lack of faith as they journey homeward. His conscience revolts against her and, with the plot of his life changing despite his passionate desire for her body, Edward comes to see Alice, and everyone else he knows, as "beings without firm substance," people "with interchangeable attitudes," and admits himself to be a mere shadow, or imitation, of them. Remorseful despite his physical attraction to her, he tells Alice that she disgusts him, and when they arrive in Prague the good-byes they say are clearly final.

Kundera ends the story and the book with images of spiritual ambivalence: Edward, done with both his desire and regret for Alice, sees Miss Chehachkova weekly, with the intent of doing so until his position at the school is secure. Meanwhile, he has begun to seek other woman, and his success with them more than satisfies his physical needs. A pensive, perhaps even monkish, Don Juan, he appreciates quiet moments alone, and his nostalgic longing for deity dramatizes the spiritual dissatisfaction in his life. Too bright to see God as real, Kundera says, Edward is yet too weak to ignore his wish for Him. In a scene of spiritual emptiness reminiscent in tone of the one that closes *The Book of Laughter and Forgetting,* he presents a theatrical tableau: Edward, in church, thoughtfully looking up at the cupola and, in his melancholy, suddenly seeing the face of God. Not mythically sexual, like the golden apple of eternal desire or a brightly colored ball tossed from a woman's outstretched hand, the image clearly, and sadly, draws everyone, including Edward, on.

So a book that begins with laughter, ends with poetry. Unlike Klima, in **"Nobody Will Laugh,"** Edward lacks an ironic sense of himself. Still, he smiles and, Kundera says, feels happy. He asks us to keep that sad fictional image of Edward (keeping that charged fictional image of spiritual longing) in our memories. It is a paradox of longing, Kundera says, and a poetry of need. In the world that neither Edward nor any of the other characters made, it is a truth whose only expression comes in the fictional world of dreams.

John O'Brien   (essay date 1995)

SOURCE: *"Laughable Loves,"* in *Milan Kundera & Feminism: Dangerous Intersections,* St. Martin's Press, 1995, pp. 79-87.

[*In the following essay, O'Brien singles out the stories "Hitchhiking Game" and "Edward and God" as illustrations of Kundera's "ability to expose the misogynistic male psychology."*]

In *The Politics of Postmodernism,* Linda Hutcheon contends that the characteristic that defines a work as postmodern is not solely whether it can be praised for its critique of representation. Instead, she maintains that it is the combination of both complicity with dominant representational strategies and critique that makes a work postmodern. With this idea in mind, it is perhaps less strange to find that the stories that most challenge oppositional thinking in Kundera's collection of short fiction are two that . . . are among the most problematic in their treatment and representation of women. On closer scrutiny, **"Hitchhiking Game"** and **"Edward and God"** specifically dramatize alternatives to the oppositional thinking they simultaneously seem to reinforce.

Before considering these two works, I would like to comment briefly on aspects of other stories in this collection that . . . contribute to the direct critique of male representations and perceptions of women. In **"Nobody Will Laugh,"** for example, when Mr. Zaturetsky goes to Klara's factory to identify the woman whom he is falsely accused of harassing, he fails because he was so "dazzled" by her beauty: "Beauty created before her some opaque screen. A screen of light, behind which she was hidden as if beneath a veil." It is a minor scene, but the "parable on the power of beauty" the narrator introduces does not so much empower beauty as underscore the obfuscating nature of oppositional thinking. Asked to describe Klara, Zaturetsky conforms to the cultural stereotype of beauty. The actual Klara escapes detection because she is neither tall nor blonde, "and so when the little man finally approached the corner where Klara, in a brown work smock, was huddled over a shirt, he didn't recognize her, because he had never seen her."

This association of oppositional extremes with a fundamental failure to see is continued in **"Let the Old Dead Make Room for the Young Dead."** The older woman in this story effectively plays a resistant role in her past and present encounters with the male protagonist in his drive to appropriate women. Her resistance occurs on two levels in two tenses. Years ago, shortly before their first and only sexual union, he is frustrated by his inability to imagine her in bed, finding at every turn that *"she absolutely defied his imagination"*: "And that was the situation, which had never since been repeated in his life. At that time he had stood face to face with the *unimaginable*." With the young man's imagination confounded, the ambiguity of the situation continues even in their most intimate moments, during which he is unable to see her or comprehend what she says:

> He looked into her face, but in the dusk her expression entirely eluded him, and he couldn't even make out her features. He regretted that it was dark, but it seemed impossible for him to get up and move away from her at that moment to turn on the switch by the door, so vainly he went on straining his eyes. But he didn't recognize her. It seemed to him that he was making love with someone else; with someone spurious or else someone quite unreal and unindividuated.
>
> Then she got on top of him (at that time he saw only her raised shadow), and moving her hips, she said something in a muffled tone, in a whisper, and it wasn't clear whether she was talking to him or to herself. He couldn't make out the words and asked her what she had said. She went on whispering, and even when he clasped her to him again, he couldn't understand what she was saying.

Speaking without being seen, heard, or understood—resisting by way of ambiguity, as with Lucie—this woman cultivates the ungraspable characteristics that the young man finds so maddeningly impenetrable.

After this one time together, she avoids him, apparently sure that she could gain some kind of immortality by his having "erected a memorial" to her within himself. And even in the present-tense time frame of the story, she is initially convinced that "we cannot allow [this memorial] to be destroyed," deciding later to transform her ambiguity into a reified memorial representing nostalgic beauty. Near the end of the story, however, she thinks again and finally comes to the decision to destroy the memorial: "There was no reason why she should give preference to memorials over life." Importantly, she not only decides to destroy the memorial, but she recognizes that it is a construction that is outside her, a representation no longer worth preserving: "If he then became disgusted with her and destroyed her memorial in his thoughts, it made no difference because her memorial was outside her, just as his thoughts and memory were outside her, and everything that was outside her made no difference." The story ends with her in a room full of light slowly unbuttoning her dress, able even to set aside her Maman-like anxiety about her scarred abdomen. Both she and he are aware that there will be absolutely no return to the memorial of beauty and youth. It is problematic, of course, that her action, which she partly considers an act of defiance against her "son-enemy," also appears to be an act of submission to his insistent plea, "don't fight me"; however, her recognition

of the constructed nature of memorials and her conviction that the memorial-as-representation is both false and "outside her" is a relatively significant discovery in a story and a collection of stories in which such perceptual sea changes in male characters are relatively rare.

Finally, the strong character of the woman doctor in **"Symposium"** deserves mention. The story presents the ambiguous circumstances of Alzhbeta's near-death and the efforts of a group of men to understand the event. More than up to the task of textualizing women, the men in the story quickly find themselves certain that she has attempted suicide. It is only the woman doctor who lucidly interprets the events in question, demonstrating that there was no suicide attempt and pointing out in passing that her insight is a result of looking around a room that the men "no longer even wanted to see." Later that night, she takes role of seducer, tempting the aged Don Juan and convincing him, again with her strong reasoning, to betray his friend, the chief physician, even though Dr. Havel has previously spoken so passionately about male friendship as "the only value I've found in life." There is no careful series of deconstructionist moves in the narrative of the woman doctor, but she nonetheless undercuts the cherished ideals of male friendship, beats the seducer at his own game, and shows the most cogent, aggressive, and pragmatic thinking in a story that is otherwise male dominated. From the margins of the story, she exposes the shortcomings of male textualization and even forces Havel to a higher level of introspection. As a result of her seduction, Havel extends his new view on male friendship to a criticism of himself: "'I guarantee that friendship is not a bit less fickle than love and it is impossible to build anything on it. Self-love? I wish it were possible,' now said Havel almost ardently, and it sounded like repentance. 'But, sir, I swear to you that I don't like myself at all.'"

The next day, the woman doctor again emerges as a strong character, recognizing that the male-propagated, deluded account of Alzhbeta's accident is the only way to keep the men content (the only way to achieve the "Happy Ending" that the title of the next section of the story announces). As a result (and as a critique), she humors their romanticized view of the alleged suicide attempt: "'My dear gentlemen,' said the woman doctor smiling, 'if it will make the world more beautiful for you and will save your souls, please, let's agree that Alzhbeta really did want to commit suicide. Agreed?'" The night before, while the men presented their specious theories to explain Alzhbeta and her actions, the woman doctor was silent, "listening attentively to both doctors" before refuting their thinking completely, presenting her own alternative theory void of stereotypes and lyrical romanticism. While the men (especially Flaishman) happily end the story by returning to their original delusions, the unnamed woman doctor moves from the margins of this symposium to become, according to Kundera in his *Salmagundi* [Winter, 1987] interview, one of a few strong women "whose thinking is the most cynical and lucid."

"The Hitchhiking Game" shares with most of the stories in *Laughable Loves* a self-conscious study of role playing. Instead of reinforcing an either/or distinction between the oppositional roles in question for women (i.e., Madonna/whore), Kundera's story deconstructs the opposition, leaving the young woman as a casualty not of her supposedly whore-like desire, but of the cultural vision of eroticism that sees the desire of a Madonna and the desires of her opposite in exclusive opposition. Though the hitchhiking game itself may seem initially somewhat implausible, as it progresses, the role-playing dynamic appears remarkably similar to the daily role playing with which everyone is familiar. In Derridian style, however, the roles of these two individuals are reversed: A shy woman admired for her purity becomes bold and provocative; a solicitous man turns rough and longs to humiliate her "as a whore." As elsewhere, Kundera's critique of oppositional thinking here initially suggests that the escape from one role too often becomes a shift to an opposite formulation instead of an abandonment or combination of both oppositional terms. In this story, however, something beyond this opposition is experienced, challenging/blurring, rather than leaving intact, oppositions like Madonna/whore.

There is no question that this opposition is a powerful one in the story. For the young man in **"Hitchhiking Game,"** Madonna-like purity is primarily seen in negative terms. It is her not being a whore that "distinguished her from the women he'd met before," which is to say that her purity is the only feature of importance to him. Along these lines, his undeconstructed aspiration is to find a woman who is wholly pure, and her aspiration until now has been to enjoy the sense of an unfragmented self that is also predicated on purity. By the end of the story, both of these extreme conceptions are destroyed in the course of their game, not just reversing the opposition that both initially use to understand their relationship, but blurring its distinctions.

Hopelessly muttering the tautology "I am me, I am me," the young woman experiences an acute crisis of identity at the end of the story when she sees herself treated as if her life were "split down the middle" in the way Helena fears in *The Joke*. It seems she ends the story with the impulse to return to the oppositions that begin **"Hitchhiking Game,"** and yet it is hard to believe she will return to perceiving of herself as a pinnacle of purity after the mix of pleasure and humiliation she has experienced. She may well go on being perceived from within this narrow opposition that bisects femininity, but for her the distinction can be no longer meaningful. After all, while she has experienced being seen as a whore, Kundera makes it clear that her view of herself is more complex. Before his vision of her turns into abuse, she conceives of the experience quite differently, as giving her "the ability to be all women," all roles, throwing the stability of the Madonna/whore opposition into serious doubt.

There is, without question, a problem in suggesting that the story chronicles liberation from a constraining opposition, especially given the degradation suffered by the young woman on the road to freedom. On the other hand, it is crucial to note that her sense of freedom is enjoyed well before his behavior gets violent. Her exhilaration is rooted in her polyvalence, her ability to embody all roles and "be all women" rather than *either* all whore *or* all

Madonna: "She smiled at the thought of how nice it was that today she was this other woman, this irresponsible, indecent other woman, one of those women of whom she was so jealous; it seemed to her that she was cutting them all out, that she had learned how to use their weapons; how to give the young man what until now she had not known how to give him: lightheartedness, shamelessness, and dissoluteness; a curious feeling of satisfaction filled her, because she alone had the ability to be all women and in this way (she alone) could completely captivate her lover and hold his interest." While she enjoys the possibility of getting his attention in ways other than being pure and shy, he, of course, reacts quite differently, but his angry denial of her attempt to transcend oppositional roles does not make her exhilaration any less real. It only brings it to a dramatic end and underscores, if anything, the male willingness to enforce limited roles for women, with force if necessary.

The chronology of her brief sense of personal freedom and self-satisfaction also stands in marked contrast to the young man's continued reluctance to see through the opposition himself. He either loves her as the essence of simplicity and purity or feels that her "*whole persona* had changed" so that "she unpalatably and faithfully resembled that type of woman whom he knew so well and for whom he felt some aversion." While she expands her perception of herself to encompass the range of roles and experiences extending from one end of the spectrum to the other, he continues to fall back on the boundary separating the opposition: "It had always seemed to him that her inward nature was *real* only within the bounds of fidelity and purity, and that beyond these bounds it simply didn't exist; beyond these bounds she would cease to be herself, as water ceases to be water beyond the boiling point. When he now saw her crossing this horrifying boundary with nonchalant elegance, he was filled with anger." Sharing Helena's belief that crossing the Madonna/whore border is "monstrous" or "horrifying," the young man punishes his companion for the transgression.

Kundera uses the hitchhiking game to deconstruct the border separating Madonnas from whores through the example of the young woman's initial celebration of freedom. Even though the ending of his story takes a tragic turn, Kundera straightforwardly identifies that it is the young man, not her, who takes offense at the ambiguity of her new role(s). In the same way that Kostka and Ludvik are unable to escape opposition-based thinking in *The Joke*, even when they may have earlier acknowledged its limitations, the young man sees relatively early into the game that the woman is not *either* a Madonna or a whore, but the image of both simultaneously. On its own, this moment of understanding serves as a powerful deconstructionist metaphor of double vision . . . : "It was as if he were looking at two images through the same lens, at two images superimposed one upon the other with the one showing through the other. These two images showing through each other were telling him that *everything* was in the girl, that her soul was terrifyingly amorphous, that it held faithfulness and unfaithfulness, treachery and innocence, flirtatiousness and chastity." Ended at this point, his observations would be insightful and even revolutionary, except that he immediately pulls away from his double vision to embrace the more familiar myopia of opposition-based misogyny. The level of his vitriol and the paranoid irrationality of his fear that women might find a place beyond his narrow oppositional perspective function to critique what Kundera represents here and throughout as a characteristically masculine impulse: "This disorderly jumble seemed disgusting to him, like the variety to be found in a pile of garbage. Both images continued to show through each other and the young man understood that the girl differed only on the surface from other women, but deep down was the same as they: full of all possible thoughts, feelings, and vices, which justified all his secret misgivings and fits of jealousy." For all his blinding anger, he acknowledges that the young woman has become "hopelessly *ambiguous*." He also seems to recognize that part of the ease with which she abandons the role of the pure Madonna is attributable to the instability of the role itself and of his construction of her within the narrative prescribed by the Madonna/whore opposition. Exactly like Ludvik, the young man eventually sees that "the girl he loved was a creation of his desire, his thoughts, and his faith," and he sees this plural image of the young woman as "the *real* girl," though it is this conviction more than anything that inspires his hatred, his return to oppositional thinking, and his abusive behavior.

By abandoning single roles instead of following the rules of the original game (exchanging one role for its opposite), the young woman dramatizes the potential for personal freedom. Her belief that "everything was permitted" and her enjoyment of the *"indecent joy caused by her body,"* as well as the violent brooding of yet another self-obsessed man, make for a well-rounded chronicle of the potential escape from oppositional extremes, but also an accurate account of the way traditional conceptions of women are desperately and violently defended. At the end of the story, the young man literally forces her to mimic the "whore narrative" he has created to offset his previous worshipful stance, making her go through the motions of conforming to the opposition she has moved beyond. Of course, his only knowledge of what a whore might be comes from literature and hearsay, but ignorance does not keep him from physically forcing her to hold the most stereotypical poses literature and hearsay might represent as whore-like (dancing on the shiny top of a piano, for example). His attempt to reconstruct by force the stereotypical simplicities of an opposition that has, as far as she is concerned, been "seen through" is the tragedy read between the lines of the "pitiful tautology" ("I am me, I am me") that ends the story. The tautology itself is hopelessly ambiguous. The easiest reading finds her longing to return to her original role, but it is perhaps just as easy to see each circular repetition/reiteration of selfhood as a gesture toward the plural roles she embraces. Instead of viewing her sobbing as nostalgia for an undeconstructed opposition that lets her play the role of an unambiguous Madonna, I believe attention to the young woman's earlier sense of freedom inspired by double vision suggests that her grief can be best explained as the result of her having to live in a world that refuses to see double.

In **"Edward and God,"** Edward, too, experiences punishment for a role initially taken on as a game of sorts, and also like **"Hitchhiking Game,"** this story ends with a complete blur of the factual "self" and the fictional mask. Both stories, then, self-consciously expose the predominance of role playing, especially concentrating on revealing the momentum of roles in the context of sexual politics. Both Edward and the young hitchhiking woman experience a strong initial sense of freedom, and both eventually suffer for it. One fundamental difference, however, is that Edward fully embraces the indeterminacy of clashing and confused roles, even when the world he lives in is receptive to neither the humor of the situation nor the possibilities of border crossing.

Even though what might be called a crisis of meaning and identity in this story is experienced by a male character, the play of gender roles is nonetheless addressed by his experiences. The beautiful and chaste Alice, whom Edward works so hard to "win," functions much as Lucie does in *The Joke,* forcing the male character to come to terms with her ambiguity, even when it is her simple Madonna-like beauty that initially attracts him. Far from a conventional Cinderella myth, with a movement from rags to riches, **"Edward and God"** tells the story of an ugly directress who stays ugly and a virginal beauty (Alice) who stays beautiful; for the most part, what changes in this story is what fails to change in **"Hitchhiking Game"**—the male character's oppositional perspective. In this regard, the story plays an important part in what I take to be Kundera's critique of the representation of women.

As with Ludvik in *The Joke* and the young man in **"Hitchhiking Game,"** indeterminacy is associated with female characters. Once he has tricked Alice into believing that he is a Christian, Edward enjoys the body that was earlier so inaccessible to him. While never losing this desire, he nonetheless rejects her soon after "winning" her because she is no is no longer "a stable and distinct being." In effect, Edward cruelly rejects her for no longer being "solid" and "coherent," but in rejecting her he finds his own world changed. Instead of physically or figuratively trying to force Alice to return to her original state of coherence and stability, as the young man in **"Hitchhiking Game"** does, he manages instead to see through his own assumptions: "[With regret he realized that] the love affair he'd experienced with Alice was derisory, made up of chance and errors, without any importance or sense whatsoever; he heard Alice's words, he saw her gestures (she squeezed his hand), and it occurred to him that these were signs devoid of meaning, currency without funds, weights made of paper, and that he couldn't grant them significance any more than God could the prayer of the naked directress." Along with seeing Alice as an "arbitrary and unstable" conjunction of "a body, thoughts, and a life's course," Edward expands this vision to the rest of the world, and, importantly, to himself:

> All of a sudden it seemed to him that, in fact, all the people whom he'd met in his new place of work were only ink lines spreading on blotting paper, beings with interchangeable attitudes, beings without firm sub-

stance; but what was worse, what was far worse (it struck him next) was that he himself was only a shadow of all these shadowy people; after all, he had been exhausting his own brain only to adjust to them and imitate them and yet, even if he imitated them with an inward laugh, unseriously, even if he made an effort to mock them secretly (and so exonerate his accommo-dation), it didn't alter the case, for even malicious imitation remains imitation, and the shadow that mocks remains a shadow, subordinate, derivative, and wretch-ed, and nothing more.

This shadow metaphor is particularly apt in characterizing the world that makes up the backdrop for Kundera's fiction, both in conveying the oppositional aspect (shadow as opposite image of an object) and in reflecting the sense of blurring, distortion, and lack of classifiable substance.

Both **"Hitchhiking Game"** and **"Edward and God"** chronicle the male response to a woman's efforts to transcend limited oppositional perspectives. Though the young man in **"Hitchhiking Game"** never becomes fully aware of the woman's challenge to his view, in **"Edward and God,"** Edward is cognizant of the challenge. Close scrutiny of these stories in *Laughable Loves* presents a clear illustration that dismissing Kundera on the basis of the mistreatment of women will be at the expense of appreciating his ability to expose the misogynistic male psychology at the heart of this collection of stories and at the heart of Kundera's critique of the oppositional basis of that psychology.

Additional coverage of Kundera's life and career is contained in the following sources published by Gale Research: *Authors and Artists for Young Adults*, Vol. 2; *Contemporary Authors*, Vols. 85-88; *Contemporary Authors New Revision Series*, Vol. 19; *Contemporary Literary Criticism*, Vols. 4, 9, 19, 32, 68; *DISCovering Authors, Novelists Module*; *and Major 20th-Century Writers*.

Joaquim Maria Machado de Assis
1839–1908

Brazilian novelist, short story writer, poet, critic, playwright, essayist, and journalist.

INTRODUCTION

Machado de Assis is thought by many to be Brazil's greatest writer. Although he wrote in many genres, he achieved his greatest literary successes in both the novel and short-story forms. A complex blend of psychological realism and symbolism, Machado's fiction is marked by pessimism, sardonic wit, an innovative use of irony, and an ambiguous narrative technique. His best known novel, *Memórias póstumas de Brás Cubas* (*Epitaph of a Small Winner*), is often cited as the first modern novel of the western hemisphere. Another, *Dom Casmurro* is thought by many to be the finest novel ever written in both Americas. But Machado is also acknowledged as the father of the modern Brazilian short story, producing more than 200 works that use a wide range of styles and forms. Earl E. Fitz has remarked that "whether we consider him primarily as a short story writer of as a novelist, Machado de Assis deserves—and is beginning to receive—recognition as one of the true modern masters of Western narrative."

Biographical Information

Machado was born in Rio de Janeiro on June 21, 1839, to a Portuguese mother, who died when he was ten, and a mulatto father. Machado had epilepsy and a speech impediment, which are thought to have made him very self-conscious. During his teens he met many prominent literary figures while working as a printer's apprentice. These acquaintances helped Machado get his first works published. He was an early success, and his work was widely acclaimed by the time he was twenty-five. In 1860 he entered the civil service, to which he dedicated himself, and he eventually attained the directorship of the Ministry of Agriculture. Over the next decade, while working for the Ministry, Machado wrote mostly poetry and several comedies—drama being his first literary passion—before he gave more serious attention to narrative fiction. During the 1880s and 1890s Machado wrote what many critics consider his greatest fiction: the novels *Epitaph of a Small Winner*, *Quincas Borba* (*Philosopher or Dog?*), and *Dom Casmurro*; and the stories in *Papeis avulsos, Historias sem data, Varias historias,* and *Paginas recolhidas*. In 1897 Machado was named the first president in perpetuity of the Brazilian Academy of Letters, of which he was a founding member. He held this title until his death on September 29, 1908, of arteriosclerosis.

Major Works of Short Fiction

Having a much broader range than his novels, Machado's short fiction is concerned with the destructiveness of time, the nature of madness, the isolation of the individual, conflicts between self-love and love for others, and human inadequacy. Often humorous, Machado's stories portray the thoughts and feelings, rather than the actions, of characters who often exemplify Brazilian social types. Machado's stories deal satirically with cultural institutions and contemporary social conditions. His short fiction eschews description or narration in favor of self-revealing dialogue and monologue. Unlike his novels, very few of Machado's more than two hundred short stories have been translated into English, but those that have represent his most accomplished works in the genre. These include "The Psychiatrist," which struggles with the twin questions of who is insane and how one can tell; "Alexandrian Tale," a satirical attack on the tendency to use science to cure human problems; "The Companion," one of Machado's most anthologized tales, in which a man hired to care for a cantankerous old invalid is driven to murder him instead; and "Midnight Mass," regarded by most as his best single story, which relates the

126

events surrounding an ambiguous love affair between the young narrator and a married woman.

Critical Reception

Outside his native Brazil, Machado's short stories are relatively unknown, and consequently they have received little international critical attention. This is due to the fact that Portuguese is not widely accepted as a literary language, and Brazilian literature, in particular, comprises a small part of the traditional Western canon. According to Fitz, "had [Machado] written in French, German, or English, for example, [he] would be as well-known today as Flaubert, Goethe, or Shakespeare." Recent comparative studies have linked his short stories with those of such masters as Henry James, Anton Chekhov, and Guy de Maupassant. Some critics have interpreted Machado's narrative art as being part of the realistic trend in literature, but most have identified his work with the modern movement, linking the style and technique of his fiction to writers such as Marcel Proust, James Joyce, and Thomas Mann. Other scholars have examined Machado's works as an influence in the construction of a postcolonial Brazilian national identity and for indications of the author's stand on racism and civil rights. As international readers have slowly discovered his fiction through translation, most agree that Machado's narrative art is the work of an unrecognized genius.

PRINCIPAL WORKS

Major Works of Short Fiction

Contos fluminenses 1869
Histórias da meia-noite 1873
Papéis avulsos 1882
Histórias sem data 1884
Várias histórias 1896
Páginas recolhidas 1899
Relíquias de casa velha 1906
Brazilian Tales 1921
The Psychiatrist, and Other Stories 1963
The Devil's Church, and Other Stories 1977

Other Major Works

"Ela" (poetry) 1855; published in journal *Marmota Fluminense*
Hoje avental, amanha luva (drama) 1860; published in journal *A Marmota*
Desencantos (drama) 1861
Quase ministro (drama) 1863
Crisalidas [*Chrysalises*] (poetry) 1864
Os deuses de casaca (verse drama) 1865
Falenas (poetry and drama) 1870
Ressurreiçao (novel) 1872
A mao e a luva [*The Hand and the Glove*] (novel) 1874

Americanas (poetry) 1875
Helena [*Helena*] (novel) 1876
Antes da missa (drama) 1878; published in journal *O Cruzeiro*
O bote de rape (drama) 1878; published in journal *O Cruzeiro*
Yaya Garcia [*Yaya Garcia*; also published as *Iaia Garcia*] (novel) 1878
†*Tu, so tu, puro amor* (drama) 1880; published in journal *Revista Brasileira*
Memorias póstumas de Bras Cubas [*Epitaph of a Small Winner*; also published as *Posthumous Reminiscences of Braz Cubas*] (novel) 1881
Quincas Borba [*Philospher or Dog?*; also published as *The Heritage of Quincas Borba*] (novel) 1891
Nao consultes medico (drama) 1896
Dom Casmurro [*Dom Casmurro*] (novel) 1900
‡*Poesias completas* (poetry) 1901
Esau e Jaco [*Esau and Jacob*] (novel) 1904
Licao de botanica (drama) 1906
Memorial de Ayres [*Counselor Ayres' Memorial*] (novel) 1908
Obra completa. 31 vols. (novels, short stories, drama, poetry, and essays) 1955

*This collection contains the drama *Uma ode de Anacreonte.*

†This play was originally titled *Tu só, tu, puro amor.*

‡Includes a section of new poems written for this volume and widely known as *Ocidentais.*

CRITICISM

Donald M. Decker (essay date 1965)

SOURCE: "Machado de Assis: Short Story Craftsman," in *Hispania*, Vol. XLVIII, No. 1, March, 1965, pp. 76-81.

[*In the following essay, Decker discusses the themes, style, and technique in Machado's later stories from* Histórias sem data *to* Várias histórias.]

The themes of Machado's short stories are subtopics of one broad basic concept of human life and the world in which men live. If there is a purpose in Machado's writing, other than simply to entertain his readers, it is to reveal to them this concept by combining fantasy, irony, and reality, blended in innumerable and original juxtapositions.

In **"Adão e Eva"** a judge explains that the earth was really created by the Devil, not by God. In **"Viver!"** the last man on earth, being weary of the world's ills, is happy to have reached the end of his existence. Although Machado appears to view the world as the Devil's creation, he does not find it perfect in its evil. In the story **"A igreja do Diabo"** the Devil establishes his own Church on earth, but its success is tempered by followers who "practice virtues on the side." The enraged Devil approaches God, who calmly replies: "—Que queres tu, meu pobre

Diabo? . . . é a eterna contradicção humana." William L. Grossman, in translating some of Machado's stories into English, has noted the writer's "curiosity about the relationship between good and evil—and always his critique, now biting, now compassionate, of human inadequacy."

In the story **"Um apólogo"** the needle works hard while the thread receives all the benefit. In **"Trio em lá menor"** the writer refers to the "technique of destiny," which proves in this case, as usual throughout his stories, to be utterly absurd. In **"Viver!"** man's vigorous hope for a better life proves to be but a foolish fancy. Thus, Machado does not envision a completely evil world, but rather one which is basically incongruous.

In her article "Machado de Assis, Encomiast of Lunacy," Clotilde Wilson refers to the writer's "deeply pessimistic philosophy" which sees "humanity struggling in vain against a relentless fate and seeking with frantic eagerness a chimerical happiness, which may fall within his grasp for one brief moment only to vanish the next with mocking laughter." Machado's characters frequently have specific yearnings for happiness both in material forms—such as, a uniform (**"O espelho"**), a pair of shoes (**"Ultimo capítulo"**), or coins (**"Anedota pecuniaria"**)—and in longings for fame (**"Fulano"**) or social success (**"Teoria do medalhão"**). Whether or not these are achieved, however, is purely a matter of incongruous fate. In any case, disease or death soon dissolves all human yearnings.

With unremitting frequency Machado's characters suddenly fall ill and die. It is evident that he had a broad knowledge of physical ailments. Never dealing emotionally with death, he briefly states that a character dies. The only commentary which he may imply is that death serves well to end a life of absurdities. Machado has Ahasverus savor this idea in **"Viver!"**: "Posso morrer. Morrer! deliciosa ideia! Seculos de seculos vivi, cansado, mortificado, andando sempre, mais eil-os que acabam e vou morrer com elles."

The mystery of a woman's age is another recurrent incongruity. In **"Uma senhora"** a lady is desperate in her campaign to appear youthful, even after becoming a grandmother. In **"O caso da vara"** a lady is described in these terms: "Sinhá Rita tinha quarenta annos na certidão de baptismo, e vinte e sete nos olhos." Similar indications of interest in the phenomenon of a woman appearing younger than she really is are common in Machado's stories.

The senseless world of man is revealed by Machado in tales both fanciful and realistic. Most of these are based on curious variations of sociological and psychological phenomena.

In considering the social aspects of an incongruous world, Machado humorously depicts the sharp contrasts between lofty sociological ideals and basic individual self-interests. He commonly deals with government, science, and philosophy in their relationships to the functioning of society.

The institution of government is mocked in **"A Sereníssima República"** through satire directed at election procedures. In **"O alienista"** a governmental institution becomes subservient to "sacred" science: "A camara recusou acceital-a, declarando que a Casa Verde era uma instituição publica, e que a sciencia não podia ser emendada por votação administrativa, . . ."

Science provides the basis for satire and ironic humor in many of Machado's stories. In **"Conto alexandrino,"** for example, scientific methods of experimentation lead to utter folly. Dr. Bacamarte, protagonist of **"O alienista,"** while carrying on absurd experiments in his insane asylum, declares: "Meus senhores, a sciencia é cousa séria, e merece ser tratada com seriedade. Não dou razão dos meus actos de alienista a ninguem, salvo aos mestres e a Deus." Weird pseudo-scientific theories are propounded in **"As academias de Sião"** (e.g., the "gender of the soul") and in **"O lapso"** ("forgetting" the concept of paying).

Imagined or existing philosophical notions are often presented in Machado's stories. In **"O segrèdo do bonzo"** the theory that belief is the equivalent of truth is treated humorously. **"Idéias de canário"** deals with the concept that a man's philosophy is entirely dependent upon his own limited experience. Most of the philosophical elements in Machado's stories are related to his idea of an incongruous world. For example, in **"Lágrimas de Xerxes"** he points out that both life and love are fleeting in spite of the strong human yearning for permanency.

The stories most nearly approaching literary realism, as it is generally regarded, are those which illustrate individual psychological phenomena. These are clearly of special interest to Machado and his writings reveal a remarkable understanding of them.

That quirk of human nature which renders love between man and woman so impermanent is an incongruity which fascinated Machado. It is the most common theme of his stories—generally cast in "eternal triangle" plot structures. A usual "triangle" consists of husband and wife and a third man (usually the husband's friend) who in time becomes the wife's "true love." In **"A cartomante"** a husband shoots his wife's lover; in **"Mariana"** a wife completely forgets her love for her original suitor; in **"A senhora do Galvão"** a wife fights for her husband's faithfulness; in **"Um erradio"** Tosta steals Estrellita from his poet friend; while in **"Três tesouros perdidos"** the main character loses his wife, friend, and a large sum of money all in one day.

Illicit love affairs appropriately constitute an essential element in Machado's inconsistent and diabolical world. In **"A igreja do Diabo"** the Devil dictates: "A unica hypothese em que elle permittia amar ão proximo era quando se tratasse de amar as damas alheias, . . ."

Other human traits vividly depicted in the stores are: sadism (**"A causa secreta"**), envy (**"Verba testamentária"**), compensation (**"Ultimo capítulo"**), selfishness (**"Na arca"**), fickleness (**"Dona Benedita"**), vanity (**"Elogio da vai-**

dade"), love of fame ("**Fulano**"), and aversion to marriage ("**A desejada das gentes**"). These are but a few of the stories illustrating clear-cut psychological phenomena or "cases," as Machado sometimes calls them: "Mas aqui vai, per exemplo, um caso bem caracteristico da influencia que a justiça dos outros póde ter no nosso procedimento." or "Pela minha parte creio ter decifrado este caso de empréstimo; ides ver se me engano."

There is a timelessness and universality in Machado's realistic stories. He constantly eschews descriptions of settings and elements of local color. The interpersonal problems which he deals with occur principally among members of the middle or upper classes of Rio de Janeiro and could easily be applicable to life in any large city of the Occident.

Another thematic source from which many of the stories are drawn is the matter of the superiority of spontaneous creativity to studied art. In "**Cantiga de esponsais**" a newly-wedded bride impulsively provides the musical phrase which a composer has sought all his life. In "**Ex cathedra**" a godfather sets up classes in love for two young persons who succeed in becoming enamored of each other on their own outside the classroom. In "**Um homem célebre**" a musician meets with success through his popular compositions in spite of a strong personal preference for classical music.

Machado's writings are a testimony of his own posession of the talent of spontaneous creativity which he admired so much. Many of his stories are pure fancies—highly original and entertaining. One marvels at his ability to conjure up an imaginary situation and to follow it along from association to association in a bold and bizarre progression. With apparent ease he begins "**As academias de Sião**" thus: "Conhecem as academias de Sião? Bem sei que em Sião nunca houve academias: mas supponhamos que sim, e que eram quatro, e escutem-me." "**Lágrimas de Xerxes**" is also initiated with a deliberate and expressed supposing: "Supponhamos (tudo é de suppor) que Julieta e Romeu, antes que Frei Lourenço os cassasse, travavam com elle este dialogo curioso: . . ."

Sometimes Machado creates characters who are creators themselves. Such a one, for example, is Elisiário, the professor in "**Um erradio**": "Essa feição era a menos sympathica; mas tudo o mais, a falla, as ideias, e principalmente a imaginação fecunda e moça, que se desfazia em ditos, anecdotas, epigrammas, versos, descripções, ora serio, quasi sublime, ora familiar, quasi rasteiro, mas sempre original, tudo attraia e prendia." Or "Não imaginas a eloquencia desse homem, callida e forte, mansa e doce, as imagens que lhe brotavam no discurso, as ideias arrojadas, as fórmas novas e graciosas." And the sailor, Deolindo, in "**Noite de almirante**" who is a gifted story-teller, and especially *o bacharel* Duarte in "**A chinela turca**," who resorts to a fanciful reverie to avoid listening to his friend's reading of a boring play—thus experiencing on the spur of the moment a marvelous imaginative adventure.

An ancient Greek returns to earth in modern times in "**Uma visita de Alcebíades**" and cannot tolerate the wearing of hats. In "**O dicionário**" the king's ministers decide to invent a dictionary with entirely new words. The protagonist of "**Idéias de canário**" is a bird that informs its owner about its concept of the world. The statues of saints in a church described in "Entre santos" come to life and engage in a discussion. In "**O cônego**" a writer supposes that nouns and adjectives occupy opposite sides of the brain, that they may come to love one another, and that their marriages produce style.

Exotic and faraway places, often of long ago, provide settings for certain tales. "**O segrêdo do bonzo**" occurs in old China; "**Conto alexandrino**," in ancient Egypt; "**As academias de Sião**," in Siam; and "**O Dicionário**," in a legendary kingdom.

These and many similar samples of Machado's remarkable flights of fancy show that he clearly champions the literary value of make-believe, as well as of realism, to develop his themes.

In designing the structure of his tales, Machado often uses the straightforward, chronological pattern of an anecdote—especially in illustrating an irony of fate or an incongruous social or psychological phenomenon. While narrating in the third person, he sometimes takes the liberty of interjecting his own remarks: "Emquanto ella compõe os babadinhos e rendas do roupão branco. . . convido a leitora a observar-lhe as feições. Vè que não lhe dou Venus; tambem não lhe dou Meduza [sic]."

Some of the realistic-type stories take the form of a straight dialogue in which one character relates his own or another's experiences to a second person. Examples of these are "**Teoria do medalhão**," "**A desejada das gentes**," and "**Singular ocorrência**."

The more fanciful narratives, such as "**O alienista**," "**Idéias de canário**," and "**O cônego**," are usually written in the third person with highly improbable plots.

Another group of stories are allegorical in form, such as "**A Seréníssima República**" (a republic of spiders), "**A igreja do Diabo**," "**Adão e Eva**" (a new version of the biblical account), "**Elogio da vaidade**" (in which Modesty and Vanity address an audience), and "**Viver!**" (in the form of a stage play).

Taking the form of documents or manuscripts, some stories are supposed to be "additions" to existing works: "**Na arca**" is an addition to the Bible; "**O segrêdo do bonzo**," to Fernão Mendes Pinto's *Peregrinação;* and "**Lágrimas de Xerxes**," to Shakespeare's *Romeo and Juliet*. "**Manuscrito de um sacristão**" is a manuscript presenting a case of human perfectionism. "**Uma visita de Alceíades**" is written as a letter to a chief of police.

Several stories are disguised as wills and the final writings of men about to die. Some examples of these are: "**Verba testamentária**," the will of an envious man; "**Ultimo capítulo**," a suicide note; "**Galeria póstuma**," a posthumous diary; and "**O enfermeiro**," a final document of confession.

In two instances the apologue structure is employed. **"Filosofia de um par de botas"** is a dialogue between two shoes; **"Um apólogo"** is a discussion between a needle and thread.

Like the Peruvian Ricardo Palma, Machado often breaks into the structure of his stories to discuss openly the methods and purposes of his story fabrication. He usually does this in a whimsical manner—as one might speak when telling a tale to a group of listening friends.

The wide variety of his basic structures is further evidence of the originality which enriches Machado's stories.

In **"Um cão de lata ão rabo"** Machado describes three different styles of writing: the "antithetic and asthmatic," the *"ab ovo,"* and the "classical." In comparing these with the author's own style, one notes that the "asthmatic" is the one most closely matching it. Machado seems to prefer a style of vigorous fancy, apparent disorder, and free association of ideas—exhibiting a minimum of limitation and system. Although his choice of plots and themes is unrestrained, his wording is controlled and "correct." It is not unusually affected. If it were, his stories might be judged excessively bizarre.

Machado's imagination finds ample play in his creation of images, similes, and metaphors. In **"Conto alexandrino"** he describes Egypt as follows: "A terra era grave como a ibis pousada n'uma só pata, pensativa como a sphynge, circumspecta como as mumias, dura como as pyramides." **"Manuscrito de um sacristão"** characterizes Father Theophilo in this way: "Já n'esse tempo era um mystico; achava em todas as cousas uma significação recondita. A vida era uma eterna missa, em que o mundo servia de altar, a alma de sacerdote e o corpo de acolyto."

These are but two instances of numerous striking images which are fruits of Machado's extraordinary power of fanciful association.

Allusions to well-known literary works occur in scattered form throughout Machado's stories. Most frequent references are those made to Shakespeare and the Bible. These works, dealing with universal human traits, evidently led Machado away from a purely "local" view of life—or perhaps they coincided with a universal viewpoint which appealed to him from the outset. He was never a "regionalist" writer.

With regard to general attitudes reflected in Machado's stories, one notes a tendency toward equanimity. Although dealing with weird aberrations, strange incongruities, and discouraging twists of fate, the author never openly expresses despair or strong emotions. If there is a trace of attitude, it is usually that of humor born of irony. The follies of fate do not seem greatly to perturb Machado as he describes their ironic absurdities.

In the handling of his themes, therefore, he strives for "objectivity" in refraining from subjective evaluations of that which he relates. The touch of humor, evident from time to time, usually appears in the guise of light satire. Like William S. Gilbert (of Gilbert and Sullivan operetta fame), Machado often uses a topsy-turvy situation to produce such humor. **"A igreja do Diabo"** is perhaps the best example of this. In **"O alienista"** first the insane, then the sane, and finally the doctor himself are committed to the asylum.

Satire is evident in the ludicrous election methods of the spiders in **"A SeReníssima República,"** in the ridiculous scientific methods of the philosophers in **"Conto alexandrino,"** and in the following chant of the contending academicians in **"As academias de Sião"**: "Vinham dentro os quatorze membros da academia (contando U-Tong) e todos em còro mandavam aos ares o velho hymno: 'Gloria a nós, que somos o arroz da sciencia e a claridade do mundo'!"

As to the language element in the author's style, highly literary or abstruse terms are infrequent. Machado writes concretely, tersely—one might say, almost in a journalistic fashion. He avoids an excessive use of adjectives and affective expressions. His language is clear, straight-forward, and restrained. It provokes thought, enjoyment, and often amusement in the reader—as the concise writings of the Chinese have done for centuries.

Although varied, the short stories of Machado de Assis, taken as a whole, have a basic unity—reflecting the same general concept of the "Devil's world." They are products of an ingenious craftsman gifted with a deep understanding of human motives, a flair for a spontaneously fanciful and original treatment, and a clear and restrained manner of expression. Reading them affords anenjoyable literary experience.

Carmelo Virgillo (essay date 1966)

SOURCE: "Love and the 'Causa Secreta' in the Tales of Machado de Assis," in *Hispania,* Vol. XLIX, No. 4, December, 1966, pp. 778-86.

[*In the following essay, Virgillo examines Machado's representation of true love in his stories, detecting even in his early "romantic" stories that true love is rarely genuine, and usually motivated by self-interest.*]

It has been observed that Machado de Assis' fiction reveals the author's preoccupation with the theme of true love versus self-love. One can add, however, that excluding perhaps *Memorial de Aires,* his last novel, true love generally appears in his works as a device concealing an ulterior motive deeply rooted in self-love. This motive Machado himself has called the "causa secreta," or the ugly side of human beings, which his fictional characters try to conceal behind a mask of selfless humanity. Machado's denial of true love, furthermore, can be observed in his short stories as well as his novels, and even in those early tales commonly taken as emotional, sentimental stories supposedly aimed at the immature, love-starved reader who delights in the triumph of true love. These earlier tales, assigned to his so-called romantic period, seem to be filled with sentimental clichés very much in keeping with the literary conventions of the times. As one looks more close-ly, however, at the stories in *Contos fluminenses* and *Histórias da meia noite,* his first collections, one finds paradoxes and ironies that should dispel the notion that these early tales among Machado's works are uncharac-teristically romantic, hence inferior to his later produc-tion. The mating game is depicted, to be sure, but as an ironical battle of wits, and a strenuous one at that, at the conclusion of which it is uncertain whether the winner really enjoys the spoils or merely gets stuck with them. In these tales Machado seems to be asking: Who is to tell what lies hidden behind people's actions even when they seem most sincere? What guarantees that love can reform self-centered people?

Self-centered love appears in a number of these early sto-ries in the form of greed, vanity, pride, jealousy, envy, lust or any combination of these. In **"Frei Simão"** selfish parents destroy their son's life out of greed and pride. Simão's parents, wishing their son to marry a wealthy heiress, more likely for a financial gain of their own than for their son's welfare, deceive Simão by telling him that Helena, the destitute orphan girl with whom he is in love, has died. Machado describes Simão's parents in a way that leaves no doubt as to their character: "Os referidos pais eram de um egoismo descomunal. Davam de boa vontade o pão da subsistència a Helena; mas lá casar o filho com a pobre órfã é o que não podiam consentir." This egoism eventually kills Simão, who after he has be-come a Benedictine monk discovers that Helena is alive and married to a peasant. Soon after, he goes out of his mind and dies. Greed is again encountered as a manifes-tation of self-love in **"Luís Soares."** Here Luís is por-trayed as an irresponsible individual incapable of loving anyone but himself, yet he almost succeeds in persuading his beautiful young cousin Adelaide that he is in love with her. This occurs when he discovers that she is to inherit a large sum of money which is to rescue him from finan-cial difficulties. Fortunately, the girl learns of Luís Soares' scheme in time to prevent an unhappy marriage.

In **"O segrêdo de Augusta,"** the "causa secreta" is envy on the part of a parent, who should be the last person to be suspected. Augusta is envious of her daughter Ade-laide's youth and beauty, which she conceals behind a mask of motherly zeal. Fearing that if her daughter were to marry and have children of her own it would make her look old, Augusta discourages her daughter's suitors by magnifying their slightest faults while feigning parental concern.

Lust is the "causa secreta" which triggers the seemingly sincere actions of a number of Machadian lovers. Machado, however, does not usually allow lust to triumph unmolest-ed over honor. His unscrupulous lovers will get away with just about anything except with a deception leading to moral degradation. In **"Confissões de uma viúva moça,"** for instance, Eugênia is led to believe by handsome Emílio that she is deeply loved by him and that she should give in to his demands. But when her husband dies and she is free to marry, her young man suddenly leaves, revealing his true, dishonorable intentions. **"Casada e viúva"** de-picts an outwardly ideal husband, Meneses, very much in love with his wife Eulália although he deceives her con-stantly. Eulália, however, going through her husband's papers, unearths some incriminating love letters that give away the man's escapades and his true character. He ends up losing his wife's love forever. Similarly, in **"O relógio de ouro"** a beautiful gold watch exposes a worthless, perfidious husband. Luís Negreiros, a typical jealous hus-band, returns home to find a gold watch on his bureau. Knowing well that it is not his, he accuses his wife, Clar-inha, of infidelity and demands a full confession. When Clarinha refuses to furnish a plausible explanation for the sudden appearance of the watch in their home, Negreiros' anger assumes homicidal proportions. Thereupon, the des-perate woman, fearing for her life, hands him the proof of his unfaithfulness, a note from his mistress accounting for the watch and betraying a secret rendevous. The lustful husbands who seem to collect mistresses to inflate their male ego while pretending to adore their wives are fre-quently encountered in Machado's short stories. They are insensitive, selfish creatures who are usually punished by their own "causa secreta" which gives them away.

Machado de Assis often portrays women as selfish crea-tures incapable of self-denial, with the result that they seem to create more problems for the men who fall in love with them than they solve. However, men in Machado's fiction cling to these women desperately as a salvation from their miserable existence or, as is usually the case, as a liberation from themselves. But when a misanthrope meets a conceited woman and expects her to reform him, the results are all but good. Indeed, many of Machado's males are weak individuals who seek in women financial and moral support. This type of man is an easy prey for self-centered women like Rosina of **"Ernesto de Tal."** She stops seeing Ernesto and takes up with a fellow re-ferred to only as "o rapaz do nariz comprido" so that she can hasten Ernesto's marriage proposal. Ernesto, described by Machado as the type who "não possuia uma só casaca nova nem velha," seeks in Rosina security and stability. Consequently, he is completely dominated by her. She lets him know that she has many suitors, which makes him furious. Yet, says Machado in his usual tongue-in-cheek humor, "a boa menina, com a sua varinha mágica, trazia o rapaz a bom caminho, escrevendo-lhe duas linhas ou dizendo-lhe quatro palavras de fogo. Ernesto confessava que tinha visto mal, e que ela era excessivamente miser-icordiosa para com êle." Realizing that in spite of her flirtation with "o rapaz do nariz comprido" Ernesto is still undecided, Rosina deceives the former into thinking that she is in love with him and succeeds in having "o rapaz do nariz comprido" propose to her. When Ernesto discov-ers this he rushes to propose to Rosina and she is only too glad to accept, at the expense of the other party. But Machado's subtle conclusion leaves the reader sure that, after all, things worked out quite nicely for all concerned. Ernesto's rival in love may have lost a wife in Rosina but won a mistress. Rosina married a semidestitute Ernesto, but through the "partnership" with "o rapaz do nariz com-prido" she still succeeded in making a financial gain. As for Ernesto himself, Machado gives the reader to under-stand that he would live happily ever after in complete ignorance of his wife's affair with his business associate. Women scheme to attain their goals by using one man to keep or win the love of another in two other of Machado's earlier tales. Again, the deceived men are portrayed as weak individuals, idealistic, immature, and contradictory; in short, perfect targets for female egocentricity. Dr. Soares of **"A mulher de preto,"** for instance, is described by Machado as a very capable logician when it comes to science and mathematics, yet a dreamer "em busca de não sei que ideal mal definido, obscuro, incerto." When he seeks companionship and affection as a way out of his lonely, meaningless existence he meets the beautiful, mysterious Adelaide, who leads him to believe that she does not resent his wooing until she is certain she can count on his unconditional devotion. Then she tells him that she is the wife of his best friend, Meneses, and that all she ever wanted was to be reunited with him. Realizing, finally, Adelaide's "causa secreta," Dr. Soares has no alternative but to intercede for her. Having reunited his former beloved with his best friend, Soares leaves the scene a noble loser. Similarly, credulous old Diogo in **"Linha reta e linha curva"** is unmercifully used by D. Emília in her effort to make Tito jealous and induce him to propose to her. When she has accomplished this she dismisses Diogo the way one disposes of an old shoe that has ceased to be useful. Like Dr. Soares, Diogo takes defeat stoically.

So far we have examined several of the narratives sometimes branded by Machadian interpreters as not fully representative of his style and the general philosophy of life that will emerge clearly with the creation of an embittered and cynical Brás Cubas. As it has been observed, however, Machado is far from presenting his readers with uncomplicated stereotypes. Everyone of his characters conceals a "causa secreta," an intimate secret triggering actions anything but altruistic.

Machado de Assis' pessimistic philosophy of life becomes even more apparent in his third collection of stories, *Papéis avulsos*. Here one difference is noticed immediately in his concern with the subject of love. Machado concentrates his efforts on a number of other aspects of this emotion, consistently tearing it down to expose the real side of his characters. The latter are portrayed as either consciously hiding a "causa secreta" or as acting according to a subconscious selfish urge. This is readily apparent in his constant presentation of seemingly legitimate acts of affection concealing self-love, frustrated love succumbing to egoism, or in the proclamation of the superiority of opportunism over altruism.

In the initial stories of *Papéis Avulsos* we immediately encounter a departure from the general pattern of *Contos fluminenses* and *Histórias da meia noite* in that the plot is not constructed around a romantic dilemma. For instance, love is not the reason Dr. Simão Bacamarte, the protagonist of **"O alienista,"** marries D. Evarista. He is in love with his work. He purposely chooses to marry a corpulent, unattractive woman so that he may have big, healthy children and yet spend very little time making love to her. Fate punishes him, however, as both his work and D. Evarista fail to bear

the desired fruits. As a result, Dr. Bacamarte dies a failure leaving behind a childless wife.

Many of Machado's characters seem to be affected by what the Brazilian writer refers to as "o enjôo" or "tédio"—boredom with life leading to apathy and withdrawal from reality. The character is usually described as an inconsistent, unreliable individual who unconsciously cannot help but think of himself. Such is D. Benedita, the protagonist of the homonymous tale. She loses her husband because, too busy thinking of herself, she cannot make up her mind to follow her magistrate husband where his new job has taken him. Her concern for her children, a son and a daughter, is quite superficial: she is more worried about what other people think of her than she is about her own children. D. Benedita hardly interferes with their lives. She ignores the boy and goes along with her daughter's every wish. As for her friends, they too serve only to inflate her ego, only to be soon forgotten when they cease to be of use to her. Following her daughter's marriage and the husband's death, D. Benedita is left to face a life of loneliness and frustration with no one to flatter and worship her.

Jealousy hidden behind a seemingly selfless act is encountered in **"Verba testamentária."** Here Nicolou B. dies holding a grudge against humanity, particularly against those whose earthly accomplishments overshadowed his. His grievance against his fellow human beings is based on the competitive role of man in society. Everyone strives for importance on earth without regard to religion or moral values. Failure to achieve importance generates hate for the luckier ones. It is for this reason that Nicolau's will and testament insists that he be given burial by the least known and least successful casket maker in town.

Frustrated parental love in the face of greed and selfishness, symbolic and universal, occurs in **"Na arca."** Here the sad parent is Noah, the Biblical patriarch who must witness broken-hearted the fratricidal anger of his children over the division of lands and seas. One might wonder what good it has done Noah to have saved so many from the flood through his great love for humanity, when he has been unable to teach his own flesh and blood how to love one another.

Life is a type of lottery where the prizes are far too few compared to the great number of players; so one generation must necessarily thrive on the misfortunes of the previous one, learn from its mistakes, and hope not to make those same mistakes: "com os suspiros de uma geração é que se amassam as esperanças de outra." This is the philosophy a father teaches his twenty-one year old son in **"Teoria do medalhão."** A life of success for one generation is born of a life of failure in another generation. Success is not an easy thing to achieve, not honestly, anyway, the father warns his boy. One must learn to cheat, to flatter, to take advantage of the weak and credulous if one expects to even the odds of life's lottery. This is not easy, indeed, "come tempo, muito tempo, leva anos, paciência, trabalho, e felizes os que chegam a entrar na terra prometida! Os que não penetram, engole-os a obscuridade. Mas os que triumfam!. . . ."

The satisfied parent concludes his man-to-man talk with his boy by saying to him that their little chat is well worth Machiavelli's *The Prince.*

Machado's continued denial of altruistic love and his exposé of man's constant attempt to hide egocentricity behind a mask of generosity reaches paradoxical proportions in **"A causa secreta."** Here what has all the appearances of a humanitarian act by Fortunato conceals instead a gruesome reality. Fortunato's only reason for caring for a wounded man and for later opening a hospital is that he enjoys watching others suffer. When he cannot observe human beings suffer he takes great pleasure in vivisecting guinea pigs in the pretext of doing scientific research.

Humanitarian love goes down in defeat once again in **"O caso da vara."** Damião is torn between conflicting feelings: compassion for a sick Negro girl who is about to be beaten by Sinhá Rita, her ruthless mistress, and the desire to win Sinhá Rita's compassion for himself. Damião's conflict between humanitarian love and selfish love is resolved quickly; he hastens to look for the whip of the mistress of the house and to hand it over to her.

Though man knows that he is selfish, he somehow feels an urge, almost an obligation to mankind, to appear otherwise. Deep inside of him, however, there lies the real reason for his superficial abnegation. In **"Galeria póstuma"** Joaquim Fidelis' own "causa secreta" or ulterior motive is to be idolized as a great philanthropist by semi-destitute friends and relatives whom he often rescues from their financial difficulties. The very person who owes old man Joaquim the highest debt of gratitude is his nephew whom he adopted after the parents' death. It is not until the old man's own death that his nephew discovers a diary in which Joaquim's secret is revealed. There, in black and white the young man unearths his benefactor's true character in the form of contemptuous statements directed against him and all those others who had benefitted by his apparent generosity.

Whenever he does not deny that man is actually capable of noble acts. Machado appears to ridicule the very essence of altruism by satirizing legitimate philanthropists. These are portrayed in his stories as lunatics or wild visionaries who take upon themselves the courageous task of saving humanity through seemingly worthy feats which in true quixotic tradition defeat their own purposes. Such is the case of Dr. Jeremias Halma, the Dutch psychiatrist of **"O lapso,"** who decided to rescue the entire town from Tomé Gonçalves whose acute amnesia is bankrupting nearly everyone through his habit of borrowing money without paying it back. Out of pure altruism, Machado ironically suggests, Dr. Halma promises each citizen that for a nominal fee he will cure Tomé Gonçalves of his costly disorder. In no time at all there is not a single creditor in town . . . except, of course, our selfless psychiatrist. Another paradoxical situation is encountered in **"Conto alexandrino"** where Herophilus appoints himself a savior of mankind and discovers the science of anatomy, which is to spare his fellow human beings the pain of malady. To carry on his merciful work our great humanitarian asks the state for and obtains live human guinea pigs whom he vivisects unmercifully in the name of science.

The theme of *Humanitas,* the antithesis, or, to be more precise, the take-off on humanitarianism as conceived by the mad protagonist of *Quincas Borba* appears in a number of tales. In them we observe egocentricity replacing altruism quite successfully, and out of necessity at that. Only the strongest and the most clever should survive, claims Quincas' philosophy. There is no such thing as death when two forces are striving for survival, only life, since death for the weaker means life for the strong. War between two starving primitive tribes is used by Quincas to illustrate *Humanitas.* . . .

> **In later stories one notices almost immediately that Machado has dropped the romantic veil of pretense which may have previously masked his sentiments on love. His new treatment of passion brings to light all kinds of illicit love affairs.**
>
> —*Carmelo Virgillio*

Let the loser find only contempt or compassion in defeat, while the winner enjoys the spoils—the potatoes, insufficient to feed both but adequate for the one that survives.

No better demonstration of the philosophy of the survival of the fittest is, it seems, to me, to be found anywhere in Machado's fiction than in a tale entitled **"Pai contra mãe."** It concerns a man, Cândido Neves, who earns his livelihood by tracking down and returning fugitive slaves to their rightful owners. Cândido feels that hunger and a family to feed are sufficient reasons for him not to feel guilty about the often inhuman job he has to perform. Other occupations, he realizes, are not easy to find in an overcrowded and competitive city. Besides, he gets a thrill from capturing slaves—it is almost a challenge to him. One day, however, when a number of able competitors move into his neighborhood business suddenly drops to nothing. Cândido's wife Clara has a baby and, completely out of funds, the family is unable to pay the rent and, consequently, is evicted. There is no alternative but to turn the baby over to the ominous *Roda* where unwanted children are abandoned every day by destitute parents. Cândido is already on his way to deliver his only child to the *Roda* when he hears of the recent escape of a mulatto girl. The reward is high and suddenly there is hope for Cândido and his baby. He finds the girl, she is pregnant and begs him to let her go lest her master's beatings cause her unborn child's death. Here, then, the conflict is presented in all its pathos. It is the life of a little mulatto against that of Cândido's own baby. One of the two must die in order that the other may live. And so, the young mother is dragged through the streets of Rio and is finally dropped exhausted at her master's feet, her child dead inside of her.

In later stories one notices almost immediately that Machado has dropped the romantic veil of pretense which may have previously masked his sentiments on love. His new treatment of passion brings to light all kinds of illicit love affairs. Only the writer's characteristic *bienséance* rescues some of his stories from immorality. Here the "causa secreta" is more present than ever. Under a coat of marital faithfulness spouses either deceive one another or wish they did. Many a time matters are greatly facilitated if the lover or the mistress is a friend of the house not likely to be suspected. Friendship is betrayed in **"A cartomante"** where Vilela offers young Camilo his "big brother" affection and his home when Camilo's parents die. Vilela's wife, Rita, is quite helpful. Hints Machado: "Vilela cuidou do entêrro, dos sufrágios e do inventário; Rita tratou especialmente do coração, e ninguém o faria melhor." Before long Rita and the adopted orphan are more than just friends; a little later they are dead—at the hands of an enraged Vilela.

In a recently published article, Donald Decker points to a number of other stories in which Machado de Assis presents us with adultery perpetuated by friends who feign the noblest intentions. Helen Caldwell points in the first page of her study to eight short stories where Shakespeare's Othello is brought into the argument. However, with the exception, perhaps, of **"A cartomante,"** where Vilela's rage results in his murdering the guilty pair, Machado's short stories show us very little similarity between the deceived Shakespearean husband or lover and the Machadian counterpart. Deception or the "causa secreta" is normally either unknown to the one deceived or is taken rather philosophically by him. In **"Mariana"** Evaristo returns to Brazil to resume his love affair with Mariana whose husband has, in the meantime, passed away. He finds her thoroughly uninterested in him, not out of love for her deceased husband whom she had loved for only a short while, but out of the desire to pass in the eyes of friends and relatives as a faithful wife. Machado's ever-present subtlety is clear in the concluding lines of this tale where his sentiments toward love seem to be clearly manifested. In short, love does not deserve to be glorified. Like anything else in life it is fickle, perishable. Only life continues unmolested and indifferent to man's suffering. To this end, he informs all those readers who may feel sorry for Evaristo that the latter, far from being crushed by Mariana's *volte-face,* returns to France to resume the life he has temporarily interrupted. Machado enables his character to reflect on life as a stage and on his unsuccessful romantic venture as very much like the theatrical fiasco of a friend: "Antes de um mês estava em Paris. Não esquecera a comédia do amigo, a cuja primeira representação no Odéon ficara de assistir. Correu a saber dela: tinha caído redondamente.—Coisas de teatro, disse Evaristo ão autor, para consolá-lo. Há peças de teatro que caem. Há outras que ficam no repertório."

Love is not worth sacrificing one's life for. One should only try to prove the contrary, and he will discover how senseless it is to pit something ephemeral—love—against something quite concrete, death. This theory is evidenced in **"Maria Cora"** where Correia risks his own life for the love of a married woman, only to be scorned and miserably rejected by her after killing on the field of battle and quite honorably a husband she despised. Theoretically Correia should be driven to desperation, Machado seems to suggest ironically. He should punish Maria Cora for first motivating the combat and then scorning the winner. But what good would it do? Is life going to stop because of the ingratitude of a fickle woman? Indeed not; Correia will just have to remember to wind his watch, a thing he seems to have overlooked the very night he thought he had finally met his true love.

People in love commonly think that love is eternal; it survives time and should not bow even to death. The marriage vows are a trifle more realistic, for the spouses promise one another love and devotion only as long as both shall live. A close examination of Machado's views on the subject as observed through his many tales appears to contrast radically with both of these views. He seems to question the validity of any institution created by human beings who are by nature selfish and inconstant. Time changes everything including love, which, like people, must also be selfish and fickle. Machado's married and unmarried lovers either give the impression of being faithful or are actually faithful as long as nothing better appears on the horizon. When time sends along a more advantageous situation they do not hesitate to trade spouses, lovers, and even their children for what they think is an improvement in their situation. This is precisely what occurs in **"O machete"** where Carlotinha leaves her musician husband and her son to follow the sound of a *machete* which her lover, Barbosa, plays more convincingly than her husband plays the violoncello. In reacting to his tragedy, which he explains to a friend, our musician Inácio, shows the stoicism typical of most Machadian Othellos:-se embora, foi-se com o machete. Não quis o violoncelo, que é grave demais. Tem razão; machete é melhor."

> It seems to me that selfless love, as opposed to self-love, is represented in Machado's stories as an illusion devised to conceal man's natural instinct of self-preservation in a world full of uncertainty and contradiction.
>
> —*Carmelo Virgillo*

Having examined a goodly number of short stories where Machado seems to have manifested his views on love, what conclusion can one draw? It seems to me that selfless love, as opposed to self-love, is represented in Machado's stories as an illusion devised to conceal man's natural instinct of self-preservation in a world full of uncertainty and contradiction. A pessimist and a true fatalist, the Brazilian writer sees in beauty and goodness something superficial and ephemeral designed to counteract the ugliness of a basically evil life. Like life itself, nearly all Machadian lovers are deceivingly ideal individuals: good-looking, healthy, well-off, yet tragic, unpredictable, often ugly in truth. Men are many a time misanthropes who expect to find in heterosexual love a way out of their misery, thus seeking a cure-all in their relationship with the opposite sex. They fail miserably in their intent, most of the time. The Machadian woman is no better than her male counterpart, if anything, worse. She is described by an interpreter as "um elemento perturbante e incerto, um ser estranho e fascinante que acentua o trágico da vida, porque é contraditória e surpreedente como a fatalidade." Most of the time she is of no help to herself, much less to the men in her life.

If life is conceived by Machado's dialectical philosophy as basically contradictory, and if man is nothing but a part of life, or life itself, then one must conclude that there must be two sides to every person. To this end the Brazilian writer presents selfless love, generosity, and a number of other positive attributes of man only to prove that they represent but one of the two sides of the individual. The other side is represented by self-love, opportunism, and all the vices imaginable which constitute the invisible "causa secreta." Therefore, assuming that Machado's fictional creations seek in beauty an escape from the ugly side of life, and if love is synonymous with beauty and everything that is good, then one must concede that behind the beautiful human beings in love or behind the altruists in Machado de Assis' fiction there must be ugly creatures in love with themselves. The two sides: the superficial, or the beautiful, and the invisible, or the ugly, complete the individual. Man, claims Jacobina, a Machadian character in **"O espelho,"** is, metaphysically speaking, nothing but an orange: there are the peelings covering the orange and then, underneath, there is the orange itself. It seems to me from a close examination of a number of the Brazilian writer's most representative short stories that his denial of selfless love as symbolic of all good in man is very real; it is Machado's way of saying that human beings must not be taken at face value. Man is basically sinful, evil, and if he expects to survive he must create the beautiful part of himself with his own hands for everyone to see. This second soul will enable others not to detect the "causa secreta" which motivates his selfish actions and which is, as I see it, his only true self.

John Nist (essay date 1968)

SOURCE: "The Short Stories of Machado de Assis," in *Arizona Quarterly*, Vol. 24, No. 1, Spring, 1968, pp. 5-22.

[*In the following overview of* The Psychiatrist, and Other Stories *, Nist discusses themes and techniques used in the stories, and praises Machado's subtle and understated style of writing.*]

Joaquim Maria Machado de Assis (1839-1908) is generally recognized as the finest novelist in all of Latin America. Indeed the epileptic quadroon who founded the Brazilian Academy of Letters in 1897 combines such deep Dionysian wisdom of life with such cool Apollonian con-

trol of his medium that his genius must rank him with Flaubert, James, Kafka, and Proust. But it was not until forty years after Machado's death that literary criticism in the United States made a first serious assessment of the creative magnitude of Brazil's number one man of letters. In 1948 Samuel Putnam devoted most of Chapter XIV of his book *Marvelous Journey* to the delineation of Machado's life and work and called for the translation into English of three supreme novels (*Dom Casmurro, Quincas Borba, Brás Cubas*) and the short stories. A modest enough challenge to American publishers when one considers that Machado's collected works run to thirty-one volumes. In 1952 Noonday Press responded to Putnam's challenge with *Epitaph of a Small Winner* (tr. William L. Grossman) and followed up this initial *succès d'estime* with *Dom Casmurro* (tr. Helen Caldwell) in 1953 and with *Philosopher or Dog?* (tr. Clotilde Wilson) in 1954. Thus the novels made their way into the mainstream of Western literature and were hailed as masterpieces of expressive economy and psychological power.

The short stories, however, had to wait a decade longer— and even then only twelve of Machado's prodigious output appeared in the lingua franca of the present-day world. In 1963 the University of California Press published *The Psychiatrist and Other Stories* (tr. Grossman and Caldwell). Despite the smallness of this collection, it is representative enough to show the Brazilian *contista* to be a master worthy of ranking with such giants of the genre as de Maupassant, Chekhov, and Joyce. In fact, the short story, more than the novel, was the ideal literary form for Machado de Assis; in it he could develop his themes "vertically," with all the subtle and meticulous precision that characterizes his classically limpid and laconic style. Such development, in turn, is the result of these three attributes of Machadian art: acuteness of perception, originality of medium, and perfection of literary execution. From these three attributes emerges Machado's esthetic gift to the spirit of modernism: *a rich ambiguity of conflicting forces held in suspension so that the tragicomic chaos of the id can be projected into the unified field of an ego that delights in plurisignificance and multivalence.* In the sorrow and wit, satire and humor, iconoclasm and passion of these stories, it is as though the mind of Pascal were joined to the sensibility of Shakespeare and ordered to see the world of man via the vision of Kierkegaard as objectified through the whimsical manner of Laurence Sterne. The result, of course, is an utterly engaging universe in which madness constitutes the ultimate innocence; detachment from all pat philosophical answers, the final commitment to the search for truth.

Committed to that search Machado is. Paradoxically, the degree of his commitment is measured by the extent of his detachment. In Yeatsian terminology, he must wear the mask of his anti-self in order that the tormented psyche that is himself may sing the universal out of the particular. Tormented that psyche was: by the knowledge of his slum origins, the poverty of his boyhood, the enslavement of the ancestors of his Negro blood (Brazil did not abolish that hateful form of human bondage until 1888), the constant fear of epileptic seizures in public, and the melancholy sterility of a childless marriage. Thus the author who ridicules the mediocre success attained by conformity and publicity in **"Education of a Stuffed Shirt"** spent most of his adult life—like Hamlet's dramatic historian—in the pursuit of personal fame, public respectability, and class status; as with Shakespeare before him, Machado always wanted to build the best house in his own Stratford—the provincial and imitative Rio de Janeiro of the late nineteenth and the early twentieth century. Build the best house he did; it was not, however, the conventional one of brick and mortar in which he died, but rather the original one of Portuguese prose in which his spirit lives forever. And one of the most brilliantly appointed rooms in that house belongs to his short stories.

In **"The Psychiatrist,"** a magnificently paced tale long enough to be a novella, Machado illustrates Pascal's famous dictum that "Men are so necessarily mad, that not to be mad would amount to another form of madness." So subtle is Machado in his pointing of forecast that it takes several indications of "scientific sanity" to establish the suspicion that the hero of the story, Dr. Simão Bacamarte, suffers from his own form of mania: the consuming desire to be a psychiatric Messiah in both theory and practice. Since science is his only office and the little Brazilian town Itaguai his universe, Bacamarte refuses the King of Portugal's offer of either the Presidency of the University of Coimbra or the position as Chief Expediter of Government Affairs. Because he demonstrates theorems with poultices, the doctor has no eye for feminine beauty; hence he marries the homely Dona Everista—after all, her digestion is perfect, her eyesight excellent, her blood pressure normal, and her urinalysis negative. But she bears Simão no children (the subject of sterility is an obsession with Machado), and so the physician of the psyche builds his Green House for the projected children of his own insecurity: the mad. Then he rationalizes his act with a quotation from the Koran, "in which Mohammed declared that the insane were holy, for Allah had deprived them of their judgment in order to keep them from sinning." Bacamarte, of course, finds this idea beautiful and profound; he has the passage engraved on the façade of the Green House, and is soon doing a thriving business in psychotherapy. His one concession to prudence is his attributing of the quotation from Mohammed to Benedict VIII. Thus he stays on good terms with the Vicar and the Bishop.

Before long, however, Bacamarte has locked up in his asylum four-fifths of the people of Itaguai, the same proportion—so Professor Grossman claims—of Manhattanites found to be emotionally ill in a recent psychological survey. Regardless of the validity of Machado's statistics, this much is certain: his psychiatrist's Green House is a symbol of the incommunicable prison of this world, through which man flees from the Reality Principle in pursuit of the Pleasure Principle. By moving this symbol through the myth of his story, Machado succeeds in X-raying the soul of man and discovers therein most of the mental illnesses that afflict the human race. So rife are these illnesses, in turn, that they force Bacamarte to theorize as follows: "Till now, madness has been thought a small island in an ocean of sanity. I am beginning to suspect that it is not an island at all but a continent." On this continent in Itaguai the grotesque becomes "ferocity in disguise," and the "Bastille of the human reason" offers the helping hand of science to a tired and mired theology.

Finally grabbed by that hand of science, Sr. Costa first undergoes a series of declensions from opulence to poverty by becoming a Quincas Borba in reverse. His maniacal charity, in which the *last* loan is always the *lost* loan, dissipates a fortune, lands him in the Green House, and jostles a cynical kaleidoscope of gossip into the weird patterns of a collective human imagination that exaggerates actual fact into the dimension of its own fictional dream. Because she believes that a curse was put on her uncle's money by a man with the star of David tattooed on his arm, Costa's niece joins the inmates in the ward for those suffering from delusions or hallucinations. Meanwhile, Machado continues, in his own inimitable way, to make the seemingly impossible become the esthetically inevitable. Thus Sr. Mateus, a semi-retired manufacturer of pack saddles, enjoys his sumptuous house, elaborate garden, and rare furniture in vain: he is committed to the asylum for the treatment of his *petrophilia,* the inordinate love of edificial masonry. Hence the highly metaphorical orator Martim Brito, who tries to flatter Dona Everista into curbing the scientific zeal of her husband, comes at last to grow beautiful thoughts in the Green House. And Machado records the typically inept response of the populace as follows: "The terror grew in intensity. One no longer knew who was sane and who was insane. When their husbands went out in the street, the women of Itaguai lit candles to Our Lady. And some of the men hired bodyguards to go around with them."

A slave to his own self-intoxicating rhetoric, the barber who is nicknamed "Stewed Corn" leads his followers into a comic-opera revolution that makes him momentarily the dictator of Itaguai. But since Bacamarte's asylum has become an "established municipal institution," the eloquent Porfírio refuses to abolish the Green House; consequently, when the good doctor learns that eleven Stewed Corners were killed and twenty-five wounded in the revolution, he seals the fate of the barber and his political adherents with this perfect coda to section IX of the story: "Two beautiful cases." João Pina, another barber even more eloquent than Stewed Corn, evidently agrees with Bacamarte, for when this tonsorial rhetorician deposes Porfírio as dictator of Itaguai, he places everybody's destiny in the hands of the psychiatrist. The result of this touching fascist loyalty to the demands of science is a mass occupation of the Green House by scores of new patients, including Dona Everista herself—her madness a dementia induced by an inability to choose between a garnet necklace and a sapphire necklace, whereby the jewel of her mind is lost.

By this time, however, Simão has begun to doubt the validity of his theory and practice. If four-fifths of the town are mentally unbalanced, then such imbalance must be the norm of psychic health. By the same token, if one-fifth of the town are mentally balanced, then such balance must be the sign of psychic illness. And so, with the blessing of the exempted members of the Town Council, Bacamarte reverses himself, releases the formerly mad, and incarcerates the formerly sane according to their various manifestations of psychotic morality: modesty, truthfulness, guilelessness, loyalty, magnanimity, and wisdom. To cure the minority in the Green House of their spiritual maladies, the psychiatrist invents an ingenious therapy: he destroys the particular virtue that put each patient in the asylum. Thus he flatters the modest into vanity, turns the truthful into liars, motivates the guileless into deception, corrupts the loyal into traitors, makes the magnanimous into misers, and restores the wise to the general folly of mankind. The irony of Machado's satire is devastating.

Although the relatives of the restored patients hail the doctor's cures as miracles, Bacamarte fears that it is only fraud that returns men to the "sanity of the world." With his motto of *plus ultra* and his desire to discover the ultimate truth underlying all psychic phenomena, Simão gradually comes to realize that mental imbalance is naturally so inherent in man that only the absolutely dedicated and heroically innocent person is truly insane. His one example in proof of his final theory is himself: "He possessed wisdom, patience, tolerance, truthfulness, loyalty, and moral fortitude—all the qualities that go to make an utter madman." As an embodiment of both the theory and the practice of the New Doctrine in psychopathology, Bacamarte commits himself to the Green House, where after seventeen futile months of "Physician, heal thyself!"— he dies. Whereupon the people of Itaguai bury his mortal remains with "great pomp and solemnity."

Within the 18,000 or so words of **"The Psychiatrist,"** Machado paints the ambiguous portrait of a microcosmic representative of the madly sane and sanely mad world of the human spirit. Man's inexhaustible capacity for insanity, Machado seems to say, is a case of hilariously sad and deliciously bittersweet *pathedy,* wherein the hero of tragedy is saddled and ridden like an ass by the fool of comedy. Pathedy (or tragicomedy, in more conventional terminology) is, in fact, the peculiar esthetic forte of Machado de Assis. Time and again, by means of a vision that brings laughter to the point of pain and pain to the point of laughter, the Olympian of Brazil shows that man achieves tragic ends by comic means and comic ends by tragic means. Because he can create this rainbow effect of sunshine and tears, Machado never succumbs to the kind of uncontrolled hysteria that mars the satire in the last voyage of *Gulliver's Travels.* In the jargon of Marshall McLuhan, his medium is cooler than Swift's.

That medium, in turn, constitutes the anti-self mask of Machado de Assis as it conflicts with the love of big-bellied bombast and condoric eloquence that is so native to the man of the tropics, and especially to the Brazilian. As the first major writer of Brazil to turn away from Portuguese and French influences, Machado drank deep from the springs of an Anglophilia that taught him the virtues of masculine self-control in a world of feminine emotionalism: concision is precision, sense of proportion is sense of humor, dramatic objectivity allows the greatest play of an antiseptic lyric subjectivity, understatement says it all, surface whimsy mirrors deep wisdom, description is

admission of narrative failure, and the only nature worth studying is human nature. Like Laurence Sterne, whose work he admired, Machado makes the "emotional aura" of the deed more important than the deed itself, because he knows that if you ask a man what he thinks, he will invariably tell you how he feels. Although Machado generally avoids such mechanical tricks as the use of asterisks, black and marble pages, blank sheets, nonconsecutive numbering, pointing index fingers, and elongated dashes (localized mannerisms of the impressionistic Sterne), he does nevertheless owe some of his brilliant method to an emulation—as distinct from mere imitation—of the creative habits of the irrepressible author of *Tristram Shandy.*

> Within the 18,000 or so words of "The Psychiatrist," Machado paints the ambiguous portrait of a microcosmic representative of the madly sane and sanely mad world of the human spirit.
>
> —*John Nist*

Many of the features of that brilliant method may be seen at work in **"The Psychiatrist."** At the heart of his method is Machado's habit of *suppression,* of suggesting more than he directly states, of evoking more than he manifests, of writing ulterior meanings between the lines. Thus his dialogues are full of mental ellipses and dramatic interruptions: there is no need to belabor the obvious once the reader's imagination has been alerted to the true facts of a situation and can therefore draw its own conclusions and through them engage in the act of creation. And so Machado draws the reader into the art of his fiction by making him guess at the exact contents of a communal inner speech shared by characters who live together in the intimate key of exteriorized thought, by palimpsesting the secondary meaning of a statement upon its primary one for the sake of ambiguous humor, by compressing the constructions of his syntax so that surface-level form points to its hidden significance, by surprising the mind with quick thrusts of oblique wit, and by constantly squeezing the norm of the context to extract the sweet juice of satiric hyperbole, ironic litotes, and philosophic punning.

Economy of means and deceptive simplicity mark the style of Machado de Assis throughout the entire range of his stories; he does not waste time in lichen-hunting or bird-watching. As one naïve reader asked, "Where are the trees?" Dissolved in the background of what is naturally given as part of the intuited reality that lies outside man's Green House. Unless the setting of fiction impresses itself upon the consciousness of the mask of the author or of one of his characters, then Machado ignores the presence of the outer world. By so doing, of course, he frees his attention for the execution of more important tasks than giving his reader a weather report or a lesson in local ecology. Thus in dramatic narrative Machado often achieves a maximum of effect with an apparent minimum of effort:

"This must not be permitted to continue."

"Down with tyranny!"

"Despot! Outlaw! Goliath!"

At first such things were said softly and indoors. Later they were shouted in the streets. . . .

The mastery shown in this brief passage from **"The Psychiatrist"** informs the form of **"Education of a Stuffed Shirt"** and turns it into an incredible performance in burlesque.

As a short story written entirely in dramatic form, **"Education of a Stuffed Shirt"** is a symbol of Machado's daring and economy. Burlesqued, of course, is the Platonic dialogue as a means of moral edification and instruction. With irony and satire, wit and implicit sarcasm, Machado has the father of his tale deliver a Polonius-like sermon to his just-come-of-age son Janjão, who answers sleepily from time to time like a straw man in a Socratic search for truth. Now that the young man has an enormous moustache and is ready for love affairs (a typical Machadian definition of manhood in Brazil), his father is bent on teaching him how to become a socially admired and respected nincompoop. The instruction is simple and direct: to become a "stuffed shirt," Janjão must cultivate a correctness and gravity of carriage; achieve the full maturity of dullness at forty-five; smother every genuine idea his mind might entertain; become eloquent on trivia; undergo a systematic course of mental impoverishment (including gin rummy, dominoes, and whist); play at billiards; avoid solitude; be a gossip-monger; court a monotony of opinions; use outworn Classical, Romantic, and Naturalistic figures of speech; quote aphorisms; become a cliché expert and be irrelevantly sententious; master mere terminology rather than methods or contents; court vulgar publicity and join every committee attending on fame; have a bust of himself made and put on display; avoid both false and genuine modesty; become an "obligatory presence" in society; woo the adjective as the soul of rhetoric; speak on political theory as a "shining cipher," with neither imagination nor any real philosophy; tell only vulgar tales for the local yokels; and above all—remain immune to irony.

But **"Education of a Stuffed Shirt"** is remarkable not only for its technique, but also for its evidence of the *sabedoria* (deep life wisdom) of Machado de Assis. Based upon his acuteness of perception and originality of theme, this *sabedoria* makes the great Brazilian writer a literary forerunner of Sigmund Freud; the psychological profundity of Machado permeates his work and gives his esthetic vision the quality of spiritual prophecy. In **"A Woman's Arms,"** for example, the love-hungry and child-starved Dona Severina suspects that her husband's fifteen-year-old apprentice Ignacio has a crush on her. Because her Jocasta complex answers the adolescent love that makes a confused sexual fetish of her voluptuous arms, Dona Severina's awakened libido becomes a mirrored image of Ignacio's dream. Asleep in a hammock, the boy entertains the fantasy of his own desire: he makes love to Dona Severina's beautiful arms, until suddenly—she bends over

and touches her eager mouth to his. And as Machado says, "Here dream coincided with reality. And the same mouths were joined in imagination and outside of it." But the drive of potential mother wins out over the drive of potential mistress: guilt and fear cause Dona Severina to cover her arms with a shawl for a week. And then she persuades her husband to dismiss his faithful legal apprentice. Unaware of the real cause for his dismissal, Ignacio leaves, carrying with him forever the fragrance of his dream:

> And down the years, in other love adventures, more real and lasting, he never again found the thrill of that Sunday on the Rua da Lapa, when he was only fifteen. To this day he often exclaims, without knowing he is mistaken, "And it was a dream! Just a dream!"

Like Keats in the "Ode to a Nightingale," Machado questions both reality and illusion: "Do I wake or sleep?"

Ultimately, however, Machado does more than merely question reality and illusion. Through the organicity of his fiction he affirms that art is the illusion of reality; life, the reality of illusion. And since these two kinds of being merge in the consciousness of man, the human psyche cannot endure the inner subjective life of the id without the outward identity of the ego as it assumes some role in objectified reality. This is the central message of **"The Looking Glass,"** a haunting story that Machado calls, in a parenthetical subtitle, the "rough draft of a new theory of the human soul." According to the character Jacobina, who does most of the talking in the tale, man has two souls: inner and outer, like the two halves of an orange. To lose one half is to risk loss of the other half and therefore of one's entire existence. To prove his point, Jacobina invokes the example of Shylock, whose exterior soul was his ducats. Then Jacobina tells the story of himself as a young Brazilian lieutenant who became his uniform and military privilege to such a degree that while isolated on his Aunt Marcolina's *fazenda* (plantation), he was reduced to a spiritual cipher until he dressed before a huge mirror and once again took on a human identity. In the course of the narrative, meanwhile, Machado demonstrates Pascal's thesis that ultimate reality is not to be found either wholly within or wholly without the consciousness of man.

In the demonstration of that thesis, Machado reveals the devastating sense of loneliness, doubt, and anxiety of the human psyche as it faces the terrible possibilities of Nothingness. Just as the inner soul is dependent on the outer soul during the role-playing of the day, so the outer soul is dependent on the inner soul during the dream fantasies of the night. Hence the final answer of man to the threat of Nothingness must be the mutual interpenetration of the Pleasure Principle with the Reality Principle in order that the Value Principle may emerge. That Value Principle, as a simple act of faith based upon the courage to be one's own finite and ephemeral being *as a particular manifestation of transcendent Being-Itself,* is what produces—so Machado seems to imply—the spiritual essence known as *person.*

Through the affirmation of that essence, the Brazilian master finds a solution for the problem of despair, which has produced so much of what Lawrence Durrell has called the "cry-baby literature"of the twentieth-century Existentialists. In **"The Secret Heart,"** for example, the sadistic husband Fortunato behaves like a miniature Caligula and feeds like a vampire upon the cruelty-induced loneliness of his wife Maria Luiza. But the more Maria Luiza suffers, the more beautiful she becomes. Her spiritual beauty, in turn, wins the chaste regard of the gentle Garcia. Because Fortunato's vanity convinces him that his wife and his friend have committed adultery together, his perverted mind relishes the shattering sorrow that racks Garcia at the death of Maria Luiza. As a human embodiment of inscrutable evil, Fortunato seems on the surface of things to represent the equally inscrutable triumph of a heartless nonbeing. Yet even as the title of the story is ironic, so is Fortunato's name. As a mad slave to the Pleasure Principle, Fortunato is self-deceived in his interpretation of the relationship between his wife and his friend. And so it is Garcia, the servant of the Value Principle, who actually prevails. His is truly the secret heart, and—paradoxically—the measure of its suffering is the measure of its triumph in love, the last light spoken by courage against the darkness of despair.

Because that light cannot be spoken by Damiã, in **"The Rod of Justice,"** the witty but cowardly runaway from a seminary ironically proves himself unworthy of the very priesthood he seeks to escape. While the Quixotic João Carneiro is off verbally battling Damião's tyrannical father for the sake of the boy's freedom, the "unruly and vicious character" of Carneiro's comical rhetoric turns out to be just that. At first resolved to protect the pitiful little tubercular slave Lucretia, whom Sinha Rita treats like a piece of furniture, Damião weakens and in order to court the favor of his godfather's mistress, hands her the hated instrument of punishment. Once again, Machado's title is a piece of cynical irony, the satirical device of a disillusioned idealism.

Such disillusioned idealism is responsible for the consummate depiction of man's tragicomic illogicality in **"The Animal Game,"** a literal and yet metaphoric name for the national passion of Brazil: gambling via legalized lottery. Literal because each player, in the words of Machado, "chooses a number that by established custom is identified with a certain animal, and if this number turns out to be the winning number in the lottery, all who risked their pennies on it win, and all who placed their trust in other numbers and other animals lose." Metaphorical because, by thematic implication, though monkeys are the craziest people, people are also the craziest monkeys—mimicking faith and reason to the point of hilarious parody. Thus the arsenal clerk Camillo, while marking time for a governmental promotion, believes that patience and perseverance are the key to victory in the lottery. And so he bets and bets and bets, only to lose and lose and lose. He has, like the general run of mankind, "a genuine talent for closing his eyes to the truth." When he does finally win, he buys food and wine to celebrate with and a "gold pin with a precious stone" to give to his longsuffering wife, not realizing that if he had kept from gambling in the first place, he could have celebrated far more often and bought many

more tokens of his husbandly care. To ask Camillo to be that sensible, however, is like trying to dip the sea in a sieve: flight from reality is the deepest reality in his psyche. If Camillo is ingenuously mad, then Sr. Nogueira, the narrator of **"Midnight Mass,"** is madly ingenuous. Nogueira recalls a Christmas Eve when he was seventeen and his beautiful and neglected landlady Conceição was thirty. As he recalls the suffocating atmosphere of onanistic sublimation, he sees all the clues of Conceição's inept attempt to seduce him, but he still does not fathom them. Perhaps the key to her ineptitude and his naïveté lies in his ironic observation that "She spoke ill of no one, she pardoned everything. She didn't know how to hate; quite possibly she didn't know how to love." Thus the lady is too gentle to be sexually aggressive, and the young man is still too innocent to understand the depth of her emotional hunger. And so he remembers, but fails to properly interpret, the signs that point to her romantic interest in him: she has lain awake hoping for a chance to be with him alone; she wears only a white negligee, loosely tied at the waist; she smiles at his protestation that she is not "getting along in years"; she cannot keep her "large, perceptive eyes" off him; she walks about the room, posing for him; she keeps returning to the fact that they are both awake and alone together; she constantly asks him to speak softly, lest he wake her mother; she finally places one of her hands on his shoulder and trembles "as if she had a chill." As suppressed desire turns to religious fervor in her, so forgotten Catholic piety turns to sexual somnolence in him. At last the spell is broken by the cry of Nogueira's neighbor, rapping at the window: "Midnight Mass! Midnight Mass!" The story closes upon two more clues: Conceição's suspended guilt and hope, and her quick remarriage to her husband's apprenticed clerk after the sudden death of the adulterous Menezes. The story, told in the limited first person throughout, is as shimmeringly subtle as the saintly heroine's negligee.

In **"Father versus Mother,"** however, Machado's ironic satire hits with all the force of a sledgehammer:

> Slavery brought with it its own trades and tools, as happens no doubt with any social institution. If I mention certain tools, it is only because they are linked to a certain trade. One of them was the iron collar, another the leg iron. There was also the mask of tin plate.

As material illustrations of the cynical adage "Sweet are the uses of virtue," these tools are the instruments of social justice as practiced by the catchers of runaway slaves. The leg iron prevents a second flight, the iron collar brands the runaway as an habitual fugitive from the tender mercies of his master, and the tin mask keeps such a fugitive from indulging in the vice of alcoholism to escape his misery. All three tools, of course, are at the disposal of Candido Neves, the ne'er-do-well protagonist of the story. As a projection of Machado's obsession with the thought of having a child, Candido Neves (white snow) and his wife Clara (bright) prove that poverty is indeed prolific: the awaited offspring of their marriage becomes a subtle blend of the Immaculate Conception and the Incarnation. Set against that motif is the dark trade that Candido follows in order to earn his meager living. The trade, in turn, brings him to the brink of having to abandon his new-born son to the Wheel, a composite symbol of Fortune and Cross. But with a superb pacing and a consummate climax, Machado shows how Neves avoids submission to this cruel fate. By capturing a pregnant runaway mulatto and returning her to her licentious master, Candido earns enough money to retain the custody of his son, but he also causes the wretched Arminda to abort: "The fruit of some months came into this world without life, between the groans of its mother and the despairing gesture of its owner." Blessing the slave for having tried to run away, Neves' heart beats out the rhythm of his own selfish love: "Not all the babies have the luck to be born!" In that evil inversion of the will, Machado strikes a powerful blow at man's inhumanity to man and creates with his child-for-a-child theme a modern secular parallel to the Biblical Slaughter of the Innocents.

With equal artistic polish, though with less emotional impact, Machado depicts the incapacity of the human heart to grieve beyond the limitations of its sense of *relation,* as distinct from its desire for *experience*. Told in first-person retrospect to age ten, **"The Holiday"** is an ironic comment on the narrator's frustrated expectation. When his Uncle Zeca comes to get him out of school, young José-Martins' first thought is that he will be taken to "a party, a picnic, or something." He goes, instead, to his father's wake. The tension between the boy-that-was's naïveté and the story-teller-that-is's integrity is what sustains the narrative suspense to the point of catastrophic revelation. Once José learns that his father is dead, his attention shifts from his dream of fun to the mechanism of sorrow that is his mother. In the ritual of mourning, he plays his somber role, helped by the fact that he is truly sorry at the loss of anticipated festival and celebration. But he cannot sustain his filial grief for the eight days of post-funeral seclusion demanded by Brazilian custom. Not that his father was not a good man, for he most certainly was, but rather that the boy soon sees him only as a remembered *It* and not as an immediate *Thou*. Bored with his mother's repetition of how his father died and temporarily shut away from the everyday world of the young and gay, José escapes his prison of enforced behavior via fantasies of imagination, in which he sets off skyrockets, listens to street organs, and dances with little girls. And so he longs to return to the larger prison of the school from which he once wanted a holiday. When he does finally return to the routine of boyhood, he is delighted that his ironic holiday has come to an end and that he is now distinguished by his black attire. As the teller of his own tale, José asks the reader not to censure him. Machado has so skillfully handled his material that the reader can do nothing but grant José's request: immaturity hath a privilege.

So hath a man's pride; so hath a woman's romantic desire. In **"Admiral's Night,"** Deolindo the Nostril has to cover the blow to his ego delivered by the infidelity of Genoveva the Golddigger by pretending to his shipmates that his reunion with her after three months at sea was the orgy of love ironically signified by the title of the story. Deolindo, alas, is but an apprentice seaman in the game of hearts; in his absence Genoveva has fallen in love with José Diogo, the cloth peddler. As amoral as the natural force of gravity that causes a rock to fall on a man's head, Genoveva accepts the pair of earrings Deolindo has brought her from Trieste—and deposits them in her jewelry case. As innocent as a whirlpool that sucks a shipwrecked sailor to his death, she is as cold as physics. What is more, she understands the warm weakness of her jilted lover: he will neither take revenge nor commit suicide. And so Machado demonstrates that human love needs constant nourishing or it dies and that many a man lives on an impossible hope. When the hope vanishes, he assumes the dramatic courage of make-believe and chooses to save face in pathetic dissembling rather than to lose his head in tragic violence.

But the most privileged condition of all is that of madness. That is why the last will and testament of Nicolau B. de C. is honored down to the last detail—namely, that he be buried in a coffin made by Joaquim Soares, a mediocre craftsman whose work is seen in its true light by Nicolau's brother-in-law: *not* "worth a damn." The brother-in-law, however, does not see the "Final Request" in its proper perspective. Neither does the reader until Machado has recounted the past life of the dead man. Then and only then does the title of this psychologically profound story take on the full burden of its awful meaning.

Born with "a hidden deformity, an organic flaw" deeply buried in his nature, Nicolau grows up a sadistic schizoid. Like the malevolent Iago, he is eaten up with spiritual envy. In a passage that subconsciously reveals Machado's obsession with his own malady of epilepsy, the author shows the physical effects of such inward turmoil: "Other times his legs grew wobbly and he reeled, or from the corner of his mouth there trickled an almost imperceptible thread of foam." Choosing friends to whom he can condescend, Nicolau goes through life banqueting on the empty air of flattery. Thus he comes to feed on inferior natures like an addict dependent upon dope. Envying in turn his wife, his Emperor, and the poet Gonçalves Dias, Nicolau finally fires his chef: the man simply cooks too well and becomes the recipient of universal praise. Literally green in his secluded old age, Nicolau undergoes the psychic excruciation of splenetic jealousy: "The least or greatest thing pulverized his nerves: a good speech, a clever artist, a carriage, a cravat, a sonnet, a witty remark, an interesting dream, everything brought on an attack." Hence the motivation behind his final request that Joaquim Soares make his coffin: so mad has Nicolau become that only the worst of anything is good enough for him.

Written at about the same time as **"The Psychiatrist"** (1881-82), the story **"Final Request"** (1882) joins with its longer companion piece as a testimonial to the prophetic genius of Machado de Assis: he was a generation or two ahead of his time—not only in Brazil, but also in the Americas at large. No other writer in New World Portuguese, Spanish, or English is his match in the sheer economy of means to ends. Comparisons, however, are indeed odious. And Machado needs none for literary criticism to acknowledge the supreme value of his work.

That value, in turn, inheres to a large degree in the modernity of its vision. Such modernity can be seen in the fact that Machado's stories, as well as his great novels, are an esthetic anticipation of the leading psychological, metaphysical, and religious ideas of the twentieth century.

As an organized objectification of the id, Machado's art helps to reclaim the wastelands of the human psyche; in such reclamation, of course, it also helps to create the moral conscience of the race. That conscience, moreover, avoids self-indulgence in the fantasies of the Pleasure Principle in order to achieve the transcendent values that have their origins in the Reality Principle. By depicting the conflicts of Jungian archetypes, Machado leads his readers into an awareness of the basis for Martin Buber's distinctions among *I, Thou,* and *It.* These distinctions ultimately reveal that man is not inherently an atheist, but rather an idolater. In the worship of such finite things as power, pleasure, wealth, fame, and knowledge, human nature performs its own happening and therefore inflicts its own punishment. By bringing man to the abyss of Nothingness, Machado—in anticipation of Tillich—also brings him to the very ground of his being: man himself is the source of both heaven and hell. So adept is the whimsically sad and apparently cynical Brazilian master at killing off the false gods of man's deterministic materialism that he leaves none to compete with the one true God of man's heroically accepted spiritual freedom. Implicit throughout the work of Machado de Assis, then, is the fact that man's courage to be himself in the blank face of cosmic nihilism constitutes the very hope which issues from despair.

If the epileptic quadroon from Rio de Janeiro had bequeathed contemporary society nothing more than this implicit legacy of hope, he would still remain a giant of a literary figure. But he has left also his own personal example, which says that since man's highest task is to convert matter into spirit, it is no wonder that from the disease of human flesh and blood should come the bright offspring of the creative act. Just as friction produces the pearl in the oyster, so psychic disturbance produces the need for artistic expression. In the expression that Machado de Assis achieves through the twelve short stories now available in English, Dionysian ecstasy projects Apollonian serenity; personal defeat, universal triumph. Although Machado makes Braz Cubas, the cynical (and posthumous!) narrator of *Epitaph of a Small Winner,* close his story on the ironic note that he is ahead in the game of human existence because he has not transmitted to anyone "the legacy of our misery," Machado himself died with this blessing on his lips: "Life is good." In that answer to his anti-self lies one more reason why the English-speaking world must become better acquainted with the genius of Brazil's greatest *contista.* He may very well be the supreme prose writer of both Americas during the late nineteenth and the early twentieth centuries.

Jack Schmitt and Lorie Ishimatsu (essay date 1977)

SOURCE: An introduction to *The Devil's Church, and Other Stories,* by Machado de Assis, translated by Jack Schmitt and Lorie Ishimatsu, University of Texas Press, 1977, pp. ix-xiii.

[*In the following essay, Schmitt and Ishimatsu examine Machado's fiction as a kind of social and literary criticism, and also discuss the ways in which it approached literary modernism.*]

The modern Brazilian short story begins with the mature works of Joaquim Maria Machado de Assis (1839-1908), acclaimed almost unanimously as Brazil's greatest writer. Between 1858 and 1906, Machado wrote more than two hundred stories, and no other writer in Brazil achieved his technical mastery of the story form before the 1930s.

Until recent years, Machado's reputation abroad was not commensurate with the quality of his remarkable stories and novels or his high position in Western letters. The Brazilian critic Antônio Cândido considered it a paradox that a writer of international stature, whose style and themes are characteristic of the twentieth century, should have remained relatively unknown outside Brazil. The obscurity of Machado's works in the United States was closely related to the fact that Portuguese was not widely known in this country, and translations of his novels and stories into English have been available only in recent years, thanks especially to the excellent translations by Helen Caldwell and William L. Grossman. . . .

Machado's fiction can be divided roughly into two periods: those works written before and those written after 1880. The early Machado is basically romantic, whereas his late works are written in the vein of psychological realism. The Brazilian writer Augusto Meyer supports this division, comparing Machado's break in evolutionary continuity to that between Herman Melville's earlier works and *Moby-Dick.* Meyer's parallel is certainly valid. There is little in Machado's early novels and stories to prepare the reader for the abrupt changes in content and technique found in *Epitaph of a Small Winner* (*Memórias Póstumas de Brás Cubas,* 1880), his first great novel, and ***Miscellaneous Papers*** (*Papéis Avulsos,* 1882), the first of five volumes in which the majority of his best stories appear. The consistently high quality of the sixty-three narratives in these five books defies comparison with the works of other Brazilian short-story writers, past or present.

Machado's stories constitute an excellent satirical portrait of middle class values and social structures in Brazil during the period of the Second Empire (1840-1890) and the first years of the Republic. If he had continued to publish the bland, moralistic love stories and parlor intrigues of the 1860s and 70s, his legacy to posterity would have been a mildly ironic but pleasant and entertaining portrait of a miniature *Belle Epoque* in a Brazilian setting. By the late 1870s, however, his fiction begins to reveal a devastatingly penetrating satirical assault on that society in particular and on humanity in general. In a moment of understatement, Helen Caldwell said that "one does not find in his writings a great deal of smug satisfaction with his own century and country" [*The Brazilian Othello of Machado de Assis,* 1960].

There is an abundance of implicit social criticism in Machado's descriptions of the life styles and the family structures of middle-class characters in his stories. One is always aware that the material comforts his characters enjoy are either the fruits of a carefully observed caste system or achieved at the expense of others: friendships and marriages are based on self-interest, financial position, or social class; government jobs and sinecures are arranged through close ties within the extended families of those who are actually forced to work for a living; upper-middle-class characters come by their leisure through inheritances, rents, or allowances from family estates; family retainers and impoverished relatives live out their lives as parasites or dependents. The sharpening of sadistic instincts and the avoidance of manual labor are possible results of the corrupting force of slavery. Many of Machado's characters seem to have a knack for avoiding useful work; they are idle, bored, passive, indifferent, and unresourceful, to the extent that they are often paralyzed when faced with the trauma of real action. The women in his stories are usually more social than domestic; they are vain, devoid of maternal instincts, and either physically, intellectually, or emotionally sterile.

We can see in Machado's critique of society that he prefers to dwell on the negative aspects of human behavior: egotism, pretentiousness, shallowness, corrosive envy and jealousy, cowardice, and intellectual lethargy. The more desirable qualities, such as philanthropy and altruism, are usually motivated by the less desirable ones.

Skeptical that the successes of science in the nineteenth century could be repeated in the areas of human values and behavior, Machado also doubts that the future has better things in store for us than the past. He is merciless in his satirization of intellectuals and scientists who offer dogmatically stated panaceas for the ills and shortcomings of humanity.

Machado's critique of literary conventions in Brazil is equally cutting. In his early literary essays and journalistic sketches, he offers constructive criticism, arguing persuasively against the Brazilian writers' emphasis on nature, the Indian, and the picturesque or exotic aspects of regionalism. After the mid-1870s, he begins to structure his critique of literary conventions within the fabric of his fiction, insulting his readers' traditional narrative expectations, satirizing romantic literary canons, and assaulting empty rhetoric, verbosity, and banality through the unimaginative flat language of his characters.

Although most of the human frailties Machado satirizes are not restricted to time and place—and thus universal—many Brazilians have taken offense at his ironic barbs, accusing him of having painted an overly pessimistic portrait of Brazilian society, even denying him literary citizenship in Brazil.

Machado does in fact reveal sympathy for many of his characters, but it is an ironic sympathy. He is not indifferent to human conflicts, but he does use humor and irony to stress the absurdity and futility of those conflicts when acted out against the backdrop of a serene universe. Such a spectacle creates a sense of helplessness and can only inspire wistful amusement. The irony-laden controversies and reversals in his stories are intellectually satisfying and speculatively responsible; the staunch aesthetic moralism revealed in his narratives refutes those who consider his skepticism and pessimism nihilistic or sterile. It is not destructive to emphasize the presence of evil, the illusory nature of truth and reality, or the quagmires upon which people build the foundations of their speculative castles.

Many of Machado's best critics have hinted that his deepest meanings are found in his technique. Augusto Meyer claimed that the analysis of themes is a useless approach with Machado and concluded that ambiguity is the predominant theme in his works. As early as 1922, the American critic Isaac Goldberg saw that "we must not hunt too eagerly for action in [Machado's] stories"; he is "sui generis, a literary law unto himself," and "his method is the most leisurely of indirection" [*Brazilian Literature*, 1922]. Years later, in 1948, Samuel Putnam recognized Machado's universal appeal and modernity and established a list of priorities for prospective readers and translators. Putnam also drew some valid parallels between Machado and Henry James: they both "deal in ideas" and are "concerned with psychological analysis, with the nebulous action that takes place behind the curtained consciousness of men"; they resemble one another in the "comparative absence of plot in their pages," as this term is commonly understood [*Marvelous Journey*, 1971]. More recently, Caldwell posed the problem of ambiguity in Machado's works when she said that his leaving the reader to pass judgment is "to be sought in Machado's artistic method" [*The Brazilian Othello of Machado de Assis*].

As a result of his aversion to the superficiality of his contemporaries' interpretation of Brazilian reality, Machado attempts to portray a less idealized and more complex notion of human behavior. He strips his characters of their deceiving surface behavior and probes beyond their lives of public conformity. By aiming at psychological truth and focusing on crucial moments of experience in the lives of his characters, he approaches the method of the moderns. His ambiguity is in part the result of his subjective, relativistic world view, in which truth and reality, which are never absolutes, can only be approximated; no character relationships are stable, no issues are clear-cut, and the nature of everything is tenuous.

By exploring the subjective musings and the illusions of his characters, Machado leaves us no rational measure by which we may judge the flow of time, expanded and contracted at will in the individual consciousness of his characters. We attempt to make sense out of our experience, but our time sense is always relative to our perception of time at any given moment. In the words of A. A. Mendilow, the sensation of openness and expansion is further aided by the fact that "feelings and associations do not come to an end; they are not felt once and then finished with; they are not amenable to arrangement in shapes" [*Time and the Novel*, 1952]. These "feelings and associations" are often the most tangible elements in Machado's better stories.

Barreto Filho makes an acute observation when he remarks that in Machado's narratives "there is a final conclusion of impotence, and that's why the evocation of the past is ironic" [*Interoduçzo a Machado de Assis*, 1947]. This evocation of the past is ironic in Machado because despite our tendency to aspire to eternity, practice self-deception, and play mental games with time to make it serve ephemeral illusions, time is in fact a cross to bear; it passes on inexorably and remorselessly, destroying everything in its wake, save art and works of the intellect. Machado's experimentation with the time element is yet another facet of his fiction that gives his readers the distinct impression of modernity.

By communicating his meanings through the use of suggestion and implication, Machado developed a shorthand style that allowed him to convey progressively more information in smaller spaces. Sean O'Faolain stresses the modern writer's aim at "general revelation by suggestion" and "making a very tiny part do for a whole." Machado, like the modern storyteller, "has not dispensed with incident or anecdote or plot and all their concomitants, but he *has* changed their nature. There is still adventure, but it is less a nervous suspense than an emotional or intellectual suspense."

In his technical mastery of the short story, Machado was decades ahead of his contemporaries and can still be considered more modern than most of the modernists themselves. He is also an obligatory point of reference for anybody interested in the development of modern Brazilian literature. The fact that his works elicit extensive and diverse reactions and opinions is a tribute to the richness, complexity, and importance of those works.

Maria Luisa Nunes (essay date 1983)

SOURCE: "An Artist's Identity versus the Social Role of the Writer: The Case for Joaquim Maria Machado de Assis," in *CLA Journal*, Vol. XXVII, No. 2, December, 1983, pp. 187-96.

[*In the following essay, Nunes defends Machado against attacks that he was unsympathetic to blacks in Brazil based on his apparant reticence on the issue of slavery. The critic cites examples from Machado's fiction that demonstrate the writer's "anti-slavery" position.*]

Joaquim Maria Machado de Assis, 1839-1908, was the greatest Brazilian writer of his time and perhaps of all time. Because he wrote in Portuguese, his works have not received the universal acclamation they merit, but in the past twenty years or so, most of his major novels have been translated into English—*Memórias Póstumas de Bras Cubas* (*Epitaph for a Small Winner*), *Quincas Borba* (*Dog or Philosopher?*), *Dom Casmurro*, *Esau e Jacó* (*Esau and Jacob*), and *Memorial de Aires* (*Ayres' Memorial*). In combination with his novels, Assis's short stories make up the corpus of imaginative literature on which his fame

rests. His great works are marked by a profound knowledge of universal literature and the innovations of an originality that was exclusively his own.

Despite his incomparable artistic achievement, there is a long tradition of speculation on Machado de Assis the man. Because he was an extremely private person who spoke little of his early years, and in his adult life dedicated himself to his writing, to his position as an upper-level civil servant, and to his wife—Carolina Xavier de Novais, with whom he enjoyed a reportedly blissful marriage—little is known about him apart from the views expressed in his work. As a result, a great deal of misinformation has been disseminated about Machado de Assis, much of it far from flattering.

According to the myth recently demolished by Raymundo Magalhães in his *Machado de Assis Desconhecido*, by Helen Caldwell in her brief Introduction to *Machado de Assis*, and particularly by Jean-Michel Massa in his *A Juventude de Machado de Assis*, Assis was the epileptic product of syphilitic blacks and mulattoes. He was an ugly street urchin who stuttered and spent his childhood in abject poverty. In his overweening desire to rise socially, he repudiated his mulatto stepmother, who had made inordinate sacrifices to educate him. He was a traitor to other men of color in Brazil and to the cause of abolition. To complete the portrait, he was self-centered and a social-climbing snob. Before examining the evidence which refutes these accusations, it would be interesting to examine some of their sources.

A black Brazilian school teacher, Hemetério dos Santos attacked Machado de Assis two months after his death in the *Gazeta de Notícias* of Rio, November 29, 1908. Not only did Santos criticize and deny Assis's artistic achievement, but he established the "black legend" of the Brazilian master's indifference to the oppression of slavery, his repudiation of his black ancestry and mulatto stepmother, and his refusal to take an interest in his suffering black brothers.

The North American Raymond Sayers, in the *The Negro in Brazilian Fiction*, reechoes the legend in questioning why Assis's early contacts and relationships with other mulattoes did not automatically translate into lending his talents to the black cause and the struggle against slavery as did José do Patrocínio and Luis Gama.

Mixed in with these allegations against Assis is a peculiar variety of Brazilian racism. Assis's biographer, Lucia Miguel Pereira, describes him in the following terms: "He was not able to hide the fact that he was a mulatto, his race screaming from the abundant and unruly head of hair falling over his ears, the thick lips toped by a coarse mustache, and flattened nostrils" [*Machado de Assis Estudo Crítico e Biogràfico*, 1955]. In Afranio Coutinho's analysis of "mulatto psychology," the subject is offered no exit. He's damned if he does, damned if he doesn't. Coutinho affirms: "They know very well the way to get accepted by society: imitation, forced discipline, purity of language which always degenerates into ridiculous pedantry, solemn and ceremonious airs, or the opposite: cordiality, mania to please and be obsequious, to get confidential, well measured and honeyed courtesy to the point of being disagreeable" [*A Filosofia de Machado de Assis e outros ensaios,* 1959]. Coutinho's conclusions about Assis are that "his color, humble origin, poverty, the anxiety to rise socially, the need to struggle, all made him see life negatively and to be delighted by the spectacle. Because he was offended in his dignity, because he was very proud, he translated his resentments into art in the form of a revolt against society and a conception of men and life without generosity."

Any attempt to view the social role of the writer objectively must conclude that the legend surrounding Assis was the product of envy and intrigue further elaborated upon by a large dose of racism. Although we are told that many mulattoes of humble origin came to occupy places of prominence in the nineteenth-century liberal empire in Brazil and that Assis's success was therefore not unusual, it is obvious that subsequent critics have dwelt on the color question inordinately if, in fact, color was an insignificant variable for a man of talent at that time and afterwards. We submit that for the person of color in Brazilian society, there is a great deal of ambiguity surrounding the question of how he sees himself and how others see him. This question has traditionally been bound up with that of class—education, family, and money—but for Machado de Assis, whose education was autodidactic and whose family was poor, his status was clearly defined as a mulatto, not black, but not white and subject to the instability and hazards of the upwardly mobile nonwhite in Brazilian society. Let us look now at what we believe to be the "reality" of Assis's life and views.

Two of the Brazilian master's paternal great grandparents were known to be black slaves according to the genealogical tree established by Massa. The unknown males in these relationships were whites or mulattoes, possibly ecclesiastics. The writer's paternal grandparents were freed mulattoes whose son, Francisco José de Assis, was father to Joaquim Maria. His mother was an Azorean of humble origin, Maria Leopoldina Machado da Camara, whose genealogical tree shows that her family was as modest as her husband's—in fact if not juridically—despite Gondim da Fonseca's claim that Assis's mother's family was noble. The Assis family members were residents on the Chacara de Livramento, whose aristocratic owner was Joaquim Maria's godmother. The family's status on the estate was similar to that of clients on an ancient Roman patriarchy as distinguished from that of the slaves. Massa deduces from this that Assis's childhood was that of a rustic who had exposure to a certain amount of culture.

As for Assis's repudiation of his mulatto stepmother, Massa asserts that the boy was ten when his mother died and fifteen when his father remarried, approximately the age at which he began to be on his own, thus precluding any debt of education of his stepmother. He was twenty-five when his father died, and the fact that he and his stepmother had separate masses said for the dead man indicates some feud between the son and the widow rather than an obligation on the part of the former to the latter. Assis's epilepsy was real as was that of Flaubert and Dostoyevsky, but his general health was good, as attested by his survival to the age of sixty-nine at a time when tuberculosis and yellow fever often reached epidemic levels in Brazil. Regarding Assis's supposed unwillingness to participate in the struggle against slavery and oppression, Raymundo Magalhães has proven conclusively through reporting on less well-known writings that this allegation was false. Each step forward in the struggle was observed and commented on by Assis. In the chronicle *The Week,* of May 14, 1883, Assis wrote of Abolition Day:

> It was sunny, very sunny on that Sunday of 1888 when the Senate voted for the law which the Regent sanctioned and we all went out on the streets. Yes, even I went, the most retiring of snails, I entered the parade in an open carriage, if you'll do me the favor, guest of an absent fat friend. We all breathed happiness, all was delirium. Really, it was the only day of public delirium I remember having seen.

We will see the distance between Assis and his narrators when we observe how this event is transformed in *Memorial de Aires.*

Although the famous abolitionist Patrocínio was reported to have lambasted Machado de Assis because of the latter's indifference to abolition, this accusation was apparently the intrigue of one disgruntled writer named Luis Murat, who was angry at Assis because of unfavorable criticism of his poetry. He is said to have dredged the libel up after forty years, but it is found nowhere in the writings of Patrocinio. Doubt has also been cast on Murat's mental faculties when he wrote it.

The major theme in Assis's fiction is self-love. Like Shakespeare, the Brazilian master believed this to be the root of all emotional problems.

—*Maria Luisa Nunes*

Throughout his chronicles, Machado de Assis broached the question of abolition. On April 4, 1965, he discussed slave owning religious corporations in Brazil. He was consistently supportive of the cause of the slaves and critical of the barbarous practices of the institution. During his old age, he recalled the abolitionist campaign in correspondence with Joaquim Nabuco, a reflection of his interest and concern rather than of indifference. As Magalhães observes, Assis contributed to the campaign according to his temperament, which was not that of the militant José do Patrocínio, but in his post at the Ministry of Agriculture, he worked quietly in favor of the slaves. In the case of Machado de Assis, it appears that his temperament, a prerequisite for his artistry, did not lend itself to mass public participation in the Abolition campaign, but in his short stories and novels, the effect of his subtlety in the treatment of the issue surpasses the most ardent oratory of the great abolitionists.

The major theme in Assis's fiction is self-love. Like Shakespeare, the Brazilian master believed this to be the root of all emotional problems. Assis treats this aspect of human nature satirically. Irony is one of his most frequent modes. He views the oppression of other human beings by the institution of slavery as only one aspect of self-love related to others such as avarice, cruelty, ambition, hypocrisy, and the transiency of human emotions. Counterpoised to this satirical world is an ideal world of love and fulfillment, but man is a creature divided against himself and will never achieve unity with an Absolute, whether it be God, the good and the beautiful, or other human beings. Love is a rare occurrence on our planet. Machado de Assis did not desire acceptance by the upper classes about whom he wrote and whose value systems he satirized. The values of his idealized selves (the implied authors of his novels) are in sharp contrast with those of his most famous narrators, the egotistical Bras Cubas, the doubt-ridden Dom Casmurro, and, to a lesser extent, the contemplative Ayres.

The relative rarity of blacks in Assis's fiction is due to the condition of most blacks in the society of his time. As Professor [Raymond] Sayers states: "The Negro could not serve as a subject for the irony of Machado, for the Negro could never determine his own conduct or fix his own position in society; he was not a free agent, and therefore he could not be made a subject for satire" [The Negro in Brazilian Literature, 1954]. Assis's literary output can be viewed as a protest to the value system of the society in which he lived. The oppression of slavery was only one of man's limitations to his own fulfillment.

In *Memórias Póstumas de Bras Cubas,* the institution of slavery comes in for Assis's typical subtle attack. While he is well aware of man's perversity, which leads him to inflict on others the punishment he has received—Prudencio, Bras's former slave playmate, becomes a slaveowner and whips his slave—he makes it clear through his irony who the original oppressor is and where the responsibility lies. Let us listen to the consummate egotist, Bras Cubas, as he reflects on his former slave's conduct:

> I left the group which looked at me in amazement and whispered its conjectures. I walked on unthreading an infinity of reflections which I am sorry to have lost entirely; furthermore, it would be material for a good and perhaps happy chapter. I like happy chapters; it's my weakness. Outwardly,the Valongo episode was appalling; but only outwardly. As soon as I got deeper into my ratiocinations I found a mischievous core, subtle and even profound. It was a way Prudencio had of making up for blows received, transmitting them to another. I, as a child, rode him, put reins in his mouth, and beat him without compassion; he moaned and suffered. Now, however, that he was free, was his own master and in control of his arms and legs, could work, relax, sleep, unfettered by his former condition, now it was that he surpassed himself. He bought a slave and was paying him with high interest the sums he had received from me. Imagine the subtlety of the rascal!

In the short story **"Father versus Mother,"** self-interest of self-love is posited against an abstract morality which does not exist in the slave-owning society. After a description of the cruel and inhuman punishments inflicted on runaway slaves related in a matter-of-fact way, the omniscient narrator ironically concludes that money hurts and that property must therefore be protected. The main action of the story consists of a search for a runaway slave. The slave hunter is characterized as an incompetent who is able to get along only as a parasite on an immoral institution. Because he must provide for his own wife and child, he does not hesitate to capture the pregnant runaway slave. Society's acceptance of the brutality involved in underscored by the narrator's comment that anyone passing by or standing in the door of a shop understood what it was and *naturally* did not come to the rescue. At the moment of being given back to her owner, the slave woman aborts. The narrator's comment opposes self-interest to human life: "Not all children have the luck to survive."

Assis treats the theme of slavery in other short stories, such as **"O Caso da Vara," "Encher Tempo,"** and **"Mariana,"** but in his final novel, *Memorial de Aires,* he dwells most lingeringly on the issue. In this novel, abolition is one of the major themes. Unlike his own spontaneous reaction to it cited above, Assis's narrator, Ayres, is much more reflective of the event. He dissociates himself from the ignominy of the institution altogether. If it can be assumed, as some critics have, that of all Assis's narrators, Ayres is the closest to the writer, we can infer from this dissociation that Machado de Assis did not consider himself responsible for the society in which he lived. The reference to the burning of records on slavery is an historian's nightmare, but it is interesting to note that the poem referred to in the following passage is the source for the name of one of Ralph Ellison's characters in *Invisible Man,* Supercargo:

> An acquaintance of mine, a journalist, offered me a place in his coach which was on the Rua Nova and was going to circulate in the parade organized to go by the palace in the city and give an ovation to the Regent. I was just about to accept, such was my commotion, but my quiet habits, my diplomatic customs, my very nature and age kept me back better than the reins of the coachman held back the horses, and I refused. I refused with regret. I let them go, him and the others who got together and left from the Rua Primeiro de Marco. They told me later that the paraders stood up in the coaches which were open and made great acclamations in front of the palace where the ministers were too. If I had gone, probably I would have done the same and even now I wouldn't have understood myself. . . . No, I wouldn't have done anything: I would have put my head between my knees.

> It's well and good that we finished with that. It was time. Even though we burned all the laws, decrees, and notices we will never be able to finish with the particular acts, deeds and inventories, nor blot out the institution from history, or even from poetry. Poetry will speak of it particularly in those verses of Heine in which our name is perpetual. In them the captain of

the slave ship recounts having left three hundred blacks in Rio de Janeiro, where the "Goncalves Pereira" house paid him one hundred ducats per slave. It isn't important that the poet corrupts the name of the buyer and calls him Gonzales Pereira; it was the rhyme or its bad pronunciation which caused this. Nor do we have ducats, but there it was the seller who changed into his language the money of the buyer.

Ayres later comments that a personal happiness is worth much more than a public job (abolition) and seems to mark distance between his value of self-interest and the social problems associated with slavery. His doubts about the panacea which abolition (and even the benefits bestowed on the freedmen) represented to his countrymen show Ayres' attitude to be far ahead of his time rather than simply distant. When the protagonist Fidelia gives her plantation to the freedmen, Ayres ends his speculations on the preparedness of the former slaves to run a plantation in an ellipsis. Its implication would seem to cast doubts not on the freedmen's capabilities, but on the expectations of a capitalistic society which had systematically and oppressively kept them from its techniques and now expected them to manage within its norms without adequate training.

Machado de Assis emerges as quite a different person from the man of the legend. What becomes immediately apparent is that he was too subtle for his detractors. It is true that he was more concerned with the perfection of his art than with taking a militant role in social causes. Nevertheless, he took his stand on the issues, and his perception of them was farsighted enough to comprehend more than their immediate implications. His art is a testimony to his success and fulfillment in his life's goal. He did not wish perhaps to be known as a black, white, or mulatto artist but as an artist. His concerns reflect a desire to be accepted in his unique identity, a desire common to all great artists and even to lesser human beings.

John Gledson (essay date 1984)

SOURCE: "Machado de Assis between Romance and Satire: 'A Parasita Azul'," in *What's Past is Prologue: A Collection of Essays in Honor of L. J. Woodward,* edited by Salvador Bacarisse, and others, Scottish Academic Press, 1984, pp. 57-69.

[*In the following essay, Gledson discusses the parallels between the story "A Parasita Azul" and the plots of Machado's major novels. The critic argues that the story, when read as satire rather than straight-forward romance, can be better understood as a forerunner of Machado's later novels, which are more overtly concerned with social and political criticism.*]

"A Parasita Azul" is the opening story of Machado de Assis' second collection, *Histórias da Meia-Noite* (1873): it was first published in the preceding year, in four parts, in the *Jornal das Famílias.* It is not an undiscovered masterpiece, but it is a surprising work which does not merit the almost complete critical neglect which has been

its lot. There are fascinating parallels between its plot and those of the great novels published after 1880—in particular, *Memórias Póstumas de Brás Cubas* (1881) and *Quincas Borba* (1885-91). Most suggestively, the novel whose plot most closely resembles that of **"A Parasita Azul"** is Machado's last, the strange and in many ways off-putting *Memorial de Aires* (1906). If this parallel can be established and explained, this long and in some ways uncharacteristic early story may well tell us more of Machado's secrets than its artistic shortcomings would lead one to imagine.

Perhaps the most disconcerting aspect of the story from the point of view of the reader is the discrepancy between the plot and the tone in which the story is told, or to put it another way, between the moral form of the story and its amoral import. The plot is simple and traditional: the most illuminating parallel is perhaps that of the Prodigal Son. In 1849, Camilo Seabra, the son of a rich *comendador* from Goiás in the far interior of Brazil, is sent by his father to study medicine in Paris: his decision, somewhat surprising at such a place and time, is inspired by a French naturalist who had visited the area at the time of Camilo's birth (1828). In Paris, Camilo is at first under the botanist's watchful eye; but after his death, he proceeds to waste his father's allowance in riotous living (though he is careful to get his degree). We first meet him on his unwilling return to Brazil in 1857, his father having finally lost patience with his procrastination. In Rio, he meets a fellow-townsman, Leandro Soares, who has stayed at home all these years. On the long journey home via Santos and São Paulo, this talkative dullard reveals himself to have three passions—hunting, politics and Isabel Matos, who however does not return his affections. Since she does not, he is determined at least that no-one else will have her: 'tinha o sestro aliás comum, de querer ver quebrada ou inútil, a taça que ele não podia levar aos lábios'. Cutting a long story short (though many of its details and digressions will be returned to), Camilo inevitably falls in love with Isabel, and marries her after it is discovered that he is the lover she has been waiting for for years. She had sworn to marry a boy who, years ago, had fallen and grazed himself while climbing a tree to get a blue parasitical plant— *a parasita azul*—for her. Leandro is contented with the fulfilment of his political ambition to be a local *deputado*.

If the Biblical story of the Prodigal Son, along with that of Esau and Jacob, seem closest to the structure of the story as a whole (Leandro is actually referred to as exchanging the 'direito de primogenitura por um prato de lentilhas', even though he is no relation of Camilo's), there are other elements in it which recall traditional romance. Naturally, they surround Isabel, who is first seen by Camilo on horseback, like a Scott heroine:

> Vira muitas amazonas elegantes e destras.
> Aquela porém tinha alguma cousa em que se
> avantajava ás outras; era talvez o
> desalinho do gesto, talvez a espontaneidade
> dos movimentos, outra cousa talvez, ou todas
> essas juntas que davam á interessante goiana
> incontestável supremacia.

The motif of waiting for the promised lover to return is common enough in romance, of course: more than Cinderella, Isabel is perhaps the Sleeping Beauty, bound by her own childhood promise, and guarded by the 'dragon' Leandro, who threatens terrible deaths to anyone else who dares approach her. She is also the lady who imposes tasks on her suitors. Even after Camilo has been revealed as the boy of the parasite incident, she refuses to marry him until he shows his affection for her in some dramatic way. This he does by disappearing, apparently distraught, for some days; Isabel's remorse at being the cause of this near-suicide finally brings her to her senses, though the reader might wonder with the *comendador* why 'uma moça apaixonada por um mancebo, e um mancebo apaixonado por uma moça, em vez de caminharem para o casamento, tratassem de separar um do outro'. His reasonable suspicion is that his son has run away 'para fugir a um enlace indispensável'.

As this summary cannot avoid indicating, these 'serious' Biblical or romance motifs are continually undermined by the tone of the story, and by its setting, which is not a mythical land, but a 'real' Goiás, where shotgun marriages are more common than suicidal lovers. When Camilo is approached in a crowd by a mysterious old man who turns out to know the secret of Isabel's passion for the parasite, his first impression (and the reader's) might well be that this is one of Leandro's toughs come to warn him off—the first thing he says is 'Veja o que faz'. Nothing of the sort, however; Camilo is right to conclude that he is in a novel:'—Um romance! disse ele; estou em pleno romance.'

He *is* right, however; none of the realism is allowed to get in the way of the conventional happy ending, in which the young man gets his girl, and even the churlish Leandro is happy with his 'prato de lentilhas'. What is perhaps most surprising is that this takes place without any conversion or repentance that the reader can be sure of. The story is completely without a moral in this sense, for Camilo remains irresponsible and lucky to the end. Admittedly, the stories of Esau and Jacob and the Prodigal Son are not the most conventionally moral in the Bible, but in each there is some final justification for Jacob's trickery and the Prodigal Son's behaviour. Here there is none. Machado goes out of his way to tell us that his disappearance in the final chapter is not caused by suffering, but is simply play-acting:

> O mésero rapaz trazia escrita no rosto a
> dor de haver escapado á morte trágica que
> procurara; pelo menos, assim o disse muitas
> vezes em caminho, ão pai de Isabel.

Faced with such incongruences, the reader may well be forced to read the story in a different sense, and to see it as satire rather than romance. This entails largely ignoring the plot with its conventional ending, and concentrating on the characters, who stand condémned as foolish and/or selfish. Many details, which go against the grain of the 'romance', suggest this; even the heroine, Isabel, is described by Padre Maciel as 'uma grande finória', who will not accept Soares 'a ver se pilha algum casamento que lhe abra as portas das grandezas políticas'. Politics is the

consuming passion of the whole community; not only does Leandro regard a place in the provincial parliament as sufficient compensation for the loss of Isabel; we meet the latter's aunt, who is a poor old woman with 'two other defects'—'era surda e gostava de política.'

At the centre of the story (Chapter IV of the seven into which it is divided) stands the festival of the Espírito Santo, introduced by Machado much as if it were a *flagrante* of traditional Brazilian life, in the style of Manuel Antônio de Almeida's *Memórias de um Sargento de Milícias* for instance:

> Vão rareando os lugares em que de todo se não apagou
> o gosto dessas festas clássicas, resto de outras eras,
> que os escritores do século futuro hão de estudar com
> curiosidade, para pintar aos seus contemporâneos um
> Brasil que eles já não hão de conhecer. No tempo em
> que esta história se passa uma das mais genuínas festas
> do Espírito Santo era a da cidade de Santa Luzia.

But the reader should not be deluded; this is not a *costumbrista* sketch, but the centre of Machado's political satire. The festival is presided over by Tenente-Coronel Veiga, whose concern, not unconnected with the desire to outshine his political rivals, is to make the festival as brilliant as possible. By a carefully constructed *crescendo,* Machado builds up to the appearance of the Tenente-Coronel, dressed up as the *Imperador do Divino:*

> Āo peito rutilava uma vasta comenda da Ordem da
> Rosa, que Ihe não ficava mal. Mas o que excedeu a
> toda a expectação, o que pintou no rosto do nosso
> Camilo a mais completa expressão de assombro, foi
> uma brilhante e vistosa coroa de papelão forrado de
> papel dourado, que o tenente-coronel trazia na cabeça.

It is impossible not to see a more generalised political satire here: the repeated references to the connexion between politics and the festival, the crown, and the *Ordem da Rosa* leave us in no doubt that Machado is making fun of the Brazilian Imperial system, of a society mesmerised by a cardboard crown. This long passage, it should be said, is only perfunctorily integrated into the main love story. It is during the festival that the mysterious old man comes up to Camilo, but it is difficult to see that he could not have done so at any other time or place.

One of the objects of **"A Parasita Azul"**, then, is plainly satirical. It is in this sense the forerunner of *Brás Cubas,* and most strikingly, of *Quincas Borba.* Quincas Borba the character, when he appears in the former novel, is shown to be a direct descendent of Tenente-Coronel Veiga: he too used to play Emperor at the Espírito Santo celebrations; and they are delusions which he passes on to his legatee in the latter novel, above all in the climactic scene in which the mad Rubião places the non-existent crown of Napoleon III on his own head. *Quincas Borba* in fact achieves what can be seen here in embryo—a picture of a totally deluded society with a deluded Emperor-figure at its centre.

At the very least, we have to conclude that this is a romantic story with a considerable element of satire. Of course, there is no literary law against such a mixture—

many of Dickens' novels are clear examples. However, I believe that many aspects of the central love-story itself show that Machado was not contented with such a solution; some hints of this (Isabel's ambition, Camilo's feigned 'suicide attempt') have already been mentioned. As we have seen, on the one hand, their affair is a childhood romance which leads to happiness ever after; on the other, it is the convenient marriage of a wastrel and a social climber. These are difficult things to reconcile in a story which is to be artistically or morally satisfying, and it must be said that Machado fails to reconcile them.

What is interesting, however, is that he attempts to do so, at at least three points in the story. The most obvious of these concerns the parasite itself which provides the title. Of course, it is the flower which represents the maiden's purity and honour; so much we can gather from the traditions of romance. But Machado's prose says something else:

> Ama . . . uma parasita. Uma parasita? É verdade, uma parasita. Deve ser então uma flor muito linda,—um milgre de frescura e de aroma. Não, senhor, é uma parasita muito feia, um cadáver de flor, seco, mirrado, uma flor que devia ter sido lindíssima há muito tempo, no pé, mas que hoje na cestinha em que ela a traz, nenhum sentimento inspira, a não ser de curiosidade. Sim, porque é realmente curioso que uma moça de vinte anos, em toda a força das paixões, pareça indiferente aos homens que a cercam, e concentre todos os seus afetos nos restos descorados e secos de uma flor.

Enough has been said before this for the reader to suspect the truth about Isabel's love—so much, in fact, that 'pergunta vivamente' can only be sarcastic. Camilo, then, *is* the parasite: if he is, of course, he is also 'um cadáver', 'os restos descorados e secos' of what he once was. The obviously symbolic scene which follows, in which the boy wounds himself going up the tree to get the plant, begins to look like a parable of lost innocence, the fall and the wound being symbols of that loss. The choice of the parasite is of course significant enough in itself. They are typical enough flowers of the Brazilian forest, often referred to without ironic intention in more conventionally Romantic descriptions of virgin American nature in the Indianist works of writers like José de Alencar or Machado himself in other moods. Here though, there can be no doubt that the other meaning is also intended, and that Camilo is also a social parasite a species in whom Machado had already shown some interest. This episode cannot but make us aware of a possible undercurrent in the story, conveyed by symbols, and whose outcome is in many ways opposite to that of the story itself. In connexion with the flower symbol, we should remember that the original decision to send Camilo to Paris is inspired by a botanist. Machado's introduction of this character is perfectly likely historically—such botanists as Auguste de Sainte-Hilaire did journey to the Brazilian interior during the early part of the 19th Century—but the symbolic overtones are fascinating. If Camilo is the parasite, once fresh, now faded and shrivelled, it may be because he has been plucked from the tree by this botanist: the journey to Europe is itself a fall from innocence. The scientific (and, possibly,

political) ideals which the naturalist imports are in some sense contrary to Brazil's 'nature'.

Such ideas may seem exceedingly unlikely for a writer like Machado; they posit a type of innocence or original state of nature which it would be very hard to find in the great novels. However, it is difficult to avoid the conclusion that the existence of such an ideal *is* posited, even if it is no more than a working hypothesis. Nor is this as unlikely as one might think, once one has found the appropriate context for the ideal itself. It seems to me that the most likely one, contrary as it may be to some conceptions of Machado's intellectual make-up, is the Romantic idealisation of virgin America, which in Brazil as in other countries became an important element in the search for an independent literature. Machado is well known to have been an opponent of simplistic nationalism—in a famous passage from a critical article written in the same period as **"A Parasita Azul",** he is sceptical of an exclusive doctrine which makes the choice of 'national' subjects obligatory:

> O que se deve exigir do escritor antes de tudo, é certo sentimento íntimo, que o torne homem do seu tempo e do seu país, ainda quando trate de assuntos remotos no tempo e no espaço. Um notável crítico da França, analisando há tempos um escritor escocês, Masson, com muito acerto diziaque do mesmo modo que se podia ser bretão sem falar sempre do tojo, assim Masson era bem escocês, sem dizer palavra do cardo, e explicava o dito acrescentando que havia nele um *scotticismo* interior, diverso e melhor do que se fora apenas superficial.

The urban setting of Machado's novels, and of the vast majority of his stories, might lead one to suspect that he was completely averse, not only to Indianist but to *sertanejo* settings, or at least regarded them as more suitable for poetry than for prose. **"A Parasita Azul",** in fact, could be regarded as proof *for* this argument, for its *sertão* is deliberately unpoetic; by and large, it is simply monotonous, and when it is poetic, the language is conventional to the joint of perfunctoriness:

> Era já noite. A fogueira do jantar alumiava um pequeno espaço em roda; mas nem era precisa, porque a lua começava a surgir de trás de um morro, pálida e luminosa, brincando nas folhas do arvoredo e nas águas tranqüilas do rio que serpeava ali ão pé.

At this level, there can be no doubt of Machado's scepticism about 'typically Brazilian' subjects; but another plainly symbolic episode reinforces the suspicion that the story depends on the tradition of literary nationalism: more specifically, on the most important novelist within that tradition, Alencar. On the journey from Rio to Goiás, Leandro has a nightmare which he recounts to Camilo the next morning. While out hunting, he catches sight of Isabel on the other side of the river. She announces that she has lost her hat in the stream, and asks him to go down and get it. He hesitates, only to find that Camilo comes up behind him, and goes down to fetch the hat. When he gets down there, however, the river suddenly rises; Isabel rushes down to help him, and the two are about to be swept away when Leandro is awoken by Camilo. The nightmare is, as Camilo says, 'uma porção de tolices', but it is unlikely that any Brazilian reader at the time could fail to be reminded of the novel which made Alencar famous, *O Guarani* (1857). At the end of this very popular work, the Indian hero, Peri, and Ceci, the blonde, blue-eyed maiden whom he has saved from death, are swept over the horizon by suddenly rising floodwaters. The link with *O Guarani* is made even more likely by the idea of going down to the river to fetch Isabel's hat; it is very likely a parody of the scene in the novel in which Peri rescues Ceci's bracelet from the snake-filled abyss surrounding the fort where she lives.

The vital comparison, however, is that involving the end of *O Guarani*. In Machado's story, the rising waters which carry the lovers off seem to cast doubt on the happy ending itself, even though the dream is told five chapters before that ending, and by a jealous fool. It is worth considering the reasons which lay behind the end of Alencar's 'romance histórico', much more romance than historical. From the beginning, the devoted Indian, the noble savage who eventually even turns Christian in order to save his lady, and Ceci, the lady herself, are obviously destined for one another. But when they are finally free from the complications involving the rest of the characters, the tensions underlying the racial differences between them come to the surface and pose delicate problems for the novelist. Where are they to go? They cannot go to Rio, for there Peri will simply be a slave, but neither will Alencar abdicate the values of civilisation as far as to allow him to carry her off to his tribe. So, the storm breaks, and, grasping a palm-tree, they are swept off into a realm where the reader can still exercise his imagination.

It seems likely that, in the dream episode in **"A Parasita Azul"**, Machado is expressing his own doubts about the fate of another couple who, in their way, represent Brazil, though his doubts are conscious, and most probably inspired by his own thoughts about Alencar, rather than being, as Alencar's themselves were, the product of his novel's own (contradictory) momentum. The parasite and the social climber may be happy at the end of the story, but on another level they are doomed.

Just as the image of the flower is given an extra twist by the introduction of the botanist, so the image of the river cannot be left here. The old man who comes up to Camilo at the Espírito Santo festival eventually tells him the story of the blue parasite, so proving that Isabel is in love with him. When he does so, Camilo not unnaturally tries to reward him for his pains:

> . . . estendeu-lhe a nota. O desconhecido riu-se desdenhosamente sem responder palavra. Depois, estendeu a mão à nota que Camilo lhe oferecia, e, com grande pasmo deste, atirou-a ão riacho. O fio d'água que ia murmurando e saltando por cima das pedras, levou consigo o bilhete, de envolta com uma folha que o vento lhe levara também.

This is a strange scene, though for readers of Roberto Schwarz's *Ão Vencedor as Batatas*, which places so much emphasis on the importance of favour in Machado's novels, it will seem less outlandish. Primarily, it seems that Machado is again determined to cast doubt on the purity and innocence of the central love-match, which cannot exist (he seems to be saying) without the cooperation of a society which it would nevertheless like to ignore, or fob off with a tip. Admittedly, if Camilo's gesture seems to sully their purity, the old man's maintains it. But that is his affair: other go-betweens—José Dias, the *agregado* in *Dom Casmurro,* and the greatest parasite of all, is the most striking example—will be less upright, and the implications for the lovers correspondingly less edifying.

The most important implications of this story, then, seem to me to lie in the ambiguity with which Machado tries to surround his central pair of lovers. If romance and satire can be mixed with relative ease in the story as a whole, their contradictory impulses issue in something else, most interestingly in a pair of symbols—the flower, fresh and corrupt at the same time, and the river, leading over (Alencar's?) horizon—which maintain a real ambiguity, and partake of both literary worlds.

As was said at the beginning, the interest of this story lies not so much in its own excellence, as on the light it casts on the plots of Machado's major works. Most obviously, *Brás Cubas* returns to the story of the spoilt wastrel of a son who returns from Europe to make his reputation: but in the novel, 'success' is much more obviously failure. Brás remains quite happily a social parasite, but married love becomes adultery, and success the series of negatives with which the novel concludes (v. Ch. 160). Machado has discovered, and embodied in the narrative voice of Brás himself, that the novelist has no need to point up the moral in the plot by punishing his hero with unhappiness, however symbolic. The different world of satire allows him, by taking on Brás's own voice, to assume simple amusement at, and even sympathy for the 'pranks' of his hero.

Quincas Borba, aside from the element of generalised political satire centring on the figure of the Emperor, repeats the basic plot pattern of our story. The provincial boor (Rubião) and the smart operator (Palha) are both in love with the same ambitious woman (Sofia): one has to be contented with delusory compensations (Napoleon III's crown), while the couple live on in morally reprehensible bliss—again, the satirist's perspective removes Machado from any of the awkwardness of tone which afflict **"A Parasita Azul"**.

It could be said, then, that the story is an experiment which failed, and that the plainly unresolved tensions between the surface and the symbolic plots had to await Machado's rejection of Romantic plots and acceptance of the healthier premises of satire to reach fruition. This is quite true; I certainly do not wish to quarrel with perfectly sensible conventional accounts of Machado's literary development. However, I do believe that the lessons to be drawn from **"A Parasita Azul"** are more interesting than that; in particular, such arguments would inevitably tend to ignore the surface, Romantic plot of the story, on which, after all, it is entirely dependent structurally. Did Machado simply see the folly of his ways, and reject such hangovers from the past?

The most striking evidence that this is not so appears in his last novel, *Memorial de Aires*. If this is not exactly ignored by critics—after all, it is a *novel*—their rejection of it as an artistic failure is unanimous. Augusto Meyer, the best of the modernist critics of Machado, calls is 'um livro bocejado e não escrito'. Again, it seems to me that value-judgements, right or wrong, should not stand in the way of a simple understanding of what Machado was trying to do. If one can dismiss this novel, or excuse it as the product of a tried, sick writer depressed by the death of his wife, one cannot thereby explain its plot.

It is this plot, as I have suggested, which has striking similarities to that of **"A Parasita Azul"**. A young man (Tristão) is brought up in Brazil, but goes to Europe (Portugal, in this case), and there forgets the old couple who brought him up (Aguiar and Dona Carmo). He comes back, for reasons which are never made explicit but may well be simply financial, and falls in love with the other adopted child of Aguiar and Dona Carmo, Fidélia, the widowed daughter of a *fazenderio*. They are married, and in spite of the hopes of the foster parents, leave for Portugal, where Tristão has a political career lined up for him (on his way to Lisbon, in fact, he is elected deputy to the Portuguese *cortes*). It is a slender structure on which to build a 150-page novel, and it is true that, in spite of the minor characters, including one Osório, a successor for Leandro Soares, and the interest provided by the narrator, Conselherio Aires himself, *Memorial de Aires* is not easy to read with pleasure; though that does not mean that it conveys nothing of value to those who persevere. The sense of desolation at the end, when the old couple who have so lovingly cared for Tristão and Fidélia are abandoned by them, hypocritically in Tristão's case at least, has no real parallel in Machado's fiction. At least Bento can still go to the theatre.

Common to **"A Parasita Azul"** and *Memorial de Aires,* then, is a plot in which a wastrel comes back from abroad, and marries a girl who plainly in some sense represents Brazil, and for whom he is in some sense destined. There is no question that Leandro or Osório are the rightful suitors, nor that the love between Tristão and Fidélia, like that between Camilo and Isabel, is real. Interestingly, *Memorial de Aires* has something of the same contradiction between plot and moral which infects **"A Parasita Azul"**: the plot is plainly about betrayal, yet the betrayers, as Aires the narrator insists, are admirable, delightful young people. The Wagnerian connotations of Tristão's name convey something of the same conflict between all-powerful love and treachery.

Machado's return to this plot-form, and re-involvement in its contradictions, seem to imply that it has a certain independent power *as* a plot. It is not too difficult to see why. It clearly has its origins in the same national obsessions mentioned above, and which necessarily haunted Brazilian literature in the 19th Century. These stories, in their common plot, dramatise the contradictions which

Brazil's real situation arguably imposed. Of the two suitors for the hand of the (female) essence, one is a provincial idiot, the other a foreign traitor: to idealise one or the other as a noble savage or representative of civilisation is unrealistic. Beyond any moral judgements we might feel inclined to make is the inevitable outcome of the situation itself. The conflict, we should notice, reflects itself not merely in the characters of the suitors, but equally in that of the central female character, who is both ideal and, possibly, self-seeking.

This conflict, whose terms are simple enough, is nevertheless not easily soluble: as with the *civilización/barbarie* opposition familiar in other contexts, and which it resembles in many ways, it is difficult to say which side is in the right. For a novelist as subtle as Machado, this could be an unexpected boon. He turned it into a dialectic whose shifting balances allowed him to explore reality without simplifying it, revealing complexities within a pattern which remains relatively simple in its major terms. If we look at the great novels—at least, *Memórias Póstumas de Brás Cubas, Quincas Borba* and *Dom Casmurro*—we can see that they all have at the centre of their plot a triangle which, with different emphases, falls quite naturally into the pattern outlined above ('foreign' traitor—'ideal' woman—'national' idiot): Brás Cubas—Virgília—Lobo Neves; Palha—Sofia—Rubião; Escobar—Capitu—Bento. *Memorias Póstumas* follows the pattern of **"A Parasita Azul"** most faithfully, by opposing the dilettante to the stupid, cuckolded politician. *Quincas Borba* shows, among other things, how an analysis of the rise of a capitalist can be fitted into the pattern. Palha (who has persuaded the gullible Rubião to buy the foreign knicknacks we encounter in the third chapter of the novel) is above all interested in linking himself to the import business, and so to foreign capital. This story of trickery and exploitation, Machado's greatest satire in the usual sense of that word, is very usefully seen as an opposition between two personalities, 'international' and 'provincial'—certainly, this fits the novel much better than any moral opposition between Palha and Rubião, who is a fool, not a saint. The opposition continues in Machado's greatest novel of all, *Dom Casmurro*. It may be, in fact, that its fascination is partly due to the unexpected weighting of the novel in the direction of the provincial boor, to whom Machado gives the narration, and indeed, to an unprecedented extent, the 'control' of the novel. If it seems inappropriate to describe this civilised, upper-class *carioca* as a provincial boor, that is a measure of what the novel, eventually, allows us to understand. Bento represents a ruling class cocooned in its own world, and mistrustful of what takes place beyond it; the stories it constructs for itself to explain that world are self-destructive as well as destructive of others. Machado's repeatedly-made observation of human envy and resentment, summed up in the description of Leandro Soares quoted earlier ('tinha o sestro aliás comum de querer quebrada ou inútil a taça que ele não podia levar aos lábios') is here taken to its logical conclusion.

This version of the development of Machado's plots is admittedly schematic, but it has the virtue of allowing one to see the structure beneath the irony; Sofia, to give only the most striking example, is not only an ambitious, ignorant and over-sexed egotist: she is also, in the novel's structure, the essence, the 'Southern Cross' which in the novel's last sentence Machado mockingly refers to. In its turn this structure depends, surprisingly enough, on the nationalist tradition which in fact Machado greatly respected in many ways. **"A Parasita Azul"** and *Memorial de Aires,* separated by more than thirty years in which Machado wrote all his greatest fiction, witness the real strength of that tradition, even if in their cases the result is partial artistic failure.

Earl E. Fitz (essay date 1989)

SOURCE: "The Short Story Collections," in *Machado de Assis,* Twayne Publishers, 1989, pp. 61-71.

[*Below, Fitz traces the development of Machado as a short story writer, commenting on each of his collections.*]

For all Machado's innovative skill and imagination as a novelist, many critics, including Lúcia Miguel Pereira, Renard Pérez, and Barreto Filho, believe he attained his highest levels of excellence in the demanding short story form, a genre Machado cultivated throughout his career. His first published story, a comic piece about mistaken identity and a spurious love affair involving the narrator's wife and best friend entitled, **"Três tesouros perdidos"** (Three lost treasures), appeared 5 January 1858, when he was eighteen years old. In all, Machado wrote more than two hundred pieces of short fiction, many of which originally appeared in literary journals and were anthologized much later; some have been discovered only very recently. During Machado's lifetime, seven collections of stories, a few of which had appeared earlier in journals, were published. Other stories have appeared posthumously, as in *Outros contos* and *Outras relíquias,* reflecting Machado's enduring popularity in Brazil and reinforcing his reputation as the father of the modern Brazilian short story.

Technically and thematically, the history of Machado's development as a story writer parallels his development as a novelist. Like the novels the stories reflect an even higher level of technical sophistication and a steady movement away from romanticism, often rendered ironically, toward a subtle and complex mixture of psychological realism and symbolism.

Even in the early works, however, several features characteristic of the Machadoan short story stand out. According to Mário Matos [in "Machado de Assis: Contador de Historias," *Obras Completas*], Machado's stories are typically urban rather than rural; they depict characters in the process of thinking and feeling rather than in action; they are orally oriented (creating the impression that the reader is hearing them rather than reading them); they feature a great deal of psychologically self-revealing dialogue and monologue as opposed to description or narration; they are told from either an epic perspective (in which they are seen to represent certain social types, traits, or problems) or a dramatic one (in which the characters reveal themselves, this being Machado's most effective and predilect manner of presentation); they often involve antithesis, irony, and surprise, or unexpected themes, revelations, and turns of events; they often lack conventional plots and instead focus on imagistically rendered revelations of character or theme; they show a strong enthusiasm for the creation of enigmatic female characters (both as protagonists and as secondary characters); they reflect an ironic or bittersweet sense of life as a tragicomic affair; they are nearly always humorous (genteelly so in the early works but, as in the novels, more mordantly, resignedly, or "pessimistically" so in the later works); they are critically self-conscious about their artifice and metafictively flout the nature of the truth they present; they are full of characters—men more than women (undoubtedly a reflection of Machado's realization that few positions of social power or authority were open to women)—who epitomize certain Brazilian social types, institutions, or conditions of their age; they develop the sea as a virtual motif of the author's work; they are full of philosophic and often sharply ironic aphorisms about life (many of which reappear throughout his work). The stories repeat Machado's basic corpus of themes: the destructiveness of time, humanity's temporally limited existence, the problems caused by our vanity, doubt, and selfishness, our frustrating inability to attain in life the state of perfection we conceive in our mind, the nature of madness, and our enthusiasm for seeking the solutions to our problems in external sources, such as science or institutionalized religion, rather than in our own need to choose between what is right and wrong (symbolized everywhere in Machado's work by the choice between love of self, or selfishness, and love of others). As Machado matured these basic characteristics gained in sophistication.

From a critical perspective, it is useful to consider Machado's first two story collections, *Contos fluminenses* (1869) and *Histórias da meia-noite* (1873), as a single unit. With only a few exceptions, such as the psychologically oriented **"Miss Dollar," "Ernesto de tal,"** and **"Linha reta e linha curva"** (straight line and curved line) or **"O relógio de ouro"** (The gold watch), **"A parasita azul"** (The blue parasite), and **"Ponto de vista"** (Point of view), respectively, the stories of these first two collections are well written but otherwise rather undistinguished. **"Miss Dollar,"** for example, an ironic and self-conscious story with a surprise revelation ("Miss Dollar" turns out to be a remarkable dog), deals with the issue of how language shapes and determines our readerly expectations in ways not immediately apparent to us. While one can in such titles as **"Straight Line and Curved Line"** and **"The Gold Watch"** (which is one of the best stories overall in the two collections) already see a tendency toward metaphorically driven narratives, the majority of these early pieces deal in various ways with the kinds of domestic parlor intrigues, including adultery, we associate with romanticism. Moreover, with the exceptions noted above, these overly long and occasionally tedious early pieces do not show the same concision and economy of means so brilliantly employed in the later works.

Like Machado's novels his stories can be divided up into early and late periods. The first of the later or mature story collections is *Papéis avulsos,* which appeared in 1882, one year after *Epitaph of a Small Winner* came out in book form. Like the novel the pieces in *Papéis avulsos* show dramatic changes in theme, form, and technique. From the late 1870s on Machado, increasingly committed to narrative, published stories that amounted to a sharp and satirically perspicacious assault on the otiose middle-class values and social structures of Brazil's Second Empire (1840-90) and the early years of the republic (established in 1889). As Jack Schmitt and Lorie Ishimatsu observe of the stories that make up *Papéis avulsos* and later works: "There is an abundance of implicit social criticism in Machado's descriptions of the life styles and the family structures of middle-class characters in his stories. One is always aware that the material comforts his characters enjoy are either the fruits of a carefully observed caste system or achieved at the expense of others" [Introduction to the collection *Devil's Church*].

One of the most famous of the narratives included in *Papéis avulsos* is "The Psychiatrist," an extended tale that satirizes the tendency to seek in science, or in the name of science, solutions to human defects. Read on its most superficial level, "The Psychiatrist" addresses the twin questions of who in this life is insane (as opposed to who is not) and how can we tell? Read deconstructively, the story centers squarely on the impossibility of knowing for certain what the word *insane* means and therefore what it means to be insane. Structurally, as in *Dom Casmurro* and James's *Ambassadors,* the story involves an ironic inversion of roles: Dr. Simão Bacamarte, the learned protagonist for whom science is the only truth, begins the story by rather sanctimoniously committing other people to an insane asylum known as the "Green House"; later, he ends it by judging these formerly insane people to be sane and committing himself. Thus the story's basic binary opposition, sanity versus insanity, is coupled with the larger epistemological problem of meaning and knowledge, with the relationship between language and existence, and our cognition of both. Since even science is forced to use language, an imprecise and ever evolving human invention to define and delineate "madness" in a person, it too proves a failure in its attempt to eliminate ambiguity, uncertainty, and contradiction from our understanding of the human condition. Bacamarte's initial definition of insanity is so comprehensive in its applicability that nearly every "normal" person can be rationally defined as "crazy," an idea echoed in many other of Machado's works when "normal," "sane" people like Felix, Braz Cubas, or Dom Casmurro consciously choose to conduct their lives in "abnormal" or "insane" ways.

Later in the story, however, Bacamarte's initial position which he developed logically and "scientifically," showing the unquestioning confidence of a zealot, is totally reversed by Bacamarte himself, who, without ever wondering about the validity of what he is doing, blithely creates a new theory of insanity in which the "sick" (formerly the well) are, absurdly, considered the "rational." As the story's narrative voice explains, "The psychiatrist informed the Council . . . that as a consequence of this reexamination in the light of the statistics, he had con-

cluded not only that his theory was unsound but also that the exactly contrary doctrine was true—that is, that normality lay in a lack of equilibrium and that the abnormal, the really sick, were the well balanced, the thoroughly rational. . . ." Ludicrously undisturbed by this sudden reversal of positions, Bacamarte, a rational paragon, eventually begins to wonder about his theory, however. Upon releasing as "cured" all the asylum's inmates, he muses to himself, "Were they all really insane? Did I really cure them? Or is not mental imbalance so natural and inherent that it was bound to assert itself with or without my help?"

After "twenty minutes" of "rational" inquiry, Bacamarte discovers—in himself—the one "undeniably well balanced, virtuous, insane man" he sought, the one who "possessed wisdom, patience, tolerance, truthfulness, loyalty, and moral fortitude—all the qualities that go to make an utter madman." Declaring that his newest "discovery" "is a matter of science, of a new doctrine" and that he embodies both its theory and practice, Bacamarte, "his eyes alight with scientific conviction, . . . set about the business of curing himself." Wryly, the omniscient narrator remarks that some of his former "patients" had ventured to suggest that, given his demise, the good doctor, "was the only madman . . . ever committed to the asylum."

Possibly inspired, as Gomes suggests [in *Influências inglêsas*], by Machado's reading of Swift's *Serious and Useful Scheme to Make a Hospital for Incurables,* "The Psychiatrist," one of the first great stories from Machado's "mature" period, is a comic masterpiece of satire and ironic inversion that, through its deliberate exposition of the arbitrary semantic codes that operate between signifier and signified, human existence and our urge to find meaning in it involves the basic precepts not only of structuralist literary analysis but those of poststructuralism as well. Along with "The Looking Glass," "The Bonzo's Secret," "The Education of a Stuffed Shirt," and "Final Request," "The Psychiatrist" numbers among Machado's most accomplished stories.

Machado's next collection of stories, *Histórias sem data* (1884), continues the artistic growth so dramatically begun in *Papéis avulsos.* Outstanding stories like "The Devil's Church," "Final Chapter," "A Strange Thing," "Alexandrian Tale," "Plus Ultra!" "Those Cousins from Sapucaia," "A Second Life," and "Admiral's Night" all reflect Machado's increasingly ironic world view, his pungent humor, his technical experimentations with point of view and structuring, and his ever more subtle use of symbolism and imagery to advance his plot structures. As is evident in these compact, concentrated stories, Machado was mastering the genial but laconic style that marked his greatest works. Striking for its sharply ironic drollery as well as for its exceptional economy of expression, "Alexandrian Tale" is like "The Psychiatrist" a satirical assault on the tendency to seek science (or any other external source) as a panacea for human problems, which, Machado's texts imply, can only be solved by individuals making choices that lead to moral rather than immoral lives. This powerful but subdued sense of the need for moral human conduct permeates Machado's work and, in addition to offsetting the charge that Machado is a bleakly nihilistic writer, also constitutes the mechanism by which Machado philosophically endows his characters with both a universal significance and a particular social or cultural dimension. Machado's basic method is to show the reader what he considers to be the truth concerning the human condition, the propensity to do evil (generally associated with egoism and selfishness), the illusory nature of truth, the transitoriness of life, and the endless hypocrisies upon which individual lives and entire societies are built, and then leave the reader, who has been actively drawn into the texts, to make his or her own decisions about how to act, about how to live.

A unique feature of **"Alexandrian Tale,"** however, is its sadism. Perpetrated in the name of science against helpless and innocent victims, first rats and then humans, the sadistic violence done to living things by those who believe they are going to save the human race is trenchantly contrasted to the serenity and sanctimoniousness with which its agents perform it: "Science, like war, has its imperious necessities. . . . Stroibus caged the rats and subjected them to the knife one by one. A less skillful surgeon would have frequently interrupted the procedure because the victims' spasms of pain and agony made the handling of the scalpel awkward. . . . But this was precisely Stroibus' superiority: he possessed the trained unflinching self-assuredness of a master surgeon.

At Stroibus' side, Pythias collected the blood and assisted with the operations, restraining the patients' convulsive movements and observing the progress of the agony in the animals' eyes." Though not frequently employed in his work, violence does appear from time to time in Machado's work. Generally its effect is to subtly remind us that, far from being benign or irrelevant, the actions we choose to take in life can under certain circumstances have direct physical consequences for other people. In addition, however, to underscoring the importance of making moral choices in life, Machado's use of violence also reminds us that we live in an absurd universe, one utterly indifferent to our fate and our conduct and one in which good and evil, like love and self-love, coexist simultaneously, with each one exerting a strong if contradictory influence on our thoughts and actions.

Physical violence also plays a role in **"The Companion,"** one of the several excellent stories in Machado's fifth anthology. *Várias histórias* (1896). Allowing modestly in his introduction that the short narratives of *Várias histórias* are "inferior" to those of Prosper Mérimée and Edgar Allan Poe (whose stories he believes to be among the best written in America), Machado with characteristic wit also avers that even his "poor" pieces have one great advantage over novels: they are short.

The brevity of the stories in *Várias histórias,* however, also demonstrates how economical Machado had become in his writing. Epitomizing Flaubert's passion for finding "the precise word," Machado shows here that he has mastered the art of making a few words do the work of many. Indeed, it is precisely from this exceptional econ-

omy of means that Machado generates the ambiguity and complexity that critics like Meyer, Caldwell and Nunes find so characteristic of his work. By building "texts" (in Derrida's sense of the term) that develop through a concise, often ironic and "minimalist" prose style and that structure themselves around certain often recurring images, motifs, and symbols, Machado's artfully controlled ambiguity is never in any sense that of a confused or uncertain story. Rather, it is the complex and dynamic relativism of stories that, involving both the author's intention (or intentions) and each reader's response to the text, open themselves up in an endless process of reader involvement and interpretation. Commenting on Machado's famous ambiguity, Schmitt and Ishimatsu [in the introduction to *Devil's Church*] observe that "by aiming at psychological truth and focusing on crucial moments of experience in the lives of his characters, he approaches the method of the moderns. His ambiguity is in part the result of his subjective, relativistic world view, in which truth and reality, which are never absolutes, can only be approximated; no character relationships are stable, no issues are clear-cut, and the nature of everything is tenuous." This intentionally generated and artistically maintained ambiguity is consistently present in such ironically charged stories as **"A Woman's Arms," "A Celebrity," "The Secret Heart," "Adam and Eve," "The Companion," "The Diplomat," "Mariana," "Dona Paula," "Life,"** and **"The Fortune-Teller,"** works that give ample evidence why Machado, along with de Maupassant, Chekhov, and James, deserves recognition as one of the true masters of the modern short story form.

> **Machado's basic method is to show the reader what he considers to be the truth concerning the human condition, the propensity to do evil (generally associated with egoism and selfishness), the illusory nature of truth, the transitoriness of life, and the endless hypocrisies upon which individual lives and entire societies are built, and then leave the reader, who has been actively drawn into the texts, to make his or her own decisions about how to act, about how to live.**
>
> —*Earl E. Fitz*

"The Companion" continues to be one of Machado's most anthologized pieces. An ironic, darkly comic tale of violence, greed, and the self-serving human balm of rationalization, **"The Companion"** tells the story of a man hired as a nurse for an irascible and malicious old invalid, a man so contentious and cantankerous that he drives his companion to murder him. The story's narrator, the man who has committed the crime, delivers his story to the reader in a fully self-conscious, metaphoric, and macabrely comic mode: "So you think what happened to me in 1860 could be put in a book? . . . Look, I could even tell you my whole life story—it has other points of interest . . . read this and wish me well. Forgive whatever appears evil to you, and don't be surprised if what I have to say gives off an odor quite distinct from that of a rose. You asked me for a human document, and here it is." The story ends ironically with the murderer not only never accused of having committed a crime but actually inheriting his victim's fortune. In addition, he is widely venerated by people who in a moment of sharp dramatic irony praise him for the "Christian patience," "loyalty," and "devotion" with which he had served the old man. The reader, however, who unlike the other characters knows what really happened, also gets to observe how the narrator's progressive self-delusion about what he did begins to move him from speaking about the murder he committed to calling it at the story's conclusion an "accident," one that in a surprising turnabout had left him quite wealthy, the legal beneficiary of the man he murdered. Thus, the human penchant for self-delusion becomes a major thematic force in the story, one reinforced by the sense of moral obtuseness shown by the narrator and his reaction to the events he describes.

Another story that brilliantly represents Machado's ability to create and sustain an ambiguous fictive world is **"Midnight Mass,"** the centerpiece of his sixth collection of stories, *Páginas recolhidas,* published in 1899 and often said to be Machado's finest overall story collection. Widely judged to be Machado's greatest single story, **"Midnight Mass"** is a masterpiece of repressed sexuality, of psychological insight, and atmospheric ambiguity. The story's basic plot involves what may or may not have been the sexual attraction between a young man, who is telling the story in retrospect, and a young married woman, Conceição. At the outset of the story, the narrator openly admits to his own "confusion" surrounding the events he will relate: "I have never quite understood a conversation that I had with a lady many years ago, when I was seventeen and she was thirty. It was Christmas Eve. I had arranged to go to Mass with a neighbor and was to rouse him at midnight for this purpose." The narrator, who, saying he lived quietly with his books in a room of the house owned by the lady in question and her husband, subtly establishes (or seeks to establish) his innocence and naiveté in matters of male and female relationships. Yet because the narrator also notes that at one point he learned both that the man Menezes was having an affair and that seemingly his wife, Conceição, not only knew of the affair but gradually came to accept it as "proper," it is possible to view him as less "innocent" than he would have the reader believe. Indeed, one very plausible reader response to his particular manner of presenting these facts is to speculate whether the narrator perhaps sensed that he and a "neglected" young wife living in such close quarters might develop a relationship from which a tryst could emerge. With his mind perhaps unconsciously cogitating on these ideas, the narrator intriguingly describes the woman: "Gentle Conceição! They called her the saint and she merited the title, so uncomplainingly did she suffer her husband's neglect. . . . Everything about her was passive and attenuated. . . . She spoke ill of no one, she pardoned everything. She didn't know how to hate; quite possibly she

didn't know how to love." By having already suggested that Conceição not only knew about but accepted her husband's infidelity, and by suggesting that she may not have known "how to love," the narrator intentionally or not continues to imply simultaneously that he was merely the detached observer of this entire scenario and that, sensing an opportunity for a sexual liaison, he could "teach" a frustrated woman—who, knowing herself to be the victim of an unfaithful husband, might well be receptive to the idea of seeking sexual fulfillment elsewhere—"how to love." The ambiguity of the story's presentation and interpretation is perfectly poised and maintained right through to the conclusion.

The story's repressed sexual tension is heightened when, after reading for a time the highly romantic *Three Musketeers* (which could easily have erotically stimulated the narrator's mind), he suddenly sees Conceição enter the room where he is reading. All alone late at night, Conceição, who, he learns, has not slept at all (possibly, one speculates, because of her sexual frustrations), and the narrator begin to chat. The narrator's description of Conceição's dramatic entrance (coming perhaps strategically after her mother had gone to bed) is crucial to the reader's interpretation of what is happening, an interpretation that may be at variance with what the narrator implies, or wishes to imply: "After a time, however, a sound from the interior of the house roused me from my book. . . . I raised my head. Soon I saw the form of Conceição appear at the door . . . Conceição, wearing her bedroom slippers, came into the room. She was dressed in a white negligee, loosely bound at the waist. Her slenderness helped to suggest a romantic apparition quite in keeping with the spirit of my novel. . . . She sat on the chair facing mine, near the sofa. . . . Her eyes were not those of a person who had just slept. . . ."

Dressed in this fashion, with a loosely bound negligee, Conceição leans forward, ostensibly to "hear better," and crosses her legs, all acts or circumstances that could be interpreted as being either deliberately seductive or as being merely very casual, domestic, and even familial in nature. Suggesting, however, that she is struggling with a conflict between an expression of her frustrated sexuality and her religious views (that sex is sinful), Conceição initiates a series of surprising comments about what she takes to be the salacious nature of two pictures (one of which is of Cleopatra) hung in the room:

> ". . . to tell the truth, I'd prefer pictures of saints. These are better for bachelors' quarters or a barber shop."

> "A barber shop! I didn't think you'd ever been to . . ."

> "But I can imagine what the customers there talk about while they're waiting—girls and flirtations, and naturally the proprietor wants to please them with pictures they'll like. But I think pictures like that don't belong in the home. That's what I think, but I have a lot of queer ideas."

Intimating that he himself was not certain what he wanted to have happen, the narrator then observes, of his own response to Conceição's apparel, conduct, and words: "I wished and I did not wish to end the conversation. I tried to take my eyes from her, and did so out of respect; but, afraid she would think I was tired of looking at her, when in truth I was not, I turned again towards her."

At this point the story abruptly begins to come to a close. Conceição and the narrator, enveloped (as the narrator presents it) in a dreamlike reverie, fall silent. A friend of the narrator then appears, rapping on the window to call the narrator off to Midnight Mass. In a deliciously ambiguous moment of plurisignation, one charged with two levels of meaning (one denotatively literal and the other sensually connotative), Conceição observes, "Hurry, hurry, don't make him wait. It was my fault. Good-bye until tomorrow." The ambiguity inherent under these circumstances in the words "don't make him wait" implies both that Conceição is referring to the person at the window and, allowing for a pronominal change (one perhaps already existing in Conceição's agitated mind) from "him" to "me," to herself. From this, one could then infer that when Conceição says "It was my fault" she is speaking both to the man at the window (whom she does not wish to keep waiting) and to her own repressed sexuality, a confused manifestation of which the genesis of the entire episode may have been.

Machado, along with de Maupassant, Cheknov, and James, deserves recognition as one of the true masters of the modern short story form.

—*Earl E. Fitz*

As in the case of *Dom Casmurro,* which appeared six years later, **"Midnight Mass"** is not simply ambiguous; it is a story meticulously structured around the inherently ambiguous nature of language, around the unresolved conflicts or "slippages" between logocentric signifieds and the ever unstable and often contradictory signifiers. Establishing a final opposition between the events (real and imagined) of a "romantic" night and those of a "realistic" day, between religion and sensuality, between life and death, and most importantly between the narrator and Conceição, the story draws to its uncertain but artistically perfect conclusion:

> And with her rocking gait Conceição walked softly down the hall. . . . During Mass, Conceição kept appearing between me and the priest; charge this to my seventeen years. Next morning at breakfast I spoke of the midnight Mass and of the people I had seen in church, without, however, exciting Conceição's interest. During the day I found her, as always, natural, benign, with nothing to suggest the conversation of the prior evening.

> A few days later I went to Mangaratiba. When I returned to Rio in March, I learned that the notary had died of apoplexy. . . . I learned later that she had married her husband's apprenticed clerk.

The story's last line provides one final tantalizing bit of information. Read one way, the fact that upon her husband's death Conceição had married his "apprentice clerk" could easily be taken as yet one more objective piece of reportage about this entire episode. Read another way, however, it could suggest either that was already having an affair with the clerk or, frustrated as she was (or thought to be), that she had indeed all along been seeking some form of sexual experience, either with the clerk or with the narrator of the story. The story's essential ambiguity then is really twofold: the narrator's "confusion" about what took place and, more importantly, Conceição's confusion over how to proceed given her husband's infidelity and her own sexual needs.

Machado's seventh collection of stories, *Relíquias de casa velha* (1906), which opens with an elegiac sonnet, "**A Carolina,**" to his beloved and recently deceased wife, Carolina, was the last of his story anthologies to be published before his death in 1908. This final collection contains a number of stories that show Machado's continuing mastery of the short narrative form. Pungently ironic and psychologically compelling yet possessed of a keen social consciousness, stories like **"Father versus Mother," "Funeral March," "The Holiday," "Evolution,"** and **"Pylades and Orestes"** experiment modernistically with time, with various types of fallible, self-conscious narrators, and with differing manners of character presentation and plot development. Intensely synecdochic and metaphoric, these wryly comic and compact tales are, like those of Joyce's *Dubliners* (1914), exercises in the artistic integration of the modes of both realism and symbolism. In terms of their structuring, their acute awareness of time's destructive passing, and their advancement of plot by symbolic and allusive means, stories like **"Funeral March," "Evolution,"** and **"Father versus Mother"** (to say nothing of **"Midnight Mass"**) compare favorably with such Joycean classics as **"Araby," "Clay,"** and **"The Dead."**

A final collection of stories, *Outros contos,* was published posthumously. The tales in this collection, notable among which are **"Marina," "The Animal Game,"** and **"Casa velha"** (The old house), were culled by critics from among those pieces that Machado had not included in his previous volumes. Ranging in date of publication from 1864 (**"Virgínius: narrativa de um advogado"**; Virgínius: the narrative of an attorney) to 1906 (**"Um in endio"**; A fire), these stories, most of which have not been translated, demonstrate in dramatic fashion Machado's continuing artistic growth and development as a writer of short narratives. Especially notable in this regard is the rather longish story **"Casa velha,"** which, appearing between 1885 and 1886, is sometimes considered Machado's tenth novel.

In general, Machado's post-1873 stories exemplify the same technical expertise, innovativeness, and psychological nuance that we associate with such better-known masters of the modern short story form as James, Poe, Chekhov, Mérimée, de Maupassant, Woolf, Kafka, and Joyce. Like James Machado found the necessarily compressed form of the short story an ideal genre in which to work and like de Maupassant he learned to present his observations accurately and without obvious moral judgments. An early pioneer in the area of dramatic characterization, that is, the process of allowing characters to reveal themselves rather than being described, Machado de Assis was also an innovator in his many experiments with self-conscious narrators and metafictional texts. His technical expertise is also apparent in his innovative implementation of a condensed, oral, and imagistic style, and in his predilection for developing tragicomic conflicts of a psychological or philosophic nature that, through the character types that express them, nevertheless generate a sharply critical social consciousness. In this regard one thinks of de Maupassant, Woolf, and Joyce, though several other modern masters could be cited as well. Machado's two most singular stylistic features, his development of plot through a closely interwoven web of symbols, images, metaphors, and in the manner of Eliot and Joyce often ironic allusions, and his Flaubert-like economy of expression, are more strikingly evident in his short narratives than in his novels. But whether we consider him primarily as a short story writer or as a novelist, Machado de Assis deserves—and is beginning to receive—recognition as one of the true modern masters of Western narrative.

FURTHER READING

Biography

Machado, Jose Bettencourt. *Machado of Brazil: The Life and Times of Machado de Assis, Brazil's Greatest Novelist,* second edition. New York: Charles Frank Publications, 1962, 246 p.
    Bio-critical study of Machado's life and work.

Bibliography

Bagby, Albert I., Jr. "Brazilian Literary and Bibliographic Studies over the Last Twenty Years." *The Modern Language Journal* LIX, No. 4 (April 1975): 186-89.
    Acquaints English-speaking readers with reference materials on Machado and Brazilian literature in general.

Criticism

Barrow, Leo L. "Ingratitude in the Works of Machado de Assis." *Hispania* XLIX, No. 2 (May 1966): 211-17.
    Studies the theme of ingratitude in Machado's works.

Brakel, Arthur. "Ambiguity and Enigma in Art: The Case of Henry James and Machado de Assis." *Comparative Literature Studies* 19, No. 4 (Winter 1982): 442-49.

Compares the ambiguous narrative techniques of Machado and Henry James.

Decker, Donald M. "Machado de Assis: Short Story Craftsman." *Hispania* XLVIII, No. 1 (March 1965): 76-81.
    Overview of the wide variety of styles, themes, and techniques in Machado's later stories, from *Historias sem data* to *Varias historias.*

Dixon, Paul B. "Feedback, Strange Loops and Machado de Assis' 'O espelho'." *Romance Quarterly* 36, No. 2 (May 1989): 213-21.
    Examines "the formal technique of doubling and symmetry" in Machado's short story "O espelho."

Fitz, Earl E. *Machado de Assis.* Boston: Twayne Publishers, 1989, 149 p.
    Comprehensive study of Machado's themes, style, and technique in his novels and short stories. Also contains overview of and commentary on Machado's canon.

Foster, David W. "Joaquim Maria Machado de Assis." In *Critical Survey of Short Fiction,* edited by Frank N. Magill, pp. 1548-53. Pasadena, Calif.: Salem Press, 1993.
    Considers the short story "A Singular Event" in terms of Machado's "concern with ambiguities of the human experience."

Haberly, David T. "A Journey through the Escape Hatch." In *Three Sad Races: Racial Identity and National Consciousness in Brazilian Literature,* pp. 70-98. Cambridge: Cambridge University Press, 1983.
    Addresses discrepancies between Machado the man and Machado the writer, noting how his life influenced his literary work.

MacNicoll, Murray Graeme. "Machado de Assis in 1878." *Luso-Brazilian Review* 19, No.1 (Summer 1982): 31-8.
    Pegs the year 1878 as the watershed in Machado's literary career.

Pimentel, A. Fonseca. "Machado de Assis—Brazilian Writer." *Journal of Inter-American Studies* 10, No. 1 (January 1968): 154-58.
    Appreciative overview of Machado's fiction.

Pritchett, V. S. "Machado de Assis." *New Statesman* 71, No. 1824 (25 February 1996): 261-62.
    Brief overview of Machado's literary career.

Putnam, Samuel. "Machado de Assis and the End-of-the-Century Realists." In *Marvelous Journey: A Survey of Four Centuries of Brazilian Writing,* pp. 176-92. New York: Alfred A. Knopf, 1948.
    Surveys Machado's canon in relation to other late-nineteenth-century realists.

Additional coverage of Machado's life and career is contained in the following sources published by Gale Research: *Black Literature Criticism*; *Contemporary Authors,* Vol. 107; and *Twentieth-Century Literary Criticism,* Vol. 10.

François Mauriac
1885–1970

(Full name François Charles Mauriac; also wrote under the pseudonym Forez) French novelist, short story writer, poet, dramatist, essayist, critic, journalist, screenwriter, and autobiographer.

INTRODUCTION

Mauriac is considered one of the most significant authors of the twentieth century. Most of his short fictional works depict individuals tormented by the absence of virtue in their lives. The trials of Mauriac's protagonists reflect his abiding concern with Catholicism's interpretations of sin, redemption, pleasure, and morality. James M. Mellard has concluded: "For Mauriac's characters, mankind's sins may rest on their shoulders, but each man, not mankind, must work out his own redemption; the communal Church seems less crucial than the individual soul."

Biographical Information

Mauriac was born in the Bordeaux region of France. His father died soon after his son's birth, and Mauriac was raised by his mother in a strict Catholic household. As a boy he was sent to Catholic schools run by Marian priests. After earning academic degrees in 1904 and 1906, Mauriac moved to Paris where he remained for most of his life. He became close friends with many writers, including André Gide. In 1913 he married Jeanne Lafon, with whom he had four children; their son Claude is also an acclaimed novelist and screenwriter. During World War I Mauriac served as a hospital orderly in Salonika, Greece. During World War II he frequently wrote on political issues and was an outspoken supporter of Charles de Gaulle. From 1954 to 1961 Mauriac was a columnist for the newspaper *L'express*; after this and until his death he was a regular contributor of reviews and articles to *Figaro littéraire*. The recipient of numerous awards and literary honors during his lifetime, Mauriac was elected in 1934 to the Académie Française—the prestigious French cultural institution established in the 1600s by Cardinal Richelieu for preservation and perfection of the French language. Mauriac was awarded the Nobel Prize for Literature in 1952.

Major Works of Short Fiction

Mauriac wrote several short novels and only ten short stories, eight of which were collected in *Trois récits* and *Plongées,* the remaining two in *Oeuvres complètes.* Critics note that these works, like Mauriac's other writings,

reflect his conservative, "Jansenist" interpretation of Catholicism. Named for the Flemish theologian Cornelis Jansen, whose strict interpretation of St. Augustine's philosophy inspired it, Jansenism was a seventeenth-century movement in French religious thought that espoused the doctrines of original sin and absolute predestination. Jansenists believe that it is impossible to be good or do good without divine grace and that God has already determined the few who will receive salvation. This theology has been called a philosophy of pessimism because of its denial of free will and its conception of the wretchedness of man's fallen state. In accordance with Jansen's idea that mankind "bears the full burden of its condemnation," Mauriac portrayed his characters as essentially evil beings who could be redeemed only after they renounced all worldly pleasures and devoted themselves to the worship of God. Significantly, much of his short fiction contains vibrant depictions of sexual desire. While he was aware of and distressed by the possibility that his work might offend Catholic readers, Mauriac was resolved, in his words, to probe "the secret source of the greatest sins." His early works are semiautobiographical studies of young people on the verge of adulthood. In his first short novel—and first work of fiction—*L'enfant chargé de chaînes (Young Man in*

Chains), the protagonist experiments with political activism and sexual promiscuity before accepting religious devotion as his true vocation. The short novel *Le baiser au lépreux* (*A Kiss to the Leper*) is considered by many commentators to be his first major exploration of religious issues. The story concerns the physical and emotional rejection of an unattractive man by his beautiful wife. After her husband's death, which Mauriac suggests was attributable in part to her years of aloofness, the wife belatedly realizes her love for him. In *Génitrix* Mauriac depicts the desperate dysfunctionality of an upper-class family. Here a weak-willed middle-aged man marries a lower-class woman who is much younger than he as a way of breaking the possessive grip of his domineering mother. Suffering an exceedingly unhappy marriage, which she entered into primarily to obtain wealth and status, the wife dies after several alcoholic binges and attempted affairs. After the death of his mother, the man is left alone, miserably trapped in old patterns of dependence.

Mauriac's most famous fictional character was introduced in the 1927 short novel *Thérèse Desqueyroux* (*Thérèse*). Feeling trapped by the conventions of her class, the provincial mores of her community, and by her circumscribed role as a woman, Thérèse unsuccessfully tries to poison her husband, explaining she just wanted "to see in his eyes a momentary flicker of uncertainty." After her crime is discovered, Thérèse becomes an outcast, tormented by guilt yet stubbornly refusing to seek God's forgiveness. Critics have noted that, for Mauriac, Thérèse's real crime appears to be a kind of spiritual arrogance more than attempted murder. Illicit passion and its attendant guilt are the subjects of *Destins* (*Destinies*), a short novel about a handsome young Parisian vacationing in Bordeaux who becomes the object of the desires of two lonely women.

Most of Mauriac's relatively few short stories were first collected in *Trois récits* and *Plongées*. Critics tend to regard these stories as studies for the novels that Mauriac was writing around the time of their composition. Among the best known of these works—and among the few that have been translated into English—are "Thérèse chez le docteur" ("Thérèse and the Doctor") and "Thérèse à l'hôtel" ("Thérèse at the Hotel"). Both were written in 1933 and continue the story of Mauriac's own favorite character; these short tales were translated and collected in 1947 as *Therese: A Portrait in Four Parts*. *Le mal* (*The Enemy*) is a short novel about a young man and his first serious love affair. The protagonist, raised in a pious, Jansenist household, goes to Paris and becomes involved with a beautiful woman who represents the sensual opposite of his upbringing. Eventually the young man's religious principals reassert themselves and he abandons the woman.

Le sagouin (*The Little Misery*), set soon after the first World War, also concerns the fate of a young man. Here, the protagonist is the unloved, somewhat slow-witted son of a middle-class woman who married into an old, no longer flourishing noble family. For a time the boy is entrusted to the care of a Communist schoolteacher, who, because he treats him kindly and gives him reasons to participate in the world, becomes his first positive parental

figure. The boy is eventually called back by his family, however, and, feeling abandoned by everyone, kills himself. Irving Howe has called this short novel "one of the few successful works of religious fiction written in our time." In *Galigaï* (*The Loved and the Unloved*), Mauriac again examines the lives of the high-born. There are four main protagonists in the story: two are described as attractive, two as particularly ugly. The novel thus concerns, as S. M. Fitz-Gerald has put it, "the effects upon a human soul of physical ugliness." *L'agneau* (*The Lamb*)—one of Mauriac's last works of fiction—is a version of the Christ story. This short novel tells the story of a young seminary student who determines to sacrifice his life in order to save the soul of a corrupt older man.

Critical Reception

Generally, Mauriac's standing among literary critics is very high, as his membership among "the immortals" of the Académie Française and his Nobel Prize attest. However, there has been serious criticism leveled against his work. Chiefly, Mauriac has been accused of promoting misogynistic views in his fiction. Critics have pointed to the roles women often play in his novels—seductresses, tempters, and murderesses—and to his depictions of sexual activity—which frequently convey a certain measure of disgust with not merely the act itself but, importantly, with female anatomy. Mauriac has also had at least one notable detractor, Jean-Paul Sartre. In his essay "M. François Mauriac et la liberté" (in *Nouvelle revue Française,* February, 1939), Sartre accused Mauriac of hypocritically denying his characters free will. Focusing mainly on the 1935 novel *La fin de la nuit* (*The End of the Night*), but extending his critique to include all of Mauriac's work, Sartre demonstrated the ways in which Mauriac violated putative laws of fiction, namely that of identifying with a character but judging him or her by criteria outside the fictional universe. Sartre argued that Mauriac imposed judgments and destinies on characters ostensibly portrayed as autonomous individuals. As Robert Speaight has written: "If Sartre's criticism was well founded, Mauriac would not have been the first Christian to be caught by the problem of predestination and free will, nor the first to find it insoluble." Nevertheless, Gerard Hopkins, the main English translator of Mauriac's fiction, has commented that "Mauriac supplies . . . a moral fervour which was once a common feature of [English] literature." Mauriac's short fiction continues to be celebrated for its distinct prose style and for its psychological insights.

PRINCIPAL WORKS

Short Stories

Trois Récits 1929
Plongées 1938

Short Novels

L'enfant chargé de chaînes [*Young Man in Chains*] 1913
*Le baiser au lépreux [*A Kiss to the Leper*] 1922; also
    published as *A Kiss for the Leper,* 1950
*Génitrix 1923
†*Thérèse Desqueyroux* [*Thérèse*] 1927
Destins [*Destinies*] 1928; also published as *Lines of Life,*
    1957
‡*Le mal* [*The Enemy*] 1935
‡*Le sagouin* [*The Little Misery*] 1951; also published as
    The Weakling, 1952
Galigaï [*The Loved and the Unloved*] 1952
L'agneau [*The Lamb*] 1954

Other Major Works

Les mains jointes (poetry) 1909
L'adieu à l'adolescence (poetry) 1911
La robe prétexte [*The Stuff of Youth*] (novel) 1914
La chair et le sang [*Flesh and Blood*] (novel) 1920
*De quelques coeurs inquiets: Petits essais de psychologie
    religieuse* (essays) 1920
Préséances [*Questions of Precedence*] (novel) 1921
Le fleuve de feu [*The River of Fire*] (novel) 1923
Le désert de l'amour [*The Desert of Love*] (novel) 1925
Dieu et Mammon [*God and Mammon*] (essay) 1929
Ce qui était perdu [*Suspicion*] (novel) 1930; also pub-
    lished as *That Which Was Lost,* 1931
Commencements d'une vie (nonfiction) 1932
Le noeud de vipères [*Viper's Tangle*] (novel) 1932; also
    published as *Knot of Vipers,* 1951
Le mystère Frontenac [*The Frontenac Mystery*] 1933
Journal. 5 vols. (journals) 1934-1953
La fin de la nuit [*The End of the Night*] (novel) 1935
Les anges noirs [*The Dark Angels*] (novel) 1936; also
    published as *The Mask of Innocence,* 1953
Vie de Jésus [*Life of Jesus*] (nonfiction) 1936
Asmodée [*Asmodee; or, The Intruder*] (drama) 1937
Les chemins de la mer [*The Unknown Sea*] (novel) 1939
La pharisienne [*The Woman of the Pharisees*] (novel)
    1941
Les mal-aimés (drama) 1945
La rencontre avec Barrès (nonfiction) 1945
§*Oeuvres complètes.* 12 vols. (complete works) 1950-
    1956
La Pierre d'achoppement [*The Stumbling Block*] (non-
    fiction) 1951
Bloc-Notes 1952-1967. 5 vols. (journalism) 1958-1971
Mémoires intérieures [*Mémoires Intérieures*] (memoirs)
    1959
Ce que je crois [*What I Believe*] (essay) 1962
Thérèse [with Claude Mauriac and Georges Franju]
    (screenplay) 1963

*These works were also published together in a volume entitled *The
Family* (1930), translated by Lewis Galantiére.

†This short novel was also published in *Therese: A Portrait in Four
Parts* (1947), translated by Gerard Hopkins, which collects all the works
Mauriac wrote dealing with the title character; the other works included

are the novel *La fin de la nuit* and the short stories "Thérèsechez le
docteur" and "Thérèse à l'hotel," both of which were first collected in
Plongées.

‡These works were published together as *The Weakling and the Enemy*
(1952).

§These volumes include the two previously uncollected short stories
"Le Visiteur nocturne" and "Le Drôle."

CRITICISM

Angel Flores (essay date 1930)

SOURCE: "Silver-Cord Motif," in *New York Herald Tribune Books,* August 10, 1930, pp. 3-4.

[*A Mexican-born educator and critic who specialized in
Spanish literature but also was an authority on Franz
Kafka, Flores published extensively in English and Spanish.
In addition, he edited more than a dozen books—including*
The Kafka Problem *(1946),* Franz Kafka Today *(1958),*
The Kafka Debate *(1977), and* Explain to Me: Some Stories
of Kafka *(1983)—and translated the works of major Spanish
and South American authors into English. In the following
review of the two short works collected in* The Family—
*"The Kiss to the Leper" and "Gentrix"—Flores lauds
Mauriac's "understanding of the heart."*]

With strange vehemence Mauriac spurs categorical imperatives on to combat. He is an Ibsenite in the grand manner—
perhaps the last of Ibsen's inheritors. Only great conflicts
concern him. By stressing metaphysical concepts the novelist
is likely to lose control of everyday contingencies, and
that is why symbolic literature fails so often to persuade
the contemporary reader.

But Mauriac's saving grace is his profound understanding
of the heart. In **"The Kiss to the Leper"** (1922), the first
part of **The Family,** the duel is between Christ and Nietzsche.
The ugly dwarf Jean, the only son of a wealthy and exalted
family, is ashamed of his puny, weak body. One day he
reads by chance a few lines in *Beyond Good and Evil*:
"What is good? Everything in man that exalts the feeling
of power, the will to power, power itself. What is evil?
Everything that has its roots in weakness. Let the weak
and the failures die! Help them to disappear! What is it
that is more injurious than any vice? The pity felt by the
strong for the dispossessed and the weak: Christianity."
This violent gospel upset the unhappy moor-dweller who
had tacitly adhered to Montaigne's "For my part I sing the
praise of a gliding, somber and mute life."

Through the machinations of the parish priest Jean is forced
to marry Noémi, the most beautiful girl of the town. For
economic reasons Noémi's parents compelled her to wed the
person who had inspired her only with repulsion. Tragedy
looms over these two characters: Jean adores Noémi, but,
ashamed of his own ugliness, he keeps away from her as

much as possible. His Nietzschean attitude does not hold because he has become the laughing-stock, the pitiable creature of the community. Noémi, on the other hand, goes toward Jean as a martyr. A good Christian, a saint, resigned to her fate, she tries to love the being she despises and abhors. She rejects the country doctor she loved, and as a final gesture of renunciation kisses the dying Jean. Jean and Noémi are two saints created by the Catholic Mauriac. Sacrifice, humility and predestination are the pivotal forces at stake. The theme is as somber as the background of the story: a sere and parched land that consumes its inhabitants with phthisis.

The second part of *The Family,* "Genitrix," was written two years after "The Kiss to the Leper," and Mauriac's craft had so improved that one could readily foretell the author of *The Desert of Love* (1925) and *Destinies* (1927). Only the D. H. Lawrence of *Sons and Lovers* surpassed Mauriac in the handling of the silver-cord motif. In "The Kiss to the Leper" we heard Felicite Cazenave prophesy: "If Fernand marries, my daughter-in-law will die." And now we witness the fulfillment of this vaticination. When the story opens, Fernand, a fifty-year-old man, has been married for almost a year. He picked up a wife as a weapon, as an instrument of warfare against his mother's immense, obsessive love. Now at the death of his wife a bitter enchantment chains him to a corpse. He has "a hunger that can no longer be assuaged, when the prey of the flesh, the perfumed prey, has dissolved." This death is a dawn, an awakening, and also a defeat. The Matriarch, the maenad of the Juno profile, dies broken hearted because she no longer can possess her son. Genitrix dies when spiritual domination ceases. And Fernand walks around in his old manorial house like a helpless ghost. The reader is haunted by the incantatory beauty in such sentences as: "The season arrived when despite the chill in the air, one hesitates to light the first fire in the grate as one might pause before an unknown fate. . . . It had rained all day and the drops fell from the trees in a supernatural silence. There was nothing in the world save this tranquil sound of tears." In "Genitrix" there is much of Attic tragedy: restraint and intensity, an exorcising and pantheistic ring, a presage of doom, a fatal palpitation as though from some dark, immense and mysterious heart.

Irving Howe (essay date 1952)

SOURCE: "The Religious Novel," in *The New Republic,* Vol. 126, No. 14, April 7, 1952, pp. 18-9.

[*An esteemed American critic, essayist, and social historian, Howe was a member of the "New York Intellectuals"—a group of liberal, socialist writers that included, among others, Philip Rahv and Lionel Trilling—and is perhaps best remembered for* World of Our Fathers (1976), *his history of Jewish-American culture and immigration to New York City. In the following excerpt from a review in which he also discusses Mauriac's work of nonfiction entitled* The Stumbling Block, *he examines the two short works collected as* The Weakling and The Enemy. *Howe describes* Le Sagouin—here translated as The Weakling—as "one of the few successful works of religious fiction written in our time."*]

[*The Weakling and the Enemy*] actually contains two long stories, *The Enemy,* published in France 17 years ago, and *The Weakling,* which came out last year. Though the idea of sewing a book together from two unrelated items is dubious, and the slyness of the jacket irritating, there is a certain value in having these two pieces together. From them one can surmise something of Mauriac's development; the first revealing his inner troubles as Catholic and artist, the second suggesting at least a partial resolution.

The Enemy is a portrait of a boy brought up in a milieu of Jansenist piety, who in late adolescence is exposed to a woman of beauty and sensuality, a woman who lives by pleasure and love. What follows is predictable to anyone who has read a dozen French novels: passion in Paris, ennui, a reappearance of the boy's religious scruples, and the hysteria of the abandoned woman.

For all its aroma of canned Proust, *The Enemy* is a competent fiction, suavely faithful to the French prescription for illicit love, persuasive in its study of the boy's emotions. Unfortunately, however, the two parts of the story remain unfused: the flesh and the faith come neither to peace nor to grips. If anything, the flesh has the better of it; and we can understand why French Catholic critics rebuked Mauriac in the twenties and thirties as a refined sensualist, who was careful to renew his option with God—and why Mauriac, in a blaze of anguish and anger, cried out, "Christianity makes no allowance for the flesh; it abolishes it."

By contrast, *The Weakling* seems to me one of the few successful works of religious fiction written in our time. The old Parisian triviality has been stripped away; nothing remains of Mauriac's earlier fondness for the decorative and voluptuous; the story is clearly allegorical yet does not hurl this fact at the reader; and the characters, neither "round" nor "flat," are appalling gargoyles—monsters come alive from a Goya picture. In a French village after the first world war, a coarse but ambitious middle-class girl marries into a crumbling noble family. Her son, slow-minded and unloved, becomes an issue of struggle between herself and the family. The boy is put out to a Communist schoolteacher, a decent man strapped by dogma; and for the first time, because the teacher treats him with kindness, the boy begins to feel himself part of a living world. But then the family pulls him back; the schoolmaster refuses responsibility for this child of the upper classes. And the boy, abandoned by the agents of the aristocracy, the middle-class and the revolution, is left entirely to himself. In a scene of gruesome power, he wanders off to a pond and drowns himself.

Mauriac renders the squalor of the village with such economy and directness that it soon comes to seem a symbol of the modern world. The intentions behind his allegory of withdrawn love are obvious enough; but *The Weakling* is an impressive work of art because it surmounts categories and, despite Mauriac's doctrinal bias, can be "translated" into any serious mode of thought or feeling. If there is to be a religious fiction in our time worthy of serious respect, I think it will take this form: brusquely allegorical, harshly written, almost uncouth in its disregard for the usual decor of the novel. . . .

In Mauriac's best works the idiosyncrasies of the characters rather than the author's biases stand out, and complex motivation is suggested by action rather than by allusion to the dark forces of evil or the mysterious workings of divine providence.

—Alexander Fischer, in Modern Language Quarterly, *December, 1979.*

Anthony West (essay date 1952)

SOURCE: "Revolt Against Nature," in *The New Yorker,* Vol. XXVIII, No. 8, April 12, 1952, pp. 129-30.

[*West was an English-born journalist and author who contributed essays and book reviews to magazines such as* The New Yorker. *The son of writers H. G. Wells and Rebecca West, he wrote a frank and revealing biography of his father titled* H. G. Wells: Aspects of a Life *(1984). In the following review of* The Weakling and The Enemy, *West discusses the misogyny evident in Mauriac's work.*]

François Mauriac, whose two short novels ***The Weakling*** and ***The Enemy*** have just been issued in a single volume, is one of the intellectual pillars of the Roman Catholic Church in France. He has been called one of the greatest living writers by many reputable European critics who have judged his work by purely literary standards. His work is, however, primarily religious, and it seems to present a case in which the aesthetic approach is too limited. In 1948 he wrote a statement of his beliefs for a French magazine called *La Table Ronde*. This statement has now been published here as *The Stumbling Block*. It was interesting at the time not only as a profession of belief but as a singular revelation of the extent of M. Mauriac's dislike of women. He referred with violence to the cult of Mary and with contempt to those women who found delight in it. He spoke of the organizers of the innocent festivals in honor of Notre Dame du Grand Retour that were widely celebrated in France in 1947 as "pious Barnums," and of the processions and masses that honored the Virgin Mother as "this abasement, this humiliation of the Church." The vigorousness of his feeling was perhaps at its clearest in his remarkable gloss of verses twenty-one to thirty-five of the fifth chapter of St. Mark and the latter part of the eighth chapter of St. Luke. M. Mauriac had been speaking harshly of those simple forms of worship that appeal to the naïve and the illiterate, and calling them superstitions and manias:

I was wrong to speak of vermin; it is necessary to enter into the charity the Church shows toward human frailty. The old woman who handles and caresses a plaster statue is the same who, nineteen centuries ago, seizing an advantage offered by the crowd, touched the mantle of the Lord without his knowing it, that she might be healed. And the Lord said in annoyance: "Somebody hath touched me; for I perceive that virtue is gone out of me." Yet the poor woman was healed, all the same.

This was the woman who had had an issue of blood for twelve years and had spent all her living on physicians, to no purpose. Neither Mark nor Luke attributes any annoyance to Jesus on this occasion, and there is no flavor of rebuke in the words He is said to have spoken to the woman: "Daughter, be of good comfort, thy faith hath made thee whole; go in peace." It is hard to feel that M. Mauriac's interpolation adds to the story; rather, it changes it, essentially and disagreeably. Since *The Stumbling Block* was written, the dogma of the Assumption of the Virgin Mary has been defined and promulgated, and M. Mauriac has been compelled to add a preface recognizing the horrid fact that a woman has been admitted to heaven. His recognition is not exactly graceful:

I am anxious to state at the beginning of this book that the reserves inspired in me by certain excesses of the Marian cult do not imply any sort of resistance to the new dogma. . . . But I also think that the Assumption of the Virgin does not legitimize, any more than do her other privileges, the manifest abuses to which I am calling attention. On the contrary, it makes them more embarrassing, more dangerous.

Indeed, if M. Mauriac's observations are to be relied upon, women are dangerous creatures, especially if they are mothers. Paula de Cernès of ***The Weakling*** is no exception. She is a commoner from Bordeaux who marries into the provincial aristocracy to satisfy her craving for a title. But if marriage brings her the satisfaction of calling herself the Baronne Galéas de Cernès, it brings her little else. The Baron is hideous and sexually inadequate. He manages to give her a child who turns out to be a cartoon of himself, with knock-knees, skinny legs, a sagging, adenoidal mouth, and a drooling lower lip. After that he lets her alone. She becomes a monster consumed by fantasies of lust, and gives herself up to secret bouts of curaçao-drinking in her bedroom.

Before her inner eye visions arose beyond the power of language to express. Now and again she got to her feet to put another log upon the fire and fill her glass. Then she lay down again. The occasional flicker of a flame played on her face, revealing alternately the mask of a criminal or of a martyr.

The morning after this particular bout she decides to take the first step toward seducing the village schoolmaster. Her tactics are unsound, as M. Mauriac makes clear. She starts off in the rain, wearing a mackintosh, heavy shoes, and a beret pulled down over her eyes. "The rain beating on her face, she thought, would wash away the telltale signs of last night's orgy." Her exceptionally hairy cheeks are unpowdered, her unwashed hair is greasy, and she has not used any scent. "Looking as bedraggled as always, she set out to try her luck for the last time." The schoolmaster does not avail himself of the opportunity so generously offered him, and Paula turns on her wretched son in her frustration and fury and makes his life a burden and a misery. The Baron is moved to pity by the boy's sufferings:

> Would he have to defend himself, at every moment of his life, against this woman who would be always there, the woman with the Gorgon's face blotched with bilious yellow? Hatred caught at his breath, but, more than hatred, shame, because it was he who had been that woman's torturer. Only once had he taken her in his arms, only once. She was, now, like a bitch confined— not for a few days only. Through all her youth it had gone on, and for years and years she would go howling for the absent male. . . . With what fantasies . . . what actions . . . had he, Galéas, cheated hunger. . . . Every night, yes, every night, and in the morning, too. . . . Such would be the lot of this abortion born of their one embrace.

Under the spell of this powerful and disagreeable soliloquy the Baron proceeds to drown himself and the boy. Paula soon after begins to die of a malignant tumor, in pain only partially alleviated by morphine, and haunted by regrets, but not for the man and boy she has destroyed.

> It was of her own free will that she had consented to share the bed of a half-impotent monster. She had allowed him to take her in his arms, and that, in her eyes, was the crime for which there was no pardon.

This is curious, because it underlines the resemblance between *The Weakling* which M. Mauriac finished in 1951, and his *A Kiss for the Leper,* which was published in 1922. The marriages described in the two books are identical, except that in the earlier novel the deformed husband was entirely impotent and the wife was physically attractive. The husband was, if anything, uglier than the Baron de Cernès:

> He was so short that the low dressing mirror reflected his pinched little face, with its hollow cheeks and long, pointed nose. It was red in color, and seemed to have been worn away like a stick of barley sugar as the result of prolonged sucking.

Marriage was fatal to him, too, and it was knowledge of his inability to satisfy his wife's sensuality that made him wish to die. And yet, closely as the two books resemble each other, it is a difference between them that is in the end most remarkable. In *A Kiss for the Leper,* the impotent monster who has crept into the bed of a woman with normal and healthy desires is in the wrong; in *The Weakling* it is the woman who is in the wrong, and it is her desires that have become monstrous. This idea can be seen in development in *Woman of the Pharisees* (published in 1941), in which M. Mauriac handled his obsession with a good

deal more subtlety; the desire for children by a woman married to an impotent husband leads her into an adultery that has a disastrous effect on her husband and her children. As usual, the satisfaction of the instinctive drive produces deadly results. In that case M. Mauriac felt a slight unease about the theme that has such a compulsive attraction for him, and after he had introduced it he addressed an unusual technical aside to the reader:

> Subjects of this kind are, as a rule, instinctively avoided by the professional novelist, . . . Renan once said that the truth may well be depressing. . . . On the level of human affairs it may be not only depressing but ridiculous and embarrassing—so much so that decency forbids us to put it into words. Hence the silence in which such things are usually shrouded.

M. Mauriac has certainly shown a rare determination to make himself heard in that particular zone of quiet.

Woman of the Pharisees deals with two abominable females, one a monster of false piety who disintegrates the lives of six people, the other a mother who destroys her son morally by spending a night at a country hotel with a gentleman to whom she happens not to be married. The affairs of this second woman present his obsession with the horror of feminine sexuality in another form:

> There are many novels that bear, or might bear, the title: "A Woman's Heart"—more than one professional psychologist has plumbed the secrets of the feminine mind. . . . The man who was sharing tonight the Comtesse de Mirbel's bed at the Hotel Garbet lived for no other object than to reduce this mystery to its true and rather squalid proportions. His victims knew precisely what they might expect of him. Those whom he had possessed all bore about them the same indelible sign—the sign of a lust that could know no satisfaction. . . . One does not often meet a saint by the roadside, but neither does one often come across anyone capable of dragging from one's vitals that particular kind of groan, that cry expressing horror no less than delight, which becomes sharper as time lays its hand upon a body already threatened by decay, already undermined as much by desire as by age. . . . No one has ever written of the torment which old age brings to women of a certain type. In it they taste of Hell before death touches them.

Aside from what M. Mauriac discloses about himself in this preliminary generalization on the squalors of the feminine mind, one may detect a certain lip-smacking pleasure, an element of gloating, in the conclusion of this passage. And the statement that no one has ever written about it is not strictly true. M. Mauriac himself had pawed it over in *The Enemy,* which was published in 1935. The central figure in this book is Fanny Barrett, a woman of considerable charm, who lives a life of frivolous grace—whatever M. Mauriac may say. She has the misfortune to be kind to a loutish young man from the Gironde, some years her junior, who has known and adored her since his boyhood. She initiates him into an international world of pleasure and of art, in which he meets musicians, poets, painters, ballet dancers, and choreographers. He is, however, irredeemable, and remains a self-centered clod. He treats her vilely, on the excuse that she has been tampering with his immortal soul, and after they have parted he goes into a decline, like a wronged Victorian heroine. She hears that her dear booby is ill and sends him flowers with a fond and forgiving note. M. Mauriac tells us, with approval, that his mother tears up the note, burns some of the flowers, and allows others to be trampled underfoot by a priest who has come to administer the last rites. The young man recovers, though, and is soon strong enough to tear up Fanny's letters himself. This is supposed to be a happy ending to the story, since he is by then determined to be unkind to Fanny but to pray for her soul. This is how M. Mauriac tells us that she has enjoyed life and kept her looks:

> The modern miracle which has given to women the seeming boon of eternal youth produces in some people, of whom Fabien Dézaymeries was one, a sense of terror and disgust. . . . She looked as she had always looked, though the flood of time had swept her on, and each passing moment had marked her as with fire; five years of exigent desires and glutted senses, of lovers lost and lovers found, of passionate abandonments and bleak awakenings; five years of late nights, of endless cigarettes, of rich food, strong drink, narcotics, and drugs. Yet there she stood, her young body apparently un-touched by the passing of the years, strong as steel, tempered and hardened and possessed. Sin, in its way, is a form of life. There is such a thing as *infernal* grace, and it can galvanize, just for as long as may be necessary, that adorable shape of moulded flesh which, according to St. Catherine of Siena, stinks in all its parts.

When one considers this rancor in relation to M. Mauriac's strained hatred for the poor Comtesse de Mirbel and for the abominable woman who gives her name to his *Thérèse,* and when one considers the peculiar vileness of the mother in his *Genetrix* and of Mme. Léonie Costadot ine value of the whole body of M. Mauriac's often beautifully written work. It may be that a fundamental flaw is revealed by the uncontrolled violence of his feelings about those who like to burn candles in little bowls of ruby glass before statues of a clear-skinned young woman dressed in blue with stars about her and a child in her arms. Archeologists and classical scholars may inform us that the attributes of this member of the Christian family show that she is older than Christianity, and warn us that her cult appears to perpetuate that of the Roman Mother of the Gods and of the Great Mother who was worshipped before God became a man in ancient Greece. If this is so, her worshippers are, without knowing it, kneeling at the altars of Ge, who was the fruitful earth itself, or at those of Themis, who seems to have been the natural order. However that may be, the fact remains that the instinct to respect fertility and creativity that lies behind the cult in its primitive and simple forms is a profoundly healthy one. In turning his back on it, and expressing the loathing of the feminine principle that inspires almost every page of his writings, M. Mauriac seems to express a loathing of life itself. It is hard to see how writing, even though rich and elaborate, that is in favor of negation and sterility and that has, in the long run, nothing more to offer than a cry of protest against the nature of man's physical being can have any real value.

S. M. FitzGerald   (essay date 1952)

SOURCE: "Hecate Revisited," in *The New Republic,* Vol. 127, No. 21, November 24, 1952, pp. 19-20.

[*In the following excerpt from a review in which he also examines* The Illusionist *by Françoise Mallet, FitzGerald discusses realism in* The Loved and the Unloved.]

Dorthe, an ugly little community petrifying in the sun somewhere near Bordeaux, is the scene [of *The Loved and the Unloved*] in which several supernaturally ugly, and two handsome, people reach crucial points simultaneously, split apart and re-combine to the fulfillment of some need in each, whether of love or hatred. Only one is unshackled in the process and able to leave Dorthe freed of idolatry and self-delusion.

Mme. Agathe, the repulsive daughter of an impoverished aristocrat, is governess to Marie, lovely young daughter of M. and Mme. Dubernet, who are personages in the town but are nevertheless somewhat awed by their high-born employee. M. Dubernet is a gluttonous old man, whose private plans form slowly and in silence while he munches through innumerable prawns and joints of mutton and tarts. He leaves to his waspish, dying wife, "a thin woman, but her protuberant stomach gave her a look of royalty," all the concerns proper to arranging a suitably creditable and profitable marriage for Marie, or preventing any other.

Marie's choice, the son of a local doctor, is despised by her mother. Gilles is a ruthless young man, without the insight to know what he is suggesting when he asks his devoted friend, Nicolas Plassac, on whom Mme. Agathe has fixed her starved eye, to deceive the governess a while, long enough at least to gain her advocacy of his own case with Mme. Dubernet. Nicolas succumbs to his selfish idol's pleading—as well as to pity for Agathe, and to a native urge in him to self-immolation. The proposed deception is intolerable to him, though, so he determines to marry her in truth, trusting that the event can be postponed as long as possible by his mother's hoped-for opposition, his own poverty, or any other convenient obstacle.

He is not prepared for the will and resources of his eager lady, however. His mother's distaste for her is instantly dispelled by Agathe's offer of housekeepership at Belmonte, her family estate. When Nicolas objects that he is too poor to marry at once, she offers gladly to live with him forever on leftover noodles warmed on a gas-ring. The waters closing over his head, Nicolas makes the desperate effort necessary to save them from what he knows will be a dreadful life both for himself and Agathe. In an exchange that nearly kills them both, he undeceives her as to his feelings. Humiliated, hopeless and full of hatred for Nicolas, for M. Dubernet, and particularly for Marie, the beautiful and young and beloved, Agathe agrees, on the night of Mme. Dubernet's funeral, eventually to marry her master. He will thereby gain Belmonte, his heart's desire, and she will gain a position from which she can hope to torture

Marie, that being the only desire left in her own heart. Nicolas is freed at last of his atrocious fiancee, but more significantly, of the romantic illusions he has cherished about himself, his friend Gilles, his home, and his awful mother. "The world I have described is the world as it appears to Nicolas when the scales fall from his eyes," writes Mauriac in a postscript to the novel. Nicolas, so released, can move toward God, as the author finally makes clear he is about to do. . . .

[Evil is hideous to Mauriac] and all his writing carries his strong religious conviction as to its reality and meaning. But apart from what he makes of it all, he simply sees and understands more of people as they are. A part of his whole aim as a writer is defined in a statement about his work which he quotes from a perceptive critic: "To set against a literature determined by metaphysics, in which man girds at everything, one based on psychology, in which man girds only at himself." *The Loved and the Unloved* is among other things a study of the effects upon a human soul of physical ugliness.

The new book of his should invite a second look by the critics who regard him as in revolt against nature and think they discern in him a near-pathological hatred of feminine sexuality as *a priori* evil. That is not at all the case. The evil depicted is spiritual: hatred, illusion, snobbery, greed, materialism of the crassest sort. The maunderings of Nicolas' mother; the contemptuous pride, coupled with abject lust, and complicated by hatred, in Agathe; the "wisdom" of toad-like M. Dubernet in his dissertation on happiness: (". . . is the knowledge that one is not dependent on others; . . . is the certainty that one occupies the leading position in the society one lives in.")—these have in them far more of realism, of the awful truth about human states of being, than any number of carefully shocking descriptions of a Lucy's Bar, or of the practices of a dashing lady of at most two dimensions [FitzGerald is refering to details in the noval *The Illusionist* by Françoise Mallet]. Mlle. Mallet keeps to the surface of human behavior and wickedness; M. Mauriac moves in darker, deeper waters.

Laurent LeSage (essay date 1956)

SOURCE: "Light for a Somber World," in *The Saturday Review,* Vol. XXXIX, No. 3, January 21, 1956, p. 17.

[*An American educator and critic specializing in French literature, LeSage is the author of* The French New Novel *(1962),* The French New Criticism *(1966), and four book-length studies of the writer Jean Giraudoux. In the following favorable review of* The Lamb, *LeSage argues that Mauriac has "reached in this novel . . . a point of unsurpassable mastery."*]

François Mauriac, often described as the outstanding novelist of the Catholic Renaissance and who, among living French writers, is surely the greatest artist in fiction, undertakes in his new novel *The Lamb* to demonstrate the most sublime of Christian concepts—that of martyrdom for the redemption of mankind.

The solemn mystery is acted out against the vineyards and pine-forests of the Landes country, where old families moulder in ancestral dwellings. We have met this family before in Mauriac's pages. Here is Brigitte Pian, the *Woman of the Pharisees,* now seventy-eight, a colossus of malevolence, who, with her young secretary Dominique, has come to stay with her stepdaughter Michèle. Here is Jean de Mirbell, now Michèle's husband, of whom Mauriac says, "All that seems strange, perhaps even monstrous, in this man of thirty, will seem less strange to those who remember the years of his youth." The childless couple have with them Rolland, a snot-nosed urchin taken on trial from a foundling home.

Into this musty household smelling of vermin and soul corruption walks Xavier Dartigelongue, turned, like a somnambulist, from the seminary he was about to enter, to follow a vocation foreordained. Secretly he has always understood what will be his lot. "Millions of Christs with tender, brooding eyes" lead him along the path that Jesus himself first trod. He too will know doubt and grow fearful. Harassed by the diabolic mockery of Jean and the cynical commonsense arguments of the curé, Xavier's faith is sorely tried. "If only," he cries out, "I had saved one single person!" Might it be for nothing more than a myth that he will end upon a cross? He will know revilement—his family's scorn, lewd insinuations about his attachment for Jean and for Rolland, the old woman's suspicion. "Like a young pine tree in the night" he stands before Brigitte Pian while she accuses him of impure intention towards Dominique. Chaste though his love be, through it he will know temptation: "Here was salvation within reach of his hand . . . True, simple, life was there for him to take and hold, . . . the lot of wedded men and women." The night little Rolland is locked supperless in the library, Xavier follows the *via crucis* as, bent under a heavy ladder, he walks barefoot through the pine needles and leaves a blood-stained trail. In his final hour he will know despair. But there is a despair that leaves hope intact and Xavier probably did not kill himself. "He was pushed," pushed by everyone, the sinners who, by his blood sacrifice, now know peace.

The Lamb may represent the pinnacle of Mauriac's career. After more than forty years of painting in gloomy novels a corrupt and abject humanity, he finally undertook to portray a saint. Impatient readers, not satisfied with his other sacrificial victims, his sinners ultimately touched by grace, and his abortive holy men, have reproached Mauriac for omitting real saints and heroes from his Christian universe. They may now contemplate virtue incarnate. Xavier's compassionate love has flooded Mauriac's somber world with radiant light. As a narrative vehicle too, *The Lamb* may represent the summit of Mauriac's attainment. Increasingly a master of ellipsis and richly significant statement, he would seem to have reached in this novel, so powerfully and yet so elegantly articulated, a point of unsurpassable mastery.

James Finn (essay date 1957)

SOURCE: "Marks of Eternity," in *The Commonweal*, Vol. LXVII, No. 4, October 25, 1957, pp. 105-07.

[*An American editor and author, Finn worked for the journals* Commonweal, Worldview, *and* Christian Century, *in succession, and published several books about war and pacificism. In the following laudatory review of* Lines of Life, *he briefly discusses the novel's place in Mauriac's body of work and then assesses it as a great work of art.*]

Lines of Life, published first in France in 1928 under the title *Destins,* is part of the "early" Mauriac, those six or seven novels that made him a standard and symbol for young writers in the thirties. It was primarily this group of novels against which the *bien pensants* leveled charges of "unwholesome" and "corrupt," these novels which M. Mauriac had in mind when he wrote his brilliant apologia, *God and Mammon.*

Readers who approach M. Mauriac for the first time through the recent, and excellent, translations of Gerard Hopkins may have some difficulty in understanding the furor which attended their first publication, the heightened criticism and praise which was once the author's regular fare. For M. Mauriac, whose literary "position" may not yet be settled, is so established an author that he is readily ignored, and temporarily overshadowed, by the new novelists, who are also, supposedly, more daring. He is a winner of the Nobel Prize and is happily accepted by readers and critics whose counterparts once eagerly pilloried him. Time and M. Mauriac's fame thus act, unfortunately, as a buffer between his early novels and the reader.

But if the literary life and atmosphere of the twenties and thirties are hard to recover, the reasons for the excited reception of the author's early works are still to be found in the works themselves. As is almost every valid work of art, *Lines of Life* is subversive. It reveals what we did not know or chose to ignore. It disturbs and unsettles easy presumptions and conventions. It challenges our complacencies.

Lines of Life is set in the famili, against the strict conventions which guide their lives, are highlighted the virtues and, even more conspicuously, the grave, unlikable failings of the middle-class. The Lagaves and the Gornacs are not born to love, despise or hate; they are less committed one to another than they are to their land, to the forests and vines. Both Maria Lagave and Jean Gornac, her employer, agree that two boys—and no more—are essential to a family, one to look after the estate, the other to be employed by the State.

These standards and goals remain unchallenged until Maria's grandson is born. Robert Lagave enters his closely bound society as a "representative of the hostile race," those who experience the pangs and pleasures of love. Very early he recognizes his body as the only god he knows. As early as his eighteenth birthday, he is conscious of his passing youth and youthful charm; each additional birthday brings sadness. Before his twenty-third birthday, however, his ephemeral charm has won him the admiring attention of a fashionable, corrupt circle of friends.

The lines of young Lagave's life cross those of many people. He arouses jealousy in those who lack his knowledge of love; dismay and repulsion in a fiancée who suddenly encounters a revelation of his corrupt life; love, and subsequent loneliness, in an older woman who had remained lethargically unaware of either; and disapproval and confusion in the minds of others.

With his customary astonishing economy Mauriac creates scenes of great intensity. The heavy summer heat presses upon the countryside. No leaf stirs; no voice breaks the silence. And upon the hot, cracked ground the lovers lie together, while those whose love is unreturned ache with loneliness. Others, concerned only with the land, remain unaware of and uninterested in the eruptions of human passion. Their lives move with the rhythm of the seasons, and are fulfilled in devotion to the land.

As the destinies of these people intersect, each leaves his mark upon the other. The direction of the novel is to show that "the marks left by one individual on another are eternal, and not with impunity can some other's destiny cross our own." Because Mauriac has attempted to show these people in all their wounded nature, because he has attempted to reflect a world where evil is palpable yet mysterious—and because he has done both so successfully—he has been severely criticized. Mauriac himself has given an answer to those charges. He acknowledges that a presence broods over the action of his early novels, that evil is a reality and many of the characters corrupt or broken. But his characters, asserts M. Mauriac, have souls. They acknowledge the eternal consequences of their actions. And he has not been tempted to the pleasant falsehoods so many readers expect to find in works by a Catholic author.

Some readers may find M. Mauriac's self-accounting unsatisfactory, however subtle and sincere. Others will accept his apologies as brilliant introspections of a true artist, but as gratuitous offerings. For these early novels are true works of art which now surpass and will surely survive their justification.

Germaine Brée and Margaret Guiton (essay date 1957)

SOURCE: "Private Worlds: François Mauriac," in *An Age of Fiction: The French Novel from Gide to Camus,* Rutgers University Press, 1957, pp. 114-15.

[*A French-born American educator and critic specializing in French literature, Brée is widely acknowledged to be an expert on the life and work of Albert Camus. In the following excerpt, Brée and Guiton discuss Mauriac's focus on the morality of material possessions and the "inner landscape" evident in his novels.*]

As a novelist, François Mauriac himself, as he has admitted,
is haunted by the secret that lies at the heart of all human
beings. In one of his last novels, *L'Agneau* (*The Lamb*),
1954, he analyzes the satanic nature of the fascination we
exercise over each other, preying one on the other to satisfy
our emotional needs. The spiritual crisis he went through
in mid-career was in part due to his own uncertainty on
that score. As Mauriac sees it, the novelist, like the priest,
is deeply concerned with the fate of human beings; but
unlike the priest, he uses them for his own ends, like a
Mephistopheles in disguise.

This somber drama, which lies at the heart of the Mauriac
novel, is played out, almost exclusively, in Mauriac's native
Guyenne, a region where he still often lives in his estate
of Malagar and to which he makes constant imaginative
reference. The Bordeaux countryside, with its vineyards
and farms and beyond them the flat stretches of pine forests
that reach down to the sea, provides the physical setting
for the novel. The characters, taken from the rich Bordeaux
estates, betray an obsessive lust for possession which is
symbolized in the autocracy of the country house set in its
own lands, the power exercised over the individual by the
family, the binding strength of provincial rituals and traditions, and the continuity assured by the patient accumulation
of wealth. Wealth in the family is not considered a source
of pleasure. It is the tangible form of a passion to possess
materially and completely, that passion which, according to
Mauriac, can never be assuaged. But the particular atmosphere of the novel comes rather from an imaginary inner
landscape that Mauriac seems to carry in his mind both as
a memory and as an image of remorse.

"Do not hope that I shall allow you to forget me," it
whispers in Mauriac's *Bordeaux*.

> The more the life you lead differs from the life I gave
> you, the more distinct I shall become inside you. And
> do not hope that the human beings which preoccupy

you now will ever penetrate your books without passing
through me. I must first draw them toward me, absorb
them, so that eventually they will be reborn in my
atmosphere, the only atmosphere in which your miserable creatures come to life.

This inner landscape pervades Mauriac's novels, imposing
a strong and simple pattern and carrying its own recognizable atmosphere. The light pouring like "liquid metal"
through the shutters of the houses, the "outer furnace," the
"torrid" summer days, the tight circle of the pine trees, the
strident cicadas, the forest trees always ready to blaze, are
characteristic of Mauriac's tales. His imaginary land can
also seize one in a glacial grip, but never can it give
relaxation or temporary comfort. There is a terrible beauty
in it, an alien, disquieting beauty, that generates disaster.
It is the purgatory of Mauriac's world, from which the
sole escape is to the indifferent "asphalt" of Paris's nonchalant hell. An inner rhythm carries Mauriac's novels,
and his characters with them, from Bordeaux to Paris. But
this movement is illusory, for Guyenne holds Mauriac's
characters as surely as it holds their creator. They must
always in the end return.

R. T. Davies (essay date 1959)

SOURCE: "Reservations about Mauriac," in *Essays in
Criticism*, Vol. IX, No. 1, January, 1959, pp. 22-36.

[*Davies is an English educator and critic specializing in
English literature of the Middle Ages. In the following
essay, he argues that Mauriac is concerned with only a
very narrow range of themes, and that, while he fails to
address certain aspects of life in his novels, the power of
his work is nevertheless at least partly related to the
concentration of its focus.*]

Reading, pondering and re-reading the novels of M. Mauriac
over the last eight years, I have not found my first and
almost unqualified love for them much diminished. M.
Mauriac speaks my language: I am immediately at home
in his world because it seems to be my world, and, to me,
what he is representing is life. The effect is one of illumination and sheer pleasure: he gets to the heart of certain
sorts of character, certain sorts of motive, certain sorts of
situation, so that I have a reassuring sense of expanded
understanding; and he evokes them so convincingly that I
am disarmed and fascinated.

Nevertheless, there are qualifications that must be made.
Mauriac communicates, characteristically, a sense that living
is a distasteful and hellish affair. His novels suggest, characteristically, that the everyday world is not to be trusted.
For example, there is uncommonly frequent mention of
the physically repulsive. In *The Knot of Vipers*, on page
sixteen of the English translation published by Eyre &
Spottiswoode, the miser says of himself in his journal:

> I am ending my life in a dressing-gown, surrounded by
> all the paraphernalia of incurable disease, sunk in the

great winged chair where my mother sat waiting for her end. There is a table beside me, as there was beside her, laden with medicine-bottles. I am ill-shaven and evil-smelling, a slave to all sorts of disgusting little habits.

Thérèse is described taking a glance at her father's 'grubby, bilious face . . . the stiff little yellowish-white bristles that covered his cheeks.' Such bilious faces, such incurable diseases—cancer, angina—such disgusting little habits, constantly recur.

As Xavier sees it, in *The Lamb,* the natural world is full of enmity. However, what follows the expression of this sentiment, so typical of M. Mauriac's sensibility, is a revulsion from it: 'But to wish for death is wicked. It is no more permitted to commit suicide in the heart than to fall into adultery. He moved on again, guided by the hall-lamp.' Such a reference to a higher calling might be thought likely to sweeten, enlighten and invigorate M. Mauriac's world: but instead of being the occasion of noble aspiration and gallant effort, it is one of conflict, miserable and frustrating, between what it is sensed should be done and a stronger predisposition to do otherwise. Divine intervention excepted, such a conflict is doomed to continue until death, as it does in *The Desert of Love* in the case of Raymond, who is so inextricably a victim of the flesh and its promptings.

> If he decided that, at no matter what cost, he must fight his way out of the dense blackness, must escape from this murderous law of gravity, what choices were there open to him but the alternatives of stupor or of sleep?—unless this star in the firmament of his heart should go suddenly dead, as all love goes dead. He carried within him a tearing, frantic capability of passion inherited from his father—of a passion that was all-powerful, that would breed, until he died, still other planetary worlds, other Maria Crosses, of which, in succession, he would become the miserable satellite.

Sex is rarely happy in Mauriac. He makes use in one way or another (but always with discretion) of some of its abnormal manifestations—paederasty, sadistic self-indulgence, that impotence some know in the presence of the beloved object. The narrator of *A Woman of the Pharisees* (speaking in character, of course) says, 'I believe that all the miseries of our human state come from our inability to remain chaste.' This character distrusts the feelings and the flesh. He would have them, he says, 'under a strict discipline'. He would have 'the movements of the heart and the promptings of the flesh' bridled. And Mauriac writes, in a Foreword to *Thérèse Desqueyroux,* with characteristic compassion but with characteristic disgust, 'I know the secrets of the hearts that are deep buried in, and mingled with, the filth of the flesh.'

The characteristic flavour of Mauriac in this respect, as in so many others, is bitter and salt. That is one thing. A second thing is that he appears sometimes to relish it so. For example, in this sentence from *The Loved and the Unloved,* there is conspicuous enjoyment of the repulsive and diseased.

She was one of those countrywomen still to be found, perhaps, even in these days, who would rather suffer agonies than reveal to the sight and touch of a man—he might be a doctor, but that made no difference—the shameful plaguespot set in the female flesh, the breeding lair of pestilence.

Moreover, the repeated recurrence of certain types of unsavoury character or situation or theme or physical phenomenon, and the general omission of many others of a more healthy sort, leads one to feel—in a total view of Mauriac—that he rather likes depicting sin and misery and disease, that this is just his cup of nasty tea.

It is certain he lacks the breadth of the greater novelists and dramatists. His range is limited indeed. There is no humour, no sheerly comic character, no really good laugh at things. All is intense, though with the intensity, certainly, of great art. Much human experience is altogether absent, and a great deal more has only a small place. Sometimes a character is presented harshly and no attempt is made to understand him, no compassion is shown for him. True, he feels compassion for Thérèse:

> I came to you [Mauriac is addressing his imagined character in a Foreword] in a country drawing-room, a young and ravaged woman plagued by the attentive care of aged relatives and a foolish husband . . . often (I) watched you prisoned behind that family barrier, prowling like a shewolf, and caught your sad, malevolent eye fixed full upon me.

He feels compassion for Thérèse, but he loathes Madame Agathe in *The Loved and the Unloved,* the governess who tries by force of will and inhuman calculation to compel a young man to love her. And yet she is a sad, unfortunate creature, a victim of the mis-shapen world, just as much as Thérèse.

But just as it is clearly not true that he is wholly lacking in compassion, so also it is not true that he has no sense of innocence, or that tenderness and generosity are human feelings never described in his pages. He is not without some characters who are described as happy, by nature, naturally innocent, and appear to be so in the novel. In *A Woman of the Pharisees* the narrator says of his sister that:

> She was one of those human beings whose temperaments are so surely balanced, their hearts so pure, that their instincts are almost always at one with their duty, so that their natural inclinations lead them to do precisely what God expects of them.

In *The Knot of Vipers,* the twisted miser describes his nephew, Luc, as one whose

> nature was purely instinctive, and what struck me more and more, as he grew older, was his purity, his unawareness of evil, his utter disregard of it. . . . If . . . humanity carries in its flesh the stigma of original sin, then, all I can say (continues the miser) is that no living eye can ever have seen the mark in Luc. He had come from the hand of the potter uncracked and lovely.

But such utterances as these are uncommon, and the characteristic spirit of a great part of most of Mauriac's novels is not overwhelmingly warm or generous. The flavour is essentially mixed, and there is involved a great deal of distaste, of coldness, of disgust, of what a Middleton Murry or a Charles Williams would call 'denial of life'.

II

M. Mauriac himself frankly admits that the world he paints is strongly coloured with his own sensibility. What he creates he allows to be distinctively his own creation. In his *Journal* he writes:

> as soon as I set to work, everything takes on a colour according to my eternal colours; even my most beautiful characters enter into a kind of sulphurous light which is natural to me and which I do not defend—for it is simply mine.

Rose, the heroine of *The Unknown Sea,* who has the most saintly selflessness, has also blackheads. A confessor, who brings God's peace to a tortured soul, brings also his sour breath.

The characters Mauriac creates are tortured, then, because he is tortured. Look at the Preface to **The End of the Night,** the last novel about Thérèse:

> The reader [says Mauriac] who demands—and quite rightly—that every literary work should mark a step forward in a spiritual pilgrimage may, perhaps, feel some surprise at finding himself once more dragged down to Hell. Him I would ask to remember that the heroine of this novel belongs to a period of my life now long past, and that she bears witness to a phase of intellectual restlessness which I have at last outgrown.

On page three of a Foreword to **Thérèse Desqueyroux,** he explains why he so rarely writes about those who appear happy and healthy:

> Many will feel surprise that I should give imagined life to a creature more odious than any character in my other books. Why, they will ask, have I never anything to say of those who ooze with virtue and wear their hearts upon their sleeves?

The reply is simple: such people 'have no story for me to tell', such people are not to Mauriac imaginatively significant. For all that there are such people in the actual world, such is his sensibility that he does not readily project them into his imagined world.

It is clear, from an open letter in the *Month* (June, 1950, p. 418) on the correspondence between Claudel and Gide, that Mauriac regards such predilections, emphases and omissions as oblique indications of the novelist's own inner life. Referring to their writers, he calls novels

> false pieces of evidence about ourselves . . . touched-up portraits in which we pose. . . . We are in truth brothers of the actor and even more of the prostitute, for we lose our own personality, put on other people's,

give ourselves to the first comer, expose our hearts as others do their bodies, and sell ourselves.

The image of the prostitute betrays how personal is Mauriac's picture of his rôle: he regards himself through the same eyes as he sees so much of the world. But, allowing for this, his view remains intact: it is, that the novel is a form of exhibitionism.

What it inevitably exhibits is the novelist's own obsession. In words used by Mr. Graham Greene of Walter de la Mare, in *Lost Childhood and Other Essays,* Mauriac, 'like any artist worthy of the name', is 'a victim: a man given over to an obsession'. His persuasiveness, intensity and compelling power are those of one obsessed. This it is, first and foremost, rather than their verisimilitude, that makes his characters convincing, and that they should convince is, as E. M. Forster has said, in *Aspects of the Novel,* more important than that they should be like ourselves.

In one major essay—a Postscript to **The Loved and the Unloved**—Mauriac disclaims all verisimilitude for his characters. Again, like Mr. Forster, he asserts a difference between Homo Fictus and Homo Sapiens and observes that, in making his characters, the novelist is in some sense describing himself.

> Living persons are never like the characters of fiction . . . these invented creatures are conditioned and circumstanced by the author . . . no matter how complex they may be, they inevitably express some tendency, some passion, or some vice, and are, to that extent, detached from the human context. . . . There is no such thing as a novel which genuinely portrays the *indetermination* of human life as we know it.

> The most, therefore, that may be conceded is that the novel, though it does not throw any revealing light on persons living in the actual world, may, and does, give us a great deal of information about the author.

Whatever may be the final effect of his work, during its composition

> The artist stresses this or that characteristic almost unconsciously, and in obedience to his creative instinct. He may even distort his material the better to give form and substance to those feelings of pity and horror which, since his earliest years, he has felt when confronted by certain persons and certain lives.

Mauriac was led to make these observations (which reveal how personal and purely artistic his genius is) in self-defence against the imagined attack of 'those of my readers who share with me a religious outlook', and he concludes his defence with the admission that 'the Christian who happens also to be a novelist must resign himself to pleading no better an excuse than that of "vocation". He writes novels because he has some reason to think that he was born into the world to write, seeing that from childhood on he has struggled endlessly to do so.'

But he allows that even against this ultimate and only defence there are two legitimate objections. One, which he mentions last, is that there can be 'A vocation for evil, no less than a vocation for good' and that the artist's impulse and its satisfaction may well be contrary to God's will.' The other, which he mentions at the beginning, is that, whatever may be said of the relationship between the novel and the novelist and whatever may be its artistic value, 'It remains true, however, that if the world which the Christian novelist portrays is noticeably denuded of Grace, that if God seems to be absent from it, the pious critic has a perfect right to hold that the work in question may fairly be used in evidence against its author'. He cites his own *The Loved and the Unloved* as a work in which, following his genius and without any other intention, he has painted a picture which 'is indeed black. It shows mankind as warped, . . . It shows humanity untouched by Grace. In favour of whom, or of what, can such a portrait bear witness? That question sums up the critical attitude of the Christian.'

Mauriac affirms, then, that other considerations than those we may loosely call 'artistic' are properly made by a Christian critic, and in the Preface to *The End of the Night* he allows that a reader may 'quite rightly' demand 'that every literary work should mark a step forward in a spiritual pilgrimage'. Praising the work of René Bazin he says, 'What joy and peace an artist must experience in the evening of his life, when he possesses the assurance that no soul has ever beenwounded by him.' Fr. Martin Jarrett-Kerr, in his little book on Mauriac, quotes these words and calls them naïve. Now it is true that a certain simplicity (and some inconsistency) are typical of Mauriac's comments inside and outside his novels. But although what may be naïve about Mauriac's conception of the specifically Christian attitude to creative art and criticism may be responsible for some of that self-defensiveness and self-depreciation which we have noticed, at the same time his simplicity has about it something that one senses to be nearer the truth than many an aesthetic sophistication, and it is supported by the practice of such a very different artist as Chaucer, who at the end of his career renounced all he had written that might be called a 'worldly vanitee', including *Troilus and Criseyde*. And it is not immature scrupulosity that prompts Mauriac's obser-vation that, 'The work which is *merely* an end in itself becomes an idol, on whose altar the artist will sacrifice everything, even if that everything shall include, as with Proust it did, life itself', but the simple acknowledgment of the mortal danger, from the Christian point of view, that not only the pure artist but all men are in if they worship anything but God. That is why, pure artist as he is, he sympathises with the pious critic who may deplore that vices have been displayed in a novel 'not, indeed, with the purpose of making them seem attractive, but at least of serving the purposes of a work of art which shall be judged as an end in itself'. From the point of view of a Christian critic, a work of art cannot be evaluated simply as an end in itself; but, on the other hand, from the point of view of any artist, to make his creation serve a superior end is to distort it since it may have to be conformed, perhaps, to an edifying pattern or trimmed against the measure of some orthodoxy. Mau-

riac is clear that, whereas the critic may well wish that, after the artist had displayed vices, he had shown also the eventual 'victory of Grace', yet 'the novelist must be constantly on his guard against trying to *prove* anything . . . his duty is to make the most of his own peculiar vision of human life and human persons'. Mauriac is clear that the artist should have no concern beyond 'painting to the best of his ability', and should certainly never 'force his talent. Mine does not easily breathe the air of sublimity'.

III

Mauriac's insistence that as an artist he must serve only the ends of his art, responding freely and fully only to the impulsions of his own imagination, whereas that as a critic one may well have other allegiances—and rightly, too—is also an acknowledgment that his own heart is divided, and that his own loyalty is not single. His position is not new: it is, as I have already suggested by my reference to Chaucer, one that was, in one way and another, in spite of what is often said of their supposed wholeness, characteristic of some outstanding artists of the Middle Ages. Mauriac's emphatic assertion that his vision is personal and the world he represents peculiarly his own world and unlike the actual one, not only guarantees his integrity as an artist, but, were it notfor his own frank admission of the opposite, might also be said to cut the ground from under the critic who maintains he lacks verisimilitude. But Mauriac allows that the critic, especially if he be a Christian critic, may not rest content, possessed by the novelist's personality communicated through his creation, simply contemplating his vision. Moreover, there is an invitation embedded in the novels themselves, despite what Mauriac says outside them, to refer what he has created to what it purports to represent—he invites us to ask ourselves whether his vision is a true vision of the actual world. For example, in the Preface to *The End of the Night,* he says of Thérèse, his own creation, 'she belongs to that class of human beings . . . for whom night can end only when life itself ends'. Naturally we ask ourselves, are there such human beings? and is Thérèse like them? Moreover, he invites us to relate his work to a specifically Christian view of the world, for God and His Grace, and the means of Grace, are frequent actors in his drama, and for example, in such a plain comment on his own work as the Foreword to *Thérèse* he says:

> I could have wished, Thérèse, that sorrow might have turned your heart to God, . . . But had I shown you thus redeemed there would have been no lack of readers to raise a cry of sacrilege, even though they may hold, as an article of Faith, the Fall and Ransom of our torn and twisted natures.

At Mauriac's instigation, then, let us evaluate the world he has created in relation to the actual world, especially as that world is interpreted by Christians; for he has, he tells us in the Postscript to *The Loved and the Unloved,* accounted in the past to his pious critics for his dark picture of human misery by saying 'that the people I set out to paint are fallen creatures, painted from birth . . . evil is a reality in this world of ours'. The unsavoury world projected by his obsessed sensibility we may regard, then, especially at his occasional suggestion, as the world the Christian knows as Fallen. Like Pascal, Mauriac presents the miserable lot of human beings without God. He depicts the degraded and hopeless state of man without Grace.

So regarded, it must be said that his picture is at least tinged with the spiritual colours of Jansenism. In several places Mauriac overtly rebuffs those inclined to that heresy but, taking his vision of the world all in all, one is left with the general sense of the powerlessness , in Mauriac, very little conspicuous evidence of the glory that God has revealed in His Creation. Such generalisations as I am making do not do justice, of course, to the peculiar ethos of individual novels, and they are certainly not without incidental exceptions. Among these are such as were noticed above in which some characters are seen as, by nature, godly and in which all flesh, despite original sin, is seen as holy; and among these, also, is that major one which Mauriac professes to have made the character of Thérèse supremely important for him, namely, that she was 'an example of that power, granted to all human beings—no matter how much they may seem to be the slaves of a hostile fate—of saying "No" to the law which beats them down'.

It is, however, usual in a novel of Mauriac's to be aware that natural inheritance, personal and collective, encounters with fellow-men, conscious or unconscious, and the inscrutable, unpredictable hand of God are disposing his characters in their tormented ways. It is also the hand of God which saves them from their slavery: Grace interposes and sets them free. If the celebration of the glory of God revealed in the natural order is not a characteristic theme of Mauriac's, the very opposite is true of man's redemption from the fascinating miseries of the Fall. He is frequently concerned—though not in order to 'prove' anything and simply because it is to him imaginatively significant—with how a man becomes aware of God, is converted and sanctified. Thus, in *A Woman of the Pharisees,* Brigitte Pian is shown learning to understand 'at last that it is not our deserts that matter but our love'. And yet, says the narrator, however apparent this change, 'People do not change . . . they do quite often turn back to what they were once and show again those very characteristics which they have striven tirelessly, through a whole lifetime, to suppress. . . . God is very often the good temptation to which many human beings in the long run yield'.

In this last comment Mauriac comes from one angle at a complex problem both in the technique of the novel and in the formulation of a theology, the problem of the immediate, local relationship of Grace and Nature. As a problem in writing a novel it is two-fold: on the one hand, the intrusion of Grace is likely to appear in some respects adventitious, so that the turn then taken in what purports to be a novel seriously concerned with living is, in some ways, rather what might be expected of one that is merely concerned with adventure; on the other hand, the operations of Grace in a soul are not readily imagined by any novelist, never mind how sincere his conscious Christian purpose in writing and living, for saints seem to feel no desire to make novels and sinners invent with most conviction characters that resemble themselves.

So far as the first part of this problem is concerned, Mauriac takes pains to trace the 'natural' psychological development of a character to the point at which Grace breaks in. It is when Nicolas has asserted his newly-conscious manhood both against Madame Agathe, who has calculated marrying him through force of will, and against his dominating and shrewd mother, and when he has achieved independence of Gilles, the friend of his adolescence, then it is that, a 'prey to a melancholy hunger which all the kingdoms of the earth could not have satisfied', his 'only companion . . . a tenderness that lay outspread like the sea beneath the mindless stars, . . . a stranger to himself, detached from all his fellows'—then it is, at this point in Nicolas' psychological development, that Mauriac ends his novel with a picture of this young man, sitting on the parapet of the bridge over the Leyrot, 'as though he had agreed with Somebody to meet him there'.

However, despite the verisimilar psychological preparation made for it, such a moment of spiritual awakening and growth has, sometimes, in Mauriac a romantic quality which is as intrusive in tone as the sudden turn of events is in the plot. Thus, in *The Unknown Sea,* the image of the Sea itself as a symbol of a truth about living seems alien and forced. In a novel which is so typically and finely concerned with concrete human relationships in concrete settings, in which each scene is itself so convincing and independently meaningful, and the portrait of each character so firm and consistent with what are apparently the laws of human nature, the reader suddenly finds the hard ground gone from under him and cobwebs about his face at the author's interjected comment that 'there are some who, even in childhood, realise that they are moving towards an unknown sea. . . . On they go, until, at length, when the last dune has been surmounted, they find themselves in a world of spume and blown sand which seems to speak to them of an infinity of passion. That is the moment when they must choose their path'.

As in **The Loved and the Unloved,** so also in *The Knot of Vipers,* the incursion of Grace is represented in close step with the careful development of the miser's state of mind. So much is this so that, should the turning of the miser inside-out from hatred to love be thought incredible, the fault must be not so much that supernature has intervened as that it is not in nature that this revolution should happen, not so much that there has been a miracle as that the psychology is wrong. The novel is unified by a theme concisely formulated at the end, 'where his treasure was, there his heart was *not',* and it is the need of this heart, which has become a knot of vipers only a sword can cut free, that makes it 'impossible to deny that a way does exist in me which might lead me to your God'. The expression Mauriac uses to describe the miser's awareness of his change of heart is a homely and unprepossessing one, forcing no theological issues—'It was borne in on me': 'It was borne in on me at that moment that my hatred was dead. . . . I thought of the fortune which, so it seemed, had been my life's obsession. . . . now I felt, suddenly, wholly detached. It no longer interested me, was no longer any concern of mine'. Whatever the ultimate cause, natural or supernatural, my judgment is that this experience, unexpected, illuminating, the end of a stifling tunnel, is true to life.

True to life, also, is the interpretation put upon the miser's conversion by his son. Commenting on his father's journal, which he has found after his death, he writes to his sister, 'All through his life he had been the enemy of his family, hated by everybody, and without a single friend. . . . Is it conceivable that, towards the end of his life, he should have felt a desire for the consolations of prayer? I don't think so. What emerges from these pages with dazzling clarity is a state of well-defined mental instability, taking the form of persecution mania and religious hallucination . . . bogus mysticism of this kind makes me feel physically sick'. This is certainly the sort of 'psychological' language that might well be used to describe what the miser himself accounts for in 'religious' terms. The presence of such a parallel interpretation of the miser's case helps to make the novel all the more convincing, countering, as it does, any feeling that what happens is merely adventitious since it does not obey such laws of cause and effect as seem normally to govern everyday living in the modern world.

Mauriac does not find it possible, however, to portray Grace in action as convincingly as he portrays evil. This is the second sort of difficulty the novelist meets in making Grace one of his protagonists. Mauriac says so openly at the end of *The Enemy*:

> But how is one to describe the secret drama of a man who struggles to subdue his earthly heritage, that drama which finds expression neither in words nor gestures? Where is the artist who may dare to imagine the processes and shifts of the great protagonist—Grace? It is the mark of our slavery and of our wretchedness that we can, without lying, paint a faithful portrait only of the passions.

Therefore he has to stop this novel at just the point where the story of his hero should really begin. Of Thérèse, too, Mauriac says in *The End of the Night* that he would have liked to have described her finding pardon and peace, but

> I could not *see* the priest who would have possessed the qualifications necessary if he was to hear her confession with understanding. Since then I have found him—in Rome, and I know now (some day, perhaps, I may tell the story) just how Thérèse entered into the eternalradiance of death.

Of course, Mauriac knows as well as anyone who has read a handbook of ascetic theology what, in theory, should be her confessor's rôle; but that is quite another thing from making it real before the reader of a novel. For that, imaginative sympathy is essential. Whether it is that there is something about the action of Grace that is not, anyway, susceptible of realisation in a novel, or whether it is that Mauriac has failed to trace the course of sanctification uniformly through all its stages—certainly, as Mr. Graham Greene has said, 'the "joins" of his plot . . . are often

oddly lacking'—or whether it is the reader feels an inhibiting uneasiness at the exhibition of virtue, or whether it is, simply, as he himself has declared, that Mauriac cannot convincingly imagine growth in holiness: certainly it is not with such unquestioning belief as I have in her in the full pride of her pharisaicism that I read of the signs of Brigitte Pian's maturing love, or as I have in him when his ministry has more obvious success that I catch glimpses of the abbè Calou's increasing saintliness in his humiliation— 'and his face was as the face of an angel'.

The ultimate holiness of Sarah in Mr. Greene's *The End of the Affair*—which is suggested by the miracles—is incredible in something of the same way. It is not because I think the salvation of such a sinner impossible, but because so little is done by Mr. Greene to persuade me that here, in the world of this particular novel, it has occurred. There is here, as I see it, not a defect in his reading of life but a fundamental deficiency in his imagination and art. At a deep level, this is tantamount to saying that there is, indeed, a defect in his reading of life, but, at the level of consciousness, my distinction will hold and, at this level, serve a useful purpose.

In one guise or another, such limitations in Mauriac's imaginative sympathy account for a certain scrappiness and discontinuity in the course of his novels. There are many of the ordinary aspects of everyday life which are opaque to his pen, so that the illusion of a continuum is absent. That apparently insignificant variety there is in life and that 'indetermination', which we have seen him assert to be irreproducible in art, are not even suggested by him. His is a markedly selective vision, over-emphasising certain constantly recurring elements and omitting much. But the jet of water is all the more powerful for the narrowness of the nozzle and Mauriac's virtue is his concentration and economy, his lucid intensity and point. Moreover, despite what we have seen to be Mauriac's own opinion that his characters are more like himself than like others, and despite his own awareness that his world is coloured in his own colours, there is about his novels, though with the major exceptions we have discussed, a characteristic sense of the objective and serene. For the greater part, however personal the vision, he has given to it the body and reality of the actual world; he has not compromised the detachment at least of art.

The Times Literary Supplement (essay date 1961)

SOURCE: "Tender Conscience," in *The Times Literary Supplement*, No. 3093, June 9, 1961, p. 353.

[*In the following review of* Young Man in Chains, *the critic suggests that the questions that have intrigued Mauriac throughout his career were present in this early short novel.*]

We all know the world of M. Francois Mauriac by now, the *landes* "steaming with prayer and fornication", the vile meannesses of the men of property (or, better, the women, for men seem to die like drones once they have fecundated the monstrous queen bees) in their shuttered villas round which even the pines are sensuous. Yet we have waited nearly forty years for the translation of *L'Enfant Chargé de Chaînes,* which was first published in 1913, when M. Mauriac was twenty-eight.

This, the last in the uniform English edition, was the novel that first revealed his sultry, tortured talent and, on reading the translation so many years later, we are struck by the technical mastery the young M. Mauriac had already achieved, the clear classical lines with no loose ends. Like Joyce's Stephen Dedalus, M. Mauriac's protagonist, Jean-Paul Johanet, is a sensitive young literary man tortured by the Beatific Vision and Hell, or, as one of his apostolic friends puts it, always "analysing his empty, complicated little mind". No one can say that Joyce's Dublin had less of that strictness and obsession with sin—especially, of course, the sins of the flesh—than the *bon-dévot* families of Bordeaux from which M. Mauriac stemmed.

Like Stephen, Jean-Paul wrestles to adjust his Catholicism and his life, though, unlike Stephen, Jean-Paul never really loses his faith. Joyce's work, of course, is on a far larger scale than M. Mauriac's, but M. Mauriac has more perfection of form. Moreover, M. Mauriac is not the intellectual Joyce was. Philosophy and theology have always left him cold, he has no interest in those "pamphlets in which scholarly clerics set out to prove that the activities of the Inquisition and the Massacre of Saint Bartholomew could not be laid to the charge of the Church." Divine grace is experienced almost physically; it threatens to withdraw even from fiancés such as Jean-Paul and Marthe when they "indulge in a voluptuous confusion of the senses in the highest degree equivocal."

Instead of the theological subtleties, then, Jean-Paul turns to a heartfelt moral cause, here called *Amour et Foi,* whose object is to inflame the ideals of democratic life with the Christian message. We cannot help linking this with those journalistic activities that M. Mauriac has pursued over the years, boldly, independently, and with a *bordelais* common sense underlying the passionate command of phrase. The Cause, we need hardly add, was somehow going to disentangle the grace and poetry of the gospels from that dead and bourgeois formalism in religion which M. Mauriac has always found so repulsive.

But the "sacristy spiders", normal butts of French as of other Catholic novelists, form only an unedifying background. The leader of the *Amour et Foi* movement, Jérome Servet himself, has vices peculiar to the chrysalis-holy. No power over others is more insidious than spiritual power and Jérome basks in the worship of his followers. In his office he looks at the photographs dedicated to him by admirers: "To Jérome my only friend", "For him who revealed the truth to me": "poor little faces whose smiles awakened no memory in his heart. . . . Jérome Servet felt within himself that exaltation from which great works may emerge. He rang the bell. His secretary came in. He began to dictate."

Such wholehearted, working-class followers naturally distrust a dilettante young bourgeois like Jean-Paul who, when pressed, admits that in the Cause he was "seeking a private happiness". Moreover what he is really doing is oscillating between his little kept woman, Liette, and the confessional: "Seven o'clock sounded. He got up in haste and hurried to the church of Saint-Francois-Xavier. In the darkness of the confessional box he cast off all his weaknesses, striking his head against the varnished wood in an excess of penitence. When he rose from his knees he felt calmer, scarcely any longer troubled by delicate scruples and sins only ill-defined."

Such a "divided consciousness" has always struck M. Mauriac's agnostic readers with a certain distaste. We find it with other Catholic novelists such as Bloy, Fogazzaro or Bernanos and it is a meaningless complication unless we grant the writer his main premise—that his faith is valid. If in M. Mauriac particularly the tension between life and faith rarely seems to allow any ease-up this is because his faith has always been that of Pascal, just as the sensuality and classical control of his art always remind us of Racine.

We see then that the problem was already stated when M. Mauriac was in his twenties and he has done no more than work it out in other ways ever since. In this early novel his religious friend Vincent Hiéron says to Jean-Paul:

> As a Catholic you have found yourself immersed in a pagan society and, seated at a banquet where all the luxuries and pleasures of the world are proffered have, nevertheless, claimed for yourself the sacred heritage of a Christian childhood. *But no man can serve two masters.* Is it not that truth which now torments you?

It was this question that M. Mauriac later tried to answer in his essay on the dilemmas of a novelist who is also a Catholic—*Dieu et Mammon;* his examination of tender conscience which was also an attempt to reply to the accusation made both by André Gide and by his co-religionists that he turned his readers into accomplices. Whether on the literary side the Catholic tension adds a dimension to M. Mauriac or not is an open question, but few will deny that he is among the most gifted of all living novelists.

K. R. Srinivasa Iyengar (essay date 1963)

SOURCE: "A Flawed Eden," in *Francois Mauriac: Novelist & Moralist,* Asia Publishing House, 1963, pp. 117-22.

[*An Indian educator and author, Iyengar has written on a wide range of subjects, variously treating English studies, education in India, religious matters, and the relation between English and Indian literature. In the following excerpt, he discusses the influence of geographical setting— primarily the Bordeaux region and Paris—on Mauriac's characters.*]

In M. Mauriac's fiction we are introduced . . . to a world not less distinctive than the crowded world of Dickens, the agonized and diseased world of Dostoevsky, the intense if also vanishing world of Hardy, or the dark nightmarish world of Faulkner. Geographically, it is the Gironde and Landes country—the region round Bordeaux facing the Bay of Biscay—marked by pine trees and marshy tracts, tall oak trees and endless sandy stretches. Lured to the 'lovely Landes' by *Therese,* Dilys Powell writes after a recent visit (*The Sunday Times,* 8 July 1962):

> The forest of Landes . . . has the beauty of a landscape in which man has taken a hand, and the variety: the clearings, oases of bright green with farms and maize-fields; the sudden, rare outcrop of silvery pipes . . . It has the curious detail too: the stripped bark of the cork-trees which line some of the roads, the cups for collecting the resin as it oozes from long ochre gashes in the pine-trunks.

The people too are of a piece with the soil that breeds and sustains them. There are the landed gentry and the workers on land, there are the wine-merchants and timber-merchants at Bordeaux, and there are also the professional men—lawyers, doctors, teachers—with their respective idiosyncracies. The rich are not superlatively rich, the poor are not demoralizingly poor. There is a recognizably cohesive society in the countryside in contrast to the sharp class-antagonisms and corrosive snobbery so typical of Bordeaux. Of the men of Argelouse we are told (in *Therese*):

> The heath-land has their hearts, and their imaginations never range beyond it. They have no thought for anything but the pleasures it can give. It would, they feel, be a base betrayal on their parts to be different from the men who work their land, to speak anything but the local patois, or abandon the crude, rough manners of their neighbours.

The women are often "markedly superior to the men", and Therese as a girl reads with avidity the novels of Paul de Kock, and books like the *Causeries du Lundi* and *l'Histoire du Consulat.* People have on the whole a strong sense of tradition still, and this and their ineradicable family pride give them the capacity to 'endure'. The feeling for property is really an expression of the desire for stability and security. For a rich Desqueyroux to marry an even richer Larrouques is the most natural thing in the world, and that is how Bernard marries Therese. When Jean Peloueyre (the 'leper') asks for the hand of Noemie d'Artiailh, it is not so much the adequacy of Jean as a man as the weight and volume of his property that clinches the issue:

> No, a son of the Peloueyres is not the sort of man a girl refuses. One didn't refuse farms—tenant and free-hold—flocks of sheep, silver plate, linen that was ten generations old and lay neatly piled in tall, deep, sweet-smelling presses. . . .

It is through marriage that property is augmented and passed on from father to son, son to grandson; and between 'family' and 'property' the compact is sealed to cheat Death itself of its dues:

To all the vanished fathers of his (Fernand Cazenave's) line marriage had meant but one single thing—an increase in worldly possessions, an assurance of the continuity of property. The certainty of the family's survival had been their challenge flung in the teeth of mortality.

For these people, then, their homesteads and farmsteads are at once a refuge and a retreat, a refuge from Nature yet untamed and a retreat from the bustle and distractions of the city. Just beyond the homestead there is, perhaps, an expanse of wet and wilderness and heath, and one could be awed as well as enchanted:

> Far away, in the country of the Frontenacs and the Peloueyres, beyond the lost lands where the tracks end, the moon was shining on the drenched and spongy heath. It kept its state especially in that clearing of the trees, left free by the resinous growths, around some five or six huge oaks, very old and very gnarled, giant children of the earth. There it was still possible for the slashed and wounded pines to raise their heads heaven-wards. Drowsy sheep-bells were tinkling at intervals in the pastures. . . .

There is a seemingly ageless quality about this world, and nations may break but one feels that this elemental life would go on for ever. Civilization might make inroads here and there, pockets of sophistication might be established in the unlikeliest places, but something of the opulence, vitality and mystery of primordial Nature might somehow survive the rages and ravages of insatiable man.

If 'family' and 'property' are the base of this society set in the background of Nature, the religious sense (the people are Catholics) is like an envelope that holds this society together, a circumambient force that like gravity keeps these men and women in a state both of tension and order. It is true their religion is often more a formality than an acutely felt experience. Some try to be neutral, a few are even violently allergic to the claims of religion; some suffer insurrections, and these battles of the soul leave them almost prostrate. But none of these characters is wholly indifferent—that is, not in the deep obscure levels of their being—to the muted ineluctable intimations of religion. Actually, for several of these men and women, the religious sense means either a call to scale inaccessible heights or the consciousness of ejection from the safe harbourage of innocence into a tempestuous sea. The Mauriac world, whatever else it might be, is thus a world that is deeply involved in the agonies, ardours and ecstasies, in the false lights, hidden lights and blinding lights of religion. The desert and the darkness are real, they have an immediately defeating quality: but we are also left with the feeling that deep underneath the desert there surely flows the life-giving spring, that the light is somewhere around, ready to burst at the very centre of the darkness and scatter it away. The teacher, Bordas, in *The Little Misery* is a revolutionary, perhaps even a Communist; but when he learns about the tragic death of the boy he had earlier rejected, he finds that his eyes are opened to a world of intensities of whose very existence he had not dreamt before:

But was it really darkness? He strained his eyes in an effort to see beyond material things, beyond the walls and furniture of this, his house, beyond the tiled roof, beyond the star-pointed night, beyond the Winter constellations. He sat there, seeking the kingdom of the spirit where, rapt away into eternity, the boy could see him still, and, on his cheek, stubby with unshaven beard, a tear he had not thought to wipe away.

The desert and the darkness are presented realistically enough by M. Mauriac's selective and suggestive art. But the hint of the spring, the promise of the tongue of flame, are achieved by the poet, the man of faith. There is no contradiction, however, nor any uneasy partnership between the novelist and the poet, nor even between the artist and the man of religion.

The Mauriac world, constricted though it seems to be and peopled by hardly more than one-tenth of the 2,000 characters that fill the crowded canvas of Balzac's *Comedie Humaine,* is neither free from inner convulsions nor is it quite insulated from outside influences. There is Paris, a centre of attraction and distraction, a lure and a trap, an 'eternal city' to escape into or a base from which to direct operations against the country. In the early novel, *The Stuff of Youth,* the scene shifts from Ousilanne to Bordeaux and on to Paris—and so back to Ousilanne. But the primacy of Paris is not readily conceded. As the narrator of *The Stuff of Youth* records:

> They (Granny and Sister Marie-Henriette) had informed me that the capital was in no way superior to other cities, and, in particular, not to Bordeaux, except in the height of its houses, and the number of carriages and pedestrians in the streets. The Seine, according to Granny, compared with the Garonne, was a wretched stream—a sewer. . . .

"'The air of Paris'", Landin warns Pierrot in *The Unknown Sea,* "was not favourable to clear-cut moral judgements". Paris is a whirlpool on which one floats giddily for a while till one is sucked in and lost. Young Jacques of *The Stuff of Youth* has his first strong taste of Parisian life, but before he succumbs to its deadening routine, "some terrible Providence" intervenes and he turns away. In *Flesh and Blood,* Edward Dupont-Gunther leaves the Chateau de Lur for Paris, explores oblivion with Edith till she tires of him, and escaping even from Paris ends his life in a hotel room at Chalous-sur-Marne. Jean Peloueyre, as a possible escape from, if not also a cure for, his frustrations at home, makes a no less frustrating trip to Paris, and makes a precipitate retreat in greater discomfiture than ever before. In *The River of Fire,* the final drama of suspense is enacted in Paris—in Versailles where Lucille waits and in Louvres where Gisele waits—till the invisible protagonist, Grace, brings about the desired end at last. In *The Desert of Love,* while the main events are merely recapitulated 17 years after their occurrence, the principal characters—Maria, the Larousselles (father and son), and Paul and Raymond Courreges—all meet in Paris, and there is a stock-taking that is nevertheless eluded by the imponderables of Love and Grace. We see Therese, having at last effected her escape from Argelouse, sitting on the terrace of the

Cafe de la Paix, in the Rue Royale, smoking and dropping the cigarettes and putting her foot on them. We see her again sitting enveloped in darkness on a bench in the Champs Elysees—we see her with Dr. Schwartz the psychiatrist—and we see her madly cantering between hope and despair in her third-floor flat in the Rue du Bac. Yet Therese, even Therese, returns to Angelouse at last, and it is there that she patiently awaits 'the end of life, the end of the night'. In *Lines of Life,* the return of Bob Lagave from Paris to Viridis starts a tragic chain-reaction which involves more than one destiny. *That Which Was Lost* is located wholly in Paris, except for the retrospective reconstruction of life at La Hume in the Gironde countryside. Paris (like any other 'city') has a catalytic effect on most men and women who are drawn to it for the first time: what is latent is suddenly forced out, and especially evil has a riotous time of it. In the companion novel, *The Dark Angels,* although the brutal murder of Aline by Gradere takes place at Liogeats, both criminal and victim are hardened Parisians; and (this is significant, too) it is a little doubtful who is the more repulsive character—Gradere the murderer with a Parisian background or Desbats the Liogeats 'man of property' and spidery weaver of diabolical plots. In *The Knot of Vipers,* part of the drama—the double-crossing by Robert, Louis's illegitimate son—takes place in Paris. In *The Frontenac Mystery,* Yves the poet, escaping from the family, is lost for a while in Paris—his infatuation for his mistress proves almost his ruin—but the contact of 'home' in the person of his brother, Jean-Louis, effects a timely rescue. Again, in *The Enemy,* young Fabien has his sense of spring-time intoxication awakened in Paris, but it is later, in Venice, that he surrenders to Fanny, a veritable Circe in her power to enchant and grapple and consume. Soon the drama shifts to Paris, and Fabien is apparently caught in her coils more irretrievably than ever. He is rescued, too, and his mother takes him to the country, and a new life begins for him. In *The Unknown Sea,* after the suicide of the lawyer, Oscar Revolou, his clerk, Landin, and young Pierrot Costadot the poet, move separately to Paris, and are there thrown together by accident, each then making a decisive impact on the other. Finally, in *The Lamb,* Jean and Xavier, although heading for Paris (Jean to escape from his wife and Xavier to join the Institut Catholique), make a determined backward movement, and the tragedy—the 'sacrifice' of the 'lamb'—is encompassed only amidst the aridities and silences of the countryside around Larjuzon.

From all this it must be clear that, while Paris is not wholly sealed out of the Mauriac world, it figures nevertheless only as an 'alien' city, at once attractive and sinister, a vanity fair with a cemetery behind. Nor is the novelist himself quite at his ease in Paris. When the scene is in the countryside or even in Bordeaux, Mauriac seems to write as if he had achieved complete comprehension and total identity, but whenever the scene shifts to Paris, we have the uneasy feeling that there is the adroit improvisation of maddening urban modes rather than the evocation of actuality. To modify a phrase of D. H. Lawrence, it is the novelist making up to the best of his ability, not the tale telling itself, carrying along, in its heady current, both reader and novelist.

In a physical sense, then, the heart of the Mauriac world is the Gironde and the Landes, which could be an Eden were it not for the subtle serpent of sophistication that has toad-like sneaked its way into this world—and were it not also for the sudden squalls that blow from distant Paris. A flawed Eden, if you will; a damaged and mangled Paradise. In this too too sullied world, there is one natural refuge for the people: mother earth. For these children of the soil (so long as they are not wholly divorced from it), Nature—notwithstanding her veering moods and seasonal fluctuations—is really the mother. When this refuge too is unavailing (as sometimes it must prove to be), another refuge is hinted at: Mother Church. While Nature is present visibly, and Supernature too is present though invisibly, our eyes are normally rivetted only on the little cluster of human beings who play their respective roles at the centre of the lighted stage, a small circle illuminated by the novelist's potent art. This alone, this little circle, is M. Mauriac's world; these alone are the actors: such might very well be our first impression. But presently we know that Nature is a protagonist too, and that Grace is the chief protagonist of all.

Philip Stratford (essay date 1964)

SOURCE: "Mauriac: Poet into Novelist," in *Faith and Fiction: Creative Process in Greene and Mauriac,* University of Notre Dame Press, 1964, pp. 65-86.

[*Stratford is a Canadian educator and critic. In the following excerpt, he discusses the development of and literary influences on Mauriac's early work.*]

In the introduction to *Commencements d'une vie* Mauriac admits that the intensity of his childhood experience was heightened by the habit of self-dramatization. "As a child I played at being solitary and misunderstood," he writes, "and it was the most fascinating of games. Perhaps I found it so because I instinctively knew that much more than a game was involved, a preparation in fact, an exercise for becoming a writer. To enjoy watching oneself suffer is the obvious sign of a literary vocation." It is the change of that instinctive sense of vocation into conscious purpose that I wish to trace in this chapter, furnishing biographical background and evidence from the novels of the period, but still focusing on those elements which determine the character of Mauriac's creative vision.

One of the forces that contributed most to its development was a passionate love of literature. "As a child books were my unique deliverance," Mauriac states, and adds, characteristically, qualifying the idea of escape, "they provided me with the image of my own confusion and anxieties" [*Commencements*]. There was nothing exceptional in his early "voracious appetite" [*Mémoires Intérieurs*] for books. Like any child, he read indiscriminately, and his mother, apart from making sure that what he read was "safe" (as often as not sanctioned by the *Bibliothèque Rose*), did nothing to guide him or shape his taste. Mauriac

thinks that among the children's classics of his time the novels of Zénaïde Fleuriot had the greatest influence. It is hard to say just what these stories of the mis-adventures and heartbreaks of little aristocrats in Brittany could have given him beyond some insight into the pleasure of invention, but they impressed him enough to set him writing numerous imitations of them at the age of ten.

Despite this precocious start, the form of the novel was not to tempt Mauriac seriously for almost twenty more years, and during this time his literary taste was being formed by his reading in French classics. At Grand-Lebrun he was introduced to Pascal and Racine who were to affect him profoundly, not so much by providing him with literary models as by furnishing him with a point of view. Referring to the strict religious practice of his mother and to the dramatic extremes of fear and love which colored family piety, Mauriac says that he was well prepared to fall under the spell of Pascal. The Brunschvicg school edition of *les Pensées* has never left his bedside, and he refers to Pascal as "the writer to whom I owe the most, who has most permanently left his mark upon me, and who has been my master since my sixteenth year" [*Ce gue je crois*].

If Pascal's influence was capital in shaping his religious attitude, Racine's was even more important in forming his artistic outlook. Mauriac states that he knows Racine "from the inside," and from his first encounter with the plays in the school curriculum he felt that he had been penetrated by Racine's tragic sense "to the very marrow-bones" ["Préface," *Oeuvres Complètes,* Vol. VIII]. He assures us that on an adolescent level the Racinian type of conflict between conscience and the passions was lived out with great intensity in a religious college like his own. And in a poem in *L'Adieu à l'adolescence* he says that at sixteen Racine's heroines awakened him to the life of the passions. When he seriously began to write, he found that his novels proceeded directly from Racine's dramas, and he has often acknowledged that Racine's characters, Phèdre in particular, have served as inspiration for his own creation. Moreover, as he advanced in his literary career he felt that Racine's problems as a Catholic writer, led by his artistic vocation to delineate the passions, tallied so closely with his own difficulties that when, in 1926, he was asked to write a biography, the method he employed was to reconstruct Racine's interior life by thinking constantly of his own.

It was really lyric poetry, however, that first captured Mauriac's imagination and fixed his desire to write. In his lonely days at Grand-Lebrun he fortified his solitude with poetry: "I interposed between myself and reality all the lyricism of the last century. Lamartine, Musset, Vigny . . . " [*Commencements*]. Mauriac's father, alone among his family, had been well-read, and it was in his library that, at fifteen, he discovered Baudelaire and Rimbaud, whose books had hitherto been classed as *les mauvais livres*. The former led him out of childhood into the fallen world, into "the world of sin." The latter represented to his growing dislike of the bourgeois climate of Bordeaux, and the indifference of his next of kin, the romantic image of the artist in revolt. Yet despite the fact that the influence of both poets came early and remained a strong undercurrent, the experience that they dealt with remained foreign to him, and their full effect on him was delayed.

When he began to write poetry himself during his last years at Grand-Lebrun, he turned to more modest regional models. In Francis Jammes he discovered tender and simple love of the Girondin countryside, of that nature which had remained his own first love, even beyond his love of books. "Nothing can change the fact of my indebtedness to him in that secret order of things that is at the very heart of one's inspiration," Mauriac writes.

> His verse . . . may not have modified my vision of the world, but it taught me that I could express it in the plainest terms without falling back on the clichés of romanticism. Jammes revealed to me that to write would mean directly expressing what I felt with all the fervour of a country-bred child. He showed me the path which was to become my own, and which was to lead me through the tangible world of nature to the world of human passion. Already at college I knew from Racine that there was nothing more wonderful than to be able to give the passions visible form in invented character. . . . But through Jammes I discovered that human feelings and the moods of nature would fuse together in the novels I would write, and that it would be my special artistic province to so combine them. [Mauriac, in his "Préface" to *Clara d'Ellébeuse* (1958) by Francis Jammes]

In the works of another poet of the southwest, Maurice de Guérin, whom Mauriac felt he knew "from the inside" ["Préface," *Oeuvres Complètes,* Vol. VIII], he found an even more intense expression of this communion with the natural world. "De Guérin not only made us sensitive to the beauty of external nature as the great romantics had done," he writes of himself and two young poet friends, André Lafon and Jean de la Ville de Mirmont, "he initiated us to the mute passions of the earth. He gave to our frail and humiliated adolescence the giddy certitude that we were the conscience of the vegetal world. It was through us that the trees tortured by the Atlantic wind and the hills shadowed by the flying clouds knew themselves . . . " ["Avant-Propos," in *Le Cahier vert* (1947) by Mauriac de Guérin].

But although Mauriac felt himself in close correspondence with nature, he was prevented by the Jansenist in him, by the influence of Pascal, from following de Guérin in his paganism. Andwhile sympathizing with de Guérin's romantic idealism and his rejection of the compromises of the adult world, one side of his nature was ambitious for success and esteem; he was drawn by the doctrine of Barrès and his *culte du moi* to exalt his own individuality and to covet the glory and influence that usually accompany the careers of professional writers in France. On the positive side of the balance he writes of Barrès: "Without the influence of this disciple of Pascal, everything human would never have become for me the object of such an ardent curiosity" ["Discours de réception à l'Académie Françaite," in *Oeuvres Complètes,* Vol. VIII]. More critically, he speaks of himself in his twenties as being "the perfect little Barrèsian ["Prè-face," *L'Élève Gilles* (1956) by André Lafon], conditioned by "the ruminations of a scrupulous

Catholicism to read Barrès's breviary of egotism like an open book" ["Mes premières années à Paris," *Le Figaro,* February 24, 1940].

Mauriac's early fiction resounds with echoes of his literary favorites and current reading. In the course of his first short novel, *Young Man in Chains* (1913), the twenty-year-old hero, Jean-Paul Johanet, finds occasion to quote from Jammes, Pascal, Verlaine, Laforgue, Balzac, LaFontaine (and Mauriac), and to refer respectfully to Chateaubriand, Lacordaire, Montalembert, Henri Perreyve, Baudelaire, Huysmans, Barrès, Maeterlinck, Romain Rolland, Gide and Claudel. Although Mauriac himself was saturated in literature at this time, he was nervously aware of the dangers of such over-exposure. In fact, the central theme of the novel is the conflict between the power of literature over the hero and the call to a life of action, and through the character of Jean-Paul, Mauriac analyzes his own situation as he hesitated in his mid-twenties on the threshold of a life of letters.

"He swims in a tide of books and spends long afternoons alone analysing his empty, complicated little mind," one of the characters says of Jean-Paul, a remark which must have given Mauriac a shiver of self-contemptuous delight. Jean-Paul who "throughout a quiet and lonely childhood . . . had got into the habit of watching himself live," believes his only happiness to lie "in examining myself by the light of what I find in the books I most adore." His cousin, Marthe, warns him that he is a victim of his reading, that he takes his books too seriously, that he talks like a book, and his only rejoinder is to assert complacently: "You're right, Marthe, I've got printer's ink in my veins instead of blood!"

Jean-Paul's infatuation with literature is not innocuous. It sustains him in a self-centered universe and in a kind of emotional vacuum which often borders on despair. One of his friends, Vincent Hiéron, a rather smug young religious zealot, analyzes Jean-Paul's trouble in the following terms: "The love of books, when all's said and done, Jean-Paul, is just love of oneself. One reads only those authors in whom one sees oneself reflected. But worshipping himself, a man fails to live because he is his own prisoner. Before any of us can truly live he must renounce self. . . . And he tries to win Jean-Paul's enthusiasm for an altruistic Christian-Socialist movement called *Amour et Foi* to which he is committed.

He briefly succeeds, and Jean-Paul becomes an ardent disciple. But accompanying, and perhaps growing out of, his love of literature is an acid self-critical sense which he finds he cannot help turning on the idealistic "Cause" of *Amour et Foi.* His cynicism results in his expulsion from the movement. Having failed "to free himself from himself" and "live" in a spiritual sense, Jean-Paul seeks escape by trying to lose himself in the pleasures of the body. He takes a mistress and lives a life of forced gaiety in Paris. But again he is too self-conscious to succeed. He experiences nothing but an "artificial passion" which is "pieced together. . . from odds and ends of literary memories," and in the end is forced to see himself as "an exile even from the world of human love."

Finally he is rescued from this impasse by an act of Grace, by "the awakening of his religious consciousness." At first, true to his habit of self-examination, he is skeptical of its validity, and wonders if he was "just yielding to it with the shrewdness, the ability he always had to fabricate emotions, to deceive himself." But this time he senses a difference: "At this moment, of all the petty dodges learnt from books, nothing remained." The conversion is a lasting one. His interior change is seconded externally by Marthe's patient love which is now revealed to him, and the young man in chains discovers that "on that day when my thoughts became centered upon Marthe with a tender and a fixed concern, I began to be delivered from myself."

The genuine part of this novel is not the liberation but the chains. Jean-Paul's conversion is literature, contrived to round out the novel. His doubts about being able to come to terms with reality, the curse of incessant introspection, and his mistrust of the literary quality of all his experience reveal the true preoccupations of the young author. These themes run like an obsessive undercurrent through the next three novels. [Note] the curious disability of Jacques, hero of *The Stuff of Youth* (1914), who cannot react spontaneously to those who love him, but must wait for the intervention of death, either real or figurative, before he can shape a suitable emotional response. The narrator in his fourth novel, *Questions of Precedence* (1921), is one of the same species and speaks of "those of my race who suffer from the melancholy mania of worshiping that part of themselves that is already dead. They are alive with memories, images, and anterior sensations like badly embalmed corpses." This same character refers to himself elsewhere as to "one whom reading has dispensed from living." And Edward Dupont-Gunther, a major figure in the intervening novel, *Flesh and Blood* (1914-1920), is a brooding, self-absorbed young man like Jean-Paul who is addicted to literature and has so feeble a hold on reality that, following his morbid penchant, he is led to commit suicide.

In these various characterizations Mauriac explored his own conscience. Unlike Jean-Paul after his conversion, he was by no means free from the prison of himself. He saw that, committed to the passive life of a writer, liberation in art or in action, as he had invented it for Jacques's father, the South Seas painter in *The Stuff of Youth*, or for Augustin, hero of *Questions of Precedence* (like Rimbaud, Augustin abandons himself to an inconspicuous and laborious life in Africa), would never be his except in imagination. At about the same time, or a little earlier, he must have given up hopes of a direct religious vocation. Jacques in *The Stuff of Youth* speaks of a Jesuit priest as having "infected me with his own passion for souls." But he adds, "his attitude was one of absolute detachment. I, on the other hand, though I did not know it, was less moved by love than by curiosity." Mauriac, aware of this distinction, decided, as for himself, that he would try to surpass Jacques's mere quisitiveness, or at any rate, if he was to remain a prisoner it would not be to the kind of listless and sickly curiosity that had ruined Edward in *Flesh and Blood*. Short of a vocation to the religious life, in his fiction he would try to give the passion for self-analysis and the "taste for the delicious pleasure which comes from

probing into the intricacies of human souls" [*Young Man in Chains*] a Christian orientation.

At the time of Jean-Paul Johanet's conversion, his friend Vincent invokes the enduring power of a Catholic childhood over one's adult life and refers to it as to an imprisonment of a different kind. "No man can serve two masters," he apostrophizes, adding in his preachy way, "Is it not that truth which now torments you? You cannot escape it. It holds you prisoner. . . ." This same truth was to torment Mauriac far into his career, as will be seen in a later chapter, but at least he had fixed a goal for himself. Years later, writing of this period in his life he expressed his attitude in these words: "I took stock of my resources. And my first decision was, whatever happened, never to let go the hand of God . . . I determined that I would no longer let questions of faith arise for me, but that my destiny should be played out in the borderland between nature and Grace, and that I would resign myself to live in the shadow that the cross throws over a human life" ["La Rencontre avec Barrès," *Oeuvres Complètes,* Vol. IV].

Resigned to his faith, he also resigned himself to a life of literary introspection. "We all belong to the heritage of Rousseau," he wrote [in "Hommage à Charles du Bos," *Qu'est-ce que la littérature* (1945)], and felt that the greatness and the peril of a literary vocation lay in audacious and sincere self-revelation which must, however, be undertaken with the maximum of lucidity and the minimum of self-indulgence. To write, for an artist of his kind, would be not so much deliverance as surrender of himself: on the one hand to the exigencies of his art, on the other to the curiosity of his public. This sort of self-exposure would require the greatest self-knowledge and the greatest self-discipline. "The perfection of art," he wrote, "is to take those morbid inclinations which threatened to destroy you, isolate them, contain them, and make them serve, on the contrary, to release in you a vital, life-giving power" ["Le Jeune homme," *Oeuvres Complètes,* Vol. IV].

It was in these terms that Mauriac began to voice the debate between the idea of a life devoted to action and a life devoted to literature. Much more of a struggle is implied in his attempts to resolve it than in the simple intervention of Grace that dispels Jean-Paul's difficulties. Not only was this sense of strain to be felt in every succeeding examination of his literary vocation, but it was also to nourish many of the conflicts of his forthcoming fiction.

Young Man in Chains is partly based on the private journal which Mauriac kept during his last year at Grand-Lebrun, and he recognizes in Jean-Paul the most authentic characterization of his four early novels. The hero's experiences not only reveal the state of his author's mind, but also provide a point of departure for a brief review of some of the actual circumstances of Mauriac's literary debut. The part of the novel which deals with *Amour et Foi* is a fictionalized account of Mauriac's association with the *Sillon* movement under the direction of Marc Sangnier (Jérôme in the novel) before its condemnation by Rome in 1906. The rest of the novel is drawn from his first impressions of Paris where he had gone in 1906, after completing a *licence ès lettres* at the University of Bordeaux, with the intention of preparing a diploma at the École des Chartes. A small inheritance made him financially independent, however, and after qualifying in the entrance examinations, he decided to abandon his studies and devote himself entirely to literature. For three years he led a leisurely and introspective life, much like that of the hero of his novel. He busied himself with the affairs of a Catholic students' group, Cercle Montalembert, and published a few poems and critical articles in its review. On the side he began to make contacts which would later permit him to enter the thorny labyrinth of Parisian literary society. During his third year in Paris he attracted the attention of C.-F. Caillard, editor of *La Revue du Temps Présent,* who gave him the job of reviewing poetry for the magazine and sponsored the publication of his first volume of verse, *Les Mains Jointes,* which appeared in November, 1909, when Mauriac had just turned twenty-four.

In later years Mauriac judged this verse very severely, writing that he had "stepped on to the literary scene an angelic cherubim, fresh from the sacristy" [*Dieu et Mammon*], and deploring the facility of its "spineless" technique, as well as the timid sentimentality of its religious outlook. When the book was reprinted in March, 1910, however, it was enthusiastically reviewed by one of Mauriac's adolescent idols, none other than Maurice Barrès, who forecast that his future would be "easy, open, assured and glorious" ["La Rencontre avec Barrès"].

Barrès's approval was an important first step in the fulfillment of this prophecy. From that time on, more and more doors were open to Mauriac; he began to frequent literary circles and to publish in better known reviews. In May, 1911, a second volume of verse, *L'Adieu à l'adolescence,* appeared; in November of the same year he contributed his first fiction (a chapter from what was to be *The Stuff of Youth*) to *La Revue Hebdomadaire.* This was followed by the serialization of *Young Man in Chains* in the *Mercure de France* in June, 1912, and by a second installment of *The Stuff of Youth* in the *Revue de Paris* in October. After this he published little more verse. By the age of twenty-six the change from poet to novelist was well begun.

This metamorphosis, for all that it is a common one, deserves some attention. "If I am first of all a poet," Mauriac wrote in the year of his Noble prize, "and that is something that I, at any rate, have never questioned, I have never deliberately betrayed poetry for the novel." And yet, though the poetic quality of Mauriac's prose is indisputable, it is a fact that, as Mauriac admits, "it was fiction and not poetry which released in me that irresistible revelation of the inmost self, that cry which a man in the grips of inspiration cannot hold back" ["Vue sur mes romans," *Le Figaro,* November 15, 1952].

What exactly is the relationship between the lyrical and the narrative mode of expression in Mauriac's experience? On the surface the change from one to the other seems largely to be an effect of age. As an adolescent, interested in nothing so much as himself, Mauriac sought to define

his sensations by finding their reflection in nature. He made a fetish of his solitude and his sense of difference, and this decided the subject and the mood for most of his early poetry. As revealed in the heroes of his first novels, he felt himself to be alone, even in love, and his soul-searching, his joys and his griefs were almost invariably private and self-centered. While with one side of himself he believed in the universal validity of his experience, with another he held as fervent a faith in his own singularity. Like the romantic poet, he remade the world in his own image and became self-consciously immanent in everything that he created, while the exterior world tended to fade or be transformed by the uniqueness of his own subjective vision.

In retrospect, Mauriac speaks of himself at this time as being under the spell of "a certain type of romanticism which at my age seems to be the very height of absurdity and foolishness"[*Mémoires intérieurs*]. Although he still acknowledges his debt to his early masters, Jammes and de Guérin, he describes the truth of their work as "the truth of sensation." And while it is too simple to suggest that his change in view from romanticism to realism was made through a transfer of allegiance from one poet to another, his description of Baudelaire, "who was my hero as a young man," points up the change in emphasis:

> Baudelaire is the poet of the real, so little romantic that the very language created by his poetry for its purpose is the nearest thing to prose that any poet has ventured to use, the most "figurative"—to use the modern jargon, always strictly controlled by the object. . . . Whatever its nature, Baudelaire saw it with an unswerving eye, smelt it, touched it, and showed it *sub specie aeternitatis* as Van Gogh did his kitchen chair. [*Mémoires intérieurs*]

A change in interest of this order stimulated Mauriac's growing interest in fiction in his mid-twenties. Though the poet in him was still very much alive, he began to shed some of his romantic self-centeredness in his first experiments in prose. He began to see his lonely childhood in perspective as an object, not just as a theme. He recalled in detail the facts and people of his early years, as well as his own moods and emotions, now somewhat objectified in memory. He remembered the fascination with which he had listened to the adult members of his family as a child. He speaks of having been "passionately interested in grown-ups," because they were, to his eyes, deeply engaged in the drama of living, and, even more—since to him they seemed to be close to death—dangerously involved in the drama of salvation. He recalled, too, their stories of local and family history, "of which I have made great use in my work," and he now feels that his own narrative instinct was cultivated by listening to these family raconteurs. From these elements he began to build up his first novels.

The transition from poet to novelist was a gradual one however. It is carried on throughout the first four novels, and in them one can observe a developing process of objectification, particularly in regard to the creation of character. *Young Man in Chains,* Mauriac's first novel, is little more than a transcription into prose of Mauriac's self-analysis in verse. Jean-Paul is patently a self-portrait and the only significant character in the novel, eclipsing all the other figures who exist only as signposts and sounding-boards for his own development. The author is not yet disengaged from his hero whose self-questionings remain fluid, imprecise, and troublesome beyond the requirements of the characterization. And although Mauriac employs the third person narrative technique in an attempt to distance himself from his subject, it is constantly being interrupted by telltale interior monologue in which the author continues his own unresolved debate. . . .

In the best of his characterizations Mauriac strikes a dynamic balance between subjectivity and objectivity, between identification with his fictional creatures and detachment from them. He might learn from the disciplines of objectivity how to create convincingly not only characters who resembled him in some way but also a wide variety of types drawn from outside his own immediate experience. But in so doing he felt he must describe these characters "from the inside," must "draw [them] out of his own substance" ["Le province," *Oeuvres Complètes,* Vol. IV]. And he brought to the most objectively conceived of the characters in these early novels—to Florence, for instance, in *Questions of Precedence*—the same intense and deeply personalconcern for his subject as marked the best of his own lyric poetry. To have gained proficiency in the technique of objectivity was, in the end, to have mastered a device which would permit him to penetrate even further into his own private world.

Harry T. Moore (essay date 1966)

SOURCE: "'The Chemistry of Conscience': François Mauriac, Georges Bernanos, Julien Green," in *Twentieth-Century French Literature to World War II,* Southern Illinois University Press, 1966, pp. 96-118.

[*An American educator, critic, and author, Moore is best remembered for his studies of the life and works of D. H. Lawrence, though he also wrote and edited books on John Steinbeck, E. M. Forster, Lawrence Durrell, Rainer Maria Rilke, and other authors. In the following excerpt, Moore surveys Mauriac's body of work and finds that, despite a predilection toward didacticism, it is populated with compelling characters and offers trenchant psychological insights.*]

Nietzsche's phrase, the chemistry of conscience, might usefully describe the work of François Mauriac, Georges Bernanos, and Julien Green. It is the Catholic conscience, in Mauriac the struggle of sensuality and passion against religion, in Bernanos of greed and lack of reason against the realization of good, in Green (especially in his later books) of assurance against emptiness.

Mauriac, eldest of the three, was born in 1885 at Bordeaux, whose area provides the sandy, pine-rimmed coast and the sloping vineyards which appear so often in his novels, as well as the old stone city itself. Mauriac, fatherless before

---

Artistic Compromise in Mauriac's fiction:

Mauriac's writing has always been for him a sort of self-exorcism. He defines his literary creations as his own monsters, the most impure part of himself. Hence the world he shows us is exclusively that of sin, his characters mortal wretches harassed by their consciences and their lusts. The freedom that Mauriac, as a Christian, is bound to give them is more apparent than real, for Christian free-will turns out in his novels to be simply a question of ambivalent feelings. Not one of his creatures is actually free, and, as one senses from the beginning, their destiny is unalterable. Even their crimes are passive crimes. Perhaps, as Jean-Paul Sartre has suggested, Mauriac's refusal to let his characters act as free agents is a basic flaw in his art as well as a metaphysical error.

Laurence LeSage, "A Catholic View of Mayhem," in Saturday Review, *April 5, 1952.*

---

he was two years old, was brought up by his stringently Catholic mother. He was educated at parochial schools and at the Bordeaux lycée. He went to Paris as a young man and began his literary career with two volumes of poetry, *Les Mains jointes* (1909; *With Clasped Hands*) and *l'Adieu à l'adolescence* (1911; *Farewell to Adolescence*). Paul Bourget and Maurice Barrès praised the writings of the new author, who soon turned to fiction, after helping to found (in 1912) a Catholic literary magazine, *Les Cahiers* (*Notebooks*). His early novels, such as *l'Enfant chargé de chaînes* (1913; *The Child in Chains*), lack the force of his postwar work; it was not until *Le Baiser au lépreux* (1922; *A Kiss for the Leper*) that he produced a novel which was at once a public and an artistic success. During the First World War, while stationed in Macedonia as a hospital assistant, he had written the material later published as *Petits Essais de psychologie religieuse* (1920; *Little Essays on Religious Psychology*), in which he worked out his moralistic determinations.

Mauriac's first two novels after the war, *La Chair et le sang* (1920; *Flesh and Blood*) and *Préséances* (1921; *Precedences*), exalted the senses and all the physical aspects of existence, as did a somewhat better book, *Le Fleuve de feu* (1923; *The River of Fire*), the story of the pleasure-seeking Daniel and the virgin Gisèle who, after giving herself to him, retires into a life of renunciation. But this was not so impressive a novel as its predecessor, *A Kiss for the Leper,* which depicts the miseries of an ugly man, Jean Peloueyre, unhappily married to a peasant girl; when he dies, partly because he is broken by life, he leaves her his money on condition that she will never remarry; Noémi, the wife who has given herself out of charity to the lust of her unattractive husband, accepts the terms of the will and piously devotes herself to his memory. In 1923, Mauriac published another story of the same family, of the Cazenave branch that had brought up Jean Péloueyre: *Genitrix,* brought out in English with the earlier book as *The Family.* In *Genitrix,* Jean's cousin Fernand, whose far younger wife dies during an unhappy marriage, has always been dominated and even obsessed by his mother. He now withdraws from her and she too dies, defeated in her autocratic selfishness. There is a bit of fine irony at the mother's funeral when Fernand, leaning over his mother's grave as her body is lowered into it, secretly tries to see, down in the darkness, the coffin of his wife. Later, Fernand is painfully alone in the dismal house, from which in a rage he even banishes the old servingwoman who, in her way, represents the earth mother, the genitrix. But at the end of the story she returns and goes to Fernand's room with a lighted lamp such as Fernand and his mother used to carry across the courtyard.

Both these books—*A Kiss for the Leper* and *Genitrix*—are heavy with the atmosphere of that bleak country house in the Bordeaux region; *A Kiss for the Leper* has some scenes in Paris, where Jean lives for a while unhappily. But Mauriac is best when dealing with characters living in les Landes, the desolate countryside around Bordeaux. Atmosphere and the psychology of sin are indeed Mauriac's strong points; sometimes the moralistic novelist intrudes, as in one of his weaker stories, *Le Mal* (1924; *The Enemy*), in which, after describing the appearance of a young woman, the novelist steps between her and the reader with a comment: "Sin is, in its fashion, a form of life. Such a thing as *infernal* Grace exists, and it can give life, as long as necessary, that attractive form which, according to St. Catherine of Siena, stinks in all its parts."

In 1925, the year in which the Académie française awarded Mauriac its Grand Prix du Roman, he brought out one of his most powerful novels, *Le Desert de l'amour (The Desert of Love)*. This begins with an important recognition: in a Paris bar, with a Negro jazz orchestra playing in the background, the thirty-five-year-old Raymond Courrèges sees a woman he had been in love with when he was an adolescent in Bordeaux. Maria Cross has aged, but is still beautiful; she is with her husband, whom Raymond remembers as a Bordelais, Victor Larousselle. Maria has identified Raymond and recalls her acquaintanceship with him. They had often traveled together on a trolley car to a Bordeaux suburb, and first saw one another in that vehicle crowded with workingmen with coal-blackened faces. Maria, then the mistress of the wealthy merchant Larousselle, liked Raymond when she came to know him, for he was sensitive and enthusiastic. Maria wasn't leading her life as a mistress out of emphatic preference, but largely out of weariness; she had never yearned for anything in life except peace and quiet. Her ennui was something which the boy helped to dispel. He saw her as a figure of evil and became obsessed with her; the relationship ended one day after he tried to force himself upon her.

All this is reflected in flashbacks as Raymond sits watching her in the bar. Years before in Bordeaux, Raymond's father, a doctor, was also in love with Maria, in a different way, more idealistically, the late love of middle age. But ultimately he was, in his own way, as futile and fumbling as his son, though Maria had a high regard for him. The doctor, reflecting the imagery of the story's landscape, at one point says that he has always been cut off from those

he has ached to possess—the region stretching between them and him is one of fetid swamp and mud.

In the Paris bar, Larousselle has drunk too much and is taken ill; Raymond helps Maria to get him to their apartment. Their own doctor can't be located, so Raymond calls his father who, he remembers, has come to a medical congress and is at a Paris hotel. While waiting for his father to arrive, Raymond is led by Maria into a side room where he must wait, isolated as always in the desert of love. His father attends to the patient, then makes a fumbling attempt to resume acquaintanceship with Maria, who politely puts him off. Father and son step out together into the Paris night to get a taxi. The father has decided to leave at once for Bordeaux; the son explains that he will soon be managing director of a factory. Later Raymond walks alone through the streets of dawn, inhabited only by the men who clean the city and by the market gardeners; he looks back across a life that has been barren because he has made every woman he has ever known pay for Maria Cross, who still obsesses him. Impulsively, Raymond goes to the railway station to see his father leave, and for a moment in the corridor of the train the two men, fellow wanderers in the desert of love, attain an understanding they have never had before.

In 1925, the year of *The Desert of Love,* Mauriac also brought out *Orages (Storms)*, one of his weaker novels, but two years later he followed this with one of his most powerful works of fiction, the novella *Thérèse Desqueyroux,* translated into English, together with several other stories about the name character—the last of them *La Fin de la Nuit* (1935; *The End of the Night*)—and put into a single novel as *Thérèse*. The volume tends to seem formless, and yet the book is more than a mere chronicle of the experiences of Thérèse, ending when she is about to die. The development of her character—or rather its very failure to develop through experience, while at the same time it deteriorates—gives the book an almost visible shape.

A girl from a well-to-do family, Thérèse Larroque has married the landowner and sportsman, Bernard Desqueyroux, who is sexually a young bull, outraging the sensibilities of his convent-schooled bride. She is something of an intellectual, while Bernard's only interests, except for his animal gratifications, which include gluttony, are the estate and duck hunting. The term of Julien Benda comes to mind—*bovarysme*, the provincial woman seeing herself in the grand image—but the troubles of Thérèse are far more complicated than this, and the author never quite diagnoses them. He prefers to remain in this case the pure novelist recording events that comprise the mystery of character. Thérèse herself, for example, never quite knows why she poisons her husband: the deed is simply part of what she is.

The poison, a prescription she forged, doesn't kill Bernard, who makes a court fight to save Thérèse, not for her own sake, but for the family's honor. After her acquittal she is kept a prisoner in one of those gloomy houses in the Guyenne countryside which supply Mauriac with so many of his settings. Her small daughter Marie is taken away from her, but Thérèse had never impressed those about her as being a devoted mother. At one point in her captivity, Thérèse starts to kill herself but the sudden occurrence of another event, the abrupt death of her aunt, stops her. Her jailers, the Desqueyroux family, know nothing of her suicide attempt, but suspect trouble and finally decide to send her to Paris. Bernard accompanies her, and as they sit together at the Café de la Paix they come closer to rapport than ever before in their married life. Bernard keeps asking her why she poisoned him, and she tries to answer, but her effort to simplify her motives by examining and explaining them drives her further into confusions, though she does once plainly say that she is sorry for what she did. Bernard leaves her, and she drifts to a restaurant in the rue Royale for lunch, to begin her life as a Parisienne. She realizes that, although her ordeal has left marks upon her, she is still young.

This section of the novel, as first published separately, ends here. The early part of it has been told in a flashback, as Thérèse sits aboard the train from Bordeaux to the provincial town where her husband and his family await her. Thérèse is not beautiful, but everyone is susceptible to her charm. She has a small nose, overlarge ears, and a high forhead several times described as magnificent.

In one of her later adventures she is seen in a climax of hysteria in a Parisian psychiatrist's office; her confession, the story of her increasingly sordid love affairs, is all the more effective because it is presented through the consciousness of the doctor's wife, who eavesdrops and judges not only Thérèse but her own ineffectual husband. In still another escapade, Thérèse is on the Riviera in a brief, not fully realized, erotic experience with a boy of twenty whose attitude to her is strikingly similar to that of the young Raymond Courrèges toward Maria Cross in *The Desert of Love.* Another young man falls in love with Thérèse in the last of the episodes relating to her, *The End of the Night.* There is a further parallel with *The Desert of Love* in that it repeats the theme of parent and child both entangled with the same person. In this case it is the youthful Georges Filhot, loved by Thérèse's daughter Marie, now entering young womanhood and escaping from the Bordeaux region to visit her mother's left-bank apartment. Georges, on meeting Thérèse, falls in love with her although she points out the folly of a boy of twenty-two loving a woman of more than forty. At the high point of the narrative—Mauriac called it "the entire intention" of the story—Thérèse sits before Georges on a low stool and pulls the hair back from her large forehead, revealing her oversize, pale ears, and suddenly he sees how ravaged with age her once-magnificent forehead is, how old her hands are that fifteen years before had tried to deal out death. This is, Mauriac said (in the preface to this last part of the Thérèse story separately published in 1935), the one gesture she was capable of making, despite her wretchedness, to fight against her power of poisoning and corrupting the lives of others.

Thérèse, who has an ailing heart, goes back to her husband's house in Guyenne, to die; even before leaving Paris she is obsessed with fears of persecution, especially from the police. As the story concludes, she is visited by Georges as she lies on what she knows will be her deathbed; address-

ing him as "my dear," she tells him she waits for "the end of life, the end of the night."

In spite of their scattered and often elliptic quality, the episodes gathered together as the novel *Thérèse* comprise a powerful story, with an intensity rarely matched in the literature of the twentieth century. Here, Mauriac doesn't intrude with moral epigrams, as in so much of his writing, but lets the adventures of Thérèse work themselves out dramatically. He fought against the temptation to let doctrine interfere, something he mentions in at least two of the prefaces in the *Thérèse* series. In one of them (1927) he says he wishes that he could have shown Thérèse in sorrow turning her heart to God and perhaps becoming another Saint Locusta, a poisoner in Nero's time who through grace reached sanctity. In the 1935 preface to *The End of the Night,* Mauriac tells how Thérèse, weary of living ten years inside his brain, longed for death, which he had hoped could be a Christian death. He confesses that he had even written pages showing this, but had destroyed them. He adds that later he had met a priest in Rome who made it possible for him to see how Thérèse could enter "into the eternal radiance of death," a story he might perhaps tell someday.

Mauriac, who was awarded the Nobel Prize in 1952, continued to write excellent novels after the Second World War, among them *Le Sagouin* (1951; *The Little Misery*) and *l'Agneau* (1954; *The Lamb*), the latter another story of the power of diabolical fascination which some human beings have for others. In the postwar years Mauriac carried on the journalistic career he had begun with the résistance, writing for *le Figaro* and then for *l'Express,* creating a new rôle for himself as a frequent commentator not only on literature but also on public events.

As a novelist, Mauriac developed into a superb technician in the classical French tradition, writing with a cool prose, marked by understatement, even when dealing with vehement subject matter. He has earned consistent praise for this fine restraint of style. But he has also been strenuously criticized, notably by the late Claude-Edmonde Magny and by Jean-Paul Sartre. Mlle. Magny delivered her objections in the magazine *Ésprit* in September, 1949, and Sartre expressed his in la *Nouvelle Revue française* in February, 1939, reprinting them in his book, *Situations,* in 1947. Sartre brought up a point frequently mentioned in connection with Mauriac, linking him with the Jansenists, that seventeenth-century sect opposed to the Jesuits and finally branded as heretical. The Jansenist doctrine had correspondences with Calvinism in that it expressed belief in predestination rather than in freedom of the will. Sartre's essay, which infuriated Mauriac and has drawn many rebuttals from him, is called "Mauriac et la liberté" ("Mauriac and Freedom"); it attempts to show that the characters of this novelist, all victims of original sin, have no freedom to develop, but are hopelessly doomed. There is certainly some truth in this criticism, but in spite of the imposition of moral doctrines, sometimes even didactically, the stories of Mauriac are compelling. Their characters have the intensity of those of the Russian novelists of the last century and are projected by someone who, for all his doctrinal bent, has a profound knowledge of modern psychological discoveries. And when the moralist hasn't interfered with the novelist, as in *A Kiss for the Leper* and *Thérèse,* and has simply shown the people and situations without the addition of moral dissertations, Mauriac has written novels of magnitude. If he is, after Gide, the most distinguished French man of letters of his time, he is, after Proust, the finest French novelist of his time.

J. E. Flower (essay date 1969)

SOURCE: "Introduction," in *Intention and Achievement: An Essay on the Novels of François Mauriac,* Oxford: Clarendon Press, 1969, pp. 1-8.

[*In the following excerpt, Flower discusses Mauriac as a "Catholic novelist."*]

With the exception of one of his earliest critics, Charles du Bos, and more recently Professor Stratford, and in spite of the apparent content of a number of critical studies, no commentators have paid adequate attention to the basic problem of the Catholic novel and to Mauriac's consideration of it. It has, to be sure, been acknowledged as a distinctive form but only in as much as it is a piece of writing which bears witness in some way to the Catholic faith. In other words it is a form of committed literature, but beyond this little attention has been given to the limiting effects of this commitment nor has the basic problem of incorporating a personal belief in a piece of imaginative literature in such a way that it does not obtrude been adequately examined. Sartre in his article 'Monsieur François Mauriac et la liberté' in which he accuses Mauriac of oversimplification and of manipulating his characters, certainly has some pertinent remarks to make, though, as Professor Stratford has pointed out, Mauriac was well aware of these difficulties and has not infrequently admitted that *La Fin de la nuit,* the target for Sartre's attack, is not one of his better novels. Professor Albert Sonnenfeld in an article 'The Catholic novelist and the Supernatural' [see *French Studies,* October, 1968] has indicated some of the characteristic features of this type of writing: the clumsy direct intervention of God's will through miraculous events or abrupt, unprepared conversions; the intervention by the author to point a moral or direct his reader's attention; the private unsolicited confession by letter or journal; the appeal made to an undefined deity or omniscient power; the more subtle use of allusion and symbol. Of these Mauriac's novels offer us many interesting examples. But it is not on account of such detail as this that the Catholic novel should be considered a distinct type in its own right,be found in literature which is in no way Catholic in inspiration. Moreover even within the relatively narrow context of French literature the term 'Catholic novel' is one to be used with some latitude and uncertainty. Indeed if we take for example Bernanos' *Sous le soleil de Satan,* a melodramatic, highly coloured clash between the forces of good and evil; Julien Green's *Moïra,* the account of the extreme effects of Protestantism on an American student; Cesbron's *Les Saints vont en enfer* which deals with the

problem of the worker priests and in some ways is little more than an elaborate form of semi-documentary writing, and *Le Nœud de vipères,* the intricate account of a personal recantation, we at once have four novels all of which have been labelled Catholic but which in style and form are quite different. The problem is clearly a large one and as far as Mauriac is concerned only Du Bos and Stratford have made any satisfactory attempts to solve it, but again each approach is limited. Du Bos' essay on the Catholic novel admits the essential problem of combining the 'éléments impurs' of human life and the revealed truth of the Catholic faith, but his *personal* acceptance of that faith at once places him in a position which will not necessarily be shared by all his fellow critics. His conviction that a Catholic has a greater understanding of life and therefore an advantage over the atheist novelist will clearly not be acceptable to all. Professor Stratford [in *Faith and Fiction,* 1963] also admits the basic problem and goes some way to analysing Mauriac's discussion of it, but he only really considers Mauriac's self-confessed Catholic novels as evidence for any claim that it may have been solved.

Mauriac's aims and intention as a novelist during some forty years of writing have been to exemplify to others his own firm conviction that mankind is assured of God's love: 'nous sommes aimés. Voilà le fond de tout.' 'Il nous dit Lui-même que le Fils de l'Homme est venu chercher et sauver ce qui était perdu, oui, *tout* ce qui était perdu, et non pas seulement tel ou tel à qui il aurait consacré en particulier une avare goutte de sang.' Yet against this stands his description of a particular segment of bourgeois society with its families decaying and doomed to extinction. This is the problem stated in its simplest terms and one of which Mauriac becomes increasingly aware in the course of his career. Implied values are not sufficient, particularly for the demanding Catholic critic, yet as a novelist Mauriac is very aware of the danger of didactic literature. His attempts to incorporate his personal faith in the public statements that are his novels are various: the semi-autobiographical account of his relationship with Social Catholicism as a young man, the harsh castigation of the attitude of mind which raises material values over spiritual ones, the idealized portrait of a family in *Le Mystère Frontenac,* or the allegory of Christ's passion in *L'Agneau.* Too frequently, however, such attempts are doomed to fail and Mauriac is open to the accusation of having implanted a particular point of view and in consequence of having falsified his picture of society. In order to avoid the charge of didacticism or of manipulation, therefore, the Catholic element of the novel must be included in such a way that it is an essential part of the structure of the book which without it would crumble. . . . . Mauriac succeeds by allowing a pagan natural cycle of events to carry a Christian message. It is not enough to argue that *Le Nœud de vipères* and *Les Anges noirs* are Catholic simply because they are 'fondés sur la Révélation'; what is essential is to ascertain how Mauriac has worked the forces of Grace into the novels in such a way that they have become an integral part of them. In this way for the critic who from the outset denies the value of the Catholic faith Mauriac's intention may remain unacceptable, but his achievement will none the less deserve acknowledgement.

On the dark quality of Mauriac's stories:

Shortly after winning the Nobel Prize for Literature in 1952, François Mauriac stated the theme of his work in an interview given to *The Paris Review:*

> I rediscover the narrow, Jansenist world of my devout, unhappy and introverted childhood. It is as though when I was twenty a door inside of me had closed forever on that which was going to become the material of my work.
>
> Grace H. Glaeck, in "A Mechanical
> Redemption," The New Republic,
> *February 6, 1956.*

Upon the world of his childhood, Mauriac, one of the best-known writers of the Catholic Renascence, has taken an epic revenge. He has rediscovered it as a stern, Augustinian sphere that fairly hisses with escaping evil, where sin is sin with no Freudian nonsense or excuse about it. Its bourgeois inhabitants, bred in guilt and nourished on despair, grope futilely for love and human communication throughout lives composed of faint-hearted marriages, vulgar spouses, sullen children, grasping land transactions, and occasional joyless bouts of the flesh in the rootless, iniquitous cities.

Though the men of his milieu are often monsters (a favorite Mauriac word) of spiritual, emotional and physical impotence, Mauriac reserves his real venom for the women. For when he is not mortifying their flesh, an art at which he is highly skilled, he is castigating them as watchdogs of the middle-class proprieties who have vulgarized religion into an empty ritual.

Maxwell A. Smith   (essay date 1970)

SOURCE: "The Short Stories," in *François Mauriac,* Twayne Publishers, 1970, pp. 121-28.

[*An American educator and critic, Smith was the author of* Short History of French Literature *(1924), the editor of* Short Stories by French Romanticists *(1929), and coedited* French Short Stories of the Second Half of the Nineteenth Century *(1932). In the following essay, he analyzes Mauriac's two short story collections,* Trois Recits *and* Plongées.]

I *Trois Récits* (1929)

Since Mauriac's most successful novels are brief or at least of medium length, it might be expected that he would find the genre of novella or *récit* appropriate to his type of composition. He has produced, however, only two volumes of short stories, *Trois Récits* (*Three Tales*) and *Plongées*. None of the first volume appear likely to add appreciably to his reputation in fiction. The first two tales in the earlier collection, **"Coups de couteau"** and **"Un Homme de lettres"** are so similar in plot that it is difficult not to confuse them in our memory.

"Coups de couteau" (**"Knife Blows"**) is less a story than the recital by a painter to his wife of his amorous desires and frustrations in regard to a young woman he had befriended and protected. Never, perhaps, has the author's irony shown itself more acerbic, never has he illustrated more convincingly his theory of the impossibility for two souls to understand and penetrate each other. Unable to comprehend why his confession of love for another and younger woman should distress the quiet serenity of his "patient Griselda" wife, the famous artist expresses his despair at being appreciated only through gratitude for his professional aid instead of having his passion reciprocated. In his preface Mauriac wonders if he has succeeded in rendering acceptable to the reader such *"muflerie"* [boorishness] on the part of the artist-husband. A short quotation, chosen almost at random, should suffice to prove that for most readers the author has not succeeded. When Louis observes to his delighted surprise that his wife has actually felt jealousy of the other woman:

> —You have then suffered a little, my poor Babeth? He repeated, "you have suffered"with a vague pleasure.

Then:

> —Andrée, *she* doesn't suffer. I have never had that happiness to see her suffer because of me. Yet nothing can be as reassuring as the tears of the other.

When at the end of **"Coups de couteau"** we witness the artist's joy at the telephone call from Andrée expressing her desire to see him again, we note the irony of his realization that her real purpose was only to confide in him the anguish another had caused her. The tragic misunderstanding of these tortured souls comes full circle in the denouement.

"He began to walk back and forth in the studio, repeating one by one each word of Andrée, until he had extracted from them all the poison that was necessary for him to suffer."

The second story in this collection, **"Un Homme de lettres,"** differs from the first only in that its hero (or anti-hero) is an author rather than a painter, and its *souffre-douleur* or victim is not a wife but a faithful mistress of fifteen years' standing. Deserted by the man whose career she had worshiped, she is tortured primarily by the question of why Jérôme had abandoned her for an older woman with sickly children. She urges Mauriac to find out from Jérôme the answer to this mystery. The latter tells his friend that it is precisely because Gabrielle has surrounded him with such tranquillity and isolation from worldly cares, whereas it is in the confusion of a household filled with noisy children that he finds inspiration for his work. Apparently, however, the man of letters does not follow his own prescription, for some days after this conversation Mauriac receives a letter of gratitude from Gabrielle, thanking him for being the agent who brought about Jérôme's decision to put his second mistress with her children on the train to a health resort so that he could return to her. Lest we assume the permanence of this happy ending however, we read between the lines in the concluding sentence that Jérôme has already found another mistress. "The raised hand of Jérôme stopped a cab driver; but I could not hear the address which he gave in a low voice."

In these two stories of Parisian life the reader's lack of emotional involvement is due in part to the unsympathetic nature of the principal protagonists, in part perhaps because, like La Bruyère and the seventeenth-century moralists, Mauriac has given us abstractions, typical portraits of *the* artist, *the* man of letters. The third story, **"Le Demon de la connaissance,"** however, is more effective, not only because it is full of personal memories of Mauriac's own boyhood and Bordeaux background, but also because its young hero moves us deeply in his solitude and quest for perfection. While critics have reproached Mauriac for not giving a portrait of a pure intellectual, he tells us in his preface that this is exactly why he called this story the demon of knowledge: "a mind invaded, troubled, blinded by the exhalations of his blood, that is what one must seek in my sad hero."

In the opening pages with their depiction of the school days of young Maryan, viewed askance by the masters and proctors for his dreamy eccentricities and inability to conform to the rigid rules of the establishment, we may glimpse, no doubt, memories of Mauriac's own rather solitary childhood. Overcome with distaste and repulsion for an active career in the prosaic business world of his family, and attracted perhaps by the opportunity for solitude and the pursuit of knowledge, young Maryan chooses the quiet and austere cell of a seminary. After a few months, however, his independence of thought and his pursuit of new truths render him suspect to the pious fathers, who show him the door.

He arranges with his friend Lange to spend Easter vacation at the estate of his sister-in-law Mone, a confirmed invalid whose husband Robert visits her occasionally on weekends. Despite the chilly rain outside, Maryan rambles through the countryside, leaving his friend alone with Mone by the fireside. Climbing the stairs to the belfry of an almost abandoned church, he encounters a pair of lovers in passionate embrace. Returning to Mone's dwelling he sees through the window a pantomime in which Mone is obviously describing to his friend an attempt that Maryan, in a fit of youthful passion, had once made to embrace her. Furious at what he considers a betrayal, Maryan quarrels with his friend, who then decides to leave on the next morning's train.

When a letter arrives on the morrow announcing Robert's arrival for the weekend, the sudden joy which lights up Mone's pallid face convinces Maryan of his unimportance in her life. Yes, it must be true as Lange had so tactlessly told him, that he was destined never to inspire love. Heartsick at the collapse of his amorous ambitions, discouraged by his consciousness that his search for God had been in vain, Maryan climbs once more to the top of the belfry, thinking of suicide to escape this world full only of emptiness. Suddenly, however, he sees resplendent before him a celestial Face; he feels that he is loved and that he is no longer alone.

As epilogue, the last sentence in the story suggests the ultimate fate of this young seeker after God: "He did not see in his mind that trench in the earth, where, a few seconds before the attack, a few minutes before being struck down, he would repeat in a medium voice the most beautiful words that the war has inspired in a man about to die: 'At last! I am going to know.'"

II *Plongées* (1938)

"Thérèse must be your favorite character, M. Mauriac, since you have made her the heroine in four of your works, besides her brief appearance in *Destins*." "No," he answered this writer, "but I feel such immense pity for her." The two short stories concerning Thérèse were written in 1933 and are the first two tales included in Mauriac's second volume of short stories which appeared five years later. In his preface, Mauriac states that he has written these two *plongées* into the obscure period of her life in answer to those who have questioned him about her fate. In **"Thérèse chez le docteur"** some ten or eleven years have elapsed since the end of *Thérèse Desqueyroux*. Thérèse calls late at night upon a psychiatrist, Dr. Schwartz, in a despairing effort to receive guidance concerning a crisis she is facing. Haggard and distraught, she relates her bohemian existence in the night life of Paris, her unhappy liaison with Jean Azévédo—whom we remember for his role of catalyst for her revolt in the novel—and her present anguished efforts to retain the affections of Phili. The latter, a sordid wastrel in the toils of some financial imbroglio, has returned to Thérèse in hopes of pecuniary aid from her estate; and in default of this, having learned of her early crime, he wants her assistance in poisoning his blackmailer. When Dr. Schwartz greets this confession with scornful laughter and cynically advises her to get what she wants from Phili without acceding to his demands, Thérèse in disgust makes a movement toward her purse which the doctor, terrified, misinterprets as a gesture toward a revolver. At his frightened outcry his wife rushes in, convinced now of his shallow cynicism and cowardice, and compassionately conducts the disillusioned Thérèse to the elevator.

The second of these short stories, **"Thérèse à l'hotel,"** takes place a few months later. Recounted in the first person by Thérèse herself, this brief anecdote shows us a Thérèse temporarily calmed by the suicide of Phili but depressed by the ravages of time which show only too clearly in her mirror. A strange rebirth of hope and tenderness surges forth in her heart as she observes the passionate gaze of a youth of eighteen resting upon her. Through a bit of feminine strategy she engages him in conversation and arranges a rendezvous for that evening. Before she can commit herself, however, she discovers that the young man's interest in her is purely spiritual and humanitarian, for he has seen in this middle-aged woman a fallen creature, a brand he would pluck from the burning. Furious at herself, even more furious with this "poor fool," Thérèse leaves in a rage to mourn the destruction of her illusions.

One critic at least found these incarnations of Thérèse possessed of more truth and carnal consistency than the earlier one. André Thérive was closer to recent critical evaluation in finding **"Thérèse chez le docteur"** melodramatic and unconvincing, as is usual when Mauriac tries to describe the fleshpots of Paris. In any case we have here a preparation for the appearance of Thérèse in *La Fin de la nuit.* Marked by Parisian dissipation and by the approach of middle age, Thérèse has become a truly pitiable personage, preserved by her intelligence from the depths of moral degradation but speaking now with an accent of coarseness and cynicism, still the prisoner of the crime committed so many years before. As pure narrative **"Thérèse chez le docteur"** is perhaps superior for the intensity with which it grips the reader, but for irony and pathos **"Thérèse à l'hotel"** is not entirely lacking in merit.

"Insomnie," written in 1927 as Mauriac tells us in the foreword to this volume, is less a short story than a *plongée* or descent "into the thickness of a life." According to the author,

> It is the chapter of a novel that I have not written, for which **"Coups de couteau"** might perhaps have been the prologue. Many destinies which are dramatic do not furnish material for a novel, because they lack events. The history of the hero of **"Insomnie"** can have only a chapter. His sorrow loses itself in the sand.

Louis (the same name as that of the hero in **"Coups de couteau,"** likewise a painter and therefore perhaps the same individual), furious at the conduct of his mistress who seems more interested in his comrades than in him, flees unceremoniously to his hotel room, hoping to escape his jealous torments through the medium of sleep. Alas, his vivid imagination forces him to toss restlessly until dawn, creating vivid pictures of his mistress in the company of a rival. He waits anxiously for the sound of the elevator which might betoken her arrival to console him, decides to break off future relations in order to allow his deep wounds to heal with time, then realizes that this solution is impossible since his fickle mistress has the rare faculty of knowing just how far she can push him before reopening his wound with protestations of tenderness. Just as we saw in **"Coups de couteau,"** a masterly analysis of masculine treachery, so in **"Insomnie"** we perceive the sharp scalpel of the author probing the depths of masculine jealousy and despair.

"Le Rang" (**"Rank"**), unlike its predecessor, is a well-constructed tale, perhaps the most successful of Mauriac's short stories. In Bordeaux or one of its suburbs, old Auguste Duprouy who has returned to the empty house after conducting the body of his sister Emma to the family vault in Langoiran where repose the remains of his father, mother, and sister Eudoxie, receives a visit of condolence from his cousin, Hector Bellade. In the act of relating calmly to Hector the tragic account of his life of frustration, he suddenly collapses in a faint. Hector, after seeking vainly any vestige of food or drink in the gloomy mansion, realizes that the old man is a victim of hunger. He takes him to a restaurant where, his vitality restored, Auguste proceeds to finish his sad tale.

His father's dying words had implored his mother to maintain her position in society at no matter what cost. This implacable old lady, who reminds us of the grim figure of Mme Cazenave in *Genitrix,* exerts a dominating role in control of the household. First she refuses to allow Emma and Eudoxie to give singing or piano lessons, since this would be considered retrogression from their social standard of respectability and decorum. Then she forces her son Auguste to renounce a brilliant career as scholar and teacher to accept a lucrative offer as traveling salesman for the great wine firm of Harry Maucoudinat. A final straw, which effectively breaks the back of Auguste's independence, is his mother's refusal to allow his marriage to the woman he loves, since this would entail the removal of mother and old-maid sisters to a comfortable nursing home.

Some months after this conversation it is discovered that Auguste had died alone in the desolate mansion three days before the neighbors found his emaciated corpse. Hector is deeply moved by the contrast with the radiant youth he had known in his childhood. A final ironic touch is afforded by his wife's decision, despite the heavy expense, to have the body transported to the family funeral vault at Langoiran. "He would have been pleased, poor old Auguste, if he had been able to foresee that he would rejoin his mother, Eudoxie, Emma for eternity." Hector asked, "Do you think so?"

In this mordant flagellation of pride and social prestige among the upper bourgeoisie Mauriac has returned to the theme of his early novel *Préséances* (in which the name of Harry Maucoudinat was also prominent).

A refreshing contrast to this stark tale of genteel poverty and bourgeois pride is the final **"Conte de Noël"** or **"Christmas Story"** which concludes the volume, with its delicate fragrance and nostalgic charm of Mauriac's own childhood in Bordeaux. As his seven-year-old comrades gather at the school preparatory to dismissal for the Christmas holidays, the overgrown bully Campagne jeers at little Jean de Blaye with his long silken tresses (which remind young Frontenac of little Lord Fauntleroy) and mocks his naïve belief that it is the little Jesus who descends in the chimney to fill his shoes with presents. Since his mother has told him this, Jean insists that it must be true, for his mother never lies. Nevertheless, Frontenac, whose skepticism has been aroused, persuades Jean to stay awake also on Christmas Eve in order to discover the truth. Little Frontenac does indeed perceive that it is his mother who performs this function, thinking him safely asleep, yet somehow he is not disillusioned for he feels in his mother the spirit of the Christ child.

On returning to school after New Year's Day, Frontenac finds a new Jean de Blaye, shorn of his curly locks, shorn also of his childlike faith. Their tender companionship has been broken, and since Jean's family soon leaves Bordeaux, Frontenac loses all contact with his chum. Many years later, when Frontenac (Mauriac) is a student in Paris celebrating Christmas Eve in a noisy bar, he encounters a youth whom he mistakes at first for Jean de Blaye, but who turns out to be his younger brother, Philippe. The latter tells him how Jean had been disillusioned, first by learning it was his mother after all who placed the presents, later that the family treasure box contained only his shorn locks, as if his mother wished always to keep him in her mind as a child. As he matured, little Jean had fallen into vice, and the last word they had received was of his death in a hospital in Saigon.

As Mauriac returned to his room, in spite of his desire for sleep he decided to write down this story of little Jean de Blaye. Creating in his imagination the details which led from that moment of disenchantment to Jean's death, after a misspent youth, in a Saigon hospital, "it is that night that I became a novelist, or at least that of this power. . . . A novelist had just been born and was opening his eyes upon this sad world."

Robert Speaight (essay date 1976)

SOURCE: "Thérèse Rediviva," in *François Mauriac: A Study of the Writer and the Man,* Chatto and Windus, 1976, pp. 116-29.

[*Speaight was a noted English actor and theater scholar. In the following excerpt, he discusses the composition of* La fin de la nuit—*a novel featuring the character Thérèse from* Thérèse Desqueyroux—*and the criticisms levelled against it by Jean-Paul Sartre.*]

[In 1933] Mauriac lifted the curtain on the creative process of the novelist in an essay, *Le Romancier et ses Personnages.* With the deliberate exception of *Le Mystère Frontenac,* he had proved that 'the novelist begins to take shape in us at the same time as we begin to detach ourselves from our own feelings.' In that conventional family of Frontenacs, he had been the spy—the traitor unconscious of his treachery—who captured, registered, and retained unawares the obscure complexity of daily life. He never conceived a novel without having clearly in his mind, down to its minutest detail, the house and surroundings where the action would take place. He admitted the monotony of atmosphere to which his choice of theme, place, and milieu condemned him; nor was it enough to reproduce, in one book after another, the properties he had known since he was a child. He invaded the houses of his neighbours, using as a theatre for some drama of intolerable tension the salon where old ladies had once offered him 'the finest muscat grapes, cream pastries, quince *pâtes,* and a large glass of slightly sickly *orgeat.*'

It was one thing to observe, another to transform. Thérèse Desqueyroux owed something to the poisoner he had watched at the Bordeaux assizes, but who had nothing in common with the character who did not herself know what had driven her to crime. If she had been living in Paris she would have known quite clearly, but in Paris it was 'difficult to imagine a rural world where a woman understands nothing of herself, once her feelings stray ever so little from the norm. Similarly, the central character of *Le Noeud de Vipères,* and the principal outlines of his story, were the fruit of observation; but once the character began to move he became totally different from his prototype. The novel was essentially the story of a recovery, and it finished

when the author had 'restored to my hero, to this son of darkness, his right to love and to illumination, and, in a word, to God'. Both he and Thérèse Desqueyroux were exempt from the one vice that Mauriac found it hard to put up with in a human being: 'complacency and self-satisfaction'.

If he were criticised for a monotony of characterization as well as of atmosphere, he accepted the charge and justified it. In Balzac and Tolstoy, Dickens and Dostoievsky, the same types recurred from one book to another. This was particularly true of *The Idiot.* And in his own case the principal character of *Le Noeud de Vipères* recalled, feature by feature, the principal character of **Génitrix**—and the echo was quite unintentional. It was the mark of a genuine novelist—the guarantee so to speak of his paternity—that the creatures of his imagination should exhibit a family likeness. Yet Mauriac was troubled by what appeared to him the inevitable bankruptcy of the novelist's art.

> On the one hand it claims to be the science of mankind— a swarming world which both persists and passes away—and all it can do is to isolate from the swarm, and fix under its magnifying glass a particular passion or virtue or vice which it amplifies out of all proportion: Père Goriot or a father's love, Cousin Bette or jealousy, Père Grandet or avarice. On the other hand—the novel claims to describe for us the life of society, and yet it never reaches individuals except by severing most of the roots which attach them to the group. In the word, the novel isolates and immobilises a passion in the individual, and it isolates and immobilises an individual in the group. And you can say that in doing so the painter of life expresses the contrary of what life really is.

This might be so, but Mauriac was encouraged by the survival—he would not have claimed the immortality—of certain of his characters. As always, he came back to Thérèse Desqueyroux. Why had she tried to poison her husband?

> The question mark has done much to preserve her melancholy shade in our midst. Several readers have looked to Thérèse for a light upon their own secret, or perhaps sought her as an accomplice. These characters are not sustained by their own life; it is our readers, and the anxiety of living hearts, that penetrate and animate these phantoms, allowing them to hover for a moment in some provincial salon, around the lamp where a young woman is lingering over her book, and pressing the paper knife against her burning cheek.

The secret of Mauriac's art was an intimacy with his characters, and like other intimacies it could not be forced. 'Why don't you draw some good people?' he was often asked; but he generally made a mess of his good people. 'Try to raise their moral stature'; but the more he did so, the more obstinately they declined even the most modest elevation; 'You never write about the people' objected the democratic reader, but Mauriac replied that it was absurd to write about a milieu that one did not know. He compared his attitude towards his characters to that of a 'strict schoolmaster' who found it hard not to show a secret preference for the more unmanageable pupils. At least he had Biblical warrant for his favouritism. The intimacies of literary creation raised problems of a moral and psychological order. The dispersal of the novelist through so many characters, and the ever closer identification with them, imperilled the unity of his personality. 'How much of him is left after these multiple and contradictory incarnations?' Proteus, in reality, was nobody, because he had the power to be everyone. Just because the novelist held himself open to every impression, at the disposal of any subject, the contradictions and the multiplicity of his creation must be organised around an 'unchanging rock'; or to be more precise, around an unchanging Person. *Le Romancier et ses Personnages* is a fascinating exercise in self-examination, but Mauriac was presently to discover that the public confession of these intimacies could not be undertaken without risk.

In his next novel, *La Fin de la Nuit* (1935), he yielded to temptation, and the temptress was Thérèse Desqueyroux. He confessed that whereas in the novel that bears her name she had imposed herself upon him, in the sequel he imposed himself upon her, and he was to pay dearly for the indiscretion. Everything essential had been said about Thérèse; what happened to her, how she lived and died, could have been left to the imagination of her many readers—just as Mauriac had left her on the pavement, powdering her nose. But he had fallen in love with her, and could not leave her alone. The book was greatly damaged by a preface, which Mauriac suppressed in the collected edition of his works. Here—with an eye on the Catholic readers who had so violently attacked him over the past twenty years—he apologised for not converting Thérèse on her death-bed. In fact, he tells us, these pages were written and then destroyed, because he could not 'see' the priest who could have heard her confession. Later on, in Rome, he did see him; and he held out the prospect of telling how Thérèse 'entered into the illumination of death'. Edward Sackville-West, who has written with keen perception about Mauriac, expressed the hope that he would do no such thing—and the hope was realised.

It is fifteen years since we last saw Thérèse, except for that momentary glimpse in *Ce qui était perdu*. Living alone in Paris, with only a maid to look after her, she is visited by her seventeen-year-old daughter Marie, who is in love with a student, Georges Filhot. He is reluctant to engage himself in marriage, and his parents—wealthy farmers in the *Landes*—do not encourage him to do so. The Desqueyroux are less prosperous than they once had been, and the cloud that still overhangs their name lowers still further the price of their daughter in the marriage market. Marie now extracts from her mother the truth of what hitherto she had only heard vaguely hinted at, and Thérèse promises at the same time to settle her private fortune on Georges and Marie, should they eventually get married. When she meets Georges he falls under her spell—for she still has the remnants of beauty beneath a skilfully applied cosmetic. The ambiguity of this brief relationship illustrates what Mauriac had written in his preface about

the power given to creatures the most burdened with fatality—the power to say no to the law that crushes

them. When Thérèse, with a hesitating gesture, brushes away the hair from her ravaged forehead, so that the boy she charms shall be horrified to look at her and shall remove himself from her presence, this gesture gives its meaning to the whole book. The unfortunate woman renews it at each encounter, never ceasing to react against her power to poison and corrupt.

As the book proceeds, her heart condition worsens and her neurasthenia turns into something not far removed from insanity. She imagines that the police are after her. Eventually Marie brings her back to her husband, and to what had once been her home in the *Landes*. It is there we take leave of her, after she has more or less forced the betrothal of Marie to Georges. One has the feeling that Thérèse should have died, if not hereafter, then at least elsewhere—though, in fact, she is still living when the novel comes to an end. It is as though Mauriac felt that she was someone about whom the last word could never be said. He certainly had great difficulty on saying it.

La Fin de la Nuit is less important for itself than for the stringent criticism it provoked from Jean-Paul Sartre. This did not appear until four years later, in February 1939; but it will be convenient to discuss it here. Twenty pages of closely reasoned, hostile dialectic in the *Nouvelle Revue Française* must have appeared to Mauriac like a betrayal in the house of his friends. The article affected, and even discouraged, him deeply, for it was a *mise en question,* not only of *La Fin de la Nuit* but of his whole practice as a novelist. Sartre was not yet the social prophet and philo-sopher he was shortly to become, but he was already a voice to reckon with; and in a climate of literary opinion that was rapidly changing under the threat of war and the stress of political tension he sounded a sharp discord amid the plaudits of the Académie française. The 'Immortal' was to receive a rude reminder of his mortality.

The article was entitled 'M. François Mauriac et la Liberté'. Sartre began, so to speak, by taking the ball into Mauriac's court. He did not hold it against him that he was a Christian novelist; on the contrary he maintained, quoting Dostoievsky to his purpose, that Christian belief should be to the novelist's advantage because it was based on a belief in free will. The novelist must create a dimension of time like that of the reader in which 'the future is yet to make . . . do you want your characters to come alive? Then see that they are free.' His business was 'not to explain but to *present* actions and passions which are unpredictable'. When Mauriac spoke in his preface of the 'fatality' that weighs upon Thérèse, and against which she recurrently reacts, he was apparently thinking of vices inherent in her nature. 'When liberty accepts Nature, fatality begins its reign. Or she may reject Nature, and remount the slope. Thérèse Desqueyroux *is* free.' Free, according to the preface; but not, as Sartre sees her, in the novel, where Mauriac switched back and forth between the notion of a creature struggling against tendencies in her own nat between the natural and the supernatural. If Sartre's criticism was well founded, Mauriac would not have been the first Christian to be caught by the problem of predestination and free will, nor the first to find it insoluble.

Sartre further accused Mauriac—and not in this novel alone—of identifying himself with a character and then considering it from outside, whether with his own eyes or those of other people. He gave the following as one example:

> She heard nine o'clock striking. She must wait a little longer, for it was too early to swallow the pill which would guarantee her a few hours of sleep; *not that this was a habit of this careful and desperate woman,* but this evening she could not deny herself the relief.

Who described Thérèse as 'careful and desperate'? Clearly not Thérèse herself. Mauriac had exchanged the liberty of his heroine for his own omniscience, and indeed he had compared the relationship of the novelist to his characters with the relationship of God to His creatures. Sartre categorically denied this. The novelist could be the witness or the accomplice of his characters, but he could not be both at the same time. And he could not be their judge. God viewed everything in the light of eternity, but once the novel escaped from the dimension of time it deserted the only atmosphere in which it could survive. In allowing his characters to do so, Mauriac destroyed their consciences; and *La Fin de la Nuit,* which he intended to be an illustration of liberty, was in fact an illustration of servitude.

Mauriac, a Catholic writer, continues in the heavy framework of determinism, as elaborated by the Naturalists, and has been described by some critics as a latter-day Jansenist, which would, of course, imply that he sees a distant spiritual force as accountable for the patterns of fate.

—*Jack Murray, "Three Murders in the Contemporary French Novel," in* Texas Studies in Literature and Language, *Autumn, 1964.*

By the time that Sartre mounted his attack, Mauriac had written his first play, *Asmodée,* and Sartre understood why the theatre had tempted him. It suited the quickness of his temperament and the classicism of his method. . . . Sartre contrasted the dramatic construction of his dialogue with the stylisation of talk proper to the novel; to the hints, stammerings, and repetitions out of which Dostoievsky, Conrad, and Faulkner had woven the illusion of life and time. French classicism was both 'eloquent and theatrical', and the reaction against it was in full swing. Sartre sympathised with the reaction where Mauriac did not; and an opposition, initially aesthetic, was to become evident in other fields as well. But whatever justice there was in Sartre's criticism, Mauriac had sinned in good company; and it was going a little far to declare that '*La Fin de la Nuit* is not a novel' and that 'M. Mauriac is not a novel-

ist'. Sartre delivered the *coup de grâce* when he turned the Divine analogy against his victim:

> A novel is written by a man for men. In the sight of God, who penetrates appearances without pausing over them, there is no such thing as the novel, and no such thing as art, because art lives by appearances. God is not an artist; and neither is M. Mauriac.

It has seemed right to give the Devil's advocate a hearing, but I think that Mauriac himself undervalued *La Fin de la Nuit,* and I prefer to endorse the opinion of Edward Sackville-West that the two books that relate the story of Thérèse compose 'a nearly faultless work of art'.

Diana Festa-McCormick (essay date 1984)

SOURCE: "Mauriac's Thérèse: An Androgynous Heroine," in *Writing in a Modern Temper: Essays on French Literature and Thought in Honor of Henri Peyre,* edited by Mary Ann Caws, ANMA Libri, 1984, pp. 174-87.

[*Festa-McCormick is an American educator and critic. In the following essay on* Thérèse Desqueyroux, *she traces Therese's motivation for murder to her unrequited passion for Anne.*]

Thérèse is a strange heroine. Her story is that of a quest and the quest is, ostensibly, for a conscience, for a confrontation with a crime that defies her understanding. Although she would like to lay bare the mechanism within her that set her on the path to murder and made it urgent to eliminate an undesired presence, Thérèse does not pursue her quest to the end, her search remains unfulfilled, and her questions unanswered. What I propose to do in the following pages is to resume that search, to follow the heroine along the digressions and the labyrinthine ways of her personality, and lay bare her secret. That secret, I believe, is hidden in her androgynous nature.

Thérèse defies definition in the framework of the novel. The story is not a narrative in the manner of *Genitrix,* nor is it a confession in the French tradition of the "roman personnel." The reader can rely neither on an omniscient author to unravel the heroine's motives, nor on the heroine's own merciless pursuit of her identity in the manner of an *Adolphe.* Both author and heroine point to signs and evidences of hidden purposes; neither clearly establishes or clarifies them. It is up to the reader to undertake the detective work, to assemble all manifest clues in order to arrive at a conclusion.

Thérèse is introduced after her crime, or attempted crime. She is a spiritual prisoner of her own impenetrable urges, caught more relentlessly by them than even by the eventual chains of family life. In a brief foreword, the author announces his intention of revealing her secret to the reader, as if that secret lay in the slow resolve to which she had surrendered, unquestioningly, to poison her "foolish husband." But he then adds almost cryptically, "I know the secrets of the hearts that are deep buried in, and mingles with, the filth of the flesh." The act of poisoning, however, is not *per se* "filth of flesh" and we are implicitly directed to look for Thérèse's secret elsewhere. Mauriac hints at the presence of a deeper problem in her than just the temptation of evil. Yet he does not reveal what is at the source of the chasm separating his heroine from the world of those around her.

The forlorn "she wolf" who will later prowl in the bleak woods of Argelouse is introduced in the opening sentence as poised between freedom and bondage. Thérèse's trip back home after the trial then emerges as a brief and sustained interlude in which the events of the past are measured against the rising consciousness of the present. A vacuum has been created where the nexus between years past and this moment remains suspended, and in that vacuum Thérèse moves hesitantly. The lawyer's words echo the uncertainty of her position. Her trial stands unresolved, her "case dismissed." She "felt the fog upon her face and took deep breaths of it." One would like to think that that avid breathing aims at dissolving the enveloping fog. But Thérèse's search never dares go beyond the boundaries of the visible. The fog is welcome, for it is the barrier she seeks against the world of man, and the mantle to which she clings against the intrusion of untenable truths. It is the symbol of her freedom, comforting and yet precarious and volatile. It is, too, the mirror of her personality, opaque and shadowy. But in the very act of deliberate breathing, Thérèse also reaches toward her nature, and the secret that lies there. Courageously, she sets out on her adventure in deciphering her actions through the invisible signs of her unavowed wishes. That she recoils at each step which could lead to a discovery only points to the impossibility of resolution in a dilemma she dares not name.

In his study of love in Mauriac's works, Emile Glénisson analyzes the sense of shame and repulsion that all physical contact with woman seems to inspire to the author's male characters [see *L'Amour dans les romans de François Mauriac*, 1970]. The psychological imbalance that pushes several of those men to abandon the conjugal bed in an unresolved tension of hatred and desire can only be viewed, he insists, as the unconscious transposition of the mother in the woman at their side. The same need for chastity in spite of the throbbing desire which Glénisson discerns in Mauriac's heroes exists and with greater violence in Thérèse. All that would be needed in order to make his assumption applicable here are a few exterior modifications. The "maternal substitute" seen in the victimized wives of Mauriac's novels would become a "paternal substitute," and the "near impotence" of the heroes would have to be translated into frigidity in Thérèse's case. But I would not insist with Glénisson on the author's own distaste for the assertive demands of the flesh, or yearnings for the primordial purity of the child at its mother's breast, in order to try and clarify Thérèse's behavior. It is not relevant to this study to ask whether Mauriac's tormented heroes were a mirror of his own personal bewilderment in relation to sexuality. All the same, I would not dismiss the link that he himself traced between his own person and the most perplexing of his creations. When writing prefaces for the

Pléiade edition of his collected works in 1950, Mauriac confessed to an affinity with Thérèse and, implicitly, to his identification with her solitude and misery.

> She is nevertheless more alive than any other of my heroines; not truly me, except in the sense in which Flaubert said "Madame Bovary is myself"—at my antipodes in more ways than one, but built all the same of all that in myself I have had to conquer, or eschew, or ignore.

It is permissible to wonder about the traits that Mauriac felt compelled to "conquer, or eschew, or ignore," and which he lent to his heroine; it is more pertinent to look at Thérèse directly.

Thérèse steps unaware into the realm of her own unconscious. Her search begins almost casually, out of the need to mend her relation with Bernard once she reaches Argelouse. Confidently, she decides that "all that was hidden must be brought into light." She will tell it all and begin at the beginning. And there, at the very start, she finds the image of Anne. Anne is the key, she intuitively knows, not only to her predicament of the moment but to what is hidden in her very nature.

> Little sister Anne, dear innocent, what an important part yours is in all this story! The really pure in heart know nothing of what goes on around them each day, each night! never realize what poisonous weeds spring up beneath their childish feet.

In her effort to uncover the truth, Thérèse evokes unhesitantly the presence of the childlike Anne, that luminous figure in the implacable summers of her adolescent years.

That Thérèse should immediately think of Anne in wanting to understand and in her desire to explain the events leading to her trial, points both to the honesty of her intentions and to an instinctive knowledge of herself. Outwardly, Anne has little bearing on what has happened; indeed, hardly any. Why then does Thérèse address her as the "pure at heart" who has played "an important part" in her story? That part was invisible, hidden within the recesses of Thérèse's wishes. Yet she must know that the beginning of her story coincides with her passionate yearnings for Anne's arrival in the torrid summers of her innocence. She calls "little sister" the slender silhouette she spied from around the bend in the heated moors, as if to conjure endowed with the rite of prayer, but the tone is one of defeat. It is to herself that she alludes in recalling the "poisonous weed" hidden behind the candor of her friend. "Each day, each night," harried by a nameless desire, Thérèse had lived the endless wait of the lover.

The ambiguity of Thérèse's determination to solve her enigma may well be due to some complicity between her and Mauriac, to what Claude-Edmonde Magny defines [in *Histoire du roman français depuis 1918*-1950)] as the author's participation in his heroine's dilemma, or his "illegitimate paternity," secret and somewhat shameful. Sartre noted, more pertinently, (in his well known chapter on "La Fin de la nuit" in *Situations,* I) that Thérèse is more in the tradition of a classical heroine of ancient Greece than in that of the modern novel. She is a tragic figure in whom reason is pitted against nature, and not a dramatic creation whose contest against bondage revolves on the pursuit of freedom in its own right. But Sartre's analysis is concerned with the philosophical and religious axioms of the author, not with investigating the heroine as such. Magny was not interested in exploring Thérèse's nature either. But Mauriac throws too many clues on the "masculinity" of that nature for it to remain thus undetected. My assumption, indeed, is that the androgynous quality in Thérèse's personality is not merely latent but obvious, though critics have been surprisingly silent on that score. I am also convinced that Mauriac intended it as such and made it, through innuendoes, the culprit for the diabolical force at the root of his heroine's actions.

Masculinity, or femininity for that matter, is a concept tied to times and social mores. It is remarkable, therefore, that a young woman's charm in that earlier part of the century and in a provincial French setting, should have been drawn not along the traditional demure and gentle stances expected by her society, but rested in her intelligence and "strong mind." Clearly, those were male prerogatives, together with a marked taste for reading (she "devoured" all she could lay hands on, from Paul de Kock's novels to the *Causeries du lundi* and Thiers' *Histoire du Consulat*) and for solitude in the vast and silent country home. Thérèse could not claim for herself the most coveted of a woman's assets, beauty; yet "it never occurs to one to wonder whether she is pretty or ugly. One just surrenders to her charm." "Charm" is to be translated into seductive intelligence here, or that superiority of intellect that captivates despite all preconceived assumptions. For Thérèse's thin lips, enormous forehead and large hands (perennially holding a cigarette) would have stood her ill in a conventional appraisal of feminine allure. Her more noticeable traits are unmistakably "masculine," both on the intellectual and physical plane. The text recurs to those qualities, to the "devastated brow" under the weight of tormenting thoughts, to the constant cigarette in a hand that was "a little too large," and thus confirms their importance in the characterization of the heroine.

The picture that emerges of Thérèse is that of a young woman who has always been at odds with her society and whose nonconformity came to be accepted as a matter of course both by the villagers of Argelouse and by herself. The former, no doubt, made concessions to her social position, and she had never known anything else. She was different, and no identification was possible between the dreams shared by other young persons of her sex and her own solitary prowlings within the vague confines of her intimate world. Only through her retrospective glance to those far away days of her immaculate youth does she understand the meaning of happiness. That past which she had attempted to hold still in the penumbra of a country room while the sun raged outside, now emerges as her only share of joy in life. Yet it was a past with no dreams, no tension toward the future, and in which each day sufficed unto itself. It was a past "unsullied, but lit by a vague and

flickering happiness." There is no doubt that the "unsullied" refers to a primordial purity here, to her untouched virginity. Later, the presence of a man at her side, her marriage, would desecrate her and obliterate happiness. Mauriac's condemnation of sexuality through what amounts to religious sophistry might explain, but only on the surface, Thérèse's revolt against the intrusion of a male presence in her life. If the author's assertion that man's love for God is to be exclusive and to remain unshared with any other human being is debatable in itself (in spite of his heavy leaning upon Bossuet's and Pascal's pronouncements) that reasoning could hardly apply to a woman who lays no claim to any religious feelings or mysticism. Nor is that all. Thérèse's nostalgic evocation of long summers past does not stress exclusively the innocence of those days. The emphasis in the text is equally shared between the beauty of "that unsullied season of her past" and another kind of allure at the basis of her "vague and flickering happiness." A question naturally arises, "whence had come all that happiness?" and the answer offers itself: Anne was there, sitting by her side on the sofa, in that "darkened drawing room set in the merciless glare of summer heat."

Desire, or one's conscious yearning for something rests on a basis of experience. Recognition of one's desires cannot occur without a retrospective glance (even if it be of a vicarious kind, through hearsay) of the thrill, or anguish, or hope that accompanies them. Thérèse had no experience and no knowledge that could allow her to identify the nature of her happiness at the side of Anne and of her anguish in Anne's absence. Her imagination was thus not involved in expectation or fear, it did not feed or dash hopes. She lived the phases of her passionate longing through violent sensations alone, surrendering in turn to appeasement or to turmoil. She was never far removed from a lingering inner sense of agitation. The cool atmosphere of the drawing room is evoked, contrasted to the fierce heat of summer at Argelouse, the appeasing presence of the blond adolescent at her side acting as balm against the tumult of the senses. Anne would get up now and then and check if the sun had paled. Thérèse remembers the constant quiver of heat that threatened to invade the room, ready to splutter and to flare like fire. "But through the half-opened shutters the blinding glare would pounce like a great stream of molten metal, till it almost burned the carpet, and all must be again shut tight while human beings went once more to earth." This is the torrid nature that furnishes what O'Donnell calls "the dramatic commentary" or the key to what is most intimate in the characters' personality [see Donat O'Donnell, *Maria Cross,* 1952]. I do not believe that it would be driving connotations too far to see in the darkened room a desire for protection against the furor of invading heat and unnamed desires.

It could be argued that Thérèse's need for Anne's presence offers nothing unusual. Friendship between girls—or boys— was and still is often passionate in societies where diversions and social relations are curtailed. But there is a tension in the atmosphere here, there are palpitations only briefly quietened for Thérèse and unshared by her friend, that go beyond the most intense feelings of friendship. In this "land of thirst" the girl's yearning knows a momentary respite only in the other's presence. The walk to the cold stream of La Hure is strenuous along the sandy heath; but there, briefly, peace reigns. These are the images that Thérèse evokes as she sits in the carriage that brings her back to Argelouse after the trial. One must remember that these are the clues she seeks to help her unravel the confusion in her being. In those images thus evoked she relives the assuaging sensation of the icy waters in which their naked feet dipped for a moment, side by side. The girls did not speak a word; time remained suspended. But the suspension appears somewhat like the holding of one's breath, condemned soon to resume the accustomed rhythm and, for Thérèse, to heighten the pervasive anguish of the protracted wait.

> To have stirred so much as a finger, so it seemed to them, would have set scurrying in fright their chaste, their formless happiness. It was Anne, always, who moved first—eager to be at the business of killing larks at sundown, and Thérèse, though she hated the sport, would follow, so hungry was she for the other's company.

The "so it seemed to them" of the quotation resembles a lover's obstinate belief in a shared experience. What makes it unconvincing that it apply to both of "them" is not merely that these are Thérèse's thoughts with not a hint of corroboration found in Anne's behavior. On the contrary, Anne is "always" the one to break the silence and so destroy the magic of the moment for Thérèse. She is quite predictably eager to move on, to kill birds with the unconscious cruelty of youth and youth's thoughtless tenderness, too. Thérèse alone is aware of the plight of those who are hunted and of their helplessness, for she has probed the dimensions of suffering. She identifies with the lark whose instant of life and "song of rapture" are already tainted by death, yet she follows her friend for she cannot do otherwise. She tries to blot away the cry of the wounded bird and her own pain at the same time, for she is "hungry for the other's company."

Those excursions in the heat of summer offer the only memory of happiness Thérèse ever experienced. But at no time did she ignore that those moments were volatile and in perpetual flight, nor was she spared the anguish of that knowledge. "Coming tomorrow?" she would ask, and the "sensible" answer would inevitably ensue, "Oh no—not every day." Thérèse recalls her dispirited walk home after her friend's silhouette had disappeared around the bend. Evening and darkness would have set in. "What was that anguish?" she asks. Why was she unable to read or do anything except wander back onto the now empty road? The hiatus of time is here evident in the use of the past tense, and with it the perspective which through distance could now afford a clearer view of events. Thérèse measures her wretchedness of those days, the morose restlessness that would bring her back to the very spot where Anne had disappeared. She asks the right question, but no sooner has she done so than she drops it. No explanation is sought for the dead silence that would suddenly engulf her when Anne was no longer visible. One cannot, however, simply ascribe Thérèse's oscillations to ignorance, let alone to innocence. It is too late for that. She wants to know, pre-

sumably, why she was seized by a pervasive anguish once her companion left. Why does she not pursue the question, the reader may ask, unless it be out of fear of finding an unbearable answer?

If Thérèse could simply be classified as a repressed lesbian, she would surely hold limited interest for us. But there exists in her, together with the unrequited need for Anne's nearness, an undeniable urgency for purity. One could argue that her attraction to a rather insipid adolescent girl who shared not a single one of her tastes is dictated by an intricate defense mechanism, which makes her yearn for somebody who must by necessity remain untouchable. This could become a circular reasoning, however, where cause and effect would be inextricably tied. "Christianity makes no allowances for the flesh; it simply abolishes it," Mauriac affirms in the famous opening words of "Souffrances du pécheur." But the turgid atmosphere in ***Thérèse*** can only be seen as a strong denial of such a precept, and thus of Christianity itself. In that case, it would of course be the absence of grace that wreaks havoc in the heroine's life. Yet that very absence would then emerge as the craving of the flesh and the stormy sensuality at the base of Thérèse's dilemma. Her nostalgia for the purity preceding her marriage is manifest, particularly in contrast to "the indelible filth" of her wedded life. But at the same time she cannot silence her doubts on her own candor as she wonders, "was I really so happy, so innocent of guile?"

Thérèse was never unaware of the need, illogical in her own sight, for being close to Anne. Bernard, on the other hand, had never set her imagination to motion. Why had she married him? "I married because. . ." and, irrepressibly, Anne's image comes again to the fore: "There had, of course, been the childish delight with which she had looked forward to becoming Anne's sister-in-law as a result of that marriage." She remembers the days preceding the wedding and her calm wait, not for the traditional fulfillment of her woman's role, but for Anne's presence: "Anne would be coming back from the Saint-Sebastian convent for the wedding." But what she had thought of as peace was only "half sleep, the torpor of the snake within her breast." One wonders what she means by "snake," what shape she would give to evil, if she pursued her search to the end and exacted an answer to her own inquiry. Her memory lingers on the oppressiveness that suddenly rushed upon her and the nightmarish quality of her wedding day. "She had entered this cage like a sleepwalker" and sensed with horror that she would inexorably join "the herd of those who have served." This is not the case of a girl's vague dreams of love being dashed by the brutality of a husband or the banality of family life. Thérèse suffered in anticipation of the fatal embrace of the flesh, of her contact with man. She had for the first time resented the presence of Anne whose visible joy made no allowance for the separation that would soon place them apart not merely in space "but by reason of what Thérèse was about to suffer—of that irreparable outrage to which her innocent body would have to submit." Again, it is not merely the case of a certain anxiety, perturbation, or even fear, which could be explained by a puritanical education (although Thérèse professed independence of mind and no submission to church dogma) or by inexperience. She felt outright horror, an irrepressible revulsion at the very thought of physical contact with the man she had chosen to marry—and who was the best she could have chosen, she still believed.

Perhaps the most revelatory signs of a certain abnormality in Thérèse's nature are to be found in her musings about her nights in Bernard's arms. She had mastered the art of feigning a pleasure she did not in fact experience. Yet her husband's embraces had made her wonder about the happiness of complete abandon: "Much as when looking at a landscape shrouded in mist, we fancy what it must be like in sunshine, so did Thérèse discover the delights of the flesh." Her sensuality was awakened but remained shrouded in the mist of her own resistance. She never considered the possibility of surrender and joy in her nuptial bed, but now found herself trying to envisage their wondrous beauty, the "sunshine" that remained elusive. She submitted to the laws of matrimony and, possibly, her body involuntarily responded to the pressures of the male at her side. Yet her vagaries pushed her toward an unknown realm of voluptuous experience where she too might discover the total fulfillment of desire. So her honeymoon passed, her "teeth clenched" as the "little pig" at her side sought pleasure in his trough: "and I was the trough" she reflects. Her only comfort during that time: a letter from Anne which she read over and over again. The girl complained that she no longer went to Vilméja so as not to run into the owner of the premises. Young Azévédo had come back and she abhorred consumptives.

For a woman who ignores or chooses to ignore all peremptory calls of the flesh, the imperatives of love must remain empty words in the dictionary of the inane. Thus it is that Anne's subsequent letters with their message of burning passion for Azévédo are found shocking. Thérèse's violent and cruel reaction against the girl who had made her own heart throb is unmistakably that of a jilted lover and not of a friend. How could it be that the foolish adolescent girl she had left behind, so lacking in imagination, should have discovered the lyrical beauty of sentiment and desire? Thérèse knew only too well how incapable of responding to the fervent longing of the heart, how indifferent to the dashed hopes of those who live in helpless wait Anne had been: "How could this song of songs have burst from the dry little heart she had known?—for it *was* dry, as she knew only too well. . . . " How else could she have known, if not through the impassiveness that had made her suffer, Anne's irresponsiveness to her tacit entreaties, the casual and repeated "Oh no—not every day" given in answer to her anxious question, "coming tomorrow?" A passion such as Thérèse nourished relies for continuity on ignorance. She must never acknowledge the nature of her desires in a world that would find them inadmissible. The key to their being rests on the secrecy that shrouds them from everybody and makes them seemingly impervious to her own investigating efforts. If ever they were allowed to the surface those desires would be condemned to perish in shame. Her anguish would have a name, her yearnings an aim. But Thérèse comes here quite close to recognizing the character of her trepidation in the hot summer afternoons at Argelouse, of the wretchedness that always seized her when Anne went away.

What follows is startling only if one refuses to see in Thérèse a would-be lover rather than a friend. She herself does not even try to explain an act performed as an ancient ritual and aiming at bending fate to will: "Two years ago, in the hotel bedroom" she reflects, "I took the pin, and I pierced the photograph of that young man just where the heart should be—not in a fit of temper, but quite calmly, as though I were doing a perfectly ordinary thing." The fact is that that kind of black magic performed with determination has from time immemorial been a last recourse from shattered hopes and unrequited passions. In that context, it is indeed "a perfectly ordinary thing" that Thérèse should yield to superstition in her bid for vengeance. She turns against the rival who had known how to inspire fiery emotions and desire in the cool adolescent she had left behind. Everything in herself revolts against that act of betrayal. Her teeth clenched, she "was surprised at her own appearance in the glass." The presence of Bernard now becomes intolerable: "She felt no hatred for him, but simply a wild desire to be alone with her pain, to discover where it was that the blow had struck her!" The language is quite explicit here. Thérèse lives the tragedy of a woman condemned to give vent neither to love nor to pain. Where was the hurt, she asks herself? Does she also wonder what the hurt was? Her questions seek no answers at any rate, except thatshe must have solitude, to dress her wounds and contemplate undisturbed the extent of her misery.

"I could have wished, Thérèse, for sorrow to have turned your heart to God," Mauriac says in his brief foreword. But creations have a way of voicing their own truth and of asserting their own inner laws, heedless of all preconceived ideas. The author, no doubt, intended the slow germination of a conscience and the coming to grips with her evil deed or his heroine. Yet Thérèse remains to the end the free spirit initially delineated in the story, unconcerned with her soul and the dimensions of evil. Her redemption would have exacted "a cry of sacrilege" from the best intentioned of readers, the author concedes. I suggest that the reason for it is that Thérèse's depravity was not in the temptation of murder as such, and the author indirectly alludes to that. Her rebellion, in fact, probably "commanded her creator's not altogether unconscious sympathy," as O'Donnell points out. Mauriac was all too aware of the wearing down of dreams and the enslaving tyranny exercised relentlessly within a home in the name of kinship and love. Murder was not the cause of Thérèse's dilemma but its result. It was the "necessary" step she had to take in order to reassert her right to her own wilderness and to the nonconformity of her desires. But she appears so caught behind "the living bars" of family life that readers may fall into the trap of believing that it was only against them that she chafed. The author manipulates us into assuming that Thérèse's unconscious if violent rebellion was against the mounting and stifling monotony and the empty rituals within the entrapping walls of her country house. But she had not been in the dark before, and her revolt had started long before those walls began to close about her. It was during her honeymoon, when she had not

yet lived in the La Trave household but had already received the jolt of Anne's betrayal, that she looked dispas-
sionately at the "country-bred fellow" she had married
and yearned, with a mind all too clear:

> If only she had not got to make such an effort to eat
> her lunch and smile, to compose her features and to
> keep her eyes from blazing. If only she could fix her
> mind freely upon the mysterious despair which seemed
> to have seized upon her.

The English translation is faithful to the original. Thérèse
talks quite literally of the mysterious despair ("désespoir
mystérieux") that had got hold of her, as her mind went
over the fiery words in Anne's letters. Bernard is no longer
merely the male who had violated the sanctity of her body,
he is the intruder into the passionate world of her feelings
and emotions. The only way she finds of converting him
into a bearable presence is to make of him a sounding
board for a name she needs to mention: "she had to talk
about Anne." Like those of all lovers, Thérèse's words,
too, coverage to the object of her desires. She needed to
evoke the only name and face that had for so long filled
the realm of her reveries.

The crime of Mauriac's heroine is presented like a living
organism with a volition of its own, a germ that, once
implanted, matures irrespective of will or consciousness.
It does not become evident until the night of the forest
fire, when Thérèse watches, mute and fascinated, Bernard
taking, unaware, a second dose of his Fowler prescription.
But murder was by then within her, an unrecognized yet
germinating embryo. Its stirring was merely a confirmation of the life that had already been infused in it. If one
could trace that life at its inception one would have to go
back to the far away days of Thérèse's honeymoon. There
was first the revulsion inspired by the cumbersome body
that shared her bed and which she forcefully pushed away
as it sought her warmth during sleep. And then there was
the prospect of squalor and emptiness, as the loss of the
only love she had ever nourished took for her the shape of
a "mysterious despair." All that followedwedness now lay forever beyond the boundaries of the possible for her, is a
manifest-ation of that awareness. Without hope there could
only be destruction for a nature without docility. Lacking
the resignation of the meek, Thérèse could only strike
back with the weapons at her disposal: her charm and her
intelligence at the service now of vengeance and her thirst
for freedom.

Nelly Cormeau whose study is somewhat too deferential
to Mauriac and to what is perhaps his technique of deception (to what I see as the author's effort to depict seething
and passionate natures under the guise of religious innuendoes) refers nevertheless to Thérèse as a creature branded
by a terrible passion and an ineluctable fate [see Nelly
Cormeau, *L'Art de François Mauriac* (1951)]. I have
chosen to call Thérèse's passion by its name, and to answer
her ill-fated search with words and thoughts shaped in her
own mind, dictated by her emotions, and yet left unacknowl-
edged. She goes meticulously over the events that followed
her return to Argelouse after the honeymoon, her meetings

with Azévédo and her cruel duplicity against the girl she
had so intensely wanted close to her. But she knows now
that she could not allow Anne to realize a dream from
which she was herself excluded. As for the arsenic she
poured drop by drop into the glass of the man who was
her avowed master, that was an act similar in its nature to
the one of pushing him away from her nupital bed. Her
vengeance, however, was not directed against that man,
for whom she had little consideration but hardly any animosity. Had she been able to isolate herself from his presence, from his touch above all, he would have played a
negligible role in her life. But Anne and the desire, which
that blond adolescent had unconsciously culled from her
heart, had ineluctably shaped her existence and condemned
it to a frightening solitude. If Mauriac leaves Thérèse at
the end on a Parisian sidewalk deprived of redemption, it
is because no redemption is possible from the imperatives
of nature and the assertive demands of the heart.

Edward J. Gallagher   (essay date 1986)

SOURCE: "Sexual Ambiguity in Mauriac's *Thérèse Desqueyroux*," in *Romance Notes,* Vol. XXVI, Spring, 1986,
pp. 215-21.

[*In the following essay, Gallagher argues that Mauriac is
purposefully ambiguous regarding the sexual orientation
of Thérèse Desqueyroux—much more so than is conveyed
by the standard English translations of the novel, which
tend to attribute gender to verb forms that in the original
French are neutral.*]

To the reader of François Mauriac's 1927 novel ***Thérèse
Desqueyroux*** the complexity of the title character's personality and motivations is readily apparent. Critics have,
in fact, suggested affinities between her and such towering
fictional women as Racine's ill-facted Phèdre and Flaubert's
insatiable dreamer Emma Bovary.

It is for this reason then all the more surprising to encounter in an otherwise sensitive and astute critical reading of
Mauriac's novel this simplistic sexual labelling of his
heroine:

> So it is that Thérèse—another Lesbian—belongs not
> to the world of Mme. Canaby (whose physical appear-
> ance she inherits) but to the inner world of the writer
> himself. . . . [Cecil Jenkins, *Mauriac* (1965). In a
> footnote, Gallagher adds: "The Mme Canaby referred
> to here, acquitted in 1906 by the Bordeaux Assizes of
> having attempted to poison her husband, was the in-
> spiration for Mauriac's plot"].

Simply to call Thérèse Desqueyroux a Lesbian—and with
a capital L—(the capitalization is Jenkins') is to resolve
a broad and subtle network of textual ambiguities which
make Mauriac's title character complex, fascinating, perplexing, and, for all these reasons, hauntingly memorable. To use the term "Lesbian" so unabashedly and un-

qualifiedly is to do nothing less than seriously distort the meaning of the novel and misrepresent the demonstrable intent of its author.

It is undeniable that Thérèse Desqueyroux views the activities of her marriage bed as physically repugnant. Returning to Argelouse after her acquittal, she recalls the day she married Bernard and the thoughts she had then of the appoaching wedding night, the significance of which was entirely lost on her sister-in-law Anne:

> . . . la joie enfantine de la jeune fille l'isolait de Thérèse: sa joie! Comme si elle eût ignoré qu'elles allaient être séparées le soir même, et non seulement dans l'espace; à cause aussi de ce que Thérèse était au moment de souffrir. . . .

Marriage represents for Thérèse life's watershed. As she begins her long examination of conscience, she describes her life thus:

> Tout ce qui précède mon mariage prend dans mon souvenir cet aspect de pureté; contraste, sans doute, avec cette ineffaçable salissure des noces.

One would be foolish to try to explain away her aversion to conjugal sex as simply a reaction to the brutish insensitivity or worse of her cloddish husband Bernard. What his sexual practices were is not at all clear. That Thérèse saw what she calls "les impatients inventions de l'ombre" as abnormal and perhaps aberrant is evident, for she asks herself: "Où avait-il appris à classer tout ce qui touche à la chair—à distinguer les caresses de l'honnête homme de celles du sadique?"

While frigid with Bernard—"je faisais la morte"—Thérèse is not unreceptive to the possibility of sexual response. In fact, her conjugal submission to Bernard presages for her the possibility of other sexual feelings:

> Un fiancé se dupe aisément; mais un mari! N'importe qui sait proférer des paroles menteuses; les mensonges du corps exigent une autre science. Mimer le désir, la joie, la fatigue bienheureuse, cela n'est pas donné à tous. Thérèse sut plier son corps à ces feintes et elle y goûtait un plaisir amer. Ce monde inconnu de sensations où un homme la forçait de pénétrer, sonimagination l'aidait à concevoir qu'il y aurait eu là, pour elle aussi peut-être, un bonheur possible—mais quel bonheur? Comme devant un paysage enseveli sous la pluie, nous nous représentons ce qu'il eût été dans le soleil, ainsi Thérèse découvrait la volupté.

While her sexual dislikes seem rather indisputable, her sexual preferences remain terribly imprecise. Four times in the novel, twice in the course of two different scenes, Thérèse imagines herself with a lover. The absolutely unresolvable question of the sex of her fantasy lover is striking and seems to have escaped the notice, not only of Mauriac's English translator, but also of those who have written on the novel, analysed its heroine, and alluded to her sexuality.

The first two of these imaginings occur during successive confrontations in the garden at Saint-Clair between Thérèse and her husband's half-sister Anne de la Trave with whom Thérèse has been intimate since childhood and whose amorous liaison with Jean Azévédo she has recently decided to frustrate. Reacting to Anne's inability to describe clearly Azévédo's personality, Thérèse muses on the effect passion would have on her own powers of observation and description: "Moi, songeait Thérèse, la passion me rendrait plus lucide, rien ne m'échapperait de *l'être* dont j'aurais envie." While there is nothing particularly unusual about Thérèse's use here of *l'être*, upon reflection, *le garçon*, which she uses several sentences earlier to refer to Azévédo, or *l'homme* might be felt in this context to be *le mot juste*. While one instance of the use of the noun *être* could be explained as a stylistic avoidance of the banal, its systematic use to the absolute exclusion of any sexually precise noun is worth noting. So it is, in a second garden conversation following hard upon the first, that Thérèse who has begun to arouse Anne's anxiety about Azévédo's commitment to her reflects:

> Qu'il doit être doux de répéter un nom, un prénom qui désigne *un certain être* auquel on est lié par le coeur étroitement! La seule pensée qu'il est vivant, qu'il respire, qu'il s'endort, le soir, la tête sur son bras replié, qu'il s'éveille à l'aube, que son jeune corps déplace la brume. . . .

Much later during her long sequestration at Argelouse she fills her time with daydreams of other lives she might lead. She sees herself in Paris declining a young man's repeated invitations to dine, for her evenings are never free and with reason:

> *Un être* était dans sa vie grâce auquel tout le reste du monde lui paraissait insignifiant; *quelqu'un* que personne de son cercle ne connaissait; *une créature* très humble, très obscure; mais toute l'existence de Thérèse tournait autopêchait de respirer; mais elle aimait mieux perdre le souffle que l'éloigner.

A mere five paragraphs farther on, she conjures up another scene. In this one too, her lover—described simply as *quelqu'un*—is again sexually undifferentiated:

> Thérèse, assise, reposait sa tête contre une épaule, se levait à l'appel de la cloche pour le repas, entrait dans la charmille noire et *quelqu'un* marchait à ses côtés qui soudain l'entourait des deux bras, l'attirait. Un baiser, songe-t-elle, doit arrêter le temps; elle imagine qu'il existe dans l'amour des secondes infinies.

At the very end of the novel too, it should be noted in addition to the four key passages just cited, as Thérèse sits alone having just explained to Bernard the two irreconcilable sides of her personality, she decides not to go see Jean Azévédo and ponders the chance rather of other encounters:

> . . . elle n'avait pas envie de le voir: causer encore! chercher des formules! Elle connaissait Jean Azévédo;

mais *les êtres* dont elle souhaitait l'approche, elle ne les connaissait pas; elle savait d'eux seulement qu'ils n'exigeraient guère de paroles. Thérèse ne redoutait plus la solitude.

This pattern of ambiguity—albeit subtle in context—can hardly be accidental or without import. [In a footnote, Gallagher adds: "It is nothing less than startling that in the standard English translation of this novel by Gerard Hopkins entitled **Therese** the first three of these incontrovertibly ambiguous passages are systematically resolved. The ambiguous *être* is made male:

'Passion,' thought Thérèse, 'would make me clearer sighted. I should take note of every detail in the *man* whom I desired.'

How sweet it must be to say a name over and over, the pet name of the *man* to whom one's heart is tightly bound!—merely to think *he* is alive and breathing; that *he* sleeps at night with *his* head upon *his* arm, and wakes at dawn; that *his* young body plunges through the morning mist. . . .

Someone was in her life who made the rest of the world seem meaningless: someone completely unknown to the rest of her circle, someone very obscure and very humble. But her whole existence revolved about this sun which she alone could see, the heat of which she only could feel upon her flesh. Paris rumbled like the sound of the wind in the pines. The sensation of her companion's body pressed against her own, light though the contact was, hindered her breathing. But rather than push *him* away she would stop breathing altogether.

It was in discussions with my former colleagues William Hendrickson and the late Richard Admussen that these mistranslations came to light. For a discussion of Mauriac's novel and the film it inspired, see R. Admussen, E. Gallagher, and L. Levin, 'Novel into Film: An Experimental Course,' *Literature/Film Quarterly* 6 (1978), 66-72. Naturally, critics relying on the flawed Hopkins English translation (which appeared in 1947) help perpetuate these egregious misreadings. See, for example, Michael F. Moloney, *François Mauriac: A Critical Study* (1958)."] It is, in fact, highly significant and suggestive, for in the sexual realm too, as in the motivational, Thérèse, it seems clear, is incapable of absolute honesty with herself. Like her sexuality, her role in Bernard's slow poisoning remains imprecise:

Mais Thérèse n'a plus rien à examiner: elle s'est engouffrée dans le crime béant; elle a été aspirée par le crime; ce qui a suivi, Bernard le connaît aussi bien qu'elle-même: cette soudaine reprise de son mal. . . .

The seemingly autonomous nature of his illness suggested by the expression "cette soudaine reprise de son mal" is echoed in the following paragraphs by two similar descriptions of his condition:

. . . vers la mi-août, après une crise plus alarmante . . .

and

Au début de décembre, une reprise de son mal terrassa Bernard.

She is unwilling or, more likely, unable to own up to her active and persistent role in attempting to murder the anemic Bernard by slowly poisoning him with overdoses of an arsenic-based medicine he regularly takes.

While Thérèse's role and responsibility in Bernard's poisoning are clearer to the reader than to her, the precise nature of her sexuality is much less clear to both character and reader. In an attempt to clarify, one could argue that the word *être*, used so regularly in her sexual fantasies, is at least once in the novel, and early on, used as a feminine substitute when Thérèse thinks in this way of the imminent loss of her virginity: "Anne demeurait sur la rive où attendaient *les êtres* intacts; Thérèse allait se confondre avec le troupeau de celles qui ont servi"; yet this single such use while suggestive of a possible feminine decoding, rather than resolving, simply underscores the sexual ambiguity of *être* when used elsewhere.

Whether Thérèse Desqueyroux is a woman with deeply repressed lesbian tendencies or, given the admitted duality of her personality, a bi-sexual is not at all certain. What she ought certainly not to be called is simply a "Lesbian" *tout court*, as Jenkins does quite matter-of-factly in the first quote cited in this essay. It is not terribly clear whether one is meant to read hers as a repressed homosexual personality, intended perhaps to complement on the internal, psychological level the constraints and limits imposed on her from without in her struggle to survive in the stiffling and oppressive atmosphere of the Desqueyroux family or as bi-sexual. If one is to see her as the latter, is it so because she is to be construed as doomed to yearn for both kinds of love, yet to face as a consequence the impossibility of ever really knowing human love at all? She herself, of course, acknowledges her view of the divided self in her final conversation with Bernard, saying that "la Thérèse qui était fière d'épouser un Desqueyroux, de tenir son rang au sein d'une bonne famille de la lande, contente enfin de se caser, comme on dit, cette Thérèse-là est aussi réelle que l'autre, aussi vivante. . . ." Even here though the nature of "l'autre" is undefined.

Rather it would seem, just as Thérèse cannot explain herself, her actions or her motivations—"Était-il vraisemblable qu'une femme de son intelligence n'arrivât pas à rendre ce drame intelligible?"—that her creator does not choose entirely to do so either. Labelling Thérèse and thus narrowly defining her sexuality simplifies what is, in fact, the richly suggestive nature of her sexuality and the complexity of the total personality which Mauriac gave her and which makes her such a memorable, disturbing and haunting character whose ambiguities resist easy resolution. To attempt to explain Thérèse Desqueyroux in terms of her sexuality alone would be an exercise as foolish and myopic as attempting, as some have, to resolve the ambiguity of her sexuality.

Richard Griffiths (essay date 1989)

SOURCE: "Mauriac and the Art of the Short Story," in *François Mauriac: Visions and Reappraisals,* edited by John E. Flower and Bernard C. Swift, Berg Publishers, 1989, pp. 77-95.

[*A Welsh educator and critic, Griffiths is the author of* The Reactionary Revolution: The Catholic Revival in French Literature, 1870-1914 *(1966), among other works. In the following essay, he examines Mauriac's short stories and argues that they should be viewed on their own terms as literary works—not simply in relation to the novels.*]

François Mauriac is famous above all as a novelist. The fact that he wrote a number of successful short stories appears, on the whole, to have been neglected by the critics. Far from being studied as a genre in their own right, these stories have tended to be studied entirely in relation to the novels, and to have aroused interest only in so far as they give greater insight into Mauriac's general literary intentions.

At times, in his own comments on his works, Mauriac appears to have given the green light to such critical attitudes. Referring to **'Insomnie',** for example, he wrote: 'C'est le chapitre d'un roman que je n' ai pas écrit' [Preface to ***Plongées,*** in *Oeuvres Complètes,* Vol. II]. This remark, if unqualified by any of Mauriac's other more ambiguous statements, has led to the belief that in a novelist of the importance of Mauriac short stories must either be *ébauches* for novels, or, at any rate, possess the same characteristics as a novel. Jacques Petit's notes to the Pléiade edition, for example, bear this out. Of **'Coups de couteau'** he writes: 'La scène décrite dans **"Coups de couteau"** pauvait conduire à une situation romanesque riche' [in *Oeuvres Complètes,* Vol. I]. From his reading of **'Thérèse chez le docteur',** he draws the following general conclusions on Mauriac's art as a writer of short stories: 'On voit que la nouvelle, pour Mauriac, est moins un récit court, ordonné autour d'un thème, qu'un épisode de roman, détaché, et qui en garde la complexité' [in *Oeuvres Complètes,* Vol. III].

Yet Mauriac himself was aware of at least some of the basic differences between a short story and a chapter of a novel. The statement quoted above about **'Insomnie'** is continued as follows: 'Beaucoup de destinées qui sont dramatiques ne fournissent pas l'étoffe d'un roman, parce qu'elles manquent de péripéties. L'histoire du héros d'*Insomnie* ne peut avoir qu'un chapitre. Sa douleur se perd dans le sable [Preface to *Plongées*].

There is more to the art of the short story, of course, than the purely negative characteristic of lacking the 'péripéties' suitable to a novel. While we do not have much in the way of positive statements by Mauriac himself about that art, we do find, in his best short stories, evidence of his consummate skill in this very different genre, and an ability to adapt, and at times to abandon, his novelist's techniques, in order to fit into a new and demanding framework. One of the best examples of this, as we shall see, is **'Thérèse**

The infuence of Catholicism on Mauriac's fiction:

Mauriac has frequently been asked if his Catholicism has exercised a limiting effect on his novels. To this question he has replied that his Catholic viewpoint has both hindered and helped his fiction. "My heart secretly nourished an insatiable curiosity about the hearts of others. On this point, never did a young Catholic feel less constrained than I by his faith," he wrote in *Écrits intimes.* However, he has admitted severe compunctions about the depiction of human passions, particularly in their most graphic forms. His favorite illustration of a writer who had made a literary reputation by washing his linen in public is André Gide, one of the *maîtres littéraires* of Mauriac's generation. And in Proust, the novelist he ranks highest, the severest fault appears to him the disintegration of the characters and consequently of the novel itself because various perverse passions eventually occupy almost all the foreground of the narrative.

Mauriac's Catholicism has been the basis for all his en restricted by his religious viewpoint in depicting the human being. Echoing a dictum common to the so-called existentialist novelists, Mauriac wrote that the novelist must "testify to man—And this testimony *must* be disinterested, gratuitous." As a Catholic novelist, he felt bound to describe man as contradictory, unfaithful to his divine origins, because he saw him thus. As a political journalist after the Liberation, Mauriac continued his critical appraisal of man on other levels. Both activities appeared to him natural functions of his religious viewpoint and as inevitable tasks demanded by his integrity as a Catholic.

Rima Drell Reck, Literature and Responsibility: The French Novelist in the Twentieth Century, *1969.*

---

chez le docteur', a short story which, because one of its protagonists appears in other works by Mauriac, has been presumed to be merely one episode in an ongoing novel, and to have no independent artistic form.

This is not to say that there are not short stories by Mauriac which fall below this standard. His small output in this genre is remarkably uneven. One can, in fact, group Mauriac's successfulstories into two groups, each written at specific points in time: **'Un Homme de lettres', 'Coups de couteau'** and **'Insomnie'** in 1926-7, **'Thérèse chez le docteur', 'Thérèse à l'hôtel'** and **'Le Rang'** in 1933-6. These periods reflect precise changes in Mauriac's attitudes as a writer: after the pre-1924 period, in which his writings had on the whole combined a desire for edification with a use of the traditional techniques of the pre-war Catholic novel, the first great trilogy of successful stories was written in the period when, in Mauriac's own words, 'Je crus résoudre les difficultés de mon état en m'appliquant à peindre la vie telle que je la voyais, et à inventer les créatures qui spontanément naissaient de mon expérience' [Preface to ***Trois Récits,*** in *Oeuvres Complètes,* Vol. I], and when, accepting all the techniques of modern narrative fiction, he turned his back on the traditional 'Catholic' techniques. With **'Le Démon de la connaissance'** (1928), however, we find Mauriac at the beginning of that return to a need for an edifying content, and for some of the traditional 'Catholic' techniques, which is epitomised by the novel *Ce qui était perdu*. Not only that, these new concerns succeed in destroying the successful short-story form which Mauriac had been developing, and substitute a work overweighted by novelistic rather than short-story concerns. By the time we come to the second group of successful stories, however, Mauriac has reached that new literary equilibrium which, from *Le Nœud de vipères* onwards, was to mark his literary creation; and, in the process, he manages once again to disentangle his short-story techniques from purely novelistic concerns, and create satisfying works of art in their own right.

These two groups of stories in fact use remarkably different techniques, each of them perfectly valid. The first group gains its effects through what has been described as 'la seule évocation, l'approfondissement d'un instant précis d'une vie' [René Godenne, *La Nouvelle française*, 1974]. The second, while homing in equally precisely on specific moments of experience, relies far more on a highly organised framework, in which economical methods of allusion convey more than acres of text might do.

Mauriac's other short stories, however, have a variety of faults. Some suffer from a desire to do what a novel should have done, and from a resultant elephantiasis of form. Others are afflicted by triteness, or by a desire for edification. A look at the faults of these lesser stories will, by contrast, pinpoint for us some of the positive qualities possessed by Mauriac's best short stories. Let us start with a youthful effort, **'Le Visiteur nocturne'** (published on 25 May 1920, in the *Revue des jeunes*).

At first sight, **'Le Visiteur nocturne'** appears to have many of the attributes of a successful short story in a traditional nineteenth-century mould. It has a simple story-line, set in a precise form, with a beginning, middle and end. It starts with the evocation of a successful writer, Octave, who has become increasingly disillusioned by the life he is leading. Late at night, when alone after a party, he is visited by an apparent stranger, poor and miserably dressed, who turns out to be a childhood friend called Gabriel. Octave lets him come in, but is grudging in his welcome, and graceless in his reception of Gabriel's remi-niscences; he hides the presence of the delicious left-overs from his evening entertainment, and gives his guest bread, cheese and water. He allows Gabriel, who is emigrating next day to Dakar on a ship sailing from Bordeaux, to spend the night in his armchair, but denies him the luxurious divan, for fear of it being spoiled. The next day Octave wakes after Gabriel's departure; he is now uneasy about the way he has treated Gabriel, and wants to make it up to him; he is full of a sense of sin. He rushes to Bordeaux, presuming because of the bad weather that the ship will not have departed; but it has, and he soon learns that it has gone down with all hands. Octave ends on his knees in the cathedral.

A satisfying shape, but a rather obvious one. For a twentieth-century story, it is almost too neat and predictable. Above

all the story is written with an obvious aim of edification. The man who has strayed from God is brought back to God by the central experience depicted; a voice from childhood returns him to purity.

This aim is underlined by the language and imagery that is used. The visitor (significantly named Gabriel) is clearly a messenger from God when, presented with a glass of water, he says: '"Voilà donc ce verre d'eau qui sera rendu au centuple . . . mais cent verres d'eau, Octave, pour éteindre un feu éternel!"' Octave, in his later remorse, uses similarly Biblical terms: '"Que ne m'avais-tu pas prévenu!" gémit Octave. Alors il se rappela qu'il est écrit que le Fils de l'Homme viendra comme un voleur, à l'heure que nous n'avons pas choisie. Heureux celui qui n'a pas une maison à mettre en ordre, un champ à ensemencer, une passion à assouvir une suprême fois.' The identification of Gabriel with Christ continues in an even more obvious way: 'Ah! le revoir une fois encore, le servir, essuyer d'un linge cette face désolée, apaiser cette faim et cette soif! [. . .] Trop tard! "Seigneur, c'est à ce croisement de route qu'il aurait fallu Vous reconnaître et que j'eusse dû sentir mon âme ardente en moi."' Finally, the sudden sense of forgiveness that Octave experiences is found to have coincided with the sinking of the ship with Gabriel aboard; it is as though Gabriel had served as a sacrifice for him. Mauriac is here using, in a rather simplistic manner, the theme of vicarious suffering, which was so central to traditional techniques of the Catholic novel.

It is, of course, possible to find in this story some aspects of Mauriac's later, more polished literary techniques. But where these later techniques are subtly and effectively used, here they are vitiated by heavy and obvious clumsiness. Thus the visual and sensuous evocation of past scenes, which is used with such subtlety in stories like **'Le Rang'**, is here merely one more heavy sack of pious offerings:

> Il chercha dans son passé: en lui, autour de ce regard, peu à peu des objets émergeaient; il vit la barrière d'une cour de récréation [. . .] En une seconde (car les images se succédaient si rapides qu'Octave les aurait pu croire simultanées) il entendit les chaînes de l'encensoir qu'ouvrait dans le chœur embrasé, embrumé, cet enfant vêtu d'écarlate. Sur l'autel de la Vierge, les lilas étaient mourants; une voix indiquait la page du cantique qui soudain jaillissait, soutenu par l'orgue[. . .]

Similarly, the opening evocation of the silent house, and the listening Octave ovserving himself in a mirror, which promises mature Mauriacian effects, declines into banal obviousness: 'Il [. . .] entendit sourdre au plus secret de son être une protestation, comme une voix étouffée, comme un appel perdu.' Above all, however, this story lacks any of the nuances, the ambiguity one expects of modern literature. It tells a moral tale with no surprises and no blurred edges.

When, after the successful 1926-7 trio, Mauriac came to write **'Le Démon de la connaissance'** (1928), he fell back into many of the same pitfalls. Again, he is concerned to edify, as certain authorial interventions make absolutely clear: 'Ainsi délire cet orgueilleux: comme il est loin du Maître humble de cœur! Mais il ne le sait pas.' But there are even more serious flaws in this story, which stem from another of Mauriac's over-riding concerns: the desire to depict in full the character and fate of the central figure, Maryan. Maryan is closely based on Mauriac's childhood friend André Lacaze; and, though many of the details of the story are imaginary, it is as though it runs in a kind of counterpoint to the actual events of Lacaze's life, which appears to have been a starting-point for a process that Jacques Petit describes as follows: 'Le romancier rêve sur un souvenir et le déforme' [*Oeuvres Complètes,* Vol. I]. As Mauriac himself said, 'Tout est inventé, mais non le personnage lui-même' [*Oeuvres Complètes,* Vol. I].

This concern with the character of his friend dominates this short story and makes Mauriac's account of the imaginary events of his life clumsy. Instead of those short-hand glimpses of aspects of human character in which the short story excels, we find a desire to tell as much as possible, and over as long a period as seems necessary. It is the attempt to compress a whole range of events, over a period of years, into one short story, which strains the form of the genre so disastrously. We see, in Chapter I, Maryan and his friend Lange in his school playground, and perceive the elements in Maryan's make-up: his intellectual violence, his physical ugliness, his strange tics, and so on. Maryan describes his intention to go into a seminary, more for negative reasons than because of a clear religious vocation. By Chapter II, Maryan has entered the seminary; Lange visits him; by the end of the chapter we have moved forward once more in time, and find a letter from Maryan announcing his departure from the seminary and asking Lange to join him on a visit to his sister-in-law's. Chapters III and IV deal dramatically with the complicated relationships and hang-ups revealed by this visit. They are the high-point of the story, and as one sequence in a complete novel would be highly successful. Finally, we have Maryan's apparent conversion, which, by a *tour de force mauriacien,* is seen to be mistaken: 'Ainsi [. . .] Maryan se parle à lui-même et déjà, à son insu, falsifie la parole de Dieu. The story ends with a look to the future, and to Maryan's eventual conversion in the trenches of the First World War:

> Se résignerait-il jamais aux longues étapes d'une recherche sans espérance? De nouveau, il regarda le ciel comme un homme qui guette un présage. Mais il n'y découvrit pas le terrible 'chemin court' qui, bien des années plus tard, lui serait proposé pour atteindre Dieu. Il ne vit pas en esprit cette tranchée dans la terre où, quelques secondes avant l'assaut, quelques minutes avant d'être abattu, il répéterait à mi-voix la plus belle parole que la guerre ait inspirée à un homme près de mourir: 'Enfin! je vais savoir'.

The ending, and much of the previous comment on Maryan's state of mind, share the main fault of *Ce qui était perdu,* which was to succeed it two years later: an omniscient narrator who perceives religious truths, including the private thoughts of his characters, and their conversions, and who judges these things from a vantage-point of moral certainty.

A swift outline of the shape of this story, such as we have given, naturally cannot do justice to the complexity of emotions and motivation depicted within it. What it does, however, is to show us how the story as a whole suffers from problems inherent in any short story written without regard to the basic problems of the genre. To move chronologically through events widely spaced in time is natural to the novel; in the short story it only works (as in certain nineteenth-century examples) if there is a clear dramatic twist involved, and if the issues can be explained simply and clearly. Far more satisfactory, when the emotional issues are complicated, is to concentrate on 'un instant précis', and to make use of flashbacks, as Mauriac does so effectively in **'Coups de couteau'** and in **'Le Rang'**. Here, Chapter III and the first part of Chapter IV of **'Le Démon de la connaissance'** would fit superbly into a novel; but unfortunately the rest of that novel has been crammed into the first two chapters and the final paragraph. Forgetting his success with short-story techniques only a year or so before, Mauriac here seems to see a short story as being merely a shortened novel.

Two remaining stories from a later date, **'Le Drôle'** and **'Conte de Noël'**, both use traditional techniques of the short story perfectly adequately, but both are vitiated by faults of another order. **'Le Drôle'** need not retain us long. Appearing in the same year (1933) as two of Mauriac's most successful stories, it was doomed from the start by the particular requirement it was expected to fulfil—'histoire pour les enfants'—as part of a series of such stories written by great writers. Unfortunately Mauriac's approach to this task was to produce a rather banal little tale which might well still arouse some enthusiasm nowadays on a children's television programme, but which is so predictable that it has very little literary merit. A governess arrives to look after a child who has been so monstrously spoiled that he terrorises his family, and is a legend in the neighbourhood; she eventually tames him partly through tough tactics, partly through kindness to his dog, and partly through the power of music. All those who wished to accuse the governess of unkindness to the child are put to confusion by his clear attachment to her. Not a handkerchief remains dry among the readers.

The banality of this little 'cautionary tale' is matched by the sheer unreality of the central figure. Spoilt children have often figured in literature, but the powers this child holds over his family and servants are so exaggerated as to appear completely unreal. The whole story would fit well into an unreal *Struwelpeter* format, but the realistic techniques used by the author only serve to heighten the reader's disbelief. Elements in those techniques, it must be noted, are at times evidence of the advances Mauriac has made in the short story; but they revolve around an unsuitable subject.

'Conte de Noël', published in 1938, is unusual among Mauriac's short stories in that it uses one of the central nineteenth-century short-story techniques: the surprise ending. The first part of the story takes place in the narrator's childhood. Christmas is approaching; in the playground a child, Jean de Blaye, who has always been persecuted because of his curls (which the narrator secretly admires because they remind him of Little Lord Fauntleroy), is this time being mocked because of his belief in Father Christmas. He and the narrator discuss the matter; Jean has implicit faith in his mother's word. However, they both decide to stay awake and see. In the event the narrator, half-asleep, ends up by half-believing. At school after the holiday, however, Jean de Blaye appears shorn of his curls. Of his mother, he says: 'Elle ne me blaguera plus' [*Oeuvres Complètes*, Vol. III]. The scene now shifts to a Paris night club, several years later, where the adult narrator, nostalgic for the Christian Christmas at home which he is missing, is drinking alone. He sees a person he believes to be Jean de Blaye, and says to him: 'On n'aurait pas dû te couper les boucles. The man, who turns out to be Jean's younger brother, is naturally bewildered. Of the curls, he tells a story: his mother had owned a silver box, which the boys were sure contained a treasure. Jean, of whom his brother says, 'Elle l'aimait plus que moi [. . .] Et au fond je crois bien qu'elle n'aimait que lui . . . Mais quelque chose les séparait, je ne sais quoi', forced the lock one day, and found— his childhood curls. Jean, furious, burned them. Jean, it is discovered, is now dead. By hints, we learn that he 'avait fini comme un mauvais garçon, comme un enfant perdu'. The narrator goes home moved by the story, but above all with his vocation as a writer made clear. 'Un romancier venait de naître et ouvrait les yeux sur ce triste monde.'

A number of subtle techniques are used to create the effects in this story, such as we shall see in Mauriac's best stories. Above all, the conversation with the brother, with its hints and reticences, is a masterpiece. And the harsh treatment of a subject with the misleading title **'Conte de Noël'** is striking and quite effective. But the story as a whole just does not work. The attempt to produce an 'effect de surprise' *à la* Maupassant is clumsy; we have already guessed that Jean's break with his mother is what has made him cut off his curls (which by the stress on them have already become central); we can guess the effect this will have on what was clearly a doting mother; as for his eventual 'bad life', the story leading up to it appears disproportionate, so that the story loses the desired effect. We find, perhaps, a clue to Mauriac's intentions in the last section; perhaps this *is* the kind of story that might have set him on the path to writing at an early stage; perhaps it *is* an early story which he has published at this late date, to make up the number of stories in *Plongées*. Certainly, unlike the other stories in this collection, this story had not been published before. From its mawkish tone, and from the self-conscious ending so typical of a young writer, it would seem to date from an earlier part of Mauriac's career.

If we turn now to Mauriac's successful trio of stories from 1926 and 1927, we find not only that the three dangers of edification, of banality, and of novel-form have been avoided, but that the traditional short-story shape, as found in **'Le Drôle'** or **'Conte de Noël'**, has also been lost. The 'beginning, middle and end' story-line, with its satisfying shape, so typical of the nineteenth-century short story, has given way to the evocation of a mood or a situation in their own right, to the depiction of an instant in time, the overtones of which can spread far and wide outside the confines of the story itself.

'Un Homme de lettres' depicts a writer's fluctuating relationships with women. Much of this *nouvelle* consists of attempts, by the writer himself and by those around him, to understand his behaviour. On the last page, as the narrator has produced what appears a convincing explanation, Jérôme (the writer) answers his enquiry as to whether this is correct with a series of questions, which seem mostly addressed to himself:

—Avouez que j'ai touché juste!

—Juste ou non, comment le saurais-je? Qu'est-ce donc que signifie: rejoindre un être? [. . .] Pourquoi l'amitié ne nous suffit-elle? [. . .] Pourquoi faut-il que, seule, une femme nous féconde? [*Oeuvres Complètes*, Vol. I]

The ending of the story remains open, with Jérôme obviously heading off for another liaison: 'La main levée de Jérôme arrêta un chauffeur; mais je n'entendis pas l'adresse qu'il luidonnait à voix basse.'

'Insomnie' is the evocation of a seemingly interminable night in which the hero, Louis, goes over and over in his mind the suffering caused him by the love he feels for a woman of whom he is morbidly jealous, and who perpetually appears to give cause for that jealousy. The story begins at a dinner-party, and is seen at this stage through the eyes of the woman herself. She is aware that she has given Louis cause for jealousy, and that he has left the party: 'La jeune femme écoute à, peine: un absent l'occupe, qu'elle torture. La douleur de Louis ressemble à un feu qu'elle entretient, dont elle ne peut s'éloigner' [*Oeuvres Complètes*, Vol. II]. The rest of the story deals with Louis's insomniac night. Finally, as dawn breaks, despite the torments he has suffered, despite his realisation of her cruelty, he awaits the telephone call that will cause it all to start again: 'Cependant Louis guette l'appel du téléphone. Ce bruit de pas? C'est peut-être une dépêche qu'on apporte. Il attend la permission de cette femme, il attend que son bourreau lui fasse un signe pour se relever, pour rentrer dans la vie.'

As with **'Un Homme de lettres'**, the ending is open; the *tranche* of Louis's existence that we have seen is self-perpetuating, and has no beginning, middle or end. The two stories we have just described thus not only provide a new type of short story, much in line with the contemporary developments in the English short story and with later developments in France; they also (particularly **'Un Homme de lettres'**) make use of the new ambiguity which Mauriac had introduced to his novels in this period, and of which *Thérèse Desqueyroux* is the outstanding example: an individual's motivation is a mystery not only to others but also to the individual him- or herself; a variety of interpretations is possible for every action; above all, people fail to communicate with one another.

'Coups de couteau' shares these qualities, and is perhaps the most outstanding short story of the three. For this reason I have chosen it for a rather closer examination of some of the more detailed techniques Mauriac uses; it must be borne in mind, however, that a similar examination of the other two would reveal many of the same characteristics.

The time-scale for '**Coups de couteau**' is only one night. It takes the form of a conversation between husband and wife, in which events outside that time-span are merely referred to, or remembered by one of the two characters. The third of the four chapters consists entirely of a flash-back, in the mind of the wife, to a specific previous event; this flashback technique is here seen to be far more effective, in the context of a concise short story, than any chronological treatment such as that in '**Le Démon de la connaissance**' could have been.

The subject is, once again, suffering in love. The husband, Louis, a famous artist, is as tormented by his love for a young woman as was his namesake, the hero of '**Insomnie**'. Yet here the whole matter is complicated by the presence, at his side, of another suffering human being, his wife Elisabeth, of whose feelings he is basically unaware. The whole story revolves about the impossibility of communication, and of ever seeing into each other's hearts.

The story starts with a brilliant evocation of the wakeful Elisabeth, who has been awaiting the return of the children's nurse before going to sleep; she becomes aware that her husband is also awake. She realises that he is distressed, and presses him to tell her the reason. She begins to realise that it is because of a woman, but still desires to know more: 'Elle pouvait être tranquille, maintenant: il parlerait, il s'abandonnerait à un flux de paroles, susciterait la présence spirituelle de l'être bien-aimé. Comment se fût-il retenu de céder à cette consolation? D'ailleurs, c'était vrai qu'on pouvait tout dire à Élisabeth: "On peut tout lui dire; elle est étonnante; elle comprend tout" [*Oeuvres Complètes*, Vol. I]. 'C'était vrai que . . . ': as so often with such phrases, for a writer like Mauriac, the truth is not so simple. The passage of *style indirect libre,* followed by direct speech, conveys merely Louis's view of Elisabeth. Gradually we will begin to realise the complexity of her emotions.

At first, this comes merely through hints, as when Louis, in full spate of his emotional outpourings, clearly hits a nerve as he discounts everything but his love:

> [. . .] un être dont soudain la valeur se découvre à nous jusqu'à nous paraître infinie, jusqu'à reléguer tout le reste, à rejeter au néant tout ce qui emplissait notre vie! . . . Qu'as-tu, Babeth?
>
> —Rien, un frisson.
>
> —Durant tout ce temps où je ne l'aimais pas[. . .]

As Louis heedlessly rattles on, Elisabeth encourages him by recalling, in her own words, Louis's own cliché about her—in other words, by taking on the character that he has imagined: 'Tu sais bien qu'on peut tout me dire, à moi. A qui donc te confierais-tu, sinon à Babeth?'

The woman whom he loves is a young artist, Andrée. Elisabeth suggests, apparently for Louis's own sake, that Andrée has made up to him for the sake of her career. Many of the actions of this 'absent' character in the story make us believe that this is quite possibly so; our main problem is that we can only see her through the eyes of either Louis or Elisabeth. As Louis, after protesting, admits that he finds it impossible to believe that Andrée loves him, Elisabeth feels it necessary to console him; and, in so doing, reveals his lack of feeling towards *her*:

> Élisabeth le serra de nouveau contre elle, répéta:
>
> —Je le sais bien, moi, que l'on peut t'adorer.
>
> —Toi, chérie, ça ne compte pas.
>
> Elle desserra un peu son étreinte, et comme elle murmurait: 'C'est affreux, ce que tu dis . . . ', il voulut expliquer sa pensée: les époux sont si mêlés l'un à l'autre, si confondus, que les lois ordinaires de l'amour ne les concernent pas.

Louis talks about suffering. Elisabeth, who 'souffrait de ne rien pouvoir pour lui', reassures him that he must be loved by Andrée, because of the jealousy that she, Elisabeth, had suffered when they were together.

Again, Louis's self-centredness comes out: '"—Tu as donc un peu souffert, ma pauvre Babeth?" Il répétait: "Tu as souffert avec un vague plaisir."' At every point, we sense Louis's capacity for hurting Elisabeth. Asked whether she has ever made him suffer (in the way Andrée does), he replies that that was impossible, because he knew that she was 'toute à lui'. (Again, a supposition produced as a truth.) When Elisabeth, faced once again by his maudlin meanderings about his love, says that if it were not for the children she would leave, and get out of the way, he protests that he could not imagine life without her and the children. At this, she 'l'embrassa dans un élan de gratitude', but she remembers at the same time how keen he has been to get away from them whenever possible. Once again words are seen to be untrustworthy, and truths to be hidden and uncertain.

From now on Mauriac starts using a technique which is habitual to him in such scenes—his characters' minds wander from what the other is saying. This has two very effective results: the persistence of the speaker is conveyed to us, without our being bored by his repetitions; and the state of mind of the listener is hinted at, without anything precise being stated: 'Depuis quelques instants, Élisabeth n'écoutait plus Louis, elle prêta l'oreille. Ah! c'était de l'autre encore qu'il parlait avec une abondance horrible. [. . .] La pensée d'Élisabeth fuit encore. Il fait étouffant dans la chambre.'

As the night wears on, and dawn breaks, Louis rattles on, and now touches on a new theme: Andrée, too, is suffering in love, and looks upon Louis as someone she can rely on. In a sense, the Louis-Elisabeth relationship is reflected in the relationship between Andrée and Louis. Andrée has said to him: 'C'est beaucoup pour moi de pouvoir souffrir auprès de vous.' Again, Louis takes Elisabeth's attitude for granted; and she does nothing to contradict him. Describing his own jealousy, he says:

> 'Que tu dois me trouver bizarre, toi, cœur tranquille! car quoi que tu en dises, c'est une justice à te rendre: tu n'es pas jalouse.'

Elle rit encore, assura que, si peu jalouse qu'elle fût, elle arrivait tout de même à se représenter assez bien ce que pouvait être cette passion.

Gradually, however, we perceive a need in Elisabeth. She needs to know that Louis could have felt jealousy for *her* in the way he does for Andrée. She asks him outright, and his response is uncomprehending:

—Je suis bien sûre que tu n'as jamais éprouvé à mon propos le moindre mouvement de jalousie?

—Voyons, Babeth, ce serait te faire injure.

Elle éclata de ce mauvais rire, mais Louis ne comprenait pas. Il ne croyait pas qu'avec Élisabeth il y eût même à essayer de comprendre.

Elisabeth now feels the need to open his eyes: 'Enfin, cette nuit, et pour la première fois monte du plus profond de son être une exigence: que Louis sache au moins qu'elle est faite de cette même chair qu'il chérit dans une autre femme.' She attempts to provoke him by allusions to having given him cause for jealousy; but this time, by a brilliant reversal of the technique, it is the self-centred Louis who is not listening:

—Rien à faire, Babeth, je suis tranquille.

Elle s'exaspérait de sentir qu'il l'écoutait à peine; il ne la vers elle, à cette minute: le petit jour éclairait assez cette figure pour qu'il y pût lire les signes d'un désordre profond. Mais il demeurait étendu et les yeux clos.

It is then that she breaks the spell (or attempts to do so) with the violent and provocative remark: 'Tu as eu tort quelquefois d'être tranquille. At last he looks at her, and realises her feelings; yet almost immediately his self-centredness relegates them once more to the sidelines:

A ces mots, pourtant, il leva les paupières, vit enfin Élisabeth. Le bref regard qu'ils échangèrent éclaira chacun d'eux sur les coups qu'il avait porté à l'autre, au long de cette nuit. Il la prit à son tour dans ses bras, fit un effort pour s'évader de sa propre douleur et pour pénétrer dans cette douleur étrangère. Mais qu'elle lui paraissait mesquine! Il n'aurait jamais cru que Babeth fût capable de ressentir ces pauvres blessures d'amourpropre.

Desperate to prove something, under his questioning she mentions the name of a man, Paul Orgère. He roars with laughter at the thought of that 'nigaud'; and it is true that this, too, had been her opinion of him. But there is something she needs to explain to Louis, and cannot: 'Comment faire entendre à Louis que son indifférence faillit un jour la livrer à cet homme?' As with Thérèse Desqueyroux, as with other Mauriac heroines, Elisabeth finds motivations and emotions impossible to explain; like them she searches her memory in vain for the key: 'Élisabeth s'efforce de se rappeler [. . .] Elle se souvient [. . .]'

Chapter III of the story is an account through Elisabeth's memory of a journey alone in a car with Paul Orgère; of the sexual excitement of the drive, and of her exultation because 'aux yeux d'un autre être, elle incarnait le monde et toutes ses délices; quelqu'un, enfin, lui reconnaissait un prix infini. Assez de vivre dans un désert d'indifférence! Why had she not fallen, when they went to a hotel? Because, when she came downstairs for dinner, the 'young god' had become a young man 'en smoking, la boutonnière fleurie d'un œillet, les cheveux lisses et qui sentaient bon', who 'avait au coin des lèvres le sourire de l'aventure'.

Typically, there is more to it than that. Elisabeth's reaction 'Sauvée! ce n'était plus qu'une affaire de verrou' hints at the fact that she *is* at heart the virtuous, dependable wife that Louis imagines. None of this, of course, can be explained to Louis. All he can see is the expression on her face as she relives the experience; and that expression arouses, for the first time, his compassion: 'Tandis qu'elle refaisait en esprit ce voyage sur une route trop chaude, souhaitant et redoutant à la fois de découvrir à son époux comme elle avait été près de se perdre, Louis l'observait dans le petit jour, plein de pitié pour cette figure exténuée, vieillie.' He attempts to reassure her; she pretends to be reassured. They both believe that, the night aiding, they have exaggerated. Yet the moment Elisabeth leaves the room, Louis shows that he is just as obsessed. Finally, he has a telephone call from Andrée. Typically, as he returns from it, he is once more self-centred, in that he cannot imagine why the telephone call has only changed *his* mood, and not that of Elisabeth. The story ends with the prospect of his suffering situation continuing *ad infinitum*: 'Louis, déjà, s'était redressé. Il commença de marcher dans l'atelier, reprenant une à une chaque parole d'Andrée, jusqu'à ce qu'il en eût extrait tout le poison qui lui était nécessaire pour souffrir.'

Like the other two stories, **'Coups de couteau'** is openended. We have witnessed an instant in two people's lives, but those lives are going to continue in the same noncommunicating, suffering manner.

All three 1926-7 stories use with great effect the techniques of ambiguity which Mauriac had perfected in the contemporary novels *Le Désert de l'amour*, **Thérèse Desqueyroux** and **Destins**. More than this, however, they also use the techniques of concision essential to the short story. Where, in a novel, a wide variety of psychological characteristics would be invoked, through a series of incidents, here the concentration is on a few clear elements in a relationship, complicated and ambiguous though they turn out to be. By concentrating on one moment in time, and on the obsessions of the characters concerned, Mauriac spotlights these aspects convincingly; it is not necessary, as in a novel, for the characters to be satisfactorily rounded.

Nothing could be more misleading than to think of these stories as potential chapters of a novel. Their open-endedness tells us that things are, in each case, going to continue exactly as they have done. The moment in time that we have witnessed is not a link in a chain of events; it is a bead in a rosary of exactly similar beads, and it is through the depiction of that bead that we have been made fully aware of the nature of the rosary, without the other beads needing to be described.

The next group of short stories is very different, but equally adapted to the genre, to the extent that one cannot imagine the subjects being treated in a different way. By now Mauriac, while still concentrating on specific moments of experience, has become less concerned with the exploration of individual consciousness, and more interested in the clash of personalities, ideas, and impressions; and in the process he creates perfectly chiselled cameos in which certain precise techniques create powerful effects.

I shall take, as the main example, **'Thérèse chez le docteur'**. But before doing so, we must clear up a widespread misapprehension. The two Thérèse stories have suffered from the presumption that, because of one character within them, their main importance for Mauriac must have been simply as a continuation of the story of the powerful heroine of *Thérèse Desqueyroux*. Yet, viewed differently, Thérèse can be seen as a useful figure for a short-story writer in that her characteristics do not need to be described at length. For similar reasons other characters, and families, recur in Mauriac's work from time to time.

This is particularly relevant to **'Thérèse chez le docteur'**, where, unlike **'Thérèse à l'hôtel',** Thérèse is not even the central figure, but serves as a catalyst for the experiences of others. If we approach **'Thérèse chez le docteur'** with an open mind, *as a short story in its own right,* we perceive that the relationship between Dr Schwartz and his wife is not merely a 'cadre' to Thérèse's interview with the psychologist, but is one of the two central points of the story (the other, intimately linked with it, as we shall see, being the attack on psychoanalysis).

The relationship between Elisée and Catherine Schwartz is stressed from the very beginning of the story. We have, first, an example of Elisée's 'plaisir de la contredire et de l'humilier' [*Oeuvres Complètes*, Vol. III]; this is followed by a section in which the background to the marriage is explained. It is clear that the reader's attention is being directed towards their problems. Once the late-night visit of an 'obsédée' is announced, 'harcelée par le désir du meurtre', Catherine decides to disregard her husband's orders and to remain at hand near his consulting-room (of which we have already conveniently heard that every sound within it could be heard outside). Throughout Thérèse's interview with Dr. Schwartz, which we hear through Catherine's ears, we are aware of Catherine's reactions. The visitor's laugh 'réveillait l'angoisse de l'épouse aux aguets'. The doctor's 'accent affectueux et grave', which he never had when speaking to her, made her realise her own situation: 'Elle se répétait que cet homme, pour elle seule, faisait étalage de sa férocité . . . oui, pour elle seule. Again, the unknown visitor's laugh makes Catherine 'tressaillir'. As the woman pours out her emotions to the doctor, Catherine feels a desire to warn her:

> Pourquoi s'adressait-elle à Élis? se demandait Catherine. Pourquoi à lui, précisément, ces confidences? Elle avait

> envie d'ouvrir la porte du cabinet, de crier à l'inconnue: 'Il n'a rien à vous donner, il ne peut rien pour vous que vous enfoncer davantage dans cette boue. J'ignore à qui il faudrait vous adresser, mais pas à lui, pas à lui!'

This reinforces the picture we have already formed of the doctor's private life, and of his night-club adventures far from his wife, in the course of which he had met Thérèse; it tells us even more about his relationship with Catherine.

There is then a significant moment when Catherine, realising that she is eavesdropping on confidences, decides to go upstairs. We, the readers, naturally go with her, and witness her communion with herself in a mirror: 'Elle s'approcha de la glace, regarda longuement cette figure ingrate avec laquelle il lui fallait traverser sa vie. La lumière, les objets familiers la rassuraient. Qu'avait-elle craint? Quel péril? D'ailleurs, cette femme n'était pas la première venue. We not only learn, here, more about Elisée and Catherine; we also, by a Mauriacian technique with which we are by now familiar, miss some of the conversation below. Raised voices bring her back to listen; but even now, 'une seconde, le bruit de l'ascenseur l'empêche de rien entendre'. From now on, Catherine listens to the whole interview, and we are left in no doubt as to the mood in which she listens:

> Catherine savait bien qu'elle n'écoutait plus par simple devoir: il ne s'agissait plus, pour elle, de secourir son mari en cas d'attaque. Non: elle cédait à une curiosité irrépressible [. . .] Cette voix inconnue la fascinait, et en même temps, elle ne pouvait supporter la pensée de la déception qui attendait cette malheureuse. Élis n'était même pas capable de la comprendre; pas même d'avoir pitié d'elle. Comme ses autres victimes, il la pousserait à s'assouvir. La délivrance de l'esprit par l'assouvissement de la chair: c'était à cela que se ramenait sa méthode. La même clé immonde lui servait pour interpréter l'héroïsme, le crime, la sainteté, le renoncement . . . Ces idées traversaient confusément l'esprit de Catherine sans qu'elle perdît un mot de ce qui se disaitdans le cabinet.

Catherine's reactions continue to be examined during the interview. Finally, because at one moment she cannot stand her husband's laugh, she 'ferma derrière elle la porte de sa chambre, tomba à genoux contre le lit, se boucha les oreilles, demeura longtemps ainsi, prostrée, abîmée, ne pensant à rien'. We thus miss the climax of the scene in the consulting-room, and it is only the terrified voice of her husband calling her name that causes her to burst into the room, to find Elisée crouching behind the desk, hidden from view, beseeching her to 'disarm' Thérèse, whose right hand, hidden within her handbag, is merely clutching a white packet, and not a weapon.

The story ends with Catherine's reaction to what she has seen or heard. For one single moment in the story we see things through the eyes of her husband: 'Il observait sa femme avec étonnement. Il ne lui avait jamais vu cette figure rayonnante de bonheur.' Her final remarks show just what has happened during the course of the story: Il m'a fallu vingt années . . . Mais enfin, c'est fini! Je suis délivrée, Élis, je ne t'aime plus.' Typically, we are left to wonder which of the many thoughts which had affected her during the story has had this effect and the extent to which her husband's ludicrous behaviour at the end had some bearing on it. As always, the meaning is ambiguous. But, when viewed without *parti pris,* this story is seen to be about the doctor and his wife, with Thérèse acting above all as an instrument. This is not to say that Thérèse's confession is not a powerful one. But it is only when placed in the *Thérèse* corpus that it can be made to appear significant in relation to events outside this story—as opposed to details of those outside events being used to give more effect to the story.

The other main theme of the story, the attack on psychoanalysis, is similarly attached to Schwartz rather than to Thérèse, who again is an instrument to make a case. As I have suggested elsewhere, this attack is part of the revulsion that Mauriac felt against the methods of his novels of the mid-1920s: it shows Mauriac turning to an explanation of human behaviour based on supernatural forces, with evil becoming a living force in its own right. Mauriac appears to have been influenced in this by Bernanos's expression of the same problem. Based clearly on the scene between Mouchette and the doctor in *Sous le soleil de Satan,* the Thérèse-Schwartz scene contains at frequent intervals the 'rire de l'inconnue', the 'rire un peu fou', the 'éclat de rire de l'inconnue (comme une étoffe déchirée)', which in Bernanos's work signify possession by the devil. And Thérèse herself asks the question which the doctor cannot answer: 'Croyez-vous au démon, docteur? Croyez-vous que le mal soit quelqu'un?' Like Bernanos, Mauriac condemns psychiatry for the false issues which, in his view, it presents. Again in the mouth of Thérèse, we hear the indictment: 'Vous faites semblant de vouloir guérir l'âme, et vous ne croyez pas à l'âme . . . Psychiâtre, ça signifie médecin de l'âme, et vous dites que l'âme n'existe pas. Catherine's assessment of her husband's methods, which we have seen above, adds to the indictment. In the other direction, the psychiatry theme adds piquancy to the Elisée-Catherine theme. They are firmly intertwined. For the two clear purposes for which the story was written, the framework and the techniques are perfect.

In **'Thérèse à l'hôtel',** where Thérèse plays the central role, the short story is again satisfying and self-sufficient. It has a perfect shape, centred on a short period in time. The relationships and misunderstandings have, indeed, very wide implications in relation to love, sin and repentance; Thérèse, by her nature, is a perfect central figure for the treatment of such themes. But, like the 'middle-period' stories, this story need not be a link in a chain: it can stand on its own. **'Le Rang',** by its skilful use of repetitive evocations of the past, by its repetitions of key phrases in relation to the characteristics of individuals, and by a panoply of the techniques we have already seen in the other stories, is a particularly good example of Mauriac's art. Psychological truths are conveyed not by the more leisurely techniques of the novel, but by a series of hints and flashbacks, which pinpoint states of mind.

It is hoped that what this study has shown is that, in his best short stories, Mauriac succeeds in making a particularly appropriate use of techniques which make of these stories works of art in their own right; and that they should never

be seen either as *romans manqués,* as *romans en préparation,* or as parts of a corpus which merely serve to throw greater light on the larger works within it.

David O'Connell   (essay date 1995)

SOURCE: "The Early Fiction and the Short Stories," in *François Mauriac Revisited,* Twayne Publishers, 1995, pp. 28-50.

[*O'Connell is an American educator and critic. In the following excerpt, he surveys Mauriac's short stories and relates them thematically to the novels he was writing at the time.*]

Mauriac's short fiction appeared during his lifetime in two principal collections: *Trois récits* (1929), (Three stories) and *Plongées* (1938), (Fathomings), which contained another five stories. In addition to these collections, there are two more stories, **"Le Visiteur nocturne"** and **"Le Drôle,"** which were published separately and not gathered into a collection until publication of the *Oeuvres complètes.* These 10 stories represent the only short fiction that Mauriac chose to pass on to posterity.

With the exception of **"Un Homme de lettres"** and **"Le Démon de la Connaissance,"** all the stories are more or less directly related to Mauriac's novels. In some cases the connection is obvious, as for instance the two stories dealing with the character of Thérèse Desqueyroux. But even here, the apparent relationship is more complex than it seems at first. In the case of **"Thérèse chez le docteur,"** for example, themes are developed that range far beyond what we usually associate with the character of Thérèse. In fact, it can be argued that she is a mere pretext for treatment of such themes.

Mauriac's short fiction, including the still unpublished stories in the Bibliothèque Jacques Doucet, are a minor, but interesting and at times important part of Mauriac's total oeuvre. They have not as yet been studied in any systematic way either on their own merits or in terms of the ways in which they help to illuminate the novels. The following discussion is a first critical and analytical attempt at such a study.

"Le Visiteur nocturne" (1920)

When Mauriac gathered together the texts to be placed in his *Oeuvres complètes,* he selected only one story from among several published immediately after World War I. **"Le Visiteur nocturne"** (The nocturnal visitor) first appeared in May 1920 in the *Revue de Jeunes.* The story seems to be a further development of the character Augustin of *Préséances,* the novel that Mauriac was working on at the same time.

In this brief story, a young would-be writer named Octave, living in a bourgeois setting in Paris, is visited late at night by a former classmate from secondary school whom he has not seen in eight years. Gabriel, who had wanted to become a seminarian but could not because of financial difficulties, is now passing through Paris on his way to Bordeaux from Charleville, a city in the north of France where Rimbaud was born. He has been exploited these last few years while working for meager wages in a private school in order to support his sickly parents. Now he is returning to Bordeaux in order to embark on a ship destined for Dakar, where he has been offered a job. He will be leaving shortly aboard *L'Afrique.* Unfortunately, Octave does not extend a very warm welcome to his old friend, who wants to reminisce about the adolescent experiences that still mean so much to him. Octave begrudgingly allows his friend to sleep on the sofa and does not even get up to wish him farewell in the morning.

It is only after Gabriel's departure that Octave begins to feel remorse. He forces his memory to overcome the obstacle of all the recent events of his life in Paris and return to the school in Bordeaux where he knew Gabriel. He realizes that in not welcoming Gabriel properly, he has turned his back on an important part of his own life. He thus boards a train for Bordeaux to catch up to his friend before he leaves, but to no avail. He not only arrives after the departure of *L'Afrique,* but learns the next day that the ship has sunk in a storm. As the story ends, Octave is hastening to visit a church. Gabriel's abrupt return into his life has clearly been an occasion of grace, for in the closing scene we find the somewhat decadent and self-absorbed Octave kneeling next to a poor man at the back of the church.

In this story, Mauriac pits the purity and innocence of Gabriel against the calculating selfishness of Octave. The references to Rimbaud are unmistakable—both Charleville and the flight to Africa—for Mauriac was still quite conscious of his debt to Rimbaud at this time and wanted to acknowledge it. The story shares the same concerns raised in *Préséances* and may be read as a companion text to that novel.

"Un Homme de lettres" (1926)

"Un Homme de lettres" (A man of letters) is one of Mauriac's most important short stories. It was first published in the *NRF* in July 1926 and later appeared in *Trois récits.* Written in 1926, at the beginning of the spiritual crisis that culminated in the publication of *Ce qui était perdu* in 1930, it tells us a great deal about the *souffrance amoureuse* that had caused so much turmoil in Mauriac's life.

This story, which is more a portrait than a true narrative, is told by an unidentified male writer about his friend Gabrielle and her lover of 15 years, the writer Jérôme, who has left her for Berthe, an older woman with two children. The narrator, through his conversations with Gabrielle, elicits testimony about her years of total sacrifice to Jérôme, a well-known playwright. She has tolerated his past escapades, knowing that he would always come back, but she is upset now because his departure seems irrevocable.

Through the narrator's separate discussions with Gabrielle and Jérôme, the monstrous selfishness of the "man of letters"

is laid bare. Critics generally agree that Mauriac to a certain extent is writing about his own selfish tendencies as he tried to expropriate the experiences that came into his life for eventual transformation into art. It is a bleak portrait of what he could have become if the "conversion" of 1928 had not taken place. The adoring female is the tortured and oppressed party, for her suffering seems to be necessary for the success of the weak and insecure writer. At the end of the story, Jérôme has also left Berthe and her two children; he is last seen going off in a taxi—with no guarantee at all that he is returning to Gabrielle. The story is not so much about the couple as about how the creative partner must use the other to nourish his art.

It is unclear whether Mauriac ever intended to develop this idea into a novel. Although it bears no direct relationship to any of the novels; the story shares a sense of atmosphere with *Ce qui était perdu,* with Jérôme, the insecure writer at the center of the story, foreshadowing Marcel, the failed poet of the novel.

"Coups de couteau" (1926)

"Coups de couteau" ("Stab Wounds") was written shortly after **"Un Homme de lettres"** and first appeared in the *Revue des Deux Mondes* in October 1926. It was later included in *Trois récits.* As he had done in **"Un Homme de lettres,"** Mauriac develops once again the theme of the selfishness and monstrosity of the creative artist. This theme, combined with the stifling Parisian atmosphere centered on the world of art and artists, links the story to *Ce qui était perdu.* Jérôme, the playwright of the earlier story, here becomes Louis, a painter. Once again, there is a couple at the center of the action. To Mauriac, the study of the couple, an enduring theme in western literature, had entered a new phase in the 1920s, with the widespread acceptance of divorce among the social elites. Thus, although divorce is an alternative for Louis, who is infatuated with Andrée (herself a wife and mother) and who no longer loves his wife, Elizabeth, he cannot bring himself to break the invisible chain that binds him.

Mauriac analyzes willpower as an important factor in love, since it can affect a conscious decision to remain committed to the lover. The same idea will be taken up later in **"Insomnie."** As the will becomes weakened, the *souffrance amoureuse* caused by longing to be with the lover and not with the spouse increases. This suffering in turn tends to isolate the couple from the rest of the world. They are so preoccupied with their own (largely self-generated) problems that they shut out the outside world.

Within the realm of love and affection, Mauriac tended to divide people into two separate groups: those who suffer in the name of love and those who impose this same suffering on others. The theme is illustrated quite well at the end of this story, when Louis receives a phone call from Andrée. It is Saturday and she must see him that very afternoon; otherwise she will be unable to survive through the weekend. Previously determined to break up with her, he now drinks in this news like a poison, as if he and his wonderful suffering had no effect on his wife (who has answered the phone). This closing scene shows how the two tendencies are inseparable, for as the masochistic Louis suffers in the name of love, he is also imposing renewed torments on his wife, who loves him.

"Insomnie" (1929)

"Insomnie" (Insomnia) was written in 1927, just after "Coups de Couteau," and was published in 1929 under the title "**La Nuit du bourreau de soi-même**" (The night of the hangman of oneself). Significantly, Mauriac deliberately held it back and did not publish it in *Trois récits*. One possible explanation for this is that he feared that if he published it together with "**Coups de couteau**" and "**Un Homme de lettres**" he would run the risk of revealing too much about his personal life.

The thematic relationship of "**Insomnie**" to "**Coups de couteau**" is evident in the opening pages of the story, for the principal protoganists represent the two groups that interested Mauriac most at this time: those who suffer in the name of love, and those who cause this suffering. He not only gives the protagonists the same names used in "**Coups de couteau**," but also points out the nature of the relationship between the two works. To him, "'**Coups de couteau**' and '**Insomnie**' are like two pieces of wreckage from an unknown vessel, from a novel that was not written, [and] that I couldn't write at that time, since I was, so to speak, too involved in the affair, too directly affected by it". On another occasion, he wrote that "**Insomnie**" is "the chapter of a novel that I didn't write, and for which '**Coups de couteau**' would have been perhaps the prologue. Many dramatic destinies still don't furnish the substance of a novel, because there isn't enough action. The story of the hero of "'**Insomnie**' can have only one chapter." Of course, it is precisely this "chapter" of his life that Mauriac was always reluctant to speak about openly. Read together, however, these two stories begin to provide an understanding of the sentimental aspects of Mauriac's religious crisis of the late 1920s.

"**Insomnie**," along with "**Coups de couteau**," stands out in Mauriac's fiction as a road explored but not quite taken. In both works there is no fully developed plot or action. Louis, once again, is a painter, as is the younger Andrée. He is married and his wife and family are away on vacation. In a nightclub Andrée shows interest in another, younger man. Louis, jealous, leaves in a huff and goes home. He knows that Andrée will be unhappy at his jealous departure, but he wants to be home alone and enjoy the feeling of being miserable. He cannot sleep, tossing and turning the whole night. The thoughts that pass through his mind constitute the essence of the story. By being home he is sure to be able to enjoy his suffering, because Andrée, for fear of giving scandal to the domestics and neighbors, cannot come to comfort him in the middle of the night. The story ends on an inconclusive note. The protoganist's suffering is in no way attenuated.

In "**Coups de couteau**," the emphasis is on the suffering that Louis imposes on his wife when he tells her of his love for Andrée. Here we see what this relationship is

doing to him and, in the process, we begin to understand why this essentially sick love attachment can lead nowhere, for Louis is really in love with himself. But he is lucid in his egotism, as he recalls how, as a boy, he had narcissistically kissed his own image in the bathroom mirror.

Just as "**Le Rang**" and "**Le Visiteur nocturne**" are related to *Préséances* by their treatment of the themes of money and social rank, "**Insomnie**," "**Coups de couteau**," (and indirectly "**Un Homme de lettres**") are all related in some way to *Ce qui était perdu*—what I call Mauriac's important, but underrated, Parisian novel—by the theme of the artist/adulterer. Mauriac was right when he stated that these stories were aborted remainders of another attempt to write a novel about Parisian artistic circles. To my mind, this apparent failure only enhances the value and interest of *Ce qui était perdu*, which does, to a certain extent, deal with this subject.

"Le Démon de la connaissance" (1928)

This story was also written during Mauriac's crisis of faith in the late 1920s. Published in the *NRF* in July and August 1928, it also appeared in *Trois récits*. In "**Coups de couteau**" and "**Insomnie**" there exists a genuine tension between the temptations of the flesh and the religious training that Louis, the protagonist, had presumably received as a young man. The incompatability between the two is stressed. In "**Le Démon de la connaissance**" (The demon of understanding), Mauriac develops this same theme from a slightly different point of view by exploring how a young man can decide to become a priest in part because he considers himself so physically unattractive as to be unlovable. This story once again shows Mauriac's obsession, during these crisis years, with the relationship between love and suffering.

Lange and Maryan share an intellectual and artistic quest. Lange is more sensitive to literature, while Maryan prefers to study philosophy.

Thus it is Lange who will become a novelist and who will recount the details of this relationship from his particular point of view. The story is a thinly veiled transposition of Mauriac's boyhood friendship with André Lacaze, who later became a priest and remained true to his calling until death. At some time during their friendship, which fluctuated over the years, Mauriac and Lacaze seem to have had an argument, during which the priest accused the novelist of convincing him as a boy that he was too unattractive to please a girl. This, claimed Lacaze, was the origin of his religious vocation. In the story Maryan (Lacaze) tells his friend: "If I made the mistake of going into the seminary, if I began life with this mistake, you alone are responsible." Mauriac later admitted in his *Bloc-Notes* that, "He reproached me later in life for having made him so conscious of his ugliness that he decided to go into the seminary."

There is little if any action in this story, which, like the others just considered, concentrates on the evocation of a state of mind. For Maryan, the great challenge in life is to understand the mystery of existence, but his philosophical and theological investigations will be inevitably flawed by the heartsickness and isolation that characterize his conviction that he is unlovable. At the end of the story Maryan is sick of life and ready to die, if only to finally know what comes after death. Like the artist Louis of **"Coups de couteau"** and **"Insomnie,"** he is at an impasse, unable to move forward, immobilized by self-absorption.

"Le Démon de la connaissance" is yet another evocation of the difficulties that Mauriac encountered during these years. Although it is not directly related to any of the novels, he would explore this theme again in *Les Chemins de la Mer* (1939) (*The Unknown Sea,* 1948), and base the entire novel *Galigaï* (1952) (*The Loved and the Unloved,* 1953) on it. In these later works, however, it is female characters who are unable to become objects of desire for the men they love.

"Le Drôle" (1933)

"Le Drôle" (The oddball), published in 1933, was specially commissioned for a series of books written by great writers for little children. It tells of a crucial episode in the life of Ernest Romazilhe, a spoiled boy in a provincial family. About 10 years old, he is so spoiled that he has never attended school and has already caused the resignation of 17 nannies. A new nanny, Mlle Thibaud, arrives in his small provincial town as the story opens. Even before she gets off the train, she learns of the challenge that awaits her when a traveler tells her what a terror the boy is. After sizing up the nature of the power that the boy exercises over the entire household, she comes to the conclusion that she will never be able to educate this boy, let alone cure him of his tyrannical ways, as long as his father, his grandmother, and the family maid are there to wait on him. Once she has persuaded the three of them to leave the house and take up residence temporarily at their country home, she is able to deal directly with Ernest. By the end of the story she has succeeded in domesticating him, first by sharing with him her love of animals and later by discovering that his love of music is his Achilles heel.

This story can be connected to Mauriac's novels in a number of ways. One possibility is that Ernest could be considered a childhood portrait of Fernand Casenave of *Génitrix.* On firmer ground, the maid, named Seconde, reminds us of Marie de Lados of *Genitrix* and Cadette of *Le Basier au lépreux.* Finally, Mlle Thibaud's taming of this little Nero through music reminds us of both *Le Sagouin,* in which Guillou's father plays the piano, and *Le Mal,* in which Fanny seduces Fabien through music.

The resemblance to *Le Sagouin* (1951), (*The Little Misery,* 1952) is the most striking, for both Ernest and Guillou are marginal figures. The one is spoiled by adults, who are largely responsible for making him what he has become, while the other is mistreated in a different way by his family. Their similarity lies in their sense of isolation within these dysfunctional families. In each case it is a teacher

from outside the family who is able to help the child. **"Le Drôle,"** unlike *Le Sagouin,* has a happy ending—a somewhat unusual occurence in Mauriac's fiction, but the story had to end like this if it was to fit into the series for which it had been commissioned. Perhaps it is in part for this reason that **"Le Drôle"** is so captivating and delightful to read. Since Mauriac did not include it in either of his two collections, and seems to have published it as an afterthought at the end of volume 10 of his *Oeuvres complètes,* it tends to be overlooked. Nonetheless the portrait that it provides of the relationship between the little Nero of the title and the dysfunctional family of which he is a part makes this a very modern work.

"Thérèse chez le docteur" (1933)

"Thérèse chez le docteur" ("Thérèse and the Doctor," 1947) first appeared in *Candide* in 1933 and was one of the five stories published in *Plongées.... Thérèse Desqueyroux* had originally been drafted in the form of a confession made by Thérèse to the parish priest. Mauriac rewrote this first draft, adopting instead a third-person point of view. In the novel, when Thérèse returns home from the courthouse, she is ready to discuss her crime and to ask her husband, Bernard, for forgiveness, but he does not want to talk. This desire for confession should be kept in mind when reading **"Thérèse chez le docteur."** In this story, ten years have passed since Thérèse left Bernard on the rue Royale. She has had a number of lovers, including Jean Azévédo and later Phili, the narrator's son-in-law from *Noeud de vipères.* Because of her feelings of guilt and anguish, she is still seeking a confessor. This is why she comes to Dr. Schwartz's apartment late at night.

Mauriac uses a framing device in this story, a rare occurrence in his work: the discussion between Thérèse and the psychiatrist is framed by another, quite different story, which probes the relationship between Dr. Schwartz and his wife. Thus, the title of the story notwithstanding, Thérèse is not the exclusive focus of this work, for the authorial voice accords as much importance to the failed love relationship of the Schwartzes.

Thérèse's late arrival at Dr. Schwartz's apartment can be explained perhaps in part because he seems to have given her assurances at an earlier meeting (in a nightclub) that she could visit him at any time if she felt the need to do so. When Thérèse comes to see Dr. Schwartz at his home, where he has his office, she is entering a form of confessional, but in a perverted form. The great doctor is professionally successful, but he has been alienated from his wife for the last 20 years. It is a rainy night and Dr. Schwartz's wife, Catherine, is upset by this sudden arrival of a patient. She tries to relax and regain her composure, but sounds from other apartments, above, below, and elsewhere on the sixth floor, not to mention traffic in the street below, disturb her. There is no silence in this particular confessional. Catherine reminds her husband that he had previously told her about this somewhat strange woman, whom he had met two years earlier, and she voices her fear at having him receive such people in their apartment so late in the evening. The friction between them reminds us of the marital strife between the spouses in **"Un Homme de letters"** and **"Coups de couteau"**. The unhappy and disunited couples in *Le Desert de l'Amour* and *Noeud de viperès* also come to mind, but here there are no children.

Dr. Schwartz refers to the couch on which he places his patients as his "confessional." His name clearly indicates that he symbolizes Freudianism as well as Freud's Germanic and Jewish backgrounds. Since the name means "black" in German, it also evokes the priest, whose traditional garb is black. As Catherine overhears Thérèse's confession, she becomes aware of the difference in the treatment that the doctor accords to her and to this particular patient. Thus, everything that Thérèse says takes on a possible double and contrastive meaning. Gradually, as she listens to Thérèse speak about her love affairs with Jean Azévédo and Phili, Catherine realizes that she is really not listening to this conversation to protect her husband in case Thérèse is carrying a gun, but to eavesdrop on his work. She realizes that she hates both her husband and his work, because he explains everything in terms of an unconscious sexual drive, even going so far as to advise that one can calm the mind by giving the body all the pleasure it wants. Thus, she thinks to herself: "thousands of unhappy people had stammered and repeated their lies, while trying to discover the secret of their existence which they claimed to know nothing of."

This is a harsh condemnation of the man who pretends to be a rival to the priest. Mauriac's grotesque caricature and simplistic reduction of psychoanalysis is no doubt unfair, but he intends to show no mercy to his adversary. The strong polemic tone that is found so often in his journalism creeps in here and becomes a major element in the story. Thus, Catherine's thoughts continue: "As with his other victims, he would encourage her to indulge all her appetites. Freeing the mind by satisfying the flesh; that's what his method was all about. The same filthy key was used to interpret heroism, crime, sanctity, self-renunciation." Through Catherine, Mauriac expresses his own fundamental reason for attacking psychoanalysis: it attacks the notion of sin by weakening the feelings of guilt that Catholic theology traditionally attaches to the sex drive, which of course he had been taught to suppress since childhood; in taking this stance, psychoanalysis threatens the sacred preeminence of the priest, who alone is able to absolve guilt through the sacrament of confession.

Mauriac skillfully intertwines the Thérèse/Dr. Schwartz narrative with the framing narrative of Dr. Schwartz/Catherine in order to contrast the parallel thoughts and feelings of the two women while allowing the narrative voice to attack the scientific claims of psychoanalysis. Since the mysterious visitor is clutching her handbag when she arrives, the doctor's wife thinks that she might be carrying a pistol. This is her excuse for listening to the confession that is about to take place. Through this device the narrative voice is able to draw out the contradictions between Dr. Schwartz as a professional and as a husband.

The first part of Thérèse's confession, in which she tells of her amorous adventures, evokes the atmosphere of both

Ce qui était perdu and **Le Mal**. The theme of drug use (alcohol, cocaine, etc.) on the fringes of a decadent bourgeois society brings to mind what I call Mauriac's Parisian novels, but it shows the self-absorbed characters in a slightly different light. Instead of seeing them in the habitual nightclubs or bars, racing their cars or stealing away to hotel rooms, we see Thérèse in the equivalent of what would become their church, the psychiatrist's office. It is this strong Parisian flavor that also serves to distance this story from the novel **Thérèse Desqueyroux,** which is thoroughly immersed in the lore and culture of les Landes, and to which the story is only superficially related.

The story ends when Catherine hears her husband cry out. She enters the room to find him hiding behind his desk while Thérèse stands against the wall with her hand in her purse. Dr. Schwartz had called for help, thinking that Thérèse was going to shoot him when in fact she was simply reaching for something in her handbag. Catherine now shows the visitor to the door, but not before Thérèse accuses Dr. Schwartz of being a thief because he charges money to treat the soul without really believing in its existence. After Thérèse leaves, Catherine can finally tell her husband that she no longer loves him, no doubt because of his cowardice, as Jacques Petit suggests, but also because of his haughty manner with the sincere and vulnerable patient.

At the time of writing the story, Mauriac took a dim view of psychoanalysis. During his career he would oscillate between acceptance and rejection of Freud's views about the human personality, but at this particular time he was clearly having quite negative thoughts. This is perhaps why he portrays Thérèse's confessor, Dr. Elisée Schwartz, in a very unsympathetic manner. Since Mauriac displayed a good deal of interest in the same subjects that Freud studied, scholars have begun in recent years to probe this possible relationship. In fact, it can be said that Mauriac's principal convictions as a novelist correspond rather well to Freud's basic doctrines on the human personality. Thus, Mauriac's belief throughout his life in theis preoccupation with the power of the church and family in the life of the young Catholic hero corresponds in a way to what Freud called the superego; and his self-conscious development of himself as a person and as an artist makes one think of the fragile Freudian ego navigating in the perilous waters between the id and superego. Mauriac and Freud, after all, were interested in the same things: the hidden forces that make people behave the way they do. But since Mauriac was a steadfast Catholic and Freud an atheist, they used completely different sets of words and images to express themselves.

One useful way to think of Mauriac's possible relationship to Freud is to picture him working between the "old" and the "new," that is, to situate him somewhere between traditional Catholic theologians on the one hand and Freud and his disciples on the other. At the same time, we must bear in mind that even if Mauriac did read Freud—and the evidence here is fragmentary, even contradictory as to what he read and when he read it—he almost certainly did not make an effort to understand Freud any more than he tried to understand the technical and specialized writings of theologians. He was simply not inclined to digest such materials, which were never able tohold his attention for very long. Mauriac's strength lay in language and style, not in philosophy and science. Thus, in his fictional work he never tried to prove or validate the theoretical work of any thinker, including Freud.

"**Thérèse chez le docteur**" is one of Mauriac's most successful pieces. From a purely artistic point of view, Mauriac's objection to psychoanalysis is perhaps best expressed when Thérèse says to the doctor: "Do you believe in the devil, doctor? Do you believe that evil is a person?" Mauriac obviously believed that the answer to this question had to be in the affirmative, since to the Catholic novelist, evil, like goodness, must be incarnate. This is why, in an edifying novel like *Ce qui était perdu,* he had created a Satan figure like Hervé de Blénauge. Likewise, both Gradère in *Les Anges noirs* (1936) and Landin in *Les Chemins de la mer* (1939), would be assigned similar roles. For Mauriac, the stakes are high in this story, for virtually his entire fictional universe depends on the reader's acceptance of evil as a personalized entity. Psychoanalysis, which sees the same human problems that Mauriac analyzed in his fiction as disorders to be treated scientifically and not as problems with metaphysical roots, seemed to him to challenge the very foundations of his art. Thus, he goes for the Freudian jugular in this story. Thanks to its concision, sophisticated framing structure, and passionate defense, however indirect, of the Catholic novelist's reason for being, "**Thérèse chez le docteur**" stands out as one of Mauriac's minor masterpieces. It deserves to be rediscovered and more widely read.

"Thérèse à l'hôtel" (1933)

"**Thérèse à l'hôtel**" ("**Thérèse at the Hotel,**" **1947**) was written sometime after "**Thérèse chez le docteur**" and first published in *Candide* in August 1933. It was later included in *Plongées*. It takes the form of a monologue in which Thérèse recounts a meeting with a young man in a hotel. The encounter leads nowhere when Thérèse, seeking to initiate a relationship with the young man when she meets him, realizes that he feels sorry for her and wants to save her. (Fanny and Fabien in *Le Mal* come to mind in this regard). Whereas the earlier story was finely structured, this one is open-ended, with no clear denouement. In addition, Thérèse's interior monologue reads like the examination of conscience that would precede a confession. The young man seems to be a future priest, the person who could eventually hear her confession, but their meeting leads nowhere. This structure suggests that "**Thérèse à l'hôtel**" might very well have been a first draft of what would eventually become *La Fin de la nuit*. As in that novel, Thérèse is paradoxically both free to pursue further adventures with still more lovers, and a prisoner held hostage by the memory of her earlier act: the attempted murder of her husband.

"Le Rang" (1936)

It is unclear when "**Le Rang**" ("**Rank**") was written, but it was first published in *Candide* in March 1936 and appeared later in *Plongées*. There is no surviving manu-

script of the story, which Jacques Petit thinks was written in 1936.

Based on a maternal grandaunt, a *genitrix* figure who had dominated her children to such an extent that they never married, this story is one of Mauriac's most pessimistic works. It is linked by this theme to *Genitrix* as well as to several other novels in which the dominating mother stifles the development of her children.

Mauriac builds this story around an image. Hector and Hortense Bellade discuss the fact that their cousin, Auguste Duprouy, has spent an unusual amount of money on his dead sister's funeral. Auguste, the last of a dying lineage, had grown up under the controlling influence of his mother, a widow. Since the Duprouy family did not have much money but still had a certain "rank" in society that they had to maintain, Hector Bellade and his wife had given them a small monthly subsidy for years. This enabled the girls to devote their time to work in the local parish. Since the Duprouys had essentially lived on handouts from their cousin and his wife, Hortense sends her husband to enquire of Auguste why he has spent so much on the funeral. The essence of the story is the conversation between the two men.

Auguste tells of his mother's domination of him and his two sisters, and describes in detail how a local priest had attempted to arrange a marriage between him and a wealthy young girl of their social rank in need of a husband. Of course, even though both Auguste and the girl wanted to marry, the plans fell through because of the mother's opposition. Before Auguste finishes telling his story he faints—from hunger, for he has no money to buy food. Hector takes him to a restaurant, brings him back home, and gives him extra money in addition to the regular monthly allowance. Several months later Hector receives word from the police that his cousin has died of natural causes, simply a lack of nourishment. When Hortense insists that they will pay to have him buried with his mother and two sisters, because then he will be happy for eternity, Hector responds ironically, "Do you think so?" On this somber note the story ends. The domineering mother of this story is one of the most monstrous in all of Mauriac's fiction. In keeping her children for herself, she forced them all to live tragically lonely and unfulfilled lives.

"Conte de Noël" (1938)

"**Conte de Noël**" ("**A Christmas story**") was the only work to appear in *Plongeés* that had not already been published elsewhere. The title is misleading, for the story has very little to do with Christmas and very much to do with what is perhaps the major theme in Mauriac's fiction: a son's struggle for emancipation from a dominating mother.

The first-person narrative is related by Yves Frontenac, the young poet of *Le Mystère Frontenac*. He is calling to mind events that took place many years before in the school playground when he was seven years old. His friend Jean de Blaye, teased by the other boys because of his long blond curls, comes in for special abuse from the class bully, Campagne, because he still believes that Jesus comes down the chimney on Christmas Eve to bring presents to children. He holds this belief because his mother told him the story was true. Two weeks later, when classes resume after Christmas, Jean's hair is cut very short. When Yves asks him about Christmas, his only response is that his mother will no longer put things over on him. The shorn curls seem to symbolize the break with the mother. A year later he and his family move away from Bordeaux.

In the last section of the story, Yves is now a student in Paris, where he meets Jean de Blaye's brother, Philippe, in a bar. He learns that Jean as an adolescent broke open the strongbox in which his mother had kept his boyhood curls. This action symbolizes a desire to free himself from his mother's control. Later, after having lived a less than exemplary life, he died in ignominy in a hospital in Saigon.

Yves Frontenac now looks back on his chance meeting with Jean de Blaye's brother as the eventthat made him decide to become a fiction writer. Since the story helped him to understand his own childhood, which was also dominated by the influence of a powerful mother, the desire to tell Jean de Blaye's story (and to make the connection between the mother's stifling love in his childhood and his unsuccessful life as an adult) confirms that he should really be a novelist and not a poet.

FURTHER READING

Criticism

Dillistone, F. W. *The Novelist and the Passion Story.* New York: Sheed & Ward, 1960, 128 p.

Discusses *L'agneau* as a form of Christian "Passion" narrative.

Fischler, Alexander. "Thematic Keys in François Mauriac's *Thérèse Desqueyroux* and *Le noeud de vipères.*" *Modern Language Quarterly* 40, No. 4 (December 1979): 376-89.

Analyzes thematic elements in the two best-known novels of Mauriac's "golden decade."

Flower, John E. "François Mauriac and Social Catholicism: An Episode in *L'enfant chargé de chaînes.*" *French Studies* 21, No. 2 (April 1967): 125-38.

Demonstrates that *L'enfant chargé de chaînes* subverted the conservative Catholic traditions of its day by associating them with the Social Catholic movement.

Gartt, Toby. *Mauriac: Thérèse Desqueyroux.* London: Grant-and Cutler, 1991, 76 p.

Closely examines the composition, main themes, and critical reaction to *Thérèse Desqueyroux.*

Murray, Jack. "Three Murders in the Contemporary French Novel." *Texas Studies in Literature and Language* 6, No. 3 (Autumn 1964): 361-75.

Compares the murderers in Mauriac's *Thérèse Desqueyroux*, Albert Camus's *L'étranger* (1942) and Alain Robbe-Grillet's *Le voyeur* (1955).

O'Connell, David. *François Mauriac Revisited.* New York: Twayne Publishers, 1995, 190 p.Surveys Mauriac's career using primary source material that became available after Mauriac's death.

Reck, Rima Drell. "François Mauriac: The Novelist and the Moral Landscape."*Literature and Responsibility: The French Novelist in the Twentieth Century*, pp. 162-89. Baton Rouge: Louisiana State University Press, 1969.

Discusses Mauriac's place in twentieth-century literature and his role as a moralist.

Mary McCarthy
1912–1989

(Full name Mary Therese McCarthy) American novelist, short story writer, and critic.

INTRODUCTION

Considered one of America's most eminent intellectuals, McCarthy was renowned for her outspokenness and her opposition to what she perceived as hypocrisy. She rose to prominence in the 1930s as part of a group of New York City intellectuals that included Edmund Wilson Philip Rahv, and Lillian Hellman, and became known for her commitment to political issues. McCarthy's writing—both fiction and non-fiction—is characterized by a spare, elegant style but also by a caustic wit that earned her both high praise and notoriety. For literary inspiration she drew from her life and from the lives of friends and acquaintances, and she made little effort to disguise her sources. Some of her stories shocked contemporary audiences with their sexual candor, and the fact that her subject matter was known to be autobiographical made McCarthy herself into something of a legendary figure. Favoring the presentation of ideas through fiction, she used her sometimes merciless character portraits to dig deeply into the philosophical basis underlying behavior and attitudes.

Biographical Information

Born in Seattle, McCarthy was orphaned at the age of six when her parents died after contracting an illness while in the process of relocating the family to Minneapolis. She spent several years in the care of abusive relatives, an experience she later recounted in the much-praised memoir *Memories of a Catholic Girlhood.* Rescued from her plight by sympathetic grandparents living in Seattle, McCarthy attended schools in the Northwest and eventually became an aspiring young writer studying at Vassar College, which she entered in 1929. This second phase of her life has been described in *How I Grew,* which some have called her intellectual autobiography. In 1933 McCarthy graduated and moved to New York City, where she quickly became a professional writer whose essays and sometimes scathing reviews appeared in many respected publications, including the *New Republic*, *Nation*, and *Partisan Review*. Her work at the *Nation* earned McCarthy some recognition. She joined the staff of the *Partisan Review* in 1937, where she worked as editor until the next year, continuing to contribute drama criticism for several years thereafter. It was during this time that McCarthy came to know the noted literary figures Edmund Wilson (who became her second husband), Philip Rahv, and Lillian Hellman, among others.

McCarthy began writing fiction at the encouragement of Wilson, shortly after their marriage in 1938. On one occasion he confined his wife to a room until she produced something, and in this manner she wrote her first short story, "Cruel and Barbarous Treatment." McCarthy's first book came about when she noticed a relationship between several stories that she had originally written separately. She worked these stories into a unified framework, and the result was *The Company She Keeps.* McCarthy's marriage to Wilson was tempestuous from the start, and it ended in divorce after seven years. Scenes from their marriage served as inspiration for short stories even while she still lived with Wilson, and later became material used in her novels. McCarthy taught for a short time at Bard College but resigned in order to devote more time to writing. By 1955 she had published the novella *The Oasis,* the short story collection *Cast a Cold Eye,* and two novels. Her early works received considerable attention in literary circles and established McCarthy as a writer with a keen critical sense and as a social satirist who focused on the intellectual elite. But it was *The Group,* a novel about eight Vassar girls in the 1930s, that became a bestseller in the U.S. and abroad, earning McCarthy much wider recognition than than she had enjoyed previously.

In the late 1960s McCarthy interrupted a novel in progress to take action against the Vietnam war. She visited Southeast Asia twice, travelling to Saigon in 1967 and to Hanoi in 1968. Her essays based on these trips were later collected in her books *Vietnam* and *Hanoi*. *Medina*, a third book of essays about the war, addresses the trial of the U.S. army captain in command of the soldiers who massacred South Vietnamese civilians in the village of My Lai in 1968. McCarthy also wrote about the Watergate scandal in *Masks of State*. She continued to publish essays and memoirs even as her health failed in the 1980s. She died of cancer in 1989.

Major Works of Short Fiction

McCarthy published her first short stories in the *Southern Review* and in the *Partisan Review* between 1939 and 1941. She then assembled these stories into *The Company She Keeps*, which is ostensibly a novel, by weaving the same female protagonist through them. Some of the individual chapters are among her best short fiction. "The Man in the Brooks Brothers Shirt" is the tale of a woman aboard a train to Reno, where she will divorce her husband. She meets a man in the club car and gets drunk with him. Waking the next morning, the woman thinks nothing has happened, then remembers in a rush having had humiliating sex with him. This has all the hallmarks of McCarthy's style—unflinching narration of deeply intimate material, often involving characters who are spiritually or psychologically adrift. William Peden has described the female protagonist of these stories in this way: "Shrewd, perceptive, intelligent, supercilious, arrogant, uncertain beneath her cockiness, coldly analytical, always the insider viewing outsiders with disdain yet simultaneously 'always wanting something exciting and romantic to happen,' Margaret is the new woman, a women's libber two decades before the term came into everyday speech." The short fiction in *Cast a Cold Eye* shares the bleak, disenchanting quality of the stories in *The Company She Keeps*. "The Weeds" is the grim portrait of a wife who fails to leave a stifling marriage. Set on a train in Italy, "The Cicerone" tells of a young American couple who meet up with an Italian gentleman. The Italian seems to detest them, but nevertheless refuses to leave them alone. They are unable to communicate clearly with him—partially because of his uncertain grasp of English, partially because the two parties have too little in common—and their failure leaves them with a dismal emptiness. The stories comprising the second half of *Cast a Cold Eye* are memoirs that were later included in *Memories of a Catholic Girlhood*. These are perhaps McCarthy's most effective short stories. "Yonder Peasant, Who Is He?" and "The Tin Butterfly" have been praised for an emotional depth unmatched in most of McCarthy's fiction. The novella *The Oasis* satirizes a failed utopian experiment set in New York. Readers readily recognized this work as a thinly veiled account of the individuals and experiences that McCarthy herself observed while participating in the founding of a commune started by intellectuals.

Critical Reception

Voicing an objection that has been directed at McCarthy's writing as a whole, several reviewers of *The Oasis* complained that McCarthy was preoccupied with intellectuals and their ideas. Nevertheless, most discussions of her short fiction has revolved around debate about the appeal of her literary style. In a review of *Cast a Cold Eye*, George Miles attributed both heartlessness and a detached analytical manner to the author when he spoke of her as "the psychologist and the executioner." Similarly, Jeffrey Walker has remarked that "The reader is aware of McCarthy's own cold eye in presenting these stories of social relationships. . . . All reveal the coldness of their central characters and form a satiric indictment of urban relationships." Ultimately, approval of McCarthy's writing style appears to depend heavily on personal preference, with critics seemingly split on the issue. *The Company She Keeps* was subject to the same dispute about artistic merit as *Cast a Cold Eye*. In addition, numerous commentators have taken issue with the book's dubious classification as a novel, finding the individual chapters much more effective when considered independent narratives.

PRINCIPAL WORKS

Short Fiction

*_The Company She Keeps_ 1942
The Oasis (novella) 1949
Cast a Cold Eye 1950
†*The Hounds of Summer, and Other Stories* 1981

Other Major Works

The Groves of Academe (novel) 1952
A Charmed Life (novel) 1955
Venice Observed (criticism) 1956
Memories of a Catholic Girlhood (memoir) 1957
Sights and Spectacles: Theatre Chronicles 1937-1956 (criticism) 1957
The Stones of Florence (criticism) 1959
On the Contrary (essays) 1961
The Group (novel) 1963
Mary McCarthy's Theatre Chronicles, 1937-1962 (criticism) 1963
Vietnam (essays) 1967
Hanoi (essays) 1968
The Writing on the Wall (essays) 1970
Birds of America (novel) 1971
Medina (essay) 1972
The Mask of State: Watergate Portraits (essays) 1974
The Seventeenth Degree (essays and memoir) 1975
Cannibals and Missionaries (novel) 1979
Ideas and the Novel (essays) 1980
Occasional Prose (essays) 1985
How I Grew (memoir) 1987
Intellectual Memoirs: New York 1936-1938 (memoir) 1992

*This work is considered by some critics as a novel and my others as a collection of stories.

†Includes seven stories from *Cast a Cold Eye* and two that had been published previously in *The New Yorker*, "The Appalachian Revolution" (1954) and "The Hounds of Summer" (1963).

CRITICISM

Malcolm Cowley (essay date 1942)

SOURCE: "Bad Company," in *The New Republic*, Vol. CVI, No. 21, May 25, 1942, p. 737.

[*A prominent American critic, Cowley made several valuable contributions to contemporary letters with his editions of important American authors (Nathaniel Hawthorne, Walt Whitman, Ernest Hemingway, F. Scott Fitzgerald, William Faulkner), his writings for the* New Republic, *and above all, his chronicles and criticism of modern American literature. In the following review, he concedes that* "The Company She Keeps *is not a likable book, nor is it very well put together, but it has the still unusual quality of having been lived."*]

In the first episode of **The Company She Keeps,** the heroine deceives and deserts her husband for no reason, apparently, except that she loves a dramatic situation. Her moment of rapture comes when she tells him what she is doing. "They walked out of the restaurant together and through the streets, hand in hand, tears streaming 'unchecked,' she whispered to herself, down their faces."

In the second episode, she is working for an art dealer who would like to swindle his customers and live outside the law, but who is forced by circumstances to be a moderately honest man. Of all the characters in the book, he is the only one she unaffectedly likes.

In the third episode, she gets herself seduced by a man in a Brooks Brothers shirt whom she doesn't like at all, but who gives her "a feeling of uniqueness and identity," not to mention a rather pleasant sense of self-sacrifice. "Quickly she helped him take off the black dress, and stretched herself out on the berth like a slab of white lamb on an altar."

In the fourth episode, she goes to dinner at a house where each of the guests has been selected, not for what he is, but for what he might be taken to represent. "Tonight there was John Peterson, who stood for criticism and also for official Communism. There was Jim Berolzheimer, a bright young man in one of the great banking houses, who represented capitalism, and his wife who painted pictures and was going to have a baby, and was therefore both art and motherhood." The heroine represents Trotskyism, and dutifully plays her part like everybody else.

In the fifth episode, she has a very brief affair with a liberal journalist from Yale, and it changes his whole career. Long afterwards, when he is drawing a big salary

from Fortune, he gets tight at a party and tries to explain what she had meant to him. "Oh, thank you," she says, widening her eyes. "I'll have a brass plaque made to hang around my neck, saying, 'Jim Barnett slept here'."

The book so far has been a comedy of life among the New York intellectuals—clever and wicked, but not quite wickedly clever; psychologically acute, but never seeming to go much below the surface. The characters have had a peculiar air of coming from nowhere, having no relatives and believing in nothing, as if their well cut opinions were delivered in a box with their clothes. Like the guests at poor Pflaumen's party, each of them is acting out an assigned role—the Liberal Editor, the Party Liner, the Publisher Who Flirts with His Authors, the Girl on the Make—but although they gesture with animation and often convince their audience, they never convince themselves. And the heroine who keeps such bad company is perhaps the worst of the lot—the most snobbish and affected and spiteful, the least certain that she has any personality of her own or even exists outside the book she keeps rewriting.

In the sixth and last episode, she is married again, this time to a prosperous architect, and is enjoying the well deserved luxury of a nervous breakdown. Lying on a couch in a psychoanalyst's study, she tells the story of her life. We hadn't even known that it was a puzzle, but now the pieces are fitted together, and the picture that emerges is a little different from anything we had been expecting.

It seems that her mother had died when Meg Sargent was still a little girl. Her father, a successful Oregon lawyer and a Protestant, had left her in care of her mother's piously Catholic sister, who made her feel like a prisoner in the second story of the big family house. Meg believed, however, that she was being justly punished for some innate fault, and she continued to love her father, even though she regarded him as her jailer. At the age of fifteen, she rebelled. She quarreled with her aunt, left the Church and came East to school, where she established a totally new life for herself; and yet in her heart she never believed it was real. Always she was trying desperately to recapture the pattern of her childhood.

After this story told in the psychoanalyst's study, the five earlier episodes assume a different meaning; they are now something more than a comedy of bad manners. Meg had deserted her first husband not only because she loved a dramatic situation but also because he was too forgiving, and because she had to do something violent to justify her lasting sense of guilt. She sympathized with the art dealer because she pictured herself in the same ambiguous relationship to society. The man in the Brooks Brothers shirt was like her father; that was why she obeyed him and then ran away. Pflaumen's parties, with their falseness, were the symbol of her life in New York. Her motive for despising the liberal journalist was that she knew him too well; his middle-class opinions were essentially her own.

But although the heroine accepts this diagnosis, she does not confuse it with a cure. She feels at the end of the novel that the mind is powerless to save her; only men could do that. "Now for the first time she saw her own extremity, saw that it was some failure in self-love that obliged her to snatch blindly at the love of others, hoping to love herself through them. . . . And yet, she thought, walking on, she could still detect her own frauds." It is this scrupulous honesty toward herself and others that is the redeeming side of her character.

It is also the redeeming side of a novel that would otherwise be only one unit in the long production line of stories about young provincials adrift in Paris or London or New York. All these books set out to tell the truth, but few of them succeed. Miss McCarthy has learned the difficult art of setting down everything as it might have happened, without telling a single self-protective lie and without even failing, in the midst of a seduction, to mention the safety pin that holds up the heroine's badly mended underwear. *The Company She Keeps* is not a likable book, nor is it very well put together, but it has the still unusual quality of having been lived.

Christopher Isherwood (essay date 1942)

SOURCE: "Her Name Is Legion," in *The Nation*, Vol. 154, June 20, 1942, p. 714.

[*Isherwood is an English-born man of letters who is known for his largely autobiographical accounts of pre-Nazi Berlin and for his detached, humorous observations on human nature and manners. As a young man during the 1930s, he was a member of the Marxist-oriented Oxford group of poets that included Stephen Spender and W. H. Auden. In the following review, Isherwood questions McCarthy's artistic intention in* The Company She Keeps *but nevertheless hails the six portraits that comprise the volume.*]

The publishers' somewhat pretentious synopsis and Miss McCarthy's amusing foreword unintentionally do their best to mislead us as to the character of [*The Company She Keeps*]. So let us begin with a synopsis of our own.

The Company She Keeps is divided into six episodes. The first, "**Cruel and Barbarous Treatment**," describes, with the disgusted objectivity of a dyspeptic anthropologist, the various stages of an adultery which lead to divorce and the decision not to marry the other man. Neither the girl, the husband, nor the lover is given a name; passion is purely algebraical; the authoress unfolds her theme with the gusto of a scientist developing a favorite thesis. The result is brilliant and highly convincing, but it is the weakest thing in the book.

In "**Rogue's Gallery**" we meet Mr. Sheer, a dealer in doubtful antiques, who gives the girl her first job. (This episode is, of course, a flashback to Margaret's earlier pre-marital life.) Mr. Sheer, with his debts and deceits and baroque imagination, is quite somebody. We see far too little of him. Miss McCarthy could easily have expanded this portrait into a short novel. That she has not done so

---

> **The malicious and shallow feel of *The Company She Keeps*:**
>
> Sharp rather than witty, malicious rather than cynical, [*The Company She Keeps*] reminds one of the early Aldous Huxley, when he was still a lost soul and rather enjoying it.
>
> The She of the title is young, pretty, neurotic, demi-intellectual, pseudo-radical, bohemian, and characterless—the familiar type that Pearl Harbor has, let us hope, dated completely. We get glimpses of her in six different mirrors. When we meet her she is having the affair which is to result in her divorce. Then, successively, we watch her as assistant to a fake art dealer, being seduced in a Pullman, attending an "intellectual" dinner party, affecting the mind and body of a young liberal writer (Yale), and finally confessing to a somewhat dull psychoanalyst.
>
> Miss McCarthy is no novelist (the book does not hold together in the least) but she has considerable talent for dissecting people and leaving a nasty mess on the table. One has the feeling that her characters are drawn from life and that all of them are really much pleasanter and decenter people than Miss McCarthy gives them credit for being. Her book, however, has the definite attraction of high-grade back-fence gossip.
>
> *Clifton Fadiman, in* The New Yorker,
> *May 16, 1942.*

---

shows either the folly of a literary spendthrift or the liberality of vast inventive wealth. Here is a figure who might have stood beside the Great Gatsby.

And now we are on a westbound train. Margaret is traveling to visit an aunt in Portland—to tell her that she is going to marry again. Once more, however, she changes her mind: this time because of her encounter with "**The Man in the Brooks Brothers Shirt**." Here is a little masterpiece, carried through in perfect detail from the come-on to the brush-off—the classic study of the Business Man conquering the Tired Bohemian Girl. Even those who have never been seduced in a railway compartment will recognize here the accents of utter and awful truth.

"**The Genial Host**" is another portrait, crueller but equally well balanced, of one of those arachnidan entertainers who weave spider's webs around their guests and exact from each a character performance in exchange for a good dinner. Margaret, growing weary of this technique, tries to walk out of her role, but is promptly lassoed and yanked back into position by a silky thread.

"**Portrait of the Intellectual as a Yale Man**" is good, too. Its central figure is Jim Barnett, the clean-limbed Bright Young Pinkist whom everybody likes; in the end, of course, he sells out to weekly pluto-imperio-reportage-journalism—accepts, in other words, the Facts of *Life*. Margaret appears here at second remove. She is seen through his eyes. She is his bad conscience: sexually, because Jim has an affair with her while his wife is in childbed; politically, because in the obstinate integrity of her Trotskyism she seems to him to symbolize loyalty, idealism, honorable poverty, and freedom.

But Margaret, when we see her last, in the consulting room of a psychoanalyst, is neither loyal, idealistic, nor free. Remarried at last to a successful architect, she is no longer even poor. "**Ghostly Father, I Confess**" is the annotated report of a typical hour spent with Dr. James—the annotations being Margaret's childhood memories. "Here," says Simon and Schuster's back flap, "for the first time, we see the girl plain and whole. . . . Psychologically she has come to a dead end and can only act and reenact the childhood drama of estrangement that has left her permanently in doubt as to her moral identity, turned her into a human chameleon who can only know herself vicariously, through those whose company she keeps."

This kind of talk seems to me, as I have said above, misleading and anyhow superficial. There is nothing special, or inviting to pity and terror, about Margaret's case; we are all "human chameleons," every one of us. The stupid are not aware of this fact, the wise accept it, and the rest make a terrible fuss. The search for what Miss McCarthy calls "the ordinary indispensable self" is as futile as the "search" for one's own reflection in a mirror: the object sought is infinitely protean, and it can never be grasped or possessed, since it moves on another plane of being. Between the eternity of the animal, which is reproduction, and the eternity of the spirit, which is awareness of its life in ultimate reality, there is nothing firm, nothing solid, nothing "indispensable." The personality, which we value so much, is only a swirling nebula, a looking-glass at a fair—or, as the Hindus put it, the skins of the onion, which, when they are peeled of leave nothing at all. "But," the reader will object, "surely you'll admit that the 'ordinary indispensable self,' however illusory it may be in our human life, is very real in fiction, Surely this is the paradox of the novelist's art: in his work he must square the convention of 'the personality' with his empirical knowledge that the personality does not, in any final sense, 'exist'."

Needless to say, I agree. And I am bound to add that this was really Miss McCarthy's original artistic intention and not a regrettable highbrow afterthought, I think she has made a very bad job of it. Margaret does *not* appear as a series of striking contrasts and apparent contradictions; in fact, this idea seems hardly to have been exploited at all. Actually, she is a somewhat colorless though sympathetic and attractive minor figure who serves as a stooge for feats of really dazzling social analysis or as second fiddle to the principal characters.

But why carp? Why be ungrateful? Never mind if the book is wrongly presented; never mind the slightly dated almost twentyish intellectualism. Miss McCarthy has given us Mr. Sheer and Mr. Breen and Pflaumen and Jim Barnes and Dr. James. She is a real novelist, a vivid original talent whose warmth and charity and insight need no pompous introductions. We should rejoice in her, and wait eagerly for more.

Alexander Klein (essay date 1949)

SOURCE: "Satirist's Utopia," in *The New Republic,* Vol. 121, No. 23, December 5, 1949, pp. 19-20.

[*In the following review, Klein asserts that the novella* The Oasis *is artificial and forced.*]

With sharp wit, high spirits and a talent for epigram and capsule characterization, Mary McCarthy offers us in this *roman à clef* a satirical portrayal of intellectuals at bay. In essence, **The Oasis** is a series of vignettes hung on a forced framework of several contrived moral crises, most of which are either basically false or far too neat and complete. The result, despite specific true elements, is not truth larger than life-size but the exaggerations of falsehood.

There is still another reason why these flareups, planned as focusing highlights, actually reveal much less than the keen bits of analysis sprinkled liberally throughout. Miss McCarthy's depiction of character suffers from the intrinsic shallowness of all chiefly cerebral fabrications, even when these are documented by carefully chosen details from observation. As long as imagination, empathy and introjection of a high order are largely absent from the creative process, what is produced is mere attitudes and figures, and crises between attitudes and figures cannot engender tension, cannot achieve emotional significance or true and universal characterization. (By contrast—I cite it for its *kind,* not degree, of achievement—there is Dostoevsky's Foma Opiskin in his short novel, *The Friend of the Family.*)

In Miss McCarthy's fable a variety of idealists and critical realists (the chief of whom are said to be modeled closely on editors of two "elite" leftist cultural periodicals), enmeshed in a continuing struggle to keep their egos and political theories afloat, form a Utopian colony vaguely dedicated to the maintenance of liberal ideals against the flood tide of war and anti-intellectualism. It is never clear to Miss McCarthy, to the reader or to the Utopians themselves precisely how they can achieve their misty, undefined objectives. I take it that this, in one sense, is the cream of the jest, the implication being that the real-life counterparts of these Utopians, both celebrated and unknown, are similarly lacking in direction. At any rate, this New England hilltop retreat is foredoomed by the dissension between its two major factions, the Realists and the Purists.

The first moral skirmish occurs when the committee on admissions almost succumbs to the sin of Sectarianism. Then comes the near-expulsion of a colonist on highly dubious grounds, an incident, unbelievable from its inception, that is too plainly *made* to occur by the author to supply the needed action and underscore a simple point. This is followed by the complete fiasco of another colonist's dream-project, "Operation Peace," as every member in puppet fashion (almost as if the episode had been written by a pro-Soviet leftist intent on proving what frauds anti-Soviet leftists invariably are) shrinks from fulfilling his pledge when concrete action is broached. The well-

---

Harsh criticism of McCarthy's novella:

[*The Oasis*] is a weak and disappointing satire, toothless, only moderately pleasant. Considering the personalities drawn from, it is unmalicious to the point of not reaching the vigor of caricature of neutral naturalism. Unfortunately it deals with a subject, the thirst for the millennial—the crisis of our dullness, that these days must be described with wild eagerness or black bile rage, or with comprehension that irrational longing is justified, these days when it is unbearable for you to continue as you are, tho you imagine it is bearable. In handling our utopian theme, at least hope, despair, or vivisection are required to achieve a light touch; Mrs. Broadwater's [McCarthy's married name by her third husband] habitual sunny friendliness and suburban ethical analyses merely erect defenses for herself—they project no object—this is not interesting enough to make a book.

Paul Goodman, in Furioso, *Winter, 1950.*

---

telegraphed, too cunningly arranged disintegrating climax is the Battle of Strawberry Patch, in which the "revolutionary" members of Utopia are found unequal (morally and physically) to the defense of the colony's strawberries against three invading members of the *Lumpenproletariat*. Several less inhibited and high-minded colonists send the three scurrying, leaving the strawberries for the Utopians, whose moral precepts and injured egos are freely stained by the ripe fruit's juice. As any reader could predict by this time, it is the lone capitalist Utopian who expresses indignation at the anti-humanitarian "violation" of the rights of the invading proletarian pickers.

This charade is narrated in a lucid, finely controlled style, shot through with a filigree of intellectual sinew and, frequently, true insights and fresh abstractions rather than psychological jargon. Miss McCarthy also displays a courageous willingness to slay dragons evidently long grazing in her own backyard, a quality seen earlier in her remarkably successful collection of stories, *The Company She Keeps*. Occasionally, however, she sticks cruel pins into pitiable, defenseless, uninteresting people, hardly fit objects for lampooning. Except for rare moments, she displays a personal animus and a lack of sympathy that limit understanding and reduce most of *The Oasis* to surface satire that depends for its full effect on the reader's successful identification of the models for her characters.

Another major flaw is highlighted by the fact that the tragedy of impending war (World War III), which forms the backdrop to and inspiration for the colony, is too close a reality today. Miss McCarthy's continued *amusement* when she finally reveals her colonists as so many disciples of Nero (though subtler fiddlers) borders on the ghoulish. The satire's narrow, personal compass becomes picayune and the tone of high-spirited burlesque and ironic comedy no longer suits her underlying subject matter: the failure of leftist intellectuals (and, by implication, of all of us) to

unite theory with practice and counteract "the resignation of a public which, despite the ballot box, looked upon wars and social catastrophes as the medieval peasant looked upon cholera and earthquake, as manifestations of fatality, afflictions from the Beyond."

Of one of her characters Miss McCarthy writes that "he lacked audience-sense to an almost fatal degree." One could justly say of Miss McCarthy that she possesses audience-sense to an almost fatal degree. In fact, she is a victim of one of the diseases of our age: the bounden necessity to be clever and tough before all else. On that score she ranks high, but the price she pays for it might, conceivably, have purchased her passage on a deeper-plowing, wider-ranging vessel. Of course, the dangers of foundering would have been greater and the odds much longer against ringing encomia greeting one at the dock. Perhaps, therefore, it would be unfair to ask one ironic soul—admittedly hardy, but more of a Utopian herself than one might at first imagine—to venture that far out of port. To this critic, however, the penchant (or is it compulsion?) of many of the better writers working today—Sylvia Townsend Warner and Ernest Hemingway, to name two disparate examples—carefully to hew to the line of their preconceived limitations is more deplorable than the frequently scored temerity of the writer who aims at the moon and lands in a fishpond.

Charles Poore (essay date 1950)

SOURCE: A review of *Cast a Cold Eye*, in *The New York Times*, September 21, 1950, p. 29.

[*In the following review, Poore judges the stories of* Cast a Cold Eye *to be brilliant character sketches.*]

Scott Fitzgerald's memorable observation on writing short stories—"begin with an individual, and before you know it you have created a type; begin with a type, and you find that you have created nothing"—comes frequently to mind as you read Mary McCarthy's new collection of rather remorselessly satiric tales, *Cast a Cold Eye*. Miss McCarthy will be remembered as that source of the southpaw intellectuals whose Utopian lampoon, *The Oasis,* drew blood all over the Marx-and-Kafka set, about a year ago. Also as the author of **"The Man in the Brooks Brothers Suit,"** and other aspects of *The Company She Keeps*.

Also as the author of **"Yonder Peasant, Who Is He?"** a profoundly moving story of orphaned childhood, last encountered in that fine anthology, *55 Short Stories from The New Yorker,* which appears again, we are happy to say, in *Cast a Cold Eye,* along with these stories: **"The Weeds," "The Friend of the Family," "C. Y. E.," "The Blackguard,"** and **"The Cicerone."**

Since Miss McCarthy's types are devastating, it is natural enough to find that sometimes they scarcely seem to exist as individuals. Yet they're never quite devastated right off the face of the earth. You keep remembering their obsessions, even if you've forgotten what they look like.

You wish, for example, that the tormented wife in **"The Weeds"** who kept trying to get away from her husband could have encountered the sad-sack man-about-town in **"The Friend of the Family"** when she made her brief and characteristically feckless flight to New York.

Those two had a lot in common. The stories they appear in, though, have a more striking affinity. For while **"The Weeds"** is busy kicking the living daylights out of a marriage, **"The Friend of the Family"** has many a brutally unkind thing to say about people who live alone and do or do not like it.

You won't find many cheery moonbeams in *Cast a Cold Eye,* but you will see that there are brilliant sketches here by a brilliant writer. Even the young man in **"The Old Men"** has to stop and ask himself in the hospital: "Am I a monster?" And the desperately puzzled convent girl of **"C. Y. E."** felt she suffered from "a kind of miserable effluvium of the spirit that the ordinary sieves of report cards and weekly confessions had been powerless to catch."

Somehow, the ultimate point of **"The Cicerone"**—a story of Americans in Italy, than which there is nothing rifer in contemporary literature, led by Mr. Hemingway, right now—seems to apply widely to the people in this book: "The relation between pursuer and pursued had been confounded, by a dialectic too subtle for their eyes."

Lorine Pruette (essay date 1950)

SOURCE: "Stories Told in Cold Fury and Disciplined Hatred," in *New York Herald Tribune Book Review,* September 24, 1950, p. 8.

[*In the following favorable review of* Cast a Cold Eye, *Pruette judges McCarthy's writing style well suited to her harsh stories.*]

Whatever Mary McCarthy writes has its own authenticity. Her veritable signature lies squarely across each of these stories as it did upon *The Company She Keeps* and *The Oasis.* Several of the stories [in *Cast a Cold Eye*] are unforgettable; all are interesting; all have the flavor that one associates with bitter aloes, without quite knowing what that is. They appear to be concerned with incidents on the periphery of existence, footnotes to the daily struggles and complications; yet in the end the reader shudders back from their impact and wonders: Is this, then, the essence, the distilled and acrid essence of man's life?

The title is excellent, for there is a coldness here. The victim in the powerful but somehow banning **"The Old Men,"** quotes from Yeats's tombstone, "Cast a cold eye on life, on death. Horseman, pass by." In exploring her deep but narrow vein of first-grade ore, Mary McCarthy records the intimate wretchedness of the solitary individu-

---

The artificiality of *Cast a Cold Eye*:

Whatever the successes or failures of *Cast A Cold Eye* may be, they are not the successes or failures of fiction. Here is a kind of pseudo-fiction, a collection of discourses in masquerade. This has to be qualified somewhat in speaking of three of the pieces, "The Weeds," "The Old Men" and "The Cicerone," which are much closer to stories in form and intention, but even these have a strong dogmatic trend.

The deception is expert, of course, and it takes a little while to realize that the characters in *Cast A Cold Eye* are only introduced in a series of exemplary tableaux designed to ornament and footnote the theory of the narrator coming to you over the public address system. They appear, verify something, fade and are forgotten. Some of them will appear in another tableau, standing silent while the author cleverly describes them, but it is only the description, not they, that will remain memorable. McCarthy's Waxworks, then, is a highly educational place, despite the unreality of its figurines.

Robie Macauley, in Furioso, *Winter,* 1951.

---

al, without pity, almost without concern. She shows no two people observing each other with tenderness or putting out a kindly hand. In fact, she shows no communication, no possibility of communication, between any two separate individuals, and in her cosmology all are separate.

The McCarthy pictures have horror in them, and all her characters live in hell, but there is nothing depressing about reading her stories. Her style has such verve and swiftness, is so compelling, that the reader follows after her, on the scavenger hunt for the revealing incident, the ultimate perception that will give away another person and deliver him, naked and quivering, into his understanding. There is an intellectual satisfaction to be found here, gratification in a style that is so perfect a tool for its purpose.

In the first story, **"The Weeds,"** the opening reads: "She would leave him, she thought, as soon as the petunia had bloomed." There follows an impalement of the neurotic female, her alibis, her false gestures toward freedom, and finally her passivity and paralysis, by which she achieves a permanent state of being injured. In **"The Friend of the Family"** Francis Cleary is "the perfect sanforized man" in a civilization where "people, like sheets, came preshrunk."

"The Cicerone" requires the two young American lovers to listen to the account of the wealthy Miss Grabbe's one night of love, if it may be called so: one of the most brutal and degraded episodes to be encountered in a long life of misspent reading. **"The Old Men"** is a magnificent exploration into the validities of personality: "To exist, he suddenly became convinced, was an act of deliberate impersonation." This ends with a sudden ferocity, as the next, **"Yonder Peasant, Who Is He?"**—also excellent, ends with a sharp Irony. Speaking of the hideously mistreated children, she writes "We thought it only natural that grandparents should know and do nothing, for did not God in the Mansions of Heaven look down upon human suffering and allow it to take its course?"

The last two stories concern the miseries and triumphs of a young girl in a convent school, the second ending with a characteristically ferocious attack upon the integrity of the personality of the young girl. It is this cold fury, this disciplined hatred, that casts an enigmatic light upon the cold title, the cold stories. There is fire in Mary McCarthy. If it could burst forth into any sort of flame it might make a light to reveal even to her some shreds of dignity in the human beings she writes about.

Seymour Krim (essay date 1951)

SOURCE: "Short Stories by Six," in *The Hudson Review,* Vol. III, No. 4, Winter, 1951, pp. 626-33.

[*Since the late 1950s Krim has been writing freewheeling, hardhitting, and deeply personal essays in which he explores the vicissitudes of his own life not only as a means of deriving therapy from art but also as a way of examining contemporary American life and literature. In spirit, style, and purpose these writings are strongly influenced by the Beats and are often openly hostile to the highly formal, analytical literary criticism of the New York intellectual elit. In the following excerpt, Krim finds* Cast a Cold Eye *pedantic.*]

Artfulness . . . is hardly a deficiency in Mary McCarthy, especially as regards her style and the way in which her material is conceived, if not in the actual working-out of the story itself. . . . *Cast A Cold Eye* is her third book; yet, thus far, she has not written one sustained book in the accustomed sense. Her first, *The Company She Keeps,* was called a novel (despite Mr. Eliot), but was only so, in any strict terminology, by virtue of the autobiographical heroine's appearance in each of the episodes; the whole was united only by her presence, and the material was not integrated to make a narrative that develops in time and meaning as well. Its merit, apart from the conspicuously articulate and finished writing, lay in the keen observations of the author, who displayed an almost masculine intelligence at work roasting the game that a female sensibility had trapped. *The Oasis,* Miss McCarthy's next book, was much less distinguished than the first; again, this was called a "novel," but was hardly novella length and showed little skill with the traditional elements of fiction. Its satire, of a political utopia mismanaged by New York intellectuals, was often ponderous and suffered from what Henry James called "the platitude of mere statement"; apparently there was relish involved if readers knew who the characters were based upon, but aside from this gossip interest, necessarily lost to non-sect members, the book did not "come off." *Cast A Cold Eye* is the third of these not-entirely-a-book books; it is composed of approximately half short stories and half *New Yorker* "I Remember Mama" pieces. In general, it may

be compared to a series of classic poses struck by a superbly composed and expensive model, so audience-conscious, however, that her face is a mask.

The esthetic emotions aroused by such a sight as that described above are considerable and in a noble tradition; but when applied to Miss McCarthy's fiction, the very flawlessness seems to vitiate mobility and interest within the context of any given story. The author's unusually keen perceptions are evident in each story, but like so much of what can most easily be called *Partisan Review* fiction, the intelligence does not seem to be worked into the narrative invention proper, but resides rather in the critical faculty of the author. The result is that readers can admire Miss McCarthy, but not her stories. When she writes in her own person it is difficult not to be struck by the balance, precision and often the weight of her thought (inflexible though her scale often is); she is never relaxed or unguarded as a writer, but her very composure is queenly enough to command attention. In the stories proper, however, Miss McCarthy's large style is not sufficient to conceal the fact that thus far she has displayed weak powers of narrative invention; more important, the author seems to have imposed upon herself none of that necessary dirty work that goes on within the lively story.

Considered in a broader perspective for a moment, Miss McCarthy might be taken as a not entirely fair example of a school of fiction-writers which *Partisan Review* has, by its temper if not its express wish, encouraged, and whose selfconscious, highly intellectualized work has regularly appeared in that magazine. (Miss McCarthy surely is not representative as regards her aristocratic air, her considered style, and her cold eye; and yet the author definitely seems to qualify by virtue of what might be called her 100 Great Books binding, which prevents her stooping to put some "story" into her stories.) Much of the tediousness of these writers seems to come from an inability, thus far, to transmute their heavy load of ideas into an appropriate art; what the reader is often presented with, in the guise of fiction, has the total effect of a Paper that might be read at the Rand School (or, as in several of Miss McCarthy's pieces, at Sarah Lawrence); the whole adds up to a genuinely new pedantry in American fiction. The pedantry seems hardly the result of too much literary intelligence, which would think twice before permitting itself to wear a beard in this culture (except the Be-bop kind). It seems rather to come from an understandable, but hardly condonable, transvestism: namely, the attempt to put European clothes on an American body. Natural as this perversion may have seemed to a generation suckled on Freud (as well as Marx, Kafka, Joyce and all the other Big Berthas of Europe), a paragraph in *Women's Wear Daily* notes that sport clothes are being worn all year round, now. . . .

Mary McCarthy with Elisabeth Niebuhr (interview date 1962)

SOURCE: An interview in *The Paris Review,* No. 27, 1962, pp. 58-94.

[*In the following excerpt from an interview that was conducted in the winter of 1961, McCarthy discusses her writing, literary influences, and politics.*]

[NIEBUHR]: *I remember that you published parts of* Memories of a Catholic Girlhood *as one section in* **Cast a Cold Eye.** *You changed the story about your nickname a great deal, reducing it to just a small incident in* Catholic Girlhood.

[MCCARTHY]: I couldn't *bear* that one! It had appeared years ago in *Mademoiselle,* and when I put it in **Cast a Cold Eye,** I didn't realize how much I disliked it. When I came to put *Catholic Girlhood* together, I simply couldn't stand it, and when I was reading the book in proof, I decided to tear it out, to reduce it to a tiny tiny incident. As it stood, it was just impossible, much too rhetorical.

When you publish chapters of a book separately on their own, do you think of them as chapters, or as independent short stories?

As chapters, but if somebody, a magazine editor, thought they were what *Partisan Review* calls a "self-contained chapter," all right, but I've never tried to make them into separate units. If one happens to be, all right—if they want to publish it as such. The *New Yorker* has given me surprises: they've printed things that I would never have thought could stand by themselves. But *they* thought so.

Did you, when you saw them in print?

Surprisingly, yes.

What about in your first novel, **The Company She Keeps?**

Those chapters were written originally as short stories. About half-way through, I began to think of them as a kind of unified story. The same character kept reappearing, and so on. I decided finally to call it a novel, in that it does in a sense tell *a* story, one story. But the first chapters were written without any idea of there being a novel. It was when I was doing the one about the Yale man that I decided to put the heroine of the earlier stories in that story too. The story of the Yale man is not a bit autobiographical, but the heroine appears anyway, in order to make a unity for the book.

Were you also interested simply in the problem of writing one story from various different points of view, in experimenting with the different voices?

There were no voices in that. I don't think I was really very much interested in the technical side of it. It was the first piece of fiction I had ever written, I mean I'd never made any experiments before. I was too inexperienced to worry about technical problems.

You hadn't written any fiction before then?

No. Well, in college I had written the tiniest amount of fiction: very bad short stories, very unrealized short sto-

---

An assessment of *The Company She Keeps*:

The Company She Keeps sets out to paint the psychological portrait of a young American woman from various angles. . . .

But Mary McCarthy's study of her heroine turns out to be neither as detailed nor as analytical as the foreword leads one to expect. . . .

What one does find is a series of snappy shots superimposed on one another and building up an entertaining, lively, rather bewildering, rather malicious picture of American life and society, somewhat in the style of a photographic montage. The last piece in the book, which glances into the heroine's stream of consciousness while she is lying on the psychoanalyst's couch, is the only one to maintain a serious tone and it is perhaps the least successful.

The writer is at her best when she is being funny, as in her very humorous sketch of the bogus art-dealer; or in **"The Man in the Brooks Brothers Shirt,"** which conveys with admirable horror the sordid dreariness of casual erotic adventure.

The psychology of the book is quite superficial, and there's a suggestion of smart slickness about the writing; but judged at *New Yorker* level it's good entertainment value.

Anna Kavan, in Horizon, *February, 1944.*

---

ries, for courses, and that was all. I once started a detective story to make money—but I couldn't get the murder to take place! At the end of three chapters I was still describing the characters and the milieu, so I thought, this is not going to work. No corpse! And that was all. Then I simply did **The Company She Keeps,** and was only interested in the technical side from the point of view of establishing the truth, of trying to recreate what happened. For instance, the art gallery story was written in the first person because that's the way you write that kind of story—a study of a curious individual.

You imply that most of the stories were distinctly autobiographical.

They all are more or less, except the one about the Yale man.

Is this distinction between autobiography and fiction clear in your mind before you begin writing a story, or does it become so as you write? Or is there no such distinction?

Well, I think it depends on what you're doing. Let's be frank. Take **"The Man in the Brooks Brothers Shirt"**: in that case it was an attempt to describe something that really happened—though naturally you have to do a bit of name-changing and city-changing. And the first story, the one about the divorce: that was a stylization—there were no proper names in it or anything—but still, it was an attempt to be as exact as possible about something that had happened. The Yale Man was based on a real person. John Chamberlain, actually, whom I didn't know very well. But there it was an attempt to make this real man a broad type. You know, to use John Chamberlain's boyish looks and a few of the features of his career, and then draw all sorts of other Yale men into it. Then the heroine was put in, in an imaginary love affair, which *had* to be because she had to be in the story. I always thought that was all very hard on John Chamberlain, who was married. But of course he knew it wasn't true, and he knew that I didn't know him very well, and that therefore in the story he was just a kind of good-looking clothes-hanger. Anything else that I've written later—I may make a mistake—has been on the whole a fiction. Though it may have autobiographical elements in it that I'm conscious of, it has been conceived as a fiction, even a thing like *The Oasis,* that's supposed to have all these real people in it. The whole story is a complete fiction. Nothing of the kind ever happened; after all, it happens in the future. But in general, with characters, I do try at least to be as exact as possible about the essence of a person, to find the key that works the person both in real life and in the fiction. . . .

Could I go back for a moment to what you said about your early writing at college? I think you said that **The Company She Keeps** *was the first fiction you ever wrote, but that was some years after you left Vassar, wasn't it?*

Oh yes. You know, I had been terribly discouraged when I was at Vassar, and later, by being told that I was really a critical mind, and that I had no creative talent. Who knows? they may have been right. This was done in a generous spirit, I don't mean that it was harsh. Anyway, I hadn't found any way at all, when I was in college, of expressing anything in the form of short stories. We had a rebel literary magazine that Elizabeth Bishop and Eleanor Clark were on, and Muriel Rukeyser and I. I wrote, not fiction, but sort of strange things for this publication.

A rebel magazine?

There was an official literary magazine, which we were all against. Our magazine was anonymous. It was called *Con Spirito*. It caused a great sort of scandal. I don't know why—it was one of these perfectly innocent undertakings. But people said, "How awful, it's anonymous." The idea of anonymity was of course to keep the judgment clear, especially the editorial board's judgment—to make people read these things absolutely on their merits. Well anyway, *Con Spirito* lasted for only a few numbers. Elizabeth Bishop wrote a wonderful story for it which I still remember called "Then Came the Poor." It was about a revolution, a fantasy that took place in modern bourgeois society, when the poor invade, and take over a house.

When you left Vassar, what then?

Well, I went to New York, and I began reviewing for the *New Republic* and the *Nation*—right away. I wrote these little book reviews. Then there was a series about the critics. The *Nation* wanted a large-scale attack on critics and book-reviewers, chiefly those in the *Herald Tribune,*

Nastiness in McCarthy's fiction:

[McCarthy's] novels have given a lot of offence. They are based closely on real people, and are merciless in their character analysis and foible-dissection—real plums in imaginary puddings' is her own formulation, but the plums have not always seen it quite that way. It is hard to open any of her books at random without encountering something one would not be at all pleased to hear said about onself. The character Randall Jarrell based on Mary McCarthy, in his novel *Pictures from an Institution,* is described as having 'a bark worse than her bite. But what am I saying? Gertrude's bark *was* her bite—and many a bite has stayed awake at night, wishing it was Gertrude's bark.' McCarthy, . . . is aware of the effect her portraits have, and regrets it, but says that 'I can't stop myself.' She and her third husband once had to sell a New England holiday home *before* publication of a novel set in the area. They knew what was coming.

John Lanchester, in London Review of Books, *October 26, 1989.*

---

the *Times,* and the *Saturday Review,* and so on. I had been doing some rather harsh reviews, so they chose me as the person to do this. But I was so young, I think I was twenty-two, that they didn't *trust* me. So they got Margaret Marshall, who was the assistant literary editor then, to do it with me: actually we divided the work up and did separate pieces. But she was older and was supposed to be— I don't know—a restraining influence on me: anyway, someone more responsible. That series was a great sensation at the time, and it made people very mad. I continued just to do book reviews, maybe one other piece about the theater, something like the one on the literary critics. And then nothing more until *Partisan Review* started. That was when I tried to write the detective story—before *Partison Review.* To be exact, *Partisan Review* had existed as a Stalinist magazine, and then it had died, gone to limbo. But after the Moscow trials, the PR boys, Rahv and Phillips, revived it, got a backer, merged with some other people—Dwight Macdonald and others—and started it again. As an anti-Stalinist magazine. I had been married to an actor, and was supposed to know something about the theater, so I began writing a theater column for them. I didn't have any other ambitions at all. Then I married Edmund Wilson, and after we'd been married about a week, he said, "I think you have a talent for writing fiction." And he put me in a little room. He didn't literally lock the door, but he said, "Stay in there!" And I did. I just sat down, and it just came. It was the first story I had ever written, really: the first story in *The Company She Keeps*. Robert Penn Warren published it in the *Southern Review.* And I found myself writing fiction to my great surprise.

This was when you became involved in politics, wasn't it?

No. Earlier. In 1936, at the time of the Moscow trials. That changed absolutely everything. I got swept into the whole Trotskyite movement. But by accident. I was at a party. I knew Jim Farrell—I'd reviewed one of his books, I think it was *Studs Lonigan*—in any case, I knew Jim Farrell, and I was asked to a party given by his publisher for Art Young, the old *Masses* cartoonist. There were a lot of Communists at this party. Anyway, Farrell went around asking people whether they thought Trotsky was entitled to a hearing and to the right of asylum. I said yes, and that was all. The next thing I discovered I was on the letterhead of something calling itself the American Committee for the Defense of Leon Trotsky. I was furious, of course, at this use of my name. Not that my name had any consequence, but still, it was mine. Just as I was about to make some sort of protest, I began to get all sorts of calls from Stalinists, telling me to get off the committee. I began to see that other people were falling off the committee, like Freda Kirchwey—she was the first to go, I think— and this cowardice impressed me so unfavorably that naturally I didn't say anything about my name having got on there by accident, or at least without my realizing. So I stayed. I began to know all the people on the committee. We'd attend meetings. It was a completely different world. Serious, you know. Anyway, that's how I got to know the PR boys. They hadn't yet revived the *Partisan Review,* but they were both on the Trotsky committee, at least Philip was. We—the committee, that is—used to meet in Farrell's apartment. I remember once when we met on St. Valentine's Day and I thought, Oh, this is so strange, because I'm the only person in this room who realizes that it's Valentine's Day. It was true! I had a lot of rather rich Stalinist friends, and I was always on the defensive with them, about the Moscow Trial question, Trotsky, and so on. So I had to inform myself, really, in order to conduct the argument. I found that I was reading more and more, getting more and more involved in this business. At the same time I got a job at Covici Friede, a rather left-wing publishing house now out of business, also full of Stalinists. I began to see Philip Rahv again because Covici Friede needed some readers' opinions on Russian books, and I remembered that he read Russian, so he came around to the office, and we began to see each other. When *Partisan Review* was revived I appeared as a sort of fifth wheel— there may have been more than that—but in any case as a kind of appendage of *Partisan Review.*

Then you hadn't really been interested in politics before the Moscow trials?

No, not really. My first husband had worked at the Theater Union, which was a radical group downtown that put on proletarian plays, and there were lots of Communists in that. Very few Socialists. And so I knew all these people; I knew that kind of person. But I wasn't very sympathetic to them. We used to see each other, and there were a lot of jokes. I even marched in May Day parades. Things like that. But it was all . . . fun. It was all done in that spirit. And I remained, as the *Partisan Review* boys said, absolutely bourgeois throughout. They always said to me very sternly, "You're really a throwback. You're really a Twenties figure."

How did you react to that?

Well, I suppose I was wounded. I was a sort of gay, good-time girl, from their point of view. And they were men of the Thirties. Very serious. That's why my position was so insecure on *Partisan Review;* it wasn't exactly insecure, but . . . lowly. I mean, in *fact.* And that was why they let me write about the theater, because they thought the theater was of absolutely no consequence.

How did the outbreak of the war affect your political opinion? The Partisan Review *group split apart, didn't it?*

At the beginning of the war we were all isolationists, the whole group. Then I think the summer after the fall of France—certainly before Pearl Harbor—Philip Rahv wrote an article in which he said in a measured sentence, "In a certain sense, this is our war." The rest of us were deeply shocked by this, because we regarded it as a useless imperialist war. You couldn't beat Fascism that way: "Fight the enemy at home," and so on. In other words, we reacted to the war rather in the manner as if it had been World War I. This was after Munich, after the so-called "Phony War." There was some reason for having certain doubts about the war, at least about the efficacy of the war. So when Philip wrote this article, a long controversy began on *Partisan Review.* It split between those who supported the war, and those who didn't. I was among those who didn't—Edmund Wilson also, though for slightly different reasons. Dwight Macdonald and Clement Greenberg split off, and Dwight founded his own magazine *Politics,* which started out as a Trotskyite magazine, and then became a libertarian, semi-anarchist one. Meyer Schapiro was in this group, and I forget who else. Edmund was really an unreconstructed isolationist. The others were either Marxist or libertarian. Of course there was a split in the Trotskyite movement at that period.

Toward the end of the war, I began to realize that there was something hypocritical about my position—that I was really supporting the war. I'd go to a movie—there was a marvelous documentary called *Desert Victory* about the British victory over Rommel's Africa Corps—and I'd find myself weeping madly when Montgomery's bagpipers went through to El Alamein. In other words, cheering the war, and on the other hand, being absolutely against Bundles for Britain, against Lend Lease—this was after Lend Lease, of course—against every practical thing. And suddenly, I remember—it must have been the summer of '45 that I first said this aloud—I remember it was on the Cape, at Truro. There were a lot of friends, Chiaromonte, Lionel Abel, Dwight, et cetera, at my house—by this time I was divorced from Edmund, or separated anyway. And I said, "You know, I think I, and all of us, are really *for* the war." This was the first time this had been said aloud by me. Dwight indignantly denied it. "I'm *not* for the war!" he said. But he was. Then I decided I wanted to give a blood transfusion. And I practically had to get cleared! Now no one was making me do this, but I felt I had to go and get cleared by my friends first. Was it wrong of me to support the war effort by giving a blood transfusion? It was agreed that it was all right. All this *fuss!* So I gave a blood transfusion, just one. Some other people were doing it too, I believe, independently, at the same time, people of more or less this tendency. That is the end of that story. Years later, I realized I really thought that Philip had been right, and that the rest of us had been wrong. Of course we didn't know about the concentration camps: the death camps hadn't started at the beginning. All that news came in fairly late. But once this news was in, it became clear—at least to me, and I still believe it—that the only way to have stopped it was in a military way. That only the military defeat of Hitler could stop this, and it had to be stopped. But it took a long, long time to come to this view. You're always afraid of making the same mistake over again. But the trouble is you can always correct an earlier mistake like our taking the attitude to World War II as if it were World War I, but if you ever try to project the correction of a mistake into the future, you may make a different one. That is, many people now are talking about World War III as if it were World War II. . . .

In speaking of your own writing, . . . you attribute its "style" to your earlier critical work—then you don't feel the influence of other writers of fiction?

I don't think I have any influences. I think my first story, the first one in *The Company She Keeps,* definitely shows the Jamesian influence—James is so terribly catching. But beyond that, I can't find any influence. That is, I can't as a detached person—as detached as I can be—look at my work and see where it came from from the point of view of literary sources.

There must be certain writers, though, that you are drawn to more than others.

Oh yes! But I don't think I write like them. The writer I really like best is Tolstoy, and I *know* I don't write like Tolstoy. I wish I did! Perhaps the best English prose is Thomas Nash. I don't write at all like Thomas Nash.

It would seem also, from hints you give us in your books, that you like Roman writers as well.

I did when I was young, very much. At least, I adored Catullus, and Juvenal; those were the two I really passionately loved. And Caesar, when I was a girl. But you couldn't say that I had been influenced by *Catullus!* No! And Stendhal I like very very much. Again, I would be happy to write like Stendhal, but I don't. There are certain sentences in Stendhal that come to mind as how to do it if one could. I can't. A certain kind of clarity and brevity—the author's attitude summed up in a sentence, and done so simply, done without patronizing. Some sort of joy.

Doris Grumbach (essay date 1967)

SOURCE: "Rare Birds of New York," in *The Company She Kept,* The Bodley Head, 1967, pp. 111-14.

[*Grumbach is an American novelist, critic, and biographer. Her novels involve a process of constant reflection and reinterpretation of facts, paralleled by the reflection of her characters upon their own lives and professions. Often placed in academic environments, these characters are intelligent but unable to use their knowledge to lead satisfying lives or enjoy fulfilling relationships. In the following excerpt from her book-length study of McCarthy, Grumbach remarks on McCarthy's treatment of emotion in "The Company Is Not Responsible" and "The Unspoiled Reaction."*]

There was considerable doubt about whether or not *The Company She Keeps* was a novel. A series of stories held together by a metamorphosing heroine seemed to some critics not to qualify. One called it "thinly disguised autobiography," a good and amusing parallel to the critic who was later to call *Memories of a Catholic Girlhood* thinly disguised fiction. Whether or not the stories added up to a novel, they stood well alone, and in the years between this book and the next, a number of other short stories appeared, among them **"The Company Is Not Responsible,"** in *The New Yorker* in 1944 and **"The Unspoiled Reaction"** two years later in the *Atlantic Monthly*. These are not especially significant; they might better be described as sketches with a slight core of emotion suggested to the reader but not fully communicated, so removed that the reader has the curious sense that he is being told at second hand about the events. The narrator stands in his way.

"The Company Is Not Responsible" tells of a bus trip the author took from New York to Wellfleet during World War II. After an initial cataloguing of the persons aboard, and a wait until the connecting bus arrives, the bus moves on toward Provincetown. The author listens to the unusual "lark" spirit of the war years, the good-naturedness of the sailor, the girls, Margie and Ann, the Harvard boys, a man named George, the driver called Mac, and the others, but she waits with some dread for the inevitable "detestable person," the "disagreeableness, the bad part" that often breaks out when diverse persons are grouped together and confined. A near-crisis is reached (although only in the mind of the author) when the Harvard boys begin to sing "Die Lorelei" in German. "'Will someone object?' I thought; 'is this where the trouble will come?' I held my breath, but no patriot censor intervened." On the contrary, the others join in singing, even the "outsider" author. The boys get off at their stop, bidding everyone good-bye by name, everyone but the author: "I felt a slight stab of envious regret that they did not know my name." Once at home, she begins to disbelieve in the brief experience, until on the return trip she hears George's voice, sees Margie in the crowded bus, and knows her short acquaintanceship with human goodness was not something she "had made up." Slight as the story is, it suggests the changing moods of dread, exultation, distrust, and relief that things are not always as bad as one expects them to be. The form of the sketch is prophetic, a group of persons sequestered for a brief span of time in a limited space, and then observed carefully for their reactions, a form to be used again in *The Oasis, The Groves of Academe, A Charmed Life* and finally in *The Group*. The location of the author is interesting too: the outsider, regretting her

---

McCarthy's moralism:

Miss McCarthy's attitude toward the people in her stories is one of contempt and outrage, but it is not just a shallow, miffed, critical attitude. It originates in a deep and almost continually disappointed moralism. She wants people with intelligence to be good and decent and productive, and that they are not arouses the furious broken-hearted chastiser in her. Once in a while, however, she gets carried away and becomes pedantic, but this is a minor fault.

Chandler Brossard, in The American Mercury, *February, 1951.*

---

stance, feeling disconnected from the group and yet harboring a yearning to be part of it, fearing its potential ugliness yet left with a nostalgia for its unexpected goodness. It is the only example, in Mary McCarthy's work, of a small Eden preserved. Her skepticism was to create a number of other idylls, but "the bad part" always comes upon them.

Another story, **"The Unspoiled Reaction,"** has, oddly enough, been reprinted in a collection called *Masters and Masterpieces of the Short Story*. Whatever the truth of the first part of this title for Mary McCarthy, the second part does not, clearly, apply to this story; it is in no sense a masterpiece. The title refers to what is expected of children at a puppet show, what indeed does occur. The sketch contains the curious, disembodied voice of the narrator, presumably the author who, with her young son, is present at a puppet performance of Little Red Riding Hood in a shabby, near-empty theatre in New York on a rainy Monday morning. The sketch is told, without internal evidence of the presence of the author, and this gives it the same removed feeling I have mentioned, as if emotion were perceived from a great distance. Here primitive fear of a mad, unexplained emotion, suddenly let loose, is felt immediately by both the children, their parents, but only at a distance by the reader. A child in the audience, urged on by his teacher, approaches the puppet and an hysterical human voice, not the falsetto of the puppet, inexplicably frightened by the child's approach, screams out, "You horrible, horrible children," and chases him from the stage. Parents and children are routed from the theatre, the sentence of the outraged teacher ringing in their ears: "That is no way to talk to a *child*." The story ends with the observation that the sentence is "pronounced by the teacher in a tone of peculiar piety and reverence, her voice genuflecting to it as to the Host."

What happens in **"The Unspoiled Reaction"** is that an erratic performer whose job is entertaining children as a puppet cracks up in full view of the audience. Her disguised madness breaks forth and shatters the air of childlike trust that had pervaded the theatre. In a way, what happens in this sketch is precisely what does not happen in **"The Company Is Not Responsible,"** where the threat of unpleasantness and evil (in this case nationalism) is contained by the workings of a spirit of goodwill; here, despite the presence of well-meaning parents and "unspoiled" children, evil (madness) breaks through, horrifyingly. **"The Unspoiled Reaction"** is close in spirit to *The Oasis,* and might almost be said to be a preparatory sketch for it. But the story. lacks direction and focus. Its suddenly revealed moment of emotion is given no explanation, no roots, and few results. It *is*, it threatens the peace of mind of those present, and ultimately the reader's. Nothing more.

Most curious of all is the final sentence I have quoted which seems a simile out of all proportion to the event. The effect of it is that at the very last moment a new note is sounded, a high reverence for the shattered children, and the sudden, new direction of the story stuns the reader. Here, perhaps, its use was incongruous, but this kind of religious imagery crops up often in Mary McCarthy's writing, under all sorts of conditions. In *The Company She Keeps* the safety pin in Meg's underwear seemed to her to be like "a symbol of moral fastidiousness, just as the sores of a mendicant saint can, if thought of in the right way, testify to his moral health." The reliance upon religious imagery . . . becomes even more frequent in the novels to come.

Francis Gillen (essay date 1972)

SOURCE: "The Failure of Ritual in 'The Unspoiled Reaction'," in *Renascence,* Vol. XXIV, No. 3, Spring, 1972, pp. 155-58.

[*In the following excerpt, Gillen explores themes of religious faith and ritual in the short story "The Unspoiled Reaction."*]

Mary McCarthy's **"The Unspoiled Reaction"** deals with the interaction between the "knowing" world of adults and the relatively unsophisticated and, to that extent, innocent world of children. Taken to attend a puppet show of Little Red Riding Hood one rainy Monday afternoon, the children find themselves warmly greeted by an entrepreneuse who asks each child's name. Separated from the parents and teachers so that the puppeteers may obtain an "unspoiled reaction" from the children, these youngsters are amazed when the puppet Sunny appears and greets each of them by name. Encouraged to participate, the boys and girls exchange repartees with Sunny and loudly take sides in the play, some choosing the part of the grandmother and others encouraging the wolf to make a good meal of her. Suddenly a child, who with his teacher and classmates from a progressive school had arrived late for the performance, reacts with the "natural" enthusiasm Sunny had encouraged, goes up on stage and attempts to touch Sunny. Sunny's falsetto voice becomes an agonized woman's scream: "Sunny doesn't like that." Startled by the reality and the aversion in the voice, the boy slips backward into the orchestra pit. After a few agonizing minutes when the boy is recovered unhurt and the parents wait to see if the show's illusion has been irremediably destroyed,

Sunny reappears, seemingly as affable as ever—"Bygones were bygones, all was forgiven, . . ." Now, however, the children's reaction is no longer unspoiled or natural. They look to their parents, find the correct reaction as the more docile begin to imitate the adults who have "screwed their own faces into grimaces of pleasure." Soon the children are caught up in the play once again and all seems to go smoothly until after the final curtain when the same boy receives his teacher's permission to go backstage and handle the puppet. There he and the other children who follow him encounter the entrepreneuse, screaming now, no longer in Sunny's, but in her own voice: "Get out, get out of here . . . You dreadful, horrible children." The children run, and they and their guardians flee in shame and silence out into the rain.

As has been noted by several critics, Miss McCarthy's story touches then on several themes: the exploitation of the children by those who care nothing for them, the concurrence of the adults in this deception, the loss of innocence and the expulsion from childhood's paradise. A further ambiguity is added by the fact that the children's "unspoiled reaction" is not wholly innocent, that some, siding with the wolf, grow so unrestrained that the rational control of the adults is not wholly unadmirable and is perhaps necessary. Beyond these important themes, however, I would like to suggest that Miss McCarthy's story deals with the idea of theatre as ritual, with the lack of genuine ritual in the modern world, and the consequence of this lack on today's theatre. What the entrepreneuse desires or seems to desire from the children is their ritualistic participation in the play, the breaking down of the fourth wall of the theatre. In commenting on this active involvement, the narrator notes that "the reciprocity between player and audience, lost to us since the medieval mysteries, and mourned by every theoretician of the drama, was here recovered. . . ." The medieval mysteries referred to, of course, are those plays depicting events from the Bible which were originally performed as part of the ritual of the Roman Catholic Mass. The difference between such ritual and the play performed for the children by the puppets lies in the matter of belief. Noting the frank, often ribald and sometimes blasphemous language of players and audience alike, Parrott and Ball in their account of these mysteries write: "People then believed so implicitly in the Bible story that they were ready to allow themselves the frankest familiarity with Bible characters" (*A Short View of Elizabethan Drama*). What was enacted before them was the panorama of God's genuine interest in man, of man's creation, original sin, expulsion from Eden, and his reconciliation with God. By contrast there is no genuine adult belief in the sincerity of Sunny's friendliness or his interest in the children. When the entrepreneuse's smiling and tender greeting of each child seems to bring the parent within the circle of "the holy miracle of his child's identity," that lady feels obliged to nudge the parent and let him in on the utilitarian motive. In the auditorium, the non-believing adults must be separated from their credulous children so that their lack of belief will not be infectious. After her reference to the medieval mysteries, the narrator continues ironically: "And what did it matter if the production was a mockery, a cartoon of the art of drama."

Several of Mary McCarthy's critical writings lend support, I believe, to this interpretation. In her description of St. Mark's in *Venice Observed*, Miss McCarthy suggests that the vivid colors in which hell is painted in the mosaic, the "Universal Judgment," imply that the Venetians took the idea of judgement and damnation as story rather than as fact. She contrasts this mosaic with the impression of solid belief one gets when one looks at the altar and continues: "Something of this obstinate faith survives in the redhaired boy who explains the mosaics. He heard me one afternoon explaining them myself to a friend, and it cannot have been professional rivalry that caused him to interrupt. 'After the Crucifixion,' I was saying, 'Christ is supposed to have gone to Limbo—.' 'Not "supposed": *He did,*' the boy cut in, peremptorily."

Similarly, in a review of three plays produced in the 1944 season, she complains that though each—*Harvey, The Streets are Guarded,* and *A Bell for Adono*—suggests a pattern of belief, external doubt and renewed faith, each play fails to stand up to intellectual analysis because, outside of the play, no one can believe in the validity of the objects of belief. She writes: "Now this is an old enough pattern of drama or fiction; it is, after all, the story of the New Testament. What is remarkable in these three plays is that the virtue resides, not in the object, but in the believer. It makes no difference, according to these authors, whether the belief is objectively a delusion." Somewhat sadly she continues:

> The truth is (and the weakness of these plays demonstrates it) that the drama is incorrigibly concrete; it cannot, like the movies, deal in shadows, or in reverie, like the novel. It demands that its conflicts be settled; it cannot, by its very nature, dissolve them away, as the camera can. It is the only one of the arts whose medium is the living flesh, and this sets a certain limit on belief—one is always more conscious of what is excessive in a stage performance than one is of the same kind of thing in a movie or a novel. In fact the very plainness, conclusiveness and realism of the stage have unfitted it to deal with this period of irresolution, evasion and ambiguity (*Theatre Chronicles, 1937-1962*).

When we return to **"The Unspoiled Reaction"** with this distinction between genuine and spurious ritual in mind, we see that many events in the story parallel the ritual of the medieval mysteries. In the theatre lobby, there exists the initial friendliness between the entrepreneuse and the children, as there existed in Eden an initial friendliness between God and man. The adults, however, are "the snake in this paradise of innocence." Lacking faith, they see the badly lighted, damp, mostly empty theatre only as "this house of death." When the boy wanders onto the stage and attempts to touch Sunny, there is a breach between Sunny and the children as there was a breach between Adam and Eve and God. Retreating from Sunny, the boy stumbles and falls into a pit. Seemingly, too, there is redemption, for when Sunny returns, he is "cordial as ever. . . . Bygones were bygones, all was forgiven." After the play, however, the validity of this redemption is tested: "The drama was not quite over; a reconciliation must follow between the puppet and the child. . . ." Only then, in the curse of the old white-haired woman, "'You dreadful, horrible children,'" and her continued rage, is the spuriousness of the apparent reconciliation revealed, and the distinction between this and effective medieval rituals revealed. In these mysteries there was no fourth wall; the forgiveness was genuine because that which was enacted was, to player and audience alike, real.

Miss McCarthy seems to suggest, then, that the loss of faith has also meant the loss of affirmative ritualistic theatre. Incurably realistic, the theatre demands faith in the objects of belief it propounds. Lacking such belief itself, the modern adult world sees faith as suitable for children—fairy tales, Santa Claus, etc.—but, in the presence of other adults, especially is embarrassed and uneasy over the fraud. Nevertheless its continued, though somewhat uneasy, investing in childhood many of the values formerly associated with belief—innocence, forgiveness, kindness, and a certain nostalgia—suggests its own feelings of separation and desire for reconciliation, for genuine ritual. "In shame and silence, it [the audience] fled out into the rain, pursued by the sound of weeping which intermingled with the word *child,* as pronounced by the teacher in a tone of peculiar piety and reverence, her voice genuflecting to it *as though to the Host*" (final emphasis mine).

Barbara McKenzie (essay date 1974)

SOURCE: "The Arid Plain of 'The Cicerone'," in *The Process of Fiction: Contemporary Stories and Criticism,* Second Edition, edited by Barbara McKenzie, Harcourt Brace Jovanovich, 1974, pp. 72-116.

[*In the following essay, McKenzie provides a detailed analysis of "The Cicerone," focusing on the story's communication of malaise.*]

"English, surely," the young American lady says, eying the "tall, straw-colored" stranger who stood smoking in the corridor of the *wagon-lit.* Unconvinced, her companion concedes, "If English, then a bounder." Their conversation continues "in an agreeable rattle-rattle" as they discuss the problems of detecting "a bounder in a foreign country." Thus Mary McCarthy begins her story about two young Americans (unnamed and unmarried) traveling together in Europe shortly after the end of World War II. For the most part, she writes from an inside point of view, using as her narrative focus the double consciousness of the American couple. Yet, in reality, this double consciousness is single. Different in their characteristic external responses, the young Americans are basically alike, having come "to think in unison" and needing "the spoken word only for a check."

Intrigued by Europe, they are also puzzled and challenged by its mystery. Although they are tourists and are ostensibly traveling in Italy for pleasure, the couple is determined to penetrate the "Continental standards" that they sense as "mysteriously different" and even, although they

question their own seriousness, "to get into European society." Architecture, they believe, provides "the most solid answer to their social curiosity." Thus they seek to understand the Sforzas "through the agency of their Castello" and "to know the Pisani" by visiting Stra, on the Brenta. Putting great stock in appearances, they find their penchant for categorizing thwarted by upper-class Europeans who, trying "to dress like English gentlemen," strike "the inevitable false notes."

But **"The Cicerone"** is less about the adventures of two Americans in search of Europe than it is about American attitudes toward the Continent. To dramatize this wider purpose, Miss McCarthy uses Rino Sciarappa, the cicerone, and introduces a third American, Polly Grabbe. Basic to the symbolic structure of the story is the assumption that Sciarappa is the personification of post-war Europe. "The mystery of Europe lay in him as solidly as in the stones of Venice, and it was somewhat less worn by previous inquisitive travelers." To the American couple, the Italian is "a city of Catacombs" whose "real life" is conducted in the "tunnel" of his mind. The cicerone's appearance underscores his identification with Europe—in particular, post-war Italy. His slenderness is cadaverous and his quick and light movements, effete. He reminds the young lady and young man "of that horror so often met in Paris, city of beauty, the well-preserved woman in her fifties." Even "the terraced fields" are "like Mr. Sciarappa's wrinkles." Moreover, the land bears "the mark of wisdom—it too had seen life." The different ways in which the young American couple and Miss Grabbe relate to Sciarappa clarify different but similar American attitudes toward Europe. Conversely, the disbelieving and contemptuous Italian expresses a conventional attitude of Europe toward America: "'Ah, you Americans,'" he remarks, "'your streets are paved with dollars.'"

Like Rino Sciarappa, the young American couple behaves in a manner that, similar to "the young lady's large black hat, long gloves, high-heeled shoes, and nylon stockings," acts as "a declaration of nationality." The young man who walks "proudly on the dilapidated streets of Europe" is unabashedly curious. Little interested in people's opinions or in their emotions, he is "passionately, madly curious as to what people did and how they made their money." Uneasy in "his small role as war-profiteer," he nonetheless avoids the black market in favor of cashing "his checks at the regular rate at the bank" for only a single week. The young lady shares the inquisitiveness of her companion. An active verbalizer, she is adept at labeling sentiments, at dissecting shades of feeling, of making subtle distinctions. She is both aggressive and gullible. Being gregarious, she "took the kindest view of everyone" and believed that "she was the only person in the world who told lies."

The relationship that develops between Rino Sciarappa and the two Americans is as deserved as it is bizarre. Since the narrator does not enter the Italian's mind, the Italian is an enigma not only to the young man and young lady but to the reader as well. Stymied by the cicerone's uncertain grasp of English syntax, the Americans seek to ascertain his place in the social hierarchy and thereby to

McCarthy's strength and weakness as a writer:

The fact that [McCarthy's] mind works logically by habit shows up in her style, which itself is a rare modern example of the fine results obtained when a writing talent is early exposed to a classical education. She can manage a trope with ease; her lightly formal vocabulary allows for degrees of wit; and she can swing a periodic sentence to a telling close. She is also a skeptic, if not by nature, by training; and she is more attached to the pleasures of method than to those of belief. It is the basic situation which interests her, not a secondary envelope of atmosphere. With this equipment, her successes are naturally those of satire.

The trouble is that as a satirist she is never quite through or relentless enough; she often stops at the moment of "scoring off," instead of making a final plunge into regions where the true roots of the matter are exposed.

Louise Bogan, in The New Republic,
November 27, 1950.

"understand" Europe not through what he says but through more tangible, external means. But neither his appearance nor his professed occupation allows them to turn him into a demonstrable abstraction. Equally unknowable are his reasons for staying with them in the role of cicerone.

The term "cicerone" derives from the name of the Roman orator Cicero and refers to his learning or eloquence. It was first applied to learned Italian antiquarians whose function was to provide visitors with information about the antiquities of a place. Subsequently, the meaning was widened to include ordinary professional guides. But in neither the original nor the later sense is Sciarappa a cicerone, and herein lies the central irony of the story at its literal and satirical levels. Not valuing the art treasures of Italy and, in fact, not valuing post-war Italy, he cannot credit tourism as a legitimate motive for the Americans' being in Italy any more than he can credit as honest their enthusiastic response to Italy's art objects and buildings: "it was as if the devaluation of the currency had, for Mr. Sciarappa's consistent thought, implicated everything Italian; cathedrals, pictures, women had dropped with the lira." Further, since cathedrals, works of art, museums, and palaces maintained by the state were free to all, Sciarappa considers them as valuable to none. Equally peculiar—for a guide—is the "one solid trait" that the two Americans discover in his character, his "rooted abhorrence of the advertised first-rate, of best hotels, top restaurants, principal shopping streets, famous vineyards." In an interplay of internal emotions and external forces, Miss McCarthy balances Sciarappa against the Americans. Neither the Italian nor the Americans can assign each other to a social class. The young man and young lady sense that Sciarappa believes himself to be the victim of an imposture. "But did he believe that they were rich pretending to be poor, or poor pretending to be rich? They could not tell." Their partial understanding of the Italian's hostility does not preclude their lessening sympathy toward him and their increasing impatience at devoting evenings to a "stranger who was continually out of sorts because he could not make up his mind whether they were worth swindling." Later, in Venice, they find themselves in the same kind of situation: "He had become a problem for them in both senses of the word: the impossibility of talking *with* him was compensated for by the possibilities of talking about him, and the detachment of their attitude was, they felt, atoned for by their neighborliness in the physical sphere."

This kind of balancing, this interplay between abhorrence and attraction, supply and demand, is apparent in other short stories by Miss McCarthy. In **"The Genial Host,"** for example, Margaret Sargent realizes that she exists in a strange symbiotic relationship with Pflaumen the host. His price for providing dinner parties where she meets eligible young men is that she inform him of resulting emotional liaisons. In **"The Friend of the Family,"** the husband and wife discover the usefulness of the unobtrusive and dull Francis Cleary. His company is not sprightly but neither is it demanding or upsetting, and thus they find themselves cultivating this mutually satisfactory friend, even to the point of wooing him in order to maintain the delicate balance of their own social relationship. Further evidence can be found in **"The Weeds,"** where the wife, after trying to break away from her husband and start a new life in New York City, returns to her husband, defeated by the inevitable changes that five years have wrought in herself, her friends, and the social patterns she had known as a single woman. Modifying her demands, she goes back to her insensitive and dogmatic husband because she needs the structured situation he offers her.

In a similar way, the Americans find themselves drawn to the distrustful and uncommunicative cicerone, despite the absence of a common meeting ground. In fact, they need him precisely because he is different from them, for they sense the mystery of Europe in his enigmatic disaffection. If they can understand Sciarappa, they reason, they can understand Europe. Consequently they try to coax the Italian "out into the open." Their bait is Polly Grabbe, a "middling but authentically rich" American whom they are to meet in Venice. Well known for her semi-annual pilgrimages to Europe in search of love and for her collection of garden statuary, the flower-bulb heiress provides a means for them to trap Sciarappa into revealing himself. If he wishes money, Polly Grabbe has enough to precipitate him into some decisive action. If he seeks a mistress, Miss Grabbe is accessible.

But the relationship that develops between Sciarappa and the American heiress fails to reveal the inner nature of the Italian. Shrewd and flighty, relentless in her search for experience and lenient in her judgments of men, Miss Grabbe fails to provoke the cicerone into disclosing his motivation. Throughout, Polly Grabbe refuses to see anything transcendent about the man and interprets his behavior on the basis of her own limitations. Instead of seeing "the problem of Sciarappa," she warns the Americans that he will spoil Venice for them. Commenting on Sciarappa's disappearance on the day of the fiesta, she says, "'I thought you wanted to get rid of him—he has probably found bigger fish.'" At another time, she tells the young man, "'My dear, he simply wants to sell us something.'"

It is inevitable, therefore, that she should relate to Sciarappa in her own way—as a convenient directory of people and places and, finally, as a lover. Her graphic confession after a night of lovemaking ("'he is much older than you think'") dramatizes the polarities between her and the young Americans. The young lady begs her to stop because she knows that "this mortal exposé" is not what they had wanted; "on the contrary, they had had in mind something more sociological, more humane—biographical details, Mr. Sciarappa's relation with his parents, his social position, his business, his connection with the Fascist state." The revelation of Miss Grabbe yields only an image of Sciarappa "hunted down, defenseless, surprised in bed by a party of intruders." The motives, status, and true public self of the Italian—"'the really interesting part about him'"—continue to elude them.

As they travel to Florence, they note that the "landscape itself seemed to wear a face baked and disabused as Mr. Sciarappa's own." Geography and man merge when they unexpectedly encounter the cicerone in Florence. Baffled, the young man admits, "'He is following us, but he is ahead.'" In Rome, where their persistent curiosity causes them to "investigate" the address of the Italian, they do so with quickened expectation. "The European enigma and its architectural solution lay just before them, around a bend in the street." Their discovery that his house is "plain and shabby" makes them feel as mortified and embarrassed as when they had listened to Polly Grabbe's confession. "This house too was an obscenity, like the shrunken skin and the scapular, but it was also a shell which Rino Sciarappa did not truly inhabit." Their shame causes them to turn away, aware that "the relation between pursuer and pursued had been confounded, by a dialectic too subtle for their eyes."

What has happened is that their net—architecture—is, like Miss Grabbe's, "too coarse to catch" the mystery of the Italian. The distaste the American couple feels for each other is really an objectifying of what each finds repugnant in himself. In their alikeness, each is subdued by the grossness he sees reflected in the other person. Thus the story folds back on itself, and the two Americans are again standing at a distance from the secrets of Europe, reduced, at least momentarily, from their hopeful curiosity on the *wagons-lits* or their naive, optimistic belief that someone would "discover them in this dark continent."

The dialectic that confounds the relation between pursuer and pursued has to do with the interchangeability of the two entities. Ostensibly Sciarappa is the pursuer. The American couple and Miss Grabbe see him as wanting something from them. What the young lady and young man discover is that they are also pursuers in a pursuit externalized by their image of the cicerone "hunted down" in Miss Grabbe's bed, by their finding him waiting for them in Florence, and by their "investigation" of his residence in Rome. The dialectic resulting from this exchange

of roles is indeed too subtle for their eyes to detect. Externals such as houses and clothes are forever incapable of explaining an entity as elusive as Rino Sciarappa, who had, quite literally, "careened away from them into the inexplicable."

The conclusion of **"The Cicerone"** makes the formal design of the story apparent. It began with the two young Americans, opened to include Rino Sciarappa (as the first sentence suggested), and then widened to encompass the flower-bulb heiress. After this relative fullness, the story closed in on itself again, finally returning to the isolated consciousness of the American couple. Such formal balancing of plot and characters parallels and enhances the delicate balance of the social relationships that form the story's content.

In commenting on her technique as a writer, Mary McCarthy has said, "With characters, I do try at least to be as exact as possible about the essence of a person, to find the key that works the person both in real life and in the fiction." Yet, despite scrupulous delineation of dress (Miss Grabbe's and the young lady's "costumes"), history (Miss Grabbe's past), mannerisms (the young man's unleashed hilarity), subtleties of feeling (the young lady is a "specialist in sentiments"), the reader remains at considerable psychic distance from the characters. This "gulf" is inevitable in the case of Polly Grabbe and the cicerone—characters whose consciousnesses are closed to us. But we are removed even from those characters whose perceptions serve as narrative focus—the young couple. This separation is widened by Miss McCarthy's failure to name her central characters: They are anonymous Americans of cultivated sensibility.

As a fiction writer, however, Miss McCarthy most often bases her characters on persons whom she has known. The facts of her life frequently supply the "facts" of her fiction. Many knowledgeable readers have noted the similarities between Mary McCarthy and the young lady, Miss McCarthy's third husband and the young man, and a famous real-life American heiress and Polly Grabbe. It is as though by drawing them from real-life models Miss McCarthy *assumes* their "life-likeness" in fiction. In truth, however, the characters in **"The Cicerone"** are little more than two-dimensional puppets maneuvered into place by the author. A consequence of their "flatness," of the *manner* in which they are made "real," is their distance from us. In turn, this distance compounds our lack of sympathy toward them.

Ironically, the "person" we are closest to in **"The Cicerone"** is the implied author—that is, the image of Mary McCarthy we construct from reading the story. In the first paragraph, it is Miss McCarthy (not the young man or young woman) who compares Sciarappa to "an English cigarette," finding that the Italian bears "the same relation to a man that a Gold Flake bears to a normal cigarette." In this same paragraph, it is Miss McCarthy, again speaking directly through her narrator, who likens the young man's eyes to "strange green headlights on an old-fashioned car." Throughout the story, various similes, meta-

---

The worldly quality of McCarthy's fiction:

The stories of Mary McCarthy sum up one side of contemporary American intellectual life better then any other writing about it. Born in Seattle, a student at Vassar, a dramatic critic, an editor of the *Partisan Review,* an instructor at Bard College and Sarah Lawrence, formerly wife of critic Edmund Wilson, she is the spokesman of the ex-Marxist double-domes, the political sophisticates, and of the circles where everything—people, gardens, love affairs, divorces, parties—are analyzed in political terms. It is a world with a humor and a language of its own, in which one point of reference is the Danish philosopher Kierkegaard and another appears to be a familiar reference to Harry's Bar in romantic Venice.

Newsweek, *September 25, 1950.*

---

phors, allusions, and turns of phrase come not from the characters but, unfiltered, from the narrator who, serving as the author's agent, displays her brilliant command of language.

Yet Miss McCarthy's unwillingness or inability to create round, sympathetic characters is basic to her method and purpose as a writer. Fundamental to her intention is the depiction of characters that are representative types as well as singular entities. Her ability to see and describe generically is partly responsible for her ability to write satirically. In **"The Cicerone,"** the Americans and Sciarappa are satirical portraits of representative types. Concomitantly, satire allows Miss McCarthy to accomplish her larger social purpose in this story.

For through Sciarappa and the American she is embodying national attributes and attitudes. Parasitic, unyielding, and nervous, Rino Sciarappa *is* Europe. Remember Polly Grabbe's confession, "'My dear, he is much older than you think.'" He is also faded and secretive. To the Americans, he is "the face of Italian history." Even his purposelessness, his lack of occupation, identifies him with a Europe recovering from a devastating war. Polly Grabbe and her flower-bulb fortune represent more than American materialism, vulgarity, and artistic pretension. Quite literally, Polly Grabbe "grabs" at Europe through the agency of the cicerone. Accepting Sciarappa as a lover, she causes him to strip himself physically in a gesture that parallels her requisitioning of Europe's art treasures. The young American couple wants to strip Europe spiritually and intellectually, but, in their persistence, they are as gross as Miss Grabbe. The tone-deaf young man and the gullible young lady differ in kind but not degree from the heiress in their quest to understand the social hierarchy and heritage of Europe and to lay bare its spiritual essence. That they fail with Sciarappa is symptomatic of their larger failure.

The life depicted in **"The Cicerone"** is bleak and hopeless. In many ways, the war-torn, humbled, unyielding Europe Miss McCarthy describes has echoes of T. S.

Eliot's *The Waste Land,* which also imagizes a parched and barren land. Like Eliot's personages, the young Americans are dry and sterile people who intellectualize their experience as they attempt, unsuccessfully, to intellectualize Europe and its mystery. In the manner of the inhabitants of *The Waste Land,* they have lost touch with the past and cannot participate in its rituals, as their inability to share in the bacchanalian experience of the fiesta suggests. Paralleling Eliot's poem, the failure in sexual relationships in **"The Cicerone"** suggests the malaise of the wider society. Having recognized the disadvantages of traveling together—"('My dear,' said the young lady, 'a couple looks so complete')"—the young Americans accept their "handicap" like "the best jockey" in a horse race who "scorns to take a lighter weight." Although Rino Sciarappa gives himself to Polly Grabbe in a night of adequate though not extraordinary lovemaking, he rejuvenates neither himself nor his partner. Instead, he leaves Venice the next morning, offering as a reminder of himself a list of second-best restaurants and hotels. That Polly Grabbe stores the devalued currency of Italy in her douchebag is a fitting and final symbol for all that is incongruous and debased in the arid plain of **"The Cicerone."**

Irvin Stock (essay date 1980)

SOURCE: "The Novels of Mary McCarthy," in *Fiction as Wisdom: From Goethe to Bellow,* The Pennsylvania State University Press, 1980, pp. 156-89.

[*In the following excerpt, Stock discusses the themes of the novella* The Oasis.]

McCarthy has defended *The Oasis* (1949) from the charge that it is not a novel by insisting that it was not intended to be, that it is a *conte philosophique.* This explains its lack of action, for instead of plot we have slight episodes explored for their large meanings and characters revealed less by what they do than in long satirical descriptions. But it cannot eliminate the sense that the tale's developments, which ought after all to arise by an inner necessity, are sometimes arbitrarily asserted, as if to get things moving. And yet the reminder of an elegant eighteenth-century prose form does point to qualities that will keep the tale, in spite of its imperfections, interesting for a long time. The satirical descriptions do not merely imitate but genuinely duplicate the qualities of eighteenth-century prose masters—the psychological insight, the general wisdom, the witty, epigrammatic, gracefully balanced sentences.

The Oasis is the story of a group of New York intellectuals—based apparently on well-known friends of the author, but to the rest of us recognizable as contemporary types—who, shortly after World War II, form a colony called Utopia in the Taconic Mountains of New York State. The colonists fall mainly into two factions. The "purists" hope the colony will illustrate "certain notions of justice, freedom, and sociability" derived from their Founder, a saintly Italian anarchist lost in "a darkened city of Europe." This group is led by Macdougal Macdermott, a man who rightly senses that he does not naturally belong to "that world of the spirit" which he yearns to enter, but who, "ten years before . . . had made the leap into faith and sacrificed $20,000 a year and a secure career as a paid journalist for the intangible values that eluded his empirical grasp. He had moved down town into Bohemia, painted his walls indigo, dropped the use of capital letters and the practice of wearing a vest" and become the editor of a "libertarian magazine." The "realists," on the other hand, have come only for a holiday from the pressures of real life. They look upon "conspicuous goodness" like the Founder's as a "form of simple-mindedness on a par with vegetarianism, and would have refused admission to Heaven on the ground that it was full of greenhorns and cranks." Moreover, they find absurd the assumption of "human freedom" which underlies all that the purists believe, for they are inheritors of Marxian "scientific socialism," and though they had discarded the dialectic and repudiated the Russian Revolution, "the right of a human being to *think* that he could resist history, environment, class structure, psychic conditioning was something they denied him with all the ferocity of their own pent-up natures and disappointed hopes." And since "ideological supremacy" has become "essential to their existence," they look forward with pleasure to the colony's failure. They do, however, wish it to fail convincingly, of its own foolishness, and this seduces them into unusually good behavior. Soon Will Taub, their leader, finds that he participates "in the forms of equity with increasing confidence, and though of course he did not take any of it *seriously,* his heavy and rather lowering nature performed the unaccustomed libertarian movements with a feeling of real sprightliness and wondering self-admiration, as if he had been learning to dance."

In Will Taub we have the first full-fledged example of the enemy in McCarthy's world, the Other to all that she values. He is one who is at home only in the realm of ideas, who is flat-footed in his behavior with children, women—in all nonintellectual relations—who feels pain at the very word "Jew" because "his Jewishness [was] a thing about himself which he was powerless to alter and which seemed to reduce him therefore to a curious dependency on the given." And this rejection of the "given," the real, on behalf of a world of ideas where he can reign supreme involves too a rejection of moral responsibility. It is for the realists a felt oddity in Utopia that "here they were answerable for their deeds to someone and not simply to an historical process." And Taub is even capable, like the later Henry Mulcahy, of beginning to believe his own lie (that an embarrassingly cowardly reaction of his is due to former police persecution) in order to maintain his cherished supremacy.

These two characters, and Joe Lockman, the go-getting businessman who comes to Utopia determined to get more spiritual profit out of it than anyone else, are the tale's most vivid portraits. But it is a fourth, Katy Norell, to whom its chief events tend to happen and out of whose responses its meanings emerge. Katy, a teacher of Greek, suffers from "a strong will and a weak character," an awkward compulsion to tell the truth even when it aggravates her problems, and a readiness to feel guilty when things go wrong. Though it was her "instinctive opinion . . . that the past could be altered and actions, like words, 'taken back,'" her husband's disgust with her, one occasion when it seems serious, gives her a frightening glimpse of life "as a black chain of consequence, in which nothing was lost, forgot, forgiven, redeemed, in which the past was permanent and the present slipping away from her." This character, weak but scrupulous, who wishes life were easy but can't shut out the perception that it is hard, is, of course, a sister of Margaret Sargent [in *The Company She Keeps*] as well as of the later Martha Sinnott [in *A Charmed Life*], though, unlike the others, she pays for representing her author's inner life by being one of the less vivid characters in her book. But it is out of her inner contradictions that the book's closing insights come. These insights are initiated by the last of several challenges to the colony's "sociability"— the stealing of their strawberries by some rough interlopers, whom Katy herself, frightened when her pleading is answered with threatening gestures, demands be ejected by force. Taub taunts her with her contradiction, her yielding to "human nature," and at this, lulled or liberated by the dinner wine, she begins to understand. They did wrong, she thinks, to cling to the strawberries without needing them—it was only the idea of the strawberries they cared about. They had let "mental images" possess them as the idea of sex dominates the mind in pornography. But the mind should stick to its own objects, "love, formal beauty, virtue"; they should not have tried to make real things dance to the mind's tune. And this is only a small example of their fundamental error. As the tale draws to an end, she realizes that Utopia is going to fail because of their wish to "*embody* virtue." If they had been content to manufacture, not virtue, but furniture, it might have survived.

It is a rueful, if not tragic, conclusion. To replace the stubborn complexity of people and society with ideas is the mistake of both parties in Utopia. The cynics who insist that our behavior is determined by history and the "idealists" who believe that man can be what he wishes to be are shown to be equally removed from the life we actually live. And yet those like Katy Norell, who see how both are wrong, who feel and suffer life up close, are better off, if at all, only because it is better to understand. For their superiority consists mainly in desiring a virtue they know they can never attain.

FURTHER READING

Biographies

Brightman, Carol. *Writing Dangerously: Mary McCarthy and Her World.* New York: C. N. Potter, 1992, 714 p.
   Depicts McCarthy in the context of her intellectual milieu.

Gelderman, Carol. *Mary McCarthy: A Life.* New York: St. Martin's Press, 1988, 430 p.
   Shows the writer in relation to her family, friends, enemies, and lovers.

Criticism

Dickstein, Morris. "A Glint of Malice." *The Threepenny Review* XV, No. 3 (Fall 1994): 29-30.

    Frequently refers to stories in McCarthy's *The Company She Keeps* while examining the reasons for the rise and gradual decline of McCarthy's literary reputation.

Eisinger, Chester E. "Mary McCarthy as the Sceptical New Liberal." In his *Fiction of the Forties*, pp. 128-35. Chicago: The University of Chicago Press, 1963.

    Contends that McCarthy was an author who displayed the attitude of a sceptical new liberal, meaning that she was suspicious not only of political creed and moral code but also of human reason. Eisinger uses *The Company She Keeps*, *Cast a Cold Eye*, and the novella *The Oasis* to support his claim.

Fitch, Robert E. "The Cold Eye of Mary McCarthy." *The New Republic* 138, No. 18 (5 May 1958): 17-19.

    Maintains that McCarthy's fiction suffers because it focuses on the intellectual and physical dimensions of humans while excluding consideration of compassion, affection, and "moral emotion." Fitch mentions several stories and the novella *The Oasis*.

Fitts, Dudley. "Portraits Cut in Acid." *The New York Times Book Review* (24 September 1950): 9.

    Favorable review of *Cast a Cold Eye*. Fitts admires the style of the writing in particular.

Gay, Robert M. A review of *The Company She Keeps*. *The Atlantic Monthly* CLXX (August 1942): 109.

    Adding to the debate about the classification of *The Company She Keeps* as a novel or short story collection, Gay states: "The method and structure give the impression that the chapters were written without reference to one another and then were somewhat highhandedly brought together by means of the tenuous theme of lost personality. The result is discontinuity and lack of cumulative effect."

Gottfried, Alex, and Davidson, Sue. "Utopia's Children: An Interpretation of Three Political Novels." *Western Political Quarterly* XV, No. 1 (March 1962): 17-32.

    Contrasts the novella *The Oasis* to Nathaniel Hawthorne's *The Blithedale Romance* and Harvey Swados's *False Coin*, all of which are about "utopian experiments carried out in an American setting contemporary with the author's time."

Halsband, Robert. "Jaundiced Eye . . . ." *The Saturday Review* 33, No. 40 (7 October 1950): 23.

    Highly complimentary assessment of *Cast a Cold Eye*, which is cited as proof that McCarthy "has a terrifying talent." Halsband states: "Miss McCarthy casts a distinctly jaundiced eye on all the characters who pass before her, including—and this is her saving grace—herself."

Hardy, Willene Schaefer. *The Company She Keeps*. New York: Frederick Ungar Publishing Co., 1981, 214 p.

    Contains chapters on *The Company She Keeps* and the novella *The Oasis*.

Marshall, Margaret. A review of *The Oasis*. *The Nation* CLXIX (17 September 1949): 281-82.

    Claims that *The Oasis* "is not serious either as a work of art or as the satiric comment it purports to be on our contemporary intellectual and political life."

Munson, Gorham. "Parlor Pinks Playing Utopia." *The Saturday Review of Literature* XXXII (20 August 1949): 12.

    Judges *The Oasis* to be a comedy. According to Munson, "Some advance readers have called it a satire but [McCarthy] seems to me too close to her material, too much identified with it herself to gain a satiric point of view toward it."

Rago, Henry. A review of *The Oasis*. *Commonweal* L (9 September 1949): 536-37.

    Faults *The Oasis* as detached and intellectualized. As Rago states: "You settle for a kind of intellectual slapstick . . . in Mary McCarthy's best fiction (except in that wonderful short story 'The Cicerone')."

Stock, Irvin. *Mary McCarthy*. Minneapolis: University of Minnesota Press, 1968, 47 p.

    Stock focuses on McCarthy's novels but does mention her other works. This study, with slight revision, was published as "The Novels of Mary McCarthy" in *Fiction as Wisdom: From Goethe to Bellow*.

Warren, Robert Penn. "Button, Button." *Partisan Review* IX, No. 6 (November-December 1942): 535-40.

    Describes *The Company She Keeps* as "a shrewd, witty, malicious, original, and often brilliantly written book" but expresses some uncertainty about the purported intention of McCarthy's satire and the heroine's search for identity.

Wilford, Hugh. "An Oasis: The New York Intellectuals in the Late 1940s." *Journal of American Studies* 28, No. 2 (August 1944): 209-23.

    Proposes that "*The Oasis* should be read not as an indictment of radicalism, but rather as a sympathetic—and very perceptive—imaginative enquiry into the causes of radical failure."

Additional coverage of McCarthy's life and career is contained in the following sources published by Gale Research: *Contemporary Authors*, Vols. 5-8 (rev. ed.), 129; *Contemporary Authors New Revision Series*, Vols. 16, 50; *Contemporary Literary Criticism*, Vols. 1, 3, 5, 14, 24, 39, 59; *Dictionary of Literary Biography*, Vol. 2; *Dictionary of Literary Biography Yearbook, 1981*; and *Major 20th-Century Writers*.

The Ballad of the Sad Café
Carson McCullers

(Full name Lula Carson Smith McCullers) American novelist, short story writer, dramatist, essayist, and poet.

The following entry presents criticism on McCullers's novella *The Ballad of the Sad Café*, first published in August, 1943 in *Harper's Bazaar*. For an overview of McCullers's short fiction, see *SSC*, Volume 9.

INTRODUCTION

The Ballad of the Sad Café (1943) is generally considered one of McCullers's best works of fiction and her most successful exploration of her signature themes: loneliness and the effects of unrequited love. McCullers was twenty-four-years-old when she began writing the novella during the winter of 1941. Citing her remark that "everything significant that has happened in my fiction has also happened to me," McCullers's biographer, Virginia Spencer Carr, noted that *The Ballad of the Sad Café* was most likely inspired by several events in her life at this time. For example, the story's depiction of unreciprocated love is often seen as a grotesque representation of her own one-sided infatuations with the Swiss journalist and novelist Annemarie Clarac-Schwarzenbach and the American writer Katherine Anne Porter. Similarly, the motif of the romantic triangle is regarded as a distorted rendering of the situation between McCullers, her husband, and the American composer David Diamond.

Plot and Major Characters

The Ballad of the Sad Café is set in a small mill town in Georgia, where Miss Amelia Evans lives alone in a boarded-up building. Most of the story is told in a flashback that explains how "Miss Amelia" came to her present situation. We learn that the building she lives in was a general store she inherited from her father. Miss Amelia is described as a tall, somewhat masculine woman who becomes the richest person in town from her earnings with the store and a very prosperous still that produces the best liquor in the county. A grim and solitary person, Miss Amelia surprises the town when she agrees to marry Marvin Macy. A handsome and apparently industrious man, Macy has a history of nefarious and sadistic activities: he used to carry with him the ear of a man he killed in a razor fight; he has chopped off the heads of squirrels; and he has abused several young girls. His marriage to Miss Amelia lasts only ten days, mainly because, having married only to gain companionship, she refuses to consummate the marriage. Disgusted by his attempts to seduce her, Miss Amelia puts him out of the house. Macy leaves town vowing revenge and quickly returns to his old ways, robbing gas stations and supermar-

kets and becoming a suspect in a murder. He is eventually arrested and sentenced to serve time in a penitentiary near Atlanta.

One April evening eleven years later, Miss Amelia and several townspeople are sitting on her porch when a hunch-backed stranger named Lymon Willis shows up. Claiming to be a distant relation of Miss Amelia, "Cousin Lymon," as he comes to be known, is a sociable if somewhat shallow character who has "an instinct which is usually only found in small children, an instinct to establish immediate and vital contact between himself and all things in the world." Miss Amelia takes him in. The next day, however, Cousin Lymon is nowhere to be seen. The third day after his arrival, Miss Amelia stays holed up inside her house, leading one of the townspeople to speculate that she has murdered Lymon for something he had in his suitcase. By nightfall, with the rumor having spread throughout the town, a number of men come to Miss Amelia's house and watch from the porch as she writes at the desk in her office. When she gets up to close her office door, the men sense that the moment has come for action and walk into the store. At that point Cousin Lymon emerges from the top of the stairs and begins chatting with everyone. Miss Amelia comes out of her office and asks if anyone needs anything. She then breaks her rule against liquor being consumed in the building and brings out some bottles and glasses and serves the men drinks. This is how the café starts. Over the course of the following four years it gradually expands: tables and chairs are brought in and meals are served. The café's growth is due largely to Miss Amelia's compassion for Cousin Lymon's fear of the night: the company and pleasure the customers bring help him pass the hours. Six years later Macy returns to town. Cousin Lymon, hearing that he has been to Atlanta and been in jail, becomes infatuated with this dangerous character and follows him around. For his part, Macy shows nothing but contempt and disgust for Lymon. Miss Amelia endures Cousin Lymon's refocused affection, tolerates his giving Macy liquor, puts up with his making fun of her gangly walk, and even bears with his asking Macy to live with them, because she knows that if she were to drive Macy away, she would lose Cousin Lymon. The climax of the story occurs when the hatred between Miss Amelia and Macy explodes in a fist fight. After thirty minutes or so of struggling, Miss Amelia is about to win the fight when Lymon suddenly leaps onto her back and claws at her throat, enabling Macy to get the upper hand. During the night Macy and Lymon destroy the café, steal Miss Amelia's belongings, and break her still; by morning, they have left town. For three years Miss Amelia waits for Cousin Lymon to return. Eventually giving up hope, Amelia boards up the house and locks herself in.

Major Themes

As many critics have pointed out, *The Ballad of the Sad Café* reflects McCullers's fascination with freaks, misfits, and grotesques. For her, such characters best embodied the loneliness and isolation that she regarded as the basic condition of human existence. Other themes—all of which bear on the novella's central concern with loneliness—include the failure of communication, the anguish of unrequited love, the psychological phenomenon that causes human beings who are worshiped to despise the worshiper, and the redemptive and transformative effects that even transitory and ultimately doomed love can have on an individual and his or her community. Critics note that McCullers was particularly interested in the paradox of shared isolation, a term that describes the relationships among the three main characters and between the three and their community as well.

Critical Reception

On the initial publication of *The Ballad of the Sad Café*, Tennessee Williams wrote that it is "assuredly among the masterpieces of our language in the form of the novella." V. S. Pritchett considered it evidence that McCullers was "the most remarkable novelist . . . to come out of America for a generation." William Clancy stated that the work's "metaphysical fusion of horror and compassion" represented "an achievement equaled by few other contemporary American writers." The critical reaction has not been unanimously favorable, however. Robert Drake has called

The Ballad of the Sad Café "ridiculous . . . with its fabricated primitivistic folkishness." Lawrence Graver has argued that while the novella is "by far the best of Mrs. McCullers's excursions into the grotesque . . . it is not without reminders of the penumbral insistence that mars her worst work," namely the sense that "too much is made of dark nights of the soul and of things going on there that only God can understand." Nonetheless, *The Ballad of the Sad Café* is generally regarded as one of her best works of fiction. The 1950s, 1960s, and 1970s saw renewed interest in McCullers's body of work. During these decades numerous studies appeared on the novella that focused on issues such as the role of the narrator, the nature of love, the relationship between the text and the traditional ballad form, its mythical qualities, its connection to the Southern Gothic tradition, and its representation of sexuality and gender.

CRITICISM

Coleman Rosenberger   (essay date 1951)

SOURCE: A review of *The Ballad of the Sad Café: The Novels and Stories of Carson McCullers*, in *The New York Herald Tribune*, June 10, 1951, pp. 1, 13.

[*In the following favorable review, Rosenberger discusses McCullers's short fiction and calls* The Ballad of the Sad Café *her most intense achievement.*]

Here in one omnibus volume, which includes her three novels, a half dozen short stories, and an unfamiliar longer one which gives the volume [*The Ballad of the Sad Café: The Novels and Stories of Carson McCullers*] its name, is the whole fabulous world of Carson McCullers: the dwarfed and the deformed, the hurt and the lonely, the defeated and the despised, the violent and the homicidal—all the masks and symbols which she has employed over a decade of writing to shock the reader into a shared experience of her own intense sense of human tragedy. When *The Heart Is a Lonely Hunter* was published in 1940 it was widely recognized as an original and mature work, and the acclaim for it was mixed with mild astonishment that the book should be the work of a twenty-three-year-old writer. Something like that first astonishment is induced by the present collection, which exhibits what an impressive and unified body of work has been produced by Mrs. McCullers at an age when many another writer has hardly started upon his career. For *The Ballad of the Sad Café* makes abundantly clear, which was not generally seen at the time of their separate publication, that *Reflections in a Golden Eye* and *The Member of the Wedding* extend and broaden the themes of her first book, as do the shorter pieces, so that each takes its place in an expanding structure in which each part augments and strengthens the rest.

A recurring theme throughout Mrs. McCullers' work—perhaps the central theme—is the human tragedy of the failure of communication between man and man, and the sense of loss and separation and loneliness which accompanies that failure. The theme is examined and illuminated through minor characters as well as major ones. We see the drunken Blout in *The Heart Is a Lonely Hunter* pouring out his torrent of words to the deaf mute and exclaiming "You are the only one in this town who catches what I mean." Or the old man of "A Tree, A Rock, A Cloud," in his wild and earnest pre-dawn monologue directed at the uncomprehending paper boy. Or Frankie in *The Member of the Wedding* running beside the man on the tractor to shout words he could not hear through the noisy excitement.

In Mrs. McCullers' world of symbols, the urgent need to communicate is most often presented in the guise of the physically maimed or deformed, who are at once the favored and the damned. Frankie ticks off the freaks she had seen at the Chattahoochee Exposition—The Giant, the Fat Lady, The Midget, The Wild Nigger, The Pin Head, the Alligator Boy, the Half-Man Half-Woman—and recalls that "it seemed to her that they had looked at her in a secret way and tried to connect their eyes with hers, is though to say: we know you." And the artist, with his own compelling need to communicate, is one of the freaks of the world. Anacleto in *Reflections in a Golden Eye* lists himself with the "people behind footlights, midgets, great artists, and such-like fabulous folk."

The establishment of communication, the breaking down of the barriers of a torturing separateness, is the ultimate achievement of Mrs. McCullers' characters. The urgency which drives Frankie to become "A Member of the Wedding" is the conviction that "All other people had a we to claim, all other except her. The soldiers in the army can say we, and even the criminals on the chain-gangs." Again the theme is stated explicitly in the Twelve Mortal Men, the brief epilogue to the story of Miss Amelia. The voices of the twelve chained convicts on the road gang join in an intricately blended music: "And what kind of gang is this that can make such music? Just twelve mortal men, seven of them black and five of them white boys from this county. Just twelve mortal men who are together."

The six short stories which are here printed in book form for the first time, and the title piece, have apparently been drawn from Mrs. McCullers' whole writing career. The stories are not dated—the earliest copyright is 1936, when Mrs. McCullers was nineteen—and there is little to suggest the possible order of composition. If one were to guess, it would be that **"Wunderkind"** is the earliest. It is the story of the heartbreak of a fifteen-year-old girl who knows that she will not be a great pianist, a Wunderkind.

Such a brief gloss can give little of the quality even of the shorter pieces, such as **"The Jockey"** or **"Madam Zilensky and the King of Finland."** The jockey, dressed carefully in his tailored suit of green Chinese silk, is seen for a moment when he is on the edge of disintegration brought on by the injury of his companion and their separation. Madam Zilensky, composer and teacher is also seen in a moment of crisis. She inhabited a private world in which she lived vicariously in the imagination, but in response to

a story of hers about seeing the King of Finland, Mr. Brooks coldly observed: "But there is no King of Finland." And "never afterward could Mr. Brooks forget the face of Madam Zilensky at that moment. In her eyes there was astonishment, dismay, and a sort of cornered horror. She had the look of one who watches his whole interior world split open and disintegrate."

"The Sojourner" and **"A Domestic Dilemma"** and **"A Tree, A Rock, A Cloud"** are, in their various ways, stories or the separateness which may exist in the "we" of man and wife. It is, however, in the title story, ***The Ballad of the Sad Café,*** that Mrs. McCullers achievement is seen at its most intense. A short novel, or long short story, or novella—it runs to some sixty pages in the present closely printed volume—it is condensed and disciplined and brilliant writing, which carries the reader along so easily on the wave of the story that he may not at first be aware how completely he has been saturated with symbolism. The story opens and closes with Miss Amelia's house as it now is, lonely, estranged, separate, boarded up. Between is an account of the coming and the departure of the hunchback and Marvin Macy. The hunchback, the deformed, the freak, the artist, was possessed of the "instinct to establish immediate and vital contact between himself and all things in the world." Before disaster came at last, Miss Amelia pushed back the barriers of separateness for a time, and the strange café was established as a place of warmth and fellowship in the desolate town. Miss Amelia and the hunchback and Marvin Macy, the instrument of the disaster, are a grotesque crew. But as Mrs. McCullers patiently explains: "The hearts of small children are delicate organs. A cruel beginning in this world can twist them into curious shapes. The heart of a child can shrink so that forever afterward it is hard and pitted as the seed of a peach. Or again, the heart of such a child may fester and swell until it is a misery to carry within the body, easily chafed and hurt by the most ordinary things." Mrs. McCullers' freaks are not to be dismissed: they are Everyman.

Robert S. Phillips   (essay date 1964)

SOURCE: "Dinesen's 'Monkey' and McCullers' 'Ballad': A Study in Literary Affinity," in *Studies in Short Fiction,* Vol. 1, No. 3, Spring, 1964, pp. 184-90.

[*In the following essay, Phillips compares Isak Dinesen's short story "The Monkey" (1934) with* The Ballad of the Sad Café *and argues that Dinesen's tale was a likely source of inspiration for McCullers.*]

Originality is the quality most remarkable in the writings of Carson McCullers. Her novels and stories, with their poetic simplicity and Gothic elements, their freakish characters and malevolent plots, hold a unique place in contemporary American literature. Because her work has been unique, the fiction of Mrs. McCullers has been subjected primarily to textual analysis. A few isolated critics have noted the correspondence between Mother Lovejoy, in the

1958 McCullers play, *The Square Root of Wonderful,* and Amanda Wingfield, of Tennessee Williams' *The Glass Menagerie* (1944). But *Square Root* has been universally acknowledged to be Mrs. McCullers' least inspired creation. No one, however, has noted the influence of Isak Dinesen upon her work. Especially revealing is a comparison of Miss Dinesen's long story, "The Monkey" [in *Seven Gothic Tales,* 1934], with Mrs. McCullers' celebrated novella, *The Ballad of the Sad Café*.

The following discussion is not to be construed as a conjecture that Mrs. McCullers has deliberately borrowed from the Danish author. But "The Monkey" can be seen as a very probable inspiration for the McCullers work, and affords a partial understanding of the sources and invention of a work which in our time has become a minor though cryptic classic. Brewster Ghiselin has noted that for any artist production . . . a process of purely conscious calculation seems never to occur. The writer uses the sum total of his past to fabricate the new. An artistic creation is an extension of life, and as such "is not an elaboration of the established, but a movement beyond the established" [Ghiselin, *The Creative Process: A Symposium,* 1955]. Such is *The Ballad of the Sad Café,* which marks a movement well beyond the established characterizations and action of "The Monkey" it resembles in many aspects. The result, of course, is another individual work of art.

We know that Mrs. McCullers is familiar with the work of the Danish author. Indeed, she was moved by the death of Miss Dinesen to write one of her infrequent essays ["Isak Dinesen: In Praise of Radiance," *Saturday Review,* March 16, 1963]. In that piece Mrs. McCullers stated that she first read *Seven Gothic Tales*—in which volume "The Monkey" was published-in 1938. (*The Ballad of the Sad Café* was published in 1943.) Mrs. McCullers praised the tales for their brilliance, control, and deliberation, three qualities very much evident in every piece she herself has written. The case is clearly one of affinity for a kindred spirit.

Part I of "The Monkey" establishes a world very analogous to that of *The Ballad*. The Prioress ruling over Closter Seven performs a role similar to that of Miss Amelia in the small Southern town. Amelia provides necessities through her store, cares for the sick, and owns most of the town's property. The Prioress' pet monkey, furthermore, is curiously reminiscent of Amelia's companion, the dwarf Lymon. Of the former we are told, "When she was at her card table, a place where she spent some of her happiest hours, the monkey was wont to sit on the back of her chair, and to follow with its glittering eyes the course of the cards as they were dealt out and taken in." Lymon continually surveys Miss Amelia and her customers in the café, and is humoured as a plaything. Both the monkey and Lymon are small love objects for strong, sexless women. The protective attitude of the Prioress toward the monkey when children bombard it with chestnuts is akin to Amelia's protection of Lymon from the scorn and derision of the town. Both stories employ a group of characters who function as a chorus, and articulated conscience. The old women of Closter Seven, sitting in the sun and commenting on the strange actions, parallel the gossips of *The Ballad,* who conjecture the existence of hideous atrocities where there are none.

Boris, of "The Monkey," is the counterpart of Marvin Macy. Both men possess fabulous reputations: Boris is described as appearing to be "a young priest of black magic." Later in the tale we find Boris being pursued by authorities as one of the "corrupters of youth." Marvin Macy, we are told, "was not a person to be envied, for he was an evil character. . . . For years, when he was a boy, he had carried about with him the dried and salted ear of a man he had killed in a razor fight. . . . Yet in spite of his well-known reputation he was the beloved of many females in this region. . . . These gentle young girls he degraded and shamed." Boris remains constant to the character and actions performed by Marvin Macy throughout the story.

The Prioress, Boris' beloved Aunt Cathinka, named after the deity of mercy, resembles Amelia in her compassion for the sly and unloved. She and Amelia, in addition, both have a fondness for property. The Prioress, determined and strong, too old to possess her handsome nephew, sees a surrogate in young Athena Hopballehus, and achieves sublimation by proposing that Boris marry her. It is at this point that the character we may recognize as a true prototype for Miss Amelia is introduced.

Athena lives in a house which is "now baroquely dilapidated and more than half a ruin." Miss Amelia's house is "very old. There is about it a curious, cracked look that is very puzzling until you suddenly realize that at one time, and long ago, the right side of the front porch had been painted, and part of the wall—but the painting was left unfinished and one portion of the house is darker and dingier than the other." Both tales take place in autumn, and the landscapes are described in images of despair, with a feeling for what Miss Dinesen calls "the sad heart of autumn."

Athena lives alone with her father, a man who is continually involved in a great lawsuit. Of Amelia we learn, "She would have been rich as a Congressman if it were not for her one great failing, and that was her passion for lawsuits and the courts." The duplication of this detail seems singularly fortuitous. The most striking parallels, however, are to be found in the appearance of the two characters. "Athena was a strong young woman of eighteen, six feet high and broad in proportion, with a pair of shoulders which could lift and carry a sack of wheat." Mrs. McCullers describes Amelia as "a dark, tall woman with bones and muscles like a man." Amelia Evans is six feet, two inches tall. Boris looked at Athena and "wondered if she had ever heard of love." Mrs. McCullers states, "Miss Amelia cared nothing for the love of men."

Both Athena and Amelia are prevented from having a normal love affair by an obstacle greater than that of physical size. Each possesses a latent incestuous desire for her father; both have been sheltered too long by the male parent. Athena is, in her father's words, "the key of my whole world." Amelia's most prized possession is a large acorn she picked off the ground on the dark day her father died. Athena and Amelia have grown up in a male world, and their dress and actions underscore their inability to accept the traditional feminine role. Insecure, they foster their great strength as a protection against the demands of the normal world.

To each of these stalwart heroines, a proposal of marriage is most alarming, and apparently unmotivated. Both stories explore what Miss Dinesen has termed "the tender and dangerous emotions of the human heart." Mrs. McCullers elaborates: "Almost everyone wants to be the lover. And the curt truth is that, in a deep secret way, the state of being beloved is intolerable to many. The beloved fears and hates the lover, and with the best of reasons. For the lover is forever trying to strip bare his beloved. The lover craves any possible relation with the beloved, even if this experience can cause him only pain." It is obvious that Amelia consents to marry Macy in hopes of securing a replacement for her deceased father. When Macy tries to consummate the marriage—thereby destroying the father-image-she rejects him. Amelia seems devoid of any sexual feeling, much less of desire. Athena likewise rejects Boris, and is shown to be totally innocent of sexual knowledge.

A key to both stories is the legend which Boris recalls, "the old ballad about the giant's daughter, who finds a man in the wood, and surprised and pleased, takes him home to play with. The giant orders her to let him go, telling her that she will only break him." In each case, the giantess is indeed capable of breaking the body as well as the spirit of the beloved. Both Athena and Amelia will not tolerate being loved by any other than their fathers. This ancient ballad recalled by Boris is, in fact, the "ballad" of the sad café. That subconscious incestuous love is the motivation here is reinforced in part VIII of "The Monkey" when the Prioress recalls a tale said to be in her great-grandmother's memoirs, a tale concerning the Duchess of Berri, who was allegedly pregnant by her father.

Cousin Lymon's appearance fosters new emotions in Amelia. She loves Lymon as a possession, a pet, a beloved object incapable of attempting the role of sexual lover. In addition to his alleged kinship to Amelia, which should prohibit cohabitation, it is clear that his twisted body and broken back make physical love an impossibility. Lymon, then, is the monkey idol of Dinesen's Gothic tale, one of those "symbols which seem to have been the common property of all pagan iconoclasts," perhaps "due to the idea of original sin." Isak Dinesen gives us a Wendish idol for the goddess of love an idol whose front is the face of a beautiful woman and whose back is the face of a monkey. This juxtaposition of beauty and ugliness, the human and the bestial, is a personification of the dual nature of love. Mrs. McCullers expands upon this theme in *The Ballad:*

> This lover about whom we speak need not necessarily
> be a young man saving for a wedding ring this lover

can be man, woman, child, or indeed any human creature on this earth.

> Now, the beloved can also be of any description. The most outlandish people can be the stimulus for love. . . . A good man may be the stimulus for a love both violent and debased, or a jabbering madman may bring about in the soul of someone a tender and simple idyll. Therefore, the value and quality of any love is determined solely by the lover himself.

The proposal of marriage, because unforeseen and unwanted, is a great shock to Amelia and to Athena. It breaks into their solitude, their proud isolation.

"Now, the beloved can also be of any description. The most outlandish people can be the stimulus for love . . . A good man may be the stimulus for a love both violent and debased, or a jabbering madman may bring about in the soul of someone a tender and simple idyll. Therefore, the value and quality of any love is determined solely by the lover himself." The proposal of marriage, since unforeseen and unwanted, is a great shock to Amelia and to Athena. It breaks into their solitude, their proud isolation.

The Prioress, eager to see Boris succeed, gives him an amber-colored love potion, which will make him forget himself for a few hours and seduce the unwilling Athena. In *The Ballad* Miss Amelia is first known for her home-brewed liquor which "has a special quality of its own . . . once down a man it glows inside him for a long time afterward. . . . Things that have gone unnoticed, thoughts that have been harbored far back in the dark mind, are suddenly recognized and comprehended."

The most salient similarity between the two stories is in the battle royal that occurs at the conclusion of each—Athena's fight with Boris when he enters her chamber to seduce her, and Amelia's fight with Macy over rights to Lymon. A brutal fistfight between lovers can scarcely be called a common conception for fiction; yet such is to be found in these two tales. In both stories, the bizarre fight is shown to be predictable and inevitable.

The fight in "The Monkey" is described to the length of three pages. A sample of the graphic scene will suffice:

> Her powerful, swift and direct fist hit him in the mouth and knocked out two of his teeth. The pain and the smell and taste of the blood which filled his mouth sent him beside himself. He let her go to try for a stronger hold, and immediately they were in each other's arms, in an embrace of life and death.

Mrs. McCullers' version is equally fierce:

> Then, like wildcats, they were suddenly on each other. There was the sound of knocks, panting, and thumpings on the floor. They were so fast that it was hard to take in what was going on—but once Miss Amelia was hurled backward so that she staggered and almost fell,

and another time Marvin Macy caught a knock on the shoulder that spun him round like a top. So the fight went on in this wild violent way with no sign of weakening on either side.

Just as Marvin Macy never succeeds in making love to Amelia, Boris' struggle to seduce Athena is equally unsuccessful.

The morning after the fight, Athena promises the Prioress she will marry Boris, but that "whenever I can do so, I shall kill him." Her regard for Boris, prior to the fantastical metamorphosis of the Prioress at the conclusion, remains identical to that of Amelia for Macy. When the monkey attacks the Prioress, and forces her to the floor, we have Cousin Lymon leaping on Amelia in the *Ballad's* terrible climax. In the transmogrification of the Prioress, the iconic face of human love once more prevails, and under its benevolent aegis, Boris and Athena become partners together in life. Mrs. McCullers' ballad has no such happy ending.

There are other important similarities between the two tales. Miss Dinesen's wandering crew of hangmen, who have seen so much horror that they can weep on command, parallel Mrs. McCullers' sad chain gang. Miss Amelia at the conclusion of the *Ballad,* her face sexless and white, resembles for all the world the old Prioress, one of those beings whom Miss Dinesen describes as "old enough to have done with the business of being women." Miss Amelia was done before she had begun.

Despite the similarities, it should be noted that both stories are constructed upon the foundation of ancient fairy tale and myth, in which the world of giants (the supernatural order) is juxtaposed with the world of men (the natural order). The "larger than life" has proved invaluable to storytellers of all ages who wish to illuminate the little world of man. Swift's Gulliver discovers in the land of the Brobdingnagians the perils of the supernatural for life when he becomes the plaything of a giantess. That his end was a happy one, like Boris', proves nothing more than that the comic mask has temporarily displaced the tragic on the face of a neutral universe. Miss Amelia, having looked upon the tragic mask, must forever wear it.

Albert J. Griffith (essay date 1967)

SOURCE: "Carson McCullers' Myth of the Sad Café," in *The Georgia Review,* Vol. XXI, No. 1, Spring, 1967, pp. 46-56.

[*In the following essay, Griffith examines the ways in which McCullers imbues* The Ballad of the Sad Café *with mythic elements.*]

Carson McCullers' *The Ballad of the Sad Café* is as grotesque in characterization and incident as anything in Ameri-

can literature. The simple summarizing of the situation reveals its perverseness: a dark, masculine, cross-eyed giant of a woman develops strange, possessive love for a dirty, mischievous, hunchbacked dwarf of a man, who in turn worships a handsome, guitar-strumming robber and seducer, who in his turn had previously so desired the giant woman that he had contracted a miserable ten-day unconsummated marriage with her.

Yet the quality of the novella most frequently cited by critics is the mysterious beauty which encompasses the whole work. Even the violence of the denouement—a primitive bare-fisted agon between the woman and her one-time bridegroom over the hunchback—fails to mar the poetic serenity of the tale for most readers. The story as a whole is neither a morbid Gothic monstrosity perpetrated for mere shock effect nor a specimen of the extreme naturalism, a la Erskine Caldwell, sometimes associated with the South. Somehow *The Ballad of the Sad Café* sublimates its unpromising ingredients.

The reason for the paradoxical charm of this grotesque story is not difficult to find. From its first appearance, critics have recognized the lyricism of the McCullers narrative style, which can render even sordid subject matter in poetic terms. They have also noted the aura of legend which surrounds the incidents recounted, embuing them with a peculiar remoteness in both time and space. They have even sensed the allegorical structure which gives significance to otherwise preverse literal details.

What has not been sufficiently noted, however, is that these elements—the quasi-poetic stylistic devices, the fairytale atmosphere, the non-literal meanings—are the marks of the mythic imagination, and their combination in this story suggests the making of a modern myth. *The Ballad of the Sad Café* may be set in a twentieth century Southern town and speak of things like Greyhound buses and brick privies and marijuana cigarettes, but the imagination which informs it is in many important ways close kin to the imagination of those ancient authors who set their stories on Olympus, in Valhalla, and in Camelot and spoke of winged sandals and golden thrones and magic potions.

This is not to say that Mrs. McCullers in *The Ballad of the Sad Café* was writing a contemporary parallel to some well-known myth, as Joyce, Faulkner, Eliot, Welty, Updike, and many other modern authors have done. Mrs. McCullers' story seems to have sprung from her own imagination, but she has invested it with some of the same qualities which distinguished the archetypal literature of past cultures. She has not parodied an old myth but created her own new one out of primitive elements.

The mythic quality, discoverable in both the characters and the incidents, does not perhaps inhere so much in the subject itself as in the author's attitude toward the subject. It is the implied presence of a personal narrator in *The Ballad of the Sad Café* which transforms the story. The bare incidents, stripped of the narrator's poetic presentation, are ugly, ludicrous, even repulsive; no paraphrase could ever begin to convey their significance, much less their beauty. The characters, presented out of context, would be unreal, aberrant, unfathomable; the setting, bizarre, contrived; the theme, sentimental, foolish. In context, the grotesqueness remains but is turned towards a purpose, becomes part of a whole which is not grotesque, transcends the human and moves into the numinous.

The trio of principal characters, for instance, seems to step right out of the world of folk imagination. Each of them has physical characteristics, personality traits, and community functions which set him off, not only from others in the story, but in some ways from all humankind. Miss Amelia, the dominating figure in the story, is perhaps the most impressive of the three. She is first presented as a face looking down on the town from the one unboarded window of the deserted café: "a face like the terrible dim faces known in dreams—sexless and white, with two gray crossed eyes which are turned inward so sharply that they seem to be exchanging with each other one long and secret gaze of grief." This phantasmagoric impression remains even in the later descriptions of Miss Amelia in the days before her withdrawal from the life of the town. "She was," we are told, "a dark, tall woman with bones and muscles like a man. Her hair was cut short and brushed back from the forehead, and there was about her sunburned face a tense, haggard quality." Throughout, she appears with a kind of barbaric regal dignity, towering above the lesser mortals of the town, always moving surely and deliberately in a "slow, gangling swagger," asserting with a "proud and stern" face her authority over all who venture near her premises.

Strong and domineering as an Amazonian queen, Miss Amelia is in personality as inscrutable as a visitant from Asgard or Olympus. Her expression has been known to have a "look that appears to be both very wise and very crazy" and her ways and habits are "too peculiar ever to reason about." Her reticence is such that the people of the town resort to wild conjectures ("I know what Miss Amelia done. She murdered that man for something in that suitcase") to explain her behavior, for she provides no explanations herself, acting always in confident self-righteousness. Her pattern of life is both solitary and independent; she makes her own schedules (often spending "whole nights back in her shed in the swamp, dressed in overalls and gum boots, silently guarding the low fire of the still") and ignores whenever she pleases the conventions of the community (not warming "her backside modestly, lifting her skirt only an inch or so, as do most women when in public," but pulling up her red dress "quite high in the back so that a piece of her strong, hairy thigh could be seen by anyone who cared to look at it"). Using everything about her with great success, she is in fact ill at ease only with people. Even here, her chagrin is that of a demiurge over the recalcitrance of creatures: "People, unless they are nilly-willy or very sick, cannot be taken into the hands and changed overnight to something more worth-while and profitable. So that the only use that Miss Amelia had for other people was to make money out of them." Her penchant for

lawsuits is reminiscent of the endless litigations the classical divinities entered into with mortals.

> *The Ballad of the Sad Café* may be set in a twentieth century Southern town and speak of things like Greyhound buses and brick privies and marijuana cigarettes, but the imagination which informs it is in many important ways close kin to the imagination of those ancient authors who set their stories on Olympus, in Valhalla, and in Camelot.
>
> —*Albert J. Griffith*

Yet Miss Amelia is not totally estranged from the life of the town. She plays, indeed, the beneficent role of a bucolic Vesta, presiding over the private and public hearth. She is the "richest woman for miles around" and, even before the founding of her café, runs a country store from which the staples of life (feed, guano, meal, and snuff) are dispensed. Furthermore, from her still three miles back in the swamp, she runs out the best liquor in the county—liquor with a "special quality of its own," "clean and sharp on the tongue" and capable of bringing out "that which is known only in the soul of a man" the way fire brings out a message written in lemon juice. Her whisky is veritably a mystic potion:

> Things that have gone unnoticed, thoughts that have been harbored far back in the dark mind, are suddenly recognized and comprehended. A spinner who has thought only of the loom, the dinner pail, the bed, and then the loom again—this spinner might drink some on a Sunday and come across a marsh lily. And in his palm he might hold this flower, examining the golden dainty cup, and in him suddenly might come a sweetness keen as pain. A weaver might look up suddenly and see for the first time the cold, weird radiance of midnight January sky, and a deep fright at his own smallness stop his heart. Such things as these, then, happen when a man has drunk Miss Amelia's liquor. He may suffer, or he may be spent with joy—but the experience has shown the truth; he has warmed his soul and seen the message hidden there.

Like a tutelary deity, too, Miss Amelia rules over the rituals at the changes of season. It is she, who, when the first frost comes, goes out to "judge the day." Already she has led the town in preparations for the new season: she has made a new and bigger condenser for her still, ground enough sorghum to dizzy her old grist mule, scalded her Mason jars, and put away pear preserves. People "come in from the country to find out what Miss Amelia thought of the weather"; they await her word for the ritual slaughtering of the first hog. When her command is given, the scene is reminiscent of a pagan sacrifice: "There was the warm smell of pig blood and smoke in the back yard, the stamp of footsteps, the ring of voices in the winter air." Only the unprecedented snowfall near the climax of the *Ballad* catches Miss Amelia unprepared; she simply shutters herself up in her house and ignores it so she will not "have to come to some decision" about it.

Miss Amelia's final attribute is also one which in folklore often attests to a superhuman status: she is a great healer. "She possessed great imagination and used hundreds of different cures," we are told. "In the face of the most dangerous and extraordinary treatment she did not hesitate, and no disease was so terrible but what she would undertake to cure it." The fact that "female complaints" are the one exception to her healing skills foreshadows another fact that the story will bring out, that Miss Amelia is helpless in dealing with her own sexual weakness, her love for the hunchback, Cousin Lymon.

Contrasted with Miss Amelia is another godlike personage, Marvin Macy, the loom-fixer destined to become first her lover, then her rival:

> . . . Marvin Macy was the handsomest man in this region—being six feet one inch tall, hard-muscled, and with slow gray eyes and curly hair. He was well off, made good wages, and had a gold watch which opened in the back to a picture of a waterfall. From the outward and worldly point of view Marvin Macy was a fortunate fellow; he needed to bow and scrape to no one and always got just what he wanted.

With hyacinthine locks and golden talisman, Marvin Macy is the composite image of the great Greek gods and heroes: a young Adonis, the beloved of all the pastoral nymphs "with tender sweet little buttocks and charming ways"; a country Orpheus, parading "up and down the road with his guitar" and descending into the underworld of the penitentiary near Atlanta; a thieving Hermes, carrying "forbidden marijuana weed to tempt those who were discouraged and drawn toward death" and holding up the A & P (Apollo's?) Store of Society City; a muscular Heracles, fighting for the girdle, as it were, of the Amazonian queen; a passionate Phoebus, finding his Daphne struck by the frigid tip of the leaden arrow.

Marvin Macy's whole personality and upbringing sets him apart from the others of the town. As one of seven unwanted children deserted by wild young parents who only "liked to fish and roam around the swamp," Marvin Macy developed early a heart "hard and pitted as the seed of a peach." He chops off the tails of squirrels in the pinewoods "just to please his fancy," degrades and shames gentle young girls, and carries with him "the dried and salted ear of a man he had killed in a razor fight." His demonic degeneracy is stressed in the imagery: the narrator says "his heart turned tough as the horns of Satan"; Miss Amelia vows he will never set his "split hoof" on her premises; Cousin Lymon is "possessed by an unnatural spirit" on first sight of him; and all the townspeople know that he never sweats even in the summer, "surely a sign worth pondering over." Furthermore, his evil is "not mea-

sured by the actual sins he had committed," for, quite apart from his innumerable crimes, "there was about him a secret meanness that clung to him almost like a smell." And to the one marvelous event in the story—the unheard-of snowfall—Marvin Macy lays claim, since he alone of the townsfolk has had the prior experience to cope with it and to use its suspected preternatural significance to his advantage. In short, Marvin Macy is also created of heroic stature, a worthy antagonist to the established tyrant of the town, Miss Amelia.

The third of the principal characters, Cousin Lymon, springs perhaps from deeper sources in the mythopoeic subconsciousness. Although he has certain affinities with the deformed gods (Haephestus, for instance) and monsters (the Sphinx, the Minotaur, the Harpies) of Greek mythology, he is most ways probably closer to the oneiric creations of the Teutonic mentality—Loki, the fickle mischief-maker of Asgard; Rumpelstiltskin, the mysterious little man who appears from nowhere and bargains for favors; and all the trolls, dwarfs, elves, and gnomes who haunt the forests of the north.

Cousin Lymon appears first as the Mysterious Stranger, the visitant from an unknown world:

> The man was a stranger, and it is rare that a stranger enters the town on foot at that hour [toward midnight]. Besides, the man was a hunchback. He was scarcely more than four feet tall and he wore a ragged, dusty coat that reached only to his knees. His crooked little legs seemed too thin to carry the weight of his great warped chest and the hump that sat on his shoulders. He had a very large head, with deep-set blue eyes and a sharp little mouth. His face was both soft and sassy—at the moment his pale skin was yellowed by dust and there were lavender shadows beneath his eyes. He carried a lopsided old suitcase which was tied with a rope.

He is mistaken at first for a calf, then for a child; later he is compared to a fly, a mosquito, a hawk, a magpie, a child of a swamphaunt. Because Cousin Lymon sniffles and weeps, the loafers on Miss Amelia's porch call him "a regular Morris Finestein," a reference to "a quick, skipping little Jew" who had lived in the town years before and moved away under the force of calamity, a reference that thus links Cousin Lymon indirectly with the saga of the Wandering Jew. Further, no one is ever able to guess his age and he himself professes not to know whether he has been on the earth for ten years or a hundred.

Cousin Lymon, bedecking himself like a little king in knee-breeches, stockings, and lime-green shawl, quickly comes to fill an important role in the town, a role unfilled before his advent. For Cousin Lymon, we are told, is "the type of person who has a quality about him that sets him apart from other and more ordinary human beings"—the instinctive ability "to establish immediate and vital contact between himself and all things in the world." His magical camaraderie brings "the air of freedom and illicit gladness" that changes Miss Amelia's business-like store into a warm and genial café. Despite the fact that he is a great "busybody" and "mischief-maker," who without a word is capable of setting people at each other "in a way that was miraculous," he is "most responsible for the great popularity of the café." "When he walked into the room," the narrator says, "there was always a quick feeling of tension, because with this busybody about there was never any telling what might descend on you, or what might suddenly be brought to happen in the room. People are never so free with themselves and so recklessly glad as when there is some possibility of commotion or calamity ahead." And commotion and calamity is, of course, exactly what Cousin Lymon brings with him.

Surrounding these three principals are the townspeople. None of these are developed as three-dimensional characters and only a few—Henry Macy, Merlie Ryan, Stumpy MacPhail, the Rainey twins—are individualized at all. The townspeople function in the story as a single character; they are, indeed, a kind of Greek chorus, reacting to and commenting on the action, occasionally forcing an issue and precipitating a crisis. Thus, when rumors circulate that Miss Amelia may have murdered the hunchback, the chorus reacts:

> Some eight or ten men had convened on the porch of Miss Amelia's store. They were silent and were indeed just waiting about. They themselves did not know what they were waiting for, but it was this: in times of tension, when some great action is impending, men gather and wait in this way. And after a time there will come a moment when all together they will act in unison, not from thought or from the will of any one man, but as though their instincts had merged together so that the decision belongs to no single one of them, but to the group as a whole. At such a time no individual hesitates. And whether the matter will be settled peaceably, or whether the joint action will result in ransacking, violence, and crime, depends on destiny.

When the time comes and the "instinct to act" is felt, the group all at once enters the store "as though moved by one will." "At that moment," we are told, "the eight men looked very much alike—all wearing blue overalls, most of them with whitish hair, all pale of face, and all with a set, dreaming look in the eye." Not only do they look alike and act in unison, they also share a common font of experience:

> Now the names of the men of the group there on that evening were as follows: Hasty Malone, Robert Calvert Hale, Merlie Ryan, Reverend T. M. Willin, Rosser Cline, Rip Wellborn, Henry Ford Crimp, and Horace Wells. Except for Reverend Willin, they are all alike in many ways as has been said—all having taken pleasure from something or other, all having wept and suffered in some way, most of them tractable unless exasperated. Each of them worked in the mill, and lived with others in a two- or three-room house for which the rent was ten dollars or twelve dollars a month. All had been paid that afternoon, for it was Saturday. So for the moment, think of them as a whole.

If the people of the town are to be thought of "as a whole," it is even more necessary to think of the "twelve mortal men" of the chain gang as a whole. Their single shared personality is emphasized by their prison uniform, the chains linking their ankles, their common labor, and their har-monious singing. The chain gang functions, then, as a kind of second chorus, more removed from the action of the story and commenting only indirectly through their song on the great issue of the story, the problem of love and alienation. The very existence of these "twelve mortal men who are together" is itself the most telling commentary possible.

The mythic aura which surrounds the characters extends to the events as well. In the first place, Mrs. McCullers sets the action in the remembered past, so that we do not see it directly as it happens but retrospectively as it is recalled, re-created, interpreted. We are allowed to glimpse first the present desolation of the town, then to have the cause of the desolation explained as the ballad unfolds. The style is presentational, however, rather than representational: we are always aware of the mediating influence of the narrator. The narrator's panoramic vision opens before us in the very first lines of the novella, those hauntingly poetic lines that merge past and present, intimacy and mystery, fact and mythic imagination in the evocative decription of the dreary town. "These August afternoons— when your shift is finished there is absolutely nothing to do; you might as well walk down to the Forks Fall Road and listen to the chain gang," we go on to read, unconsciously being affected by the colloquial tone, the second person address, the intruding interpretations of a personalized viewpoint. In Percy Lubbock's terms, this is a "pictorial" work in which we face toward the story-teller and listen to him, instead of a "scenic" work in which we would turn toward the story and watch it. "So let the slow years pass and come to a Saturday evening six years after the time when Cousin Lymon came first to the town," the narrator will say, reminding us that the story has its primary existence in his memory and imagination.

The events as narrated seem, furthermore, to be fore-ordained, the result of destiny, not free will. Motivation for the peculiar actions of the characters is sometimes suggested, but never clearly specified. Why Marvin Macy loves Amelia, or Amelia, Lymon, or Lymon, Marvin Macy can only be conjectured. The famous disquisition on love—"Now some explanation is due for all this behavior. The time has come to speak about love," etc.—is no psychological explanation at all; at best it is a philosophic hypothesis which only begs the question.

Moreover, the characters often seem helplessly impelled toward a certain course of events. The chorus moves because "the time had come" or "the instinct to act" came upon them. Cousin Lymon behaves as if bewitched by Marvin Macy. Miss Amelia seems "to have lost her will" when she reacts to Marvin Macy's charming of the hunchback, makes no protest when Marvin Macy moves in on her, and stands "helpless" when Marvin Macy bounces her curses back upon herself. The climactic brawl at the end of the story comes precisely at seven o'clock in the evening—a time instinctively "known to everyone, not by announcement or words, but understood in the unquestioning way that rain is understood, or an evil odor from the swamp." Each of the three principals fills his role as if the whole action had been "arranged in some manner beforehand."

Omens and natural portents provide clues to what destiny has in store. When Cousin Lymon first comes upon the scene, a dog begins "a wild, hoarse howl." When Miss Amelia is suspected of murdering Cousin Lymon, it is noticed that the lamps in the houses make "mournful, wavering flickers" and that the wind comes not from the swamp but from the cold black pinewoods to the north. At Miss Amelia's wedding the sun shining through the ruby windows of the church puts a "curious glow" on the bridal pair. On the day that Henry Macy gets word his brother is out of the penitentiary on parole, little children are fretful, Cousin Lymon compulsively tells a weird lie about stepping on an alligator in Rotten Lake, Henry Macy himself develops a nervous tic, and somewhere in the darkness a woman sings "in a high wild voice" a tune that has "no start and no finish" and is "made up of only three notes" repeated endlessly. Marvin Macy brings back with him "bad fortune, right from the first, as could be expected"; the weather turns suddenly and unseasonably hot, the freshly slaughtered pork spoils, and an entire family dies from infected meat at a reunion. Sadly, it is "a time of waste and confusion" and Marvin Macy is "the cause of all this."

The most impressive of all the ominous signs that winter is the unprecedented snowfall that covers the town the day Marvin Macy moves into Miss Amelia's house. The snow makes most people "humble and glad about this marvel" so that they speak in "hushed voices" and say "'thank you' and 'please'" more than is necessary. The day of the violent denouement turns out to be Ground Hog Day and the ground hog sees his shadow: a sign bad weather is ahead. Further, a "hawk with a bloody breast" flies over the town and circles twice around the property of Miss Amelia. Significantly, the happenings at the sad café have reverberations in the whole chain of being.

Most of the major events of the **Ballad** are carried out in a solemn and ceremonious manner, suggestive of rituals, both sacred and satanic. The gossiping about Miss Amelia has the quality of an "evil festival" or an "unholy holiday." The opening of the café provides a primitive agape in which bottles of Miss Amelia's whisky shared among friends create an almost eucharistic bond; the people respond to the love feast with dignified circumspection, allowing no "rambunctiousness, indecent giggles, or misbehavior whatsoever," becoming "polite even to the point of a certain timidness," and exemplifying the atmosphere of a proper café: "fellowship, the satisfactions of the belly, and a certain gaiety and grace of behavior." Marvin Macy's courting of Miss Amelia is preceded by a two-year period of reform and atonement and accomplished by the chivalric presentation of symbolic gifts—"a bunch of swamp flowers, a sack of chitterlins, and a silver ring." Miss Amelia likewise gives talismanic presents to Cousin Lymon, including her own kidney stones which she has had set as ornaments in a watch chain.

The violent clash which ends the story is no private skirmish entered into in the heat of passion but a public encounter with all the ceremony of a gladiatorial contest or a knightly joust. It is prepared for by several ritualistic confrontations in which the antagonists take their fighting postures without actually coming to blows. As if on cue, the whole town automatically gathers for the fray at the mystically chosen hour. Cousin Lymon, the proximate cause of it all, hops onto the counter where he sits like a victor's trophy until he awards himself at the last minute to Marvin Macy by attacking the nearly triumphant Miss Amelia. The rubrics of destruction are fulfilled by the final ritualistic devastation of the café, the surrogate enemy, the avatar of Miss Amelia herself.

Both the characters and the events in **The Ballad of the Sad Café,** then, have the remoteness, the mystery, the numinousness of myth. This is not gratuitous, however, for Mrs. McCullers' central insight in this work—that the operations of love are not amenable to nor explainable by reason-is not one to be demonstrated scientifically, but by an appeal to those very sources of irrational knowledge from which love itself springs. To treat of love "wild, extravagant, and beautiful as the poison lilies of the swamp," Mrs. McCullers has elevated her primitive characters and their grotesque actions to the wild, extravagant, and beautiful level of myth.

Lawrence Graver (essay date 1969)

SOURCE: *Carson McCullers,* University of Minnesota Press, 1969, pp. 24-33.

[*In the following excerpt, Graver argues that* The Ballad of the Sad Café *is McCullers's best work of "grotesque" fiction. He concludes, however, that this novella is not quite as fully realized as* The Member of the Wedding.]

The Ballad of the Sad Café is a good deal more rewarding [than *Reflections in a Golden Eye*]. Instead of trying to compete with writers of much greater psychological awareness and architechtonic skill, Mrs. McCullers here wisely moves in a limited area more suited to her talents—the alien, elemental world of legend and romance. Like all good ballads, her story is urgent, atmospheric, and primitive, and yet, in its melodramatic swiftness and simplicity, tells us more things memorable about human life than all the devious sophisticated posturings of *Reflections in a Golden Eye.*

In the background are the physical facts of life that count for so much in the ballad world: a dingy southern town cut off from the accommodations of civilized society, boundaries of swamps and cold black pinewood, weather that is raw in winter and white with the glare of heat in summer. Only those who must come here: the tax collector to bother the rich; an investigator to refuse credit to Ryan, the weaver; a lost traveler to find his way back to his destination. Decayed buildings lean in imminent collapse and intimations of mortality are everywhere. The moon makes "dim, twisted shadows on the blossoming peach trees," and the odor of sweet spring grass mingles with the warm, sour smell of a nearby lagoon. Strangers arrive suddenly, often at night, and they have intimate ties with the twilight world of animals. The hunchback's hands are like "dirty sparrow claws," and he perches on a railing the way "a sick bird huddles on a telephone wire," to "grieve publicly." Much depends on the cycle of the seasons and the climactic events of the plot often have their effective climatic correspondences. Autumn begins with cool days of a "clean bright sweetness," but when the villain comes home from prison, the weather turns sticky, sultry, and rotten. A month before the famous wrestling match that brings the story to a close, snow falls for the first time in living memory.

The boldness and precision with which she creates the sense of a town estranged from the rest of the world is the first of Mrs. McCullers' successes in *The Ballad of the Sad Café.* Unlike those narrators in the earlier novels who move uneasily from realism to myth and back again, the invented voice in this story has an obvious authority and grace. Beginning simply in the present, she tells us that things are dismal now but once upon a time there was gaiety and color in the human landscape. No attempt is made to mask the calamitous outcome; ruin is announced at the start; our interest will be entirely in how it was accomplished. Since she is confident in her grasp of the moment and the milieu, Mrs. McCullers assumes a relaxed, colloquial style, punctuating the narrative with phrases like "time must pass" and "so do not forget."

Knowing that her gruesome story might, if too solemnly told, seem wildly melodramatic, she skillfully uses folk humor to sweeten the Gothic tale. When the shambling, toothless Merlie Ryan spreads the rumor that Amelia has murdered the newly arrived Lymon, Mrs. McCullers casually reports: "It was a fierce and sickly tale the town built up that day. In it were all the things which cause the heart to shiver—a hunchback, a midnight burial in the swamp, the dragging of Miss Amelia through the streets of the town . . ." But then, moments later, she parades her little peacock proudly down the stairs. Throughout the narrative, understatement and playfulness humanize the actors and make their behavior seem less morbid. Often, in dialogue, they use an idiom full of the comic hyperbole so common in country speech. Amelia claims to have slept as soundly as if she were drowned in axle grease, and when she is dizzy with apprehension and love, the neighbors speak of her being "well on her way . . . up fools' hill," and they can't wait to see how the affair will turn out.

It turns out badly. *The Ballad of the Sad Café* is the story of Miss Amelia Evans, a quirky amazon who sells feed, guano, and domestic staples in the town's only thriving store. Tall, dark, and unapproachable in a rough, masculine way, Amelia is an uncompromising merchant with a passion for vindictive lawsuits and a beneficent witch doctor with a genuine desire to ease human pain. Both her business acumen and her healing powers are legendary; what she shrewdly extracts in trade she gives back in the free and effective dispensation of a hundred different cures. Since her liquors relieve melancholy, her foods hunger, and her folk remedies pain, this perverse cross between Ceres, Bacchus, and the neighborhood medicine man is the one indispensable person in town.

That the hard-fisted Amelia has the living touch is demonstrated at the arrival of a sniveling hunchbacked dwarf who asks for food and shelter. His worth, he claims, is based on the urgency of kinship, and his weird unraveling of cousins, half sisters, and third husbands is a neat parody of the mysterious genealogical links in ballad and romance. Miss Amelia immediately acknowledges the tie, lightly touches his hump, and offers him liquor, dinner, and a bed. Soon, Cousin Lymon is installed in Amelia's sanctuary, sharing rooms rarely seen by living eyes, and a bizarre relationship, very much like love, transforms them both. As lover, she becomes softened, graceful, communicative, eager to extend the rewards of companionship to others; he, the beloved, becomes proud, perky, aristocratic. Even the townspeople benefit. The liquor that Miss Amelia used to dispense on her doorstep is now served inside, and gradually the store evolves into a café featuring the exotic hunchback and some palatable food and drink. Warmth, affectionate fellowship, "a certain gaiety and grace of behavior," momentarily replace suspicion, loneliness, egotism, and rough-hewn malice—the rigorous truths of the world outside. Niggardly Amelia puts free crackers on the counter, customers share their liquor, and the flourishing café provides the one bright page in the history of this melancholy town.

Unhappily, the festive interlude lasts only six years before the sins of the past exact their tribute and the catastrophe announced at the start is set in motion. Some years before the appearance of Lymon, the young Amelia had been married for ten stormy days to Marvin Macy. Handsome, mercurial, vicious, and cunning, Macy had been a most notable young scoundrel, the demon lover of every "soft-eyed" young girl in town. Miraculously enough, *he* had fallen passionately in love with the haggard Amelia and became her long-suffering romantic knight. As a disdainful mistress, Amelia needed little instruction; after their marriage, she rejected his advances, sold his presents, and battered his face with her punches. Macy, disconsolate and swearing vengeance, ran off to a life of crime and an eventual stretch in the Atlanta penitentiary. Afterwards, Miss Amelia cut up his Klansman's robe to cover her tobacco plants.

Once Macy reappears in town, the tempo quickens and everyone prepares for the inevitable confrontation of the two epic antagonists. Most of the wise money is on Amelia, for she had beaten more than her weight several times before. The twist, however, in this tale is provided by Cousin Lymon, who completes the eccentric triangle of love relationships by falling desperately for the roguish Macy. This time it is Amelia's turn to suffer at the hands of a capricious beloved. While Lymon slavishly follows the scornful Macy about town, she becomes increasingly distraught at the turn in his affections; but nothing can be done. Lymon announces that Macy will move in with them and Amelia comes to the mournful recognition that "once you have lived with another . . . it is better to take in your mortal enemy than face the terror of living alone."

Step by step, Amelia and Macy prepare for the hand-to-hand combat that everyone knows must come. On the second of February, when a bloody-breasted hawk gives the signal by flying over Amelia's house, all the towns-people move as spectators toward the café. At seven o'clock, the two contestants begin to pound one another with hundreds of bone-cracking blows. After a savage half-hour, when boxing has turned to wrestling, Amelia puts her triumphant hands to the throat of her fallen adversary; but with astonishing swiftness, Cousin Lymon flies at her back, pulls her off, and gives the victory to Macy. That night, to celebrate their triumph, the two men smash up Amelia's property and disappear. In the months that follow, Amelia lets the café and her healing practice fall into ruin, and she eventually becomes a recluse. The town returns to its desolate, mechanical ways; "the soul rots with boredom"; and the tale ends with the swelling song of a chain gang.

Much of what is permanently haunting in this grotesque little story is the product of Mrs. McCullers' easy rela-tionship with the properties of the ballad world. Experi-ence heightened far beyond the realm of plausibility is given a valid, poetic truth by the propriety of those con-ventions that make the miraculous seem oddly real. Dreams, superstitions, omens, numbers, musical motifs, all operate here to provide an authentic atmosphere for this perverse triangle of passions, and to make the inexplicable long-ings of the characters seem like dark elemental forces in the natural world. Enigmatic melodies are heard in the night: wild, high voices singing songs that never end. Macy, the demon lover, plays the guitar, and when he sings the tunes glide "slowly from his throat like eels." As a doctor, Amelia depends on a stunning variety of secret herbs; her Kroup Kure, made from whiskey, rock candy, and an unnamed third power, is a wonder drug, while her liquor has been known to bring up messages from the bottom of the human soul. When she guards the low fire of her ritual still, Amelia likes to untie knots in rope, and in her parlor cabinet she keeps an acorn and two small stones. The acorn she picked from the ground the day her father died, and the stones had once been removed from her kidney. If she wants Lymon to come along to Cheehaw, she asks him seven times and when he continually refuses, she draws a heavy line with a stick around the barbecue pit and orders him not to trespass that limit. Naturally, when the time must be set for the epic fight, seven o'clock is chosen. Miss Amelia is not the only character to be given a pow-erful armory of signs and talismans. Lymon sits regularly on a sack of guano and is rarely without his snuffbox. Years earlier, Macy had courted his love with a bunch of swamp flowers, a sack of chitterlings, and a silver ring; and when he returns from prison the neighbors fear him as more dangerous than ever because while put away he "must have learned the method of laying charms." Always called devilish, Macy never sweats, not even in August, and that—Mrs. McCullers reminds us—is surely "a sign worth pon-dering."

By relying so heavily on charms and rituals, the characters emphasize the fated, irrational quality of so many of their decisive acts. Like most works in its traditional genre, *The Ballad of the Sad Café* illustrates the consequences of moral choice but does not probe it; analysis is less vital than the starkness of dramatic presentation. Yet an evoca-tive atmosphere and a strong story line would not in them-selves ensure success if the illustration were not themati-cally absorbing as well. The richly patterned, sinister dance in which Macy, Amelia, and Lymon play at different times the roles of lover and beloved dramatizes the wayward nature of human passion and the irreconcilable antagonism inherent in every love relationship.

At one point in his poem "Prayer for My Daughter," William Butler Yeats, speaking of the splendid contrariety with which females choose their lovers, describes how beautiful women sometimes eat "a crazy salad with their meat." *The Ballad of the Sad Café* is about the "crazy salad" of every man: ugly and beautiful, heiress and outlaw, dwarf and amazon—they all choose love objects in ways that demonstrate that passion is the most permanent and amazing of all the human mysteries. In the McCullers world, the lover occupies the highest seat in the pantheon, for he has the restlessness and imagination to wish to break free from the constrictive prison of ego and connect with another person. His choices are often arbitrary and improb-able, but once made he worships them with a constancy that can only inspire amazement. Everyone wants to be a lover because the lover is the archetypal creative spirit: dreamer, quester, romantic idealist. If love compels, it can also soften. When Macy is smitten with Amelia, he becomes improved in civility; and Amelia's passion for Lymon not only refines her temperament and reduces her lawsuits, but results in the establishment of the café. Product of her love, the café is the symbol of the ability of human affection to create intimacy and delight where only barrenness existed before. Yet, if love can sweeten and refine, it can also leave the lover defenseless. Having created the beloved in the image of his own desperate desire, the lover is open to rebuff and betrayal, for he tempts the one permanent quality of any beloved—his cruelty. In *The Ballad of the Sad Café,* the beloved is a static figure, chosen by some-one else. Easily resentful of being considered a token, he is also quick to recognize the assailability of his admirer and the extent of his own manipulative powers.

In Mrs. McCullers' triangle, each character is revealed successively in the roles of lover and beloved. In his suit of Amelia, Macy is meek with longing and easily swayed by others: he saves his wages, abandons fornication, and goes regularly to church. But in response to Amelia's chilling rejection, he becomes more brutally antisocial than he had ever been before. On his return to town, cast as his wife's revenger and Lymon's beloved, he alternates be-tween abusiveness and complete indifference, calling the sullen dwarf "Brokeback" at one moment and ignoring him the next. Like Macy, Lymon is also violently contra-dictory in both roles. Admired by Amelia, he gains force-ful self-assurance, but also learns to exercise the hateful tyranny of a spoiled child. Finicky, boastful, self-absorbed, he becomes wildly obsessive in his demands for personal gratification. Yet when he falls for Macy, his reversal is perhaps even more disagreeable. Obsessed now by his desire to attract Macy's attention, he flaps his ears and mopes about pathetically like a small dog sick for love.

The most memorable metamorphosis, however, is experienced by Amelia. Chosen by Macy at nineteen, she spits in contempt and strikes out fiercely at every opportunity. Hardhearted, peremptory, and self-sufficient, she does not let her rage affect her capacity to turn a deal in her own favor, and she quickly strips her husband of everything he owns. At thirty, however, when she chooses Lymon, a remarkable change occurs. The rudest misanthrope in town turns genial, even cheerful, moving easily among people, sharing her liquor, forgetting to bolt the door at night. Instead of overalls and swampboots, she occasionally dons a soft red dress, and as she rubs Lymon twice a day with pot liquor to give him strength, her hatred of physicality relaxes. Suddenly nostalgic about the past, she turns candid about the present, confiding in the dwarf about trade secrets and the size of her bank account. As lover for the first time in her life, Amelia takes emotional risks by putting herself in a position of extreme vulnerability. Staring at Lymon, her face wears the fascinating expression of "pain, perplexity, and uncertain joy"—the lonesome look of the lover. When she learns that Macy may return, she—in her pride—miscalculates Lymon's fickleness and her own power over his life; and after his affection is alienated, she becomes frightfully distracted, pursuing those contradictory courses that lead to her downfall.

Because she has the capacity to change and the energy to pursue her awakened desire for companionship, Amelia turns from a harridan evoking awe to a woman worthy of compassion. By learning to love she has become more human—more tender, gracious, amiable, perceptive; but also more obviously exposed to the inevitable stings of loneliness, betrayal, and suffering. As healer, hostess, and lover, she is—despite her rudeness and suspicion—a force for good in the community, and the destruction of her dream is a cause for genuine mourning. *The Ballad of the Sad Café* is an elegy for Amelia Evans, and it has all the brooding eloquence and eccentricity to stand as a fitting tribute to that very peculiar lady.

Although *The Ballad of the Sad Café* is by far the best of Mrs. McCullers' excursions into the grotesque, it is not without reminders of the penumbral insistence that marks her worst work. Too much is occasionally made of dark nights of the soul and of things going on there that only God can understand. Because the things that go on in *The Member of the Wedding* are available to everyone and are recorded with vivacity by an artist who understands them, it is the best of all her books.

Dawson F. Gaillard (essay date 1972)

SOURCE: "The Presence of the Narrator in Carson Mc-Cullers' *The Ballad of the Sad Café*," in *The Mississippi Quarterly,* Vol. XXV, Fall, 1972, pp. 419-27.

[*In the following essay, Gaillard argues that it is through the consciousness of the narrator in* The Ballad of the Sad Café *that the reader experiences the mythic qualities of the depicted characters and events.*]

> The poet's voice need not merely be the record of man, it can be one of the props, the pillars to help him endure and prevail.
>
> —William Faulkner, Nobel Prize Acceptance Speech.

A voice speaks to us in the first paragraph of Carson McCullers' *The Ballad of the Sad Café,* a flat, inflectionless voice, adjusted to the dreariness it describes as we go on a walking tour with the speaker to the center of town. There, we find an old house leaning dangerously near collapse. The voice changes. No longer flat and inflectionless, it describes a face which looks down on the town, a face "sexless and white" like those "terrible dim faces known in dreams." And then the voice is flat again as it recalls the present dreariness of the August afternoon when, having nothing to do after work, "you might as well walk down to the Forks Falls Road and listen to the chain gang."

The voice continues. It tells us of a time when things were not always dreary, a time when "this very town" had a café, "unlike any other place for many miles around." The reader-listener is now captured, not by a glittering eye, but by the warm presence of the narrator, reliving his memory, telling us what we want to know: why has the town changed? The ballad has begun.

In *The Classic Line* [1966], Albert Cook says, "Like epic, the ballad refers to the communal life amid which it is originally performed. Like epic, it characteristically tells a story, of the human spirit persisting through and beyond mortality. . . ." That the narrator of McCullers' *Ballad* is a member of the community where changes for the worse have occurred is central to the power of the novel. To these changes (the sadness of the "Sad Café") the narrator responds with a spirit that persists "through and beyond mortality." The spirit is contained in his telling, a telling characterized by wisdom and reflections that give to the ballad a sense of timelessness, moving the story out of history (the record of irreversible events) into tradition, or myth.

That the narrator is a member of the town and, therefore, a part of its history is suggested, as I have already implied, in the beginning paragraphs of the story. Also his descriptions suggest a sense of place, which results from having lived in that place for a long while. First, the similes he chooses have their source in the rural community. Cousin Lymon's hands are compared to "dirty sparrow claws"; his fluttering eyelids look like "pale, trapped moths"; two old people resemble "two little walking peanuts"; Miss Amelia's voice is "soft, and sad as the wheezy whine of the church pump-organ." Secondly, his description of the landscape reveals a response and knowledge of detail that come from personal experience:

The sky was the color of a blue swamp iris, the moon clear and bright. The crops that spring promised well and in the past weeks the mill had run a night shift. Down by the creek the square brick factory was yellow with light, and there was the faint, steady hum of the looms. It was such a night when it is good to hear from faraway, across the dark fields, the slow song of a Negro on his way to make love. Or when it is pleasant to sit quietly and pick a guitar, or simply to rest alone and think of nothing at all.

That he may very well have been on the spot where the history of the sad café occurred as surely as were Merlie Ryan, Horace Wells, and Rosser Cline causes the reader to regard the narrator as convincing. However, says Wayne Booth [in *The Rhetoric of Fiction,* 1961],

> No narrator or central intelligence or observer is *simply* convincing: he is convincingly decent or mean, brilliant or stupid, informed, ignorant, or muddled. Since there are few such qualities that even the most tolerant of us can observe in full neutrality, we usually find our emotional and intellectual reactions to him as a character affecting our reactions to the events he relates.

McCullers' speaker is neither neutral nor ignorant. He takes sides. He treats with respect the rituals of the people in his area. For example, recalling the verbal battle between Marvin Macy and Miss Amelia, the narrator accepts as fitting Marvin Macy's means of winning:

> "Bust a gut!" she would repeat, in a shout.
>
> But always Marvin Macy had the answer ready for her. He would . . . reply with slow, sure insolence.
>
> "Everything you holler at me bounces back on yourself. Yah! Yah!"
>
> Miss Amelia would have to stand there helpless, as no one has ever invented a way out of this trap. She could not shout out abuse that would bounce back on herself. He had the best of her. . . .

The narrator's wisdom is evident in the homey reflections regarding what has occurred in the town. He is particularly perceptive in his observations of the secrets of the human heart and common experiences of man. Characteristically, the speaker uses the pronoun "you" as if he is assured that he speaks to a sympathetic audience from a reservoir of common experience: "Once you have lived with another, it is a great torture to have to live alone. The silence of a firelit room when suddenly the clock stops ticking, the nervous shadows in an empty house it is better to take in your mortal enemy than face the terror of living alone." He knows what brings despair to the human heart:

> Life could become one long dim scramble just to get the things needed to keep alive. And the confusing point is this: All useful things have a price, and are bought only with money, as that is the way the world

is run. You know without having to reason about it the price of a bale of cotton, or a quart of molasses. But no value has been put on human life; it is given to us free and taken without being paid for. What is it worth? If you look around, at times the value may seem to be little or nothing at all. Often after you have sweated and tried and things are not better for you, there comes a feeling deep down in the soul that you are not worth much.

The narrator's seriousness, empathy, and sympathy for man's soul-pains and his assurance that he speaks from common experience bring to the telling the presence of a human being trying to make sense of the events he recalls. Because of this presence, the reader cannot, I feel, distance himself from the emotional impact of the action. Such is the magic of the oral quality in literature.

What the speaker relates is the story of a town, which found one period of time when "the deep bitter knowing that you are not worth much in this world could be laid low," the golden age of Miss Amelia's café. The reflections of the narrator give to that café a special quality: it is an archetypal place of renewal in his mind.

He perceives what its value was to the townspeople, whose lives before the café had been devoted to work and an awareness of damnation only: "They met to work in the mill. Or on Sunday there would be an all-day camp meeting—and though that is a pleasure, the intention of the whole affair is to sharpen your view of Hell and put into you a keen fear of the Lord Almighty." The people were without those activities that could relieve the dull sameness of their lives, a sameness manifest in their collective life style: "Each of them worked in the mill, and lived with others in a two- or three-room house for which the rent was ten dollars or twelve dollars a month."

The café changed these dull lives. It became a sanctuary from dullness and, particularly, from the "deep, bitter knowing" by providing the townspeople with "a certain pride that had not hitherto been known in these parts." For Cousin Lymon, who "had a deep fear of death," the café was a refuge of light and activity. For Miss Amelia, it was the outward creation to share that which cannot, ultimately, be shared—"a whole new inward world," a world of strangeness in which a lover must suffer alone, for

> love is a joint experience between two persons—but the fact that it is a joint experience does not mean that it is a similar experience to the two people involved. . . . Often the beloved is only a stimulus for all the stored-up love which has lain quiet within the lover for a long time hitherto. And somehow every lover knows this. He feels in his soul that his love is a solitary thing. He comes to know a new, strange loneliness and it is this knowledge which makes him suffer. So there is only one thing for the lover to do. He must house his love within himself as best he can; he must create for himself a whole new inward world— a world intense and strange, complete in himself.

It is the outward model which is in danger. It is subject to time.

As the narrator says, "Now time must pass." The recognition of necessity is present in the narrator's word choice, "must." With time's passing comes inevitable change.

The change began with the return of Marvin Macy, whom earlier the narrator has asked us to remember, "as he is to act a terrible part in the story which is yet to come." When Miss Amelia heard that he was out of prison, "she shivered although the night was warm." The narrator's flair for dramatic detail prepares the listener for a conflict which has hints of unpleasant results. In causing these results, Miss Amelia's beloved played a central role. When Cousin Lymon and Marvin Macy first confronted each other, it was with "a peculiar stare . . . like the look of two criminals who recognize each other." About this first evening of Marvin Macy's return, the narrator recalls other details, seemingly from having been an eyewitness: "It had grown late. The red winter sun was setting, and to the west the sky was deep gold and crimson. Ragged chimney swifts flew to their nests; lamps were lighted. Now and then there was the smell of smoke, and the warm rich odor of the barbecue slowly cooking in the pit behind the cafe." The tension of the scene is recreated by the narrator's focus on the vivid sensory impressions which contrast with the silence of the crowd that gathered slowly in Miss Amelia's backyard with heavy hearts. "Not a living soul in all the town was glad to see him [Marvin Macy]."

He is the evil principle, which myth and folk tales include. He is Frankenstein's monster and Milton's Satan, but given a rural identity by the vernacular of a back-country narrator. Alienated, his heart twisted into a curious shape, shrunk as "hard and pitted as the seed of a peach," Marvin Macy wanted, like the monster of Frankenstein, to express his rage. And Miss Amelia was his target. Like Frankenstein's monster, he took the beloved of that person who denied him a companion. Like Milton's Satan, he destroyed the pleasant existence of others. The center of the universe, the café, "the warm center point of the town," was destroyed by the battle between Marvin Macy and Miss Amelia.

Their battle occurred during a winter people still remember, says the narrator, a winter when "[a] great thing happened. People woke up on the second of January and found the whole world about them altogether changed. Little ignorant children looked out of the windows, and they were so puzzled that they began to cry." The phenomenon was snow. To the people in this section of the country it was as if the apocalyptic signs had begun.

The reactions to the phenomenon were varied. The narrator, as is characteristic of him, recalls sensory impressions—"soft colors of blue and silver" in the snow, the "gentle shining gray" of the sky, and "the dreamy quietness of falling snow—when had the town been so silent?" Miss Amelia closed her shutters; Marvin Macy sneered at the timid; Reverend Willin tried to use the

phenomenon in his sermon, and a "few weak characters, of course, were demoralized and got drunk." The sign of change had forecast truly, for after the snowfall, Marvin Macy "crowded into Miss Amelia's home." The narrator's reflection about man's terror of living alone, a reflection I have already mentioned, makes sense of such an unbelievable event.

And after the snow melted another sign of coming change appeared: Miss Amelia's punching bag. The narrator recalls the day of the fight, which "took place on Ground Hog Day," a day of "neutral temperature" that year. He says, "A hawk with a bloody breast flew over the town and circled twice around the property of Miss Amelia." The signs were in keeping with the tension of the atmosphere, tension created by an awareness that something of major significance was to be decided that day.

As the daylight became twilight people gathered for the fight. And serving as an eyewitness, the narrator mentions the three boys from Society City who usually appeared at gatherings of violence or emotional fervor: they "wore yellow rayon shirts and caps put on backwards—they were as much alike as triplets, and could always be seen at cock fights and camp meetings."

At the stroke of seven (the apocalyptic number of Revelation), Miss Amelia and Marvin Macy appeared. The narrator describes how Miss Amelia looked—"she had an iron strength band around her right wrist"—and how the fight progressed "in this wild violent way with no sign of weakening on either side." The impression he creates is that this was a fight between two Titans. During such a fight, says the narrator, "it is worth-while to turn from the confusion of the fight itself and observe the spectators," which is what he did. He recalls, for example, that Merlie Ryan swallowed a fly before he realized it. Such details, in addition to relieving the tenseness with recollections of humor, keep the reader simultaneously on the spot of the specific back-country event and in the perspective of mythology with its recurring patterns and archetypal figures. We witness the metamorphosis of time into timelessness taking place in the mind of the narrator, a happening which dramatizes man's way of dealing with time and change.

With the overthrow of Miss Amelia, the world she had created was at an end. The narrator's reflection indicates the seriousness with which the people responded to the outcome of the battle, as if they were aware of the future to come: "This was not a fight to hash over and talk about afterward; people went home and pulled the covers up over their heads."

The story of the café is a story of irreversible changes, which result in the loss of more than goods or a physical gathering place. The changes in the story lead to a loss the soul must bear—Miss Amelia's, the townspeople's, the narrator's, whose "soul rots with boredom." With the loss of the café, the narrator almost instinctively seeks to fill the dark void of his soul by listening to the singing of the twelve mortal men of the chain gang. Their music is the music of life itself, being "both somber and joyful." This moment cannot last, but like the café, it can provide, for a short time, a sanctuary from total darkness of the soul. And like the music of the twelve mortal men, the balladeer's tale can cause the heart of the reader-listener "to broaden and the listener to grow cold with ecstasy and fright."

The narrator's presence, his telling, lifts the story beyond the commonplace facts, beyond the immediate, and beyond history. He recreates in his own image the events which caused a sad change in his world by responding to those events with sympathy and thoughtful reflections. He finds serious significance in the events, now that he has his present perspective; the significance makes the events larger than history. His vision is like that of his fellow townspeople, who see in "a quick skipping little Jew who cried if you called him Christ-killer, and ate light bread and canned salmon every day" a representative type of man: "if a man were prissy in any way, or if a man ever wept, he was known as a Morris Finestein." Morris Finestein, the factual, historical person, has become less important than his essential qualities; we see the mythmaking imagination at work.

Similarly, the café, because of the narrator's response to it, takes on mythic proportions. It is placed in the perspective of the ideal when the narrator calls it a "proper café" and then describes such a café: "[T]he atmosphere of a proper café implies these qualities: fellowship, the satisfactions of the belly, and a certain gaiety and grace of behavior." His perspective transforms the café from a physical place into a state of mind. Thus, the demise of the café results in the loss of what it signified, not just the physical place alone. The pattern of gain and loss goes beyond the specific irreversible history of Miss Amelia's café. It is a pattern of loss which man has experienced throughout time; and the repetition of the pattern makes it not easier to bear, but harder because it must be accepted as a condition of life.

The presence of the narrator dramatizes for us the human spirit in action, bearing the burden it must because of time and mortality. Just as Miss Amelia, without exactly knowing why, picked up an acorn the day her father died, the narrator listens to the music of the chain gang. He also tells his story, as a balladeer sings his song, and in these actions of vocalizing the spirit of man, the speaker or singer dramatizes one moment of victory over time and mortality, one period of time when "the deep bitter knowing that you are not worth much in this world could be laid low." It is the sound of the human voice, the action of a human mind coming to grips with what has occurred in time that provide the power of *The Ballad of the Sad Café*.

Joseph R. Millichap (essay date 1973)

SOURCE: "Carson McCullers' Literary Ballad," in *The Georgia Review,* Vol. XXVII, No. 3, Fall, 1973, pp. 329-39.

[*In the following essay, Millichap argues that the musical ballad form provides the key to understanding* The Ballad of the Sad Café.]

Carson McCullers' novels, particularly *The Heart Is a Lonely Hunter* (1940) and *Member of the Wedding* (1946), often have been misread as Gothic and grotesque fictions, categories derived by critics from her works in these modes, *Reflections in a Golden Eye* (1941) and *Ballad of the Sad Café* (1943). Strangely enough, the same critics, intent on demonstrating their Procrustean theories in all of her work, often misunderstand *Ballad* by insisting on the universality of elements which are obviously peculiar to the point of aberration. The use of the bizarre theory of love offered by the narrator of *Ballad* as a formula for interpreting all of McCullers' fiction has hampered analysis not only of the *novella* itself but of her other works as well. The description of her narrative as a ballad, so obviously presented in the title, provides a key to understanding which unlocks the novella's difficulties of literary mode, point-of-view, characterization, and plot structure.

The literary ballad evolved from the ballad of tradition, which in turn is rooted in folklore, because the literary artist wished to exploit the archetypal energy of the ballad world and the formal simplicity of the ballad structure. Professor Gerould, the best known authority on the ballad, has provided in *The Ballad of Tradition* a succinct definition based on a wide knowledge of the *genre*. "The ballad is a folk song that tells a story with stress on the crucial situation, tells it by letting the action unfold itself in event and speech, and tells it objectively with little comment or intrusion of personal bias." Though McCullers' ballad is neither song nor folk art, and though its narrator certainly intrudes a great deal of personal opinion, the narrative also presents many of the characteristics Professor Gerould mentions in his definition and develops in his elaboration of it. McCullers' ballad concentrates on the strange love triangle formed by a manly giantess, a selfish dwarf, and a demonic bandit. The action unfolds in a few weird events which culminate in an epic battle waged purposely on Groundhog Day to decide the death or rebirth of love. The setting is a romantic wasteland where piney woods and swamps counterpoint the stunning heat of August afternoons. The concrete symbols of the ballad world both explain and motivate the action; buildings lean in precarious decay; trees twist grotesquely in the moonlight; birds and animals provide mysterious analogues to human action.

Clearly this is the traditional world of the ballad, a world of passion and violence, of omens and portents, of the full wild impulsiveness of archetypal human behavior. The particular world of this ballad is a Georgia mill village, a place like all the Southern back country, "a place that is far off and estranged from all other places in the world." The Southern hinterlands preserved the folk qualities as well as the folk songs of the Scotch border country. Therefore, the line between the real world and the ballad world is often indistinct in the American South and in McCullers' fictions which are set there. Unlike the larger mill city which serves as the setting of most of her fiction, the mill village is not used to probe economic conditions or regional problems in a realistic manner. Even the chronological setting is unimportant; it might be 1920 or 1940; for the village in *Ballad* exists in the temporally imprecise world of human passion.

Of course, McCullers' ballad is a literary one, wrought by a modern, conscious artistry not by the folk mind or by an artless imagination. The literary ballad has always been a difficult form; it can be hauntingly effective, as in Keats' "La Belle Dame Sans Merci," resoundingly dull, as with many of Scott's attempts, or unintentionally humorous, as Longfellow's "The Wreck of the Hesperus." The structural and stylistic integrity of the story, especially of narrative voice marks her literary ballad as an unqualified success. McCullers presents a narrator who can spin the fine fabric of romantic fiction from the raw materials of mill-village life without violating either realm. In *Ballad* a ballad-maker evokes from the world of the Georgia backcountry a timeless, compelling story of human passion. His voice fixes the style of the novel—a perfect blend of the literate and colloquial, the objective and personal, talky observation. The existence of this filtering personality assures the novella's achievement.

Neither McCullers nor the typical third person omniscient voice, narrates; the ballad-maker tells the tale. A part of the town himself, he knows people, places, and history, often commenting like a chorus of spectators from the village (the refrain of the ballad sometimes has this same function). At the same time he is possessed of knowledge that only an omniscient author could have. Therefore, he must be creating the narrative from the history of this particular mill-village and demonstrating the operations of human passion to his listeners.

This device also releases McCullers from responsibility for the universalization of the fantastic observations on the mutual exclusiveness of love so often ascribed to her by earlier critics (such as Oliver Evans, Ihab Hassan, and Klaus Lubbers). The narrator defines love as "joint experience between two persons," the lover and the beloved. The experience between them is not necessarily the same for each party, for the lover and the beloved "come from two different countries." The lover attaches his love to some person, often without rational purpose. He creates an imaginary world surrounding the beloved and then releases his stored creative energies on this dream vision. "Therefore, the value and quality of any love is determined solely by the lover himself." The narrator continues: "It is for this reason that most of us would rather love than be loved. Almost everyone wants to be the lover. And the curt truth is that, in a deep secret way, the state of being beloved is intolerable to many. The beloved fears and hates the lover, and with the best of reasons. For the lover is forever trying to strip bare his beloved. The lover craves any possible relation with the beloved, even if this experience can cause him only pain."

The ballad-maker's theory of love is substantiated by the character relationships in the novella, but the limited number of cases prevents immediate acceptance of it as a universal law of human nature; it clearly remains the narrator's hypothesis, not McCullers'. The theory depicts one facet of the love's dynamics, but other loves have other patterns. In her later novels and stories love does live for a few people, at least for a time. Yet the earlier novels have partially demonstrated this pattern. In *Heart,* Singer often lashes out against the lonely hearts, who have forced themselves on him as lovers, though he is most often simply puzzled by their behavior. The tangled relationships of *Reflections* are sometimes marked by hate, for example, Leonora's hatred of Capt. Penderton, but most often by indifference. In the limited context of this novella, the ballad world, this one tragic aspect of love is exaggerated to the point where it looms as its totality. The ballad creates a picture without delicate shading; therefore, the projection of one tragic aspect of love can be accepted romantically as the whole definition of this complex human phenomena. The same fascinating effect exists in many of the traditional ballads, in "Barbara Allen" for instance, where an analogous love-hate relationship exists between the courtly lover and the disdainful beloved.

The narrator's theory of love arises out of the weird triangle that forms the structural center of this novella. There are three characters of importance: Miss Amelia Evans, Cousin Lymon, and Marvin Macy. Miss Amelia is loved by Marvin Macy whom she rejects; she loves Cousin Lymon; he turns from her to an idolatrous love for Marvin Macy, who despi-ses the dwarf. A neat triangular diagram is formed. . . . The ballad relates the story of this diagram, and the story aptly illustrates the ballad-maker's generalizations about love. As in both *Heart* and *Reflections* a geometrically patterned rela-tionship of characters is the basis of symbolism and structure.

The description of *The Ballad of the Sad Cafe* as a ballad, so obviously presented in the title, provides a key to understanding which unlocks the novella's difficulties of literary mode, point-of-view, characterization, and plot structure.

—*Joseph R. Millichap*

After the description of the town, which opens the tale, the narrator introduces Miss Amelia. On the hot, empty afternoons of August, the season when the town seems most desolate and isolated, her strange face peers down crazily from an upper window of the town's largest structure which is now boarded up and fast decaying. The building has "a curious, cracked look that is very puzzling," and Miss Amelia's haunted face with her severely crossed eyes provides the human analogue of the structure. The ballad-maker is also the Southern storyteller, the courthouse or country store loafer who will pass this dull

August day retelling the story of the building and its strange inmate. The third paragraph introduces the history of the café, and of Miss Amelia, Cousin Lymon, and Marvin Macy. The narrator wanders back to the misty times before the café even existed; the ballad is being spun.

Earlier the café had been a store which Miss Amelia had inherited from her widowed father; "Big Papa" had raised the motherless girl almost like a son. The big-muscled Amazon easily assumed her masculine role and even surpassed her daddy in becoming the leading entrepreneur of the region. She supplies the mill workers and the surrounding farmers with groceries, hardware, and sundries. She also produces for sale her own chitterlings, sausage, sorghum, and whiskey. The quality of her versions of these Southern staples, especially her whiskey, is superior to any others; in fact the liquor becomes almost a magic potion which creates joy and insight. "For the liquor of Miss Amelia has a special quality of its own. It is clean and sharp on the tongue, but once down a man it glows inside him for a long time afterward. And that is not all. It is known that if a message is written with lemon juice on a clean sheet of paper there will be no sign of it. But if the paper is held for a moment to the fire then the letters turn brown and the meaning becomes clear. Imagine that the whiskey is the fire and the message is that which is known only in the soul of a man—then the worth of Miss Amelia's liquor can be understood." Miss Amelia is also the doctor, sawmill operator, and major property owner of the mill-village. Supernatural elements are present in her doctoring, as Miss Amelia's cures are drawn from the folk medicine of the region and her own mysterious researches into the properties of roots and herbs. Her benevolent or white witchcraft adds to the magical atmosphere of the tale. (An example is her use of "pot liquor," the juices left in the pot after cooking vegetables, as a rub for Lymon's frail body; Southern folk superstition still attaches magical healing powers to this brew.) Her whiskey and her medicine are also representative of a basically human, creative nature. Yet there is another side of her always competing with these generous instincts. She is acquisitive and avaricious in all her business dealings, quick to "go to law" or to use her big fists to defend her property rights. The store stands as her citadel; its transition into a café is essentially the story of Miss Amelia's humanization through love.

She has an earlier chance for human contact in her marriage, but it proved a dismal failure. Marvin Macy, her husband, is another larger-than-life character, as legendary in the mill town and its environs as Miss Amelia. An unhappy childhood caused by irresponsible parents made him into a figure of evil. His corruption is belied by his physical appearance. "For Marvin Macy was the handsomest man in this region—being six feet one inch tall, hardmuscled, and with slow gray eyes and curly hair." Moreover he is materially successful with a good job as a loom-fixer at the mill. Yet beneath these bright surfaces some dark force implies him to acts of outrageous evil. He carries as a talisman the salted ear of a man he killed in a razor duel, while another pocket contains

"marijuana weed." As the demon lover of the region, he has degraded the sweetest young virgins, performing these depredations as coolly as he cuts the tails off squirrels in the pine woods. Yet Miss Amelia, because she is essentially unfeminine, cannot be seduced; Marvin confuses her asexuality and father fixation with personal strength, and this mistake makes him love her. He imagines that her self-sufficient strength can turn him from his dissolute ways, make him a responsible person, and restore the happiness he lost in childhood. In fact, he is asking her to be a mother to him, to replace his own lost mother.

The incestuous undertones of his love are mirrored in Miss Amelia's acceptance of him; she simply wants someone to take Big Papa's place as a companion and business partner. Both Amelia and Marvin project their unconscious desires onto the other, and both will be mightily disappointed. Marvin's love for Amelia does have an immediately reformative effect, and, until she rejects him, he is serious and well-behaved. Miss Amelia, hating him for his love, despising her own feminine role, and always driving a hard bargain, never allows their marriage to be consummated, not even when Marvin wills her all his possessions, and after ten days she drives him off her property.

Cousin Lymon is the strangest member of this outlandish trio. His past is mysteriously clouded; there can be no proof of his own version of his history, and even the village loafers regard it suspiciously. He does not elaborate in any way on his first revelation. When asked where he has come from, he replies uncertainly, "I was traveling." Even his appearance conceals the past of this mysterious stranger.

> His eyes were blue and steady as a child's but there were lavender crepy shadows beneath these blue eyes that hinted of age. It was impossible to guess his age by his hunched queer body. And even his teeth gave no clue—they were all still in his head (two were broken from cracking pecans), but he had stained them with so much sweet snuff that it was impossible to decide whether they were old teeth or young teeth. When questioned directly about his age the hunchback professed to know absolutely nothing—he had no idea how long he had been on the earth, whether for ten years or a hundred! So his age remained a puzzle.

The dwarf has much of the child about him. He possesses ". . . an instinct to establish immediate and vital contact between himself and all things in the world." His child's love of treats and spectacles movies, fairs, cock-fights, revivals—provides insight into his personality, as does his child's curiosity and quarrelsomeness. Thus in many ways Cousin Lymon seems akin to the fairy children of folk tale and ballad—pixies, elves, leprechauns.

Miss Amelia is attracted to him by these childish qualities. Among people she likes only "the nilly-willy and the very sick," those she can see as easily molded and changed by her strong hands. In a sense the sickly, childish dwarf appears pliable. His physical deformities are also part of his attraction for Amelia and the others; touching a hunchback's hump is regarded as good luck in folk tradition. He becomes a strange combination of man, child, and pet that Amelia can love as she could not love her husband. He is a man loved without sex, a child acquired without pain, and a companion which her limited personality finds more acceptable than a husband or a child. Their relationship, like Amelia's marriage, is symbolically incestuous and immaturely formed.

The very nature of her attitude toward him ultimately causes his rejection of her for Marvin Macy. Some bond of natural kinship exists between the two adolescent men. When they first see each other they exchange a stare, ". . . like the look of two criminals who recognize each other." Cousin Lymon has a child's fascination with outlaws and an adolescent's admiration of the rebel and outcast. More importantly, the criminal is a father figure; Marvin Macy's tall, straight body and masculine swagger are qualities opposite to Lymon's, qualities which are not a part of the child's role he must play with Amelia. Therefore, he begins to reject Amelia, just as Marvin Macy hates him as representative of his failed marriage. A new dimension of hate is added to the love triangle [involving Amelia, Macy, and Lymon].

Plot is developed tightly and economically so as to dramatize the creation of these triangles and to emphasize the role of the balladeer-narrator. After beginning in the "present" with the description of the town, the narrator shifts back many years to the arrival of Cousin Lymon, the mysterious stranger who completes the triangle. The movement is natural; he switches to the beginning of the café in the relationship between Lymon and Amelia. This movement also initiates the temporal and seasonal motifs which form an important part of the novella's symbolism. Cousin Lymon arrives in April with the spring, symbolic of creation, youth, and love. When the villagers suspect that Amelia has murdered the tiny stranger the weather turns cold once again, but winter's gloom is dispelled by the warmth of the café when Lymon is discovered alive and well. Amelia's marriage took place in winter and the groundhog sees his shadow before the final battle, a portent of the triumph of hate over love and six more weeks of winter. The temporal shift at the opening is to the "once upon a time" past when things were happier, and the season is appropriate for Amelia's love creates the café and both flourish for the following six years.

The narrator quickly moves the story through these years of human growth for Miss Amelia, symbolized by the emergence of the café. Since the events of these years are ordinary and repetitive he merely summarizes them. The seasons pass in their regular order, and the passage of time is productive of joy and love. The store evolves into a real café with tables and chairs, decorations, and a mechanical piano. Like Biff Brannon's New York Café in *Heart,* Miss Amelia's place has a spiritual function as well as a material one. At the café there were at least a few hours when "the deep bitter knowing that you are not worth much in this world could be laid low." Miss Amelia even neglects to lock the door; clearly a change has taken place.

The years pass in this fruitful manner until Marvin Macy comes back to the village; bad luck follows him to his home town. Though it is autumn the weather turns hot again at his return, spoiling the barbecue and chitterlings just made. A whole family dies from eating spoiled pork. The natural rhythms of the seasons are broken for the first time in six years, when Marvin Macy arrives with the fall like some Hades of Dixie bringing death, desolation, and waste. As the fall turns to winter Marvin Macy's fearful reputation increases, and in direct proportion so does Cousin Lymon's adoration of him. On January 2 it snows, a strange occurrence in the mill-village, and Marvin Macy somehow assumes credit for this meteorological miracle. Miss Amelia in her agitation comes to hate Macy even more deeply than she has in the past. They often circle each other, fists clenched, in ritualistic fashion, and the community waits tensely for the conflict to explode. Miss Amelia's degeneration is symbolized by the poison she puts in Marvin's food; her witchcraft is now destructive, her magic black with hate. After the snow Cousin Lymon brings his beloved to stay in the rooms over the café; this final displacement of Amelia precipitates the total collapse on February 2, Groundhog Day. The date proves significant because Cousin Lymon sees the groundhog observe his shadow, an indication of six more weeks of winter ahead and prefiguration of Marvin Macy's destructive triumph. Other portents are observed on this ominous day: "A hawk with a bloody breast flew over the town and circled twice around the property of Miss Amelia."

The climactic battle begins at seven o'clock, as Miss Amelia sets great store by the mystical number seven. Significantly the fight takes place in the café; the center of companionship and symbol of love has become a place of hatred and combat. The two fighters are evenly matched, and they lunge at each other like wildcats. After a half hour of stunning punches and wild kicks, they become locked in a fearsome wrestling hold.

The ballad-maker points out that this is the style of fighting natural to country people and that the heroic struggle will be decided by this contest of raw strength and will power. After several agonizing moments Miss Amelia emerges as stronger; slowly, she bends her opponent to the floor and gets a strangle hold on him. She has won. But at this instant of victory Cousin Lymon springs onto her back, flying across the room like "a hawk," and turns the advantage to his beloved Marvin. Before the crowd can react Miss Amelia is severely beaten, and left in disgrace. She drags herself into the office, and the crowd disperses. Cousin Lymon and Marvin Macy leave that night, but, before they go, they completely wreck the café: food, whiskey, decorations, the mechanical piano. The café ends as Miss Amelia's love ends. Slowly she shrivels into an old maid; her muscles shrink and her eyes cross to look inward. After three years of lonesome waiting for Cousin Lymon to return, she has the store-café boarded up. Retreating into the upstairs rooms, she remains there alone and isolated. The town takes on a new loneliness also; a perpetual August drought envelops it in a claustrophobic malaise. Time hangs heavy and dull.

Yes, the town is dreary. On August afternoons the road is empty, white with dust, and the sky above is bright as glass. Nothing moves—there are no children's voices, only the hum of the mill. The peach trees seem to grow more crooked every summer, and the leaves are dull gray and of a sickly delicacy. The house of Miss Amelia leans so much to the right that it is now only a question of time when it will collapse completely and people are careful not to walk around the yard. There is no good liquor to be bought in the town; the nearest still is eight miles away, and the liquor is such that those who drink it grow warts on their livers the size of goobers, and dream themselves into a dangerous inward world. There is absolutely nothing to do in the town. Walk around the millpond, stand kicking at a rotten stump, figure out what you can do with the old wagon wheely by the side of the road near the church. The soul rots with boredom. You might as well go down to the Forks Falls highway and listen to the chain gang.

The chain gang illustrates the prison house aspect of the human condition. The coda, entitled "Twelve Mortal Men," emphasizes how man can achieve creativity, in this case the beautiful work songs and ballads of the gang, even in the most difficult situations if there is harmony and cooperation. The last sentence of the novella points out that they are only ". . . twelve mortal men who are together." The picture of the chain gang contrasts with the reader's final vision of Miss Amelia. She could release her creative efforts when she was "to-gether" with Cousin Lymon; alone she can accomplish nothing. Where love and harmony exist much can be created; sadly enough, they exist in few places and for short times—human failings quickly frustrate them, and they are often replaced by hate and isolation. McCullers' other novels demonstrate this condition in the modern social world; the strange ballad of the café that becomes sad traces the roots of these difficulties in the timeless province of the lonely human heart.

John McNally (essay date 1973)

SOURCE: "The Introspective Narrator in *The Ballad of the Sad Café*," in *South Atlantic Bulletin*, Vol. XXXVIII, No. 4, November, 1973, pp. 40-4.

[*In the following essay, McNally examines the point-of-view of the narration in* The Ballad of the Sad Café, *arguing that when the reader views the narrator as "a character in the story, he notices a subtle but significant shift in the story's form and subsequent themes."*]

Carson McCullers' novella, *The Ballad of the Sad Café,* is intriguing for a number of reasons. First there is the incredibly grotesque gallery of characters who people the little dreary town in which the story takes place. Then, of course, there is the enigmatic epilogue, "The Twelve Mortal Men," which seems at first glance to have been an afterthought of the author. And there is the disturbing plot with its love triangle so reminiscent of Sartre's curious *ménage*

à trois in *No Exit*. But perhaps the most disturbing feature of the whole novella is the point of view which informs the piece.

On the surface of it, the narration of *The Ballad of the Sad Café* is third-person omniscient with an occasional authorial intrusion. The narration employs the present tense for three introductory paragraphs, shifts to the past tense for the whole flashback section—virtually the whole story unfolds in this section and returns to the present tense for the final three paragraphs, two of which comprise the chain-gang epilogue. Simple? Yes. And no.

Yes, the point of view is simple at first glance; however, a careful examination of the tense-shifts, the so-called intrusions and digressions, and the appended "Twelve Mortal Men" shows that McCullers has fashioned a very complicated fictive narrator from whom the reader receives the details of the story and about whom he is left to speculate. When one reads the novella in the understanding that the narrator is a character in the story, he notices a subtle but significant shift in the story's form and subsequent themes. Such a reader finds himself absorbed not so much with the bizarre goings-on in the old café as with the changing perceptions of a person in the process of intense introspection—a process he shares with his listen-er-reader.

The first clue to the actual point of view is the fact that the story begins and ends in the present tense. In itself, the present tense does not a fictive narrator make. Considered in the context of the references to "here" and "now," though, the use of the present suggests a person who is describing the café "on the spot." For example, in the first paragraph the narrator says "the winters *here* are short and raw," and "*here in this very town* there was once a café," suggesting his presence on the scene he is describing (italics mine throughout). Then, speaking of the café which "has long since been closed," he says that "it is still remembered." In not pointing out who specifically in the town remembers the café, he suggests that it is he, the narrator, who remembers it as he sits there looking at its boarded up remains. A further suggestion of the narrator's actual physical presence comes from the comment that on "*These* August afternoons— . . . there is absolutely nothing to do; you might as well walk down to the Fork Falls Road and listen to the chain-gang." In referring to "*these* August afternoons" the narrator places himself in a more or less specific time; in suggesting that you "*walk down* to the Fork Falls Road and listen," he fixes himself in space. He *is in* the town, most probably right in front of the café on an August afternoon which is "white with glare and humming hot."

To perceive the narrator as an actual person who is in the little town on a hot August afternoon is not merely to observe one of the story's nicer nuances. To read the story in the light of this perception is to read a very different story indeed—it is to read a story in which, for one thing, the apparent authorial intrusions and digressions are no longer flaws in the narrative but actually key passages in the story's curious network of meanings.

When the narrator "digresses" to explain the significance of the whisky, for example, he now takes on the credibility of one who has actually tasted of it and felt its effects. Now he is one who knows from experience that the whisky is "clean and sharp on the tongue" and that "once down a man it glows inside him for a long time afterward." He is one who *knows* that the experience of drinking Miss Amelia's liquor is one in which a person is "shown the truth;" he, himself, is a person who has "warmed his soul and seen the message hidden there." As an actual character, then, the narrator is less to be faulted for digressing than would a simple omniscient narrator—for *real* people do digress when they tell stories.

But there is more to this than mere verisimilitude. As the concern of a character-narrator, the "digression" is more clearly related to the later section in the story in which the narrator describes the effects of the music of the chain gang. For, just as Miss Amelia's liquor had once "warmed his soul," "shown the truth" and the "message hidden there," so now the music causes his "heart to broaden," his soul to "grow cold with ecstasy and fright." The café he had once visited gone, the narrator seeks truth in the music of "the earth itself," of the "twelve mortal men who are together."

Besides the liquor "digression" and the enigmatic chain-gang passage, there are other frequent points in the narrative at which the narrator asserts his personality—points at which he speaks directly to the reader (or, perhaps, a fictive listener) to tell him, in effect, to pay attention, to remember this detail or that, to see things this way or that. Fairly early in the flashback section of the story, the narrator says "Now this was the beginning of the café. . . . It was as simple as that. *Recall* that the night was gloomy as in wintertime." Somewhat later he says, "for the moment regard these years from random and disjointed views. *See* the hunchback marching in Miss Amelia's footsteps. . . . *See* them working on her properties. . . . So *compose* from such flashes an image of these years as a whole and for a moment *let* it rest." Still later, the narrator says "So *do not forget* this Marvin Macy as he is to act a terrible part in the story which is yet to come." In each of these instances the tone is clearly conversational, the mild imperatives suggesting direct address. We may not *see* the narrator as a character at this point, but it is virtually impossible not to *hear* him as one.

If in these passages the narrator reveals something of himself, what is it? In other words, who is he? What does he mean?

It should be remembered that in the second paragraph of the story, the narrator suggests that "you might as well walk down to the Fork Falls Road and listen to the chain-gang." At this point the comment smacks of cynicism: given the choices of staying or leaving, one might as well leave, for, after all, there is nothing to do. But the narrator doesn't leave—not yet. Intrigued by the setting or, perhaps, merely discouraged by the August heat, he stays to reminisce (To himself? To a listener? Who can be sure?) about the café that once was. It is here that the verbs shift tense and the café and its people come back to life—but they are seen through the filter of the narrator's power of recollection. The whole story he remembers—digressions and all—has the effect of changing his perceptions of himself and his present predicament. He realizes, for example, that the characters he has recalled were incapable of sharing love, that each was the other's hell. He recalls a pageant of grotesquery and violence that eventually turns the nostalgia to bitterness and pain. More than anything else, though, he experiences the contrast between the proprietress in her prime and the bent, broken and inward-turned terrible face she now shows at the window.

The recollection done, he is a man who sees himself in the town in which he sits, who sees the town—like the remembered café—as a reflection of his own static image. It is here—after the flashback—that he repeats "Yes, the town *is* dreary. . . ." It is so dreary that "the soul rots with boredom." It is so dreary that he "might as well go down to the Fork Falls highway and listen to the chain-gang." This last paragraph suggests, then, that the narrator is a man who realizes he has refused to obey his impulse to move—to go listen to the chain-gang. It shows him to be a man who has wrestled with the past and who has used the past to reinterpret the present. It shows that he knows that when nothing moves—the spirit dies; "the soul rots with boredom."

The so-called epilogue, "The Twelve Mortal Men," seen in the context of the character-narrator's struggle becomes not a cryptic appendix to a gothic tale but, instead, the positive act of a man of changed perspective. In this section the narrator fulfills his own earlier inchoate suggestion to "go down to Fork Falls highway and listen to the chain-gang." This time, though, there is less of the cynicism which characterized the initial suggestion—for now to go to listen is to save one's soul from rotting. The whole section is seen in direct contrast to the flashback section of the story. Where in the café reminiscences the narrator found free people unwilling or incapable to share love with one another, in the epilogue he finds people in chains who share their suffering and who, in sharing, bring music from the earth and sky. Such music is what keeps the narrator's soul alive.

It has not been my purpose here to insist that the inside story—the flashback about the café that is still remembered—is of minor significance. On the contrary, that story is an intriguing one: it is a grotesque delineation of love's power to destroy. It *has* been my purpose, though, to show that its chief significance lies in what it reveals about the character who, in recalling it, gives it its shape and who, in reaction to it, finds new meaning in his own existence.

Let me call on the narrator in just two more instances to help make my position clear. At one point in the story, the narrator says something which could easily be taken as a key to this story's significance. "There are great changes," he says, "but these changes are brought about bit by bit, in single steps which in themselves do not appear to be important." Then, later, speaking of Marvin Macy, he provides what, I believe, is a clue to his own situation. "But though the outward facts of this love [read: story] are indeed sad and ridiculous, it must be remembered that the real story was that which took place in the soul of the lover [read: narrator] himself."

What we have in *The Ballad of the Sad Café*, then, is a beautifully sculptured piece of writing in which we over-hear the internal monologue of a character whose haunting recollections enable him to overcome his own *ennui* and to resist the atrophying pressures of the familiar world; a character to whom, like Marlow in Conrad's *Heart of Darkness,* the "meaning of an episode was not inside like a kernel but outside, enveloping the tale which brought it out only as a glow brings out a haze, in the likeness of one of those misty halos that sometimes are made visible by the spectral illumination of moonshine." The *Ballad* is a song of the human spirit.

Panthea Reid Broughton (essay date 1974)

SOURCE: "Rejection of the Feminine in Carson McCullers' *The Ballad of the Sad Café*," in *Twentieth Century Literature,* Vol. 20, No. 1, January, 1974, pp. 34-43.

[*In the following essay, Broughton asserts that the characters in* The Ballad of the Sad Café *regard tenderness and the expression of emotion as inherently feminine and, for that reason, "weak" qualities. She argues that their attitudes toward the feminine cause them to reject qualities that are essential to the survival of the human community.*]

Well over a century has passed since Alexis de Tocqueville astutely observed that compulsive individualism, so idealized in America, might indeed foster personal isolation. Tocqueville surmised that the inescapable isolation of the individual American was as much economic as political and that, though its causes might indeed be material, its ultimate significance was spiritual; for Tocqueville concluded that, as it throws a man "back forever upon himself alone, [democracy] threatens in the end to confine [that man] entirely within the solitude of his own heart" [*Democracy in America,* Vol. II, edited by Phillips Bradley, 1963].

The spiritual solitude Tocqueville sensed in the America of the 1830's has hardly lessened with the passage of years. Indeed, as our literature of alienation abundantly testifies, man's sense of isolation has been exacerbated in the intervening years. But the so-called literature of alienation frequently is so lacerated with hatred and self-pity that it fails to offer any really mature understanding of the phenomena of alienation. Not so with the fiction of Carson McCullers; for McCullers, who made personal alienation the explicit single concern of all her fiction, treats the solitude of the heart with both objectivity and compassion and, ultimately, with an understanding born of the blending of head and heart.

Mrs. McCullers once said of her work "my central theme is the theme of spiritual isolation. Certainly I have always felt alone" ["Preface," *The Square Root of Wonderful,* 1958]. In her *The Ballad of the Sad Café,* the setting itself serves as metaphor for such spiritual isolation. She begins this novella by establishing the dreariness, lonesomeness, and sadness of a setting which seems "estranged from all other places in the world." The largest building in the town, we are told, is old, boarded up, and leans far to one side. The house has "about it a curious, cracked look" which results, we discover, from its having once been haphazardly half-painted. The house is not, however, uninhabited. On hot afternoons a face may linger at the window for an hour or so before the shutters are closed once more: "It is a face like the terrible dim faces known in dreams—sexless and white, with two gray crossed eyes which are turned inward so sharply that they seem to be exchanging with each other one long and secret gaze of grief."

All of this sounds curiously gothic. We have the impression that the town itself is a grotesque, warped by its isolation, and that the building, with its cracked appearance, its dilapidated one-sided construction, and its boarded-up façade, might serve as symbol for whatever life remains in it and in the town. For life here is hopelessly inward, separated, and estranged. Selfhood means only confinement in the solitude of one's own heart.

With D. H. Lawrence, Carson McCullers believed that "we need one another" and that we attain our very individuality itself in living contact, the give-and-take of human relations. Lawrence felt that without such relationships, we are nonentities. In *The Ballad* McCullers presents us with an unnamed Southern town and with a woman, Miss Amelia Evans, who together almost manage to escape aloneness and nonentity. The effort, however, is as abortive as the abandoned paint job on the front porch of her house.

When the building Miss Amelia owns becomes a café rather than a dry goods store, Miss Amelia and the townspeople as well almost succeed in breaking out of their separateness. On the occasion when Miss Amelia first breaks her rule and allows liquor to be drunk on the premises, an atmosphere of "company and genial warmth" suddenly emerges. "For," McCullers writes, "the atmosphere of a proper café implies these qualities: fellowship, the satisfactions of the belly, and a certain gaiety and grace of behavior."

In other words, through the café people do manage to overcome their aloneness. They begin to share their liquor, and when the café closes, Miss Amelia for the first time forgets to bolt her door. Trust in one another, founded on a new sense of human dignity, pervades. The change may best be seen in Miss Amelia who, along with Cousin Lymon, becomes actually sociable and is "not so quick to cheat her fellow man and to exact cruel payments."

Most studies of *The Ballad* emphasize only McCullers' theme of spiritual alienation and irreparable loneliness;

they seem to disregard the fact that aloneness was, for a time at least, actually overcome. But Carson McCullers is very explicit about the achievement of "an air of intimacy . . . and a vague festivity" in the café. Her theorizing about the café is crucial enough to deserve quoting at some length:

> But it was not only the warmth, the decorations, and the brightness, that made the café what it was. There is a deeper reason why the café was so precious to this town. And this deeper reason has to do with a certain pride that had not hitherto been known in these parts. To understand this new pride the cheapness of human life must be kept in mind. There were always plenty of people clustered around a mill—but it was seldom that every family had enough meal, garments, and fat back to go the rounds. Life could become one long dim scramble just to get the things needed to keep alive. And the confusing point is this: All useful things have a price, and are bought only with money, as that is the way the world is run. You know without having to reason about it the price of a bale of cotton, or a quart of molasses. But no value has been put on human life; it is given to us free and taken without being paid for. What is its worth? If you look around, at times the value may seem to be a little or nothing at all. Often after you have sweated and tried and things are not better for you, there comes a feeling deep down in the soul that you are not worth much.

> But the new pride that the café brought to this town had an effect on almost everyone, even the children. . . . Children love to sleep in houses other than their own, and to eat at a neighbor's table; on such occasions they behave themselves decently and are proud. The people in the town were likewise proud when sitting at the tables in the café. They washed before coming to Miss Amelia's, and scraped their feet very politely on the threshold as they entered the café. There, for a few hours at least, the deep bitter knowing that you are not worth much in this world could be laid low.

Although, then, the "people in this town were unused to gathering together for the sake of pleasure," they do manage for a time to do so and consequently to escape the humdrum everydayness of their lives and the sense of their own worthlessness. But the effort cannot be maintained; the café is closed and the people retreat once again into their own separateness and aloneness. The convivial nights in the café end ostensibly because Marvin Macy and Cousin Lymon have ransacked the place, carving obscene words on the tables and bringing shame and sadness to Miss Amelia. But I should like to suggest that the café's violent end was already inherent in the consciousness of Amelia and her patrons.

McCullers makes a comparison between useful commodities which have a clearly established value and human lives which do not. The comparison is seminal here because it is a lack of confidence in their own human worth which renders the townspeople incapable of sustaining the transcendent affirmation which was the café. For the dreary desperation of the town with its one-industry economy has conditioned the people to hoard themselves as well as their money. As Tocqueville long ago surmised, spiritual isolation is closely aligned with competitive capitalism. Here the normative pattern for dealing with the world and its people is the transaction. Now the transaction may be efficient, abstract, uninvolved, and profitable, but it is also dehumanized. In the business transaction people are used, not respected. Their worth is calculated in terms of dollars and cents. Of course, as McCullers writes, there is "no feeling of joy in the transaction," only the determination not to risk too much. And so, among a people "unused to gathering together for the sake of pleasure" the experience of joy cannot be sustained. To expend the soul in an open give-and-take relationship with another is too much of a risk; it seems safer, and more expedient, to approach another only to take rather than to risk being taken.

Mrs. McCullers once said of her work "my central theme is the theme of spiritual isolation. Certainly I have always felt alone. In her *The Ballad of the Sad Cafe,* the setting itself serves as metaphor for such spiritual isolation.

—*Pathea Reid Broughton*

The three central characters exemplify this habit of defining human relationships pragmatically. Ravishing the young girls in the town, Marvin Macy has exploited human relationships to assert his will. Miss Amelia has exploited them to make a profit. (We learn that until the arrival of Cousin Lymon, she has never invited anyone to eat with her, "unless she were planning to trick them in some way, or make money out of them.") And even Cousin Lymon, who has "an instinct to establish immediate and vital contact between himself and all things in the world," exploits these contracts for excitement; for Lymon, who loves a spectacle, tries to create tension in the café by badgering and setting hostilities on edge. Furthermore, each of these characters, when he is the beloved, only exploits the other's affection. Amelia appraises Marvin's gifts and then shrewdly puts them up for sale; Lymon uses his sickliness, like his trick of wiggling his ears, whenever he wants "to get something special out of Miss Amelia." And Marvin, of course, uses Lymon's devotion to get his own back from Amelia.

Now, John B. Vickery may suggest that there is comedy in the characters' inability to synchronize their successive roles as lover and beloved ["Carson McCullers: A Map of Love," *Wisconsin Studies in Contemporary Literature,* Wintes, 1960]; I would insist, on the other hand, that the situation is tragic. For these characters simply do not know how to love. As the lover, each is a slave; as the beloved, each is a tyrant. None can achieve a satisfactorily balanced human relationship. He cannot love without sacrificing his own individual integrity, nor can he be beloved without exerting his power and superiority. His problem directly results from the deeply ingrained assumption that one approaches a human relationship only to exploit, not to enjoy. These characters cannot overcome a value system in which it is better to subjugate than to share, better to use than to love. They live in the world that McCullers describes in her poem "Saraband:"

> The world that jibs your tenderness
> Jails your lusts.
>
> [*The Mortgaged Heart*]

In this world, the virtues of openness, receptivity, tenderness, and compassion are held in such contempt that no one can comfortably express them.

In this town if a man shows his feelings he is labeled contemptuously a "Morris Finestein," Finestein, we are told, was a little Jew sensitive enough to cry whenever people called him a Christ-killer and foolish enough to live in this town (before, that is, an unnamed but easily imagined calamity overcame Finestein and he was compelled to move away to Society City). The reference to Finestein is important because it reveals the town's concept of sexual roles. McCullers writes "if a man were prissy in any way, or if a man ever wept, he was known as a Morris Finestein." In other words to be sensitive, to weep, is to be effeminate. The human virtues of tenderness and sensitivity are considered to be exclusively feminine and decidedly superfluous and downright contemptible by a pragmatic and rationalistic society. The human psyche has then been split, "cracked," if you will, into qualities which are feminine and contemptible on the one hand and masculine and admirable on the other.

Sexual characteristics, then, are so rigidly dichotomized that they cannot be held in balance. One is either servile and feminine, or, preferably, dominant and masculine. Ideally, as the psychoanalyst Karl Stern writes in his study entitled *The Flight from Woman*, "Man in his fullness is bisexual" or, as Carson McCullers herself puts it, "By nature all people are both sexes" [*"The Heart is a Lonely Hunter": the Novels and Stories of Carson McCullers*, 1951]. But here, in this novella, people cannot be both sexes at once. Marvin Macy, for instance, who is described as the "cause" of all the trouble, is ruthlessly masculine. With his razor and knife and the sharpened stick he uses to pick his teeth, he is viciously phallic. McCullers describes him as an "evil character" with a "secret meanness" about him. She explains:

> For years, when he was a boy, he had carried about with him the dried and salted ear of a man he had killed in a razor fight. He had chopped off the tails of squirrels in the pinewoods just to please his fancy, and in his left hip pocket he carried forbidden marijuana weed to tempt those who were discouraged and drawn toward death. Yet in spite of his well-known reputation he was the beloved of many females in this region—and there were at the time several young girls who were clear-haired and soft-eyed, with tender sweet little buttocks and charming ways. These gentle young girls he degraded and shamed.

Macy, then, dominates and destroys others in order to enhance his own ego. To admit his need of another is equivalent, in this frame of mind, to abolishing his own ego. That is why Marvin Macy's attachment to Miss Amelia is such a pathetic thing. Her indifference only provokes further, more desperate, acts of self-abasement from him, but to no avail. Miss Amelia continues to ignore the man Macy and to turn his gifts to profit. It is only normative though, as McCullers remarks in one of her short stories, that "you hate people you have to need so badly." [In *The Mortgaged Heart*]. Thus Macy cannot but resent Amelia, not only for spurning him, but for making him so despicably servile. And so Marvin Macy vows to get even, and he does.

Macy's behavior represents the extremes of sadism and masochism which Erich Fromm tells us are not emotionally dissimilar. And I should like further to suggest that his unhealthy behavior, whether aggressively masculine or servilely feminine, results from a social ethos which has destroyed a human sense of balance. Karl Stern describes this contemporary psychic phenomenon as a "Flight from Woman" and explains that, with modern men and women "The very possibility of being in the least dependent or protected, or even being loved, amounts to nothing less than a phantasy of mutilation or destruction."

Certainly, with Miss Amelia, the experience of having an operation for kidney stones was an experience of mutilation. She seems to have been unable to survive the experience of being totally helpless and dependent, unless she could justify it in pragmatic, business-like terms. Thus she kept the kidney stones and later has them set as ornaments in a watch chain for Cousin Lymon. McCullers writes, "It had been a terrible experience, from the first minute to the last, and all she had got out of it were those two little stones; she was bound to set great store by them, or else admit to a mighty sorry bargain." Miss Amelia, then, has real difficulty in justifying any experience unless, that is, she can extract from it something practical and tangible, preferably in the shape of a profit. And so that is why the café and love seem doomed from the start. The pattern of pragmatism is too deeply entrenched for these people to sustain, for long, the experience of delight for its own sake.

Here each person has such a deep-seated fear of tenderness that he cannot admit his need of another without self-effacement, followed by hatred of the self and resentment of the needed one as well. Karl Stern describes this psychic phenomenon as "an undue emphasis on the technical and the rational, and a rejection of what for want of a better term we call 'feeling,' [which] go with a neurotic dread of receiving, a fear of tenderness and of protection, and are invariably associated with an original maternal conflict." Now both Marvin Macy and Amelia Evans, and apparently Lymon too, have been deprived of the security of motherly love, and each of them has a real dread of receiving and an inability to show tenderness or love except at the price of self-abandonment.

With her father, himself described as a "solitary man," Amelia may have been, despite her six-foot-two-inch stature, known as "Little" but with everyone else she is the big one, the dominant force. Amelia is "like a man," then, not because she wears overalls and swamp boots, nor because she is six feet two inches tall (though McCullers does remark that Amelia's height is indeed "not natural for a woman"), nor even because Amelia settles her disputes with men by a wrestling match; Amelia is "like a man," instead, simply because of her insatiable need to dominate. The assumption here is that it is masculine to dominate, to force one's shape upon matter, whereas it is feminine to be receptive and malleable. In these terms, Miss Amelia is as masculine as Marvin Macy; for we learn that "with all things which could be made by the hands, Miss Amelia prospered." But also, that "It was only with people that Miss Amelia was not at ease. People, unless they are willy-nilly or very sick, cannot be taken into the hands and changed overnight to something more worthwhile and profitable. So that the only use that Miss Amelia had for other people was to make money out of them. And in this she succeeded." Unless they are sick, she deals with people only to make a profit (until, that is, the café opens). And she deals with sick people because they are malleable. With them she can achieve a symbiotic union which confirms her sense of power even more than litigations and profit-making do. Thus this fiercely materialistic woman need charge no fees for doctoring, for power is its own reward. Miss Amelia, however, is incapable of dealing with female complaints. At the mention of a female problem she reacts "like a great, shamed, dumb-tongued child;" she is then, as much as the cruelly phallic Marvin Macy, in flight from the feminine.

With the coming of Lymon and the opening of the café, of course, Miss Amelia tries to change, to become female. She still wears overalls and swamp boots, but on Sundays she now wears a dress. She is "not so quick to cheat her fellow man." She becomes more sociable and even takes Lymon into her confidence about "the most delicate and vital matters." But these matters are mostly details about her property—where she keeps bankbook, keys, and whisky barrels. Certainly she never confides in Lymon about her ten-day marriage to Marvin Macy.

Miss Amelia tries very hard to be open and tender, for she does love Lymon, but she simply does not know how to show that love. She gives him presents when he is cross, and she spoils him as a foolish mother does a child, but she is unable to maintain a reciprocal relationship with him. Instead she smothers him in a symbiotic relationship which must itself be the cause of his deep fear of death, for, as McCullers explains, "the lover is forever trying to strip bare his beloved."

Miss Amelia is then no more capable of manifesting a healthy femininity than Marvin Macy is. She is alternately hard and soft, but cannot manage to balance the qualities or to be both at once. She is, as McCullers explains, "divided between two emotions." Thus when Marvin Macy returns, she puts aside her overalls and wears always the dark red dress as symbol of her accessibility. She tries giving Marvin free drinks and smiling at him in

a "wild, crooked way." But she also sets a terrible trap for him and tries to poison him. And she is no more successful at destroying him than she is at attracting him. She remains then the figure in the boarded-up house, white and sexless, the eyes turning increasingly inward upon themselves.

Amelia is left in the prison of her aloneness because the stereotyped patterns by which she encountered others were exclusively those of dominance or subjugation. She has known no way to love without self-abasement. Nor has Marvin Macy. Nor has Cousin Lymon. And self-abasement can only result in resentment and eventual retaliation, so Marvin Macy has his turn taking from Amelia and then, with Lymon's help, destroys the café in order to get his own back from her.

All these relationships are organically incomplete because no one knows how to give without vitiating his own integrity and no one knows how to take without enhancing his sense of personal power. These characters need to dismiss the sexual stereotypes of extremity and to learn to be strong without cruelty, tender without servility. The problem, then, is to reclaim the virtues of tenderness and receptivity from their exclusive association with whatever is female and weak, and to reinstate them as virtues which are essential to all humanity; for, without accepting these virtues as a dignified aspect of mankind, the human community cannot survive.

In a recent article entitled, "The Hard and the Soft: The Force of Feminism in Modern Times," Theodore Roszak quotes from the Tao Te Ching:

> What is hard and stiff
> Belongs to death;
> The soft and tender belong to life.

The soft and tender, therefore, may not be excluded or rejected from life. Roszak's thesis is that "Saving the compassionate virtues is not the peculiar duty of women. On the contrary; the sooner we have done with the treacherous nonsense of believing that the human personality must be forced into masculine and feminine molds, the better" [Roszak, "The Hard and the Soft," in *Masculine/Feminine: Readings in Sexual Mythology and the Liberation of Women,* edited by Betty Roszak and Theodore Roszak, 1969]. The feminine virtues must not be rejected; they must be reclaimed by all humankind.

Once toward the end of McCullers' story, Marvin Macy laughs at Miss Amelia and says, "'Everything you holler at me bounces back on yourself.'" His denunciation provides an apt image for the entire novella. For *The Ballad of the Sad Café* may be interpreted as a fable which shows us that rejecting those characteristics labeled as exclusively feminine bounces back on the rejector and renders men and women alike incapable of loving and thereby escaping the prisons of their own spiritual isolation.

Now, we may have learned from contemporary cinema that we have "a failure to communicate" and from the popular song that "what the world needs now is luv, luv, luv," but only modern fiction has, to date, been subtle and serious enough to bring us to some understanding of why we have a communication gap and of how love can bridge that gap. In this tradition, McCullers' *Ballad* is especially significant; for to read it is to experience the solitude of the heart and to understand how misconceptions of love only reinforce that solitude.

Richard M. Cook   (essay date 1975)

SOURCE: *"The Ballad of the Sad Café,"* in *Carson McCullers,* Frederick Unger, 1975, pp. 84-104.

[*In the following excerpt, Cook suggests that* The Ballad of the Sad Café *celebrates the capacity of love to transform a community and is an elegy to the ephemerality of such love.*]

After working on drafts of *The Member of the Wedding* for two years, in the fall of 1943 Carson McCullers interrupted her work, took a trip to Saratoga Springs and in six weeks' time wrote what is now her best-known work, *The Ballad of the Sad Café*. Like McCullers's other novels, *The Ballad of the Sad Café* is the story of lonely people falling in love; but it is more than that. It is a celebration of the power of love itself and an elegy on its passing. It is, as the title indicates, a ballad, a short oral tale, transcribed into written prose, that in Frankie's words has a beginning and an end, a shape like a song—a song about love and its miraculous effect on a town and its inhabitants. Using such traditional ballad motifs as natural and supernatural signs, magic potions, and grotesque characters resembling birds and animals, McCullers tells the story of a strange and tragic love affair between a mannish giant of a woman, Miss Amelia Evans, and a hunchback dwarf, Cousin Lymon, that turns a small backwater town in Georgia into a stage of high, albeit bizarre, drama and romance. The extreme physical grotesquery of the story's characters, the remoteness of its setting—"the town . . . is like a place that is far off and estranged from all other places in the world"—and the quaint, almost childish story-telling language of the narrator, combine to remove the events of the tale from the realm of most of McCullers's fiction, the South in the 1930s and 1940s, to a mythic, timeless realm of elemental passion and violence. Love in this archetypal, fairy-tale world is not merely a matter of a private susceptibility or idiosyncrasy; rather it is shown to be a "stored up," almost magical power within all human beings, which if triggered by the right circumstances—and it is impossible to say what those circumstances will be—will effect a complete transformation of the lover and make itself dramatically felt in the world at large.

The miraculous power of love in *The Ballad of the Sad Café* to change people and places is implicit in its nostalgic, flashback structure. The novel begins with a brief description of the town as it is now, a dreary desolate place, "a place where there is absolutely nothing to do,"

and moves quickly back into the history of Miss Amelia's past love affair with the hunchback, Cousin Lymon. This love affair, now long since over, lasted six years and created in the duration Miss Amelia's wonderful café, which turned the town into an exciting, lively place where people came from miles around on a Saturday night to talk and have a good time. The love affair and the café both came to a disastrous end, however, when Miss Amelia's former husband, "a terrible character," returned to the town, caused ruin and then went on his way again. *The Ballad* concludes where it began, back in the present, the love affair long passed, the café boarded up, and the town so wearisome and dull that "the soul rots with boredom." Like a gold-rush town out West, the town in *The Ballad* now sits in the hot sun, abandoned and falling to ruin. Yet the very extensiveness of its dilapidation and the occasional appearance of a "terrible dim" face in the upstairs window of the boarded-up café suggest a past in which something extraordinary once happened—in which love, not gold, brought an intense if temporary life.

Though Miss Amelia's love for Cousin Lymon is the energizing force in *The Ballad of the Sad Café* their strange affair is only part of the larger story of the café itself. The café is the true subject of *The Ballad,* for it is in the café's miraculous growth and sudden destruction that we see the dramatic changes brought about by love—changes in the personality of Miss Amelia and of the town. The café is the creation of love, a rare external blossoming of love's inwardness tying the happiness of the community to the fate of private desire. But the café is also a measure of love's fragility. Its appearance marks the narrow limits within which love is possible. Its fall evokes again that tragic sense of loss encountered in *The Heart Is a Lonely Hunter.*

The birth of the café comes suddenly and unexpectedly— the result of a surprise of encounter at midnight. Standing on her front porch late one summer evening, Miss Amelia and a number of the local mill workers see a misshapen, solitary figure coming down the road into town. As it slowly approaches they realize that it is not a lost calf, as they had at first supposed, but a hunchbacked dwarf carrying a lopsided suitcase. The hunchback moves haltingly toward the company on the porch and then introduces himself as Lymon Willis, cousin to Miss Amelia Evans. Miss Amelia has never claimed kin to anyone. Thus when the hunchback produces a faded-out photograph of "two pale, withered-up children" to back his claim, he gets only empty stares from everyone present. Miss Amelia stares too. But when the hunchback suddenly begins to cry, she takes two great strides across the porch and "gingerly with one long brown forefinger . . . touched the hump on his back." She then does something that shocks everyone present. She offers the hunchback a drink of free liquor out of her hip flask and invites him in for a meal and a bed.

Miss Amelia has never been one to offer free food and lodging to anyone. Since her father died when she was nineteen, she has lived alone spurning all company. Except for a short, disastrous marriage soon after her father's death, she has especially avoided the company of men. A tall, dark masculine woman "with bones and muscles like a man," who wears swamp boots all day long, Miss Amelia through hard work and cutthroat business practices has become the richest person in town. She carpenters, runs a still in the swamp, and makes a handsome profit in her feed store. She is also a fine doctor, but if a woman comes to her with a "female complaint," she only rubs her swamp boots together in an embarrassed way and turns her away. Except for the doctoring, which she does free, Miss Amelia has nothing to do with people whom she cannot make a profit out of. Certainly she has never "invited anyone to eat with her unless she was planning to trick them in some way, or make money out of them." Taking in an itinerant hunchback thus makes no sense to the townspeople, who begin to think she plans to murder him for something he has in his suitcase. The real reason, as it soon becomes obvious, is more mysterious. She has fallen in love with him.

The café begins three days after Miss Amelia offers Cousin Lymon bed and board. That Saturday evening a self-appointed delegation visits Miss Amelia's store to find out what has happened to the hunchback. But instead of discovering a murder victim, they find Cousin Lymon alive and thriving and Miss Amelia strangely changed. The crowd of men are at first surprised, then fascinated—fascinated especially by Cousin Lymon, who, after looking at each of them carefully, struts over to a full sack of guano, sits down, and begins to talk. What he says is mostly nonsense: lies, bragging, and idle gossip, but there gradually comes over the gawking group as they stand awkwardly around an unusual feeling, like "an air of intimacy in the room and a vague festivity."

The hunchback is partly the cause of this feeling. He has what the narrator describes as "an instinct which is usually found only in small children, an instinct to establish immediate and vital contact between himself and all things in the world." He is "extremely sociable." But Miss Amelia also contributes to the odd sociable feeling in the air. She is behaving in an extraordinary fashion. Instead of staring at the company until they become uncomfortable and leave her premises, she seems to accept them. She even goes back into the kitchen and brings out glasses to serve liquor in the store. (Before she had only sold it secretly by the bottle in her dark backyard.) She then opens up two boxes of crackers "so that they were there hospitably on the counter and anyone who wished could take one free."

Such is the start of the café. For the next six years it grows steadily. Miss Amelia begins cooking catfish dinners for fifteen cents a plate. Cousin Lymon entertains. The café quickly becomes the "warm center point of the town," "the only place of pleasure for miles around."

The growth of the café is rapid and astonishing—the more astonishing in that it obviously reflects the profound changes that have occurred in Miss Amelia's personality. Miss Amelia has become sociable. She acts pleasantly to people, and occasionally she and Cousin Lymon go out on the weekends—to a funeral or a revival meeting.

She starts looking after her appearance, and, though she still wears overalls and swamp boots during the week, on Sundays she puts on a red dress. She even moderates her tough business practices and is "not so quick to cheat her fellow man." Above all she continues to idolize Cousin Lymon. Stingy and mean all her life, she can refuse him nothing. It is for him alone that she has turned her feed store into a café. The café is her most elaborate gesture of affection.

But the growth of the café also reflects a new feeling among the townspeople. A change of heart in a town's most powerful citizen has its inevitable effect on everybody else around. Everyone seems more sociable, and the café becomes the place for general gossip and excitement. Just as Miss Amelia finds in her love for Cousin Lymon an interest in life beyond making money, the people of the town find in the society of the café a "freedom and illicit gladness" that makes them forget their dull work in the factory and their grinding poverty. At the café the people enjoy themselves as social human beings. Instinctively they act with a "certain gaiety and grace of behavior," taking pride in the fellowship the café offers as well as in "the satisfactions of the belly."

The effect of Cousin Lymon's arrival in town is thus little short of miraculous. The hard-hearted Miss Amelia has fallen in love. A café has been started where there was once a feed store. An inert, boring town has been brought to life. Miss Amelia's feed store turned café symbolizes a profound shift in values that has occurred within the community. Following the example of the all-powerful Miss Amelia, the people have become less concerned with matters of economic and practical necessity and more concerned with matters of larger social interest. They have begun to talk to each other and to find each other interesting. More importantly, they have begun to take pride in the fact that there is more to their lives than mere survival. "It was not only the warmth, the decorations, and the brightness that made the café what it was. There is a deeper reason why the café was so precious to this town. And this deeper reason has to do with a certain pride that had not hitherto been known in these parts." That certain pride is the pride in knowing that as human beings they have a special value above and beyond what can be measured in financial terms. It is a pride that makes them act with dignity and finds expression in social ceremony:

> The people in the town were . . . proud when sitting at the tables in the café. They washed before coming to Miss Amelia's and scraped their feet very politely on the threshold as they entered the café. There, for a few hours at least, the deep bitter knowing that you are not worth much in the world could be laid low.

Oliver Evans has described the townspeople in *The Ballad of the Sad Café* as "a symbol of suspicion" and "among the least sympathetic of Mrs. McCullers's characters" [*The Ballad of Carson McCullers: A Biography*, 1966]. They are, I think, more complicated than that. To be sure, many of them are gossips and heartily enjoy the spectacle of someone being done in "by some scandalous and terrible means." But they can be generous as well: "people in this town will as often as not be kindly if they have a chance." For the most part they welcome the happy change that has come over Miss Amelia, and they hope her good influence on the town will continue. As the ballad-narrator McCullers asks us to think of them "as a whole"; and, as a whole, it is obvious from their activity in the café, that they can behave with unexpected dignity and grace. Like Miss Amelia herself, they show a more human side to their personalities than had hitherto been seen. The café has revealed their own and Miss Amelia's better self.

But the café is doomed. It is doomed by the mysterious force that brought it into being, by the perverse powers of love. In the final reckoning the love felt by Miss Amelia for Cousin Lymon is an unbalanced, disorderly love, containing in its single-minded intensity the seeds of its own destruction. Like the love felt by Singer for Antonapoulos, the love Miss Amelia feels for Cousin Lymon is a possessive, irrational, nonreciprocal love and therefore tragic and doomed. At one point in *The Ballad of the Sad Café*, the narrator provides an extended, prophetic definition of the love felt by Miss Amelia a definition which doubles as a death warrant for the café and the town:

> First of all, love is a joint experience between two persons—but the fact that it is a joint experience does not mean that it is a similar experience to the two people involved. There are the lover and the beloved, but these two come from different countries. Often the beloved is only a stimulus for all the stored-up love which has lain quiet within the lover for a long time hitherto. And somehow every lover knows this. He feels in his soul that his love is a solitary thing. He comes to know a new, strange loneliness and it is this knowledge which makes him suffer. So there is only one thing for the lover to do. He must house his love within himself as best he can; he must create for himself a whole new inward world—a world intense and strange, complete in himself. . . .
>
> Now, the beloved can also be of any description. The most outlandish people can be the stimulus for love. . . . A most mediocre person can be the object of a love which is wild, extravagant, and beautiful as the poison lilies of the swamp. A good man may be the stimulus for a love both violent and debased, or a jabbering madman may bring about in the soul of someone a tender and simple idyll. Therefore, the value and quality of any love is determined solely by the lover himself.
>
> It is for this reason that most of us would rather love than be loved. Almost everyone wants to be the lover. And the curt truth is that, in a deep secret way, the state of being beloved is intolerable to many. The beloved fears and hates the lover, and with the best of reasons. For the lover is forever trying to strip bare his beloved, even if this experience can cause him only pain.

This description of love is the best-known, most frequently quoted passage from Mrs. McCullers's oeuvre. In a more realistic mode of fiction, such a forthright explanation of love's secrets might have the effect of making love appear mechanical or obvious. In *The Ballad,* however, it retains the mystery and force of a magic formula.

At the heart of love's mystery, as expressed in this passage, is the blunt, cruel fact that love is a private rather than a mutual experience. The lover, instead of breaking out of his isolation and sharing his experiences with the beloved, creates a charged, illusory world of his own, "a world, intense, and strange, complete in himself," a world in which he blindly idolizes the beloved. One thinks of Mick, Jake Blount, and Dr. Copeland turning Singer into a "chimerical" god and friend, of Frankie turning her brother's wedding into a wedding of her own, and of Berenice turning three of her husbands into replicas of the dead Ludy Freeman. McCullers further emphasizes the absolute separateness of the lover and the beloved, in this passage, by describing the beloved as a mere "stimulus" for the "stored-up love" within the lover. Like a chemical catalyst, the beloved merely precipitates a reaction that was all ready to go off and that runs its course without involving or changing his own interests and needs. There is, in fact, no apparent relation between the personality and appearance of the beloved and the nature of the love experienced: "the value and quality of any love is determined solely by the lover himself."

The final paragraph of this description is in many ways the most interesting one. Certainly, it has the most dire implications for the future of the café: "The beloved fears and hates the lover, and with the best of reasons. For the lover is forever trying to strip bare his beloved." The beloved's fear and hatred of the lover injects a new destructive element into Mrs. McCullers's love relationships. In her other novels the beloved is either indifferent to, or, at worst, mildly irritated by the lover. Singer misunderstands his visitors and thinks some of them "half crazy," but he does not hate or fear them. Private Williams ignores Captain Penderton; it is doubtful that he even suspects he is beloved. And Janice and Jarvis evidently have no idea that Frankie wants to be part of the marriage. But the love possessing Miss Amelia is a love to excite fear. It is an elementary force, too mysterious, too demanding, even too savage, to ignore or shrug off with indifference. Like the love described in the following two stanzas from W. H. Auden's poem, "The More Loving One," it is a love to inspire dread:

> Looking up at the stars, I know quite well
> That, for all they care, I can go to hell,
> But on earth indifference is the least
> We have to dread from man or beast.
>
> How should we like it were stars to burn
> With a passion for us we could not return?
> If equal affection cannot be,
> Let the more loving one be me.

Unable to return love, the beloved fears love's unknown powers. He fears "with the best of reasons" that the lover will strip him of his individuality, will possess him. It is partly for this reason that Cousin Lymon eventually turns on "the more loving" Miss Amelia and helps destroy the café.

McCullers uses this long passage on the nature of love to introduce Marvin Macy, Miss Amelia's former husband. Marvin Macy's early marriage to Miss Amelia and his return to town are thus to be seen as a working out of lover's contradictions as stated in this elaborate definition. Marvin Macy is the wronged lover and the avenger of love's imbalance. He is the one most responsible for the eventual destruction of the café.

When Miss Amelia was nineteen years old, Marvin Macy had fallen hopelessly and unaccountably in love with her. At that time he was the handsomest and most dangerous man in town. His reputation "was as bad if not worse than that of any young man in the county." But falling in love had "reversed the character of Marvin Macy," just as it was to reverse Miss Amelia's character years later. He changed from being a brutal no-good, who, among other things, "carried about with him the dried and salted ear of a man he had killed in a razor fight," to a perfectly behaved gentleman: "He was good to his brother and foster mother. . . . saved his wages and learned thrift. . . . He attended church and was present at all religious meetings." But he changed to no avail. "The lover and the beloved come from different countries," and though Miss Amelia married him, she did so only to reject him. During the ten days of their "scandalous" marriage, she managed to bilk her husband of all his property without letting him come near her. She then threw him out of her house. Disgraced and desperate, Marvin Macy had left town and shortly afterward was arrested and sentenced to prison in Atlanta for robbing three filling stations and an A&P store in Society City. He had evidently reverted to his old self. Miss Amelia could not have been happier. "Deeply gratified," she sold all the gifts he had given her and cut up his Klansman's robe to cover her tobacco plants.

This "grotesque affair" between Marvin Macy and Miss Amelia reveals a more menacing side to love than that evidenced by the "warm" café; a side, moreover, that cannot stay hidden forever. Housed with Marvin Macy in his Atlanta cell were those darker mysteries of love, which no one in the town was able to forget: "The thought of him trapped in his cell in the penitentiary, was like a troubling undertone beneath the happy love of Miss Amelia and the gaiety of the café." Thus it is no surprise that when Marvin Macy returns home after his release, "not a living soul in all the town was glad to see him"—not a living soul, that is, except Cousin Lymon.

The moment Cousin Lymon catches sight of Marvin Macy strolling idly through town with his tin suitcase, he too falls in love. Before he has been only the "beloved." Like a petted and fawned-over child, he has cried for and got everything he wanted from the foolishly indulgent Miss Amelia. But with Marvin Macy's arrival, Cousin Lymon becomes the lover. As passionate and devoted in his own way as Miss Amelia has been in hers and Marvin Macy

had been in his, Cousin Lymon will not let Marvin Macy out of his sight. Whining plaintively, waiting patiently and wiggling his ears (his most enticing gesture of affection), Cousin Lymon follows the handsome ex-convict about as a dog follows its master. When Macy ignores him or treats him rudely, as he often does, Cousin Lymon would then "perch himself on the bannister of the front porch much as a sick bird huddles on a telephone wire, and grieve publicly." Cousin Lymon becomes in effect Marvin Macy's slave, and Macy uses him for his own revenge on Miss Amelia. He encourages Cousin Lymon to sass and ridicule his former wife, and sometimes to please Macy, Cousin Lymon would cross his eyes as Miss Amelia's were crossed and strut around imitating her gestures in a manner that was "so terrible that even the silliest customer of the café . . . did not laugh." Marvin Macy also got Cousin Lymon to serve him free meals at the café, and eventually he moved in on both of them, forcing Miss Amelia out of her own bedroom just as she had forced him out years before.

Marvin Macy's return thus brings the fortunes of love full circle. The wronged husband returns to steal his wife's lover. Miss Amelia, caught between her love for Cousin Lymon and her hatred for Marvin Macy, can only grit her teeth and glare at her husband "in a wild and crooked way." The love that had saved her now traps her. She dares not throw out Macy for fear of losing Cousin Lymon, and the thought of the house silent and empty again is more than she can bear: "Once you have lived with another, it is a great torture to have to live alone. The silence of a firelit room when suddenly the clock stops ticking, the nervous shadows in an empty house—it is better to take in your mortal enemy than face the terror of living alone." She has never been so vulnerable. The comforts of love have opened up depths of terror she could hardly have suspected before. Love's tragic formula is working itself out.

The final event of the novel is a terrific fight between Miss Amelia and Marvin Macy. The fight follows a period filled with strange portents: sudden changes in the weather, erratic behavior from Miss Amelia, a growing intensity in the conversation of Cousin Lymon, and the smell of "a secret meanness" that comes off Marvin Macy. Everywhere in the ballad world there are "signs too plain to be overlooked," signs that make the fate of Miss Amelia's love and the café a matter of apocalyptic importance.

The fight takes place on Ground Hog Day. It is a day in which "there was every sign." The ground hog, according to a report from Cousin Lymon, had seen his shadow, meaning bad weather ahead, and at noon a hawk with a bloody breast had circled twice around the property of Miss Amelia. That evening at seven, "a number of mingled possibilities," Miss Amelia and Marvin Macy enter the crowded café, greased and ready for battle. The fight lasts half an hour. After an exchange of blows Miss Amelia grabs Marvin Macy around the waist, bends him slowly backward to the floor, and goes for his throat. Suddenly, Cousin Lymon, who has been perched on the café counter, springs twelve feet through the air, lands on Miss Amelia's back and clutches at her neck "with his clawed little fingers." After that Marvin Macy easily wins: "because of the hunchback the fight was won by Marvin Macy." Helped by Cousin Lymon, Marvin Macy spends the rest of the night wrecking the place. They broke the piano, "carved terrible words on the café tables," poured syrup over the kitchen floor and went out in the swamp and destroyed Miss Amelia's still. The two then leave town together never to be heard from again.

The café thus comes to its end, a victim to the forces that created it. Its flourishing had always been temporary and problematical, occurring in that uncertain period between love's initial creativity and its inevitable failure. It was only a matter of time before the imbalance of passion that destroyed Marvin Macy's marriage would wreck the café as well. It had happened before; it would happen again. The "signs . . . were too plain to be overlooked."

The events leading up to and following the fight in the café run a dramatic course encountered before in McCullers's novels. It may be described as one of rising hope leading to a sharp, violent confrontation with reality, followed by disillusionment and despair—the pattern of the interrupted fantasy or daydream, of emotional intoxication plummeting into emotional withdrawal. The arrival of Marvin Macy, the uncertain behavior of Miss Amelia, the increasing restlessness of the townspeople, and the myriad signs, all combine to create a charged atmosphere, an "atmosphere of imminent explosion," to use David Madden's characterization of all McCullers's fiction, that threatens to break down the fragile structure of relationships making life in the town so intense and interesting [see Madden, "Transfixed among the Self-Inflicted Ruins: Carson McCullers's *The Mortgaged Heart*," *Southern Literary Journal* 5 (Fall 1972)]. The fight, like the death of Singer, the shooting of Private Williams, and Frankie's "wrecked" wedding, brings the long-expected and feared return to boredom and isolation.

Only now it is an isolation made the more unbearable by the loss of past hope. Miss Amelia goes into immediate decline. She becomes "thin as old maids are thin when they grow crazy," and her eyes which had always been crossed, "slowly day by day . . . were more crossed, and it was as though they sought each other out to exchange a little glance of grief and lonely recognition." The café is boarded up and now "leans so far to the right that it is . . . only a question of time when it will collapse completely." The town has become oppressively, hopelessly dull:

> There is absolutely nothing to do in the town. Walk around the mill pond, stand kicking at a rotten stump, figure out what you can do with the old wagon wheel by the side of the road near the church. The soul rots with boredom. You might as well do down to the Forks Falls highway and listen to the chain gang.

Without love the town is thus left in a state of living death. Miss Amelia's passion may have been unhealthy, possessive, and unbalanced, but it was a temporary salva-

tion from isolation and the boredom of being alone. For better or for worse, it brought people together, gave them something to talk about, and established new relations among them. And it seems that any relationship between people, even one that turns to jealousy and hate, is better than no relationship at all—or one based on the mechanical necessities of money and work. Early in the novel the narrator describes the wonderful whiskey that Miss Amelia made in her still. When drunk, the whiskey acted on the heart in the way fire acted on a piece of paper written on in lemon juice—it revealed its secret message: "Things that have gone unnoticed, thoughts that have been harbored far back in the dark mind are suddenly recognized and comprehended." Love is shown to work in a similar fashion. It too acts as a magic potion, awakening hidden feelings and revealing people to each other as people—not things or blank pieces of paper. What is revealed is not always pleasant: "a love [could be] both violent and debased." It could and did result in jealousy, anger, and violence. But it also brought people out of their solitude, intensified their experiences, and filled their lives with what Robert Frost has called "the shocks and changes that keep us sane" ["On Looking up by Chance at the Constellations"]. It made life complicated, but it made it interesting as well.

The Ballad of the Sad Café does not end, however, with the death of Miss Amelia's love, the vanishing of Cousin Lymon, and the boarding up of the café. In an epilogue entitled "The Twelve Mortal Men," McCullers adds a coda or envoy to her ballad, which, as Ihab Hassan has suggested, speaks out its hidden refrain [*Radical Innocence: Studies in the Contemporary American Novel*, 1961]. It is, in fact, a description of the chain gang singing in chorus on the Forks Falls highway, a chorus, which, like *The Ballad* itself, celebrates a sad joy springing out of boredom, pain, and death:

> All day there is the sound of the picks striking into the clay earth, hard sunlight, the smell of sweat. And everyday there is music. One dark voice will start a phrase, half-sung, and like a question. And after a moment another voice will join in, soon the whole gang will be singing. The voices are dark in the golden glare, the music intricately blended, both somber and joyful. The music will swell until at last it seems that the sound does not come from the twelve men on the gang, but from the earth itself, or the wide sky. It is music that causes the heart to broaden and the listener to grow cold with ecstasy and fright. Then slowly the music will sink down until at last there remains one lonely voice, then a great hoarse breath, the sun, the sound of the picks in the silence.

> And what kind of gang is this that can make music? Just twelve mortal men, seven of them black and five of them white boys from this county. Just twelve mortal men who are together.

Here again we see McCullers using music to express the underlying message of her story. Trapped in the cruelest and most hopeless of physical conditions, the prisoners display an elemental capacity for joy that transcends and changes, if only for a moment, the miserable conditions of their lives. Like the café, which takes form amidst the white dust of the dreary, bored town, the music "intricately blended, both somber and joyful," rises from the chain gang at their endless labor—a joy apart, celebrating the fact that they are men together. The beauty of their song, that quality "that causes the heart to broaden and the listener to grow cold with ecstasy and fright," is the more intense and upsetting for the extraordinary pain and despair out of which it grows. We are moved by the contradictions in this scene just as we are moved by the contradiction of a giantess falling in love with a hunchback dwarf. *The Ballad of the Sad Café* is, in fact, Carson McCullers's most daring excursion into the contradictory and the grotesque. It is composed of material so disparate; comic, ugly, drab, and bizarre, as seemingly to defy harmonious organization into art. Yet the strangeness of the mixture is undoubtedly what makes *The Ballad* so startlingly, hauntingly beautiful. Like the watch chain Miss Amelia gives to Cousin Lymon, that she has had decorated with her own kidney stones, like the table in the café decorated with "a bouquet of swamp lilies in a Coca-Cola bottle," *The Ballad* and its envoy reveal through all the surface contradictions and incongruities a deeper beauty of shared human feeling, of people who are together.

Oliver Evans has written that "*The Ballad of the Sad Café* must be among the saddest stories in any language—not merely on the surface level of narrative . . . but also, and far more importantly (because it makes a generalization about mankind), on the level of parable." But if Mr. Evans means by the parable of the story the inevitable failure of love, *The Ballad of the Sad Café* is not unusual in its parable; rather it is typical of many of the great love stories in Western literature, typical in that such love as Miss Amelia feels for Cousin Lymon can never be fulfilled, can never last, that its end is always woe or, at best, a sweet sadness and never a permanent satisfaction. The love experienced by Miss Amelia resembles in some ways the kind of love we find in fairy tales and folklore, a magical love that might attract a princess to a frog or a beautiful girl to a beast. But it also resembles the love found in ancient romances, the love described by Denis de Rougemont in *Love in the Western World,* that brings an "exquisite anguish," that heightens life's feelings against its "mechanical boredom," that denies terrestial bliss for spiritual transcendence. Such love is too intense and too fragile to survive into an ordinary present and must therefore be recollected nostalgically from the legendary past. "The happiness of lovers," de Rougemont writes:

> stirs our feelings only on account of the unhappiness which lies in wait for it. We must feel that life is imperiled, and also feel the hostile realities that drive happiness away into some beyond. What moves us is not its presence, but its nostalgia and recollection. Presence is inexpressible and has no perceptible duration; it can only be a *moment* of grace—

And the love described in *The Ballad of the Sad Café* did have its moment of grace—a sustained moment, that for a period of six years actually transformed the dreary town and its "mechanical boredom" into a place of excitement

and heightened life. It may be that *The Ballad of the Sad Café* is less sad than Carson McCullers's other stories. The café was not, after all, like Singer's friendship with Antonapoulos or Frankie's dream of joining the wedding, an illusion. It was, for a time, anyway, a miraculous if temporary reality.

The Ballad of the Sad Café was reprinted along with Mrs. McCullers's first three novels and six short stories in the spring of 1951. The book, which was essentially a collected edition of Mrs. McCullers's works, going under the title of *The Ballad of the Sad Café,* proved to be a milestone in the history of Carson McCullers's critical reputation. Critics, who had previously been uneasy about the bizarre, or what they called the "gothic," quality of her work, began to see that the oddities and incongruities in her fiction served a more legitimate artistic purpose than the creation of sensational effects. The extraordinary achievement of *The Ballad of the Sad Café* forced them to realize the truth of what Carson McCullers had written some ten years earlier in her essay, "The Russian Realists and Southern Literature"—that the strange and the incongruous can be extremely helpful in exposing irrational and inexplicable patterns in all human behavior, that the grotesque can serve the purposes of a more exact moral and psychological realism in art. By abjuring moral judgment and exaggerating rather than resolving contradictions in human experience, the writer, according to McCullers, could reveal the hidden abnormalities in "normal" life. Russian writers had been doing this for some time, and as she noted, it was a technique prevalent in the best of recent Southern literature, especially in the fiction of William Faulkner:

> The technique briefly is this: a bold and outwardly callous juxtaposition of the tragic with the humourous, the immense with the trivial, the sacred with the bawdy, the whole soul of man with a materialistic detail.

It is, as I suggested before, a technique that predominates throughout *The Ballad of the Sad Café,* not only in the obvious area of characterization and plot, an amazon falling in love with a dwarf, but in the homely and shocking details that contribute so much to the tragic, comic, haunting tone of the book. One thinks of Miss Amelia's pathetic, almost freakish, white face appearing in the upstairs window of the café "with two gray crossed eyes which are turned inward so sharply that they seem to be exchanging with each other one long and secret gaze of grief," of Marvin Macy carrying round with him "the dried and salted ear of a man he had killed in a razor fight," of Cousin Lymon riding through the swamp on Miss Amelia's broad back holding to her ears for balance, and of those nights when the café was lively with jokes and gossip while outside "in the darkness a woman sang in a high wild voice and the tune had no start and no finish and was made up of only three notes which went on and on and on."

Persuaded by "the bold, outwardly callous, juxtaposition[s]" found in *The Ballad of the Sad Café,* critics began to reconsider all of Carson McCullers's novels, most of them concluding, in the words of the reviewer from *Com-*

monweal, that "'the gothic' label misses the point," that the grotesque and the abnormal in her fiction point not to the exceptional but the universal:

> Behind the strange and horrible in her world there are played out the most somber tragedies of the human spirit; her mutes, her hunchbacks, speak of complexities and frustrations which are so native to man that they can only be recognized, perhaps in the shock which comes from seeing them dressed in the robes of the grotesque. They pass us on the street everyday, but we only notice them when they drag a foot as they go by [William P. Clancy, *Commonweal* (15 June 1951)].

V. S. Pritchett said much the same thing as this *Commonweal* reviewer when in *The New Statesman* he praised Carson McCullers for "a courageous imagination . . . bold enough to consider the terrible in human nature without loss of nerve, calm dignity or love [*The New Statesman* (2 August 1952)]. The source of this courage and love, which sought no reconciliation between the comic and the tragic, the beautiful and the horrible, is not, however, to be found in any sophisticated theories about human behavior, but rather in what Carson McCullers herself has called (again in "The Russian Realists and Southern Literature") an almost naive acceptance of the facts of life, a humility before experience, a refusal to judge. Perhaps she stated it most succinctly in *The Ballad of the Sad Café* when she wrote:

> Well, all this happened a long time ago, and it is the story of Miss Amelia's marriage. The town laughed a long time over this grotesque affair. But though the outward facts of this love are indeed sad and ridiculous, it must be remembered that the real story was that which took place in the soul of the lover himself. So who but God can be the final judge of this or any other love?

Richard Gray (essay date 1977)

SOURCE: "Moods and Absences," in *Carson McCullers,* Chelsea House Publishers 1986, pp. 77-85.

[*In the following essay, originally published in 1977, Gray argues that the sense of isolation that permeates McCullers's fiction—which he claims has often been commented upon but never satisfactorily accounted for—is attributable to her having produced most of her fiction in a transitory period between the "renaissance" in Southern fiction and its "new wave," as well as to specifics of her childhood. He further states that* The Ballad of the Sad Café *exemplifies the ways in which McCullers created a new kind of fiction, one cut off from recognizable tradition, out of what was familiar to her.*]

There is a peculiar quality of isolation about Carson McCullers's work, frequently remarked upon but never properly explained, that owes some of its intensity perhaps to her own status vis-à-vis the South. She does not belong to the great generation of the "renaissance," that is

clear enough: indeed, she was only twelve years old when *The Sound and the Fury* was published, and her first novel, *The Heart Is a Lonely Hunter,* did not appear until after the beginning of the Second World War. But she does not really belong to the new wave of southern writers either, since apart from *Clock Without Hands*—a book dealing, among other things, with the issue of desegregation, which was not published until 1961—all of her more important fiction had been written by 1946; and was collected into a uniform edition some five years later. Her major period of creativity was very brief, consisting of about five years in all; and the last twenty or so years of her life were so marred by ill health that, in retrospect, it seems remarkable she was able to write the little, during the period, that she did. Certainly, illness offers a sufficient explanation for her gradual lapse into silence. Coming after the great fiction and poetry of the twenties and thirties, but before the more recent examples of southern Gothic (before *Wise Blood* and *Lie Down in Darkness,* for example, before even *Other Voices, Other Rooms* and *A Streetcar Named Desire*) her novels and short stories occupy, consequently, a particular transitional moment of their own in the tradition. Theirs is a special, and especially separate, place in the history of southern literature, which makes their author seem occasionally like one of her own characters—alone, cut off from all normal channels of communication, and strangely vulnerable.

Other factors, quite apart from her unusual literary situation, probably contributed to McCullers's interest in the dimensions of loneliness. Her childhood, for example, seems to have been a very quiet one. "Almost singularly lacking," as her biographer has put it, "in the excitement of external events," it reflected the particular milieu into which she was born; shabbily genteel, the Smith family of Columbus, Georgia, were inordinately embarrassed by their fallen circumstances and actively discouraged contact or intercourse with anybody from outside the home. Then, when Carson did grow up and move away (to New York and, later, to Europe) her aloof and rather prickly personality tended to complete the process thus begun. Always afraid of a full commitment to others, searching for the possibility of betrayal and claiming to find it even when it was not there, she seemed to draw a magic circle around herself for much of the time, and live in an inner world that was compounded equally of memory and imagination. "I . . . have my own reality," she said once toward the end of her life, made out "of language and voices and foliage"; and it was this reality, I believe, her ghostly, private world, that she tried to reproduce in most of her fiction. She gave it many names, over the years, and placed it consistently in the South. Southern though its geographical location might be, however, it was like no South anybody had ever seen before. It was not the South of newspaper articles and political speeches, nor the South of country humor or magnolia-blossom romance; it was not even the South described so extensively in the Yoknapatawpha novels. In effect, it was another country altogether, created out of all that the author had found haunting, soft, and lonely in her childhood surroundings—a new place offering a new perspective on the experience from which it had been drawn.

Perhaps we can gain a better idea of this new place, the unique map that McCullers offered of her home, by looking at one of her characteristic attempts at depicting it. Her novella, *The Ballad of the Sad Café*, for example, begins with this memorable description of a town without a name and, in doing so, establishes the climate, physical and emotional, in which all its characters are to move.

> The town itself is dreary; not much is there except the cotton-mill, the two-room houses where the workers live, a few peach trees, a church with two colored windows, and a miserable main street only a hundred yards long. On Saturdays the tenants from the near-by farms come in for a day of talk and trade. Otherwise the town is lonesome, sad, and like a place that is far off and estranged from all other places in the world. The nearest train stop is Society City, and the Greyhound and White Bus Lines use the Fork Falls Road which is three miles away. The winters here are short and raw, the summers white with glare and fiery hot.
>
> If you walk along the main street on an August afternoon there is nothing whatsoever to do. The largest building . . . is boarded up . . . and . . . looks completely deserted. Nevertheless, on the second floor there is one window which is not boarded; sometimes in the late afternoon . . . a hand will slowly open the shutter and a face will look down on the town . . . as likely as not there will not be another soul to be seen along the . . . street. These August afternoons—when your shift is finished there is absolutely nothing to do; you might as well walk down to the Fork Falls Road and listen to the chain gang.

I have quoted a fairly long passage from the book because, it seems to me, the effect of McCullers's prose is accumulative. She does not work in a series of detached, glittering phrases as, say, Truman Capote does. Nor does she, imitating Faulkner, write sentences that coil up snakelike and then strike, suddenly, before the period. Her language is cool and lucid, almost classical in its precision, her descriptions clipped and occasionally cryptic. A nuance in one place, a repetition or a shading somewhere else: this is all she needs really because, like the painter Edward Hopper, she tends to rely on the resonance given to a detail by its total context—and to use concealment almost as a medium of communication. The inertia, the desolation, and the brooding violence of the small-town South are caught in images that are hermetic, despite their apparent candor, and in incidents brimming with undisclosed biography.

The act is performed so quietly that it may tend to go unnoticed: what McCullers has created here, in effect, is a world where emotion and vision can coalesce—in which, through the agency of her prose, her own particular sense of life can be externalized. The town is no dream kingdom, that is clear enough. It is anchored in this world, in a firm if understated way, by such details as the references to the bus and train services and by an implicit understanding of its economic function. But it is no ordinary place, either—the kind of town we might easily come across in Georgia, in the South, or anywhere else. Why? Because, quite apart from establishing this anchorage, the

writer has used every means at her disposal to reorder, rearrange, and so metamorphose; in a way that must be familiar to us by now, she has created another country out of her own known home. In this respect, the anonymity of the prose ties in with the evasiveness of the narrator, the hermeticism of the imagery with the apparent emptiness of the scene. For together they direct our attention to precisely the same subject; a feeling of "lonesomeness" or loss seems to result from them all. This feeling, needless to say, is not imposed on the material: as other writers like Thomas Wolfe could testify, it is there in the Deep South already, waiting to be acknowledged. McCullers has, however, emphasized it almost to the exclusion of everything else and, in doing so, cleverly established a nexus, a point of connection between the geometry of her self and the geography of her childhood surroundings. Gently, she has nudged the regional landscape into the expression of a fresh mood.

McCullers's aims are, of course, not just personal. Quite apart from externalizing her own state she is trying also, through the medium of the South, to anatomize human nature, to chart, in her plan of her region, the coordinates of all our lives. And in order to make this clear she will occasionally punctuate her narrative with little explanatory passages, like the following, which suggest that, remembering her own doubts about the possibility of proper contact between man and man—and, perhaps, experiencing some misgivings about her oblique methods elsewhere—the author is afraid the reader will otherwise miss the point.

> There are the lover and the beloved, but these two come from different countries. Often the beloved is only a stimulus for all the stored-up love which has lain quiet within the lover for a long time hitherto. And somehow every lover knows this. He feels in his soul that his love is a solitary thing. He comes to know a new, strange loneliness. . . . So there is only one thing for the lover to do. He must house his love within himself . . . ; he must create for himself a whole new inward world—a world intense and strange, complete in itself.

The longing to communicate and the difficulty of ever properly communicating, the delusions attendant upon the human need to love: the themes could hardly be presented more explicitly than they are here (indeed, the existence of a triangular relationship between personal feeling, regional landscape, and moral reference is virtually insisted upon) and this does, naturally, tend to carry its own dangers with it. The "message" may, as a result, seem a little too pat to be convincing, too limited and limiting even for the purpose of fable. The writer may, in short, end up with didacticism of the crudest possible kind. McCullers is saved from such dangers most of the time, I think, though; and what saves her more than anything else is her constant awareness of the *human* situation—the specifically emotional and imaginative terms into which her ideas have to be translated. Her landscapes, for all their initial sparseness, *are* inhabited. More to the point, the figures inhabiting them possess a special kind of resonance, that sense of roots and a definite history which marks them out as the descendants of recognizable southern types. They have the substance and immediate credibility of people long brooded over, and so well understood—and to this is added that freshness, the sense of surprise and valuable discovery, which can only come when someone as well known as this is seen from a radically altered standpoint. We may suspect, while we read a McCullers story, that we have seen characters like hers before; in fact, if we have read much earlier southern fiction we are sure we have. But until now, she makes us feel, we have never been properly acquainted with them: there is something about them, some crucial side of them we have somehow managed to miss.

The major characters in *The Ballad of the Sad Café* offer a perfect illustration of this, the way in which the familiar is suddenly turned into the strange and new. And the nature of their *familiarity,* at least, is suggested by a bare summary of the *Ballad*'s plot, which is like something borrowed from the comic legends of the old Southwest. There is a kind of crazy, comic logic of frustration behind everything that happens: the beloved is always turning away from the lover to create a false idol of his or her own. So "Miss Amelia" Evans, the central character and the owner of the "terrible, dim" face which appears in the opening portrait of the town, refuses the love of her husband, Marvin Macy, and, having done so, falls in love with a newcomer to the district, the hunchback "Cousin" Lymon. Cousin Lymon, in turn, despises Miss Amelia and worships Marvin Macy—who despises *him.* Nobody gets what he wants in the story. Everybody is thwarted and, in the process, made to look utterly grotesque. This, for example, is how Miss Amelia is described before the charade has properly begun:

> She was a dark, tall woman with bones and muscles like a man. Her hair was cut short and brushed back from the forehead, and there was about her sunburned face a tense, haggard quality. She might have been a handsome woman if, even then, she was not slightly cross-eyed.

By reducing her appearance to a series of conflicting angles, by emphasizing her physical defects and her masculinity (or, rather, her sexual ambivalence), McCullers effectively transforms Miss Amelia into a freak here as much of a caricature in her own way as Sut Lovingood is, say, or any of the subhumans populating *Tobacco Road.* At least one of the strategies for presenting the character to us, in other words, seems to have been learned from Longstreet, Harris, and their imitators: we are distanced from Miss Amelia, made to inspect her and her country home with a clinical detachment, and then invited to consider her frustrations, such as they are—her utter failure to realize her ambitions in her given world—as at the very least potentially comic. As if to confirm McCullers's debt, there is even an epic fight at the end of the *Ballad,* between Miss Amelia and Marvin Macy, which in its combination of the macabre and the grotesque (Macy greases himself, for instance, so that he can keep slipping through Miss Amelia's fingers) must remind us of those almost operatic trials of strength which enliven so many of the tales of the southwestern school.

That is not the whole story, though. If it were, we could hardly talk about McCullers making her characters new. Miss Amelia is a grotesque, perhaps, but she is a grotesque for the same reason that most of McCullers's subjects are—because, as the author herself once put it, her "physical incapacity" is being used primarily as "a symbol of [her] spiritual incapacity . . . —[her] spiritual isolation." She is not just the comic loser, nor is she economically deprived in the way that Jeeter Lester and Ty Ty Walden are. She is, to use that word again, "lonesome," and her lonesomeness is intended eventually to figure our own. Like an image seen in a carnival mirror, she is meant to offer us an exaggerated, comically distorted, and yet somehow sadly accurate reflection of ourselves. Exactly what this means, in terms of the total effect she has upon us, will perhaps become clear if we look at the way she is described toward the end of the story, when both Marvin Macy and Cousin Lymon have deserted her.

> Miss Amelia let her hair grow ragged, and it was turning grey. Her face lengthened, and the great muscles of her body shrank until she was thin as old maids are thin when they go crazy. And those grey eyes—slowly day by day they were more crossed, . . . as though they sought each other out to exchange a little glance of grief and lonely recognition.

This, surely, is to give the familiar caricature a fresh dimension. The details of Miss Amelia's appearance are just as grotesque as they ever were, but they appear to be placed now in a changed, and more sympathetic, context. We are drawn to the woman even while she still seems a little odd to us. The knowledge we have of her by this time has, of course, something to do with this development: we understand why she is odd and, understanding, we perhaps suspect that her oddity touches upon ours. And certain fragments of descriptive detail, which hint at pity as much as ridicule, are possibly relevant as well— the comparison with "crazy" old maids, for example, or the partly funny, partly moving account that McCullers now gives us of Miss Amelia's crossed eyes. But of immeasurably more significance than either of these things, I think, is something almost indefinable—which, for want of a better phrase, we must call the sheer texture of her prose. It goes back, in fact, to what I was saying earlier about McCullers's style, that it manages to be lyrical and colloquial, lucid and enigmatic, at one and the same time. For it is as a direct consequence of this strange combination, really, that we find ourselves held back from Miss Amelia here—and brought close up into a special kind of intimacy with her as well. She is distanced from us by a certain lingering freakishness of expression, a mysterious image, it may be, or a quirky turn of phrase; and yet she is also brought into an immediate contact with us by our sense that this is, after all, a conventional idiom we are listening to—that the language Miss Amelia inhabits, so to speak, belongs to normal, everyday conversation. This is an extraordinarily subtle relationship to set up between character and reader far subtler than anything we are likely to come across elsewhere, in the work of other writers who have experimented with the southern comic mode. It has its origins, of course, in McCullers's belief that a paradox lurks at the heart of experience, naturally attaching itself to the idea of a *shared* isolation. As for its issue, that we find in the mood or *ambiance* to which our minds first return when recalling a McCullers novel—our memories of a quiet, but peculiarly inclusive, pathos.

Pathos; it is an unfashionable term partly because, through bad use, it has acquired an odor of sentimentality—become associated with what Ezra Pound once called that most inhumane of emotions, an indiscriminate sympathy. The unlucky man wallowing in his own bad luck, the account of poverty or suffering that begins and ends in moral posturing, without any reference being made to the possible agencies of change: these are the sort of things to which we tend to apply the word "pathetic" now. Nor are matters helped much, I suppose, by the memories most of us have of films that have been described as pathetic—where, more often than not, a patently contrived series of events is used as a pretext for self-indulgence. Pathos, in such cases, becomes the emotional equivalent of beating one's head against the wall—an exquisitely painful way of preparing for the moment when the pain stops, and the release offered by the inevitable happy ending arrives. Still, there is no reason why misuse of a word should blind us to its proper uses; and I would like to suggest that McCullers's fiction, at its best (by which I mean **The Ballad of the Sad Café,** *The Member of the Wedding,* and parts of *The Heart is a Lonely Hunter*), can supply us with a valuable corrective to all this. For it shows, I think, how tough and really critical an emotion pathos can be. Her characters are pathetic, but they are pathetic in the finest sense—in the same way that, to continue an earlier analogy, a good Chaplin film is. That is to say, the melancholy we experience while contemplating Miss Amelia Evans or Frankie Addams in *The Member of the Wedding* stems principally from the shock of recognition, our feeling that part of our own lives has been accurately defined. It encourages us not to escape from problems, still less to accept them, but simply to become more aware—to understand, fully to understand, their general scope. In this way the pathetic is used as an agent of moral instruction more than anything else, a means of telling us, quietly and sadly, what we are and the most we can do and of advising us, by inference, as to how we should behave.

McCullers's is, then, the definitive use of a specific emotional effect—a pathos that at once lends a strange atmosphere to landscape and character, and helps establish an intimate, unusually searching relationship between tale and reader. This is an impressive achievement—showing the kind of subtlety and even deviousness of intent we are perhaps more inclined to associate with more "difficult" fiction—and its very impressiveness has, I believe, led one or two of McCullers's critics into overestimating her. For there is a tendency, noticeable especially among those with a bias toward the New Criticism, to assume that because her work represents a perfect adaptation of means to ends she is, therefore, more or less unsurpassed among writers of her own region. So Walter Allen, in his standard history of the modern English and American novel,

places her second only to Faulkner; and Gore Vidal, going one characteristic step further than this, insists, "of all our southern writers Carson McCullers is the one most likely to endure." Such commentary, I think, is exaggerated and unhelpful: the very perfection of McCullers's work depends, after all, upon her own levelheaded acceptance of her limitations. She knows that she can describe, quite subtly, one particular dilemma or area of life and she concentrates almost her entire resources on that. There is no place in her fiction, really, for the rich "overplus" of experience—by which I mean any aspects of behavior that cannot be included under the heading of theme, or any dimensions of feeling that cannot be reconciled with the major effect of pathos. And recognizing this she demonstrates little interest in such matters as the historical and social context, and no commitment either to the idea of a developing consciousness. Her people walk around and around within the circle of their own personalities, their inner world of thought and desire hardly engaging with the outer world at all. They seldom change, except physically, they never reflect more than one aspect of our experience (admittedly, it is a significant one); and to inflate them, their world, or indeed their creator to a major status—to suppose, in fact, that McCullers's novels and short stories are any more important to the tradition than they genuinely are—is, I believe, to be guilty of what used to be called "overkill." It is, in other words, to smother a quiet but effective talent by heaping upon it unearned and patently unacceptable praise.

As for McCullers's actual achievement, though, setting aside all such exaggeration, that surely is certain and secure. She is not a major writer, despite anything that Allen, Vidal, or any other critic may say to the contrary. But she is a very good minor one—so good, indeed, that she seems to reap a definite advantage from her minor status and turn her limitations into virtues. The absence of the historical dimension is a useful illustration of this. With many other writers, and especially southern ones, such an absence might prove fatal—indeed it *has* proved fatal, I think, in the case of Tennessee Williams and the earlier Capote. With McCullers, however, just the opposite is true; and this because in some strange way she manages to make history function as an *absent presence* in her work. It seems to be not so much omitted from her writing as concealed, made to disappear, and in such a way that the disappearance itself, like the disappearance of the religious perspective from later Victorian fiction, encourages our active comment. McCullers's characters, we infer, have not even this, the mere possibility of a tradition, to sustain them; they can only hang as Lowell's Czar Lepke does, "oas[es] in . . . [the] air/of lost connections"—so disoriented as to have no point of reference really, no common denominator with which to chart their disorientation. They may suffer pangs of nostalgia; in fact most of them do, it is a natural consequence of their loneliness. But that nostalgia is for a condition they can hardly define. They may be adrift, homesick; but that homesickness is for a place that has never, personally, been theirs. Just as space seems to recede from them even while it is being described, to try to hide from them in a way, so time in its larger dimension appears somehow to mock them by remaining hidden; the vacuum its departure creates is, we sense, *there* as a positive force in the narrative contributing to their despair. One sometimes wonders if, in all this, McCullers is not trying to add her own idiosyncratic footnote to Nietzsche by suggesting that not only God, that traditional comforter of the lonely and spiritually disfigured, is dead now—history, as a common secular resource and the modern substitute for God, is as well.

Margaret B. McDowell   (essay date 1980)

SOURCE: *"The Ballad of the Sad Café,"* in *Carson McCullers,* Twayne Publishers, 1980, pp. 65-79.

[*In the following excerpt, McDowell provides an overview of* The Ballad of the Sad Café, *addressing topics such as the novella's combination of comic and tragic elements, the relation between the story and McCullers's personal life, and its mythical, Gothic, and ballad-like features.*]

In *The Ballad of the Sad Café* McCullers achieved an intricate blending of the real and the mythic, of the comic and the desolate, and of the provincial and the universal. She attained in this short novel an extraordinary compression, control, objectivity, and sense of proportion. The narrative voice speaks at times in archaic diction and at times in a tone of leisured elegance; at still other times, in a pithy colloquial idiom. Though the three principal characters are grotesques, rather than fully-developed human beings and the villagers are not individualized, the "balladeer's" compassion for them pervades this book, as does his quiet humor when he pauses in the narrative to comment upon their inexplicable, eccentric, and often perverse behavior.

I. A Turbulent Relationship

Kay Boyle declared *The Ballad of the Sad Café* a work in which an author "accepted the responsibility of being artisan as well as sensitive artist" ["I Wish I Had Written *The Ballad of the Sad Café*," *I Wish I Had Written That,* edited by Eugene J. Woods, 1946]. As in *Reflections in a Golden Eye,* McCullers attains in this novel an allegorical or "fairy-tale" exaggeration in her characters. Their freakishness, Boyle suggests, moves them beyond the range of ordinary human experience. Nevertheless, the thematic content of *The Ballad of the Sad Café* is not so remote as Boyle intimates from McCullers' personal life, her search for self-identification, and her exploration of unusual sexual experience. In creating intricate emotional diversities as characteristic of the life of Miss Amelia Evans, McCullers reflects, to a degree, the turbulence of her own life at the time she wrote this work, a turbulence emerging from the compounding of deep conflicts and complex relationships—the love and hate she felt for Reeves, whom she was divorcing; the strong, but frustrated, love she felt for her new friend Annemarie Clarac-Schwarzenbach; and the bewildering, but warm, affection she was discovering for David Diamond, who

was attracted both to her and to Reeves. In *The Ballad of the Sad Café* McCullers assimilated all of these confused loves and disappointments when she conceived and almost completed the tale in the summer of 1941 at Yaddo and announced to Diamond that she would dedicate it to him.

The fact that *Reflections in a Golden Eye* was dedicated to Annemarie Clarac-Schwarzenbach in the summer of 1940 and *The Ballad of the Sad Café* to David Diamond the following summer suggests how fully McCullers had by this time confronted her bisexuality and that of her husband, who was during these months living with Diamond in New York. In this novel McCullers explores such themes as sexual ambivalence, destructive infatuation, the pain of being rejected by the beloved, the problematical configur-ations implied in any love triangle, and the paradoxical closeness of love and hate.

McCullers, hoping to return with renewed creativity to the uncompleted *The Bride* (later *The Member of the Wedding*), expected, for a time, to publish both of these short works in the same volume. However, the subtle balance of mood, theme, and image she sought in the story of Frankie Adams' adolescence continued to evade her until 1945. In the meantime, she published *The Ballad of the Sad Café* in *Harper's Bazaar,* August 1943.

> In *The Ballad of the Sad Cafe* McCullers explores such themes as sexual ambivalence, destructive infatuation, the pain of being rejected by the beloved, the problematical configurations implied in any love triangle, and the paradoxical closeness of love and hate.
>
> —Margaret B. McDowell

Though Carson McCullers ostensibly used a southern mill town as setting for *The Ballad of the Sad Café,* the locale is also an imaginatively created milieu inhabited by grotesque and improbable characters—a milieu, for example, in which a female giant, Miss Amelia Evans, possesses, in the eyes of the villagers, awesome powers. As the tale opens and as it closes, life in the village is so static that "the soul rots with boredom," but for a short time between the opening of the story and its final sequence, the town becomes a place where strange and unbelievable events occur and where the three principal participants exist in some indefinable state between the human and the supernatural.

McCullers exhibits in this novel many of the properties of the ballad. Its plot is direct and swift; the action is familiar, rooted in folk tradition; and the language, stylized and intense, derives a quality of artifice from McCullers' studied use of archaic words and phrases. The narrator presents himself as a balladeer with much starkness of vision, an individual who establishes a desolate beginning and end for his tale, before he expands upon the intervening action, which he summarizes quickly in his opening words:

> The owner of the place was Miss Amelia Evans. But the person most responsible for the success and gaiety of the place was a hunchback called Cousin Lymon. One other person had a part in the story of this cafe—he was the former husband of Miss Amelia, a terrible character who returned to the town after a long term in the penitentiary, caused ruin, and then went on his way again. The cafe has long since been closed, but it is still remembered.

Although he is responsible for the lively atmosphere in the cafe and provides his townsmen with food, drink, and fellowship, Lymon accentuates the sinister, as well as the comic, tone of the novel. One evening at dusk this dwarf hunchback trudges into the town and identifies himself as Miss Amelia's cousin. The villagers sitting on Miss Amelia's steps find him repulsive: "His hands were like dirty sparrow claws." (McCullers, in fact, uses bird imagery throughout the novel to describe Lymon.) Because Miss Amelia thought that she had no relatives—a situation which sets her apart from other people—she is filled with wonder by the dwarf's insistent claim of kinship. She offers him a drink from the bottle in her overalls pocket "to liven his gizzard" (she owns the best still in the whole region), and she receives the weeping little man into her house.

Miss Amelia is a sorceress of reputation and establishes by her acts and attributes the ineffable atmosphere and eerie tone of the novel. She heals the diseases of the townfolk with her magical potions, and she regulates important events in their lives by telling them, for example, when the weather or the moon will be right for planting crops or for slaughtering hogs. Whenever her hated ex-husband, Marvin Macy, or her beloved dwarfed companion, Cousin Lymon, challenges her power and omniscience, the townspeople grow fearful and surly. While they respect her, they reveal curiosity and excitement about her, rather than deep concern. In their lack of affection, they become a vaguely malevolent force and, as it were, a sinister chorus to comment on the action. Consequently, when the townspeople do not see Lymon for the next three days, they assume that Amelia has murdered him. A self-appointed contingent arrives to investigate, and at this dramatic moment, Lymon makes a grand entrance from the top of the staircase, dressed in Amelia's fancy green shawl, which trails to the floor. He carries what the townsmen, astonished, recognize as the snuff box Amelia treasures because it belonged to her father. Lymon has filled it with cocoa and sugar, which he uses throughout the novel to sweeten his mouthful of decayed teeth.

McCullers' juxtaposition of past and present is notable. The narrator, soon after the opening sequence, moves back in time to reveal Amelia as she was at twenty, ten years before, when her father was still alive and cherished her. He had protected her, talked philosophically to her, and ridiculously nicknamed her "Little"; she slept calmly ev-

ery night, as if covered with "warm axle grease." The narrator then dwells upon Amelia's present wealth, her ability to brew a liquor with magical properties, and her knowledge of folk medicine. Handsome enough to attract men, she is dark, tall, and muscular. She is a personage to be respected, not to be loved or pitied. Her chief recreation—bringing a lawsuit whenever she has a gambler's hunch that she may win it—suggests her selfishness and her shrewd eye for business.

A solitary individual, Amelia lacks any genuine basis for communication with either men or women. She has never cared for men, nor does she in this tale ever have a conversation with a woman; in fact, this book contains little direct conversation, the narrator more often summarizing the action. Amelia will not treat "female complaints," and blushes whenever talk of them arises. She also wears men's overalls. Though she denies her own femininity, she expresses maternal concern for children and is infinitely gentle in her treatment of them, making sure they are thoroughly anesthetized by drinking enough of her best liquor before she performs any painful operation.

Amelia's unconsummated marriage to Marvin Macy suggests that her denial of feminine identity may prevent her response to physical love from any man. In a large family of unwanted and abused children, Marvin Macy grew up with a stone in place of a heart, and as a young man he violated virgins throughout the land. Inexplicably, he falls in love with Amelia, reforms, and becomes suddenly humble. To the further astonishment of the townspeople, Amelia, soon after the death of her father, agrees to marry Macy. Awkward and uncomfortable in her wedding dress, Amelia amuses the guests as she reaches for the pockets of her overalls to rest her hands in them. In the days after the wedding, the mood of the villagers shifts dramatically from surprise and amusement to shock when they recognize that Amelia denies Macy access to her bedroom, abuses her lovesick groom, and finally orders him off her property.

If Amelia gains some sympathy at the beginning and the end of the book, at the point of her marriage she is almost monstrous, the female who preys upon the male whom she has lured to her abode. Though the townspeople react with disbelief to her humiliation of Macy, they also derive perverse pleasure from the fact that "someone has been thoroughly done in by some scandalous and terrible means." They are tainted by the evil that Amelia herself seems to have let loose in the community.

Vengeance pervades the latter part of the tale when Macy returns to inflict vengeance upon the woman who has betrayed his love. In building toward the physical struggle between Amelia and Macy, which provides the climax for the book, the narrator slows the pace. About six years altogether pass between Lymon's appearance in town and his departure. Lymon immediately falls in love with Amelia's ex-husband and, because Macy does not accept this love, Lymon sits mourning on the porch rail, "like a bird on a telephone wire." Amelia must bury her pride and give Macy the best room in her house, to prevent Lymon's leaving with him. She concludes: "It is better to take in your mortal enemy than face the terror of living alone."

Tension builds from August to Ground Hog Day, when the great confrontation takes place between Macy and Amelia, a struggle with overtones of the Grendel-Beowulf encounter. The townspeople are "recklessly glad" as they anticipate the battle between Amelia and Macy, a struggle of interminable length because of the mythical strength possessed by each antagonist. Only the intercession of the demonic Lymon, a still more powerfully mythical figure, finally defeats Amelia in the agonizingly protracted wrestling contest. A creature who vaguely possesses the characteristics of a pet, as well as human (or subhuman) attributes, Lymon now, like a hawk propelling himself through the air, leaps on Amelia's back, digs his birdlike claws into her shoulders, and helps to overcome her. Victorious after battle, Macy and Lymon steal Amelia's treasures and pillage her home and her still. Amelia waits three lonely years for Lymon to return at dusk before she boards up forever the windows of her dilapidated building. As at the beginning of the novel, the men of the prison chain gang can be heard singing as they work on the highway—twelve people who have escaped the solitary existence—but who are together only because they are in chains. Spontaneous and lasting fellowship is an impossibility in this novel. The forced and uneasy fellowship in the cafe, like the harmony and solidarity of the chain gang, lacks genuineness.

The novel is remarkable for its sweep over wide reaches of time while it also achieves much compression and concentration. Four years elapse between Part I, when Lymon arrives, and Part II when he and Amelia are seen operating the cafe and talking in the long evenings together. Two years elapse between Part II and Part III, when trouble settles in upon Amelia as Lymon falls in love with her enemy.

II. Gothic, Mythical, and Ballad Aspects of the Novel

McCullers claimed that in *The Ballad of the Sad Café* she tried to illustrate the superiority of Agapé (communal affection) over Eros (passionate love). Actually, the novel demonstrates the destructive nature of Eros in the lives of the three main characters, Miss Amelia Evans, Cousin Lymon, and Marvin Macy. McCullers' suggestion of Agapé is at best minimal, and appears only in the brief and uncertain pleasure the villagers enjoy at the cafe. Even more elusive than the fickle Eros, Agapé provides a joy to be savored in passing, rather than a durable influence through which one might shape a lifetime. The townspeople develop no continuing sense of community but remain easily frightened and suspicious of Amelia and Cousin Lymon. They rise to no significant realization of Agapé, even if the tenuous fellowship they find at the cafe provides a few moments of satisfaction in the meaningless repetition of their days. But perhaps Agapé does win out by implication, for it is surely superior to the destructiveness of Eros as it is dramatized in this book.

In demonstrating the destructive nature of Eros in the lives of Amelia, Macy, and Lymon, McCullers implies that any three-sided love affair, particularly a bisexual one, can be expected to fail, and, beyond this, most love affairs between two people will not endure.

McCullers' theme of the isolated individual seeking escape from loneliness through love, which had inspired *The Heart Is a Lonely Hunter,* became exceedingly complex by the time she wrote this third novel. In her first novel, she had presented loneliness as an affliction of the solitary "hunter," who may possibly be cured by love and certainly can be cured by nothing else. But she indicated even in that novel, through the other characters' attraction to Singer, that love is often mere narcissism and that any individual craves response from an admiring lover primarily to reinforce his or her self-esteem. Such characters want not so much to love as to be loved. Only Antonapoulos eludes Singer's love, and ironically only he is beloved by Singer. In McCullers' second novel, *Reflections in a Golden Eye,* lust rather than love dominates the vortex of sadism, masochism, self-pity, and violence so dramatically presented. In *The Ballad of the Sad Café* she again addressed the dominant theme of her first novel: the ambiguity in love. The beloved resents and fears the lover, though he also needs him and craves his presence. Love, because it reveals one's inmost identity, causes the lover and the beloved to be psychologically vulnerable to each other and even more accessible to betrayal by any third person who may gain access to their private world. In a forthright passage, the narrator acknowledges the inescapable power of such paradoxical attraction and repulsion: "There are the lover and the beloved, but these two come from different countries. . . . The beloved fears and hates the lover, and with the best of reasons. For the lover is forever trying to strip bare his beloved."

Thus love becomes in this novel a force which drives the lover into deeper isolation by driving him in on himself. Love is the dreadful result of an individual's isolation and its intensifier, rather than its cure. Eros, if frustrated, leads to hatred and destruction; Agapé is an ideal, an inspiriting influence seldom to be attained as a pure and lasting force, though it alone can give order and meaning to our chaotic lives.

Because it embodies qualities of the gothic as McCullers defined them in "The Russian Realists and Southern Literature," *The Ballad of the Sad Café,* like *Reflections in a Golden Eye,* is interesting to consider as evidence that she herself turned rapidly toward the gothic mode after she wrote this essay. The kind of novel written in this mode, she continued, is antithetical to the meticulous and reportorial depiction of character and milieu which she found, perhaps mistakenly, typical of most contemporary Southern fiction. In her view, it was imprecise and simplistic to apply the term "gothic" to such complex works as William Faulkner's *As I Lay Dying* largely on the basis of their combination of beauty and the sinister and their juxtaposition of the comic and the tragic, although Faulk-ner's works contain elements of the gothic as she defined them and as she began to use them in her own work.

In her presentation of situation and characters in *The Ballad of the Sad Café* McCullers herself dramatically blends realistic detail with romantic and supernatural elements. Like gothic novelists, as she defined them, she herself attains striking effects of ambivalence in her work through presenting Amelia's tragic betrayal by Lymon within a comic frame and through the use of everyday phrases, perhaps more typical of the comic mode, to convey the despair reflected in the latter part of the book.

Gothic fiction writers in England at the close of the eighteenth century maintained that fear distorts the perceptions of the psyche and that a phenomenon ordinarily discerned by the rational mind as trivial can become, under stress, momentarily overpowering both for the character and the reader. These early gothic authors often deliberately chose medieval settings, because they could thus embed their credulous characters in an age and milieu wherein unquestioning belief in miracles, visions, necromancy, and dreams was common. Such a world predisposes the characters to be sensitive to extrasensory perceptions and to see the normal as through a distorting lens. Frequently, these individuals confuse the probable with the improbable.

In *Reflections in a Golden Eye* McCullers localized the action by limiting it to a military base, in order to suggest the presence of a closed society. The characters are further enclosed by their lack of emotional and intellectual development. They are limited by their intense obsessions or "simple-mindedness." Their personal limitations and their narrowed environment predispose them to irrational fear when they are under pressure. Thus, even in writing *Reflections in a Golden Eye,* McCullers showed her understanding that fundamental to the gothic mode of fiction is the creation of psychic stress in the characters that will distort their perceptions and also will, in turn, communicate intimations of a psychic realm that transcends the ordinary.

By the time she produced *The Ballad of the Sad Café,* she thoroughly understood the "gothic" principle that irrational impulses of all sorts distort an individual's perception of reality. The result is that in extreme circumstances the character will find a trivial or harmless phenomenon overpowering. In both *Reflections in a Golden Eye* and *The Ballad of the Sad Café,* McCullers renders states of inner turmoil in terms of outward stress or in terms of the terrifying, the macabre, or the bizarre. Another aspect of traditional gothic fiction that now appealed to McCullers was the dramatization of forces of evil at large in the universe, beyond the control and understanding of the characters. Evil in both McCullers' second and third books appears as an unmotivated, irrational, or inexplicable phenomenon. She appreciated, furthermore, the power of such forces and probed their psychological effects on the individual more fully than did earlier romantic novelists exploring this mode. Her characters react irrationally in their frustrations or their anxiety and seem as fascinated by evil

as repelled by it. She also assumes, as did many early gothic writers, that a close relationship exists between evil and human solitude or loneliness.

Although in McCullers' first novel Singer cannot survive his anguish, she emphasized the optimism of Mick Kelly and Portia Copeland in the face of suffering. In *Reflections in a Golden Eye* and in *The Ballad of the Sad Café* she recognized more decisively that irrationality and evil lie as close to the heart of human experience as do the hunger for love and its possible redemptive influence. Whoever acknowledges that the cosmos is malign (or even sees that it is indifferent to the individual human being) may learn to laugh at it, she felt, may also learn to accept the fact that life is strange, uncomfortable, and never fully meaningful in human and rational terms, and may further realize that effort and inertia are equally powerless to change the universe.

In *The Ballad of the Sad Café,* as in her first novel, the principal character remains a lonely hunter after a brief period of love expended upon an unlovable and unresponsive person. Pity for others and the desire to achieve a meaningful communion with them is absent, moreover, as the isolation in the lives of Amelia, Macy, and Lymon intensifies. In *The Ballad of the Sad Café* isolation, fear, and guilt also return to the lives of the townspeople after the struggle between Amelia and Macy leaves her defeated.

Even though McCullers in *The Ballad of the Sad Café* projects her characters more decidedly into a fantastic milieu than she did in *Reflections in a Golden Eye,* paradoxically the figures in *The Ballad of the Sad Café* emerge as more individualized figures and as people more often worthy of sympathy than those presented in the earlier book. In addition to being grotesques or eccentrics, Amelia, Lymon, and Macy sometimes reach universal and archetypal dimensions, as they reflect certain complexities in human relationships and the strong individual's insight into his or her own situation.

All the characters illustrate these challenging complexities. The giantlike Amelia, foolishly but lovingly nicknamed "Little" by her father, is, as an adult, afraid to assume her full sexual identity and remains his little child. Lymon, the hunchbacked dwarf, openly weeps for himself, longs for a male lover, and finds pleasure in inciting trouble among other individuals, but he also has a shrewd sense of the realities that encompass him. Of all the characters, Lymon's behavior is the least predictable; his motivation, the most paradoxical and ironic. He is both more and less than a man, neither adult nor child, neither sparrow and hawk nor quite human. Injured irreparably as a small child by poverty and by his parents' mistreatment, Macy, in his turn, regresses to rebellion, self-destruction, and vengefulness when he encounters rejection in his marriage; but he also elicits sympathy as a victim of forces which are too powerful for him to control. His behavior, likewise, is at times far from the ordinary, since he exists with only a stone where his heart had been; he cannot react in the usual human mode when his emotions are involved.

Amelia is also an unusual and complicated individual. In spite of the comic means used by McCullers to characterize her, she becomes a figure capable of deep and poignant suffering. She is the one who symbolizes most forcibly the inevitable isolation experienced by most persons—an isolation which may be the result of their self-centered behavior. She has been set apart at the beginning by the townspeople as a woman with special understandings and powers, and at the end she is isolated as one who, through a series of peculiar incidents and relationships, has been overcome by incomprehensible forces of evil.

Like the anonymous townspeople, the three chief characters, in spite of their legendary powers, are intense, irrational, superstitious, and naive. Amelia hides her uncertainty behind her shrewd business activity and her ability to take risks in her law suits, but even she is fearful of what she perceives as supernatural messages manifested in natural events or objects. The townspeople are childlike, simplistic, easily frightened by events or objects which they do not understand but also easily delighted by small pleasures, like the bright decorations in the cafe. Such lack of sophistication makes McCullers' presentation of them as superstitious and suspicious all the more credible. They are bound by long traditions of folk-knowledge, some of which are terrifying, some of which are amusing, and some of which provide colorful language and imagery for McCullers' tale.

The cafe becomes a joyous place where poor people, trapped in monotonous work in the textile mill, can see themselves as individuals of some worth; but this sense of worth grows in them only through the potency of Miss Amelia's liquor, which provides warmth and which also has the magical power to heal, to kill pain, and even to produce sexual potency. Amelia herself does not seem to know the exact significance of the acorn that she picked up the afternoon her father died when Cousin Lymon questions her about it, but the narrator hints that perhaps it symbolizes masculinity, her father's love, or his death. Likewise, the significance of the kidney stone removed from Amelia's body assumes special awesomeness for her, perhaps because it caused her the greatest pain she experienced before the agony of Lymon's desertion. Throughout the book, the villagers perceive various phenomena as mysterious portents. For example, the snowfall which bewilders Amelia, as well as the townsfolk, freezes her spirit into silence so that her speech sounds muffled—her aborted speech reflects her benumbed inner being. The snowfall is surely an omen, but one she cannot interpret to her satisfaction.

Most dramatic in its resemblance to folk legends which glorify the heroic is the climactic fight between Amelia and Macy, which achieves dimensions far beyond the natural and the ordinary. Bird imagery presages this struggle: "A hawk with a bloody breast flew over the town and circled twice around the property of Miss Amelia." The conquest occurs on Ground Hog Day, a day of portent. Lymon early that morning takes a solitary journey into the swampland to see whether the animal sees his shadow, much as a character in mythology might sojourn into the netherworld to gain knowledge about his own fate and destiny. Because the weather is "neither rainy nor sunny but with a neutral temperature," the groundhog casts an indeterminate image and so foreshadows the long impasse of the wrestling match. The deliberate, ceremonial decorum of the antagonists lends solemnity to the event: "They walked toward each other with no haste, their fists already gripped, and their eyes like the eyes of dreamers." At one point, the narrator turns from the deadlocked belligerents to describe imperturbably the other spectators. When he finally returns to the match, he soberly exaggerates the length of time in which the struggle has hung in balance: "Perhaps it was half an hour before the course of the fight shifted. Hundreds of blows had been exchanged, and there was still a deadlock." Little dramatic action occurs in the book except for this great event of extraordinary violence. Anticipation, memory, and long anxiety are far more important in creating intensity and ominousness than the incidents themselves.

As later in *The Member of the Wedding,* the frequent, unexplained, and incantatory repetition of the numbers *three* and *seven* suggests magical or religious ritual. The numbers appear in many connections. For three days and three nights after Lymon's arrival, the townspeople do not see him. Repeatedly, the narrator claims three good persons live in town, but their identity remains secret, as does that of the three persons who are said to come from Society City to see the fight. After her dramatic fight, Amelia knocks her fist on her desk three times and then begins to sob. Three years she waits for Lymon to return before boarding up her house. Her medicines may be efficacious because the number *seven* appears in the directions: seven swallows of water for hiccups, seven runs around the millpond for crick in the neck, and seven doses of Amelia's Miracle Mover for curing worms. Macy's cruelty derives from his upbringing as one of seven unwanted children. Seven times Amelia invites Lymon to go with her to Cheehaw, on the fateful day that he stays home alone, meets Macy, and falls in love with him. The townfolk know intuitively that the climactic and brutal struggle which forces Amelia to acknowledge Macy's mastery will take place at 7:00 that evening.

The attribution of magical properties to certain numbers occurs in folklore of many cultures. This ritualistic use of numbers suggests a universal significance to this tale that extends it far beyond the life of one woman in an obscure village. The narrator's archaic formality also hints at a wider significance in the story he tells.

The novel contains relatively little dialogue. Hence, the narrator's voice becomes particularly important in establishing shifts in tone or mood. His acknowledgment of the efficacy of incantatory rhythms in the repetition of certain numbers reflects his willingness to share the superstitions of the naive villagers. He thus gives credence to the villagers' beliefs, and he himself seems to believe in the gossip that they pass about, exaggerated and malicious as it may be. The narrator shifts unpredictably from using the voice of a laborer at the mill, talking after work with an audience of other bored mill hands, to using the voice of a mystical balladeer who speaks in a poetic, archaic, and stylized pattern. The balladeer's omniscience and his primitive sensibility seem inconsistent with the colloquial voice of the millworker, though they both ultimately reveal a folk origin. As poetic singer, he remarks, for instance, that Macy upon his return from prison "caused ruin." But the colloquial idiom, comic in its emphasis, dominates most of the narrative passages. The humor in them gains much of its ludicrous effect from a colorful vocabulary, a curious phrasing, or a use of surprising illustrations. In his simple and direct sentences, the narrator, on the other hand, often eloquently expresses his philosophy as oracular wisdom. He moves in a moment from the comic to the profound.

The contrast between the comic idiom and the poetic expression in the narrative voice may be illustrated in the descriptions of Amelia's wonderful brew. When her liquor is not available, the narrator complains sadly that all other whiskey in the region is of such poor quality that "those who drink it grow warts on their liver the size of goobers." In contrast to such colloquial comic imagery, the narrator elsewhere describes Amelia's liquor in highly poetic context. For instance, it can make the spinner or weaver, whose sensitivity is long dulled by monotonous work, take a marsh lily in the palm of his hand and discover in it a significance that warms his soul. As an invisible message written in lemon juice becomes visible when held under the warmth of a lamp, so the mysteries of the universe, the narrator asserts, can be seen through the magical warmth of Amelia's brew. Her liquor opens astonishing worlds to the townspeople. Beyond "the loom, the dinner pail, the bed and then the loom again," a man can "see for the first time the cold, weird radiance of a midnight January sky, and a deep fright at his own smallness stops his heart."

In addition to the narrator's continual shifting between the colloquial and the formal or poetic, his style is characterized throughout the book by an extensive use of lists, as if his credibility could best be increased by piling up factual details. After the climactic fight, for example, the narrator takes time to itemize the damage done to Amelia's property by Lymon and Macy. Whenever a meal is eaten, the narrator lists the menu, which includes the regional favorites: "fried chicken . . . mashed rootabeggars, collard greens, and hot pale golden sweet potatoes." He lists the names of all the eight men who call on Amelia early in the story to investigate the rumor that she has murdered Lymon, although we hear of none of them elsewhere in the tale. (Some of the details in these lists may be humorously irrelevant to the rest of the items in the series, a comic device used by McCullers in *Reflections in a Golden Eye*.)

The explicitness by which the narrator establishes Amelia's milieu helps him gain credence for Amelia as an inhabitor of that milieu and as an extraordinary personage. Though the exact sources of her remarkable power remain mysterious, that power is so carefully demonstrated and her fabulous reputation is so convincingly documented that one cannot question the validity of her leg-

endary accomplishments. The narrator always presents her behavior, her feelings, her thoughts, her appearance, and her words concretely rather than in the abstract. For instance, instead of remarking that Amelia was energetic and extremely busy in the autumn before Macy's return, the narrator recites a long series of her activities, comic in its specificity and variety:

> She made a new and bigger condenser for her still, and in one week ran off enough liquor to souse the whole country. Her old mule was dizzy from grinding so much sorghum, and she scalded her Mason jars and put away pear preserves. . . . She had traded for three tremendous hogs, and intended to make much barbecue, chitterlins, and sausage. . . . One day she sat down to her typewriter and wrote a story—a story in which there were foreigners, trap doors, and millions of dollars.

Such a passage, with its celebration of a woman possessing remarkable vitality and zest, renders more poignant the effect of both the first and the last pages of this work, wherein the languor of life in the late summer afternoon town dominates. The narrator closes the tale, as he began it, by commenting quietly upon the twelve men on the chain gang, who represent, in part, the dull existence and the tragic boredom that ordinarily prevail in this town. As they sing, they leave behind them, for the moment, their misery. They begin to work in the early dawn. The ordinary daily routine of hard work and a suggestion of the eerie in their music—sounds which seem to emanate from both earth and air—contrast strangely, as do the black sky and the streaks of the golden sunrise and the skin of the black men and white. Disaster in their lives and peacefulness in their monotonous activity find expression in this "music intricately blended, both somber and joyful."

Even more a prisoner now than these men, Amelia exists as an idle and remote presence behind the shutters of the dilapidated house on the now deserted street. At the close, she thus becomes more abstract, a mythic figure representing the deep, chronic isolation which McCullers saw at the center of human life. Her face, dimly peering out from the darkness, is "sexless" because loneliness surrounds men and women alike. Because the most isolated people may become almost invisible, her face is like "the terrible dim faces" one sees only in dreams.

Barbara C. Gannon (essay date 1982)

SOURCE: "McCullers' *Ballad of the Sad Café*," in *The Explicator*, Vol. 41, No. 1, Fall, 1982, pp. 59-60.

[*In the following essay, Gannon argues that the final paragraph in* The Ballad of the Sad Café—*in which the chain gang from the beginning of the novella reappears— "recounts, in the manner of an envoy, the whole ballad."*]

Carson McCullers' *Ballad of the Sad Café* is bracketed with the observation that the town is dreary. The narrator suggests in the introduction and again in the closing lines that one listen to the chain gang, presumably for diversion. But in the introduction the gang's appearance is a promise; in the final paragraph the gang actually recounts, in the manner of an envoy, the whole ballad. The envoy sketches successive concepts of an empty or fallow time, a time of incipience, increase, crest, and a relapse and return to greater emptiness. The overall concept of the ballad and of the envoy is cyclical; the beginning and ending of both are congruent.

The ballad opens in uneventful monotony. There is no way even to guess what effect any change would have. The envoy's counterpoint is morning at the work station, with no oral evidence of the men—only the sound of their tools. In the ballad, the distant appearance one evening of the small figure of the hunchback is echoed by the envoy's solitary, inquiring voice which begins to sing. There are no words in the music of the singer. The melody is an inarticulate sound, a herald rather than a message and as unclear of portent as the arrival of Lymon Willis.

Elements of the plot move along: incipience and increase follow quickly, and the crest is prolonged. Cousin Lymon establishes himself and reigns. Miss Amelia mellows toward her neighbors and caters to her strange kin in every way. The cafe brightens the life of the whole town, strengthening the residents against the drudgery of life and a sense of personal insignificance. In the envoy this aspect is repeated by the high point at which the whole group of prisoners is singing a swelling and intricate blend of music that dilates the heart and mightily affects those who hear it.

The ballad slips abruptly from the point of crest with news of Marvin Macy's release from prison, and then his sudden appearance. With Miss Amelia's disastrous attempt to regain what is slipping away from her, all traces of the good times are destroyed. She is decisively and foully beaten, and sprawls on the floor of the cafe. She drags herself to her office and sobs with grating, winded breath. Her numbness turns to pain and all the rest is anticlimactic. The envoy notes that "the music will sink down . . . at last there remains one lonely voice, then a great hoarse breath, . . . silence." The very means that Miss Amelia thinks will solve her problems brings about her desolation. She and the whole town are worse off than before the arrival of Lymon.

The envoy encapsulates the *Ballad of the Sad Café*. At the outset of the former, there is the "sound of the picks striking into the clay earth." The singers then sing, reach a climax, and relapse into silence. Their brief song is an expressed communing and an aspiring and temporarily successful effort. But when it ends, the void and the sense of loss are a keener pain. The presence of the singers is known again only by the "sound of the picks in the silence." Earlier they had nothing to miss, but now a greater misery settles upon them than was theirs prior to the song. This is the compounded situation of Miss Amelia as her loneliness of loss is underlined by the images of the "hand [that] will slowly open the shutter," and the "face [that] will look down on the town."

Louise Westling (essay date 1982)

SOURCE: "Carson McCullers' Amazon Nightmare," in *Modern Fiction Studies,* Vol. 28, No. 3, Autumn, 1982, pp. 465-73.

[*In the following essay, Westling argues that while many feminist critics have demonstrated an interest in androgynous characters, the nature of McCullers's Miss Amelia has not been adequately examined. She argues that this character's "freakishness" represents an ambivalence McCullers's part toward female identity.*]

Miss Amelia Evans is a monstrous creature, really, and yet Carson McCullers lavished admiring care in picturing her many talents, her forbidding strength, and her control of the squalid village world of *The Ballad of the Sad Café* (1943). Despite a good bit of critical attention to the novella and recent feminist interest in androgynous characters in literature, Miss Amelia's freakishness has not been seriously examined. It is crucial to the meaning of this grotesque fable, relating it closely to *The Heart Is a Lonely Hunter* and *The Member of the Wedding.* McCullers [in *The Mortgaged Heart*] said that "Love, and especially love of a person who is incapable of returning or receiving it, is at the heart of my selection of grotesque figures to write about—people whose physical incapacity is a symbol of their spiritual incapacity to love or receive lov— their spiritual isolation." But Miss Amelia's peculiarities are more specific than mere "spiritual incapacity"; they reflect McCullers' ambivalence about female identity. Miss Amelia is a grown-up tomboy whose physical proportions symbolize her exaggerated masculine self-image.

Louis Rubin is perceptive in suggesting that McCullers destroys Mick Kelley and Frankie Addams as characters when she tries to force them beyond the pain of adolescent sexual awakening into an acceptance of womanhood [see Rubin, "Carson McCullers: The Aesthetic of Pain," *Virginia Quarterly Review,* 53 (1977)]. She cannot really imagine such acceptance because she never found it herself. Friends often commented on her childlike manner, and her adult photos present images of the same kind of fierce boyishness she described in both Mick and Frankie. Virginia Spencer Carr's biography amply documents the sexual ambivalence revealed most explicitly in McCullers' declaration to Nelson Algren, "I was born a man" [Carr, *The Lonely Hunter,* 1976]. It is this identification with the masculine that stimulates her imagination to explore the dangerous psychological territory of *The Ballad of the Sad Café.*

One critic calls McCullers' flat, childlike narrative tone "a kind of buffer to fend off what would otherwise be unbearable" [Robert Rechnitz, "The Failure of Love: The Grotesque in Two Novels by Carson McCullers," *Georgia Review,* 22 (1968)], but I would instead describe it as a strategy for placing the action at a safe enough remove from ordinary life to allow forbidden impulses free scope— at least for awhile. The form of *The Ballad of the Sad Café* allows McCullers to indulge the impulse to appropriate male power and thus escape the culturally inferior role of woman. There can be no other explanation for Miss Amelia's strapping physique, her skill at masculine trades, or her rejection of everything female, most apparent in her indignant refusal to play the physical part of a woman in her ten-day marriage to Marvin Macy. Her later relationship with Cousin Lymon is never threatening because he is not a real man who sees her as female. Behind the dream of independence represented by Miss Amelia's "masculinity," however, lies the fear of male vengeance which triumphs in the story's conclusion, as Marvin Macy and Cousin Lymon join forces to destroy the usurper. The formerly invincible Amazon is left shrunken and imprisoned in the slowly collapsing shell of her once prosperous cafe.

The folk tale atmosphere of *The Ballad of the Sad Café* may owe something to Isak Dinesen's *Seven Gothic Tales* (1934), whose strange ambience Carson McCullers never ceased to praise after a first reading in 1938. Dinesen's work remained very close to her, and it is quite understandable that three years later, while she struggled to resolve Frankie Addams' anxiety about growing too tall, she might have remembered Dinesen's portrait of six-foot Athena Hopballehus in "The Monkey." Probably this process was not conscious; her imagination simply revived the motif of the Amazon in order to explore for herself some of the problems of sexual identity and female independence which Dinesen treats in her exotic fable. Robert S. Phillips [in "Dinesen's 'Monkey' and McCullers's 'Ballad,'" *Studies in Short Fiction* 1 (1963-1964)] was the first to comment on the similarities between *The Ballad of the Sad Café* and "The Monkey," but I think he overstates their extent. The only clear parallels are the motifs of the Amazon and her bitter hand-to-hand combat with a hated male suitor. These motifs are developed in very different ways by the two writers, and the stories move through entirely different atmospheres to almost opposite conclusions about the sources of female autonomy. Because McCullers' novella is a kind of challenge to the arguments implied by Dinesen's story, it is useful to remind ourselves of the significance of the Amazon maiden in "The Monkey."

The fairy tale world of "The Monkey" is centered in the female dominion of Cloister Seven, a wealthy retreat for unmarried ladies and widows of noble birth. It is ruled by a virgin Prioress with mysterious powers who resembles a sybil, the Chinese goddess Kuan-Yin, and the Wendish goddess of love. To all of the Cloister's inhabitants it is "a fundamental article of faith that woman's loveliness and charm, which they themselves represented in their own sphere and according to their gifts, must constitute the highest inspiration and prize of life."

Athena Hopballehus embodies this ideal femininity in heroic form. She is a motherless only child who has been raised by her father in a nearby castle, surrounded by "an atmosphere of incense burnt to woman's loveliness." The father admits, however, that "she has been to me *both* son and daughter, and I have in my mind seen her wearing the old coats of armor of Hopballehus" (my italics). The problem implied in this reference to androgynous childhood

training is never explored in the story, but perhaps it is meant to suggest an excess of independence. At eighteen, Athena is six feet tall, powerful and broad-shouldered, with flaming red hair and the eyes of a young lioness or eagle. Athena is what her name suggests, a human type of the warrior goddess, whom Dinesen also associates with the virgin huntress Diana and "a giant's daughter who unwittingly breaks men when she plays with them." When a proposal of marriage is made by a handsome young cavalry officer named Boris, the Prioress' nephew and Athena's childhood playmate, Athena's fierce autonomy sparks an indignant refusal.

Although forceful womanhood dominates the world of "The Monkey," the story's central problem is not Athena's fate but rather the decadent weakness of the Prioress' nephew Boris. This overcultivated young man is the central consciousness of the narrative, and the plot follows his reluctant entrance into normal manhood through the manipulations of his aunt. The old ladies of Cloister Seven, having heard rumors of Boris' implication in a homosexual scandal, give him an ambiguous welcome when he arrives from the capital city. They think of him as "a young priest of black magic, still within hope of conversion." A sort of conversion is indeed accomplished by the end of the story, but only because the Prioress uses deception and magic to force the resisting bride and groom together. Threatening Boris by revealing her knowledge of the scandal, she induces him to drink a love potion and to force himself upon Athena. The maiden responds with her fist and knocks out two of his teeth. Dinesen tells us that all the young women Boris had previously rejected "would have felt the pride of their sex satisfied in the contemplation of his mortal pursuit of this maiden who now strove less to escape than to kill him." A fierce battle ensues, and she is about to dispatch him with a death grip on his throat when he transforms the nature of the conflict by forcing his mouth against hers. Instantly her whole body registers the terrible effect of his kiss. "As if he had run a rapier straight through her, the blood sank from her face, her body stiffened in his arms," her strength dissolved away, and she collapsed. Both Boris' and Athena's faces express "a deadly disgust" with the kiss.

In her ability to overcome even this revulsion, the Prioress emerges as the very incarnation of the Wendish goddess of love, half-monkey and half-human. Because Boris and Athena witness the Prioress' grotesque exchange of shapes with her monkey on the morning after the seduction attempt, they are united as initiates to the mystery of her power. They submit to her insistence that the sexes cannot remain separate; Boris must pay homage to female power, and the proud young Athena must renounce her heroic virginity in an alliance with him.

No union of male and female, however reluctant, occurs in *The Ballad of the Sad Café*. In contrast to Athena's essentially female power, Miss Amelia's remarkable strength depends on her masculinity in a world devoid of feminine qualities. All the characters who have speaking parts are males, except for Miss Amelia, who never betrays even a hint of conventionally feminine behavior.

Like Dinesen's Athena, Miss Amelia is a motherless only child raised by an adoring father, but McCullers gives her Amazon a more exaggerated physique and a mysterious authority. At the height of her adult pride, Miss Amelia is the central personality of her town. An imposing figure, she is "a dark, tall woman with bones and muscles like a man," hairy thighs, and short-cropped hair brushed back from her forehead like Mick Kelley's and Frankie Addams'. In the building she inherited from her father, she operates a profitable general store which gradually becomes the town's only cafe. She produces the best liquor in the county from her secret still in a nearby swamp; sells chitterlins, sausage, and golden sorghum molasses; owns farms in the vicinity; and is adept at all manual skills, such as carpentry, masonry, and butchery. The most impressive of all her powers, however, and the one that with the magical properties of her whiskey best reveals her nearly supernatural dimensions, is her ability to heal the sick. Like a sorceress or witch, she brews her own secret remedies from roots and herbs. "In the face of the most dangerous and extraordinary treatment she did not hesitate, and no disease was so terrible but what she would undertake to cure it."

There is one notable exception to Miss Amelia's healing powers:

> If a patient came with a female complaint she could do nothing. Indeed at the mere mention of the words her face would slowly darken with shame, and she would stand there craning her neck against the collar of her shirt, or rubbing her swamp boots together, for all the world like a great, shamed, dumb-tongued child.

Her embarrassed confusion is a natural consequence of her total identification with masculinity and her childlike sexual innocence. Even in adulthood, Miss Amelia preserves the tomboy attitudes we encounter in Mick Kelley and Frankie Addams. For all of these characters, the first physical encounters with men are unpleasant surprises. We remember Mick's distaste for her one experience of lovemaking with Harry Minowitz and Frankie's terrified escape from the soldier who tried to seduce her. For both Mick and Frankie, sexual experience brought the necessary renunciation of childhood boyish freedom and a reluctant accept-ance of adult femininity. But Miss Amelia refuses to accept the diminished status of woman. When she rather absentmindedly marries Marvin Macy, the whole town is relieved, expecting marriage to soften her character and physique "and to change her at last into a calculable woman." Instead, after the bridegroom follows her upstairs to bed on their wedding night, Miss Amelia stamps downstairs in a rage, wearing breeches and a khaki jacket. Until dawn she reads the Farmer's Almanac, smokes her father's pipe, and practices on her new typewriter. During the ensuing ten days of the abortive marriage, she sleeps downstairs and continues to ignore her husband unless he comes within striking range, when she socks him with her fist. Macy disappears from town in disgrace, leaving Amelia victorious in her Amazon virginity.

For ten uneventful years Miss Amelia goes about her solitary life, aloof, stingy, maintaining her strange control of the town. Then one night the little hunchbacked Cousin Lymon mysteriously appears on her doorstep, wins her heart, and causes momentous changes both in her life and in the life of the town for six years before the sinister return of Marvin Macy. The question is why Miss Amelia should have rejected a vigorous normal man, only to fall in love with a twisted midget. Joseph Millichap sees traditional folk tale elements in the characters of Marvin Macy and Cousin Lymon: Macy is a sort of demon lover, and Cousin Lymon is reminiscent of the figures of mysterious stranger and elf. But Millichap comes closer to answering our question when he says that Cousin Lymon "is a man loved without sex, a child acquired without pain, and a companion which her [Amelia's] limited personality finds more acceptable than a husband or a child" ["Carson McCullers's Literary Ballad," *Georgia Review*, 27 (1973)]. Marvin Macy had been sufficiently ennobled by his love for Miss Amelia so that he might have been a tolerable mate for her, but, by accepting her feminine part in the marriage, Amelia would have had to renounce the masculine sources of her strength. Such a capitulation to the female mysteries that she has avoided all her life would be unthinkable. Her enraged reaction to Macy's forlorn attempts at lovemaking clearly expresses the insult they represent to her pride. Cousin Lymon, on the other hand, represents no threat to her power. He is a sickly, deformed mannikin whom she could crush with one blow of her first, and, from all we can see, he makes no sexual demands. His warped, childlike form clearly indicates his masculine impotence, just as Amelia's grotesquely masculine appearance expresses her inability to function as a woman. With Lymon she feels safe in revealing affection, for she can baby and pet him without any threat of sexuality.

At the heart of Miss Amelia's relationship with Cousin Lymon, there is actually an inversion of traditional roles of male and female. Miss Amelia is physically dominant and provides a living for the household as a husband would. Cousin Lymon is the pampered mate who struts about in finery, is finicky about food and accommodations, and gads about town socializing and gossiping. He functions as a hostess would in the cafe, while Miss Amelia stands aloof and silent in the background. In their intimate conversations before the parlor fire, Miss Amelia sits with her "long legs stretched out before the hearth" contemplating philosophical problems and reminiscing about her father, while Cousin Lymon sits wrapped in a blanket or green shawl on a low chair and chatters endlessly about petty details.

Despite his physical weakness and his vanity, Cousin Lymon seems to embody the spirit of spring and renewal. He has drifted mysteriously into town in April, in a year when the crops promise well and conditions at the local mill are relatively prosperous. Once accepted as Miss Amelia's intimate, he becomes a catalyst for the release of her genial impulses. Her devotion to him brightens her face and gradually engenders a hospitality she had never expressed before. Before the hunchback's arrival, she sold her moonshine by the bottle, handing it out through her back door in the dark. Never was anyone allowed to open or to drink this liquor inside the building. But once Cousin Lymon is installed in her house, she begins selling it inside, providing glasses and plates of crackers for consumption on the premises. Gradually the store is transformed into a cafe with tables where Miss Amelia sells liquor by the drink and serves fried catfish suppers for fifteen cents a plate. Miss Amelia grows more sociable and less inclined to cheat her business associates. Even her special powers for healing and for brewing her marvelous liquor are enhanced. All these positive developments of her character expand themselves in the communal warmth which her cafe comes to provide for the town.

Though Cousin Lymon brings fruitful changes in the lives of Miss Amelia and her town, his own physical state suggests a fatal limitation to prosperity. He remains "weakly and deformed" despite Amelia's pampering and the exercise of her fullest healing abilities. He is also personally malicious, even though he has generally served as an agent for gaiety and warmth. Thus he is naturally drawn to the cruel strength of Marvin Macy, a force which complements his own unpleasant traits. When Macy suddenly returns to town from years in the state penitentiary, Cousin Lymon is immediately infatuated.

Macy embodies all the qualities of "normal" masculinity, but McCullers has cast them in an evil, destructive light throughout the story. Macy may be tall, brawny, and good-looking, but he is also violent and viciously lustful. He is the devil male who mutilates animals for fun and has ruined the tenderest young girls in the region. Amelia refers to Macy's cloven hoof, and the Satanic is also suggested by his red shirt and the fact that he never sweats. Throughout the story he is allied with winter. Even though he had been temporarily reformed by his love for Miss Amelia, their wedding took place on a winter day rather than in the traditionally propitious season of spring or of summer. His revengeful return to town sixteen years later comes in autumn and brings sinister portents of unseasonable weather, ruining the normally festive ritual of hogbutchering: "there was everywhere the smell of slowly spoiling meat, and an atmosphere of dreary waste." Macy lays claim to the unprecedented snowfall in January that gives the town "a drawn, bleak look." The climactic battle between Miss Amelia and Marvin Macy occurs exactly one month later, on ground-hog day. Its issue is foreordained by Cousin Lymon's report that the groundhog has seen its shadow and, therefore, that more winter lies ahead.

Understanding at once that Macy's return to town is a challenge, Miss Amelia begins preparations for a fight, taunting Macy by wearing her red dress as a flagrant reminder of his failure to make her act the part of a woman during their marriage. While she wears the dress, she pokes her biceps constantly, practices lifting heavy objects, and works out with a punching bag in her yard. In the climactic battle between the two antagonists, the question to be decided is not, as in Dinesen, whether a powerful young woman can be subdued so that a union of the sexes can occur. For McCullers, the contest will decide whether a woman can deny her sex and dominate men with a strength analogous to their own.

> Now the test had come, and in these moments of terrible effort, it was Miss Amelia who was the stronger. Marvin Macy was greased and slippery, tricky to grasp, but she was stronger. Gradually she bent him over backward, and inch by inch she forced him to the floor. . . . At last she had him down, and straddled; her strong big hands were on his throat.

Suddenly, at this moment of Miss Amelia's triumph, Cousin Lymon leaps across the room from his perch on the bar to aid his adored male friend. He lands on Amelia's back and changes the balance of force to Macy's advantage. Miss Amelia is destroyed.

The sexual dynamics of *The Ballad of the Sad Café* are an inversion of traditional heterosexual patterns. Contrasts with Dinesen's "The Monkey" help reveal the masculine sources of Miss Amelia's autonomous strength and point up McCullers' complete rejection of heterosexual union. Rather than accepting her femininity by consummating her marriage to the aggressively masculine Marvin Macy, Miss Amelia focuses her affections on the little hunchback who seems to function simultaneously as child, pet, and rather feminine companion. But Cousin Lymon is much less devoted to Miss Amelia than she is to him, and this gives him an emotional advantage over her which proves ultimately disastrous. It seems inevitable that the foppish dwarf should fall helplessly in love with Marvin Macy, thus completing the destructive triangular relationship which McCullers used to develop her theory that "almost everyone wants to be the lover" and that "in a deep secret way, the state of being loved is intolerable to many." But this theory and McCullers' statement that *Ballad* was intended to show the inferiority of passionate individual love to *agape* [see *The Mortgaged Heart*] fail to account for the individual peculiarities of her characters and for the sexual dimensions of their problems in love. The real force of *The Ballad of the Sad Café* lies in its depiction of a masculine Amazon whose transgression of conventional sexual boundaries brings catastrophic male retribution. Unlike Dinesen, who portrayed an uneasy compromise between proud female autonomy and reluctant masculine homage, McCullers sought to deny the feminine entirely and to allow a woman to function successfully as a man. She could not sustain her vision because she knew it was impossible. I believe that the consequences of her experiment in this novella play a part in determining the final form of *The Member of the Wedding*, which, as I have argued elsewhere ["Carson McCullers's Tomboys," *Southern Humanities Review* 14 (1980)], inexorably moves Frankie toward an acceptance of conventional femininity. After writing *The Ballad of the Sad Café* in only a few months, when McCullers returned to her six-year struggle with the materials of *The Member of the Wedding*, she knew that Frankie would have to submit as Miss Amelia had not.

Mary Ann Dazey (essay date 1985)

SOURCE: "Two Voices of the Single Narrator in *The Ballad of the Sad Café*," in *The Southern Literary Journal*, Vol. XVII, No. 2, Spring, 1985, pp. 33-40.

[*In the following essay, Dazey argues that the narrator of* The Ballad of the Sad Café *has two distinct voices: one that interprets the story and laments the town and the actions of the characters, and one that tells the story in a relatively objective manner.*]

When ***The Ballad of the Sad Café*** was first published in *Harper's Bazaar* in 1943, Carson McCullers was twenty-six, and at that time most critics pointed to the work as evidence of the great promise of the young writer. Today, however, it is ranked along with *The Member of the Wedding* as her most successful work. McCullers' choosing to call the sad, romantic tale a ballad has caused many to discuss her ballad style in some fashion. In his work *Carson McCullers,* Lawrence Graver, for example, concludes that ***The Ballad of the Sad Café*** is one of her most "rewarding works" in part because she employed "a relaxed colloquial style, punctuating the narrative with phrases like 'time must pass' and 'so do not forget.'" Ironically, Dayton Kohler, eighteen years earlier [in "Carson McCullers: Variations on a Theme," *College English,* 13 (1951)], had selected these identical lines as evidence of McCullers' "stylistic coyness," which he called "poetically false and out of the context with the objective drama." He further determined that the passages where the narrator stops the flow of the story to make "wise observations" indicate McCullers' own feelings that her story was "too weak to carry unsupported its burden of theme and sensibility." Both critics are reacting to what Dawson F. Gaillard determines is the changing voice of the narrator. Gaillard points out that in the first paragraph of the story, for example, the narrator's voice is "flat" and "inflectionless" and is "adjusted" to the "dreariness" of the town; then it changes and loses the flatness to become the ballad teller ["The Presence of the Narrator in Carson McCullers' *The Ballad of the Sad Café,*" *Mississippi Quarterly* 25 (1972)]. This ballad maker, Joseph R. Millichap concludes, "fixes the style of the novel." His voice permits McCullers to weave her literary ballad into a perfect blend of the "literate and colloquial" ["Carson McCullers' Literary Ballad," *Georgia Review,* 27 (1973)].

A stylistic analysis of ***The Ballad of the Sad Café*** reveals that McCullers has created a single narrator with two distinctly different voices. In the first voice the narrator places the characters and their actions in the mainstream of human existence. This voice begins, "The town itself is dreary" and ends, "Yes, the town is dreary." This voice concludes the introduction, "You might as well walk down to the Forks Falls Road and listen to the chain gang" and ends the story, "You might as well go down to the Forks Falls highway and listen to the chain gang." Not only does this voice provide the frame for the drama, but it also flows throughout the story as a second voice of the single narrator. In this voice the reader is sometimes addressed directly and even commanded to respond to the narration.

For the voice of the ballad maker, who actually tells the tale of Miss Amelia, her ten-day bridegroom, and her cousin Lymon, McCullers chooses past tense verb forms. When the first voice, the voice of the lamenter, encountered at the beginning of the novel, speaks, McCullers chooses present tense verb forms. The first shift occurs after Cousin Lymon has appeared and has been offered a drink of Miss Amelia's whiskey. The narrator explains:

> The whiskey they drank that evening (two big bottles of it) is important. Otherwise, it would be hard to account for what followed. Perhaps without it there would never have been a café. For the liquor of Miss Amelia has a special quality of its own. It is clean and sharp on the tongue, but once down a man it glows inside him for a long time afterward. And that is not all. It is known that if a message is written with lemon juice on a clean sheet of paper there will be no sign of it. But if the paper is held for a moment to the fire then the letters turn brown and the meaning becomes clear.

Next this voice draws the reader into the experience, and McCullers employs the first of eight imperatives that run throughout the first half of the novel (italics in quotations mine):

> *Imagine* that the whiskey is the fire and that the message is that which is known only in the soul of a man—then the worth of Miss Amelia's liquor can be understood. Things that have gone unnoticed, thoughts that have been harbored far back in the dark mind are suddenly recognized and comprehended.

The second of the eight imperatives occurs after the regular group of townsmen has been named and described. The ballad maker says, "Each of them worked in the mill, and lived with others in a two- or three-room house for which the rent was ten dollars or twelve dollars a month. All had been paid that afternoon, for it was Saturday." And the lamenting voice adds, "So, for the present, *think* of them as a whole."

In the third imperative, the narrator becomes a camera which provides a long shot of Miss Amelia and Cousin Lymon as the two establish a pattern of behavior over the years:

> So for the moment *regard* these years from random and disjointed views. *See* the hunchback marching in Miss Amelia's footsteps when on a red winter morning they set out for the pinewoods to hunt. *See* them working on her properties—with Cousin Lymon standing by and doing absolutely nothing, but quick to point out any laziness among the hands. On autumn afternoons they sat on the back steps chopping sugar cane. The glaring summer days they spent back in the swamp where the water cypress is a deep black green, where beneath the tangled swamp trees there is a drowsy gloom. When the path leads through a bog or a stretch of blackened water *see* Miss Amelia bend

down to let Cousin Lymon scramble on her back—and *see* her wading forward with the hunchback settled on her shoulders, clinging to her ears or to her broad forehead.

. . . . .

For the hunchback was sickly at night and dreaded to lie looking into the dark. He had a deep fear of death. And Miss Amelia would not leave him by himself to suffer with this fright. It may even be reasoned that the growth of the café came about mainly on this account; it was a thing that brought him through the night. So *compose* from such flashes an image of these years as a whole. And for a moment *let* it rest.

The next imperative instructs the reader in his understanding of Miss Amelia's peculiar behavior and prepares him for the story of Marvin Macy and Miss Amelia's ten-day marriage: "*Remember* that it all happened long ago, and that it was Miss Amelia's only personal contact, before the hunchback came to her, with this phenomenon—love." And at the end of the recital of events concerning the brief marriage and Marvin Macy's departure from town, this voice again addresses the reader, "So *do* not *forget* this Marvin Macy, as he is to act a terrible part in the story which is yet to come." The final instructions to the reader are delivered when Marvin Macy is about to return to town and change the lives of Miss Amelia and Cousin Lymon forever: "So *let* the slow years pass and come to a Saturday evening six years after the time when Cousin Lymon came first to the town."

That the two distinctly different narrative voices in *The Ballad of the Sad Café* are not in discord is a tribute to the author's ability to convey these voices in two recognizably different yet compatible rhetorical styles.

—Mary Ann Dazey

Constantly flowing alongside these imperatives and the lively voice of the ballad maker are the generalizations made by the lamenting voice about the specific actions of the characters. The specific action of a character is told in past tense, but the interpretation is always in the present tense. Of Cousin Lymon, the subjective narrator explains, "There is a type of person who *has* a quality about him that sets him apart from other and more ordinary human beings. Such a person *has* an instinct to establish immediate and vital contact between himself and all things in the world." And the ballad maker observes, "Certainly the hunchback *was* of this type." And after the ballad maker tells the story of the miserable lives of the Macy children, the lamenting voice explains what this background does to Henry Macy:

But the hearts of small children *are* delicate organs. A cruel beginning in this world *can twist* them into curious shapes. The heart of a hurt child *can shrink* so that forever afterward it is hard and pitted as the seed of a peach. Or again, the heart of such a child *may fester* and *swell* until it is a misery to carry within the body, easily chafed and hurt by the most ordinary things. This last *is* what happened to Henry Macy, who *is* so opposite to his brother, *is* the kindest and gentlest man in town.

Of the two voices of the narrator, the one which tells the love story, the actual narrative, is the dominant one. This voice is the objective voice of the literary ballad maker. On this level, McCullers chooses past tense verb forms, simple diction, a large percentage of simple sentences, often as short as three or four words, compound sentences with short members, and realistic dialog. The dialog is in rural Georgia dialect and comprises a very small percentage of the total narrative, actually less than one hundred and fifty lines. Like Eudora Welty, McCullers relies entirely on syntax and local idiom to convey the speech patterns of these rural milltown people. She does not employ distortion of spelling to convey variances in pronunciation. Although the narrator implies that long hours of the long, hot summers and dreary winters were spent in telling tall tales, little actual evidence of any prolonged conversation exists in the novel. Only once is there a sustained conversation between Miss Amelia and Cousin Lymon:

"Amelia, what does it signify?" Cousin Lymon asked her. "Why, it's just an acorn," she answered. "Just an acorn I picked up on the afternoon Big Papa died."

"How do you mean?" Cousin Lymon insisted.

"I mean it's just an acorn I spied on the ground that day. I picked it up and put it in my pocket. But I don't know why."

"What a peculiar reason to keep it," Cousin Lymon said.

In an apparent imitation of the poetic ballad, McCullers constructs paragraphs which are rather uniform in length, about one hundred and fifty words each. Many of these paragraphs begin with very short simple sentences in subject-verb order:

The place was not always a cage.

Dark came on.

And Miss Amelia married him.

They were wrong.

The hunchback chattered on.

Henry Macy was still silent.

The hunchback was impatient.

The autumn was a happy time.

No one answered.

Miss Amelia made no protest.

The snow did not last.

So things went on like this.

The rest is confusion.

Additionally in the literary ballad form McCullers employs alliteration, repetition, and poetic imagery. Running throughout the narrative are repeated references to Miss Amelia's "ten-day marriage," "the loom-fixer," "the August white heat," "the peach trees," "the golden dust." She paints her background canvas with color imagery:

The *red* winter sun was setting, and to the west the sky was deep *gold* and *crimson*.

The next morning was serene, with a sunrise of warm *purple* mixed with *rose*. In the fields around the town the furrows were newly plowed, and very early the tenants were at work setting out the young, deep *green* tobacco plants. The wild crows flew down close to the fields, making swift *blue* shadows on the earth. In the town the people set out early with their dinner pails, and the windows of the mill were blinding *gold* in the sun.

McCullers most frequently employs alliteration and sensory images, often combining the two:

The moon made dim, twisted shadows of the blossoming peach trees along the side of the road. In the air the odor of blossoms and *s*weet *s*pring grass mingled with the warm, *s*our *s*mell of the near-by lagoon.

The night was silent and the moon *s*till *s*hone with a *s*oft, clear light—it was getting colder.

The lamp on the table was well-trimmed, *b*urning *b*lue at the edges of the wick and *c*asting a *c*heerful light in the kitchen.

The two voices of the single narrator alternate and together weave the tale of the lover, the beloved and of love betrayed. The ballad voice tells the story, and the second voice provides the sad background music. The styles of the two voices are distinctly different in syntax also. In the ballad teller's voice, McCullers rarely employs complex sentences. When they are used, they are almost always in normal order with single right-branching clauses. The most common of these structures is the noun modifier rather than an adverbial modifier. Unlike the simple sentences which often have tricolon verb structures with the last member expanded, the complex sentences usually employ either a single verb or a compound verb. On the other hand, the lamenting voice is related in complex sentences in periodic order with multiple clauses that are

both adverbial and adjectival. These structures often employ self-embeddings along with multiple nominals and verbals.

This analysis would seem to imply that one voice is entirely separate from the other; that, however, is not the case. The transitions from one voice to the other are smooth, almost unnoticeable. One of the transitional devices that McCullers employs to move from one to the other is the question and answer. The ballad teller asks a question, and the lamenting voice answers it:

What sort of thing, then was this love?

First of all, love is a joint experience between two persons—but the fact that it is a joint experience to the two people involved. There are the lover and the beloved, but these two come from different countries. Often the beloved is only a stimulus for all the stored-up love which has lain quiet within the lover for a long time hitherto. And somehow every lover knows this. He feels in his soul that his love is a solitary thing. He comes to know a new, strange loneliness and it is this knowledge which makes him suffer. So there is only one thing for the lover to do. He must house his lover within himself as best he can; he must create for himself a whole new inward world—a world intense and strange, complete in himself.

The most frequently used device is the shift from the particular action of the mill-town group to the lamenting voice's generalization about that pattern of behavior among all people, as when McCullers moves from a description of Henry Macy as a child to her generalization about all such miserable children, or from Miss Amelia's liquor to the effects of liquor in general. This particular technique also permits transition again to the narrative in the reverse pattern of general to particular. For example, after the ballad teller has described the birth of the café, the lamenting voice comments on the general behavior of people in cafés, and the ballad teller follows this philosophical comment with the behavior of Miss Amelia's customers:

But the spirit of a café is altogether different. Even the richest, greediest old rascal will behave himself, insulting no one in a proper café. And poor people look about them gratefully and pinch up the salt in a dainty and modest manner. For the atmosphere of a proper café implies these qualities: fellowship, the satisfactions of the belly, and a certain gaiety and grace of behavior.

This had never been told to the gathering in Miss Amelia's store that night. But they knew it of themselves, although never, of course, until that time had there been a café in the town.

The third method of transition from one voice to the other employed by McCullers is the time shift from the past of the story to the present. Of course the novel begins and ends in the present in the "dreary" mill town, but constantly within the frame of this time, the reader is swept back from the lively past into the present. The reader is carefully reminded that "it all happened long ago."

After the narrator's two voices are silent, after the sad story has been told, McCullers attaches the epilogue "Twelve Mortal Men." Barbara Nauer Folk believes that this epilogue serves to remind the reader that the story is both a "literary ballad and a folk dirge ["The Sad Sweet Music of Carson McCullers," *Georgia Review* 16 (1962)]. What Folk is isolating in form as "dual-level usage of the ballad form" is stylistically the dual voices of the single narrator. The harmony of the voices of the "twelve mortal men, seven of them black and five of them white boys from this county" is precisely the kind of harmony McCullers achieves in the blending of the two voices of her single narrator. For the objective voice that relates the sequence of events of the narrative, McCullers chooses short, almost choppy sentences in normal order and casts the verbs in the past tense. For the subjective, lamenting voice, she employs long sentences with multiple embeddings, present tense verb forms, and frequent imperatives that order the reader to interpret the bare details given by the other voice. These two voices serve McCullers in the same way that various instruments within an orchestra serve the conductor. The harmony is not achieved because the various musicians are reacting to the same notes; it relies upon the instructions of that conductor. That the two distinctly different narrative voices in *The Ballad of the Sad Café* are not in discord is a tribute to the author's ability to convey these voices in two recognizably different yet compatible rhetorical styles.

Todd Stabbins (essay date 1988)

SOURCE: "McCullers' *The Ballad of the Sad Café*," in *The Explicator*, Vol. 46, No. 2, Winter, 1988, pp. 36-8.

[*In the following essay, Stebbins briefly discusses the final section of* The Ballad of the Sad Café, *arguing that this "coda" demonstrates the harmony that is possible, however temporarily, between human beings.*]

In *The Ballad of the Sad Café*, Carson McCullers shows us a carefully crafted world where people struggle to escape the isolation that oppresses each of them. *The Ballad*'s famous love passage predicts that each person will use love for another as his or her means of escape. McCullers' skillful use of settings—the town, the cafe with its upper rooms, the ventures away from the cafe—further the theme of isolation and this quest for love. Everything in *The Ballad*, save the key final scene in which McCullers offers a note of hope, centers around the cafe. As the protagonist, Miss Amelia, is finally left alone inside her inner rooms, so the cafe is left alone, slowly deteriorating. The relationships initiated by Cousin Lymon cannot last. As the love passage explains, the lover who must escape to the outer world through love does so by attempting to absorb and enclose the beloved, as Miss Amelia attempts to enclose Cousin Lymon in her inner world. This in itself is a paradox. These relationships, essentially social, are doomed. Individual relationships die, the social cafe dies, and the town pride dies. McCullers does, however, show

us in the final scene that the attempt is not a futile one. She uses the unlikely setting of the Fork Falls highway, away from the cafe, to show that escape from the solitary loneliness is possible, albeit temporary.

In this final scene, it is important to notice that while the twelve mortal men are working outside, they are nonetheless trapped in an inner world. The fact that they are chained together shows that they, too, are confined. In spite of the absence of any rooms, a cafe, or other enclosures, these men are, through no choice of their own, linked to one another. It is this social confinement that allows them to achieve some harmony in their music. Their situation reflects the life of Miss Amelia because their harmony is also temporary. The music begins with one voice, alone, as Miss Amelia was alone. That solitary voice reaches out and is joined by others, as Cousin Lymon touches Miss Amelia's life. But finally, only one voice remains, isolated before fading into silence.

> And every day there is music. One dark voice will start a phrase, half-sung, and like a question. And after a moment another voice will join in, soon the whole gang will be singing. The voices are dark in the golden glare, the music intricately blended, both somber and joyful. The music will swell until at last it seems that the sound does not come from the twelve men on the gang, but from the earth itself, or the wide sky. . . . Then slowly the music will sink down until at last there remains one lonely voice, then a great hoarse breath, the sun, the sound of the picks in the silence.

As these twelve mortal men are together, so have Miss Amelia and Cousin Lymon been together. The gang's music is temporary, as was the "music" of Miss Amelia and Cousin Lymon. The emotional description of the music points to a parallel with love. "It is music that causes the heart to broaden and the listener to grow cold with ecstasy and fright." That we are talking about love as well as music is clear. This understood, we are asked: "And what kind of gang is this that can make such music?" and the answer comes: "Just twelve mortal men who are together." But they are only together temporarily. The music sinks down to one lonely voice. As their unified music is tempor-ary this day, so the gang's days together are also short-lived. These men will serve their time and move on.

McCullers shows us that, whether we see two people like Miss Amelia and Cousin Lymon in a room trying to communicate, or we see townspeople in a cafe feeling a social sense of pride, or we see twelve mortal men chained together in the countryside, all rely on contact with another a social setting to expand outside the lonely self. At the same time, it is the nature of these social relationships that they disintegrate. Private rooms deteriorate, cafes are boarded up, friendships fade, and men move on. McCullers' careful use of setting indicates the fragility of these relationships and portends their destruction; yet, there is a real sense of hope in *The Ballad*. McCullers' message seems pessimistic because relationships die and Miss Amelia is completely isolated, but the story does not end there. The optimism, as shown clearly in the final scene, is that relationships do occur, harmony can be reached. McCullers is using the twelve mortal men to illustrate the fact that any two people, or a group of people, can make music, no matter how unlikely the match, as long as they are together: together in a private room, in a town cafe, roaming the country, or even together on the Fork Falls highway under the wide sky.

Sandra M. Gilbert and Susan Gubar (essay date 1988)

SOURCE: "Fighting for Life: The Women's Cause," in *No Man's Land: The Place of the Woman Writer in the Twentieth Century, Volume 1: The War of the Words,* Yale University Press, 1988, pp. 104-12.

[*In the following excerpt, Gilbert and Gubar argue that* The Ballad of the Sad Café *dramatizes the retribution exacted on a woman who attempts to rebel against patriarchal social conventions.*]

McCullers shows in her dreamlike mythic narrative of *The Ballad of the Sad Cafe* the culturally determined psychic logic that condemns the autonomous woman as a freak who must necessarily be sentenced to the defeat that is femininity. In fact, like her friend and contemporary Tennessee Williams, Carson McCullers seems to stand outside the constructs of gender in order to demonstrate, as Williams did in *Streetcar,* the pain of what Adrienne Rich has called "compulsory heterosexuality" ["Compulsory Heterosexuality and Lesbian Existence," *Signs* (1980)]. But even more than Williams does in *Streetcar,* McCullers focuses in "Ballad" on the terrifying revenge that the law of the phallus inflicts on those (women) who defy its imperatives. Specifically, she dramatizes the punishment meted out to a woman who has arrogantly supposed that she could live in a no man's land—first without a real man, and then with a dwarfish no-man.

At the beginning of *Ballad,* Miss Amelia Evans has the kind of physical power, intellectual authority, and personal autonomy that characterize Rebecca West's Evadne Silverton, but, unlike Evadne, she does not need men at all, even as instruments of her own pleasure. Six feet two inches tall, frequently "dressed in overalls and gumboots," the thirty-year-old Amelia Evans is "a woman with bones and muscles like a man," who has parlayed an inheritance from her father into a fortune that makes her "the richest woman for miles around," for she is the proprietor of a store and a still (where she makes "the best liquor in the county") and the possessor of "mortgages on crops and property, a sawmill [and] money in the bank." In addition, she is an extraordinarily skillful healer, a kind of self-taught general practitioner about whom McCullers observes that "no disease was so terrible but what she would undertake to cure it."

That Miss Amelia's success is associated with a culturally problematic eccentricity is shown not only by her masculine and peculiar physical appearance (besides being unusually tall and strong for a woman, she is cross-eyed, "dark and somewhat queer of face") but also by her antisocial nature (it is "only with people that Miss Amelia [is] not at ease"), by her litigiousness (only her proclivity for lawsuits keeps her from being "as rich as a congressman"), and, most important, by her one failing as a "doctor":

> If a patient came with a female complaint she could do nothing. Indeed, at the mere mention of the words her face would slowly darken with shame, and she would stand there craning her neck against the collar of her shirt, or rubbing her swamp boots together, for all the world like a great, shamed, dumb-tongued child.

Taken together, all these traits illustrate this woman's rebellious desire to rule rather than to be ruled. Alienated from the community which she in some sense governs, the indomitable Miss Amelia manipulates social law in order to transcend it, and she refuses to acknowledge the biological law that governs her own body.

Inevitably, then, when Miss Amelia marries one Marvin Macy—for reasons that remain mysterious to the townsfolk as well as to the reader but which seem to have the inexplicable force that motivates actions in fairy tales—the wedding leads to immediate disaster. During the ceremony itself, Miss Amelia rubs "the palm of her right hand down the side of her satin wedding gown" as if "reaching for the pocket of her overalls," and afterwards she hurries out of the church, "walking at least two paces ahead" of her bridegroom. But the couple's wedding night is even more catastrophic. Though the townsfolk had "counted on the marriage to tone down Miss Amelia's temper, to put a bit of bride-fat on her, and to change her at last into a calculable woman," this incalculable bride refuses to sleep with her husband, instead "stomp[ing] down the stairs in breeches and a khaki jacket" and spending the night, "feet up on the kitchen stove," smoking her father's pipe. Worse still, when the humiliated Marvin Macy—who has for love of her transformed himself from the handsome town ne'er-do-well to an exemplary suitor—seeks to placate his resistant wife with presents from "Society City," she offers them for sale in her store; when he signs "over to her the whole of his worldly goods . . . ten acres of timberland," she studies the paper "sternly" and files it away "soberly"; and when, driven to drunkenness by her recalcitrance, he approaches her humbly, she swings "once with her fist and hit[s] his face so hard that he [is] thrown back against the wall and one of his front teeth [is] broken." After ten days of marriage, she turns him off her property and, following much public suffering, he leaves town, writing her a "wild love letter" in which "were also included threats" and vows of revenge.

At this point, Miss Amelia seems invincible, not only in her battle with her groom but also in her social and sexual eccentricity. Yet, oddly enough, she can only speak of Marvin Macy "with a terrible and spiteful bitterness" that would not appear to be the natural response of the victor to the vanquished. Given Miss Amelia's fierce independence, along with her excessive hostility to Marvin Macy, it is almost predictable that, having rejected a he-man, she now embraces a no-man like Lymon Willis, the mysterious hunchbacked dwarf who claims to be her cousin. Coming out of nowhere from no one but asserting common ancestry with hers, this physically deformed and spiritually dissolute but emotionally compelling creature is destined, in his consumptive way, to consume most of Miss Amelia's worldly goods, and, significantly, he resembles not only the dwarfish "sewer rat" Loerke in Lawrence's *Women in Love* but also the spiteful cripple Doyle in Nathanael West's *Miss Lonelyhearts,* both paradigmatic no-men who represent for their authors all that is socially bankrupt in contemporary culture.

But while Lawrence and West characterize the dwarf as from first to last a decadent whose perversity signals the end of the species of man, McCullers implies that, at least in the beginning of their relationship, Miss Amelia's Cousin Lymon is an empowering figure for her. Knitting her into the community, he facilitates her creation of the cafe in which her rare liquor can teach its drinkers how to read the truths of their own souls. Offering her (or, more accurately, allowing her to offer) love and friendship, he functions as the family, and hence the identity, she lost when her "Big Papa" died; and that she gives him not only her father's snuff box but her father's (master) bedroom suggests again the dwarf's connection with her patrilineage. Tiny as a child yet charismatic as any gigolo, he seems to be her son and her lover, a link to the ancestral past who might provide her with the future she repudiated when she rejected Marvin Macy. Yet, as McCullers's text gradually and grimly reveals, Miss Amelia's Cousin Lymon is, in the deepest sense, a lie-man, a no-man whose manhood is really a lie. In fact, nebulously related to her mother (ostensibly the son of her mother's half-sister), he is not in any way associated with her patrilineage. Rather, pale and vampiric, he is in Freudian terms the (false) baby as false phallus, whose deformity and fake masculinity represent the deform-ity and fakery that (as Miss Amelia must learn) are associated with her own self-deluding male impersonation. If she wants a member instead of a wedding, she has to discover that this treacherous imposter is what she will get.

That Lymon as phallus is a lie becomes clear with the liberation of Marvin Macy from the penitentiary where, after Miss Amelia's rejection, he had been incarcerated for a number of years. Unlike George Silverton in Rebecca West's "Indissoluble Matrimony," who had been pruriently obsessed with his wife's supposed adultery and whose no-manhood had led him to the edge of madness, Lymon becomes instantly enthralled to his patroness's unknown husband, with whom he exchanges a look "like the look of two criminals who recognize each other." But once the no-man Lymon, who as the fake thing recognizes the real thing, weds himself to the he-man Marvin, Miss Amelia begins to go into a bizarre decline, a decline that presages a defeat even more radical than Evadne's victory. Relin-quishing her overalls for the red dress that she had previously reserved only for Sundays, Miss Amelia has lost her falsely instrumental Lymon Willis and is now,

therefore, will-less. Moreover, caught between two phallic beings the one exploitative, the other vengeful—she tries to please one and poison the other, but in both cases she fails: mendacious cousin Lymon becomes a mad man who is increasingly flirtatious toward Marvin Macy, while Marvin Macy becomes a bad man whose gradual usurpation of the very house and grounds she had granted to the dwarf signifies that, even if the rebellious woman desires the false phallus that she can control, the true phallus will eventually repossess her and all her worldly goods in an ultimate act of masculinist retribution. Indeed, as McCullers shows, though Miss Amelia tries to resist her "mortal enemy," "everything she trie[s] to do against Marvin Macy rebound[s] on herself."

Since the terms of the psychodrama unfolding in McCullers's sad cafe are so inexorable, Miss Amelia is doomed from the start to lose the physical battle with Macy which constitutes the novella's climax. Because she has given up her bed to Lymon (who has given up his to Marvin Macy), her only bed has been an uncomfortable sofa, and perhaps, we are told, "lack of sleep . . . clouded her wits." But in itself, as McCullers makes clear, neither sleeplessness nor the stress of having her house invaded would necessarily have been enough to guarantee Miss Amelia's defeat. "A fine fighter," this powerful woman "know[s] all manner of mean holds and squeezes," so that "the town [is] betting on" her victory, remembering "the great fight between Miss Amelia and a Forks Falls lawyer who had tried to cheat her . . . a huge strapping fellow [who] was left three quarters dead when she had finished with him. And it was not only her talent as a boxer that had impressed everyone—she could demoralize her enemy by making terrifying faces and fierce noises." In spite of Miss Amelia's unnatural strength, though, the sexual subtext represented by the grotesque triangle in which she is involved dooms her to defeat.

For, as McCullers describes it, the spectacular fight in which Marvin Macy and Miss Amelia engage before a mass of spectators in the cleared cafe at seven P.M. on Ground Hog Day is not just a jealous struggle for power over Lymon, it is the primal scene of sexual consummation which did not take place on their wedding night. Stripped for action—Miss Amelia barefoot in overalls rolled up to the knees, Marvin Macy "naked to the waist and heavily greased"—the combatants present themselves as the central figures in a bizarre but ancient ritual, "walk[ing] toward each other with no haste, their fists already gripped, and their eyes like the eyes of dreamers." But as they come together in the match, the specifically sexual nature of this ritual becomes clear, for McCullers's language, whether intentionally or not, is heavy with double entendres. At the beginning of the fight, when the strange and estranged husband and wife are said to produce "the sound of knocks, panting, and thumpings on the floor" as they are "experimenting with various positions," McCullers evokes the idiom of foreplay. Then, when Miss Amelia gets "a grasp around [Marvin Macy's] waist" and "the real fight" begins, the wrestling couple's thrashings not only recall the wrestling match between the unnaturally virile Bertha Mason Rochester and her captor husband but also plainly suggest that, besides being sexual, the battle *is* sex: "For a while the fighters grappled muscle to muscle, their hipbones braced against each other. Backward and forward, from side to side, they swayed in this way."

Unlike Rochester, however, who is so confident in his mastery that he will not "strike," he will "only wrestle," Marvin Macy appears to be on the verge of losing the fight and his manhood, for though he is "tricky to grasp," Miss Amelia is "stronger." In fact, as their bout reaches its climax, she bends "him over backward, and inch by inch she force[s] him to the floor" until she has "him down, and straddled; her strong big hands . . . on his throat." At just this moment of imminent female victory, however, the phallic retribution that must punish Miss Amelia's transgressive behavior is exacted. The hunchback, who has been watching the fight from an elevated position on the counter of the cafe, suddenly utters "a cry . . . that caused a shrill bright shiver to run down the spine" and sails "through the air as though he had grown hawk wings" to land like an incubus on Miss Amelia's back and to allow Marvin Macy to leave her "sprawled on the floor, her arms flung outward and motionless."

Why is the hunchback the agent of Miss Amelia's symbolic defloration as well as her literal defeat and thus the instrument of Marvin Macy's sexual triumph? And why is his leap into the fray accompanied by a mysterious cry? McCullers's text is so complex that we have to read it as overdetermined. From one perspective, if we take the hunchback to represent the false phallus associated with Miss Amelia's presumptuous usurpation of masculine privilege—with, that is, what Freud would call her "penis envy" and her "masculinity complex"—then his intervention in the fight signals the moment when she must be forced to confront the delusional quality of her pseudo-virility. Deformed himself, Lymon lands on her back to dramatize the way in which his physical deformity echoes her sexual deformity. In this reading, then, as Miss Amelia is made to surrender her pretensions to power, true masculinity reasserts itself with a victorious war whoop that sends a shiver down the spines of the onlookers, who realize that they are present at a solemn cultural event.

From another perspective, if we see the hunchback as representing the "little man" that is the female clitoris or, in a more generalized sense, the authentic if truncated female libido that Miss Amelia has refused to acknowledge, then the intervention of the hunchback in the fight signals the moment when she has been forced to confront her desire for Marvin Macy. Certainly from the day Macy returned to town, her behavior has notably changed: abandoning overalls for a dress, feeding Macy at her table, and finally bedding him down in her private quarters, she might almost "[seem] to have lost her will" because she is in a kind of erotic trance, and the hunchback's open flirtation with Marvin Macy might well express her own secret enthrallment. In this reading, therefore, the mysterious cry is a cry of female orgasmic surrender which sends a shiver down the spine of on-

lookers because they realize that they are voyeurs witnessing a ceremonial sexual event.

Finally, from yet a third perspective, if we define the hunchback not simply as an anatomical or allegorical aspect of Miss Amelia but rather as an autonomous male character, then his intervention in the fight signals the moment when, by eliminating Amelia as a rival, he achieves a homosexual union with the man whom he has been trying to seduce since the moment when they exchanged their first gaze of secret complicity. In this reading, then—a reading that supposes McCullers's text to be haunted by female anxiety about male social and sexual bonding—Miss Amelia is simply the medium whose house and flesh provide the opportunity for Lymon and Marvin Macy to come together, and the mysterious cry at the end of the fight expresses their homoerotic orgasm while sending a shiver down the spines of onlookers because they realize they are witnessing a perverse and subversive event. Moreover, that the two men leave town together after destroying most of Miss Amelia's property reiterates the point that she not only is no longer necessary to them but that their union requires her obliteration.

Whether one subscribes to all or none of these readings, it is clear that at the conclusion of **Ballad** Miss Amelia has been metamorphosed from a woman warrior to a helpless madwoman. Her very body has shriveled, for she is "thin as old maids are thin when they go crazy"; her eyes emphasize her isolation because they are "more crossed . . . as though they sought each other out to exchange a little glance of grief and lonely recognition"; and her voice is "broken, soft, and sad." Bereft of her once legendary physical strength, she has also lost her social, intellectual, and economic authority; her cafe is closed; her house is boarded up; and all her "wise doctoring" is over, for she tells "one-half of her patients that they [are] going to die outright, and to the remaining half she recommend[s] cures so far-fetched and agonizing that no one in his right mind would consider them for a moment." Incarcerated in a wasteland of a town where "the soul rots with boredom," she resembles not only such paradigmatic mad spinsters as Miss Havisham in Dickens's *Great Expectations* and Miss Emily in Faulkner's "A Rose for Emily" but also a female version of T. S. Eliot's wounded Fisher King.

Even the male prisoners in the novella's mysterious epilogue—a brief coda entitled "THE TWELVE MORTAL MEN"—are happier on their chain gang than is this prisoner of sex in her sad cafe, for as she sits in silence beside the one window of her house "which is not boarded" and turns toward the empty street "a face like the terrible dim faces known in dreams," their voices swell together "until at last it seems that the sound does not come from the twelve men on the gang, but from the earth itself, or the wide sky." Even in the penitentiary, McCullers implies, men are sustained by their own community while a woman like Miss Amelia—who, even at her most powerful, never had a community of women—has been inexorably condemned to the solitary confinement such a singular anomaly deserves.

Virginia Spencer Carr (essay date 1990)

SOURCE: *"The Ballad of the Sad Café,"* in *Understanding Carson McCullers,* University of South Carolina Press, 1990, pp. 53-71.

[*In the following essay, Carr introduces* The Ballad of the Sad Café, *discussing, among other things, thematic parallels between the novella and McCullers's other fiction, connections between McCullers's life and work, and the critical response to the novella.*]

The monotony and boredom that permeated [McCullers's] life with her husband in 1939 before their move from Fayetteville, North Carolina, contributed not only to the completion of *Reflections in a Golden Eye,* but also to her novella, *The Ballad of the Sad Café,* published for the first time in 1943 in a single issue of *Harper's Bazaar.* More important to the story line of the tale than McCullers's southern discomfort, however, was her predicament in New York in 1940 and 1941. She had hoped for a committed relationship with her new friend Annemarie Clarac-Schwarzenbach, having fallen deeply in love with her, but it became apparent to McCullers soon after their involvement that nothing further would develop.

To suffer in despair was her destiny as a mortal, she reasoned, turning once more to fiction to express what she saw as her truths. Although McCullers had been working for many months on a manuscript that she referred to as "The Bride and Her Brother," its design and technique had not yet revealed themselves to her (a metaphysical experience McCullers described later as "the grace of labor") ["The Flowering Dream: Notes on Writing," in *The Mortgaged Heart* (1971)]. She realized while in the nurturing environment of her native Columbus that she could put off no longer the strange tale of thwarted love that had grown out of her tangled relationships with her husband and her Swiss friend. That winter she wrote her editor (Robert Linscott) that passion and tension in her life were necessary if she were to write at all, but that she needed it in smaller doses. With her husband, there had been too much tension, and passion had been replaced by disillusionment, ennui, and disgust. But now, removed

physically from the two people with whom she had been most deeply involved, she found herself writing well once more. Her new tale was better than anything else she had done, she reported.

McCullers told a number of friends while she was at work on her "folk tale" during the summer of 1941 at Yaddo Artists Colony that she had written the "music" for it years earlier as a result of her experiences with people she loved. Her lyrics, however, were more recently inspired. In the first week of her stay at Yaddo, she became enamored of Katherine Anne Porter, a fellow guest and the reputed grande dame of the colony, a crush that added still another dimension to her tale. According to Porter, McCullers lost no time in making her infatuation known and followed her about the colony in the very manner in which the characters she was creating moon over one another in *The Ballad of the Sad Café*.

Although the pivotal character in the tale that McCullers was writing bears a resemblance to any number of individuals in her life (and even, to some extent, to the author herself), Cousin Lymon owes his creation, in part, to an actual hunchback whom McCullers saw in a Sand Street bar that she frequented in Brooklyn Heights when she lived at 7 Middagh Street, near the old Brooklyn Naval Yard. In her essay "Brooklyn Is My Neighborhood," McCullers described him as "a little hunchback who struts in proudly every evening, and is petted by everyone, given free drinks, and treated as a sort of mascot by the proprietor" [*Vogue* (March 1, 1941)]. But even more relevant to his development as a character was McCullers's wry humor and sheer delight in reading and hearing recounted tales of folk epic and classical mythology, as well as of bizarre situations found within her contemporary world. Mary A. Gervin has written convincingly of certain "frames of reference" and mythic parallels between Amelia/Macy and Artemis/Orion ["McCullers' Frames of Reference in *The Ballad of the Sad Café*," *Pembroke Magazine* 20 (1988)].

Still another situation in McCullers's life found its way into her tale that summer, too: her abandonment by Reeves and his love affair with their best friend, David Diamond. McCullers wrote Diamond from Yaddo when she finished her "strange fairy tale," as she repeatedly described it, that it was for him. (Diamond, in turn, dedicated his ballet *The Dream of Audubon* to both McCullers and Reeves and set to music her recently published poem, "The Twisted Trinity," yet another handling of her troubled life.) In the fictional tale, Amelia is abandoned by Cousin Lymon— whom she loves inordinately—in favor of Marvin Macy. The two men team up against her, steal her treasures, wreck her café and distillery, and leave town together.

Critic Margaret Walsh has argued cogently that *The Ballad of the Sad Café* is not a "fairy tale" but an "anti-fairy tale," for "unlike the redeeming love of fairy tales, love in McCullers's tale is the spell that weakens the will, the enchantment that can dwarf giants"; thus to "lay oneself bare to love is to be open to disloyalty, to be meek, powerless, and defenseless, to be at the mercy of love's unpredictability" ["Carson McCullers' Anti-Fairy Tale: *The Ballad of the Sad Café*," *Pembroke Magazine* 20 (1988)].

The twisted, ill-fated triangles that haunt the lives of McCullers's fictional characters repeatedly haunted the author in reality as well. The theme of abandonment (that had prevailed in *The Heart Is a Lonely Hunter*) is important not only to *The Ballad of the Sad Café,* but even more so to the longer work in progress that summer, the novel that eventually became *The Member of the Wedding.* McCullers finished her novella at Yaddo during the summer of 1941, then put it away for two years, intending to write two more tales of about the same length and to publish them as a trilogy in one volume. Caught up in the writing of *The Member of the Wedding,* however, she never worked on the other tales she envisioned, and *The Ballad of the Sad Café* was published in 1943 in a single issue of *Harper's Bazaar.* Eight years later, it became the title story in her omnibus collection, *"The Ballad of the Sad Café" and Other Works,* which included all of the long fiction published to date and six of her short stories.

The narrator of McCullers's novella maintains a relatively objective distance from the scene and situation that he (or she) describes in much the same manner as the narrator does in *Reflections in a Golden Eye.* He is not a specific character within any scene, but his commentary and subtle forewarnings function like a Greek chorus. He sees the dangers inherent in the triangle of Amelia, Lymon, and Macy, but is powerless to act. He does not pretend to know everything, but his omniscient voice sets the mood and pace of the action to follow, shifting from formal, stylized, poetic, and at times archaic, to the colorful and colloquial folk patterns of the simple mill people who frequent Miss Amelia's café.

Over the years McCullers's narrator has evoked more critical discussion than has any other aspect of the tale. Robert Rechnitz argued cogently in 1968 that the author's "childlike style" served her especially well in *The Ballad of the Sad Café,* for it enabled the narrator to hide behind a facade of childlike innocence that became a "kind of buffer to fend off what would otherwise be unbearable" ["The Failure of Love: The Grotesque in Two Novels by Carson McCullers," *Georgia Review* 22 (Winter 1968)]. A later essay, Dawson F. Gaillard's "The Presence of the Narrator in McCullers' *Ballad of the Sad Café*," posits that the empathetic presence of the narrator makes it impossible for the reader "to distance himself from the emotional impact of the act," and that it is the oral quality of the tale and the personal balladeer's response to the café that lifts the café to mythic proportions. ["The Presence of the Narrator in Carson McCullers' *Ballad of the Sad Café*," *Mississippi Quarterly* (Fall, 1972)]. Critics have generally agreed that the narrator's most striking characteristic is his (or her) compassion for the three principal characters, whose traits are employed by McCullers as symbols of the moral isolation and pain to which one inevitably falls heir in the absence of any kind of meaningful communication with another human being.

Told as one long flashback, the story actually begins at the end. Unlike her first two books with their three- and four-part divisions, *The Ballad of the Sad Café* is tightly compressed into one continuous narrative that relies upon narration alone and an occasional space break to emphasize passage of time or an extraordinary turn of events.

When the reader first encounters Amelia Evans, by far the most pitiful and tragic figure in the tale, she is living alone behind boarded-up windows in a large, sagging house on the main street of a small town in what appears to be the hills of North Georgia. It is August, and "sometimes in the late afternoon when the heat is at its worst a hand will slowly open the shutter and a face will look down on the town. It is a face like the terrible dim faces known in dreams—sexless and white." The solitary Miss Amelia is a freakishly tall, pale woman whose "two gray crossed eyes" are turned so sharply inward that they seem to be exchanging with each other "one long and secret gaze of grief." Amelia is six feet two inches tall and has bones and muscles like a man's. She cares "nothing for the love of men," although she identifies with them in her labors of sausage making, bricklaying, and carpentry. The town's only general practitioner, she doles out her homemade medicines, but is uncomfortable with women and refuses to treat any "female complaint." Like Private Williams in *Reflections in a Golden Eye,* Amelia was reared in a motherless home. She had no idea what might be expected of her in a romantic relationship and had no basis for remorse over her violent expulsion of Marvin Macy from the bridal bed-chamber or of her abuse of him later. When Amelia, in turn, is abandoned by Lymon, she evokes the townspeople's pity.

The town itself is dreary and undistinguished, for "not much is there except the cotton mill, the two-room houses where the workers live, a few peach trees, a church with two colored windows, and a miserable main street only a hundred yards long. On Saturdays the tenants from the nearby farms come in for a day of talk and trade. Otherwise the town is lonesome, sad, and like a place that is far off and estranged from all other places in the world." Nature imposes itself upon the hapless people with short, raw winters and summers that are "white with glare and fiery hot." In such a godforsaken place, the "soul rots with boredom," and one's only relief, suggests the balladeer, is "to walk down the Forks Falls Road and listen to the chain gang."

In the process of telling his tale, the narrator overcomes his boredom and, as critic John McNally has carefully demonstrated, adds a meaningful dimension to his own banal existence ["The Introspective Narrator in *The Ballad of the Sad Café*," *South Atlantic Bulletin* 28 (November 1973)]. But the town was once quite different, and so was Amelia, insists the narrator. In addition to having been the richest woman in town, she also ran the only local general store and made the best liquor in the county from an illegal still deep in the nearby swamp. Obviously displeased over the state of affairs in the community, she was ill at ease with the rest of the townspeople because they could not "be taken into the hands and changed overnight to something more worthwhile and profitable." Amelia's indifference to others was seen most clearly in her strange, ten-day unconsummated marriage to Macy, whom she drove out of her house—and out of town—after getting him to turn over all of his worldly possessions to her. Macy's humiliation by Amelia caused him to revert fiercely to his old, cruel habits that had shocked the town and gained him notoriety throughout the state. Captured, finally, he was charged for murder and any number of shotgun robberies and sent off to the penitentiary outside of Atlanta.

The narrator explains that some eleven years have passed since that event, however, and that Miss Amelia's independence and meanspiritedness are legendary. Thus the townspeople are amazed beyond belief when a tubercular and repulsive-looking hunchback struts into town one day and claims distant kinship with her. She calls him Cousin Lymon, and overnight he becomes the focus of her world. Lymon looks like a sick pelican with his thin crooked legs, oversized head, and great warped chest, and he is described repeatedly through distasteful bird imagery. For the first time in Amelia's life she feels pity, moved first by his tears, then by a love—a love that she offers freely, having intuited that the little hunchback is no threat to her sexuality. Critic Joseph R. Millichap has aptly described Lymon as "a man loved without sex, a child acquired without pain, and a companion" whom Amelia found "more acceptable than a husband or a child." ["Carson McCullers' Literary Ballad," *Georgia Review* 27 (Fall 1973)].

In one of the most frequently quoted passages from McCullers's entire canon, the narrator addresses mankind (and womankind) in general regarding the nature of the lover and the beloved:

> First of all, love is a joint experience between two persons—but the fact that it is a joint experience does not mean that it is a similar experience to the two people involved. There are the lover and the beloved, but these two come from different countries. Often the beloved is only a stimulus for all the stored-up love which has lain quiet within the lover for a long time hitherto. And somehow every lover knows this. He feels in his soul that his love is a solitary thing. He comes to know a new, strange loneliness and it is this knowledge which makes him suffer. So there is only one thing for the lover to do. He must house his love within himself as best he can; he must create for himself a whole new inward world—a world intense and strange, complete in himself.

McCullers's balladeer makes it clear that the lover can be "any human creature on this earth," and that "the most outlandish people can be the stimulus for love":

> A most mediocre person can be the object of a love which is wild, extravagant, and beautiful as the poison lilies of the swamp. A good man may be the stimulus for a love both violent and debased, or a jabbering madman may bring about in the soul of someone a tender and simple idyll. Therefore, the value and quality

of any love is determined solely by the lover himself. It is for this reason that most of us would rather love than be loved. Almost everyone wants to be the lover. And the curt truth is that, in a deep secret way, the state of being beloved is intolerable to many. The beloved fears and hates the lover, and with the best of reasons. For the lover is forever trying to strip bare his beloved. The lover craves any possible relation with the beloved, even if this experience can cause him only pain.

When *The Ballad of the Sad Café* first appeared in *Harper's Bazaar*, McCullers sent a copy of the magazine to a young army private she had recently met, Robert Walden, and in the margin beside her treatise on the failure of *eros,* she scribbled in pencil: "This is true, Bob, only when you are *not* in love." Later, McCullers insisted in her essay "The Flowering Dream: Notes on Writing" that the "passionate, individual love the old Tristan-Isolde love—the Eros love—is inferior to the love of God, to fellowship, to the love of Agape—the Greek god of the feast, the God of brotherly love—and of man. This is what I tried to show in *The Ballad of the Sad Café* in the strange love of Miss Amelia for the little hunchback, Cousin Lymon." Whereas McCullers does reveal the eventual failure of *eros* and its destructive powers upon the trio in her tale, the characters achieve no redemption through *agape* (in the sense of communal affection), except for the temporal relief afforded by the café.

One could argue that McCullers's claim regarding her intentions in a work written fifteen years earlier when her emotions were deeply involved in the fiction is not wholly true. Louise Westling has pointed out that McCullers's statement that *The Ballad of the Sad Café* "was intended to show the inferiority of passionate individual love to *agape*" by no means accounted "for the individual peculiarities of her characters and the sexual dimensions of their problems in love" [*Sacred Groves and Ravaged Gardens: The Fiction of Eudora Welty, Carson McCullers, and Flannery O'Connor* (1985)]. Just as McCullers herself had experienced abject grief upon her painful discovery of the transitory nature of love and the impossibility of a lasting relationship with her Swiss friend, so, too, does Amelia suffer profoundly through her extraordinary love for Lymon, and for the café itself.

Six years after Lymon became ensconced in the café, Marvin Macy returns to town bent on revenge. The two men stare at one another with "the look of two criminals who recognize each other," and Lymon becomes instantly transformed into a spirited lover. He performs every trick he knows to get Macy's attention, while Macy, in turn, alternately ignores and insults his suitor. The strange triangle takes its final turn when Amelia is reduced to accepting the role of the frustrated lover, and this time it is Lymon who cruelly spurns *her,* choosing instead the swaggering, revengeful husband who puts up with the hunchback merely to gain an ally against his wife. Lymon flirts shamelessly with Macy, apes and insults the grieving Amelia to her face, and invites her husband to move in with them. Amelia does not rebel, knowing that if she drives her rival away, Lymon will follow. The thought of being alone again, having abandoned the last vestige of her strident independence to the dwarf, is intolerable. The narrator intercedes at this point to declare that "it is better to take in your mortal enemy than face the terror of living alone." Amelia's futile efforts to regain Lymon's favor parallel Macy's former attempts to woo her. Until he courted Amelia and was mysteriously transfigured by love, Macy's meanness was legendary throughout the region.

A bitter confrontation between Amelia and Macy is inevit-able, an event that McCullers describes in mock-heroic fashion. The couple square off one evening in the center of the café before all the townspeople, who have watched the trio fearfully since the day Macy arrived. It is the dead of winter after an extraordinary snow, and there have been countless strange interruptions to nature's rhythms that the townspeople attribute to Macy. Along with other ominous signs a few hours before the fight begins, "a hawk with a bloody breast" flies over the town and circles "twice around the property of Miss Amelia." Thirty minutes after the fight commences, Amelia's advantage is unmistakable. She pins Macy to the floor and straddles him, her strong, big hands at his throat, but the hunchback intervenes. From the counter twelve feet away where he has perched to watch the fight, Lymon sails through the air "as though he had grown hawk wings," lands upon Amelia's back, and claws furiously at her neck. When the townsfolk come to their senses, Amelia lies motionless on the floor. The narrator explains that "this was not a fight to hash over and talk about afterward; people went home and pulled the covers up over their heads."

Amelia's pathetic defeat echoes the scene at the close of *Reflections in a Golden Eye,* but Amelia is not afforded the release of death. Trapped in the abyss of loneliness and isolation, she sobs fitfully "with the last of her grating, winded breath," her head in the crook of her arm. The destruction of her café and still, the theft of her worldly possessions, the sausage and grits laced with poison left behind—all mean nothing compared to the physical and spiritual decay that sets in irrevocably with the hunchback's sweeping leap. A victim of complete abandonment, the pathetic woman sits every night for three years on the front steps of her sagging house and gazes forlornly down the road upon which Lymon had first appeared. At last, in an admission of defeat, Amelia lets her hair grow ragged, and day by day her gray eyes become more crossed, "as though they sought each other out to exchange a little glance of grief and lonely recognition." Finally, she hires a carpenter to board up the premises of the café, and there is, as a result, no good liquor to be had anywhere. It is rumored that those who drink from the still eight miles away will "grow warts on their livers the size of goobers" and "dream themselves into a dangerous inward world." The rest of the townsfolk, in their boredom, have little to do except "walk around the millpond, stand kicking at a rotten stump, figure out what [one] can do with the old wagon wheel by the side of the road near the church," and as a last

resort, "go down to the Forks Falls highway and listen to the chain gang." But Amelia allows herself no such relief. She does not go to the highway like the others to seek solace in the voices of the chain gang. Yet McCullers's coda, "The Twelve Mortal Men," stands as a paean to survival and a moving illustration of the power of brotherhood, even when the union is brought on by chains of bondage.

For a recording made in 1958—seventeen years after writing *The Ballad of the Sad Café*—McCullers read the final passage of the novel, the coda of the chain gang. Although her spirits were low and her health wretched, McCullers's voice was steady and strong until she reached the final line. "Just twelve mortal men who are together," wept McCullers, her breaking voice a vital part of the recording. In her canon, the word *just* had a special connotation that heightened its irony. "*Just* is too small a word for pity," explained Mollie Lovejoy, a character she had created some fifteen years after *The Ballad of the Sad Café*. "It's like saying *just* food, *just* God. [See McCullers's *The Square Root of Wonderful,* 1958.]

The Ballad of the Sad Café provoked no serious attention from reviewers until its appearance in the 1951 omnibus edition. In a front-page review in the Sunday *New York Herald Tribune* [June 10, 1951], Coleman Rosenberger declared the title story "condensed and brilliant writing, which carries the reader along so easily on the waves of the story that he may not at first be aware how completely he has been saturated with symbolism." William P. Clan-cey, reviewing for *Commonweal* [June 15, 1951], called McCullers's work "metaphysical fusion of horror and compassion" by the author whose "young American talent" was of the "very first order." Robert Kee informed readers of the British *Spectator* [September 12, 1952] that McCullers's style had an "Olympian dispassionateness which is designed to strengthen the violence of the human emotions with which she is often concerned. It is the same sort of effect which Hardy achieved for his characters in far more clumsily contrived sentences." V. S. Pritchett insisted that McCullers was the "most remarkable novelist to come out of America for a generation" and declared that her compassion gives her characters "a Homeric moment in a universal tragedy." ["Books in General," *The New Statesman and Nation* (August 2, 1952)].

In his notable argument, "The Myth of the Sad Café," Albert J. Griffith contrasted McCullers's impressive mythic imagination with that of such moderns as James Joyce, T. S. Eliot, William Faulkner, Eudora Welty, and John Updike, stressing that her fellow writers had created contemporary parallels to various well-known myths, whereas McCullers shaped "her own new myth out of primitive elements." [*Georgia Review* 21 (Spring 1967)].

A strong body of feminist criticism of *The Ballad of the Sad Café,* as well as of McCullers's other works, emerged in the mid-1970s. Panthea Reid Broughton provided the first significant feminist reading, which viewed the tale as a fable that "shows us that rejecting those characters labeled as exclusively feminine bounces back on the rejecter and renders men and women alike incapable of love," ["Rejection of The Feminine in Carson McCullers' *The Ballad of The Sad Café*," *Twentieth Century Literature* 20 (January 1994)]. Charlene Clark's study of "male-female pairs" in both *The Ballad of the Sad Café* and *The Member of the Wedding* demonstrates effectively how McCullers's aggressive females dominate the passive males with whom they are paired and that these women vent their aggression through violence as a means of dominating the men ["Male-Female Pairs in Carson McCullers's *The Ballad of the Sad Café* and *The Member of the Wedding*," *Notes on Contemporary Literature* 11 (September 1979)]. Another notable feminist reading is Claire Kahane's "Gothic Mirrors and Feminine Identity," which treats *The Ballad of the Sad Café* as a "redefined modern Gothic fiction" and places McCullers closer to Flannery O'Connor than to any of her other contemporaries [*Centennial Review* 24 (1980)]. Both Robert S. Phillips and Louise Westling have addressed Isak Dinesen's considerable influence through her tale "The Monkey" upon *The Ballad of the Sad Café* [Phillips, "Dinesen's 'Monkey' and McCullers' 'Ballad': A Study in Literary Affinity," *Studies in Short Fiction* 1 (Spring 1964); Westling, "Carson McCullers' Amazon Nightmare," *Modern Fiction Studies* 28 (Autumn 1982)]. Westling perceives a significant difference between the work of the two writers, noting McCullers's attempt to deny the feminine entirely and to allow a woman to function successfully as a man.

The Ballad of the Sad Café has continued to stand up well under the scrutiny of critics. Many contend that, all things considered, it is still her best work.

FURTHER READING

Criticism

Allen, Walter. "Welty, McCullers, Taylor, Flannery O'Connor." In *The Short Story in English,* pp. 313-18. Oxford: Clarendon Press, 1981.

    Argues that McCullers's "extremely idiosyncratic view of human beings" is most successfully articulated in *The Ballad of the Sad Café.*

Baldanza, Frank. "Plato in Dixie." *The Georgia Review* 12 (Summer 1958): 151-67.

    Discusses the use of Platonic parables in southern fiction, remarking that the theory of love expounded by the narrator of *The Ballad of the Sad Café* is reminiscent of Plato's Socratic dialogue, *Phaedrus* (c. 5th-4th century BC.).

Dodd, Wayne D. "The Development of Theme through Symbol in the Novels of Carson McCullers." *The Georgia Review* XVII, No. 2 (Summer 1963): 206-13.

Argues that there is "a suggestive and developmental symbolism" in McCullers's work that "always emphasizes the discreteness of individuals from each other and from God himself." Dodd notes that the half-painted house in *The Ballad of the Sad Café* is symbolic of McCullers's contention that human beings can have only an incomplete and partial understanding of others.

Edmonds, Dale. *Carson McCullers,* pp. 19-23. Austin, TX: Steck-Vaughn Company, 1969.

    Discusses the musical, ballad-like elements of *The Ballad of the Sad Café,* arguing that the "coda" at the end counters the previous parts of the story that suggest the impossibility of love.

Evans, Oliver. "The Theme of Spiritual Isolation in Carson McCullers." *New World Writing* 1 (1952): 297-310.

    Argues that all of McCullers's fiction reflects the essential loneliness of the human condition, and that McCullers gives this theme its most impressive treatment in *The Ballad of the Sad Café.*

Folk, Barbara Nauer. "The Sad Sweet Music of Carson McCullers." *The Georgia Review* XVI, No.1 (Spring 1962): 202-09.

    Discusses the function of musical allusions in McCullers's fiction and argues that in *The Ballad of the Sad Café,* the prisoners in the final "coda" section transcend their chained existence through song.

Hoffman, Frederick J. "Eudora Welty and Carson McCullers." In *The Art of Southern Fiction: A Study of Some Modern Novelists,* pp. 68-71. Carbondale: Southern Illinois University Press, 1967.

    Suggests that *The Ballad of the Sad Café* recapitulates "the theme of willed and wilful loneliness in Mrs. McCullers's work" and that the story is superior to her earlier treatments of this theme.

Kohler, Dayton. "Carson McCullers: Variations on a Theme." *College English* 13 (October 1951): 1-8. Printed simultaneously in *English Journal* 40 (October 1951): 415-22.

    Argues that *The Ballad of the Sad Café* reveals the structural and thematic unity of McCullers's earlier fiction.

Vande Keift, Ruth M. "The Love Ethos of Porter, Welty, and McCullers." In *The Female Tradition in Southern Literature,* edited by Carol S. Manning, pp. 250-56. Urbana: University of Illinois Press, 1993.

    Discusses McCullers's bisexuality and the figuring of sexual ambivalence in her fiction.

Vickery, John B. "Carson McCullers: A Map of Love." *Wisconsin Studies in Contemporary Literature* 1 (Winter 1960): 13-24.

    Argues that *The Ballad of the Sad Café* is a parody of romantic love.

Walsh, Margaret. "Carson McCullers' Anti-Fairy Tale: *The Ballad of the Sad Café.*" *Pembroke Magazine* 20 (1988): 43-8.

Outlines the similarities between *The Ballad of the Sad Café* and the fairy tale genre. Walsh argues, however, that the story ultimately subverts the notion of the redemptive power of love that informs fairy tales, commenting that the "moral seems to be that a visitor to the Sad Café should not plan to live happily ever after."

Additional coverage of McCullers's life and career is contained in the following sources published by Gale Research: *Contemporary Authors*, Vols. 5-8 (rev. ed.), 25-28 (rev. ed.); *Contemporary Authors Bibliographical Series*, Vol. 1; *Concise Dictionary of American Literary Biography*, 1941-1968; *Contemporary Literary Criticism*, Vols. 1, 4, 10, 12, 48; *DISCovering Authors*; *DISCovering Authors: British*; *Dictionary of Literary Biography*, Vols. 2, 7; *Major 20th-Century Authors*; *Something about the Author*, Vol. 27; *Short Story Criticism*, Vol. 9; and *World Literature Criticism.*

Sinclair Ross
1908–1996

Canadian novelist and short story writer.

INTRODUCTION

Ross is best known for his novels and short stories about life on the prairies of western Canada. Much of his work is set during the Depression era and depicts the severity of frontier life and the destructive power of natural forces. Generally considered naturalistic, Ross's fiction is characterized by distinctive regional language, economical prose, powerful descriptions of western Canadian landscapes, and a lack of sentimentality. In his most notable works, *As For Me and My House* and *The Lamp at Noon and Other Stories*, Ross's characters struggle to remain hopeful despite the universe's apparent indifference to their sufferings.

Biographical Information

Ross was born on a 160-acre homestead twelve miles from the town of Shellbrook, Saskatchewan. His parents separated when he was seven, and his mother, the daughter of Scottish-born clergyman, supported the family by working as a housekeeper. After finishing the eleventh grade Ross began a lifelong career at the Royal Bank of Canada, intermittently living in such Canadian cities as Abbey, Lancer, Arcola, Winnipeg, and Montreal. He served in the army during World War II from 1942 to 1946. After retiring from the Royal Bank in 1968 Ross lived in Greece and Spain before returning to Canada in 1980. He died in 1996.

Major Works of Short Fiction

Ross became interested in writing when he was ten and first submitted a story for publication at age sixteen. In 1934 his short story "No Other Way" was published by the English magazine *Nash's Pall-Mall*. Between 1934 and 1952 Ross published fifteen short stories that were later revised and collected in *The Lamp at Noon and Other Stories*. These stories realistically depict rural life in Saskatchewan during the 1930s and are centered around familial relationships. In "The Lamp at Noon," for instance, a three-day dust storm quells a farm woman's determination to overcome her extreme poverty and ultimately causes her to go insane. In "A Field of Wheat" a family's entire crop is destroyed by a sudden hailstorm, and the husband, unable to exhibit his emotions to his family, retreats to the isolation of the barn to cry in anguish.

Critical Reception

Although his short stories are widely anthologized, critical reaction to Ross's work has been limited. Because much of his fiction has been associated with nature and the struggle of humans against it, critics have labelled Ross a naturalist. Some commentators, however, have underscored his realistic and deft portrayal of human relationships amidst the isolation and physical hardships of the prairie. In recent years Ross's reputation has undergone a mild resurgence within Canada, though his work has not yet sparked recognition outside of the Canadian context.

PRINCIPAL WORKS

Short Fiction

The Lamp at Noon and Other Stories 1968
The Race and Other Stories 1982

Other Major Works

As For Me and My House (novel) 1957
The Well (novel) 1958
Whir of Gold (novel) 1970
Sawbones Memorial (novel) 1974

CRITICISM

Margaret Laurence (essay date 1968)

SOURCE: An introduction to *The Lamp at Noon and Other Stories* by Sinclair Ross, McClelland and Stewart, 1968, pp. 7-12.

[*Laurence was a Canadian novelist, short story writer, essayist, memoirist, editor, and translator. She is considered a prominent figure in contemporary Canadian literature. In the essay, she acknowledges Ross as an early influence upon her work and describes his style as "spare, lean, and honest."*]

Although Sinclair Ross's stories and two novels have appeared over a period of some twenty-five years, most of his writing has been done out of the background of the prairie drought and depression of the Thirties, and as a chronicler of that era, he stands in a class by himself. When I first read his extraordinary and moving novel, *As For Me And My House,* at about the age of eighteen, it had an enormous impact on me, for it seemed the only completely genuine one I had ever read about my own people, my own place, my own time. It pulled no punches about life in the stultifying atmosphere of small and ingrown towns, and yet it was illuminated with compassion.

In Ross's short stories, the same society is portrayed, the same themes explored, with the difference that these stories all have completely rural settings. The farms stand far apart, only distantly related to whatever town is the focal point for buying and selling. The human community is, for most of the time, reduced to its smallest unit, one family. The isolation is virtually complete. It is within this extreme condition of human separateness and in the extremes of summer drought and winter blizzard that Ross's characters grapple with their lives and their fate, a fate partly imposed upon them by an uncaring and fickle natural order and partly compelled by their own spiritual inheritance, the pride and the determination which enable them to refuse defeat, but which also cut them off from nearly all real contact with others.

Appearing almost as chief protagonist is the land itself. In spite of its deceptive moments of calm promise, it is an essentially violent and unpredictable land, quixotic, seeming to bestow grace and favour, then suddenly attacking with arrows of snow, shrieking armies of wind, bludgeons of hail, or the quiet lethal assault of the sun. Indeed, the land sometimes assumes a character as harsh as that of the vengeful God who sorely tried Job, and the farmers who stay on, year after year, seeing their crops spoiled and themselves becoming old in youth, yet still maintaining their obsessive faith in the land, are reminiscent of Job himself—*Though He slay me, yet will I trust in Him.*

Characteristically, and in keeping with his themes, Ross describes the land in strong, broad strokes, and I do not believe that anyone has ever given a better impressionistic view of the prairies. I think, for example, of his description of drought in **"Not by Rain Alone"**:

> The days were still, brassy, pitiless. Swift little whirlwinds scoured across the field; in their wake there closed a hushed, oppressive immobility. On wheat and fallow land and ripening rye alike lay a dusty-yellow monochrome of haze. . . .

Or the hard, sharp description of winter as seen by Ann in **"The Painted Door"**:

> The sun was risen above the frost mists now, so keen and hard a glitter on the snow that instead of warmth its rays seemed shedding cold. One of the two-year-old colts that had cantered away when John turned the horses out for water stood covered with rime at the stable door again, head down and body hunched, each breath a little plume of steam against the frosty air. She shivered, but did not turn. In the clear, bitter light the long white miles of prairie landscape seemed a region alien to life. Even the distant farmsteads she could see served only to intensify a sense of isolation. Scattered across the face of so vast and bleak a wilderness it was difficult to conceive them as a testimony of human hardihood and endurance. Rather they seemed futile. Rather they seemed to cower before the implacability of snow-swept earth and clear pale sun-chilled sky.

Ross's style is always beautifully matched to his material—spare, lean, honest, no gimmicks, and yet in its very simplicity setting up continuing echoes in the mind.

The women in these stories have their own personal dilemmas, but they also have many qualities in common. They are farmers' wives, most of them still fairly young, trying to resign themselves to lives of unrelieved drabness. They are without exception terrifyingly lonely, shut into themselves, shut out of their husbands' inner lives. Ann, in **"The Painted Door,"** is trapped both by John's blunt devotion and by his total lack of perception of her real needs. Ellen, in **"The Lamp At Noon,"** feels caged and cannot communicate her feelings to Paul. Their separate pain remains separate, until she, in a final madness of concern about their baby, tries to escape and walks into the windstorm in which the child, ironically and tragically, is smothered both by dust and by his mother's hysterical efforts to protect him.

These women are intensely loyal, and as driven by work-compulsion as their men, but they still long, hopelessly, for communication and tenderness with their husbands—who desperately need the same thing but can never permit or accept it lest it reflect unmanfully upon themselves.

Martha, in **"A Field Of Wheat,"** thinks that ". . . love was gone; there was only wheat." In lieu of expressed love towards their men, these prairie women take refuge in attempting to instil small, rigid, meaningless and usually tasteless portions of "culture" into their children's lives. In **"A Field Of Wheat,"** Martha's ambitions are described. They are heartbreakingly limited. She would like to see her husband for once unclenched with worry, and to have him shave twice a week, as he used to do when they were first married, and she would like her children to be able to have music lessons. The mother in **"Cornet At Night"** forces her son to spend dreary hours in the stuffy plush parlour, playing hymns on the piano so that he will not grow up rough. (In this same story, interestingly enough, there is some adumbration of Ross's first novel, for on the parlour wall is a pansy-bordered motto which reads *As For Me And My House We Will Serve The Lord*.)

Ross's style is always beautifully matched to his material—spare, lean, honest, no gimmicks, and yet in its very simplicity setting up continuing echoes in the mind.

—*Margaret Laurence*

The men who are portrayed here are painfully inarticulate. They are not able to make themselves known, not even to their women—perhaps especially not to their women. They are basically men with great uncertainties, great inner doubts. But because they believe that a man must be strong, both physically and spiritually, it is quite beyond them to acknowledge any vulnerability to any other human. They must maintain faith in the land's ability to yield, and in their own ability to coax or force it, for in this encounter their essential manhood lies in the balance. They cannot desert the land in its drought because in some way they would die as male beings if they did. Yet their helplessness in the face of drought and blizzard gives them a recurring sense of importance against which they can only rage inwardly.

Paul, in **"The Lamp At Noon,"** refuses to leave his land, although it is dying all around him. Consciously, the one thing he could not bear would be to become dependent upon his town store-owning in-laws. But at a deeper level, one feels that what he really could not stand would be to prove inadequate to the land. He cannot express his torment verbally. He cannot appeal to his wife for help or reassurance, and in the end his self-imposed isolation and his shutting-out of Ellen are decisive factors in her final crackup. In **"September Snow,"** Will meets the challenge of wind and snow, only to fail utterly in the area of human contact, for he refuses to admit into his consciousness the realization of his wife's desperation. Her horrifying death in childbirth seems bizarrely similar to retribution. These prairie men fail consistently in close rela-

tionships. They never perceive what is being asked of them, nor do they see what they themselves might have gained by allowing someone to get close to them. When they suffer, it is doggedly alone. John, in **"A Field Of Wheat,"** consoles his wife after the crop has been destroyed by hail, and assumes a mask of unbreakable strength. It is only by chance that she goes later to the barn and finds him there, sobbing. She goes away without letting him see her, knowing this is the kindest thing she can do for him. The real issues will never be mentioned between them, for she is too afraid of being brushed away, and he is too afraid of appearing weak in her eyes.

With the character of Vickers, in **"One's A Heifer,"** there is a sense of real evil, and yet even this sinister man's madness is pictured as a direct result of unbearable isolation. This is where it can sometimes end, this total noncontact—in a man who, when another human being attempted to touch him even slightly by coming in and cooking his meals, responded by killing her.

The children in Ross's stories are only half aware of the deprivation of their lives, but they long for the colour and excitement which are missing. Tommy, in **"Cornet At Night,"** listens to the unsuitable hired hand playing his cornet, a voice quite literally out of another world. "A harvest, however lean, is certain every year; but a cornet at night is golden only once." He does not know at all what the rest of the world holds, but the notes of the cornet suggest marvels to him, and he will never forget.

Fantasy is these children's solace and place of retreat. For many of the imaginative youngsters in these stories, horses symbolize freedom, escape, faroff glamour. In **"The Outlaw,"** the mare Isabel is infinitely more feminine and more sophisticated than the prissy girl child Millie, and to the thirteen-year-old boy, the horse represents adventure and the conquering of worlds.

> She was one horse, and she was all horses. Thundering battle chargers, fleet Arabians, untamed mustangs—sitting beside her on her manger I knew and rode them all. I charged with her at Balaklava, Waterloo, scoured the deserts of Africa and the steppes of the Ukraine. Conquest and carnage, trumpets and glory—she understood, and carried me triumphantly.

The horse represents something quite different to the men whom the boys grow up to be. Paul, in **"The Lamp At Noon,"** turns to his horses, strokes their necks, for the comfort which he cannot seek from his wife. When John, in **"A Field Of Wheat,"** goes to the stable after his wheat has been ruined, he rests his face against the flanks of one of his horses, and sobs his anguish there.

Throughout Ross's stories, the outer situation always mirrors the inner. The emptiness of the landscape, the bleakness of the land, reflect the inability of these people to touch another with assurance and gentleness. In **"The Painted Door,"** Ann finally makes love with Steven, the young bachelor, out of her need to be noticed once more as a woman and to be allowed to express tenderness. When her husband discovers what has happened, and in his shock and pain allows himself to freeze to death, his act, as well as being an appallingly unanswerable reproach to her, is in a sense only a final and terrible externalization, for the process of emotionally freezing to death was begun long before. Ross never takes sides, and this is one admirable quality of his writing. Blame is not assigned. Men and women suffer equally. The tragedy is not that they suffer, but that they suffer alone.

The patterns are those of isolation and loneliness, and gradually, through these, the underlying spiritual goals of an entire society can be perceived. The man must prove absolutely strong, in his own eyes. The woman must silently endure all. If either cannot, then they have failed to themselves. With these impossible and cruel standards, and in circumstances of drought and depression, it is no wonder that individuals sometimes crack under the strain.

The real wonder is that so many of these men and women continue somehow—stumbling, perhaps, but still going on. Hope never quite vanishes. In counterpoint to desolation runs the theme of renewal. Tomorrow it may rain. The next spring will ultimately come. Despite the sombre tone and the dark themes of Sinclair Ross's short stories, man emerges as a creature who can survive—and survive with some remaining dignity—against both outer and inner odds which are almost impossible.

Sandra Djwa (essay date 1971)

SOURCE: "No Other Way: Sinclair Ross's Stories and Novels," in *Canadian Literature*, Vol. 47, 1971, pp. 49-66.

[*In the following essay, Djwa determines the quintessential Canadian nature of Ross's short fiction.*]

As a Newfoundlander, I have always felt a great fondness for the writings of Sinclair Ross. I do not quite understand the nature of the attraction, whether it is his concept of a prairie nature—hard, with overtones of fatalism—which corresponds to my own view of Newfoundland, or whether it is simply his wry observations of the circumlocutions of the Puritan way—a sensibility which also strikes a familiar note. In any event, whenever the term "Canadian novel" comes to mind, I find myself gravitating towards Ross and particularly towards his sometimes puzzling first novel, *As For Me and My House.*

Reading through *Queen's Quarterly* of the late 30's and early 40's, it is not too difficult to recognize branches of the novel. Here are the familiar characters and concerns of Ross's world: the Steves, the Philips, the Pauls, the young boy with the horse ("**A Day with Pegasus,**" 1938); the chance intrusion of the artist into the prairie town ("**Cornet at Night,**" 1939); the paralyzing lack of communication between husband and wife ("**The Lamp at Noon,**" 1938, "**The Painted Door,**" 1939); or, for that matter, between friends ("**Jug and Bottle,**" 1939) which leads inevitably to further betrayal;

the "unappetizing righteousness" and pansy-embroidered motto, "As For Me and My House We Will Serve the Lord" of "**Cornet at Night.**" Here, too, in the short story, as in "**No Other Way,**" first published in *Nash's* magazine (London, 1938), is the unmistakable silhouette of Mrs. Bentley. Older, more haggard than the protagonist of *As for Me and My House,* Hatty Glenn is equally dependent on the love of her still-elusive husband of over twenty years.

Reviewing the short stories and novels, I seem to find that character recedes into the emotional landscape; the primary impression is of those short paragraphs which establish the natural landscape and its relation to perceiving consciousness. Throughout Ross's work, there is a sense of a bleak, hard nature—the loneliness and isolation of the prairie winter, the indifferent sun which scorches the summer wheat. Against this nature, man is insignificant:

> In the clear bitter light the long white miles of prairie landscape seemed a region strangely alien to life. Even the distant farmsteads she could see served only to intensify a sense of isolation. Scattered across the face of so vast and bleak a wilderness it was difficult to conceive them as a testimony of human hardihood and endurance. Rather they seemed futile, lost, to cower before the implicability of snowswept earth and clear pale sun-chilled sky. ("**Lamp at Noon**")

Mrs. Bentley, looking across the open prairies and towards the Alberta foothills, recognizes both man's insignificance and his need to project human meaning into the natural landscape:

> We've all lived in a little town too long. The wilderness here makes us uneasy. I felt it the first night I walked alone on the river bank—a queer sense of something cold and fearful, something inanimate, yet aware of us. A Main Street is such a self-sufficient little pocket of existence, so smug, compact, that here we feel abashed somehow before the hills, their passiveness, the unheeding way they sleep. We climb them, but they withstand us, remain as serene and unrevealed as ever. The river slips past us, unperturbed by our coming and going, stealthily confident. We shrink from our insignificance. The stillness and solitude—we think a force or presence into it—even a hostile presence, deliberate, aligned against us—for we dare not admit an indifferent wilderness, where we may have no meaning at all. (*As For Me and My House*)

This is a nature against which man must struggle—not just to become a man—but simply to exist and perhaps, if he is particularly fortunate and determined, to exist in some meaningful way. Most of these stories are a legacy of the drought years of the thirties on the prairies—the depression moving imperceptibly into the war years. Even in Ross's second novel, *The Well,* where the protagonist, Chris Howe, is given an urban childhood, the primary emphasis is still placed on the essentials of survival: "to outwit, score, defeat, survive—Boyle Street had permitted nothing else." However, as is later suggested in this novel and throughout the first novel, existence of some meaningful way becomes the ultimate goal. For Philip Bentley this search for meaning involves the attempt to find dignity and purpose in nature and in himself through his art:

> Tonight Philip made a sketch of Joe Lawson. . . . He's sitting at a table, half-hunched over it, his hands lying heavy and inert in front of him like stones. The hands are mostly what you notice. Such big, disillusioned, steadfast hands, so faithful to the earth and seasons that betray them. I didn't know before what drought was really like, watching a crop dry up, going on again. I didn't know that Philip knew either.

In many of the short stories and also in some of the entries in Mrs. Bentley's journal, human action is presented as the reaction to natural events. The young farm boy of **"One's a Heifer"** is sent out into the open prairie because a blizzard has caused the cattle to stray; Ellen, the young wife of **"The Lamp at Noon,"** is driven to madness by the incessant wind and dust beating against the walls of the house and stable, "as if the fingers of a giant hand were tightening to collapse them." This reaction to the natural event can precipitate a quarrel, most often between husband and wife, sometimes with a young boy as the interested bystander, and the development of the plot quite often lies in the working out of the emotional tension that has been generated by the conflict.

Because this conflict is intimately connected with the struggle for survival, the tragedy of these stories is that there is often no possible reconciliation of any kind. When an author's horizon is composed of "the bare essentials of a landscape, sky and earth," there are no compromises open: if land and weather fail man, the struggle for survival can only end tragically, the extent of the tragedy being largely determined by the strength of the person concerned. Will, the young farmer of **"Not by Rain Alone"**, has a moment of bleak recognition when he suddenly sees the future which must surely lie ahead of himself and his sweetheart, Eleanor:

> He was thinking of other dry spells—other wheat that had promised thirty bushels and yielded ten. It was such niggard land. At the best they would grub along painfully, grow tired and bitter, indifferent to each other. It was the way of the land. For a farmer like him there could be no other way. (**"Lamp at Noon"**)

As in the poetry of Pratt, this struggle against nature becomes a test of endurance in which only the very strong such as Paul of **"The Lamp at Noon"** survive, but with such heart-breaking self awareness as to make it almost unendurable, while those who are weaker, such as his wife Ellen, are destroyed. As Laurence notes, Ross's men seem to know by instinct and by habit that strength, if not actual, at least apparent, is demanded, and each of them refuses to communicate to his wife those admissions of failure and of helplessness which would undermine the appearance of strength until the final, irreversible betrayal. John, the good but stolid farmer of **"The Painted Door,"** is simply unable to communicate; his wife's tragedy is that she can see but not accept the fact until it is too late. Paul of **"The Lamp at Noon"** cannot accept his wife's anguish; even after the final devastating betrayal when he realizes that compromise with the land is no longer possible, when his crops are completely destroyed and he is stripped of "vision and purpose, faith in the land, in the future, in himself," he is still attempting to find a way to withstand his wife and to go on: "For so deep were his instincts of loyalty to the land that still, even with the images of his betrayal stark upon his mind, his concern was how to withstand her, how to go on again and justify himself." For a farmer such as Paul or Will or the John of **"A Field of Wheat,"** there is "no other way" than to go on, and this continued struggle against tremendous odds becomes a revelation of the real self, as is suggested in Ross's description of the stripping down of Paul's character to "a harsh and clenched virility . . . at the cost of more engaging qualities . . . a fulfillment of his inmost and essential nature."

Unlike Huckleberry Finn, the characteristic American hero who determines "to light out for the territory" when civilization becomes too pressing, the characteristic Canadian hero is the one who stays and endures— the farmers of Ross's prairie.

—Sandra Djwa

For other characters of Ross's fictional world, the stripping down which leads to self discovery is equally important. Often made in terms of a sudden discovery of one's essential nature, it delimits the path that this nature must follow. For the country boy of **"Cornet at Night,"** a chance meeting with a musician, Philip, makes him aware of his vocation as an artist: "This way of the brief lost gleam against the night was my way too. And alone I cowered a moment, understanding that there could be no escape, no other way." For the Bentleys, the gradual stripping away of the "false fronts" of dishonest life leads to the realization that they must get away from the kind of world that the small town of Horizon imposes, to a community where essential self can be safely revealed: "I asked him didn't he want to get out of the Church, didn't he admit that saving a thousand dollars was the only way."

Ross's earliest references to the "way" which character and environment impose are found in his first published story, **"No Other Way."** Hatty Glenn, the female protagonist of this story, is a simpler character than Mrs. Bentley, as she is most strongly motivated by the habit of parsimony. After a lifetime of "grubbing" while her husband "schemed," she is weather-beaten while he is still comparatively attractive; to make matters worse, he now ignores her. In a moment of insight, she recognizes that nothing in the world can better her relationship with her husband, and that for her there is "no other way" than to continue along in the same tragi-comic fashion:

> She glanced over her shoulder and saw the half-chewed turnips being slobbered into the dirt. December— January—a pail a day.

And then in a flash she was clutching a broom and swooping into the garden. 'Get out, you greedy old devils! After them, Tubbie!'

Butter twenty five cents a pound. There was no other way.

In Ross's more sober stories, character and environment can combine like a vise to grip a character and set up a course of direction that even repeated failure does not change. His characters appear to be driven, like those of Grove in *Settlers of the Marsh,* to act as they do until one or another of a partnership is destroyed. When Paul is finally willing to make some compromises with the land, he finds his wife mad and his child dead. Having betrayed her husband, Ann of **"The Painted Door"** has a revelation of his intrinsic strength and determines to make it up to him. He, however, has already walked out into the blizzard where he freezes to death. Coulter, the inept recruit who has been repeatedly befriended by the soldier narrator of **"Jug and Bottle,"** is accidentally let down by his friend. Crushed by an overwhelming burden of guilt and despair, and with no one to turn to, Coulter kills himself: ". . . caught helpless in some primitive mechanism of conscience like a sheaf in the gear of a thresher, borne on inexorably by the chain of guilt to the blade of punishment." Many such scenes of human despair and futility suggest that the President of the Immortals also has his sport with the people of Ross's prairie. Mrs. Bentley comments on this when observing the work-torn country congregation which is still waiting and praying after five years without a crop: "And tonight again the sun went down through a clear, brassy sky. Surely it must be a very great faith that such indifference on the part of its deity cannot weaken—a very great faith, or a very foolish one."

On the whole, despite the suggestion of naturalism, particularly in the metaphor used to describe Coulter, Ross is not a naturalist in the sense of Norris's *The Octopus* or even in the modified sense of Stead's *Grain.* There is a strong streak of determinism running through Ross's work, but it is most often kept firmly within a Christian context through a respectful address to "Providence," albeit with some irony as suggested by the title, **"Not by Rain Alone,"** of one short story where the crops fail. Philip of *As For Me and My House* ". . . keeps on believing that there's a will stronger than his own deliberately pitted against him . . . a supreme being interested in him, opposed to him, arranging with tireless concern the details of his life. . . ." The good man of **"The Runaway"** finds himself troubled by God's justice, especially when the scales are eventually weighed in his favour: "What kind of reckoning was it that exacted life and innocence for an old man's petty greed? Why, if it was retri-bution, had it struck so clumsily?" (**"Lamp at Noon"**). . . .

The significance of Ross's achievement, and I fully agree with those critics who suggest that *As For Me and My House* is in the mainstream of the English Canadian novel, is that in nature, ethos and hero, Ross has captured all of these qualities which we attempt to invoke when we want to talk about Canadian writing. It is Ross's hard nature

given tongue by Mrs. Bentley when she observes that the wilderness frightens us:

> We've all lived in a little town too long. . . . We shrink from our insignificance. The stillness and solitude— we think a force or presence into it. . . . for we dare not admit an indifferent wilderness, where we may have no meaning at all . . . .

which also recurs in Bruce Hutchison's book, *The Unknown Country* and which is given the status of a literary myth in Northrop Frye's rationale for the "garrison mentality" of Canadian writing.

Yet, in significant difference from the nature which leads to the formulation of Frye's "garrison mentality" or, for that matter, from the mental "pallisade" of William Carlos Williams's *In The American Grain,* Ross does not seem to be suggesting that there is no god in nature if for no other reason than that his people would not allow it. It may very well be the Old Testament vengeful God, the Nemesis of Philip's guilty conscience, or simply the psychological projection of the will to believe. Nonetheless, the people of Ross's prairie appear to keep on waiting and believing that beyond the individual tragedies of such as **"Not by Rain Alone,"** such endurance does have value. And, certainly, in the larger structure of the first novel, there is a kind of grace bestowed: Mrs. Bentley is supported in her struggle to find the way by the Old Testament metaphor of the pointing finger: "It was like a finger pointing again, clear and peremptory, to keep on pretending ignorance just as before." Ross gives an explicit psychological basis for this metaphor; yet, as it springs from the inner recesses of self and is associated with her desire to find the "way," it is not without implications of a transcendent function. Then, too, Philip undergoes a kind of salvation through grace. He does find other-directed subjects for his art and he is given a child which he so desperately wants. Most importantly, it is a child with all of the New Testament implications of "a little child shall lead them."

It would appear that the religious frame of reference, even if only in terms of residual response, is still a very important part of the Canadian novel. It was with considerable surprise that I realized recently that a surprisingly large number of our twentieth century novels refer to specifically moral, often explicitly religious concerns, as is suggested in the following titles: Grove's *Our Daily Bread, Fruits of the Earth*; much of Callaghan, including *Such is my Beloved, They Shall Inherit the Earth, More Joy in Heaven*, and *The Loved and the Lost*; Mitchell's *Who has Seen the Wind?*; Klein's *The Second Scroll*; MacLennan's *Each Man's Son* and *The Watch that Ends the Night*; Buckler's *The Mountain and the Valley*; Wiseman's *The Sacrifice*; Watson's *The Double Hook*; Laurence's *A Jest of God*; Wiebe's *Peace Shall Destroy Many*; Horwood's *Tomorrow Will Be Sunday* and Kriesel's *The Betrayal*.

Why might this be so? There does not appear to be a comparable movement in the American novel of the last twenty years, although a successful argument might be made for the preceding three decades. There is the obvious fact of the unpopulated land itself: Canada, particularly the prairie, is still largely open space. In the midst of land and sky, as is explicitly suggested at the start of Mitchell's *Who Has Seen the Wind?*, it is difficult not to feel the cosmic setting. Then, too, the country is still basically regional; in the smaller communities religion still remains a strong force. Furthermore, our great wave of immigration was at the turn of the twentieth century rather than in the late eighteenth or nineteenth, as it was in the United States. This turn-of-the century immigration, particularly of Scotch Presbyterians and European Jews, has greatly strengthened the Old Testament concerns of our literature.

Another possibility may be inferred from the fact that naturalism did not take hold in Canada as it did in the United States. R. E. Watters, in an address to the Third Congress of the International Comparative Literature Association (Utrecht, 1961), gives a convincing rationale for this fact. He further notes that as Canada experienced no wars of emancipation and liberation, Canadian fictional characters do not usually see existing social conditions in Zolaesque terms, nor are they particularly concerned with leaving established communities for a place where they might be more free, as is suggested in the American myth of the journey west. Rather, as the historical fact of the United Empire Loyalists would suggest, and as Frye and Watters both note, the Canadian hero is concerned basically with maintaining his own integrity within a chosen community. I would add to this that the works of Ross would suggest that naturalism cannot flourish where there is even a remnant of divine providence. Religion, even if largely residual or seemingly converted to demonism as it is in *As For Me and My House,* invokes another set of values which even if psychologically internalized, still supports the individual in his struggle:

> A trim, white, neat-gabled little schoolhouse, just like Partridge Hill. There's a stable at the back, and some buggies in the yard. It stands up lonely and defiant on a landscape like a desert. . . . The distorted, barren landscape makes you feel the meaning of its persistence there. As Paul put it last Sunday when we drove up, it's *Humanity in Microcosm.* Faith, ideals, reason—all the things that really are humanity—like Paul you feel them there, their stand against the implacable blunderings of Nature . . .

And it was just a few rough pencil strokes, and he [Philip] had it buried among some notes he'd been making for next Sunday's sermon.

Unlike Huckleberry Finn, the characteristic American hero who determines "to light out for the territory" when civilization becomes too pressing, the characteristic Canadian hero is the one who stays and endures—the farmers of Ross's prairie. If and when there is to be some way as there is for the Bentleys of Horizon, it must be an honourable way and one which is sanctioned by community.

Robert D. Chambers   (essay date 1975)

SOURCE: "The Lamp at Noon and Other Stories," in *Sinclair Ross & Ernest Buckler,* McGill-Queen's University Press, 1975, pp. 9-24.

[*In the following essay, Chambers explores the pervasive sense of isolation, claustrophobia, and cramped imagination found in Ross's short fiction, particularly "A Field of Wheat," "Cornet at Night," and "The Painted Door."*]

Between 1934 and 1952, Sinclair Ross published sixteen short stories, all but three of them in the *Queen's Quarterly.* Great credit is owing to this distinguished university journal for such faithful encouragement of a fledgling Canadian writer. These stories, especially those collected in *The Lamp At Noon and Other Stories,* comprise perhaps the most consistently excellent literary pieces to appear in Canada during the 1930s and 1940s.

Since limitation of space precludes discussing each of Ross' stories in turn, it has been necessary to treat them under general headings. Yet each repays close scrutiny, and at least three are superb little masterpieces.

Literary Techniques

A number of the stories are narrated from the viewpoint of a young boy between the ages of ten and fifteen. While he seldom felt inclined to use a distinctive idiom or dialect, such as Twain adopted for Huck Finn, Ross nonetheless wanted this youthful narrative voice to seem fresh and natural. He was also aware, from his own experience, that prairie farm boys in the 1930s entered early into the world of adult responsibility. The grim facts of the Depression required a maturity of outlook far beyond their years. Ross sought to combine the natural impulsiveness of youth with the tempered understanding and quiet acceptance of the adult world. Yet the meanings which the stories unfolded often demanded a kind of insight—and a phrasing of that insight—far beyond the limited powers of a young boy:

> And Scripture we did read, Isaiah, verse about, my mother in her black silk dress and rhinestone brooch, I in my corduroys and Sunday shoes that pinched. It was a very august afternoon, exactly like the tone that had persisted in my mother's voice since breakfast time. I think I might have openly rebelled, only for the hope that by compliance I yet might win permission for the trip to town with Rock. I was inordinately proud that my father had suggested it, and for his faith in me forgave him even Isaiah and the plushy afternoon. Whereas with my mother, I decided, it was a case of downright bigotry.
>
> **("Cornet at Night")**

Almost immediately we recognize the general territory of Huck Finn, but Twain would not have allowed Huck such big words as "august," "compliance," "inordinately proud" or "downright bigotry." When Twain wants to do bigotry he has a drunken Pap tongue-lash a coloured university professor. Huck simply doesn't know what the word "bigotry" means, though he clearly recognizes the bigot that his father is. Ross has additional things to accomplish. Notice, for example, how this whole passage is shaded in meaning by the exquisite choice of "august" and "plushy," so that in the boy's clear-sighted judgment the ritual of a Sunday afternoon reflects a beautifully light satirical tone.

Here and there, we may feel that the narrative voice grows slightly strained:

> I have always been tethered to reality, always compelled by an unfortunate kind of probity in my nature to prefer a bare-faced disappointment to the luxury of a future I have no just claims upon.
>
> **("Cornet at Night")**

A boy may well develop such an outlook on life, but no eleven year old could phrase it as perceptively. Ross overcomes this problem by consistent use of the past tense, and by such useful devices as the repetition in this passage of "always." The narrative voice takes on a retrospective quality, a distancing which makes us forget for a moment that we are listening to a youth. Ross adopted this rather complex narrative voice—youthful but also quietly sage— for several of his best stories: **"The Outlaw," "Cornet at Night," "The Runaway," "One's a Heifer,"** and, more recently, **"The Flowers That Killed Him."**

A second distinctive narrative voice is that of the prairie farm woman. Two of Ross' finest stories, **"A Field of Wheat"** and **"The Painted Door,"** employ this approach, thus allowing us to experience at first hand lives of terrible loneliness and isolation. Ross was particularly attracted to this narrative mode, and the novel *As for Me and My House* combines his two strongest forms of story-telling— the vivid intimacy of first-person narration combined with the prairie woman's point of view.

Occasionally the stories use a shifting narrative pattern. **"The Lamp at Noon,"** for example, alternates the viewpoint between Paul and Ellen, an appropriate device since the story involves a husband/wife debate about the value of prairie farm life. A similar narrative mode appears in **"Not by Rain Alone"**: Part I shows events from Will's point of view; Part II (originally published separately as **"September Snow"**) gives frightening glances into the demented mind of Will's wife.

Ross is equally diverse and skilful when describing landscape, weather, and the seasons. The prairie writer is here faced with a special problem; to the outsider, the prairie appears empty, featureless, almost without character. It is thus a major triumph for Ross that the land comes to life so magnificently in these stories. But it is a particular kind of life. Here the landscape has a brooding, threatening quality, as though just beyond the horizon a malevolent God is preparing horrors of nature to hurl against an embattled people. Weather here is cursed, at first flattering human hopes, then mockingly dashing them asunder.

There is, of course, nothing made-up or fanciful about Ross' use in these stories of wind and storm, dust, hail, and snow. During the time that he lived the experiences which

became the raw material of his art, the Canadian prairies were a gigantic dust bowl for years on end. To the farmers it seemed that nature had turned against them forever, exacting a terrible price for some unknown crime. At the heart of the stories is an unequal, but nonetheless heroic, struggle between tenacious man and relentless nature.

Personification is of primary use in making nature seem hostile to his prairie farm characters. Wind doesn't merely blow in these stories; it pries into the very houses and lives of a people besieged:

> Tense; she fixed her eyes upon the clock, listening. There were two winds: the wind in flight, and the wind that pursued. The one sought refuge in the eaves, whimpering, in fear; the other assailed it there, and shook the eaves apart to make it flee again. Once as she listened this first wind sprang inside the room, distraught like a bird that has felt the graze of talons on its wing; while furious the other wind shook the walls, and thudded tumbleweeds against the window till its quarry glanced away again in fright. But only to return—to return and quake among the feeble eaves, as if in all this dust-mad wilderness it knew no other sanctuary.
>
> **("The Lamp at Noon")**

This paragraph is beautifully conceived and executed. The wind becomes diabolically alive, with the dominant image of a hunt carried superbly throughout the passage. But the personification works in two directions: we feel the savage attack of the wind but are never allowed to forget that a woman, alone and tensely watching a clock, listens to a predatory drama, which will go on and on and on . . . until she cracks.

At other moments, Ross works this same effect using a landscape of snow:

> Then she wheeled to the window, and with quick short breaths thawed the frost to see again. The glitter was gone. Across the drifts sped swift and snakelike little tongues of snow. She could not follow them, where they sprang from, or where they disappeared. It was as if all across the yard the snow were shivering awake— roused by the warnings of the wind to hold itself in readiness for the impending storm. The sky had become a sombre, whitish grey. It, too, as if in readiness, had shifted and lay close to earth. Before her as she watched a mane of powdery snow reared up breast-high against the darker background of the stable, tossed for a moment angrily, and then subsided again as if whipped down to obedience and restraint. But another followed, more reckless and impatient than the first. Another reeled and dashed itself against the window where she watched. Then ominously for a while there were only the angry little snakes of snow. The wind rose, creaking the troughs that were wired beneath the eaves. In the distance, sky and prairie now were merged into one another linelessly. All round her it was gathering; already in its press and whimpering there strummed a boding of eventual fury.
>
> **("The Painted Door")**

This powerful build-up to storm is described in no neutral way. Rather, some live but hostile force has selected this desolate farm house as a target for its assault. With the outside world completely cut off, it begins to try its strength, and release its wrath, upon the lonely woman who stares unmoving through the frozen window.

Many of the finest moments in Ross' stories combine these few but simple elements: menacing nature, lonely humans, a tightening claustrophobia. The dominant mood is one of attrition, with a terrible harmony between the working of wind upon soil and snow and the slow undermining of human stamina and strength.

Prairie Life and Prairie People

Knowledge is valuable no matter where we find it, and one aspect of literary criticism is an assessment of what we learn about life at a particular time and place. The historian and economist can give us the statistical data about prairie farm life in the 1930s, but literature alone can render these hard facts in an imaginative or creative way. Indeed, the Depression years in the Canadian west have been represented in a variety of evocative ways, from the impressive National Film Board production called *The Drylanders* (1962) to Michiel Horn's brilliant anthology, *The Dirty Thirties: Canadians in the Great Depression* (Toronto: Copp Clark, 1972). But it remains for writers like Sinclair Ross, who actually lived through those years, to illuminate them.

In Ross' stories, knowledge of prairie life is revealed in many ways. While the social historian or economist can usefully record that farm income dropped dramatically, and therefore drastically curtailed consumer purchasing, perhaps only the imaginative writer can communicate the effect, as in this passage from **"Cornet at Night"** in which the boy is instructed what to do when he takes the eggs to market in town:

> By the time they had both finished with me there were a great many things to mind. Besides repairs for my father's binder, I was to take two crates of eggs each containing twelve dozen eggs to Mr. Jenkins' store and in exchange have a list of groceries filled. And to make it complicated, both quantity and quality of some of the groceries were to be determined by the price of eggs. Thirty cents a dozen, for instance, and I was to ask for coffee at sixty-five cents a pound. Twenty-nine cents a dozen and coffee at fifty cents a pound. Twenty-eight and no oranges. Thirty-one and bigger oranges. It was like decimals with Miss Wiggins, or two notes in the treble against three in the bass. For my father a tin of special blend tobacco, and my mother not to know. For my mother a box of face powder at the drugstore, and my father not to know.
>
> **("Cornet at Night")**

Sometimes Ross' knowledge reveals itself in brief but precise instinctive reactions—a glance at a man's hands conveys the certainty that he won't be any good at setting up wheat stooks; or humiliation comes from thinking, against one's better judgment, that a balky horse can be cured:

> Of course he was wrong. He should have known what every horseman knows, that a balky horse is never

cured. If you're unscrupulous, you'll trade it off or sell it. If you're honest, you'll shoot it. Promptly, humanely, before it exasperates you to moments of rage and viciousness from which your self-respect will never quite recover. For weeks and months on end it will be a model horse, intelligent, cooperative, and then one fine day, when you're least expecting trouble, it will be a balky one again. You'll waste time and patience on it. You'll try persuasion first, then shouts and curses. You'll go back to persuasion, then degrade yourself to blows. And at last, weary and ashamed, you'll let the traces down and lead it to its stall.

("The Outlaw")

This exact and detailed knowledge of horses runs throughout Ross' fiction, and some of his best writing has been concerned with the relationship of boy and horse—for example, from the early story **"A Day with Pegasus,"** through the better known **"The Outlaw,"** to sequences in both *The Well* and *Whir of Gold.*

Ross's male characters, especially the farmers in the short stories, share with their creator this accumulated knowledge of prairie farm life. They can best be defined, not in relation to any society or to the universe, but simply in relation to nature. They think crop. They learn to read the skies. They are men who gauge and calculate, who play endlessly, as it were, a desperate game of chance with the weather and the seasons. And it is well to understand the effect of these obsessions upon themselves, their wives, and their children.

Many of the finest moments in Ross' stories combine these few but simple elements: menacing nature, lonely humans, a tightening claustrophobia. The dominant mood is one of attrition, with a terrible harmony between the working of wind upon soil and snow and the slow undermining of human stamina and strength.

—*Robert D. Chambers*

Ross' farmers are big, silent men who go about their work with a dogged fortitude that is truly impressive. Working farms which are at best marginally viable as economic units, and engaged as they are in a desperate duel with the land, it is hardly surprising that their inner lives reveal some terrible tensions. As heads of families they must grow the crops which buy the clothes and put the food on the kitchen table; failure to do this means more than the possibility of poverty or the ignominy of going on relief, for the vast majority of Saskatchewan farmers were on some form of relief during the Depression years. Failure entails, too, a loss of moral authority, the inability to retain what has traditionally been seen as a man's chief role, the support of his wife and children. Because of these pressures many of these prairie farmers suffered terrible strains, or broke under the unequal struggle against the unyielding seasons. Ross records, with both power and compassion, the heroic lives of these simple but good men, and celebrates their intense loyalty to a land which had apparently gone bad forever.

The farm wives form a distant point of this impossible prairie triad: men, women, and land. A typical moment in a Ross story finds the wife alone in the farm house, straining for a glimpse through the window of her husband ploughing in far off fields or struggling through mountainous drifts of snow. These are the loneliest women in Canadian fiction, and Ross has an especial understanding of their unjust plight. They are basically good and faithful mates, with an instinctive awareness of the severe tensions under which their husbands labour. But the desolation and hopelessness of prairie farm life occasionally gets to them, often against their own wills and desires. Then they come face to face with reality and with pained awareness count the toll of their way of life:

> There was a dark resentment in her voice now that boded another quarrel. He waited, his eyes on her dubiously as she mashed a potato with her fork. The lamp between them threw strong lights and shadows on their faces. Dust and drought, earth that betrayed alike his labour and his faith, to him the struggle had given sternness, an impressive courage. Beneath the whip of sand his youth had been effaced. Youth, zest, exuberance—there remained only a harsh and clenched virility that yet became him, that seemed at the cost of more engaging qualities to be fulfilment of his inmost and essential nature. Whereas to her the same debts and poverty had brought a plaintive indignation, a nervous dread of what was still to come. The eyes were hollowed, the lips pinched dry and colourless. It was the face of a woman that had aged without maturing, that had loved the little vanities of life, and lost them wistfully.

("The Lamp at Noon")

Sometimes the bleak face of despair leads to desperate acts. Ellen, in **"The Lamp at Noon,"** flees into a prairie dust storm and unwittingly suffocates the child whom she is trying to free from such a terrible life. In **"Not by Rain Alone"** (Part II), Eleanor dies when a winter blizzard invades the house and freezes her in the act of childbirth. It is the sense of being utterly cut off from the world (both women are alone) which vividly characterizes their lives. Neighbours are far distant through swirling dust or across frozen prairie; no radios or phones bring the outside world into these bare parlours and kitchens; husbands come for meals or to sleep. Even a rare trip to town may become a traumatic experience, as in the fine story, **"Nell,"** with its lovely symbol of fidelity in a remembered ketchup bottle. Indeed, the overall testimony of these stories suggests only a single motivating force which keeps these prairie farm women struggling on—the hope that their children will one day enjoy a better way of life.

The children in the stories are a fascinating group. They share with their parents the discipline and hard work of prairie farm life, and their lives are likewise not without

tensions. The pressure to be "good" and "nice" comes largely from their mothers, the children becoming the objects of their mothers cultural aspirations:

> It was the children now, Joe and Annabelle: this winter perhaps they could send them to school in town and let them take music lessons. Annabelle, anyway. At a pinch Joe could wait a while; he was only eight. It wouldn't take Annabelle long to pick up her notes; already she played hymn tunes by ear on the organ. She was bright, a real little lady for manners; among town people she would learn a lot. The farm was no place to bring her up. Running wild and barefoot, what would she be like in a few years? Who would ever want to marry her but some stupid country lout?

("A Field of Wheat")

With significant frequency the drive for culture takes the form in these stories of music lessons; to play the piano is a sure sign that one has risen above the level of chickens and crops. (The nature of these lessons is nicely detailed in Chapter 11 of *Whir of Gold*.) Equally impressive is the belief in the benefits of formal schooling, as though education were the one certain way of delivering the next generation from the hardships and heartbreaks of prairie farm life.

The children, moreover, often find themselves caught between two different value systems. Fathers, needing help with the farm work, encourage the useful skills; mothers insist upon religion, good manners, and those dreary piano lessons! Somehow, between chores and cultural workouts, the youngsters find moments for exotic dreams or brave fantasies. The climactic moments of their young lives occur, however, when parental pressures subside, when both parents gladly hand over some adult sphere of responsibility to the proudly waiting child. And while we naturally welcome this initiation into the adult community, we also sense that this parental dream of a better future may never be realized for these children. We come away haunted by the thought that, as with their mothers and fathers before them, these children will in time yield to this lonely and harsh environment.

Three Stories

Many of the themes and techniques discussed above appear in three of Ross' masterly stories: **"A Field of Wheat," "Cornet at Night,"** and **"The Painted Door."**

"A Field of Wheat" (Ross' first story published in Canada) opens on a strong note of hope. After years of blight and failure, a great crop of wheat is ripening for John. For his wife Martha, little dreams of the future begin to form, better schooling for the children, perhaps even something left over for herself and John. Ross creates in Martha's mind a quietly musing quality which parallels the outer scene of the great crop shimmering in the summer sun. This is one of the story's strong points—the subtle equation between the human world and the world of nature. Indeed, after sixteen years of marriage, Martha has come to see John almost in terms of the land—dried out and without hope. But this once, with the great crop coming on, she dreams that it (not herself) will restore John to his former self. This balanced tension between inner weather and outer weather is beautifully caught again in the symbol of the poppies, that most fragile of flowers, which the daughter Annabelle grows in the garden behind the house:

> Sitting down on the doorstep to admire the gaudy petals, she complained to herself, "They go so fast—the first little winds blow them all away." On her face, lengthening it, was bitten deeply the enigma of the flowers and the naked seed-pods. Why did the beauty flash and the bony stalks remain?

Ross thus establishes the terrible fragility of prairie farm life, the extraordinary beauty followed by sudden destruction and loss. And with this symbolic touch Ross begins the horrible prelude to storm.

The description of the hail storm—from Martha's first sensing it through its savage length—is one of the finest set pieces Ross has written, and takes its authority from his first-hand experience of prairie storms. This shows especially in Martha's frantic efforts at defence—throwing open the barn door for John and the horses, the children holding pillows against the exposed windows. And then the breaking ferocity of the storm, "like a weapon that has sunk deep into flesh," invading the house, smashing windows, lamps, dishes, and leaving the poor mutt Nipper beaten to death by the door. And after the storm has passed, they walk out into the fields:

> Nothing but the glitter of sun on hailstones. Nothing but their wheat crushed into little rags of muddy slime. Here and there an isolated straw standing bolt upright in headless defiance.

This is the farthest point of endurance, with the great promise of the season stretched dead before them. Both John and Martha are at the breaking point, but mask their agony before the children. It is only later, with anger and frustration and rage in her eyes and on her lips, that Martha seeks John in the barn, and finds him sobbing against the mane of a horse. Watching him cry is the most terrible moment of her life—a reaction which indicates the price exacted on these prairie farmers by the code of tough masculinity. Without letting him know that she has witnessed his agony, Martha creeps back to the house to clear up the mess left in the wake of the storm:

> Martha hurried inside. She started the fire again, then nailed a blanket over the broken window and lit the big brass parlour lamp—the only one the storm had spared. Her hands were quick and tense. John would need a good supper tonight. The biscuits were water soaked, but she still had the peas. He liked peas. Lucky that they had picked them when they did. This winter they wouldn't have so much as an onion or potato.

There is a fantastic strength of character in these final acts and thoughts of Martha (notice how the clipped rhythm of the sentences seems to keep the deeper emotions temporarily at bay), and the story's ending sees love and compassion

wrenched from the potential chaos of human despair. The will to go on never completely dies in the world of Ross' fiction, and some of his finest moments show the little lights of hope burning bravely against the black and massive forces of negation.

"Cornet at Night" is narrated by Tommy Dickson, an eleven-year-old prairie farm boy. It is a story which celebrates at least two firsts in Tommy's life—his first trip to town alone (his father is too busy with the harvest to find another hand, so Tommy is sent on the mission) and, secondly, his first awareness of a world of strange and beauty which exists outside the narrow compass of farm life. It is thus a story in which practical responsibility comes in conflict with aesthetic impulse.

Tommy is one of those prairie lads caught between the different values of his parents. His father's great compulsion is the crop; ripe wheat *will* be harvested, Sunday or not. Tommy's mother warns of the vengeance that will be reaped by breaking the Sabbath, or keeping Tommy home from school to help with the harvest. Ross sketches these parental values in a quietly satirical tone in the early part of the story:

> He slammed out at that to harness his horses and cut his wheat, and away sailed my mother with me in her wake to spend an austere half-hour in the dark, plushy little parlour. It was a kind of vicarious atonement, I suppose, for we both took straight-backed chairs, and for all of the half-hour stared across the room at a big pansy-bordered motto on the opposite wall: *As for Me and My House We Will Serve the Lord.*

But the male forces win out, and Tommy goes off to town to hire another hand. Tommy finds a young man named Philip, with shabby clothes but gentle manners, whose delicate hands hardly suggest the kind of man his father wants:

> His hands were slender, almost a girl's hands, yet vaguely with their shapely quietness they troubled me, because, however slender and smooth, they were yet hands to be reckoned with, strong with a strength that was different from the rugged labour-strength I knew.

On the ride home, Tommy discovers that Philip is a musician (Ross skilfully withholds the symbolic cornet until after the middle point of the story). Philip turns out to be a hopeless worker and, after one glorious evening of cornet music. Tommy's father drives him back to town.

From the mid point of the story, Ross develops a powerful tension between two sets of values, already prefigured in Tommy's parents. In one sense, Tommy has shown poor judgment and thus failed the test of his father's work ethic. The father nicely diverts the blame for this onto Tommy's mother—with all her nonsense about music lessons! On this count Tommy has been humiliated, but he has learned in the process that you don't judge every man by the toughness of his hands, or his ability to set up stooks. Tommy defends Philip as a musician, and about that there could be no argument:

There were no answers, but presently he reached for his cornet. In the dim, soft darkness I could see it glow and quicken. And I remember still what a long and fearful moment it was, crouched and steeling myself, waiting for him to begin.

And I was right: when they came the notes were piercing, golden as the cornet itself, and they gave life expanse that it had never known before.

Nor is Tommy the only one listening. His parents also respond to this extraordinary and unexpected beauty, as though realizing that the endless drudgery of farm life had almost closed their ears forever to the possibility of such unearthly loveliness. Once Philip has gone, Tommy's anger at the world flares briefly and then subsides into the pattern of acceptance which prairie life demands: "It's like that on a farm. You always have to put the harvest first."

Ross handles the theme of this story with great delicacy. Despite the temporary defeat of Tommy's pride, and the apparent triumph of his father's values, we see a process of growth—a developing awareness in Tommy that farm values are not the only values. (The story of Tommy's later life is, in a sense, transferred to Sonny in *Whir of Gold*.) Moreover, the resolution of this story's tensions is supported throughout by a subtle deployment of diction. One notes, for example, how the word "lesson" threads through the story in a variety of contrasting contexts. There are the overt lessons—Tommy's music lessons, and the lesson he tries to give Philip in stooking. And there are the hidden ones—the lesson which the Lord, so his mother claims, will teach Tommy's father for desecrating the Sabbath with work (Philip embodies that particular lesson); the lesson which Tommy's parents sense from the beauty of cornet music by night; the lesson Tommy learns about the potential beauty of the world outside the farm.

Towards the end of the story, Ross plays with equally skilful effect on the word "golden." Its usual form is in such phrases as "golden harvest," but a rival connotation emerges in the beauty of the gleaming instrument which Philip raises to his lips. The quiet and subtle meaning of the story—an ironical probing into the value systems of prairie farm life—is superbly caught in the final sentence, where the different sets of values are brought together powerfully and established, once and for all, in their proper relationship: "A harvest, however lean, is certain every year; but a cornet at night is golden only once."

"The Painted Door" is perhaps Ross' most dramatic story. It is told almost entirely from the woman's point of view, and spans a single day and night in her life—a fateful time, nonetheless, which brings her first act of sexual infidelity since her marriage, and the death of her husband. Ann and John have together struggled with prairie farm life for seven years. They have only two close neighbours—Steven, a bachelor, who farms alone about a mile away, and John's father, five miles across the hills. It is winter and the story opens with an ominous reference—to be repeated throughout the story—to "a double wheel around the moon," a certain prelude to storm.

Moreover, the early pages make it clear that Ann is undergoing a crisis in her relationship with both John and the prairie. A caustic quality colours her exchanges with John as he prepares to set out across the hills to visit his aging father: "'Plenty to eat—plenty of wood to keep me warm—what more could a woman ask for?'" What, indeed?—except company—she hasn't seen anyone but John for two whole weeks—and love; but John really loves the battle for survival with the land:

> Year after year their lives went on in the same little groove. He drove his horses in the field; she milked the cows and hoed potatoes. By dint of his drudgery he saved a few months' wages, added a few dollars more each fall to his payments on the mortgage; but the only real difference that it all made was to deprive her of his companionship, to make him a little duller, older, uglier than he might otherwise have been.

The middle section of the story, before Steven arrives, is a brilliant depiction of the lonely winter day of a prairie farm wife. Even the familiar noises of the house—crackling stove and ticking clock—grate on her taut nerves, and the rising blizzard slowly builds the atmosphere into a terrible tension. Ann's few attempts at relief somehow fail to bring any comfort—touching up the interior with white paint, returning in memory to happier days, when John was younger and more alive, when she danced with the youthful Steven (the recurring reference to Steven shows Ross' skill at creating dramatic suspense). Ann simply faces the hard truth that life has passed her by.

Then Steven comes. But his coming brings no lessening of the tension. Alone now with this younger man, whose calm assurance contrasts strongly with John's dullness, Ann is forced to admit an attraction:

> She felt eager, challenged. Something was at hand that hitherto had always eluded her, even in the early days with John, something vital, beckoning, meaningful. She didn't understand, but she knew. The texture of the moment was satisfyingly dreamlike: an incredibility perceived as such, yet acquiesced in. She was John's wife—she knew—but also she knew that Steven standing here was different from John.

As Ann and Steven put in the long hours until John's return (five miles across the hills in a blizzard), the tension continues to build inside this desolate farm house. Finally, they respond to both the attraction and the desire.

However, the presence of John, not in person but in thought, dominates the relationship of Ann and Steven throughout the long winter night. Ross' handling of John's off-stage presence is masterly. For example, we notice a subtle transition in the way John is referred to. The phrasing of Ann's doubt that John would attempt to return home through the blizzard is vaguely threatening: "'. . . he wouldn't dare . . . he wouldn't dare . . .'" Steven's judgments are more ominous: "'—it would be suicide to try,'" and "'A man couldn't live in it.'" Finally, in a splendidly symbolic moment, Ann imagines that she has dreamed of John's return, that he has stood over her menacingly just as the shadows from the stove mass above the sleeping lovers:

> There was one great shadow that struggled towards her threateningly, massive and black and engulfing all the room. Again and again it advanced, about to spring, but each time a little whip of light subdued it to its place among the others on the wall.

One cannot sufficiently praise the suggestive brilliance of this passage: words such as "struggled" and "advanced" force us to imagine John making his slow way through the blizzard, and the play of shadows on the wall beautifully parallels Ann's unsuccessful attempts to put John completely from her mind.

The final pages of the story bring a resolution to Ann's agony, and a totally unexpected dénouement. Ann's dark night of the soul—she suffers terrible pangs of guilt while Steven slumbers contentedly beside her—is finally dissolved by the coming of day. Ann now stands convinced of two certainties—that John is the man she really loves, and that somehow he has made his way home through the blizzard. In a surprise ending of great dramatic power—one which sends our minds reeling back across the whole length of the story—Ross finally reveals the rightness of Ann's intuition.

Ken Mitchell (essay date 1981)

SOURCE: "The Stories," in *Sinclair Ross: A Reader's Guide,* Thunder Creek Publishing, 1981, pp. 3-27.

[*In the following excerpt, Mitchell surveys the major themes of Ross's short fiction.*]

The short stories of Sinclair Ross are worth examining first because of what they tell us about his craft and moral purpose. As a group, the 16 stories published indicate his development as a prose writer, and provide some key insights to the world of psychological violence he depicts in his longer fictions. On the whole, the stories are simpler and more precise—although Ross himself is inclined to see them as "apprentice" works of fiction.

When his first story, **"No Other Way,"** was published in the English magazine *Nash's* in 1934, Ross wrote, "I am now starting to work on short stories, hoping gradually to build up a better technique without the cramping grind that writing a novel after hours demands." At that time, he was working for the bank in Winnipeg and had written two novels which he described as "failures."

The stories from Ross's "early" period, roughly 1935 to 1945, are his most successful—that is, during the time when he was giving them close artistic attention. He virtually stopped writing short stories after 1950.

Most of the stories have a remarkably similar pattern: a direct narrative simplicity and lack of stylistic excess.

Occasionally, there is a first-person narrator. The characters are usually simple people, either rural or small-town; "sophisticates" never appear, even peripherally. Ross's technique of characterization, however, is never simple. It shows a careful accretion of physical and psychological detail through the course of a well-plotted story. His pieces are, in other words, models of the "classic" story, and show much similarity to the stories of James Joyce and Stephen Crane. Ross's particular strength is the use of external forces, such as weather and landscape, to create symbolic patterns around the internal lives of his characters; he also shows a highly developed eye for the significantly vivid detail in a commonplace world.

Except for **"No Other Way,"** Ross's stories have been published in small Canadian magazines, and it was many years before they were widely available or read. They are unusual in Canadian fiction, in that the best of them achieve an exhilarating fusion of the classic elements of short fiction: character, plot and theme. By not fearing to rig out a strong plot—a "populist" rather than literary approach—Ross has succeeded while many of his more "polished" contemporaries have already faded from view.

It has taken a long time for Sinclair Ross's fiction to be appreciated, no doubt in part because he is averse to interviews and publicity—but also because his very qualities of simplicity, directness and a thematic concern with "ordinary" people, have placed his work below the dignity of Canadian academics and critics. History is the final judge of literature, however—and it is a rare anthology of Canadian stories these days that does not include at least one of his stories.

In 1968, nine of the stories were selected by the editors of McClelland and Stewart to be published in paperback, the first time any of them would appear in book form. This followed the successful paperback reprint of *As For Me and My House,* in 1957—sixteen years after its first publication. This selection of stories for inclusion is curious, as some of those omitted are superior, but perhaps the unifying principle of *The Lamp at Noon and Other Stories* is simply one of agricultural setting. All of these stories take place on farms, and the characters are all rural.

As these nine are the only stories generally available to readers, I will examine them first. They can—for the purpose of discussion—be divided into two groups. The strongest stories are in the first group, one marked by an intense conflict between husband and wife—that is, a sexual conflict. This is a theme which dominated Ross's first story (**"No Other Way"**); elements of it appear in nearly all his written works.

In each of these stories, the husband is a wheat farmer. He is usually tight-lipped and physically powerful, almost brutal. As an archetype, he could be seen as a slave of the earth-goddess Demeter, toiling to satisfy the demands of his farm and crops. The wife is generally characterized as sensitive and refined, often well-educated. She is subjected to a life of suffering and emotional deprivation in this harsh existence of rural isolation, fearing that worldly and cultural pleasures will be denied to her forever.

While these stories are not specifically located, it appears obvious that Ross has drown on his observations of Saskatchewan during the "Dirty Thirties."

"A Field of Wheat" is one of Sinclair Ross's finest achievements and illustrates this thematic conflict perfectly. John and Martha (surnames are rarely given in any of Ross's stories) live with their children, Annabelle and Joe, on a farm somewhere in the Great Plains. From the number of crop failures they have suffered, the period could be assumed to be the 1930s. There are no other characters, and their world becomes reduced to one of the simplest elements: family, animals, farm, weather. They are in conflict with the universe, and among themselves, but it is this starkness of detail which provides the story with its beauty. There is no attempt to provide social history, or any kind of documentary realism. The effect is to give us a microcosm of suffering mankind, caught in the grinding wheels of a universe beyond understanding or control.

> John has never been to school himself; he knew what it meant to go through life with nothing but his muscles to depend upon; and that was it, dread that Annabelle and Joe would be handicapped as he was, that was what had darkened him, made him harsh and dour. That was why he breasted the sun and dust a frantic, dogged fool, to spare them, to help them to a life that offered more than sweat and debts. Martha knew. He was a slow, inarticulate man, but she knew. Sometimes it even vexed her, brought a wrinkle of jealousy, his anxiety about the children, his sense of responsibility where they were concerned. He never seemed to feel that he owed her anything, never worried about her future. She could sweat, grow flat-footed and shapeless, but that never bothered him.

The girl Annabelle is the repository of Martha's dreams. In the coming winter she will, perhaps, take music lessons. "The farm was no place to bring her up. Running wild and barefoot, what would she be like in a few years? Who would ever want to marry her but some stupid country lout?" Martha is terrified that her daughter will follow her own pattern, despite a real love she has for her husband.

Martha's dream of the future is, naturally, centred on the crop of wheat, "the best crop of wheat John had ever grown," and she goes continually out to the field to examine its progress. It is three hundred acres of dreams: "Beautiful, more beautiful than Annabelle's poppies, than her sunsets. Theirs—all of it."

However, on the mid-summer day when the story is set, there is an oppressive atmosphere building in the air. The children are quarrelling around her feet in the hot kitchen, and when she suddenly looks outside, "there was no sky, only a gulf of blackness. . . . Above, almost overhead, a heavy, hard-lined bank of cloud swept its way across the sun-white blue in august, impassive fury."

Martha screams at the children to stay inside as the hail storm suddenly strikes. The description of the storm is one of the most effective passages Ross has written, opening with:

> a sharp, crunching blow on the roof, its sound abruptly dead, sickening, like a weapon that has sunk deep into flesh. Wildly she shook her hands, motioning Annabelle back to the window, and started for the stairs. Again the blow came; then swiftly a stuttered dozen of them.

> She reached the kitchen just as John burst in. With their eyes screwed up against the pommelling roar of the hail they stared at each other. They were deafened, pinioned, crushed. His face was a livid blank, one cheek smeared with blood where a jagged stone had struck him. Taut with fear, her throat aching, she turned away and looked through Joe's legs again. It was like a furious fountain, the stones bouncing high and clashing with those behind them. They had buried the earth, blotted out the horizon; there was nothing but their crazy spew of whiteness.

The effect of the storm is catastrophic; it breaks the windows and invades the house, heaping hailstones on the beds and floors. The dog Nipper is forgotten outside and "beaten lifeless." When it subsides, Martha and John walk out to their field of wheat:

> Nothing but the glitter of sun on hailstones. Nothing but their wheat crushed into little rags of muddy slime. Here and there an isolated straw standing bolt upright in headless defiance. Martha and John walked to the far end of the field. There was no sound but their shoes slipping and rattling on the pebbles of ice. Both of them wanted to speak, to break the atmosphere of calamity that hung over them, but the words they could find were too small for the sparkling serenity of wasted field. Even as waste it was indomitable. It tethered them to itself, so that they could not feel or comprehend. It had come and gone, that was all; before its tremendousness and havoc they were prostrate. They had not yet risen to cry out or protest.

Up to this point the story, though well-written, is fairly conventional and, it might be said, typically Canadian in its grim presentation of the power of nature. Ross, however, is more concerned with the human dynamics of this archetypal family. Martha, devastated, whimpers that she cannot go on any longer. John pleads with her to put on a brave front for the sake of the children, which she does, though vowing to herself she will leave the farm. Unable to take the strain, she runs to the stable to "unloose the fury that clawed within her, strike back a blow for the one that had flattened her." Her intention is to attack her husband, but she cannot find him at first; and when she does, she is startled to find him "pressed against one of the horses," sobbing in private anguish. It is a shock to her, "the strangest, most frightening moment in her life. He had always been so strong and grim; had just kept on as if he couldn't feel, as if there were a bull's hide over him, and now he was beaten." Like an intruder she creeps away, an unwilling witness to his humiliation.

The story concludes on a curious note of triumph and hope, when Annabelle cries to her mother, "Look at the sky!"

> Withdrawn now in the eastern sky the storm clouds towered, gold-capped and flushed in the late sunlight,

high still pyramids of snowiness and shadow. And one that Annabelle pointed to, apart, the farthest away of them all, this one in bronzed slow splendour spread up mountains high to a vast, plateau-like summit.

Martha hurries indoors to prepare a "good supper" for John, with the peas she had picked before the storm. The image of the gold-capped clouds towering in the east suggests that life will go beyond this stormy moment in their lives, despite the terrible burden of defeat and despair, which threatens to crush their hopes. Martha's faith in self, at least, is somehow renewed—and a story drenched in pathos somehow becomes a parable of existential hope.

"The Lamp at Noon," another dust-bowl story, is considerably bleaker. This time, the external force is the shrieking wind. For three days it has hurled dust at a struggling young farm couple, Paul and Ellen. Again, the storm symbolizes the conflict between man and wife, or at least the suffocating blast of circumstances which threatens Ellen's equilibrium. A former school-teacher, she has been struggling against deep emotional depression, perhaps a result of her recent birth-giving as much as farm life. It is the isolation which abrades her nerves, but she focuses her bitterness on the helpless Paul.

The story begins at noon on the third day of the dust storm. Even at noon, the obscuring dust has brought on such darkness that Ellen must light their kitchen lamp. The description of the farm quickly becomes more universal:

> In dim, fitful outline the stable and oat granary still were visible; beyond, obscuring fields and landmarks, the lower of the dust clouds made the farmyard seem an isolated acre, poised aloft above a sombre void. At each blast of wind, it shook, as if to topple and spin hurtling with the dust-reel into space.

Alone with the baby inside the claustrophobic shack, she recalls her recent arguments with Paul, bitter exchanges of angry words which neither of them understands. When he finally comes in for lunch, the quarrel picks up where it left off, as she pleads with her husband to give up the futile struggle against the wind.

> The lamp between them threw strong lights and shadows on their faces. Dust and drought, earth that betrayed alike his labour and his faith, to him the struggle had given sternness, an impassive courage. Beneath the whip of sand his youth had been effaced.

> He sat staring at the lamp without answering, his mouth sullen. It seemed indifference now, as if he were ignoring her, and stung to anger again she cried, "Do you ever think what my life is? . . . I'm still young—I wasn't brought up this way."

> "You're a farmer's wife now. It doesn't matter what you used to be, or how you were brought up. You get enough to eat and wear. Just now that's all I can do. I'm not to blame that we've been dried out five years."

As the storm intensifies its violence around them, Paul refuses to sympathize, seeing her hysteria as female weakness. Finally his preoccupation with the waiting farmwork overwhelms any need for talk, and "with a jerk" he frees his smock from her clutch.

Like John in **"A Field of Wheat,"** he goes to the stable to find comfort in the company of his work-horse. Even there, the walls "creaked and sawed as if the fingers of a giant hand were tightening to collapse them; the empty loft sustained a pipelike cry that rose and fell but never ended." As in so much of Sinclair Ross's fiction, the external world seems alive with malignant rage. Once alone, however, Paul becomes filled with remorse for his cruelty, seeing his wife's face in front of him with "its staring eyes and twisted suffering."

As the afternoon wears on, the storm gradually expires and Paul returns to the house. "But she was gone. . . . The door was open, the lamp blown out, the crib empty. The dishes from their meal at noon were still on the table." Terrified, he stumbles for hours through the piles of dirt around their farm until he finds her "crouched against a drift of sand as if for shelter, her hair in matted strands around her neck and face, the child clasped tightly in her arms."

The baby is dead, suffocated either by her frantic arms or by the dust. The horror is that Ellen does not realize that the child is dead, and her eyes show only "an immobile stare." Although the storm is over and she whispers "tomorrow will be fine," the conclusion is one of unrelieved despair, so that Ellen's final utterance is tragically ironic. For this couple there is no tomorrow. Yet Ross is careful to assign no blame to either of the characters; like the unnamed baby, they are victims of their own frailty.

"Not By Rain Alone" is a story in two parts, called **"Summer Thunder"** and **"September Snow."** These were originally published separately (the latter section two years before the former) in *Queen's Quarterly,* where most of Ross's stories first appeared. They were unified in the collection with slight revisions, to greatly enhanced effect. The cycle of the seasons and years becomes—like the storms of the other stories—a symbol of the changing lives of the central characters, Will and Eleanor.

In **"Summer Thunder,"** Will is a bachelor farmer, very poor and fighting a drought. He hopes to marry Eleanor, the daughter of a wealthy neighbour, but they are thwarted by the "still, brassy, pitiless" weather. His farm is full of stones which appear every spring as fast as he can clear them, the frost heaving "another litter from the bitch-like earth." His black mare Bess is beginning "to sag a little now," and his shack is a "stench of heat and a sickening drone of flies." All in all, a rather unattractive proposition for Eleanor. "At the best they would grub along painfully, grow tired and bitter, indifferent to each other. It was the way of the land."

The couple meets in the field to look at their hopeless crop, but they determine to marry after harvest in the fall. As they talk the distant thunder grows closer, like tumbling stones. . . . flare after flare of lightning lit the clouds, yellow and soft like the flickerings of a lamp; and they saw what dark and threatening clouds they were, yet how they still hung in the distance, as if at a pause, uncertain of their way.

In **"September Snow"** a year later, the couple is married. Eleanor is pregnant, and, with a snowstorm coming, she does not want Will to go out into the fields at night to collect his cattle. Yet the cattle must be brought in, or they will be lost, so he goes into the storm. When he finds them, huddled against a fence, they prove impossible to drive back against the wind. When Will loses his temper and strikes his horse Bess, she jerks away and disappears into the night.

Will sets out walking back to the farm, sometimes "backwards, sometimes with one shoulder thrust out, his head tilted, the way a swimmer meets a wave." Finally he can go no further and seeks refuge in a straw-stack. As though trying to reverse his child's impending birth, Will attempts to escape from the world back into the womb-like warmth.

> He tunnelled into it, lengthwise, feet first, kicking and burrowing until he could stretch his legs. And now the warmth was real, but wide awake from the effort it had cost him to pull out the straw he began to think of Eleanor, and to feel troubled and even guilty because he was lying here comfortable and idle. . . . She would be waiting for him, pacing through the house. . . . afraid he might be lost. Sometimes a woman did queer things when she was expecting a baby. She might even start out to look for him, or try to make her way to a neighbour's.

Panic stricken, he tries the storm once again, but is driven back by a wind "like a needled wall." Surrendering to its fury, he retreats into the warm shelter of the stack and dozes until morning. When he wakes, the storm is over, and the world has become "colourless and blank, without balance or orientation." He trudges home, anticipating a quarrel with his wife.

The house, however, is empty except for an invasion of snow "mounded right across the kitchen, curled up like a wave against the far wall, piled on table and chairs. Even on the stove—" He finds Eleanor on the bed, "her face twisted into a kind of grin, the forehead shining as if the skullbones were trying to burst through the skin." She dies in the process of childbirth; the cattle wander home by themselves. Eleanor's death has been completely absurd, and Will must live a future knowing that his devotion to the farm has killed her. Yet once again, there is at the conclusion of this utterly bleak scene a curious trumpet-note of hope:

> They talked to him about the baby, somebody held it up for him to see, but he went to the door and stood blinking at the glitter of the sun. . . . It was like a spring day, warm and drowsy. . . . There was a hushed, breathless silence, as if sky and snow and sunlight were self-consciously poised, afraid to wrinkle or dishevel their serenity. Then through it, a faint, jagged little

saw of sound, the baby started to cry. He felt a twinge of recognition. He seemed to be listening to the same plaintiveness and protest that had been in Eleanor's voice of late. An impulse seized him to see and hold his baby; but just for a minute longer he stood there, looking out across the sun-spangled snow, listening.

What is Will listening for? What does he wish to hear? The voice of God, providing an explanation for this cruel joke? Why should he, of all men, be made to suffer in this sharp exchange of life and death? As in all of Sinclair Ross's stories, there are no answers. Man simply must go on. The new generation is at hand, maintaining the cycle, just as Will himself has taken on the endless toil of moving rocks from his parents' harsh land. Here is a Sisyphean parable indeed.

> Ross's technique of characterization is never simple. It shows a careful accretion of physical and psychological detail through the course of a well-plotted story. His pieces are, in other words, models of the "classic" story, and show much similarity to the stories of James Joyce and Stephen Crane.
>
> *—Ken Mitchell*

The sexual conflict in these stories, obviously, is not of the conventional boy-meets-girl, man-takes-mistress variety. Here the sexual roles are very basically defined. The male is the physical half of the human animal, imbued with grim determination to provide and compete. The female is the spiritual half, trying to make sense of it all, victimized by her physical weakness just as the man is victimized by his lack of "common sense." The source of Ross's vision lies as much in the ancient mythology of Egypt as it does in Canadian geography. The primal conflict is demonstrated most brilliantly in Ross's finest story, **"The Painted Door,"** a piece which has been anthologized dozens of times but was virtually unknown for years after its first publication in 1939.

Here again, we have John, "a slow, unambitious man, content with his farm and cattle, naively proud of Ann. He had been bewildered by it once, her caring for a dull-witted fellow like him." They have no children, and like the other doomed couples, they toil out their lives in the same vast and lonely land.

John's father lives a few miles away and needs help in the middle of winter. Ann is terrified of being alone, with a blizzard threatening, but John promises he will return no matter how bad the storm gets. His promises, it is assumed, are absolutely reliable. But to allay her fears, he says he will ask Steven, their neighbour, to drop by for a visit.

As the day wears on, Ann paints the kitchen woodwork to keep her mind off the weather and solitude. Like the other women, she reflects on their long years of drudgery to pay off the mortgage, their sacrifice to a future that will never arrive. Painting onward, accompanied by the ominous ticking of her clock, the silence grows unbearable. She thaws the frost on the window to see the storm beginning, its drifts

> swift and snakelike little tongues of snow. . . . It was as if all across the yard the snow were shivering awake—roused by the warnings of the wind to hold itself in readiness for the impending storm. . . . Before her as she watched a mane of powdery snow reared up breast-high against the darker background of the stable, tossed for a moment angrily, and then subsided again as if whipped down to obedience and restraint. But another followed, more reckless and impatient than the first. Another reeled and dashed itself against the window where she watched. Then ominously for a while there were only the angry little snakes of snow. The wind rose, creaking the troughs that were wired beneath the eaves. . . . All around her it was gathering; already in its press and whimpering there strummed a boding of eventual fury. Again she saw a mane of snow spring up, so dense and high this time that all the sheds and stables were obscured.

The sustained intensity in the description of the blizzard is one of the most effective passages in Ross's canon. He is, of course, describing the storm within Ann—complete with deft touches of sexual imagery—as well as the one which assaults from without. The elements rage like demons, threatening her soul as they do the walls of the house with "sharp, savage blows." For relief, she keeps turning to the stove to warm herself—that is, to the domestic hearth. But gradually she begins to doubt that John will return through this ferocious storm. She goes outside to feed the animals in the stable and encounters the blizzard head-on:

> A gust of wind spun her forward a few yards, then plunged her headlong against a drift that in the dense white whirl lay invisible across her path. For nearly a minute she huddled still, breathless and dazed. The snow was in her mouth and nostrils, inside her scarf and up her sleeves. . . . The wind struck from all sides, blustering and furious. It was as if the storm had discovered her, as if all its forces were concentrated upon her extinction. . . . Suddenly [with] a comprehension so clear and terrifying that it struck all thoughts of the stable from her mind, she realized in such a storm her puniness.

She retreats back to the house, shortly before Steven arrives to calm her hysteria. She collapses against him, "hushed by a sudden sense of lull and safety." Steven is a swaggering opportunist who exploits Ann's loneliness and seduces her, after convincing her that John could not possibly travel through such a storm.

As she lies in bed with Steven asleep beside her, Ann has a frightening nightmare in which a great shadow

> struggled towards her threateningly, massive and black and engulfing all the room. Again and again it advanced,

about to spring, but each time a little whip of light subdued it to its place. . . . Still she cowered, feeling that gathered there was all the frozen wilderness, its heart of terror and invincibility.

In this world where sexual infidelity is more than a sin, but approaches the vilest evil, she is tormented with a vision of John standing at the bedroom doorway, gazing on her transgression. As she looks on the sleeping Steven, "half-smiling still, his lips relaxed in the conscienceless complacency of his achievement," she knows she was wrong to see anything in his smooth appearance that was preferable to her rough, unshaven—and entirely faithful—John. To make it up to him, she resolves, "John was the man. With him lay all the future."

It is already too late, however, John is found in the morning a mile away, clutching the wire on the fence past the house. It appears he missed the house, returning in the storm, and got caught up in the wire. Later, when left alone with his corpse, Anne sees a "little smear of paint" on the palm of his hand, paint he could only have gotten from the bedroom door as he watched his own nightmare in the bedroom. He has killed himself in the storm, rather than return to a home he could no longer tolerate.

The ending employs an unexpected twist of plot, yet its impact is totally convincing. Ann is left as Will was, facing an indescribably tormented future of guilt, for her one lapse of conviction. It is a tough moral world that Ross's characters occupy.

The second group of stories in *The Lamp at Noon* shows a slightly different perspective. They reveal an element in Sinclair Ross's writing which appears, so far, only in the stories. This is the story seen from a child's point of view, though often narrated by the child grown-adult. Here the themes are less tragic—though never whimsical—as the child learns how to deal with the confusing adult world of farm life. The horse as both character and symbol is important in all of Ross's work, but there is an especially strong link in this group of stories between child and horse.

For example, in **"The Outlaw,"** a 13-year-old unnamed boy has two loves which dominate his life: Millie Dickson, a sweet little thing "from town," and Isabel, his "beautiful but dangerous" pony. It is a touching and often funny triangle, for Millie comes to the farm one day and taunts the boy into riding the "outlaw" horse, against the specific commands of his parents. He has already fantasized riding Isabel to the school house to impress Millie, "whose efforts to be loyal to me were always defeated by my lack of verve and daring."

In a moment of heroic exhilaration, he gallops across the fields—a horseman at last, among the strawstacks "luminous and clear as drops of gum on fresh pine lumber"—before Isabel throws him off head-first into a snowdrift, almost at the feet of her watching rival. Millie is wickedly amused at the punishment which will follow—but it never comes. His father is pleased after all at his daring, and silences the mother's disapproval. "Now, in their peculiar parental idiom, they had just given their permission, and Isabel and the future were all mine. Isabel *and* Millie Dickson."

"Circus in Town" is probably the lightest story in the collection, concerning an 11-year-old girl, Jenny, who is denied the circus because of the family's poverty. Worse, she must endure her parents' recurring bickering over finances, making her feel "exasperated and guilty that there should be a quarrel about it, her father looking so frightened and foolish, her mother so savage and red." Jenny flees with her bright circus poster to the barn loft—another womb-like sanctuary of privacy and innocence—where she proceeds to enjoy the circus in her fantasies: "All night long she wore her purple tights and went riding Billie round and round the pasture in them. A young, fleet-footed Billie. Caparisoned in blue and gold and scarlet, silver bells on reins and bridle—neck arched proudly to the music of the band." Like most of these sad children, Jenny fights to retain her sense of beauty and romance by retreating inward, away from the cruel world of practical adulthood.

A much more densely plotted story is **"The Runaway,"** a tale of moral justice in the Faulkerian mode. Here a boy tells of the conflict between his father, a rather unsuccessful farmer, and Luke Taylor, a highly successful breeder of "Black Diamond" horses, and a man with a reputation for sharp dealing. When Father acquires a team of Black Diamonds, over Mother's objections, they are horrified to discover they own a "balky" team—that is, a team which, at unpredictable moments, refuses to move. Father is completely humiliated on Main Street when the Diamonds "instead of springing away with flying manes and foaming mouths, striking sparks of envy and wonder from the heart of every beholder, simply stood there, chewed their bits and trembled."

Father, a Christian optimist, keeps hoping to change them, but loses control of himself when he is further goaded by Luke Taylor. (Taylor is described in generally Satanic terms, especially by Mother). Father finally employs Luke's taunting suggestion and builds a fire under the balky team while they are hitched to a straw stack. Frightened, the horses pull the strawrack over the fire and take off for home—not to their new home, but to Luke Taylor's big hip-roofed barn. They gallop off with "terror in their hearts, hitched to a load of fire," while the boy chases behind on his pony Gopher.

Like a pair of rebellious black imps, the Diamonds set Luke's barn on fire. The herd of Diamonds inside *all* balk when the boy tries to remove them; Luke runs into the barn as the floor of the burning loft collapses. "You sow the wind and you reap whirlwind," Mother comments knowingly, while Father continues to dream of a pair of Black Diamond colts "[the] prettiest horses a man ever set eyes on."

The most unusual story in the collection is **"One's a Heifer,"** a mysterious tale which pits a young boy of thirteen against one of the most sinister and crudely appealing characters in Canadian fiction, Arthur Vickers.

Vickers runs "a poor, shiftless-looking place" a few miles distant from the boy's uncle's farm. They meet when the boy is out late searching for some stray cattle. Vickers denies seeing them, although he is extremely evasive about a closed box-stall in his ramshackle barn. Nonetheless, he invites the boy to stay for supper and a game of checkers in his crude bachelor's shack. "The table in the centre was littered with tools and harness. On a rusty cookstove were two big steaming pots of bran. . . . At the end opposite the bed, weasel and coyote skins were drying. There were guns and traps on the wall. . . . In a corner squatted a live owl with a broken wing." In explanation, Vickers, say, "You get careless, living alone like this. It takes a woman anyway."

A little later, however, he reveals he had a woman there a few weeks the previous summer, "but it didn't last. Just a cow she was—just a big stupid cow—and she wanted to stay on. . . . I had to send her home."

All the time, the boy is plotting how he can slip out to the barn, round up his uncle's yearlings and start the long trek home. He decides to accept Vickers' invitation to stay overnight, and they get involved in a series of checker games which Vickers transparently allows the boy to win. "Sometimes I used to ask her to play," he says, "but I had to tell her every move to make. If she didn't win she'd upset the board and go off and sulk." Eventually Vickers begins talking about the girl, who wanted to marry him, or at least stay on with him in the shack. Vickers could not be trapped so easily, especially by an inferior checker-player.

His "glassy, cold" eyes are deeply disturbing to the young narrator, filling him with "a vague and overpowering dread." Pretending to sleep, the boy is distracted by Vickers, who remains sitting at the checker-board,

> staring fixedly across the table as if he had a partner sitting there. His hands were clenched in front of him, there was a sharp, metallic glitter in his eyes. . . . then suddenly wrenching himself to action he hurled the checkers with such vicious fury that they struck the wall and clattered back across the room.

When Vickers finally goes to sleep, the boy has a nightmare in which he goes to the stable, with the owl "sitting over the door with his yellow eyes like a pair of lanterns. The calves, he told me, were in the other stall with the sick colt. I looked and they were there all right, but Tim [his horse] came up and said it might be better not to start for home till morning. . . . I agreed, realizing now that it wasn't the calves I was looking for after all, and that I still had to see inside the stall that was guarded by the owl."

In the morning, Vickers is very tense, and the boy employs a trick to get into the mysterious stall to find his calves. Vickers returns and grabs him violently by the throat, then knocks him down to the floor. "But it wasn't the blow that frightened me. It was the fierce wild light in his eyes."

When he finally makes his escape on his horse, by lashing Vickers across the face with the reins, he gets home to discover that the calves had come home by themselves. Vickers didn't have them in the stall at all, and we are left to conclude that Vickers kept the corpse of the "stupid cow" in there. It is not indicated how or when this nightmare will end, either for Vickers or for the boy.

"Cornet at Night" is probably Ross's most popular story, widely anthologized and adapted to a short film. It is the most optimistic in the collection, despite the theme of intense sexual conflict. The Dicksons represent the same family again: a hard-working father, a cultured, even Puritan mother. Tommy, the boy, is sent into town to hire a man to help with the harvest, against his mother's wishes.

> "But Monday's his music lesson day—and when will we have another teacher like Miss Wiggins who can teach him music too?"
>
> "A dollar for lessons and the wheat shelling! When I was his age I didn't even get to school."
>
> "Exactly," my mother scored, "and look at you today. Is it any wonder I want him to be different?"

Like the other children, Tommy is the battleground for his parents' obsessions. He is torn between his is father, who is demanding and surly, and his mother, who makes him wear "knicker corduroys" and practise hymns on the piano.

However, a compromise is wrung, and Tommy is sent with Rock, the plodding reliable work-horse, to hire a hand. Mr. Dickson wants "somebody big and husky"; Mrs. Dickson wants one who looks clean. On his first solo flight to town, even with Rock, Tommy is ecstatic. "For a farm boy is like that. Alone with himself and his horse he cuts a fine figure. He is the measure of the universe. . . . His horse never contradicts."

In town, however, it is very different, and his "little bubble of self-importance" is soon burst. On an impulse, he selects from the candidates a young well-dressed man with slender hands, "almost a girl's hands, yet vaguely with their shapely quietness they troubled me, because, however slender and smooth, they were yet hands to be reckoned with, strong with a strength that was different from the rugged labour-strength I knew."

The young man, named Phil, turns out to be a musician who has never worked on a farm before. He is a disaster, and even Mrs. Dickson is contemptuous. Mr. Dickson attempts to blame her for Tommy's misjudgement: "It's your fault—you and your nonsense about music lessons. If you'd listen to me sometimes, and try to make a man of him."

Completely shattered, Tommy is compensated that night when Phil plays his cornet in the bunk-house.

> . . . when they came the notes were piercing, golden as the cornet itself, and they gave life expanse that it

had never known before. They floated up against the night, and each for a moment hung there clear and visible. Sometimes they mounted poignant and sheer. Sometimes they soared and then, like a bird alighting, fell and brushed earth again.

The next day, after failing miserably in the fields, Phil is cast back again into the stream of unemployment just as Tommy comes home from school. Moved by the mysterious outburst of music, his mother shows some sympathy for the haggard Phil, giving him "a box of lunch and some ointment for his sunburn." "My father looked uncomfortable, feeling, no doubt, that we were all unjustly blaming everything on him. It's like that on a farm. You always have to put the harvest first."

This is what Tommy learns, apparently, although the parents' bickering continues long after Phil has gone. Mrs. Dickson says the misfortune came about as retribution for her husband harvesting on Sunday. It is back to painful piano marches and a life of brutal toil, but Tommy has transcended for one moment into the world of the spirit. He concludes, "A harvest, however lean, is certain every year; but a cornet at night is golden only once."

The uncollected stories show many of the same themes. **"No Other Way,"** Ross's first story, is a somewhat melodramatic account of Hatty Glenn, an unfortunate farm wife who tends cattle and turnips while her husband runs off to town to dally with the undertaker's wife. She is humiliated on the one occasion when she insists on going with him to a dance. She contemplates killing herself as "an ugly, crabbed old woman," but when the endless farmwork demands her presence, she once again takes up her burdens for "there was no other way."

It is apparent, then, that even in his first story, Sinclair Ross was depicting his farm characters as existential antiheroes, winding the plot around the battle of the sexes. This is again demonstrated in **"Nell,"** a later story that is, if possible, even more depressing. Nell is a "tall, spare, rawboned woman" who struggles in resentment over her husband's Saturday night jaunt to town. He plays poker in the back of the poolroom while she maintains her vigil in the general store, finally walking home with her son Tommy and a bottle of ketchup she had purchased especially for her husband's enjoyment.

It is hard to understand why **"A Day with Pegasus"** was not included in *The Lamp at Noon,* as it is not only a superior story, but is remarkable for its positive outlook. For once, the farm family is harmonious and prosperous. The emphasis is on romantic fantasy, rather than despair.

Peter Parker is a young boy with a vivid imagination, in the process of being shackled by a prosaic school teacher. Inspired by a new colt he has been given by his father, he writes a school composition about rodeos and a fictitious cowboy friend named Slim. Miss Kinley is outraged at the "lies" and demands that he writes a "true" composition on how he spent the previous Saturday planting potatoes.

At home again, Peter recovers his dignity with the companionship of his colt, and retreats to the barn loft to gaze at the prairie, lit by the setting sun:

> For a few miles it fell gently, then with a long slow swell slipped over the horizon. There was a state of mind, a mood, a restfulness, in which one could skim along this curve of prairie floor and, gathering momentum from the downward swing, glide up again and soar away from earth. He succeeded now, borne by a white-limbed steed again. And as they soared the mystery was not solved, but gradually absorbed, a mystery still but intimate, a heartening gleam upon the roof of life to let him see its vault and spaciousness.

This "magic crystal globe" of transcending imagination is a key motif in Sinclair Ross's writing that lies as a counterbalance to the harsh and stringent realism of the psychic conflicts he otherwise explores. Treated here with thematic purity, it puts **"A Day with Pegasus"** in a class by itself.

Two stories which derive from Ross's army experiences during World War Two appeared in magazines just after the war, **"Barrack Room Fiddle Tune"** and **"Jug and Bottle."** These may be surviving fragments from an abandoned novel which Ross has said he was working on during the war years "about a young soldier from Manitoba." **"Barrack Room Fiddle Tune"** is a slight tale about a group of soldiers who destroy the fiddle of a pathetic character because he torments them with his awful playing. **"Jug and Bottle"** is a far more substantial morality tale, rather Conradian in structure and density. Of all of Ross's stories, it is the most remote from his prairie landscape. It resists summarizing, being essentially a character study of Private Coulter, an ungainly man, a misfit who keeps trying to kill himself for unexplained reasons. The narrator finds himself keeping the man alive, becoming friendly with him, and finally assuming responsibility for his life. Gradually, it evolves that Coulter has previously married an invalid girl out of pity. When she did not die as expected, he could not keep up his false mask of love and now he is tormenting himself with guilt.

Gradually, the narrator realizes that he has put himself in a similar position, that Coulter "had a special claim on me, as if sympathizing with him in his misfortune was my special job." He attempts to back out of the friendship, avoiding him because there is a difference "between helping a man through a tough spot, and turning yourself into a crutch for him to lean on permanently."

The conclusion is complicated, but effective. Coulter's estranged wife dies; the narrator agrees finally to meet him at an English pub called *The Jug and Bottle*. Too late, he discovers that the name is simply the description of a pub entrance, and he waits at the door of the wrong pub. As a result, Coulter has slashed his wrists and died, his burden of guilt unrelieved. Now the narrator must carry Coulter's burden.

Another later story is **"Saturday Night,"** about a young man who is painfully pursuing a Saturday night date in his old home town with a girl who had charmed him the week before. But his illusion of great romance is shattered; when he finally tracks her down, she is out with a fancy rival. The point of the story is his recovery from the disappointment—the rhythm of life going on with or without him.

The most recently published (1972) of Ross's stories, **"The Flowers that Killed Him,"** is also his most experimental in structure. If anything, however, it is even more somber than his rural stories. Were it not for the odd twist of plot at its conclusion, it would not be recognized as a story by the same author.

The narrative technique is rather sophisticated, as the story is told by a young boy who is obviously disturbed by something he does not reveal. His two friends—13-year-olds like himself—have recently been sexually assaulted and murdered. Together they were known as "the inseparables," although the other boys had come from deprived backgrounds, and were considered outcasts.

The narrator's father is the town's school principal, known as "Old Creeper" because of his fascination with plants and flowers. It is the father who brought the boys together, and when the narrator discovers that his father is the murderer—through a complex series of plot turns and character revelations—he is revolted. His father had used him like a piece of bait to bring the other boys into his reach. He waits until his father comes out onto the balcony of their apartment building, "because to reach one of the boxes you've got to lean out over the railing and stretch." When he does, the boy pushes him over, hurtling him five floors down onto the pavement and a broken milk bottle the son has placed there in preparation—"to be sure that nobody, even after they'd straightened him out and washed off the blood and makeup, would notice the scratches that had been there before he hit the pavement."

It is a particularly gruesome and gothic story, combining the outraged innocence evident in Ross's earlier work with the demands of magazines for more sophisticated material and techniques. If nothing else, it proves Sinclair Ross's continuing adaptability as a writer, and that his ability to write short fiction has not waned over the years.

F. H. Whitman (essay date 1982)

SOURCE: "The Case of Ross's Mysterious Barn," in *Canadian Literature,* No. 94, Autumn, 1982, pp. 168-69.

[*In the following essay, Whitman contends that the little girl in Ross's "One's a Heifer" is an imaginary construct of Vickers's "schizoid personality."*]

When discussing Sinclair Ross' **"One's a Heifer,"** most readers seem drawn to essentially two considerations: why Vickers would not allow the boy to look into the stall and what he kept there. Over the years one popular explanation has emerged to the exclusion of others—namely, the boy was denied access to the stall because Vickers kept there the girl who used to visit him, and that she was possibly dead, but more probably confined as a prisoner. In my opinion this explanation is totally unsatisfactory, for the very good reason that the whole story of the girl is nothing more than a fiction in Vickers' mind. I see no grounds for believing that the stall contains anything or for rejecting Vickers' own explanation of his conduct: "There's a hole in the floor—that's why I kept the door closed. If you didn't know, you might step into it—twist your foot."

The clues that Vickers' girl is purely imaginary may be found in both what Vickers tells us about the girl and his behaviour in the light of what he has said. Our suspicions ought to be aroused by the very first mention of the girl ("Last summer I had a girl cooking for a few weeks, but it didn't last. Just a cow she was—just a big stupid cow"), and, if not, then certainly by the account of her performances at the checkerboard: her inability to make decisions ("I had to tell her every move to make"), or remember ("she'd forget whether she was black or red"), or even speak ("This one . . . couldn't even talk like anybody else"). What puts the issue beyond doubt is the description of Vickers playing checkers with himself:

> Most of the time he played checkers with himself, moving his lips, muttering words I couldn't hear, but once I woke to find him staring fixedly across the table as if he had a partner sitting there. His hands were clenched in front of him, there was a sharp, metallic glitter in his eyes. I lay transfixed, unbreathing. His eyes as I watched seemed to dilate, to brighten, to harden like a bird's. For a long time he sat contracted, motionless, as if gathering himself to strike, then furtively he slid his hand an inch or two along the table towards some checkers that were piled beside the board. It was as if he were reaching for a weapon, as if his invisible partner were an enemy. He clutched the checkers, slipped slowly from his chair and straightened. . . .

> It was a long time . . . then suddenly wrenching himself to action he hurled the checkers with such vicious fury that they struck the wall and clattered back across the room.

The change that Vickers undergoes, the impression he creates of playing with "an invisible partner," someone he is angry with, the final description of the game, the consequent release of tension—all of these things call to mind what Vickers has previously told the boy of his games with the girl, in particular that "If she didn't win she'd upset the board and go off and sulk." Significantly Vickers would always sit rigidly before the checkerboard, staring fixedly before him, his eyes not on the door but the window. The reason for this is obvious: his "visitor" never came through the door but always "appeared" in the window, and when she "appeared" was unmoving: "night after night she'd be sitting there—right there where you are, looking at me, not even trying to play." Such odd behaviour, it is worth pointing out, does not escape the boy. After the game has been disrupted and Vickers has calmed down, the boy sums up the episode with the observation, "I relaxed gradually, telling myself that he'd just been seeing things."

Clearly the most important cause of these "appearances" is the extreme loneliness of Vickers' life. As Vickers himself explains in one revealing passage, "You don't know how bad it is sometimes. Weeks on end and no one to talk to. You're not yourself—you're not sure what you're going to say or do." Worst of all is apparently the summer ("it's worse even than this in the summer. No time for meals— and the heat and flies"). Evidently this is when Vickers feels loneliness the most; by no coincidence, it is also the time the girl has "stayed" the longest. Significantly, the girl disappears when Vickers goes to town and has social contact: "I went to town for a few days—and when I came back she was gone." Solitude, then, is a primary factor in Vickers' condition; but it is not the only one. Another would seem to be Vickers' belief in the need for a feminine presence to handle the domestic work. As he says, "You get careless living alone like this. It takes a woman." So strong is this sense that in the absence of a woman he himself takes on a feminine role. This tendency comes out in a number of small ways, most notably perhaps in the scene where Vickers is helping the boy dress ("He [Vickers] held my sheepskin for me while I put it on, and tied the scarf around the collar with a solicitude and determination equal to Aunt Ellen's"); its culmination of course is the girl's "appearance" for given periods of time. So it is, I think, that in Vickers we may find a rather sharp portrait of a schizoid personality, whose duality is expressed in the title of the story (**"One's a Heifer"**), which itself is excerpted from the boy's description of the calves ("Yearlings . . . red with white spots and faces. *The same except that one's a heifer and the other isn't"*—my italics). There is a nice symmetry to this—this equation between the calves and Vickers: the boy does not find the two almost identical calves that he is looking for, but in Vickers, particularly when the "big stupid cow" of a girl appears, he happens upon a striking human parallel; and in both matters, identification of the calves and analysis of Vickers' behaviour, the boy misinterprets what he sees by a wide margin.

As I see it, the business of the barn, what might or might not be there, is not only unimportant but is even an impediment to any appreciation of what the story—a study of illusion—is about. Interest in this matter only arises when the reader is seduced into an unwitting acceptance of the values and opinions of a narrator who believes in Vicker's guilt but whose judgements throughout are unfortunately unreliable. For such an elementary critical error there can be no excuse. We are told explicitly that the boy is only thirteen; we know that he has not been away from home all night before and never visited these parts; we can see from his reactions on the way to Vickers' place, as his disappointment at not finding the calves mounts and his sense of alienation increases, that he is highly impressionable; and what is more important, we cannot escape the fact that in charging Vickers with theft of the calves he is simply wrong. Given this, I find it surprising that any reader would entertain the boy's suspicions seriously. Aunt Ellen obviously knows better.

Lorraine McMullen (essay date 1982)

SOURCE: An introduction to *The Race and Other Stories,* by Sinclair Ross, University of Ottawa Press, 1982, pp. 15-21.

[*In the following essay, McMullen provides a stylistic and thematic analysis of Ross's short fiction.*]

The Race and Other Stories includes all of Sinclair Ross's previously uncollected short stories and a chapter from *Whir of Gold,* here titled **"The Race,"** which stands on its own as a short story. Heralded as a prairie writer and best known for his stories of the bleak dust-bowl prairie of the Great Depression, Ross has also written of urban life and, briefly, of army life, as these stories demonstrate.

Not a prolific writer, Ross has published only four novels and eighteen stories. He spends much time rewriting and revising, and he destroys much of what he writes. His work indicates that the discipline and control essential to survival on the prairie can be adapted to the achievement of a controlled art. His taut, economical, rhythmic prose reflects the bleak, spare landscape of the prairie. He achieves economy of style largely through metaphor and through a diction both simple and precise, suggestive and resonant. The concerns of his novels are equally evident in his stories: loneliness and alienation, the sense of entrapment, the imaginative and artistic struggle. Ross's bleakest stories were published between 1934 and 1941, the year he published *As For Me and My House*. During these years Ross was living in Winnipeg and working for the Royal Bank of Canada. In 1933 he had left Saskatchewan, where as a bank clerk in small prairie towns he had witnessed the combination of economic and climatic disasters of the Great Depression.

Ross's first story, **"No Other Way,"** appeared in *Nash's Pall-Mall* in October 1934, selected for third prize from among eight thousand entries in the magazine's short-story competition. The story foreshadows many of the stylistic characteristics and thematic preoccupations Ross develops in later work. Ross reveals his concern with personal relationships, especially the interplay between husband and wife against a setting that has an important effect on their relationship. In **"No Other Way,"** as in later stories, he shows the effect on a marriage of years of exhausting struggle. The portrait of Hatty Glenn is the first of many portraits of prairie farm wives. Hatty has made a success of the farm by dint of hard physical labour while her husband has devoted his time to wheat and land speculations. Hatty has become wrinkled and worn as well as shrewish, bitter, and parsimonious, and her still youthful-looking husband has grown away from her. Facing her situation, Hatty contemplates suicide only to realize that for her there is "no other way" but to continue, stoically, working, as she has done for twenty years. In **"No Other Way"** Ross does not present the drought-ridden farm we come to know in **"A Lamp at Noon"** and other stories of this period but the successful farm. The theme of antimaterialism he develops twenty-

four years later in *The Well* is evident here. As in *The Well* the protagonist looks back to the struggling past as happier than the materially successful present. As in *The Well* an abandoned well becomes the focal point for recollections of past happiness:

> . . . she came to the bleached cribbing of an old, unused well.
>
> She looked at it reflectively, remembering how her arms used to ache when she had to pull up water with a rope and pail, before they drilled the new well and could afford a windmill. There was an old roan cow that used to drink eight pailfuls, night and morning, and then leave the trough reluctantly.
>
> And yet, that had been the vital, solid time of her life. The work had a purpose behind it: there had been something to look forward to. It used to seem that a windmill, and a big house with carpets and a gramophone, were all that was needed to make life perfect: and now, after all the old wishes had been realised, here she was, back at the well.

Though the well as a symbol of vital, meaningful activity and shared love, and as a link between past and present, hope and disillusion, is more skilfully woven into the fabric of the novel, this first story shows us the early development of Ross's concern with the contrast between past and present, illusion and reality, a contrast that recurs throughout the canon. We also find in **"No Other Way"** the endurance so characteristic of many of Ross's later protagonists and the theme of entrapment so prevalent in much of his later work.

Stylistically, the story provides an indication of the course Ross follows in future works. The first sentence prefigures one of the most outstanding characteristics of his style, his metaphoric use of nature: "Out of a sprawling sunset, ragged and unkempt, as if in a sullen mood it had grown careless of itself, the October wind dragged a clamping resolute night." The image itself and the symbol are awkward in comparison with Ross's later more subtle use of imagery and smoother, less stilted phrasing, yet it is an appropriate image for this account of a bitter, unkempt, and sullen woman and her attempt to influence her resolutely indifferent husband. Except for one brief revelation of her husband's thoughts, the third-person narrative is told from the point of view of the wife, the narrative point of view which characterizes most of the later stories of prairie farmers and their wives. The momentary shift in viewpoint is unexpected and inappropriate, the technical failing of a less experienced writer. The irony present in most of Ross's writings is evident in the dilemma of Hatty Glenn, who realizes that she has lost her husband through her excessive devotion to the farm she had considered to be their shared concern. The story is cyclic; it begins and ends with Hatty chasing cows out of the turnips, a scene not without humour, but a scene signifying her entrapment. Her situation at the end of the story is the same as it was at the beginning.

"No Other Way" lacks the subtlety and psychological complexity which are major sources of strength in Ross's later writing: the emotion is less intense, the handling of voice is less skillful, and the style is not always as graceful as in succeeding stories. Nevertheless, the story points the direction Ross will take.

Ross's work indicates that the discipline and control essential to survival on the prairie can be adapted to the achievement of a controlled art. His taut, economical, rhythmic prose reflects the bleak, spare landscape of the prairie.

—Lorraine McMullen

"Nell," published seven years later, is similar in theme to "No Other Way." Again a woman is trying to win back the love of her husband. Eight years married, Nell recognizes her own rawboned ugliness in contrast with her husband's slight build and fine features. She cuts a ridiculous figure when she wears a silk dress and high-heeled shoes to accompany her husband to town one hot Saturday evening. Ross recalls that "Nell" had its origin in an incident in which a man did forget to pick up his wife waiting for him at the store but, unlike Nell's husband, he returned to town to get her. The ketchup Nell buys because her husband likes it becomes a symbol of her continuing devotion to him despite his neglect of her. Again, as in "No Other Way," communication between husband and wife is virtually impossible. For Nell, "Words were always a labor. The task of explanation now was beyond her." Reticence, stubbornness, insensitivity, and the kind of inarticulateness demonstrated here, cause rifts between such women and their husbands. Nell and Hatty are isolated on their farms, lacking the freedom of their husbands to find diversion or solace elsewhere, and hence are more dependent on their husbands than their husbands are on them. Unlike the wives in some of Ross's stories who are better educated and more intelligent than their husbands, Nell and Hatty feel their husbands to be superior.

In Ross's world, dreaming is necessary to sustain hope. Nowhere is dreaming as escape from reality more in evidence than in his stories of children. Ross's children are imaginative and hopeful. In "A Day with Pegasus," eight-year-old Peter Parker is propelled into a fantasy world by the fulfillment of his dream of having his own horse. Even a detention from his uncomprehending teacher, who mistakes his imaginative composition for a lie, fails to quench his delight. The colt becomes a Pegasus carrying Peter into an exciting new world:

> There was a state of mind, a mood, a restfulness, in which one could skim along this curve of prairie floor

and, gathering momentum from the downward swing, glide up again and soar away from earth. He succeeded now, borne by a white-limbed steed again. And as they soared the mystery was not solved but gradually absorbed, a mystery still but intimate, a heartening gleam upon the roof of life to let him see its vault and spaciousness.

This story not only reveals the excitement and wonder of childhood but also contrasts this excitement and wonder with the overliteral and unimaginative attitude of the adult unable to comprehend or value a child's fantasies. The colt is Peter's agent of escape from the dreary and restricted everyday world. Though Ross later uses the first-person point of view in stories of childhood, in this early story he uses the third person, as he does in most early stories, and he gets inside the mind of his young protagonist by using him as the centre of intelligence. In later works, such as "Cornet at Night" and "Circus in Town," Ross continues to contrast the imaginative child with the adult who because of lack of opportunity or stimulus has lost the gift of transcending reality. This theme is linked with Ross's conception of the struggling artist which he develops in *As For Me and My House* and in *Whir of Gold*.

"A Day with Pegasus" is one of several stories centred on the same boy which Ross at one time planned as a group. "At the beginning," Ross writes, "I had *in mind* a group of short stories having to do with the same boy. In "Cornet at Night" he becomes really aware, for the first time, of the wonder of music—I suppose you could call it an aesthetic wakening. "One's a Heifer" is his first contact with evil (although the man in the story, Vickers, is not evil, of course, but deranged). There was to have been one about death—he loses his parents in a fire, which is why in "One's a Heifer" he is living with an aunt and uncle. "A Day with Pegasus," the mystery of life and beginning, etc."

"The Race" continues the adventures of what could be considered the same young boy. Sonny is a prairie farm boy, now a clarinetist in Montreal. In the novel, the race is one of several flashbacks to his prairie childhood. In Sonny's mind, music is joined with his spirited horse Isabel; both were stimuli to his imaginative life in the bleak environment of his childhood. Throughout this adventure, Isabel remains her cocky, assured self, a fitting ally for her confident young rider. Isabel's arrogance and pride are a projection of Sonny's own arrogance and pride.

"The Race" is closely linked with the earlier story "The Outlaw." In fact, Isabel is described in almost the same words as in "The Outlaw":

> One horse and all horses—somehow representative. Chargers, mustangs, Arabians, standing beside her in the stall, I knew and rode them all. In the neigh and eyes and forelock there was history. Battle and carnage, trumpets and glory—she understood and carried me triumphantly.

> She was coal-black, gleaming, queenly. Her mane had a ripple and her neck an arch. And somehow, softly and mysteriously, she was always burning. The reflection

on her glossy hide, sun or lantern, seemed the glow of some secret passion. There were moments when you felt the whole stable charged with her, as if she were the priestess of her kind, in communion with her deity.

The self-contained incident of **"The Race"** possesses the characteristics we are accustomed to find in Ross's stories: humour, economy, skilful combination of dialogue with retrospective narration, and an introductory conversation which leads directly into the action. Since the story is a flashback, the point of view is the dual perspective Ross uses in most of his stories of young boys. The adult Sonny, recalling his past, relives the childhood event while retaining his adult perspective on his younger self. The narrative voice speaks for the two points of view simultaneously.

As a result of his wartime experience, Ross started a novel of a Canadian soldier from Manitoba, but he was never satisfied with it and eventually destroyed it. All that remains of his army years are two stories, both based partly on experience. **"Barrack Room Fiddle Tune"** is a light story stemming from Ross's having had as a barrack mate a country boy who played the fiddle. The boy's off-key playing irritated his mates, but nothing untoward happened, Ross tells us, except for the occasional boot flung in his direction. The idea for **"Jug and Bottle"** occurred to Ross when, like the protagonist in the story, he mistakenly assumed early in his tour of duty in England that the words "Jug and Bottle" on a pub signified its name. The element of chance in this story of a suicidal young soldier is akin to the element of determinism in several of the prairie stories where an indifferent nature plays a large part in deciding man's fate.

"Spike," read on CBC radio, is published here for the first time in English. The panic of a man terrorized by a teenage hitch-hiker depends largely on the clipped, terse rhythm of the language. The man's terror is accentuated by the bored tone of his teenage daughter when he calls home. In the earlier story **"Saturday Night,"** the teenager is a naive adolescent from a simpler world. Like Spike, he is coming home to see his girl friend. The myth of romantic love he had built up around the girl is destroyed when he sees that her interpretation of their relationship is very different from his. To her, he was just another date. His story is an initiation.

With **"The Flowers that Killed Him,"** a story of perversion and murder, Ross demonstrates his fascination with the criminal mind which he explores at greater length in *The Well* and *Whir of Gold*. An unexpected ending adds an extra dimension to the story. Ross does not attempt to get into the mind of the killer, but views him from outside, from the perspective of a thirteen-year-old boy. Thus we see only the mask the murderer wears to the world.

"The Flowers that Killed Him" is Ross's last published story. It is written with the same skill and economy that distinguish his earlier stories. He has since published one novel, *Sawbones Memorial*. Like his last story, the novel demonstrates that Ross has not lost the artistry he displayed in earlier stories and in *As For Me and My House*.

Karen Bishop (essay date 1985)

SOURCE: "The Pegasus Symbol in the Childhood Stories of Sinclair Ross," in *Ariel,* Vol. 167, No. 3, July, 1985, pp. 67-87.

[*In the following essay, Bishop traces the metaphor of the horse in Ross's childhood stories, maintaining that the image of the horse "becomes the enspiriting essence of the imagination."*]

> It's all over and it's all beginning, there's nothing more required of you. April and the smell of April just as it was that day too . . .

These are Doc Hunter's final words in *Sawbones Memorial,* Sinclair Ross's latest novel, published in 1974. On an April day forty-five years earlier, Doc Hunter had arrived in Upward, Saskatchewan to practice medicine. On this day in April, he has retired and his son will take his place. It's all over *and* it's all beginning.

This sense of ending-and-beginning is present in most of Sinclair Ross's short stories and novels. The endings may be devastating, as in **"The Lamp at Noon,"** or tentatively hopeful, as in *As For Me and My House,* but, in all cases, the possibility of a new beginning results from the ending of a one-sided experience of life dominated by either happiness or suffering, creativity or destruction. Awareness of reality is refocused or expanded to encompass both values, to acknowledge a duality in life. In his work, then, Ross is not "affirming polarities of good and bad . . . but exploring what is real in the world." In order to begin again, a recognition of both halves of the whole—insight into the interplay of creative and destructive elements—is necessary to understand and come to terms with life. Doc Hunter capsulizes this theme, of "what is real in the world," toward the conclusion of *Sawbones Memorial*:

> The Great Mother and The Evil Mother, maybe one and the same, creating life only to turn and destroy it. . . . As if the potter got his wheel going and then couldn't stop it—and not knowing what to do with all the jugs and bottles piling up, no storage space, no markets, had to rig up another machine to grind them into dust again.

An inkling of this cycle produces new beginnings from endings, because hope need never die. The pots ground to dust do not remain dust. Instead, they are moulded again into beautiful perfect vessels. Creativity and destruction, beginnings and endings, are inextricably linked. The group of stories to be discussed here, **"A Day with Pegasus," "Cornet at Night," "Circus in Town," "The Outlaw,"** and **"One's a Heifer,"** deal with Ross's most optimistic and hopeful endings-and-beginnings. In each story, a child discovers the dimension of the imagination and the one dimensional understanding of life anchored in every day reality ends. Each child is awakened to a world of new possibilities and experiences—a phase in the potter's cycle when creativity dominates and the life-sustaining, benevolent side of the duality of life shows itself.

Until quite recently, studies of the works of Sinclair Ross have overlooked such purely literary aspects of Ross's art to focus on his place among those writers whose time and place is the Canadian prairie during the Depression. Largely because critical attention has been centred on *As For Me and My House* and **The Lamp at Noon and Other Stories,** most Ross criticism is an outgrowth of the impression of Ross as prairie realist, portraying the human suffering and environmental effects of the dustbowl prairie environment. As a result, the role of the prairie landscape as it reflects character or as it moulds character receives much emphasis in this criticism. However, as attention shifts from Ross's earliest work to considerations of his total literary output, the role of the landscape becomes secondary. More formalist study of Ross has yielded patterns of image, symbol, and theme which emerge from his novels and short stories to inform the vision of reality, which happens to have a prairie setting but also exists independent of it. Ross's writing is a unit in which he expresses his understanding of life as a cyclical duality of endings and beginnings, of combinations of creativity and destruction, which make up the whole of life. Although recent criticism has dealt with a range of symbols, such as the lamp as symbol of hope, the colour gold as symbol of beauty, the mirrors, false fronts, and the house in *As For Me and My House* as symbols of hypocrisy, no one has yet undertaken a complete study of the imagery and symbolism and how they contribute to the meaning of Ross's fiction. One important aspect of Ross's imagery is his use of the horse as symbol of the hopeful creative, imaginative half of the duality of life.

Horses, in the works of Sinclair Ross, are recognized by recent critics, such as Lorraine McMullen [in *Sinclair Ross,* 1979] and Robert Chambers, as more than realistic props in the dustbowl prairie setting. The horse is a recurring image in Ross's works, always "linked to the imaginative life." The sensitive reader is immediately aware of a special relationship between Ross's children and their horses. This closeness gives the horses personalities of their own, independent of the children, so that as nearly separate characters, they initiate experiences which go beyond the normal child-horse relationship. The horse, which is more than a peripheral link to the imagination, becomes the enspiriting essence of the imagination. Without their horses, the children are at a loss to discover the dimension of the imagination which awakens their dreams of fulfilment, creativity, and happiness for the future by ending their one-sided view of life.

Each horse becomes a Pegasus, soaring above everyday reality to a light-filled dimension of perfection and beauty. In Greek mythology, Pegasus, the white, winged horse born from the blood of the beheaded Medusa, created the fountain of Hippocrene, which was sacred to the Muses as the source of poetic inspiration. The only man to ride this magical horse was Perseus, who captured and gently tamed him with a golden bridle provided by Athena. He successfully rode Pegasus to kill the Chimera, but when he pridefully attempted to join the gods on Olympus, Pegasus threw him back to earth, where Perseus remained, while Pegasus became the thunder and lightning bearer of Zeus.

As for Perseus, the Pegasus propels Ross's children into flights of the imagination, in which they soar above earthly reality. Specific elements associated with the dimension of the ima-gination recur in these stories. Extreme clarity of vision is possible in this dimension, beauty and light are prominent sense impressions, and a sense of timelessness is experienced. Like Perseus, with his golden bridle, the children tame their imaginations by combination with everyday reality, and channel them into, in some cases, specifically artistic creation and, in all cases, a new awareness or perception of the world. Although these flights of imagination are momentary and these children could, like Perseus, be thrown back to earth forever, all are aware of having seen an otherworldly dimension, of having had a "glimpse of the unknown," that is, a glimpse of the possibilities or opportunities of life.

"A Day with Pegasus," published in 1938, Ross's second published work, is the prototype for his use of the horse as symbol of the spirit of imagination, symbol of the creative half of the duality. With the birth of his long-awaited colt, Peter Parker discovers the tangibility of dreams:

> It was a strange, almost unbearable moment. The horse that for five months had served the extravagances of his imagination, that he had lived with, gloried in, and underneath it all, never quite expected to come true— it was a reality now—alive, warm and breathing—two white stockings and a star.

Because this incredible dream has come true, Peter is transported by degrees into a world of pure imagination, where anything is possible. The newborn colt quickly outstrips even Peter's dreams of its speed:

> The colt ran with him, more swiftly now than it had ever run before. With no earth beneath their feet they leaped across the garden and around the house—around the house and across the garden—then back to stand a moment eager and irresolute before the stable door.

Soon the spirit of the dream possesses him, kindling his imagination further:

> His colt, grown fleet of limb, possessed a fire and beauty that enslaved him now, that he could not abandon for the blear-eyed reality in Biddy's stall.

Peter's vision expands yet again. His colt becomes the Pegasus which carries him into the world of the imagination:

> But it was a mile to school, and the reality could not last so far. The white-stockinged legs began to flash more quickly, the long limp neck to arch, the stubby tail to flow. Then suddenly as if by magic he was mounted, and the still May morning sprang in whistling wind around his ears. Field after field reeled up and fell away. The earth resounded thundering, then dimmed and dropped until it seemed they cleaved their way through flashing light. Until at last he stood quite still, impaled with a kind of wonder-fear that life should yield him such divinity, while the sun poured blazing,

and the road stretched white and dusty through the fields of early wheat.

Peter is no longer conscious of the material colt; he rides a spirited, mystical horse through the barrier separating earthbound reality and the realm of the imagination. Like Perseus, he has been transported into a new dimension above earthly reality where he sees divinity, perfection, and purity.

Also like Perseus, Peter's flight is abruptly grounded by earth-bound reality. First, his farm chores break the spell of his imagination:

> It was the colt, the colt he had raced with before breakfast across the garden, that made the feeding of the calves this morning such a humiliation. . . . Nigger—Daisy—Dot—as stupid and silly as their names, gurgling and blowing at him until there was no colt left at all—until for beginnings again he had to steal back to the stable, and pay another visit to the box-stall.

Next, he is reprimanded by Miss Kinley, his teacher, when he attempts to share his excitement with his friends, but her anger is lost on him. Possessed by the spirit of his new colt, he is involuntarily pulled out of the classroom reality into the dimension of his earlier flight:

> Hammer of mortification—of despairing foreknowledge that he would never solve the [arithmetic] problem— and gradually at last of galloping hooves. . . . The rhythm persisted, was stronger even that [sic] the implacability of Miss Kinley's tapping ruler. . . . Gradually the class-room fell away from him. The light flashed golden in his eyes again. The fields sped reeling young and green.

Also, Peter's friends, firmly rooted in farm reality, are untouched by the spirit of the imagination embodied by the colt. When Peter must defend the colt from their insults, his faith in its tangible spirit is strengthened:

> The colt, now that he had actually championed it, seemed more real, more dependable—seemed even reaching out to assure him that the flights of his imagination this morning had been something more than mere fantasy.

Such incidents cannot permanently ground or defeat the spirit stimulated for the first time by his Pegasus. In each case, Peter is renewed and reaffirmed in his new beginning by the spirit of the imagination.

Peter's dilemma is, instead, that he is unable to convey to others the tangibility of the spirit of the imagination and, at the same time, this spirit prevents him from descending completely into reality. His short, but actual, friendship with a cowboy named Slim and his sensitized imagination combine into a daydream over which he has little control. Imagination overpowers reality and an improbable fantasy results:

Slim must have another name, and fancifully it began to grow in Peter's mind that some day he might take horse and ride out seeking him again. . . . Then on again all four of them—unequal, yet in total virtue equalling: himself on the horse that was to be called whatever Slim's real name was—and a great cowboy riding Tony.

Later, the spirit of the imagination works in him so that he is consciously able to unite imagination and reality in a composition for Miss Kinley. He thinks of his colt and is again transported above the earth to the dimension of the imagination:

> [T]here was a moment's stillness round him, clear and isolating like a globe of magic crystal; and then suddenly he was writing. As he had never written before. With the glow and enthusiasm of sheer inspiration.

Rather than reproduce the Saturday which he considers "a limbo of unworthy dullness," "he transformed it—redeemed it with an inner, potential reality—rose suddenly like a master above the limitations of mere time and distance." Now for the first time, Peter reproduces in a controlled manner the experiences of his flight above the earth. He gives his Saturday the freedom of possibility, the inner, potential reality which pushes his experience in the sheer joy of being alive into the timeless, universal sphere of perfection.

Miss Kinley, like Peter's friends, demands pure earthbound reality. She insists that he write a completely accurate account of how he spent his Saturday and destroys the imaginative one, filled with possibility, hope for the future, and excitement. Peter is again thrown to earth in mid-flight. In confusion and frustration, he again seeks renewal from his colt, the embodiment of the spirit of the imagination: "all his pride in a peerless horse had become a humble need to see again and draw comfort from a wobbly-legged one." He enters Biddy's stall "in fearful hope of what awaited him," but the spirit of the imagination is still strong: "There was the same hush, the same solemnity," which he has felt on first discovering the colt. In addition, as he seeks renewal from the material horse, his dream expands once more from being merely a childish wish for a fast horse to become a dream of understanding, of seeing and knowing the mysteries which life offers.

Peter slips into the hay loft to interpret the awakening which has been inspired by the birth of his colt. Instinctively, he senses that this moment is the beginning of the fulfilment of his own destiny. With the birth of his colt, which inspired the birth of his imagination, Peter was born anew: "It was imperative to be alone a few minutes, to feel his way through and beyond this mystery of beginning." As he looks out over the prairie from the stable loft, Peter is able to describe this new awareness:

> There was a state of mind, a mood, a restfulness, in which one could skim along this curve of prairie floor, and gathering momentum from the downward swing, glide up again and soar away from earth. He succeeded

now. Borne by a white-limbed steed again, but smoothly, as if their passage were a flight: no rush of wind, no beat of thundering hooves. And in the flight the mystery was not solved, but gradually absorbed, a mystery still but intimate, a heartening gleam upon the roof of life to let him see its vault and spaciousness.

He laments the fact that he has only just awakened to the possibilities of his future and has wasted time, unlike his colt which is "[a]ble to go into and explore a whole new waiting world. . . . It seemed a pity that a boy was never born that way."

As Peter's awareness of the power of the imagination grows and he gains control over its influence, he becomes an artist uniting reality and imagination in a new way of perceiving the world around him. This is Peter's beginning, his first experience with the side of the duality of life which he had not known existed, and the first step toward the mature vision of the whole of the potter's cycle. The earthly horse acts as a Muse, the spirit in its purest form, to inspire in Peter recognition of an inner, potential reality, an awareness of the numberless possibilities life holds. Since the colt lived up to his expectations, the spirit of the imagination suggests that his hopes for the future are also possible. However, Peter's awareness advances one step further to make him an artist and bring him closer to affirming the duality. He still has no experience with the soul-destroying side of darkness which dominates in the stories about the dustbowl prairie. While Pegasus transports the boy into a dimension of crystal clarity, light, divinity, and beauty, he does, through the story of his Saturday, unite this creative side of life with its opposite, dreary, ordinary reality.

> The sensitive reader is immediately aware of a special relationship between Ross's children and their horses. This closeness gives the horses personalities of their own, independent of the children, so that as nearly separate characters, they initiate experiences which go beyond the normal child horse relationship.
>
> —*Karen Bishop*

While Peter Parker has his knowledge of the two-sidedness of life expanded by the Pegasus spirit at the birth of his colt, some children are inspired to begin seeking life's possibilities by other manifestations of the same spirit. The earthly manifestation of Peter's flight to the dimension of the imagination was his inspired story about his adventurous Saturday. Similarly, music, the earthly manifestation of another artist's flight in the creative dimension, is the enspiriting force which begins Tommy Dickson's new awareness of the duality of life in **"Cornet at Night."**

In this story, the musical composition, *Sons of Liberty,* is Tommy's counterpart to Peter's cowboy adventure day dream. The Pegasus spirit of this music, unfortunately, is not under Tommy's control:

> There was a fine swing and vigor in this piece, but it was hard. Hard because it was so alive, so full of youth and head-high rhythm. It was a march, and it did march. I couldn't take time to practise the hard spots slowly till I got them right, for I had to march too. I had to let my fingers sometimes miss a note or strike one wrong. Again and again this afternoon I started carefully, resolving to count right through, the way Miss Wiggins did, and as often I sprang ahead to lead my march a moment or two all dash and fire, and then fall stumbling in the bitter dust of dissonance.

Unlike Peter, Tommy cannot control the Pegasus spirit, and rather than open to him a new perception of life, such inspiration is frustrating and confusing. In addition, he does not confront life with Peter's vigour, like an adventurous Perseus. For example, in a departure from the usual farm routine, Tommy's father sends him to town to hire a hand for the harvest. Cautious of hoping for too much, Tommy will not submit himself entirely to the sheer joy of this new opportunity:

> For while it was always my way to exploit the future, I liked to do it rationally, within the limits of the sane and probable. On my way to the cows I wanted to live the trip to town tomorrow many times, with variations, but only on the explicit understanding that tomorrow there was to be a trip to town. I have always been tethered to reality, always compelled by an unfortunate kind of probity in my nature to prefer a barefaced disappointment to the luxury of a future I have no just claims upon.

The spirit of Pegasus, the luxury of a future, is a disruptive force in Tommy's life. He is not a dreamer on the possibilities of life, even though he has been touched by the spirit of the imagination through his music.

Significantly, Tommy is sent to town in the care of an old farm horse named Rock, which is outwardly not of the race of Pegasus. However, with Rock, Tommy knows the feeling of control, confidence, and superiority that a horse, a Pegasus, inspires. Like Peter Parker riding his dream horse on Saturday rodeo adventures, Tommy and Rock together are a match for the world, and Tommy, under Rock's influence, is awakened to his own capabilities and potential:

> Alone with himself and his horse he [a boy] cuts a fine figure. He is the measure of the universe. He foresees a great many encounters with life, and in them all acquits himself a little more than creditably. He is fearless, resourceful, a bit of a brag. His horse never contradicts.

Therefore, even stolid Rock belongs to the spirit of the imagination for helping Tommy experience, if only momentarily, how his life could be.

Naturally, under Rock's influence, Tommy is attracted to a man whose presence proclaims that he *is* the measure of the universe. Although the man is obviously not the farm hand his father needs to help with the harvest, he is "strong with a strength that was different from the rugged labour-strength I knew." Drawn by this inner strength, which he does not possess, Tommy hires Philip Coleman knowing he is unacceptable for harvest work. He *is* suitable, however, for Tommy's purpose. He corrects Tommy's impression that by subduing his flights of feeling, inspired by his music, by "keep[ing] slow and steady like Miss Wiggins" when he plays, he would be less frustrated and perplexed. Philip disagrees. What Tommy needs to do is learn to control his imagination.

To illustrate his point, Philip plays his cornet. "[O]nly one fragment of a note" from the cornet "like pure and mellow gold" is necessary to transform the plodding Rock into a spirited Pegasus. At the briefest sound from the cornet, Rock leaves the road, carrying the wagon on a jolting gallop across the open prairie. Although his flight never becomes airborne, Rock responds to the spirit of the imagination and breaks out of routine reality. For Tommy, too, the stranger's cornet is the agent of the imaginative spirit which lifts him out of earthly reality, the notes flying and soaring like Pegasus, to expand his limited understanding of life for new awareness:

> And I was right: when they came the notes were piercing, golden as the cornet itself, and they gave life expanse that it had never known before. They floated up against the night, and each for a moment hung there clear and visible. Sometimes they mounted poignant and sheer. Sometimes they soared and then, like a bird alighting, fell and brushed earth again.

Tommy feels the influence, not only of having found a kindred spirit, but of the spirit of the imagination ordering his life and giving him a destiny, a place to begin:

> I could still feel the cornet's presence as if it were a living thing. Somehow its gold and shapeliness persisted, transfiguring the day, quickening the dusty harvest fields to a gleam and lustre like its own. And I felt assured, involved. Suddenly there was a force in life, a current, an inevitability, carrying me along too.

This is how Peter Parker felt at the end of **"A Day with Pegasus."** He was awake to explore and know the world. Now the awakened artistic spirit in Tommy has a purpose. The march Philip plays, which is controlled and disciplined, as *Sons of Liberty* should have been, inspires him to take advantage of life's possibilities: "It said that life was worth the living and bright as morning shone ahead to show the way."

However, Tommy's beginning is not as assured as Peter's is. Life on a farm dictates that artistry like Philip's is insignificant. He merely delays the harvest and leaves a bittersweet memory of his short intrusion: "A harvest, however lean, is certain every year: but a cornet at night is golden only once." This conclusion is ambivalent, and

Ross's revisions of this story indicate that he meant it to be so. As McMullen comments, "Ross eliminated the lines which specifically indicate that Tommy now sees he too must be a musician—or at least an artist. Ross has no successful artists in his work, only those who are beginning to pursue that dream with "tentative self-knowledge." Indeed, after **"A Day with Pegasus,"** the potter's cycle of "creation one day, destruction the next," imposes itself more strongly in Ross's fictional world, as is evident in **"Cornet at Night."** An intimate knowledge of the dimension of the imagination is strictly balanced with a bitter taste of the dimension of destruction, a more extreme version of the everyday reality which opposed Peter's flight.

The strengthening of the destructive side of the duality is evident in **"Circus in Town,"** even though the child, Jenny, does have her awareness of life expanded by a flight with Pegasus. A torn poster advertising a circus transports Jenny from the reality of her bickering parents into a flight of imagination.

> The bit of poster had spun a new world before her, excited her, given wild, soaring impetus to her imagination; and now, without in the least understanding herself, she wanted the excitement and the soaring, even though it might stab and rack her, rather than the barren satisfaction of believing that in life there was nothing better, nothing more vivid or dramatic than her own stableyard.

Jenny's awareness of life's possibilities grows out of her initial wish merely to prolong the wonder and excitement of her fantasy-circus. Under the influence of the Pegasus spirit, she sees life going in two directions:

> This sudden dilation of life—it was like a bubble blown vast and fragile. In time it might subside, slowly, safely, or it might even remain full-blown, gradually building up the filmy tissues to make its vastness durable, but tonight she was afraid. Afraid that before the hack of her mother's voice it might burst and crumble.

To prevent the bubble of this beginning awareness from bursting, she retreats from the world to remain untouched by reality in her imaginative reverie:

> [F]or once the threats of what would happen next time failed to touch her. The circus went on. All night long she wore her new purple tights and went riding Billie round and round the pasture in them.

While Jenny's dream-circus seems unforgettable, it also appears to be only a momentary escape from the bickering and unhappiness of her family life, rather than a permanent beginning leading to fulfilment outside the farm. Like Tommy Dickson, Jenny's insight into the possibilities of life is not as complete as the awareness of Peter Parker, perhaps because of the encroachment of the destructive dimension of the duality.

Jenny and Tommy Dickson wander in their imagination-states, enjoying the freedom and emotional intensity, but have no concrete goals formulated from their flights of imagination, no clear beginnings initiated. Only Peter Parker is able to articulate what he has learned from his flight with Pegasus. He is an artist, able to synthesize the dimension of earthly reality and the dimension of the imagination to explore the world. However, Peter McAlpine, in **"The Outlaw,"** is thirteen, older than Peter, Tommy, and Jenny, and the first child to be confronted with the harsher, dark side of the duality which is dominant in the stories about adults coping with the dustbowl prairie. In short, Peter McAlpine is the first child to experience the polar opposites of the duality, the extremes of experience which correspond to the images in the potter's cycle, for the most complete perception of life in Ross's childhood stories.

Peter McAlpine and Isabel and Peter Parker and his new colt have much in common. Both boys ride exquisitely beautiful and spirited horses into the dimension of the imagination. The imagery used to describe their flights connotes a realm of pristine beauty, crystal clarity, absolute timelessness, and an aura of the magical or mystical. However, the exotic, black Isabel is much more complex than the purely spiritual white-limbed creature in **"A Day with Pegasus."** Initially, she is described as "beautiful but dangerous," a killer which no one expects the thirteen-year-old Peter to ride. She is kindred to the destructive elements of the prairie evironment:

> [S]he was a captive, pining her heart away. Week after week she stamped and pawed, nosed the hay out of her manger contemptuously, flung up her head and poured out wild, despairing neighs into the prairie winds and blizzards streaming past.

For Peter, she is the composite of equine beauty and spirit:

> She was one horse, and she was all horses. Thundering battle chargers, fleet Arabians, untamed mustangs—sitting beside her on her manger I knew and rode them all. There was a history in her shapely head and burning eyes. I charged with her at Balaklava, Waterloo, scoured the deserts of Africa and the steppes of the Ukraine. Conquest and carnage, trumpets and glory—she understood and carried me triumphantly.

Isabel embodies all time and all experience. She understands and transmits to Peter the mystery of life, its potential and its dreams:

> To approach her was to be enlarged, transported. She was coal-black, gleaming, queenly. Her mane had a ripple and her neck an arch. And somehow, softly and mysteriously, she was always burning. The reflection on her glossy hide, whether of winter sunshine or yellow lantern light, seemed the glow of some fierce, secret passion. There were moments when I felt the whole stable charged with her, as if she were the priestess of her kind, in communion with her diety [sic].

Isabel glows golden like Philip's cornet, but much more sensually. She too has a presence of her own, an electrical charge, "a force in life, a current, an inevitability."

Isabel's personality, then, adds another dimension to the imaginative spirit which initiates Peter's new awareness of life. Peter must fight the temptation to ride Isabel because her reputation is tainted with evil, not just disobedience. In a scene which, as McMullen suggests, echoes the temptation of Christ by Satan, Isabel shows how, as co-conspirator, she could raise him to a respected position among his peers:

> And then, temptress, she bore me off to the mountain top of my vanity, and with all the world spread out before my gaze, talked guilefully of prestige and acclaim.

> Over there, three miles away, was the school house. What a sensation to come galloping up on her, the notorious outlaw, instead of jogging along as usual on bandy-legged old Pete. . . . How sweet to wipe out all the ignominy of my past, to be deferred to by the older boys, to bask in Millie's smiles of favour.

> Over there, seven miles away . . . was town. Where fairs were sometimes held, and races run. On such a horse I naturally would win . . .

Peter childishly attempts to keep the boundary between good and evil sharply defined, while Isabel would blur the focus because true awareness of the mystery of life requires experience with both. As a result, Peter will be confronted with a two-sided reality. Isabel *is* a killer, but, because she is so dangerous, she can provide the self-respect which Peter so desires. She *is* a temptress, coaxing him toward disobeying his parents' order not to ride her, but she also offers knowledge of the unknown. In describing Isabel as "one horse, and . . . all horses," Peter unwittingly acknow-ledges this duality. He has ridden Isabel in wars, situations of life and death, carnage and glory, where destinies are decided. In addition, Isabel in her very essence, burning with sensual devotion to her deity, combining sensuality and spirituality is not, according to W. H. New, "affirming polarities of good and bad, but . . . exploring what is real in the world." True understanding of the mystery of life is gained from knowledge of both good and evil. Since Isabel represents all experience in the potential, inner reality of life, Peter must conclude that life will bring his worst fears as well as his most desired dreams to fruition. By resisting Isabel, Peter remains a child, resisting a complete awareness of the two-sided mystery of life.

As the imaginative spirit, Isabel's motive for Peter's ride is to share with him the secrets of her deity. As she has promised, the actual ride is more spectacular than Peter has ever imagined. She is Pegasus, the flying horse:

> She didn't drop to a trot or walk as an ordinary horse would have done, but instead, with the clean grace and precision of a bird alighting on a branch, came smoothly to a halt.

She shows him beauty he has never seen before, a deeper awareness of the landscape not possible without the influence of the spirit of the imagination:

And I too, responsive to her bidding, was aware as never before of its austere, unrelenting beauty. There were the white fields and the blue, metallic sky; the little splashes here and there of yellow strawstack, luminous and clear as drops of gum on fresh pine lumber; the scattered farmsteads brave and wistful in their isolation; the gleam of the sun and snow.

All the elements of Peter Parker's dimension of the imagination are here, but Isabel adds more. She insists Peter see the world as it really is, two-sided:

> Look, she said firmly, while it's here before you, so that to the last detail it will remain clear. For you, too, some day there may be stalls and halters, and it will be a good memory.

Isabel directs his awareness to the future, but just as Peter suspected, not only do dreams come true, but also fears and a harsher reality. She heightens this cruel, dark, fear-inspiring side of the mystery on the return ride:

> She disdained and rebelled against her stall, but the way she whipped the wind around my ears you would have thought she had suddenly conceived a great affection for it. It was a strong wind, fierce and cold. . . . Her mane blew back and lashed my face. Before the steady blast of wind my forehead felt as if the bone were wearing thin.

Peter manages to stay mounted while Isabel gives him a taste of this destructive side of life. He suffers frozen ears for the experience. However, more significantly, like prideful Perseus who attempted to ride Pegasus to Olympus to place himself among the gods, the moment Peter thinks *he* is in control of this experience, Isabel throws him into a snow drift:

> Being able to ride an outlaw was not the same thing at all as being accorded the privilege of riding one, and for the good of my soul, it was high time I appreciated the distinction.

Riding Pegasus is an opportunity not to be missed or taken for granted. Other such chances will be available to Peter, but he must take responsibility for his actions. As Pegasus, she naturally explains this through the metaphor of horsemanship:

> From the bottom of her heart she hoped I wouldn't be so unfortunate another time. So far as she was concerned, however, she could make no promises. There had been one fall, she explained . . . and there might easily be another. The future was entirely up to me. She couldn't be responsible for my horsemanship.

Within this experience, then, Isabel shows Peter both sides of the mystery of life. By riding this two-faceted Pegasus, he accepts the challenge of a new beginning, the challenge to encounter life as a duality of light and dark, creativity and destruction, and to deal with the phases of the potter's cycle. Therefore, Peter has not, as McMullen suggests,

"move[d] from the fantasy world of the child to the real world of the adult," but has linked the two for a new awareness of life. Peter McAlpine's flights of the imagination with Isabel are not replaced by tangible, realistic dreams of impressing his friends at school, as if the tangible reality were superior to the imaginative reality. Isabel shows him the calm, perfect beauty of the landscape from a Pegasus point of view and qualifies this insight with: "Someday there may be stalls and halters, and it will be a good memory," because full complete awareness of the mystery of life depends on knowledge of both sides of the duality.

A much more intense manifestation of the destructive dimension of life is experienced by an unnamed boy in **"One's a Heifer."** Like Peter, he is thirteen and takes a horseback ride which changes his awareness of life. In **"The Outlaw,"** Isabel rewards Peter with a glimpse of exquisite beauty when he takes charge of his own life by doing a thing forbidden by parents who think he is still a child. The boy in **"One's a Heifer"** voluntarily takes on the adult duty of searching for lost calves, but rather than ascending to a lofty vision of perfection and beauty, he descends to a dark, hellish atmosphere which, nevertheless, accords him a new awareness. Both boys are passive participants in this growth toward insight; neither boy looks voluntarily at the unknown. Peter is forced to appreciate the beauty of the landscape by Isabel, and the boy in **"One's a Heifer"** is drawn involuntarily and fearfully to the dark mystery in the boxstall by an uncontrollable urge. Both forces, light and dark, beauty and terror, are equally strong as manifestations of the unknown.

While the boy's visions expand in opposite directions, one toward light and the other toward darkness, the role of the horse remains constant. Like Isabel, Billie, and Peter Parker's colt, Tim is also associated with the warmth, light, and clarity of vision of the creative dimension. For example, Tim reluctantly leaves the farmyard, where perception is clear:

> After the storm the drifts lay clear and unbroken to the horizon. Distant farm-buildings stood out distinct against the prairie as if the thin sharp atmosphere were a magnifying glass.

He naturally becomes disheartened as the cold saps the warmth which associates him with Isabel and the cornet as manifestations of the spirit of the imagination: "despite the cold his flanks and shoulders soon were steaming." Tim and the boy follow the calves to "a poor, shiftless-looking place," which is devoid of light and comfort: "Darkness was beginning to close in, but there was no light in the windows." Tim has carried his rider to a place of insight into the dark side of the duality, just as Isabel carried Peter McAlpine to an awareness of the light-filled dimension of the imagination.

This boy cannot respond to the experiences of this newly discovered dimension with joy and spontaneity as the other children reacted to their flights in the creative dimension. Vickers, the man who lives in this dark, cold environment, is threatening. Furthermore, his unlit barn has a presence which seems the essence of darkness and evil:

> Behind the light from his lantern the darkness hovered vast and sinister. It seemed to hold its breath, to watch and listen. . . . My eyes were fixed on him so intently that he seemed to lose substance, to loom up close a moment, then recede. At last he disappeared completely, and there was only the lantern like a hard hypnotic eye.

This looming and receding movement has been experienced by the children associated with the bright side of the mystery as their focus on reality weakened or dilated and they were overcome by the quiet, timeless clarity of the dimension of the imagination. Rather than an expanded vision, however, the oppressive, dark presence has focused the boy's awareness onto the lantern, a yellow glow, which is almost defeated by the darkness: "It held me. It held me rooted against my will." Peter Parker is also unable to shake off his imaginative vision, but this boy's glimpse at the unknown has a sinister quality from which he wishes to escape:

> I wanted to run from the stable, but I wanted even more to see inside the stall. Wanting to see and afraid of seeing.

This mystery is not carefree and prolonged with enthusiasm; the boy willingly escapes when Vickers offers an excuse to leave the boxstall uninvestigated.

The boy spends the night with Vickers rather than return home through the darkness without his calves, which he believes are locked in Vickers's stall. He spends an uneasy night. At first, he and Vickers play checkers and Vickers talks about his former housekeeper. When he does go to bed, the boy dozes and dreams, waking to find Vickers's owl starting at him and Vickers still at the checkerboard, apparently in combat with an invisible enemy. The boy dreams about rising and going to look in the boxstall:

> There was a bright light suddenly and the owl was sitting over the door with his yellow eyes like a pair of lanterns. The calves, he told me were in the other stall with the sick colt. I looked and they were there all right, but Tim came up and said it might be better not to start for home till morning. . . . I agreed, realizing now it wasn't the calves I was looking for after all, and that I still had to see inside the stall that was guarded by the owl.

The owl is Vickers. His eyes have seen the secret contents of the boxstall and he guards others from such knowledge. In the dream, the boy realizes that this knowledge, not the calves, is what he searches for.

In the morning, despite this dream, the boy still believes the calves are hidden in the boxstall. When he goes to the barn to get Tim, he uses a nervous horse as a diversion to distract Vickers long enough to attempt to look in the stall. As he tries to open the door, he comes to realize his desire to see inside has nothing to do with the calves or Vickers. His search is now focused on knowledge of the essence of darkness, the side of the duality which is unknown to him:

> Terrified of the stall though, not of Vickers. Terrified of the stall, yet compelled by a frantic need to get inside. For the moment I had forgotten Vickers, forgotten even the danger of his catching me. I worked blindly, helplessly, as if I were confined and smothering. For a moment I yielded to panic. . . . Then, collected again, I forced back the lower bolt, and picking up the whiffle-tree tried to pry the door out a little at the bottom.

The boy escapes and returns home cold, exhausted, and emotionally distraught. The calves, he learns, had returned shortly after he had set out. The boy is stunned to silence by the realization that the secret Vickers guarded was that he had murdered his housekeeper and hidden her body in the stall. Though the boy has not actually seen into the stall, he has glimpsed this dark divinity of death through his experiences with Vickers.

The other children, Peter Parker, Jenny, and Tommy Dickson, experience flights to the light-filled imaginative realm, the opposite dimension to the one experienced by this boy. As with Peter McAlpine, in **"The Outlaw,"** who faced the destructive dimension by making his own decision to ride Isabel, the boy in **"One's a Heifer,"** by searching for the calves, also comes into contact with the potentially dangerous side of life. However, for both boys, the urge to experience both sides of the mystery, the light and the dark, is strong. Rather than grow increasingly more frightened the longer he stays with Vickers, the boy becomes more and more determined to look into the boxstall. When an initially pride-inspiring ride becomes the opposite, the dimension of destruction and the dimension of the imagination are linked in one experience. The boy becomes disturbingly aware that a mature understanding of life includes knowledge of both light and darkness, that elements of both sides make up the true essence of life. For this child, as for Ross's other child characters, "it's all over and it's all beginning." A childish one-sided understanding of life ends and a sometimes dangerous, potentially disappointing and painful world of new possibilities and challenge begins.

David Carpenter (essay date 1992)

SOURCE: "Horsey Comedy in the Fiction of Sinclair Ross," in *From the Heart of the Heartland: The Fiction of Sinclair Ross,* edited by John Moss, University of Ottawa Press, 1992, pp. 67-80.

[*In the following essay, Carpenter offers an overview of the critical reaction to Ross's short fiction and notes the comic elements in eight of his stories.*]

I began reading Sinclair Ross's work around 1970, a bit before the publication of his last story, **"The Flowers**

That Killed Him" (1972). At the time there seemed to be a hunt in progress to find our cultural heroes, who in turn would articulate for us that elusive thing called "The Canadian Identity." The word was out: return to your roots, scour the countryside, haul those skeletons out of the closet. The grimmer the better. As a graduate student in search of a thesis, I canvassed the bookshelves in search of the most unsparing realism I could find. What I sought would have as many broken teeth as Faulkner's stories, as many corpses as Hemingway's. It would vibrate with existential angst and vomit, just like Sartre's *La Nausée*. It would seethe with all the trapped futility of Joyce's *Dubliners*. When I found whatever it was I was looking for, I would feel a shudder in my soul and cry, "The horror! The horror!" And it would be politically relevant too.

I became a card-carrying proselytizer for stark realism, a grim reality snob in the Saskatchewan tradition: grimmer than thou. But was I alone in my glorification of despair, deprivation, and defeat? I think not.

When I came across **"The Painted Door"** by Sinclair Ross, I knew I had come home. Several other narratives in *The Lamp at Noon and Other Stories* confirmed my discovery: **"Not by Rain Alone," "One's a Heifer,"** and the title story, **"The Lamp at Noon." "A Field of Wheat"** was powerfully written, but in those days I was like Atwood's surfacer: I was corpse hunting. And as far as I was concerned, **"A Field of Wheat"** should have ended paragraphs earlier with the dog Nipper lying mutilated on the ground.

I had become a Rosselyte, what critic Morton Ross refers to as the "gladly suffering reader." Looking back at the critics of *As for Me and My House* in this same era, Morton Ross observes, "It is, I suspect, natural for literary critics to recommend books on the same grounds that castor oil is prescribed; the experience is not pleasant, but it may be good for you".

I felt that to be a true Rosselyte, you had to suffer willingly through these stories; that was part of the aesthetic pleasure. And as I intimated earlier, I was not alone. Here is Laurie Ricou [from *Sinclair Ross and Ernest Buckler*, 1975] summing up his impressions of *As for Me and My House* and the grimmest stories in *The Lamp at Noon*: "An empty, unproductive, and oppressive existence in an empty, unproductive and oppressive landscape makes an intense fictional impact. The discovery of meaning in this existence . . . makes Sinclair Ross one of Canada's best novelists." And here is Robert Chambers [from *Vertical Man/Horizontal World: Man and Landscape in Canadian Prairie Fiction*, 1973], commenting on the same short stories referred to by Ricou: "Many of the finest moments in Ross' stories combine these few elements: menacing nature, lonely humans, a tightening claustrophobia. The dominant mood is one of attrition, with a terrible harmony between the working of wind upon soil and snow and the slow undermining of human stamina and strength."

Re-reading all 18 of Ross's stories has been a disturbing process for me. So has my reading of the dozen or so critics who have done studies of Ross's short fiction.

Virtually every major study seems to emphasize what Margaret Laurence refers to as the "lives of unrelieved drabness" chronicled in these stories. Perhaps she speaks for all the Rosselytes in her ground-breaking preface to *The Lamp at Noon and Other Stories* (1968):

> Throughout Ross's stories, the outer situation always mirrors the inner. The emptiness of the landscape, the bleakness of the land, reflect the inability of these people to touch another with assurance and gentleness. . . . Ross never takes sides, and this is one admirable quality of his writing. Blame is not assigned. Men and women suffer equally. The tragedy is not that they suffer, but that they suffer alone.

Laurence's remark here seems to speak for all the stories in *A Lamp at Noon,* but she has very little to say about Ross's *other* stories in this volume, the comic pieces: **"The Runaway," "Circus in Town," "The Outlaw,"** and **"Cornet at Night."** Her sombre essay seems to have set the tone for all subsequent treatments of Ross's later volume, *The Race and Other Stories* (1982). Ross's comic work in the short story is either ignored by subsequent Rosselytes or cast in such a dubious light that the stories seem unduly severe in the critical interpretations. Typical of these readers is Paul Comeau, who claims that Ross's short fiction between 1934 and 1952 is written in "the tragic mode [*Canadian Literature,* Winter, 1984]. This position forces Comeau to paint Ross's comic stories with a strangely grey brush. After all, these characters in Ross's lighter work "come from the same pioneer stock and cling to variations of the same dream [as the characters in Ross's grim tragedies]. For example, Martha's ambition to have her children properly educated is realized by Tom's mother in 'Cornet at Night,' mainly because she has sufficient time and funds to maintain an orderly household and supervise his music and Bible studies." Stories like **"Cornet,"** which I now claim to be richly comic, are seen by Comeau as merely less severe reflections of Ross's "hostile environment."

Keath Fraser's essay on Ross's stories [which was published in *Queen's Quarterly,* Spring, 1970] is much more perceptive than the studies of Comeau, Djwa, Chambers, Mitchell, Friesen, and McCourt. Like Lorraine McMullen, he devotes some serious consideration to these comic stories—as comedy. And even more than McMullen he demonstrates a rich awareness of Ross's comic talents.

My problem with Fraser's essay is one I've seen in the work of most of the Rosselytes: he reads each story within the pervasive context of all the stories in *A Lamp at Noon.* In his treatment of them, the comic stories come across as though they were part of a formally constituted story cycle, such as *Jake and the Kid* or *Go Down, Moses*. According to Forrest Ingram, a short story cycle is "a book of short stories so linked to each other by their author that the reader's successive experience on various levels of the pattern of the whole significantly modifies his experience of each of its component parts." Fraser reads all of Ross's stories in *The Lamp at Noon* "as part of the futility cycle" he claims Ross has established:

The futile cycle of eking existence from an indifferent world predominates [in] this collection of stories—a kind of rural *Dubliners* in which the same adult impotence replaces a similar childish Araby. Overall, the book spawns variations on the theme of isolation and its haunting melody is unmistakable. . . . These prairie inhabitants . . . can retreat nowhere that is not whirling vainly in an absurd seasonal cycle. . . .

There is nothing wrong with reading these stories as a unified collection as most critics have done. They are unified by their setting and their time. Indeed, two of these stories were altered by Ross to form a linked sequence. The two-part story we now know as **"Not by Rain Alone"** was first published as two stories six years apart: **"Not by Rain Alone"** and **"September Snow."** In her pioneering study *Sinclair Ross* (1979), Lorraine McMullen notes: "For consistency the original names of the man and wife in **'September Snow,'** Mark and Ann, were changed to Will and Eleanor (the names of the man and wife in **'Not by Rain Alone')**".

Ross's comic work in the short story is either ignored by subsequent Rosselytes or cast in such a dubious light that the stories seem unduly severe in the critical interpretations.

—David Carpenter

Lorraine McMullen's lengthy treatment of Ross's stories has the advantage of allowing some of them their own separate integrity. Reading them as Comeau or Fraser or Chambers do, as a unified cycle, occasionally forces these critics into a discussion of the comic stories as though they were written to a theme: the impact of the drought on farm economy, or how farm debt affects interpersonal relationships. These stories deserve to be read as individual works that maintain their own comic integrity without the cloudlike encumbrance of an overall scheme or a theme that prefigures their significance.

One story badly neglected and distorted by the readings of the Rosselytes is **"The Runaway."** Chambers claims it is one of Ross's "best stories," but says nothing about it. Paul Comeau seems to think it has something to do with the price of prosperity exacted by the land, and dismisses it. So does McMullen with the passing thought that "sometimes nature or coincidence works hand in hand with divine retribution. . . . In **'The Runaway'** Luke Taylor's own meanness and cheating lead indirectly to his own death and that of all his magnificent horses." By grouping **"The Runaway"** with Ross's truly tragic stories under the theme of "Nature as Impassive Agent," she obscures the story's comic vitality. McMullen and Fraser are better geared to Ross's comic vision than the other Rosselytes, but even

Fraser doesn't know what to say about **"The Runaway."** His only words on it are: "Sometimes it seems enough that the bad among them are punished (as is Luke Taylor in **'The Runaway'** when he dies in his burning barn, and the wife of the man he cheated calls upon her Biblical clichés that justify his death). But when are the good rewarded? Not really ever. . . .'"

The only critic bold enough to comment on this story is Ken Mitchell. He gives it a page in his book *Sinclair Ross*. His reflection on the story is only a plot summary, but he does manage to locate it as "a tale of moral justice in the Faulknerian mode." By "Faulknerian mode" I assume Mitchell means the Faulkner of the *Snopes* trilogy. The story's antagonist, Luke Taylor, is a dishonest horse trader who, like Faulkner's Flem Snopes, becomes the richest landowner in the district. And like Flem, he meets his nemesis, dies violently, and not a tear is shed. I like Mitchell's phrase, "a *tale* of moral justice." Perhaps because this story is a tale, it fits less securely into Ross's collection *A Lamp at Noon* than those praised by the Rosselytes for their unsparing portrayal of bleak lives. By "tale" I assume Mitchell means a narrative that is not realistic but has its own kind of brilliance and charm. [In his *The Art of Fiction,* 1985] John Gardner is helpful on this distinction between stories like **"The Painted Door"** and others like **"The Runaway"**:

> The realistic writer's way of making events convincing is verisimilitude. The tale writer, telling stories of ghosts, or shape-shifters . . . uses a different approach: By the quality of his voice, and by means of various devices that distract the critical intelligence, he gets what Coleridge called . . . "the willing suspension of disbelief for the moment, which constitutes poetic faith."

Nevertheless, the tale writer, like the realist, must document his story from time to time in some way that gives credibility to his narrative voice. We believe the narrative "not just because the tale voice has charmed us but also, and more basically, because the character's gestures, his precisely described expression, and the reaction of others to his oddity all seem to us exactly what they would be in this strange situation." The reader of **"The Runaway,"** then, is from time to time given proofs (closely observed details of farm life and human intercourse) that generate a compelling sense of reality—however fantastic or illusory.

Ross uses a nameless boy to tell his tale. This boy obviously loves a good yarn. In the heat of the story's climax, the narrator thinks, "I knew that for months to come the telling of [this tale] would be listened to." He begins in this fashion:

> You would have thought that old Luke Taylor was a regular and welcome visitor, the friendly, unconcerned way he rode over that afternoon, leading two of his best Black Diamond mares.

> "Four-year-olds," he said with a neighbourly smile. "None better in my stable. But I'm running short of

stall room—six more foals last spring—so I thought if you were interested we might work out a trade in steers."

My father was interested. We were putting a load of early alfalfa in the loft, and he went on pitching a minute, aloof, indifferent, but between forkfuls he glanced down stealthily at the Diamonds, and at each glance I could see his suspicion and resistance ebb.

So far, we have a realistic story grounded in the conventions of verisimilitude. But note how, in the next passage, the narrator's tone and diction modulate when he comes to his description of Luke Taylor's Black Diamonds and their impact on all who behold them:

> For more than twenty years old Luke had owned a stableful of Diamonds. They were his special pride, his passion. He bred them like a man dedicated to an ideal, culling and matching tirelessly. A horse was a credit to the Black Diamond Farm, a justification of the name, or it disappeared. There were broad-rumped, shaggy-footed work horses, slim-legged runners, serviceable in-betweens like the team he had with him now, suitable for saddle or wagon—at a pinch, even for a few days on the plough—but all, whatever their breed, possessed a flawless beauty, a radiance of pride and spirit, that quickened the pulse and brought a spark of wonder to the dullest eye. When they passed, you turned from what you were doing and stood motionless, transfixed. When you met them on the road you instinctively gave them the right of way. And it didn't wear off. The hundredth time was no different from the first.

Note the closely observed details here, the "broad-rumped, shaggy-footed work horses, slim-legged runners," the sort of things one might associate with any group of normal horses. Then note the intangibles, that "flawless beauty, a radiance of pride and spirit, that quickened the pulse," rendering all who saw them "motionless, transfixed." Note, too, the extravagance of the boy's claims—that all people were affected by these magic steeds, even those with "the dullest eye."

Luke Taylor's Black Diamonds turn out to be "balky," which means that at unpredictable times, the very worst times even, they will refuse to move. Once again Luke Taylor has triumphed. The boy narrator's mother, who in this story is always right, had predicted Taylor would manage in some way to swindle them. This was her warning to her husband:

> "But there are things you can't check. All the years we've known [Luke] has he once done what was right or decent? Do you know a man for twenty miles who'd trust him? Didn't he get your own land away from you for half what it was worth?" And she went on, shrill and exasperated, to pour out instance upon instance of his dishonesty and greed, everything from foreclosures on mortgages and bribes at tax and auction sales to the poker games in which, every fall for years, he had been fleecing his harvest-hands right after paying them.

We have in Luke Taylor, of course, the classic villain of romance. Martha Ostenso's Caleb Gare comes to mind as well as Flem Snopes. And Taylor's victims provide an interesting contrast to him in this intensely moral struggle. Here is the boy narrator's description of his father:

> According to his lights my father was a good man, and his bewilderment [over Luke's successful swindle] was in proportion to his integrity. For years he had been weakened and confused by a conflict, on the one hand resentment at what Luke had done and got away with, on the other sincere convictions imposing patience and restraint; but through it all he had been sustained by the belief that scores were being kept, and that he would live to see a Day of Reckoning. Now, though, he wasn't sure. You could see in his glance and frown that he was beginning to wonder which he really was: the upright, God-fearing man that he had always believed himself to be, or a simple, credulous dupe.

The boy's father is in fact in the throes of a spiritual crisis that has been precipitated by envy. His envy is not simply for Luke's handsome greystone house and hip-roofed barn, the "abode of guile" as the narrator calls it, but is a much deeper, more forbidden envy, focused on Luke Taylor's Black Diamonds but eating away at his own soul. So when he trades his four fat steers for the team of Diamonds, he and his wife are suddenly, mysteriously, young again. Our narrator explains it this way: "My father had a team of Diamonds, and my mother had something that his envious passion for them had taken from her twenty years ago."

Seen on its own terms, then, **"The Runaway"** is a tale told by an ideal teller in the (slightly) hyperbolic tradition about an upright man in danger of losing his soul to a comic embodiment of the devil. Had Ross taken his hyperbole much further, he would have had a yarn in the tradition of "The Devil and Daniel Webster" or "The Black Bonspiel of Wullie MacCrimmon." But like William Faulkner's narrator Ratliff of *The Hamlet,* Ross's narrator reins in his hyperbole so that on the surface, for the most part, this moral conflict remains fairly realistic. I say *fairly* realistic. Note how, even in realistic passages, the innuendoes spread like superstition throughout the narrative. Here is an example. The boy's father loses his hat in a gust of wind. Just as Luke Taylor approaches on horseback, the father reins in his new team of Diamonds so that he can retrieve his hat.

> And after weeks without a single lapse, that had to be the moment for [the Diamonds] to balk again. Was it the arrival of Taylor, I have often wondered, something about his smell or voice, that revived colthood memories? Or was it my father's anger that flared at the sight of him, and ran out through his fingers and along the reins like an electric current, communicating to them his own tensions, his conflicting impulses of hatred and forbearance? No matter—they balked, and as if to enjoy my father's mortification, old Luke too reined in and sat watching. "Quite a man with horses," he laughed across at me. "One of the finest teams for miles and just look at the state he's got them in. Better see what you can do, son, before he ruins them completely." And then, squinting over his shoulder as he

rode off, he added, "I'll tell you how to get a balky horse going. It's easy—just build a little fire under him."

"I wouldn't put it past him at that," my father muttered, as he climbed down and started to unhitch. "Being what he is, the idea of fire comes natural."

Just as envy of Luke Taylor's Black Diamonds has apparently robbed the narrator's father of his virility, so too have the horses responded, apparently, to his spiritual conflict, "his conflicting impulses of hatred and forbearance," by humiliating him. And we are teased, rather than informed, in wondering at the cause of this humiliation: a man to whom the idea of fire "comes natural."

If we read Sinclair Ross critics and not the story itself, we might at this point be tempted to predict the ending of **"The Runaway."** Will Christian forbearance and God-fearing piety win out over evil? Will the devil (or his emissary) and his demonic charges be destroyed on a Day of Judgement? Of course not. Ross's blind and uncaring universe, the indifference of his deity that critics often associate with all of his early work, all these resolutely bleak emanations from an absentee or uncaring God will determine the fate of Ross's God-fearing family. [In *Canadian Literature,* Winter, 1971] Sandra Djwa puts it very well when she says the following: "Because this conflict is intimately connected with the struggle for survival, the tragedy of these stories is that there is often no possible reconciliation of any kind. When an author's horizon is composed of the bare essentials of a landscape, sky and earth, there are no compromises open: if land and weather fail man, the struggle for survival can only end tragically, the extent of the tragedy being largely determined by the strength of the person concerned."

But this is not what happens in **"The Runaway."** It is not even close. What happens is that Luke Taylor is destroyed, along with his demonic horses, in a fiery inferno. No tears are shed, not even for the horses, and there is only a perfunctory sort of mourning after this apocalyptic incident. In fact, Luke Taylor's death is rather funny. His advice to the narrator and his father is Luke Taylor's undoing. The horses balk again with a load of straw on a cold and windy November afternoon. And this time, exasperated, the father says to his son, ". . . I think I'll take old Luke's advice, and see what a fire will do." The narrator tells it this way:

> I closed my eyes a moment. When I opened them he had straightened and stepped back, and there on the ground between the Diamonds' feet, like something living that he had slipped out of his coat, was a small yellow flame, flickering up nervously against the dusk.

> For a second or two, feeling its way slowly round the straw, it remained no larger than a man's outspread hand. Then, with a spurt of sparks and smoke, it shot up right to the Diamonds' bellies.

They gave a frightened snort, lunged ahead a few feet, stopped short again. The fire now, burning briskly, was directly beneath the load of straw, and even as I shouted to warn my father a tongue of flame licked up the front of the rack, and the next instant, sudden as a fan being flicked open, burst into a crackling blaze.

The Diamonds bolt, the boy jumps on his entirely ordinary horse Gopher, and the chase is on. "Riding close behind, my head lowered against the smoke and sparks, I didn't realize, till the wagon took the little ditch onto the highway at a sickening lurch, that the Diamonds were going home. Not to their new home, where they belonged now, but to old Luke Taylor's place."

These stories deserve to be read as individual works that maintain their own comic integrity without the cloudlike encumbrance of an overall scheme or a theme that prefigures their significance.

—David Carpenter

Note how our narrator has personified the fire, with its nervous flickering, "like something living." Note too how the narrator characterizes the Black Diamonds in Luke Taylor's stable. When the flaming wagon is drawn home by the terrified team, it overturns and sets fire to Luke Taylor's barn. His Black Diamonds are inside, and the boy tries to save them from immolation. Instead of fleeing their stalls to safety, they *all* balk. Instead of being portrayed by our narrator as the innocent victims of an uncaring fate, the Black Diamonds are presented to us as monsters. The narrator describes them as follows:

> I ran forward and squeezed in past [the] heels [of the first Diamond I saw], then untied the halter-shank, but when I tried to lead [the horse] out it trembled and crushed its body tight against the side of the stall. I climbed into the manger, struck it hard across the nose; it only stamped and tossed its head. Then I tried the next stall, then the next and the next. Each time I met the same fear-crazed resistance. One of the Diamonds lashed out with its heels. Another caught me such a blow with a swing of its head that I leaned half-stunned for a minute against the manger. Another, its eyes rolling white and glassy, slashed with its teeth as I turned, and ripped my smock from shoulder to shoulder.

This is the point at which Luke Taylor shows up. He heads straight for his huge burning barn, evading those well-meaning neighbours who try to head him off. He goes through the door. "The same moment that he disappeared, the floor of the loft collapsed. It was as if when running through the door he had sprung a trap, the way the great, billowy masses of burning hay plunged down behind him."

It doesn't take long. Luke returns to his element, and the two remaining Diamonds whose fateful trip "home" started the fire mysteriously return to a prosaically horsey identity. The narrator fears that they will balk again. He "mounted Gopher as usual and rode through the gate ahead of them, but at the first click of the reins they trotted off obediently. Obediently and dully, like a team of reliable old plough-horses. Riding along beside them, listening to the soft creak and jingle of the harness, I had the feeling that we, too, had lost our Diamonds."

The story closes with the mother (who in this story, as I have said, is always right) and the father (whose judgement is usually questionable where horses are concerned) trying to place their own construction upon the events of the day:

> "It's as I've always said [the mother argues] . . . *Though the mills of God grind slowly, yet they grind exceeding small.* His own balky Diamonds, and look what they carried home to him." She hadn't been there to see it— that was why she could say such things. "You sow the wind and you reap the whirlwind. Better for him today if he had debts and half-a-section like the rest of us." But my father sat staring before him as though he hadn't heard her, There was a troubled, old look in his eyes, and I knew that for him it was not so simple as that to rule off a man's account and show it balanced. Leave Luke out of it now—say that so far as he was concerned the scores were settled—but what about the Diamonds? *What kind of reckoning was it that exacted life and innocence for an old man's petty greed? Why, if it was retribution, had it struck so clumsily?*

These last words, which I italicized, are the ones Djwa quotes to arrive at her sombre conclusion about this work. "The good man of '**The Runaway**' finds himself troubled by God's justice, especially when the scales are eventually weighed in his favour." But "**The Runaway**" does not end with the man's words; it ends with the narrator's response to the impact of his mother's words. Here are the last lines of the story:

> "All of them," he said at last, "all of them but the team he was driving and my own two no-good balky ones. Prettiest horses a man ever set eyes on. It wasn't coming to them."

> "But you'll raise colts," my mother said quickly, pouring him a fresh cup of coffee, "and there'll be nothing wrong with them. Five or six years—why you'll have a stableful."

> He sipped his coffee in silence a moment and then repeated softly, "Prettiest horses a man ever set eyes on. No matter what you say, it wasn't coming to them." But my mother's words had caught. Even as he spoke his face was brightening, and it was plain that he too, now, was thinking of the colts.

Note how the conversation in this closing scene goes in one way, but how the tone moves like an undertow in the opposite direction, away from any possibility of tragedy.

And if the father has undergone a spiritual crisis (which might reappear with the birth of Black Diamond colts), so too, perhaps, has Sinclair Ross. To write "**The Runaway**" he has forfeited that bleak nihilism he has been branded with in all of his early work.

In the above reading, I have characterized "**The Runaway**" as a tale rich in comic detail. It is much less about the fate of a man and his horses that "wasn't coming to them" than about the damnation of a diabolical schemer and his demonic steeds. Luke Taylor's fire unites the settlement in a common cause. His death restores normality and hope to the characters.

A re-reading of all of Ross's stories has served to focus my attention upon his talents as a comic writer. I hesitate to say what kind of a comic writer, because the very moment I make a formulation of his comedy, I will begin to recall stories in his canon that refuse, like Luke's horses, to conform to a theoretically "normal" category. "**Spike**" has the structure but not the texture of romantic comedy. "**The Race**" (an excerpt from Ross's novella *Whir of Gold*) reads like a long joke or a boy's adventure, full of good spirits and friendly contempt for the strictures of the adult world. "**A Day with Pegasus**," written in what critics would like us to think of as Ross's early black period, is a realistic story about a boy's fantasy lie, and it reads a bit like a Miracle Play. "**Barrack Room Fiddle Tune**" is Ross's only story written in the first person plural, an anecdote about the impact of a farm boy's terrible fiddle-playing on a group of army recruits. There is really only one character in this story, so again it defies easy classification.

"**The Outlaw**," "**Cornet at Night**," and "**Circus in Town**" have all received fair attention from critics. The only thing I would add to the comments I have read is that these three stories work by means of subversion. The subversive victory in each has something to do with a child's attainment of a vision which is antithetical to that of his or her parents. In each case the child manages to invert the value system that oppresses her or him.

It is interesting to note that the comedy in almost every one of these eight stories is inextricably bound up with horses. For example, in "**Cornet at Night**" the story proceeds with quiet, almost detached, irony. Our narrator, Tommy Dickson, has tried to remain obedient to the strictures of his parents' parsimony. His orders for his first ever trip to town alone are to hitch Rock (an old, utterly reliable horse) to the wagon, do the shopping, and bring back a hired man to help his father with the stooking.

> "Mind you pick somebody big and husky," said my father as he started for the field. "Go to Jenkins' store, and he'll tell you who's in town. Whoever it is, make sure he's stooked before."

> "And mind it's somebody who looks like he washes himself," my mother warned, "I'm going to put clean sheets and pillowcases on the bunkhouse bed, but not for any dirty tramp or hobo."

By the time they had both finished with me there were a great many things to mind. Besides repairs for my father's binder, I was to take two crates of eggs each containing twelve dozen eggs to Mr. Jenkins' store and in exchange have a list of groceries filled. And to make it complicated, both quantity and quality of some of the groceries were to be determined by the price of eggs. Thirty cents a dozen, for instance, and I was to ask for coffee at sixty-five cents a pound. Twenty-nine cents a dozen and coffee at fifty cents a pound. Twenty-eight and no oranges. Thirty-one and bigger oranges. It was like decimals with Miss Wiggins, or two notes in the treble against three in the bass. For my father a tin of special blend tobacco, and my mother not to know. For my mother a box of face powder at the drugstore, and my father not to know. Twenty-five cents from my father on the side for ice-cream and licorice. Thirty-five from my mother for my dinner at the Chinese restaurant. And warnings, of course, to take good care of Rock, speak politely to Mr. Jenkins, and see that I didn't get machine oil on my corduroys.

All things considered, Tommy doesn't do too badly. His only major deviation from the rule of the adults is to bring home a trumpet player with slender and smooth white hands to do the stooking. The young musician's name is Philip Coleman. Philip, lover of horses, Paul Kirby might remind us. Tommy cannot keep his eyes off Philip's cornet case, but other than this, he keeps his enthusiasms and old Rock dutifully reined in—until Philip takes his cornet out of the case:

It was a very lovely cornet, shapely and eloquent, gleaming in the August sun like pure and mellow gold. I couldn't restrain myself. I said, "Play it—play it now—just a little bit to let me hear." And in response, smiling at my earnestness, he raised it to his lips.

But there was only one note—only one fragment of a note—and then away went Rock. I'd never have believed he had it in him. With a snort and plunge he was off the road and into the ditch—then out of the ditch again and off at a breakneck gallop across the prairie. There were stones and badger holes, and he spared us none of them.

Note how, when Philip puts the cornet to his lips and Rock explodes, the comedy takes off as well, from a nicely modulated irony in the first 11 pages to a wonderful moment of farce which effectively destroys the parental hold over Tommy's mission. The carefully garnered supplies fly out of the wagon, an egg crate is smashed, items are lost or ruined, and best of all (or worst of all, depending on your politics), Tommy has been seduced into a new vision of soaring possibilities by Philip's cornet.

Ross returns again and again in his comic works to these moments of subversive joy brought about by a young person whose feelings are catalyzed and released by a horse. Even the relatively horseless **"Barrack Room Fiddle Tune"** does this when the farm boy protagonist jumps a fence to have a conversation with a horse.

Horses in Ross's work are usually associated with freedom, self-sufficiency, release, and sometimes male pride. They are the Pegasus vehicles for a child's dream of freedom and adventure. And in a society in which sexual desire is suppressed so relentlessly, the horse is often the adolescent's substitute for a true object of desire. Isabel, the horse in **"The Outlaw"** and **"The Ride,"** for example, is a temptress. The horse is the trigger for the body's ecstatic release, so a horse out of control (as in Ovid's story about Phaëthon or Pindar's version of Bellerophon and Pegasus) is a moment of high celebration in the life of a prairie youth. When I re-read my own summary of **"Cornet at Night,"** I can't help but notice how the images I have cast this story in are charged with erotic innuendoes. The story seems to carry this subcurrent.

It is not my purpose here to offer firm value judgements about Ross's comic work. But I have reached the point where I can urge all the Rosselytes to read his eight short comic pieces *as comedy*. Reading these works will remind us most obviously that Ross has unsung talents as a writer of comedy. It does not, as some critics imply, show up only in Ross's later works; it is there right from the beginning. Also, if we read Ross's short stories without the constrictions imposed by a prearranged scheme—some form of thematic criticism, for example—we can begin to appreciate Ross's subversive sense of the ridiculous, his buoyant affirmations. And best of all, we can rid ourselves of the excesses of the Rosselytes: their insistence upon suffering as a salutory element of aesthetic pleasure.

I have re-read these stories after the rise and fall of postmodernism in North American fiction, after the theatre of the absurd, after Beckett and Pinter, after the quest for the Canadian identity when stark realism was the unchallenged orthodoxy, and I am returning to something Shakespeare must have known a long time ago: that a balanced diet of comic and tragic renderings is healthier than a strict regimen of one without the other. When I think of modern Canadian works that might fit some acceptable definition of tragedy, I can think of very few: *The Stone Angel,* perhaps, or *Under the Volcano.* Both are written by people who had, by my reckoning, a pretty good sense of humour. So did Sinclair Ross.

FURTHER READING

Criticism

Bowen, Gail. "The Fiction of Sinclair Ross." *Canadian Literature* No. 80, Spring, 1979, pp. 37-48.
    Discusses the main themes of Ross's fiction.

Chapman, Marilyn. "Another Case of Ross' Mysterious Barn," *Canadian Literature*, No. 103, Winter, 1984, pp. 184-186.

Provides an alternative interpretation of "One's a Heifer," contending that the girl does in fact exist and acts as an ironic counterpoint to the narrator.

Comeau, Paul. "Sinclair Ross's Pioneer Fiction," *Canadian Literature*, No. 103, Winter, 1984, pp. 174-84.

Examines Ross's use of tragedy, irony, and comedy as a response to the Canadian pioneering experience.

Fraser, Keath. "Futility at the Pump: The Short Stories of Sinclair Ross." *Queen's Quarterly* LXXVII, No. 1 (Spring 1970): 72-80.

Examines the characters of Ross's short fiction, noting the common aspiration to prevail amid the harsh prairie conditions.

McCourt, Edward. "Sinclair Ross (1908-)." In *The Canadian West in Fiction*, pp. 100-05. Toronto: The Ryerson Press, 1970.

Asserts that Ross's short stories are superior to his novels. McCourt also ranks "The Painted Door" as one of the most finely crafted stories in all of Canadian fiction.

Ricou, Lawrence. "The Prairie Internalized: The Fiction of Sinclair Ross." In his *Vertical Man/Horizontal World: Man and Landscape in Canadian Prairie Fiction*, pp. 81-94. Vancouver: University of British Columbia Press, 1973.

Explores the theme of alienation in Ross's short fiction.

Additional coverage of Ross's life and career is contained in the following sources published by Gale Research: *Contemporary Authors*, Vols. 73-76; *Contemporary Literary Criticism*, Vol. 13; and *Dictionary of Literary Biography*, Vol. 88.

Joan Vinge
1948–

(Full name Joan Carol Dennison Vinge) American short story writer and novelist.

INTRODUCTION

Vinge has written award-winning science fiction stories, novelettes, and novels predominantly featuring the theme of alienation. Her work is known for their strong female characters, often outcasts or otherwise isolated. These figures typically find redemption through love and communication, and as a result, they discover the potential to change the world.

Biographical Information

Vinge became interested in science fiction at a young age. She has recalled that science fiction writer Andre Norton "started me reading science fiction, and although I never suspected it at the time, her writing would directly or indirectly influence almost every major life choice I made from then on." Calling science fiction the "the anthropology of the future," Vinge received a degree in anthropology in 1971. The following year she married Vernor Vinge, also a science fiction writer, who encouraged his wife's writing. For an early work, *Eyes of Amber,* Vinge received the Hugo Award for best science fiction novelette. Her book *The Snow Queen* won the Hugo in 1981 for best science fiction novel.

Major Works of Short Fiction

The stories in Vinge's first collection, *Fireship*, reflect her sense of humor as well as her wish to explore a diversity of moods and styles. The title story chronicles the adventures of Ethan Ring, a human/computer amalgam. *Mother and Child* is a more serious work from this collection; it is an example of Vinge's "anthropological" science fiction, which emphasizes the interactions between different cultures and the importance of communication. The author's first notable success as a writer of short fiction came when she won the Hugo for *Eyes of Amber.* This story has been compared to the story of "Cinderella" because of its fairy-tale elements. Among the stories in *Phoenix in the Ashes*, the title story depicts the love between Amanda and Hoffman, two characters who achieve closeness in a harsh, brutal world. Vinge's short stories share similar treatments of character and setting with her novels. Major novels include *The Outcasts of Heaven Belt* and *The Snow Queen*.

Critical Reception

Vinge has enjoyed significant critical acclaim for her characterizations of women and relationships and her use of the theme of alienation versus communication. Her fiction is complex and skillfully wrought. Although some critics have found the stories flawed in their evocations of multi-layered meanings, most have judged her work thematically rich, tightly constructed, and psychologically and sociologically intricate.

PRINCIPAL WORKS

Short Fiction

*Fireship 1978
"Eyes of Amber" and Other Stories 1979
Tarzan, King of Apes (novella) 1983
The "Santa Claus—The Movie" Storybook (novella) 1985

Other Major Works

The Outcasts of Heaven Belt (novel) 1978
The Snow Queen (novel) 1980
Psion (novel) 1982
†*Return of the Jedi Storybook* (novel) 1983
World's End (novel) 1984
†*Ladyhawke* (novel) 1985
†*Return to Oz* (novel) 1985
†*Santa Claus* (novel) 1985
Catspaw (novel) 1988
Willow (novel) 1988
Heaven Chronicles (novel) 1991
The Summer Queen (novel) 1991

*This work contains the novellas *Fireship* and *Mother and Child.*
†These works are novelizations of screenplays.

CRITICISM

Anthony R. Lewis (essay date 1979)

SOURCE: A review of *Fireship,* in *Analog Science Fiction/Science Fact,* Vol. XCIX, No. 10, October, 1979, pp. 165-66.

[*In the following excerpt, Lewis favorably reviews* Fireship, *describing it as a story of "love and loyalty and integrity and courage."*]

Here are two novellas: *Fireship* [and] *Mother and Child* . . . The cover blurbs say that these are short novels, but I say they're novellas. The first, which appeared here (December 1978), and from which the book takes its title is a competent adventure story. The protagonist, whom we do not meet until late in the story, has by his existence called into being an antagonist. This antagonist would normally be considered the hero. He is a human/computer symbiosis, not a cyborg. The computer personality is more appealing than the human in most aspects. The "hero" gets involved in interplanetary intrigue, fights assorted villians, wins in the end, and gets to bed a female. But the culmination is not that of the typical super-agent story. Victory is achieved by the (not-quite Hegelian) synthesis of the protagonist (villain) and the antagonist (our hero) which suggests a higher order of human/computer symbiosis is possible. . . .

The second novella, *Mother and Child,* more than justifies the existence of this book. It should have been the title story but marketing has shown that the average SF book buyer is more likely to purchase something called *Fireship* than *Mother and Child.* The story is this: an alien planet, with two cultures. One is agricultural worshipping the Mother Goddess (the Kotaane), the other is urban and patriarchal (the Neaane). The Kotaane have an additional sense, which is either absent in the Neaane or is suppressed by deliberate mutilation. These cultures are coming into conflict. Mixing into this is a second group of aliens, the Colonial Service. A Kotaane priestess, pregnant by her smith husband, is stolen by Neaane forces and becomes concubine to their king. Her subsequent life, childbirth, exile, and recovery form the story. It is a good story. As for the plot; you may have read something similar called the *Iliad* (by Homer's time all the major plots were known).

This story has aliens; two types of aliens. They don't act alien: they seem to be human beings. This is not a failure of imagination on the writer's part. It is, rather, a recognition of the existence of certain universals necessary to build a culture. These are needed if you are discoid, amorphous, felinoid, or even humanoid. Could this story have been about Earth humans at different technological levels? Yes. Why then is it SF? Operationally, almost no short fiction is published these days outside of SF and mystery magazines. I enjoyed reading this story; if it has to be called SF to be published, then it is an SF story. (It says Dell SF on the cover; would a publisher lie?) The story is about love and loyalty and integrity and courage. Perhaps it is the inclusion of these characteristics that makes it SF; these qualities are rarely found in the current mainstream novels. There are villains but they are not completely evil; their good is a different and conflicting good from that of the protagonists. Be it understood, there is evil in the Neaane culture; the evil of suppressing abilities and human qualities, of persecuting people for what they are, rather than what they do. If you keep working at it, good wins in the end because evil is intrinsically weak. Again, maybe that's why this got labelled SF instead of mainstream.

Carl Yoke (essay date 1982)

SOURCE: "From Alienation to Personal Triumph: The Science Fiction of Joan D. Vinge," in *The Feminine Eye: Science Fiction and the Women Who Write It,* edited by Tom Staicar, Frederick Ungar Publishing Co., 1982, pp. 103-30.

[*In the following excerpt, Yoke examines the theme of alienation in Vinge's stories.*]

> But she wore the nomad's tunic she had brought back
> with her from Persiponë's, the only clothing she owned,
> its gaudy color as alien as she suddenly felt herself,
> among the people who should have been her own.

These lines from the "footrace" scene in Joan Vinge's *The Snow Queen* clearly express the psychological alienation of Dawn Moontreader Summer, the novel's heroine. Though she stands in a crowd of people from her own clan, she feels that she is an outsider, that she is somehow divorced from the very culture in which she was raised. This is the fundamental experience of a person alienated, estranged, or disenfranchised. Any doubts about the nature of Moon's feelings are quickly erased by a closer examination of the scene, which Vinge has skillfully filled with clues to induce such a conclusion.

The first comes as Moon waits for the race to begin. She suddenly feels a "tension" wrap around her "like tentacles," and to avoid it, she moves to the front of the forming field of runners. Though she believes the tension has been generated by a "certainty" that she will be chosen Summer Queen, that very possibility is born from the differences between her and the Summers. The tension she feels is symptomatic of the anxiety felt by an alienated person, and withdrawal from it is the typical reaction to it.

But there are other clues to establish Moon's alienation. While struggling to maintain her balance amid "the jostling mob of colored ribbons and eager Summer faces," for example, she describes them as "strangers." Moreover, while they are dressed in traditional Summer holiday garments, she is not. She wears instead a heavy Winter's nomad tunic. Though she is struck by the irony of the situation, she somehow feels it is appropriate. Further, to disguise her resemblance to Arienrhod, the reigning Winter Queen and her biological mother, she covers her head with a scarf. The other runners are bareheaded. And, since she displays no family totem as the others do, some of the Summers challenge her right to run, which forces her to bare the sibyl symbol tattooed on her throat. In addition to identifying the sibyls, the tattoo, a barbed trefoil, is the ancient symbol for biological contamination.

If nothing else, the fact that she is a sibyl would alienate her from everyone else. Viewed as seers by some and as witches by others, sibyls are simultaneously revered and feared. Obscured by time and superstition, the actual function of the sibyls is as vehicles for the transmission of Old Empire culture. When the Empire collapsed because of civil war, a group of selfless scientists, hoping for a rapid return to civilization, created a massive databank of knowledge in every area of human concern and genetically altered certain humans so they could tap into it. Able to pass this ability on to their children, these individuals (sibyls when trained in the use of their gift) suffer from a peculiar side effect. They can infect other humans with their blood, producing madness in some and death in others. This effect has given rise to the legend that it is death both to kill a sibyl and to love one. In turn, this has caused the Winters to ban all sibyls from the capital city of Carbuncle.

Yet another mark of Moon's alienation occurs when she is struck by the irony of her parentage as she waits for the race to begin. She was neither her mother's child nor Arienrhod's. As the clone of Arienrhod, she was raised by another, a Summer. Thus, she has roots in both cultures. This, plus the fact that she is a child without a father, makes her unlike anyone else in the crowd. It is the sudden recognition of her uniqueness and her divorce from both cultures that prompts her to question what she is doing there.

Another clue to Moon's alienation is found in her reaction as Fate Ravenglass performs the final bit of ritual in the choosing of the Summer Queen at the end of the scene. A part of her mind separates from the rest, and while she participates in the ceremony, she also experiences near

panic from her sudden doubt that she will be chosen. Momentarily, she falls into "Transfer," that state sibyls experience when they are in contact with the Old Empire computer, then she is snapped to wakefulness and finds herself in Fate's body. She watches the candidates for Summer Queen file by, but she is barely able to see them because of Fate's near blindness. Then, she sees herself stumbling forward, supported by two other women, and she reaches out and masks herself. Immediately she is snapped back into her own body, and she realizes that Fate is also a sibyl. This experience of separateness is schizophrenic and that is exactly where modern psychiatry classifies cases of extreme self-alienation. Moreover, she also realizes that indeed she is being controlled, that she is being programmed through her experiences, and that her destiny is truly not hers to control.

Moon's portrayal as an alienated being is no accident. She is but one of several such characters in *The Snow Queen*. Equally estranged are Sparks, Moon's cousin and lover; Jerusha, a highly capable but emotionally tortured police inspector; BZ Gundhalinu, Jerusha's prideridden and rigidly structured aide; and Arienrhod, the beautiful but power-crazed Winter Queen. Moreover, these characters reflect a pattern that predominates in Vinge's writing. Most of her major works contain at least one alienated character, usually the protagonist. There are, for example, Betha Torgussen and Wadie Abdhiamal of *The Outcasts of Heaven Belt*, Mythili Fukinuki and Chaim Dartagnan of **"Legacy,"** Amanda Montoya and Cristoval Hoffmann of **"Phoenix in the Ashes,"** Etaa of *Mother and Child,* T'uupieh of *Eyes of Amber,* and Tarawassie and Moon Shadow of **"The Crystal Ship."**

To find alienation the major theme of Vinge's writing is no surprise, for as critic Blanche Gelfant has indicated, it "is the inextricable theme of modern American fiction." Indeed, it may well be the major theme of modern world fiction, for in addition to notable American writers like Theodore Dreiser, Ernest Hemingway, John Dos Passos, and Saul Bellow, it is also the primary subject of such foreign writers as Jean-Paul Sartre, Albert Camus, Andre Malraux, Franz Kafka, and Herman Hesse, and as a literary form, it can be traced back directly to Fyodor Dostoevsky's *Notes from the Underground.* While the characteristics of the alienated human have existed independently for centuries, their crystallization into a major phenomenon is primarily the result of the events of the last century: rapid industrialization, global wars, deterioration of the cities, pollution of the environment, dilution of culture, dehumanization of art, refinement of the establishment, mass anaesthetization of humans, and so on. Regardless of the causes, however, the result has been to create societies that are maladjusted and comprised of individuals who accept these maladjustments as normal without realizing that they will eventually find themselves alienated from them without knowing why.

Since the term alienation was first introduced into English with the publication of Erich Fromm's *Marx's Concept of Man,* it has been so overused that its meaning is often unclear. It may be defined metaphysically, for example, as

G. W. F. Hegel does, or psychologically as Ludwig Feuerbach does, or economically as Karl Marx does. Despite this breadth of concept and its subsequent dilution, however, all the definitions have a common ground best set forth perhaps by F. H. Heinemann:

> The facts to which the term "alienation" refer, are, objectively different kinds of disassociation, break or rupture between human beings and their objects, whether the latter be other persons, or the natural world, or their own creations in art, science and society; and subjectively, the corresponding states of disequilibrium, disturbance, strangeness and anxiety.... There is one point common to all of them, i.e., the belief that a preceding unity and harmony has been transformed into disunity and disharmony.

And, the psychological characteristics of an alienated person can be identified. In describing the "Underground Man," a neurotic extension of the alienated man, Edward Abood lists the following. (1) He is usually at odds with the prevailing norms of the society in which he lives and the forces that perpetuate it. This animosity may extend to Nature, Being, or God. (2) He may either be in active revolt against the society, or he may have turned in upon himself with such ferocity that he has been reduced to despair and a longing for death. (3) His commitments are subjective, and thus he is isolated and estranged. (4) Emotionally, he is lonely, frustrated, anxious, and tense. Sometimes, this is aggravated by a keen, often morbid sensibility. (5) His attitude is typically negative. If he does develop a positive philosophy, it begins with and is conditioned by a denial of the codes of conduct, especially the values, by which those in his culture live. To these we can add the feeling of being manipulated, used, or exploited, a characteristic identified by Marx and several psychologists. Taken together, these qualities comprise the prototype of an individual alienated to the point of being psychotic. It is important to remember, however, that there are differences of degree involved. Not all alienated individuals will display all the qualities that comprise the prototype, nor will they suffer them severely enough to be classified psychotic.

While being alienated certainly implies being neurotic, it does not inevitably spell psychological disaster. Some individuals do struggle and fail in their attempts to cope with their cultures. Others succeed. The latter group first began to appear in American fiction at the end of the 1960s when many authors started producing works in which the protagonists transcend their conditions: loneliness, estrangement from the world and from self. Inevitably, success is impelled by love, for it is characters who love themselves, another, and the world who do transcend. Abood confirms that alienation need not be fatal when he points out that Camus, Sartre, and Malraux all use the condition as a foundation for constructing new and positive value systems that permit their characters to reach some reconciliation with their cultures. The belief that man can transcend his alienation is held by several philosophers and psychologists, who have been termed "utopian existentialists." While accepting that estrangement is a condition of present-day society, they believe that it can

be overcome by future sociological and psychological developments.

If Vinge's characters are not at odds with their own societies, they are at odds within the societies they find themselves and are alienated from them.

—Carl Yoke

Among this group, psychologist Erich Fromm, in particular, believes that transcendence is possible. He sees alienation as evolutionary. "Human nature drives toward unity with the 'all,' with nature; but unity on the highest level requires a temporary separation, and consequent loneliness. One goes out in order to return enriched. Separation, though painful, is a progressive step." To accomplish the transcendence, man must establish a sense of identity based upon his experience of self as the subject and agent of his own powers. This will occur when he grasps reality both inside and outside himself. Transcendence is characterized by a productive orientation in which the ability to love and create is predominant.

Though there is no evidence that Vinge has consciously based her characters in Fromm's psychology, the fact is that they closely parallel his thinking. They exhibit the qualities of alienated individuals. Then, by virtue of their experiences, they form new value systems and manage to transcend their estrangement. They do this by learning to love, and they learn to love by learning to communicate. In maturing, some of them even develop the potential to change their cultures. A close examination of Vinge's stories will demonstrate this pattern.

Mythili Fukinuki and Chaim Dartagnan of **"Legacy"** both exhibit characteristics of alienation. They are at odds with the norms of their culture, they are lonely, tense, and frustrated. Chaim is a "media man," which forces him to survive by flattering the wealthy and powerful. It is a position of high esteem in the fragile Heaven Belt culture. Yet, his self-loathing produces such disgust in him that it is "transmuted into physical self-punishment" and his stomach "pays the price of too many false smiles." Still, he persists until the attempted murder of Mythili, whom he has come to care for, forces him to acknowledge his integrity and suffer the consequences of the action he must take to preserve it.

Mythili is equally at odds with her culture. She is a female spaceship pilot in a society that will not honorably permit its women any role other than childbearer. Moreover, she has voluntarily undergone sterility. She is resented both for her burning desire to succeed as a pilot and for choosing to eliminate her breeding capability when the Heaven Belt culture needs all the healthy children it can get to maintain its faltering technology. Steven Spruill writes: "She burns with inner integrity, a dedication to her *self* at the other extreme of Dartagnan's utter, if unintended, self-abnegation. By trying so hard to exist on her own terms, to resist the malicious pressures of maledom and the passive restricted example of her society's women, she courts paranoia and madness." Mythili's breech of Heaven Belt values is an active revolt against them. Dartagnan, on the other hand, has turned in on himself with such ferocity that he has been reduced nearly to despair. The commitments of both characters are subjective and their attitudes negative.

Both are also frustrated and lonely. This is most evident in the scene where they are just completing the exploration of a planetoid in the Main Belt. It had promised salvagable goods, but all they found were masses of old printouts and plastic packing crates and a pair of mummified bodies. Disappointed, Chaim returns to their ship and once inside begins to retch, a reaction to his ulcer. Concerned, Mythili follows and in the exchange that follows, he compares himself to "those crazy bastards down in the rock, drowning in garbage, dying by centimeters—just like this goddamned system!"

She suggests that they are not at all like that reclusive couple they found. He counters that they are worse because they had a chance to be something more, hinting of course that they could be lovers. She rejects the idea angrily. She still cannot forgive him for suggesting to Demarch Siamang, a man who tried to kill her because she was unwilling to help him cover up a murder he committed, that he abandon her on the surface of a hostile planet even though she knows that Chaim's suggestion was the only way to save her life. Defeated and frustrated, he replies, "Get the hell out of here, then. Let me be alone by myself." Other evidence of Dartagnan's loneliness is found earlier in the story. His relationship with Mythili seems very promising, and it suddenly occurs to him that the reason he has always hated prospecting was because of its loneliness. A moment later a book of poems falls open in his hands to a page where Mythili has written: "*It will be lonely to be dead; but it cannot be much more lonely than it is to be alive!*" Next to her plain, back-slanted writing, he pens, "Yes, yes, yes."

Moon Shadow and Tarawassie of **"The Crystal Ship"** suffer the same characteristics of alienation that Dartagnan and Mythili do. They are at odds with the norms of their society, lonely, frustrated, and tense. Moon Shadow, a kangaroolike creature, is initially divorced from his own kind, called the Real People, because he is the last offspring produced by the mating of one of his own kind and one of the humans who came to colonize his planet. He has been ostracized from his kith because he insists upon trying to teach his people that change offered through the superior technology of the humans is preferable to their current stagnation. But they want no part of it. They remember too vividly how they were decimated and exploited by the humans. Moon Shadow, on the other hand, cannot help trying to teach them, for he is a repository for the memories of all his ancestors, and a special organ inside

his pouch permits him to draw an outside mind into his own and down into his racial consciousness. Nonetheless, his compulsion to teach the ways of the humans is an active breach of Real People values. He has been hounded into a solitary, half-fugitive existence, spied on and abused, and denied the rituals of the clan.

Tarawassie, a young girl who lives in a starship orbiting high above the planet, is equally alienated. Like most of the other remaining humans, she is completely removed from reality, living initially only for the highs induced by *chitta,* a native drug that when introduced to the colonists five hundred years earlier caused the society to collapse. Happy and unaware at first, the deaths of a friend and then her mother stir her curiosity to wakefulness. Both committed suicide in the mysterious Star Well of the ship. When no one can satisfactorily explain what the Star Well is and why she has begun to have nightmares, she seeks an answer in the ruined city below because that is where Andar, her dead friend, had found it.

When she becomes lost in the city and cut off from any chitta, her long-suppressed emotions begin to take over, and she is overwhelmed by loneliness. As she continues to withdraw from the drug, she encounters Fromm's reality both inside and outside herself:

> She remembered the sight of her own starved body, the reflection of a terrible truth. Because it was true, she was certain of it now. The self and the reality that she had always known had been a dream, a dream. But not a fantasy. She remembered her mother's death, the Star Well. Were this ruined world and her own wretchedness what her mother had seen without chitta? And was this what Andar had seen?

Moon Shadow tries to help her find an answer, and in the process she learns to read. This only increases her divorce from her own kind. When at last she is fully aware of how the colony fell and the insufferable dead end that now presents itself as her future, she thinks: "But even knowing that they [she and Moon Shadow] were valued by one another, she knew that they would both always feel isolated, alienated, lost, because they had no purpose here, no reason for existing in an alien world." Passive at first, Tarawassie actively revolts against her system's values and eventually steps into the Star Well to escape her living death. The Star Well, she believes, is a transporter that can create duplicate bodies at its terminus on Earth, and when Tarawassie steps into it she performs the ultimate rejection of her society's values.

Perhaps the purest and most direct example of a character at odds with the norms of her society, lonely, tense, and frustrated occurs in Amanda Montoya of **"Phoenix in the Ashes."** Like Moon Shadow she too has been ostracized. She chose love over a marriage arranged by her father, but when the sailor she promised to wait for fails to return, she is forced from her father's home and her dowry is distributed between her two sisters. Now she lives in an adobe cottage on her father's land but far from the main house, and gleans his fields for food. Though he refuses to acknowledge her existence, he has not so completely forgotten her that he would force her to become a beggar or a whore, the only occupations left to a woman of San Pedro who has lost her family sponsorship. In this rigid, male-dominated society, women are regarded as valuable property. From birth they are impressed with the need for obedience and chastity; their role is to serve their husbands and fathers blindly. They weave and cook but do not read.

Amanda's rebellion costs her dearly. Even though other pockets of civilization remain in this postbomb world, San Pedro maintains only limited trading relationships. Because of religious stringency, leaving the society is nearly impossible. So, eight years after her rebellion, Amanda survives at a minimum level. She is bitter, she is lonely, and she finds that "the staid ritual life in San Pedro [is] suffocating her, and her dreams [are] dying."

Amanda's rebellion extends beyond the defiance of her father. She rebels in fact against her God when she gives refuge to Cristoval Hoffmann, a prospector whose helicopter crashed into her father's field. Believing him to have been struck from the sky by God because he was an agent of evil, the villagers invoke their "Angel of the Prophet" to ward off any powers he might have and leave him to die. Amanda explains to him later that the villagers thought that by flying he was performing sorcery. He asks if she were not afraid of God's punishment for helping him, and she replies, "There's little more that God could do to me or I to God. . . ."

Hoffmann, a prospector of rare scrap metals for the Brazilian government, is as alienated as Amanda. He enjoys his profession because it takes him away from the greed and exploitation of his own society. During the exchange when Cohelo, his boss, asks him to take the assignment that brings him eventually to San Pedro, he says, "I use you, you use me. . . ." When Hoffmann crashes, his alienation is increased twofold because he not only loses his only means of returning to Brazil but also suffers amnesia, which prevents him from even remembering his previous life.

If Vinge's characters are not at odds with their own societies, they are at odds within the societies they find themselves and are alienated from them. This displacement occurs, for example, to Etaa, the Kotaane priestess of the powerful novelette *Mother and Child.* While she never loses faith with her own native Nature cult, Etaa is twice removed from it physically. First, she is kidnapped by Meron, King of Tramaine. Then, she is kidnapped from Tramaine by Wic'owoyake, one of the silicon-based life forms believed to be gods by Meron and his people. Nicknamed Tam by Etaa, Wic'owoyake actually removes her from her home, a moon circling a giant, gaseous planet called Cyclops, to Laa Merth, another moon now uninhabited. Physical displacement and isolation are, of course, symbols of alienation, but there are other signs as well. Believed to be a witch and too uncouth to be a consort of the King, Etaa is rejected by the Tramanians. Her rape by Meron speeds her withdrawal and virtually eliminates all communication with him, but her disgust with the Trama-

nians is more fundamental. She believes them to be pitiful and cursed because they do not believe in the Earth-Mother goddess that dominates her religion.

When Tam removes her to Laa Merth for political reasons, Etaa withdraws even farther. Not only does she cease virtually all communications with Tam, she never ventures outside their shelter again by choice. Though estranged, manipulated by an outside source, and literally isolated, Etaa never falls into despair. She has Alfilere, her infant son, to think about and to care for. His welfare prevents her from becoming completely subjective, and more importantly he is a symbol of her love for Hywel, her husband. That her love for him still lives is confirmed by the fact that she kept the silver-bell earring he gave her close to her during her entire ordeal even though she believed him to be dead. . . ."

Eyes of Amber, Vinge's Hugo Award winning novella, presents an interesting variation of the alienation theme. T'uupieh the protagonist, is an excellent example of what Erich Fromm calls "socially patterned defect." As a female assassin among the winged creatures of Saturn's moon, Titan, she accepts the values of her culture, at least at the conscious level, even though her people are treacherous, devious, dangerous, unethical, and immoral by our standards. T'uupieh not only embraces those values but, in fact, promotes them. When she is dispossessed of her lands by the Overlord and is forced to live by her wits, for example, she resolves to become the best thief and cutthroat in the land. She succeeds amazingly well until a space probe introduces her indirectly to Shannon Wyler, an ex-rock musician with a facility for computers. T'uupieh is an excellent example of a person who has learned "to live with a defect without becoming ill" because her culture provides patterns that act as opiates.

The acceptance of Titan's values does not, however, prevent T'uupieh from becoming alienated and lonely. The loss of her lands and her wealth brings a radical change in her life-style and a subsequent loss of prestige and security. The marriage of her sister, Ahtseet, to the man who stole their lands and property, eliminates her closest companion and confidante. Her subsequent rise to leadership of a band of outcasts like herself forces her to maintain her distance from them in order to control them. And, when she finds the probe, it only serves to alienate her further:

> She looked away again, toward the fire, toward the cloak-wrapped form of her outlaws. Since the demon had come to her she had felt both the physical and emotional space that she had always kept between herself as leader and her band of followers gradually widening. She was still completely their leader, perhaps more firmly so because she had tamed the demon, and their bond of shared danger and mutual respect had never weakened. But there were other needs, which her people might fill for each other, but never for her.

The more she relies on the probe, her demon, the greater her degree of alienation will become, for Shannon is weaning her from her values and toward ours. The process is aided by her perception of the probe as a supernatural thing. Her reaction is greatly influenced by her fear and awe of its powers.

T'uupieh is neither despairing nor longing for death. Her commitments are selfish, at least up until the time she is forced to admit to herself that her sister's escape from death pleased her. In fact, despite the loneliness, she feels good about herself. She is successful, but she does not realize that her feeling occurs because defect has been raised to a virtue by her culture.

From these illustrations, it is clear that alienation is a major component of Vinge's characterization. It does produce withdrawal from one's own kind, rebellion against a society's values, loneliness (the affective corollary of alienation), tension, anxiety, frustration, even physical illness, but it is not an irreversible condition like Sören Kierkegaard's "sickness unto death." Rather, it is evolutionary. It is a stage a personality must pass through on its way to transcendence. From this point of view, it parallels Erich Fromm's position and is much like what an adolescent passes through in his search for identity.

For Vinge alienation is the result of the compelling drive of her characters toward the realization of their potentials. Completing their quests for fulfillment brings them into conflict with the values of the societies in which they find themselves because the societies themselves are neurotic and unrealized. Yet, Vinge's characters escape their alienation with both dignity and integrity because they persevere in their attempts to grasp reality, both inside and outside themselves. They continue to strive to understand themselves, to align themselves with nature, and to communicate with all things, especially in emotional terms. Moon realizes this as she tries to make friends with Blodwed's caged pets in *The Snow Queen*. "She lost track of time or any purpose beyond the need to communicate even to the smallest degree with every creature, and earn for herself the reward of its embryonic trust. . . ." Like Moon, Vinge's other characters also succeed in achieving something like Fromm's "productive orientation characterized by the ability to love and create." For Vinge, communication and love are psychologically opposed to alienation and loneliness.

Because love is the ultimate communication, and communication, in the broadest and deepest sense of the word, is the means for breaking down alienation, Vinge frequently focuses her stories on love relationships. In particular, she brings together an alienated man and an alienated woman and lets them work at communicating. Bound together by their loneliness and prompted by the events of the story that continuously force them together, they eventually break down the barriers between them and achieve a love relationship based upon mutual trust. Their common enemy is often the values of the society in which they find themselves. From the exertion of their mutual struggle, they forge new value systems and come to a more complete realization of their own potentials. Battling to survive at both the physical and psychological levels, they do produce or promise to produce changes in the value system of the society itself.

Such is the case in **"Legacy."** Mythili and Chaim are both alienated. When he is chosen as media man and she as pilot of Sabu Siamang's rescue mission to Planet Two, a sequence of events forces them not only to communicate with but to trust one another. When Siamang kills Sekka-Olefin, the prospector he is supposed to be rescuing, for the computer software he controls and subsequently tries to cover up the crime, both Mythili and Chaim are forced to recognize the fact that the values of their society are not only undesirable but psychologically unhealthy. Mythili's refusal to cover up the crime forces Siamang to try to kill her. The incident makes Chaim aware of the limits of his own integrity and forces him to make a realistic choice in order to save them both: he convinces Siamang to abandon Mythili on the planet's surface rather than "spacing" her on the way home. He argues that she will either freeze or suffocate if they jam the oxygen valve on her suit. Either way, her death will look like an accident. But Dartagnan knows something that neither Mythili nor the drug-crazed Siamang knows—the air of Planet Two is breathable, at least for a short time. Olefin told him that when Siamang was out of the shelter. Chaim's choice is difficult but realistic. He also knows that Mythili can make it back to Olefin's shelter and fix his landing module, if she does not panic. Under the existing conditions, it is the best possible decision. When they finally land on Mecca, their home asteroid, Dartagnan publicly charges Siamang with the murder, knowing full well that he may also be charged with Mythili's death if she fails to escape. She does escape, however, and he ruins his career as a media man, but he has learned something valuable about himself and his world. So has she. Subsequent situations force greater understanding, eventually permitting them to build new, more healthy value systems and to fall in love.

The pattern recurs in **"The Crystal Ship."** Impelled by her desire to understand the Star Well, Tarawassie is forced to rely upon Moon Shadow. After an accidental meeting, she learns that he can help her to understand the terrible conditions of their society. In learning of the reality surrounding her, however, she increases her alienation from the remaining humans on the Crystal Ship. Through Moon Shadow's ability to draw her into his mind and thus allow her to become the ancestors who inhabit it, she not only learns the truth but experiences a schizophrenia similar to what Moon experiences when she invades the mind of Fate Ravenglass. While it is a symbol of alienation, it is also means for Tarawassie to develop a deep understanding of both Moon Shadow and humans who are not addicted to chitta. Their relationship, on the other hand, alleviates his loneliness. A genuine affection develops between them, one based in reality and in the new value systems each forms.

In **"Phoenix in the Ashes,"** the pattern occurs again. When Hoffmann's 'copter crashes in Amanda's father's field, events are set in motion that make Amanda and Cristoval communicate with and rely upon one another. He needs her to nurse him back to health; she needs him to reaffirm her independence and integrity. Their continuous reliance upon one another forges a relationship based upon values different from San Pedro's and brings both of them a new perception of reality. Eventually they marry, and Amanda learns that a realistic love relationship is very different from the romance she sought with the sailor who abandoned her.

The pattern is varied somewhat in *Mother and Child.* Etaa's psychological journey is cyclical: from love and communication through alienation and loneliness and back to love again. But the love she feels by the end of her journey is much different than what she felt at the beginning. It is a love based in maturity and reality rather than one based in innocence. It is broader, deeper, and wiser. Events again force her to rely on alienated individuals: Hywel, her husband; Meron, the King of Tramaine; and Tam, the shape-changing, alien, xenobiologist. Each of them is initially alienated and lonely, but their experiences with her change them. Each achieves a new perception of reality, new understanding, and new value systems because they learn to love her.

She too is changed by her ordeal. Believing Hywel to be dead, Etaa finds solace in her responsibility to her infant son. But she is forced to rely first on Meron and then on Tam for her physical survival. She grows from her experiences with them. She matures; she broadens her understanding of reality; she forms new values:

> "I am not what I was. And neither is the world." Her hands dropped; her eyes found my face again. "One's truth is another's lie, Tam; how can we say what is right, when it's always changing? We only know what we feel . . . that's all we ever know. . . ."

Eyes of Amber presents yet another variation on the pattern. While both T'uupieh and Shannon Wyler are alienated and lonely, there is never any physical contact between them. In fact, T'uupieh is not even aware that she is in contact with another intelligent being. In her highly superstitious society, she believes the probe through which they communicate to be a demon. It brings her power, so she relies on it more and more to accomplish her ends. In the process, however, she becomes more and more alienated from her own kind. Because the probe is animated, she develops a relationship with it analogous to love. In replying to a question from one of her band at the end of the story, for instance, she says, "'The Wheel of Change carries us all, but not with equal ease. Is that not so, my beautiful Shang'ang [her name for the probe].' She stroked its day-warmed carapace tenderly, and settled down on the softening ground to wait for its reply." Communication between T'uupieh and the probe has eased her loneliness and altered her values. While she has begun to accept Wyler's values, he has learned that communication can indeed make a difference. He did prevent T'uupieh from murdering her sister. In the process, he has reached an understanding with his mother that promises to alleviate his own alienation from her.

The Snow Queen presents an even more complicated variation on the pattern. It is similar to *Mother and Child* in that it moves cyclically, from innocent love through alienation to mature love, and it involves more than one other alienated individual. As the novel begins, Moon and Sparks are naively happy, but when they both seek acceptances as sibyls and Sparks is rejected, he leaves his warm, southern homeland for Carbuncle, the capital, in the north. As Moon's selection for training overtly marks the beginning of her alienation (she is unaware that the very nature of her birth has already marked her), Sparks's rejection marks his alienation. Instead of being forced together to learn to understand each other, themselves, nature, God, and their people, they are torn apart. Reality is thrust upon them through their experiences and relationships with the outside world. Into the mix, Vinge inserts Arienrhod, the Winter Queen. She is Moon's mother, by cloning, though the two do not know one another, and she is Moon's mirror image: evil, insensitive, power mad, and accomplished in the ways of the world.

As events unfold, Arienrhod permits Starbuck, her right hand and lover, to be ousted by Sparks and then takes him as lover. The relationship is logical. Arienrhod possesses the secret of longevity, so age is not a factor, and as Moon's genetic equivalent, she bears the physical and mental characteristics that attracted Sparks to Moon in the first place. But her power over Sparks is so complete that she corrupts him, and as he becomes more dependent upon her, his alienation deepens.

The relationship among Moon, Sparks, and Arienrhod is broadly defined by Hans Christian Andersen's fairy tale, also entitled "The Snow Queen" and one of the novel's sources. In Andersen's story, Kay, a young boy, is struck in the eye and the heart by silvers from a magic mirror invented by a wicked hobgoblin and then shattered. The mirror's power is to distort all that is beautiful and to turn the heart cold. Kay wanders off to live with the Snow Queen, oblivious to the cares and concerns of Gerda, a young girl who loves him. She is persistent, and she learns what is wrong with him, finds him, and heals him with a kiss whose power is drawn from her innocence.

Moon's psychological journey, however, is not that simple. While Sparks is writhing uncomfortably in the clutches of Arienrhod, she must first solve the problem of her own alienation. Her destiny is not her own; she is manipulated by the Old Empire computer, which places her inevitably into conflict with the values of both the Winters and the Summers. While she is trying to realize her personality, she is also gaining experience that broadens her perception of reality. Though she bears the same genetic program as Arienrhod, environment has shaped her differently.

In the other stories, communication between the alienated female and the alienated male mutually brought them to a better understanding of reality and fostered new value systems that brought love, but in *The Snow Queen* it is Moon who must force the personality transcendences. Not until she finally locates Sparks and sleeps with him is he even aware that he is under some kind of "spell." Only then, and after his father has acknowledged his parentage, is Sparks's alienation resolved. In a conversation with Moon about the pledge they made to always love one another but subsequently broke, Sparks dismisses his need for a festival mask by saying, "No . . . I don't need one. I've already taken mine off." His literal reference is to the mask he was required to wear as Starbuck, but his symbolic reference is to the persona he has shed in casting off his alienation.

While the pattern of an alienated woman forced through a series of experiences with an alienated man expresses Vinge's concern for communication, the enlarged perception of reality that each character aquires also brings a benefit with it. It is that each transcended protagonist finds herself with the ability to change the values of her society or the promise to do so. As the Summer Queen, for example, Moon will integrate the values of the Winter and Summer peoples and through the power of the sibyl computer, will begin to recreate the Old Empire civilization on Tiamat. Where Arienrhod has failed because of her insensitivity and alienation, Moon will succeed because of her ability to love in a psychologically healthy way. With the power of the probe, T'uupieh possesses the capability to change her culture's values. With the fusion reactor engine of the *Ranger*, Betha possesses a tool to teach the Heaven Belt peoples the value of cooperation. Because of her unique relationship with Tam and the belief that her son is the heir to the Tramaine throne, Etaa possesses the means to change not only the societies of her own world but also those of the aliens. Amanda's rebellion has brought San Pedro Hoffmann's knowledge of crop rotation and the promise of a more productive agriculture. And though not made clear until Vinge wrote the "Afterword" to the story, Tarawassie and Moon Shadow do eventually set in motion the forces that will bring understanding to both the humans and the Real People of their world.

In order to frame the fight her characters must wage against the values of the various societies in which they find themselves, Vinge usually sets her stories in worlds that are either very primitive or have been destroyed by some disaster. This permits her to create societies that have values that are obviously unhealthy and that suffer from Fromm's socially patterned defect. The distopic worlds, where created by technology, also suggest the dangers of human folly.

"Legacy" and *The Outcasts of Heaven Belt,* for example, are set in an asteroid system whose civilizations have been virtually destroyed by a civil war that killed a hundred million people. What remains are fragile societies slowly disintegrating into chaos. Natural resources are scarce. Radiation has produced sterility and a high number of cripples. The will to survive has given preeminence to greed and selfishness. The Demarchy is marked by lying, cheating, distrust, convenience, and suffering. People must scavenge to live. Women are valued only for their fertility. Cooperation has been replaced by division. It is a society that is psychologically unhealthy and one that easily breeds estrangement.

The planet upon which Tarawassie and Moon Shadow live, in **"The Crystal Ship,"** contains the remains of a society destroyed by drugs. Its population has been depleted of both humans and Real People. Its cities are crumbling, its machines lie rusting, its libraries gather dust, its people are starving. Fear and superstition prevail. Progress is ignored. Technology is distrusted. Even the purposes of the books and machines have been forgotten by all but a few, and the humans, who do apathetically survive, dream away their lives in drug-induced trances, some of them in the beautiful crystal ship that orbits endlessly above the pinwheel-clouded world. The Real People have returned to the ways of the past and reject any suggestion of progress, regardless of how difficult living may become. Because it is a world whose peoples refuse to recognize reality, it is a world that promotes alienation.

The setting for **"Phoenix in the Ashes"** is Earth of the future, devastated by an atomic holocaust that has left isolated pockets of civilization. The San Pedro group, to which Amanda Montoya belongs, is primitive and fundamentalistic. Wrapped in religious superstition, it values its women only as servants to its men. Agriculture dominates, technology is feared, contact with other surviving cultures is limited because of distrust. Morality is strictly regulated. It is a rigid and conservative culture that suppresses personal development except through prescribed and narrow channels.

The world of *Mother and Child* has been ravaged by a plague that left most of its people either infertile or crippled by mutations. Vision and hearing, in particular, have been severely affected. The two principal societies of the world have developed along lines dictated by these impairments. Their religions especially reflect them. People with perfect vision, for example, are said to have "second sight" and become priestesses among the Kotaane. On the other hand, the church of the Neaane believes hearing to be a curse and punctures the eardrums of any child born with that ability. Rather than working toward some reconciliation beneficial to both societies, however, the Kotaane and the Neaane have developed a deep distrust of one another. Their cultural stagnation has been encouraged by the shape-changing aliens, thought to be gods by the Neaane because they fear the potential destructiveness of humans. While living in primitive harmony with Nature is the principal concern of the Kotaane culture, the Neaane's concerns are more material. Both groups are ignorant of their true situations. Therefore, their values breed an unhealthy psychology and eventual alienation.

Though no specific cause is given, the Titanian civilization of *Eyes of Amber* is also dystopic. It is primitive compared to Earth, with knowledge of even the basest technology almost nonexistent. Fear and superstition dominate. Murder, thievery, deceit, and other acts regarded as sins on Earth are held in high regard. Indeed, the better one practices these vices, the better one's chances of surviving, and survival is the ultimate goal of Titan's population. Greed, selfishness, and distrust are the dominant values of this society and the enemies of psychologically healthy communication. So, alienation and loneliness are inevitable. Since the Titanians know nothing else, they learn to live with it. . . .

[One] supportive device is the fertility theme. It has obvious connections to the archetype because the death and subsequent revival of vegetation implies infertility and fertility, respectively. Except for *Eyes of Amber,* where no particular emphasis is given to it other than the fact that Titan is just entering its spring season, all the stories place a premium on fertility. In *Mother and Child,* for example, it is expressed through motherhood. The plague that struck the planet not only produced undesirable mutations but more importantly limited the ability of humans to reproduce. Lack of fertility thus gives birth a special emphasis. A respect for fertility is also apparent in the Kotaane religion, which makes "Mother Earth," and therefore "Mother Nature," its center and engages in a variety of fertility rituals.

In "Legacy" and *The Outcasts of Heaven Belt,* fertility is again conspicuous by its absence. Atomic spillage and the normal radiation from space have left most of the asteroid belt people either genetically defective, so that they fear to have children, or sterile. So concerned are they about their falling population (their failing technology requires a certain manpower level to maintain it), that they value their women almost exclusively for their ability to reproduce. Wadie Abdhiamal sums up the fate of a sterile woman in his society quite nicely when he says, she "had only two alternatives: to work at a menial, unpleasant job, exposed to radiation from the dirty postwar atomic batteries; or to work as a geisha, entertaining the clients of a corporation."

San Pedro, the primitive, agricultural village of "Phoenix in the Ashes," treats its women with equal defensiveness. Amanda Montoya's ostracism is an example of the punishment inflicted upon one who places herself outside the rigid mores of the community. Women are viewed as property, and their proper role is as servants to their fathers and husbands. They are expected to marry and raise families. The San Pedro religion is nature-centered. Their prophet, the son of God, who led them to the Los Angeles Basin from the south, revealed "that the only true and righteous life is one within the pattern of nature, the life all creatures were meant to live." And a seasonal cycle runs through the story. Hoffmann, who will increase their agricultural productivity by introducing them to crop rotation, comes to Amanda and the community from the field where he crashed while suffering from amnesia. Figuratively, he is reborn. Through the winter, he and Amanda lie fallow, and then in the spring they both bloom: "Amanda had blossomed with the spring, the ache of hunger forgotten. . . ." When Hoffmann's experiment at crop rotation produces wheat that grew taller than ever before, Amanda's father rewards him with the gift of a cow. Vinge leaves no doubt that the fertility images are to mirror the psychological development of her characters.

In *The Snow Queen,* fertility is treated more subtly. The shift of power to the Summers, after the ritual destruction of the Winter Queen, certainly suggests it since summer is the season of lush vegetation. But equally important is the symbolic value of Moon who becomes the Summer Queen and who is identified with the New Moon of the "White Goddess" symbol. It is the aspect of regeneration, growth, and rebirth. It is also important to note that Arienrhod is sterile. This is a side effect from taking the "waters of life," which though they extend life and suppress the effects of aging, do cause other problems. In "The Crystal Ship," there are no specific references to either fertility or motherhood, but fertility again becomes conspicuous by its absence. The preoccupation of the remaining human population with drugs has virtually ended all breeding, and from a simple lack of interest, the humans are now in danger of extinction.

Vinge's characters escape their alienation with both dignity and integrity because they persevere in their attempts to grasp reality, both inside and outside themselves. They continue to strive to understand themselves, to align themselves with nature, and to communicate with all things, especially in emotional terms.

—Carl Yoke

In addition to the fertility theme, Vinge also uses a cluster of images suggesting coldness to support the dying and reviving vegetation archetype. Snow is the most prominent image, but also included in the cluster are ice and winter and adjectives like frozen and white, which suggest coldness. As a symbol, the cold cluster signifies the winter season, that season when the Earth is devoid of most vegetation. Psychologically, it signifies that period when the character is alienated and lonely. But, like winter it holds the promise of rebirth, renewal, and regeneration.

In *Mother and Child,* for example, Hywel is orphaned near the end of winter, which marks the beginning of his alienation and loneliness, relieved only when he falls in love with Etaa, who as the priestess of the clan is the symbol of summer and fertility. When they are separated, it is at a cliff where "snow-water dashed itself down, down to oblivion." And Hywel, while relating the first part of the story, lies, his back broken in the leap from the cliff to escape King Meron's soldiers, in cold, drizzling rain under gray skies. Later, when Etaa is kidnapped by Tam and taken to Laa Merth, they arrive in a cold, gusting wind, and they spend the winter inside the shelter with virtually no communication between them. It is not until spring that a breakthrough comes.

In *Eyes of Amber* the spring melt is just beginning, and both the world and the characters are described in cold images. Chwiel compliments T'uupieh, for example, when he says, "You are carved from ice, T'uupieh," and later when she is speaking, Vinge describes her voice as one "which snapped like a frozen branch." Moreover, the frozen landscape of Titan stands in sharp contrast to the warm, interior scenes in the laboratory on Earth where Shannon Wyler works. The contrast marks the antithesis in values between the two cultures, and the cold images of Titan signify the alienation that exists in its people.

In **"Legacy"** and *The Outcasts of Heaven Belt,* the cold symbol takes a subtle and pervasive form. Integrated fully into the world of the stories, its primary manifestations are the near absolute cold of space and the "cold" fire of radiation. The people of Heaven Belt live inside asteroids with no atmospheres to protect them. Cold literally surrounds them as it surrounds the spaceships upon which most of the scenes of both stories are set. Vinge establishes the vastness and coldness of space as a symbol of alienation at the beginning of *The Outcasts of Heaven Belt* when she merges the icy images of Morningside's dark side with those of space and likens the *Ranger*'s flight to a moth drawn to the candleflame of the stars. But the cold symbol is also amplified by radiation, the heatless fire, which is everywhere in the system. Because of the failing technology, dampening screens no longer protect the people from it, either on the surface of the asteroids where many are forced to work or on their ships.

Snow does appear in both stories. In **"Legacy,"** Planet Two, where Chaim, Mythili, and Siamang go to rescue Olefin, features snow and deep cold. Mythili is abandoned there and figuratively dies only to be reborn later from her alienation. The planet also offers hope for the Belters as a habitable world. In *The Outcasts of Heaven Belt,* the "Snows-of-Salvation" is a Ringer plant that processes snow into hydrogen and oxygen. Hydrogen is an important fuel. Snow itself, while symbolizing the alienation of the Belters, also holds out the promise of salvation.

Richard Law (essay date 1983)

SOURCE: "Science Fiction Women: Victims, Rebels, Heroes," in *Patterns of the Fantastic,* edited by Donald M. Hassler, Starmont House, 1983, pp. 11-20.

[*In the following excerpt, Law determines all Vinge's short fiction to be, in individual ways, love stories.*]

Joan D. Vinge is another science fiction writer attuned to Existentialism, but her isolated or beleaguered characters. survive what William Barrett calls the modern "encounter with Nothingness" [*Irrational Man: A Study in Existential Philosophy*]. A representative character is Emmylou Stewart in the homiletic story, **"View from a Height."** Lacking natural immunities essential for life on Earth, Emmylou volunteered for permanent duty as an explorer isolated in an observatory in space. Being "trapped in the arc of blackness . . . meaningless, so insignificant," she falls into depression but recovers and expresses valiant acquiescence:

"We're all on a one-way trip into infinity. If we're lucky we're given some life's work we care about, or some person. Or both, if we're very lucky."

Optimistic fatalism is the prevailing attitude in the work of Vinge. Her strength is the romance, a genre older than the novel—"a fact which has developed," in Northrop Frye's words, "the historical illusion that it is something to be outgrown, a juvenile and undeveloped form." [*Anatomy of Criticism,* 1965] Without denying the existence of evil or the data of suffering, this tender-minded author highlights innocence and beauty, which belong to human experience as surely as do their opposites. She recalls treasured impressions—allusions to fairy tales and childhood memories are frequent—and commends the endearing or admirable traits in men, women, and children. Underlying her sentimental science fiction fables is a steadfast belief in the power of the human spirit to endure pain, promote decency, and preserve love.

> **Nearly every work by Joan Vinge is a love story, sentimental and idealized, but not to be confused with silly television and film servings. Love is not a panacea, not perpetual ecstasy, and not a magic charm in Vinge's fiction. It is emotional interdependence, mutual commitment, caring and sacrifice shared.**
>
> **—Richard Law**

Whether it is a reflective piece, a long exotic fantasy like *The Snow Queen,* or a juvenile space adventure, nearly every work by Joan Vinge is a love story, sentimental and idealized, but not to be confused with silly television and film servings. Most of her characters who love are not glamorous or handsome; some are permanently disabled, some are deformed, some are freaks. They have been losers and might never be much better than survivors; and their love, no matter how poetic, will not dissolve the hard conditions, of existence. Love is not a panacea, not perpetual ecstasy, and not a magic charm in Vinge's fiction. It is emotional interdependence, mutual commitment, caring and sacrifice shared. *The Outcasts of Heaven Belt* (1978) is a light space-adventure entertainment. It also is designed to address its epigraph from *Ecclesiastes*: "Two are better than one, because they have a good reward for their labours. For if they fall, the one will lift up his fellow: but woe to him that is alone when he falleth; for he hath not another to help him up." The ideal of unity in adversity is sensitively exhibited by two fugitives, Shadow Jack, a certified defective, and Bird Alyn, rejected as an ugly, ungainly cripple. Mutual empathy upholds them: "She had comforted him, out of compassion and her own need; his need had bound him to her, and made them friends." They and other couples in Joan Vinge's works illustrate the concept that "the unifying element, the common bond of need that join[s] every human being, could be used as a force against disintegration and decay. . . .

The Outcasts of Heaven Belt is a marriage and family fairy tale. It is true that for sentimental style of expression, the poetic allusions, soothing reflections, the regard for innocence and domesticity, for children and gentle animals, nearly all of Vinge's science fiction has a fairy tale ambience. But the need for faith and hope and the benefits of human interdependence reflected in her works are true-to-life. Joan Vinge speaks to the imagination in a transitional age that psychotherapist Rollo May diagnoses as suffering "bankruptcy of inner values." For lack of love and will, the contemporary world is schizoid. Those attributes are necessary for people who yearn to exercise "the conjunctive emotions and processes." The source of love and will is care, concern, compassion:

> Care is a state composed of the recognition of another, a fellow human being like one's self; of identification of one's self with the pain or joy of the other; of guilt, pity, and the awareness that we all stand on the base of a common humanity. . . . Care is given power by nature's sense of pain. . . . and care must become a conscious psychological fact [Rollo May, in *Love and Will,* 1979].

[Vinge idealizes] the conjugal relationship in which a woman and man, with or without children, are united in care. But care is an attribute that seems so rare historically and today that its efficacy is dubious to [some other writers]. They depict the consequent alienation and aggression in a society that continues to assume that woman's place is subordinate to man's. The tough-minded science fiction writers expose the thoughtless assumptions and philosophical rationalizations supporting the age-old sexist order. The tender-minded imagine models of love in a better order—at least a retreat—wherein harmony between the sexes is cultivated.

Carolyn Wendell (essay date 1984)

SOURCE: "Second Rate Vinge," in *Fantasy Review,* Vol. 7, No. 11, December, 1984, pp. 29-30.

[*Here, Wendell offers a mixed review of* Phoenix in the Ashes.]

Joan Vinge provides some of the better science fiction reading available today. Her interest in human emotion and motivation usually results in recognizable people and some of the most intriguing aliens around [I particularly recall those in her first collection, *Eyes of Amber,* 1979].

The six stories in this volume [*Phoenix in the Ashes*] are good reads, but not quite up to the standards set by that earlier volume. For example, the title story is a gripping and compelling tale of two isolated individuals who meet despite the odds and come to love and need each other. Hoffman, a metals prospector in a post-nuclear

war world, crashes in a backwards village. Amanda, disinherited by her father for not marrying the man selected for her, nurses Hoffman back to health. They are both fascinating characters—but the story's end has Hoffman deciding to stay in the village. Although it is suggested that his world is brutal, it is graphically depicted that her world is harsh and repressive. One wants them both to escape it. Until that point, Hoffman and Amanda live and breathe as real people, but are reduced to cardboard cutouts by the last page.

Mother and Child, the longest and earliest offering [originally published in *Orbit 16* in 1975, one of Vinge's earliest short stories, antedating those in *Eyes of Amber* as well as those in *Phoenix in the Ashes,* most of which date from 1980], is also a mix of strong and weak. A deaf society where hearing is an aberration is original, and her depiction of an alien who is producing offspring is breathtaking. But the heroine is too sweet, too strong to be credible. And people in an all-deaf society would not move their lips in any way that could be "read"—for that [an inefficient process anyway], you need speech, and for speech, you need hearing people.

"Peddler's Apprentice" was written with Vernor Vinge, Joan's first husband [and it lacks her usual attention to emotional chaacter]. "The Storm King" is a variant on the fairy tale motif of wish-granting. "Voices from the Dust" is an adventure-thriller that does not go anywhere. "Psiren," on the other hand, is one of the best stories here, a tale of telepathic aliens in an non-telepathic human colony [it is a sequel to *Psion* and will whet your appetite for the novel].

The volume must be recommended because it is better than most science fiction on the market, but it is a rather strange hodge-podge and not Vinge at her best.

Audrey Eaglen (essay date 1985)

SOURCE: A review of *Phoenix in the Ashes,* in *Voice of Youth Advocates,* Vol. 7, No. 6, February, 1985, p. 340.

[*In the following negative review, Eaglen deems* Phoenix in the Ashes *a disappointing collection.*]

Vinge fans who expect to find any of the qualities that made her *The Snow Queen* a Hugo winner will be sorely disappointed in this collection of six previously unpublished short stories [*Phoenix in the Ashes*]. The first, the title story, is about a plain Jane living in post-nuclear holocaust California and disowned by her feudal, traditionally rigid father in the agricultural society which that part of the world has become. Then a helicopter (which no one in the village has ever seen) crashes in her father's wheat fields. Surely it's a curse! No one will help the pilot, but Amanda does and nurses him back to health. As might be expected he falls in love with her and marries her. When a search party from his home (Brazil) finds him, they ask him to return with them, but he chooses Amanda and the rural life instead. The whole thing is apparently supposed to sound elegiac, but reads like warmed-over Barbara Cartland. Then we have interfering aliens who, in their attempts to help humans left crippled, blind, and deaf by a series of plagues, end up hurting rather than helping.

Four more stories deal with human explorers on Mars, a dragon defeated by human goodness, human/alien half-breeds, and finally a story written with Vinge's husband Vernon that is nothing short of embarrassing for a writer of Vinge's talent. The six tales are not only unfocussed and over-written, but are mawkish and largely written along the lines of the final passage from the title story: "She [Amanda] nodded, resting her head on his shoulder. 'Yes, my husband; I'd like that [taking a trip sometime] very much.' 'Amanda . . .' he said, surprised, wonderingly. 'My wife. My wife.'" Good grief.

Gerald Jones (essay date 1985)

SOURCE: A review of *Phoenix in the Ashes,* in *The New York Times Book Review,* April 28, 1985, pp. 20-1.

[*In the following favorable review, Jones briefly discusses thematic and stylistic characteristics of Vinge's short fiction.*]

Joan D. Vinge writes the kind of science fiction that might appear in a family magazine of tomorrow. Her themes are the common currency of modern science fiction—first contact with alien intelligences, post-nuclear-holocaust survival, the mixed blessings of extrasensory powers, the unpredictable outcome when more advanced beings interfere in the affairs of "lesser" species. In plot outline, some of these stories resemble old-fashioned adventure-oriented science fiction but the pace is invariably slower, the texture of the prose richer. Instead of looking for new twists on old themes, Miss Vinge concentrates on people. She is interested, if you will, in sensibility. Caught in situations not of their own making, her characters feel pain, sorrow, ecstasy.

The title story [of *Phoenix in the Ashes*] not in a post-holocaust community fearful of all technology, exemplifies Miss Vinge's virtues: attractive people, believable conflicts, readable dialogue. It also reveals her shortcomings. She looks too hard for cosmic significance in each situation. Too often, her endings dissolve into uplifting lessons. A hint of what might happen if her characters were freed from the obligation of making points for the author can be found in a story called **"Pairen"** about a blocked telepath. Perhaps because this story is a sequel to the novel *Psion,* the motives of the principal characters are never quite clear; events crucial to our understanding have taken place off-stage. Instead of more action. We get reactions. Instead of cosmic significance, we get the slow healing of a deep wound—which is all the more remarkable because the hurt is felt in a sensory channel, which we do not share with the protagonist. A fine, disturbing story.

Richard Law (essay date 1986)

SOURCE: "'*Eyes of Amber' and Other Stories* and *Phoenix in the Ashes* and 'The Hunt of the Unicorn'," in *Suzy McKee Charnas, Octavia Butler, Joan Vinge,* by Marleen S. Barr, Ruth Salvaggio, and Richard Law, Starmont House, 1986, pp. 11-21, 52-9.

[*In the following excerpt, Law analyzes the principal themes in Vinge's short fiction.*]

Joan D. Vinge's *"Eyes of Amber" and Other Stories* (1979) includes six short works that appeared originally in different science-fiction publications between 1974 and 1977. One of the works, **"Media Man,"** subsequently was incorporated by Vinge into a novella, **"Legacy"** (which will be discussed in the next chapter). *"Eyes of Amber" and Other Stories* exhibits Vinge's versatility. The diverse topics and themes, depth of understanding, fresh invention, engaging style and evocative power, and the uniform high quality of the works attest to her rich creative resources. This collection also signaled the increasing recognition of the talent of one of the most promising young writers in science fiction. A year later, *The Snow Queen* fulfilled the promise.

Vinge is among the science-fiction authors whose brief comments on their own work are luminous. Her knack probably stems from her deliberate craftsmanship, along with her intuitive grasp of correspondences between themes and symbols. Speaking figuratively, Vinge called her 1978 Hugo-winning novelette, *Eyes of Amber,* a Cinderella story. Actually, its design resembles the fairy tale's, and shares with it the motifs of sibling rivalry, benevolent mother, rescue device, and ultimate exaltation of the ill-treated heroine.

In the exotic novelette, the central character is the chiropteran Lady T'uupieh, who lives on Saturn's main moon, Titan, site of chilling treachery. She had been dispossessed by a wicked nobleman, Klovhiri. However, her sister, Ahtseet, discarded family honor to marry him and stay rich. In the end, T'uupieh's estate and noble station are recovered. Instrumental in securing the prosperous ending is Shannon, musician and crack linguist on the Titan project at Coos Bay, Oregon. (He corresponds to the prince in "Cinderella.") The pivotal device for undoing the enemies of T'uupieh, the probe through which she and Shannon communicate, is like the symbolic slipper that fits only Cinderella's petite foot. (With an IBM synthesizer, Shannon translates and reproduces the musical chords of T'uupieh's speech.)

In "Cinderella," a white bird is the emblem of the girl's dead mother—in Perrault's rendition, a fairy godmother appears—that gives Cinderella a dress and the precious slippers to wear to the ball. By means of displacement, Shannon's mother corresponds to the maternal spirit (or fairy godmother) in "Cinderella." (Displacement is adopting symbolic elements from a literary or artistic source and altering them to function appositely in a new context or genre.) Shannon's mother, Dr. Wyler, a communication engineer on the Titan project, uplifts her son after he fails to dissuade T'uupieh from seeking blood-revenge (as per Titan's code) on her sister and Klovhiri. Dr. Wyler explains that T'uupieh disbelieves the power of self-conscious effort to influence destiny but that the alien woman had conceded to her demon, i.e., the probe, the right to intervene. Following Dr. Wyler's plan, the probe is located where it detects an ambush and, with its electrical defense system, kills T'uupieh's assailant. Forthwith, T'uupieh recovers her lands, pardons her sister, and awaits further communication with Shannon via her amber-eyed demon.

Among the novelette's several themes, the concept of change is prominent. On the personal and moral level, for instance, T'uupieh changes from victim to victor and from avenger to forgiver. The seemingly futile efforts of Shannon are brought to success by his mother's strategy. Shannon and Dr. Wyler's professional association, one characterized by mutual respect and restraint, becomes a truly sympathetic mother-son relationship. Essential for the changes is communication (for which the probe/demon is an apt symbol). However, the communication is efficacious precisely because, in every case, warm personal signals are transmitted, e.g., signs of encouragement, care, and assistance.

Change is important as a metaphysical theme, too. T'uupieh espouses determinism: "We can change nothing, our lives are preordained." The issue of free will vs. destiny or necessity is underscored by repeated mention of the Wheel of Change, a dominant motif on Titan. At a crucial moment, T'uupieh perceives "the gibbous disc of greenish gold, cut across by a line of silver and a band of shadow-black. It seems then to foretell death, the final state after the last turn of the wheel. Without doubt, the Wheel of Change signifies inconstant and implacable fortune. An exemplar of the Fortune archetype is *Carmina Burana,* with medieval lyrics echoing ancient Roman sentiments and given modern orchestration by Carl Orff: "O Fortune, variable as the moon, always dost thou wax and wane. . . . Monstrous and empty fate, thou, turning wheel, art mean." T'uupieh's view of inescapable fate reflects the traits of instability, fickleness, contrary, and perverseness imputed to Fate in the age-old vision. On Titan, conspiracies, betrayals, and treachery are ample reminders of that vision. T'uupieh herself travels disguised as an old beggar. She has served Titan's Overlord as his hired bandit and assassin, and she is nearly ambushed while laying a trap for her enemies. The atmosphere on Titan befits the faithless society: chill air, misty landscapes, and swampy terrain where "treacherous sinks and pools opened like blossoms to swallow the unwary. The sinister power of fate seems invincible on Titan. However, ultimately, the Wheel of Change, symbol of inconstancy, is opposed by human effort expressive of fortitude. By refusing to acquiesce, Shannon and his mother manage to rescue T'uupieh and reform her cynical view. The major philosophical alteration is T'uupieh's: she who had maintained that "The Wheel of Change carries us all" acquires the gentler understanding that it does not carry everyone "with equal ease." In *Eyes of Amber,* meliorism and mediation supersede fatalism and alienation. In the final picture of Lady

T'uupieh and her demon, "She stroked its day-warmed carapace tenderly, and settled down on the softening ground to wait for its reply."

The original inspiration for **"The Crystal Ship"** was a song of the same title by The Doors, a 1960's rock group. The first part of the novelette is imbued with the ennui, despair, and self-indulgent melancholy that the late Jim Morrison's lyrics evoke: "Before you slip into unconsciousness, I'd like to have another kiss"; "Deliver me from reasons why you'd rather cry, I'd rather fly." On an orbiting starship fifty passengers languish, addicted to chitta syrup, a poisonous narcotic. Tarawassie, a young woman with raven locks and blue-green eyes, is wrenched out of a drug dream by a companion's suicide. After Andar wails some formulaic lines, he plunges into the mysterious blue-green Star Well, "the thing at the heart of all beauty." The Star Well's mortuary power perturbs Tarawassie; later, her infirm mother repeats Andar's words and slips through Tarawassie's arms into the Star Well. "There is a heaven, and it is death"—the formula becomes an obsession for the forlorn and remorseful daughter. Sick of the narcotic wreckage on the "crystal coffin" and aching to die but afraid to, she descends alone to the city in search of answers that only experience can give. Tarawassie's thanatopsis is prologue to her rite of passage.

The departure of Tarawassie to the world below to begin her quest is tantamount to the first of the three parts of Joseph Campbell's monomythic rite of passage: separation—initiation—return. In this archetypal pattern, the hero, as Campbell explains, undertakes a journey that symbolizes everyone's experience of going through a crisis or a crucial period (e.g., puberty, illness, bereavement) that changes one's status, role, and self-image. Passing the threshold of adventure, the hero

> journeys through a world of unfamiliar yet strangely intimate forces, some of which severely threaten him (tests), some of which give magical aid (helpers). When he arrives at the nadir of the mythological round, he undergoes a supreme ordeal and gains his reward.

The helper for Tarawassie braving initiation is a gentle alien, Moon Shadow, one of the natives (the Real People) of this world discovered by humans (the Star People) five centuries earlier. His name denotes that he was born during a lunar eclipse; the tribe declares him "strange. . . . last of Starman kith . . . born with evil spirit." Although Moon Shadow has the kangaroo form of the natives, he is ostracized by them for being the last living halfbreed and for advocating sexual integration between the Real People and the Star People for the mutual benefit of both species.

The companionship of Tarawassie and Moon Shadow is beautifully affecting because each answers the other's appeal with care and respect. He is her comforter and guide; she is his needed and dear friend. The relationship between sympathetic aliens is more engaging by virtue of the Amerindian ambience that Vinge creates. Images and phraseology evoke Indian legend: names such as Hunter's Luck and Beautiful Sky; Moon Shadow, his moccasins, loincloth, and string of beads; the shaman, Swift Springer; ritual "spirit fire"; and ceremonies to help the ancestral spirit find rest. The dramatic narrative is enchanted by this veil of Indian lore. It makes key moments fetching, such as one when Moon Shadow tries to diagnose Tarawassie's despondency: ' "Bad . . . here?' The tip of his tail swept down his crouching form. 'Or bad . . . here?' The tail tapped his head; he drooped into a perfect image of despair." Intimations of the occult enhance suspense when several tribesmen led by the shaman form a personal chain for testing the outcast: "Swift Springer reached out, as though he approached something unclean, to make contact with Moon Shadow. A muttering passed through the crowd. Moon Shadow closed his eyes, his face enraptured. The crowd fell silent."

Moon Shadow sustains Tarawassie; he also is her mentor, guiding her through alarming racial history. He engages her in "showing"; i.e., by means of transgenerational ESP, she reenacts in her mind the ancestral experiences that Moon Shadow vividly recalls. She learns that centuries ago her ancestors from the overcrowded Homeworld had journeyed through space, landed here, and conquered and oppressed the natives. But the invaders' addiction to chitta infected them with "a malignant death ecstasy." In Vinge's science fiction-Amerindian fable, these phrases are electric with nemesis: "How many countless times throughout human history had 'primitive' groups like the Real People been decimated and demoralized by the vices of a superior technology? And this time, this *once,* it had gone the other way."

The psychic dramatizations give Tarawassie answers to her original questions about death and immortality. Paramountly, she learns that she could atone for her past failure to exercise love for her mother and perhaps could be reunited with her by valiantly entering the Star Well. It dissolves the body and transmits the spirit into a new body at a remote destination. Ambivalent with yearning and fear, Tarawassie is inspired by Moon Shadow to risk annihilation for the "mystical experience of a rite of passage." He too would benefit from it, for she might induce other humans on Homeworld to begin a new colony here, thus enabling him to restore ties with his interspecies ancestors.

Contemplating the formula of death and heaven, "Silently, without motion, she entered the ocean." At last trusting in reincarnation, Tarawassie completes the rite of separation—initiation—return (and reward). Yet **"The Crystal Ship"** ends only half in triumph. After many years of solitary wait, Moon Shadow dies unattended. The poignant epilogue concludes with a prayer: "So is shown the legend of Tarawassie and Moon Shadow. May their souls show our peoples the way to true understanding." Vinge's artful legend ends paradoxically. It extols the ideal of integration, yet elicits regret that the envoys of that ideal are denied reunion based in spiritual belief.

Echoes of Indian legend, tribal rituals, the shaman, spirit and soul, psychic and mystical states, and the Star Well as a "gateway" to afterlife—these terms and tropes signal the mythic dimension of Vinge's novelette. The racial memories that Moon Shadow shares with Tarawassie bring to mind the archetypal concepts of Carl G. Jung. Jung incorporates the psychological and mystical elements in myth. Originating and residing in the "collective unconscious" shared by all humanity, myth constitutes the archaic structure of psychic life, the matrix of deepest felt-beliefs, the well of enduring wisdom. On the affirmative side, **"The Crystal Ship"** is a myth of eternal life (the reincarnation and reunion of Tarawassie and her mother). However, the theme of tribal incompatibility is more powerfully lamentable because it is reinforced by means of opposition between affectionate understanding on the personal conscious level and species (or racial) estrangement on the deepest level of belief. Moon Shadow and Tarawassie desire personal and spiritual union. However, her belief-system posits a communion of saints whose souls have transmigrated:

> But she remembered that this body was no more than a vessel for the pattern, the code, the essence that would be transmitted, poured forth into the universe—a vessel that would be re-created in perfection, surely . . . She saw her mother waiting for her, well and strong.

And alas, Moon Shadow belongs to a tribe dedicated to ancestor worship, the belief that the spirits of the dead remain kin and will reward acts of homage by visiting the living who remember them:

> He was the last, the last Starman, and his people had destroyed his ancestors. . . . Only she could save his ancestors or make him real again. If she never brought her people back, never returned to him, he would die too, . . . forever. She was his kith-friend, his only friend, and she had promised. . . .

Tarawassie had resolved to be faithful. And she entered the Star Well bearing a part of him in "the essence of her being." Moon Shadow waited for her, "for thirty years, scorned and shunned among the Real People of the ruined city. But in that time she never came." And after Moon Shadow died, no one was there to "give his spirit rest, for he was the last Starman." It is regrettable that personal expressions of love and faith are thwarted by irreconcilable tribal (or racial) beliefs. In their caring relationship, Tarawassie and Moon Shadow are exemplary, yet Vinge's coordination of the complex themes in **"The Crystal Ship"** produces an ultimate effect that is wistful.

In its 7,500-17,500 words, the novelette develops character and action more than the short story does, but without rejecting the compact structure that characterizes the short story. However, **"Tin Soldier,"** Vinge's first science-fiction publication (1974), is a novelette that resists compactness and seems to telescope certain properties of the *Bildungsroman.* This kind of novel covers the central character's journey from innocence to understanding as he or she advances from childhood or adolescence to young adulthood. Along the way, there are crises through which the mind and character of the protagonist are developed. The *Bildungsroman* reveals that maturation implies disillusionment; it is acquired through experiences that dissolve misconceptions or unrealistic expectations of life.

In **"Tin Soldier,"** Brandy travels as far away from home as any other innocent in transition. She is a technician on a starship that navigates "the Quadrangle run," three years cruising AAFAL (almost as fast as light) to ports adjacent to the Pleiades. The restlessness of adolescence had induced Brandy to leave Calicho, her home planet. However, after her first long trip *ad astra,* the homesick eighteen-year old bewails being so far from her loving parents, probably forever. She asks Maris, who owns the Tin Soldier tavern in the port of New Piraeus, to be her steadfast friend. He gives her a paternal pledge that his home will always be hers, too, when her ship harbors in New Piraeus.

In four successive episodes, Brandy and Maris rendezvous after every twenty-five year space flight. It is by dint of AAFAL-travel that Brandy becomes only three years older each time. As for Maris, the extensive prosthetics that saved his body, which had been savagely mutilated by a bomb explosion long ago, cause him to age only a year or so between meetings. The uniqueness of the principals and their ambiguous relationship—as youth and surrogate parent as well as two persons falling in love—calls for considerably more analytical development than the novelette affords. Structurally, there is trouble with this exercise in "double time," as characters belonging to different generations close the chronological gap through their series of meetings. However, **"Tin Soldier"** succeeds as a sequence of sentimental vignettes whose essential action is the process of thought and feeling that unites a young woman disillusioned after renouncing conventional society, and a man of perseverance who is looked upon as a perpetual freak. These sympathetic aliens merit the benefits of the enduring love that they cultivate together.

Like sailors celebrated in song—one such song is "Brandy"—the spacer women are devoted to their transient vocations. They are an exclusive corps, envied and also scorned because they *appear* to resist aging. In addition and in Lothario fashion, they have random flings, shunning commitments and avoiding emotional ties. In contrast to this code, is the mutual interdependence that Brandy and Maris reinforce during their brief sojourns together. Hence, after Brandy is totally disabled in a fiery crash, she is granted extraordinary recompense. Prosthetic modifications convert her into a cyborg, and she relies on Maris to teach her the wisdom acquired through decades of forbearance. The promise of unique longevity distinguishes them from the analogous figures in Hans Christian Andersen's tale. At the end of "The Steadfast Tin Soldier," the toy ballerina and one-legged soldier are accidentally blown into an open stove and destroyed in its fire. Respectively, Maris and Brandy are survivors of war and fire. The peace and love that they come to embody are opposite to the values signified by the proper name each had been given: "Maris" commemorates the ancient Roman god of war; "Brandy" is for *Branduin,* which is derived from the Dutch, *brandewijn,* meaning "burnt wine."

There is no need to apply Freudian or Jungian postulates to this tale for theoretical validation. Like Andersen's fairy tales, Vinge's **"Tin Soldier"** is so make-believe and unabashedly sentimental that it recalls human dreams and ideals and for the moment precludes realistic objections. Also, the ingenuous vision is enhanced by poetic allusion. Vinge is versatile in the art of expert reappropriation. Recognizable echoes and allusions introduce resources from traditional literature and legend that amplify the meanings and associated feelings in her fiction. The allusive manner gives **"Tin Soldier"** a range of implications far beyond the obvious limits of the narrative.

Maris (Mars), New Piraeus, the Pleiades—these and other proper names suggest the classical world. So also does the name that Maris affectionately gives to Brandy: "Diana, like the silver Lady of the Moon." He is Endymion to the silver-haired namesake of the goddess. **"Tin Soldier"** gives a happy turn to the myth, for at the end Brandy has descended from the sky to stay with her sublunary lover permanently. Symbolically, the happy ending also hints at eternity, surely for love, if not for its disciples as well. In a previous conversation, Brandy and Maris take pleasure in a line from Wordsworth's great "Ode on Intimations of Immortality": "Though inland far we be, our souls have sight of that immortal sea which brought us hither." The spiritual dimension of the novelette is confirmed by the lines that come to Maris' mind while he is reading Brandy's poetry manuscript: "Attired with stars we shall forever sit, triumphing over Death, and Chance, and thee, O Time." These lines are from John Milton's poem, "On Time," and convey the poet's belief that after earthly death there is personal immortality in God's presence. Vinge's piece is not a Christian allegory or a pagan myth. Collectively, however, the religious and the classical allusions invite an interpretation imbued with absolute idealism. That is, as cyborgs Brandy and Maris will endure; their contact with the underlying spirit of the universe will last for centuries. Their phenomenal duration metaphorically implies that the ultimate reality is spirit or mind. **"Tin Soldier"** projects a vision resembling that which, in the immortality ode, Wordsworth calls "the faith that looks through death."

Again, allusion expands the imagination in **"To Bell the Cat."** The title denotes the medieval fable—recalled in *Piers Plowman,* B (1377)—of the rats who planned to protect themselves from the cat by hanging a bell around its neck. In Vinge's story, ratlike troglodytes, a highly intelligent and cooperative species on an unfamiliar planet, are threatened with extinction by a human research expedition. The particular cat-figure is Piper Alvarian Jary. As punishment for his part in a certain tyrant's crimes against humanity, Jary now is Dr. Hoban Orr's slave, subjected to inhuman experiments and forced to descend into a hellish radioactive gorge to collect the trogs for Orr's cruel and fatal laboratory analyses. Jary is Orr's "catspaw," hence, the link to another old fable, that of the monkey (or fox) using the paw of a cat to rake roasted chestnuts out of burning coals. Both fables infuse additional danger, cruelty, and pain into this horror story about how merciless some rational and technological men can be to aliens and to their own species.

The vivid spectacle of atrocity also is a shrewdly shaped psychological study. Continually monitored is an argument among the expedition wardens over Dr. Orr's revolting experiments, particularly the torture of Jary, ostensibly for research purposes. Xena (trans. "alien"), the sympathetic one, cannot persuade her callous husband to denounce Orr's activities. But Juah-u Corouda, brought over to decency, encourages Jary to seek release from his grotesque life sentence. The story does not lead to a predictable outcome, however, for in the universe of life forms another value means more to Jary than human acquittal.

Although reduced to subnormal behavior and through surgery deprived of neural sensations, except in his hands, Jary is supersensitive and scrupulous. He sees himself in human society bearing "the mark of Cain," never able to atone for his past sins. However, in the alien domain, he can prove himself worthy of the trogs' trust by warning them to withdraw whenever he approaches their chamber in "the tormented underworld." Instead of a bell, the radiant mud on his protective suit is his signal to the trogs. Thus, Jary becomes "the shining one", the trogs' protector, a new model of the fallen Lucifer—not reigning in Hell, but earning deliverance in radioactive depths.

"Le silence éternel de ces espaces infinis m'effraie"—Pascal. Joan Vinge ponders the silent infinite spaces in **"View from a Height,"** one of her few short stories. It is a science-fiction parable on the tragic paradox that human beings are endowed with intelligence and free will, yet know that their choices are made within a system that rules and limits their lives. The story covers nine days of solitary meditation by Emmylou Stewart, an astrophysicist who for twenty years has been on an interstellar probe designed to remain in space permanently. She had volunteered to be isolated in the space observatory because she lacked the natural immunities needed for living on Earth and she wanted to make worthwhile use of her insulated life. On the second day recorded in her journal, Emmylou learns, through a video message from mission control, of a recent breakthrough in immunology research. It would enable her to lead a normal life—if only it were not impossible for her to return to Earth.

Emmylou is overcome by depression for five days. The refrain, "You can't go home again," underscores the anguish of her humble but unattainable desire. It recalls Thomas Wolfe's famous novel, of course, as well as John Milton's immortal elegy, "Lycidas"; "Look homeward, Angel, now, and melt with ruth" is an eloquent caption for this picture of forsakenness. Emmylou calls herself "only a bird in a gilded cage." Her endless imprisonment is signified also by her parrot (a long-lived bird) whose name is "Ozymandias," after the ancient ruler in Shelley's sonnet who craved immortality. And Emmylou pictures herself eventually expiring in her "computerized tomb," her corpse "lying like Snow White's in inviolate sleep."

In this piece, as in others, Vinge's dramatic and lyrical portrayal of characters is engaging. The thoughts, feelings, and idiom of Emmylou's monologue denote gentle idealism. She is intrepid, but nevertheless vulnerable. Whatever fears and regrets she had repressed for two decades nearly overwhelm her during this crisis. Inherent bad luck notwithstanding, Emmylou feels responsible for her life and combats depression with her sense of duty. She risks death climbing outside the vessel to repair the telescope and then feels the calming effect of being absorbed in the task: "One step at a time," she thinks, "the way we get through life." When Ozymandias announces, "Awk. Food time!" she treats him like a comrade in distress, knowing "that he's worried, and he cares." She regrets that he was "Stolen away from his own kind, raised in a sterile bubble to be a caged bird for a caged human." And Emmylou cannot forget all the joys denied her since childhood because she had to be sealed off from normal experiences: "In all my life I've never smelled the sea wind, or plucked berries from a bush and eaten them, right there! Or felt my parents' kisses against my skin, or a man's body." She laments being separated from her loving parents and from Jeffrey, the young man she meets now in frustrating amorous dreams.

Emmylou goes through depression of life-threatening severity. For awhile she is disabled, scorning her isolation, reproaching herself, taking sleeping pills, pondering ultimate escape: "When we die, do we wake out of reality at last, and all our dreams come true?" Still, she never enters suicide's vestibule, the condition of despair that Robert Jay Lifton defines as "a sense of radical absence of meaning and purpose, and of the impossibility of human connection," which precedes "an attempt to transform own's existence radically." Even across the abyss of one-thousand astronomical units. Emmylou is sustained by the bond of communication and friendship with Harvey Weems, the project director.

In this interstellar parable, Emmylou is conscious of being "trapped in the arc of blackness . . . meaningless, so insignificant." Confined forever, but undefeated, she speaks authentically on the Absurd, which the late Albert Camus called our "intellectual malady." It is the condition of human longing to grasp the purpose of life being answered by "the unreasonable silence of the world." One can surrender to the Absurd and decide that since life is senseless, it is not worth continuing. Or one can trust that the meaning of life will be made manifest sometime. But doomed Emmylou, who rejects despair, suicide, and illusions, is the Absurd hero. She determines to live in a position of revolt in the presence of mortality. That revolt is not aspiration. Instead, as Camus wrote, it is "the certainty of a crushing fate, without the resignation that ought to accompany it."

Emmylou realizes that she is "lost for eternity in an unknown sea" but finds comfort in humility: "When you confront the absolute indfference of magnitudes and vistas so overwhelming, the swollen ego of your self-important suffering is diminished." Her soliloquy reflects Camus' view of unaccommodated human existence and also his conviction that life, however distressing, is invaluable. In Vinge's story, the dialectic over the irrepressible spirit and inexorable mortality is essentially affirmative. Camus' mythical hero is Sisyphus; Emmylou alludes to a mythical hero, too: "Even Atlas tried to get rid of his burden; because no matter how vital his function was, the responsibility was still a burden to him. But he took his burden back again too, . . . for better or worse." Forever exiled from her home on Earth, Emmylou still advocates being grateful if there is some person and some work that "we care about" on our "one-way trip into infinity." **"View from a Height"** observes the austere metaphorical journey by starlight.

. . . . .

In a column on Joan D. Vinge that was written prior to the publication of *The Snow Queen, Psion,* and *World's End,* Anne Hudson Jones declares Vinge "a major talent," whose best works are in the novella form she favors." A new collection of six of Vinge's shorter works that were first published between 1975 and 1981 verifies that Jones's judgment was well-founded. *Phoenix in the Ashes* (1984) reinforces the evidence in *"Eyes of Amber" and Other Stories* (1979) that Vinge is an expert hand at the novella and novelette.

With plain elemental characters, the title piece, **"Phoenix in the Ashes,"** charms like a folktale. Its warm lyricism and artful impressions disclose earned truths of the heart that relieve the somber atmosphere of a primitive southern California village two centuries after nuclear ruin. Vinge intended to call this novelette "Take Me out of Pity," after an old folk song (also called "The Old Maid's Lament"). But on the advice of her editor, she dropped that title. Pity, sympathetic grief for someone in distress, pervades the tale, but all too often the term connotes condescension or maudlinness.

Amanda is the disowned and disinherited daughter, less prudent than her married sisters, one sympathetic, one unkind. Amanda had defied her matchmaking father; so, for eight years she has lived in a poor cottage, barely supporting herself weaving cloth and bartering it. The folktale ambience is confirmed by her faithful old ragged dog. A key to Amanda's character (and prefigurement of her coming partnership) is that she had taken "Dog" in through remorse after throwing a stone that broke the stray mongrel's leg when he was stealing eggs.

Compassionate Amanda preserves the phoenix figure, Cristoval Hoffmann, after his escape from the burning wreckage of his copter from Brazil, which crashed after "the umbilical of vibrating roar that gave him life within his glass-and-metal womb was cut." Hoffmann, under Amanda's care, comes through his nearly fatal ordeal. This tableau is central in the tale (and in Vinge's idealistic vision):

> She put her arms around him and let him find the comfort of her own warmth. He sighed and quieted, touching her in his delirium as a child seeks its mother, as a husband seeks his wife. Amanda heard the steeple bells sound midnight in the town below, remembered them on too many nights, when she lay alone with sleepless sorrow.

Amanda had repudiated the hard patriarchal survival-mentality that converted every available thing, including marriageable women, into negotiable property. In the narrow-minded village, even the model couple respected the sovereignty of husband and father. Although she and Hoffmann developed a different ideal of mutual cooperation, once they were wed Amanda immediately became subservient until he admonished her to resume her independence, "a source of pride and integrity, a defense against the indignities of life."

Management of time in **"Phoenix in the Ashes"** is Vinge's technical coup. The crucial process of thought and feeling uniting Amanda and Hoffmann unfolds through close-up scenes that occupy but a few days and nights. Yet their complete understanding and union in love evolve over nearly a year's time. And through flashbacks, reveries, and dreams, significant events that shaped their past lives come into focus.

Finally, gentleness, justness, freedom, and reason prevail in the personal love story. But the romantic exaltation of the tale does not obscure the fact that the native culture is crude and superstitious, and the advanced society in Brazil, which Hoffmann renounces, is aggressive. The rival South American nations that had recovered after the nuclear war two centuries earlier covet wealth and power in ways that bode familiar consequences.

> **Joan Vinge ponders the tragic paradox that human beings are endowed with intelligence and free will, yet know that their choices are made within a system that rules and limits their lives.**
>
> —*Richard Law*

For the realistic setting on Mars in her short story, **"Voices from the Dust,"** Vinge drew on information from the Mariner mission. The action reflects her interest in psychic phenomena, an intriguing concept that is also prominent in Arthur C. Clarke's and Andre Norton's work. In the Mariner Valley in the year 2001, geologist Petra Greenfeld discovers a metal artifact that exerts on her mind a strong influence which she attributes to an alien intelligence. The leader of the expedition, an Iranian named Shiraz Mitradati, wants to return Petra to Earth for rest; he makes her idea "sound like something out of a Grade Z science fiction movie." But later he admits that the strange force affects him, too.

At the moment when Petra is pondering the thought that this experience was fated for her, Shiraz utters, "Kismet." The coincidence marks the turning point in their relationship. Sensing that the artifact has sinister and ruthless power, they blow it up, but the explosion rips Shiraz's spacesuit. Petra seals the rip and saves him from suffocation. The dust cloud raised by the explosion signals their location to a rescue party. Afterwards, while Shiraz is recuperating in the hospital, Petra laughingly invites him up to her place to see a tape of *2001*. By happy coincidence, this fatalistic story appeared in a 1980 collection entitled *Destinies*.

Vinge tells **"The Storm King"** in the impersonal way of a legend, in which the unnatural warrants matter-of-fact notice: "They said that in those days the lands were cursed that lay in the shadow of the Storm King." In the tropological prelude, the personification of the dormant volcano includes images of past potency: "The peak thrust up"; "a brooding finger probing the secrets of heaven"; "the mountain lay quiet" after "the Earth had spent Her fury." Later, the Storm King shared its fire spirit with its namesake, a powerful dragon dwelling there which scourged the countryside, defying the sky gods that the people had begun to worship instead of the Earth.

This geomythical beginning implies that power is both essential and problematic. The power of Mother Earth is indispensable, but she is a jealous provider. Demonic power (the dragon) is invincible until someone learns or dares to use the means to control it. The main character in Vinge's highly figurative construct is Lassan-din, who was wounded in the spine by his uncle, the usurper of his royal power. He learns from a witch how to use Mother Earth's hydropower to control the fiery dragon. From the dragon, he gets a skin of scales to protect him in the battle to recover his domain. But his subjects come to hate him, the new Storm King, a tyrant in dragonskin.

Fallatha, "the Earth's Own," guided Lassan-din now and again, and salved his wounded body and spirit. From her, he learns that his brave, aggressive exercise of power must be tempered by gentler traits to win the allegiance of his subjects and to shed his hideous dragonskin. He must help Fallatha, too. Prior to his confronting the dragon, she had seduced him, for she wanted a baby; the "new soul" enabled her to retrieve her own from the witch. Now she persuades Lassan-din to save his soul by using his power to help others through expelling the dragon and by taking Fallatha and her daughter as his own with love, respect, and gratitude. The legend ends, but Vinge's polysemous romantic novelette invites further exegesis.

Joan D. Vinge and her first husband, Vernor, collaborated on the novelette, **"The Peddler's Apprentice."** In it, Lord Buckry I of Fyffe, the astute, middle-aged lord of the Flatlands, learns that the sea kingdoms have suspended their usual hostilities to wage war against Buckry for his rich farmlands. This is the frame for the central action, Buckry's long flashback recalling a phenomenal adventure when he was seventeen-year-old Wim, leading a clan in the Highlands. The first third of the narrative (drafted by Vernor) is a droll tale of frontier feuds between yokels. Joan Vinge picks up the account where Wim, after being ambushed, is rescued by a mysterious peddler who learned some tricks from true magicians at the wondrous place called Sharn. The peddler is Jagit Katchetooriantz, called "Jagged" by his new apprentice, Wim. They go to Fyffe

(on Jagit's pretext that he will find a market for his wares there). In the ensuing "debate of warlocks" between Jagit and a world governor, Charl Aydricks, it is revealed that for ten-thousand years the World Government has stilled the cyclical rise and decline of human civilizations. The government's exclusive technological system has kept the world unchanged and stable. Jagit objects: "Stasis is a coma—no lows, but no highs either, no *choice*." After some associate governors, communicating via satellite, warn Aydricks that Jagit can upset their system, he makes to kill the peddler. But Wim dispatches Aydricks "and, unknowingly, helped to destroy an empire."

After a fantastic fight and return to the Highlands, Jagit discloses that he is a human time traveler who employs suspended animation and emerges from his cave every ten- or fifteen-thousand years to check on the condition of Earth and its inhabitants. The flashback ends, and Lord Buckry sighs nostalgically, then—thanks to the subtlety he had learned from Jagit—he plans a strategy for sabotaging the fragile alliance between the sea kingdoms. Causing his perennial enemies to renew their feuding will nullify the latest threat to Buckry. So ends **"The Peddler's Apprentice,"** a diverting apprentice piece by Joan D. Vinge.

In the novella, **"Psiren"** Cat, the hydran-human adolescent telepath, is still emotionally incapacitated a year after events in the novel, *Psion* (1982). Having the non-violent nature of a Hydran, he is still guilt-ridden over killing Rubiy, although he acted in self-defense. He has been solitary since then, staying dismal in a room above Jule and Ardan's Center for Psionic Research in Oldcity. The action begins when Jule coaxes Cat to go out for an evening and they find themselves in a sinister night club, the Haven.

The "psiren" to whom Cat is strongly attracted is an alien called the Dreamweaver, who can spellbind audiences telepathically. She is Ineh, a Hydran whose psionic powers and desperate need together revive Cat's desire to actualize his telepathic potential. But she is addicted to trihannobin, known as "nightmare" (a lethal nerve poison), which makes her prey to underworld figures who mindrape her at their vile soirees. The appalling abuse is not unfamiliar to Cat, who had once been a "boytoy" and a slave in the mines on Cinder (in *Psion*).

As in the novel, Vinge focuses realistically on criminal exploitation of aliens and societal neglect of them. She continues the depiction of the miserable existence of abused, demoralized inhabitants—many addicted to drugs and hardened by crime—in the slums of Oldcity. She adds further reflections on the damage that prejudice, oppression, perversion, sickness, and guilt do to the mind and spirit. Amid all the poverty, malaise, abuse, and vice, there are few agencies of hope, such as the Center with its small staff of caring people. Along with human services, Vinge also endorses a salutary theme from *Psion*: trust between individuals, the essential bond of mutual reliance based on personal expressions of integrity.

After Ineh and Cat are rescued from the criminals, the dramatic narrative reaches a climax of rhetorical intensity: Ineh and Cat's psycho-coalescence through her agonizing withdrawal from "nightmare." Earlier, Cat had thought that Jule and he "learned to trust each other more than any two human beings had the right to." Now the bond of trust between tormented addict and imperiled comrade is radically tested—and proves sufficient. Cat saves Ineh's sanity. And he admits that when the stress became too severe for his mind, Ineh's dragged him "out of [his] own death wish." Vinge again exalts the ideal of shared sacrifice by partners in need.

Mother and Child is a future-world narrative set in another planetary system. Conditions there are primitive because a plague decimated the civilization, leaving the surviving population nearly sterile and with disabled sensory modes. (In a perceptive discussion of *Mother and Child, The Snow Queen,* **"Phoenix in the Ashes,"** and other works, Carl Yoke relates Vinge's symbolic imagery of sickness/health and sterility/fertility to death and revival motifs in the myths of many cultures.) The three narrators of Vinge's novella were edified by Etta, the chosen priestess of Mother Earth who, having unimpaired sense functions, seems gifted with magical perceptions. The first part is a bucolic love story. Two young herders of the Kotaane tribe, Hywel (the narrator, an orphan) and Etaa, fell in love and later were married (her being "blessed" notwithstanding). A highly significant event during their wooing time was the landslide that fell on Hywel. After Etaa dug him out, he acknowledged that the Mother had chastized him for lacking faith. But after eight years, the idyllic romance ended when Etaa and Hywel were pursued by enemy tribesmen, the Neaane, who worship sky gods. To escape capture, the couple chose to leap off a cliff. Hywel leaped, but Etaa, pregnant, held back momentarily and was caught. Lying broken on the rocks, Hywel implored the chthonic goddess to heal him so he could avenge the Neaane misdeeds.

The action in Part 2, which covers the next year, is recalled by Meron, the Neaane warrior-king, on the eve of a battle with the Kotaane. King Meron, whose loveless fifteen-year marriage was barren, had had Etaa captured for him, primarily to sire a prince, but he fell in love with her. His cousin, Archbishop Shappistre, aimed to unseat Meron and mount a theocracy. (The church's gods are offworld aliens, a silicon-based life form; these "starfolk" manifest themselves as comely men and keep the populace comfortable and ignorant and thus content where they are.) An attempt on Meron's life was foiled when Etaa blocked Shappistre's hired assailant (her act of valor prompting parturition). Meron assumed he was the baby's father and named it Alfilere. Soon afterwards, mother and child vanished. It was thought that they fled back to Hywel, who after mending had become Kotaane leader.

The third part is told by Tam, one of the worshipped starfolk. Disguised as the king's coachman, Tam had transported Etaa and Alfilere to the outside moon, Laa Merth. In a desolate town there (abandoned since a futile colonization attempt by the humans), they stayed until the tribal war on Earth was over. An asexual being, Tam, inspired by love for the devoted young mother, gave birth to S'elec'eca (that

Etaa called "Silver"). After the war in which Meron was killed, Tam persuaded Etaa to give him Alfilere to be reared by the "gods" to become king in order to unite the tribes and blend their religions. The brave sorrowful mother found comfort in her reunion with Hywel.

Mother and Child is captivating. With many poignant effects, Vinge develops Etaa from girl to woman, from ritual priestess to noble mediator. It is an evocative piece teeming with absorbing details released directly from the author's unconscious mind. Vinge adumbrates many themes here, which she unfolds dramatically in *The Snow Queen*. These include cooperation in the ecosystem, unification of cultures, mutual respect between women and men, and the value of communication (as shown through different modes of expression: sign language, lip-reading, conventional speech, kinesics, and intuition). The most embracing theme is given in the title.

The outstanding instance of a human being's essentiality, Erich Neumann explains, is that of "the Great Mother," on whom the infant and child depend for shelter, nourishment, and security. In conjunction with this archetype, which *Mother and Child* celebrates, there is also Neumann's observation that "the matriarchal spirit," unlike "the Apollonian-solar-patriarchal spirit," does not claim absolute and eternal existence but acknowleges "its bond with the Earth Mother." Etaa, the perfect giver, "who represented everything a Human could be . . . or should be," is a science-fiction reminder of imperishable feminine images in the psychohistory of the world.

Besides the sheer talents of imagination, judgment, and verbal facility that accomplish "recreation of thought into feeling"—T. S. Eliot's apt phrase—others, including stylistic versatility and diversity of themes and tropes, belong to the distinguished writer. Vinge succeeds—and in many diverse genres and modes: novel, novella, novelette, short story, romance, folktale, legend, naturalistic discourse. Collectively, her works dissolve the lines between realistic literature, science fiction, and fantasy; between hard science, behavioral science, and lyrical vision. The blends are pleasingly manifest in *Phoenix in the Ashes* (just as they are in *"Eyes of Amber" and Other Stories* and in the grand romance, *The Snow Queen*).

Vinge's incorporation of the rational and intuitive, the fantastic and psychological-realistic appears in a model of another kind, too. **"The Hunt of the Unicorn,"** in *Basilisk* (1980), is Vinge's full venture into categorical fantasy and prompted the editor, Ellen Kushner, to remark, understandably, that Vinge "has finally given in to what I always suspected were sorcerous sympathies." Obviously, Vinge is comfortable molding mythical concepts.

The novelette has a distinct basic plot (in keeping with the kind of fable or legend it imitates). Caedwyn, a unicorn wounded by hunters, changes shape into a man and is given protection by Jehane, a young woman invested as Rider of the Order of the Unicorn. Later, all of her troops are killed in a treacherous attack. But she is rescued by Caedwyn who shapeshifts into a unicorn again and risks his life for her. Before he can shift back, she spellbinds him, making him her new steed in place of Suntear, her beloved unicorn that was killed in the ambush. Jehane rides Caedwyn to Dorne, High City of the Order, to seek retribution on the perpetrators of the massacre.

The allegorical aspects of **"The Hunt of the Unicorn"** make it richly provocative. On a political level, the work addresses the problem of reconciling Freedom and Order (forces constantly in tension and delicately balanced in most societies, especially in democracies). Repeatedly, figures who lack self-control or who break rules (even bad ones) suffer dire consequences, e.g., Caedwyn and his sister, Arwyn, were born with "an affinity for magic, a sensitivity to the earth and air"—aspects of liberty which their stepfather admired. Yet he restricted them completely. Seeking freedom, they were corrupted by Braide, a twisted sorcerer who, before being slain by the stepfather, cursed them into being unicorn and raven. Adding insult to injury, Braide declared, "There is no answer in the Order, no order in the world." This is an enigma that teases Caedwyn as he and Arwyn search for another sorcerer to restore their freedom. In the meantime, Caedwyn's inherent shape-shifting power continually resists Braide's curse. Caedwyn is sometimes unicorn, sometimes man until finally Jehane winds the golden chain of her Order around his neck and arrests him as a unicorn.

On a behavioral level, **"The Hunt of the Unicorn"** concerns Truth and Illusion. For example, the villain, Guillarme, who failed to qualify as a Rider in the Order because he was undisciplined—allegorical patterns usually are intertwined—was able to betray Jehane because she had loved him and still remembered the man of her dream. Jehane's mother (a model of Order and Wisdom) clearly warned Jehane to be careful dealing with the former sweetheart. (Mother had also reminded Jehane of the temptations of Dharsun. In the belief-system, Dharsun, the Creator, personified unharnessed power, "more strength than wisdom" and the mother deity, Talath, grew in power because she was uncorrupted by it, and "she was the symbol of the Order's ultimate triumph over wild magic.") Nevertheless, as Jehane rode to her meeting with Guillarme, "Birds called and twittered, sounds of love and nesting that stirred a vague spring envy deep inside her."

Needless to say, this is an allegory of Love and Betrayal, too. Arwyn and Caedwyn, loving sister and brother, are victims from beginning to end. Guillarme betrayed Jehane. She loved her unicorn, Suntear; yet Caedwyn saw the beast as "poor prisoner." After he admonished Jehane, "Willing captivity is still captivity," she "uncharitably" wished harm on him. The most crucial Love problem is that of Jehane and Caedwyn. The fantasy closes on this melancholy *tableau vivant*: "Emotions writhed like snakes inside her chest," for Jehane knows she has imprisoned a man. As Rider and mount depart, "A raven flew above their path, croaking mournfully; the stallion reared suddenly as it circled his head, answered its harsh calling, with an almost human cry." Perhaps more than any other piece by Vinge, **"The Hunt of the Unicorn"** cries out for a sequel. It would be meet for the sake of allegorical and artistic completeness. Psychologically, too, a sequel could resolve the Love and Betrayal opposition and still its subliminal longing.

Gregory M. Shreve (essay date 1987)

SOURCE: "A Lesson in Xenolinguistics: Congruence, Empathy, and Computers in Joan Vinge's *Eyes of Amber*," in *The Fantastic in World Literature and the Arts,* edited by Donald E. Morse, Greenwood Press, 1987, pp. 21-9.

[*In the following essay, Shreve examines the themes of language and understanding in* Eyes of Amber.]

The great difficulty with using language to communicate is, simply, that one does not always know whether one has communicated effectively. Between the word as it is meant and the word as it is understood lies a universe of difference. The "semantic gap" between speaker and hearer is a very real aspect of human communication; even as speakers of the same language, we are accustomed to a constant and familiar drizzle of misunderstandings and miscommunications. Problems of meaning and understanding are only compounded when the communicative act is complicated by crosscultural aspects and bilingualism. Speakers of the same language may, at least, attempt to elucidate their "messages" by interpreting the many cues of context and paralanguage that accompany the spoken word. A shared cultural experience places the transmitted message in a familiar matrix of assumptions and presuppositions, from which the most likely meanings of a given act of communication may be deduced. Even when the Kung bushman delivers a clicking message to the Aleutian Eskimo, a shared context of universal human experience informs and illuminates the act of speech.

Imagine, then, the profound difficulties that might confront two intelligent beings, not of the same culture, not of the same species, not even of the same line of evolution on the same planet, as they attempt to communicate. They would attempt to send messages not only through the emptiness of space, but into a void of shared experience. The lack of shared experience would place their act of communication in peril.

This fragility and uncertainty of communicating with the alien is a major theme of Joan Vinge's excellent short story, *Eyes of Amber*. On the human side is Shannon Wyler, musician and linguist; on the alien side is Lady T'uupieh of Titan, noblewoman, outlaw, and assassin. Ultimately a message passes between the two, overcoming the seemingly insurmountable obstacles of place and experience. This exchange highlights Vinge's message in the story—that communication is always possible—because at some level all intelligent life is kindred. Some aspect of being alive, some quality of moving, breathing, and thinking creates a matrix of common experience that can serve as the medium from which meanings may be plucked.

In the story a probe of Titan's surface discovers intelligent life; its remote reconnaissance devices establish a communication link; now the only problems are to communicate and to understand. The difficulties are many. Some are mechanical and, hence, perhaps ultimately solvable; others are less yielding. Vinge brings some new insights into the linguistic arena, but their actual applications may be more difficult than she imagines. Ever since scientists in the mid-1950s first thought that communication with another species might be possible (in this case, the bottle-nosed dolphin, *Tursiops truncatus*), several thorny areas have arisen in a discipline that we might, for lack of a better term, call *xenolinguistics,* the linguistics of interspecies communication. Most of the problems of xenolinguistics center on three major areas: recognition, translation, and empathy. Vinge deals with each of these areas in her short story, and a discussion of each provides a simple format for the remainder of this text.

The xenolinguist undoubtedly must deal with a variety of obstacles. Certainly one of the major obstacles will be the problem of recognizing and reproducing the alien voice; that is, of course, if sound turns out to be the means by which the first extraterrestrial contact communicates. In his *Kirlian Quest* trilogy, and in the novel *Viscous Circle,* Piers Anthony speculates on a great variety of communication modes, from tinkling bells to flashing laser lights and odor languages. Clearly the majority of the extraterrestrial community cannot be expected to communicate in an auditory mode, much less an audible one. The problem of recognition is bipolar. First, the hearer (a human being) must be able to recognize that communication is taking place—without any foreknowledge of the mode of communication, recognition could be very difficult. Second, even if the hearer manages to recognize communication, he or she must be able to reply in such a way that the speaker is able to determine the same thing. In *Eyes of Amber,* the aliens communicate in a fashion that is more congruent with the human mode than might be some other mode that is popular in the universe. Titanide and human both use sound and the nuances of sound to communicate; thus, a quality of congruence reduces the difficulty of the xenocommunicative act. Speaker and hearer, however, use audible languages at different levels of phonetic complexity. As Shannon Wyler comments, "Every phoneme was formed of two or three superposed sounds, and every morpheme was a blend of phonemes, flowing together like water. They spoke in chords, and the result was a choir. . . . " This difference in complexity is, in itself, a problem that might require computer assistance to resolve.

The machine processing of languages can be an important part of xenolinguistics. Although Vinge appears to discount the importance of the computer in the recognition, translation, and interpretation of alien languages, it is still an important tool, without which communication with a completely alien species could be impossible.

Automated language processors will be particularly important in the area of recognition. Human beings will be unable, without the prosthetic help of computers and computer-directed instrumentation, to deal with languages that are distinctly noncongruent, that are very highly phonetically or kinetically complex. The "synthesizer" that Shannon Wyler uses to communicate with T'uupieh could not have been used without the prior involvement of computers. In Wyler's hands the synthesizer "speaks" to T'uupieh in her own musical language, yet it is difficult to conceive of Wyler learning the language in the first place without the intervention of computers. In the initial stages of search and contact certain conditions will prevail: (1) communication will be taking place in modes that will probably be noncongruent; and (2) the patterning of signals in those modes most likely will resist discovery without complex pattern recognition programs. Only computers will be able to scan the wide range of possible communication modes over the requisite (long) periods of time, and only computers will be able to discern the subtle regularities that comprise the patterns of language.

At this point, of course, the computer has merely recognized and identified patterns of sound, light, or scent; the simple recognition of regularity does not determine the existence of a language. Many natural phenomena emit regular patterns of various kinds of energy; some patterns of activity are languages by virtue of their ability to act as a vehicle for meaning. The Titan Probe attaches meaning to T'uupieh's musical chords (sentences) only because it is able to enter into a communicative relationship in which the patterns of action and reaction in the joint act of communication begin to attach meaning to the heretofore meaningless patterns of sound. Unless the alien languages we first learn are isomorphs of human language, based on sound waves, at our levels of phonetic complexity, and embedded in congruent life experience, human beings will encounter great difficulty in constructing a lexicon or dictionary without computer assistance.

Entering into the actual communicative relationship will require that at least one partner adopt the communication mode of the other (as there will be, one assumes, no galactic *lingua franca* for them to use). Thus, after we recognize an alien language, we must reproduce it. Shannon Wyler's synthesizer is, ultimately, not a translating device, but a reproducing device, neither creating nor extracting meaning, only carrying it. Reproducing an alien language is a mechanical problem that, quite possibly, could be handled by human beings via natural or mechanical means, without computer assistance.

However, some caveats exist here. If an alien language is at a sufficiently high level of complexity, a human being will be unable to process all of the information in the message fast enough or completely enough to engage in communication. Does the fact that Shannon Wyler is able to engage in fluent conversation with the Titanides on his synthesizer make a negative statement about the ability of computers to process and reproduce language, or does it imply that Titanese language is in the same league as human language in its level of complexity? The point at which a human being would be unable, without assistance, to process the information in a single, complex, alien utterance, is unknown.

The recognition and reproduction of the patterns of alien language are, as we have said, only two of the problems of xenolinguistics. Translation, the process of mapping the tokens of one language to the types of the other, is another, perhaps more difficult obstacle. The ability to attach meaning to the sound, light, or scent tokens of an alien language requires interaction between communicating partners, but the process of compiling an English-Titanese lexicon could be a monstrous undertaking if done unassisted. During the early stages of capturing the details of an alien language, a computer would be quite indispensable. Shannon Wyler, through the probe's many "demon eyes," prompts his informant, Lady T'uupieh, for her worldview. Through his voice, the IBM synthesizer, he channels messages via a language already captured by computer. Indeed, his entry into the Titan Project is his ability to *use* the language, not necessarily his ability to translate and compile it.

The word *translate* is used here in a fairly technical sense, to refer to the initial cross-mapping of languages when the types of each are linked to the tokens of the other. Machine "translation" is one of the oldest areas of computer application in linguistics. Translation is a problem in pattern recognition and pattern matching. An incoming "word" or language "token" from the source language is matched against a list of known words in that language; each word in the list has pointers to memory locations that contain the corresponding language tokens of the object language. The compilation of such a list is an arduous task and has occupied the lives of many anthropological linguists. Alien languages are unlikely to succumb to linguistic techniques without computer assistance. A true translating program must, of course, do more than simply match source and object language tokens. It must store and apply various rules of structure; the "meanings" of words alter as a function of context, inflection, pitch, and position. A translating program must parse an alien "sentence" into its constituent parts, apply the rules of the alien grammar—discovered via a pattern recognition procedure—and develop a likely translation for the sentence. Human beings, of course, go through a similar process when they learn a language; the difference is that with an alien language our ability to recognize and correctly parse sentences is likely to be severely limited. Indeed, one might go so far as to suggest that there will exist in the universe "spheres" of linguistic congruence. Some alien races may be very similar to ours, and their languages might be learned as one now learns French, for example. Other races may be profoundly, perhaps disturbingly different; our ability to process their languages will be constrained by the level of that difference. The higher the level of complexity, the greater the disjunction between communicative modes; the greater the level of incompatibility in life experience, the less likely we will be able to communicate without computer assistance. Shannon Wyler and T'uupieh have their difficulties in communication but are ultimately enough alike to allow communication to occur in a more direct mode.

Even after recognizing, reproducing, and, perhaps, translating an alien language, no guarantee exists that we will *understand* what is being said to us. Every language is embedded in a culture, in a particular worldview. Years ago Edward Sapir understood well the relationship between language and culture when he said, "The relation between language and experience is often misunderstood. Language is not merely a more or less systematic inventory of the various items of experience which seem relevant to the individual . . . but is also a self-contained creative symbolic organization, which not only refers to experience . . . but actually defines experience for us. . . ."

An alien language will both express and constrain the alien worldview. The language was formed by, and in turn forms, the alien culture in which it is embedded. Perhaps of all the obstacles facing the xenolinguist this is the most imposing. Sapir's words intimate that a true understanding of a language requires an understanding of its cultural matrix, and vice versa.

Thus, the meaning of any sentence uttered by an alien will be bounded entirely by the alien's life experience. If we cannot share in that experience, can we ever extract from the utterance a meaning understandable to us? The ability to understand another being requires a certain level of identification, a kind of semantic empathy. Each being is reasonably secure that a common domain of reference bounds the meanings he or she seeks to express in words. The alien has no such assurances. Only insofar as evolution and cultural history match, will our languages be isomorphic; only then can we communicate on common ground.

A major theme of *Eyes of Amber* is that the problem of understanding an alien being may not be insurmountable. In the opening paragraphs of the story, Lady T'uupieh, parting from Lord Chwiul, brother of the man she is to assassinate, says, "I shall certainly get rid of your watchman. He doesn't know a lady from a beggar." These seemingly innocuous words underscore a running thread in the story, that the world is changeable, a thing of mist and appearance, where all are bound to play their parts as the great "wheel of life" turns. Thus, a beggar is a noblewoman who is an assassin; a demon is a human being who is a rock star who is a linguist. T'uupieh, on the eve of the planned assassination, says to her "demon": "The world melts and flows, it rises into mist, it returns again to ice, only to melt and flow once more. A wheel has no beginning and no end; no starting place." If it is true, as T'uupieh says, that death is the only absolute, then what basis exists for communication between a demon and a lady? Shannon Wyler keeps trying to interpret T'uupieh as if she were a human being, ascribing to her words and actions meanings derived from human experience. As he laments: "T'uupieh, whenever I think I love you, you decide to cut somebody's throat. . . ." Is T'uupieh a Robin Hood or a brutal barbarian? Is Shannon Wyler a demon or an angel?

Ultimately, Vinge sees common bonds, and believes beneath the mist and meltwater of experience are some constants. The bedrock of all experience, alien or human, is a set of universal morals, a value system embedded in life itself, that provides a foundation for communication and for the empathy that is required for full understanding. Living beings must reach down and bring forth those core values, that animus that transcends the shell of evolution and biology, what Shannon Wyler ultimately identifies as a soul. If souls exist, then Vinge's contention that computers are not up to the job of handling the "translation" of alien language and experience is probably true. Being inanimate, at least for the present, computers have no bedrock, no basis for the empathy that is so necessary to communication. At one point in the story T'uupieh tells her demon, "You are immortal, you have the power to twist the wheel.'... What T'uupieh means is that the demon is not part of the universe of life and is not subject to its laws. As long as the demon remains "outside" (like the computer), there can be no understanding. Yet, ultimately T'uupieh and Wyler do communicate; their success stems from the demon's entrance into the realm of the wheel. When Shannon Wyler tells T'uupieh his name, he is saying to T'uupieh: I too am bound to the wheel, I too can hurt and suffer and live and die. In the end, real communication is between beings who live and die—regardless of biology or the random turnings of evolution and culture.

Is mortality, then, the common bond that will ultimately allow understanding among the creatures of the universe? If Vinge is right, we will, with and without computers, be able to converse with even the strangest life-forms. But is mortality really universal? Do there exist transcendent value systems whose commandments draw the line between "trust and betrayal, right and wrong, good and evil"? Could the community of mortal beings be inside a sphere of congruence, while outside, occupying yet other spheres, reside beings so incalculably different that the concept of mortality scarcely applies to them? What will be the basis for communication with these beings? Neither humans nor computers may ever make contact with these beings, and by that act share in the beings' unique world-experience.

Xenolinguistics and xenoanthropologists must ultimately view the universe as being comprised of nested spheres of congruence. In the center of any sphere is the individual human being surrounded by fellow humans. Races of similar biology and evolution are in a larger, encompassing sphere. In yet larger, outer spheres are races that begin to diverge profoundly from our own; as we move out from the center, computers and other prosthetic devices will be necessary to establish communication. But, as we move even further out and away, no device can help us, because the bases of our experience will be so far removed that no foundations, no linguistic levers of Archimedes, will exist upon which to found our discourse. Even with her optimism, Vinge is not entirely sure of herself in the final analysis. Was the message that Shannon Wyler sent, the message that Lady T'uupieh understood? Clear indications in the final pages of the short story suggest that T'uupieh has understood a portion of her demon's message, but just which portion is not entirely clear. Wyler thinks he has communicated a message about the universal value of life and the need for compassion. T'uupieh may or may not have understood this. She

might also have interpreted the demon's message as a surrender—a gift of power to uphold the "brutal philosophy" by which she lives. Thus, Vinge concludes enigmatically, with a problem that linguists and translators have struggled with for years, a problem that will only compound as we go out into the great dark between the stars: the ambiguity and uncertainty of language; the omnipresent division between hearer and speaker.

Joan Vinge (essay date 1988)

SOURCE: "The Restless Urge to Write," in *Women of Vision,* edited by Denise Dupont, St. Martin's Press, 1988, 109-27.

[*In the following essay, Vinge discusses the origins of and the influences on her fiction, the creative process, and the role of women writers in the science fiction genre.*]

There used to be an ad for the Famous Writers School that ran on matchbook covers. It read, *Do You Have the Restless Urge to Write?* Whenever I think about my career as a writer, it always comes back into my mind, because it seems to sum up creativity better than anything I've seen. I never expected to become a science-fiction writer; probably no one was more surprised about it than I was. And yet I've had a restless urge to create *something*—not always in the form of writing—and share it, ever since childhood.

My mother discovered that when I was barely three I lay in bed at night making up stories to put myself to sleep. (A habit I continued into adulthood.) I remember that most of the stories were about cowboys; sometimes I tried to make their action fit the background music of whatever show my parents were watching on the television downstairs. (I am a "night person," and always had trouble getting to sleep at night, even as a child. My daily period of peak creativity generally runs between three in the afternoon and three in the morning, which can be inconvenient in a nine-to-five world.)

When I was about eight years old I fell in love with horses, and also began to draw, suddenly and rather compulsively. From then on I drew and painted pictures of horses and people and other things, but mostly horses. In junior high school, my horse-crazy friends and I used to spend our spare time in the library, reading about horses and writing our own stories about them, which we rarely finished. I would illustrate everyone's stories with my pictures. The drawing was more important to me then than the writing, and I began to imagine rather vaguely that I wanted to be an artist when I grew up.

I also met my lifelong best friend when I was eight. Over the years, every time we got together, we played role-playing games, which in those days consisted of reading books you liked, maybe making some costumes, and then going outside and pretending with all your imagination that you were someone else. We specialized in the Pony

Express, the French and Indian War, and the Civil War—we were always reading the sort of books that listed "other books boys will enjoy" on the back flap. We each had a male alter ego/"secret identity" we used when playing pretend, because we were all too aware that boys had all the fun in the books we read. (We also sewed for and played very happily with dolls, but the dolls frequently had hair-raising adventures.) My parents never made any attempt to interfere with what I read; probably they were just glad that I liked to read.

When I was very young my father had a telescope out in the backyard; on summer evenings we used to go out and look at the moon and planets through it. That was probably the beginning of my fascination with space, and eventually with science fiction. I still remember the haunting paintings by Chesley Bonestall in a *Life* magazine feature on space back in the Fifties. (I learned the meaning of the word "hypothetical" from one of the captions: "a double star viewed from a hypothetical planet." I was crushed to learn that "hypothetical" meant "imaginary"; that the planet, with its stunning crags and craters, orbiting that mysterious double sun wasn't real.) When I was six my parents took me on a vacation to New York state. By far my most vivid memories of the trip are still of the Hayden Planetarium at the Museum of Natural History. (It still looks just as I remember it.)

Most people who are going to become science-fiction readers seem to stumble on the genre when they're fairly young; usually between the ages of eight and fourteen. I suspect that this is because science fiction is often filled with unfamiliar terminology. It's easier for children, who find a lot of things confusing or unfamiliar, to accept that they won't understand everything they read. An adult has a harder time being patient with a book filled with strange concepts. Andre Norton novels and the Robert Heinlein juveniles seem to be the books that get most science-fiction fans addicted. I was always fascinated by Sputnik and astronauts and news about "new discoveries" like transistors and lasers, but I didn't know science fiction existed until I was in ninth grade; barely within the "window." By then I had already picked up the message that girls weren't supposed to be interested in science or math, and I had begun to avoid them as subjects in school.

Then one day, looking through the book rack at the local grocery store, I found Andre Norton's book *Storm over Warlock*. I liked the hero's picture on the cover, and although I had no idea what a "Terran Survey Team" was (I was afraid "Terrans" would turn out to be some sort of weird aliens), I decided to try it. It changed my life. It turned my head around. It took me on the most wonderful trip to somewhere else I'd ever experienced. Finally I realized that a way existed to get back to that "hypothetical planet" beneath its strange, haunting sky; that writers existed who actually seemed to believe someday we might all get there. Andre Norton started me reading science fiction, and although I never suspected it at the time, her writing would directly or indirectly influence almost every major life choice I made from then on.

After that, I gave up reading about horses (though not drawing or riding them) and read almost nothing but science fiction. Science fiction helped me remain sane during high school (just like a lot of other people) by releasing me from the miseries of high school's rigid peer structure and the stifling early Sixties. I was tall, intellectual, and painfully shy—born to be part of the nerd pack. But, like a lot of other science-fiction fans, I learned through reading science fiction that The Way Things Were was not necessarily The Way Things Had to Be. It was probably the most important lesson I learned in school. If I ever need reassurance that writers can have an effect on the lives of their readers, I have only to think about my own experience.

For some reason, I didn't try very often to draw or paint other worlds, although art was still my main compulsion. But I continued to experiment with writing stories, and the stories I wrote were suddenly all science fiction. Most writers of science fiction get their start that way; you have to love reading the stuff, to begin with, or you are unlikely to want to write it. But I did what a lot of science fiction fans apparently do: I began things and never finished them; tossed them into a drawer when I got stuck, maybe taking them out later but usually just starting something new and not finishing that. I often wrote late at night, when I was supposed to be sleeping, by the dim glow of the television set in my room so that my mother wouldn't realize I was still up. Writing was my very private hobby in high school; I rarely showed my stories to anyone, even my friends. Art and poetry were my "serious" creative outlets.

Then I went to college, intending to major in art and become a commercial artist. I ran afoul of the kind of people who often wind up teaching art at state schools—artists who were only there because they couldn't make a living from their art, and lacked the sensitivity of a real teacher. Three semesters was enough to destroy my "restless urge to draw" completely. I went on through a series of other majors, including English, finally graduating with a degree in anthropology/archeology . . . thanks to my continuing interest in science fiction.

Andre Norton was not only responsible for my interest in science fiction, but in anthropology as well. Her book *The Time Traders* had recreated Northern Europe in about 2000 B.C. so vividly that I had been haunted by it for years, the way I had once been haunted by a hypothetical planet. I finally realized that regular history courses would never get me there, and signed up for a European prehistory course. (I actually hoped, for the first and only time, that I would have to do a term paper.) I did my term paper on the Beaker Folk from Norton's novel. And, much to my surprise, I discovered that anthropology affected me the way science fiction did: it turned my head around, made me wonder "where has anthropology been . . . ?" I'd always enjoyed reading fantasy as well as science fiction (when I refer to "science fiction" I mentally include fantasy, just as they do at the bookstore), and anthropology seemed to set off the same kind of excitement in me. My motto became, "Archeology is the anthropology of the past, and science fiction is the anthropology of the future."

"Broadening" is a word that I am generally reluctant to use, but it's the only one I know of that expresses the thing I find appealing about both science fiction and anthropology: they prove to me over and over again that the way I live life in twentieth-century America is not the only way there is; that people in other places and times on Earth (and probably off of it) have dealt with the universe and its perversities in very different ways, many of which work equally well. A B.A. in anthropology is not generally a terribly useful degree (I had originally planned on getting a Ph.D.), but I have found it to be extremely useful in my writing. Not only did it teach me to look at human behavior from a fresh perspective, with a kind of parallax view, but it also gave me the ethnographer's structural tools for creating imaginary societies, for building worlds that I wanted to write about. It has also given me a rich mine of real-world cultures and myths to mix and match when I'm creating new worlds. I generally write what has been called "world-building" fiction, a branch of the field that has grown as more social-science-trained writers have broadened the science base in "science fiction."

I was in college in the late Sixties, a time that seemed to be very much in sync with the world view I'd started to form from reading science fiction, specifically Andre Norton's work. My support of the peace, ecology, and equal-rights movements grew naturally out of the values I'd found in her books, and the kind of person that reading them had made me want to become. These values also inspired my support of one more thing—the women's movement. Way back in junior high school I'd discovered that "Andre" Norton was actually a woman, and it had made a deep impression on me. It did not immediately suggest to me that I could grow up to be a science-fiction writer myself, but it made her more real—and somehow more wonderful—to me. In the early mid-Sixties, well before the women's movement became widespread, I read her *Ordeal in Otherwhere,* the first book I'd ever read with an honest-to-God liberated woman as the protagonist. Not only were female protagonists extremely unusual at the time, but this character came from a world on which sexual equality was the norm. I never forgot that, and in the late Sixties, when I began to see articles on feminism, something fell into place for me in a very profound way.

A great deal of the science fiction I read while growing up was *not* socially progressive or forward looking, even if it was high tech. Science fiction has historically had a reputation for sociopolitical conservatism that is not unjustified. It didn't bother me much at the time. I accepted the party line; I was still young, and so caught up in the "forest" of cultural norms that I couldn't see "trees" such as sexism. The exotic locales and strange customs (as far as they went) of science fiction still offered me escape from my limited visibility, and the few writers like Norton were a breath of fresh air. But I remember reading Heinlein's *Podkayne of Mars* only a few months before I read my first article on feminism (in the *Saturday Review*), and thinking with a sigh that "I would never be as feminine as Podkayne. . . ."

A few months later I read that article, and then more like it. And it struck me at last that *I* wasn't the one with the problem—Podkayne was. There was more than one way to look at the relationship between the sexes, and what was good and bad, valid or invalid, about it. I experienced a great deal of anger then, but more than that a feeling of pride, and a sense of profound relief. I realized that I didn't have to pretend to be a man in fantasies to do all the things I wanted to do; and that it wasn't my fault, or my failure, if I didn't wear the straitjacket of "femininity" gracefully. I still wanted to marry and have a family, but I also wanted a career, and the support of a man who wanted an equal partner, not a five-foot, ten-inch "little woman."

But at that point I still felt no ambition to become a published writer. Despite my "restless urge," I was afraid to show my work around seriously, for fear of getting my creativity crushed the way I had with my art. I had begun to understand that I had an inborn need to create something; I was afraid that if my urge, which had already been transferred from art to writing, was beaten down again, there would be no outlet left for it.

But then I met my first husband, Vernor Vinge, who was already a published science-fiction writer (another way in which Andre Norton and science fiction changed my life). He gave me the encouragement I needed to work seriously on a story and send it out. I actually sold the story (**"Tin Soldier"**), and after that there was no turning back. My career had found me. (It is possible to take quite a bit of rejection without losing courage once you have actually sold a story.)

When I look back at the odd course that led me to become a writer, there is really no way I could have predicted the outcome. But having become a writer, I have given thought over the years to the things that have shaped and affected my work. In the beginning it was only the "restless urge," the blind, instinctive need to create something, and a fascination with the strange that was science fiction, that drove me to write. But as I continued to work, and saw that my writing was not a fluke, I realized there were other forces, both conscious and unconscious, influencing everything I did.

I still write primarily for myself, and I find it difficult if not impossible to work on a story I'm not completely interested in. But beyond that, I am unquestionably affected by what is going on around me, whether I like it or not. The peace or chaos in my personal life affects the lightness or darkness of my prose; the sociopolitical climate affects how I regard my characters' actions (because science fiction is really about the present, no matter how much we try to pretend that it is about the past or future); music and images inspire me constantly, striking directly the creative, nonverbal part of my brain where story ideas take from; and other writers' works suggest new areas I want to explore myself (when I have the time to read them).

The response of readers and/or critics has an influence, for better or worse, on what I write, as well; although generally I prefer to work with an editor I trust, and disregard other critics as much as is humanly possible. I believe a writer's work can be considerably strengthened by the input of a knowledgeable editor; it is too easy to become so close to your own work that you can't see it clearly. But for input to be meaningful, it must come from someone with whom the writer shares a bond of mutual respect and creative vision; preferably it should occur before the book or story is published, since criticism after the fact is, for the most part, moot.

Science fiction is a unique field in that the writers actually have an opportunity to meet their fans and editors (and critics) face to face, at the numerous science-fiction conventions that are held around the country. The feedback is generally gratifying, and it can affect what a writer works on subsequently as well—if everbody, including the publisher, wants "the next book about so-and-so," sometimes the temptation to write it becomes overwhelming. I find myself writing a lot of sequels lately, and knowing that there is a ready audience for them helps when you're concerned with making a living—a consideration all professionals have to keep in mind. I have also found that, as a mother with two small children, new and unique ideas do not come to my mind as easily as they used to, so I am grateful to have "future histories" that I'm already familiar with, and characters that I already know and like, to give me a springboard to new books.

But the bottom line still remains the same: if the actual idea for the book leaves me cold, I will not be able to write it. Each book has to have its own reason for being, and its own integrity in my own mind, or else I might as well not write it. I am easily blocked as a writer and lack of interest in a subject is one of the surest ways I know of to keep me from getting something done. (I am not a fast writer anyway; I have found that I am able to supplement my income by doing movie novelizations, which I *can* do quickly, and even have some fun with.)

Although in the beginning and end I am writing for myself as my own "ideal audience," I am also aware that I'm writing to a real audience, and imagine—or hope—that I am having some effect on them, as Andre Norton and science fiction generally had on me. I choose to write science fiction instead of mainstream fiction because I enjoy the freedom the field gives me to experiment. Good characters are extremely important to me when I read, and also when I write; there was a time when I almost stopped reading science fiction (which happens to a lot of people somewhere around college age) because so much of it was poorly written, with cardboard characters pushed around the landscape simply to make the plot go. My first husband told me that the point was to read for the ideas, so I tried to do that; but in time I realized the two things did not have to be mutually exclusive.

And yet I also realized that it *was* the ideas I loved about science fiction, as opposed to mainstream fiction. Taking characters I am interested in getting to know, putting them into strange and different situations, allowing them

(and the reader) to discover something about human nature and their own individual natures—to see what the story teaches me, along with my characters—is more satisfying and gives me more pleasure than anything I know.

But at the same time I can't help being aware of the potential I have for teaching my readers certain things. Feminism, which for me is more a specific kind of humanism, is an inescapable part of my world view and my writing. I try not to preach when I write, for writers who set out primarily to preach quickly end up preaching only to the converted. I think of myself basically as an entertainer, and embrace the philosophy that "a spoonful of suger helps the medicine go down." Andre Norton served as a profound role model for me while entertaining me endlessly with the humanity and variety of her characters and stories; I hope that I may have the same sort of effect on at least a few of my readers. I attempt to let my characters speak for themselves, letting them interact and butt heads and learn—along with the reader, I hope—and through my characters I try not only to make female readers more aware of the possibilities open to them in their lives, but make male readers see that strong, competent women and sensitive, thoughtful men are not anathema. If a man can read a satisfying science-fiction novel in which "liberated" characters appear, and enjoy it anyway, it is my hope (and it has been borne out occasionally) that the experience might lessen the reader's fear of meeting similar people in the real world.

I choose to write science fiction instead of mainstream fiction because I enjoy the freedom the field gives me to experiment.

—Joan Vinge

I have never found it more difficult to write about male characters than female characters; I try to respect my characters' individual integrity, just as I would if they were people I met in the real world. In fact, being able to "play God" and create characters who answer to me, I am able to write about a higher percentage of men who are the kind of man I would like to know than I might actually encounter in the real world.

If anything, I sometimes feel that I have more difficulty writing successfully about women characters, simply because I am more aware of them as role models, and have to fight against the urge to keep them on their good behavior when they honestly and realistically should be covering as much of the spectrum of good and evil as any man. (I think women may have an easier time "getting into the heads" of male characters than vice versa because historically women, as an underclass, have been forced to know what was on a man's mind almost before he did, or suffer for it. Men, on the other hand, had less reason to understand "what it is women want," because to understand is to sympathize, which makes continued exploitation difficult. And on a personal level, having done so much "boy's book" role-playing as a girl, it has never been hard for me to "pretend" I was seeing things through the eyes of a male character when I write. It's all part of the "speculative fiction.")

I do not think of my writing style as being specifically "female" as opposed to "male," however. I used to be aware of what I thought of as "male" and "female" prose styles while reading science fiction when I was in college; the characteristic styles, however, were not invariably linked to writers of the appropriate sex. (At the time I thought of Le Guin as having a "male" style because her prose was spare and straightforward; I did not think of Norton's style as specifically either male or female.) Over the years I have come to feel that such distinctions are largely artificial, and that they tend to become less pronounced as male and female stereotypes break down. In any case, I feel that a well-written work will transcend such basically stereotypical categories.

In the same way, the treatment of women characters as peculiar, incomprehensible, or less than human in a lot of "classic" works of Golden Age science fiction seems to me to be a result of stereotypical attitudes (on the part of both male and female writers), prejudices of the sort I blindly accepted during much of my life. Occasionally I deal in my stories with characters who regard women that way (since such people are still at large in my universe, and I expect they always will be), but I write from the position that such an attitude is bigoted or blind, and hope that my readers (if not always my characters) will reach the same conclusion.

I have often felt fortunate that I work in the science-fiction field, because the field has proved to be far more open to the kind of points I want to make with my work than most of society is. The science-fiction field was, for a long time, a particular stronghold of male chauvinism, but I entered it during a period of general social change, when some of the groundwork of opening up the field to women writing as women (and not forced to hide their light behind male or androgynous names) had been done by other women, writers like Ursula Le Guin, Joanna Russ, and Anne McCaffrey. There was a period in the mid-Seventies when women were a novelty act (my friend joked about the all-women issue of *Analog* in which I had a story, calling it "Joan D. Vinge and Her All-Girl Band"). But because of the ongoing changes in the field, I experienced an almost utopian atmosphere of acceptance for my work. I believed that if readers were exposed to stories by women writers, even in all-women anthologies, the quality of the work would be recognized, and the "freakish" aspect would quickly fade; and that was basically what happened. I was fortunate, and I was not alone, because many other women began writing science fiction during that same period.

I believed that if women were given an honest chance to show how well they wrote, they would gain real acceptance; and through the Seventies and into the Eighties that appeared to happen. I was proud of the people in the field for proving that they were not only on the cutting edge of progress technologically, but also socially—that they believed just as strongly in social change. In interviews I was often asked why so many women had started writing science fiction all at once, and my answer was that feminism had made the real difference, making those women who had always been readers stop and say, "If I want to do that, I can." It was true for me, and every woman writer I knew considered herself to be a feminist. (So did many of the new male writers; and even the most hidebound of the older male authors actually seemed to be making some effort to raise their consciousnesses—with mixed results.) I think that women who had always been receptive to science fiction were particularly likely to be open to feminism as well; because we already had the ability to accept a new and different perspective on life.

There was a time when I would have ended an essay like this here, on an uplifting and positive note that reflected my pride at being a part of a field where I am free to realize my human potential to the fullest, without limitations or penalties. Unfortunately, as I remarked before, science fiction does not reflect the future so much as it reflects the present. My husband tells me of conversations on the train not just with men but with businesswomen for whom feminists are "some bunch of lesbians and weirdos"; who express surprise when he tells them that their goals are feminist goals, or that they wouldn't be riding that train, briefcases clutched in their hands, if their (older) sisters hadn't fought for their right to do it.

Our society has gone through a period of major backsliding after the social progress of the Sixties and Seventies; and this has been reflected in the science-fiction field. Jeanne Gomoll, a reader and fan who has written a great deal on feminism and science fiction, recently published an article detailing the move by certain (male) critics within the field to deny and belittle the work of the "world-building," humanist/feminist writers of the Seventies as inferior and/or aberrant. The trend depresses me, but it does not surprise me, any more than it changes my attitudes or goals. It only reflects what I have experienced in my own life; that reality is more complicated and ultimately more disappointing than our dreams. Trying to continue a writing career and raise a family *is* more difficult for a woman than for a man. Although my husband is both an editor in the field and an avowed feminist, still I am the one on whom most of the family responsibilities fall, which is not the case with most of the male writers I know. (Most of the women writers I know are not married, although a few are, and now have babies and conflicts of their own.)

But all that does not change the genuine progress that women have made in and out of the field; we have won a foothold in science fiction as well as in the real world, and we are not about to give it up. And it does not change a very personal truth for me: however much I treasure my children and my family life (and I honestly do not regret the ways in which children have limited certain aspects of my career, because they have enriched my life so much, both as a human being and as a writer), if I could not fulfill my *need* to write, my restless urge, I would lose myself. My work is my soul; it is what I do for *me* and no one else. Self-expression is a need that is as vital for a woman as it is for a man. And now I believe more strongly than ever in the potential that science fiction has for opening minds and spirits, in the importance of its writers continuing to serve up a little healthy humanity in a "spoonful of sugar."

It is, quite honestly, something of a surprise to me to find myself at this point in ending my essay—realizing that I am not so much writing a kind of memoir as a cautionary tale. But experience has proven for me the saying, "The price of freedom is eternal vigilance." And that old feminists never die; they just say, "Write On."

Additional coverage of Vinge's life and career is contained in the following sources published by Gale Research: *Contemporary Authors*, Vols. 93-96; *Contemporary Literary Criticism*, Vol. 30; and *Something about the Author*, Vol 36.

Appendix:

Select Bibliography of General Sources on Short Fiction

BOOKS OF CRITICISM

Allen, Walter. *The Short Story in English*. New York: Oxford University Press, 1981, 413 p.

Aycock, Wendell M., ed. *The Teller and the Tale: Aspects of the Short Story* (Proceedings of the Comparative Literature Symposium, Texas Tech University, Volume XIII). Lubbock: Texas Tech Press, 1982, 156 p.

Averill, Deborah. *The Irish Short Story from George Moore to Frank O'Connor*. Washington, D.C.: University Press of America, 1982, 329 p.

Bates, H. E. *The Modern Short Story: A Critical Survey*. Boston: Writer, 1941, 231 p.

Bayley, John. *The Short Story: Henry James to Elizabeth Bowen*. Great Britain: The Harvester Press Limited, 1988, 197 p.

Bennett, E. K. *A History of the German Novelle: From Goethe to Thomas Mann*. Cambridge: At the University Press, 1934, 296 p.

Bone, Robert. *Down Home: A History of Afro-American Short Fiction from Its Beginning to the End of the Harlem Renaissance*. Rev. ed. New York: Columbia University Press, 1988, 350 p.

Bruck, Peter. *The Black American Short Story in the Twentieth Century: A Collection of Critical Essays*. Amsterdam: B. R. Grüner Publishing Co., 1977, 209 p.

Burnett, Whit, and Burnett, Hallie. *The Modern Short Story in the Making*. New York: Hawthorn Books, 1964, 405 p.

Canby, Henry Seidel. *The Short Story in English*. New York: Henry Holt and Co., 1909, 386 p.

Current-García, Eugene. *The American Short Story before 1850: A Critical History*. Twayne's Critical History of the Short Story, edited by William Peden. Boston: Twayne Publishers, 1985, 168 p.

Flora, Joseph M., ed. *The English Short Story, 1880-1945: A Critical History*. Twayne's Critical History of the Short Story, edited by William Peden. Boston: Twayne Publishers, 1985, 215 p.

Foster, David William. *Studies in the Contemporary Spanish-American Short Story*. Columbia, Mo.: University of Missouri Press, 1979, 126 p.

George, Albert J. *Short Fiction in France, 1800-1850*. Syracuse, N.Y.: Syracuse University Press, 1964, 245 p.

Gerlach, John. *Toward an End: Closure and Structure in the American Short Story*. University, Ala.: The University of Alabama Press, 1985, 193 p.

Hankin, Cherry, ed. *Critical Essays on the New Zealand Short Story*. Auckland: Heinemann Publishers,

1982, 186 p.

Hanson, Clare, ed. *Re-Reading the Short Story*. London: MacMillan Press, 1989, 137 p.

Harris, Wendell V. *British Short Fiction in the Nineteenth Century*. Detroit: Wayne State University Press, 1979, 209 p.

Huntington, John. *Rationalizing Genius: Ideological Strategies in the Classic American Science Fiction Short Story*. New Brunswick: Rutgers University Press, 1989, 216 p.

Kilroy, James F., ed. *The Irish Short Story: A Critical History*. Twayne's Critical History of the Short Story, edited by William Peden. Boston: Twayne Publishers, 1984, 251 p.

Lee, A. Robert. *The Nineteenth-Century American Short Story*. Totowa, N. J.: Vision / Barnes & Noble, 1986, 196 p.

Leibowitz, Judith. *Narrative Purpose in the Novella*. The Hague: Mouton, 1974, 137 p.

Lohafer, Susan. *Coming to Terms with the Short Story*. Baton Rouge: Louisiana State University Press, 1983, 171 p.

Lohafer, Susan, and Clarey, Jo Ellyn. *Short Story Theory at a Crossroads*. Baton Rouge: Louisiana State University Press, 1989, 352 p.

Mann, Susan Garland. *The Short Story Cycle: A Genre Companion and Reference Guide*. New York: Greenwood Press, 1989, 228 p.

Matthews, Brander. *The Philosophy of the Short Story*. New York, N.Y.: Longmans, Green and Co., 1901, 83 p.

May, Charles E., ed. *Short Story Theories*. Athens, Oh.: Ohio University Press, 1976, 251 p.

McClave, Heather, ed. *Women Writers of the Short Story: A Collection of Critical Essays*. Englewood Cliffs, N. J.: Prentice-Hall, 1980, 171 p.

Moser, Charles, ed. *The Russian Short Story: A Critical History*. Twayne's Critical History of the Short Story, edited by William Peden. Boston: Twayne Publishers, 1986, 232 p.

New, W. H. *Dreams of Speech and Violence: The Art of the Short Story in Canada and New Zealand*. Toronto: The University of Toronto Press, 1987, 302 p.

Newman, Frances. *The Short Story's Mutations: From Petronius to Paul Morand*. New York: B. W. Huebsch, 1925, 332 p.

O'Connor, Frank. *The Lonely Voice: A Study of the Short Story*. Cleveland: World Publishing Co., 1963, 220 p.

O'Faolain, Sean. *The Short Story*. New York: Devin-Adair Co., 1951, 370 p.

Orel, Harold. *The Victorian Short Story: Development and Triumph of a Literary Genre*. Cambridge: Cambridge University Press, 1986, 213 p.

O'Toole, L. Michael. *Structure, Style and Interpretation in the Russian Short Story*. New Haven: Yale University Press, 1982, 272 p.

Pattee, Fred Lewis. *The Development of the American Short Story: An Historical Survey*. New York: Harper and Brothers Publishers, 1923, 388 p.

Peden, Margaret Sayers, ed. *The Latin American Short Story: A Critical History*. Twayne's Critical History of the Short Story, edited by William Peden. Boston: Twayne Publishers, 1983, 160 p.

Peden, William. *The American Short Story: Continuity and Change, 1940-1975*. Rev. ed. Boston: Houghton Mifflin Co., 1975, 215 p.

Reid, Ian. *The Short Story*. The Critical Idiom, edited by John D. Jump. London: Methuen and Co., 1977, 76 p.

Rhode, Robert D. *Setting in the American Short Story of Local Color, 1865-1900*. The Hague: Mouton, 1975, 189 p.

Rohrberger, Mary. *Hawthorne and the Modern Short Story: A Study in Genre*. The Hague: Mouton and Co., 1966, 148 p.

Shaw, Valerie. *The Short Story: A Critical Introduction*. London: Longman, 1983, 294 p.

Stephens, Michael. *The Dramaturgy of Style: Voice in Short Fiction*. Carbondale, Ill.: Southern Illinois University Press, 1986, 281 p.

Stevick, Philip, ed. *The American Short Story, 1900-1945: A Critical History*. Twayne's Critical History of the Short Story, edited by William Peden. Boston: Twayne Publishers, 1984, 209 p.

Summers, Hollis, ed. *Discussion of the Short Story*. Boston: D. C. Heath and Co., 1963, 118 p.

Vannatta, Dennis, ed. *The English Short Story, 1945-1980: A Critical History*. Twayne's Critical History of the Short Story, edited by William Peden. Boston: Twayne Publishers, 1985, 206 p.

Voss, Arthur. *The American Short Story: A Critical Survey*. Norman, Okla.: University of Oklahoma Press, 1973, 399 p.

Walker, Warren S. *Twentieth-Century Short Story Explication: New Series, Vol. 1: 1989-1990*. Hamden, Conn.: Shoe String, 1993, 366 p.

Ward, Alfred C. *Aspects of the Modern Short Story: English and American*. London: University of London Press, 1924, 307 p.

Weaver, Gordon, ed. *The American Short Story, 1945-1980: A Critical History*. Twayne's Critical History of the Short Story, edited by William Peden. Boston: Twayne Publishers, 1983, 150 p.

West, Ray B., Jr. *The Short Story in America, 1900-1950*. Chicago: Henry Regnery Co., 1952, 147 p.

Williams, Blanche Colton. *Our Short Story Writers*. New York: Moffat, Yard and Co., 1920, 357 p.

Wright, Austin McGiffert. *The American Short Story in the Twenties*. Chicago: University of Chicago Press, 1961, 425 p.

CRITICAL ANTHOLOGIES

Atkinson, W. Patterson, ed. *The Short-Story*. Boston: Allyn and Bacon, 1923, 317 p.

Baldwin, Charles Sears, ed. *American Short Stories*. New York, N.Y.: Longmans, Green and Co., 1904, 333 p.

Charters, Ann, ed. *The Story and Its Writer: An Introduction to Short Fiction*. New York: St. Martin's Press, 1983, 1239 p.

Current-García, Eugene, and Patrick, Walton R., eds. *American Short Stories: 1820 to the Present*. Key Editions, edited by John C. Gerber. Chicago: Scott, Foresman and Co., 1952, 633 p.

Fagin, N. Bryllion, ed. *America through the Short Story*. Boston: Little, Brown, and Co., 1936, 508 p.

Frakes, James R., and Traschen, Isadore, eds. *Short Fiction: A Critical Collection*. Prentice-Hall English Literature Series, edited by Maynard Mack. Englewood Cliffs, N.J.: Prentice-Hall, 1959, 459 p.

Gifford, Douglas, ed. *Scottish Short Stories, 1800-1900*. The Scottish Library, edited by Alexander Scott. London: Calder and Boyars, 1971, 350 p.

Gordon, Caroline, and Tate, Allen, eds. *The House of Fiction: An Anthology of the Short Story with Commentary*. Rev. ed. New York: Charles Scribner's Sons, 1960, 469 p.

Greet, T. Y., et. al. *The Worlds of Fiction: Stories in Context*. Boston, Mass.: Houghton Mifflin Co., 1964, 429 p.

Gullason, Thomas A., and Caspar, Leonard, eds. *The World of Short Fiction: An International Collection*. New York: Harper and Row, 1962, 548 p.

Havighurst, Walter, ed. *Masters of the Modern Short Story*. New York: Harcourt, Brace and Co., 1945, 538 p.

Litz, A. Walton, ed. *Major American Short Stories*. New York: Oxford University Press, 1975, 823 p.

Matthews, Brander, ed. *The Short-Story: Specimens Illustrating Its Development*. New York: American Book Co., 1907, 399 p.

Menton, Seymour, ed. *The Spanish American Short Story: A Critical Anthology*. Berkeley and Los Angeles: University of California Press, 1980, 496 p.

Mzamane, Mbulelo Vizikhungo, ed. *Hungry Flames, and Other Black South African Short Stories*. Longman African Classics. Essex: Longman, 1986, 162 p.

Schorer, Mark, ed. *The Short Story: A Critical Anthology*. Rev. ed. Prentice-Hall English Literature Series, edited by Maynard Mack. Englewood Cliffs, N. J.: Prentice-Hall, 1967, 459 p.

Simpson, Claude M., ed. *The Local Colorists: American Short Stories, 1857-1900*. New York: Harper and Brothers Publishers, 1960, 340 p.

Stanton, Robert, ed. *The Short Story and the Reader*. New York: Henry Holt and Co., 1960, 557 p.

West, Ray B., Jr., ed. *American Short Stories*. New York: Thomas Y. Crowell Co., 1959, 267 p.

Short Story Criticism Indexes

Literary Criticism Series
Cumulative Author Index

SSC Cumulative Nationality Index
SSC Cumulative Title Index

How to Use This Index

The main references

Calvino, Italo
1923-1985.....CLC 5, 8, 11, 22, 33, 39,
73; SSC 3

---

list all author entries in the following Gale Literary Criticism series:

BLC = Black Literature Criticism
CLC = Contemporary Literary Criticism
CLR = Children's Literature Review
CMLC = Classical and Medieval Literature Criticism
DA = DISCovering Authors
DAB = DISCovering Authors: British
DAC = DISCovering Authors: Canadian
DC = Drama Criticism
HLC = Hispanic Literature Criticism
LC = Literature Criticism from 1400 to 1800
NCLC = Nineteenth-Century Literature Criticism
PC = Poetry Criticism
SSC = Short Story Criticism
TCLC = Twentieth-Century Literary Criticism
WLC = World Literature Criticism, 1500 to the Present

The cross-references

See also CANR 23; CA 85-88;
obituary CA 116

---

list all author entries in the following Gale biographical and literary sources:

AAYA = Authors & Artists for Young Adults
AITN = Authors in the News
BEST = Bestsellers
BW = Black Writers
CA = Contemporary Authors
CAAS = Contemporary Authors Autobiography Series
CABS = Contemporary Authors Bibliographical Series
CANR = Contemporary Authors New Revision Series
CAP = Contemporary Authors Permanent Series
CDALB = Concise Dictionary of American Literary Biography
CDBLB = Concise Dictionary of British Literary Biography
DAM = DISCovering Authors: Modules
    DRAM: Dramatists Module; MST: Most-Studied Authors Module;
    MULT: Multicultural Authors Module; NOV: Novelists Module;
    POET: Poets Module; POP: Popular Fiction and Genre Authors Module
DLB = Dictionary of Literary Biography
DLBD = Dictionary of Literary Biography Documentary Series
DLBY = Dictionary of Literary Biography Yearbook
HW = Hispanic Writers
JRDA = Junior DISCovering Authors
MAICYA = Major Authors and Illustrators for Children and Young Adults
MTCW = Major 20th-Century Writers
NNAL = Native North American Literature
SAAS = Something about the Author Autobiography Series
SATA = Something about the Author
YABC = Yesterday's Authors of Books for Children

Literary Criticism Series
Cumulative Author Index

Andier, Pierre
See Desnos, Robert

Andouard
See Giraudoux, (Hippolyte) Jean

Andrade, Carlos Drummond de ...... **CLC 18**
See also Drummond de Andrade, Carlos

Andrade, Mario de 1893-1945 ..... **TCLC 43**

Andreae, Johann V(alentin)
1586-1654 .... **LC 32**
See also DLB 164

Andreas-Salome, Lou 1861-1937 ... **TCLC 56**
See also DLB 66

Andrewes, Lancelot 1555-1626 .... **LC 5**
See also DLB 151, 172

Andrews, Cicily Fairfield
See West, Rebecca

Andrews, Elton V.
See Pohl, Frederik

Andreyev, Leonid (Nikolaevich)
1871-1919 .... **TCLC 3**
See also CA 104

Andric, Ivo 1892-1975 .... **CLC 8**
See also CA 81-84; 57-60; CANR 43;
DLB 147; MTCW

Angelique, Pierre
See Bataille, Georges

Angell, Roger 1920- .... **CLC 26**
See also CA 57-60; CANR 13, 44; DLB 171

Angelou, Maya
1928- .... **CLC 12, 35, 64, 77; BLC; DA;
DAB; DAC; DAM MST, MULT, POET,
POP**
See also AAYA 7; BW 2; CA 65-68;
CANR 19, 42; DLB 38; MTCW;
SATA 49

Annensky, Innokenty Fyodorovich
1856-1909 .... **TCLC 14**
See also CA 110

Anon, Charles Robert
See Pessoa, Fernando (Antonio Nogueira)

Anouilh, Jean (Marie Lucien Pierre)
1910-1987 ...... **CLC 1, 3, 8, 13, 40, 50;
DAM DRAM**
See also CA 17-20R; 123; CANR 32;
MTCW

Anthony, Florence
See Ai

Anthony, John
See Ciardi, John (Anthony)

Anthony, Peter
See Shaffer, Anthony (Joshua); Shaffer,
Peter (Levin)

Anthony, Piers 1934- .. **CLC 35; DAM POP**
See also AAYA 11; CA 21-24R; CANR 28;
DLB 8; MTCW; SAAS 22; SATA 84

Antoine, Marc
See Proust, (Valentin-Louis-George-Eugene-)
Marcel

Antoninus, Brother
See Everson, William (Oliver)

Antonioni, Michelangelo 1912- ..... **CLC 20**
See also CA 73-76; CANR 45

Antschel, Paul 1920-1970
See Celan, Paul
See also CA 85-88; CANR 33; MTCW

Anwar, Chairil 1922-1949 .... **TCLC 22**
See also CA 121

Apollinaire, Guillaume
1880-1918 .... **TCLC 3, 8, 51;
DAM POET; PC 7**
See also Kostrowitzki, Wilhelm Apollinaris
de
See also CA 152

Appelfeld, Aharon 1932- .... **CLC 23, 47**
See also CA 112; 133

Apple, Max (Isaac) 1941- .... **CLC 9, 33**
See also CA 81-84; CANR 19, 54; DLB 130

Appleman, Philip (Dean) 1926- ..... **CLC 51**
See also CA 13-16R; CAAS 18; CANR 6,
29

Appleton, Lawrence
See Lovecraft, H(oward) P(hillips)

Apteryx
See Eliot, T(homas) S(tearns)

Apuleius, (Lucius Madaurensis)
125(?)-175(?) .... **CMLC 1**

Aquin, Hubert 1929-1977 .... **CLC 15**
See also CA 105; DLB 53

Aragon, Louis
1897-1982 ..... **CLC 3, 22; DAM NOV,
POET**
See also CA 69-72; 108; CANR 28;
DLB 72; MTCW

Arany, Janos 1817-1882 .... **NCLC 34**

Arbuthnot, John 1667-1735 .... **LC 1**
See also DLB 101

Archer, Herbert Winslow
See Mencken, H(enry) L(ouis)

Archer, Jeffrey (Howard)
1940- .... **CLC 28; DAM POP**
See also AAYA 16; BEST 89:3; CA 77-80;
CANR 22, 52; INT CANR-22

Archer, Jules 1915- .... **CLC 12**
See also CA 9-12R; CANR 6; SAAS 5;
SATA 4, 85

Archer, Lee
See Ellison, Harlan (Jay)

Arden, John
1930- ..... **CLC 6, 13, 15; DAM DRAM**
See also CA 13-16R; CAAS 4; CANR 31;
DLB 13; MTCW

Arenas, Reinaldo
1943-1990 ...... **CLC 41; DAM MULT;
HLC**
See also CA 124; 128; 133; DLB 145; HW

Arendt, Hannah 1906-1975 ..... **CLC 66, 98**
See also CA 17-20R; 61-64; CANR 26;
MTCW

Aretino, Pietro 1492-1556 .... **LC 12**

Arghezi, Tudor .... **CLC 80**
See also Theodorescu, Ion N.

Arguedas, Jose Maria
1911-1969 .... **CLC 10, 18**
See also CA 89-92; DLB 113; HW

Argueta, Manlio 1936- .... **CLC 31**
See also CA 131; DLB 145; HW

Ariosto, Ludovico 1474-1533 .... **LC 6**

Aristides
See Epstein, Joseph

Aristophanes
450B.C.-385B.C. .... **CMLC 4; DA;
DAB; DAC; DAM DRAM, MST; DC 2**

Arlt, Roberto (Godofredo Christophersen)
1900-1942 ..... **TCLC 29; DAM MULT;
HLC**
See also CA 123; 131; HW

Armah, Ayi Kwei
1939- .... **CLC 5, 33; BLC;
DAM MULT, POET**
See also BW 1; CA 61-64; CANR 21;
DLB 117; MTCW

Armatrading, Joan 1950- .... **CLC 17**
See also CA 114

Arnette, Robert
See Silverberg, Robert

**Arnim, Achim von (Ludwig Joachim von
Arnim)** 1781-1831 .... **NCLC 5**
See also DLB 90

Arnim, Bettina von 1785-1859 .... **NCLC 38**
See also DLB 90

Arnold, Matthew
1822-1888 ..... **NCLC 6, 29; DA; DAB;
DAC; DAM MST, POET; PC 5; WLC**
See also CDBLB 1832-1890; DLB 32, 57

Arnold, Thomas 1795-1842 ...... **NCLC 18**
See also DLB 55

Arnow, Harriette (Louisa) Simpson
1908-1986 .... **CLC 2, 7, 18**
See also CA 9-12R; 118; CANR 14; DLB 6;
MTCW; SATA 42; SATA-Obit 47

Arp, Hans
See Arp, Jean

Arp, Jean 1887-1966 .... **CLC 5**
See also CA 81-84; 25-28R; CANR 42

Arrabal
See Arrabal, Fernando

Arrabal, Fernando 1932- ... **CLC 2, 9, 18, 58**
See also CA 9-12R; CANR 15

Arrick, Fran .... **CLC 30**
See also Gaberman, Judie Angell

Artaud, Antonin (Marie Joseph)
1896-1948 ... **TCLC 3, 36; DAM DRAM**
See also CA 104; 149

Arthur, Ruth M(abel) 1905-1979 .... **CLC 12**
See also CA 9-12R; 85-88; CANR 4;
SATA 7, 26

Artsybashev, Mikhail (Petrovich)
1878-1927 .... **TCLC 31**

Arundel, Honor (Morfydd)
1919-1973 .... **CLC 17**
See also CA 21-22; 41-44R; CAP 2;
CLR 35; SATA 4; SATA-Obit 24

Arzner, Dorothy 1897-1979 .... **CLC 98**

Asch, Sholem 1880-1957 .... **TCLC 3**
See also CA 105

Ash, Shalom
See Asch, Sholem

Ashbery, John (Lawrence)
1927- ...... **CLC 2, 3, 4, 6, 9, 13, 15, 25,
41, 77; DAM POET**
See also CA 5-8R; CANR 9, 37; DLB 5,
165; DLBY 81; INT CANR-9; MTCW

Ashdown, Clifford
See Freeman, R(ichard) Austin

Ashe, Gordon
See Creasey, John

Ashton-Warner, Sylvia (Constance)
1908-1984 .... **CLC 19**
See also CA 69-72; 112; CANR 29; MTCW

Asimov, Isaac
1920-1992 ...... **CLC 1, 3, 9, 19, 26, 76,
92; DAM POP**
See also AAYA 13; BEST 90:2; CA 1-4R;
137; CANR 2, 19, 36; CLR 12; DLB 8;
DLBY 92; INT CANR-19; JRDA;
MAICYA; MTCW; SATA 1, 26, 74

Assis, Joaquim Maria Machado de
See Machado de Assis, Joaquim Maria

Astley, Thea (Beatrice May)
1925- .... **CLC 41**
See also CA 65-68; CANR 11, 43

Aston, James
See White, T(erence) H(anbury)

Asturias, Miguel Angel
1899-1974 .... **CLC 3, 8, 13;
DAM MULT, NOV; HLC**
See also CA 25-28; 49-52; CANR 32;
CAP 2; DLB 113; HW; MTCW

Atares, Carlos Saura
See Saura (Atares), Carlos

Atheling, William
See Pound, Ezra (Weston Loomis)

Atheling, William, Jr.
See Blish, James (Benjamin)

Atherton, Gertrude (Franklin Horn)
1857-1948 .... **TCLC 2**
See also CA 104; DLB 9, 78

Atherton, Lucius
See Masters, Edgar Lee

Atkins, Jack
See Harris, Mark

Attaway, William (Alexander)
1911-1986 .... **CLC 92; BLC;
DAM MULT**
See also BW 2; CA 143; DLB 76

Atticus
See Fleming, Ian (Lancaster)

Atwood, Margaret (Eleanor)
1939- ..... **CLC 2, 3, 4, 8, 13, 15, 44,
84; DA; DAB; DAC; DAM MST, NOV,
POET; PC 8; SSC 2; WLC**
See also AAYA 12; BEST 89:2; CA 49-52;
CANR 3, 24, 33; DLB 53;
INT CANR-24; MTCW; SATA 50

Aubigny, Pierre d'
See Mencken, H(enry) L(ouis)

Aubin, Penelope 1685-1731(?) .... **LC 9**
See also DLB 39

Auchincloss, Louis (Stanton)
1917- .... **CLC 4, 6, 9, 18, 45;
DAM NOV; SSC 22**
See also CA 1-4R; CANR 6, 29, 55; DLB 2;
DLBY 80; INT CANR-29; MTCW

Auden, W(ystan) H(ugh)
1907-1973 ..... **CLC 1, 2, 3, 4, 6, 9, 11,
14, 43; DA; DAB; DAC; DAM DRAM,
MST, POET; PC 1; WLC**
See also AAYA 18; CA 9-12R; 45-48;
CANR 5; CDBLB 1914-1945; DLB 10,
20; MTCW

Audiberti, Jacques
1900-1965 ...... **CLC 38; DAM DRAM**
See also CA 25-28R

Audubon, John James
1785-1851 .... **NCLC 47**

Auel, Jean M(arie)
1936- .... **CLC 31; DAM POP**
See also AAYA 7; BEST 90:4; CA 103;
CANR 21; INT CANR-21; SATA 91

Auerbach, Erich 1892-1957 ...... **TCLC 43**
See also CA 118

Augier, Emile 1820-1889 .... **NCLC 31**

August, John
See De Voto, Bernard (Augustine)

Augustine, St. 354-430 ..... **CMLC 6; DAB**

Aurelius
See Bourne, Randolph S(illiman)

Aurobindo, Sri 1872-1950 .... **TCLC 63**

Austen, Jane
1775-1817 ..... **NCLC 1, 13, 19, 33, 51;
DA; DAB; DAC; DAM MST, NOV;
WLC**
See also AAYA 19; CDBLB 1789-1832;
DLB 116

Auster, Paul 1947- .... **CLC 47**
See also CA 69-72; CANR 23, 52

Austin, Frank
See Faust, Frederick (Schiller)

Austin, Mary (Hunter)
1868-1934 .... **TCLC 25**
See also CA 109; DLB 9, 78

Autran Dourado, Waldomiro
See Dourado, (Waldomiro Freitas) Autran

Averroes 1126-1198 .... **CMLC 7**
See also DLB 115

Avicenna 980-1037 .... **CMLC 16**
See also DLB 115

Avison, Margaret
1918- .... **CLC 2, 4, 97; DAC;
DAM POET**
See also CA 17-20R; DLB 53; MTCW

Axton, David
See Koontz, Dean R(ay)

Ayckbourn, Alan
1939- ...... **CLC 5, 8, 18, 33, 74; DAB;
DAM DRAM**
See also CA 21-24R; CANR 31; DLB 13;
MTCW

Aydy, Catherine
See Tennant, Emma (Christina)

Ayme, Marcel (Andre) 1902-1967... **CLC 11**
See also CA 89-92; CLR 25; DLB 72;
SATA 91

Ayrton, Michael 1921-1975 .... **CLC 7**
See also CA 5-8R; 61-64; CANR 9, 21

Azorin .... **CLC 11**
See also Martinez Ruiz, Jose

Azuela, Mariano
1873-1952 ..... **TCLC 3; DAM MULT;
HLC**
See also CA 104; 131; HW; MTCW

Baastad, Babbis Friis
See Friis-Baastad, Babbis Ellinor

Bab
See Gilbert, W(illiam) S(chwenck)

Babbis, Eleanor
See Friis-Baastad, Babbis Ellinor

Babel, Isaak (Emmanuilovich)
1894-1941(?) ...... **TCLC 2, 13; SSC 16**
See also CA 104

Babits, Mihaly 1883-1941 .... **TCLC 14**
See also CA 114

Babur 1483-1530 .... **LC 18**

Bacchelli, Riccardo 1891-1985 ..... **CLC 19**
See also CA 29-32R; 117

Bach, Richard (David)
1936- ...... **CLC 14; DAM NOV, POP**
See also AITN 1; BEST 89:2; CA 9-12R;
CANR 18; MTCW; SATA 13

Bachman, Richard
See King, Stephen (Edwin)

Bachmann, Ingeborg 1926-1973..... **CLC 69**
See also CA 93-96; 45-48; DLB 85

Bacon, Francis 1561-1626 .... **LC 18, 32**
See also CDBLB Before 1660; DLB 151

Bacon, Roger 1214(?)-1292 ...... **CMLC 14**
See also DLB 115

Bacovia, George .... **TCLC 24**
See also Vasiliu, Gheorghe

Badanes, Jerome 1937- .... **CLC 59**

Bagehot, Walter 1826-1877 ...... **NCLC 10**
See also DLB 55

Bagnold, Enid
1889-1981 ...... **CLC 25; DAM DRAM**
See also CA 5-8R; 103; CANR 5, 40;
DLB 13, 160; MAICYA; SATA 1, 25

Bagritsky, Eduard 1895-1934 ..... **TCLC 60**

Bagrjana, Elisaveta
See Belcheva, Elisaveta

Bagryana, Elisaveta .... **CLC 10**
See also Belcheva, Elisaveta
See also DLB 147

Bailey, Paul 1937- .... **CLC 45**
See also CA 21-24R; CANR 16; DLB 14

Baillie, Joanna 1762-1851 .... **NCLC 2**
See also DLB 93

Bainbridge, Beryl (Margaret)
1933- .... **CLC 4, 5, 8, 10, 14, 18, 22, 62;
DAM NOV**
See also CA 21-24R; CANR 24, 55;
DLB 14; MTCW

Baker, Elliott 1922- .... **CLC 8**
See also CA 45-48; CANR 2

Baker, Jean H. .... **TCLC 3, 10**
See also Russell, George William

Baker, Nicholson
1957- .... **CLC 61; DAM POP**
See also CA 135

Baker, Ray Stannard 1870-1946... **TCLC 47**
See also CA 118

Baker, Russell (Wayne) 1925- . . . . . . **CLC 31**
See also BEST 89:4; CA 57-60; CANR 11,
41; MTCW

Bakhtin, M.
See Bakhtin, Mikhail Mikhailovich

Bakhtin, M. M.
See Bakhtin, Mikhail Mikhailovich

Bakhtin, Mikhail
See Bakhtin, Mikhail Mikhailovich

Bakhtin, Mikhail Mikhailovich
1895-1975 . . . . **CLC 83**
See also CA 128; 113

Bakshi, Ralph 1938(?)- . . . . **CLC 26**
See also CA 112; 138

Bakunin, Mikhail (Alexandrovich)
1814-1876 . . . . **NCLC 25, 58**

Baldwin, James (Arthur)
1924-1987 . . . . . . **CLC 1, 2, 3, 4, 5, 8, 13,
15, 17, 42, 50, 67, 90; BLC; DA; DAB;
DAC; DAM MST, MULT, NOV, POP;
DC 1; SSC 10; WLC**
See also AAYA 4; BW 1; CA 1-4R; 124;
CABS 1; CANR 3, 24;
CDALB 1941-1968; DLB 2, 7, 33;
DLBY 87; MTCW; SATA 9;
SATA-Obit 54

Ballard, J(ames) G(raham)
1930- . . . . **CLC 3, 6, 14, 36; DAM NOV,
POP; SSC 1**
See also AAYA 3; CA 5-8R; CANR 15, 39;
DLB 14; MTCW

Balmont, Konstantin (Dmitriyevich)
1867-1943 . . . . **TCLC 11**
See also CA 109

Balzac, Honore de
1799-1850 . . . . **NCLC 5, 35, 53; DA;
DAB; DAC; DAM MST, NOV; SSC 5;
WLC**
See also DLB 119

Bambara, Toni Cade
1939-1995 . . . . . . **CLC 19, 88; BLC; DA;
DAC; DAM MST, MULT**
See also AAYA 5; BW 2; CA 29-32R; 150;
CANR 24, 49; DLB 38; MTCW

Bamdad, A.
See Shamlu, Ahmad

Banat, D. R.
See Bradbury, Ray (Douglas)

Bancroft, Laura
See Baum, L(yman) Frank

Banim, John 1798-1842 . . . . **NCLC 13**
See also DLB 116, 158, 159

Banim, Michael 1796-1874 . . . . . . **NCLC 13**
See also DLB 158, 159

Banks, Iain
See Banks, Iain M(enzies)

Banks, Iain M(enzies) 1954- . . . . **CLC 34**
See also CA 123; 128; INT 128

Banks, Lynne Reid . . . . **CLC 23**
See also Reid Banks, Lynne
See also AAYA 6

Banks, Russell 1940- . . . . **CLC 37, 72**
See also CA 65-68; CAAS 15; CANR 19,
52; DLB 130

Banville, John 1945- . . . . **CLC 46**
See also CA 117; 128; DLB 14; INT 128

Banville, Theodore (Faullain) de
1832-1891 . . . . **NCLC 9**

Baraka, Amiri
1934- . . . . **CLC 1, 2, 3, 5, 10, 14, 33;
BLC; DA; DAC; DAM MST, MULT,
POET, POP; DC 6; PC 4**
See also Jones, LeRoi
See also BW 2; CA 21-24R; CABS 3;
CANR 27, 38; CDALB 1941-1968;
DLB 5, 7, 16, 38; DLBD 8; MTCW

Barbauld, Anna Laetitia
1743-1825 . . . . **NCLC 50**
See also DLB 107, 109, 142, 158

Barbellion, W. N. P. . . . . **TCLC 24**
See also Cummings, Bruce F(rederick)

Barbera, Jack (Vincent) 1945- . . . . . . **CLC 44**
See also CA 110; CANR 45

Barbey d'Aurevilly, Jules Amedee
1808-1889 . . . . **NCLC 1; SSC 17**
See also DLB 119

Barbusse, Henri 1873-1935 . . . . **TCLC 5**
See also CA 105; 154; DLB 65

Barclay, Bill
See Moorcock, Michael (John)

Barclay, William Ewert
See Moorcock, Michael (John)

Barea, Arturo 1897-1957 . . . . **TCLC 14**
See also CA 111

Barfoot, Joan 1946- . . . . **CLC 18**
See also CA 105

Baring, Maurice 1874-1945 . . . . **TCLC 8**
See also CA 105; DLB 34

Barker, Clive 1952- . . . **CLC 52; DAM POP**
See also AAYA 10; BEST 90:3; CA 121;
129; INT 129; MTCW

Barker, George Granville
1913-1991 . . . . . **CLC 8, 48; DAM POET**
See also CA 9-12R; 135; CANR 7, 38;
DLB 20; MTCW

Barker, Harley Granville
See Granville-Barker, Harley
See also DLB 10

Barker, Howard 1946- . . . . **CLC 37**
See also CA 102; DLB 13

Barker, Pat(ricia) 1943- . . . . **CLC 32, 94**
See also CA 117; 122; CANR 50; INT 122

Barlow, Joel 1754-1812 . . . . **NCLC 23**
See also DLB 37

Barnard, Mary (Ethel) 1909- . . . . . . **CLC 48**
See also CA 21-22; CAP 2

Barnes, Djuna
1892-1982 . . . **CLC 3, 4, 8, 11, 29; SSC 3**
See also CA 9-12R; 107; CANR 16, 55;
DLB 4, 9, 45; MTCW

Barnes, Julian (Patrick)
1946- . . . . **CLC 42; DAB**
See also CA 102; CANR 19, 54; DLBY 93

Barnes, Peter 1931- . . . . **CLC 5, 56**
See also CA 65-68; CAAS 12; CANR 33,
34; DLB 13; MTCW

Baroja (y Nessi), Pio
1872-1956 . . . . **TCLC 8; HLC**
See also CA 104

Baron, David
See Pinter, Harold

Baron Corvo
See Rolfe, Frederick (William Serafino
Austin Lewis Mary)

Barondess, Sue K(aufman)
1926-1977 . . . . **CLC 8**
See also Kaufman, Sue
See also CA 1-4R; 69-72; CANR 1

Baron de Teive
See Pessoa, Fernando (Antonio Nogueira)

Barres, Maurice 1862-1923 . . . . . . **TCLC 47**
See also DLB 123

Barreto, Afonso Henrique de Lima
See Lima Barreto, Afonso Henrique de

Barrett, (Roger) Syd 1946- . . . . **CLC 35**

Barrett, William (Christopher)
1913-1992 . . . . **CLC 27**
See also CA 13-16R; 139; CANR 11;
INT CANR-11

Barrie, J(ames) M(atthew)
1860-1937 . . . . **TCLC 2; DAB;
DAM DRAM**
See also CA 104; 136; CDBLB 1890-1914;
CLR 16; DLB 10, 141, 156; MAICYA;
YABC 1

Barrington, Michael
See Moorcock, Michael (John)

Barrol, Grady
See Bograd, Larry

Barry, Mike
See Malzberg, Barry N(athaniel)

Barry, Philip 1896-1949 . . . . **TCLC 11**
See also CA 109; DLB 7

Bart, Andre Schwarz
See Schwarz-Bart, Andre

Barth, John (Simmons)
1930- . . . . . . **CLC 1, 2, 3, 5, 7, 9, 10, 14,
27, 51, 89; DAM NOV; SSC 10**
See also AITN 1, 2; CA 1-4R; CABS 1;
CANR 5, 23, 49; DLB 2; MTCW

Barthelme, Donald
1931-1989 . . . . . . **CLC 1, 2, 3, 5, 6, 8, 13,
23, 46, 59; DAM NOV; SSC 2**
See also CA 21-24R; 129; CANR 20;
DLB 2; DLBY 80, 89; MTCW; SATA 7;
SATA-Obit 62

Barthelme, Frederick 1943- . . . . **CLC 36**
See also CA 114; 122; DLBY 85; INT 122

Barthes, Roland (Gerard)
1915-1980 . . . . **CLC 24, 83**
See also CA 130; 97-100; MTCW

Barzun, Jacques (Martin) 1907- . . . . **CLC 51**
See also CA 61-64; CANR 22

Bashevis, Isaac
See Singer, Isaac Bashevis

Bashkirtseff, Marie 1859-1884 . . . **NCLC 27**

Basho
See Matsuo Basho

Bass, Kingsley B., Jr.
See Bullins, Ed

Bass, Rick 1958- . . . . **CLC 79**
See also CA 126; CANR 53

Belser, Reimond Karel Maria de 1929-
See Ruyslinck, Ward
See also CA 152

Bely, Andrey .... TCLC 7; PC 11
See also Bugayev, Boris Nikolayevich

Benary, Margot
See Benary-Isbert, Margot

Benary-Isbert, Margot 1889-1979... CLC 12
See also CA 5-8R; 89-92; CANR 4;
CLR 12; MAICYA; SATA 2;
SATA-Obit 21

Benavente (y Martinez), Jacinto
1866-1954 ..... TCLC 3; DAM DRAM,
MULT
See also CA 106; 131; HW; MTCW

Benchley, Peter (Bradford)
1940- ..... CLC 4, 8; DAM NOV, POP
See also AAYA 14; AITN 2; CA 17-20R;
CANR 12, 35; MTCW; SATA 3, 89

Benchley, Robert (Charles)
1889-1945 .... TCLC 1, 55
See also CA 105; 153; DLB 11

Benda, Julien 1867-1956 .... TCLC 60
See also CA 120; 154

Benedict, Ruth 1887-1948 .... TCLC 60

Benedikt, Michael 1935- .... CLC 4, 14
See also CA 13-16R; CANR 7; DLB 5

Benet, Juan 1927-............... CLC 28
See also CA 143

Benet, Stephen Vincent
1898-1943 ...... TCLC 7; DAM POET;
SSC 10
See also CA 104; 152; DLB 4, 48, 102;
YABC 1

Benet, William Rose
1886-1950 ...... TCLC 28; DAM POET
See also CA 118; 152; DLB 45

Benford, Gregory (Albert) 1941-.... CLC 52
See also CA 69-72; CANR 12, 24, 49;
DLBY 82

Bengtsson, Frans (Gunnar)
1894-1954 .... TCLC 48

Benjamin, David
See Slavitt, David R(ytman)

Benjamin, Lois
See Gould, Lois

Benjamin, Walter 1892-1940 ...... TCLC 39

Benn, Gottfried 1886-1956......... TCLC 3
See also CA 106; 153; DLB 56

Bennett, Alan
1934- ... CLC 45, 77; DAB; DAM MST
See also CA 103; CANR 35, 55; MTCW

Bennett, (Enoch) Arnold
1867-1931 .... TCLC 5, 20
See also CA 106; CDBLB 1890-1914;
DLB 10, 34, 98, 135

Bennett, Elizabeth
See Mitchell, Margaret (Munnerlyn)

Bennett, George Harold 1930-
See Bennett, Hal
See also BW 1; CA 97-100

Bennett, Hal .... CLC 5
See also Bennett, George Harold
See also DLB 33

Bennett, Jay 1912-.............. CLC 35
See also AAYA 10; CA 69-72; CANR 11,
42; JRDA; SAAS 4; SATA 41, 87;
SATA-Brief 27

Bennett, Louise (Simone)
1919- ..... CLC 28; BLC; DAM MULT
See also BW 2; CA 151; DLB 117

Benson, E(dward) F(rederic)
1867-1940 .... TCLC 27
See also CA 114; DLB 135, 153

Benson, Jackson J. 1930-.......... CLC 34
See also CA 25-28R; DLB 111

Benson, Sally 1900-1972 .... CLC 17
See also CA 19-20; 37-40R; CAP 1;
SATA 1, 35; SATA-Obit 27

Benson, Stella 1892-1933........ TCLC 17
See also CA 117; 154; DLB 36, 162

Bentham, Jeremy 1748-1832 ..... NCLC 38
See also DLB 107, 158

Bentley, E(dmund) C(lerihew)
1875-1956 .... TCLC 12
See also CA 108; DLB 70

Bentley, Eric (Russell) 1916-...... CLC 24
See also CA 5-8R; CANR 6; INT CANR-6

Beranger, Pierre Jean de
1780-1857 .... NCLC 34

Berdyaev, Nicolas
See Berdyaev, Nikolai (Aleksandrovich)

Berdyaev, Nikolai (Aleksandrovich)
1874-1948 .... TCLC 67
See also CA 120

Berendt, John (Lawrence) 1939-.... CLC 86
See also CA 146

Berger, Colonel
See Malraux, (Georges-)Andre

Berger, John (Peter) 1926- ...... CLC 2, 19
See also CA 81-84; CANR 51; DLB 14

Berger, Melvin H. 1927-.......... CLC 12
See also CA 5-8R; CANR 4; CLR 32;
SAAS 2; SATA 5, 88

Berger, Thomas (Louis)
1924- .... CLC 3, 5, 8, 11, 18, 38;
DAM NOV
See also CA 1-4R; CANR 5, 28, 51; DLB 2;
DLBY 80; INT CANR-28; MTCW

Bergman, (Ernst) Ingmar
1918- .... CLC 16, 72
See also CA 81-84; CANR 33

Bergson, Henri 1859-1941 .... TCLC 32

Bergstein, Eleanor 1938-.......... CLC 4
See also CA 53-56; CANR 5

Berkoff, Steven 1937-............. CLC 56
See also CA 104

Bermant, Chaim (Icyk) 1929- ...... CLC 40
See also CA 57-60; CANR 6, 31

Bern, Victoria
See Fisher, M(ary) F(rances) K(ennedy)

Bernanos, (Paul Louis) Georges
1888-1948 .... TCLC 3
See also CA 104; 130; DLB 72

Bernard, April 1956- .... CLC 59
See also CA 131

Berne, Victoria
See Fisher, M(ary) F(rances) K(ennedy)

Bernhard, Thomas
1931-1989 .... CLC 3, 32, 61
See also CA 85-88; 127; CANR 32;
DLB 85, 124; MTCW

Berriault, Gina 1926-............. CLC 54
See also CA 116; 129; DLB 130

Berrigan, Daniel 1921-............. CLC 4
See also CA 33-36R; CAAS 1; CANR 11,
43; DLB 5

Berrigan, Edmund Joseph Michael, Jr.
1934-1983
See Berrigan, Ted
See also CA 61-64; 110; CANR 14

Berrigan, Ted..................... CLC 37
See also Berrigan, Edmund Joseph Michael,
Jr.
See also DLB 5, 169

Berry, Charles Edward Anderson 1931-
See Berry, Chuck
See also CA 115

Berry, Chuck .... CLC 17
See also Berry, Charles Edward Anderson

Berry, Jonas
See Ashbery, John (Lawrence)

Berry, Wendell (Erdman)
1934- .... CLC 4, 6, 8, 27, 46;
DAM POET
See also AITN 1; CA 73-76; CANR 50;
DLB 5, 6

Berryman, John
1914-1972 ...... CLC 1, 2, 3, 4, 6, 8, 10,
13, 25, 62; DAM POET
See also CA 13-16; 33-36R; CABS 2;
CANR 35; CAP 1; CDALB 1941-1968;
DLB 48; MTCW

Bertolucci, Bernardo 1940- .... CLC 16
See also CA 106

Bertrand, Aloysius 1807-1841 .... NCLC 31

Bertran de Born c. 1140-1215..... CMLC 5

Besant, Annie (Wood) 1847-1933 ... TCLC 9
See also CA 105

Bessie, Alvah 1904-1985........... CLC 23
See also CA 5-8R; 116; CANR 2; DLB 26

Bethlen, T. D.
See Silverberg, Robert

Beti, Mongo.... CLC 27; BLC; DAM MULT
See also Biyidi, Alexandre

Betjeman, John
1906-1984 .... CLC 2, 6, 10, 34, 43;
DAB; DAM MST, POET
See also CA 9-12R; 112; CANR 33;
CDBLB 1945-1960; DLB 20; DLBY 84;
MTCW

Bettelheim, Bruno 1903-1990 ...... CLC 79
See also CA 81-84; 131; CANR 23; MTCW

Betti, Ugo 1892-1953 .... TCLC 5
See also CA 104

Betts, Doris (Waugh) 1932-.... CLC 3, 6, 28
See also CA 13-16R; CANR 9; DLBY 82;
INT CANR-9

Bevan, Alistair
See Roberts, Keith (John Kingston)

Bialik, Chaim Nachman
1873-1934 .... TCLC 25

Bickerstaff, Isaac
See Swift, Jonathan

Bidart, Frank 1939- . . . . **CLC 33**
See also CA 140

Bienek, Horst 1930- . . . . **CLC 7, 11**
See also CA 73-76; DLB 75

Bierce, Ambrose (Gwinett)
1842-1914(?) . . . . **TCLC 1, 7, 44; DA;**
DAC; DAM MST; SSC 9; WLC
See also CA 104; 139; CDALB 1865-1917;
DLB 11, 12, 23, 71, 74

Biggers, Earl Derr 1884-1933 . . . . . **TCLC 65**
See also CA 108; 153

Billings, Josh
See Shaw, Henry Wheeler

Billington, (Lady) Rachel (Mary)
1942- . . . . **CLC 43**
See also AITN 2; CA 33-36R; CANR 44

Binyon, T(imothy) J(ohn) 1936- . . . . **CLC 34**
See also CA 111; CANR 28

Bioy Casares, Adolfo
1914- . . . . **CLC 4, 8, 13, 88;**
DAM MULT; HLC; SSC 17
See also CA 29-32R; CANR 19, 43;
DLB 113; HW; MTCW

Bird, Cordwainer
See Ellison, Harlan (Jay)

Bird, Robert Montgomery
1806-1854 . . . . **NCLC 1**

Birney, (Alfred) Earle
1904- . . . . **CLC 1, 4, 6, 11; DAC;**
DAM MST, POET
See also CA 1-4R; CANR 5, 20; DLB 88;
MTCW

Bishop, Elizabeth
1911-1979 . . . . . . **CLC 1, 4, 9, 13, 15, 32;**
DA; DAC; DAM MST, POET; PC 3
See also CA 5-8R; 89-92; CABS 2;
CANR 26; CDALB 1968-1988; DLB 5,
169; MTCW; SATA-Obit 24

Bishop, John 1935- . . . . **CLC 10**
See also CA 105

Bissett, Bill 1939- . . . . **CLC 18; PC 14**
See also CA 69-72; CAAS 19; CANR 15;
DLB 53; MTCW

Bitov, Andrei (Georgievich) 1937- . . . **CLC 57**
See also CA 142

Biyidi, Alexandre 1932-
See Beti, Mongo
See also BW 1; CA 114; 124; MTCW

Bjarme, Brynjolf
See Ibsen, Henrik (Johan)

Bjornson, Bjornstjerne (Martinius)
1832-1910 . . . . **TCLC 7, 37**
See also CA 104

Black, Robert
See Holdstock, Robert P.

Blackburn, Paul 1926-1971 . . . . . . **CLC 9, 43**
See also CA 81-84; 33-36R; CANR 34;
DLB 16; DLBY 81

Black Elk
1863-1950 . . . . . **TCLC 33; DAM MULT**
See also CA 144; NNAL

Black Hobart
See Sanders, (James) Ed(ward)

Blacklin, Malcolm
See Chambers, Aidan

Blackmore, R(ichard) D(oddridge)
1825-1900 . . . . **TCLC 27**
See also CA 120; DLB 18

Blackmur, R(ichard) P(almer)
1904-1965 . . . . **CLC 2, 24**
See also CA 11-12; 25-28R; CAP 1; DLB 63

Black Tarantula
See Acker, Kathy

Blackwood, Algernon (Henry)
1869-1951 . . . . **TCLC 5**
See also CA 105; 150; DLB 153, 156

Blackwood, Caroline 1931-1996 . . . **CLC 6, 9**
See also CA 85-88; 151; CANR 32;
DLB 14; MTCW

Blade, Alexander
See Hamilton, Edmond; Silverberg, Robert

Blaga, Lucian 1895-1961 . . . . **CLC 75**

Blair, Eric (Arthur) 1903-1950
See Orwell, George
See also CA 104; 132; DA; DAB; DAC;
DAM MST, NOV; MTCW; SATA 29

Blais, Marie-Claire
1939- . . . . **CLC 2, 4, 6, 13, 22; DAC;**
DAM MST
See also CA 21-24R; CAAS 4; CANR 38;
DLB 53; MTCW

Blaise, Clark 1940- . . . . **CLC 29**
See also AITN 2; CA 53-56; CAAS 3;
CANR 5; DLB 53

Blake, Nicholas
See Day Lewis, C(ecil)
See also DLB 77

Blake, William
1757-1827 . . . . **NCLC 13, 37, 57; DA;**
DAB; DAC; DAM MST, POET; PC 12;
WLC
See also CDBLB 1789-1832; DLB 93, 163;
MAICYA; SATA 30

Blake, William J(ames) 1894-1969 . . . **PC 12**
See also CA 5-8R; 25-28R

Blasco Ibanez, Vicente
1867-1928 . . . . **TCLC 12; DAM NOV**
See also CA 110; 131; HW; MTCW

Blatty, William Peter
1928- . . . . **CLC 2; DAM POP**
See also CA 5-8R; CANR 9

Bleeck, Oliver
See Thomas, Ross (Elmore)

Blessing, Lee 1949- . . . . **CLC 54**

Blish, James (Benjamin)
1921-1975 . . . . **CLC 14**
See also CA 1-4R; 57-60; CANR 3; DLB 8;
MTCW; SATA 66

Bliss, Reginald
See Wells, H(erbert) G(eorge)

Blixen, Karen (Christentze Dinesen)
1885-1962
See Dinesen, Isak
See also CA 25-28; CANR 22, 50; CAP 2;
MTCW; SATA 44

Bloch, Robert (Albert) 1917-1994 . . . **CLC 33**
See also CA 5-8R; 146; CAAS 20; CANR 5;
DLB 44; INT CANR-5; SATA 12;
SATA-Obit 82

Blok, Alexander (Alexandrovich)
1880-1921 . . . . **TCLC 5**
See also CA 104

Blom, Jan
See Breytenbach, Breyten

Bloom, Harold 1930- . . . . **CLC 24**
See also CA 13-16R; CANR 39; DLB 67

Bloomfield, Aurelius
See Bourne, Randolph S(illiman)

Blount, Roy (Alton), Jr. 1941- . . . . . **CLC 38**
See also CA 53-56; CANR 10, 28;
INT CANR-28; MTCW

Bloy, Leon 1846-1917 . . . . **TCLC 22**
See also CA 121; DLB 123

Blume, Judy (Sussman)
1938- . . . **CLC 12, 30; DAM NOV, POP**
See also AAYA 3; CA 29-32R; CANR 13,
37; CLR 2, 15; DLB 52; JRDA;
MAICYA; MTCW; SATA 2, 31, 79

Blunden, Edmund (Charles)
1896-1974 . . . . **CLC 2, 56**
See also CA 17-18; 45-48; CANR 54;
CAP 2; DLB 20, 100, 155; MTCW

Bly, Robert (Elwood)
1926- . . . . **CLC 1, 2, 5, 10, 15, 38;**
DAM POET
See also CA 5-8R; CANR 41; DLB 5;
MTCW

Boas, Franz 1858-1942 . . . . **TCLC 56**
See also CA 115

Bobette
See Simenon, Georges (Jacques Christian)

Boccaccio, Giovanni
1313-1375 . . . . **CMLC 13; SSC 10**

Bochco, Steven 1943- . . . . **CLC 35**
See also AAYA 11; CA 124; 138

Bodenheim, Maxwell 1892-1954 . . . **TCLC 44**
See also CA 110; DLB 9, 45

Bodker, Cecil 1927- . . . . **CLC 21**
See also CA 73-76; CANR 13, 44; CLR 23;
MAICYA; SATA 14

Boell, Heinrich (Theodor)
1917-1985 . . . . **CLC 2, 3, 6, 9, 11, 15, 27,**
32, 72; DA; DAB; DAC; DAM MST,
NOV; SSC 23; WLC
See also CA 21-24R; 116; CANR 24;
DLB 69; DLBY 85; MTCW

Boerne, Alfred
See Doeblin, Alfred

Boethius 480(?)-524(?) . . . . **CMLC 15**
See also DLB 115

Bogan, Louise
1897-1970 . . . . **CLC 4, 39, 46, 93;**
DAM POET; PC 12
See also CA 73-76; 25-28R; CANR 33;
DLB 45, 169; MTCW

Bogarde, Dirk . . . . **CLC 19**
See also Van Den Bogarde, Derek Jules
Gaspard Ulric Niven
See also DLB 14

Bogosian, Eric 1953- . . . . **CLC 45**
See also CA 138

Bograd, Larry 1953- . . . . **CLC 35**
See also CA 93-96; SAAS 21; SATA 33, 89

Boiardo, Matteo Maria 1441-1494 . . . . **LC 6**

Boileau-Despreaux, Nicolas
1636-1711 . . . . **LC 3**

Bojer, Johan 1872-1959 . . . . **TCLC 64**

Boland, Eavan (Aisling)
1944- . . . . **CLC 40, 67; DAM POET**
See also CA 143; DLB 40

Bolt, Lee
See Faust, Frederick (Schiller)

Bolt, Robert (Oxton)
1924-1995 . . . . . . **CLC 14; DAM DRAM**
See also CA 17-20R; 147; CANR 35;
DLB 13; MTCW

Bombet, Louis-Alexandre-Cesar
See Stendhal

Bomkauf
See Kaufman, Bob (Garnell)

Bonaventura . . . . **NCLC 35**
See also DLB 90

Bond, Edward
1934- . . . **CLC 4, 6, 13, 23; DAM DRAM**
See also CA 25-28R; CANR 38; DLB 13;
MTCW

Bonham, Frank 1914-1989 . . . . **CLC 12**
See also AAYA 1; CA 9-12R; CANR 4, 36;
JRDA; MAICYA; SAAS 3; SATA 1, 49;
SATA-Obit 62

Bonnefoy, Yves
1923- . . . . . . **CLC 9, 15, 58; DAM MST,**
POET
See also CA 85-88; CANR 33; MTCW

Bontemps, Arna(ud Wendell)
1902-1973 . . . . **CLC 1, 18; BLC;**
DAM MULT, NOV, POET
See also BW 1; CA 1-4R; 41-44R; CANR 4,
35; CLR 6; DLB 48, 51; JRDA;
MAICYA; MTCW; SATA 2, 44;
SATA-Obit 24

Booth, Martin 1944- . . . . **CLC 13**
See also CA 93-96; CAAS 2

Booth, Philip 1925- . . . . **CLC 23**
See also CA 5-8R; CANR 5; DLBY 82

Booth, Wayne C(layson) 1921- . . . . . **CLC 24**
See also CA 1-4R; CAAS 5; CANR 3, 43;
DLB 67

Borchert, Wolfgang 1921-1947 . . . . . **TCLC 5**
See also CA 104; DLB 69, 124

Borel, Petrus 1809-1859 . . . . **NCLC 41**

Borges, Jorge Luis
1899-1986 . . . **CLC 1, 2, 3, 4, 6, 8, 9, 10,**
13, 19, 44, 48, 83; DA; DAB; DAC;
DAM MST, MULT; HLC; SSC 4; WLC
See also AAYA 19; CA 21-24R; CANR 19,
33; DLB 113; DLBY 86; HW; MTCW

Borowski, Tadeusz 1922-1951 . . . . . . **TCLC 9**
See also CA 106; 154

Borrow, George (Henry)
1803-1881 . . . . **NCLC 9**
See also DLB 21, 55, 166

Bosman, Herman Charles
1905-1951 . . . . **TCLC 49**

Bosschere, Jean de 1878(?)-1953 . . . **TCLC 19**
See also CA 115

Boswell, James
1740-1795 . . . . . **LC 4; DA; DAB; DAC;**
DAM MST; WLC
See also CDBLB 1660-1789; DLB 104, 142

Bottoms, David 1949- . . . . **CLC 53**
See also CA 105; CANR 22; DLB 120;
DLBY 83

Boucicault, Dion 1820-1890 . . . . . . **NCLC 41**

Boucolon, Maryse 1937(?)-
See Conde, Maryse
See also CA 110; CANR 30, 53

Bourget, Paul (Charles Joseph)
1852-1935 . . . . **TCLC 12**
See also CA 107; DLB 123

Bourjaily, Vance (Nye) 1922- . . . . **CLC 8, 62**
See also CA 1-4R; CAAS 1; CANR 2;
DLB 2, 143

Bourne, Randolph S(illiman)
1886-1918 . . . . **TCLC 16**
See also CA 117; DLB 63

Bova, Ben(jamin William) 1932- . . . . **CLC 45**
See also AAYA 16; CA 5-8R; CAAS 18;
CANR 11; CLR 3; DLBY 81;
INT CANR-11; MAICYA; MTCW;
SATA 6, 68

Bowen, Elizabeth (Dorothea Cole)
1899-1973 . . . . . . **CLC 1, 3, 6, 11, 15, 22;**
DAM NOV; SSC 3
See also CA 17-18; 41-44R; CANR 35;
CAP 2; CDBLB 1945-1960; DLB 15, 162;
MTCW

Bowering, George 1935- . . . . **CLC 15, 47**
See also CA 21-24R; CAAS 16; CANR 10;
DLB 53

Bowering, Marilyn R(uthe) 1949- . . . **CLC 32**
See also CA 101; CANR 49

Bowers, Edgar 1924- . . . . **CLC 9**
See also CA 5-8R; CANR 24; DLB 5

Bowie, David . . . . **CLC 17**
See also Jones, David Robert

Bowles, Jane (Sydney)
1917-1973 . . . . **CLC 3, 68**
See also CA 19-20; 41-44R; CAP 2

Bowles, Paul (Frederick)
1910- . . . . **CLC 1, 2, 19, 53; SSC 3**
See also CA 1-4R; CAAS 1; CANR 1, 19,
50; DLB 5, 6; MTCW

Box, Edgar
See Vidal, Gore

Boyd, Nancy
See Millay, Edna St. Vincent

Boyd, William 1952- . . . . **CLC 28, 53, 70**
See also CA 114; 120; CANR 51

Boyle, Kay
1902-1992 . . . . . **CLC 1, 5, 19, 58; SSC 5**
See also CA 13-16R; 140; CAAS 1;
CANR 29; DLB 4, 9, 48, 86; DLBY 93;
MTCW

Boyle, Mark
See Kienzle, William X(avier)

Boyle, Patrick 1905-1982 . . . . **CLC 19**
See also CA 127

Boyle, T. C. 1948-
See Boyle, T(homas) Coraghessan

Boyle, T(homas) Coraghessan
1948- . . . . . **CLC 36, 55, 90; DAM POP;**
SSC 16
See also BEST 90:4; CA 120; CANR 44;
DLBY 86

Boz
See Dickens, Charles (John Huffam)

Brackenridge, Hugh Henry
1748-1816 . . . . **NCLC 7**
See also DLB 11, 37

Bradbury, Edward P.
See Moorcock, Michael (John)

Bradbury, Malcolm (Stanley)
1932- . . . . **CLC 32, 61; DAM NOV**
See also CA 1-4R; CANR 1, 33; DLB 14;
MTCW

Bradbury, Ray (Douglas)
1920- . . . . . **CLC 1, 3, 10, 15, 42, 98; DA;**
DAB; DAC; DAM MST, NOV, POP;
WLC
See also AAYA 15; AITN 1, 2; CA 1-4R;
CANR 2, 30; CDALB 1968-1988; DLB 2,
8; INT CANR-30; MTCW; SATA 11, 64

Bradford, Gamaliel 1863-1932 . . . . . **TCLC 36**
See also DLB 17

Bradley, David (Henry, Jr.)
1950- . . . . . **CLC 23; BLC; DAM MULT**
See also BW 1; CA 104; CANR 26; DLB 33

Bradley, John Ed(mund, Jr.)
1958- . . . . **CLC 55**
See also CA 139

Bradley, Marion Zimmer
1930- . . . . **CLC 30; DAM POP**
See also AAYA 9; CA 57-60; CAAS 10;
CANR 7, 31, 51; DLB 8; MTCW;
SATA 90

Bradstreet, Anne
1612(?)-1672 . . . . . . **LC 4, 30; DA; DAC;**
DAM MST, POET; PC 10
See also CDALB 1640-1865; DLB 24

Brady, Joan 1939- . . . . **CLC 86**
See also CA 141

Bragg, Melvyn 1939- . . . . **CLC 10**
See also BEST 89:3; CA 57-60; CANR 10,
48; DLB 14

Braine, John (Gerard)
1922-1986 . . . . **CLC 1, 3, 41**
See also CA 1-4R; 120; CANR 1, 33;
CDBLB 1945-1960; DLB 15; DLBY 86;
MTCW

Brammer, William 1930(?)-1978 . . . . **CLC 31**
See also CA 77-80

Brancati, Vitaliano 1907-1954 . . . . . **TCLC 12**
See also CA 109

Brancato, Robin F(idler) 1936- . . . . . **CLC 35**
See also AAYA 9; CA 69-72; CANR 11,
45; CLR 32; JRDA; SAAS 9; SATA 23

Brand, Max
See Faust, Frederick (Schiller)

Brand, Millen 1906-1980 . . . . **CLC 7**
See also CA 21-24R; 97-100

Branden, Barbara . . . . **CLC 44**
See also CA 148

Brown, George Mackay
1921-1996 .... CLC **5, 48**
See also CA 21-24R; 151; CAAS 6;
CANR 12, 37; DLB 14, 27, 139; MTCW;
SATA 35

Brown, (William) Larry 1951-...... CLC **73**
See also CA 130; 134; INT 133

Brown, Moses
See Barrett, William (Christopher)

Brown, Rita Mae
1944- ..... CLC **18, 43, 79; DAM NOV,
POP**
See also CA 45-48; CANR 2, 11, 35;
INT CANR-11; MTCW

Brown, Roderick (Langmere) Haig-
See Haig-Brown, Roderick (Langmere)

Brown, Rosellen 1939-............ CLC **32**
See also CA 77-80; CAAS 10; CANR 14, 44

Brown, Sterling Allen
1901-1989 .... CLC **1, 23, 59; BLC;
DAM MULT, POET**
See also BW 1; CA 85-88; 127; CANR 26;
DLB 48, 51, 63; MTCW

Brown, Will
See Ainsworth, William Harrison

Brown, William Wells
1813-1884 .... NCLC **2; BLC;
DAM MULT; DC 1**
See also DLB 3, 50

Browne, (Clyde) Jackson 1948(?)-... CLC **21**
See also CA 120

Browning, Elizabeth Barrett
1806-1861 ..... NCLC **1, 16; DA; DAB;
DAC; DAM MST, POET; PC 6; WLC**
See also CDBLB 1832-1890; DLB 32

Browning, Robert
1812-1889 .... NCLC **19; DA; DAB;
DAC; DAM MST, POET; PC 2**
See also CDBLB 1832-1890; DLB 32, 163;
YABC 1

Browning, Tod 1882-1962 .... CLC **16**
See also CA 141; 117

Brownson, Orestes (Augustus)
1803-1876 .... NCLC **50**

Bruccoli, Matthew J(oseph) 1931- .. CLC **34**
See also CA 9-12R; CANR 7; DLB 103

Bruce, Lenny.................... CLC 21
See also Schneider, Leonard Alfred

Bruin, John
See Brutus, Dennis

Brulard, Henri
See Stendhal

Brulls, Christian
See Simenon, Georges (Jacques Christian)

Brunner, John (Kilian Houston)
1934-1995 ...... CLC **8, 10; DAM POP**
See also CA 1-4R; 149; CAAS 8; CANR 2,
37; MTCW

Bruno, Giordano 1548-1600........ LC **27**

Brutus, Dennis
1924- ..... CLC **43; BLC; DAM MULT,
POET**
See also BW 2; CA 49-52; CAAS 14;
CANR 2, 27, 42; DLB 117

Bryan, C(ourtlandt) D(ixon) B(arnes)
1936- .... CLC **29**
See also CA 73-76; CANR 13;
INT CANR-13

Bryan, Michael
See Moore, Brian

Bryant, William Cullen
1794-1878 ..... NCLC **6, 46; DA; DAB;
DAC; DAM MST, POET**
See also CDALB 1640-1865; DLB 3, 43, 59

Bryusov, Valery Yakovlevich
1873-1924 .... TCLC **10**
See also CA 107

Buchan, John
1875-1940 .... TCLC **41; DAB;
DAM POP**
See also CA 108; 145; DLB 34, 70, 156;
YABC 2

Buchanan, George 1506-1582 .... LC **4**

Buchheim, Lothar-Guenther 1918- ... CLC **6**
See also CA 85-88

Buchner, (Karl) Georg
1813-1837 .... NCLC **26**

Buchwald, Art(hur) 1925-.......... CLC **33**
See also AITN 1; CA 5-8R; CANR 21;
MTCW; SATA 10

Buck, Pearl S(ydenstricker)
1892-1973 .... CLC **7, 11, 18; DA; DAB;
DAC; DAM MST, NOV**
See also AITN 1; CA 1-4R; 41-44R;
CANR 1, 34; DLB 9, 102; MTCW;
SATA 1, 25

Buckler, Ernest
1908-1984 .. CLC **13; DAC; DAM MST**
See also CA 11-12; 114; CAP 1; DLB 68;
SATA 47

Buckley, Vincent (Thomas)
1925-1988 .... CLC **57**
See also CA 101

Buckley, William F(rank), Jr.
1925- .... CLC **7, 18, 37; DAM POP**
See also AITN 1; CA 1-4R; CANR 1, 24,
53; DLB 137; DLBY 80; INT CANR-24;
MTCW

Buechner, (Carl) Frederick
1926- .... CLC **2, 4, 6, 9; DAM NOV**
See also CA 13-16R; CANR 11, 39;
DLBY 80; INT CANR-11; MTCW

Buell, John (Edward) 1927-........ CLC **10**
See also CA 1-4R; DLB 53

Buero Vallejo, Antonio 1916- ... CLC **15, 46**
See also CA 106; CANR 24, 49; HW;
MTCW

Bufalino, Gesualdo 1920(?)-........ CLC **74**

Bugayev, Boris Nikolayevich 1880-1934
See Bely, Andrey
See also CA 104

Bukowski, Charles
1920-1994 .... CLC **2, 5, 9, 41, 82;
DAM NOV, POET**
See also CA 17-20R; 144; CANR 40;
DLB 5, 130, 169; MTCW

Bulgakov, Mikhail (Afanas'evich)
1891-1940 .... TCLC **2, 16;
DAM DRAM, NOV; SSC 18**
See also CA 105; 152

Bulgya, Alexander Alexandrovich
1901-1956 .... TCLC **53**
See also Fadeyev, Alexander
See also CA 117

Bullins, Ed
1935- .... CLC **1, 5, 7; BLC;
DAM DRAM, MULT; DC 6**
See also BW 2; CA 49-52; CAAS 16;
CANR 24, 46; DLB 7, 38; MTCW

Bulwer-Lytton, Edward (George Earle Lytton)
1803-1873 .... NCLC **1, 45**
See also DLB 21

Bunin, Ivan Alexeyevich
1870-1953 .... TCLC **6; SSC 5**
See also CA 104

Bunting, Basil
1900-1985 .... CLC **10, 39, 47;
DAM POET**
See also CA 53-56; 115; CANR 7; DLB 20

Bunuel, Luis
1900-1983 .... CLC **16, 80;
DAM MULT; HLC**
See also CA 101; 110; CANR 32; HW

Bunyan, John
1628-1688 ...... LC **4; DA; DAB; DAC;
DAM MST; WLC**
See also CDBLB 1660-1789; DLB 39

Burckhardt, Jacob (Christoph)
1818-1897 .... NCLC **49**

Burford, Eleanor
See Hibbert, Eleanor Alice Burford

Burgess, Anthony
. CLC **1, 2, 4, 5, 8, 10, 13, 15, 22, 40, 62,
81, 94; DAB**
See also Wilson, John (Anthony) Burgess
See also AITN 1; CDBLB 1960 to Present;
DLB 14

Burke, Edmund
1729(?)-1797 ...... LC **7, 36; DA; DAB;
DAC; DAM MST; WLC**
See also DLB 104

Burke, Kenneth (Duva)
1897-1993 .... CLC **2, 24**
See also CA 5-8R; 143; CANR 39; DLB 45,
63; MTCW

Burke, Leda
See Garnett, David

Burke, Ralph
See Silverberg, Robert

Burke, Thomas 1886-1945........ TCLC **63**
See also CA 113

Burney, Fanny 1752-1840 .... NCLC **12, 54**
See also DLB 39

Burns, Robert 1759-1796............ PC **6**
See also CDBLB 1789-1832; DA; DAB;
DAC; DAM MST, POET; DLB 109;
WLC

Burns, Tex
See L'Amour, Louis (Dearborn)

Burnshaw, Stanley 1906-..... CLC **3, 13, 44**
See also CA 9-12R; DLB 48

Burr, Anne 1937- .... CLC **6**
See also CA 25-28R

Capote, Truman
1924-1984 ...... **CLC 1, 3, 8, 13, 19, 34, 38, 58; DA; DAB; DAC; DAM MST, NOV, POP; SSC 2; WLC**
See also CA 5-8R; 113; CDALB 1941-1968; DLB 2; DLBY 80, 84; MTCW; SATA 91

Capra, Frank 1897-1991.......... **CLC 16**
See also CA 61-64; 135

Caputo, Philip 1941-.............. **CLC 32**
See also CA 73-76; CANR 40

Card, Orson Scott
1951- ...... **CLC 44, 47, 50; DAM POP**
See also AAYA 11; CA 102; CANR 27, 47; INT CANR-27; MTCW; SATA 83

Cardenal, Ernesto
1925- .... **CLC 31; DAM MULT, POET; HLC**
See also CA 49-52; CANR 2, 32; HW; MTCW

Cardozo, Benjamin N(athan)
1870-1938 .... **TCLC 65**
See also CA 117

Carducci, Giosue 1835-1907....... **TCLC 32**

Carew, Thomas 1595(?)-1640....... **LC 13**
See also DLB 126

Carey, Ernestine Gilbreth 1908-.... **CLC 17**
See also CA 5-8R; SATA 2

Carey, Peter 1943-......... **CLC 40, 55, 96**
See also CA 123; 127; CANR 53; INT 127; MTCW

Carleton, William 1794-1869...... **NCLC 3**
See also DLB 159

Carlisle, Henry (Coffin) 1926-...... **CLC 33**
See also CA 13-16R; CANR 15

Carlsen, Chris
See Holdstock, Robert P.

Carlson, Ron(ald F.) 1947-......... **CLC 54**
See also CA 105; CANR 27

Carlyle, Thomas
1795-1881 .... **NCLC 22; DA; DAB; DAC; DAM MST**
See also CDBLB 1789-1832; DLB 55; 144

Carman, (William) Bliss
1861-1929 .... **TCLC 7; DAC**
See also CA 104; 152; DLB 92

Carnegie, Dale 1888-1955 .... **TCLC 53**

Carossa, Hans 1878-1956......... **TCLC 48**
See also DLB 66

Carpenter, Don(ald Richard)
1931-1995 .... **CLC 41**
See also CA 45-48; 149; CANR 1

Carpentier (y Valmont), Alejo
1904-1980 .... **CLC 8, 11, 38; DAM MULT; HLC**
See also CA 65-68; 97-100; CANR 11; DLB 113; HW

Carr, Caleb 1955(?)-.............. **CLC 86**
See also CA 147

Carr, Emily 1871-1945........... **TCLC 32**
See also DLB 68

Carr, John Dickson 1906-1977 ...... **CLC 3**
See also CA 49-52; 69-72; CANR 3, 33; MTCW

Carr, Philippa
See Hibbert, Eleanor Alice Burford

Carr, Virginia Spencer 1929-....... **CLC 34**
See also CA 61-64; DLB 111

Carrere, Emmanuel 1957- .... **CLC 89**

Carrier, Roch
1937- ... **CLC 13, 78; DAC; DAM MST**
See also CA 130; DLB 53

Carroll, James P. 1943(?)-......... **CLC 38**
See also CA 81-84

Carroll, Jim 1951- .... **CLC 35**
See also AAYA 17; CA 45-48; CANR 42

Carroll, Lewis .... **NCLC 2, 53; WLC**
See also Dodgson, Charles Lutwidge
See also CDBLB 1832-1890; CLR 2, 18; DLB 18, 163; JRDA

Carroll, Paul Vincent 1900-1968.... **CLC 10**
See also CA 9-12R; 25-28R; DLB 10

Carruth, Hayden
1921- ...... **CLC 4, 7, 10, 18, 84; PC 10**
See also CA 9-12R; CANR 4, 38; DLB 5, 165; INT CANR-4; MTCW; SATA 47

Carson, Rachel Louise
1907-1964 .... **CLC 71; DAM POP**
See also CA 77-80; CANR 35; MTCW; SATA 23

Carter, Angela (Olive)
1940-1992 ...... **CLC 5, 41, 76; SSC 13**
See also CA 53-56; 136; CANR 12, 36; DLB 14; MTCW; SATA 66; SATA-Obit 70

Carter, Nick
See Smith, Martin Cruz

Carver, Raymond
1938-1988 .... **CLC 22, 36, 53, 55; DAM NOV; SSC 8**
See also CA 33-36R; 126; CANR 17, 34; DLB 130; DLBY 84, 88; MTCW

Cary, Elizabeth, Lady Falkland
1585-1639 .... **LC 30**

Cary, (Arthur) Joyce (Lunel)
1888-1957 .... **TCLC 1, 29**
See also CA 104; CDBLB 1914-1945; DLB 15, 100

Casanova de Seingalt, Giovanni Jacopo
1725-1798 .... **LC 13**

Casares, Adolfo Bioy
See Bioy Casares, Adolfo

Casely-Hayford, J(oseph) E(phraim)
1866-1930 .... **TCLC 24; BLC; DAM MULT**
See also BW 2; CA 123; 152

Casey, John (Dudley) 1939-....... **CLC 59**
See also BEST 90:2; CA 69-72; CANR 23

Casey, Michael 1947-.............. **CLC 2**
See also CA 65-68; DLB 5

Casey, Patrick
See Thurman, Wallace (Henry)

Casey, Warren (Peter) 1935-1988... **CLC 12**
See also CA 101; 127; INT 101

Casona, Alejandro................. **CLC 49**
See also Alvarez, Alejandro Rodriguez

Cassavetes, John 1929-1989........ **CLC 20**
See also CA 85-88; 127

Cassill, R(onald) V(erlin) 1919-... **CLC 4, 23**
See also CA 9-12R; CAAS 1; CANR 7, 45; DLB 6

Cassirer, Ernst 1874-1945 .... **TCLC 61**

Cassity, (Allen) Turner 1929- .... **CLC 6, 42**
See also CA 17-20R; CAAS 8; CANR 11; DLB 105

Castaneda, Carlos 1931(?)-......... **CLC 12**
See also CA 25-28R; CANR 32; HW; MTCW

Castedo, Elena 1937- .... **CLC 65**
See also CA 132

Castedo-Ellerman, Elena
See Castedo, Elena

Castellanos, Rosario
1925-1974 ...... **CLC 66; DAM MULT; HLC**
See also CA 131; 53-56; DLB 113; HW

Castelvetro, Lodovico 1505-1571..... **LC 12**

Castiglione, Baldassare 1478-1529 ... **LC 12**

Castle, Robert
See Hamilton, Edmond

Castro, Guillen de 1569-1631........ **LC 19**

Castro, Rosalia de
1837-1885 ...... **NCLC 3; DAM MULT**

Cather, Willa
See Cather, Willa Sibert

Cather, Willa Sibert
1873-1947 .... **TCLC 1, 11, 31; DA; DAB; DAC; DAM MST, NOV; SSC 2; WLC**
See also CA 104; 128; CDALB 1865-1917; DLB 9, 54, 78; DLBD 1; MTCW; SATA 30

Catton, (Charles) Bruce
1899-1978 .... **CLC 35**
See also AITN 1; CA 5-8R; 81-84; CANR 7; DLB 17; SATA 2; SATA-Obit 24

Catullus c. 84B.C.-c. 54B.C. ..... **CMLC 18**

Cauldwell, Frank
See King, Francis (Henry)

Caunitz, William J. 1933-1996 ..... **CLC 34**
See also BEST 89:3; CA 125; 130; 152; INT 130

Causley, Charles (Stanley) 1917-..... **CLC 7**
See also CA 9-12R; CANR 5, 35; CLR 30; DLB 27; MTCW; SATA 3, 66

Caute, David 1936-.... **CLC 29; DAM NOV**
See also CA 1-4R; CAAS 4; CANR 1, 33; DLB 14

Cavafy, C(onstantine) P(eter)
1863-1933 .... **TCLC 2, 7; DAM POET**
See also Kavafis, Konstantinos Petrou
See also CA 148

Cavallo, Evelyn
See Spark, Muriel (Sarah)

Cavanna, Betty .... **CLC 12**
See also Harrison, Elizabeth Cavanna
See also JRDA; MAICYA; SAAS 4; SATA 1, 30

Cavendish, Margaret Lucas
1623-1673 .... **LC 30**
See also DLB 131

Caxton, William 1421(?)-1491(?)..... **LC 17**
See also DLB 170

Cayrol, Jean 1911-............... **CLC 11**
See also CA 89-92; DLB 83

Cela, Camilo Jose
1916- ..... **CLC 4, 13, 59; DAM MULT;**
HLC
See also BEST 90:2; CA 21-24R; CAAS 10;
CANR 21, 32; DLBY 89; HW; MTCW

Celan, Paul ...... **CLC 10, 19, 53, 82; PC 10**
See also Antschel, Paul
See also DLB 69

Celine, Louis-Ferdinand
.... **CLC 1, 3, 4, 7, 9, 15, 47**
See also Destouches, Louis-Ferdinand
See also DLB 72

Cellini, Benvenuto 1500-1571 .... **LC 7**

Cendrars, Blaise .... **CLC 18**
See also Sauser-Hall, Frederic

Cernuda (y Bidon), Luis
1902-1963 .... **CLC 54; DAM POET**
See also CA 131; 89-92; DLB 134; HW

Cervantes (Saavedra), Miguel de
1547-1616 .... **LC 6, 23; DA; DAB;**
DAC; DAM MST, NOV; SSC 12; WLC

Cesaire, Aime (Fernand)
1913-.............. **CLC 19, 32; BLC;**
DAM MULT, POET
See also BW 2; CA 65-68; CANR 24, 43;
MTCW

Chabon, Michael 1963- .... **CLC 55**
See also CA 139

Chabrol, Claude 1930-............. **CLC 16**
See also CA 110

Challans, Mary 1905-1983
See Renault, Mary
See also CA 81-84; 111; SATA 23;
SATA-Obit 36

Challis, George
See Faust, Frederick (Schiller)

Chambers, Aidan 1934- .... **CLC 35**
See also CA 25-28R; CANR 12, 31; JRDA;
MAICYA; SAAS 12; SATA 1, 69

Chambers, James 1948-
See Cliff, Jimmy
See also CA 124

Chambers, Jessie
See Lawrence, D(avid) H(erbert Richards)

Chambers, Robert W. 1865-1933... **TCLC 41**

Chandler, Raymond (Thornton)
1888-1959 .... **TCLC 1, 7; SSC 23**
See also CA 104; 129; CDALB 1929-1941;
DLBD 6; MTCW

Chang, Jung 1952-............... **CLC 71**
See also CA 142

Channing, William Ellery
1780-1842 .... **NCLC 17**
See also DLB 1, 59

Chaplin, Charles Spencer
1889-1977 .... **CLC 16**
See also Chaplin, Charlie
See also CA 81-84; 73-76

Chaplin, Charlie
See Chaplin, Charles Spencer
See also DLB 44

Chapman, George
1559(?)-1634 ..... **LC 22; DAM DRAM**
See also DLB 62, 121

Chapman, Graham 1941-1989 ...... **CLC 21**
See also Monty Python
See also CA 116; 129; CANR 35

Chapman, John Jay 1862-1933..... **TCLC 7**
See also CA 104

Chapman, Lee
See Bradley, Marion Zimmer

Chapman, Walker
See Silverberg, Robert

Chappell, Fred (Davis) 1936-.... **CLC 40, 78**
See also CA 5-8R; CAAS 4; CANR 8, 33;
DLB 6, 105

Char, Rene(-Emile)
1907-1988 .... **CLC 9, 11, 14, 55;**
DAM POET
See also CA 13-16R; 124; CANR 32;
MTCW

Charby, Jay
See Ellison, Harlan (Jay)

Chardin, Pierre Teilhard de
See Teilhard de Chardin, (Marie Joseph)
Pierre

Charles I 1600-1649 .... **LC 13**

Charyn, Jerome 1937- .... **CLC 5, 8, 18**
See also CA 5-8R; CAAS 1; CANR 7;
DLBY 83; MTCW

Chase, Mary (Coyle) 1907-1981 ...... **DC 1**
See also CA 77-80; 105; SATA 17;
SATA-Obit 29

Chase, Mary Ellen 1887-1973....... **CLC 2**
See also CA 13-16; 41-44R; CAP 1;
SATA 10

Chase, Nicholas
See Hyde, Anthony

Chateaubriand, Francois Rene de
1768-1848 .... **NCLC 3**
See also DLB 119

Chatterje, Sarat Chandra 1876-1936(?)
See Chatterji, Saratchandra
See also CA 109

Chatterji, Bankim Chandra
1838-1894 .... **NCLC 19**

Chatterji, Saratchandra .... **TCLC 13**
See also Chatterje, Sarat Chandra

Chatterton, Thomas
1752-1770 .... **LC 3; DAM POET**
See also DLB 109

Chatwin, (Charles) Bruce
1940-1989 .. **CLC 28, 57, 59; DAM POP**
See also AAYA 4; BEST 90:1; CA 85-88;
127

Chaucer, Daniel
See Ford, Ford Madox

Chaucer, Geoffrey
1340(?)-1400 .... **LC 17; DA; DAB;**
DAC; DAM MST, POET
See also CDBLB Before 1660; DLB 146

Chaviaras, Strates 1935-
See Haviaras, Stratis
See also CA 105

Chayefsky, Paddy .... **CLC 23**
See also Chayefsky, Sidney
See also DLB 7, 44; DLBY 81

Chayefsky, Sidney 1923-1981
See Chayefsky, Paddy
See also CA 9-12R; 104; CANR 18;
DAM DRAM

Chedid, Andree 1920-............. **CLC 47**
See also CA 145

Cheever, John
1912-1982 ...... **CLC 3, 7, 8, 11, 15, 25,**
64; DA; DAB; DAC; DAM MST, NOV,
POP; SSC 1; WLC
See also CA 5-8R; 106; CABS 1; CANR 5,
27; CDALB 1941-1968; DLB 2, 102;
DLBY 80, 82; INT CANR-5; MTCW

Cheever, Susan 1943-.......... **CLC 18, 48**
See also CA 103; CANR 27, 51; DLBY 82;
INT CANR-27

Chekhonte, Antosha
See Chekhov, Anton (Pavlovich)

Chekhov, Anton (Pavlovich)
1860-1904 ..... **TCLC 3, 10, 31, 55; DA;**
DAB; DAC; DAM DRAM, MST; SSC 2;
WLC
See also CA 104; 124; SATA 90

Chernyshevsky, Nikolay Gavrilovich
1828-1889 .... **NCLC 1**

Cherry, Carolyn Janice 1942-
See Cherryh, C. J.
See also CA 65-68; CANR 10

Cherryh, C. J. .... **CLC 35**
See also Cherry, Carolyn Janice
See also DLBY 80

Chesnutt, Charles W(addell)
1858-1932 .... **TCLC 5, 39; BLC;**
DAM MULT; SSC 7
See also BW 1; CA 106; 125; DLB 12, 50,
78; MTCW

Chester, Alfred 1929(?)-1971....... **CLC 49**
See also CA 33-36R; DLB 130

Chesterton, G(ilbert) K(eith)
1874-1936 .... **TCLC 1, 6, 64;**
DAM NOV, POET; SSC 1
See also CA 104; 132; CDBLB 1914-1945;
DLB 10, 19, 34, 70, 98, 149; MTCW;
SATA 27

Chiang Pin-chin 1904-1986
See Ding Ling
See also CA 118

Ch'ien Chung-shu 1910-........... **CLC 22**
See also CA 130; MTCW

Child, L. Maria
See Child, Lydia Maria

Child, Lydia Maria 1802-1880 .... **NCLC 6**
See also DLB 1, 74; SATA 67

Child, Mrs.
See Child, Lydia Maria

Child, Philip 1898-1978 .... **CLC 19, 68**
See also CA 13-14; CAP 1; SATA 47

Childers, (Robert) Erskine
1870-1922 .... **TCLC 65**
See also CA 113; 153; DLB 70

Childress, Alice
1920-1994 .... **CLC 12, 15, 86, 96; BLC;**
DAM DRAM, MULT, NOV; DC 4
See also AAYA 8; BW 2; CA 45-48; 146;
CANR 3, 27, 50; CLR 14; DLB 7, 38;
JRDA; MAICYA; MTCW; SATA 7, 48,
81

Chislett, (Margaret) Anne 1943- .... **CLC 34**
See also CA 151

Chitty, Thomas Willes 1926- .... **CLC 11**
See also Hinde, Thomas
See also CA 5-8R

Chivers, Thomas Holley
1809-1858 .... **NCLC 49**
See also DLB 3

Chomette, Rene Lucien 1898-1981
See Clair, Rene
See also CA 103

Chopin, Kate
.... **TCLC 5, 14; DA; DAB; SSC 8**
See also Chopin, Katherine
See also CDALB 1865-1917; DLB 12, 78

Chopin, Katherine 1851-1904
See Chopin, Kate
See also CA 104; 122; DAC; DAM MST,
NOV

Chretien de Troyes
c. 12th cent. - .... **CMLC 10**

Christie
See Ichikawa, Kon

Christie, Agatha (Mary Clarissa)
1890-1976 ...... **CLC 1, 6, 8, 12, 39, 48;**
DAB; DAC; DAM NOV
See also AAYA 9; AITN 1, 2; CA 17-20R;
61-64; CANR 10, 37; CDBLB 1914-1945;
DLB 13, 77; MTCW; SATA 36

Christie, (Ann) Philippa
See Pearce, Philippa
See also CA 5-8R; CANR 4

Christine de Pizan 1365(?)-1431(?) .... **LC 9**

Chubb, Elmer
See Masters, Edgar Lee

Chulkov, Mikhail Dmitrievich
1743-1792 .... **LC 2**
See also DLB 150

Churchill, Caryl 1938- ... **CLC 31, 55; DC 5**
See also CA 102; CANR 22, 46; DLB 13;
MTCW

Churchill, Charles 1731-1764........ **LC 3**
See also DLB 109

Chute, Carolyn 1947- .... **CLC 39**
See also CA 123

Ciardi, John (Anthony)
1916-1986 .... **CLC 10, 40, 44;**
DAM POET
See also CA 5-8R; 118; CAAS 2; CANR 5,
33; CLR 19; DLB 5; DLBY 86;
INT CANR-5; MAICYA; MTCW;
SATA 1, 65; SATA-Obit 46

Cicero, Marcus Tullius
106B.C.-43B.C. .... **CMLC 3**

Cimino, Michael 1943- .... **CLC 16**
See also CA 105

Cioran, E(mil) M. 1911-1995....... **CLC 64**
See also CA 25-28R; 149

Cisneros, Sandra
1954- ..... **CLC 69; DAM MULT; HLC**
See also AAYA 9; CA 131; DLB 122, 152;
HW

Cixous, Helene 1937- .... **CLC 92**
See also CA 126; CANR 55; DLB 83;
MTCW

Clair, Rene...................... **CLC 20**
See also Chomette, Rene Lucien

Clampitt, Amy 1920-1994 .... **CLC 32**
See also CA 110; 146; CANR 29; DLB 105

Clancy, Thomas L., Jr. 1947-
See Clancy, Tom
See also CA 125; 131; INT 131; MTCW

Clancy, Tom..... **CLC 45; DAM NOV, POP**
See also Clancy, Thomas L., Jr.
See also AAYA 9; BEST 89:1, 90:1

Clare, John
1793-1864 .... **NCLC 9; DAB;**
DAM POET
See also DLB 55, 96

Clarin
See Alas (y Urena), Leopoldo (Enrique
Garcia)

Clark, Al C.
See Goines, Donald

Clark, (Robert) Brian 1932-........ **CLC 29**
See also CA 41-44R

Clark, Curt
See Westlake, Donald E(dwin)

Clark, Eleanor 1913-1996 .... **CLC 5, 19**
See also CA 9-12R; 151; CANR 41; DLB 6

Clark, J. P.
See Clark, John Pepper
See also DLB 117

Clark, John Pepper
1935- .... **CLC 38; BLC; DAM DRAM,**
MULT; DC 5
See also Clark, J. P.
See also BW 1; CA 65-68; CANR 16

Clark, M. R.
See Clark, Mavis Thorpe

Clark, Mavis Thorpe 1909-........ **CLC 12**
See also CA 57-60; CANR 8, 37; CLR 30;
MAICYA; SAAS 5; SATA 8, 74

Clark, Walter Van Tilburg
1909-1971 .... **CLC 28**
See also CA 9-12R; 33-36R; DLB 9;
SATA 8

Clarke, Arthur C(harles)
1917- .... **CLC 1, 4, 13, 18, 35;**
DAM POP; SSC 3
See also AAYA 4; CA 1-4R; CANR 2, 28,
55; JRDA; MAICYA; MTCW; SATA 13,
70

Clarke, Austin
1896-1974 ...... **CLC 6, 9; DAM POET**
See also CA 29-32; 49-52; CAP 2; DLB 10,
20

Clarke, Austin C(hesterfield)
1934- .... **CLC 8, 53; BLC; DAC;**
DAM MULT
See also BW 1; CA 25-28R; CAAS 16;
CANR 14, 32; DLB 53, 125

Clarke, Gillian 1937- .... **CLC 61**
See also CA 106; DLB 40

Clarke, Marcus (Andrew Hislop)
1846-1881 .... **NCLC 19**

Clarke, Shirley 1925-............. **CLC 16**

Clash, The
See Headon, (Nicky) Topper; Jones, Mick;
Simonon, Paul; Strummer, Joe

Claudel, Paul (Louis Charles Marie)
1868-1955 .... **TCLC 2, 10**
See also CA 104

Clavell, James (duMaresq)
1925-1994 .... **CLC 6, 25, 87;**
DAM NOV, POP
See also CA 25-28R; 146; CANR 26, 48;
MTCW

Cleaver, (Leroy) Eldridge
1935- ..... **CLC 30; BLC; DAM MULT**
See also BW 1; CA 21-24R; CANR 16

Cleese, John (Marwood) 1939- ..... **CLC 21**
See also Monty Python
See also CA 112; 116; CANR 35; MTCW

Cleishbotham, Jebediah
See Scott, Walter

Cleland, John 1710-1789 .... **LC 2**
See also DLB 39

Clemens, Samuel Langhorne 1835-1910
See Twain, Mark
See also CA 104; 135; CDALB 1865-1917;
DA; DAB; DAC; DAM MST, NOV;
DLB 11, 12, 23, 64, 74; JRDA;
MAICYA; YABC 2

Cleophil
See Congreve, William

Clerihew, E.
See Bentley, E(dmund) C(lerihew)

Clerk, N. W.
See Lewis, C(live) S(taples)

Cliff, Jimmy...................... **CLC 21**
See also Chambers, James

Clifton, (Thelma) Lucille
1936- .... **CLC 19, 66; BLC;**
DAM MULT, POET
See also BW 2; CA 49-52; CANR 2, 24, 42;
CLR 5; DLB 5, 41; MAICYA; MTCW;
SATA 20, 69

Clinton, Dirk
See Silverberg, Robert

Clough, Arthur Hugh 1819-1861.. **NCLC 27**
See also DLB 32

Clutha, Janet Paterson Frame 1924-
See Frame, Janet
See also CA 1-4R; CANR 2, 36; MTCW

Clyne, Terence
See Blatty, William Peter

Cobalt, Martin
See Mayne, William (James Carter)

Cobbett, William 1763-1835 ..... **NCLC 49**
See also DLB 43, 107, 158

Coburn, D(onald) L(ee) 1938- ...... **CLC 10**
See also CA 89-92

Cocteau, Jean (Maurice Eugene Clement)
1889-1963 .... **CLC 1, 8, 15, 16, 43; DA;**
DAB; DAC; DAM DRAM, MST, NOV;
WLC
See also CA 25-28; CANR 40; CAP 2;
DLB 65; MTCW

Copeland, Stewart (Armstrong)
1952- . . . . **CLC 26**

Coppard, A(lfred) E(dgar)
1878-1957 . . . . **TCLC 5; SSC 21**
See also CA 114; DLB 162; YABC 1

Coppee, Francois 1842-1908 . . . . . . **TCLC 25**

Coppola, Francis Ford 1939- . . . . **CLC 16**
See also CA 77-80; CANR 40; DLB 44

Corbiere, Tristan 1845-1875 . . . . . **NCLC 43**

Corcoran, Barbara 1911- . . . . **CLC 17**
See also AAYA 14; CA 21-24R; CAAS 2;
CANR 11, 28, 48; DLB 52; JRDA;
SAAS 20; SATA 3, 77

Cordelier, Maurice
See Giraudoux, (Hippolyte) Jean

Corelli, Marie 1855-1924 . . . . **TCLC 51**
See also Mackay, Mary
See also DLB 34, 156

Corman, Cid . . . . **CLC 9**
See also Corman, Sidney
See also CAAS 2; DLB 5

Corman, Sidney 1924-
See Corman, Cid
See also CA 85-88; CANR 44; DAM POET

Cormier, Robert (Edmund)
1925- . . . . **CLC 12, 30; DA; DAB; DAC;**
DAM MST, NOV
See also AAYA 3, 19; CA 1-4R; CANR 5,
23; CDALB 1968-1988; CLR 12; DLB 52;
INT CANR-23; JRDA; MAICYA;
MTCW; SATA 10, 45, 83

Corn, Alfred (DeWitt III) 1943- . . . . **CLC 33**
See also CA 104; CAAS 25; CANR 44;
DLB 120; DLBY 80

Corneille, Pierre
1606-1684 . . . . **LC 28; DAB; DAM MST**

Cornwell, David (John Moore)
1931- . . . . **CLC 9, 15; DAM POP**
See also le Carre, John
See also CA 5-8R; CANR 13, 33; MTCW

Corso, (Nunzio) Gregory 1930- . . . **CLC 1, 11**
See also CA 5-8R; CANR 41; DLB 5, 16;
MTCW

Cortazar, Julio
1914-1984 . . . . . . **CLC 2, 3, 5, 10, 13, 15,**
33, 34, 92; DAM MULT, NOV; HLC;
SSC 7
See also CA 21-24R; CANR 12, 32;
DLB 113; HW; MTCW

CORTES, HERNAN 1484-1547 . . . . . **LC 31**

Corwin, Cecil
See Kornbluth, C(yril) M.

Cosic, Dobrica 1921- . . . . **CLC 14**
See also CA 122; 138

Costain, Thomas B(ertram)
1885-1965 . . . . **CLC 30**
See also CA 5-8R; 25-28R; DLB 9

Costantini, Humberto
1924(?)-1987 . . . . **CLC 49**
See also CA 131; 122; HW

Costello, Elvis 1955- . . . . **CLC 21**

Cotter, Joseph Seamon Sr.
1861-1949 . . . . **TCLC 28; BLC;**
DAM MULT
See also BW 1; CA 124; DLB 50

Couch, Arthur Thomas Quiller
See Quiller-Couch, Arthur Thomas

Coulton, James
See Hansen, Joseph

Couperus, Louis (Marie Anne)
1863-1923 . . . . **TCLC 15**
See also CA 115

Coupland, Douglas
1961- . . . . **CLC 85; DAC; DAM POP**
See also CA 142

Court, Wesli
See Turco, Lewis (Putnam)

Courtenay, Bryce 1933- . . . . **CLC 59**
See also CA 138

Courtney, Robert
See Ellison, Harlan (Jay)

Cousteau, Jacques-Yves 1910- . . . . . . **CLC 30**
See also CA 65-68; CANR 15; MTCW;
SATA 38

Coward, Noel (Peirce)
1899-1973 . . . . **CLC 1, 9, 29, 51;**
DAM DRAM
See also AITN 1; CA 17-18; 41-44R;
CANR 35; CAP 2; CDBLB 1914-1945;
DLB 10; MTCW

Cowley, Malcolm 1898-1989 . . . . **CLC 39**
See also CA 5-8R; 128; CANR 3, 55;
DLB 4, 48; DLBY 81, 89; MTCW

Cowper, William
1731-1800 . . . . . . **NCLC 8; DAM POET**
See also DLB 104, 109

Cox, William Trevor
1928- . . . . **CLC 9, 14, 71; DAM NOV**
See also Trevor, William
See also CA 9-12R; CANR 4, 37, 55;
DLB 14; INT CANR-37; MTCW

Coyne, P. J.
See Masters, Hilary

Cozzens, James Gould
1903-1978 . . . . **CLC 1, 4, 11, 92**
See also CA 9-12R; 81-84; CANR 19;
CDALB 1941-1968; DLB 9; DLBD 2;
DLBY 84; MTCW

Crabbe, George 1754-1832 . . . . **NCLC 26**
See also DLB 93

Craddock, Charles Egbert
See Murfree, Mary Noailles

Craig, A. A.
See Anderson, Poul (William)

Craik, Dinah Maria (Mulock)
1826-1887 . . . . **NCLC 38**
See also DLB 35, 163; MAICYA; SATA 34

Cram, Ralph Adams 1863-1942 . . . . **TCLC 45**

Crane, (Harold) Hart
1899-1932 . . . . **TCLC 2, 5; DA; DAB;**
DAC; DAM MST, POET; PC 3; WLC
See also CA 104; 127; CDALB 1917-1929;
DLB 4, 48; MTCW

Crane, R(onald) S(almon)
1886-1967 . . . . **CLC 27**
See also CA 85-88; DLB 63

Crane, Stephen (Townley)
1871-1900 . . . . . . **TCLC 11, 17, 32; DA;**
DAB; DAC; DAM MST, NOV, POET;
SSC 7; WLC
See also CA 109; 140; CDALB 1865-1917;
DLB 12, 54, 78; YABC 2

Crase, Douglas 1944- . . . . **CLC 58**
See also CA 106

Crashaw, Richard 1612(?)-1649 . . . . . . **LC 24**
See also DLB 126

Craven, Margaret
1901-1980 . . . . **CLC 17; DAC**
See also CA 103

Crawford, F(rancis) Marion
1854-1909 . . . . **TCLC 10**
See also CA 107; DLB 71

Crawford, Isabella Valancy
1850-1887 . . . . **NCLC 12**
See also DLB 92

Crayon, Geoffrey
See Irving, Washington

Creasey, John 1908-1973 . . . . **CLC 11**
See also CA 5-8R; 41-44R; CANR 8;
DLB 77; MTCW

Crebillon, Claude Prosper Jolyot de (fils)
1707-1777 . . . . **LC 28**

Credo
See Creasey, John

Creeley, Robert (White)
1926- . . . . . **CLC 1, 2, 4, 8, 11, 15, 36, 78;**
DAM POET
See also CA 1-4R; CAAS 10; CANR 23, 43;
DLB 5, 16, 169; MTCW

Crews, Harry (Eugene)
1935- . . . . **CLC 6, 23, 49**
See also AITN 1; CA 25-28R; CANR 20;
DLB 6, 143; MTCW

Crichton, (John) Michael
1942- . . . . **CLC 2, 6, 54, 90; DAM NOV,**
POP
See also AAYA 10; AITN 2; CA 25-28R;
CANR 13, 40, 54; DLBY 81;
INT CANR-13; JRDA; MTCW; SATA 9,
88

Crispin, Edmund . . . . **CLC 22**
See also Montgomery, (Robert) Bruce
See also DLB 87

Cristofer, Michael
1945(?)- . . . . **CLC 28; DAM DRAM**
See also CA 110; 152; DLB 7

Croce, Benedetto 1866-1952 . . . . . . **TCLC 37**
See also CA 120

Crockett, David 1786-1836 . . . . **NCLC 8**
See also DLB 3, 11

Crockett, Davy
See Crockett, David

Crofts, Freeman Wills
1879-1957 . . . . **TCLC 55**
See also CA 115; DLB 77

Croker, John Wilson 1780-1857 . . **NCLC 10**
See also DLB 110

Crommelynck, Fernand 1885-1970 . . **CLC 75**
See also CA 89-92

Davies, (William) Robertson
1913-1995 ..... **CLC 2, 7, 13, 25, 42, 75, 91; DA; DAB; DAC; DAM MST, NOV, POP; WLC**
See also BEST 89:2; CA 33-36R; 150; CANR 17, 42; DLB 68; INT CANR-17; MTCW

Davies, W(illiam) H(enry)
1871-1940 .... **TCLC 5**
See also CA 104; DLB 19, 174

Davies, Walter C.
See Kornbluth, C(yril) M.

Davis, Angela (Yvonne)
1944- .... **CLC 77; DAM MULT**
See also BW 2; CA 57-60; CANR 10

Davis, B. Lynch
See Bioy Casares, Adolfo; Borges, Jorge Luis

Davis, Gordon
See Hunt, E(verette) Howard, (Jr.)

Davis, Harold Lenoir 1896-1960.... **CLC 49**
See also CA 89-92; DLB 9

Davis, Rebecca (Blaine) Harding
1831-1910 .... **TCLC 6**
See also CA 104; DLB 74

Davis, Richard Harding
1864-1916 .... **TCLC 24**
See also CA 114; DLB 12, 23, 78, 79; DLBD 13

Davison, Frank Dalby 1893-1970 ... **CLC 15**
See also CA 116

Davison, Lawrence H.
See Lawrence, D(avid) H(erbert Richards)

Davison, Peter (Hubert) 1928- ..... **CLC 28**
See also CA 9-12R; CAAS 4; CANR 3, 43; DLB 5

Davys, Mary 1674-1732 .... **LC 1**
See also DLB 39

Dawson, Fielding 1930- .... **CLC 6**
See also CA 85-88; DLB 130

Dawson, Peter
See Faust, Frederick (Schiller)

Day, Clarence (Shepard, Jr.)
1874-1935 .... **TCLC 25**
See also CA 108; DLB 11

Day, Thomas 1748-1789 .... **LC 1**
See also DLB 39; YABC 1

Day Lewis, C(ecil)
1904-1972 .... **CLC 1, 6, 10; DAM POET; PC 11**
See also Blake, Nicholas
See also CA 13-16; 33-36R; CANR 34; CAP 1; DLB 15, 20; MTCW

Dazai, Osamu .... **TCLC 11**
See also Tsushima, Shuji

de Andrade, Carlos Drummond
See Drummond de Andrade, Carlos

Deane, Norman
See Creasey, John

de Beauvoir, Simone (Lucie Ernestine Marie Bertrand)
See Beauvoir, Simone (Lucie Ernestine Marie Bertrand) de

de Brissac, Malcolm
See Dickinson, Peter (Malcolm)

de Chardin, Pierre Teilhard
See Teilhard de Chardin, (Marie Joseph) Pierre

Dee, John 1527-1608 .... **LC 20**

Deer, Sandra 1940- .... **CLC 45**

De Ferrari, Gabriella 1941- .... **CLC 65**
See also CA 146

Defoe, Daniel
1660(?)-1731 .... **LC 1; DA; DAB; DAC; DAM MST, NOV; WLC**
See also CDBLB 1660-1789; DLB 39, 95, 101; JRDA; MAICYA; SATA 22

de Gourmont, Remy(-Marie-Charles)
See Gourmont, Remy (-Marie-Charles) de

de Hartog, Jan 1914- .... **CLC 19**
See also CA 1-4R; CANR 1

de Hostos, E. M.
See Hostos (y Bonilla), Eugenio Maria de

dc Hostos, Eugenio M.
See Hostos (y Bonilla), Eugenio Maria de

Deighton, Len .... **CLC 4, 7, 22, 46**
See also Deighton, Leonard Cyril
See also AAYA 6; BEST 89:2; CDBLB 1960 to Present; DLB 87

Deighton, Leonard Cyril 1929-
See Deighton, Len
See also CA 9-12R; CANR 19, 33; DAM NOV, POP; MTCW

Dekker, Thomas
1572(?)-1632 ..... **LC 22; DAM DRAM**
See also CDBLB Before 1660; DLB 62, 172

Delafield, E. M. 1890-1943 .... **TCLC 61**
See also Dashwood, Edmee Elizabeth Monica de la Pasture
See also DLB 34

de la Mare, Walter (John)
1873-1956 .... **TCLC 4, 53; DAB; DAC; DAM MST, POET; SSC 14; WLC**
See also CDBLB 1914-1945; CLR 23; DLB 162; SATA 16

Delaney, Franey
See O'Hara, John (Henry)

Delaney, Shelagh
1939- .... **CLC 29; DAM DRAM**
See also CA 17-20R; CANR 30; CDBLB 1960 to Present; DLB 13; MTCW

Delany, Mary (Granville Pendarves)
1700-1788 .... **LC 12**

Delany, Samuel R(ay, Jr.)
1942- .... **CLC 8, 14, 38; BLC; DAM MULT**
See also BW 2; CA 81-84; CANR 27, 43; DLB 8, 33; MTCW

De La Ramee, (Marie) Louise 1839-1908
See Ouida
See also SATA 20

de la Roche, Mazo 1879-1961 ...... **CLC 14**
See also CA 85-88; CANR 30; DLB 68; SATA 64

Delbanco, Nicholas (Franklin)
1942- .... **CLC 6, 13**
See also CA 17-20R; CAAS 2; CANR 29, 55; DLB 6

del Castillo, Michel 1933- .... **CLC 38**
See also CA 109

Deledda, Grazia (Cosima)
1875(?)-1936 .... **TCLC 23**
See also CA 123

Delibes, Miguel .... **CLC 8, 18**
See also Delibes Setien, Miguel

Delibes Setien, Miguel 1920-
See Delibes, Miguel
See also CA 45-48; CANR 1, 32; HW; MTCW

DeLillo, Don
1936- ..... **CLC 8, 10, 13, 27, 39, 54, 76; DAM NOV, POP**
See also BEST 89:1; CA 81-84; CANR 21; DLB 6, 173; MTCW

de Lisser, H. G.
See De Lisser, H(erbert) G(eorge)
See also DLB 117

De Lisser, H(erbert) G(eorge)
1878-1944 .... **TCLC 12**
See also de Lisser, H. G.
See also BW 2; CA 109; 152

Deloria, Vine (Victor), Jr.
1933- .... **CLC 21; DAM MULT**
See also CA 53-56; CANR 5, 20, 48; MTCW; NNAL; SATA 21

Del Vecchio, John M(ichael)
1947- .... **CLC 29**
See also CA 110; DLBD 9

de Man, Paul (Adolph Michel)
1919-1983 .... **CLC 55**
See also CA 128; 111; DLB 67; MTCW

De Marinis, Rick 1934- .... **CLC 54**
See also CA 57-60; CAAS 24; CANR 9, 25, 50

Dembry, R. Emmet
See Murfree, Mary Noailles

Demby, William
1922- ..... **CLC 53; BLC; DAM MULT**
See also BW 1; CA 81-84; DLB 33

Demijohn, Thom
See Disch, Thomas M(ichael)

de Montherlant, Henry (Milon)
See Montherlant, Henry (Milon) de

Demosthenes 384B.C.-322B.C. .... **CMLC 13**

de Natale, Francine
See Malzberg, Barry N(athaniel)

Denby, Edwin (Orr) 1903-1983 ..... **CLC 48**
See also CA 138; 110

Denis, Julio
See Cortazar, Julio

Denmark, Harrison
See Zelazny, Roger (Joseph)

Dennis, John 1658-1734 .... **LC 11**
See also DLB 101

Dennis, Nigel (Forbes) 1912-1989 .... **CLC 8**
See also CA 25-28R; 129; DLB 13, 15; MTCW

De Palma, Brian (Russell) 1940-.... **CLC 20**
See also CA 109

De Quincey, Thomas 1785-1859 ... **NCLC 4**
See also CDBLB 1789-1832; DLB 110; 144

Deren, Eleanora 1908(?)-1961
See Deren, Maya
See also CA 111

Deren, Maya .... **CLC 16**
See also Deren, Eleanora

Derleth, August (William)
1909-1971 .... **CLC 31**
See also CA 1-4R; 29-32R; CANR 4;
DLB 9; SATA 5

Der Nister 1884-1950............ **TCLC 56**

de Routisie, Albert
See Aragon, Louis

Derrida, Jacques 1930-........ **CLC 24, 87**
See also CA 124; 127

Derry Down Derry
See Lear, Edward

Dersonnes, Jacques
See Simenon, Georges (Jacques Christian)

Desai, Anita
1937- .... **CLC 19, 37, 97; DAB;
DAM NOV**
See also CA 81-84; CANR 33, 53; MTCW;
SATA 63

de Saint-Luc, Jean
See Glassco, John

de Saint Roman, Arnaud
See Aragon, Louis

Descartes, Rene 1596-1650 ...... **LC 20, 35**

De Sica, Vittorio 1901(?)-1974 ..... **CLC 20**
See also CA 117

Desnos, Robert 1900-1945........ **TCLC 22**
See also CA 121; 151

Destouches, Louis-Ferdinand
1894-1961 .... **CLC 9, 15**
See also Celine, Louis-Ferdinand
See also CA 85-88; CANR 28; MTCW

Deutsch, Babette 1895-1982 .... **CLC 18**
See also CA 1-4R; 108; CANR 4; DLB 45;
SATA 1; SATA-Obit 33

Devenant, William 1606-1649 .... **LC 13**

Devkota, Laxmiprasad
1909-1959 .... **TCLC 23**
See also CA 123

De Voto, Bernard (Augustine)
1897-1955 .... **TCLC 29**
See also CA 113; DLB 9

De Vries, Peter
1910-1993 .... **CLC 1, 2, 3, 7, 10, 28, 46;
DAM NOV**
See also CA 17-20R; 142; CANR 41;
DLB 6; DLBY 82; MTCW

Dexter, John
See Bradley, Marion Zimmer

Dexter, Martin
See Faust, Frederick (Schiller)

Dexter, Pete
1943- .... **CLC 34, 55; DAM POP**
See also BEST 89:2; CA 127; 131; INT 131;
MTCW

Diamano, Silmang
See Senghor, Leopold Sedar

Diamond, Neil 1941- .... **CLC 30**
See also CA 108

Diaz del Castillo, Bernal 1496-1584 .. **LC 31**

di Bassetto, Corno
See Shaw, George Bernard

Dick, Philip K(indred)
1928-1982 .... **CLC 10, 30, 72;
DAM NOV, POP**
See also CA 49-52; 106; CANR 2, 16;
DLB 8; MTCW

Dickens, Charles (John Huffam)
1812-1870 ...... **NCLC 3, 8, 18, 26, 37,
50; DA; DAB; DAC; DAM MST, NOV;
SSC 17; WLC**
See also CDBLB 1832-1890; DLB 21, 55,
70, 159, 166; JRDA; MAICYA; SATA 15

Dickey, James (Lafayette)
1923- .... **CLC 1, 2, 4, 7, 10, 15, 47;
DAM NOV, POET, POP**
See also AITN 1, 2; CA 9-12R; CABS 2;
CANR 10, 48; CDALB 1968-1988;
DLB 5; DLBD 7; DLBY 82, 93;
INT CANR-10; MTCW

Dickey, William 1928-1994 ...... **CLC 3, 28**
See also CA 9-12R; 145; CANR 24; DLB 5

Dickinson, Charles 1951-......... **CLC 49**
See also CA 128

Dickinson, Emily (Elizabeth)
1830-1886 .... **NCLC 21; DA; DAB;
DAC; DAM MST, POET; PC 1; WLC**
See also CDALB 1865-1917; DLB 1;
SATA 29

Dickinson, Peter (Malcolm)
1927-.................... **CLC 12, 35**
See also AAYA 9; CA 41-44R; CANR 31;
CLR 29; DLB 87, 161; JRDA; MAICYA;
SATA 5, 62

Dickson, Carr
See Carr, John Dickson

Dickson, Carter
See Carr, John Dickson

Diderot, Denis 1713-1784 .... **LC 26**

Didion, Joan
1934- .. **CLC 1, 3, 8, 14, 32; DAM NOV**
See also AITN 1; CA 5-8R; CANR 14, 52;
CDALB 1968-1988; DLB 2, 173;
DLBY 81, 86; MTCW

Dietrich, Robert
See Hunt, E(verette) Howard, (Jr.)

Dillard, Annie
1945- .... **CLC 9, 60; DAM NOV**
See also AAYA 6; CA 49-52; CANR 3, 43;
DLBY 80; MTCW; SATA 10

Dillard, R(ichard) H(enry) W(ilde)
1937-....................... **CLC 5**
See also CA 21-24R; CAAS 7; CANR 10;
DLB 5

Dillon, Eilis 1920-1994............ **CLC 17**
See also CA 9-12R; 147; CAAS 3; CANR 4,
38; CLR 26; MAICYA; SATA 2, 74;
SATA-Obit 83

Dimont, Penelope
See Mortimer, Penelope (Ruth)

Dinesen, Isak....... **CLC 10, 29, 95; SSC 7**
See also Blixen, Karen (Christentze
Dinesen)

Ding Ling...................... **CLC 68**
See also Chiang Pin-chin

Disch, Thomas M(ichael) 1940-... **CLC 7, 36**
See also AAYA 17; CA 21-24R; CAAS 4;
CANR 17, 36, 54; CLR 18; DLB 8;
MAICYA; MTCW; SAAS 15; SATA 54

Disch, Tom
See Disch, Thomas M(ichael)

d'Isly, Georges
See Simenon, Georges (Jacques Christian)

Disraeli, Benjamin 1804-1881 .. **NCLC 2, 39**
See also DLB 21, 55

Ditcum, Steve
See Crumb, R(obert)

Dixon, Paige
See Corcoran, Barbara

Dixon, Stephen 1936-..... **CLC 52; SSC 16**
See also CA 89-92; CANR 17, 40, 54;
DLB 130

Dobell, Sydney Thompson
1824-1874 .... **NCLC 43**
See also DLB 32

Doblin, Alfred .... **TCLC 13**
See also Doeblin, Alfred

Dobrolyubov, Nikolai Alexandrovich
1836-1861 .... **NCLC 5**

Dobyns, Stephen 1941-............ **CLC 37**
See also CA 45-48; CANR 2, 18

Doctorow, E(dgar) L(aurence)
1931- ..... **CLC 6, 11, 15, 18, 37, 44, 65;
DAM NOV, POP**
See also AITN 2; BEST 89:3; CA 45-48;
CANR 2, 33, 51; CDALB 1968-1988;
DLB 2, 28, 173; DLBY 80; MTCW

Dodgson, Charles Lutwidge 1832-1898
See Carroll, Lewis
See also CLR 2; DA; DAB; DAC;
DAM MST, NOV, POET; MAICYA;
YABC 2

Dodson, Owen (Vincent)
1914-1983 .... **CLC 79; BLC;
DAM MULT**
See also BW 1; CA 65-68; 110; CANR 24;
DLB 76

Doeblin, Alfred 1878-1957....... **TCLC 13**
See also Doblin, Alfred
See also CA 110; 141; DLB 66

Doerr, Harriet 1910- .... **CLC 34**
See also CA 117; 122; CANR 47; INT 122

Domecq, H(onorio) Bustos
See Bioy Casares, Adolfo; Borges, Jorge
Luis

Domini, Rey
See Lorde, Audre (Geraldine)

Dominique
See Proust, (Valentin-Louis-George-Eugene-)
Marcel

Don, A
See Stephen, Leslie

Donaldson, Stephen R.
1947- .... **CLC 46; DAM POP**
See also CA 89-92; CANR 13, 55;
INT CANR-13

Donleavy, J(ames) P(atrick)
1926- .... **CLC 1, 4, 6, 10, 45**
See also AITN 2; CA 9-12R; CANR 24, 49;
DLB 6, 173; INT CANR-24; MTCW

Donne, John
　　1572-1631 ...... **LC 10, 24; DA; DAB;**
　　　　　DAC; DAM MST, POET; PC 1
See also CDBLB Before 1660; DLB 121,
151

Donnell, David 1939(?)- .... **CLC 34**

Donoghue, P. S.
See Hunt, E(verette) Howard, (Jr.)

Donoso (Yanez), Jose
　　1924- .... **CLC 4, 8, 11, 32;**
　　　　　　　　　DAM MULT; HLC
See also CA 81-84; CANR 32; DLB 113;
HW; MTCW

Donovan, John 1928-1992 .... **CLC 35**
See also CA 97-100; 137; CLR 3;
MAICYA; SATA 72; SATA-Brief 29

Don Roberto
See Cunninghame Graham, R(obert)
B(ontine)

Doolittle, Hilda
　　1886-1961 ..... **CLC 3, 8, 14, 31, 34, 73;**
　　　　　DA; DAC; DAM MST, POET; PC 5;
　　　　　　　　　　　　　　WLC
See also H. D.
See also CA 97-100; CANR 35; DLB 4, 45;
MTCW

Dorfman, Ariel
　　1942- .... **CLC 48, 77; DAM MULT;**
　　　　　　　　　　　　　　HLC
See also CA 124; 130; HW; INT 130

Dorn, Edward (Merton) 1929-... **CLC 10, 18**
See also CA 93-96; CANR 42; DLB 5;
INT 93-96

Dorsan, Luc
See Simenon, Georges (Jacques Christian)

Dorsange, Jean
See Simenon, Georges (Jacques Christian)

Dos Passos, John (Roderigo)
　　1896-1970 ...... **CLC 1, 4, 8, 11, 15, 25,**
　　　　　34, 82; DA; DAB; DAC; DAM MST,
　　　　　　　　　　　NOV; WLC
See also CA 1-4R; 29-32R; CANR 3;
CDALB 1929-1941; DLB 4, 9; DLBD 1;
MTCW

Dossage, Jean
See Simenon, Georges (Jacques Christian)

Dostoevsky, Fedor Mikhailovich
　　1821-1881 ...... **NCLC 2, 7, 21, 33, 43;**
　　　　　DA; DAB; DAC; DAM MST, NOV;
　　　　　　　　　　　SSC 2; WLC

Doughty, Charles M(ontagu)
　　1843-1926 .... **TCLC 27**
See also CA 115; DLB 19, 57, 174

Douglas, Ellen .... **CLC 73**
See also Haxton, Josephine Ayres;
Williamson, Ellen Douglas

Douglas, Gavin 1475(?)-1522 .... **LC 20**

Douglas, Keith 1920-1944 .... **TCLC 40**
See also DLB 27

Douglas, Leonard
See Bradbury, Ray (Douglas)

Douglas, Michael
See Crichton, (John) Michael

Douglass, Frederick
　　1817(?)-1895 .... **NCLC 7, 55; BLC; DA;**
　　　　　DAC; DAM MST, MULT; WLC
See also CDALB 1640-1865; DLB 1, 43, 50,
79; SATA 29

Dourado, (Waldomiro Freitas) Autran
　　1926- .... **CLC 23, 60**
See also CA 25-28R; CANR 34

Dourado, Waldomiro Autran
See Dourado, (Waldomiro Freitas) Autran

Dove, Rita (Frances)
　　1952- .... **CLC 50, 81; DAM MULT,**
　　　　　　　　　　POET; PC 6
See also BW 2; CA 109; CAAS 19;
CANR 27, 42; DLB 120

Dowell, Coleman 1925-1985 .... **CLC 60**
See also CA 25-28R; 117; CANR 10;
DLB 130

Dowson, Ernest (Christopher)
　　1867-1900 .... **TCLC 4**
See also CA 105; 150; DLB 19, 135

Doyle, A. Conan
See Doyle, Arthur Conan

Doyle, Arthur Conan
　　1859-1930 .... **TCLC 7; DA; DAB;**
　　　　　DAC; DAM MST, NOV; SSC 12; WLC
See also AAYA 14; CA 104; 122;
CDBLB 1890-1914; DLB 18, 70, 156;
MTCW; SATA 24

Doyle, Conan
See Doyle, Arthur Conan

Doyle, John
See Graves, Robert (von Ranke)

Doyle, Roddy 1958(?)- .... **CLC 81**
See also AAYA 14; CA 143

Doyle, Sir A. Conan
See Doyle, Arthur Conan

Doyle, Sir Arthur Conan
See Doyle, Arthur Conan

Dr. A
See Asimov, Isaac; Silverstein, Alvin

Drabble, Margaret
　　1939- .... **CLC 2, 3, 5, 8, 10, 22, 53;**
　　　　　DAB; DAC; DAM MST, NOV, POP
See also CA 13-16R; CANR 18, 35;
CDBLB 1960 to Present; DLB 14, 155;
MTCW; SATA 48

Drapier, M. B.
See Swift, Jonathan

Drayham, James
See Mencken, H(enry) L(ouis)

Drayton, Michael 1563-1631 .... **LC 8**

Dreadstone, Carl
See Campbell, (John) Ramsey

Dreiser, Theodore (Herman Albert)
　　1871-1945 .... **TCLC 10, 18, 35; DA;**
　　　　　DAC; DAM MST, NOV; WLC
See also CA 106; 132; CDALB 1865-1917;
DLB 9, 12, 102, 137; DLBD 1; MTCW

Drexler, Rosalyn 1926- .... **CLC 2, 6**
See also CA 81-84

Dreyer, Carl Theodor 1889-1968.... **CLC 16**
See also CA 116

Drieu la Rochelle, Pierre(-Eugene)
　　1893-1945 .... **TCLC 21**
See also CA 117; DLB 72

Drinkwater, John 1882-1937...... **TCLC 57**
See also CA 109; 149; DLB 10, 19, 149

Drop Shot
See Cable, George Washington

Droste-Hulshoff, Annette Freiin von
　　1797-1848 .... **NCLC 3**
See also DLB 133

Drummond, Walter
See Silverberg, Robert

Drummond, William Henry
　　1854-1907 .... **TCLC 25**
See also DLB 92

Drummond de Andrade, Carlos
　　1902-1987 .... **CLC 18**
See also Andrade, Carlos Drummond de
See also CA 132; 123

Drury, Allen (Stuart) 1918-........ **CLC 37**
See also CA 57-60; CANR 18, 52;
INT CANR-18

Dryden, John
　　1631-1700 .... **LC 3, 21; DA; DAB;**
　　　　　DAC; DAM DRAM, MST, POET;
　　　　　　　　　　　　DC 3; WLC
See also CDBLB 1660-1789; DLB 80, 101,
131

Duberman, Martin 1930- .... **CLC 8**
See also CA 1-4R; CANR 2

Dubie, Norman (Evans) 1945-...... **CLC 36**
See also CA 69-72; CANR 12; DLB 120

Du Bois, W(illiam) E(dward) B(urghardt)
　　1868-1963 .... **CLC 1, 2, 13, 64, 96;**
　　　　　BLC; DA; DAC; DAM MST, MULT,
　　　　　　　　　　　NOV; WLC
See also BW 1; CA 85-88; CANR 34;
CDALB 1865-1917; DLB 47, 50, 91;
MTCW; SATA 42

Dubus, Andre
　　1936-........ **CLC 13, 36, 97; SSC 15**
See also CA 21-24R; CANR 17; DLB 130;
INT CANR-17

Duca Minimo
See D'Annunzio, Gabriele

Ducharme, Rejean 1941- .... **CLC 74**
See also DLB 60

Duclos, Charles Pinot 1704-1772 ..... **LC 1**

Dudek, Louis 1918- .... **CLC 11, 19**
See also CA 45-48; CAAS 14; CANR 1;
DLB 88

Duerrenmatt, Friedrich
　　1921-1990 ...... **CLC 1, 4, 8, 11, 15, 43;**
　　　　　　　　　　DAM DRAM
See also CA 17-20R; CANR 33; DLB 69,
124; MTCW

Duffy, Bruce (?)-.................. **CLC 50**

Duffy, Maureen 1933- .... **CLC 37**
See also CA 25-28R; CANR 33; DLB 14;
MTCW

Dugan, Alan 1923- .... **CLC 2, 6**
See also CA 81-84; DLB 5

du Gard, Roger Martin
See Martin du Gard, Roger

Duhamel, Georges 1884-1966 .... **CLC 8**
See also CA 81-84; 25-28R; CANR 35;
DLB 65; MTCW

Dujardin, Edouard (Emile Louis)
1861-1949 .... **TCLC 13**
See also CA 109; DLB 123

Dumas, Alexandre (Davy de la Pailleterie)
1802-1870 .... **NCLC 11; DA; DAB;**
DAC; DAM MST, NOV; WLC
See also DLB 119; SATA 18

Dumas, Alexandre
1824-1895 .... **NCLC 9; DC 1**

Dumas, Claudine
See Malzberg, Barry N(athaniel)

Dumas, Henry L. 1934-1968 ..... **CLC 6, 62**
See also BW 1; CA 85-88; DLB 41

du Maurier, Daphne
1907-1989 .... **CLC 6, 11, 59; DAB;**
DAC; DAM MST, POP; SSC 18
See also CA 5-8R; 128; CANR 6, 55;
MTCW; SATA 27; SATA-Obit 60

Dunbar, Paul Laurence
1872-1906 ..... **TCLC 2, 12; BLC; DA;**
DAC; DAM MST, MULT, POET; PC 5;
SSC 8; WLC
See also BW 1; CA 104; 124;
CDALB 1865-1917; DLB 50, 54, 78;
SATA 34

Dunbar, William 1460(?)-1530(?) .... **LC 20**
See also DLB 132, 146

Duncan, Lois 1934- .... **CLC 26**
See also AAYA 4; CA 1-4R; CANR 2, 23,
36; CLR 29; JRDA; MAICYA; SAAS 2;
SATA 1, 36, 75

Duncan, Robert (Edward)
1919-1988 .... **CLC 1, 2, 4, 7, 15, 41, 55;**
DAM POET; PC 2
See also CA 9-12R; 124; CANR 28; DLB 5,
16; MTCW

Duncan, Sara Jeannette
1861-1922 .... **TCLC 60**
See also DLB 92

Dunlap, William 1766-1839 .... **NCLC 2**
See also DLB 30, 37, 59

Dunn, Douglas (Eaglesham)
1942- .... **CLC 6, 40**
See also CA 45-48; CANR 2, 33; DLB 40;
MTCW

Dunn, Katherine (Karen) 1945- ..... **CLC 71**
See also CA 33-36R

Dunn, Stephen 1939- .... **CLC 36**
See also CA 33-36R; CANR 12, 48, 53;
DLB 105

Dunne, Finley Peter 1867-1936.... **TCLC 28**
See also CA 108; DLB 11, 23

Dunne, John Gregory 1932- .... **CLC 28**
See also CA 25-28R; CANR 14, 50;
DLBY 80

Dunsany, Edward John Moreton Drax
Plunkett 1878-1957
See Dunsany, Lord
See also CA 104; 148; DLB 10

Dunsany, Lord .... **TCLC 2, 59**
See also Dunsany, Edward John Moreton
Drax Plunkett
See also DLB 77, 153, 156

du Perry, Jean
See Simenon, Georges (Jacques Christian)

Durang, Christopher (Ferdinand)
1949- .... **CLC 27, 38**
See also CA 105; CANR 50

Duras, Marguerite
1914-1996 .. **CLC 3, 6, 11, 20, 34, 40, 68**
See also CA 25-28R; 151; CANR 50;
DLB 83; MTCW

Durban, (Rosa) Pam 1947-......... **CLC 39**
See also CA 123

Durcan, Paul
1944- .... **CLC 43, 70; DAM POET**
See also CA 134

Durkheim, Emile 1858-1917 ...... **TCLC 55**

Durrell, Lawrence (George)
1912-1990 .... **CLC 1, 4, 6, 8, 13, 27, 41;**
DAM NOV
See also CA 9-12R; 132; CANR 40;
CDBLB 1945-1960; DLB 15, 27;
DLBY 90; MTCW

Durrenmatt, Friedrich
See Duerrenmatt, Friedrich

Dutt, Toru 1856-1877........... **NCLC 29**

Dwight, Timothy 1752-1817...... **NCLC 13**
See also DLB 37

Dworkin, Andrea 1946- .... **CLC 43**
See also CA 77-80; CAAS 21; CANR 16,
39; INT CANR-16; MTCW

Dwyer, Deanna
See Koontz, Dean R(ay)

Dwyer, K. R.
See Koontz, Dean R(ay)

Dylan, Bob 1941- ...... **CLC 3, 4, 6, 12, 77**
See also CA 41-44R; DLB 16

Eagleton, Terence (Francis) 1943-
See Eagleton, Terry
See also CA 57-60; CANR 7, 23; MTCW

Eagleton, Terry .... **CLC 63**
See also Eagleton, Terence (Francis)

Early, Jack
See Scoppettone, Sandra

East, Michael
See West, Morris L(anglo)

Eastaway, Edward
See Thomas, (Philip) Edward

Eastlake, William (Derry) 1917-..... **CLC 8**
See also CA 5-8R; CAAS 1; CANR 5;
DLB 6; INT CANR-5

Eastman, Charles A(lexander)
1858-1939 ..... **TCLC 55; DAM MULT**
See also NNAL; YABC 1

Eberhart, Richard (Ghormley)
1904- .. **CLC 3, 11, 19, 56; DAM POET**
See also CA 1-4R; CANR 2;
CDALB 1941-1968; DLB 48; MTCW

Eberstadt, Fernanda 1960-......... **CLC 39**
See also CA 136

Echegaray (y Eizaguirre), Jose (Maria Waldo)
1832-1916 .... **TCLC 4**
See also CA 104; CANR 32; HW; MTCW

Echeverria, (Jose) Esteban (Antonino)
1805-1851 .... **NCLC 18**

Echo
See Proust, (Valentin-Louis-George-Eugene-)
Marcel

Eckert, Allan W. 1931- .... **CLC 17**
See also AAYA 18; CA 13-16R; CANR 14,
45; INT CANR-14; SAAS 21; SATA 29,
91; SATA-Brief 27

Eckhart, Meister 1260(?)-1328(?) .. **CMLC 9**
See also DLB 115

Eckmar, F. R.
See de Hartog, Jan

Eco, Umberto
1932- ... **CLC 28, 60; DAM NOV, POP**
See also BEST 90:1; CA 77-80; CANR 12,
33, 55; MTCW

Eddison, E(ric) R(ucker)
1882-1945 .... **TCLC 15**
See also CA 109; 154

Edel, (Joseph) Leon 1907-...... **CLC 29, 34**
See also CA 1-4R; CANR 1, 22; DLB 103;
INT CANR-22

Eden, Emily 1797-1869 .... **NCLC 10**

Edgar, David
1948- .... **CLC 42; DAM DRAM**
See also CA 57-60; CANR 12; DLB 13;
MTCW

Edgerton, Clyde (Carlyle) 1944- .... **CLC 39**
See also AAYA 17; CA 118; 134; INT 134

Edgeworth, Maria 1768-1849... **NCLC 1, 51**
See also DLB 116, 159, 163; SATA 21

Edmonds, Paul
See Kuttner, Henry

Edmonds, Walter D(umaux) 1903- .. **CLC 35**
See also CA 5-8R; CANR 2; DLB 9;
MAICYA; SAAS 4; SATA 1, 27

Edmondson, Wallace
See Ellison, Harlan (Jay)

Edson, Russell .... **CLC 13**
See also CA 33-36R

Edwards, Bronwen Elizabeth
See Rose, Wendy

Edwards, G(erald) B(asil)
1899-1976 .... **CLC 25**
See also CA 110

Edwards, Gus 1939- .... **CLC 43**
See also CA 108; INT 108

Edwards, Jonathan
1703-1758 .... **LC 7; DA; DAC;**
DAM MST
See also DLB 24

Efron, Marina Ivanovna Tsvetaeva
See Tsvetaeva (Efron), Marina (Ivanovna)

Ehle, John (Marsden, Jr.) 1925-..... **CLC 27**
See also CA 9-12R

Ehrenbourg, Ilya (Grigoryevich)
See Ehrenburg, Ilya (Grigoryevich)

Ehrenburg, Ilya (Grigoryevich)
1891-1967 .... **CLC 18, 34, 62**
See also CA 102; 25-28R

Ehrenburg, Ilyo (Grigoryevich)
See Ehrenburg, Ilya (Grigoryevich)

Eich, Guenter 1907-1972 .... **CLC 15**
See also CA 111; 93-96; DLB 69, 124

Eichendorff, Joseph Freiherr von
   1788-1857 .... NCLC 8
   See also DLB 90

Eigner, Larry .... CLC 9
   See also Eigner, Laurence (Joel)
   See also CAAS 23; DLB 5

Eigner, Laurence (Joel) 1927-1996
   See Eigner, Larry
   See also CA 9-12R; 151; CANR 6

Einstein, Albert 1879-1955 .... TCLC 65
   See also CA 121; 133; MTCW

Eiseley, Loren Corey 1907-1977 ..... CLC 7
   See also AAYA 5; CA 1-4R; 73-76;
      CANR 6

Eisenstadt, Jill 1963- .... CLC 50
   See also CA 140

Eisenstein, Sergei (Mikhailovich)
   1898-1948 .... TCLC 57
   See also CA 114; 149

Eisner, Simon
   See Kornbluth, C(yril) M.

Ekeloef, (Bengt) Gunnar
   1907-1968 .... CLC 27; DAM POET
   See also CA 123; 25-28R

Ekelof, (Bengt) Gunnar
   See Ekeloef, (Bengt) Gunnar

Ekwensi, C. O. D.
   See Ekwensi, Cyprian (Odiatu Duaka)

Ekwensi, Cyprian (Odiatu Duaka)
   1921- ...... CLC 4; BLC; DAM MULT
   See also BW 2; CA 29-32R; CANR 18, 42;
      DLB 117; MTCW; SATA 66

Elaine .... TCLC 18
   See also Leverson, Ada

El Crummo
   See Crumb, R(obert)

Elia
   See Lamb, Charles

Eliade, Mircea 1907-1986 .... CLC 19
   See also CA 65-68; 119; CANR 30; MTCW

Eliot, A. D.
   See Jewett, (Theodora) Sarah Orne

Eliot, Alice
   See Jewett, (Theodora) Sarah Orne

Eliot, Dan
   See Silverberg, Robert

Eliot, George
   1819-1880 ..... NCLC 4, 13, 23, 41, 49;
      DA; DAB; DAC; DAM MST, NOV;
         WLC
   See also CDBLB 1832-1890; DLB 21, 35, 55

Eliot, John 1604-1690 .... LC 5
   See also DLB 24

Eliot, T(homas) S(tearns)
   1888-1965 ..... CLC 1, 2, 3, 6, 9, 10, 13,
      15, 24, 34, 41, 55, 57; DA; DAB; DAC;
         DAM DRAM, MST, POET; PC 5;
            WLC 2
   See also CA 5-8R; 25-28R; CANR 41;
      CDALB 1929-1941; DLB 7, 10, 45, 63;
         DLBY 88; MTCW

Elizabeth 1866-1941 .... TCLC 41

Elkin, Stanley L(awrence)
   1930-1995 ..... CLC 4, 6, 9, 14, 27, 51,
      91; DAM NOV, POP; SSC 12
   See also CA 9-12R; 148; CANR 8, 46;
      DLB 2, 28; DLBY 80; INT CANR-8;
         MTCW

Elledge, Scott .... CLC 34

Elliot, Don
   See Silverberg, Robert

Elliott, Don
   See Silverberg, Robert

Elliott, George P(aul) 1918-1980 ..... CLC 2
   See also CA 1-4R; 97-100; CANR 2

Elliott, Janice 1931- .... CLC 47
   See also CA 13-16R; CANR 8, 29; DLB 14

Elliott, Sumner Locke 1917-1991 ... CLC 38
   See also CA 5-8R; 134; CANR 2, 21

Elliott, William
   See Bradbury, Ray (Douglas)

Ellis, A. E. .... CLC 7

Ellis, Alice Thomas .... CLC 40
   See also Haycraft, Anna

Ellis, Bret Easton
   1964- .... CLC 39, 71; DAM POP
   See also AAYA 2; CA 118; 123; CANR 51;
      INT 123

Ellis, (Henry) Havelock
   1859-1939 .... TCLC 14
   See also CA 109

Ellis, Landon
   See Ellison, Harlan (Jay)

Ellis, Trey 1962- .... CLC 55
   See also CA 146

Ellison, Harlan (Jay)
   1934- ...... CLC 1, 13, 42; DAM POP;
      SSC 14
   See also CA 5-8R; CANR 5, 46; DLB 8;
      INT CANR-5; MTCW

Ellison, Ralph (Waldo)
   1914-1994 .... CLC 1, 3, 11, 54, 86;
      BLC; DA; DAB; DAC; DAM MST,
         MULT, NOV; WLC
   See also AAYA 19; BW 1; CA 9-12R; 145;
      CANR 24, 53; CDALB 1941-1968;
         DLB 2, 76; DLBY 94; MTCW

Ellmann, Lucy (Elizabeth) 1956-.... CLC 61
   See also CA 128

Ellmann, Richard (David)
   1918-1987 .... CLC 50
   See also BEST 89:2; CA 1-4R; 122;
      CANR 2, 28; DLB 103; DLBY 87;
         MTCW

Elman, Richard 1934-.............. CLC 19
   See also CA 17-20R; CAAS 3; CANR 47

Elron
   See Hubbard, L(afayette) Ron(ald)

Eluard, Paul .... TCLC 7, 41
   See also Grindel, Eugene

Elyot, Sir Thomas 1490(?)-1546 ..... LC 11

Elytis, Odysseus
   1911-1996 .... CLC 15, 49; DAM POET
   See also CA 102; 151; MTCW

Emecheta, (Florence Onye) Buchi
   1944- .. CLC 14, 48; BLC; DAM MULT
   See also BW 2; CA 81-84; CANR 27;
      DLB 117; MTCW; SATA 66

Emerson, Ralph Waldo
   1803-1882 ..... NCLC 1, 38; DA; DAB;
      DAC; DAM MST, POET; WLC
   See also CDALB 1640-1865; DLB 1, 59, 73

Eminescu, Mihail 1850-1889 ..... NCLC 33

Empson, William
   1906-1984 .... CLC 3, 8, 19, 33, 34
   See also CA 17-20R; 112; CANR 31;
      DLB 20; MTCW

Enchi Fumiko (Ueda) 1905-1986.... CLC 31
   See also CA 129; 121

Ende, Michael (Andreas Helmuth)
   1929-1995 .... CLC 31
   See also CA 118; 124; 149; CANR 36;
      CLR 14; DLB 75; MAICYA; SATA 61;
         SATA-Brief 42; SATA-Obit 86

Endo, Shusaku
   1923-1996 .... CLC 7, 14, 19, 54;
      DAM NOV
   See also CA 29-32R; 153; CANR 21, 54;
      MTCW

Engel, Marian 1933-1985.......... CLC 36
   See also CA 25-28R; CANR 12; DLB 53;
      INT CANR-12

Engelhardt, Frederick
   See Hubbard, L(afayette) Ron(ald)

Enright, D(ennis) J(oseph)
   1920- .... CLC 4, 8, 31
   See also CA 1-4R; CANR 1, 42; DLB 27;
      SATA 25

Enzensberger, Hans Magnus
   1929- .... CLC 43
   See also CA 116; 119

Ephron, Nora 1941-........... CLC 17, 31
   See also AITN 2; CA 65-68; CANR 12, 39

Epsilon
   See Betjeman, John

Epstein, Daniel Mark 1948- .... CLC 7
   See also CA 49-52; CANR 2, 53

Epstein, Jacob 1956- .... CLC 19
   See also CA 114

Epstein, Joseph 1937-............. CLC 39
   See also CA 112; 119; CANR 50

Epstein, Leslie 1938- .... CLC 27
   See also CA 73-76; CAAS 12; CANR 23

Equiano, Olaudah
   1745(?)-1797 .... LC 16; BLC;
      DAM MULT
   See also DLB 37, 50

Erasmus, Desiderius 1469(?)-1536.... LC 16

Erdman, Paul E(mil) 1932- .... CLC 25
   See also AITN 1; CA 61-64; CANR 13, 43

Erdrich, Louise
   1954- .... CLC 39, 54; DAM MULT,
      NOV, POP
   See also AAYA 10; BEST 89:1; CA 114;
      CANR 41; DLB 152; MTCW; NNAL

Erenburg, Ilya (Grigoryevich)
   See Ehrenburg, Ilya (Grigoryevich)

Feinstein, Elaine 1930-........... **CLC 36**
See also CA 69-72; CAAS 1; CANR 31;
DLB 14, 40; MTCW

Feldman, Irving (Mordecai) 1928-.... **CLC 7**
See also CA 1-4R; CANR 1; DLB 169

Fellini, Federico 1920-1993 ..... **CLC 16, 85**
See also CA 65-68; 143; CANR 33

Felsen, Henry Gregor 1916- .... **CLC 17**
See also CA 1-4R; CANR 1; SAAS 2;
SATA 1

Fenton, James Martin 1949-....... **CLC 32**
See also CA 102; DLB 40

Ferber, Edna 1887-1968........ **CLC 18, 93**
See also AITN 1; CA 5-8R; 25-28R; DLB 9,
28, 86; MTCW; SATA 7

Ferguson, Helen
See Kavan, Anna

Ferguson, Samuel 1810-1886..... **NCLC 33**
See also DLB 32

Fergusson, Robert 1750-1774 .... **LC 29**
See also DLB 109

Ferling, Lawrence
See Ferlinghetti, Lawrence (Monsanto)

Ferlinghetti, Lawrence (Monsanto)
1919(?)-............. **CLC 2, 6, 10, 27;**
DAM POET; PC 1
See also CA 5-8R; CANR 3, 41;
CDALB 1941-1968; DLB 5, 16; MTCW

Fernandez, Vicente Garcia Huidobro
See Huidobro Fernandez, Vicente Garcia

Ferrer, Gabriel (Francisco Victor) Miro
See Miro (Ferrer), Gabriel (Francisco
Victor)

Ferrier, Susan (Edmonstone)
1782-1854 .... **NCLC 8**
See also DLB 116

Ferrigno, Robert 1948(?)-......... **CLC 65**
See also CA 140

Ferron, Jacques 1921-1985 ... **CLC 94; DAC**
See also CA 117; 129; DLB 60

Feuchtwanger, Lion 1884-1958 ..... **TCLC 3**
See also CA 104; DLB 66

Feuillet, Octave 1821-1890 ...... **NCLC 45**

Feydeau, Georges (Leon Jules Marie)
1862-1921 ..... **TCLC 22; DAM DRAM**
See also CA 113; 152

Ficino, Marsilio 1433-1499 .... **LC 12**

Fiedeler, Hans
See Doeblin, Alfred

Fiedler, Leslie A(aron)
1917-................. **CLC 4, 13, 24**
See also CA 9-12R; CANR 7; DLB 28, 67;
MTCW

Field, Andrew 1938-.............. **CLC 44**
See also CA 97-100; CANR 25

Field, Eugene 1850-1895 .... **NCLC 3**
See also DLB 23, 42, 140; DLBD 13;
MAICYA; SATA 16

Field, Gans T.
See Wellman, Manly Wade

Field, Michael .... **TCLC 43**

Field, Peter
See Hobson, Laura Z(ametkin)

Fielding, Henry
1707-1754 ...... **LC 1; DA; DAB; DAC;**
DAM DRAM, MST, NOV; WLC
See also CDBLB 1660-1789; DLB 39, 84,
101

Fielding, Sarah 1710-1768 .... **LC 1**
See also DLB 39

Fierstein, Harvey (Forbes)
1954- ..... **CLC 33; DAM DRAM, POP**
See also CA 123; 129

Figes, Eva 1932-.................. **CLC 31**
See also CA 53-56; CANR 4, 44; DLB 14

Finch, Robert (Duer Claydon)
1900- .... **CLC 18**
See also CA 57-60; CANR 9, 24, 49;
DLB 88

Findley, Timothy
1930- .... **CLC 27; DAC; DAM MST**
See also CA 25-28R; CANR 12, 42;
DLB 53

Fink, William
See Mencken, H(enry) L(ouis)

Firbank, Louis 1942-
See Reed, Lou
See also CA 117

Firbank, (Arthur Annesley) Ronald
1886-1926 .... **TCLC 1**
See also CA 104; DLB 36

Fisher, M(ary) F(rances) K(ennedy)
1908-1992 .... **CLC 76, 87**
See also CA 77-80; 138; CANR 44

Fisher, Roy 1930-................. **CLC 25**
See also CA 81-84; CAAS 10; CANR 16;
DLB 40

Fisher, Rudolph
1897-1934 .... **TCLC 11; BLC;**
DAM MULT
See also BW 1; CA 107; 124; DLB 51, 102

Fisher, Vardis (Alvero) 1895-1968.... **CLC 7**
See also CA 5-8R; 25-28R; DLB 9

Fiske, Tarleton
See Bloch, Robert (Albert)

Fitch, Clarke
See Sinclair, Upton (Beall)

Fitch, John IV
See Cormier, Robert (Edmund)

Fitzgerald, Captain Hugh
See Baum, L(yman) Frank

FitzGerald, Edward 1809-1883 .... **NCLC 9**
See also DLB 32

Fitzgerald, F(rancis) Scott (Key)
1896-1940 ...... **TCLC 1, 6, 14, 28, 55;**
DA; DAB; DAC; DAM MST, NOV;
SSC 6; WLC
See also AITN 1; CA 110; 123;
CDALB 1917-1929; DLB 4, 9, 86;
DLBD 1; DLBY 81; MTCW

Fitzgerald, Penelope 1916-... **CLC 19, 51, 61**
See also CA 85-88; CAAS 10; DLB 14

Fitzgerald, Robert (Stuart)
1910-1985 .... **CLC 39**
See also CA 1-4R; 114; CANR 1; DLBY 80

FitzGerald, Robert D(avid)
1902-1987 .... **CLC 19**
See also CA 17-20R

Fitzgerald, Zelda (Sayre)
1900-1948 .... **TCLC 52**
See also CA 117; 126; DLBY 84

Flanagan, Thomas (James Bonner)
1923-.................... **CLC 25, 52**
See also CA 108; CANR 55; DLBY 80;
INT 108; MTCW

Flaubert, Gustave
1821-1880 .... **NCLC 2, 10, 19; DA;**
DAB; DAC; DAM MST, NOV; SSC 11;
WLC
See also DLB 119

Flecker, Herman Elroy
See Flecker, (Herman) James Elroy

Flecker, (Herman) James Elroy
1884-1915 .... **TCLC 43**
See also CA 109; 150; DLB 10, 19

Fleming, Ian (Lancaster)
1908-1964 ...... **CLC 3, 30; DAM POP**
See also CA 5-8R; CDBLB 1945-1960;
DLB 87; MTCW; SATA 9

Fleming, Thomas (James) 1927- .... **CLC 37**
See also CA 5-8R; CANR 10;
INT CANR-10; SATA 8

Fletcher, John 1579-1625...... **LC 33; DC 6**
See also CDBLB Before 1660; DLB 58

Fletcher, John Gould 1886-1950 ... **TCLC 35**
See also CA 107; DLB 4, 45

Fleur, Paul
See Pohl, Frederik

Flooglebuckle, Al
See Spiegelman, Art

Flying Officer X
See Bates, H(erbert) E(rnest)

Fo, Dario 1926-..... **CLC 32; DAM DRAM**
See also CA 116; 128; MTCW

Fogarty, Jonathan Titulescu Esq.
See Farrell, James T(homas)

Folke, Will
See Bloch, Robert (Albert)

Follett, Ken(neth Martin)
1949- ...... **CLC 18; DAM NOV, POP**
See also AAYA 6; BEST 89:4; CA 81-84;
CANR 13, 33, 54; DLB 87; DLBY 81;
INT CANR-33; MTCW

Fontane, Theodor 1819-1898..... **NCLC 26**
See also DLB 129

Foote, Horton
1916- .... **CLC 51, 91; DAM DRAM**
See also CA 73-76; CANR 34, 51; DLB 26;
INT CANR-34

Foote, Shelby
1916- ...... **CLC 75; DAM NOV, POP**
See also CA 5-8R; CANR 3, 45; DLB 2, 17

Forbes, Esther 1891-1967.......... **CLC 12**
See also AAYA 17; CA 13-14; 25-28R;
CAP 1; CLR 27; DLB 22; JRDA;
MAICYA; SATA 2

Forche, Carolyn (Louise)
1950- .... **CLC 25, 83, 86; DAM POET;**
PC 10
See also CA 109; 117; CANR 50; DLB 5;
INT 117

Ford, Elbur
See Hibbert, Eleanor Alice Burford

Ford, Ford Madox
1873-1939 .... **TCLC 1, 15, 39, 57;**
DAM NOV
See also CA 104; 132; CDBLB 1914-1945;
DLB 162; MTCW

Ford, John 1895-1973............ **CLC 16**
See also CA 45-48

Ford, Richard 1944-.............. **CLC 46**
See also CA 69-72; CANR 11, 47

Ford, Webster
See Masters, Edgar Lee

Foreman, Richard 1937-.......... **CLC 50**
See also CA 65-68; CANR 32

Forester, C(ecil) S(cott)
1899-1966 .... **CLC 35**
See also CA 73-76; 25-28R; SATA 13

Forez
See Mauriac, Francois (Charles)

Forman, James Douglas 1932-...... **CLC 21**
See also AAYA 17; CA 9-12R; CANR 4,
19, 42; JRDA; MAICYA; SATA 8, 70

Fornes, Maria Irene 1930-...... **CLC 39, 61**
See also CA 25-28R; CANR 28; DLB 7;
HW; INT CANR-28; MTCW

Forrest, Leon 1937- .... **CLC 4**
See also BW 2; CA 89-92; CAAS 7;
CANR 25, 52; DLB 33

Forster, E(dward) M(organ)
1879-1970 ..... **CLC 1, 2, 3, 4, 9, 10, 13,**
15, 22, 45, 77; DA; DAB; DAC;
DAM MST, NOV; WLC
See also AAYA 2; CA 13-14; 25-28R;
CANR 45; CAP 1; CDBLB 1914-1945;
DLB 34, 98, 162; DLBD 10; MTCW;
SATA 57

Forster, John 1812-1876 .... **NCLC 11**
See also DLB 144

Forsyth, Frederick
1938- .. **CLC 2, 5, 36; DAM NOV, POP**
See also BEST 89:4; CA 85-88; CANR 38;
DLB 87; MTCW

Forten, Charlotte L. .... **TCLC 16; BLC**
See also Grimke, Charlotte L(ottie) Forten
See also DLB 50

Foscolo, Ugo 1778-1827.......... **NCLC 8**

Fosse, Bob .... **CLC 20**
See also Fosse, Robert Louis

Fosse, Robert Louis 1927-1987
See Fosse, Bob
See also CA 110; 123

Foster, Stephen Collins
1826-1864 .... **NCLC 26**

Foucault, Michel
1926-1984 .... **CLC 31, 34, 69**
See also CA 105; 113; CANR 34; MTCW

Fouque, Friedrich (Heinrich Karl) de la Motte
1777-1843 .... **NCLC 2**
See also DLB 90

Fourier, Charles 1772-1837 ...... **NCLC 51**

Fournier, Henri Alban 1886-1914
See Alain-Fournier
See also CA 104

Fournier, Pierre 1916-............ **CLC 11**
See also Gascar, Pierre
See also CA 89-92; CANR 16, 40

Fowles, John
1926- ...... **CLC 1, 2, 3, 4, 6, 9, 10, 15,**
33, 87; DAB; DAC; DAM MST
See also CA 5-8R; CANR 25; CDBLB 1960
to Present; DLB 14, 139; MTCW;
SATA 22

Fox, Paula 1923-................. **CLC 2, 8**
See also AAYA 3; CA 73-76; CANR 20,
36; CLR 1; DLB 52; JRDA; MAICYA;
MTCW; SATA 17, 60

Fox, William Price (Jr.) 1926- ..... **CLC 22**
See also CA 17-20R; CAAS 19; CANR 11;
DLB 2; DLBY 81

Foxe, John 1516(?)-1587 .... **LC 14**

Frame, Janet
1924- .... **CLC 2, 3, 6, 22, 66, 96**
See also Clutha, Janet Paterson Frame

France, Anatole .... **TCLC 9**
See also Thibault, Jacques Anatole Francois
See also DLB 123

Francis, Claude 19(?)- .... **CLC 50**

Francis, Dick
1920- .... **CLC 2, 22, 42; DAM POP**
See also AAYA 5; BEST 89:3; CA 5-8R;
CANR 9, 42; CDBLB 1960 to Present;
DLB 87; INT CANR-9; MTCW

Francis, Robert (Churchill)
1901-1987 .... **CLC 15**
See also CA 1-4R; 123; CANR 1

Frank, Anne(lies Marie)
1929-1945 .... **TCLC 17; DA; DAB;**
DAC; DAM MST; WLC
See also AAYA 12; CA 113; 133; MTCW;
SATA 87; SATA-Brief 42

Frank, Elizabeth 1945-........... **CLC 39**
See also CA 121; 126; INT 126

Frankl, Viktor E(mil) 1905-........ **CLC 93**
See also CA 65-68

Franklin, Benjamin
See Hasek, Jaroslav (Matej Frantisek)

Franklin, Benjamin
1706-1790 ..... **LC 25; DA; DAB; DAC;**
DAM MST
See also CDALB 1640-1865; DLB 24, 43,
73

Franklin, (Stella Maraia Sarah) Miles
1879-1954 .... **TCLC 7**
See also CA 104

Fraser, (Lady) Antonia (Pakenham)
1932- .... **CLC 32**
See also CA 85-88; CANR 44; MTCW;
SATA-Brief 32

Fraser, George MacDonald 1925-.... **CLC 7**
See also CA 45-48; CANR 2, 48

Fraser, Sylvia 1935-.............. **CLC 64**
See also CA 45-48; CANR 1, 16

Frayn, Michael
1933- .... **CLC 3, 7, 31, 47;**
DAM DRAM, NOV
See also CA 5-8R; CANR 30; DLB 13, 14;
MTCW

Fraze, Candida (Merrill) 1945-..... **CLC 50**
See also CA 126

Frazer, J(ames) G(eorge)
1854-1941 .... **TCLC 32**
See also CA 118

Frazer, Robert Caine
See Creasey, John

Frazer, Sir James George
See Frazer, J(ames) G(eorge)

Frazier, Ian 1951-................ **CLC 46**
See also CA 130; CANR 54

Frederic, Harold 1856-1898...... **NCLC 10**
See also DLB 12, 23; DLBD 13

Frederick, John
See Faust, Frederick (Schiller)

Frederick the Great 1712-1786 ...... **LC 14**

Fredro, Aleksander 1793-1876..... **NCLC 8**

Freeling, Nicolas 1927- .... **CLC 38**
See also CA 49-52; CAAS 12; CANR 1, 17,
50; DLB 87

Freeman, Douglas Southall
1886-1953 .... **TCLC 11**
See also CA 109; DLB 17

Freeman, Judith 1946-............ **CLC 55**
See also CA 148

Freeman, Mary Eleanor Wilkins
1852-1930 .... **TCLC 9; SSC 1**
See also CA 106; DLB 12, 78

Freeman, R(ichard) Austin
1862-1943 .... **TCLC 21**
See also CA 113; DLB 70

French, Albert 1943- .... **CLC 86**

French, Marilyn
1929- .... **CLC 10, 18, 60;**
DAM DRAM, NOV, POP
See also CA 69-72; CANR 3, 31;
INT CANR-31; MTCW

French, Paul
See Asimov, Isaac

Freneau, Philip Morin 1752-1832.. **NCLC 1**
See also DLB 37, 43

Freud, Sigmund 1856-1939 .... **TCLC 52**
See also CA 115; 133; MTCW

Friedan, Betty (Naomi) 1921-...... **CLC 74**
See also CA 65-68; CANR 18, 45; MTCW

Friedlander, Saul 1932-........... **CLC 90**
See also CA 117; 130

Friedman, B(ernard) H(arper)
1926-........................ **CLC 7**
See also CA 1-4R; CANR 3, 48

Friedman, Bruce Jay 1930-.... **CLC 3, 5, 56**
See also CA 9-12R; CANR 25, 52; DLB 2,
28; INT CANR-25

Friel, Brian 1929-........... **CLC 5, 42, 59**
See also CA 21-24R; CANR 33; DLB 13;
MTCW

Friis-Baastad, Babbis Ellinor
1921-1970 .... **CLC 12**
See also CA 17-20R; 134; SATA 7

Frisch, Max (Rudolf)
1911-1991 ..... **CLC 3, 9, 14, 18, 32, 44;**
DAM DRAM, NOV
See also CA 85-88; 134; CANR 32;
DLB 69, 124; MTCW

Fromentin, Eugene (Samuel Auguste)
1820-1876 .... **NCLC 10**
See also DLB 123

Frost, Frederick
See Faust, Frederick (Schiller)

Frost, Robert (Lee)
1874-1963 .... **CLC 1, 3, 4, 9, 10, 13, 15,**
26, 34, 44; DA; DAB; DAC; DAM MST,
POET; PC 1; WLC
See also CA 89-92; CANR 33;
CDALB 1917-1929; DLB 54; DLBD 7;
MTCW; SATA 14

Froude, James Anthony
1818-1894 .... **NCLC 43**
See also DLB 18, 57, 144

Froy, Herald
See Waterhouse, Keith (Spencer)

Fry, Christopher
1907- ..... **CLC 2, 10, 14; DAM DRAM**
See also CA 17-20R; CAAS 23; CANR 9,
30; DLB 13; MTCW; SATA 66

Frye, (Herman) Northrop
1912-1991 .... **CLC 24, 70**
See also CA 5-8R; 133; CANR 8, 37;
DLB 67, 68; MTCW

Fuchs, Daniel 1909-1993 .... **CLC 8, 22**
See also CA 81-84; 142; CAAS 5;
CANR 40; DLB 9, 26, 28; DLBY 93

Fuchs, Daniel 1934- .... **CLC 34**
See also CA 37-40R; CANR 14, 48

Fuentes, Carlos
1928- ...... **CLC 3, 8, 10, 13, 22, 41, 60;**
DA; DAB; DAC; DAM MST, MULT,
NOV; HLC; SSC 24; WLC
See also AAYA 4; AITN 2; CA 69-72;
CANR 10, 32; DLB 113; HW; MTCW

Fuentes, Gregorio Lopez y
See Lopez y Fuentes, Gregorio

Fugard, (Harold) Athol
1932- .... **CLC 5, 9, 14, 25, 40, 80;**
DAM DRAM; DC 3
See also AAYA 17; CA 85-88; CANR 32,
54; MTCW

Fugard, Sheila 1932- .... **CLC 48**
See also CA 125

Fuller, Charles (H., Jr.)
1939- .... **CLC 25; BLC; DAM DRAM,**
MULT; DC 1
See also BW 2; CA 108; 112; DLB 38;
INT 112; MTCW

Fuller, John (Leopold) 1937- .... **CLC 62**
See also CA 21-24R; CANR 9, 44; DLB 40

Fuller, Margaret .... **NCLC 5, 50**
See also Ossoli, Sarah Margaret (Fuller
marchesa d')

Fuller, Roy (Broadbent)
1912-1991 .... **CLC 4, 28**
See also CA 5-8R; 135; CAAS 10;
CANR 53; DLB 15, 20; SATA 87

Fulton, Alice 1952- .... **CLC 52**
See also CA 116

Furphy, Joseph 1843-1912 .... **TCLC 25**

Fussell, Paul 1924- .... **CLC 74**
See also BEST 90:1; CA 17-20R; CANR 8,
21, 35; INT CANR-21; MTCW

Futabatei, Shimei 1864-1909 ...... **TCLC 44**

Futrelle, Jacques 1875-1912 ...... **TCLC 19**
See also CA 113

Gaboriau, Emile 1835-1873 ...... **NCLC 14**

Gadda, Carlo Emilio 1893-1973 .... **CLC 11**
See also CA 89-92

Gaddis, William
1922- ..... **CLC 1, 3, 6, 8, 10, 19, 43, 86**
See also CA 17-20R; CANR 21, 48; DLB 2;
MTCW

Gage, Walter
See Inge, William (Motter)

Gaines, Ernest J(ames)
1933- .... **CLC 3, 11, 18, 86; BLC;**
DAM MULT
See also AAYA 18; AITN 1; BW 2;
CA 9-12R; CANR 6, 24, 42;
CDALB 1968-1988; DLB 2, 33, 152;
DLBY 80; MTCW; SATA 86

Gaitskill, Mary 1954- .... **CLC 69**
See also CA 128

Galdos, Benito Perez
See Perez Galdos, Benito

Gale, Zona
1874-1938 ...... **TCLC 7; DAM DRAM**
See also CA 105; 153; DLB 9, 78

Galeano, Eduardo (Hughes) 1940-... **CLC 72**
See also CA 29-32R; CANR 13, 32; HW

Galiano, Juan Valera y Alcala
See Valera y Alcala-Galiano, Juan

Gallagher, Tess
1943- .. **CLC 18, 63; DAM POET; PC 9**
See also CA 106; DLB 120

Gallant, Mavis
1922- .... **CLC 7, 18, 38; DAC;**
DAM MST; SSC 5
See also CA 69-72; CANR 29; DLB 53;
MTCW

Gallant, Roy A(rthur) 1924- .... **CLC 17**
See also CA 5-8R; CANR 4, 29, 54;
CLR 30; MAICYA; SATA 4, 68

Gallico, Paul (William) 1897-1976 ... **CLC 2**
See also AITN 1; CA 5-8R; 69-72;
CANR 23; DLB 9, 171; MAICYA;
SATA 13

Gallo, Max Louis 1932- .... **CLC 95**
See also CA 85-88

Gallois, Lucien
See Desnos, Robert

Gallup, Ralph
See Whitemore, Hugh (John)

Galsworthy, John
1867-1933 ...... **TCLC 1, 45; DA; DAB;**
DAC; DAM DRAM, MST, NOV;
SSC 22; WLC 2
See also CA 104; 141; CDBLB 1890-1914;
DLB 10, 34, 98, 162

Galt, John 1779-1839 .... **NCLC 1**
See also DLB 99, 116, 159

Galvin, James 1951- .... **CLC 38**
See also CA 108; CANR 26

Gamboa, Federico 1864-1939 ...... **TCLC 36**

Gandhi, M. K.
See Gandhi, Mohandas Karamchand

Gandhi, Mahatma
See Gandhi, Mohandas Karamchand

Gandhi, Mohandas Karamchand
1869-1948 ..... **TCLC 59; DAM MULT**
See also CA 121; 132; MTCW

Gann, Ernest Kellogg 1910-1991.... **CLC 23**
See also AITN 1; CA 1-4R; 136; CANR 1

Garcia, Cristina 1958- .... **CLC 76**
See also CA 141

Garcia Lorca, Federico
1898-1936 ... **TCLC 1, 7, 49; DA; DAB;**
DAC; DAM DRAM, MST, MULT,
POET; DC 2; HLC; PC 3; WLC
See also CA 104; 131; DLB 108; HW;
MTCW

Garcia Marquez, Gabriel (Jose)
1928- .... **CLC 2, 3, 8, 10, 15, 27, 47, 55,**
68; DA; DAB; DAC; DAM MST,
MULT, NOV, POP; HLC; SSC 8; WLC
See also AAYA 3; BEST 89:1; 90:4;
CA 33-36R; CANR 10, 28, 50; DLB 113;
HW; MTCW

Gard, Janice
See Latham, Jean Lee

Gard, Roger Martin du
See Martin du Gard, Roger

Gardam, Jane 1928- .... **CLC 43**
See also CA 49-52; CANR 2, 18, 33, 54;
CLR 12; DLB 14, 161; MAICYA;
MTCW; SAAS 9; SATA 39, 76;
SATA-Brief 28

Gardner, Herb(ert) 1934- .... **CLC 44**
See also CA 149

Gardner, John (Champlin), Jr.
1933-1982 ..... **CLC 2, 3, 5, 7, 8, 10, 18,**
28, 34; DAM NOV, POP; SSC 7
See also AITN 1; CA 65-68; 107;
CANR 33; DLB 2; DLBY 82; MTCW;
SATA 40; SATA-Obit 31

Gardner, John (Edmund)
1926- .... **CLC 30; DAM POP**
See also CA 103; CANR 15; MTCW

Gardner, Miriam
See Bradley, Marion Zimmer

Gardner, Noel
See Kuttner, Henry

Gardons, S. S.
See Snodgrass, W(illiam) D(e Witt)

Garfield, Leon 1921-1996.......... **CLC 12**
See also AAYA 8; CA 17-20R; 152;
CANR 38, 41; CLR 21; DLB 161; JRDA;
MAICYA; SATA 1, 32, 76;
SATA-Obit 90

Garland, (Hannibal) Hamlin
1860-1940 .... **TCLC 3; SSC 18**
See also CA 104; DLB 12, 71, 78

Garneau, (Hector de) Saint-Denys
1912-1943 .... **TCLC 13**
See also CA 111; DLB 88

Garner, Alan
1934- .... **CLC 17; DAB; DAM POP**
See also AAYA 18; CA 73-76; CANR 15;
CLR 20; DLB 161; MAICYA; MTCW;
SATA 18, 69

Garner, Hugh 1913-1979 .... **CLC 13**
See also CA 69-72; CANR 31; DLB 68

Garnett, David 1892-1981 .... **CLC 3**
See also CA 5-8R; 103; CANR 17; DLB 34

Garos, Stephanie
See Katz, Steve

Garrett, George (Palmer)
1929- .... **CLC 3, 11, 51**
See also CA 1-4R; CAAS 5; CANR 1, 42;
DLB 2, 5, 130, 152; DLBY 83

Garrick, David
1717-1779 .... **LC 15; DAM DRAM**
See also DLB 84

Garrigue, Jean 1914-1972 .... **CLC 2, 8**
See also CA 5-8R; 37-40R; CANR 20

Garrison, Frederick
See Sinclair, Upton (Beall)

Garth, Will
See Hamilton, Edmond; Kuttner, Henry

Garvey, Marcus (Moziah, Jr.)
1887-1940 .... **TCLC 41; BLC;**
DAM MULT
See also BW 1; CA 120; 124

Gary, Romain .... **CLC 25**
See also Kacew, Romain
See also DLB 83

Gascar, Pierre .... **CLC 11**
See also Fournier, Pierre

Gascoyne, David (Emery) 1916- .... **CLC 45**
See also CA 65-68; CANR 10, 28, 54;
DLB 20; MTCW

Gaskell, Elizabeth Cleghorn
1810-1865 .. **NCLC 5; DAB; DAM MST**
See also CDBLB 1832-1890; DLB 21, 144,
159

Gass, William H(oward)
1924- ... **CLC 1, 2, 8, 11, 15, 39; SSC 12**
See also CA 17-20R; CANR 30; DLB 2;
MTCW

Gasset, Jose Ortega y
See Ortega y Gasset, Jose

Gates, Henry Louis, Jr.
1950- .... **CLC 65; DAM MULT**
See also BW 2; CA 109; CANR 25, 53;
DLB 67

Gautier, Theophile
1811-1872 ...... **NCLC 1; DAM POET;**
SSC 20
See also DLB 119

Gawsworth, John
See Bates, H(erbert) E(rnest)

Gay, Oliver
See Gogarty, Oliver St. John

Gaye, Marvin (Penze) 1939-1984 ... **CLC 26**
See also CA 112

Gebler, Carlo (Ernest) 1954- .... **CLC 39**
See also CA 119; 133

Gee, Maggie (Mary) 1948- .... **CLC 57**
See also CA 130

Gee, Maurice (Gough) 1931- .... **CLC 29**
See also CA 97-100; SATA 46

Gelbart, Larry (Simon) 1923- ... **CLC 21, 61**
See also CA 73-76; CANR 45

Gelber, Jack 1932- .... **CLC 1, 6, 14, 79**
See also CA 1-4R; CANR 2; DLB 7

Gellhorn, Martha (Ellis) 1908- .. **CLC 14, 60**
See also CA 77-80; CANR 44; DLBY 82

Genet, Jean
1910-1986 ...... **CLC 1, 2, 5, 10, 14, 44,**
46; DAM DRAM
See also CA 13-16R; CANR 18; DLB 72;
DLBY 86; MTCW

Gent, Peter 1942- .... **CLC 29**
See also AITN 1; CA 89-92; DLBY 82

Gentlewoman in New England, A
See Bradstreet, Anne

Gentlewoman in Those Parts, A
See Bradstreet, Anne

George, Jean Craighead 1919- ...... **CLC 35**
See also AAYA 8; CA 5-8R; CANR 25;
CLR 1; DLB 52; JRDA; MAICYA;
SATA 2, 68

George, Stefan (Anton)
1868-1933 .... **TCLC 2, 14**
See also CA 104

Georges, Georges Martin
See Simenon, Georges (Jacques Christian)

Gerhardi, William Alexander
See Gerhardie, William Alexander

Gerhardie, William Alexander
1895-1977 .... **CLC 5**
See also CA 25-28R; 73-76; CANR 18;
DLB 36

Gerstler, Amy 1956- .... **CLC 70**
See also CA 146

Gertler, T. .... **CLC 34**
See also CA 116; 121; INT 121

gfgg .... **CLC XvXzc**

Ghalib .... **NCLC 39**
See also Ghalib, Hsadullah Khan

Ghalib, Hsadullah Khan 1797-1869
See Ghalib
See also DAM POET

Ghelderode, Michel de
1898-1962 .... **CLC 6, 11; DAM DRAM**
See also CA 85-88; CANR 40

Ghiselin, Brewster 1903- .... **CLC 23**
See also CA 13-16R; CAAS 10; CANR 13

Ghose, Zulfikar 1935- .... **CLC 42**
See also CA 65-68

Ghosh, Amitav 1956- .... **CLC 44**
See also CA 147

Giacosa, Giuseppe 1847-1906 ...... **TCLC 7**
See also CA 104

Gibb, Lee
See Waterhouse, Keith (Spencer)

Gibbon, Lewis Grassic .... **TCLC 4**
See also Mitchell, James Leslie

Gibbons, Kaye
1960- .... **CLC 50, 88; DAM POP**
See also CA 151

Gibran, Kahlil
1883-1931 .... **TCLC 1, 9; DAM POET,**
POP; PC 9
See also CA 104; 150

Gibran, Khalil
See Gibran, Kahlil

Gibson, William
1914- .... **CLC 23; DA; DAB; DAC;**
DAM DRAM, MST
See also CA 9-12R; CANR 9, 42; DLB 7;
SATA 66

Gibson, William (Ford)
1948- .... **CLC 39, 63; DAM POP**
See also AAYA 12; CA 126; 133; CANR 52

Gide, Andre (Paul Guillaume)
1869-1951 .... **TCLC 5, 12, 36; DA;**
DAB; DAC; DAM MST, NOV; SSC 13;
WLC
See also CA 104; 124; DLB 65; MTCW

Gifford, Barry (Colby) 1946- .... **CLC 34**
See also CA 65-68; CANR 9, 30, 40

Gilbert, W(illiam) S(chwenck)
1836-1911 ..... **TCLC 3; DAM DRAM,**
POET
See also CA 104; SATA 36

Gilbreth, Frank B., Jr. 1911- .... **CLC 17**
See also CA 9-12R; SATA 2

Gilchrist, Ellen
1935- .... **CLC 34, 48; DAM POP;**
SSC 14
See also CA 113; 116; CANR 41; DLB 130;
MTCW

Giles, Molly 1942- .... **CLC 39**
See also CA 126

Gill, Patrick
See Creasey, John

Gilliam, Terry (Vance) 1940- .... **CLC 21**
See also Monty Python
See also AAYA 19; CA 108; 113;
CANR 35; INT 113

Gillian, Jerry
See Gilliam, Terry (Vance)

Gilliatt, Penelope (Ann Douglass)
1932-1993 .... **CLC 2, 10, 13, 53**
See also AITN 2; CA 13-16R; 141;
CANR 49; DLB 14

Gilman, Charlotte (Anna) Perkins (Stetson)
1860-1935 .... **TCLC 9, 37; SSC 13**
See also CA 106; 150

Gilmour, David 1949- .... **CLC 35**
See also CA 138, 147

Gilpin, William 1724-1804 .... **NCLC 30**

Gilray, J. D.
See Mencken, H(enry) L(ouis)

Gilroy, Frank D(aniel) 1925- .... **CLC 2**
See also CA 81-84; CANR 32; DLB 7

Ginsberg, Allen
1926- ...... **CLC 1, 2, 3, 4, 6, 13, 36, 69;**
DA; DAB; DAC; DAM MST, POET;
PC 4; WLC 3
See also AITN 1; CA 1-4R; CANR 2, 41;
CDALB 1941-1968; DLB 5, 16, 169;
MTCW

Ginzburg, Natalia
1916-1991 .... **CLC 5, 11, 54, 70**
See also CA 85-88; 135; CANR 33; MTCW

Giono, Jean 1895-1970 .... **CLC 4, 11**
See also CA 45-48; 29-32R; CANR 2, 35;
DLB 72; MTCW

Giovanni, Nikki
  1943- ...... **CLC 2, 4, 19, 64; BLC; DA;**
    DAB; DAC; DAM MST, MULT, POET
  See also AITN 1; BW 2; CA 29-32R;
    CAAS 6; CANR 18, 41; CLR 6; DLB 5,
    41; INT CANR-18; MAICYA; MTCW;
    SATA 24

Giovene, Andrea 1904-............. **CLC 7**
  See also CA 85-88

Gippius, Zinaida (Nikolayevna) 1869-1945
  See Hippius, Zinaida
  See also CA 106

Giraudoux, (Hippolyte) Jean
  1882-1944 .... **TCLC 2, 7; DAM DRAM**
  See also CA 104; DLB 65

Gironella, Jose Maria 1917- .... **CLC 11**
  See also CA 101

Gissing, George (Robert)
  1857-1903 .... **TCLC 3, 24, 47**
  See also CA 105; DLB 18, 135

Giurlani, Aldo
  See Palazzeschi, Aldo

Gladkov, Fyodor (Vasilyevich)
  1883-1958 .... **TCLC 27**

Glanville, Brian (Lester) 1931- ...... **CLC 6**
  See also CA 5-8R; CAAS 9; CANR 3;
    DLB 15, 139; SATA 42

Glasgow, Ellen (Anderson Gholson)
  1873(?)-1945 .... **TCLC 2, 7**
  See also CA 104; DLB 9, 12

Glaspell, Susan 1882(?)-1948...... **TCLC 55**
  See also CA 110; 154; DLB 7, 9, 78;
    YABC 2

Glassco, John 1909-1981 .... **CLC 9**
  See also CA 13-16R; 102; CANR 15;
    DLB 68

Glasscock, Amnesia
  See Steinbeck, John (Ernst)

Glasser, Ronald J. 1940(?)-........ **CLC 37**

Glassman, Joyce
  See Johnson, Joyce

Glendinning, Victoria 1937-........ **CLC 50**
  See also CA 120; 127; DLB 155

Glissant, Edouard
  1928- .... **CLC 10, 68; DAM MULT**
  See also CA 153

Gloag, Julian 1930- .... **CLC 40**
  See also AITN 1; CA 65-68; CANR 10

Glowacki, Aleksander
  See Prus, Boleslaw

Gluck, Louise (Elisabeth)
  1943- .... **CLC 7, 22, 44, 81;**
    DAM POET; PC 16
  See also CA 33-36R; CANR 40; DLB 5

Gobineau, Joseph Arthur (Comte) de
  1816-1882 .... **NCLC 17**
  See also DLB 123

Godard, Jean-Luc 1930-........... **CLC 20**
  See also CA 93-96

Godden, (Margaret) Rumer 1907-... **CLC 53**
  See also AAYA 6; CA 5-8R; CANR 4, 27,
    36, 55; CLR 20; DLB 161; MAICYA;
    SAAS 12; SATA 3, 36

Godoy Alcayaga, Lucila 1889-1957
  See Mistral, Gabriela
  See also BW 2; CA 104; 131; DAM MULT;
    HW; MTCW

Godwin, Gail (Kathleen)
  1937- .... **CLC 5, 8, 22, 31, 69;**
    DAM POP
  See also CA 29-32R; CANR 15, 43; DLB 6;
    INT CANR-15; MTCW

Godwin, William 1756-1836...... **NCLC 14**
  See also CDBLB 1789-1832; DLB 39, 104,
    142, 158, 163

Goethe, Johann Wolfgang von
  1749-1832 ....**NCLC 4, 22, 34; DA;**
    DAB; DAC; DAM DRAM, MST,
    POET; PC 5; WLC 3
  See also DLB 94

Gogarty, Oliver St. John
  1878-1957 .... **TCLC 15**
  See also CA 109; 150; DLB 15, 19

Gogol, Nikolai (Vasilyevich)
  1809-1852 .... **NCLC 5, 15, 31; DA;**
    DAB; DAC; DAM DRAM, MST; DC 1;
    SSC 4; WLC

Goines, Donald
  1937(?)-1974 .... **CLC 80; BLC;**
    DAM MULT, POP
  See also AITN 1; BW 1; CA 124; 114;
    DLB 33

Gold, Herbert 1924-....... **CLC 4, 7, 14, 42**
  See also CA 9-12R; CANR 17, 45; DLB 2;
    DLBY 81

Goldbarth, Albert 1948-........ **CLC 5, 38**
  See also CA 53-56; CANR 6, 40; DLB 120

Goldberg, Anatol 1910-1982 .... **CLC 34**
  See also CA 131; 117

Goldemberg, Isaac 1945- .... **CLC 52**
  See also CA 69-72; CAAS 12; CANR 11,
    32; HW

Golding, William (Gerald)
  1911-1993 .... **CLC 1, 2, 3, 8, 10, 17, 27,**
    58, 81; DA; DAB; DAC; DAM MST,
    NOV; WLC
  See also AAYA 5; CA 5-8R; 141;
    CANR 13, 33, 54; CDBLB 1945-1960;
    DLB 15, 100; MTCW

Goldman, Emma 1869-1940...... **TCLC 13**
  See also CA 110; 150

Goldman, Francisco 1955-........ **CLC 76**

Goldman, William (W.) 1931-.... **CLC 1, 48**
  See also CA 9-12R; CANR 29; DLB 44

Goldmann, Lucien 1913-1970 ...... **CLC 24**
  See also CA 25-28; CAP 2

Goldoni, Carlo
  1707-1793 .... **LC 4; DAM DRAM**

Goldsberry, Steven 1949-.......... **CLC 34**
  See also CA 131

Goldsmith, Oliver
  1728-1774 ...... **LC 2; DA; DAB; DAC;**
    DAM DRAM, MST, NOV, POET;
    WLC
  See also CDBLB 1660-1789; DLB 39, 89,
    104, 109, 142; SATA 26

Goldsmith, Peter
  See Priestley, J(ohn) B(oynton)

Gombrowicz, Witold
  1904-1969 .... **CLC 4, 7, 11, 49;**
    DAM DRAM
  See also CA 19-20; 25-28R; CAP 2

Gomez de la Serna, Ramon
  1888-1963 .... **CLC 9**
  See also CA 153; 116; HW

Goncharov, Ivan Alexandrovich
  1812-1891 .... **NCLC 1**

Goncourt, Edmond (Louis Antoine Huot) de
  1822-1896 .... **NCLC 7**
  See also DLB 123

Goncourt, Jules (Alfred Huot) de
  1830-1870 .... **NCLC 7**
  See also DLB 123

Gontier, Fernande 19(?)- .... **CLC 50**

Goodman, Paul 1911-1972.... **CLC 1, 2, 4, 7**
  See also CA 19-20; 37-40R; CANR 34;
    CAP 2; DLB 130; MTCW

Gordimer, Nadine
  1923- .... **CLC 3, 5, 7, 10, 18, 33, 51, 70;**
    DA; DAB; DAC; DAM MST, NOV;
    SSC 17
  See also CA 5-8R; CANR 3, 28;
    INT CANR-28; MTCW

Gordon, Adam Lindsay
  1833-1870 .... **NCLC 21**

Gordon, Caroline
  1895-1981 ... **CLC 6, 13, 29, 83; SSC 15**
  See also CA 11-12; 103; CANR 36; CAP 1;
    DLB 4, 9, 102; DLBY 81; MTCW

Gordon, Charles William 1860-1937
  See Connor, Ralph
  See also CA 109

Gordon, Mary (Catherine)
  1949- .... **CLC 13, 22**
  See also CA 102; CANR 44; DLB 6;
    DLBY 81; INT 102; MTCW

Gordon, Sol 1923-................. **CLC 26**
  See also CA 53-56; CANR 4; SATA 11

Gordone, Charles
  1925-1995 ..... **CLC 1, 4; DAM DRAM**
  See also BW 1; CA 93-96; 150; CANR 55;
    DLB 7; INT 93-96; MTCW

Gorenko, Anna Andreevna
  See Akhmatova, Anna

Gorky, Maxim......... **TCLC 8; DAB; WLC**
  See also Peshkov, Alexei Maximovich

Goryan, Sirak
  See Saroyan, William

Gosse, Edmund (William)
  1849-1928 .... **TCLC 28**
  See also CA 117; DLB 57, 144

Gotlieb, Phyllis Fay (Bloom)
  1926- .... **CLC 18**
  See also CA 13-16R; CANR 7; DLB 88

Gottesman, S. D.
  See Kornbluth, C(yril) M.; Pohl, Frederik

Gottfried von Strassburg
  fl. c. 1210-................. **CMLC 10**
  See also DLB 138

Gould, Lois .... **CLC 4, 10**
  See also CA 77-80; CANR 29; MTCW

Gourmont, Remy (-Marie-Charles) de
1858-1915 . . . . TCLC 17
See also CA 109; 150

Govier, Katherine 1948- . . . . CLC 51
See also CA 101; CANR 18, 40

Goyen, (Charles) William
1915-1983 . . . . CLC 5, 8, 14, 40
See also AITN 2; CA 5-8R; 110; CANR 6;
DLB 2; DLBY 83; INT CANR-6

Goytisolo, Juan
1931- . . . . . CLC 5, 10, 23; DAM MULT;
HLC
See also CA 85-88; CANR 32; HW; MTCW

Gozzano, Guido 1883-1916 . . . . PC 10
See also CA 154; DLB 114

Gozzi, (Conte) Carlo 1720-1806 . . NCLC 23

Grabbe, Christian Dietrich
1801-1836 . . . . NCLC 2
See also DLB 133

Grace, Patricia 1937- . . . . CLC 56

Gracian y Morales, Baltasar
1601-1658 . . . . LC 15

Gracq, Julien . . . . CLC 11, 48
See also Poirier, Louis
See also DLB 83

Grade, Chaim 1910-1982 . . . . CLC 10
See also CA 93-96; 107

Graduate of Oxford, A
See Ruskin, John

Graham, John
See Phillips, David Graham

Graham, Jorie 1951- . . . . CLC 48
See also CA 111; DLB 120

Graham, R(obert) B(ontine) Cunninghame
See Cunninghame Graham, R(obert)
B(ontine)
See also DLB 98, 135, 174

Graham, Robert
See Haldeman, Joe (William)

Graham, Tom
See Lewis, (Harry) Sinclair

Graham, W(illiam) S(ydney)
1918-1986 . . . . CLC 29
See also CA 73-76; 118; DLB 20

Graham, Winston (Mawdsley)
1910- . . . . CLC 23
See also CA 49-52; CANR 2, 22, 45;
DLB 77

Grahame, Kenneth
1859-1932 . . . . TCLC 64; DAB
See also CA 108; 136; CLR 5; DLB 34, 141;
MAICYA; YABC 1

Grant, Skeeter
See Spiegelman, Art

Granville-Barker, Harley
1877-1946 . . . . . . TCLC 2; DAM DRAM
See also Barker, Harley Granville
See also CA 104

Grass, Guenter (Wilhelm)
1927- . . . . . CLC 1, 2, 4, 6, 11, 15, 22, 32,
49, 88; DA; DAB; DAC; DAM MST,
NOV; WLC
See also CA 13-16R; CANR 20; DLB 75,
124; MTCW

Gratton, Thomas
See Hulme, T(homas) E(rnest)

Grau, Shirley Ann
1929- . . . . CLC 4, 9; SSC 15
See also CA 89-92; CANR 22; DLB 2;
INT CANR-22; MTCW

Gravel, Fern
See Hall, James Norman

Graver, Elizabeth 1964- . . . . CLC 70
See also CA 135

Graves, Richard Perceval 1945- . . . . CLC 44
See also CA 65-68; CANR 9, 26, 51

Graves, Robert (von Ranke)
1895-1985 . . . . . . CLC 1, 2, 6, 11, 39, 44,
45; DAB; DAC; DAM MST, POET;
PC 6
See also CA 5-8R; 117; CANR 5, 36;
CDBLB 1914-1945; DLB 20, 100;
DLBY 85; MTCW; SATA 45

Graves, Valerie
See Bradley, Marion Zimmer

Gray, Alasdair (James) 1934- . . . . . . CLC 41
See also CA 126; CANR 47; INT 126;
MTCW

Gray, Amlin 1946- . . . . CLC 29
See also CA 138

Gray, Francine du Plessix
1930- . . . . CLC 22; DAM NOV
See also BEST 90:3; CA 61-64; CAAS 2;
CANR 11, 33; INT CANR-11; MTCW

Gray, John (Henry) 1866-1934 . . . . TCLC 19
See also CA 119

Gray, Simon (James Holliday)
1936- . . . . CLC 9, 14, 36
See also AITN 1; CA 21-24R; CAAS 3;
CANR 32; DLB 13; MTCW

Gray, Spalding 1941- . . CLC 49; DAM POP
See also CA 128

Gray, Thomas
1716-1771 . . . . . . LC 4; DA; DAB; DAC;
DAM MST; PC 2; WLC
See also CDBLB 1660-1789; DLB 109

Grayson, David
See Baker, Ray Stannard

Grayson, Richard (A.) 1951- . . . . CLC 38
See also CA 85-88; CANR 14, 31

Greeley, Andrew M(oran)
1928- . . . . CLC 28; DAM POP
See also CA 5-8R; CAAS 7; CANR 7, 43;
MTCW

Green, Anna Katharine
1846-1935 . . . . TCLC 63
See also CA 112

Green, Brian
See Card, Orson Scott

Green, Hannah
See Greenberg, Joanne (Goldenberg)

Green, Hannah . . . . CLC 3
See also CA 73-76

Green, Henry 1905-1973 . . . . . CLC 2, 13, 97
See also Yorke, Henry Vincent
See also DLB 15

Green, Julian (Hartridge) 1900-
See Green, Julien
See also CA 21-24R; CANR 33; DLB 4, 72;
MTCW

Green, Julien . . . . CLC 3, 11, 77
See also Green, Julian (Hartridge)

Green, Paul (Eliot)
1894-1981 . . . . . . CLC 25; DAM DRAM
See also AITN 1; CA 5-8R; 103; CANR 3;
DLB 7, 9; DLBY 81

Greenberg, Ivan 1908-1973
See Rahv, Philip
See also CA 85-88

Greenberg, Joanne (Goldenberg)
1932- . . . . CLC 7, 30
See also AAYA 12; CA 5-8R; CANR 14,
32; SATA 25

Greenberg, Richard 1959(?)- . . . . CLC 57
See also CA 138

Greene, Bette 1934- . . . . CLC 30
See also AAYA 7; CA 53-56; CANR 4;
CLR 2; JRDA; MAICYA; SAAS 16;
SATA 8

Greene, Gael . . . . CLC 8
See also CA 13-16R; CANR 10

Greene, Graham
1904-1991 . . . . CLC 1, 3, 6, 9, 14, 18, 27,
37, 70, 72; DA; DAB; DAC; DAM MST,
NOV; WLC
See also AITN 2; CA 13-16R; 133;
CANR 35; CDBLB 1945-1960; DLB 13,
15, 77, 100, 162; DLBY 91; MTCW;
SATA 20

Greer, Richard
See Silverberg, Robert

Gregor, Arthur 1923- . . . . CLC 9
See also CA 25-28R; CAAS 10; CANR 11;
SATA 36

Gregor, Lee
See Pohl, Frederik

Gregory, Isabella Augusta (Persse)
1852-1932 . . . . TCLC 1
See also CA 104; DLB 10

Gregory, J. Dennis
See Williams, John A(lfred)

Grendon, Stephen
See Derleth, August (William)

Grenville, Kate 1950- . . . . CLC 61
See also CA 118; CANR 53

Grenville, Pelham
See Wodehouse, P(elham) G(renville)

Greve, Felix Paul (Berthold Friedrich)
1879-1948
See Grove, Frederick Philip
See also CA 104; 141; DAC; DAM MST

Grey, Zane
1872-1939 . . . . TCLC 6; DAM POP
See also CA 104; 132; DLB 9; MTCW

Grieg, (Johan) Nordahl (Brun)
1902-1943 . . . . TCLC 10
See also CA 107

Grieve, C(hristopher) M(urray)
1892-1978 . . . . CLC 11, 19; DAM POET
See also MacDiarmid, Hugh; Pteleon
See also CA 5-8R; 85-88; CANR 33;
MTCW

Griffin, Gerald 1803-1840 .... **NCLC 7**
See also DLB 159

Griffin, John Howard 1920-1980.... **CLC 68**
See also AITN 1; CA 1-4R; 101; CANR 2

Griffin, Peter 1942- .... **CLC 39**
See also CA 136

Griffiths, Trevor 1935-......... **CLC 13, 52**
See also CA 97-100; CANR 45; DLB 13

Grigson, Geoffrey (Edward Harvey)
1905-1985 .... **CLC 7, 39**
See also CA 25-28R; 118; CANR 20, 33;
DLB 27; MTCW

Grillparzer, Franz 1791-1872...... **NCLC 1**
See also DLB 133

Grimble, Reverend Charles James
See Eliot, T(homas) S(tearns)

Grimke, Charlotte L(ottie) Forten
1837(?)-1914
See Forten, Charlotte L.
See also BW 1; CA 117; 124; DAM MULT,
POET

Grimm, Jacob Ludwig Karl
1785-1863 .... **NCLC 3**
See also DLB 90; MAICYA; SATA 22

Grimm, Wilhelm Karl 1786-1859 .. **NCLC 3**
See also DLB 90; MAICYA; SATA 22

Grimmelshausen, Johann Jakob Christoffel
von 1621-1676 .... **LC 6**
See also DLB 168

Grindel, Eugene 1895-1952
See Eluard, Paul
See also CA 104

Grisham, John 1955- .. **CLC 84; DAM POP**
See also AAYA 14; CA 138; CANR 47

Grossman, David 1954- .... **CLC 67**
See also CA 138

Grossman, Vasily (Semenovich)
1905-1964 .... **CLC 41**
See also CA 124; 130; MTCW

Grove, Frederick Philip .... **TCLC 4**
See also Greve, Felix Paul (Berthold
Friedrich)
See also DLB 92

Grubb
See Crumb, R(obert)

Grumbach, Doris (Isaac)
1918- .... **CLC 13, 22, 64**
See also CA 5-8R; CAAS 2; CANR 9, 42;
INT CANR-9

Grundtvig, Nicolai Frederik Severin
1783-1872 .... **NCLC 1**

Grunge
See Crumb, R(obert)

Grunwald, Lisa 1959-............. **CLC 44**
See also CA 120

Guare, John
1938- .... **CLC 8, 14, 29, 67;
DAM DRAM**
See also CA 73-76; CANR 21; DLB 7;
MTCW

Gudjonsson, Halldor Kiljan 1902-
See Laxness, Halldor
See also CA 103

Guenter, Erich
See Eich, Guenter

Guest, Barbara 1920-............. **CLC 34**
See also CA 25-28R; CANR 11, 44; DLB 5

Guest, Judith (Ann)
1936- .... **CLC 8, 30; DAM NOV, POP**
See also AAYA 7; CA 77-80; CANR 15;
INT CANR-15; MTCW

Guevara, Che............... **CLC 87; HLC**
See also Guevara (Serna), Ernesto

Guevara (Serna), Ernesto 1928-1967
See Guevara, Che
See also CA 127; 111; DAM MULT; HW

Guild, Nicholas M. 1944-......... **CLC 33**
See also CA 93-96

Guillemin, Jacques
See Sartre, Jean-Paul

Guillen, Jorge
1893-1984 ...... **CLC 11; DAM MULT,
POET**
See also CA 89-92; 112; DLB 108; HW

Guillen, Nicolas (Cristobal)
1902-1989 .... **CLC 48, 79; BLC;
DAM MST, MULT, POET; HLC**
See also BW 2; CA 116; 125; 129; HW

Guillevic, (Eugene) 1907-......... **CLC 33**
See also CA 93-96

Guillois
See Desnos, Robert

Guillois, Valentin
See Desnos, Robert

Guiney, Louise Imogen
1861-1920 .... **TCLC 41**
See also DLB 54

Guiraldes, Ricardo (Guillermo)
1886-1927 .... **TCLC 39**
See also CA 131; HW; MTCW

Gumilev, Nikolai Stephanovich
1886-1921 .... **TCLC 60**

Gunesekera, Romesh.............. **CLC 91**

Gunn, Bill .... **CLC 5**
See also Gunn, William Harrison
See also DLB 38

Gunn, Thom(son William)
1929- .... **CLC 3, 6, 18, 32, 81;
DAM POET**
See also CA 17-20R; CANR 9, 33;
CDBLB 1960 to Present; DLB 27;
INT CANR-33; MTCW

Gunn, William Harrison 1934(?)-1989
See Gunn, Bill
See also AITN 1; BW 1; CA 13-16R; 128;
CANR 12, 25

Gunnars, Kristjana 1948-......... **CLC 69**
See also CA 113; DLB 60

Gurganus, Allan
1947- .... **CLC 70; DAM POP**
See also BEST 90:1; CA 135

Gurney, A(lbert) R(amsdell), Jr.
1930- .... **CLC 32, 50, 54; DAM DRAM**
See also CA 77-80; CANR 32

Gurney, Ivor (Bertie) 1890-1937... **TCLC 33**

Gurney, Peter
See Gurney, A(lbert) R(amsdell), Jr.

Guro, Elena 1877-1913.......... **TCLC 56**

Gustafson, Ralph (Barker) 1909-.... **CLC 36**
See also CA 21-24R; CANR 8, 45; DLB 88

Gut, Gom
See Simenon, Georges (Jacques Christian)

Guterson, David 1956-............ **CLC 91**
See also CA 132

Guthrie, A(lfred) B(ertram), Jr.
1901-1991 .... **CLC 23**
See also CA 57-60; 134; CANR 24; DLB 6;
SATA 62; SATA-Obit 67

Guthrie, Isobel
See Grieve, C(hristopher) M(urray)

Guthrie, Woodrow Wilson 1912-1967
See Guthrie, Woody
See also CA 113; 93-96

Guthrie, Woody................... **CLC 35**
See also Guthrie, Woodrow Wilson

Guy, Rosa (Cuthbert) 1928-........ **CLC 26**
See also AAYA 4; BW 2; CA 17-20R;
CANR 14, 34; CLR 13; DLB 33; JRDA;
MAICYA; SATA 14, 62

Gwendolyn
See Bennett, (Enoch) Arnold

H. D. .... **CLC 3, 8, 14, 31, 34, 73; PC 5**
See also Doolittle, Hilda

H. de V.
See Buchan, John

Haavikko, Paavo Juhani
1931- .... **CLC 18, 34**
See also CA 106

Habbema, Koos
See Heijermans, Herman

Hacker, Marilyn
1942- .... **CLC 5, 9, 23, 72, 91;
DAM POET**
See also CA 77-80; DLB 120

Haggard, H(enry) Rider
1856-1925 .... **TCLC 11**
See also CA 108; 148; DLB 70, 156, 174;
SATA 16

Hagiosy, L.
See Larbaud, Valery (Nicolas)

Hagiwara Sakutaro 1886-1942 .... **TCLC 60**

Haig, Fenil
See Ford, Ford Madox

Haig-Brown, Roderick (Langmere)
1908-1976 .... **CLC 21**
See also CA 5-8R; 69-72; CANR 4, 38;
CLR 31; DLB 88; MAICYA; SATA 12

Hailey, Arthur
1920- .... **CLC 5; DAM NOV, POP**
See also AITN 2; BEST 90:3; CA 1-4R;
CANR 2, 36; DLB 88; DLBY 82; MTCW

Hailey, Elizabeth Forsythe 1938-... **CLC 40**
See also CA 93-96; CAAS 1; CANR 15, 48;
INT CANR-15

Haines, John (Meade) 1924-....... **CLC 58**
See also CA 17-20R; CANR 13, 34; DLB 5

Hakluyt, Richard 1552-1616........ **LC 31**

Haldeman, Joe (William) 1943-..... **CLC 61**
See also CA 53-56; CAAS 25; CANR 6;
DLB 8; INT CANR-6

Hart, Josephine
1942(?)-.......... CLC 70; DAM POP
See also CA 138

Hart, Moss
1904-1961 ...... CLC 66; DAM DRAM
See also CA 109; 89-92; DLB 7

Harte, (Francis) Bret(t)
1836(?)-1902 .... TCLC 1, 25; DA; DAC;
DAM MST; SSC 8; WLC
See also CA 104; 140; CDALB 1865-1917;
DLB 12, 64, 74, 79; SATA 26

Hartley, L(eslie) P(oles)
1895-1972 .... CLC 2, 22
See also CA 45-48; 37-40R; CANR 33;
DLB 15, 139; MTCW

Hartman, Geoffrey H. 1929-....... CLC 27
See also CA 117; 125; DLB 67

Hartmann von Aue
c. 1160-c. 1205 .... CMLC 15
See also DLB 138

Hartmann von Aue 1170-1210.... CMLC 15

Haruf, Kent 1943- .... CLC 34
See also CA 149

Harwood, Ronald
1934- .... CLC 32; DAM DRAM, MST
See also CA 1-4R; CANR 4, 55; DLB 13

Hasek, Jaroslav (Matej Frantisek)
1883-1923 .... TCLC 4
See also CA 104; 129; MTCW

Hass, Robert 1941-..... CLC 18, 39; PC 16
See also CA 111; CANR 30, 50; DLB 105

Hastings, Hudson
See Kuttner, Henry

Hastings, Selina................... CLC 44

Hatteras, Amelia
See Mencken, H(enry) L(ouis)

Hatteras, Owen................... TCLC 18
See also Mencken, H(enry) L(ouis); Nathan,
George Jean

Hauptmann, Gerhart (Johann Robert)
1862-1946 ...... TCLC 4; DAM DRAM
See also CA 104; 153; DLB 66, 118

Havel, Vaclav
1936-............... CLC 25, 58, 65;
DAM DRAM; DC 6
See also CA 104; CANR 36; MTCW

Haviaras, Stratis.................. CLC 33
See also Chaviaras, Strates

Hawes, Stephen 1475(?)-1523(?) ..... LC 17

Hawkes, John (Clendennin Burne, Jr.)
1925-...... CLC 1, 2, 3, 4, 7, 9, 14, 15,
27, 49
See also CA 1-4R; CANR 2, 47; DLB 2, 7;
DLBY 80; MTCW

Hawking, S. W.
See Hawking, Stephen W(illiam)

Hawking, Stephen W(illiam)
1942-............................ CLC 63
See also AAYA 13; BEST 89:1; CA 126;
129; CANR 48

Hawthorne, Julian 1846-1934 ..... TCLC 25

Hawthorne, Nathaniel
1804-1864 ...... NCLC 39; DA; DAB;
DAC; DAM MST, NOV; SSC 3; WLC
See also AAYA 18; CDALB 1640-1865;
DLB 1, 74; YABC 2

Haxton, Josephine Ayres 1921-
See Douglas, Ellen
See also CA 115; CANR 41

Hayaseca y Eizaguirre, Jorge
See Echegaray (y Eizaguirre), Jose (Maria
Waldo)

Hayashi Fumiko 1904-1951....... TCLC 27

Haycraft, Anna
See Ellis, Alice Thomas
See also CA 122

Hayden, Robert E(arl)
1913-1980 ...... CLC 5, 9, 14, 37; BLC;
DA; DAC; DAM MST, MULT, POET;
PC 6
See also BW 1; CA 69-72; 97-100; CABS 2;
CANR 24; CDALB 1941-1968; DLB 5,
76; MTCW; SATA 19; SATA-Obit 26

Hayford, J(oseph) E(phraim) Casely
See Casely-Hayford, J(oseph) E(phraim)

Hayman, Ronald 1932-............ CLC 44
See also CA 25-28R; CANR 18, 50;
DLB 155

Haywood, Eliza (Fowler)
1693(?)-1756 .... LC 1

Hazlitt, William 1778-1830...... NCLC 29
See also DLB 110, 158

Hazzard, Shirley 1931- .... CLC 18
See also CA 9-12R; CANR 4; DLBY 82;
MTCW

Head, Bessie
1937-1986 .... CLC 25, 67; BLC;
DAM MULT
See also BW 2; CA 29-32R; 119; CANR 25;
DLB 117; MTCW

Headon, (Nicky) Topper 1956(?)- ... CLC 30

Heaney, Seamus (Justin)
1939-...... CLC 5, 7, 14, 25, 37, 74, 91;
DAB; DAM POET
See also CA 85-88; CANR 25, 48;
CDBLB 1960 to Present; DLB 40;
DLBY 95; MTCW

Hearn, (Patricio) Lafcadio (Tessima Carlos)
1850-1904 .... TCLC 9
See also CA 105; DLB 12, 78

Hearne, Vicki 1946-.............. CLC 56
See also CA 139

Hearon, Shelby 1931-............. CLC 63
See also AITN 2; CA 25-28R; CANR 18,
48

Heat-Moon, William Least.......... CLC 29
See also Trogdon, William (Lewis)
See also AAYA 9

Hebbel, Friedrich
1813-1863 .... NCLC 43; DAM DRAM
See also DLB 129

Hebert, Anne
1916-............ CLC 4, 13, 29; DAC;
DAM MST, POET
See also CA 85-88; DLB 68; MTCW

Hecht, Anthony (Evan)
1923-...... CLC 8, 13, 19; DAM POET
See also CA 9-12R; CANR 6; DLB 5, 169

Hecht, Ben 1894-1964 .... CLC 8
See also CA 85-88; DLB 7, 9, 25, 26, 28, 86

Hedayat, Sadeq 1903-1951........ TCLC 21
See also CA 120

Hegel, Georg Wilhelm Friedrich
1770-1831 .... NCLC 46
See also DLB 90

Heidegger, Martin 1889-1976...... CLC 24
See also CA 81-84; 65-68; CANR 34;
MTCW

Heidenstam, (Carl Gustaf) Verner von
1859-1940 .... TCLC 5
See also CA 104

Heifner, Jack 1946-................ CLC 11
See also CA 105; CANR 47

Heijermans, Herman 1864-1924 ... TCLC 24
See also CA 123

Heilbrun, Carolyn G(old) 1926-..... CLC 25
See also CA 45-48; CANR 1, 28

Heine, Heinrich 1797-1856 .... NCLC 4, 54
See also DLB 90

Heinemann, Larry (Curtiss) 1944- ... CLC 50
See also CA 110; CAAS 21; CANR 31;
DLBD 9; INT CANR-31

Heiney, Donald (William) 1921-1993
See Harris, MacDonald
See also CA 1-4R; 142; CANR 3

Heinlein, Robert A(nson)
1907-1988 ...... CLC 1, 3, 8, 14, 26, 55;
DAM POP
See also AAYA 17; CA 1-4R; 125;
CANR 1, 20, 53; DLB 8; JRDA;
MAICYA; MTCW; SATA 9, 69;
SATA-Obit 56

Helforth, John
See Doolittle, Hilda

Hellenhofferu, Vojtech Kapristian z
See Hasek, Jaroslav (Matej Frantisek)

Heller, Joseph
1923- .... CLC 1, 3, 5, 8, 11, 36, 63; DA;
DAB; DAC; DAM MST, NOV, POP;
WLC
See also AITN 1; CA 5-8R; CABS 1;
CANR 8, 42; DLB 2, 28; DLBY 80;
INT CANR-8; MTCW

Hellman, Lillian (Florence)
1906-1984 ...... CLC 2, 4, 8, 14, 18, 34,
44, 52; DAM DRAM; DC 1
See also AITN 1, 2; CA 13-16R; 112;
CANR 33; DLB 7; DLBY 84; MTCW

Helprin, Mark
1947-.............. CLC 7, 10, 22, 32;
DAM NOV, POP
See also CA 81-84; CANR 47; DLBY 85;
MTCW

Helvetius, Claude-Adrien
1715-1771 .... LC 26

Helyar, Jane Penelope Josephine 1933-
See Poole, Josephine
See also CA 21-24R; CANR 10, 26;
SATA 82

Hemans, Felicia 1793-1835 ...... NCLC 29
See also DLB 96

Hemingway, Ernest (Miller)
1899-1961 .... CLC 1, 3, 6, 8, 10, 13, 19,
30, 34, 39, 41, 44, 50, 61, 80; DA; DAB;
DAC; DAM MST, NOV; SSC 1; WLC
See also AAYA 19; CA 77-80; CANR 34;
CDALB 1917-1929; DLB 4, 9, 102;
DLBD 1; DLBY 81, 87; MTCW

Hempel, Amy 1951- .... CLC 39
See also CA 118; 137

Henderson, F. C.
See Mencken, H(enry) L(ouis)

Henderson, Sylvia
See Ashton-Warner, Sylvia (Constance)

Henley, Beth .... CLC 23; DC 6
See also Henley, Elizabeth Becker
See also CABS 3; DLBY 86

Henley, Elizabeth Becker 1952-
See Henley, Beth
See also CA 107; CANR 32; DAM DRAM,
MST; MTCW

Henley, William Ernest
1849-1903 .... TCLC 8
See also CA 105; DLB 19

Hennissart, Martha
See Lathen, Emma
See also CA 85-88

Henry, O. .... TCLC 1, 19; SSC 5; WLC
See also Porter, William Sydney

Henry, Patrick 1736-1799 .... LC 25

Henryson, Robert 1430(?)-1506(?).... LC 20
See also DLB 146

Henry VIII 1491-1547 .... LC 10

Henschke, Alfred
See Klabund

Hentoff, Nat(han Irving) 1925- ..... CLC 26
See also AAYA 4; CA 1-4R; CAAS 6;
CANR 5, 25; CLR 1; INT CANR-25;
JRDA; MAICYA; SATA 42, 69;
SATA-Brief 27

Heppenstall, (John) Rayner
1911-1981 .... CLC 10
See also CA 1-4R; 103; CANR 29

Herbert, Frank (Patrick)
1920-1986 ...... CLC 12, 23, 35, 44, 85;
DAM POP
See also CA 53-56; 118; CANR 5, 43;
DLB 8; INT CANR-5; MTCW; SATA 9,
37; SATA-Obit 47

Herbert, George
1593-1633 .... LC 24; DAB;
DAM POET; PC 4
See also CDBLB Before 1660; DLB 126

Herbert, Zbigniew
1924- .... CLC 9, 43; DAM POET
See also CA 89-92; CANR 36; MTCW

Herbst, Josephine (Frey)
1897-1969 .... CLC 34
See also CA 5-8R; 25-28R; DLB 9

Hergesheimer, Joseph
1880-1954 .... TCLC 11
See also CA 109; DLB 102, 9

Herlihy, James Leo 1927-1993 ...... CLC 6
See also CA 1-4R; 143; CANR 2

Hermogenes fl. c. 175- .... CMLC 6

Hernandez, Jose 1834-1886 ...... NCLC 17

Herodotus c. 484B.C.-429B.C. .... CMLC 17

Herrick, Robert
1591-1674 ..... LC 13; DA; DAB; DAC;
DAM MST, POP; PC 9
See also DLB 126

Herring, Guilles
See Somerville, Edith

Herriot, James
1916-1995 .... CLC 12; DAM POP
See also Wight, James Alfred
See also AAYA 1; CA 148; CANR 40;
SATA 86

Herrmann, Dorothy 1941- .... CLC 44
See also CA 107

Herrmann, Taffy
See Herrmann, Dorothy

Hersey, John (Richard)
1914-1993 .... CLC 1, 2, 7, 9, 40, 81, 97;
DAM POP
See also CA 17-20R; 140; CANR 33;
DLB 6; MTCW; SATA 25;
SATA-Obit 76

Herzen, Aleksandr Ivanovich
1812-1870 .... NCLC 10

Herzl, Theodor 1860-1904 .... TCLC 36

Herzog, Werner 1942- .... CLC 16
See also CA 89-92

Hesiod c. 8th cent. B.C.- .... CMLC 5

Hesse, Hermann
1877-1962 .... CLC 1, 2, 3, 6, 11, 17, 25,
69; DA; DAB; DAC; DAM MST, NOV;
SSC 9; WLC
See also CA 17-18; CAP 2; DLB 66;
MTCW; SATA 50

Hewes, Cady
See De Voto, Bernard (Augustine)

Heyen, William 1940- .... CLC 13, 18
See also CA 33-36R; CAAS 9; DLB 5

Heyerdahl, Thor 1914- .... CLC 26
See also CA 5-8R; CANR 5, 22; MTCW;
SATA 2, 52

Heym, Georg (Theodor Franz Arthur)
1887-1912 .... TCLC 9
See also CA 106

Heym, Stefan 1913- .... CLC 41
See also CA 9-12R; CANR 4; DLB 69

Heyse, Paul (Johann Ludwig von)
1830-1914 .... TCLC 8
See also CA 104; DLB 129

Heyward, (Edwin) DuBose
1885-1940 .... TCLC 59
See also CA 108; DLB 7, 9, 45; SATA 21

Hibbert, Eleanor Alice Burford
1906-1993 .... CLC 7; DAM POP
See also BEST 90:4; CA 17-20R; 140;
CANR 9, 28; SATA 2; SATA-Obit 74

Hichens, Robert S. 1864-1950 ..... TCLC 64
See also DLB 153

Higgins, George V(incent)
1939- .... CLC 4, 7, 10, 18
See also CA 77-80; CAAS 5; CANR 17, 51;
DLB 2; DLBY 81; INT CANR-17;
MTCW

Higginson, Thomas Wentworth
1823-1911 .... TCLC 36
See also DLB 1, 64

Highet, Helen
See MacInnes, Helen (Clark)

Highsmith, (Mary) Patricia
1921-1995 .... CLC 2, 4, 14, 42;
DAM NOV, POP
See also CA 1-4R; 147; CANR 1, 20, 48;
MTCW

Highwater, Jamake (Mamake)
1942(?)- .... CLC 12
See also AAYA 7; CA 65-68; CAAS 7;
CANR 10, 34; CLR 17; DLB 52;
DLBY 85; JRDA; MAICYA; SATA 32,
69; SATA-Brief 30

Highway, Tomson
1951- ..... CLC 92; DAC; DAM MULT
See also CA 151; NNAL

Higuchi, Ichiyo 1872-1896....... NCLC 49

Hijuelos, Oscar
1951- .... CLC 65; DAM MULT, POP;
HLC
See also BEST 90:1; CA 123; CANR 50;
DLB 145; HW

Hikmet, Nazim 1902(?)-1963....... CLC 40
See also CA 141; 93-96

Hildesheimer, Wolfgang
1916-1991 .... CLC 49
See also CA 101; 135; DLB 69, 124

Hill, Geoffrey (William)
1932- ... CLC 5, 8, 18, 45; DAM POET
See also CA 81-84; CANR 21;
CDBLB 1960 to Present; DLB 40;
MTCW

Hill, George Roy 1921- .... CLC 26
See also CA 110; 122

Hill, John
See Koontz, Dean R(ay)

Hill, Susan (Elizabeth)
1942- .. CLC 4; DAB; DAM MST, NOV
See also CA 33-36R; CANR 29; DLB 14,
139; MTCW

Hillerman, Tony
1925- .... CLC 62; DAM POP
See also AAYA 6; BEST 89:1; CA 29-32R;
CANR 21, 42; SATA 6

Hillesum, Etty 1914-1943 .... TCLC 49
See also CA 137

Hilliard, Noel (Harvey) 1929-...... CLC 15
See also CA 9-12R; CANR 7

Hillis, Rick 1956- .... CLC 66
See also CA 134

Hilton, James 1900-1954 .... TCLC 21
See also CA 108; DLB 34, 77; SATA 34

Himes, Chester (Bomar)
1909-1984 .... CLC 2, 4, 7, 18, 58; BLC;
DAM MULT
See also BW 2; CA 25-28R; 114; CANR 22;
DLB 2, 76, 143; MTCW

Hinde, Thomas .... CLC 6, 11
See also Chitty, Thomas Willes

Hindin, Nathan
See Bloch, Robert (Albert)

Hine, (William) Daryl 1936- .... **CLC 15**
See also CA 1-4R; CAAS 15; CANR 1, 20;
DLB 60

Hinkson, Katharine Tynan
See Tynan, Katharine

Hinton, S(usan) E(loise)
1950- .... **CLC 30; DA; DAB; DAC;**
DAM MST, NOV
See also AAYA 2; CA 81-84; CANR 32;
CLR 3, 23; JRDA; MAICYA; MTCW;
SATA 19, 58

Hippius, Zinaida .... **TCLC 9**
See also Gippius, Zinaida (Nikolayevna)

Hiraoka, Kimitake 1925-1970
See Mishima, Yukio
See also CA 97-100; 29-32R; DAM DRAM;
MTCW

Hirsch, E(ric) D(onald), Jr. 1928-... **CLC 79**
See also CA 25-28R; CANR 27, 51;
DLB 67; INT CANR-27; MTCW

Hirsch, Edward 1950- .... **CLC 31, 50**
See also CA 104; CANR 20, 42; DLB 120

Hitchcock, Alfred (Joseph)
1899-1980 .... **CLC 16**
See also CA 97-100; SATA 27;
SATA-Obit 24

Hitler, Adolf 1889-1945 .... **TCLC 53**
See also CA 117; 147

Hoagland, Edward 1932- .... **CLC 28**
See also CA 1-4R; CANR 2, 31; DLB 6;
SATA 51

Hoban, Russell (Conwell)
1925- .... **CLC 7, 25; DAM NOV**
See also CA 5-8R; CANR 23, 37; CLR 3;
DLB 52; MAICYA; MTCW; SATA 1,
40, 78

Hobbes, Thomas 1588-1679 .... **LC 36**
See also DLB 151

Hobbs, Perry
See Blackmur, R(ichard) P(almer)

Hobson, Laura Z(ametkin)
1900-1986 .... **CLC 7, 25**
See also CA 17-20R; 118; CANR 55;
DLB 28; SATA 52

Hochhuth, Rolf
1931- ..... **CLC 4, 11, 18; DAM DRAM**
See also CA 5-8R; CANR 33; DLB 124;
MTCW

Hochman, Sandra 1936- .... **CLC 3, 8**
See also CA 5-8R; DLB 5

Hochwaelder, Fritz
1911-1986 ...... **CLC 36; DAM DRAM**
See also CA 29-32R; 120; CANR 42;
MTCW

Hochwalder, Fritz
See Hochwaelder, Fritz

Hocking, Mary (Eunice) 1921- ..... **CLC 13**
See also CA 101; CANR 18, 40

Hodgins, Jack 1938- .... **CLC 23**
See also CA 93-96; DLB 60

Hodgson, William Hope
1877(?)-1918 .... **TCLC 13**
See also CA 111; DLB 70, 153, 156

Hoeg, Peter 1957- .... **CLC 95**
See also CA 151

Hoffman, Alice
1952- .... **CLC 51; DAM NOV**
See also CA 77-80; CANR 34; MTCW

Hoffman, Daniel (Gerard)
1923- .... **CLC 6, 13, 23**
See also CA 1-4R; CANR 4; DLB 5

Hoffman, Stanley 1944- .... **CLC 5**
See also CA 77-80

Hoffman, William M(oses) 1939- ... **CLC 40**
See also CA 57-60; CANR 11

Hoffmann, E(rnst) T(heodor) A(madeus)
1776-1822 .... **NCLC 2; SSC 13**
See also DLB 90; SATA 27

Hofmann, Gert 1931- .... **CLC 54**
See also CA 128

Hofmannsthal, Hugo von
1874-1929 .... **TCLC 11; DAM DRAM;**
DC 4
See also CA 106; 153; DLB 81, 118

Hogan, Linda
1947- .... **CLC 73; DAM MULT**
See also CA 120; CANR 45; NNAL

Hogarth, Charles
See Creasey, John

Hogarth, Emmett
See Polonsky, Abraham (Lincoln)

Hogg, James 1770-1835 .... **NCLC 4**
See also DLB 93, 116, 159

Holbach, Paul Henri Thiry Baron
1723-1789 .... **LC 14**

Holberg, Ludvig 1684-1754 .... **LC 6**

Holden, Ursula 1921- .... **CLC 18**
See also CA 101; CAAS 8; CANR 22

Holderlin, (Johann Christian) Friedrich
1770-1843 .... **NCLC 16; PC 4**

Holdstock, Robert
See Holdstock, Robert P.

Holdstock, Robert P. 1948- .... **CLC 39**
See also CA 131

Holland, Isabelle 1920- .... **CLC 21**
See also AAYA 11; CA 21-24R; CANR 10,
25, 47; JRDA; MAICYA; SATA 8, 70

Holland, Marcus
See Caldwell, (Janet Miriam) Taylor
(Holland)

Hollander, John 1929- ...... **CLC 2, 5, 8, 14**
See also CA 1-4R; CANR 1, 52; DLB 5;
SATA 13

Hollander, Paul
See Silverberg, Robert

Holleran, Andrew 1943(?)- .... **CLC 38**
See also CA 144

Hollinghurst, Alan 1954- .... **CLC 55, 91**
See also CA 114

Hollis, Jim
See Summers, Hollis (Spurgeon, Jr.)

Holly, Buddy 1936-1959 .... **TCLC 65**

Holmes, John
See Souster, (Holmes) Raymond

Holmes, John Clellon 1926-1988.... **CLC 56**
See also CA 9-12R; 125; CANR 4; DLB 16

Holmes, Oliver Wendell
1809-1894 .... **NCLC 14**
See also CDALB 1640-1865; DLB 1;
SATA 34

Holmes, Raymond
See Souster, (Holmes) Raymond

Holt, Victoria
See Hibbert, Eleanor Alice Burford

Holub, Miroslav 1923- .... **CLC 4**
See also CA 21-24R; CANR 10

Homer
c. 8th cent. B.C.- ..... **CMLC 1, 16; DA;**
DAB; DAC; DAM MST, POET

Honig, Edwin 1919- .... **CLC 33**
See also CA 5-8R; CAAS 8; CANR 4, 45;
DLB 5

Hood, Hugh (John Blagdon)
1928- .... **CLC 15, 28**
See also CA 49-52; CAAS 17; CANR 1, 33;
DLB 53

Hood, Thomas 1799-1845........ **NCLC 16**
See also DLB 96

Hooker, (Peter) Jeremy 1941-...... **CLC 43**
See also CA 77-80; CANR 22; DLB 40

hooks, bell .... **CLC 94**
See also Watkins, Gloria

Hope, A(lec) D(erwent) 1907- .... **CLC 3, 51**
See also CA 21-24R; CANR 33; MTCW

Hope, Brian
See Creasey, John

Hope, Christopher (David Tully)
1944- .... **CLC 52**
See also CA 106; CANR 47; SATA 62

Hopkins, Gerard Manley
1844-1889 .... **NCLC 17; DA; DAB;**
DAC; DAM MST, POET; PC 15; WLC
See also CDBLB 1890-1914; DLB 35, 57

Hopkins, John (Richard) 1931-...... **CLC 4**
See also CA 85-88

Hopkins, Pauline Elizabeth
1859-1930 .... **TCLC 28; BLC;**
DAM MULT
See also BW 2; CA 141; DLB 50

Hopkinson, Francis 1737-1791 ...... **LC 25**
See also DLB 31

Hopley-Woolrich, Cornell George 1903-1968
See Woolrich, Cornell
See also CA 13-14; CAP 1

Horatio
See Proust, (Valentin-Louis-George-Eugene-)
Marcel

Horgan, Paul (George Vincent O'Shaughnessy)
1903-1995 ...... **CLC 9, 53; DAM NOV**
See also CA 13-16R; 147; CANR 9, 35;
DLB 102; DLBY 85; INT CANR-9;
MTCW; SATA 13; SATA-Obit 84

Horn, Peter
See Kuttner, Henry

Hornem, Horace Esq.
See Byron, George Gordon (Noel)

Hornung, E(rnest) W(illiam)
1866-1921 .... **TCLC 59**
See also CA 108; DLB 70

Horovitz, Israel (Arthur)
1939- .... **CLC 56; DAM DRAM**
See also CA 33-36R; CANR 46; DLB 7

Horvath, Odon von
See Horvath, Oedoen von
See also DLB 85, 124

Horvath, Oedoen von 1901-1938... **TCLC 45**
See also Horvath, Odon von
See also CA 118

Horwitz, Julius 1920-1986......... **CLC 14**
See also CA 9-12R; 119; CANR 12

Hospital, Janette Turner 1942-..... **CLC 42**
See also CA 108; CANR 48

Hostos, E. M. de
See Hostos (y Bonilla), Eugenio Maria de

Hostos, Eugenio M. de
See Hostos (y Bonilla), Eugenio Maria de

Hostos, Eugenio Maria
See Hostos (y Bonilla), Eugenio Maria de

Hostos (y Bonilla), Eugenio Maria de
1839-1903 .... **TCLC 24**
See also CA 123; 131; HW

Houdini
See Lovecraft, H(oward) P(hillips)

Hougan, Carolyn 1943- .... **CLC 34**
See also CA 139

Household, Geoffrey (Edward West)
1900-1988 .... **CLC 11**
See also CA 77-80; 126; DLB 87; SATA 14;
SATA-Obit 59

Housman, A(lfred) E(dward)
1859-1936 ...... **TCLC 1, 10; DA; DAB;**
DAC; DAM MST, POET; PC 2
See also CA 104; 125; DLB 19; MTCW

Housman, Laurence 1865-1959..... **TCLC 7**
See also CA 106; DLB 10; SATA 25

Howard, Elizabeth Jane 1923- ... **CLC 7, 29**
See also CA 5-8R; CANR 8

Howard, Maureen 1930- ..... **CLC 5, 14, 46**
See also CA 53-56; CANR 31; DLBY 83;
INT CANR-31; MTCW

Howard, Richard 1929- ...... **CLC 7, 10, 47**
See also AITN 1; CA 85-88; CANR 25;
DLB 5; INT CANR-25

Howard, Robert Ervin 1906-1936... **TCLC 8**
See also CA 105

Howard, Warren F.
See Pohl, Frederik

Howe, Fanny 1940- .... **CLC 47**
See also CA 117; SATA-Brief 52

Howe, Irving 1920-1993.......... **CLC 85**
See also CA 9-12R; 141; CANR 21, 50;
DLB 67; MTCW

Howe, Julia Ward 1819-1910 ..... **TCLC 21**
See also CA 117; DLB 1

Howe, Susan 1937-.............. **CLC 72**
See also DLB 120

Howe, Tina 1937-.............. **CLC 48**
See also CA 109

Howell, James 1594(?)-1666 .... **LC 13**
See also DLB 151

Howells, W. D.
See Howells, William Dean

Howells, William D.
See Howells, William Dean

Howells, William Dean
1837-1920 .... **TCLC 7, 17, 41**
See also CA 104; 134; CDALB 1865-1917;
DLB 12, 64, 74, 79

Howes, Barbara 1914-1996 .... **CLC 15**
See also CA 9-12R; 151; CAAS 3;
CANR 53; SATA 5

Hrabal, Bohumil 1914-......... **CLC 13, 67**
See also CA 106; CAAS 12

Hsun, Lu
See Lu Hsun

Hubbard, L(afayette) Ron(ald)
1911-1986 .... **CLC 43; DAM POP**
See also CA 77-80; 118; CANR 52

Huch, Ricarda (Octavia)
1864-1947 .... **TCLC 13**
See also CA 111; DLB 66

Huddle, David 1942- .... **CLC 49**
See also CA 57-60; CAAS 20; DLB 130

Hudson, Jeffrey
See Crichton, (John) Michael

Hudson, W(illiam) H(enry)
1841-1922 .... **TCLC 29**
See also CA 115; DLB 98, 153, 174;
SATA 35

Hueffer, Ford Madox
See Ford, Ford Madox

Hughart, Barry 1934-.............. **CLC 39**
See also CA 137

Hughes, Colin
See Creasey, John

Hughes, David (John) 1930- .... **CLC 48**
See also CA 116; 129; DLB 14

Hughes, Edward James
See Hughes, Ted
See also DAM MST, POET

Hughes, (James) Langston
1902-1967 ..... **CLC 1, 5, 10, 15, 35, 44;**
BLC; DA; DAB; DAC; DAM DRAM,
MST, MULT, POET; PC 1;
SSC 6; WLC
See also AAYA 12; BW 1; CA 1-4R;
25-28R; CANR 1, 34; CDALB 1929-1941;
CLR 17; DLB 4, 7, 48, 51, 86; JRDA;
MAICYA; MTCW; SATA 4, 33

Hughes, Richard (Arthur Warren)
1900-1976 ...... **CLC 1, 11; DAM NOV**
See also CA 5-8R; 65-68; CANR 4;
DLB 15, 161; MTCW; SATA 8;
SATA-Obit 25

Hughes, Ted
1930- .... **CLC 2, 4, 9, 14, 37; DAB;**
DAC; PC 7
See also Hughes, Edward James
See also CA 1-4R; CANR 1, 33; CLR 3;
DLB 40, 161; MAICYA; MTCW;
SATA 49; SATA-Brief 27

Hugo, Richard F(ranklin)
1923-1982 .... **CLC 6, 18, 32;**
DAM POET
See also CA 49-52; 108; CANR 3; DLB 5

Hugo, Victor (Marie)
1802-1885 .... **NCLC 3, 10, 21; DA;**
DAB; DAC; DAM DRAM, MST, NOV,
POET; WLC
See also DLB 119; SATA 47

Huidobro, Vicente
See Huidobro Fernandez, Vicente Garcia

Huidobro Fernandez, Vicente Garcia
1893-1948 .... **TCLC 31**
See also CA 131; HW

Hulme, Keri 1947- .... **CLC 39**
See also CA 125; INT 125

Hulme, T(homas) E(rnest)
1883-1917 .... **TCLC 21**
See also CA 117; DLB 19

Hume, David 1711-1776............. **LC 7**
See also DLB 104

Humphrey, William 1924-......... **CLC 45**
See also CA 77-80; DLB 6

Humphreys, Emyr Owen 1919-..... **CLC 47**
See also CA 5-8R; CANR 3, 24; DLB 15

Humphreys, Josephine 1945-.... **CLC 34, 57**
See also CA 121; 127; INT 127

Huneker, James Gibbons
1857-1921 .... **TCLC 65**
See also DLB 71

Hungerford, Pixie
See Brinsmead, H(esba) F(ay)

Hunt, E(verette) Howard, (Jr.)
1918- .... **CLC 3**
See also AITN 1; CA 45-48; CANR 2, 47

Hunt, Kyle
See Creasey, John

Hunt, (James Henry) Leigh
1784-1859 ...... **NCLC 1; DAM POET**

Hunt, Marsha 1946-.............. **CLC 70**
See also BW 2; CA 143

Hunt, Violet 1866-1942 .... **TCLC 53**
See also DLB 162

Hunter, E. Waldo
See Sturgeon, Theodore (Hamilton)

Hunter, Evan
1926- .... **CLC 11, 31; DAM POP**
See also CA 5-8R; CANR 5, 38; DLBY 82;
INT CANR-5; MTCW; SATA 25

Hunter, Kristin (Eggleston) 1931-... **CLC 35**
See also AITN 1; BW 1; CA 13-16R;
CANR 13; CLR 3; DLB 33;
INT CANR-13; MAICYA; SAAS 10;
SATA 12

Hunter, Mollie 1922 .... **CLC 21**
See also McIlwraith, Maureen Mollie
Hunter
See also AAYA 13; CANR 37; CLR 25;
DLB 161; JRDA; MAICYA; SAAS 7;
SATA 54

Hunter, Robert (?)-1734............. **LC 7**

Hurston, Zora Neale
1903-1960 .... **CLC 7, 30, 61; BLC; DA;**
DAC; DAM MST, MULT, NOV; SSC 4
See also AAYA 15; BW 1; CA 85-88;
DLB 51, 86; MTCW

Huston, John (Marcellus)
1906-1987 .... **CLC 20**
See also CA 73-76; 123; CANR 34; DLB 26

Hustvedt, Siri 1955-.............. **CLC 76**
See also CA 137

Hutten, Ulrich von 1488-1523....... **LC 16**

Huxley, Aldous (Leonard)
1894-1963 ..... **CLC 1, 3, 4, 5, 8, 11, 18, 35, 79; DA; DAB; DAC; DAM MST, NOV; WLC**
See also AAYA 11; CA 85-88; CANR 44; CDBLB 1914-1945; DLB 36, 100, 162; MTCW; SATA 63

Huysmans, Charles Marie Georges
1848-1907
See Huysmans, Joris-Karl
See also CA 104

Huysmans, Joris-Karl............. **TCLC 7**
See also Huysmans, Charles Marie Georges
See also DLB 123

Hwang, David Henry
1957- .... **CLC 55; DAM DRAM; DC 4**
See also CA 127; 132; INT 132

Hyde, Anthony 1946-............. **CLC 42**
See also CA 136

Hyde, Margaret O(ldroyd) 1917-... **CLC 21**
See also CA 1-4R; CANR 1, 36; CLR 23; JRDA; MAICYA; SAAS 8; SATA 1, 42, 76

Hynes, James 1956(?)-............ **CLC 65**

Ian, Janis 1951- .... **CLC 21**
See also CA 105

Ibanez, Vicente Blasco
See Blasco Ibanez, Vicente

Ibarguengoitia, Jorge 1928-1983.... **CLC 37**
See also CA 124; 113; HW

Ibsen, Henrik (Johan)
1828-1906 .... **TCLC 2, 8, 16, 37, 52; DA; DAB; DAC; DAM DRAM, MST; DC 2; WLC**
See also CA 104; 141

Ibuse Masuji 1898-1993........... **CLC 22**
See also CA 127; 141

Ichikawa, Kon 1915-.............. **CLC 20**
See also CA 121

Idle, Eric 1943-................. **CLC 21**
See also Monty Python
See also CA 116; CANR 35

Ignatow, David 1914-...... **CLC 4, 7, 14, 40**
See also CA 9-12R; CAAS 3; CANR 31; DLB 5

Ihimaera, Witi 1944- .... **CLC 46**
See also CA 77-80

Ilf, Ilya........................ **TCLC 21**
See also Fainzilberg, Ilya Arnoldovich

Illyes, Gyula 1902-1983............ **PC 16**
See also CA 114; 109

Immermann, Karl (Lebrecht)
1796-1840 .... **NCLC 4, 49**
See also DLB 133

Inclan, Ramon (Maria) del Valle
See Valle-Inclan, Ramon (Maria) del

Infante, G(uillermo) Cabrera
See Cabrera Infante, G(uillermo)

Ingalls, Rachel (Holmes) 1940-..... **CLC 42**
See also CA 123; 127

Ingamells, Rex 1913-1955 .... **TCLC 35**

Inge, William (Motter)
1913-1973 .. **CLC 1, 8, 19; DAM DRAM**
See also CA 9-12R; CDALB 1941-1968; DLB 7; MTCW

Ingelow, Jean 1820-1897........ **NCLC 39**
See also DLB 35, 163; SATA 33

Ingram, Willis J.
See Harris, Mark

Innaurato, Albert (F.) 1948(?)- .. **CLC 21, 60**
See also CA 115; 122; INT 122

Innes, Michael
See Stewart, J(ohn) I(nnes) M(ackintosh)

Ionesco, Eugene
1909-1994 .... **CLC 1, 4, 6, 9, 11, 15, 41, 86; DA; DAB; DAC; DAM DRAM, MST; WLC**
See also CA 9-12R; 144; CANR 55; MTCW; SATA 7; SATA-Obit 79

Iqbal, Muhammad 1873-1938 ..... **TCLC 28**

Ireland, Patrick
See O'Doherty, Brian

Iron, Ralph
See Schreiner, Olive (Emilie Albertina)

Irving, John (Winslow)
1942- ..... **CLC 13, 23, 38; DAM NOV, POP**
See also AAYA 8; BEST 89:3; CA 25-28R; CANR 28; DLB 6; DLBY 82; MTCW

Irving, Washington
1783-1859 ..... **NCLC 2, 19; DA; DAB; DAM MST; SSC 2; WLC**
See also CDALB 1640-1865; DLB 3, 11, 30, 59, 73, 74; YABC 2

Irwin, P. K.
See Page, P(atricia) K(athleen)

Isaacs, Susan 1943- ... **CLC 32; DAM POP**
See also BEST 89:1; CA 89-92; CANR 20, 41; INT CANR-20; MTCW

Isherwood, Christopher (William Bradshaw)
1904-1986 .... **CLC 1, 9, 11, 14, 44; DAM DRAM, NOV**
See also CA 13-16R; 117; CANR 35; DLB 15; DLBY 86; MTCW

Ishiguro, Kazuo
1954- ...... **CLC 27, 56, 59; DAM NOV**
See also BEST 90:2; CA 120; CANR 49; MTCW

Ishikawa, Hakuhin
See Ishikawa, Takuboku

Ishikawa, Takuboku
1886(?)-1912 .... **TCLC 15; DAM POET; PC 10**
See also CA 113; 153

Iskander, Fazil 1929-............. **CLC 47**
See also CA 102

Isler, Alan .... **CLC 91**

Ivan IV 1530-1584 .... **LC 17**

Ivanov, Vyacheslav Ivanovich
1866-1949 .... **TCLC 33**
See also CA 122

Ivask, Ivar Vidrik 1927-1992....... **CLC 14**
See also CA 37-40R; 139; CANR 24

Ives, Morgan
See Bradley, Marion Zimmer

J. R. S.
See Gogarty, Oliver St. John

Jabran, Kahlil
See Gibran, Kahlil

Jabran, Khalil
See Gibran, Kahlil

Jackson, Daniel
See Wingrove, David (John)

Jackson, Jesse 1908-1983 .... **CLC 12**
See also BW 1; CA 25-28R; 109; CANR 27; CLR 28; MAICYA; SATA 2, 29; SATA-Obit 48

Jackson, Laura (Riding) 1901-1991
See Riding, Laura
See also CA 65-68; 135; CANR 28; DLB 48

Jackson, Sam
See Trumbo, Dalton

Jackson, Sara
See Wingrove, David (John)

Jackson, Shirley
1919-1965 .... **CLC 11, 60, 87; DA; DAC; DAM MST; SSC 9; WLC**
See also AAYA 9; CA 1-4R; 25-28R; CANR 4, 52; CDALB 1941-1968; DLB 6; SATA 2

Jacob, (Cyprien-)Max 1876-1944 ... **TCLC 6**
See also CA 104

Jacobs, Jim 1942-................. **CLC 12**
See also CA 97-100; INT 97-100

Jacobs, W(illiam) W(ymark)
1863-1943 .... **TCLC 22**
See also CA 121; DLB 135

Jacobsen, Jens Peter 1847-1885 .. **NCLC 34**

Jacobsen, Josephine 1908-........ **CLC 48**
See also CA 33-36R; CAAS 18; CANR 23, 48

Jacobson, Dan 1929- .... **CLC 4, 14**
See also CA 1-4R; CANR 2, 25; DLB 14; MTCW

Jacqueline
See Carpentier (y Valmont), Alejo

Jagger, Mick 1944-.............. **CLC 17**

Jakes, John (William)
1932- ...... **CLC 29; DAM NOV, POP**
See also BEST 89:4; CA 57-60; CANR 10, 43; DLBY 83; INT CANR-10; MTCW; SATA 62

Jalal al-Din Rumi 1297-1373..... **CMLC 20**

James, Andrew
See Kirkup, James

James, C(yril) L(ionel) R(obert)
1901-1989 .... **CLC 33**
See also BW 2; CA 117; 125; 128; DLB 125; MTCW

James, Daniel (Lewis) 1911-1988
See Santiago, Danny
See also CA 125

James, Dynely
See Mayne, William (James Carter)

James, Henry Sr. 1811-1882..... **NCLC 53**

James, Henry
1843-1916 . . . . . TCLC 2, 11, 24, 40, 47, 64; DA; DAB; DAC; DAM MST, NOV; SSC 8; WLC
See also CA 104; 132; CDALB 1865-1917; DLB 12, 71, 74; DLBD 13; MTCW

James, M. R.
See James, Montague (Rhodes)
See also DLB 156

James, Montague (Rhodes)
1862-1936 . . . . TCLC 6; SSC 16
See also CA 104

James, P. D. . . . . CLC 18, 46
See also White, Phyllis Dorothy James
See also BEST 90:2; CDBLB 1960 to Present; DLB 87

James, Philip
See Moorcock, Michael (John)

James, William 1842-1910 . . . . . TCLC 15, 32
See also CA 109

James I 1394-1437 . . . . LC 20

Jameson, Anna 1794-1860 . . . . NCLC 43
See also DLB 99, 166

Jami, Nur al-Din 'Abd al-Rahman
1414-1492 . . . . LC 9

Jandl, Ernst 1925- . . . . CLC 34

Janowitz, Tama
1957- . . . . CLC 43; DAM POP
See also CA 106; CANR 52

Japrisot, Sebastien 1931- . . . . CLC 90

Jarrell, Randall
1914-1965 . . . . CLC 1, 2, 6, 9, 13, 49; DAM POET
See also CA 5-8R; 25-28R; CABS 2; CANR 6, 34; CDALB 1941-1968; CLR 6; DLB 48, 52; MAICYA; MTCW; SATA 7

Jarry, Alfred
1873-1907 . . . . TCLC 2, 14; DAM DRAM; SSC 20
See also CA 104; 153

Jarvis, E. K.
See Bloch, Robert (Albert); Ellison, Harlan (Jay); Silverberg, Robert

Jeake, Samuel, Jr.
See Aiken, Conrad (Potter)

Jean Paul 1763-1825 . . . . NCLC 7

Jefferies, (John) Richard
1848-1887 . . . . NCLC 47
See also DLB 98, 141; SATA 16

Jeffers, (John) Robinson
1887-1962 . . . . CLC 2, 3, 11, 15, 54; DA; DAC; DAM MST, POET; WLC
See also CA 85-88; CANR 35; CDALB 1917-1929; DLB 45; MTCW

Jefferson, Janet
See Mencken, H(enry) L(ouis)

Jefferson, Thomas 1743-1826 . . . . NCLC 11
See also CDALB 1640-1865; DLB 31

Jeffrey, Francis 1773-1850 . . . . NCLC 33
See also DLB 107

Jelakowitch, Ivan
See Heijermans, Herman

Jellicoe, (Patricia) Ann 1927- . . . . . . CLC 27
See also CA 85-88; DLB 13

Jen, Gish . . . . CLC 70
See also Jen, Lillian

Jen, Lillian 1956(?)-
See Jen, Gish
See also CA 135

Jenkins, (John) Robin 1912- . . . . CLC 52
See also CA 1-4R; CANR 1; DLB 14

Jennings, Elizabeth (Joan)
1926- . . . . CLC 5, 14
See also CA 61-64; CAAS 5; CANR 8, 39; DLB 27; MTCW; SATA 66

Jennings, Waylon 1937- . . . . CLC 21

Jensen, Johannes V. 1873-1950 . . . . TCLC 41

Jensen, Laura (Linnea) 1948- . . . . . . CLC 37
See also CA 103

Jerome, Jerome K(lapka)
1859-1927 . . . . TCLC 23
See also CA 119; DLB 10, 34, 135

Jerrold, Douglas William
1803-1857 . . . . NCLC 2
See also DLB 158, 159

Jewett, (Theodora) Sarah Orne
1849-1909 . . . . TCLC 1, 22; SSC 6
See also CA 108; 127; DLB 12, 74; SATA 15

Jewsbury, Geraldine (Endsor)
1812-1880 . . . . NCLC 22
See also DLB 21

Jhabvala, Ruth Prawer
1927- . . . . CLC 4, 8, 29, 94; DAB; DAM NOV
See also CA 1-4R; CANR 2, 29, 51; DLB 139; INT CANR-29; MTCW

Jibran, Kahlil
See Gibran, Kahlil

Jibran, Khalil
See Gibran, Kahlil

Jiles, Paulette 1943- . . . . CLC 13, 58
See also CA 101

Jimenez (Mantecon), Juan Ramon
1881-1958 . . . . . TCLC 4; DAM MULT, POET; HLC; PC 7
See also CA 104; 131; DLB 134; HW; MTCW

Jimenez, Ramon
See Jimenez (Mantecon), Juan Ramon

Jimenez Mantecon, Juan
See Jimenez (Mantecon), Juan Ramon

Joel, Billy . . . . CLC 26
See also Joel, William Martin

Joel, William Martin 1949-
See Joel, Billy
See also CA 108

John of the Cross, St. 1542-1591 . . . . LC 18

Johnson, B(ryan) S(tanley William)
1933-1973 . . . . CLC 6, 9
See also CA 9-12R; 53-56; CANR 9; DLB 14, 40

Johnson, Benj. F. of Boo
See Riley, James Whitcomb

Johnson, Benjamin F. of Boo
See Riley, James Whitcomb

Johnson, Charles (Richard)
1948- . . . . CLC 7, 51, 65; BLC; DAM MULT
See also BW 2; CA 116; CAAS 18; CANR 42; DLB 33

Johnson, Denis 1949- . . . . CLC 52
See also CA 117; 121; DLB 120

Johnson, Diane 1934- . . . . CLC 5, 13, 48
See also CA 41-44R; CANR 17, 40; DLBY 80; INT CANR-17; MTCW

Johnson, Eyvind (Olof Verner)
1900-1976 . . . . CLC 14
See also CA 73-76; 69-72; CANR 34

Johnson, J. R.
See James, C(yril) L(ionel) R(obert)

Johnson, James Weldon
1871-1938 . . . . TCLC 3, 19; BLC; DAM MULT, POET
See also BW 1; CA 104; 125; CDALB 1917-1929; CLR 32; DLB 51; MTCW; SATA 31

Johnson, Joyce 1935- . . . . CLC 58
See also CA 125; 129

Johnson, Lionel (Pigot)
1867-1902 . . . . TCLC 19
See also CA 117; DLB 19

Johnson, Mel
See Malzberg, Barry N(athaniel)

Johnson, Pamela Hansford
1912-1981 . . . . CLC 1, 7, 27
See also CA 1-4R; 104; CANR 2, 28; DLB 15; MTCW

Johnson, Samuel
1709-1784 . . . . . LC 15; DA; DAB; DAC; DAM MST; WLC
See also CDBLB 1660-1789; DLB 39, 95, 104, 142

Johnson, Uwe
1934-1984 . . . . CLC 5, 10, 15, 40
See also CA 1-4R; 112; CANR 1, 39; DLB 75; MTCW

Johnston, George (Benson) 1913- . . . CLC 51
See also CA 1-4R; CANR 5, 20; DLB 88

Johnston, Jennifer 1930- . . . . CLC 7
See also CA 85-88; DLB 14

Jolley, (Monica) Elizabeth
1923- . . . . CLC 46; SSC 19
See also CA 127; CAAS 13

Jones, Arthur Llewellyn 1863-1947
See Machen, Arthur
See also CA 104

Jones, D(ouglas) G(ordon) 1929- . . . . CLC 10
See also CA 29-32R; CANR 13; DLB 53

Jones, David (Michael)
1895-1974 . . . . CLC 2, 4, 7, 13, 42
See also CA 9-12R; 53-56; CANR 28; CDBLB 1945-1960; DLB 20, 100; MTCW

Jones, David Robert 1947-
See Bowie, David
See also CA 103

Jones, Diana Wynne 1934- . . . . CLC 26
See also AAYA 12; CA 49-52; CANR 4, 26; CLR 23; DLB 161; JRDA; MAICYA; SAAS 7; SATA 9, 70

Jones, Edward P. 1950- . . . . CLC 76
See also BW 2; CA 142

Jones, Gayl
　1949- . . . . **CLC 6, 9; BLC; DAM MULT**
　See also BW 2; CA 77-80; CANR 27;
　DLB 33; MTCW

Jones, James 1921-1977. . . . **CLC 1, 3, 10, 39**
　See also AITN 1, 2; CA 1-4R; 69-72;
　CANR 6; DLB 2, 143; MTCW

Jones, John J.
　See Lovecraft, H(oward) P(hillips)

Jones, LeRoi . . . . **CLC 1, 2, 3, 5, 10, 14**
　See also Baraka, Amiri

Jones, Louis B. . . . . **CLC 65**
　See also CA 141

Jones, Madison (Percy, Jr.) 1925- . . . **CLC 4**
　See also CA 13-16R; CAAS 11; CANR 7,
　54; DLB 152

Jones, Mervyn 1922- . . . . **CLC 10, 52**
　See also CA 45-48; CAAS 5; CANR 1;
　MTCW

Jones, Mick 1956(?)- . . . . **CLC 30**

Jones, Nettie (Pearl) 1941- . . . . **CLC 34**
　See also BW 2; CA 137; CAAS 20

Jones, Preston 1936-1979 . . . . **CLC 10**
　See also CA 73-76; 89-92; DLB 7

Jones, Robert F(rancis) 1934- . . . . **CLC 7**
　See also CA 49-52; CANR 2

Jones, Rod 1953- . . . . **CLC 50**
　See also CA 128

Jones, Terence Graham Parry
　1942- . . . . **CLC 21**
　See also Jones, Terry; Monty Python
　See also CA 112; 116; CANR 35; INT 116

Jones, Terry
　See Jones, Terence Graham Parry
　See also SATA 67; SATA-Brief 51

Jones, Thom 1945(?)- . . . . **CLC 81**

Jong, Erica
　1942- . . . . **CLC 4, 6, 8, 18, 83;**
　　　　　　　　　　　　　　　　DAM NOV, POP
　See also AITN 1; BEST 90:2; CA 73-76;
　CANR 26, 52; DLB 2, 5, 28, 152;
　INT CANR-26; MTCW

Jonson, Ben(jamin)
　1572(?)-1637 . . . . . . **LC 6, 33; DA; DAB;**
　　　　　　　　　　DAC; DAM DRAM, MST, POET;
　　　　　　　　　　　　　　　　　　　DC 4; WLC
　See also CDBLB Before 1660; DLB 62, 121

Jordan, June
　1936- . . . . . **CLC 5, 11, 23; DAM MULT,**
　　　　　　　　　　　　　　　　　　　　　　　POET
　See also AAYA 2; BW 2; CA 33-36R;
　CANR 25; CLR 10; DLB 38; MAICYA;
　MTCW; SATA 4

Jordan, Pat(rick M.) 1941- . . . . **CLC 37**
　See also CA 33-36R

Jorgensen, Ivar
　See Ellison, Harlan (Jay)

Jorgenson, Ivar
　See Silverberg, Robert

Josephus, Flavius c. 37-100 . . . . . **CMLC 13**

Josipovici, Gabriel 1940- . . . . **CLC 6, 43**
　See also CA 37-40R; CAAS 8; CANR 47;
　DLB 14

Joubert, Joseph 1754-1824 . . . . **NCLC 9**

Jouve, Pierre Jean 1887-1976 . . . . . . **CLC 47**
　See also CA 65-68

Joyce, James (Augustine Aloysius)
　1882-1941 . . . . **TCLC 3, 8, 16, 35, 52;**
　　　　　　　　DA; DAB; DAC; DAM MST, NOV,
　　　　　　　　　　　　　　　　POET; SSC 3; WLC
　See also CA 104; 126; CDBLB 1914-1945;
　DLB 10, 19, 36, 162; MTCW

Jozsef, Attila 1905-1937 . . . . **TCLC 22**
　See also CA 116

Juana Ines de la Cruz 1651(?)-1695 . . . **LC 5**

Judd, Cyril
　See Kornbluth, C(yril) M.; Pohl, Frederik

Julian of Norwich 1342(?)-1416(?) . . . . **LC 6**
　See also DLB 146

Juniper, Alex
　See Hospital, Janette Turner

Junius
　See Luxemburg, Rosa

Just, Ward (Swift) 1935- . . . . **CLC 4, 27**
　See also CA 25-28R; CANR 32;
　INT CANR-32

Justice, Donald (Rodney)
　1925- . . . . **CLC 6, 19; DAM POET**
　See also CA 5-8R; CANR 26, 54;
　DLBY 83; INT CANR-26

Juvenal c. 55-c. 127 . . . . **CMLC 8**

Juvenis
　See Bourne, Randolph S(illiman)

Kacew, Romain 1914-1980
　See Gary, Romain
　See also CA 108; 102

Kadare, Ismail 1936- . . . . **CLC 52**

Kadohata, Cynthia . . . . **CLC 59**
　See also CA 140

Kafka, Franz
　1883-1924 . . . . **TCLC 2, 6, 13, 29, 47, 53;**
　　　　　　　　　DA; DAB; DAC; DAM MST, NOV;
　　　　　　　　　　　　　　　　　　　SSC 5; WLC
　See also CA 105; 126; DLB 81; MTCW

Kahanovitsch, Pinkhes
　See Der Nister

Kahn, Roger 1927- . . . . **CLC 30**
　See also CA 25-28R; CANR 44; DLB 171;
　SATA 37

Kain, Saul
　See Sassoon, Siegfried (Lorraine)

Kaiser, Georg 1878-1945 . . . . **TCLC 9**
　See also CA 106; DLB 124

Kaletski, Alexander 1946- . . . . **CLC 39**
　See also CA 118; 143

Kalidasa fl. c. 400- . . . . **CMLC 9**

Kallman, Chester (Simon)
　1921-1975 . . . . **CLC 2**
　See also CA 45-48; 53-56; CANR 3

Kaminsky, Melvin 1926-
　See Brooks, Mel
　See also CA 65-68; CANR 16

Kaminsky, Stuart M(elvin) 1934- . . . **CLC 59**
　See also CA 73-76; CANR 29, 53

Kane, Francis
　See Robbins, Harold

Kane, Paul
　See Simon, Paul (Frederick)

Kane, Wilson
　See Bloch, Robert (Albert)

Kanin, Garson 1912- . . . . **CLC 22**
　See also AITN 1; CA 5-8R; CANR 7;
　DLB 7

Kaniuk, Yoram 1930- . . . . **CLC 19**
　See also CA 134

Kant, Immanuel 1724-1804 . . . . . . **NCLC 27**
　See also DLB 94

Kantor, MacKinlay 1904-1977 . . . . . . **CLC 7**
　See also CA 61-64; 73-76; DLB 9, 102

Kaplan, David Michael 1946- . . . . . . **CLC 50**

Kaplan, James 1951- . . . . **CLC 59**
　See also CA 135

Karageorge, Michael
　See Anderson, Poul (William)

Karamzin, Nikolai Mikhailovich
　1766-1826 . . . . **NCLC 3**
　See also DLB 150

Karapanou, Margarita 1946- . . . . **CLC 13**
　See also CA 101

Karinthy, Frigyes 1887-1938 . . . . . . **TCLC 47**

Karl, Frederick R(obert) 1927- . . . . . **CLC 34**
　See also CA 5-8R; CANR 3, 44

Kastel, Warren
　See Silverberg, Robert

Kataev, Evgeny Petrovich 1903-1942
　See Petrov, Evgeny
　See also CA 120

Kataphusin
　See Ruskin, John

Katz, Steve 1935- . . . . **CLC 47**
　See also CA 25-28R; CAAS 14; CANR 12;
　DLBY 83

Kauffman, Janet 1945- . . . . **CLC 42**
　See also CA 117; CANR 43; DLBY 86

Kaufman, Bob (Garnell)
　1925-1986 . . . . **CLC 49**
　See also BW 1; CA 41-44R; 118; CANR 22;
　DLB 16, 41

Kaufman, George S.
　1889-1961 . . . . . . **CLC 38; DAM DRAM**
　See also CA 108; 93-96; DLB 7; INT 108

Kaufman, Sue . . . . **CLC 3, 8**
　See also Barondess, Sue K(aufman)

Kavafis, Konstantinos Petrou 1863-1933
　See Cavafy, C(onstantine) P(eter)
　See also CA 104

Kavan, Anna 1901-1968 . . . . . . **CLC 5, 13, 82**
　See also CA 5-8R; CANR 6; MTCW

Kavanagh, Dan
　See Barnes, Julian (Patrick)

Kavanagh, Patrick (Joseph)
　1904-1967 . . . . **CLC 22**
　See also CA 123; 25-28R; DLB 15, 20;
　MTCW

Kawabata, Yasunari
　1899-1972 . . . . **CLC 2, 5, 9, 18;**
　　　　　　　　　　　　　DAM MULT; SSC 17
　See also CA 93-96; 33-36R

Kaye, M(ary) M(argaret) 1909- . . . . . **CLC 28**
　See also CA 89-92; CANR 24; MTCW;
　SATA 62

King, Martin Luther, Jr.
  1929-1968 .... CLC 83; BLC; DA; DAB;
                            DAC; DAM MST, MULT
  See also BW 2; CA 25-28; CANR 27, 44;
  CAP 2; MTCW; SATA 14

King, Stephen (Edwin)
  1947- .... CLC 12, 26, 37, 61;
                            DAM NOV, POP; SSC 17
  See also AAYA 1, 17; BEST 90:1;
  CA 61-64; CANR 1, 30, 52; DLB 143;
  DLBY 80; JRDA; MTCW; SATA 9, 55

King, Steve
  See King, Stephen (Edwin)

King, Thomas
  1943- ..... CLC 89; DAC; DAM MULT
  See also CA 144; NNAL

Kingman, Lee..................... CLC 17
  See also Natti, (Mary) Lee
  See also SAAS 3; SATA 1, 67

Kingsley, Charles 1819-1875 ..... NCLC 35
  See also DLB 21, 32, 163; YABC 2

Kingsley, Sidney 1906-1995 .... CLC 44
  See also CA 85-88; 147; DLB 7

Kingsolver, Barbara
  1955- .... CLC 55, 81; DAM POP
  See also AAYA 15; CA 129; 134; INT 134

Kingston, Maxine (Ting Ting) Hong
  1940- .... CLC 12, 19, 58; DAM MULT,
                                              NOV
  See also AAYA 8; CA 69-72; CANR 13,
  38; DLB 173; DLBY 80; INT CANR-13;
  MTCW; SATA 53

Kinnell, Galway
  1927- .... CLC 1, 2, 3, 5, 13, 29
  See also CA 9-12R; CANR 10, 34; DLB 5;
  DLBY 87; INT CANR-34; MTCW

Kinsella, Thomas 1928- .... CLC 4, 19
  See also CA 17-20R; CANR 15; DLB 27;
  MTCW

Kinsella, W(illiam) P(atrick)
  1935- .... CLC 27, 43; DAC;
                            DAM NOV, POP
  See also AAYA 7; CA 97-100; CAAS 7;
  CANR 21, 35; INT CANR-21; MTCW

Kipling, (Joseph) Rudyard
  1865-1936 ...... TCLC 8, 17; DA; DAB;
                    DAC; DAM MST, POET; PC 3; SSC 5;
                                              WLC
  See also CA 105; 120; CANR 33;
  CDBLB 1890-1914; CLR 39; DLB 19, 34,
  141, 156; MAICYA; MTCW; YABC 2

Kirkup, James 1918- .... CLC 1
  See also CA 1-4R; CAAS 4; CANR 2;
  DLB 27; SATA 12

Kirkwood, James 1930(?)-1989 ...... CLC 9
  See also AITN 2; CA 1-4R; 128; CANR 6,
  40

Kirshner, Sidney
  See Kingsley, Sidney

Kis, Danilo 1935-1989 .... CLC 57
  See also CA 109; 118; 129; MTCW

Kivi, Aleksis 1834-1872 .... NCLC 30

Kizer, Carolyn (Ashley)
  1925- ..... CLC 15, 39, 80; DAM POET
  See also CA 65-68; CAAS 5; CANR 24;
  DLB 5, 169

Klabund 1890-1928 .... TCLC 44
  See also DLB 66

Klappert, Peter 1942- .... CLC 57
  See also CA 33-36R; DLB 5

Klein, A(braham) M(oses)
  1909-1972 .... CLC 19; DAB; DAC;
                                    DAM MST
  See also CA 101; 37-40R; DLB 68

Klein, Norma 1938-1989 .... CLC 30
  See also AAYA 2; CA 41-44R; 128;
  CANR 15, 37; CLR 2, 19;
  INT CANR-15; JRDA; MAICYA;
  SAAS 1; SATA 7, 57

Klein, T(heodore) E(ibon) D(onald)
  1947- .... CLC 34
  See also CA 119; CANR 44

Kleist, Heinrich von
  1777-1811 .... NCLC 2, 37;
                            DAM DRAM; SSC 22
  See also DLB 90

Klima, Ivan 1931- ..... CLC 56; DAM NOV
  See also CA 25-28R; CANR 17, 50

Klimentov, Andrei Platonovich 1899-1951
  See Platonov, Andrei
  See also CA 108

Klinger, Friedrich Maximilian von
  1752-1831 .... NCLC 1
  See also DLB 94

Klopstock, Friedrich Gottlieb
  1724-1803 .... NCLC 11
  See also DLB 97

Knebel, Fletcher 1911-1993 .... CLC 14
  See also AITN 1; CA 1-4R; 140; CAAS 3;
  CANR 1, 36; SATA 36; SATA-Obit 75

Knickerbocker, Diedrich
  See Irving, Washington

Knight, Etheridge
  1931-1991 .... CLC 40; BLC;
                            DAM POET; PC 14
  See also BW 1; CA 21-24R; 133; CANR 23;
  DLB 41

Knight, Sarah Kemble 1666-1727 ..... LC 7
  See also DLB 24

Knister, Raymond 1899-1932 ...... TCLC 56
  See also DLB 68

Knowles, John
  1926- ...... CLC 1, 4, 10, 26; DA; DAC;
                            DAM MST, NOV
  See also AAYA 10; CA 17-20R; CANR 40;
  CDALB 1968-1988; DLB 6; MTCW;
  SATA 8, 89

Knox, Calvin M.
  See Silverberg, Robert

Knye, Cassandra
  See Disch, Thomas M(ichael)

Koch, C(hristopher) J(ohn) 1932- ... CLC 42
  See also CA 127

Koch, Christopher
  See Koch, C(hristopher) J(ohn)

Koch, Kenneth
  1925- .... CLC 5, 8, 44; DAM POET
  See also CA 1-4R; CANR 6, 36; DLB 5;
  INT CANR-36; SATA 65

Kochanowski, Jan 1530-1584 .... LC 10

Kock, Charles Paul de
  1794-1871 .... NCLC 16

Koda Shigeyuki 1867-1947
  See Rohan, Koda
  See also CA 121

Koestler, Arthur
  1905-1983 .... CLC 1, 3, 6, 8, 15, 33
  See also CA 1-4R; 109; CANR 1, 33;
  CDBLB 1945-1960; DLBY 83; MTCW

Kogawa, Joy Nozomi
  1935- ...... CLC 78; DAC; DAM MST,
                                              MULT
  See also CA 101; CANR 19

Kohout, Pavel 1928- .... CLC 13
  See also CA 45-48; CANR 3

Koizumi, Yakumo
  See Hearn, (Patricio) Lafcadio (Tessima
  Carlos)

Kolmar, Gertrud 1894-1943 .... TCLC 40

Komunyakaa, Yusef 1947- ...... CLC 86, 94
  See also CA 147; DLB 120

Konrad, George
  See Konrad, Gyoergy

Konrad, Gyoergy 1933- ...... CLC 4, 10, 73
  See also CA 85-88

Konwicki, Tadeusz 1926- ..... CLC 8, 28, 54
  See also CA 101; CAAS 9; CANR 39;
  MTCW

Koontz, Dean R(ay)
  1945- ...... CLC 78; DAM NOV, POP
  See also AAYA 9; BEST 89:3, 90:2;
  CA 108; CANR 19, 36, 52; MTCW

Kopit, Arthur (Lee)
  1937- ..... CLC 1, 18, 33; DAM DRAM
  See also AITN 1; CA 81-84; CABS 3;
  DLB 7; MTCW

Kops, Bernard 1926- .... CLC 4
  See also CA 5-8R; DLB 13

Kornbluth, C(yril) M. 1923-1958.... TCLC 8
  See also CA 105; DLB 8

Korolenko, V. G.
  See Korolenko, Vladimir Galaktionovich

Korolenko, Vladimir
  See Korolenko, Vladimir Galaktionovich

Korolenko, Vladimir G.
  See Korolenko, Vladimir Galaktionovich

Korolenko, Vladimir Galaktionovich
  1853-1921 .... TCLC 22
  See also CA 121

Korzybski, Alfred (Habdank Skarbek)
  1879-1950 .... TCLC 61
  See also CA 123

Kosinski, Jerzy (Nikodem)
  1933-1991 .... CLC 1, 2, 3, 6, 10, 15, 53,
                                    70; DAM NOV
  See also CA 17-20R; 134; CANR 9, 46;
  DLB 2; DLBY 82; MTCW

Kostelanetz, Richard (Cory) 1940- .. CLC 28
  See also CA 13-16R; CAAS 8; CANR 38

Kostrowitzki, Wilhelm Apollinaris de
  1880-1918
  See Apollinaire, Guillaume
  See also CA 104

Kotlowitz, Robert 1924- .... CLC 4
  See also CA 33-36R; CANR 36

Landon, Letitia Elizabeth
1802-1838 .... NCLC **15**
See also DLB 96

Landor, Walter Savage
1775-1864 .... NCLC **14**
See also DLB 93, 107

Landwirth, Heinz   1927-
See Lind, Jakov
See also CA 9-12R; CANR 7

Lane, Patrick
1939- .... CLC **25; DAM POET**
See also CA 97-100; CANR 54; DLB 53;
INT 97-100

Lang, Andrew   1844-1912 .... TCLC **16**
See also CA 114; 137; DLB 98, 141;
MAICYA; SATA 16

Lang, Fritz   1890-1976 .... CLC **20**
See also CA 77-80; 69-72; CANR 30

Lange, John
See Crichton, (John) Michael

Langer, Elinor   1939- .... CLC **34**
See also CA 121

Langland, William
1330(?)-1400(?) ...... LC **19; DA; DAB;
DAC; DAM MST, POET**
See also DLB 146

Langstaff, Launcelot
See Irving, Washington

Lanier, Sidney
1842-1881 ...... NCLC **6; DAM POET**
See also DLB 64; DLBD 13; MAICYA;
SATA 18

Lanyer, Aemilia   1569-1645 ...... LC **10, 30**
See also DLB 121

Lao Tzu .... CMLC **7**

Lapine, James (Elliot)   1949- .... CLC **39**
See also CA 123; 130; CANR 54; INT 130

Larbaud, Valery (Nicolas)
1881-1957 .... TCLC **9**
See also CA 106; 152

Lardner, Ring
See Lardner, Ring(gold) W(ilmer)

Lardner, Ring W., Jr.
See Lardner, Ring(gold) W(ilmer)

Lardner, Ring(gold) W(ilmer)
1885-1933 .... TCLC **2, 14**
See also CA 104; 131; CDALB 1917-1929;
DLB 11, 25, 86; MTCW

Laredo, Betty
See Codrescu, Andrei

Larkin, Maia
See Wojciechowska, Maia (Teresa)

Larkin, Philip (Arthur)
1922-1985 .... CLC **3, 5, 8, 9, 13, 18, 33,
39, 64; DAB; DAM MST, POET**
See also CA 5-8R; 117; CANR 24;
CDBLB 1960 to Present; DLB 27;
MTCW

Larra (y Sanchez de Castro), Mariano Jose de
1809-1837 .... NCLC **17**

Larsen, Eric   1941- .... CLC **55**
See also CA 132

Larsen, Nella
1891-1964 .... CLC **37; BLC;
DAM MULT**
See also BW 1; CA 125; DLB 51

Larson, Charles R(aymond)   1938-... CLC **31**
See also CA 53-56; CANR 4

Las Casas, Bartolome de   1474-1566.. LC **31**

Lasker-Schueler, Else   1869-1945 .. TCLC **57**
See also DLB 66, 124

Latham, Jean Lee   1902-........... CLC **12**
See also AITN 1; CA 5-8R; CANR 7;
MAICYA; SATA 2, 68

Latham, Mavis
See Clark, Mavis Thorpe

Lathen, Emma .... CLC **2**
See also Hennissart, Martha; Latsis, Mary
J(ane)

Lathrop, Francis
See Leiber, Fritz (Reuter, Jr.)

Latsis, Mary J(ane)
See Lathen, Emma
See also CA 85-88

Lattimore, Richmond (Alexander)
1906-1984 .... CLC **3**
See also CA 1-4R; 112; CANR 1

Laughlin, James   1914-........... CLC **49**
See also CA 21-24R; CAAS 22; CANR 9,
47; DLB 48

Laurence, (Jean) Margaret (Wemyss)
1926-1987 .... CLC **3, 6, 13, 50, 62;
DAC; DAM MST; SSC 7**
See also CA 5-8R; 121; CANR 33; DLB 53;
MTCW; SATA-Obit 50

Laurent, Antoine   1952- .... CLC **50**

Lauscher, Hermann
See Hesse, Hermann

Lautreamont, Comte de
1846-1870 .... NCLC **12; SSC 14**

Laverty, Donald
See Blish, James (Benjamin)

Lavin, Mary   1912-1996 .. CLC **4, 18; SSC 4**
See also CA 9-12R; 151; CANR 33;
DLB 15; MTCW

Lavond, Paul Dennis
See Kornbluth, C(yril) M.; Pohl, Frederik

Lawler, Raymond Evenor   1922- .... CLC **58**
See also CA 103

Lawrence, D(avid) H(erbert Richards)
1885-1930 .... TCLC **2, 9, 16, 33, 48, 61;
DA; DAB; DAC; DAM MST, NOV,
POET; SSC 4, 19; WLC**
See also CA 104; 121; CDBLB 1914-1945;
DLB 10, 19, 36, 98, 162; MTCW

Lawrence, T(homas) E(dward)
1888-1935 .... TCLC **18**
See also Dale, Colin
See also CA 115

Lawrence of Arabia
See Lawrence, T(homas) E(dward)

Lawson, Henry (Archibald Hertzberg)
1867-1922 .... TCLC **27; SSC 18**
See also CA 120

Lawton, Dennis
See Faust, Frederick (Schiller)

Laxness, Halldor .... CLC **25**
See also Gudjonsson, Halldor Kiljan

Layamon   fl. c. 1200-............ CMLC **10**
See also DLB 146

Laye, Camara
1928-1980 .... CLC **4, 38; BLC;
DAM MULT**
See also BW 1; CA 85-88; 97-100;
CANR 25; MTCW

Layton, Irving (Peter)
1912- .... CLC **2, 15; DAC; DAM MST,
POET**
See also CA 1-4R; CANR 2, 33, 43;
DLB 88; MTCW

Lazarus, Emma   1849-1887........ NCLC **8**

Lazarus, Felix
See Cable, George Washington

Lazarus, Henry
See Slavitt, David R(ytman)

Lea, Joan
See Neufeld, John (Arthur)

Leacock, Stephen (Butler)
1869-1944 .. TCLC **2; DAC; DAM MST**
See also CA 104; 141; DLB 92

Lear, Edward   1812-1888 .... NCLC **3**
See also CLR 1; DLB 32, 163, 166;
MAICYA; SATA 18

Lear, Norman (Milton)   1922- ...... CLC **12**
See also CA 73-76

Leavis, F(rank) R(aymond)
1895-1978 .... CLC **24**
See also CA 21-24R; 77-80; CANR 44;
MTCW

Leavitt, David   1961-... CLC **34; DAM POP**
See also CA 116; 122; CANR 50; DLB 130;
INT 122

Leblanc, Maurice (Marie Emile)
1864-1941 .... TCLC **49**
See also CA 110

Lebowitz, Fran(ces Ann)
1951(?)- .... CLC **11, 36**
See also CA 81-84; CANR 14;
INT CANR-14; MTCW

Lebrecht, Peter
See Tieck, (Johann) Ludwig

le Carre, John .... CLC **3, 5, 9, 15, 28**
See also Cornwell, David (John Moore)
See also BEST 89:4; CDBLB 1960 to
Present; DLB 87

Le Clezio, J(ean) M(arie) G(ustave)
1940- .... CLC **31**
See also CA 116; 128; DLB 83

Leconte de Lisle, Charles-Marie-Rene
1818-1894 .... NCLC **29**

Le Coq, Monsieur
See Simenon, Georges (Jacques Christian)

Leduc, Violette   1907-1972......... CLC **22**
See also CA 13-14; 33-36R; CAP 1

Ledwidge, Francis   1887(?)-1917 ... TCLC **23**
See also CA 123; DLB 20

Lee, Andrea
1953- ..... CLC **36; BLC; DAM MULT**
See also BW 1; CA 125

Lee, Andrew
See Auchincloss, Louis (Stanton)

Lee, Chang-rae 1965- .... CLC 91
See also CA 148

Lee, Don L. .... CLC 2
See also Madhubuti, Haki R.

Lee, George W(ashington)
1894-1976 .... CLC 52; BLC;
DAM MULT
See also BW 1; CA 125; DLB 51

Lee, (Nelle) Harper
1926- .... CLC 12, 60; DA; DAB; DAC;
DAM MST, NOV; WLC
See also AAYA 13; CA 13-16R; CANR 51;
CDALB 1941-1968; DLB 6; MTCW;
SATA 11

Lee, Helen Elaine 1959(?)- .... CLC 86
See also CA 148

Lee, Julian
See Latham, Jean Lee

Lee, Larry
See Lee, Lawrence

Lee, Laurie
1914- .... CLC 90; DAB; DAM POP
See also CA 77-80; CANR 33; DLB 27;
MTCW

Lee, Lawrence 1941-1990 .... CLC 34
See also CA 131; CANR 43

Lee, Manfred B(ennington)
1905-1971 .... CLC 11
See also Queen, Ellery
See also CA 1-4R; 29-32R; CANR 2;
DLB 137

Lee, Stan 1922- .... CLC 17
See also AAYA 5; CA 108; 111; INT 111

Lee, Tanith 1947- .... CLC 46
See also AAYA 15; CA 37-40R; CANR 53;
SATA 8, 88

Lee, Vernon .... TCLC 5
See also Paget, Violet
See also DLB 57, 153, 156, 174

Lee, William
See Burroughs, William S(eward)

Lee, Willy
See Burroughs, William S(eward)

Lee-Hamilton, Eugene (Jacob)
1845-1907 .... TCLC 22
See also CA 117

Leet, Judith 1935- .... CLC 11

Le Fanu, Joseph Sheridan
1814-1873 .... NCLC 9, 58; DAM POP;
SSC 14
See also DLB 21, 70, 159

Leffland, Ella 1931- .... CLC 19
See also CA 29-32R; CANR 35; DLBY 84;
INT CANR-35; SATA 65

Leger, Alexis
See Leger, (Marie-Rene Auguste) Alexis
Saint-Leger

Leger, (Marie-Rene Auguste) Alexis
Saint-Leger
1887-1975 .... CLC 11; DAM POET
See also Perse, St.-John
See also CA 13-16R; 61-64; CANR 43;
MTCW

Leger, Saintleger
See Leger, (Marie-Rene Auguste) Alexis
Saint-Leger

Le Guin, Ursula K(roeber)
1929- ...... CLC 8, 13, 22, 45, 71; DAB;
DAC; DAM MST, POP; SSC 12
See also AAYA 9; AITN 1; CA 21-24R;
CANR 9, 32, 52; CDALB 1968-1988;
CLR 3, 28; DLB 8, 52; INT CANR-32;
JRDA; MAICYA; MTCW; SATA 4, 52

Lehmann, Rosamond (Nina)
1901-1990 .... CLC 5
See also CA 77-80; 131; CANR 8; DLB 15

Leiber, Fritz (Reuter, Jr.)
1910-1992 .... CLC 25
See also CA 45-48; 139; CANR 2, 40;
DLB 8; MTCW; SATA 45;
SATA-Obit 73

Leibniz, Gottfried Wilhelm von
1646-1716 .... LC 35
See also DLB 168

Leimbach, Martha 1963-
See Leimbach, Marti
See also CA 130

Leimbach, Marti .... CLC 65
See also Leimbach, Martha

Leino, Eino .... TCLC 24
See also Loennbohm, Armas Eino Leopold

Leiris, Michel (Julien) 1901-1990 ... CLC 61
See also CA 119; 128; 132

Leithauser, Brad 1953- .... CLC 27
See also CA 107; CANR 27; DLB 120

Lelchuk, Alan 1938- .... CLC 5
See also CA 45-48; CAAS 20; CANR 1

Lem, Stanislaw 1921- .... CLC 8, 15, 40
See also CA 105; CAAS 1; CANR 32;
MTCW

Lemann, Nancy 1956- .... CLC 39
See also CA 118; 136

Lemonnier, (Antoine Louis) Camille
1844-1913 .... TCLC 22
See also CA 121

Lenau, Nikolaus 1802-1850 ...... NCLC 16

L'Engle, Madeleine (Camp Franklin)
1918- .... CLC 12; DAM POP
See also AAYA 1; AITN 2; CA 1-4R;
CANR 3, 21, 39; CLR 1, 14; DLB 52;
JRDA; MAICYA; MTCW; SAAS 15;
SATA 1, 27, 75

Lengyel, Jozsef 1896-1975 .... CLC 7
See also CA 85-88; 57-60

Lenin 1870-1924
See Lenin, V. I.
See also CA 121

Lenin, V. I. .... TCLC 67
See also Lenin

Lennon, John (Ono)
1940-1980 .... CLC 12, 35
See also CA 102

Lennox, Charlotte Ramsay
1729(?)-1804 .... NCLC 23
See also DLB 39

Lentricchia, Frank (Jr.) 1940- ...... CLC 34
See also CA 25-28R; CANR 19

Lenz, Siegfried 1926- .... CLC 27
See also CA 89-92; DLB 75

Leonard, Elmore (John, Jr.)
1925- ...... CLC 28, 34, 71; DAM POP
See also AITN 1; BEST 89:1, 90:4;
CA 81-84; CANR 12, 28, 53; DLB 173;
INT CANR-28; MTCW

Leonard, Hugh .... CLC 19
See also Byrne, John Keyes
See also DLB 13

Leonov, Leonid (Maximovich)
1899-1994 .... CLC 92; DAM NOV
See also CA 129; MTCW

Leopardi, (Conte) Giacomo
1798-1837 .... NCLC 22

Le Reveler
See Artaud, Antonin (Marie Joseph)

Lerman, Eleanor 1952- .... CLC 9
See also CA 85-88

Lerman, Rhoda 1936- .... CLC 56
See also CA 49-52

Lermontov, Mikhail Yuryevich
1814-1841 .... NCLC 47

Leroux, Gaston 1868-1927 .... TCLC 25
See also CA 108; 136; SATA 65

Lesage, Alain-Rene 1668-1747 ...... LC 28

Leskov, Nikolai (Semyonovich)
1831-1895 .... NCLC 25

Lessing, Doris (May)
1919- ..... CLC 1, 2, 3, 6, 10, 15, 22, 40,
94; DA; DAB; DAC; DAM MST, NOV;
SSC 6
See also CA 9-12R; CAAS 14; CANR 33,
54; CDBLB 1960 to Present; DLB 15,
139; DLBY 85; MTCW

Lessing, Gotthold Ephraim
1729-1781 .... LC 8
See also DLB 97

Lester, Richard 1932- .... CLC 20

Lever, Charles (James)
1806-1872 .... NCLC 23
See also DLB 21

Leverson, Ada 1865(?)-1936(?) .... TCLC 18
See also Elaine
See also CA 117; DLB 153

Levertov, Denise
1923- ...... CLC 1, 2, 3, 5, 8, 15, 28, 66;
DAM POET; PC 11
See also CA 1-4R; CAAS 19; CANR 3, 29,
50; DLB 5, 165; INT CANR-29; MTCW

Levi, Jonathan .... CLC 76

Levi, Peter (Chad Tigar) 1931- ..... CLC 41
See also CA 5-8R; CANR 34; DLB 40

Levi, Primo
1919-1987 .... CLC 37, 50; SSC 12
See also CA 13-16R; 122; CANR 12, 33;
MTCW

Levin, Ira 1929- ..... CLC 3, 6; DAM POP
See also CA 21-24R; CANR 17, 44;
MTCW; SATA 66

Levin, Meyer
1905-1981 .... CLC 7; DAM POP
See also AITN 1; CA 9-12R; 104;
CANR 15; DLB 9, 28; DLBY 81;
SATA 21; SATA-Obit 27

Levine, Norman 1924- . . . . **CLC 54**
See also CA 73-76; CAAS 23; CANR 14;
DLB 88

Levine, Philip
1928- . . . . **CLC 2, 4, 5, 9, 14, 33;**
                                          DAM POET
See also CA 9-12R; CANR 9, 37, 52;
DLB 5

Levinson, Deirdre 1931- . . . . **CLC 49**
See also CA 73-76

Levi-Strauss, Claude 1908- . . . . **CLC 38**
See also CA 1-4R; CANR 6, 32; MTCW

Levitin, Sonia (Wolff) 1934- . . . . **CLC 17**
See also AAYA 13; CA 29-32R; CANR 14,
32; JRDA; MAICYA; SAAS 2; SATA 4,
68

Levon, O. U.
See Kesey, Ken (Elton)

Lewes, George Henry
1817-1878 . . . . **NCLC 25**
See also DLB 55, 144

Lewis, Alun 1915-1944 . . . . **TCLC 3**
See also CA 104; DLB 20, 162

Lewis, C. Day
See Day Lewis, C(ecil)

Lewis, C(live) S(taples)
1898-1963 . . . . . **CLC 1, 3, 6, 14, 27; DA;**
      DAB; DAC; DAM MST, NOV, POP;
                                                     WLC
See also AAYA 3; CA 81-84; CANR 33;
CDBLB 1945-1960; CLR 3, 27; DLB 15,
100, 160; JRDA; MAICYA; MTCW;
SATA 13

Lewis, Janet 1899- . . . . **CLC 41**
See also Winters, Janet Lewis
See also CA 9-12R; CANR 29; CAP 1;
DLBY 87

Lewis, Matthew Gregory
1775-1818 . . . . **NCLC 11**
See also DLB 39, 158

Lewis, (Harry) Sinclair
1885-1951 . . . . . **TCLC 4, 13, 23, 39; DA;**
      DAB; DAC; DAM MST, NOV; WLC
See also CA 104; 133; CDALB 1917-1929;
DLB 9, 102; DLBD 1; MTCW

Lewis, (Percy) Wyndham
1884(?)-1957 . . . . **TCLC 2, 9**
See also CA 104; DLB 15

Lewisohn, Ludwig 1883-1955 . . . . . . **TCLC 19**
See also CA 107; DLB 4, 9, 28, 102

Leyner, Mark 1956- . . . . **CLC 92**
See also CA 110; CANR 28, 53

Lezama Lima, Jose
1910-1976 . . . . **CLC 4, 10; DAM MULT**
See also CA 77-80; DLB 113; HW

L'Heureux, John (Clarke) 1934- . . . . **CLC 52**
See also CA 13-16R; CANR 23, 45

Liddell, C. H.
See Kuttner, Henry

Lie, Jonas (Lauritz Idemil)
1833-1908(?) . . . . **TCLC 5**
See also CA 115

Lieber, Joel 1937-1971 . . . . **CLC 6**
See also CA 73-76; 29-32R

Lieber, Stanley Martin
See Lee, Stan

Lieberman, Laurence (James)
1935- . . . . **CLC 4, 36**
See also CA 17-20R; CANR 8, 36

Lieksman, Anders
See Haavikko, Paavo Juhani

Li Fei-kan 1904-
See Pa Chin
See also CA 105

Lifton, Robert Jay 1926- . . . . **CLC 67**
See also CA 17-20R; CANR 27;
INT CANR-27; SATA 66

Lightfoot, Gordon 1938- . . . . **CLC 26**
See also CA 109

Lightman, Alan P. 1948- . . . . **CLC 81**
See also CA 141

Ligotti, Thomas (Robert)
1953- . . . . **CLC 44; SSC 16**
See also CA 123; CANR 49

Li Ho 791-817 . . . . **PC 13**

Liliencron, (Friedrich Adolf Axel) Detlev von
1844-1909 . . . . **TCLC 18**
See also CA 117

Lilly, William 1602-1681 . . . . **LC 27**

Lima, Jose Lezama
See Lezama Lima, Jose

Lima Barreto, Afonso Henrique de
1881-1922 . . . . **TCLC 23**
See also CA 117

Limonov, Edward 1944- . . . . **CLC 67**
See also CA 137

Lin, Frank
See Atherton, Gertrude (Franklin Horn)

Lincoln, Abraham 1809-1865 . . . . . **NCLC 18**

Lind, Jakov . . . . **CLC 1, 2, 4, 27, 82**
See also Landwirth, Heinz
See also CAAS 4

Lindbergh, Anne (Spencer) Morrow
1906- . . . . **CLC 82; DAM NOV**
See also CA 17-20R; CANR 16; MTCW;
SATA 33

Lindsay, David 1878-1945 . . . . **TCLC 15**
See also CA 113

Lindsay, (Nicholas) Vachel
1879-1931 . . . . **TCLC 17; DA; DAC;**
                          DAM MST, POET; WLC
See also CA 114; 135; CDALB 1865-1917;
DLB 54; SATA 40

Linke-Poot
See Doeblin, Alfred

Linney, Romulus 1930- . . . . **CLC 51**
See also CA 1-4R; CANR 40, 44

Linton, Eliza Lynn 1822-1898 . . . . **NCLC 41**
See also DLB 18

Li Po 701-763 . . . . **CMLC 2**

Lipsius, Justus 1547-1606 . . . . **LC 16**

Lipsyte, Robert (Michael)
1938- . . . . **CLC 21; DA; DAC;**
                                          DAM MST, NOV
See also AAYA 7; CA 17-20R; CANR 8;
CLR 23; JRDA; MAICYA; SATA 5, 68

Lish, Gordon (Jay) 1934- . . **CLC 45; SSC 18**
See also CA 113; 117; DLB 130; INT 117

Lispector, Clarice 1925-1977 . . . . **CLC 43**
See also CA 139; 116; DLB 113

Littell, Robert 1935(?)- . . . . **CLC 42**
See also CA 109; 112

Little, Malcolm 1925-1965
See Malcolm X
See also BW 1; CA 125; 111; DA; DAB;
DAC; DAM MST, MULT; MTCW

Littlewit, Humphrey Gent.
See Lovecraft, H(oward) P(hillips)

Litwos
See Sienkiewicz, Henryk (Adam Alexander
Pius)

Liu E 1857-1909 . . . . **TCLC 15**
See also CA 115

Lively, Penelope (Margaret)
1933- . . . . **CLC 32, 50; DAM NOV**
See also CA 41-44R; CANR 29; CLR 7;
DLB 14, 161; JRDA; MAICYA; MTCW;
SATA 7, 60

Livesay, Dorothy (Kathleen)
1909- . . . . **CLC 4, 15, 79; DAC;**
                                          DAM MST, POET
See also AITN 2; CA 25-28R; CAAS 8;
CANR 36; DLB 68; MTCW

Livy c. 59B.C.-c. 17 . . . . **CMLC 11**

Lizardi, Jose Joaquin Fernandez de
1776-1827 . . . . **NCLC 30**

Llewellyn, Richard
See Llewellyn Lloyd, Richard Dafydd
Vivian
See also DLB 15

Llewellyn Lloyd, Richard Dafydd Vivian
1906-1983 . . . . **CLC 7, 80**
See also Llewellyn, Richard
See also CA 53-56; 111; CANR 7;
SATA 11; SATA-Obit 37

Llosa, (Jorge) Mario (Pedro) Vargas
See Vargas Llosa, (Jorge) Mario (Pedro)

Lloyd Webber, Andrew 1948-
See Webber, Andrew Lloyd
See also AAYA 1; CA 116; 149;
DAM DRAM; SATA 56

Llull, Ramon c. 1235-c. 1316 . . . . . **CMLC 12**

Locke, Alain (Le Roy)
1886-1954 . . . . **TCLC 43**
See also BW 1; CA 106; 124; DLB 51

Locke, John 1632-1704 . . . . **LC 7, 35**
See also DLB 101

Locke-Elliott, Sumner
See Elliott, Sumner Locke

Lockhart, John Gibson
1794-1854 . . . . **NCLC 6**
See also DLB 110, 116, 144

Lodge, David (John)
1935- . . . . **CLC 36; DAM POP**
See also BEST 90:1; CA 17-20R; CANR 19,
53; DLB 14; INT CANR-19; MTCW

Loennbohm, Armas Eino Leopold 1878-1926
See Leino, Eino
See also CA 123

Loewinsohn, Ron(ald William)
1937- . . . . **CLC 52**
See also CA 25-28R

Logan, Jake
See Smith, Martin Cruz

Logan, John (Burton) 1923-1987..... **CLC 5**
See also CA 77-80; 124; CANR 45; DLB 5

Lo Kuan-chung 1330(?)-1400(?)...... **LC 12**

Lombard, Nap
See Johnson, Pamela Hansford

London, Jack.. **TCLC 9, 15, 39; SSC 4; WLC**
See also London, John Griffith
See also AAYA 13; AITN 2;
CDALB 1865-1917; DLB 8, 12, 78;
SATA 18

London, John Griffith 1876-1916
See London, Jack
See also CA 110; 119; DA; DAB; DAC;
DAM MST, NOV; JRDA; MAICYA;
MTCW

Long, Emmett
See Leonard, Elmore (John, Jr.)

Longbaugh, Harry
See Goldman, William (W.)

Longfellow, Henry Wadsworth
1807-1882..... **NCLC 2, 45; DA; DAB;
DAC; DAM MST, POET**
See also CDALB 1640-1865; DLB 1, 59;
SATA 19

Longley, Michael 1939-........... **CLC 29**
See also CA 102; DLB 40

Longus fl. c. 2nd cent. -.......... **CMLC 7**

Longway, A. Hugh
See Lang, Andrew

Lonnrot, Elias 1802-1884........ **NCLC 53**

Lopate, Phillip 1943-............. **CLC 29**
See also CA 97-100; DLBY 80; INT 97-100

Lopez Portillo (y Pacheco), Jose
1920-...................... **CLC 46**
See also CA 129; HW

Lopez y Fuentes, Gregorio
1897(?)-1966................. **CLC 32**
See also CA 131; HW

Lorca, Federico Garcia
See Garcia Lorca, Federico

Lord, Bette Bao 1938-............ **CLC 23**
See also BEST 90:3; CA 107; CANR 41;
INT 107; SATA 58

Lord Auch
See Bataille, Georges

Lord Byron
See Byron, George Gordon (Noel)

Lorde, Audre (Geraldine)
1934-1992......... **CLC 18, 71; BLC;
DAM MULT, POET; PC 12**
See also BW 1; CA 25-28R; 142; CANR 16,
26, 46; DLB 41; MTCW

Lord Jeffrey
See Jeffrey, Francis

Lorenzini, Carlo 1826-1890
See Collodi, Carlo
See also MAICYA; SATA 29

Lorenzo, Heberto Padilla
See Padilla (Lorenzo), Heberto

Loris
See Hofmannsthal, Hugo von

Loti, Pierre .... **TCLC 11**
See also Viaud, (Louis Marie) Julien
See also DLB 123

Louie, David Wong 1954-......... **CLC 70**
See also CA 139

Louis, Father M.
See Merton, Thomas

Lovecraft, H(oward) P(hillips)
1890-1937 .... **TCLC 4, 22; DAM POP;
SSC 3**
See also AAYA 14; CA 104; 133; MTCW

Lovelace, Earl 1935-............. **CLC 51**
See also BW 2; CA 77-80; CANR 41;
DLB 125; MTCW

Lovelace, Richard 1618-1657........ **LC 24**
See also DLB 131

Lowell, Amy
1874-1925 .... **TCLC 1, 8; DAM POET;
PC 13**
See also CA 104; 151; DLB 54, 140

Lowell, James Russell 1819-1891 .. **NCLC 2**
See also CDALB 1640-1865; DLB 1, 11, 64,
79

Lowell, Robert (Traill Spence, Jr.)
1917-1977 ... **CLC 1, 2, 3, 4, 5, 8, 9, 11,
15, 37; DA; DAB; DAC; DAM MST,
NOV; PC 3; WLC**
See also CA 9-12R; 73-76; CABS 2;
CANR 26; DLB 5, 169; MTCW

Lowndes, Marie Adelaide (Belloc)
1868-1947 .... **TCLC 12**
See also CA 107; DLB 70

Lowry, (Clarence) Malcolm
1909-1957 .... **TCLC 6, 40**
See also CA 105; 131; CDBLB 1945-1960;
DLB 15; MTCW

Lowry, Mina Gertrude 1882-1966
See Loy, Mina
See also CA 113

Loxsmith, John
See Brunner, John (Kilian Houston)

Loy, Mina .... **CLC 28; DAM POET; PC 16**
See also Lowry, Mina Gertrude
See also DLB 4, 54

Loyson-Bridet
See Schwob, (Mayer Andre) Marcel

Lucas, Craig 1951-............... **CLC 64**
See also CA 137

Lucas, George 1944-............. **CLC 16**
See also AAYA 1; CA 77-80; CANR 30;
SATA 56

Lucas, Hans
See Godard, Jean-Luc

Lucas, Victoria
See Plath, Sylvia

Ludlam, Charles 1943-1987..... **CLC 46, 50**
See also CA 85-88; 122

Ludlum, Robert
1927-... **CLC 22, 43; DAM NOV, POP**
See also AAYA 10; BEST 89:1, 90:3;
CA 33-36R; CANR 25, 41; DLBY 82;
MTCW

Ludwig, Ken..................... **CLC 60**

Ludwig, Otto 1813-1865.......... **NCLC 4**
See also DLB 129

Lugones, Leopoldo 1874-1938..... **TCLC 15**
See also CA 116; 131; HW

Lu Hsun 1881-1936 ...... **TCLC 3; SSC 20**
See also Shu-Jen, Chou

Lukacs, George .... **CLC 24**
See also Lukacs, Gyorgy (Szegeny von)

Lukacs, Gyorgy (Szegeny von) 1885-1971
See Lukacs, George
See also CA 101; 29-32R

Luke, Peter (Ambrose Cyprian)
1919-1995 .... **CLC 38**
See also CA 81-84; 147; DLB 13

Lunar, Dennis
See Mungo, Raymond

Lurie, Alison 1926-........ **CLC 4, 5, 18, 39**
See also CA 1-4R; CANR 2, 17, 50; DLB 2;
MTCW; SATA 46

Lustig, Arnost 1926-.............. **CLC 56**
See also AAYA 3; CA 69-72; CANR 47;
SATA 56

Luther, Martin 1483-1546........... **LC 9**

Luxemburg, Rosa 1870(?)-1919.... **TCLC 63**
See also CA 118

Luzi, Mario 1914-................. **CLC 13**
See also CA 61-64; CANR 9; DLB 128

L'Ymagier
See Gourmont, Remy (-Marie-Charles) de

Lynch, B. Suarez
See Bioy Casares, Adolfo; Borges, Jorge
Luis

Lynch, David (K.) 1946-........... **CLC 66**
See also CA 124; 129

Lynch, James
See Andreyev, Leonid (Nikolaevich)

Lynch Davis, B.
See Bioy Casares, Adolfo; Borges, Jorge
Luis

Lyndsay, Sir David 1490-1555 ...... **LC 20**

Lynn, Kenneth S(chuyler) 1923-.... **CLC 50**
See also CA 1-4R; CANR 3, 27

Lynx
See West, Rebecca

Lyons, Marcus
See Blish, James (Benjamin)

Lyre, Pinchbeck
See Sassoon, Siegfried (Lorraine)

Lytle, Andrew (Nelson) 1902-1995 .. **CLC 22**
See also CA 9-12R; 150; DLB 6; DLBY 95

Lyttelton, George 1709-1773........ **LC 10**

Maas, Peter 1929-............... **CLC 29**
See also CA 93-96; INT 93-96

Macaulay, Rose 1881-1958 ..... **TCLC 7, 44**
See also CA 104; DLB 36

Macaulay, Thomas Babington
1800-1859 .... **NCLC 42**
See also CDBLB 1832-1890; DLB 32, 55

MacBeth, George (Mann)
1932-1992 .... **CLC 2, 5, 9**
See also CA 25-28R; 136; DLB 40; MTCW;
SATA 4; SATA-Obit 70

MacCaig, Norman (Alexander)
1910-..... **CLC 36; DAB; DAM POET**
See also CA 9-12R; CANR 3, 34; DLB 27

MacCarthy, (Sir Charles Otto) Desmond
1877-1952 .... **TCLC 36**

MacDiarmid, Hugh
.... **CLC 2, 4, 11, 19, 63; PC 9**
See also Grieve, C(hristopher) M(urray)
See also CDBLB 1945-1960; DLB 20

MacDonald, Anson
See Heinlein, Robert A(nson)

Macdonald, Cynthia 1928- ...... **CLC 13, 19**
See also CA 49-52; CANR 4, 44; DLB 105

MacDonald, George 1824-1905 ..... **TCLC 9**
See also CA 106; 137; DLB 18, 163;
MAICYA; SATA 33

Macdonald, John
See Millar, Kenneth

MacDonald, John D(ann)
1916-1986 .... **CLC 3, 27, 44;**
DAM NOV, POP
See also CA 1-4R; 121; CANR 1, 19;
DLB 8; DLBY 86; MTCW

Macdonald, John Ross
See Millar, Kenneth

Macdonald, Ross ..... **CLC 1, 2, 3, 14, 34, 41**
See also Millar, Kenneth
See also DLBD 6

MacDougal, John
See Blish, James (Benjamin)

MacEwen, Gwendolyn (Margaret)
1941-1987 .... **CLC 13, 55**
See also CA 9-12R; 124; CANR 7, 22;
DLB 53; SATA 50; SATA-Obit 55

Macha, Karel Hynek 1810-1846 .. **NCLC 46**

Machado (y Ruiz), Antonio
1875-1939 .... **TCLC 3**
See also CA 104; DLB 108

Machado de Assis, Joaquim Maria
1839-1908 ..... **TCLC 10; BLC; SSC 24**
See also CA 107; 153

Machen, Arthur .... **TCLC 4; SSC 20**
See also Jones, Arthur Llewellyn
See also DLB 36, 156

Machiavelli, Niccolo
1469-1527 .... **LC 8, 36; DA; DAB;**
DAC; DAM MST

MacInnes, Colin 1914-1976 ...... **CLC 4, 23**
See also CA 69-72; 65-68; CANR 21;
DLB 14; MTCW

MacInnes, Helen (Clark)
1907-1985 ..... **CLC 27, 39; DAM POP**
See also CA 1-4R; 117; CANR 1, 28;
DLB 87; MTCW; SATA 22;
SATA-Obit 44

Mackay, Mary 1855-1924
See Corelli, Marie
See also CA 118

Mackenzie, Compton (Edward Montague)
1883-1972 .... **CLC 18**
See also CA 21-22; 37-40R; CAP 2;
DLB 34, 100

Mackenzie, Henry 1745-1831 .... **NCLC 41**
See also DLB 39

Mackintosh, Elizabeth 1896(?)-1952
See Tey, Josephine
See also CA 110

MacLaren, James
See Grieve, C(hristopher) M(urray)

Mac Laverty, Bernard 1942- .... **CLC 31**
See also CA 116; 118; CANR 43; INT 118

MacLean, Alistair (Stuart)
1922-1987 .... **CLC 3, 13, 50, 63;**
DAM POP
See also CA 57-60; 121; CANR 28; MTCW;
SATA 23; SATA-Obit 50

Maclean, Norman (Fitzroy)
1902-1990 .... **CLC 78; DAM POP;**
SSC 13
See also CA 102; 132; CANR 49

MacLeish, Archibald
1892-1982 .... **CLC 3, 8, 14, 68;**
DAM POET
See also CA 9-12R; 106; CANR 33; DLB 4,
7, 45; DLBY 82; MTCW

MacLennan, (John) Hugh
1907-1990 .... **CLC 2, 14, 92; DAC;**
DAM MST
See also CA 5-8R; 142; CANR 33; DLB 68;
MTCW

MacLeod, Alistair
1936- ...... **CLC 56; DAC; DAM MST**
See also CA 123; DLB 60

MacNeice, (Frederick) Louis
1907-1963 ...... **CLC 1, 4, 10, 53; DAB;**
DAM POET
See also CA 85-88; DLB 10, 20; MTCW

MacNeill, Dand
See Fraser, George MacDonald

Macpherson, James 1736-1796 ...... **LC 29**
See also DLB 109

Macpherson, (Jean) Jay 1931- ...... **CLC 14**
See also CA 5-8R; DLB 53

MacShane, Frank 1927- .... **CLC 39**
See also CA 9-12R; CANR 3, 33; DLB 111

Macumber, Mari
See Sandoz, Mari(e Susette)

Madach, Imre 1823-1864 .... **NCLC 19**

Madden, (Jerry) David 1933- .... **CLC 5, 15**
See also CA 1-4R; CAAS 3; CANR 4, 45;
DLB 6; MTCW

Maddern, Al(an)
See Ellison, Harlan (Jay)

Madhubuti, Haki R.
1942- .... **CLC 6, 73; BLC;**
DAM MULT, POET; PC 5
See also Lee, Don L.
See also BW 2; CA 73-76; CANR 24, 51;
DLB 5, 41; DLBD 8

Maepenn, Hugh
See Kuttner, Henry

Maepenn, K. H.
See Kuttner, Henry

Maeterlinck, Maurice
1862-1949 ...... **TCLC 3; DAM DRAM**
See also CA 104; 136; SATA 66

Maginn, William 1794-1842 .... **NCLC 8**
See also DLB 110, 159

Mahapatra, Jayanta
1928- .... **CLC 33; DAM MULT**
See also CA 73-76; CAAS 9; CANR 15, 33

Mahfouz, Naguib (Abdel Aziz Al-Sabilgi)
1911(?)-
See Mahfuz, Najib
See also BEST 89:2; CA 128; CANR 55;
DAM NOV; MTCW

Mahfuz, Najib .... **CLC 52, 55**
See also Mahfouz, Naguib (Abdel Aziz
Al-Sabilgi)
See also DLBY 88

Mahon, Derek 1941- .... **CLC 27**
See also CA 113; 128; DLB 40

Mailer, Norman
1923- ...... **CLC 1, 2, 3, 4, 5, 8, 11, 14,**
28, 39, 74; DA; DAB; DAC; DAM MST,
NOV, POP
See also AITN 2; CA 9-12R; CABS 1;
CANR 28; CDALB 1968-1988; DLB 2,
16, 28; DLBD 3; DLBY 80, 83; MTCW

Maillet, Antonine 1929- ...... **CLC 54; DAC**
See also CA 115; 120; CANR 46; DLB 60;
INT 120

Mais, Roger 1905-1955 .... **TCLC 8**
See also BW 1; CA 105; 124; DLB 125;
MTCW

Maistre, Joseph de 1753-1821 .... **NCLC 37**

Maitland, Frederic 1850-1906 ..... **TCLC 65**

Maitland, Sara (Louise) 1950- ...... **CLC 49**
See also CA 69-72; CANR 13

Major, Clarence
1936- .... **CLC 3, 19, 48; BLC;**
DAM MULT
See also BW 2; CA 21-24R; CAAS 6;
CANR 13, 25, 53; DLB 33

Major, Kevin (Gerald)
1949- .... **CLC 26; DAC**
See also AAYA 16; CA 97-100; CANR 21,
38; CLR 11; DLB 60; INT CANR-21;
JRDA; MAICYA; SATA 32, 82

Maki, James
See Ozu, Yasujiro

Malabaila, Damiano
See Levi, Primo

Malamud, Bernard
1914-1986 ...... **CLC 1, 2, 3, 5, 8, 9, 11,**
18, 27, 44, 78, 85; DA; DAB; DAC;
DAM MST, NOV, POP; SSC 15; WLC
See also AAYA 16; CA 5-8R; 118; CABS 1;
CANR 28; CDALB 1941-1968; DLB 2,
28, 152; DLBY 80, 86; MTCW

Malaparte, Curzio 1898-1957 ..... **TCLC 52**

Malcolm, Dan
See Silverberg, Robert

Malcolm X .... **CLC 82; BLC**
See also Little, Malcolm

Malherbe, Francois de 1555-1628 ..... **LC 5**

Mallarme, Stephane
1842-1898 .... **NCLC 4, 41;**
DAM POET; PC 4

Mallet-Joris, Francoise 1930- ...... **CLC 11**
See also CA 65-68; CANR 17; DLB 83

Malley, Ern
See McAuley, James Phillip

Mallowan, Agatha Christie
See Christie, Agatha (Mary Clarissa)

Maloff, Saul 1922- . . . . CLC 5
See also CA 33-36R

Malone, Louis
See MacNeice, (Frederick) Louis

Malone, Michael (Christopher)
1942- . . . . CLC 43
See also CA 77-80; CANR 14, 32

Malory, (Sir) Thomas
1410(?)-1471(?) . . . . . . LC 11; DA; DAB;
DAC; DAM MST
See also CDBLB Before 1660; DLB 146;
SATA 59; SATA-Brief 33

Malouf, (George Joseph) David
1934- . . . . CLC 28, 86
See also CA 124; CANR 50

Malraux, (Georges-)Andre
1901-1976 . . . . . . CLC 1, 4, 9, 13, 15, 57;
DAM NOV
See also CA 21-22; 69-72; CANR 34;
CAP 2; DLB 72; MTCW

Malzberg, Barry N(athaniel) 1939-. . . CLC 7
See also CA 61-64; CAAS 4; CANR 16;
DLB 8

Mamet, David (Alan)
1947- . . . . CLC 9, 15, 34, 46, 91;
DAM DRAM; DC 4
See also AAYA 3; CA 81-84; CABS 3;
CANR 15, 41; DLB 7; MTCW

Mamoulian, Rouben (Zachary)
1897-1987 . . . . CLC 16
See also CA 25-28R; 124

Mandelstam, Osip (Emilievich)
1891(?)-1938(?) . . . . . . TCLC 2, 6; PC 14
See also CA 104; 150

Mander, (Mary) Jane 1877-1949. . . TCLC 31

Mandeville, John fl. 1350- . . . . CMLC 19
See also DLB 146

Mandiargues, Andre Pieyre de. . . . . . CLC 41
See also Pieyre de Mandiargues, Andre
See also DLB 83

Mandrake, Ethel Belle
See Thurman, Wallace (Henry)

Mangan, James Clarence
1803-1849 . . . . NCLC 27

Maniere, J.-E.
See Giraudoux, (Hippolyte) Jean

Manley, (Mary) Delariviere
1672(?)-1724 . . . . LC 1
See also DLB 39, 80

Mann, Abel
See Creasey, John

Mann, (Luiz) Heinrich 1871-1950. . . TCLC 9
See also CA 106; DLB 66

Mann, (Paul) Thomas
1875-1955 . . . . TCLC 2, 8, 14, 21, 35, 44,
60; DA; DAB; DAC; DAM MST, NOV;
SSC 5; WLC
See also CA 104; 128; DLB 66; MTCW

Mannheim, Karl 1893-1947 . . . . . . TCLC 65

Manning, David
See Faust, Frederick (Schiller)

Manning, Frederic 1887(?)-1935 . . . TCLC 25
See also CA 124

Manning, Olivia 1915-1980 . . . . . . CLC 5, 19
See also CA 5-8R; 101; CANR 29; MTCW

Mano, D. Keith 1942- . . . . CLC 2, 10
See also CA 25-28R; CAAS 6; CANR 26;
DLB 6

Mansfield, Katherine
. . TCLC 2, 8, 39; DAB; SSC 9, 23; WLC
See also Beauchamp, Kathleen Mansfield
See also DLB 162

Manso, Peter 1940- . . . . CLC 39
See also CA 29-32R; CANR 44

Mantecon, Juan Jimenez
See Jimenez (Mantecon), Juan Ramon

Manton, Peter
See Creasey, John

Man Without a Spleen, A
See Chekhov, Anton (Pavlovich)

Manzoni, Alessandro 1785-1873 . . NCLC 29

Mapu, Abraham (ben Jekutiel)
1808-1867 . . . . NCLC 18

Mara, Sally
See Queneau, Raymond

Marat, Jean Paul 1743-1793 . . . . LC 10

Marcel, Gabriel Honore
1889-1973 . . . . CLC 15
See also CA 102; 45-48; MTCW

Marchbanks, Samuel
See Davies, (William) Robertson

Marchi, Giacomo
See Bassani, Giorgio

Margulies, Donald. . . . . CLC 76

Marie de France c. 12th cent. -. . . . CMLC 8

Marie de l'Incarnation 1599-1672. . . . LC 10

Mariner, Scott
See Pohl, Frederik

Marinetti, Filippo Tommaso
1876-1944 . . . . TCLC 10
See also CA 107; DLB 114

Marivaux, Pierre Carlet de Chamblain de
1688-1763 . . . . LC 4

Markandaya, Kamala . . . . CLC 8, 38
See also Taylor, Kamala (Purnaiya)

Markfield, Wallace 1926-. . . . . CLC 8
See also CA 69-72; CAAS 3; DLB 2, 28

Markham, Edwin 1852-1940 . . . . . TCLC 47
See also DLB 54

Markham, Robert
See Amis, Kingsley (William)

Marks, J
See Highwater, Jamake (Mamake)

Marks-Highwater, J
See Highwater, Jamake (Mamake)

Markson, David M(errill) 1927-. . . . CLC 67
See also CA 49-52; CANR 1

Marley, Bob. . . . . CLC 17
See also Marley, Robert Nesta

Marley, Robert Nesta 1945-1981
See Marley, Bob
See also CA 107; 103

Marlowe, Christopher
1564-1593 . . . . . LC 22; DA; DAB; DAC;
DAM DRAM, MST; DC 1; WLC
See also CDBLB Before 1660; DLB 62

Marlowe, Stephen 1928-
See Queen, Ellery
See also CA 13-16R; CANR 6, 55

Marmontel, Jean-Francois
1723-1799 . . . . LC 2

Marquand, John P(hillips)
1893-1960 . . . . CLC 2, 10
See also CA 85-88; DLB 9, 102

Marques, Rene
1919-1979 . . . . . . CLC 96; DAM MULT;
HLC
See also CA 97-100; 85-88; DLB 113; HW

Marquez, Gabriel (Jose) Garcia
See Garcia Marquez, Gabriel (Jose)

Marquis, Don(ald Robert Perry)
1878-1937 . . . . TCLC 7
See also CA 104; DLB 11, 25

Marric, J. J.
See Creasey, John

Marrow, Bernard
See Moore, Brian

Marryat, Frederick 1792-1848 . . . . NCLC 3
See also DLB 21, 163

Marsden, James
See Creasey, John

Marsh, (Edith) Ngaio
1899-1982 . . . . . . CLC 7, 53; DAM POP
See also CA 9-12R; CANR 6; DLB 77;
MTCW

Marshall, Garry 1934-. . . . . CLC 17
See also AAYA 3; CA 111; SATA 60

Marshall, Paule
1929- . . . . CLC 27, 72; BLC;
DAM MULT; SSC 3
See also BW 2; CA 77-80; CANR 25;
DLB 157; MTCW

Marsten, Richard
See Hunter, Evan

Marston, John
1576-1634 . . . . LC 33; DAM DRAM
See also DLB 58, 172

Martha, Henry
See Harris, Mark

Martial c. 40-c. 104 . . . . PC 10

Martin, Ken
See Hubbard, L(afayette) Ron(ald)

Martin, Richard
See Creasey, John

Martin, Steve 1945- . . . . CLC 30
See also CA 97-100; CANR 30; MTCW

Martin, Valerie 1948-. . . . . CLC 89
See also BEST 90:2; CA 85-88; CANR 49

Martin, Violet Florence
1862-1915 . . . . TCLC 51

Martin, Webber
See Silverberg, Robert

Martindale, Patrick Victor
See White, Patrick (Victor Martindale)

Martin du Gard, Roger
1881-1958 . . . . TCLC 24
See also CA 118; DLB 65

Martineau, Harriet 1802-1876. . . . NCLC 26
See also DLB 21, 55, 159, 163, 166;
YABC 2

Martines, Julia
See O'Faolain, Julia

Martinez, Jacinto Benavente y
See Benavente (y Martinez), Jacinto

Martinez Ruiz, Jose 1873-1967
See Azorin; Ruiz, Jose Martinez
See also CA 93-96; HW

Martinez Sierra, Gregorio
1881-1947 . . . . TCLC **6**
See also CA 115

Martinez Sierra, Maria (de la O'LeJarraga)
1874-1974 . . . . TCLC **6**
See also CA 115

Martinsen, Martin
See Follett, Ken(neth Martin)

Martinson, Harry (Edmund)
1904-1978 . . . . CLC **14**
See also CA 77-80; CANR 34

Marut, Ret
See Traven, B.

Marut, Robert
See Traven, B.

Marvell, Andrew
1621-1678 . . . . . . LC **4**; DA; DAB; DAC;
DAM MST, POET; PC **10**; WLC
See also CDBLB 1660-1789; DLB 131

Marx, Karl (Heinrich)
1818-1883 . . . . NCLC **17**
See also DLB 129

Masaoka Shiki . . . . TCLC **18**
See also Masaoka Tsunenori

Masaoka Tsunenori 1867-1902
See Masaoka Shiki
See also CA 117

Masefield, John (Edward)
1878-1967 . . . . CLC **11, 47**; DAM POET
See also CA 19-20; 25-28R; CANR 33;
CAP 2; CDBLB 1890-1914; DLB 10, 19,
153, 160; MTCW; SATA 19

Maso, Carole 19(?)- . . . . CLC **44**

Mason, Bobbie Ann
1940- . . . . CLC **28, 43, 82**; SSC **4**
See also AAYA 5; CA 53-56; CANR 11,
31; DLB 173; DLBY 87; INT CANR-31;
MTCW

Mason, Ernst
See Pohl, Frederik

Mason, Lee W.
See Malzberg, Barry N(athaniel)

Mason, Nick 1945- . . . . CLC **35**

Mason, Tally
See Derleth, August (William)

Mass, William
See Gibson, William

Masters, Edgar Lee
1868-1950 . . . . . . TCLC **2, 25**; DA; DAC;
DAM MST, POET; PC **1**
See also CA 104; 133; CDALB 1865-1917;
DLB 54; MTCW

Masters, Hilary 1928- . . . . CLC **48**
See also CA 25-28R; CANR 13, 47

Mastrosimone, William 19(?)- . . . . . . CLC **36**

Mathe, Albert
See Camus, Albert

Matheson, Richard Burton 1926- . . . CLC **37**
See also CA 97-100; DLB 8, 44; INT 97-100

Mathews, Harry 1930- . . . . CLC **6, 52**
See also CA 21-24R; CAAS 6; CANR 18,
40

Mathews, John Joseph
1894-1979 . . . . . . CLC **84**; DAM MULT
See also CA 19-20; 142; CANR 45; CAP 2;
NNAL

Mathias, Roland (Glyn) 1915- . . . . . . CLC **45**
See also CA 97-100; CANR 19, 41; DLB 27

Matsuo Basho 1644-1694 . . . . PC **3**
See also DAM POET

Mattheson, Rodney
See Creasey, John

Matthews, Greg 1949- . . . . CLC **45**
See also CA 135

Matthews, William 1942- . . . . CLC **40**
See also CA 29-32R; CAAS 18; CANR 12;
DLB 5

Matthias, John (Edward) 1941- . . . . . . CLC **9**
See also CA 33-36R

Matthiessen, Peter
1927- . . . . CLC **5, 7, 11, 32, 64**;
DAM NOV
See also AAYA 6; BEST 90:4; CA 9-12R;
CANR 21, 50; DLB 6, 173; MTCW;
SATA 27

Maturin, Charles Robert
1780(?)-1824 . . . . NCLC **6**

Matute (Ausejo), Ana Maria
1925- . . . . CLC **11**
See also CA 89-92; MTCW

Maugham, W. S.
See Maugham, W(illiam) Somerset

Maugham, W(illiam) Somerset
1874-1965 . . . . CLC **1, 11, 15, 67, 93**;
DA; DAB; DAC; DAM DRAM, MST,
NOV; SSC **8**; WLC
See also CA 5-8R; 25-28R; CANR 40;
CDBLB 1914-1945; DLB 10, 36, 77, 100,
162; MTCW; SATA 54

Maugham, William Somerset
See Maugham, W(illiam) Somerset

Maupassant, (Henri Rene Albert) Guy de
1850-1893 . . . . . NCLC **1, 42**; DA; DAB;
DAC; DAM MST; SSC **1**; WLC
See also DLB 123

Maupin, Armistead
1944- . . . . CLC **95**; DAM POP
See also CA 125; 130; INT 130

Maurhut, Richard
See Traven, B.

Mauriac, Claude 1914-1996 . . . . CLC **9**
See also CA 89-92; 152; DLB 83

Mauriac, Francois (Charles)
1885-1970 . . . . CLC **4, 9, 56**; SSC **24**
See also CA 25-28; CAP 2; DLB 65;
MTCW

Mavor, Osborne Henry 1888-1951
See Bridie, James
See also CA 104

Maxwell, William (Keepers, Jr.)
1908- . . . . CLC **19**
See also CA 93-96; CANR 54; DLBY 80;
INT 93-96

May, Elaine 1932- . . . . CLC **16**
See also CA 124; 142; DLB 44

Mayakovski, Vladimir (Vladimirovich)
1893-1930 . . . . TCLC **4, 18**
See also CA 104

Mayhew, Henry 1812-1887 . . . . . . NCLC **31**
See also DLB 18, 55

Mayle, Peter 1939(?)- . . . . CLC **89**
See also CA 139

Maynard, Joyce 1953- . . . . CLC **23**
See also CA 111; 129

Mayne, William (James Carter)
1928- . . . . CLC **12**
See also CA 9-12R; CANR 37; CLR 25;
JRDA; MAICYA; SAAS 11; SATA 6, 68

Mayo, Jim
See L'Amour, Louis (Dearborn)

Maysles, Albert 1926- . . . . CLC **16**
See also CA 29-32R

Maysles, David 1932- . . . . CLC **16**

Mazer, Norma Fox 1931- . . . . CLC **26**
See also AAYA 5; CA 69-72; CANR 12,
32; CLR 23; JRDA; MAICYA; SAAS 1;
SATA 24, 67

Mazzini, Guiseppe 1805-1872 . . . . NCLC **34**

McAuley, James Phillip
1917-1976 . . . . CLC **45**
See also CA 97-100

McBain, Ed
See Hunter, Evan

McBrien, William Augustine
1930- . . . . CLC **44**
See also CA 107

McCaffrey, Anne (Inez)
1926- . . . . . . CLC **17**; DAM NOV, POP
See also AAYA 6; AITN 2; BEST 89:2;
CA 25-28R; CANR 15, 35, 55; DLB 8;
JRDA; MAICYA; MTCW; SAAS 11;
SATA 8, 70

McCall, Nathan 1955(?)- . . . . CLC **86**
See also CA 146

McCann, Arthur
See Campbell, John W(ood, Jr.)

McCann, Edson
See Pohl, Frederik

McCarthy, Charles, Jr. 1933-
See McCarthy, Cormac
See also CANR 42; DAM POP

McCarthy, Cormac 1933- . . . . . CLC **4, 57, 59**
See also McCarthy, Charles, Jr.
See also DLB 6, 143

McCarthy, Mary (Therese)
1912-1989 . . . . . . CLC **1, 3, 5, 14, 24, 39,
59**; SSC **24**
See also CA 5-8R; 129; CANR 16, 50;
DLB 2; DLBY 81; INT CANR-16;
MTCW

McCartney, (James) Paul
1942- . . . . CLC **12, 35**
See also CA 146

Merezhkovsky, Dmitry Sergeyevich
1865-1941 .... **TCLC 29**

Merimee, Prosper
1803-1870 .... **NCLC 6; SSC 7**
See also DLB 119

Merkin, Daphne 1954- .... **CLC 44**
See also CA 123

Merlin, Arthur
See Blish, James (Benjamin)

Merrill, James (Ingram)
1926-1995 .... **CLC 2, 3, 6, 8, 13, 18, 34,**
91; DAM POET
See also CA 13-16R; 147; CANR 10, 49;
DLB 5, 165; DLBY 85; INT CANR-10;
MTCW

Merriman, Alex
See Silverberg, Robert

Merritt, E. B.
See Waddington, Miriam

Merton, Thomas
1915-1968 .. **CLC 1, 3, 11, 34, 83; PC 10**
See also CA 5-8R; 25-28R; CANR 22, 53;
DLB 48; DLBY 81; MTCW

Merwin, W(illiam) S(tanley)
1927- ...... **CLC 1, 2, 3, 5, 8, 13, 18, 45,**
88; DAM POET
See also CA 13-16R; CANR 15, 51; DLB 5,
169; INT CANR-15; MTCW

Metcalf, John 1938- .... **CLC 37**
See also CA 113; DLB 60

Metcalf, Suzanne
See Baum, L(yman) Frank

Mew, Charlotte (Mary)
1870-1928 .... **TCLC 8**
See also CA 105; DLB 19, 135

Mewshaw, Michael 1943- .... **CLC 9**
See also CA 53-56; CANR 7, 47; DLBY 80

Meyer, June
See Jordan, June

Meyer, Lynn
See Slavitt, David R(ytman)

Meyer-Meyrink, Gustav 1868-1932
See Meyrink, Gustav
See also CA 117

Meyers, Jeffrey 1939- .... **CLC 39**
See also CA 73-76; CANR 54; DLB 111

Meynell, Alice (Christina Gertrude Thompson)
1847-1922 .... **TCLC 6**
See also CA 104; DLB 19, 98

Meyrink, Gustav .... **TCLC 21**
See also Meyer-Meyrink, Gustav
See also DLB 81

Michaels, Leonard
1933- .... **CLC 6, 25; SSC 16**
See also CA 61-64; CANR 21; DLB 130;
MTCW

Michaux, Henri 1899-1984 ...... **CLC 8, 19**
See also CA 85-88; 114

Michelangelo 1475-1564 .... **LC 12**

Michelet, Jules 1798-1874 .... **NCLC 31**

Michener, James A(lbert)
1907(?)- .... **CLC 1, 5, 11, 29, 60;**
DAM NOV, POP
See also AITN 1; BEST 90:1; CA 5-8R;
CANR 21, 45; DLB 6; MTCW

Mickiewicz, Adam 1798-1855 ..... **NCLC 3**

Middleton, Christopher 1926- ...... **CLC 13**
See also CA 13-16R; CANR 29, 54;
DLB 40

Middleton, Richard (Barham)
1882-1911 .... **TCLC 56**
See also DLB 156

Middleton, Stanley 1919- .... **CLC 7, 38**
See also CA 25-28R; CAAS 23; CANR 21,
46; DLB 14

Middleton, Thomas
1580-1627 .... **LC 33; DAM DRAM,**
MST; DC 5
See also DLB 58

Migueis, Jose Rodrigues 1901- ..... **CLC 10**

Mikszath, Kalman 1847-1910 ..... **TCLC 31**

Miles, Josephine (Louise)
1911-1985 .... **CLC 1, 2, 14, 34, 39;**
DAM POET
See also CA 1-4R; 116; CANR 2, 55;
DLB 48

Militant
See Sandburg, Carl (August)

Mill, John Stuart 1806-1873 .. **NCLC 11, 58**
See also CDBLB 1832-1890; DLB 55

Millar, Kenneth
1915-1983 .... **CLC 14; DAM POP**
See also Macdonald, Ross
See also CA 9-12R; 110; CANR 16; DLB 2;
DLBD 6; DLBY 83; MTCW

Millay, E. Vincent
See Millay, Edna St. Vincent

Millay, Edna St. Vincent
1892-1950 .... **TCLC 4, 49; DA; DAB;**
DAC; DAM MST, POET; PC 6
See also CA 104; 130; CDALB 1917-1929;
DLB 45; MTCW

Miller, Arthur
1915- .... **CLC 1, 2, 6, 10, 15, 26, 47, 78;**
DA; DAB; DAC; DAM DRAM, MST;
DC 1; WLC
See also AAYA 15; AITN 1; CA 1-4R;
CABS 3; CANR 2, 30, 54;
CDALB 1941-1968; DLB 7; MTCW

Miller, Henry (Valentine)
1891-1980 .... **CLC 1, 2, 4, 9, 14, 43, 84;**
DA; DAB; DAC; DAM MST, NOV;
WLC
See also CA 9-12R; 97-100; CANR 33;
CDALB 1929-1941; DLB 4, 9; DLBY 80;
MTCW

Miller, Jason 1939(?)- .... **CLC 2**
See also AITN 1; CA 73-76; DLB 7

Miller, Sue 1943- ..... **CLC 44; DAM POP**
See also BEST 90:3; CA 139; DLB 143

Miller, Walter M(ichael, Jr.)
1923- .... **CLC 4, 30**
See also CA 85-88; DLB 8

Millett, Kate 1934- .... **CLC 67**
See also AITN 1; CA 73-76; CANR 32, 53;
MTCW

Millhauser, Steven 1943- .... **CLC 21, 54**
See also CA 110; 111; DLB 2; INT 111

Millin, Sarah Gertrude 1889-1968 .. **CLC 49**
See also CA 102; 93-96

Milne, A(lan) A(lexander)
1882-1956 .... **TCLC 6; DAB; DAC;**
DAM MST
See also CA 104; 133; CLR 1, 26; DLB 10,
77, 100, 160; MAICYA; MTCW;
YABC 1

Milner, Ron(ald)
1938- ..... **CLC 56; BLC; DAM MULT**
See also AITN 1; BW 1; CA 73-76;
CANR 24; DLB 38; MTCW

Milosz, Czeslaw
1911- .... **CLC 5, 11, 22, 31, 56, 82;**
DAM MST, POET; PC 8
See also CA 81-84; CANR 23, 51; MTCW

Milton, John
1608-1674 ...... **LC 9; DA; DAB; DAC;**
DAM MST, POET; WLC
See also CDBLB 1660-1789; DLB 131, 151

Min, Anchee 1957- .... **CLC 86**
See also CA 146

Minehaha, Cornelius
See Wedekind, (Benjamin) Frank(lin)

Miner, Valerie 1947- .... **CLC 40**
See also CA 97-100

Minimo, Duca
See D'Annunzio, Gabriele

Minot, Susan 1956- .... **CLC 44**
See also CA 134

Minus, Ed 1938- .... **CLC 39**

Miranda, Javier
See Bioy Casares, Adolfo

Mirbeau, Octave 1848-1917 ...... **TCLC 55**
See also DLB 123

Miro (Ferrer), Gabriel (Francisco Victor)
1879-1930 .... **TCLC 5**
See also CA 104

Mishima, Yukio
.... **CLC 2, 4, 6, 9, 27; DC 1; SSC 4**
See also Hiraoka, Kimitake

Mistral, Frederic 1830-1914 ...... **TCLC 51**
See also CA 122

Mistral, Gabriela .... **TCLC 2; HLC**
See also Godoy Alcayaga, Lucila

Mistry, Rohinton 1952- ...... **CLC 71; DAC**
See also CA 141

Mitchell, Clyde
See Ellison, Harlan (Jay); Silverberg, Robert

Mitchell, James Leslie 1901-1935
See Gibbon, Lewis Grassic
See also CA 104; DLB 15

Mitchell, Joni 1943- .... **CLC 12**
See also CA 112

Mitchell, Joseph (Quincy)
1908-1996 .... **CLC 98**
See also CA 77-80; 152

Mitchell, Margaret (Munnerlyn)
1900-1949 ...... **TCLC 11; DAM NOV,**
POP
See also CA 109; 125; CANR 55; DLB 9;
MTCW

Mitchell, Peggy
See Mitchell, Margaret (Munnerlyn)

Mitchell, S(ilas) Weir 1829-1914 .. **TCLC 36**

Morris, William 1834-1896 ...... NCLC 4
See also CDBLB 1832-1890; DLB 18, 35,
57, 156

Morris, Wright 1910-... CLC 1, 3, 7, 18, 37
See also CA 9-12R; CANR 21; DLB 2;
DLBY 81; MTCW

Morrison, Chloe Anthony Wofford
See Morrison, Toni

Morrison, James Douglas 1943-1971
See Morrison, Jim
See also CA 73-76; CANR 40

Morrison, Jim .... CLC 17
See also Morrison, James Douglas

Morrison, Toni
1931- .... CLC 4, 10, 22, 55, 81, 87;
BLC; DA; DAB; DAC; DAM MST,
MULT, NOV, POP
See also AAYA 1; BW 2; CA 29-32R;
CANR 27, 42; CDALB 1968-1988;
DLB 6, 33, 143; DLBY 81; MTCW;
SATA 57

Morrison, Van 1945- .... CLC 21
See also CA 116

Mortimer, John (Clifford)
1923- ...... CLC 28, 43; DAM DRAM,
POP
See also CA 13-16R; CANR 21;
CDBLB 1960 to Present; DLB 13;
INT CANR-21; MTCW

Mortimer, Penelope (Ruth) 1918-.... CLC 5
See also CA 57-60; CANR 45

Morton, Anthony
See Creasey, John

Mosher, Howard Frank 1943-...... CLC 62
See also CA 139

Mosley, Nicholas 1923-........ CLC 43, 70
See also CA 69-72; CANR 41; DLB 14

Mosley, Walter
1952- ..... CLC 97; DAM MULT, POP
See also AAYA 17; BW 2; CA 142

Moss, Howard
1922-1987 .... CLC 7, 14, 45, 50;
DAM POET
See also CA 1-4R; 123; CANR 1, 44;
DLB 5

Mossgiel, Rab
See Burns, Robert

Motion, Andrew (Peter) 1952-...... CLC 47
See also CA 146; DLB 40

Motley, Willard (Francis)
1909-1965 .... CLC 18
See also BW 1; CA 117; 106; DLB 76, 143

Motoori, Norinaga 1730-1801 .... NCLC 45

Mott, Michael (Charles Alston)
1930-................... CLC 15, 34
See also CA 5-8R; CAAS 7; CANR 7, 29

Mountain Wolf Woman
1884-1960 .... CLC 92
See also CA 144; NNAL

Moure, Erin 1955- .... CLC 88
See also CA 113; DLB 60

Mowat, Farley (McGill)
1921- ...... CLC 26; DAC; DAM MST
See also AAYA 1; CA 1-4R; CANR 4, 24,
42; CLR 20; DLB 68; INT CANAR-24;
JRDA; MAICYA; MTCW; SATA 3, 55

Moyers, Bill 1934-.............. CLC 74
See also AITN 2; CA 61-64; CANR 31, 52

Mphahlele, Es'kia
See Mphahlele, Ezekiel
See also DLB 125

Mphahlele, Ezekiel
1919- ..... CLC 25; BLC; DAM MULT
See also Mphahlele, Es'kia
See also BW 2; CA 81-84; CANR 26

Mqhayi, S(amuel) E(dward) K(rune Loliwe)
1875-1945 .... TCLC 25; BLC;
DAM MULT
See also CA 153

Mrozek, Slawomir 1930-........ CLC 3, 13
See also CA 13-16R; CAAS 10; CANR 29;
MTCW

Mrs. Belloc-Lowndes
See Lowndes, Marie Adelaide (Belloc)

Mtwa, Percy (?)-................. CLC 47

Mueller, Lisel 1924-.......... CLC 13, 51
See also CA 93-96; DLB 105

Muir, Edwin 1887-1959 .... TCLC 2
See also CA 104; DLB 20, 100

Muir, John 1838-1914 .... TCLC 28

Mujica Lainez, Manuel
1910-1984 .... CLC 31
See also Lainez, Manuel Mujica
See also CA 81-84; 112; CANR 32; HW

Mukherjee, Bharati
1940- .... CLC 53; DAM NOV
See also BEST 89:2; CA 107; CANR 45;
DLB 60; MTCW

Muldoon, Paul
1951- .... CLC 32, 72; DAM POET
See also CA 113; 129; CANR 52; DLB 40;
INT 129

Mulisch, Harry 1927-............. CLC 42
See also CA 9-12R; CANR 6, 26

Mull, Martin 1943-............... CLC 17
See also CA 105

Mulock, Dinah Maria
See Craik, Dinah Maria (Mulock)

Munford, Robert 1737(?)-1783 .... LC 5
See also DLB 31

Mungo, Raymond 1946-........... CLC 72
See also CA 49-52; CANR 2

Munro, Alice
1931- ...... CLC 6, 10, 19, 50, 95; DAC;
DAM MST, NOV; SSC 3
See also AITN 2; CA 33-36R; CANR 33,
53; DLB 53; MTCW; SATA 29

Munro, H(ector) H(ugh) 1870-1916
See Saki
See also CA 104; 130; CDBLB 1890-1914;
DA; DAB; DAC; DAM MST, NOV;
DLB 34, 162; MTCW; WLC

Murasaki, Lady................ CMLC 1

Murdoch, (Jean) Iris
1919- ...... CLC 1, 2, 3, 4, 6, 8, 11, 15,
22, 31, 51; DAB; DAC; DAM MST,
NOV
See also CA 13-16R; CANR 8, 43;
CDBLB 1960 to Present; DLB 14;
INT CANR-8; MTCW

Murfree, Mary Noailles
1850-1922 .... SSC 22
See also CA 122; DLB 12, 74

Murnau, Friedrich Wilhelm
See Plumpe, Friedrich Wilhelm

Murphy, Richard 1927-........... CLC 41
See also CA 29-32R; DLB 40

Murphy, Sylvia 1937-............. CLC 34
See also CA 121

Murphy, Thomas (Bernard) 1935-... CLC 51
See also CA 101

Murray, Albert L. 1916-.......... CLC 73
See also BW 2; CA 49-52; CANR 26, 52;
DLB 38

Murray, Les(lie) A(llan)
1938- .... CLC 40; DAM POET
See also CA 21-24R; CANR 11, 27

Murry, J. Middleton
See Murry, John Middleton

Murry, John Middleton
1889-1957 .... TCLC 16
See also CA 118; DLB 149

Musgrave, Susan 1951- .... CLC 13, 54
See also CA 69-72; CANR 45

Musil, Robert (Edler von)
1880-1942 .... TCLC 12; SSC 18
See also CA 109; CANR 55; DLB 81, 124

Muske, Carol 1945- .... CLC 90
See also Muske-Dukes, Carol (Anne)

Muske-Dukes, Carol (Anne) 1945-
See Muske, Carol
See also CA 65-68; CANR 32

Musset, (Louis Charles) Alfred de
1810-1857 .... NCLC 7

My Brother's Brother
See Chekhov, Anton (Pavlovich)

Myers, L. H. 1881-1944.......... TCLC 59
See also DLB 15

Myers, Walter Dean
1937- ..... CLC 35; BLC; DAM MULT,
NOV
See also AAYA 4; BW 2; CA 33-36R;
CANR 20, 42; CLR 4, 16, 35; DLB 33;
INT CANR-20; JRDA; MAICYA;
SAAS 2; SATA 41, 71; SATA-Brief 27

Myers, Walter M.
See Myers, Walter Dean

Myles, Symon
See Follett, Ken(neth Martin)

Nabokov, Vladimir (Vladimirovich)
1899-1977 ..... CLC 1, 2, 3, 6, 8, 11, 15,
23, 44, 46, 64; DA; DAB; DAC;
DAM MST, NOV; SSC 11; WLC
See also CA 5-8R; 69-72; CANR 20;
CDALB 1941-1968; DLB 2; DLBD 3;
DLBY 80, 91; MTCW

Nagai Kafu.................... TCLC 51
See also Nagai Sokichi

Nagai Sokichi 1879-1959
See Nagai Kafu
See also CA 117

Nagy, Laszlo 1925-1978........... CLC 7
See also CA 129; 112

Naipaul, Shiva(dhar Srinivasa)
1945-1985 ..... CLC 32, 39; DAM NOV
See also CA 110; 112; 116; CANR 33;
DLB 157; DLBY 85; MTCW

Naipaul, V(idiadhar) S(urajprasad)
1932- .... CLC 4, 7, 9, 13, 18, 37; DAB;
DAC; DAM MST, NOV
See also CA 1-4R; CANR 1, 33, 51;
CDBLB 1960 to Present; DLB 125;
DLBY 85; MTCW

Nakos, Lilika 1899(?)-............. CLC 29

Narayan, R(asipuram) K(rishnaswami)
1906-........CLC 7, 28, 47; DAM NOV
See also CA 81-84; CANR 33; MTCW;
SATA 62

Nash, (Frediric) Ogden
1902-1971 .... CLC 23; DAM POET
See also CA 13-14; 29-32R; CANR 34;
CAP 1; DLB 11; MAICYA; MTCW;
SATA 2, 46

Nathan, Daniel
See Dannay, Frederic

Nathan, George Jean 1882-1958 ... TCLC 18
See also Hatteras, Owen
See also CA 114; DLB 137

Natsume, Kinnosuke 1867-1916
See Natsume, Soseki
See also CA 104

Natsume, Soseki .... TCLC 2, 10
See also Natsume, Kinnosuke

Natti, (Mary) Lee 1919-
See Kingman, Lee
See also CA 5-8R; CANR 2

Naylor, Gloria
1950- ..... CLC 28, 52; BLC; DA; DAC;
DAM MST, MULT, NOV, POP
See also AAYA 6; BW 2; CA 107;
CANR 27, 51; DLB 173; MTCW

Neihardt, John Gneisenau
1881-1973 .... CLC 32
See also CA 13-14; CAP 1; DLB 9, 54

Nekrasov, Nikolai Alekseevich
1821-1878 .... NCLC 11

Nelligan, Emile 1879-1941....... TCLC 14
See also CA 114; DLB 92

Nelson, Willie 1933-.............. CLC 17
See also CA 107

Nemerov, Howard (Stanley)
1920-1991 .... CLC 2, 6, 9, 36;
DAM POET
See also CA 1-4R; 134; CABS 2; CANR 1,
27, 53; DLB 5, 6; DLBY 83;
INT CANR-27; MTCW

Neruda, Pablo
1904-1973 ..... CLC 1, 2, 5, 7, 9, 28, 62;
DA; DAB; DAC; DAM MST, MULT,
POET; HLC; PC 4; WLC
See also CA 19-20; 45-48; CAP 2; HW;
MTCW

Nerval, Gerard de
1808-1855 ..... NCLC 1; PC 13; SSC 18

Nervo, (Jose) Amado (Ruiz de)
1870-1919 .... TCLC 11
See also CA 109; 131; HW

Nessi, Pio Baroja y
See Baroja (y Nessi), Pio

Nestroy, Johann 1801-1862..... NCLC 42
See also DLB 133

Neufeld, John (Arthur) 1938- ...... CLC 17
See also AAYA 11; CA 25-28R; CANR 11,
37; MAICYA; SAAS 3; SATA 6, 81

Neville, Emily Cheney 1919-...... CLC 12
See also CA 5-8R; CANR 3, 37; JRDA;
MAICYA; SAAS 2; SATA 1

Newbound, Bernard Slade 1930-
See Slade, Bernard
See also CA 81-84; CANR 49;
DAM DRAM

Newby, P(ercy) H(oward)
1918- ...... CLC 2, 13; DAM NOV
See also CA 5-8R; CANR 32; DLB 15;
MTCW

Newlove, Donald 1928- .... CLC 6
See also CA 29-32R; CANR 25

Newlove, John (Herbert) 1938-..... CLC 14
See also CA 21-24R; CANR 9, 25

Newman, Charles 1938-.......... CLC 2, 8
See also CA 21-24R

Newman, Edwin (Harold) 1919- .... CLC 14
See also AITN 1; CA 69-72; CANR 5

Newman, John Henry
1801-1890 .... NCLC 38
See also DLB 18, 32, 55

Newton, Suzanne 1936-........... CLC 35
See also CA 41-44R; CANR 14; JRDA;
SATA 5, 77

Nexo, Martin Andersen
1869-1954 .... TCLC 43

Nezval, Vitezslav 1900-1958 ..... TCLC 44
See also CA 123

Ng, Fae Myenne 1957(?)-......... CLC 81
See also CA 146

Ngema, Mbongeni 1955- .... CLC 57
See also BW 2; CA 143

Ngugi, James T(hiong'o)........ CLC 3, 7, 13
See also Ngugi wa Thiong'o

Ngugi wa Thiong'o
1938- ..... CLC 36; BLC; DAM MULT,
NOV
See also Ngugi, James T(hiong'o)
See also BW 2; CA 81-84; CANR 27;
DLB 125; MTCW

Nichol, B(arrie) P(hillip)
1944-1988 .... CLC 18
See also CA 53-56; DLB 53; SATA 66

Nichols, John (Treadwell) 1940- .... CLC 38
See also CA 9-12R; CAAS 2; CANR 6;
DLBY 82

Nichols, Leigh
See Koontz, Dean R(ay)

Nichols, Peter (Richard)
1927- .... CLC 5, 36, 65
See also CA 104; CANR 33; DLB 13;
MTCW

Nicolas, F. R. E.
See Freeling, Nicolas

Niedecker, Lorine
1903-1970 .... CLC 10, 42; DAM POET
See also CA 25-28; CAP 2; DLB 48

Nietzsche, Friedrich (Wilhelm)
1844-1900 .... TCLC 10, 18, 55
See also CA 107; 121; DLB 129

Nievo, Ippolito 1831-1861 .... NCLC 22

Nightingale, Anne Redmon 1943-
See Redmon, Anne
See also CA 103

Nik. T. O.
See Annensky, Innokenty Fyodorovich

Nin, Anais
1903-1977 ...... CLC 1, 4, 8, 11, 14, 60;
DAM NOV, POP; SSC 10
See also AITN 2; CA 13-16R; 69-72;
CANR 22, 53; DLB 2, 4, 152; MTCW

Nishiwaki, Junzaburo 1894-1982 .... PC 15
See also CA 107

Nissenson, Hugh 1933-.......... CLC 4, 9
See also CA 17-20R; CANR 27; DLB 28

Niven, Larry .... CLC 8
See also Niven, Laurence Van Cott
See also DLB 8

Niven, Laurence Van Cott 1938-
See Niven, Larry
See also CA 21-24R; CAAS 12; CANR 14,
44; DAM POP; MTCW

Nixon, Agnes Eckhardt 1927-...... CLC 21
See also CA 110

Nizan, Paul 1905-1940........... TCLC 40
See also DLB 72

Nkosi, Lewis
1936- ..... CLC 45; BLC; DAM MULT
See also BW 1; CA 65-68; CANR 27;
DLB 157

Nodier, (Jean) Charles (Emmanuel)
1780-1844 .... NCLC 19
See also DLB 119

Nolan, Christopher 1965-.......... CLC 58
See also CA 111

Noon, Jeff 1957-................. CLC 91
See also CA 148

Norden, Charles
See Durrell, Lawrence (George)

Nordhoff, Charles (Bernard)
1887-1947 .... TCLC 23
See also CA 108; DLB 9; SATA 23

Norfolk, Lawrence 1963-.......... CLC 76
See also CA 144

Norman, Marsha
1947-.......... CLC 28; DAM DRAM
See also CA 105; CABS 3; CANR 41;
DLBY 84

Norris, Benjamin Franklin, Jr.
1870-1902 .... TCLC 24
See also Norris, Frank
See also CA 110

Norris, Frank
See Norris, Benjamin Franklin, Jr.
See also CDALB 1865-1917; DLB 12, 71

Norris, Leslie 1921-.............. CLC 14
See also CA 11-12; CANR 14; CAP 1;
DLB 27

North, Andrew
  See Norton, Andre

North, Anthony
  See Koontz, Dean R(ay)

North, Captain George
  See Stevenson, Robert Louis (Balfour)

North, Milou
  See Erdrich, Louise

Northrup, B. A.
  See Hubbard, L(afayette) Ron(ald)

North Staffs
  See Hulme, T(homas) E(rnest)

Norton, Alice Mary
  See Norton, Andre
  See also MAICYA; SATA 1, 43

Norton, Andre 1912- .... CLC 12
  See also Norton, Alice Mary
  See also AAYA 14; CA 1-4R; CANR 2, 31;
    DLB 8, 52; JRDA; MTCW; SATA 91

Norton, Caroline 1808-1877...... NCLC 47
  See also DLB 21, 159

Norway, Nevil Shute 1899-1960
  See Shute, Nevil
  See also CA 102; 93-96

Norwid, Cyprian Kamil
  1821-1883 .... NCLC 17

Nosille, Nabrah
  See Ellison, Harlan (Jay)

Nossack, Hans Erich 1901-1978 ..... CLC 6
  See also CA 93-96; 85-88; DLB 69

Nostradamus 1503-1566............ LC 27

Nosu, Chuji
  See Ozu, Yasujiro

Notenburg, Eleanora (Genrikhovna) von
  See Guro, Elena

Nova, Craig 1945-.............. CLC 7, 31
  See also CA 45-48; CANR 2, 53

Novak, Joseph
  See Kosinski, Jerzy (Nikodem)

Novalis 1772-1801 .... NCLC 13
  See also DLB 90

Nowlan, Alden (Albert)
  1933-1983 .. CLC 15; DAC; DAM MST
  See also CA 9-12R; CANR 5; DLB 53

Noyes, Alfred 1880-1958 .... TCLC 7
  See also CA 104; DLB 20

Nunn, Kem 19(?)-................ CLC 34

Nye, Robert
  1939- .... CLC 13, 42; DAM NOV
  See also CA 33-36R; CANR 29; DLB 14;
    MTCW; SATA 6

Nyro, Laura 1947- .... CLC 17

Oates, Joyce Carol
  1938- ......CLC 1, 2, 3, 6, 9, 11, 15, 19,
    33, 52; DA; DAB; DAC; DAM MST,
    NOV, POP; SSC 6; WLC
  See also AAYA 15; AITN 1; BEST 89:2;
    CA 5-8R; CANR 25, 45;
    CDALB 1968-1988; DLB 2, 5, 130;
    DLBY 81; INT CANR-25; MTCW

O'Brien, Darcy 1939-............. CLC 11
  See also CA 21-24R; CANR 8

O'Brien, E. G.
  See Clarke, Arthur C(harles)

O'Brien, Edna
  1936- .... CLC 3, 5, 8, 13, 36, 65;
    DAM NOV; SSC 10
  See also CA 1-4R; CANR 6, 41;
    CDBLB 1960 to Present; DLB 14;
    MTCW

O'Brien, Fitz-James 1828-1862... NCLC 21
  See also DLB 74

O'Brien, Flann........ CLC 1, 4, 5, 7, 10, 47
  See also O Nuallain, Brian

O'Brien, Richard 1942- .... CLC 17
  See also CA 124

O'Brien, Tim
  1946- .... CLC 7, 19, 40; DAM POP
  See also AAYA 16; CA 85-88; CANR 40;
    DLB 152; DLBD 9; DLBY 80

Obstfelder, Sigbjoern 1866-1900... TCLC 23
  See also CA 123

O'Casey, Sean
  1880-1964 ...... CLC 1, 5, 9, 11, 15, 88;
    DAB; DAC; DAM DRAM, MST
  See also CA 89-92; CDBLB 1914-1945;
    DLB 10; MTCW

O'Cathasaigh, Sean
  See O'Casey, Sean

Ochs, Phil 1940-1976............. CLC 17
  See also CA 65-68

O'Connor, Edwin (Greene)
  1918-1968 .... CLC 14
  See also CA 93-96; 25-28R

O'Connor, (Mary) Flannery
  1925-1964 .... CLC 1, 2, 3, 6, 10, 13, 15,
    21, 66; DA; DAB; DAC; DAM MST,
    NOV; SSC 1, 23; WLC
  See also AAYA 7; CA 1-4R; CANR 3, 41;
    CDALB 1941-1968; DLB 2, 152;
    DLBD 12; DLBY 80; MTCW

O'Connor, Frank........... CLC 23; SSC 5
  See also O'Donovan, Michael John
  See also DLB 162

O'Dell, Scott 1898-1989........... CLC 30
  See also AAYA 3; CA 61-64; 129;
    CANR 12, 30; CLR 1, 16; DLB 52;
    JRDA; MAICYA; SATA 12, 60

Odets, Clifford
  1906-1963 .... CLC 2, 28, 98;
    DAM DRAM; DC 6
  See also CA 85-88; DLB 7, 26; MTCW

O'Doherty, Brian 1934-........... CLC 76
  See also CA 105

O'Donnell, K. M.
  See Malzberg, Barry N(athaniel)

O'Donnell, Lawrence
  See Kuttner, Henry

O'Donovan, Michael John
  1903-1966 .... CLC 14
  See also O'Connor, Frank
  See also CA 93-96

Oe, Kenzaburo
  1935- ..... CLC 10, 36, 86; DAM NOV;
    SSC 20
  See also CA 97-100; CANR 36, 50;
    DLBY 94; MTCW

O'Faolain, Julia 1932-....... CLC 6, 19, 47
  See also CA 81-84; CAAS 2; CANR 12;
    DLB 14; MTCW

O'Faolain, Sean
  1900-1991 .... CLC 1, 7, 14, 32, 70;
    SSC 13
  See also CA 61-64; 134; CANR 12;
    DLB 15, 162; MTCW

O'Flaherty, Liam
  1896-1984 .... CLC 5, 34; SSC 6
  See also CA 101; 113; CANR 35; DLB 36,
    162; DLBY 84; MTCW

Ogilvy, Gavin
  See Barrie, J(ames) M(atthew)

O'Grady, Standish James
  1846-1928 .... TCLC 5
  See also CA 104

O'Grady, Timothy 1951-.......... CLC 59
  See also CA 138

O'Hara, Frank
  1926-1966 .... CLC 2, 5, 13, 78;
    DAM POET
  See also CA 9-12R; 25-28R; CANR 33;
    DLB 5, 16; MTCW

O'Hara, John (Henry)
  1905-1970 .... CLC 1, 2, 3, 6, 11, 42;
    DAM NOV; SSC 15
  See also CA 5-8R; 25-28R; CANR 31;
    CDALB 1929-1941; DLB 9, 86; DLBD 2;
    MTCW

O Hehir, Diana 1922- .... CLC 41
  See also CA 93-96

Okigbo, Christopher (Ifenayichukwu)
  1932-1967 .... CLC 25, 84; BLC;
    DAM MULT, POET; PC 7
  See also BW 1; CA 77-80; DLB 125;
    MTCW

Okri, Ben 1959- .... CLC 87
  See also BW 2; CA 130; 138; DLB 157;
    INT 138

Olds, Sharon
  1942- ..... CLC 32, 39, 85; DAM POET
  See also CA 101; CANR 18, 41; DLB 120

Oldstyle, Jonathan
  See Irving, Washington

Olesha, Yuri (Karlovich)
  1899-1960 .... CLC 8
  See also CA 85-88

Oliphant, Laurence
  1829(?)-1888 .... NCLC 47
  See also DLB 18, 166

Oliphant, Margaret (Oliphant Wilson)
  1828-1897 .... NCLC 11
  See also DLB 18, 159

Oliver, Mary 1935-........ CLC 19, 34, 98
  See also CA 21-24R; CANR 9, 43; DLB 5

Olivier, Laurence (Kerr)
  1907-1989 .... CLC 20
  See also CA 111; 150; 129

Olsen, Tillie
  1913- ..... CLC 4, 13; DA; DAB; DAC;
    DAM MST; SSC 11
  See also CA 1-4R; CANR 1, 43; DLB 28;
    DLBY 80; MTCW

Olson, Charles (John)
  1910-1970 ..... CLC 1, 2, 5, 6, 9, 11, 29;
    DAM POET
  See also CA 13-16; 25-28R; CABS 2;
    CANR 35; CAP 1; DLB 5, 16; MTCW

Parker, Robert B(rown)
1932- . . . . . . **CLC 27; DAM NOV, POP**
See also BEST 89:4; CA 49-52; CANR 1,
26, 52; INT CANR-26; MTCW

Parkin, Frank 1940- . . . . **CLC 43**
See also CA 147

Parkman, Francis, Jr.
1823-1893 . . . . **NCLC 12**
See also DLB 1, 30

Parks, Gordon (Alexander Buchanan)
1912- . . . **CLC 1, 16; BLC; DAM MULT**
See also AITN 2; BW 2; CA 41-44R;
CANR 26; DLB 33; SATA 8

Parnell, Thomas 1679-1718 . . . . **LC 3**
See also DLB 94

Parra, Nicanor
1914- . . . . . . **CLC 2; DAM MULT; HLC**
See also CA 85-88; CANR 32; HW; MTCW

Parrish, Mary Frances
See Fisher, M(ary) F(rances) K(ennedy)

Parson
See Coleridge, Samuel Taylor

Parson Lot
See Kingsley, Charles

Partridge, Anthony
See Oppenheim, E(dward) Phillips

Pascal, Blaise 1623-1662 . . . . **LC 35**

Pascoli, Giovanni 1855-1912 . . . . . . **TCLC 45**

Pasolini, Pier Paolo
1922-1975 . . . . **CLC 20, 37**
See also CA 93-96; 61-64; DLB 128;
MTCW

Pasquini
See Silone, Ignazio

Pastan, Linda (Olenik)
1932- . . . . **CLC 27; DAM POET**
See also CA 61-64; CANR 18, 40; DLB 5

Pasternak, Boris (Leonidovich)
1890-1960 . . . . . . **CLC 7, 10, 18, 63; DA;**
DAB; DAC; DAM MST, NOV, POET;
PC 6; WLC
See also CA 127; 116; MTCW

Patchen, Kenneth
1911-1972 . . . **CLC 1, 2, 18; DAM POET**
See also CA 1-4R; 33-36R; CANR 3, 35;
DLB 16, 48; MTCW

Pater, Walter (Horatio)
1839-1894 . . . . **NCLC 7**
See also CDBLB 1832-1890; DLB 57, 156

Paterson, A(ndrew) B(arton)
1864-1941 . . . . **TCLC 32**

Paterson, Katherine (Womeldorf)
1932- . . . . **CLC 12, 30**
See also AAYA 1; CA 21-24R; CANR 28;
CLR 7; DLB 52; JRDA; MAICYA;
MTCW; SATA 13, 53

Patmore, Coventry Kersey Dighton
1823-1896 . . . . **NCLC 9**
See also DLB 35, 98

Paton, Alan (Stewart)
1903-1988 . . . . . . **CLC 4, 10, 25, 55; DA;**
DAB; DAC; DAM MST, NOV; WLC
See also CA 13-16; 125; CANR 22; CAP 1;
MTCW; SATA 11; SATA-Obit 56

Paton Walsh, Gillian 1937-
See Walsh, Jill Paton
See also CANR 38; JRDA; MAICYA;
SAAS 3; SATA 4, 72

Paulding, James Kirke 1778-1860 . . **NCLC 2**
See also DLB 3, 59, 74

Paulin, Thomas Neilson 1949-
See Paulin, Tom
See also CA 123; 128

Paulin, Tom . . . . **CLC 37**
See also Paulin, Thomas Neilson
See also DLB 40

Paustovsky, Konstantin (Georgievich)
1892-1968 . . . . **CLC 40**
See also CA 93-96; 25-28R

Pavese, Cesare
1908-1950 . . . . . **TCLC 3; PC 13; SSC 19**
See also CA 104; DLB 128

Pavic, Milorad 1929- . . . . **CLC 60**
See also CA 136

Payne, Alan
See Jakes, John (William)

Paz, Gil
See Lugones, Leopoldo

Paz, Octavio
1914- . . . . **CLC 3, 4, 6, 10, 19, 51, 65;**
DA; DAB; DAC; DAM MST, MULT,
POET; HLC; PC 1; WLC
See also CA 73-76; CANR 32; DLBY 90;
HW; MTCW

p'Bitek, Okot
1931-1982 . . . . **CLC 96; BLC;**
DAM MULT
See also BW 2; CA 124; 107· DLB 125;
MTCW

Peacock, Molly 1947- . . . . **CLC 60**
See also CA 103; CAAS 21; CANR 52;
DLB 120

Peacock, Thomas Love
1785-1866 . . . . **NCLC 22**
See also DLB 96, 116

Peake, Mervyn 1911-1968 . . . . **CLC 7, 54**
See also CA 5-8R; 25-28R; CANR 3;
DLB 15, 160; MTCW; SATA 23

Pearce, Philippa . . . . **CLC 21**
See also Christie, (Ann) Philippa
See also CLR 9; DLB 161; MAICYA;
SATA 1, 67

Pearl, Eric
See Elman, Richard

Pearson, T(homas) R(eid) 1956- . . . . **CLC 39**
See also CA 120; 130; INT 130

Peck, Dale 1967- . . . . **CLC 81**
See also CA 146

Peck, John 1941- . . . . **CLC 3**
See also CA 49-52; CANR 3

Peck, Richard (Wayne) 1934- . . . . . . **CLC 21**
See also AAYA 1; CA 85-88; CANR 19,
38; CLR 15; INT CANR-19; JRDA;
MAICYA; SAAS 2; SATA 18, 55

Peck, Robert Newton
1928- . . **CLC 17; DA; DAC; DAM MST**
See also AAYA 3; CA 81-84; CANR 31;
JRDA; MAICYA; SAAS 1; SATA 21, 62

Peckinpah, (David) Sam(uel)
1925-1984 . . . . **CLC 20**
See also CA 109; 114

Pedersen, Knut 1859-1952
See Hamsun, Knut
See also CA 104; 119; MTCW

Peeslake, Gaffer
See Durrell, Lawrence (George)

Peguy, Charles Pierre
1873-1914 . . . . **TCLC 10**
See also CA 107

Pena, Ramon del Valle y
See Valle-Inclan, Ramon (Maria) del

Pendennis, Arthur Esquir
See Thackeray, William Makepeace

Penn, William 1644-1718 . . . . **LC 25**
See also DLB 24

Pepys, Samuel
1633-1703 . . . . . **LC 11; DA; DAB; DAC;**
DAM MST; WLC
See also CDBLB 1660-1789; DLB 101

Percy, Walker
1916-1990 . . . . **CLC 2, 3, 6, 8, 14, 18, 47,**
65; DAM NOV, POP
See also CA 1-4R; 131; CANR 1, 23;
DLB 2; DLBY 80, 90; MTCW

Perec, Georges 1936-1982 . . . . **CLC 56**
See also CA 141; DLB 83

Pereda (y Sanchez de Porrua), Jose Maria de
1833-1906 . . . . **TCLC 16**
See also CA 117

Pereda y Porrua, Jose Maria de
See Pereda (y Sanchez de Porrua), Jose
Maria de

Peregoy, George Weems
See Mencken, H(enry) L(ouis)

Perelman, S(idney) J(oseph)
1904-1979 . . . . . . **CLC 3, 5, 9, 15, 23, 44,**
49; DAM DRAM
See also AITN 1, 2; CA 73-76; 89-92;
CANR 18; DLB 11, 44; MTCW

Peret, Benjamin 1899-1959 . . . . **TCLC 20**
See also CA 117

Peretz, Isaac Loeb 1851(?)-1915 . . . **TCLC 16**
See also CA 109

Peretz, Yitzkhok Leibush
See Peretz, Isaac Loeb

Perez Galdos, Benito 1843-1920 . . . **TCLC 27**
See also CA 125; 153; HW

Perrault, Charles 1628-1703 . . . . **LC 2**
See also MAICYA; SATA 25

Perry, Brighton
See Sherwood, Robert E(mmet)

Perse, St.-John . . . . **CLC 4, 11, 46**
See also Leger, (Marie-Rene Auguste) Alexis
Saint-Leger

Perutz, Leo 1882-1957 . . . . **TCLC 60**
See also DLB 81

Peseenz, Tulio F.
See Lopez y Fuentes, Gregorio

Pesetsky, Bette 1932- . . . . **CLC 28**
See also CA 133; DLB 130

Peshkov, Alexei Maximovich 1868-1936
See Gorky, Maxim
See also CA 105; 141; DA; DAC;
DAM DRAM, MST, NOV

Pessoa, Fernando (Antonio Nogueira)
1888-1935 . . . . **TCLC 27; HLC**
See also CA 125

Peterkin, Julia Mood 1880-1961. . . . **CLC 31**
See also CA 102; DLB 9

Peters, Joan K. 1945- . . . . **CLC 39**

Peters, Robert L(ouis) 1924- . . . . **CLC 7**
See also CA 13-16R; CAAS 8; DLB 105

Petofi, Sandor 1823-1849. . . . . . . **NCLC 21**

Petrakis, Harry Mark 1923- . . . . **CLC 3**
See also CA 9-12R; CANR 4, 30

Petrarch
1304-1374 . . . . **CMLC 20; DAM POET;**
PC 8

Petrov, Evgeny . . . . **TCLC 21**
See also Kataev, Evgeny Petrovich

Petry, Ann (Lane) 1908- . . . . . . **CLC 1, 7, 18**
See also BW 1; CA 5-8R; CAAS 6;
CANR 4, 46; CLR 12; DLB 76; JRDA;
MAICYA; MTCW; SATA 5

Petursson, Halligrimur 1614-1674 . . . . **LC 8**

Philips, Katherine 1632-1664. . . . . . . **LC 30**
See also DLB 131

Philipson, Morris H. 1926- . . . . **CLC 53**
See also CA 1-4R; CANR 4

Phillips, Caryl
1958- . . . . **CLC 96; DAM MULT**
See also BW 2; CA 141; DLB 157

Phillips, David Graham
1867-1911 . . . . **TCLC 44**
See also CA 108; DLB 9, 12

Phillips, Jack
See Sandburg, Carl (August)

Phillips, Jayne Anne
1952- . . . . **CLC 15, 33; SSC 16**
See also CA 101; CANR 24, 50; DLBY 80;
INT CANR-24; MTCW

Phillips, Richard
See Dick, Philip K(indred)

Phillips, Robert (Schaeffer) 1938- . . . **CLC 28**
See also CA 17-20R; CAAS 13; CANR 8;
DLB 105

Phillips, Ward
See Lovecraft, H(oward) P(hillips)

Piccolo, Lucio 1901-1969. . . . . **CLC 13**
See also CA 97-100; DLB 114

Pickthall, Marjorie L(owry) C(hristie)
1883-1922 . . . . **TCLC 21**
See also CA 107; DLB 92

Pico della Mirandola, Giovanni
1463-1494 . . . . **LC 15**

Piercy, Marge
1936- . . . . **CLC 3, 6, 14, 18, 27, 62**
See also CA 21-24R; CAAS 1; CANR 13,
43; DLB 120; MTCW

Piers, Robert
See Anthony, Piers

Pieyre de Mandiargues, Andre 1909-1991
See Mandiargues, Andre Pieyre de
See also CA 103; 136; CANR 22

Pilnyak, Boris . . . . **TCLC 23**
See also Vogau, Boris Andreyevich

Pincherle, Alberto
1907-1990 . . . . . **CLC 11, 18; DAM NOV**
See also Moravia, Alberto
See also CA 25-28R; 132; CANR 33;
MTCW

Pinckney, Darryl 1953- . . . . **CLC 76**
See also BW 2; CA 143

Pindar 518B.C.-446B.C. . . . . **CMLC 12**

Pineda, Cecile 1942- . . . . **CLC 39**
See also CA 118

Pinero, Arthur Wing
1855-1934 . . . . . **TCLC 32; DAM DRAM**
See also CA 110; 153; DLB 10

Pinero, Miguel (Antonio Gomez)
1946-1988 . . . . **CLC 4, 55**
See also CA 61-64; 125; CANR 29; HW

Pinget, Robert 1919- . . . . **CLC 7, 13, 37**
See also CA 85-88; DLB 83

Pink Floyd
See Barrett, (Roger) Syd; Gilmour, David;
Mason, Nick; Waters, Roger; Wright,
Rick

Pinkney, Edward 1802-1828 . . . . . **NCLC 31**

Pinkwater, Daniel Manus 1941- . . . . **CLC 35**
See also Pinkwater, Manus
See also AAYA 1; CA 29-32R; CANR 12,
38; CLR 4; JRDA; MAICYA; SAAS 3;
SATA 46, 76

Pinkwater, Manus
See Pinkwater, Daniel Manus
See also SATA 8

Pinsky, Robert
1940- . . **CLC 9, 19, 38, 94; DAM POET**
See also CA 29-32R; CAAS 4; DLBY 82

Pinta, Harold
See Pinter, Harold

Pinter, Harold
1930- . . . . . **CLC 1, 3, 6, 9, 11, 15, 27, 58,**
73; DA; DAB; DAC; DAM DRAM,
MST; WLC
See also CA 5-8R; CANR 33; CDBLB 1960
to Present; DLB 13; MTCW

Piozzi, Hester Lynch (Thrale)
1741-1821 . . . . **NCLC 57**
See also DLB 104, 142

Pirandello, Luigi
1867-1936 . . . . . . **TCLC 4, 29; DA; DAB;**
DAC; DAM DRAM, MST; DC 5;
SSC 22; WLC
See also CA 104; 153

Pirsig, Robert M(aynard)
1928- . . . . **CLC 4, 6, 73; DAM POP**
See also CA 53-56; CANR 42; MTCW;
SATA 39

Pisarev, Dmitry Ivanovich
1840-1868 . . . . **NCLC 25**

Pix, Mary (Griffith) 1666-1709 . . . . . . **LC 8**
See also DLB 80

Pixerecourt, Guilbert de
1773-1844 . . . . **NCLC 39**

Plaidy, Jean
See Hibbert, Eleanor Alice Burford

Planche, James Robinson
1796-1880 . . . . **NCLC 42**

Plant, Robert 1948- . . . . **CLC 12**

Plante, David (Robert)
1940- . . . . **CLC 7, 23, 38; DAM NOV**
See also CA 37-40R; CANR 12, 36;
DLBY 83; INT CANR-12; MTCW

Plath, Sylvia
1932-1963 . . . . . **CLC 1, 2, 3, 5, 9, 11, 14,**
17, 50, 51, 62; DA; DAB; DAC;
DAM MST, POET; PC 1; WLC
See also AAYA 13; CA 19-20; CANR 34;
CAP 2; CDALB 1941-1968; DLB 5, 6,
152; MTCW

Plato
428(?)B.C.-348(?)B.C. . . . . . **CMLC 8; DA;**
DAB; DAC; DAM MST

Platonov, Andrei . . . . **TCLC 14**
See also Klimentov, Andrei Platonovich

Platt, Kin 1911- . . . . **CLC 26**
See also AAYA 11; CA 17-20R; CANR 11;
JRDA; SAAS 17; SATA 21, 86

Plautus c. 251B.C.-184B.C. . . . . **DC 6**

Plick et Plock
See Simenon, Georges (Jacques Christian)

Plimpton, George (Ames) 1927- . . . . . **CLC 36**
See also AITN 1; CA 21-24R; CANR 32;
MTCW; SATA 10

Plomer, William Charles Franklin
1903-1973 . . . . **CLC 4, 8**
See also CA 21-22; CANR 34; CAP 2;
DLB 20, 162; MTCW; SATA 24

Plowman, Piers
See Kavanagh, Patrick (Joseph)

Plum, J.
See Wodehouse, P(elham) G(renville)

Plumly, Stanley (Ross) 1939- . . . . . . **CLC 33**
See also CA 108; 110; DLB 5; INT 110

Plumpe, Friedrich Wilhelm
1888-1931 . . . . **TCLC 53**
See also CA 112

Poe, Edgar Allan
1809-1849 . . . . **NCLC 1, 16, 55; DA;**
DAB; DAC; DAM MST, POET; PC 1;
SSC 1, 22; WLC
See also AAYA 14; CDALB 1640-1865;
DLB 3, 59, 73, 74; SATA 23

Poet of Titchfield Street, The
See Pound, Ezra (Weston Loomis)

Pohl, Frederik 1919- . . . . **CLC 18**
See also CA 61-64; CAAS 1; CANR 11, 37;
DLB 8; INT CANR-11; MTCW;
SATA 24

Poirier, Louis 1910-
See Gracq, Julien
See also CA 122; 126

Poitier, Sidney 1927- . . . . **CLC 26**
See also BW 1; CA 117

Polanski, Roman 1933- . . . . **CLC 16**
See also CA 77-80

Poliakoff, Stephen 1952- . . . . **CLC 38**
See also CA 106; DLB 13

Police, The
See Copeland, Stewart (Armstrong);
Summers, Andrew James; Sumner,
Gordon Matthew

Polidori, John William
1795-1821 .... NCLC 51
See also DLB 116

Pollitt, Katha 1949- .... CLC 28
See also CA 120; 122; MTCW

Pollock, (Mary) Sharon
1936- .... CLC 50; DAC; DAM DRAM,
MST
See also CA 141; DLB 60

Polo, Marco 1254-1324 .... CMLC 15

Polonsky, Abraham (Lincoln)
1910- .... CLC 92
See also CA 104; DLB 26; INT 104

Polybius c. 200B.C.-c. 118B.C.... CMLC 17

Pomerance, Bernard
1940- .... CLC 13; DAM DRAM
See also CA 101; CANR 49

Ponge, Francis (Jean Gaston Alfred)
1899-1988 ..... CLC 6, 18; DAM POET
See also CA 85-88; 126; CANR 40

Pontoppidan, Henrik 1857-1943 ... TCLC 29

Poole, Josephine .... CLC 17
See also Helyar, Jane Penelope Josephine
See also SAAS 2; SATA 5

Popa, Vasko 1922-1991 .... CLC 19
See also CA 112; 148

Pope, Alexander
1688-1744 ...... LC 3; DA; DAB; DAC;
DAM MST, POET; WLC
See also CDBLB 1660-1789; DLB 95, 101

Porter, Connie (Rose) 1959(?)- ..... CLC 70
See also BW 2; CA 142; SATA 81

Porter, Gene(va Grace) Stratton
1863(?)-1924 .... TCLC 21
See also CA 112

Porter, Katherine Anne
1890-1980 ...... CLC 1, 3, 7, 10, 13, 15,
27; DA; DAB; DAC; DAM MST, NOV;
SSC 4
See also AITN 2; CA 1-4R; 101; CANR 1;
DLB 4, 9, 102; DLBD 12; DLBY 80;
MTCW; SATA 39; SATA-Obit 23

Porter, Peter (Neville Frederick)
1929- .... CLC 5, 13, 33
See also CA 85-88; DLB 40

Porter, William Sydney 1862-1910
See Henry, O.
See also CA 104; 131; CDALB 1865-1917;
DA; DAB; DAC; DAM MST; DLB 12,
78, 79; MTCW; YABC 2

Portillo (y Pacheco), Jose Lopez
See Lopez Portillo (y Pacheco), Jose

Post, Melville Davisson
1869-1930 .... TCLC 39
See also CA 110

Potok, Chaim
1929- .... CLC 2, 7, 14, 26; DAM NOV
See also AAYA 15; AITN 1, 2; CA 17-20R;
CANR 19, 35; DLB 28, 152;
INT CANR-19; MTCW; SATA 33

Potter, Beatrice
See Webb, (Martha) Beatrice (Potter)
See also MAICYA

Potter, Dennis (Christopher George)
1935-1994 .... CLC 58, 86
See also CA 107; 145; CANR 33; MTCW

Pound, Ezra (Weston Loomis)
1885-1972 ...... CLC 1, 2, 3, 4, 5, 7, 10,
13, 18, 34, 48, 50; DA; DAB; DAC;
DAM MST, POET; PC 4; WLC
See also CA 5-8R; 37-40R; CANR 40;
CDALB 1917-1929; DLB 4, 45, 63;
MTCW

Povod, Reinaldo 1959-1994 .... CLC 44
See also CA 136; 146

Powell, Adam Clayton, Jr.
1908-1972 .... CLC 89; BLC;
DAM MULT
See also BW 1; CA 102; 33-36R

Powell, Anthony (Dymoke)
1905- .... CLC 1, 3, 7, 9, 10, 31
See also CA 1-4R; CANR 1, 32;
CDBLB 1945-1960; DLB 15; MTCW

Powell, Dawn 1897-1965 .... CLC 66
See also CA 5-8R

Powell, Padgett 1952- .... CLC 34
See also CA 126

Power, Susan .... CLC 91

Powers, J(ames) F(arl)
1917- .... CLC 1, 4, 8, 57; SSC 4
See also CA 1-4R; CANR 2; DLB 130;
MTCW

Powers, John J(ames) 1945-
See Powers, John R.
See also CA 69-72

Powers, John R. .... CLC 66
See also Powers, John J(ames)

Powers, Richard (S.) 1957- .... CLC 93
See also CA 148

Pownall, David 1938- .... CLC 10
See also CA 89-92; CAAS 18; CANR 49;
DLB 14

Powys, John Cowper
1872-1963 .... CLC 7, 9, 15, 46
See also CA 85-88; DLB 15; MTCW

Powys, T(heodore) F(rancis)
1875-1953 .... TCLC 9
See also CA 106; DLB 36, 162

Prager, Emily 1952- .... CLC 56

Pratt, E(dwin) J(ohn)
1883(?)-1964 .... CLC 19; DAC;
DAM POET
See also CA 141; 93-96; DLB 92

Premchand .... TCLC 21
See also Srivastava, Dhanpat Rai

Preussler, Otfried 1923- .... CLC 17
See also CA 77-80; SATA 24

Prevert, Jacques (Henri Marie)
1900-1977 .... CLC 15
See also CA 77-80; 69-72; CANR 29;
MTCW; SATA-Obit 30

Prevost, Abbe (Antoine Francois)
1697-1763 .... LC 1

Price, (Edward) Reynolds
1933- .... CLC 3, 6, 13, 43, 50, 63;
DAM NOV; SSC 22
See also CA 1-4R; CANR 1, 37; DLB 2;
INT CANR-37

Price, Richard 1949- .... CLC 6, 12
See also CA 49-52; CANR 3; DLBY 81

Prichard, Katharine Susannah
1883-1969 .... CLC 46
See also CA 11-12; CANR 33; CAP 1;
MTCW; SATA 66

Priestley, J(ohn) B(oynton)
1894-1984 .... CLC 2, 5, 9, 34;
DAM DRAM, NOV
See also CA 9-12R; 113; CANR 33;
CDBLB 1914-1945; DLB 10, 34, 77, 100,
139; DLBY 84; MTCW

Prince 1958(?)- .... CLC 35

Prince, F(rank) T(empleton) 1912- ... CLC 22
See also CA 101; CANR 43; DLB 20

Prince Kropotkin
See Kropotkin, Peter (Aleksieevich)

Prior, Matthew 1664-1721 .... LC 4
See also DLB 95

Pritchard, William H(arrison)
1932- .... CLC 34
See also CA 65-68; CANR 23; DLB 111

Pritchett, V(ictor) S(awdon)
1900- .... CLC 5, 13, 15, 41;
DAM NOV; SSC 14
See also CA 61-64; CANR 31; DLB 15,
139; MTCW

Private 19022
See Manning, Frederic

Probst, Mark 1925- .... CLC 59
See also CA 130

Prokosch, Frederic 1908-1989.... CLC 4, 48
See also CA 73-76; 128; DLB 48

Prophet, The
See Dreiser, Theodore (Herman Albert)

Prose, Francine 1947-............. CLC 45
See also CA 109; 112; CANR 46

Proudhon
See Cunha, Euclides (Rodrigues Pimenta) da

Proulx, E. Annie 1935- .... CLC 81

**Proust, (Valentin-Louis-George-Eugene-)
Marcel**
1871-1922 .... TCLC 7, 13, 33; DA;
DAB; DAC; DAM MST, NOV; WLC
See also CA 104; 120; DLB 65; MTCW

Prowler, Harley
See Masters, Edgar Lee

Prus, Boleslaw 1845-1912 .... TCLC 48

Pryor, Richard (Franklin Lenox Thomas)
1940- .... CLC 26
See also CA 122

Przybyszewski, Stanislaw
1868-1927 .... TCLC 36
See also DLB 66

Pteleon
See Grieve, C(hristopher) M(urray)
See also DAM POET

Puckett, Lute
See Masters, Edgar Lee

Puig, Manuel
1932-1990 . . . . CLC 3, 5, 10, 28, 65;
DAM MULT; HLC
See also CA 45-48; CANR 2, 32; DLB 113;
HW; MTCW

Purdy, Al(fred Wellington)
1918- . . . . CLC 3, 6, 14, 50; DAC;
DAM MST, POET
See also CA 81-84; CAAS 17; CANR 42;
DLB 88

Purdy, James (Amos)
1923- . . . . CLC 2, 4, 10, 28, 52
See also CA 33-36R; CAAS 1; CANR 19,
51; DLB 2; INT CANR-19; MTCW

Pure, Simon
See Swinnerton, Frank Arthur

Pushkin, Alexander (Sergeyevich)
1799-1837 . . . . . NCLC 3, 27; DA; DAB;
DAC; DAM DRAM, MST, POET;
PC 10; WLC
See also SATA 61

P'u Sung-ling 1640-1715 . . . . LC 3

Putnam, Arthur Lee
See Alger, Horatio, Jr.

Puzo, Mario
1920- . . . . . CLC 1, 2, 6, 36; DAM NOV,
POP
See also CA 65-68; CANR 4, 42; DLB 6;
MTCW

Pygge, Edward
See Barnes, Julian (Patrick)

Pym, Barbara (Mary Crampton)
1913-1980 . . . . CLC 13, 19, 37
See also CA 13-14; 97-100; CANR 13, 34;
CAP 1; DLB 14; DLBY 87; MTCW

Pynchon, Thomas (Ruggles, Jr.)
1937- . . . . . CLC 2, 3, 6, 9, 11, 18, 33, 62,
72; DA; DAB; DAC; DAM MST, NOV,
POP; SSC 14; WLC
See also BEST 90:2; CA 17-20R; CANR 22,
46; DLB 2, 173; MTCW

Qian Zhongshu
See Ch'ien Chung-shu

Qroll
See Dagerman, Stig (Halvard)

Quarrington, Paul (Lewis) 1953- . . . . CLC 65
See also CA 129

Quasimodo, Salvatore 1901-1968 . . . CLC 10
See also CA 13-16; 25-28R; CAP 1;
DLB 114; MTCW

Quay, Stephen 1947- . . . . CLC 95

Quay, The Brothers
See Quay, Stephen; Quay, Timothy

Quay, Timothy 1947- . . . . CLC 95

Queen, Ellery . . . . CLC 3, 11
See also Dannay, Frederic; Davidson,
Avram; Lee, Manfred B(ennington);
Marlowe, Stephen; Sturgeon, Theodore
(Hamilton); Vance, John Holbrook

Queen, Ellery, Jr.
See Dannay, Frederic; Lee, Manfred
B(ennington)

Queneau, Raymond
1903-1976 . . . . CLC 2, 5, 10, 42
See also CA 77-80; 69-72; CANR 32;
DLB 72; MTCW

Quevedo, Francisco de 1580-1645 . . . . LC 23

Quiller-Couch, Arthur Thomas
1863-1944 . . . . TCLC 53
See also CA 118; DLB 135, 153

Quin, Ann (Marie) 1936-1973 . . . . . . CLC 6
See also CA 9-12R; 45-48; DLB 14

Quinn, Martin
See Smith, Martin Cruz

Quinn, Peter 1947- . . . . CLC 91

Quinn, Simon
See Smith, Martin Cruz

Quiroga, Horacio (Sylvestre)
1878-1937 . . . . . TCLC 20; DAM MULT;
HLC
See also CA 117; 131; HW; MTCW

Quoirez, Francoise 1935- . . . . CLC 9
See also Sagan, Francoise
See also CA 49-52; CANR 6, 39; MTCW

Raabe, Wilhelm 1831-1910 . . . . TCLC 45
See also DLB 129

Rabe, David (William)
1940- . . . . . . CLC 4, 8, 33; DAM DRAM
See also CA 85-88; CABS 3; DLB 7

Rabelais, Francois
1483-1553 . . . . . . LC 5; DA; DAB; DAC;
DAM MST; WLC

Rabinovitch, Sholem 1859-1916
See Aleichem, Sholom
See also CA 104

Rachilde 1860-1953 . . . . TCLC 67
See also DLB 123

Racine, Jean
1639-1699 . . . . LC 28; DAB; DAM MST

Radcliffe, Ann (Ward)
1764-1823 . . . . NCLC 6, 55
See also DLB 39

Radiguet, Raymond 1903-1923 . . . . TCLC 29
See also DLB 65

Radnoti, Miklos 1909-1944 . . . . TCLC 16
See also CA 118

Rado, James 1939- . . . . CLC 17
See also CA 105

Radvanyi, Netty 1900-1983
See Seghers, Anna
See also CA 85-88; 110

Rae, Ben
See Griffiths, Trevor

Raeburn, John (Hay) 1941- . . . . CLC 34
See also CA 57-60

Ragni, Gerome 1942-1991 . . . . CLC 17
See also CA 105; 134

Rahv, Philip 1908-1973 . . . . CLC 24
See also Greenberg, Ivan
See also DLB 137

Raine, Craig 1944- . . . . CLC 32
See also CA 108; CANR 29, 51; DLB 40

Raine, Kathleen (Jessie) 1908- . . . CLC 7, 45
See also CA 85-88; CANR 46; DLB 20;
MTCW

Rainis, Janis 1865-1929 . . . . TCLC 29

Rakosi, Carl . . . . CLC 47
See also Rawley, Callman
See also CAAS 5

Raleigh, Richard
See Lovecraft, H(oward) P(hillips)

Raleigh, Sir Walter 1554(?)-1618 . . . . LC 31
See also CDBLB Before 1660; DLB 172

Rallentando, H. P.
See Sayers, Dorothy L(eigh)

Ramal, Walter
See de la Mare, Walter (John)

Ramon, Juan
See Jimenez (Mantecon), Juan Ramon

Ramos, Graciliano 1892-1953 . . . . . TCLC 32

Rampersad, Arnold 1941- . . . . CLC 44
See also BW 2; CA 127; 133; DLB 111;
INT 133

Rampling, Anne
See Rice, Anne

Ramsay, Allan 1684(?)-1758 . . . . LC 29
See also DLB 95

Ramuz, Charles-Ferdinand
1878-1947 . . . . TCLC 33

Rand, Ayn
1905-1982 . . . . . . CLC 3, 30, 44, 79; DA;
DAC; DAM MST, NOV, POP; WLC
See also AAYA 10; CA 13-16R; 105;
CANR 27; MTCW

Randall, Dudley (Felker)
1914- . . . . . . CLC 1; BLC; DAM MULT
See also BW 1; CA 25-28R; CANR 23;
DLB 41

Randall, Robert
See Silverberg, Robert

Ranger, Ken
See Creasey, John

Ransom, John Crowe
1888-1974 . . . . CLC 2, 4, 5, 11, 24;
DAM POET
See also CA 5-8R; 49-52; CANR 6, 34;
DLB 45, 63; MTCW

Rao, Raja 1909- . . . CLC 25, 56; DAM NOV
See also CA 73-76; CANR 51; MTCW

Raphael, Frederic (Michael)
1931- . . . . CLC 2, 14
See also CA 1-4R; CANR 1; DLB 14

Ratcliffe, James P.
See Mencken, H(enry) L(ouis)

Rathbone, Julian 1935- . . . . CLC 41
See also CA 101; CANR 34

Rattigan, Terence (Mervyn)
1911-1977 . . . . CLC 7; DAM DRAM
See also CA 85-88; 73-76;
CDBLB 1945-1960; DLB 13; MTCW

Ratushinskaya, Irina 1954- . . . . CLC 54
See also CA 129

Raven, Simon (Arthur Noel)
1927- . . . . CLC 14
See also CA 81-84

Rawley, Callman 1903-
See Rakosi, Carl
See also CA 21-24R; CANR 12, 32

Rawlings, Marjorie Kinnan
1896-1953 . . . . TCLC 4
See also CA 104; 137; DLB 9, 22, 102;
JRDA; MAICYA; YABC 1

Rosa, Joao Guimaraes 1908-1967 ... **CLC 23**
See also CA 89-92; DLB 113

Rose, Wendy
1948- .... **CLC 85; DAM MULT; PC 13**
See also CA 53-56; CANR 5, 51; NNAL;
SATA 12

Rosen, Richard (Dean) 1949-....... **CLC 39**
See also CA 77-80; INT CANR-30

Rosenberg, Isaac 1890-1918....... **TCLC 12**
See also CA 107; DLB 20

Rosenblatt, Joe .... **CLC 15**
See also Rosenblatt, Joseph

Rosenblatt, Joseph 1933-
See Rosenblatt, Joe
See also CA 89-92; INT 89-92

Rosenfeld, Samuel 1896-1963
See Tzara, Tristan
See also CA 89-92

Rosenstock, Sami
See Tzara, Tristan

Rosenstock, Samuel
See Tzara, Tristan

Rosenthal, M(acha) L(ouis)
1917-1996 .... **CLC 28**
See also CA 1-4R; 152; CAAS 6; CANR 4,
51; DLB 5; SATA 59

Ross, Barnaby
See Dannay, Frederic

Ross, Bernard L.
See Follett, Ken(neth Martin)

Ross, J. H.
See Lawrence, T(homas) E(dward)

Ross, Martin
See Martin, Violet Florence
See also DLB 135

Ross, (James) Sinclair
1908- ...... **CLC 13; DAC; DAM MST;
SSC 24**
See also CA 73-76; DLB 88

Rossetti, Christina (Georgina)
1830-1894 ..... **NCLC 2, 50; DA; DAB;
DAC; DAM MST, POET; PC 7; WLC**
See also DLB 35, 163; MAICYA; SATA 20

Rossetti, Dante Gabriel
1828-1882 .... **NCLC 4; DA; DAB;
DAC; DAM MST, POET; WLC**
See also CDBLB 1832-1890; DLB 35

Rossner, Judith (Perelman)
1935- .... **CLC 6, 9, 29**
See also AITN 2; BEST 90:3; CA 17-20R;
CANR 18, 51; DLB 6; INT CANR-18;
MTCW

Rostand, Edmond (Eugene Alexis)
1868-1918 ...... **TCLC 6, 37; DA; DAB;
DAC; DAM DRAM, MST**
See also CA 104; 126; MTCW

Roth, Henry 1906-1995 .... **CLC 2, 6, 11**
See also CA 11-12; 149; CANR 38; CAP 1;
DLB 28; MTCW

Roth, Joseph 1894-1939.......... **TCLC 33**
See also DLB 85

Roth, Philip (Milton)
1933- ...... **CLC 1, 2, 3, 4, 6, 9, 15, 22,
31, 47, 66, 86; DA; DAB; DAC;
DAM MST, NOV, POP; WLC**
See also BEST 90:3; CA 1-4R; CANR 1, 22,
36, 55; CDALB 1968-1988; DLB 2, 28,
173; DLBY 82; MTCW

Rothenberg, Jerome 1931-....... **CLC 6, 57**
See also CA 45-48; CANR 1; DLB 5

Roumain, Jacques (Jean Baptiste)
1907-1944 .... **TCLC 19; BLC;
DAM MULT**
See also BW 1; CA 117; 125

Rourke, Constance (Mayfield)
1885-1941 .... **TCLC 12**
See also CA 107; YABC 1

Rousseau, Jean-Baptiste 1671-1741 ... **LC 9**

Rousseau, Jean-Jacques
1712-1778 .... **LC 14, 36; DA; DAB;
DAC; DAM MST; WLC**

Roussel, Raymond 1877-1933 ..... **TCLC 20**
See also CA 117

Rovit, Earl (Herbert) 1927-........ **CLC 7**
See also CA 5-8R; CANR 12

Rowe, Nicholas 1674-1718.......... **LC 8**
See also DLB 84

Rowley, Ames Dorrance
See Lovecraft, H(oward) P(hillips)

Rowson, Susanna Haswell
1762(?)-1824 .... **NCLC 5**
See also DLB 37

Roy, Gabrielle
1909-1983 .... **CLC 10, 14; DAB; DAC;
DAM MST**
See also CA 53-56; 110; CANR 5; DLB 68;
MTCW

Rozewicz, Tadeusz
1921- .... **CLC 9, 23; DAM POET**
See also CA 108; CANR 36; MTCW

Ruark, Gibbons 1941- .... **CLC 3**
See also CA 33-36R; CAAS 23; CANR 14,
31; DLB 120

Rubens, Bernice (Ruth) 1923-... **CLC 19, 31**
See also CA 25-28R; CANR 33; DLB 14;
MTCW

Rubin, Harold
See Robbins, Harold

Rudkin, (James) David 1936- ...... **CLC 14**
See also CA 89-92; DLB 13

Rudnik, Raphael 1933-............. **CLC 7**
See also CA 29-32R

Ruffian, M.
See Hasek, Jaroslav (Matej Frantisek)

Ruiz, Jose Martinez............... **CLC 11**
See also Martinez Ruiz, Jose

Rukeyser, Muriel
1913-1980 .... **CLC 6, 10, 15, 27;
DAM POET; PC 12**
See also CA 5-8R; 93-96; CANR 26;
DLB 48; MTCW; SATA-Obit 22

Rule, Jane (Vance) 1931-......... **CLC 27**
See also CA 25-28R; CAAS 18; CANR 12;
DLB 60

Rulfo, Juan
1918-1986 .... **CLC 8, 80; DAM MULT;
HLC**
See also CA 85-88; 118; CANR 26;
DLB 113; HW; MTCW

Runeberg, Johan 1804-1877...... **NCLC 41**

Runyon, (Alfred) Damon
1884(?)-1946 .... **TCLC 10**
See also CA 107; DLB 11, 86, 171

Rush, Norman 1933-.............. **CLC 44**
See also CA 121; 126; INT 126

Rushdie, (Ahmed) Salman
1947- ..... **CLC 23, 31, 55; DAB; DAC;
DAM MST, NOV, POP**
See also BEST 89:3; CA 108; 111;
CANR 33; INT 111; MTCW

Rushforth, Peter (Scott) 1945- ..... **CLC 19**
See also CA 101

Ruskin, John 1819-1900.......... **TCLC 63**
See also CA 114; 129; CDBLB 1832-1890;
DLB 55, 163; SATA 24

Russ, Joanna 1937-.............. **CLC 15**
See also CA 25-28R; CANR 11, 31; DLB 8;
MTCW

Russell, George William 1867-1935
See Baker, Jean H.
See also CA 104; 153; CDBLB 1890-1914;
DAM POET

Russell, (Henry) Ken(neth Alfred)
1927- .... **CLC 16**
See also CA 105

Russell, Willy 1947-.............. **CLC 60**

Rutherford, Mark .... **TCLC 25**
See also White, William Hale
See also DLB 18

Ruyslinck, Ward 1929-............ **CLC 14**
See also Belser, Reimond Karel Maria de

Ryan, Cornelius (John) 1920-1974 ... **CLC 7**
See also CA 69-72; 53-56; CANR 38

Ryan, Michael 1946- .... **CLC 65**
See also CA 49-52; DLBY 82

Rybakov, Anatoli (Naumovich)
1911- .... **CLC 23, 53**
See also CA 126; 135; SATA 79

Ryder, Jonathan
See Ludlum, Robert

Ryga, George
1932-1987 .. **CLC 14; DAC; DAM MST**
See also CA 101; 124; CANR 43; DLB 60

S. S.
See Sassoon, Siegfried (Lorraine)

Saba, Umberto 1883-1957 .... **TCLC 33**
See also CA 144; DLB 114

Sabatini, Rafael 1875-1950 .... **TCLC 47**

Sabato, Ernesto (R.)
1911- .... **CLC 10, 23; DAM MULT;
HLC**
See also CA 97-100; CANR 32; DLB 145;
HW; MTCW

Sacastru, Martin
See Bioy Casares, Adolfo

Sacher-Masoch, Leopold von
1836(?)-1895 .... **NCLC 31**

Sachs, Marilyn (Stickle) 1927- ..... **CLC 35**
See also AAYA 2; CA 17-20R; CANR 13,
47; CLR 2; JRDA; MAICYA; SAAS 2;
SATA 3, 68

Sachs, Nelly 1891-1970 .... **CLC 14, 98**
See also CA 17-18; 25-28R; CAP 2

Sackler, Howard (Oliver)
1929-1982 .... **CLC 14**
See also CA 61-64; 108; CANR 30; DLB 7

Sacks, Oliver (Wolf) 1933- .... **CLC 67**
See also CA 53-56; CANR 28, 50;
INT CANR-28; MTCW

Sade, Donatien Alphonse Francois Comte
1740-1814 .... **NCLC 47**

Sadoff, Ira 1945-................... **CLC 9**
See also CA 53-56; CANR 5, 21; DLB 120

Saetone
See Camus, Albert

Safire, William 1929-............. **CLC 10**
See also CA 17-20R; CANR 31, 54

Sagan, Carl (Edward) 1934-........ **CLC 30**
See also AAYA 2; CA 25-28R; CANR 11,
36; MTCW; SATA 58

Sagan, Francoise .... **CLC 3, 6, 9, 17, 36**
See also Quoirez, Francoise
See also DLB 83

Sahgal, Nayantara (Pandit) 1927-... **CLC 41**
See also CA 9-12R; CANR 11

Saint, H(arry) F. 1941- .... **CLC 50**
See also CA 127

St. Aubin de Teran, Lisa 1953-
See Teran, Lisa St. Aubin de
See also CA 118; 126; INT 126

Sainte-Beuve, Charles Augustin
1804-1869 .... **NCLC 5**

Saint-Exupery, Antoine (Jean Baptiste Marie
Roger) de
1900-1944 .... **TCLC 2, 56; DAM NOV;
WLC**
See also CA 108; 132; CLR 10; DLB 72;
MAICYA; MTCW; SATA 20

St. John, David
See Hunt, E(verette) Howard, (Jr.)

Saint-John Perse
See Leger, (Marie-Rene Auguste) Alexis
Saint-Leger

Saintsbury, George (Edward Bateman)
1845-1933 .... **TCLC 31**
See also DLB 57, 149

Sait Faik .... **TCLC 23**
See also Abasiyanik, Sait Faik

Saki .... **TCLC 3; SSC 12**
See also Munro, H(ector) H(ugh)

Sala, George Augustus .... **NCLC 46**

Salama, Hannu 1936-............. **CLC 18**

Salamanca, J(ack) R(ichard)
1922-..................... **CLC 4, 15**
See also CA 25-28R

Sale, J. Kirkpatrick
See Sale, Kirkpatrick

Sale, Kirkpatrick 1937-........... **CLC 68**
See also CA 13-16R; CANR 10

Salinas, Luis Omar
1937- ..... **CLC 90; DAM MULT; HLC**
See also CA 131; DLB 82; HW

Salinas (y Serrano), Pedro
1891(?)-1951 .... **TCLC 17**
See also CA 117; DLB 134

Salinger, J(erome) D(avid)
1919- ...... **CLC 1, 3, 8, 12, 55, 56; DA;
DAB; DAC; DAM MST, NOV, POP;
SSC 2; WLC**
See also AAYA 2; CA 5-8R; CANR 39;
CDALB 1941-1968; CLR 18; DLB 2, 102,
173; MAICYA; MTCW; SATA 67

Salisbury, John
See Caute, David

Salter, James 1925- .... **CLC 7, 52, 59**
See also CA 73-76; DLB 130

Saltus, Edgar (Everton)
1855-1921 .... **TCLC 8**
See also CA 105

Saltykov, Mikhail Evgrafovich
1826-1889 .... **NCLC 16**

Samarakis, Antonis 1919- .... **CLC 5**
See also CA 25-28R; CAAS 16; CANR 36

Sanchez, Florencio 1875-1910 ..... **TCLC 37**
See also CA 153; HW

Sanchez, Luis Rafael 1936-........ **CLC 23**
See also CA 128; DLB 145; HW

Sanchez, Sonia
1934- ...... **CLC 5; BLC; DAM MULT;
PC 9**
See also BW 2; CA 33-36R; CANR 24, 49;
CLR 18; DLB 41; DLBD 8; MAICYA;
MTCW; SATA 22

Sand, George
1804-1876 .... **NCLC 2, 42, 57; DA;
DAB; DAC; DAM MST, NOV; WLC**
See also DLB 119

Sandburg, Carl (August)
1878-1967 .... **CLC 1, 4, 10, 15, 35; DA;
DAB; DAC; DAM MST, POET; PC 2;
WLC**
See also CA 5-8R; 25-28R; CANR 35;
CDALB 1865-1917; DLB 17, 54;
MAICYA; MTCW; SATA 8

Sandburg, Charles
See Sandburg, Carl (August)

Sandburg, Charles A.
See Sandburg, Carl (August)

Sanders, (James) Ed(ward) 1939- ... **CLC 53**
See also CA 13-16R; CAAS 21; CANR 13,
44; DLB 16

Sanders, Lawrence
1920- .... **CLC 41; DAM POP**
See also BEST 89:4; CA 81-84; CANR 33;
MTCW

Sanders, Noah
See Blount, Roy (Alton), Jr.

Sanders, Winston P.
See Anderson, Poul (William)

Sandoz, Mari(e Susette)
1896-1966 .... **CLC 28**
See also CA 1-4R; 25-28R; CANR 17;
DLB 9; MTCW; SATA 5

Saner, Reg(inald Anthony) 1931- .... **CLC 9**
See also CA 65-68

Sannazaro, Jacopo 1456(?)-1530...... **LC 8**

Sansom, William
1912-1976 ...... **CLC 2, 6; DAM NOV;
SSC 21**
See also CA 5-8R; 65-68; CANR 42;
DLB 139; MTCW

Santayana, George 1863-1952 ..... **TCLC 40**
See also CA 115; DLB 54, 71; DLBD 13

Santiago, Danny .... **CLC 33**
See also James, Daniel (Lewis)
See also DLB 122

Santmyer, Helen Hoover
1895-1986 .... **CLC 33**
See also CA 1-4R; 118; CANR 15, 33;
DLBY 84; MTCW

Santos, Bienvenido N(uqui)
1911-1996 ...... **CLC 22; DAM MULT**
See also CA 101; 151; CANR 19, 46

Sapper .... **TCLC 44**
See also McNeile, Herman Cyril

Sappho
fl. 6th cent. B.C.- .... **CMLC 3;
DAM POET; PC 5**

Sarduy, Severo 1937-1993 .... **CLC 6, 97**
See also CA 89-92; 142; DLB 113; HW

Sargeson, Frank 1903-1982 .... **CLC 31**
See also CA 25-28R; 106; CANR 38

Sarmiento, Felix Ruben Garcia
See Dario, Ruben

Saroyan, William
1908-1981 ..... **CLC 1, 8, 10, 29, 34, 56;
DA; DAB; DAC; DAM DRAM, MST,
NOV; SSC 21; WLC**
See also CA 5-8R; 103; CANR 30; DLB 7,
9, 86; DLBY 81; MTCW; SATA 23;
SATA-Obit 24

Sarraute, Nathalie
1900- .... **CLC 1, 2, 4, 8, 10, 31, 80**
See also CA 9-12R; CANR 23; DLB 83;
MTCW

Sarton, (Eleanor) May
1912-1995 .... **CLC 4, 14, 49, 91;
DAM POET**
See also CA 1-4R; 149; CANR 1, 34, 55;
DLB 48; DLBY 81; INT CANR-34;
MTCW; SATA 36; SATA-Obit 86

Sartre, Jean-Paul
1905-1980 .... **CLC 1, 4, 7, 9, 13, 18, 24,
44, 50, 52; DA; DAB; DAC;
DAM DRAM, MST, NOV; DC 3; WLC**
See also CA 9-12R; 97-100; CANR 21;
DLB 72; MTCW

Sassoon, Siegfried (Lorraine)
1886-1967 .... **CLC 36; DAB;
DAM MST, NOV, POET; PC 12**
See also CA 104; 25-28R; CANR 36;
DLB 20; MTCW

Satterfield, Charles
See Pohl, Frederik

Saul, John (W. III)
1942- ...... **CLC 46; DAM NOV, POP**
See also AAYA 10; BEST 90:4; CA 81-84;
CANR 16, 40

Saunders, Caleb
See Heinlein, Robert A(nson)

Sheridan, Richard Brinsley
1751-1816 .... NCLC 5; DA; DAB;
DAC; DAM DRAM, MST; DC 1; WLC
See also CDBLB 1660-1789; DLB 89

Sherman, Jonathan Marc .... CLC 55

Sherman, Martin 1941(?)- .... CLC 19
See also CA 116; 123

Sherwin, Judith Johnson 1936-... CLC 7, 15
See also CA 25-28R; CANR 34

Sherwood, Frances 1940- .... CLC 81
See also CA 146

Sherwood, Robert E(mmet)
1896-1955 ...... TCLC 3; DAM DRAM
See also CA 104; 153; DLB 7, 26

Shestov, Lev 1866-1938 .... TCLC 56

Shevchenko, Taras 1814-1861 .... NCLC 54

Shiel, M(atthew) P(hipps)
1865-1947 .... TCLC 8
See also CA 106; DLB 153

Shields, Carol 1935- .... CLC 91; DAC
See also CA 81-84; CANR 51

Shields, David 1956- .... CLC 97
See also CA 124; CANR 48

Shiga, Naoya 1883-1971... CLC 33; SSC 23
See also CA 101; 33-36R

Shilts, Randy 1951-1994 .... CLC 85
See also AAYA 19; CA 115; 127; 144;
CANR 45; INT 127

Shimazaki, Haruki 1872-1943
See Shimazaki Toson
See also CA 105; 134

Shimazaki Toson .... TCLC 5
See also Shimazaki, Haruki

Sholokhov, Mikhail (Aleksandrovich)
1905-1984 .... CLC 7, 15
See also CA 101; 112; MTCW;
SATA-Obit 36

Shone, Patric
See Hanley, James

Shreve, Susan Richards 1939- ...... CLC 23
See also CA 49-52; CAAS 5; CANR 5, 38;
MAICYA; SATA 46; SATA-Brief 41

Shue, Larry
1946-1985 ...... CLC 52; DAM DRAM
See also CA 145; 117

Shu-Jen, Chou 1881-1936
See Lu Hsun
See also CA 104

Shulman, Alix Kates 1932- ...... CLC 2, 10
See also CA 29-32R; CANR 43; SATA 7

Shuster, Joe 1914- .... CLC 21

Shute, Nevil .... CLC 30
See also Norway, Nevil Shute

Shuttle, Penelope (Diane) 1947- ..... CLC 7
See also CA 93-96; CANR 39; DLB 14, 40

Sidney, Mary 1561-1621 .... LC 19

Sidney, Sir Philip
1554-1586 ..... LC 19; DA; DAB; DAC;
DAM MST, POET
See also CDBLB Before 1660; DLB 167

Siegel, Jerome 1914-1996 .... CLC 21
See also CA 116; 151

Siegel, Jerry
See Siegel, Jerome

Sienkiewicz, Henryk (Adam Alexander Pius)
1846-1916 .... TCLC 3
See also CA 104; 134

Sierra, Gregorio Martinez
See Martinez Sierra, Gregorio

Sierra, Maria (de la O'LeJarraga) Martinez
See Martinez Sierra, Maria (de la
O'LeJarraga)

Sigal, Clancy 1926-................ CLC 7
See also CA 1-4R

Sigourney, Lydia Howard (Huntley)
1791-1865 .... NCLC 21
See also DLB 1, 42, 73

Siguenza y Gongora, Carlos de
1645-1700 .... LC 8

Sigurjonsson, Johann 1880-1919 ... TCLC 27

Sikelianos, Angelos 1884-1951 .... TCLC 39

Silkin, Jon 1930- .... CLC 2, 6, 43
See also CA 5-8R; CAAS 5; DLB 27

Silko, Leslie (Marmon)
1948- .... CLC 23, 74; DA; DAC;
DAM MST, MULT, POP
See also AAYA 14; CA 115; 122;
CANR 45; DLB 143; NNAL

Sillanpaa, Frans Eemil 1888-1964... CLC 19
See also CA 129; 93-96; MTCW

Sillitoe, Alan
1928- .... CLC 1, 3, 6, 10, 19, 57
See also AITN 1; CA 9-12R; CAAS 2;
CANR 8, 26, 55; CDBLB 1960 to
Present; DLB 14, 139; MTCW; SATA 61

Silone, Ignazio 1900-1978 .... CLC 4
See also CA 25-28; 81-84; CANR 34;
CAP 2; MTCW

Silver, Joan Micklin 1935- .... CLC 20
See also CA 114; 121; INT 121

Silver, Nicholas
See Faust, Frederick (Schiller)

Silverberg, Robert
1935- .... CLC 7; DAM POP
See also CA 1-4R; CAAS 3; CANR 1, 20,
36; DLB 8; INT CANR-20; MAICYA;
MTCW; SATA 13, 91

Silverstein, Alvin 1933- .... CLC 17
See also CA 49-52; CANR 2; CLR 25;
JRDA; MAICYA; SATA 8, 69

Silverstein, Virginia B(arbara Opshelor)
1937- .... CLC 17
See also CA 49-52; CANR 2; CLR 25;
JRDA; MAICYA; SATA 8, 69

Sim, Georges
See Simenon, Georges (Jacques Christian)

Simak, Clifford D(onald)
1904-1988 .... CLC 1, 55
See also CA 1-4R; 125; CANR 1, 35;
DLB 8; MTCW; SATA-Obit 56

Simenon, Georges (Jacques Christian)
1903-1989 .... CLC 1, 2, 3, 8, 18, 47;
DAM POP
See also CA 85-88; 129; CANR 35;
DLB 72; DLBY 89; MTCW

Simic, Charles
1938- .... CLC 6, 9, 22, 49, 68;
DAM POET
See also CA 29-32R; CAAS 4; CANR 12,
33, 52; DLB 105

Simmel, Georg 1858-1918 .... TCLC 64

Simmons, Charles (Paul) 1924-..... CLC 57
See also CA 89-92; INT 89-92

Simmons, Dan 1948-... CLC 44; DAM POP
See also AAYA 16; CA 138; CANR 53

Simmons, James (Stewart Alexander)
1933- .... CLC 43
See also CA 105; CAAS 21; DLB 40

Simms, William Gilmore
1806-1870 .... NCLC 3
See also DLB 3, 30, 59, 73

Simon, Carly 1945-................ CLC 26
See also CA 105

Simon, Claude
1913- .... CLC 4, 9, 15, 39; DAM NOV
See also CA 89-92; CANR 33; DLB 83;
MTCW

Simon, (Marvin) Neil
1927- .... CLC 6, 11, 31, 39, 70;
DAM DRAM
See also AITN 1; CA 21-24R; CANR 26,
54; DLB 7; MTCW

Simon, Paul (Frederick) 1941(?)- ... CLC 17
See also CA 116; 153

Simonon, Paul 1956(?)- .... CLC 30

Simpson, Harriette
See Arnow, Harriette (Louisa) Simpson

Simpson, Louis (Aston Marantz)
1923- .... CLC 4, 7, 9, 32; DAM POET
See also CA 1-4R; CAAS 4; CANR 1;
DLB 5; MTCW

Simpson, Mona (Elizabeth) 1957-... CLC 44
See also CA 122; 135

Simpson, N(orman) F(rederick)
1919- .... CLC 29
See also CA 13-16R; DLB 13

Sinclair, Andrew (Annandale)
1935- .... CLC 2, 14
See also CA 9-12R; CAAS 5; CANR 14, 38;
DLB 14; MTCW

Sinclair, Emil
See Hesse, Hermann

Sinclair, Iain 1943-................ CLC 76
See also CA 132

Sinclair, Iain MacGregor
See Sinclair, Iain

Sinclair, Mary Amelia St. Clair 1865(?)-1946
See Sinclair, May
See also CA 104

Sinclair, May................. TCLC 3, 11
See also Sinclair, Mary Amelia St. Clair
See also DLB 36, 135

Sinclair, Upton (Beall)
1878-1968 ...... CLC 1, 11, 15, 63; DA;
DAB; DAC; DAM MST, NOV; WLC
See also CA 5-8R; 25-28R; CANR 7;
CDALB 1929-1941; DLB 9;
INT CANR-7; MTCW; SATA 9

Singer, Isaac
See Singer, Isaac Bashevis

Singer, Isaac Bashevis
1904-1991 .... CLC 1, 3, 6, 9, 11, 15, 23,
38, 69; DA; DAB; DAC; DAM MST,
NOV; SSC 3; WLC
See also AITN 1, 2; CA 1-4R; 134;
CANR 1, 39; CDALB 1941-1968; CLR 1;
DLB 6, 28, 52; DLBY 91; JRDA;
MAICYA; MTCW; SATA 3, 27;
SATA-Obit 68

Singer, Israel Joshua 1893-1944 ... TCLC 33

Singh, Khushwant 1915- .... CLC 11
See also CA 9-12R; CAAS 9; CANR 6

Sinjohn, John
See Galsworthy, John

Sinyavsky, Andrei (Donatevich)
1925- .... CLC 8
See also CA 85-88

Sirin, V.
See Nabokov, Vladimir (Vladimirovich)

Sissman, L(ouis) E(dward)
1928-1976 .... CLC 9, 18
See also CA 21-24R; 65-68; CANR 13;
DLB 5

Sisson, C(harles) H(ubert) 1914- ..... CLC 8
See also CA 1-4R; CAAS 3; CANR 3, 48;
DLB 27

Sitwell, Dame Edith
1887-1964 .... CLC 2, 9, 67;
DAM POET; PC 3
See also CA 9-12R; CANR 35;
CDBLB 1945-1960; DLB 20; MTCW

Sjoewall, Maj 1935- .... CLC 7
See also CA 65-68

Sjowall, Maj
See Sjoewall, Maj

Skelton, Robin 1925- .... CLC 13
See also AITN 2; CA 5-8R; CAAS 5;
CANR 28; DLB 27, 53

Skolimowski, Jerzy 1938- .... CLC 20
See also CA 128

Skram, Amalie (Bertha)
1847-1905 .... TCLC 25

Skvorecky, Josef (Vaclav)
1924- .... CLC 15, 39, 69; DAC;
DAM NOV
See also CA 61-64; CAAS 1; CANR 10, 34;
MTCW

Slade, Bernard .... CLC 11, 46
See also Newbound, Bernard Slade
See also CAAS 9; DLB 53

Slaughter, Carolyn 1946- .... CLC 56
See also CA 85-88

Slaughter, Frank G(ill) 1908- ...... CLC 29
See also AITN 2; CA 5-8R; CANR 5;
INT CANR-5

Slavitt, David R(ytman) 1935- .... CLC 5, 14
See also CA 21-24R; CAAS 3; CANR 41;
DLB 5, 6

Slesinger, Tess 1905-1945 .... TCLC 10
See also CA 107; DLB 102

Slessor, Kenneth 1901-1971 .... CLC 14
See also CA 102; 89-92

Slowacki, Juliusz 1809-1849 ..... NCLC 15

Smart, Christopher
1722-1771 ... LC 3; DAM POET; PC 13
See also DLB 109

Smart, Elizabeth 1913-1986 .... CLC 54
See also CA 81-84; 118; DLB 88

Smiley, Jane (Graves)
1949- .... CLC 53, 76; DAM POP
See also CA 104; CANR 30, 50;
INT CANR-30

Smith, A(rthur) J(ames) M(arshall)
1902-1980 .... CLC 15; DAC
See also CA 1-4R; 102; CANR 4; DLB 88

Smith, Adam 1723-1790 .... LC 36
See also DLB 104

Smith, Anna Deavere 1950- .... CLC 86
See also CA 133

Smith, Betty (Wehner) 1896-1972 ... CLC 19
See also CA 5-8R; 33-36R; DLBY 82;
SATA 6

Smith, Charlotte (Turner)
1749-1806 .... NCLC 23
See also DLB 39, 109

Smith, Clark Ashton 1893-1961 .... CLC 43
See also CA 143

Smith, Dave .... CLC 22, 42
See also Smith, David (Jeddie)
See also CAAS 7; DLB 5

Smith, David (Jeddie) 1942-
See Smith, Dave
See also CA 49-52; CANR 1; DAM POET

Smith, Florence Margaret 1902-1971
See Smith, Stevie
See also CA 17-18; 29-32R; CANR 35;
CAP 2; DAM POET; MTCW

Smith, Iain Crichton 1928- .... CLC 64
See also CA 21-24R; DLB 40, 139

Smith, John 1580(?)-1631 .... LC 9

Smith, Johnston
See Crane, Stephen (Townley)

Smith, Joseph, Jr. 1805-1844 .... NCLC 53

Smith, Lee 1944- .... CLC 25, 73
See also CA 114; 119; CANR 46; DLB 143;
DLBY 83; INT 119

Smith, Martin
See Smith, Martin Cruz

Smith, Martin Cruz
1942- ..... CLC 25; DAM MULT, POP
See also BEST 89:4; CA 85-88; CANR 6,
23, 43; INT CANR-23; NNAL

Smith, Mary-Ann Tirone 1944- ..... CLC 39
See also CA 118; 136

Smith, Patti 1946- .... CLC 12
See also CA 93-96

Smith, Pauline (Urmson)
1882-1959 .... TCLC 25

Smith, Rosamond
See Oates, Joyce Carol

Smith, Sheila Kaye
See Kaye-Smith, Sheila

Smith, Stevie .... CLC 3, 8, 25, 44; PC 12
See also Smith, Florence Margaret
See also DLB 20

Smith, Wilbur (Addison) 1933- ..... CLC 33
See also CA 13-16R; CANR 7, 46; MTCW

Smith, William Jay 1918- .... CLC 6
See also CA 5-8R; CANR 44; DLB 5;
MAICYA; SAAS 22; SATA 2, 68

Smith, Woodrow Wilson
See Kuttner, Henry

Smolenskin, Peretz 1842-1885 .... NCLC 30

Smollett, Tobias (George) 1721-1771 .. LC 2
See also CDBLB 1660-1789; DLB 39, 104

Snodgrass, W(illiam) D(e Witt)
1926- .... CLC 2, 6, 10, 18, 68;
DAM POET
See also CA 1-4R; CANR 6, 36; DLB 5;
MTCW

Snow, C(harles) P(ercy)
1905-1980 ...... CLC 1, 4, 6, 9, 13, 19;
DAM NOV
See also CA 5-8R; 101; CANR 28;
CDBLB 1945-1960; DLB 15, 77; MTCW

Snow, Frances Compton
See Adams, Henry (Brooks)

Snyder, Gary (Sherman)
1930- .. CLC 1, 2, 5, 9, 32; DAM POET
See also CA 17-20R; CANR 30; DLB 5, 16,
165

Snyder, Zilpha Keatley 1927- ...... CLC 17
See also AAYA 15; CA 9-12R; CANR 38;
CLR 31; JRDA; MAICYA; SAAS 2;
SATA 1, 28, 75

Soares, Bernardo
See Pessoa, Fernando (Antonio Nogueira)

Sobh, A.
See Shamlu, Ahmad

Sobol, Joshua .... CLC 60

Soderberg, Hjalmar 1869-1941 .... TCLC 39

Sodergran, Edith (Irene)
See Soedergran, Edith (Irene)

Soedergran, Edith (Irene)
1892-1923 .... TCLC 31

Softly, Edgar
See Lovecraft, H(oward) P(hillips)

Softly, Edward
See Lovecraft, H(oward) P(hillips)

Sokolov, Raymond 1941- .... CLC 7
See also CA 85-88

Solo, Jay
See Ellison, Harlan (Jay)

Sologub, Fyodor .... TCLC 9
See also Teternikov, Fyodor Kuzmich

Solomons, Ikey Esquir
See Thackeray, William Makepeace

Solomos, Dionysios 1798-1857 ... NCLC 15

Solwoska, Mara
See French, Marilyn

Solzhenitsyn, Aleksandr I(sayevich)
1918- ...... CLC 1, 2, 4, 7, 9, 10, 18, 26,
34, 78; DA; DAB; DAC; DAM MST,
NOV; WLC
See also AITN 1; CA 69-72; CANR 40;
MTCW

Somers, Jane
See Lessing, Doris (May)

Somerville, Edith 1858-1949 ...... TCLC 51
See also DLB 135

Somerville & Ross
See Martin, Violet Florence; Somerville,
Edith

Sommer, Scott 1951- . . . . **CLC 25**
See also CA 106

Sondheim, Stephen (Joshua)
1930- . . . . **CLC 30, 39; DAM DRAM**
See also AAYA 11; CA 103; CANR 47

Sontag, Susan
1933- . . . . **CLC 1, 2, 10, 13, 31;**
DAM POP
See also CA 17-20R; CANR 25, 51; DLB 2,
67; MTCW

Sophocles
496(?)B.C.-406(?)B.C. . . . . . **CMLC 2; DA;**
DAB; DAC; DAM DRAM, MST; DC 1

Sordello 1189-1269 . . . . **CMLC 15**

Sorel, Julia
See Drexler, Rosalyn

Sorrentino, Gilbert
1929- . . . . **CLC 3, 7, 14, 22, 40**
See also CA 77-80; CANR 14, 33; DLB 5,
173; DLBY 80; INT CANR-14

Soto, Gary
1952- . . . . **CLC 32, 80; DAM MULT;**
HLC
See also AAYA 10; CA 119; 125;
CANR 50; CLR 38; DLB 82; HW;
INT 125; JRDA; SATA 80

Soupault, Philippe 1897-1990 . . . . . . **CLC 68**
See also CA 116; 147; 131

Souster, (Holmes) Raymond
1921- . . . **CLC 5, 14; DAC; DAM POET**
See also CA 13-16R; CAAS 14; CANR 13,
29, 53; DLB 88; SATA 63

Southern, Terry 1924(?)-1995 . . . . **CLC 7**
See also CA 1-4R; 150; CANR 1, 55;
DLB 2

Southey, Robert 1774-1843 . . . . **NCLC 8**
See also DLB 93, 107, 142; SATA 54

Southworth, Emma Dorothy Eliza Nevitte
1819-1899 . . . . **NCLC 26**

Souza, Ernest
See Scott, Evelyn

Soyinka, Wole
1934- . . . . **CLC 3, 5, 14, 36, 44; BLC;**
DA; DAB; DAC; DAM DRAM, MST,
MULT; DC 2; WLC
See also BW 2; CA 13-16R; CANR 27, 39;
DLB 125; MTCW

Spackman, W(illiam) M(ode)
1905-1990 . . . . **CLC 46**
See also CA 81-84; 132

Spacks, Barry (Bernard) 1931- . . . . . **CLC 14**
See also CA 154; CANR 33; DLB 105

Spanidou, Irini 1946- . . . . **CLC 44**

Spark, Muriel (Sarah)
1918- . . . . . **CLC 2, 3, 5, 8, 13, 18, 40, 94;**
DAB; DAC; DAM MST, NOV; SSC 10
See also CA 5-8R; CANR 12, 36;
CDBLB 1945-1960; DLB 15, 139;
INT CANR-12; MTCW

Spaulding, Douglas
See Bradbury, Ray (Douglas)

Spaulding, Leonard
See Bradbury, Ray (Douglas)

Spence, J. A. D.
See Eliot, T(homas) S(tearns)

Spencer, Elizabeth 1921- . . . . **CLC 22**
See also CA 13-16R; CANR 32; DLB 6;
MTCW; SATA 14

Spencer, Leonard G.
See Silverberg, Robert

Spencer, Scott 1945- . . . . **CLC 30**
See also CA 113; CANR 51; DLBY 86

Spender, Stephen (Harold)
1909-1995 . . . . . . **CLC 1, 2, 5, 10, 41, 91;**
DAM POET
See also CA 9-12R; 149; CANR 31, 54;
CDBLB 1945-1960; DLB 20; MTCW

Spengler, Oswald (Arnold Gottfried)
1880-1936 . . . . **TCLC 25**
See also CA 118

Spenser, Edmund
1552(?)-1599 . . . . **LC 5; DA; DAB; DAC;**
DAM MST, POET; PC 8; WLC
See also CDBLB Before 1660; DLB 167

Spicer, Jack
1925-1965 . . . . **CLC 8, 18, 72;**
DAM POET
See also CA 85-88; DLB 5, 16

Spiegelman, Art 1948- . . . . **CLC 76**
See also AAYA 10; CA 125; CANR 41, 55

Spielberg, Peter 1929- . . . . **CLC 6**
See also CA 5-8R; CANR 4, 48; DLBY 81

Spielberg, Steven 1947- . . . . **CLC 20**
See also AAYA 8; CA 77-80; CANR 32;
SATA 32

Spillane, Frank Morrison 1918-
See Spillane, Mickey
See also CA 25-28R; CANR 28; MTCW;
SATA 66

Spillane, Mickey . . . . **CLC 3, 13**
See also Spillane, Frank Morrison

Spinoza, Benedictus de 1632-1677 . . . . **LC 9**

Spinrad, Norman (Richard) 1940- . . . **CLC 46**
See also CA 37-40R; CAAS 19; CANR 20;
DLB 8; INT CANR-20

Spitteler, Carl (Friedrich Georg)
1845-1924 . . . . **TCLC 12**
See also CA 109; DLB 129

Spivack, Kathleen (Romola Drucker)
1938- . . . . **CLC 6**
See also CA 49-52

Spoto, Donald 1941- . . . . **CLC 39**
See also CA 65-68; CANR 11

Springsteen, Bruce (F.) 1949- . . . . . . **CLC 17**
See also CA 111

Spurling, Hilary 1940- . . . . **CLC 34**
See also CA 104; CANR 25, 52

Spyker, John Howland
See Elman, Richard

Squires, (James) Radcliffe
1917-1993 . . . . **CLC 51**
See also CA 1-4R; 140; CANR 6, 21

Srivastava, Dhanpat Rai 1880(?)-1936
See Premchand
See also CA 118

Stacy, Donald
See Pohl, Frederik

Stael, Germaine de
See Stael-Holstein, Anne Louise Germaine
Necker Baronn
See also DLB 119

Stael-Holstein, Anne Louise Germaine Necker
Baronn 1766-1817 . . . . **NCLC 3**
See also Stael, Germaine de

Stafford, Jean 1915-1979 . . . **CLC 4, 7, 19, 68**
See also CA 1-4R; 85-88; CANR 3; DLB 2,
173; MTCW; SATA-Obit 22

Stafford, William (Edgar)
1914-1993 . . . **CLC 4, 7, 29; DAM POET**
See also CA 5-8R; 142; CAAS 3; CANR 5,
22; DLB 5; INT CANR-22

Staines, Trevor
See Brunner, John (Kilian Houston)

Stairs, Gordon
See Austin, Mary (Hunter)

Stannard, Martin 1947- . . . . **CLC 44**
See also CA 142; DLB 155

Stanton, Maura 1946- . . . . **CLC 9**
See also CA 89-92; CANR 15; DLB 120

Stanton, Schuyler
See Baum, L(yman) Frank

Stapledon, (William) Olaf
1886-1950 . . . . **TCLC 22**
See also CA 111; DLB 15

Starbuck, George (Edwin)
1931-1996 . . . . **CLC 53; DAM POET**
See also CA 21-24R; 153; CANR 23

Stark, Richard
See Westlake, Donald E(dwin)

Staunton, Schuyler
See Baum, L(yman) Frank

Stead, Christina (Ellen)
1902-1983 . . . . **CLC 2, 5, 8, 32, 80**
See also CA 13-16R; 109; CANR 33, 40;
MTCW

Stead, William Thomas
1849-1912 . . . . **TCLC 48**

Steele, Richard 1672-1729 . . . . **LC 18**
See also CDBLB 1660-1789; DLB 84, 101

Steele, Timothy (Reid) 1948- . . . . **CLC 45**
See also CA 93-96; CANR 16, 50; DLB 120

Steffens, (Joseph) Lincoln
1866-1936 . . . . **TCLC 20**
See also CA 117

Stegner, Wallace (Earle)
1909-1993 . . . **CLC 9, 49, 81; DAM NOV**
See also AITN 1; BEST 90:3; CA 1-4R;
141; CAAS 9; CANR 1, 21, 46; DLB 9;
DLBY 93; MTCW

Stein, Gertrude
1874-1946 . . . . . . **TCLC 1, 6, 28, 48; DA;**
DAB; DAC; DAM MST, NOV, POET;
WLC
See also CA 104; 132; CDALB 1917-1929;
DLB 4, 54, 86; MTCW

Strummer, Joe 1953(?)- . . . . CLC 30

Stuart, Don A.
    See Campbell, John W(ood, Jr.)

Stuart, Ian
    See MacLean, Alistair (Stuart)

Stuart, Jesse (Hilton)
    1906-1984 . . . . CLC 1, 8, 11, 14, 34
    See also CA 5-8R; 112; CANR 31; DLB 9,
    48, 102; DLBY 84; SATA 2;
    SATA-Obit 36

Sturgeon, Theodore (Hamilton)
    1918-1985 . . . . CLC 22, 39
    See also Queen, Ellery
    See also CA 81-84; 116; CANR 32; DLB 8;
    DLBY 85; MTCW

Sturges, Preston 1898-1959 . . . . . . TCLC 48
    See also CA 114; 149; DLB 26

Styron, William
    1925- . . . . CLC 1, 3, 5, 11, 15, 60;
                                          DAM NOV, POP
    See also BEST 90:4; CA 5-8R; CANR 6, 33;
    CDALB 1968-1988; DLB 2, 143;
    DLBY 80; INT CANR-6; MTCW

Suarez Lynch, B.
    See Bioy Casares, Adolfo; Borges, Jorge
    Luis

Su Chien 1884-1918
    See Su Man-shu
    See also CA 123

Suckow, Ruth 1892-1960 . . . . SSC 18
    See also CA 113; DLB 9, 102

Sudermann, Hermann 1857-1928 . . TCLC 15
    See also CA 107; DLB 118

Sue, Eugene 1804-1857 . . . . NCLC 1
    See also DLB 119

Sueskind, Patrick 1949- . . . . CLC 44
    See also Suskind, Patrick

Sukenick, Ronald 1932- . . . . . CLC 3, 4, 6, 48
    See also CA 25-28R; CAAS 8; CANR 32;
    DLB 173; DLBY 81

Suknaski, Andrew 1942- . . . . CLC 19
    See also CA 101; DLB 53

Sullivan, Vernon
    See Vian, Boris

Sully Prudhomme 1839-1907 . . . . . . TCLC 31

Su Man-shu . . . . TCLC 24
    See also Su Chien

Summerforest, Ivy B.
    See Kirkup, James

Summers, Andrew James 1942- . . . . . CLC 26

Summers, Andy
    See Summers, Andrew James

Summers, Hollis (Spurgeon, Jr.)
    1916- . . . . CLC 10
    See also CA 5-8R; CANR 3; DLB 6

Summers, (Alphonsus Joseph-Mary Augustus)
    Montague 1880-1948 . . . . TCLC 16
    See also CA 118

Sumner, Gordon Matthew 1951- . . . . CLC 26

Surtees, Robert Smith
    1803-1864 . . . . NCLC 14
    See also DLB 21

Susann, Jacqueline 1921-1974 . . . . . . CLC 3
    See also AITN 1; CA 65-68; 53-56; MTCW

Su Shih 1036-1101 . . . . CMLC 15

Suskind, Patrick
    See Sueskind, Patrick
    See also CA 145

Sutcliff, Rosemary
    1920-1992 . . . . CLC 26; DAB; DAC;
                                          DAM MST, POP
    See also AAYA 10; CA 5-8R; 139;
    CANR 37; CLR 1, 37; JRDA; MAICYA;
    SATA 6, 44, 78; SATA-Obit 73

Sutro, Alfred 1863-1933 . . . . TCLC 6
    See also CA 105; DLB 10

Sutton, Henry
    See Slavitt, David R(ytman)

Svevo, Italo . . . . TCLC 2, 35
    See also Schmitz, Aron Hector

Swados, Elizabeth (A.) 1951- . . . . . . CLC 12
    See also CA 97-100; CANR 49; INT 97-100

Swados, Harvey 1920-1972 . . . . CLC 5
    See also CA 5-8R; 37-40R; CANR 6;
    DLB 2

Swan, Gladys 1934- . . . . CLC 69
    See also CA 101; CANR 17, 39

Swarthout, Glendon (Fred)
    1918-1992 . . . . CLC 35
    See also CA 1-4R; 139; CANR 1, 47;
    SATA 26

Sweet, Sarah C.
    See Jewett, (Theodora) Sarah Orne

Swenson, May
    1919-1989 . . . . CLC 4, 14, 61; DA; DAB;
                                          DAC; DAM MST, POET; PC 14
    See also CA 5-8R; 130; CANR 36; DLB 5;
    MTCW; SATA 15

Swift, Augustus
    See Lovecraft, H(oward) P(hillips)

Swift, Graham (Colin) 1949- . . . . CLC 41, 88
    See also CA 117; 122; CANR 46

Swift, Jonathan
    1667-1745 . . . . . . LC 1; DA; DAB; DAC;
                                          DAM MST, NOV, POET; PC 9; WLC
    See also CDBLB 1660-1789; DLB 39, 95,
    101; SATA 19

Swinburne, Algernon Charles
    1837-1909 . . . . . . TCLC 8, 36; DA; DAB;
                                          DAC; DAM MST, POET; WLC
    See also CA 105; 140; CDBLB 1832-1890;
    DLB 35, 57

Swinfen, Ann . . . . CLC 34

Swinnerton, Frank Arthur
    1884-1982 . . . . CLC 31
    See also CA 108; DLB 34

Swithen, John
    See King, Stephen (Edwin)

Sylvia
    See Ashton-Warner, Sylvia (Constance)

Symmes, Robert Edward
    See Duncan, Robert (Edward)

Symonds, John Addington
    1840-1893 . . . . NCLC 34
    See also DLB 57, 144

Symons, Arthur 1865-1945 . . . . TCLC 11
    See also CA 107; DLB 19, 57, 149

Symons, Julian (Gustave)
    1912-1994 . . . . CLC 2, 14, 32
    See also CA 49-52; 147; CAAS 3; CANR 3,
    33; DLB 87, 155; DLBY 92; MTCW

Synge, (Edmund) J(ohn) M(illington)
    1871-1909 . . . . TCLC 6, 37;
                                          DAM DRAM; DC 2
    See also CA 104; 141; CDBLB 1890-1914;
    DLB 10, 19

Syruc, J.
    See Milosz, Czeslaw

Szirtes, George 1948- . . . . CLC 46
    See also CA 109; CANR 27

Tabori, George 1914- . . . . CLC 19
    See also CA 49-52; CANR 4

Tagore, Rabindranath
    1861-1941 . . . . TCLC 3, 53;
                                          DAM DRAM, POET; PC 8
    See also CA 104; 120; MTCW

Taine, Hippolyte Adolphe
    1828-1893 . . . . NCLC 15

Talese, Gay 1932- . . . . CLC 37
    See also AITN 1; CA 1-4R; CANR 9;
    INT CANR-9; MTCW

Tallent, Elizabeth (Ann) 1954- . . . . . CLC 45
    See also CA 117; DLB 130

Tally, Ted 1952- . . . . CLC 42
    See also CA 120; 124; INT 124

Tamayo y Baus, Manuel
    1829-1898 . . . . NCLC 1

Tammsaare, A(nton) H(ansen)
    1878-1940 . . . . TCLC 27

Tan, Amy (Ruth)
    1952- . . . . CLC 59; DAM MULT, NOV,
                                          POP
    See also AAYA 9; BEST 89:3; CA 136;
    CANR 54; DLB 173; SATA 75

Tandem, Felix
    See Spitteler, Carl (Friedrich Georg)

Tanizaki, Jun'ichiro
    1886-1965 . . . . . . CLC 8, 14, 28; SSC 21
    See also CA 93-96; 25-28R

Tanner, William
    See Amis, Kingsley (William)

Tao Lao
    See Storni, Alfonsina

Tarassoff, Lev
    See Troyat, Henri

Tarbell, Ida M(inerva)
    1857-1944 . . . . TCLC 40
    See also CA 122; DLB 47

Tarkington, (Newton) Booth
    1869-1946 . . . . TCLC 9
    See also CA 110; 143; DLB 9, 102;
    SATA 17

Tarkovsky, Andrei (Arsenyevich)
    1932-1986 . . . . CLC 75
    See also CA 127

Tartt, Donna 1964(?)- . . . . CLC 76
    See also CA 142

Tasso, Torquato 1544-1595 . . . . LC 5

Tate, (John Orley) Allen
    1899-1979 . . . . CLC 2, 4, 6, 9, 11, 14, 24
    See also CA 5-8R; 85-88; CANR 32;
    DLB 4, 45, 63; MTCW

Tate, Ellalice
See Hibbert, Eleanor Alice Burford

Tate, James (Vincent) 1943- ... CLC 2, 6, 25
See also CA 21-24R; CANR 29; DLB 5,
169

Tavel, Ronald 1940- .... CLC 6
See also CA 21-24R; CANR 33

Taylor, C(ecil) P(hilip) 1929-1981... CLC 27
See also CA 25-28R; 105; CANR 47

Taylor, Edward
1642(?)-1729 .... LC 11; DA; DAB;
DAC; DAM MST, POET
See also DLB 24

Taylor, Eleanor Ross 1920- .... CLC 5
See also CA 81-84

Taylor, Elizabeth 1912-1975 ... CLC 2, 4, 29
See also CA 13-16R; CANR 9; DLB 139;
MTCW; SATA 13

Taylor, Henry (Splawn) 1942- ...... CLC 44
See also CA 33-36R; CAAS 7; CANR 31;
DLB 5

Taylor, Kamala (Purnaiya) 1924-
See Markandaya, Kamala
See also CA 77-80

Taylor, Mildred D. .... CLC 21
See also AAYA 10; BW 1; CA 85-88;
CANR 25; CLR 9; DLB 52; JRDA;
MAICYA; SAAS 5; SATA 15, 70

Taylor, Peter (Hillsman)
1917-1994 ..... CLC 1, 4, 18, 37, 44, 50,
71; SSC 10
See also CA 13-16R; 147; CANR 9, 50;
DLBY 81, 94; INT CANR-9; MTCW

Taylor, Robert Lewis 1912- .... CLC 14
See also CA 1-4R; CANR 3; SATA 10

Tchekhov, Anton
See Chekhov, Anton (Pavlovich)

Teasdale, Sara 1884-1933.......... TCLC 4
See also CA 104; DLB 45; SATA 32

Tegner, Esaias 1782-1846........ NCLC 2

Teilhard de Chardin, (Marie Joseph) Pierre
1881-1955 .... TCLC 9
See also CA 105

Temple, Ann
See Mortimer, Penelope (Ruth)

Tennant, Emma (Christina)
1937- .... CLC 13, 52
See also CA 65-68; CAAS 9; CANR 10, 38;
DLB 14

Tenneshaw, S. M.
See Silverberg, Robert

Tennyson, Alfred
1809-1892 ...... NCLC 30; DA; DAB;
DAC; DAM MST, POET; PC 6; WLC
See also CDBLB 1832-1890; DLB 32

Teran, Lisa St. Aubin de .... CLC 36
See also St. Aubin de Teran, Lisa

Terence 195(?)B.C.-159B.C....... CMLC 14

Teresa de Jesus, St. 1515-1582 ...... LC 18

Terkel, Louis 1912-
See Terkel, Studs
See also CA 57-60; CANR 18, 45; MTCW

Terkel, Studs .... CLC 38
See also Terkel, Louis
See also AITN 1

Terry, C. V.
See Slaughter, Frank G(ill)

Terry, Megan 1932- .... CLC 19
See also CA 77-80; CABS 3; CANR 43;
DLB 7

Tertz, Abram
See Sinyavsky, Andrei (Donatevich)

Tesich, Steve 1943(?)-1996...... CLC 40, 69
See also CA 105; 152; DLBY 83

Teternikov, Fyodor Kuzmich 1863-1927
See Sologub, Fyodor
See also CA 104

Tevis, Walter 1928-1984 .... CLC 42
See also CA 113

Tey, Josephine .... TCLC 14
See also Mackintosh, Elizabeth
See also DLB 77

Thackeray, William Makepeace
1811-1863 .... NCLC 5, 14, 22, 43; DA;
DAB; DAC; DAM MST, NOV; WLC
See also CDBLB 1832-1890; DLB 21, 55,
159, 163; SATA 23

Thakura, Ravindranatha
See Tagore, Rabindranath

Tharoor, Shashi 1956- .... CLC 70
See also CA 141

Thelwell, Michael Miles 1939- ..... CLC 22
See also BW 2; CA 101

Theobald, Lewis, Jr.
See Lovecraft, H(oward) P(hillips)

Theodorescu, Ion N. 1880-1967
See Arghezi, Tudor
See also CA 116

Theriault, Yves
1915-1983 .. CLC 79; DAC; DAM MST
See also CA 102; DLB 88

Theroux, Alexander (Louis)
1939- .... CLC 2, 25
See also CA 85-88; CANR 20

Theroux, Paul (Edward)
1941- .... CLC 5, 8, 11, 15, 28, 46;
DAM POP
See also BEST 89:4; CA 33-36R; CANR 20,
45; DLB 2; MTCW; SATA 44

Thesen, Sharon 1946- .... CLC 56

Thevenin, Denis
See Duhamel, Georges

Thibault, Jacques Anatole Francois
1844-1924
See France, Anatole
See also CA 106; 127; DAM NOV; MTCW

Thiele, Colin (Milton) 1920- .... CLC 17
See also CA 29-32R; CANR 12, 28, 53;
CLR 27; MAICYA; SAAS 2; SATA 14,
72

Thomas, Audrey (Callahan)
1935- .... CLC 7, 13, 37; SSC 20
See also AITN 2; CA 21-24R; CAAS 19;
CANR 36; DLB 60; MTCW

Thomas, D(onald) M(ichael)
1935- .... CLC 13, 22, 31
See also CA 61-64; CAAS 11; CANR 17,
45; CDBLB 1960 to Present; DLB 40;
INT CANR-17; MTCW

Thomas, Dylan (Marlais)
1914-1953 ... TCLC 1, 8, 45; DA; DAB;
DAC; DAM DRAM, MST, POET;
PC 2; SSC 3; WLC
See also CA 104; 120; CDBLB 1945-1960;
DLB 13, 20, 139; MTCW; SATA 60

Thomas, (Philip) Edward
1878-1917 ...... TCLC 10; DAM POET
See also CA 106; 153; DLB 19

Thomas, Joyce Carol 1938- .... CLC 35
See also AAYA 12; BW 2; CA 113; 116;
CANR 48; CLR 19; DLB 33; INT 116;
JRDA; MAICYA; MTCW; SAAS 7;
SATA 40, 78

Thomas, Lewis 1913-1993 .... CLC 35
See also CA 85-88; 143; CANR 38; MTCW

Thomas, Paul
See Mann, (Paul) Thomas

Thomas, Piri 1928- .... CLC 17
See also CA 73-76; HW

Thomas, R(onald) S(tuart)
1913- .... CLC 6, 13, 48; DAB;
DAM POET
See also CA 89-92; CAAS 4; CANR 30;
CDBLB 1960 to Present; DLB 27;
MTCW

Thomas, Ross (Elmore) 1926-1995 .. CLC 39
See also CA 33-36R; 150; CANR 22

Thompson, Francis Clegg
See Mencken, H(enry) L(ouis)

Thompson, Francis Joseph
1859-1907 .... TCLC 4
See also CA 104; CDBLB 1890-1914;
DLB 19

Thompson, Hunter S(tockton)
1939- .... CLC 9, 17, 40; DAM POP
See also BEST 89:1; CA 17-20R; CANR 23,
46; MTCW

Thompson, James Myers
See Thompson, Jim (Myers)

Thompson, Jim (Myers)
1906-1977(?) .... CLC 69
See also CA 140

Thompson, Judith .... CLC 39

Thomson, James
1700-1748 ..... LC 16, 29; DAM POET
See also DLB 95

Thomson, James
1834-1882 ..... NCLC 18; DAM POET
See also DLB 35

Thoreau, Henry David
1817-1862 ..... NCLC 7, 21; DA; DAB;
DAC; DAM MST; WLC
See also CDALB 1640-1865; DLB 1

Thornton, Hall
See Silverberg, Robert

Thucydides c. 455B.C.-399B.C.... CMLC 17

Thurber, James (Grover)
1894-1961 .... CLC **5, 11, 25; DA; DAB;**
DAC; DAM DRAM, MST, NOV; SSC 1
See also CA 73-76; CANR 17, 39;
CDALB 1929-1941; DLB 4, 11, 22, 102;
MAICYA; MTCW; SATA 13

Thurman, Wallace (Henry)
1902-1934 .... TCLC **6; BLC;**
DAM MULT
See also BW 1; CA 104; 124; DLB 51

Ticheburn, Cheviot
See Ainsworth, William Harrison

Tieck, (Johann) Ludwig
1773-1853 .... NCLC **5, 46**
See also DLB 90

Tiger, Derry
See Ellison, Harlan (Jay)

Tilghman, Christopher 1948(?)- ..... CLC **65**

Tillinghast, Richard (Williford)
1940- .... CLC **29**
See also CA 29-32R; CAAS 23; CANR 26,
51

Timrod, Henry 1828-1867 .... NCLC **25**
See also DLB 3

Tindall, Gillian 1938- .... CLC **7**
See also CA 21-24R; CANR 11

Tiptree, James, Jr. .... CLC **48, 50**
See also Sheldon, Alice Hastings Bradley
See also DLB 8

Titmarsh, Michael Angelo
See Thackeray, William Makepeace

Tocqueville, Alexis (Charles Henri Maurice
Clerel Comte) 1805-1859..... NCLC **7**

Tolkien, J(ohn) R(onald) R(euel)
1892-1973 .... CLC **1, 2, 3, 8, 12, 38;**
DA; DAB; DAC; DAM MST, NOV,
POP; WLC
See also AAYA 10; AITN 1; CA 17-18;
45-48; CANR 36; CAP 2;
CDBLB 1914-1945; DLB 15, 160; JRDA;
MAICYA; MTCW; SATA 2, 32;
SATA-Obit 24

Toller, Ernst 1893-1939 .... TCLC **10**
See also CA 107; DLB 124

Tolson, M. B.
See Tolson, Melvin B(eaunorus)

Tolson, Melvin B(eaunorus)
1898(?)-1966 .... CLC **36; BLC;**
DAM MULT, POET
See also BW 1; CA 124; 89-92; DLB 48, 76

Tolstoi, Aleksei Nikolaevich
See Tolstoy, Alexey Nikolaevich

Tolstoy, Alexey Nikolaevich
1882-1945 .... TCLC **18**
See also CA 107

Tolstoy, Count Leo
See Tolstoy, Leo (Nikolaevich)

Tolstoy, Leo (Nikolaevich)
1828-1910 ...... TCLC **4, 11, 17, 28, 44;**
DA; DAB; DAC; DAM MST, NOV;
SSC 9; WLC
See also CA 104; 123; SATA 26

Tomasi di Lampedusa, Giuseppe 1896-1957
See Lampedusa, Giuseppe (Tomasi) di
See also CA 111

Tomlin, Lily .... CLC **17**
See also Tomlin, Mary Jean

Tomlin, Mary Jean 1939(?)-
See Tomlin, Lily
See also CA 117

Tomlinson, (Alfred) Charles
1927- .... CLC **2, 4, 6, 13, 45;**
DAM POET
See also CA 5-8R; CANR 33; DLB 40

Tonson, Jacob
See Bennett, (Enoch) Arnold

Toole, John Kennedy
1937-1969 .... CLC **19, 64**
See also CA 104; DLBY 81

Toomer, Jean
1894-1967 ...... CLC **1, 4, 13, 22; BLC;**
DAM MULT; PC 7; SSC 1
See also BW 1; CA 85-88;
CDALB 1917-1929; DLB 45, 51; MTCW

Torley, Luke
See Blish, James (Benjamin)

Tornimparte, Alessandra
See Ginzburg, Natalia

Torre, Raoul della
See Mencken, H(enry) L(ouis)

Torrey, E(dwin) Fuller 1937- .... CLC **34**
See also CA 119

Torsvan, Ben Traven
See Traven, B.

Torsvan, Benno Traven
See Traven, B.

Torsvan, Berick Traven
See Traven, B.

Torsvan, Berwick Traven
See Traven, B.

Torsvan, Bruno Traven
See Traven, B.

Torsvan, Traven
See Traven, B.

Tournier, Michel (Edouard)
1924- .... CLC **6, 23, 36, 95**
See also CA 49-52; CANR 3, 36; DLB 83;
MTCW; SATA 23

Tournimparte, Alessandra
See Ginzburg, Natalia

Towers, Ivar
See Kornbluth, C(yril) M.

Towne, Robert (Burton) 1936(?)- .... CLC **87**
See also CA 108; DLB 44

Townsend, Sue 1946- .. CLC **61; DAB; DAC**
See also CA 119; 127; INT 127; MTCW;
SATA 55; SATA-Brief 48

Townshend, Peter (Dennis Blandford)
1945- .... CLC **17, 42**
See also CA 107

Tozzi, Federigo 1883-1920 .... TCLC **31**

Traill, Catharine Parr
1802-1899 .... NCLC **31**
See also DLB 99

Trakl, Georg 1887-1914 .... TCLC **5**
See also CA 104

Transtroemer, Tomas (Goesta)
1931- .... CLC **52, 65; DAM POET**
See also CA 117; 129; CAAS 17

Transtromer, Tomas Gosta
See Transtroemer, Tomas (Goesta)

Traven, B. (?)-1969............. CLC **8, 11**
See also CA 19-20; 25-28R; CAP 2; DLB 9,
56; MTCW

Treitel, Jonathan 1959- .... CLC **70**

Tremain, Rose 1943- .... CLC **42**
See also CA 97-100; CANR 44; DLB 14

Tremblay, Michel
1942- ...... CLC **29; DAC; DAM MST**
See also CA 116; 128; DLB 60; MTCW

Trevanian .... CLC **29**
See also Whitaker, Rod(ney)

Trevor, Glen
See Hilton, James

Trevor, William
1928- ..... CLC **7, 9, 14, 25, 71; SSC 21**
See also Cox, William Trevor
See also DLB 14, 139

Trifonov, Yuri (Valentinovich)
1925-1981 .... CLC **45**
See also CA 126; 103; MTCW

Trilling, Lionel 1905-1975 .... CLC **9, 11, 24**
See also CA 9-12R; 61-64; CANR 10;
DLB 28, 63; INT CANR-10; MTCW

Trimball, W. H.
See Mencken, H(enry) L(ouis)

Tristan
See Gomez de la Serna, Ramon

Tristram
See Housman, A(lfred) E(dward)

Trogdon, William (Lewis) 1939-
See Heat-Moon, William Least
See also CA 115; 119; CANR 47; INT 119

Trollope, Anthony
1815-1882 ..... NCLC **6, 33; DA; DAB;**
DAC; DAM MST, NOV; WLC
See also CDBLB 1832-1890; DLB 21, 57,
159; SATA 22

Trollope, Frances 1779-1863 ..... NCLC **30**
See also DLB 21, 166

Trotsky, Leon 1879-1940 .... TCLC **22**
See also CA 118

Trotter (Cockburn), Catharine
1679-1749 .... LC **8**
See also DLB 84

Trout, Kilgore
See Farmer, Philip Jose

Trow, George W. S. 1943- .... CLC **52**
See also CA 126

Troyat, Henri 1911- .... CLC **23**
See also CA 45-48; CANR 2, 33; MTCW

Trudeau, G(arretson) B(eekman) 1948-
See Trudeau, Garry B.
See also CA 81-84; CANR 31; SATA 35

Trudeau, Garry B. .... CLC **12**
See also Trudeau, G(arretson) B(eekman)
See also AAYA 10; AITN 2

Truffaut, Francois 1932-1984...... CLC **20**
See also CA 81-84; 113; CANR 34

Trumbo, Dalton 1905-1976 .... CLC **19**
See also CA 21-24R; 69-72; CANR 10;
DLB 26

Van Druten, John (William)
1901-1957 .... **TCLC 2**
See also CA 104; DLB 10

Van Duyn, Mona (Jane)
1921- .... **CLC 3, 7, 63; DAM POET**
See also CA 9-12R; CANR 7, 38; DLB 5

Van Dyne, Edith
See Baum, L(yman) Frank

van Itallie, Jean-Claude 1936-....... **CLC 3**
See also CA 45-48; CAAS 2; CANR 1, 48;
DLB 7

van Ostaijen, Paul 1896-1928 ..... **TCLC 33**

Van Peebles, Melvin
1932- .... **CLC 2, 20; DAM MULT**
See also BW 2; CA 85-88; CANR 27

Vansittart, Peter 1920-........... **CLC 42**
See also CA 1-4R; CANR 3, 49

Van Vechten, Carl 1880-1964 ...... **CLC 33**
See also CA 89-92; DLB 4, 9, 51

Van Vogt, A(lfred) E(lton) 1912-..... **CLC 1**
See also CA 21-24R; CANR 28; DLB 8;
SATA 14

Varda, Agnes 1928- .... **CLC 16**
See also CA 116; 122

Vargas Llosa, (Jorge) Mario (Pedro)
1936- .... **CLC 3, 6, 9, 10, 15, 31, 42, 85;**
DA; DAB; DAC; DAM MST, MULT,
NOV; HLC
See also CA 73-76; CANR 18, 32, 42;
DLB 145; HW; MTCW

Vasiliu, Gheorghe 1881-1957
See Bacovia, George
See also CA 123

Vassa, Gustavus
See Equiano, Olaudah

Vassilikos, Vassilis 1933-........ **CLC 4, 8**
See also CA 81-84

Vaughan, Henry 1621-1695......... **LC 27**
See also DLB 131

Vaughn, Stephanie................ **CLC 62**

Vazov, Ivan (Minchov)
1850-1921 .... **TCLC 25**
See also CA 121; DLB 147

Veblen, Thorstein (Bunde)
1857-1929 .... **TCLC 31**
See also CA 115

Vega, Lope de 1562-1635........... **LC 23**

Venison, Alfred
See Pound, Ezra (Weston Loomis)

Verdi, Marie de
See Mencken, H(enry) L(ouis)

Verdu, Matilde
See Cela, Camilo Jose

Verga, Giovanni (Carmelo)
1840-1922 .... **TCLC 3; SSC 21**
See also CA 104; 123

Vergil
70B.C.-19B.C..... **CMLC 9; DA; DAB;**
DAC; DAM MST, POET; PC 12

Verhaeren, Emile (Adolphe Gustave)
1855-1916 .... **TCLC 12**
See also CA 109

Verlaine, Paul (Marie)
1844-1896 .... **NCLC 2, 51;**
DAM POET; PC 2

Verne, Jules (Gabriel)
1828-1905 .... **TCLC 6, 52**
See also AAYA 16; CA 110; 131; DLB 123;
JRDA; MAICYA; SATA 21

Very, Jones 1813-1880........... **NCLC 9**
See also DLB 1

Vesaas, Tarjei 1897-1970......... **CLC 48**
See also CA 29-32R

Vialis, Gaston
See Simenon, Georges (Jacques Christian)

Vian, Boris 1920-1959 .... **TCLC 9**
See also CA 106; DLB 72

Viaud, (Louis Marie) Julien 1850-1923
See Loti, Pierre
See also CA 107

Vicar, Henry
See Felsen, Henry Gregor

Vicker, Angus
See Felsen, Henry Gregor

Vidal, Gore
1925- ..... **CLC 2, 4, 6, 8, 10, 22, 33, 72;**
DAM NOV, POP
See also AITN 1; BEST 90:2; CA 5-8R;
CANR 13, 45; DLB 6, 152;
INT CANR-13; MTCW

Viereck, Peter (Robert Edwin)
1916-........................ **CLC 4**
See also CA 1-4R; CANR 1, 47; DLB 5

Vigny, Alfred (Victor) de
1797-1863 ...... **NCLC 7; DAM POET**
See also DLB 119

Vilakazi, Benedict Wallet
1906-1947 .... **TCLC 37**

Villiers de l'Isle Adam, Jean Marie Mathias
Philippe Auguste Comte
1838-1889 .... **NCLC 3; SSC 14**
See also DLB 123

Villon, Francois 1431-1463(?) .... **PC 13**

Vinci, Leonardo da 1452-1519....... **LC 12**

Vine, Barbara .... **CLC 50**
See also Rendell, Ruth (Barbara)
See also BEST 90:4

Vinge, Joan D(ennison)
1948-............... **CLC 30; SSC 24**
See also CA 93-96; SATA 36

Violis, G.
See Simenon, Georges (Jacques Christian)

Visconti, Luchino 1906-1976....... **CLC 16**
See also CA 81-84; 65-68; CANR 39

Vittorini, Elio 1908-1966...... **CLC 6, 9, 14**
See also CA 133; 25-28R

Vizinczey, Stephen 1933-.......... **CLC 40**
See also CA 128; INT 128

Vliet, R(ussell) G(ordon)
1929-1984 .... **CLC 22**
See also CA 37-40R; 112; CANR 18

Vogau, Boris Andreyevich 1894-1937(?)
See Pilnyak, Boris
See also CA 123

Vogel, Paula A(nne) 1951-......... **CLC 76**
See also CA 108

Voight, Ellen Bryant 1943-........ **CLC 54**
See also CA 69-72; CANR 11, 29, 55;
DLB 120

Voigt, Cynthia 1942- .... **CLC 30**
See also AAYA 3; CA 106; CANR 18, 37,
40; CLR 13; INT CANR-18; JRDA;
MAICYA; SATA 48, 79; SATA-Brief 33

Voinovich, Vladimir (Nikolaevich)
1932-.................... **CLC 10, 49**
See also CA 81-84; CAAS 12; CANR 33;
MTCW

Vollmann, William T.
1959- ...... **CLC 89; DAM NOV, POP**
See also CA 134

Voloshinov, V. N.
See Bakhtin, Mikhail Mikhailovich

Voltaire
1694-1778 ..... **LC 14; DA; DAB; DAC;**
DAM DRAM, MST; SSC 12; WLC

von Bingen, Hildegard
1098(?)-1179 .... **CMLC 20**

von Daeniken, Erich 1935- .... **CLC 30**
See also AITN 1; CA 37-40R; CANR 17,
44

von Daniken, Erich
See von Daeniken, Erich

von Heidenstam, (Carl Gustaf) Verner
See Heidenstam, (Carl Gustaf) Verner von

von Heyse, Paul (Johann Ludwig)
See Heyse, Paul (Johann Ludwig von)

von Hofmannsthal, Hugo
See Hofmannsthal, Hugo von

von Horvath, Odon
See Horvath, Oedoen von

von Horvath, Oedoen
See Horvath, Oedoen von

von Liliencron, (Friedrich Adolf Axel) Detlev
See Liliencron, (Friedrich Adolf Axel)
Detlev von

Vonnegut, Kurt, Jr.
1922- ...... **CLC 1, 2, 3, 4, 5, 8, 12, 22,**
40, 60; DA; DAB; DAC; DAM MST,
NOV, POP; SSC 8; WLC
See also AAYA 6; AITN 1; BEST 90:4;
CA 1-4R; CANR 1, 25, 49;
CDALB 1968-1988; DLB 2, 8, 152;
DLBD 3; DLBY 80; MTCW

Von Rachen, Kurt
See Hubbard, L(afayette) Ron(ald)

von Rezzori (d'Arezzo), Gregor
See Rezzori (d'Arezzo), Gregor von

von Sternberg, Josef
See Sternberg, Josef von

Vorster, Gordon 1924-............. **CLC 34**
See also CA 133

Vosce, Trudie
See Ozick, Cynthia

Voznesensky, Andrei (Andreievich)
1933- ...... **CLC 1, 15, 57; DAM POET**
See also CA 89-92; CANR 37; MTCW

Waddington, Miriam 1917-........ **CLC 28**
See also CA 21-24R; CANR 12, 30;
DLB 68

Wagman, Fredrica 1937-........... **CLC 7**
See also CA 97-100; INT 97-100

Watkins, Gloria 1955(?)-
See hooks, bell
See also BW 2; CA 143

Watkins, Paul 1964-............. **CLC 55**
See also CA 132

Watkins, Vernon Phillips
1906-1967 .... **CLC 43**
See also CA 9-10; 25-28R; CAP 1; DLB 20

Watson, Irving S.
See Mencken, H(enry) L(ouis)

Watson, John H.
See Farmer, Philip Jose

Watson, Richard F.
See Silverberg, Robert

Waugh, Auberon (Alexander) 1939-.. **CLC 7**
See also CA 45-48; CANR 6, 22; DLB 14

Waugh, Evelyn (Arthur St. John)
1903-1966 ...... **CLC 1, 3, 8, 13, 19, 27,**
44; DA; DAB; DAC; DAM MST, NOV,
POP; WLC
See also CA 85-88; 25-28R; CANR 22;
CDBLB 1914-1945; DLB 15, 162; MTCW

Waugh, Harriet 1944- .... **CLC 6**
See also CA 85-88; CANR 22

Ways, C. R.
See Blount, Roy (Alton), Jr.

Waystaff, Simon
See Swift, Jonathan

Webb, (Martha) Beatrice (Potter)
1858-1943 .... **TCLC 22**
See also Potter, Beatrice
See also CA 117

Webb, Charles (Richard) 1939-...... **CLC 7**
See also CA 25-28R

Webb, James H(enry), Jr. 1946-.... **CLC 22**
See also CA 81-84

Webb, Mary (Gladys Meredith)
1881-1927 .... **TCLC 24**
See also CA 123; DLB 34

Webb, Mrs. Sidney
See Webb, (Martha) Beatrice (Potter)

Webb, Phyllis 1927-............... **CLC 18**
See also CA 104; CANR 23; DLB 53

Webb, Sidney (James)
1859-1947 .... **TCLC 22**
See also CA 117

Webber, Andrew Lloyd............. **CLC 21**
See also Lloyd Webber, Andrew

Weber, Lenora Mattingly
1895-1971 .... **CLC 12**
See also CA 19-20; 29-32R; CAP 1;
SATA 2; SATA-Obit 26

Webster, John
1579(?)-1634(?) ...... **LC 33; DA; DAB;**
DAC; DAM DRAM, MST; DC 2; WLC
See also CDBLB Before 1660; DLB 58

Webster, Noah 1758-1843 .... **NCLC 30**

Wedekind, (Benjamin) Frank(lin)
1864-1918 ...... **TCLC 7; DAM DRAM**
See also CA 104; 153; DLB 118

Weidman, Jerome 1913-............ **CLC 7**
See also AITN 2; CA 1-4R; CANR 1;
DLB 28

Weil, Simone (Adolphine)
1909-1943 .... **TCLC 23**
See also CA 117

Weinstein, Nathan
See West, Nathanael

Weinstein, Nathan von Wallenstein
See West, Nathanael

Weir, Peter (Lindsay) 1944- .... **CLC 20**
See also CA 113; 123

Weiss, Peter (Ulrich)
1916-1982 .... **CLC 3, 15, 51;**
DAM DRAM
See also CA 45-48; 106; CANR 3; DLB 69,
124

Weiss, Theodore (Russell)
1916- .... **CLC 3, 8, 14**
See also CA 9-12R; CAAS 2; CANR 46;
DLB 5

Welch, (Maurice) Denton
1915-1948 .... **TCLC 22**
See also CA 121; 148

Welch, James
1940-..... **CLC 6, 14, 52; DAM MULT,**
POP
See also CA 85-88; CANR 42; NNAL

Weldon, Fay
1933-......... **CLC 6, 9, 11, 19, 36, 59;**
DAM POP
See also CA 21-24R; CANR 16, 46;
CDBLB 1960 to Present; DLB 14;
INT CANR-16; MTCW

Wellek, Rene 1903-1995........... **CLC 28**
See also CA 5-8R; 150; CAAS 7; CANR 8;
DLB 63; INT CANR-8

Weller, Michael 1942-......... **CLC 10, 53**
See also CA 85-88

Weller, Paul 1958-............... **CLC 26**

Wellershoff, Dieter 1925-.......... **CLC 46**
See also CA 89-92; CANR 16, 37

Welles, (George) Orson
1915-1985 .... **CLC 20, 80**
See also CA 93-96; 117

Wellman, Mac 1945-............. **CLC 65**

Wellman, Manly Wade 1903-1986 .. **CLC 49**
See also CA 1-4R; 118; CANR 6, 16, 44;
SATA 6; SATA-Obit 47

Wells, Carolyn 1869(?)-1942 ...... **TCLC 35**
See also CA 113; DLB 11

Wells, H(erbert) G(eorge)
1866-1946 .... **TCLC 6, 12, 19; DA;**
DAB; DAC; DAM MST, NOV; SSC 6;
WLC
See also AAYA 18; CA 110; 121;
CDBLB 1914-1945; DLB 34, 70, 156;
MTCW; SATA 20

Wells, Rosemary 1943-............ **CLC 12**
See also AAYA 13; CA 85-88; CANR 48;
CLR 16; MAICYA; SAAS 1; SATA 18,
69

Welty, Eudora
1909- ...... **CLC 1, 2, 5, 14, 22, 33; DA;**
DAB; DAC; DAM MST, NOV; SSC 1;
WLC
See also CA 9-12R; CABS 1; CANR 32;
CDALB 1941-1968; DLB 2, 102, 143;
DLBD 12; DLBY 87; MTCW

Wen I-to 1899-1946 .... **TCLC 28**

Wentworth, Robert
See Hamilton, Edmond

Werfel, Franz (V.) 1890-1945 ...... **TCLC 8**
See also CA 104; DLB 81, 124

Wergeland, Henrik Arnold
1808-1845 .... **NCLC 5**

Wersba, Barbara 1932-............ **CLC 30**
See also AAYA 2; CA 29-32R; CANR 16,
38; CLR 3; DLB 52; JRDA; MAICYA;
SAAS 2; SATA 1, 58

Wertmueller, Lina 1928- .... **CLC 16**
See also CA 97-100; CANR 39

Wescott, Glenway 1901-1987....... **CLC 13**
See also CA 13-16R; 121; CANR 23;
DLB 4, 9, 102

Wesker, Arnold
1932- .... **CLC 3, 5, 42; DAB;**
DAM DRAM
See also CA 1-4R; CAAS 7; CANR 1, 33;
CDBLB 1960 to Present; DLB 13;
MTCW

Wesley, Richard (Errol) 1945-....... **CLC 7**
See also BW 1; CA 57-60; CANR 27;
DLB 38

Wessel, Johan Herman 1742-1785 .... **LC 7**

West, Anthony (Panther)
1914-1987 .... **CLC 50**
See also CA 45-48; 124; CANR 3, 19;
DLB 15

West, C. P.
See Wodehouse, P(elham) G(renville)

West, (Mary) Jessamyn
1902-1984 .... **CLC 7, 17**
See also CA 9-12R; 112; CANR 27; DLB 6;
DLBY 84; MTCW; SATA-Obit 37

West, Morris L(anglo) 1916-..... **CLC 6, 33**
See also CA 5-8R; CANR 24, 49; MTCW

West, Nathanael
1903-1940 ..... **TCLC 1, 14, 44; SSC 16**
See also CA 104; 125; CDALB 1929-1941;
DLB 4, 9, 28; MTCW

West, Owen
See Koontz, Dean R(ay)

West, Paul 1930- .... **CLC 7, 14, 96**
See also CA 13-16R; CAAS 7; CANR 22,
53; DLB 14; INT CANR-22

West, Rebecca 1892-1983 .. **CLC 7, 9, 31, 50**
See also CA 5-8R; 109; CANR 19; DLB 36;
DLBY 83; MTCW

Westall, Robert (Atkinson)
1929-1993 .... **CLC 17**
See also AAYA 12; CA 69-72; 141;
CANR 18; CLR 13; JRDA; MAICYA;
SAAS 2; SATA 23, 69; SATA-Obit 75

Westlake, Donald E(dwin)
1933- .... **CLC 7, 33; DAM POP**
See also CA 17-20R; CAAS 13; CANR 16,
44; INT CANR-16

Westmacott, Mary
See Christie, Agatha (Mary Clarissa)

Weston, Allen
See Norton, Andre

Wetcheek, J. L.
See Feuchtwanger, Lion

Wetering, Janwillem van de
See van de Wetering, Janwillem

Wetherell, Elizabeth
See Warner, Susan (Bogert)

Whale, James 1889-1957 .... **TCLC 63**

Whalen, Philip 1923- .... **CLC 6, 29**
See also CA 9-12R; CANR 5, 39; DLB 16

Wharton, Edith (Newbold Jones)
1862-1937 ...... **TCLC 3, 9, 27, 53; DA;**
DAB; DAC; DAM MST, NOV; SSC 6;
WLC
See also CA 104; 132; CDALB 1865-1917;
DLB 4, 9, 12, 78; DLBD 13; MTCW

Wharton, James
See Mencken, H(enry) L(ouis)

Wharton, William (a pseudonym)
.... **CLC 18, 37**
See also CA 93-96; DLBY 80; INT 93-96

Wheatley (Peters), Phillis
1754(?)-1784 .... **LC 3; BLC; DA; DAC;**
DAM MST, MULT, POET; PC 3; WLC
See also CDALB 1640-1865; DLB 31, 50

Wheelock, John Hall 1886-1978 .... **CLC 14**
See also CA 13-16R; 77-80; CANR 14;
DLB 45

White, E(lwyn) B(rooks)
1899-1985 .. **CLC 10, 34, 39; DAM POP**
See also AITN 2; CA 13-16R; 116;
CANR 16, 37; CLR 1, 21; DLB 11, 22;
MAICYA; MTCW; SATA 2, 29;
SATA-Obit 44

White, Edmund (Valentine III)
1940- .... **CLC 27; DAM POP**
See also AAYA 7; CA 45-48; CANR 3, 19,
36; MTCW

White, Patrick (Victor Martindale)
1912-1990 .. **CLC 3, 4, 5, 7, 9, 18, 65, 69**
See also CA 81-84; 132; CANR 43; MTCW

White, Phyllis Dorothy James 1920-
See James, P. D.
See also CA 21-24R; CANR 17, 43;
DAM POP; MTCW

White, T(erence) H(anbury)
1906-1964 .... **CLC 30**
See also CA 73-76; CANR 37; DLB 160;
JRDA; MAICYA; SATA 12

White, Terence de Vere
1912-1994 .... **CLC 49**
See also CA 49-52; 145; CANR 3

White, Walter F(rancis)
1893-1955 .... **TCLC 15**
See also White, Walter
See also BW 1; CA 115; 124; DLB 51

White, William Hale 1831-1913
See Rutherford, Mark
See also CA 121

Whitehead, E(dward) A(nthony)
1933- .... **CLC 5**
See also CA 65-68

Whitemore, Hugh (John) 1936- ..... **CLC 37**
See also CA 132; INT 132

Whitman, Sarah Helen (Power)
1803-1878 .... **NCLC 19**
See also DLB 1

Whitman, Walt(er)
1819-1892 ..... **NCLC 4, 31; DA; DAB;**
DAC; DAM MST, POET; PC 3; WLC
See also CDALB 1640-1865; DLB 3, 64;
SATA 20

Whitney, Phyllis A(yame)
1903- .... **CLC 42; DAM POP**
See also AITN 2; BEST 90:3; CA 1-4R;
CANR 3, 25, 38; JRDA; MAICYA;
SATA 1, 30

Whittemore, (Edward) Reed (Jr.)
1919- .... **CLC 4**
See also CA 9-12R; CAAS 8; CANR 4;
DLB 5

Whittier, John Greenleaf
1807-1892 .... **NCLC 8**
See also DLB 1

Whittlebot, Hernia
See Coward, Noel (Peirce)

Wicker, Thomas Grey 1926-
See Wicker, Tom
See also CA 65-68; CANR 21, 46

Wicker, Tom .... **CLC 7**
See also Wicker, Thomas Grey

Wideman, John Edgar
1941- .... **CLC 5, 34, 36, 67; BLC;**
DAM MULT
See also BW 2; CA 85-88; CANR 14, 42;
DLB 33, 143

Wiebe, Rudy (Henry)
1934- .... **CLC 6, 11, 14; DAC;**
DAM MST
See also CA 37-40R; CANR 42; DLB 60

Wieland, Christoph Martin
1733-1813 .... **NCLC 17**
See also DLB 97

Wiene, Robert 1881-1938 .... **TCLC 56**

Wieners, John 1934- .... **CLC 7**
See also CA 13-16R; DLB 16

Wiesel, Elie(zer)
1928- ...... **CLC 3, 5, 11, 37; DA; DAB;**
DAC; DAM MST, NOV
See also AAYA 7; AITN 1; CA 5-8R;
CAAS 4; CANR 8, 40; DLB 83;
DLBY 87; INT CANR-8; MTCW;
SATA 56

Wiggins, Marianne 1947- .... **CLC 57**
See also BEST 89:3; CA 130

Wight, James Alfred 1916-
See Herriot, James
See also CA 77-80; SATA 55;
SATA-Brief 44

Wilbur, Richard (Purdy)
1921- ... **CLC 3, 6, 9, 14, 53; DA; DAB;**
DAC; DAM MST, POET
See also CA 1-4R; CABS 2; CANR 2, 29;
DLB 5, 169; INT CANR-29; MTCW;
SATA 9

Wild, Peter 1940- .... **CLC 14**
See also CA 37-40R; DLB 5

Wilde, Oscar (Fingal O'Flahertie Wills)
1854(?)-1900 .... **TCLC 1, 8, 23, 41; DA;**
DAB; DAC; DAM DRAM, MST, NOV;
SSC 11; WLC
See also CA 104; 119; CDBLB 1890-1914;
DLB 10, 19, 34, 57, 141, 156; SATA 24

Wilder, Billy .... **CLC 20**
See also Wilder, Samuel
See also DLB 26

Wilder, Samuel 1906-
See Wilder, Billy
See also CA 89-92

Wilder, Thornton (Niven)
1897-1975 ...... **CLC 1, 5, 6, 10, 15, 35,**
82; DA; DAB; DAC; DAM DRAM,
MST, NOV; DC 1; WLC
See also AITN 2; CA 13-16R; 61-64;
CANR 40; DLB 4, 7, 9; MTCW

Wilding, Michael 1942- .... **CLC 73**
See also CA 104; CANR 24, 49

Wiley, Richard 1944- .... **CLC 44**
See also CA 121; 129

Wilhelm, Kate .... **CLC 7**
See also Wilhelm, Katie Gertrude
See also CAAS 5; DLB 8; INT CANR-17

Wilhelm, Katie Gertrude 1928-
See Wilhelm, Kate
See also CA 37-40R; CANR 17, 36; MTCW

Wilkins, Mary
See Freeman, Mary Eleanor Wilkins

Willard, Nancy 1936- .... **CLC 7, 37**
See also CA 89-92; CANR 10, 39; CLR 5;
DLB 5, 52; MAICYA; MTCW;
SATA 37, 71; SATA-Brief 30

Williams, C(harles) K(enneth)
1936- .... **CLC 33, 56; DAM POET**
See also CA 37-40R; DLB 5

Williams, Charles
See Collier, James L(incoln)

Williams, Charles (Walter Stansby)
1886-1945 .... **TCLC 1, 11**
See also CA 104; DLB 100, 153

Williams, (George) Emlyn
1905-1987 ...... **CLC 15; DAM DRAM**
See also CA 104; 123; CANR 36; DLB 10,
77; MTCW

Williams, Hugo 1942- .... **CLC 42**
See also CA 17-20R; CANR 45; DLB 40

Williams, J. Walker
See Wodehouse, P(elham) G(renville)

Williams, John A(lfred)
1925- ... **CLC 5, 13; BLC; DAM MULT**
See also BW 2; CA 53-56; CAAS 3;
CANR 6, 26, 51; DLB 2, 33;
INT CANR-6

Williams, Jonathan (Chamberlain)
1929- .... **CLC 13**
See also CA 9-12R; CAAS 12; CANR 8;
DLB 5

Williams, Joy 1944- .... **CLC 31**
See also CA 41-44R; CANR 22, 48

Williams, Norman 1952- .... **CLC 39**
See also CA 118

Williams, Sherley Anne
1944- ..... **CLC 89; BLC; DAM MULT,**
POET
See also BW 2; CA 73-76; CANR 25;
DLB 41; INT CANR-25; SATA 78

Williams, Shirley
See Williams, Sherley Anne

Williams, Tennessee
1911-1983 ..... **CLC 1, 2, 5, 7, 8, 11, 15, 19, 30, 39, 45, 71; DA; DAB; DAC; DAM DRAM, MST; DC 4; WLC**
See also AITN 1, 2; CA 5-8R; 108; CABS 3; CANR 31; CDALB 1941-1968; DLB 7; DLBD 4; DLBY 83; MTCW

Williams, Thomas (Alonzo)
1926-1990 .... **CLC 14**
See also CA 1-4R; 132; CANR 2

Williams, William C.
See Williams, William Carlos

Williams, William Carlos
1883-1963 .... **CLC 1, 2, 5, 9, 13, 22, 42, 67; DA; DAB; DAC; DAM MST, POET; PC 7**
See also CA 89-92; CANR 34; CDALB 1917-1929; DLB 4, 16, 54, 86; MTCW

Williamson, David (Keith) 1942-.... **CLC 56**
See also CA 103; CANR 41

Williamson, Ellen Douglas 1905-1984
See Douglas, Ellen
See also CA 17-20R; 114; CANR 39

Williamson, Jack................. **CLC 29**
See also Williamson, John Stewart
See also CAAS 8; DLB 8

Williamson, John Stewart 1908-
See Williamson, Jack
See also CA 17-20R; CANR 23

Willie, Frederick
See Lovecraft, H(oward) P(hillips)

Willingham, Calder (Baynard, Jr.)
1922-1995 .... **CLC 5, 51**
See also CA 5-8R; 147; CANR 3; DLB 2, 44; MTCW

Willis, Charles
See Clarke, Arthur C(harles)

Willy
See Colette, (Sidonie-Gabrielle)

Willy, Colette
See Colette, (Sidonie-Gabrielle)

Wilson, A(ndrew) N(orman) 1950- .. **CLC 33**
See also CA 112; 122; DLB 14, 155

Wilson, Angus (Frank Johnstone)
1913-1991 .. **CLC 2, 3, 5, 25, 34; SSC 21**
See also CA 5-8R; 134; CANR 21; DLB 15, 139, 155; MTCW

Wilson, August
1945- .... **CLC 39, 50, 63; BLC; DA; DAB; DAC; DAM DRAM, MST, MULT; DC 2**
See also AAYA 16; BW 2; CA 115; 122; CANR 42, 54; MTCW

Wilson, Brian 1942-............. **CLC 12**

Wilson, Colin 1931-............ **CLC 3, 14**
See also CA 1-4R; CAAS 5; CANR 1, 22, 33; DLB 14; MTCW

Wilson, Dirk
See Pohl, Frederik

Wilson, Edmund
1895-1972 .... **CLC 1, 2, 3, 8, 24**
See also CA 1-4R; 37-40R; CANR 1, 46; DLB 63; MTCW

Wilson, Ethel Davis (Bryant)
1888(?)-1980 .... **CLC 13; DAC; DAM POET**
See also CA 102; DLB 68; MTCW

Wilson, John 1785-1854......... **NCLC 5**

Wilson, John (Anthony) Burgess 1917-1993
See Burgess, Anthony
See also CA 1-4R; 143; CANR 2, 46; DAC; DAM NOV; MTCW

Wilson, Lanford
1937- ..... **CLC 7, 14, 36; DAM DRAM**
See also CA 17-20R; CABS 3; CANR 45; DLB 7

Wilson, Robert M. 1944-......... **CLC 7, 9**
See also CA 49-52; CANR 2, 41; MTCW

Wilson, Robert McLiam 1964- ..... **CLC 59**
See also CA 132

Wilson, Sloan 1920-............. **CLC 32**
See also CA 1-4R; CANR 1, 44

Wilson, Snoo 1948-............. **CLC 33**
See also CA 69-72

Wilson, William S(mith) 1932- ... **CLC 49**
See also CA 81-84

Winchilsea, Anne (Kingsmill) Finch Counte
1661-1720 .... **LC 3**

Windham, Basil
See Wodehouse, P(elham) G(renville)

Wingrove, David (John) 1954-...... **CLC 68**
See also CA 133

Winters, Janet Lewis .... **CLC 41**
See also Lewis, Janet
See also DLBY 87

Winters, (Arthur) Yvor
1900-1968 .... **CLC 4, 8, 32**
See also CA 11-12; 25-28R; CAP 1; DLB 48; MTCW

Winterson, Jeanette
1959-............ **CLC 64; DAM POP**
See also CA 136

Winthrop, John 1588-1649......... **LC 31**
See also DLB 24, 30

Wiseman, Frederick 1930-......... **CLC 20**

Wister, Owen 1860-1938 .... **TCLC 21**
See also CA 108; DLB 9, 78; SATA 62

Witkacy
See Witkiewicz, Stanislaw Ignacy

Witkiewicz, Stanislaw Ignacy
1885-1939 .... **TCLC 8**
See also CA 105

Wittgenstein, Ludwig (Josef Johann)
1889-1951 .... **TCLC 59**
See also CA 113

Wittig, Monique 1935(?)-.......... **CLC 22**
See also CA 116; 135; DLB 83

Wittlin, Jozef 1896-1976 .... **CLC 25**
See also CA 49-52; 65-68; CANR 3

Wodehouse, P(elham) G(renville)
1881-1975 ... **CLC 1, 2, 5, 10, 22; DAB; DAC; DAM NOV; SSC 2**
See also AITN 2; CA 45-48; 57-60; CANR 3, 33; CDBLB 1914-1945; DLB 34, 162; MTCW; SATA 22

Woiwode, L.
See Woiwode, Larry (Alfred)

Woiwode, Larry (Alfred) 1941-... **CLC 6, 10**
See also CA 73-76; CANR 16; DLB 6; INT CANR-16

Wojciechowska, Maia (Teresa)
1927- .... **CLC 26**
See also AAYA 8; CA 9-12R; CANR 4, 41; CLR 1; JRDA; MAICYA; SAAS 1; SATA 1, 28, 83

Wolf, Christa 1929- .... **CLC 14, 29, 58**
See also CA 85-88; CANR 45; DLB 75; MTCW

Wolfe, Gene (Rodman)
1931-............ **CLC 25; DAM POP**
See also CA 57-60; CAAS 9; CANR 6, 32; DLB 8

Wolfe, George C. 1954-........... **CLC 49**
See also CA 149

Wolfe, Thomas (Clayton)
1900-1938 ..... **TCLC 4, 13, 29, 61; DA; DAB; DAC; DAM MST, NOV; WLC**
See also CA 104; 132; CDALB 1929-1941; DLB 9, 102; DLBD 2; DLBY 85; MTCW

Wolfe, Thomas Kennerly, Jr. 1931-
See Wolfe, Tom
See also CA 13-16R; CANR 9, 33; DAM POP; INT CANR-9; MTCW

Wolfe, Tom .... **CLC 1, 2, 9, 15, 35, 51**
See also Wolfe, Thomas Kennerly, Jr.
See also AAYA 8; AITN 2; BEST 89:1; DLB 152

Wolff, Geoffrey (Ansell) 1937- ..... **CLC 41**
See also CA 29-32R; CANR 29, 43

Wolff, Sonia
See Levitin, Sonia (Wolff)

Wolff, Tobias (Jonathan Ansell)
1945-........................ **CLC 39, 64**
See also AAYA 16; BEST 90:2; CA 114; 117; CAAS 22; CANR 54; DLB 130; INT 117

Wolfram von Eschenbach
c. 1170-c. 1220 .... **CMLC 5**
See also DLB 138

Wolitzer, Hilma 1930-............. **CLC 17**
See also CA 65-68; CANR 18, 40; INT CANR-18; SATA 31

Wollstonecraft, Mary 1759-1797...... **LC 5**
See also CDBLB 1789-1832; DLB 39, 104, 158

Wonder, Stevie .... **CLC 12**
See also Morris, Steveland Judkins

Wong, Jade Snow 1922-........... **CLC 17**
See also CA 109

Woodcott, Keith
See Brunner, John (Kilian Houston)

Woodruff, Robert W.
See Mencken, H(enry) L(ouis)

Woolf, (Adeline) Virginia
1882-1941 .... **TCLC 1, 5, 20, 43, 56; DA; DAB; DAC; DAM MST, NOV; SSC 7; WLC**
See also CA 104; 130; CDBLB 1914-1945; DLB 36, 100, 162; DLBD 10; MTCW

Woollcott, Alexander (Humphreys)
1887-1943 .... **TCLC 5**
See also CA 105; DLB 29

Woolrich, Cornell 1903-1968...... CLC 77
See also Hopley-Woolrich, Cornell George

Wordsworth, Dorothy
1771-1855 .... NCLC 25
See also DLB 107

Wordsworth, William
1770-1850 .... NCLC 12, 38; DA; DAB;
DAC; DAM MST, POET; PC 4; WLC
See also CDBLB 1789-1832; DLB 93, 107

Wouk, Herman
1915- .. CLC 1, 9, 38; DAM NOV, POP
See also CA 5-8R; CANR 6, 33; DLBY 82;
INT CANR-6; MTCW

Wright, Charles (Penzel, Jr.)
1935- .... CLC 6, 13, 28
See also CA 29-32R; CAAS 7; CANR 23,
36; DLB 165; DLBY 82; MTCW

Wright, Charles Stevenson
1932- .... CLC 49; BLC 3;
DAM MULT, POET
See also BW 1; CA 9-12R; CANR 26;
DLB 33

Wright, Jack R.
See Harris, Mark

Wright, James (Arlington)
1927-1980 .... CLC 3, 5, 10, 28;
DAM POET
See also AITN 2; CA 49-52; 97-100;
CANR 4, 34; DLB 5, 169; MTCW

Wright, Judith (Arandell)
1915- .... CLC 11, 53; PC 14
See also CA 13-16R; CANR 31; MTCW;
SATA 14

Wright, L(aurali) R. 1939-........ CLC 44
See also CA 138

Wright, Richard (Nathaniel)
1908-1960 .... CLC 1, 3, 4, 9, 14, 21, 48,
74; BLC; DA; DAB; DAC; DAM MST,
MULT, NOV; SSC 2; WLC
See also AAYA 5; BW 1; CA 108;
CDALB 1929-1941; DLB 76, 102;
DLBD 2; MTCW

Wright, Richard B(ruce) 1937- ...... CLC 6
See also CA 85-88; DLB 53

Wright, Rick 1945-............... CLC 35

Wright, Rowland
See Wells, Carolyn

Wright, Stephen Caldwell 1946- .... CLC 33
See also BW 2

Wright, Willard Huntington 1888-1939
See Van Dine, S. S.
See also CA 115

Wright, William 1930-............ CLC 44
See also CA 53-56; CANR 7, 23

Wroth, LadyMary 1587-1653(?) ..... LC 30
See also DLB 121

Wu Ch'eng-en 1500(?)-1582(?)........ LC 7

Wu Ching-tzu 1701-1754 .... LC 2

Wurlitzer, Rudolph 1938(?)- ... CLC 2, 4, 15
See also CA 85-88; DLB 173

Wycherley, William
1641-1715 ..... LC 8, 21; DAM DRAM
See also CDBLB 1660-1789; DLB 80

Wylie, Elinor (Morton Hoyt)
1885-1928 .... TCLC 8
See also CA 105; DLB 9, 45

Wylie, Philip (Gordon) 1902-1971... CLC 43
See also CA 21-22; 33-36R; CAP 2; DLB 9

Wyndham, John.................. CLC 19
See also Harris, John (Wyndham Parkes
Lucas) Beynon

Wyss, Johann David Von
1743-1818 .... NCLC 10
See also JRDA; MAICYA; SATA 29;
SATA-Brief 27

Xenophon
c. 430B.C.-c. 354B.C......... CMLC 17

Yakumo Koizumi
See Hearn, (Patricio) Lafcadio (Tessima
Carlos)

Yanez, Jose Donoso
See Donoso (Yanez), Jose

Yanovsky, Basile S.
See Yanovsky, V(assily) S(emenovich)

Yanovsky, V(assily) S(emenovich)
1906-1989 .... CLC 2, 18
See also CA 97-100; 129

Yates, Richard 1926-1992 ..... CLC 7, 8, 23
See also CA 5-8R; 139; CANR 10, 43;
DLB 2; DLBY 81, 92; INT CANR-10

Yeats, W. B.
See Yeats, William Butler

Yeats, William Butler
1865-1939 ..... TCLC 1, 11, 18, 31; DA;
DAB; DAC; DAM DRAM, MST,
POET; WLC
See also CA 104; 127; CANR 45;
CDBLB 1890-1914; DLB 10, 19, 98, 156;
MTCW

Yehoshua, A(braham) B.
1936- .... CLC 13, 31
See also CA 33-36R; CANR 43

Yep, Laurence Michael 1948- ...... CLC 35
See also AAYA 5; CA 49-52; CANR 1, 46;
CLR 3, 17; DLB 52; JRDA; MAICYA;
SATA 7, 69

Yerby, Frank G(arvin)
1916-1991 .... CLC 1, 7, 22; BLC;
DAM MULT
See also BW 1; CA 9-12R; 136; CANR 16,
52; DLB 76; INT CANR-16; MTCW

Yesenin, Sergei Alexandrovich
See Esenin, Sergei (Alexandrovich)

Yevtushenko, Yevgeny (Alexandrovich)
1933- .... CLC 1, 3, 13, 26, 51;
DAM POET
See also CA 81-84; CANR 33, 54; MTCW

Yezierska, Anzia 1885(?)-1970 ..... CLC 46
See also CA 126; 89-92; DLB 28; MTCW

Yglesias, Helen 1915-........... CLC 7, 22
See also CA 37-40R; CAAS 20; CANR 15;
INT CANR-15; MTCW

Yokomitsu Riichi 1898-1947 ...... TCLC 47

Yonge, Charlotte (Mary)
1823-1901 .... TCLC 48
See also CA 109; DLB 18, 163; SATA 17

York, Jeremy
See Creasey, John

York, Simon
See Heinlein, Robert A(nson)

Yorke, Henry Vincent 1905-1974 ... CLC 13
See also Green, Henry
See also CA 85-88; 49-52

Yosano Akiko 1878-1942 .. TCLC 59; PC 11

Yoshimoto, Banana .... CLC 84
See also Yoshimoto, Mahoko

Yoshimoto, Mahoko 1964-
See Yoshimoto, Banana
See also CA 144

Young, Al(bert James)
1939- ..... CLC 19; BLC; DAM MULT
See also BW 2; CA 29-32R; CANR 26;
DLB 33

Young, Andrew (John) 1885-1971.... CLC 5
See also CA 5-8R; CANR 7, 29

Young, Collier
See Bloch, Robert (Albert)

Young, Edward 1683-1765.......... LC 3
See also DLB 95

Young, Marguerite (Vivian)
1909-1995 .... CLC 82
See also CA 13-16; 150; CAP 1

Young, Neil 1945-................. CLC 17
See also CA 110

Young Bear, Ray A.
1950- .... CLC 94; DAM MULT
See also CA 146; NNAL

Yourcenar, Marguerite
1903-1987 .... CLC 19, 38, 50, 87;
DAM NOV
See also CA 69-72; CANR 23; DLB 72;
DLBY 88; MTCW

Yurick, Sol 1925-................. CLC 6
See also CA 13-16R; CANR 25

Zabolotskii, Nikolai Alekseevich
1903-1958 .... TCLC 52
See also CA 116

Zamiatin, Yevgenii
See Zamyatin, Evgeny Ivanovich

Zamora, Bernice (B. Ortiz)
1938- ..... CLC 89; DAM MULT; HLC
See also CA 151; DLB 82; HW

Zamyatin, Evgeny Ivanovich
1884-1937 .... TCLC 8, 37
See also CA 105

Zangwill, Israel 1864-1926........ TCLC 16
See also CA 109; DLB 10, 135

Zappa, Francis Vincent, Jr. 1940-1993
See Zappa, Frank
See also CA 108; 143

Zappa, Frank.................... CLC 17
See also Zappa, Francis Vincent, Jr.

Zaturenska, Marya 1902-1982.... CLC 6, 11
See also CA 13-16R; 105; CANR 22

Zelazny, Roger (Joseph)
1937-1995 .... CLC 21
See also AAYA 7; CA 21-24R; 148;
CANR 26; DLB 8; MTCW; SATA 57;
SATA-Brief 39

Zhdanov, Andrei A(lexandrovich)
1896-1948 .... TCLC 18
See also CA 117

Cumulative Nationality Index

SSC Cumulative Title Index

Title Index

Title Index

Title Index

Title Index

Title Index

ISBN 0-7876-0756-8